THE FIRST WORLD WAR

Volume I

To Arms

THE FIRST WORLD WAR

Volume I
To Arms

HEW STRACHAN

OXFORD
UNIVERSITY PRESS

OXFORD
UNIVERSITY PRESS

Great Clarendon Street, Oxford OX2 6DP

Oxford University Press is a department of the University of Oxford.
It furthers the University's objective of excellence in research, scholarship,
and education by publishing worldwide in

Oxford New York

Auckland Bangkok Buenos Aires Cape Town Chennai
Dar es Salaam Delhi Hong Kong Istanbul Karachi Kolkata
Kuala Lumpur Madrid Melbourne Mexico City Mumbai Nairobi
São Paulo Shanghai Taipei Tokyo Toronto

Oxford is a registered trade mark of Oxford University Press
in the UK and certain other countries

Published in the United States
by Oxford University Press Inc., New York

First published 2001
First published in paperback 2003

British Library Cataloguing in Publication Data

Data available

Library of Congress Cataloging in Publication Data

Strachan, Hew.
The First World War / Hew Strachan.
p. cm.
Includes bibliographical references and index.
Contents: v. 1. To arms.
1. World War, 1914–1918. I. Title.
D521. S86 2001   940.3—dc21   00–057122

ISBN 0–19–820877–4 (hbk.)
ISBN 0–19–926191–1 (pbk.)

10 8 6 4 2

Typeset by Kolam Information Services Pvt. Ltd, Pondicherry, India
Printed in Great Britain
on acid-free paper by
T.J. International Ltd,
Padstow, Cornwall

In memory of my grandfather, Captain F. W. Strachan, wounded, Givenchy, 14 January 1915; of his brother, Second-Lieutenant E. S. Strachan, missing presumed killed, Loos, 14 October 1915; and of Major R. B. Talbot Kelly, M C, wounded, Ypres, 5 August 1917

CONTENTS

LIST OF MAPS

INTRODUCTION

This book was commissioned, far too long ago, by Oxford University Press, as a one-volume replacement for C. R. M. F. Cruttwell's *A history of the Great War*, first published in 1934 and regularly reprinted thereafter. One of its admirers, Tim Travers, has described his book and Liddell Hart's *The real war* (1930) as the founding volumes of what he calls the 'objective tradition' in British military history.[1] Cruttwell did indeed achieve a remarkable degree of detachment. Nonetheless, both Cruttwell and Liddell Hart were describing events in which they themselves had participated, albeit at a comparatively humble level, and whose consequences continued to affect them for the rest of their lives.

Having been born after the Second World War, I fancied that I belonged to an age-group that could at last claim some distance from the events of 1914–18. The films and fiction of my childhood drew their inspiration from the deeds of my father's generation, not of my grandfather's. As the twentieth century closed, few who fought on the Somme or at Ypres still survived. If part of a historian's function is to put the events of the past into perspective, the ability to do so should increase year on year.

And yet I am not so untouched by the First World War as I once imagined. One of the three men to whose memory this volume is dedicated is my grandfather. On the birthdays and Christmases of my early childhood the postman would bring a box of W. Britain's toy soldiers. These presents, ordered by my grandfather from Hamleys, were no doubt a formative influence. The army that I assembled as a result was not arrayed in khaki, steel helmets, and gas masks. These were not the soldiers of industrialized war but of Queen Victoria's empire, clad in scarlet tunics and spiked helmets. My grandfather's toy soldiers were the toys of his own childhood rather than a reflection of his experiences as an adult.

Herein lies a wholly understandable ambivalence. His London club was a military one and he used his army rank. His wife's brothers embraced military careers, and he had met her through one of them, a fellow officer. But he was

---

[1] Tim Travers, 'The development of British military historical writing and thought from the eighteenth century to the present', in Charters, Milner, Wilson (eds.), *Military history and the military profession*, 34; see also Hew Strachan ' "The Real War": Liddell Hart, Cruttwell, and Falls', in Bond (ed.), *The First World War and British military history*. (Full references to works cited in the notes will be found in the Bibliography.)

not a professional soldier. He had joined up in 1914 as a private in the London Scottish, and had gone to France in November, as one of a draft sent to make up the battalion's losses at Messines. In the failing light of 21 December the London Scottish attacked Givenchy, and established a line on the edge of the village. They occupied it for four weeks, over Christmas and New Year, in rain and sleet, the overnight frosts followed in the morning by thaw and dampness. The routines of trench warfare, designed to manage a hostile environment, had not yet established themselves. The exchange of fire was continuous. [2] On 14 January 1915, three days before the London Scottish came out of the line, my grandfather was severely wounded in the lung. He was brought back to Britain, recovered, and, although deemed unfit for further active service, commissioned. While convalescing he heard the news of the death of his elder brother, a New Army subaltern aged 36, reported as missing at Loos on 14 October 1915. Although he never served with them again, he remained a devoted London Scot. Shortly before his death my mother (and his daughter-in-law) discovered his kilt, now moth-eaten but its hodden grey stained with blood. She suggested that I might like to have it. His response was to consign it to the fire.

At school I was taught to draw by R. B. Talbot Kelly. 'T.K.' was famous as a bird painter, his watercolours and washes capturing geese in flight or waders picking their way along the shore. He offered to teach me to draw birds, but I wanted to paint soldiers. Much to my surprise, he acquiesced. T.K. had been commissoned from Woolwich into the Royal Artillery in 1915; his first career was that of a soldier rather than of an artist, though no doubt his experiences as a forward observation officer in 1915–16 honed his eye for landscape. Although I tended to depict the same sorts of soldiers as those toys my grandfather had given me, T.K. showed me his own watercolours of the First World War. The sketches which he made at the front were worked up into larger pictures later. At the time the BBC had begun its pioneering documentary series The Great War, broadcast in 1964 for the fiftieth anniversary of its outbreak.[3] T.K. appeared in it, stressing, on the screen as he did in private life, the intensity of the experience and his gratitude for having undergone it. Later I came to interpret these responses as those of an old man, remembering his youth and endowing it with a romance that it may never have possessed in reality. But I was wrong. In 1980 T.K.'s memoir of the war, illustrated with some of his own pictures, was published posthumously as A subaltern's odyssey. The book revealed that his enthusiasm for war expressed itself as forcefully in letters to his family in 1916 as it had been to me fifty years later. [4]

---

[2] Lindsay, The London Scottish in the Great War, 48–53.
[3] See Alex Danchev, '"Bunking" and debunking: the controversies of the 1960s', in Bond (ed.), The First World War and British military history, 263, 279–81.
[4] Talbot Kelly, A subaltern's odyssey, 19.

Thus my first impressions of the western front were not derived from the war memoirs of Siegfried Sassoon or the poetry of Wilfred Owen. They came later. Indeed, it required the combination of Benjamin Britten's *War requiem* (1961) and student outrage at America's involvement in Vietnam to elevate Owen to canonical status. Today in Britain most schoolchildren learn about the war through its literary legacy. The differences in approach are profound. The war's association with adventure, excitement, courage, and even purpose has been replaced by its connotations of suffering, waste, and tragedy. In truth, as my grandfather recognized—at least implicitly—neither is exclusive of the other.

Moreover, these themes are, by virtue of their metaphysical nature, universal and timeless. The emphasis on the experience of the war has made it more immediate than could any discussion of grand strategy or industrial mobilization. Or at least, that was the case in the 1970s and 1980s. But the end of the Cold War gave even the political events of 1914–18 a relevance. The First World War broke the Austro-Hungarian empire, and so unleashed the nationalisms of south-eastern Europe, creating volatility in the inter-war period and chronic instability at the century's end. The result has been to clothe the Habsburgs not only with nostalgia but even with far-sightedness. From the collapse of another empire, that of Russia, emerged the Soviet Union, a child not just of revolution but of the war itself. The end of communism in 1989–90 gave birth to the notion of the 'short' twentieth century, an idea which brings the war closer, at times making it seem even more relevant to our lives today than the events of 1939–45.

Thus, the fact that my approach to the war has changed is in part a reflection of the length of time it has taken me to write this volume. It is now much longer than Cruttwell's. Some explanations, if not excuses, are required.

The major general histories of the war in English available in the 1980s were, above all, military histories, narrowly defined. Even Cruttwell, by training a historian of international relations, devoted, according to Liddell Hart's calculations, only 16 per cent of his book to non-military aspects.[5] Therefore, when I began my own work I assumed that I could take as read the military history of the war. My task was to graft on to it the historiographical developments of the 1960s and 1970s—the war's social history, the debate on causes and war aims, the mobilization of the economies. That agenda remains. But I also soon discovered the omissions in the English-language military histories of the war.

Liddell Hart's is more important than Cruttwell's in understanding the background. 'For most of the world', according to H. G. Wells in his novel of 1916, *Mr Britling sees it through*, the war 'came as an illimitable multitude of

[5] Strachan, '"The Real War"', in Bond (ed.), *First World War and British military history*, 59.

incoherent, loud, and confusing expressions.' However, Mr Britling, Wells's semi-autobiographical hero, spent its early weeks 'doing his utmost to see the war, to simplify it and extract the essence of it until it could be apprehended as something epic and explicable, as a stateable issue'.[6] Of course, he failed. But in 1930 Liddell Hart succeeded. Much of his agenda still preoccupies English-language historians. *The real war* posed as an objective analysis of military operations. In truth it is a sustained critique of the British high command, and its purpose is more didactic than historical. Recent scholars have done much to answer Liddell Hart, using primary sources to confirm him when he was right, to correct him when he was wrong, and above all to write analyses that are more dispassionate without being apologetic. The result is that today our understanding of Britain's conduct of the war on land is probably more profound than it is for that of any other belligerent.

But in pursuing this story British military historians have corrected only one of Liddell Hart's failings, and in doing so have still marched to the beat of his drum. They have not broken the bounds of his own Anglocentricism. A major premiss of this volume is that the First World War was global from its outset, and its treatment aims to reflect that. Those geared to the biases of the anglophone tradition will find the western front less dominant than they have come to expect, and the British army's role within it (especially for this early stage of the war) correspondingly reduced.

The real war concludes with a long and comprehensive bibliography in a range of languages. It conveys the impression that it is an authoritative synthesis of the literature on the war then available. In reality Liddell Hart could not read German, and there is little evidence that he used what had been published in French. Moreover, by 1930 the main official histories of the war had got no further than the year 1914; neither the British nor German histories of land operations were completed until after 1939. One of the delights of my own research has been discovering the variety and richness of the publications of the inter-war period. The Carnegie series on the war's social and economic history remains unsurpassed. No subsequent French publications on the military history of the war begin to overtake in importance the serried ranks of *Les Armées françaises dans la grande guerre*, with its supplementary volumes of documents. And the availability, since the end of the Cold War, of the working papers of the *Reichsarchiv*, the body responsible for the German official history, has done much to confirm the value of its published work. The reluctance to use the inter-war German histories on the grounds that they are tainted by Nazism is not only chronological nonsense in some cases (much was in print before 1933) but also an absurd self-denying ordinance, given the destruction of the bulk of the German military archives in 1945. The *Reichs-*

---

[6] Wells, *Mr Britling sees it through*, 206.

archiv historians saw material we can never see; not to refer to their output is a cloak for little more than laziness or monolingualism.

Thus, military history has assumed a priority in writing this book as insistent as every other historical sub-discipline. The project has consequently grown to embrace three volumes. They are to be divided as follows. This, the first, focuses on 1914 itself. The second, to be called *No quarter*, will cover 1915 and 1916. It will embrace the crisis for liberalism with which the war confronted the belligerent powers by summer of the latter year, and it will conclude with the failure of the peace moves (and the war aims associated with them) at the year's end. The third volume, *Fall out*, will begin with the economic and strategic strains of the winter of 1916–17, which formed the background to revolution and pacifism in 1917. It will review the collapse of Russia and the entry of the United States, and the consequences of both for the events of 1918. The volume, and the trilogy, will close not just with the peace settlement but also with an assessment of the war's cultural and social legacy.

The chronological structure is provided by a military historical narrative for the major theatres of war, including the Balkans, Italy, and the Ottoman empire. The western and eastern fronts are considered in turn and year by year. But connected to this spine are a series of themes, developed as independent chapters at the point where chronology makes their consideration most pressing, but analysed for a longer period and in some cases for the entire war. This first volume, for example, contains in Chapter 10 a discussion of war finance throughout the war. It is treated here because it was a pressing issue in August 1914 itself. It is treated as a whole for the sake of coherence. By contrast, the story of industrial mobilization is only taken to 1916, on the grounds that in that year a second 're-mobilization' took place which must be set in the context of the battles of Verdun and the Somme. Blockade, although instituted by the British in 1914, will not be discussed in its own right until the third volume, the point at which it could be deemed significant to the war's outcome and at which comparisons with U-boat war are instructive.

Of course such a structure imposes penalties. The decision to delay consideration of propaganda until later means that the issue of German atrocities in Belgium, a key feature of the 1914 debate, is only mentioned indirectly in this first volume. The soldiers' experience of the war and the maintenance of morale feed into the mutinies of 1917; they will therefore be discussed at that point, although clearly they are crucial to any understanding of the fighting from the war's outbreak.

The purpose of the thematic chapters is above all comparative. This, I would claim, is what is 'new' about 'yet another history of the war' (to answer the inevitable questions of friends and colleagues). The effect of such comparisons is to put what have been seen as peculiarly national events in context; for example, the shells crisis which brought down Britain's last Liberal government was reflected in every other belligerent. Comparative history both highlights gaps in the state of our knowledge and helps to cover them. This is not just a plea for a new generation to maximize the opportunities presented by the opening of archives in Russia and the former German Democratic Republic, but also a recognition of how little has been done with some of the archives which have been open much longer. Shell production in Britain *after* the establishment of the Ministry of Munitions is a case in point; so too is the manufacture of arms in France. When I wrote the first version of this volume's Chapter 2, that on war enthusiasm, the only careful and archivally based study of the subject was Jean-Jacques Becker's for France; in the last decade we have found out much more about Germany, but we still know far too little about most of the other belligerents, including Russia, Austria-Hungary, and Britain.

I began the actual writing of this volume in 1988–9, when given a year's sabbatical leave by Corpus Christi College, Cambridge, and I had virtually completed a first draft in 1993 when, as a consequence of my appointment to the chair of modern history at Glasgow in 1992, I became head of department. Since then I have been rewriting and incorporating fresh material, a process completed thanks to the generosity of the British Academy, which elected me its Thank Offering to Britain Fellow for 1998–9. In general I have taken the eightieth anniversary of the armistice, November 1998, as the cut-off point for bibliographical purposes.

Most of the research and writing for this book was therefore completed while I was in Cambridge, serving for over a decade first as Admissions Tutor and then as Senior Tutor of my college. I could not have sustained serious scholarship against the demands of teaching, but above all administration, without the support of Sally Braithwaite, a secretary without peer. Her ability to head off callers, deal with crises, and yet determine what was urgent and what not, was matched by her cheerfulness and her capacity to read not only my writing but also my mind. Most of the college came to realize what I knew from the outset: that tutorial business would function just the same whether I was there or not.

Cambridge was then a centre of First World War scholarship. But I developed a particular debt to two Fellows of Pembroke. Clive Trebilcock taught me about the relationship between economic history and military history: Chapter 11 is its reflection. Jay Winter, in getting me to take part in the teaching of 'European society and the First World War: Britain, France and Germany, 1914–1920', widened my horizons immeasurably, as did many of the undergraduates whom I taught as a result.

In Glasgow, those who have taken my special subject 'Strategy and Society: Britain and Germany in the First World War' have performed a similar function. Unfortunately secretarial support has been replaced by computers, an inadequate substitute in my case. Before that process got fully under way Patricia Ferguson typed Chapters 10 and 11, a penance which no doubt gave her retirement an even greater aura of relief. The in-built obsolescence of computers and their software has considerably increased the obstacles in completing a long-running project such as this. In under a decade Word Star, Word Perfect, Word, and Word for Windows have succeeded each other without being fully compatible. Patrik Andell put the entire book into a single system, an achievement which eluded the university's computing system, but even he could not rescue much of the formatting.

All my debts to others cannot be fully conveyed here. Those who have suggested books, sent me material, exchanged ideas, or provided other support include: Holger Afflerbach, Ross Anderson, Christopher Andrew, Annette Becker, Geoffrey Best, Matthew Buck, Deborah Cohen, Wilhelm Deist, Simon Dixon, Michael Epkenhans, Martin Farr, Niall Ferguson, Robert Foley, Stig Förster, David French, Peter Gatrell, John Gooch, Dominick Graham, Keith Grieves, David Hermann, Holger Herwig, Gerhard Hirschfeld, Nicholas Hope, Sir Michael Howard, Gregory Martin, Evan Mawdsley, Michael Moss, Harold Nelson, Avner Offer, Maurice Pearton, Daniel Segesser, Dennis Showalter, David Stevenson, Norman Stone, and Tim Travers. I have benefited from the stimulus of several conferences, but should mention in particular the series of seminars organized by Brian Bond, which resulted in the volume which he edited, *The First World War and British military history* (1991). Alan and Sue Warner have put me up, and put up with me, on countless occasions in London, and Peter and Angelina Jenkins were as welcoming in Paris. To those I have failed to mention I apologize.

My family has of course had to bear the lot of all authors' families—physical absence when away writing or researching, and mental absence when physically present. I am conscious of the opportunities lost, and even now cannot claim it is over. Claire Blunden said in 1981 of her husband, Edmund, author of *Undertones of war,* that until he died in 1976 no day passed in which he did not refer to the war.[7] When I repeated that story in my own wife's hearing, she remarked that she knew how Claire Blunden felt. Another writer of one of the best war memoirs, albeit one whose marital life was not quite as complex as that of Blunden, Guy Chapman, author of *A passionate prodigality,* likened the war to a mistress; I hope that my wife, however demanding she may feel the writing of this book to have been, will not see its history in the same light.

Hew Strachan

[7] *The Times,* 9 Nov. 1981.

1

THE ORIGINS OF
THE WAR

GERMANY AS A WORLD POWER

To begin at the end.[1] At Versailles, on 28 June 1919, the Germans, albeit reluctantly, acceded to the peace terms imposed upon them by the victorious powers. Although Britain, France, and the United States had made most of the running, twenty-five other states were signatory to the treaty. By it, in article 231, they asserted not only the responsibility of the defeated for the loss and damage incurred as a result of the war, but also that the war had been 'imposed upon them by the aggression of Germany and her allies'.

The Germans had already made clear their rejection of the charge. On 27 May, in a fruitless endeavour to overcome the intransigence of the victors, four distinguished professors—two of them of seminal importance in the world of scholarship: Hans Delbrück, the effective founder of academic military history, and Max Weber, the political theorist—signed a memorandum claiming that Germany had fought a defensive war against Russian tsarism. Although beaten in the short-term debate, the German government fought back. A long-term project, examining not merely the immediate causes of the war but the entire range of international relations since 1871, was put in train. The Foreign Office assumed responsibility for the volumes, and ensured that the activities which it sponsored and the publications which it produced became the basis for all

---

[1] In addition to books specified in subsequent footnotes, the following works have been of general assistance throughout this chapter: Albertini, *Origins of the war*; Berghahn, *Germany and the approach of war*; Bridge and Bullen, *Great powers and the European states system*; Droz, *Les causes*; Fischer, *War of illusions*; Jarausch, *Enigmatic chancellor*; Joll, *Origins*; Kaiser, *Journal of modern history*, LV (1983), 442–74; Keiger, *France and the origins*; Kennedy, *Rise*; Koch (ed.), *Origins*; Krumeich, *Armaments*; Steiner, *Britain and the origins*; Williamson, *Politics of grand strategy*.

serious research working on the war's causes. Access to the documents once
they had been published was denied to subsequent and possibly more independent scholars; a separate Reichstag inquiry—designed originally by the left
to put the blame on the right, and then by the right to blame the left—dragged
on and was overtaken; and the tactic of placing the events of July 1914 in the
context of the previous decades successfully muddied the precise issue of war
guilt.[2] Gradually the Germans' rejection of article 231 gained ground, although
more conspicuously in Britain and America than in France. The Versailles
Treaty itself was not ratified by the United States Senate and it became
abundantly clear that the peace settlement had not resolved the frontier
problems of eastern and central Europe in a convincing manner. In particular,
the injustices done to Germans residing in the successor states of the Austro-
Hungarian empire came to be widely recognized.

In Britain in 1933 Lloyd George, who in July 1911—three years before the
outbreak of the war—had as chancellor of the exchequer delivered a clear
warning to Germany, and who in December 1918 had been returned to power
as prime minister on a wave of anti-German sentiment, began his war memoirs
by stating that nobody in July 1914 had wanted European war, that nobody had
expected it, and that 'the nations slithered over the brink'.[3] In the United States
Sidney B. Fay, professor of history at Harvard, wrote in *The origins of the world
war*, first published in 1928, that 'all the powers were more or less responsible',
and that 'the War was caused by the system of international anarchy involved
in alliances, armaments and secret diplomacy'.[4] By shifting the blame to '-isms'
rather than individuals, to militarism, nationalism, and economic imperialism, Fay exculpated Germany. Only by re-emphasizing the immediate causes
of the war, by stating that it was the resolve of Germany and Austria-Hungary
during the crisis of July 1914 that enabled the war to occur, could the doyen of
France's war historians, Pierre Renouvin, put across a Germanophobe perspective.[5] In the 1930s, for most of the English-speaking world, as indeed for
Germany, the arguments of Fay and Lloyd George were the current orthodoxy.

The Second World War changed this perspective, albeit gradually rather
than immediately. From the vantage-point of the second half of the century the
two world wars could be seen as part of a whole, the years 1918 to 1939
representing a truce rather than a definitive break. Furthermore, given the
relative lack of controversy about the origins of the second war, that it was
caused by German aggression, and that Hitler—whether as leader of an
enraptured German people or as embodiment of a deeply-rooted national
will—was the prime culprit, it became possible to project back onto Germany

[2] Langdon, *July 1914*, 20–65; Herwig, *International Security*, XII (1972), 5–44; Droz, *Les causes*, 12–19.
[3] Lloyd George, *War memoirs*, i. 32.
[4] Fay, *Origins of the world war*, i. 2.
[5] Renouvin, *La Crise européenne*, 1939 edn., 183.

before 1933 the insights and continuities derived from a study of Nazi Germany.

In particular, the causes of the First World War could be re-examined in the light of those of the Second. The debate was also set in a general context, that of the peculiarities of Germany history, of Germany's *Sonderweg* (special path). Simply put, Germany was portrayed as a state where militarism and authoritarianism—partly owing to its Prussian origins, partly to its strategically vulnerable position—had been more easily exploited by leaders of a conservative and expansionist bent. The political thought of the Enlightenment and the bourgeois legacy of industrialization, which in west European states left a grounding of constitutionalism, in Germany was suborned by nationalism. The right used nationalism for its own conservative ends, and liberalism—in 1813, 1848, and 1919—did not take strong root. Hitler was presented as the climax of what went before.

It was against this background that the more specific controversy over the origins of the First World War was renewed. The key works, *Griff nach der Weltmacht* (*Germany's aims in the First World War*) and *Krieg der Illusionen* (*The war of illusions*), both by Fritz Fischer and published in 1961 and 1969 respectively, placed the burden of war guilt once again at the feet of Germany. Much of the detail of Fischer's case will be considered later in this book. Despite their opaque and dense presentation and despite the lack of a succinct argument, Fischer's books rent German historians into deeply entrenched camps. For them, more than for historians of other nationalities, the issue was fraught, since the overall thesis—the arguments about *Sonderweg* and the ongoing preoccupation with the effect of Hitler—concerned continuity in German history, and therefore was as much about Germany's current identity as about its past. The subtleties and differences of the interpretations put forward within the two camps were subsumed by the fundamental divide. Fischer's opponents, who constituted the majority, had to accept combat on Fischer's terms: in other words, they had to address the question of German expansionism before 1914, to ask whether Germany was prepared to go to war in fulfilment of its aims, to decide whether all the dominant groups in pre-war German society could be found culpable, and to consider whether their motivation was to use foreign policy to avert an internal social and political crisis. Fischer himself, in the foreword to *Krieg der Illusionen*, spelled out the primacy of domestic policy:

the aim was to consolidate the position of the ruling classes with a successful imperialist foreign policy, indeed it was hoped a war would resolve the growing social tensions.... By 1912 at any rate the domestic crisis was apparent. The decision to go to war in 1914 was, in addition to the domestic considerations, based above all on military reflections which in turn depended on economic and political objectives. All these factors—and as regards both the masses and the Emperor there were also the psychological elements—the Government was forced to consider. If one looks at all these forces it is possible to see a clear continuity of aim before and during the war.[6]

In 1967 Immanuel Geiss, a pupil of Fischer, put it more pithily:

The determination of the German Empire—the most powerful conservative force in the world after Tsarist Russia—to uphold the conservative and monarchic principles by any means against the rising flood of democracy, plus its *Weltpolitik*, made war inevitable.[7]

In practice, this sort of argument is very hard to substantiate in precise terms from the evidence now available. But the challenge that Fischer, Geiss, and others issued compels historians—in addition to undertaking a fundamental reconsideration of the role of Germany—to make two connections not so readily made in the 1930s. Both are connections which come more easily to a generation to whom nuclear weapons—by finding their role as deterrents rather than as weapons of war—link more closely the issues of war and peace, and at the same time obscure the divisions between purely military functions and those of civilian society. First, the Fischer controversy forces historians to dispense with their traditional division between the causes of a war, a long-standing interest of academics and exhaustively worked over in undergraduate essays, and its course, the task of military historians and all too often neglected by those same undergraduates. Fischer's revisionism began with the development of German war aims during the war itself, and worked backwards to the war's origins, finding continuity between the two and using one to illuminate the other. In 1934, by contrast, C. R. M. F. Cruttwell's history of the war, reprinted as recently as 1991, felt it unnecessary to discuss the war's origins. Secondly, Fischer restated the interconnection between domestic policy and foreign policy. The point was well taken: recent studies of other nations and the origins of the war, and of their subsequent aims, have not been able to treat foreign policy as a discrete entity. Even more must this apply to the conduct of the war itself, frequently described as the first total war and entailing the mobilization of all the belligerents' industrial and economic resources.

Therefore, the initial task must be—as it was for the peacemakers of 1919—to consider Germany and its role in the origins of the war.

On 18 January 1871, at Versailles, in the same hall where, almost five decades later, the leaders of the new republic would have to accept defeat and humiliation, the king of Prussia was declared emperor of a united Germany. Technically the new nation was a federation: the independent German states retained

---

[6] Fischer, *War of illusions*, pp. viii–ix; on Fischer's reaction to the debate, see Fisher *World power or decline*; Droz, *Les causes*, provides an excellent historiographical survey.
[7] I. Geiss, 'Origins of the first world war', in Koch (ed.), *Origins*, 46.

their own monarchs, assemblies, taxation, and—in the cases of Saxony, Württemberg, and Bavaria (as well as Prussia)—their own armed forces. To balance the national parliament, the Reichstag, which was elected by universal manhood suffrage and by a secret ballot, there was an upper chamber, the Bundesrat, made up of representatives of the individual federal states. But in practice the achievement of unification, although long sought by liberal nationalists, was not a triumph for constitutionalism but for the monarchical-aristocratic principle on the one hand and for Prussia on the other. In ousting Austria from Germany, and in effecting unification, Bismarck and Prussian junkerdom had made fellow-travellers of the national liberals, had usurped nationalism for conservative ends, and had thus split liberal loyalties. Furthermore, universal suffrage, by linking the lower classes more closely as allies of the monarchy, was designed to isolate the liberals yet further. The Reichstag was therefore weak because its political parties were weak; furthermore, even should they manage to co-operate effectively, the constitution was so designed that Prussia would act as a counterweight. Prussia held seventeen out of fifty-eight votes in the Bundesrat: it was therefore in a position to block legislation. And the Prussian Chamber of Deputies was elected not by universal suffrage, but by a complicated three-class franchise weighted according to the amount of tax paid. The majority of federal ministers either held office by virtue of their Prussian appointment (the Prussian minister of war was de facto minister for all Germany) or were themselves Prussian: including the chancellor, they were accountable not to the Reichstag but to the Kaiser. The Kaiser himself, in addition to being the king of Prussia, had direct control of those areas of government where Germany most manifested itself as a nation, in foreign policy and in control of the army.

Implicit, therefore, within the new Germany was a host of interlocking structural tensions that required the mollifications of national success and victory on the battlefield. Fundamental was Germany's status as an industrializing power: Germany industrialized late but very rapidly, the value of her output increasing well over six times between 1855 and 1913. In 1870 agriculture still contributed 40 per cent of the total national product and employed 45 per cent of the total active population, but by 1910 it constituted 25 per cent of the total national product and as early as 1895 employed only 36 per cent of the workforce.[8] A political structure designed to meet the needs of an agricultural aristocracy abetted by a compliant peasantry increasingly did not reflect the true range of German society. Economic power shifted from Westphalia to the Ruhr, from East Prussia to Silesia; the contrast between Germany's ill-adapted constitution on the one hand and the envy of western liberals for the quality and rigour of its secondary and higher education on the other became more

[8] Tables in Trebilcock, *Industrialisation*, 433–5.

pronounced. With the growth of the urban working class, the device of universal suffrage posed a new threat to the Bismarckian settlement, that of socialism. A united and effective majority in the Reichstag could upset the checks and balances so carefully built into the constitution. If this were to happen, the highly personalized nature of Germany's government and the latent differences between the states could be exposed. Germany in 1871 was sufficiently centralized to upset the feelings of individual states, particularly those of Bavaria but also of Prussia, and yet insufficiently united to get the true benefits of central government. Given the divisions within the Reichstag, the chancellor's role was to manage the parties, to play one off against another; and yet he himself remained without a true party base. His authority rested on the support of the Kaiser and on the personal relationship between the two of them. This combination of socio-economic trends at one extreme and of individual primacy at the other highlighted the central ambiguity with regard to the constitution itself: because it was given from above, it could as easily be taken away. Political rights were not axiomatic.

In 1888 Wilhelm II ascended the throne, his father's reign cut short by cancer of the throat. The new Kaiser was young, energetic, and for many the representative of the waxing vigour of Germany itself. But the immaturity concomitant with these qualities was never outgrown, never supplemented with the wisdom of experience. 'Not quite sane' was a description that readily occurred to observers. His withered arm had prompted the withdrawal of his mother's love, leaving him deeply insecure, with a strong animosity towards her and towards her native land of Britain. He constantly asserted his personality and prejudices, but proved himself unable to sustain the hard work or the serious thought required to endow them with consistency. Anxious to be the shining leader, he succeeded only in endowing his decisions with theatricality rather than substance. The aged Bismarck concluded that, 'The Kaiser is like a balloon. If you do not hold fast to the string, you never know where he will be off to.'[9]

The Kaiser was the public image of Germany: both before and during the war his upturned moustache and spiked helmet shaped foreigners' perceptions. Nor was the image without reality. The Kaiser exercised personal rule, in which he devoutly believed, and which was allowed him by the ambiguities of the constitution, in two key ways. First, he had the right of appointment to all major governmental and service posts; and secondly, once appointed, a large number of those officials had the privilege of direct audience with the monarch. The army was the main buttress to Wilhelm's idea of monarchical

---

[9] Quoted by Paul Kennedy, in Röhl and Sombart (eds.), *Kaiser Wilhelm II*, 155. Much of what follows rests on the essays in this book, particularly those of Röhl and Deist, and on Isabel V. Hull, *The entourage of Kaiser Wilhelm II*.

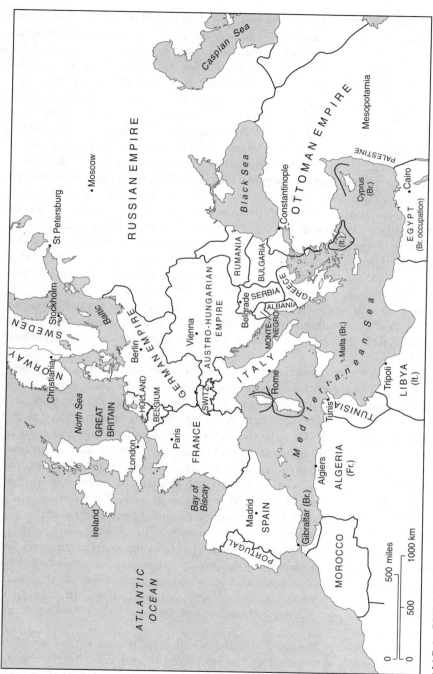

MAP 1. EUROPE IN 1914

authority, and by 1914 over forty officers—including all those commanding the military districts of Germany—had access to him. In addition, his personal entourage at court was increasingly dominated by military influences. Wilhelm himself said that it was in regimental life that he found the security, the family and friends that he had hitherto lacked. But the officers with whom he surrounded himself were even more conservative and traditional than the officer corps as a whole. Nine out of ten came from noble families, and nineteen out of twenty from landowning or military backgrounds; the cavalry dominated over the technical arms, and the guards over other types of infantry. Furthermore, once attached to the court an officer might stay a very long time: 108 served continuously throughout the reign. The entourage constituted a cocoon into which the influences of industry and commerce, western and southern Germany could only rarely penetrate. The dominance of these military and traditional influences was never complete, but gradually— and especially after 1906–8—it grew. And as it grew the contrast between it and the rest of the army increased also. A major plank of the Kaiser's personal rule was his supreme command of the armed forces, but his grasp of the complexities of exercising that command remained rudimentary.

Moreover, it was in foreign policy that the Kaiser's personal rule remained most clearly untrammelled by constitutional considerations, and it was through imperialism that the Kaiser sought to legitimize the authority which he craved.

Germany's position in Europe after 1871 was at once threatening and vulnerable—threatening because central Europe was now dominated by a major power, casting shadows over Russia to the east and France to the west, and vulnerable because the new state had long, exposed land frontiers in the same directions. For Germany the danger of a revivified France, anxious to revenge the defeat of 1870–1 and to regain the provinces of Alsace-Lorraine, was real enough: the memory of Napoleon's victories and the subsequent French occupation of Germany coloured Bismarck's determination that France should be weak and isolated as long as possible. But simultaneously Bismarck sought to reassure the states of Europe, to accustom them to the presence of a united and powerful Germany. The alliance with Austria-Hungary of 1879, guaranteeing mutual support in the event of an attack by Russia, therefore had stability as its primary objective. Bismarck hoped to restrain Austria in its dealings with Russia, and to persuade Russia that, rather than war with Germany, it should seek better relations. In 1882 Italy joined Germany and Austria-Hungary, and thus the Triple Alliance came into being.

In 1890 Wilhelm dismissed Bismarck—with good reason, as the chancellor was increasingly dominated by his own vanities and decreasingly able to manage the Reichstag. The situation which Bismarck left was in large measure the legacy of the settlement which he had achieved in 1871. Agricultural depression and economic recession had highlighted the differences between East Elbian grain producers anxious to protect their frontier with high tariffs against imported food (particularly from Russia) on the one hand, and the representatives of new industry keen to free trade so as to secure markets for their manufactured goods on the other. The mutually reinforcing weaknesses of the Reichstag and of its parties encouraged these economic interest groups to form extra-parliamentary pressure groups, which themselves confirmed the weakness of the political structures. Within the Reichstag the effects of universal suffrage began to be felt as the social democrat vote almost trebled between 1877 and 1890, and reached over 2 million—or 27 per cent of the whole—in 1898. The split in the liberal vote, already exploited by Bismarck, was deepened as the national liberals supported the interests of industry, while the left-wing liberals, the Progressives, lacked organization and were unclear in their response to social democracy. The independent peasant farmer, the small shopkeeper, the white-collar worker—the so-called *Mittelstand* of Germany— alienated by big business and hence by national liberalism, turned to conservatism, or—if Catholic—to the Catholic Centre party. To combat these fissiparous tendencies and, above all, to rally industry and agriculture to a common cause and to oppose socialism, Germany needed—it was argued increasingly from 1895—a policy that would unite and reconcile rather than divide, a *Sammlungspolitik*.

The instrument chosen to effect the rallying of Germany was one that lay specifically within the Kaiser's competence, a more nationalist and imperialist foreign policy. It was Wilhelm who appointed the main architect of *Weltpolitik*, Bernhard von Bülow, first as foreign minister in 1897 and then in 1900 as chancellor, and in 1897 Bülow himself stated that he would be a 'tool' of the Kaiser's personal rule.[10] Bülow subscribed to the feeling of inevitability associated with German overseas expansion, the product of Germany's status as a major power and of the need for markets to satisfy its burgeoning manufacturing industry. In the late nineteenth century interstate relations frequently employed the vocabulary of social Darwinism. The belief that man's environment, rather than his individuality, determined his behaviour challenged liberal views of the relationship between the individual and the state. Rather than a minimalist role for the latter to allow the fruition of the former, social Darwinism suggested the subordination of the first to the second, and went on to clothe the nation with an identity and vitality of its own. States were dynamic entities, rising or declining according to fitness. Max Weber, in his inaugural lecture as professor of political economy at the University of Freiburg in 1895, reminded his countrymen:

[10] Hull, *The entourage of Kaiser Wilhelm II*, 97; see also Craig, *Modern Germany*, 273.

We must understand that the unification of Germany was a youthful prank performed by the nation in its old age and that, because of its expensiveness, it would have been better left undone if it was meant to be the end and not the beginning of a German policy of world power.[11]

But the connection between *Weltpolitik* and the war's outbreak is not a direct one. What *Weltpolitik* certainly did not imply was territorial expansion within Europe: the incorporation of subordinate non-national groupings into a greater *Reich* could only promote the fissiparous tendencies *Weltpolitik* was designed to dampen. Rather, the first focus of *Weltpolitik* could not have been geographically more distant—its hub was China and its apogee the acquisition of Kiaochow in 1897.[12] That Germany should wish to obtain colonies did not in itself surprise or alarm to an excessive degree the power most likely to be affected by that decision, Great Britain. In 1890 the two countries collaborated to the extent of exchanging Heligoland and Zanzibar. But as the disparate threads of domestic, colonial, and naval policy were woven together, so the whole acquired a vocabulary that was much more threatening to the status quo. The notion of pax Germanica replacing the pax Britannica, however irenic in theory, promised radical revisionism in practice. By 1914 the reality had not come close to matching the rhetoric. The empire which Germany had acquired barely deserved the title: it covered a million square miles, attracted one in a thousand of Germany's emigrants, absorbed a paltry 3.8 per cent of Germany's overseas investment, and accounted for 0.5 per cent of its overseas trade.[13] It was the manner of German foreign policy more than its objects, let alone its achievements, which was to provoke the other powers before 1914.

Nor was the conclusion that German objectives remained consonant with peace a misplaced one. For all the provocative phrases of Weber or his publicist, Friedrich Naumann, Bülow's objectives remained domestic. The purpose of *Weltpolitik* was to achieve integration within Germany, to reconcile agriculture and industry, to woo social democracy. By pointing liberalism overseas, in the pursuit of markets, Bülow hoped to minimize the friction with conservatism, and to produce the economic benefits which might still the political demands of the workers. Politically, *Weltpolitik* manifested itself in a series of bargains between interest groups; externally, it aimed at a sequence of minor successes. It spoke the language of a grand design but practised short-term expediency. However, the longer it survived the more its rhetoric created exaggerated popular expectations. And, given that *Sammlungspolitik* rested on

---

[11] Quoted by Craig, in *New York Review of Books*, 18 Feb. 1988 (referring to Mommsen, *Weber*).

[12] Peter Winzen, 'Zur Genesis von Weltmacht—Konzept und Weltpolitik', in Röhl (ed.), *Der Ort Kaiser Wilhelms II.*

[13] Steiner, *Britain and the origins*, 68–71; Herwig, *Luxury fleet*, ch. 6, esp. pp. 106–7.

ad hoc compromise, it had constantly to present itself with new targets.[14] Furthermore, the principal method used to implement *Weltpolitik*, the creation of a sizeable German navy, carried with it all the elements that would generate fresh problems—the challenge to Britain as a seapower, the need for hyperbolic and expansionist propaganda to get financial support for ship construction, and the potential subordination of diplomacy to arms policy. Much of Bülow's effort in foreign policy was to be directed to providing the cover for the fleet's creation.

As with *Weltpolitik* and Bülow, so with the navy and its architect, Alfred von Tirpitz, the Kaiser's role was direct and vital. Wilhelm's personal passion for his fleet was the customary blend of absurdity and energetic enthusiasm. He felt it appropriate to wear his admiral's uniform to performances of Wagner's *Der fliegende Holländer*, and yet was fired by technical interests in the ships of the British navy and in 1894 read Alfred Thayer Mahan's influential book *The influence of seapower upon history*. Seeing Germany as a potential colonial power, Wilhelm at first advocated the construction of cruisers, but in 1895 the naval high command recommended the creation of a battle fleet able to meet the French or the Russians in a major action in home waters. It argued that Germany's ability to flex its oceanic muscles was entirely dependent on its capacity to break out of the North Sea, and thus cruisers could not be effective in isolation but only as adjuncts to battleships. The Kaiser was convinced and ordered the planning of a fleet of twenty-five battleships. The Reichstag was less easily persuaded, and so in 1896–7 the need for a press campaign to popularize the navy and thus win over the Reichstag had become clear. In June 1897 the Kaiser appointed Tirpitz, still a relatively junior admiral, to head the Imperial Naval Office; his was the responsibility of guiding the naval programme through the Reichstag.[15]

The domestic functions of the navy laws were conciliatory. The navy was above all a creature of the new Germany, not of the old Prussia: unlike the army, it was a product of unification, an armed service that belonged to all the nation, and particularly to the industrialized middle class. Its officer corps was more bourgeois than that of the army (although its members were socially divided from within, and its middle-class origins did not prevent it from aping the mannerisms of the Prussian aristocracy). The creation of a regular building pattern was designed to please heavy industry, to provide a buffer against cyclical depression, and to take the sting out of socialism by ensuring full employment. These were the strengths on which Tirpitz could base his propaganda effort: he established an information service in the naval office to

---

[14] Amidst the vast literature on this subject, Kaiser, *Journal of Modern History*, LV (1983), 442–74, speaks much sense.

[15] The main works in English on the naval programme are Herwig, *Luxury fleet*, and Steinberg, *Yesterday's deterrent*.

liaise with the press, and by 1914 the Navy League—which was founded in 1898—could boast a membership of over a million. Tirpitz proved a consummate manager of the Reichstag, of its parties and its parliamentary committees, persuading its deputies that the fleet was a vital auxiliary to the expansion of German overseas trade, that its size would be modest and its purpose defensive, and that a fixed programme which would tie the Reichstag was not a programme without controls. When opposition within parliament became too strong, when liberal imperialism began to smell a rat, Tirpitz cowed it with the popular support of the pressure groups—the Colonial Society and the Pan-German League, and in due course the Navy League. The broad lines of his policy—the emphasis on battleships rather than cruisers, and the calculation of the fleet's overall size on the basis of arithmetic rather than combat efficiency—had already been established before he took up office. In 1898 the Reichstag approved a target of nineteen battleships, eight armoured cruisers, and twelve large and thirty light cruisers, to be completed by April 1904; it also agreed that battleships should be replaced every twenty-five years. In 1900 a new law aimed for thirty-eight battleships, twenty armoured cruisers, and thirty-eight light cruisers. Tirpitz planned that Germany should possess sixty capital ships by 1920, and hoped to have the cycle of their replacement so fixed that the Reichstag's approval would be redundant and the Kaiser's whims irrelevant.

Tirpitz had hoodwinked the Reichstag, both as to his domestic objectives and as to his international aims. The naval staff continued to plan for war with France or Russia, and viewed the possibility of hostilities against Britain with horror. But from the outset Tirpitz's putative enemy was the Royal Navy. He shared the Anglophobia of his royal master, and he linked commercial rivalry with Britain to the navalist propaganda emanating from the Imperial Naval Office. Tirpitz hoped to create a sufficiently large fleet to ensure that the Royal Navy would not risk a naval battle with the Germans for fear that—even if it won the engagement—it would then be too weak to face a third naval power. He recognized the possibility of a pre-emptive strike by the British before the German fleet was complete, a rerun of Nelson's sinking of the Danish fleet in harbour at Copenhagen, and so required Bülow's foreign policy to create the right conditions to cover the period of vulnerability by mollifying the British and even seeking agreement with them. On almost every count, Tirpitz's calculations with regard to likely British responses proved to be wrong.

Britain put its foreign policy through a rapid and dramatic reorientation after 1900. However, this was less the product of the new circumstances in Europe, and more a response to an accumulation of older and more global pressures. Until the middle years of the nineteenth century Britain led the world in industrial production; free trade guaranteed access to world markets because no other country could manufacture so much so cheaply. But from then on other countries—particularly the United States and Germany—began to catch up: in 1870 Britain commanded 32 per cent of the world's manufacturing capacity, but by 1910 it had only 14.7 percent, behind both Germany (15.9 per cent) and the United States (35.3 per cent).[16] London remained the hub of the world's banking, insurance, and shipping markets until 1914, and Britain's invisible exports therefore helped mask its relative industrial decline. Nonetheless, it followed that for some the doctrinaire commitment to free trade—appropriate to the days of easy industrial supremacy—became an increasing, if self-imposed, burden. Given British opposition to protection, formal empire, the direct control of territory, with its guaranteed markets made more economic sense in 1900 than it had in 1850. However, the empire itself was enormously expensive, particularly in relation to the costs of its defence. The colonial ambitions of the other, now industrialized, European powers meant that the yardsticks by which the forces had to be judged were not simply—if they ever had been—the technological and military margin sufficient to defeat Zulus or Pathans. Seapower was the primary means by which free trade had been sustained, and by which both the home country and the colonies guarded against external attack. But what had been a source of stability before the industrialization of the continental powers became a well-spring for insecurity thereafter. Other nations transformed their financial administration and their banking systems, and proved willing to contract debts to fund naval programmes. The introduction of the iron-clad, steam-powered battleship in 1860, and the decision in 1889 that the Royal Navy should be maintained at sufficient strength to be at least equal to the next two ranking naval powers assumed that Britain's maritime rivals would restrain themselves. They did not, and Britain's defence spending soared. In 1884 British naval expenditure was £10.7 million; by 1899—in a period of relatively constant prices—it was £24.1 million (and it was to double again by 1914). Britain's total expenditure on the navy in the seven-year period 1897 to 1904 was 78 per cent higher than in the previous septennium.[17] Britain had perforce to adopt policies which eased the fiscal burdens of naval and imperial responsibility. The Boer War, which had cost £200 million and in which not far short of half a million men had served, vividly highlighted in double fashion the precarious nature of Britain's position. The war had been marked by early defeats and had been protracted; the commitment to it had left Britain's other possessions vulnerable and exposed. In 1901 Britain eased its problems in the western hemisphere with an agreement with the United States. In January 1902 it followed this up with a treaty with Japan, like America a rising naval power: the purpose of the treaty

---

[16] Kennedy, *Anglo-German antagonism*, 291.
[17] Offer, *First World War*, 6; Sumida, *In defence of naval supremacy*, 7, 13–23.

was limited and local, to help Britain balance Russia in the Far East and to ease the Royal Navy of its burdens in Chinese waters.

The German naval laws and the tub-thumping Teutonic exploitation of British embarrassment in South Africa did not at this stage produce a Euro-centric reconstruction of British strategy and diplomacy. German behaviour between 1898 and 1901 did mean that whatever attractions an Anglo-German alliance might have had for Britain were dissipated. But the end of British isolation in relation to Europe was determined by the relative position of the European powers in Africa and Asia, not within Europe itself. Improved relations with France and Russia, the former aspiring to control of North Africa and the Mediterranean, and thus challenging British control of Egypt and the Suez route to India, and the latter expanding south and east, also towards India, were the keys of future imperial policy.

Russia, spurned by a Germany focusing its foreign policy on the simplicities of the Triple Alliance after Bismarck's fall in 1890, and anxious for French loans to finance its industrialization, had come to terms with France between 1891 and 1894. The two powers ratified a military convention by which each agreed to defend the other in the event of a German attack, or of a German-supported attack by Austria-Hungary on Russia or by Italy on France: French and Russian mobilization was to follow immediately on the mobilization of any member of the Triple Alliance. Thus, in 1904 the Russo-Japanese War in Manchuria found France allied to the former and Britain to the latter; one pressure for an Anglo-French rapprochement was that both were wedded to a policy of mutual restraint in relation to Manchuria. However, the key motivation for France behind the affirmation of the *entente cordiale*, effected on 8 April of that year, was—as for Britain—imperial. After the drubbing of 1870, French ambi-tions—or those in France possessed of ambition—had looked away from the metropolis to North Africa. Delcassé, foreign minister from 1898, was anxious to expand France's influence from its colony, Algeria, into Morocco, to the exclusion of Germany. Britain, by agreement with France on the Moroccan question, in return secured its own controls over the gates of the Mediterra-nean, Gibraltar and Egypt, and hence over the route to India, the focus of the empire. The Entente was intended to affect the naval balance here and not in the North Sea.[18]

By 1904, therefore, the context in which Bülow's *Weltpolitik* was set seemed very different from that of 1897. The composing of French and British differ-ences, the existence of secret clauses in this agreement (which actually con-cerned the division of Morocco), and the more formal Franco-Russian alliance, conjoined to play on German insecurities. Convinced that France wanted revenge for the loss of Alsace-Lorraine, determined that Britain

---

[18] Williamson, *Politics of Grand Strategy*, chs. 1 and 2.

would be challenged by the naval programme, and terrified by the strategic dilemma of a war on both its western and eastern fronts simultaneously, Germany projected its fears onto its putative opponents and in due course gave its imaginings a reality which in origin they need not have had.

German policy therefore aimed to woo Russia from France or to split France from Britain. Given Russia's weakness in 1904–5, its defeat at the hands of the Japanese and its subsequent revolution, the opportunities for the former seemed somewhat greater. In the event Russia saw any treaty with Germany as incompatible with its commitments to France, resisting the German offer of a defensive alliance in October 1904 and refusing to ratify the agreement reached between the Kaiser and the Tsar at Björkö in July 1905. The opportunity to divide Britain and France was presented by French policy in Morocco. Moroccan independence was guaranteed by the 1880 Madrid Convention. Delcassé's advancement of French interests was hardly compatible with Moroccan integrity, and on 31 March 1905 the Kaiser landed at Tangiers and declared his support for the Sultan's bid to maintain his independence.

On the face of it, despite its provocative nature, the Kaiser's action was fully justified and deserving of success. Both the French prime minister and French public opinion seemed to think so, and Delcassé—the author of France's Moroccan policy—was ousted by June. But divided counsels within Germany, themselves a reflection of the lack of centralized control, and the absence of diplomatic sensitivity turned success into humiliation.

What it seems fairly clear that Germany did *not* want was war. Many of those who argue that Germany did not plan for war in 1914 point to the 1905 crisis and show how much more favourable to Germany the international position was at that juncture. The French army was still reeling from the Dreyfus affair and from the Third Republic's continuing uncertainty as to its political loyalties. The British army was both small and focused on India. Above all, Russia's preoccupation with Japan removed the threat of a war on two fronts. The chief of the German general staff, Alfred von Schlieffen, recognized the opportunity for a preventive war. But the focus of the general staff's planning was German security in Europe; whatever German objectives in Morocco, they were not in the first instance concerned with that. Furthermore, Schlieffen's was not necessarily the dominant voice in German military counsels, let alone in Germany more generally. Of late the navy had enjoyed the higher profile, and yet Tirpitz did not regard the German fleet as ready to take on the Royal Navy. Indeed, the German navy in 1905 had no operational plan for war with Britain or with Britain and France.[19] Schlieffen recognized that the army did not have the means to attack Britain should Britain support France. Moreover,

[19] On German naval plans, see Lambi, *Navy and German power politics*, esp. 242–4, 257–60.

both Germany's allies, Italy and Austria-Hungary, looked as militarily weak as did Germany's putative opponents. In these circumstances, the caution uttered by the Prussian minister of war, von Einem, was compelling—and gained force when Schlieffen fell sick in the summer. Von Einem was particularly concerned by the fact that France had completed the re-equipment of its army with quick-firing field artillery but Germany had not.[20]

Weltpolitik, in other words a diplomatic success, not war, was Germany's purpose in 1905. But, behind the overall aim of disrupting the Entente, middle-distance German objectives diverged. Wilhelm stood for little more than he had publicly declared: an open door to Morocco was necessary given the volume of German trade. But others saw the opportunity to exchange concessions to the French for German gains elsewhere, and Friedrich von Holstein of the Foreign Ministry—to whom Bülow gave a free hand—wanted to emphasize to France the dangers of disregarding Germany.[21] The foreign office realized that militarizing the crisis, threatening war, albeit with no intention of going to war, could help it achieve these wider objectives. Delcassé regarded this posturing as bluff, but others in France, all too conscious of their military weakness, were less sure. Germany insisted on the summoning of a conference at Algeçiras in January 1906 to discuss the Moroccan question. But at the same time the Kaiser made it clear that Germany would not fight. Thus, in the subsequent deliberations Germany harvested all the disadvantages and none of the benefits that its earlier high-handedness had promised. Britain was provoked into hardening its support of France; furthermore, the Triple Alliance showed its weakness, Italy backing the Entente (and thus reflecting its own awareness of the relative naval balance in the Mediterranean) and Austria-Hungary urging Germany to be more conciliatory. The conference left France in a dominant position in Morocco.

The consequence of this, the first Moroccan crisis, was thus the reverse of that intended by Germany. The Entente gained a dynamism which it had hitherto lacked. Germany was plainly using colonial questions as an instrument in European and great power politics. Such an approach found a ready response within France. French colonial activity had been in part a substitute for the loss of status in Europe, the acquisition of empire a compensation for forfeiting Alsace-Lorraine. Popular enthusiasm for colonialism was therefore yoked to continental rivalries. Delcassé had, after all, sought out an alliance with Britain precisely to enable France the better to counter Germany. Many of the permanent civil servants within the Foreign Ministry, particularly those of the younger generation, were characterized by a blend of nationalism, colonialism, and anti-Germanism: with Delcassé's fall, French foreign policy lacked a

---

[20] Bucholz, *Moltke, Schlieffen, and Prussian war planning*, 207–8; Herrmann, *Arming of Europe*, 30–5, 37–41, 52–5; Stevenson, *Armaments and the coming of war*, 68–75.
[21] Balfour, *Kaiser*, 252–4.

guiding ministerial hand, and the civil servants became correspondingly more powerful.[22]

But it was the change in British attitudes that was really decisive in confirming the shift, and in directing colonial rivalries back into a European context. Late-nineteenth-century colonial rivalry has often been portrayed as an extra-European safety valve for the tensions of the great powers. In 1898 the French Colonel Marchand and Britain's General Kitchener had glared at each other at Fashoda, but both countries had treated their competition for the Upper Nile as a purely African problem. In 1902 and 1904 Britain had settled with Japan and France at least in order to remain isolated from Europe. But during the course of 1905 German behaviour caused the British to see the Moroccan crisis less as a colonial issue and increasingly as a European one. The Anglo-German rivalry, whose roots extended back over the previous three decades, and which had been nurtured by economic competition, now found clear political expression.

Germany's naval challenge was only a part, although the most concrete manifestation, of the two powers' mutual antagonism. The build-up of the Royal Navy pre-dated the 1898 German naval law: it was a product of the introduction of the iron-clad battleship, the two-power standard, and the need to sustain a consistent pattern of orders in order to use shipyard and industrial capacity effectively. But by 1901 the Admiralty was seriously worried by Germany's plans, and thereafter Germany provided the thrust to British naval policy. On the day before Trafalgar Day 1904 'Jackie' Fisher was appointed First Sea Lord. His brief was to cut naval spending, an objective which he believed he could achieve while simultaneously delivering gains in efficiency. By December the main outlines of his reforming programme were already clear. The combination of a steam-powered fleet with the Japanese and French agreements allowed Britain's battleships to concentrate on the North Sea without sacrificing their global mission. The redistribution scheme, which used the Atlantic Fleet at Gibraltar as a potential support for the Channel Fleet, meant that three-quarters of Britain's battleships were available to face the Germans.[23] Secondly, Fisher decided to begin work on a new and revolutionary class of battleship, the Dreadnought. In so doing he rendered obsolete Britain's existing naval superiority, but in practice he had little choice since other powers were on the brink of taking comparable decisions. Fisher's early thinking on warships was conditioned by rivalry with France and Russia, and put speed ahead of armour. Envisaging war in the Atlantic or the Pacific, he wanted a vessel whose speed would enable the Royal Navy to keep its opponents at a distance and so defeat them through long-range gunnery: he

[22] Keiger, *France and the origins*, ch. 2; Hayne, *French foreign office*, 139–40.
[23] Marder, *From the Dreadnought*, i. 40–2.

dubbed this the 'battle cruiser'. But by 1905, when the first Dreadnought was laid down, the likely enemy was Germany and the probable theatre of operations the more confined spaces of the North Sea. The ship that therefore resulted was a battleship, and her most striking feature was not her speed of 22 knots but her armament.[24] Her size enabled her to mount five twin-turrets with 12-inch guns: her broadside and her effective range were double those of a pre-Dreadnought. The battleship had secured a fresh lease of life by being able to operate outside torpedo range. Fisher's anti-Germanism was as pronounced as Tirpitz's Anglophobia, and his hopes for a preventive war with Germany in 1905 were quite sufficient to justify German fears of another Copenhagen. But in his calmer moments Fisher, like Tirpitz, rationalized his fleet as a deterrent.[25]

Simultaneous with the anti-German shift in British naval thought was a comparable and similar growth within the British Foreign Office. Some members of the diplomatic service, like Eyre Crowe, were not immune to the navalism which accompanied Fisher's reforms. But most important was a belief in the balance of power in Europe, and the conviction after 1905 that Germany represented a threat to it. In the British case, ministerial direction from December 1905 was firm and continuous. Henry Campbell-Bannerman, who became prime minister when the Liberals were returned to power that month, appointed Sir Edward Grey as his foreign secretary. Grey, a liberal imperialist, used a cross-party appeal to win Conservative support for his policies, and to remove foreign policy from party-political debate and endow it with consistency and direction. Indeed, he managed to remain remarkably independent of his own cabinet, and thus minimize any challenge from the government's own left wing. The Liberals' programme of social reform, and after 1910 the preoccupations of domestic problems, meant that both parliament and cabinet were happy to collude in the separation of Britain's foreign policy from the mainstream. Thus Grey was left free to pursue a design that aimed at maintaining peace in Europe by preparing for war, and that saw Britain's role as the arbitrator in balancing power in Europe. Grey's stance was moral and high-minded, but it was also shrewdly realistic: a dominant power in Europe would threaten Britain's command of the sea at its most vulnerable point—the Channel—and so the European balance was an integral component in imperial security.[26]

The immediate threat to European stability, it was clear by 1906, came from Germany. Thus British policy leaned towards France and towards giving the Entente firmer shape and direction, albeit without a formal commitment. Paul

---

[24] Sumida, *In defence of naval supremacy*, 37–61.
[25] Marder (ed.), *Fear God and dread nought*, ii. 51, 55.
[26] Howard, *Continental commitment*, 51–2; on the British position in general, see Steiner, *Britain and the origins*.

Cambon, France's ambassador in London, picked up the mood in 1905, and worried that the Liberals might back-pedal encouraged the French to seek ways of making the Entente a defensive alliance. In December 1905 and January 1906 the two powers arranged and conducted military staff talks which continued until May 1906. Grey was a driving force in these conversations, but he insisted to the French that they did not compromise British neutrality, and to begin with set them directly in the context of the Moroccan crisis. Even when he later acknowledged that the maintenance of the Entente would itself be a cause for war, he omitted to inform the cabinet of the talks.[27]

Therefore, when in 1907 Britain settled its differences with Russia, the treaty could not, like the earlier agreements with Japan and France, remain set solely in a local and colonial context. The arena for British and Russian rivalry was Asia, and for Britain the worry of Russian penetration through Persia and Afghanistan to the frontiers of India itself. In November 1904 fears of Russians at the Khyber led the viceroy in India to demand a potential reinforcement of 143,686 men in addition to the army already in India.[28] Therefore, Britain's rapprochement with Russia was not a revolution in British foreign policy: it was a diplomatic conclusion determined by strategic and financial common sense, and one which Grey himself had espoused ever since he had been parliamentary under-secretary at the Foreign Office in the early 1890s. The main domestic obstacle had been Liberal sentiment, averse to any agreement with a reactionary autocracy. Such sensibilities were eased by the constitutional reforms introduced in Russia after the 1905 revolution, and were further consoled by the treaty's Asiatic context, which rendered it the solution to a long-standing imperial rivalry. But the implications were much greater than the fact that not so many troops would have to go to India. The Anglo-Russian convention was the coping-stone of the Anglo-French Entente. The Triple Entente had become simultaneously the means by which Britain could contain Germany in Europe, and also a contrivance for moderating relations with France and Russia. If Britain wanted to support France, it had also to accommodate Russia. French capital was increasingly—by 1914 it would be a quarter of all French investments—committed to Russia; the falling French birth rate—the lowest of the major powers in Europe—rendered France reliant on Russia's military manpower. Thus, for Conservatives the settlement was the first stage in facing a fresh threat, that of Germany.

What made the Anglo-Russian convention possible was less change in Britain than change in Russia. The twin blows of defeat in Manchuria and revolution at home convinced the Tsar's advisers that war prompted domestic upheaval. The principal objective of P. A. Stolypin, the chairman of the

[27] Williamson, *Politics of grand strategy*, ch. 3, esp. 72–4, 81–3.
[28] Gooch, *Plans of war*, 217.

Council of Ministers from 1906 to 1911, was the corollary of this point: peace was necessary to enable domestic consolidation. Thus, both Stolypin and Russia's foreign minister, A. P. Izvolsky, were anxious not merely to end Russia's forward policy in the Far East but also to secure its frontiers elsewhere. Settlement with Britain in Central Asia was one element in a package that might also embrace Germany in the Baltic and Austria-Hungary in the Balkans. But Russia lacked the strength to shape its own policy. Although in certain senses both Britain and France needed Russia more than Russia needed them, the latter was handicapped by its inability to set and follow its own agenda. As the first Moroccan crisis had shown, it had to choose between the emerging blocs. Although Russia would persist in seeking understandings with Germany and Austria-Hungary, in the last resort it remained wedded to France and Britain, finding on each occasion that it did so that the Entente tightened.[29]

In Germany, therefore, the overriding consequence of the 1905 Moroccan crisis was an unravelling of *Weltpolitik*. There can be no greater indictment of German diplomacy than the fact that the deep-seated hostilities of Britain, France and Russia had been resolved so rapidly. The constellation which faced it in 1907 had seemed unimaginable: before 1904 a Franco-British Entente was improbable, then in 1904–5 it had been hoped that the *entente cordiale* would weaken the Franco-Russian convention, and throughout there had remained the assumption that Britain and Russia were irreconcilable. More specifically, the false assumptions which Tirpitz's naval policy had made of Britain were now writ large. The calculations of German naval deficiency had not reckoned on Fisher's redistribution of the British fleet; the gradualism of the naval build-up was no longer tenable with the commissioning of the first Dreadnought; and Britain—despite a hiccough in 1907—declared its determination to continue building to the two-power standard, which meant that Germany could never reach a sufficient level for effective deterrence. To use epithets like 'paranoid' and 'fatalistic' of Germany after 1905—adjectives more appropriate to individuals than nations—does not seem so misplaced. German expansion, conceived in limited terms and apparently no more ambitious than that allowed to other powers, had triggered the creation of a power bloc which not only seemed to prevent the flexing of Germany's own industrial and commercial muscle but also to encircle Germany by land to the east and west and by sea to the north.

The vocabulary of personal emotion is of course rendered more appropriate in the context of personal rule. Bülow and *Weltpolitik*, Tirpitz and the navy— these were the creatures by which the Kaiser had attempted to legitimize his

---

[29] McDonald, *United government and foreign policy in Russia*, 4, 97–110; Neilson, *Britain and the last Tsar*, pp. xiv, 11–12, 267–9; D. W. Spring, *Slavonic and East European Review*, LXVI (1988), 583–91.

own position; Wilhelm himself had been Germany's emissary in Tangiers. His principal adviser, and indeed the architect of the means by which the Kaiser's personal rule might be effected, was Philipp von Eulenburg. In 1908 Eulenburg was arraigned on a charge of homosexuality. The implications for the imperial court as a whole went beyond scandal and loss of prestige; Eulenburg's departure left the Kaiser's entourage dominated by the military. Furthermore, in November of the same year Wilhelm gave a typically vainglorious interview to the London *Daily Telegraph*, which aroused the fury of all parties in the Reichstag and opened a split between the monarch and his foreign office. The accumulation of these blows marks the point at which personal rule can be accounted to have failed. Given the fact that Germany's constitution was designed to rest on the Kaiser's command—above all in the areas of war and diplomacy—Wilhelm's subsequent loss of confidence left a vacuum which was probably even more dangerous to Germany than his earlier assertions of authority.

No comparable self-doubts seem to have assailed Tirpitz. In 1906 he used the mood generated by the Moroccan crisis to pass a supplementary naval bill, increasing the annual spending on the fleet by 35 per cent. However, it was the 1908 bill that accepted the acceleration of the German programme in the light of the Dreadnought, and which institutionalized a naval arms race between the two powers. The life of a capital ship was reduced from twenty-five years to twenty, so that Germany would build not three but four ships a year between 1908 and 1911, and would therefore have a total of fifty-eight capital ships by 1920. Privately, Tirpitz was aiming at a rate of three—not the agreed two—ships a year in the period 1912–17.

The cost of such a programme revealed the fragility of any compromise on which *Sammlungspolitik* might rest. In the 1907 elections Bülow fought a successful campaign on an appeal to *Weltpolitik*, convincing the left-liberals, the Progressives, that they should join his bloc so as to balance reactionary influences within it and avoid the threat of a Centre party–socialist coalition; the socialists actually lost thirty-six seats. But Bülow had little with which he could hold the Progressives over the long term. Even more importantly, the financing of the navy would split conservatives and national liberals. The additional cost per ship when built to Dreadnought standards was 7 million marks, and a further 60 million marks were required for improved port facilities.[30] The deficit anticipated by the 1908 naval programme was 500 million gold marks. The national debt was almost double that of 1900. To put federal finances on a sound footing Bülow had to diminish the powers of the individual states, which were still largely responsible for their own taxation: he would therefore expose a sore which *Weltpolitik* had been designed to

---

[30] Epkenhans, *Wilhelminische Flottenrüstung*, 26.

heal. To meet part of the deficit he planned to increase inheritance tax; thus the navy came home to roost, directly challenging the interests of conservative landowners. The Centre party joined with the Conservatives in calling for a tax on mobile capital: together they crushed the inheritance tax proposal, and passed the burden of taxation on to business and urban interests. The economic consequences of *Weltpolitik* had divided, not united, the different forms of property-ownership. In June 1909 Bülow, no longer able to manage the Reichstag and held responsible by the Kaiser for the *Daily Telegraph* affair, resigned the chancellorship.

Bülow had the satisfaction of nominating his successor, Theodor von Bethmann Hollweg, a Prussian bureaucrat and former secretary of state for the interior. Bethmann Hollweg was a cabinet politician, not a popular national leader. Reserved, conscientious, and honest, he never mastered the office of which he was to be the incumbent until 1917. Fritz Fischer has bracketed Bethmann with the military and Prussian influences that were to dominate Germany during the war; by contrast, Sir Edward Grey and other contemporary observers imagined that in him rested Germany's hopes for liberalism and true parliamentary government. Neither view is wholly correct. Bethmann Hollweg was a conservative and saw the position of government as above—not dependent on—the political parties. But he was also pragmatic enough to recognize that reform, albeit limited, of the Prussian suffrage was required: typically, the measure he proposed in 1910 was sufficient to alienate the right and insufficient to please the left. Thus, even more than was the case with Bülow, his management of the Reichstag constituted a succession of short-lived compromises. Not even the conservatives, who now acted as an agrarian interest group rather than as the supporters of the political status quo, were reliable. In any case, in the 1912 elections all the parties of the right and centre lost ground to the socialists, who won sixty-seven seats to become the largest party in the Reichstag. Bethmann Hollweg's power, therefore, rested to an increasing degree on external pressure groups and on his relationship— always lukewarm—with the Kaiser himself.[31]

Bülow had managed the Reichstag by use of *Weltpolitik*. But when Bethmann Hollweg became chancellor the financial implications of the navy's expansion ensured that *Weltpolitik* was deeply divisive in its effects. Bethmann therefore forswore *Weltpolitik*, at least in its more aggressive forms, for a policy of détente. He did so for reasons not of foreign policy, a field in which he had no previous experience, but of domestic political necessity. Indeed, even had he tried to manipulate the parties by the use of nationalist appeals, he might well not have succeeded. The 1909 budget had still not resolved Germany's economic problems. Nor was it only among conservatives—with their fears of

[31] Jarausch, *Enigmatic chancellor*, 71–91.

increased inheritance taxes—that opposition to naval spending was now to be found. Industry itself was divided: between 1904 and 1914 Britain was Germany's best overseas customer, and Germany was Britain's second best; twenty-two out of forty international producer cartels were Anglo-German organizations.[32] Thus, while some German concerns welcomed the steady orders which the naval arms race generated, others—including not only bankers but also iron and steel exporters—stood to lose by any further deterioration in Germany's relations with Britain.

An Anglo-German naval agreement was therefore the main means by which Bethmann sought to extricate himself from his problems. By 1908 Bülow had already been thinking along similar lines, but Tirpitz had proved strongly opposed and he had been abetted by the Kaiser. The argument that naval construction might browbeat the British into a German agreement was no longer deemed relevant. This is not to say that Tirpitz now wanted war with Britain. He recognized full well that such a conflict would be futile. The opportunity to exploit the *tabula rasa* which the Dreadnought revolution had, at least in theory, created had not been seized; Germany's implementation of it lagged three years behind Britain's, and its building targets still did not aspire to equivalence. However, Tirpitz did aim to break Britain's commitment to the two-power standard. He proposed a formula under which ostensibly Germany would build two ships a year for every three built by Britain, but whose effects in practice would produce three and four. Germany would not reduce its programme, and Britain would have to increase its own if it wished to maintain its lead. Furthermore, because Britain had a larger fleet in the first place, more of its new construction would be replacing obsolete ships rather than adding to the total size of the fleet. Thus the gap in the effective size of the two forces would be narrowed. Tirpitz derived some comfort from the fact that radical pressures on Britain's Liberal government produced a rationale for the fleet that eschewed reference to the two-power standard, but in reality the talks held out little prospect of a successful outcome. Bethmann Hollweg wished to use the specific issue of a naval agreement to secure a much wider objective, that of British neutrality. In April 1910 the Germans actually proposed that Britain commit itself to neutrality before a naval agreement was concluded: to the Foreign Office in London it seemed that Germany was using a naval lever to secure British isolation and German domination of the continent.[33]

Bethmann Hollweg's efforts at détente were not limited to Britain. Germany's rivalry with France and Russia found its focus in Europe and not further afield; the roots of the Triple Entente were to be traced to colonial questions, and thus the chances that long-term imperial tensions between the Entente

---

[32] Steiner, *Britain and the origins*, 60–4.
[33] Ibid. 54–6; Epkenhans, *Wilhelminische Flottenrüstung*, 32–91.

partners might reappear seemed good. Bilateral arrangements with France and Russia on extra-European questions promised some loosening of the Entente. Furthermore, they accorded well with Bethmann's increasing personal sense that Germany needed colonies of its own. The détente which France and Germany achieved between 1909 and 1910 was limited, and primarily motivated by economic links (German exports to France increased 38 per cent in 1905–9), which the governments—and particularly Jules Cambon, France's ambassador in Berlin—endeavoured to clothe with political formulae. In February 1909 the Germans recognized French political interests in Morocco, and France recognized Germany's economic interests; discussions took place about possible co-operation in the Congo and the Cameroons, and French short-term capital was loaned to Germany for the construction of the Baghdad railway.[34] The latter also provided the basis, in November 1910, of an agreement between Germany and Russia: Russia approved of the extension of the Baghdad railway, while Germany undertook to help in the opening of railways in Russia's sphere of interest in Persia.

By early 1911 France was worried by the implications of Bethmann's policy for Entente unity, although it does not seem to have conceived of its next step in that light. Indubitably, however, one of the repercussions of the 1911 Moroccan crisis was a reinvigoration of Anglo-French links. The resumption of a forward French policy in Morocco was largely the responsibility of the younger generation of French Foreign Ministry bureaucrats, who dominated a weak and inexperienced foreign minister.[35] Their target was as much Germany and an end to the détente which Jules Cambon had fostered as it was an expansion of French influence in North Africa. 'The solution of the Moroccan crisis', Charles Maurras wrote in Action française, 'is not to be found in Fez but among the pines of the Vosges. What is afoot in Morocco makes sense only if we are prepared to fight in the Vosges.'[36] The second Moroccan crisis made explicit what had been implicit in the first: colonial questions were not to be dealt with simply on their own terms but were projected back into European rivalries. Indeed, the geographical position of Morocco—affecting as it did the balance of power in the Mediterranean—was bound to make the isolation of problems here from problems in Europe that much more difficult than it was for any disputes over spheres of responsibility in Central Asia or Equatorial Africa.

Using the excuse of riots against the Sultan in Fez, the French ordered troops into Morocco on 17 April 1911. Once in, the soldiers were slow to depart. The French were clearly in contravention of the Algéciras act. Neither the Spanish nor the British were very pleased, and the Germans gave the French a specific warning. However, the French having reopened the Moroccan question, the

[34] Duroselle, *La France*, 12–19; Keiger, *France and the origins*, 37–40; Kaiser, *Politics and war*, 321–2.
[35] Keiger, *France and the origins*, 34; Hayne, *French foreign office*, 199–214.
[36] Quoted in Morris, *The Scaremongers*, 286.

Germans, and specifically Kiderlen-Wächter, the foreign minister, saw the opportunity for a diplomatic success in true *Weltpolitik* style. Joseph Caillaux, France's prime minister from June, was conscious of the weakness of the French position, and was more conciliatory than his Foreign Office. Through secret negotiations—which bypassed the Foreign Office—he encouraged Kiderlen in the pursuit of German objectives. Kiderlen wished to trade German recognition of the French position in Morocco for concessions in the Congo. On 1 July, on the pretext of protecting German commercial interests, the German warship, *Panther*, appeared at Agadir.

Such sabre-rattling—although the Germans had no intention of going to war, and indeed were still without a naval plan for operations against Britain—could only provoke. Germany had seen the issue as one between France and Germany only. The employment of sea-power, however limited, immediately raised the hackles of Britain. Paramount was the fear of Germany acquiring an Atlantic port. The inadequacy of British naval and military intelligence only served to reinforce Germanophobe prejudice: the whereabouts of the German fleet was uncertain in July, and in September false indications of German preparations on the Belgian frontier suggested imminent invasion.[37] During July Grey's attitude hardened: the crisis was no longer concerned with the irresponsibility of French imperial policy but with the survival of the Entente. On this occasion the cabinet was involved: evidence of the degree of Britain's commitment would be calculated to infuriate the radicals and pacifists within the Liberal party, and increase the reliance of a government that lacked an overall parliamentary majority on Conservative support. On 21 July Lloyd George, as chancellor of the exchequer, spoke in the Mansion House: without naming Germany, he clearly stated that Britain would fight rather than let its status as a great power go unacknowledged. The Mansion House speech was designed above all for domestic purposes: by supporting Grey's foreign policy, Lloyd George—the hero of the left and the author of the Liberals' package of social reforms—split the radicals and assured the Liberal imperialists of support in the cabinet and in the party. But it also had an international effect. It faced Germany with the threat of war, however veiled, and Kiderlen-Wächter could not command the support either of Germany's ally, Austria-Hungary, or of the Kaiser to play for such stakes. In the event Kiderlen got what he had asked for; Caillaux continued to bypass his foreign ministry and on 4 November Germany—in exchange for recognizing a French protectorate over Morocco—was guaranteed respect for its economic interests and received a slice of the French Congo. But popular feeling in Germany was characterized by a sense of humiliation. The iron and steel industries had hoped for concessions to mine the ores of southern Morocco itself. Expectations had been roused and

---

[37] Hiley, *Historical Journal*, XXVI (1983), 881–4.

then disappointed. Both the Kaiser and Bethmann Hollweg lost credit. The frustration at diplomacy's failure to gain for Germany the status its power warranted grew apace.

Much of this feeling was directed against Britain, and in Britain too the crisis had the effect of hardening popular sentiment. Britain was the power that had taken the initiative in elevating a colonial dispute into a European crisis: henceforth it was not to be deflected from having Europe, rather than the empire, as the focus of its foreign policy. At the Committee of Imperial Defence on 23 August 1911 strategy followed suit.

It is tempting to argue that British military thought had already anticipated diplomacy in assuming a continental thrust. In 1903 and 1908 the Committee of Imperial Defence had concluded that British naval supremacy ensured that there was little prospect of a successful hostile invasion of Britain. Furthermore, the succession of alliances, ending with the 1907 Anglo-Russian convention, lessened the number of strategic options which the newly created general staff had to consider. The possibility of operations against Germany in Europe, first adumbrated in 1902 and the object of a war game in 1905, gradually grew in importance. But until 1907 any major continental operations which the army envisaged were centred on India, not—despite the 1906 Anglo-French staff talks—on Europe. The purpose of the latter was diplomatic, not strategic. They were fostered by the politicians, Grey and the secretary of war, Haldane, rather than by the soldiers, who had formed a low estimate of the French army.[38] The British Expeditionary Force of six divisions, ready to be dispatched to any quarter of the globe, and fashioned by Haldane, was the fruit of cash constraints, not strategic reappraisal. The burgeoning costs of the navy, plus the Liberals' domestic reforms, necessitated savings: between 1905/6 and 1909/10 Haldane had lopped £2.5 million from the army estimates. Haldane's army was still the projectile of the navy, relying on sea-power for ubiquity and concentration, and so gaining in effectiveness and in flexibility while remaining small.[39]

Two factors contributed to the emerging dominance of continentalism in British military thought. First, the navy itself showed little interest in amphibious operations: the fleet wanted a big sea battle in the event of European war not the more mundane tasks of transporting and supplying limited land warfare on the European periphery. The one plan it did develop, that for a landing on the Baltic coast, was dismissed as unworkable by the army as early as the winter of 1908–9.[40] Secondly, Henry Wilson, a noted Francophile,

---

[38] Herrmann, *Arming of Europe*, 55–6, 84.
[39] Gooch, *Plans of war*, 165–73; Gooch, *Prospect of war*, pp. vii–viii, 93–112; Spiers, *Haldane*, 3–4, 9, 38–44, 64–5, 71–3, 77–81, 193–5.
[40] Paul Hayes, 'Britain, Germany and the Admiralty's plans for attacking German territory 1906–1915', in Freedman *et al.* (eds.), *War, strategy and international politics*.

convinced that war in Europe was inevitable and possessed of political instincts few British soldiers could match, became director of military operations in August 1910. Wilson promptly began to give substance to the 1906 staff talks; he conveniently calculated that the British contribution of six divisions was sufficient to swing the balance in a Franco-German conflict, and set about planning the transport of those divisions to France. Thus, when in the wake of the Agadir crisis the Committee of Imperial Defence met on 23 August 1911 to review British strategy in the event of a European war, the army's case was well developed and specific. By contrast, the presentation of Sir A. K. Wilson, Fisher's successor as First Sea Lord, was shambling and ill-thought-out. The navy's potential supporters were not present at the meeting; instead, Lloyd George and Winston Churchill—representatives of the radicals in the government—were convinced by the arguments for rapid continental intervention in the event of a Franco-German war. In the wake of that meeting Churchill was appointed First Lord of the Admiralty. The effect was to divide Churchill from Lloyd George, so weakening the radicals' voice in the cabinet. The significance of this move became increasingly evident in late 1913 and early 1914, by which stage the chancellor of the exchequer regarded the European scene as increasingly peaceful and the case for a reduction in naval spending in 1915 as correspondingly stronger.[41] Ostensibly Churchill's task was to create a naval staff, so that the senior service could prepare itself as well as the army had done for strategic discussions, but it was also to bring the navy into line with continental thought. The French navy in 1906 had already decided to concentrate its strength in the Mediterranean, and Fisher's redistribution had weighted the British navy towards the Atlantic and the Channel; these independent decisions were made complementary by the institution of Anglo-French naval talks in 1912. The Royal Navy was prepared to accept operational plans that confirmed its existing deployment, and consigned what was seen as a subsidiary theatre to the secondary naval power.

Although the consequence of the second Moroccan crisis was a closer identification between British strategy and French, no formal alliance resulted. The cabinet was informed in November 1911 of the Anglo-French staff talks, and a year later agreed, as the culmination of the naval discussions, that the two powers would consult each other in the event of an attack by a third party. In German eyes British diplomacy was now focused on the Entente, not on the concert of Europe, with the Foreign Office too ready to interpret every crisis, however fomented, as the consequence of a Berlin-driven conspiracy.[42] Nonetheless, Grey warded off French pressure for an even tighter commitment,

[41] Grigg, *Lloyd George*, 133; Gilbert, *Lloyd George*, 76.
[42] Gregor Schöllgen, 'Germany's foreign policy in the age of imperialism: a vicious circle?', 129–30, and Gustav Schmidt, 'Contradictory postures and conflicting objectives: the July crisis', 138, in Schöllgen (ed.), *Escape into war?*.

citing his fear of radical opposition in parliament and the accompanying danger that even these limited agreements could thus be undermined. The concert of Europe remained his ideal means of managing the continent; the Entente was a device by which Britain could maintain its free hand, while simultaneously cautioning the Germans and moderating French and German behaviour.[43] Britain's refusal to align itself unequivocally created an ambiguity in great power relations between 1911 and 1914, for Grey's faith in the concert system was not reciprocated elsewhere. Conferences had, after all, not proved to be to Germany's advantage.

French foreign policy, while not pursuing an entirely straight course after 1911, gained considerably in coherence and direction. Caillaux's secret communications with Germany were intercepted and deciphered by the intelligence service of the very Foreign Ministry he was trying to bypass. In January 1912 the Germanophobe and radical, Georges Clemenceau, used this information to engineer the fall of Caillaux's government. Raymond Poincaré, who formed the new ministry, had been rapporteur of the Senate commission to examine the Franco-German treaty of 4 November 1911, and assumed the foreign office portfolio himself. In January 1913 Poincaré became president, an office that he was to hold until 1920. He was thus able to provide the continuity which proved so elusive, given the endemic ministerial instability of the Third Republic. Partly by sheer hard work, partly by creating his own administrative structure, and partly by his direct access to intercepted diplomatic messages, he contrived to be independent of the machinations of the bureaux of the foreign ministry, and to a considerable degree to insulate foreign policy from the seven changes of government experienced by France between 1912 and 1914.

Poincaré himself was a Lorrainer; he was a patriot and he distrusted Germany. But it would be mistaken to conclude that France either sought war or did so to recover Alsace-Lorraine. If Germany and France found themselves at war for other reasons, the lost provinces would, quite clearly, become a war aim for France. *Révanche* figured large in German projections of French ambitions, but in practice mattered little to most Frenchmen. The provinces increasingly identified themselves with Germany, and not even the Zabern incident of 1913, which made abundantly clear the high-handedness of the German military presence, evoked an official French response.

Poincaré's foreign policy had two main aims. Domestically, he hoped to establish a political consensus, drawing support from the left and right of the centre, and weakening *Action française* on the extreme right and socialism on the left. His chances of success were boosted by the fact that radicalism, like liberalism in Germany, was being split between left and right: at the beginning

---

[43] Steiner, *Britain and the origins*, 244–5; also 113, 117.

of the century anticlericalism had sponsored a fusion of the radicals and socialists, but after 1906 the socialists had been pulled away from the bourgeois radicals by the need to respond to the trades-union movement. Externally, Poincaré saw the Triple Alliance and the Triple Entente as creating a European balance of power and fostering continental security through mutual rivalry. To that end, the coalition of the opposing alliance was as important as that of his own. The activities of Jules Cambon in Berlin, fostering Franco-German détente, were rebuffed as a threat to Entente solidarity; but so too were the efforts of Barrère, France's ambassador in Rome, to draw Italy out of the Triple Alliance by exploiting Italian hostility for Austria-Hungary. One of the paradoxes of European security before 1914 was that each of the major players— Grey, Bethmann Hollweg, and Poincaré himself—sought to create stability, but each used different means as appropriate to its achievement.

It followed from Poincaré's commitment to the Entente that Franco-Russian relations, as well as Anglo-French, should be strengthened in 1912. From the German perspective such moves were far from reassuring: they cut across Bethmann Hollweg's policy of détente and they confirmed fears of a two-front war. Poincaré's policy did nothing to lessen the tensions in European relations, and to that extent he promoted war rather than averted it.[44] Moreover, his policy in relation to Russia in 1912 was open to more than one interpretation. Poincaré's defenders argue that his object was to manage Russia, not egg her on: the lack of Russian support for France during the 1911 crisis and German efforts to woo Russia combined with a desire to restrain Russia in her policies towards the Ottoman empire and the Balkans. But to the Russians themselves, and even to Henry Wilson, Poincaré could seem an adventurist.[45] In July 1912 the French and Russian general staffs met, as they had been doing since 1892 under the terms of the military convention. The following month Poincaré visited Russia in order to learn more of Russian involvement in the Balkans. He assured the Russians that should Russia and Austria-Hungary come to blows over the Balkans, and should the Germans then support the Austrians, they could rely on French support. Poincaré gave this undertaking knowing that in all probability the Germans would strike against France first, in order to secure their rear before turning east. The commitment did not, therefore, represent a major shift in the French position; rather, it was vital to the plans of the French general staff who hoped thus to secure Russian support against any German attack on France. On 17 November 1912 Poincaré reiterated his undertaking to Russia: France's concern for its own defence therefore allowed Russia to be more adventurous—not less so—in the Balkans. Poincaré reaffirmed his Russian policy by appointing Delcassé as

[44] Hayne, *French foreign policy*, 242–3.
[45] Stevenson, *Armaments and the coming of war*, 239–41.

France's ambassador in St Petersburg in February 1913.[46] In the summer, the French government intervened in Russian negotiations on the French stock market for a loan to finance railway construction. The French objective was to bring pressure to bear on the speed of Russian mobilization, so as to co-ordinate mutually supporting attacks on Germany from east and west: the French said they would concentrate 200,000 more troops than they had undertaken to do in 1892.[47]

All the threads of Poincaré's foreign policy were brought together during the course of 1913 by the debate on the extension of the period of military service to three years. At one level this was a purely technical question. In 1905 the term of service was set at two years: loud and long were the complaints of regular soldiers, who felt that all their time was taken up with basic training and that the level of training then acquired was inadequate. Force was given to their arguments by the relative decline in the French population (France in 1910 had to take 83 per cent of her available manpower to produce the same size army as Germany did with 57.3 per cent),[48] and by the need to match the increases authorized for the Germany army in 1912–13. Professional military wisdom therefore calculated that a longer period of service would produce an army that was both larger and more competent. The domestic arguments of the French army were of course at one with the strategy which the alliance with Russia now demanded: both Poincaré and the French general staff had committed France to taking the offensive against Germany if need be. The alliance and the three-year law therefore interlocked.[49] So powerful were these arguments that the radicals could not unite on the issue, but split, some acknowledging the threat posed by the level of German military preparedness and others accepting the socialists' preference for a short-term citizen army. The debate showed how relatively little French politics were polarized when foreign policy was employed in a domestic context: the radicals and socialists did form a fresh bloc in October 1913, but the issue that united them was less opposition to three-year service and more the advocacy of income tax as a means to finance it. Finally, although set in the context of popular nationalism, the three-year service law was presented by the government as a means of reassurance and of deterrence in Franco-German relations. The minister of war, addressing the army committee of the Chamber of Deputies on 11 March 1913, accepted that defensive requirements necessitated German manpower increases, given the threats to east and west: 'Quite frankly, and I mean this most sincerely,' he declared, 'I do not think that at this moment, as I utter these words, or even yesterday, Germany has or had the intention to pounce upon France.'[50]

[46] On Poincaré's policy in general, see Keiger, *France and the origins*; on the importance of the 1912 guarantees, L. C. F. Turner, 'Russian mobilisation in 1914' in Kennedy (ed.), *War plans*, 252–6.
[47] Krumeich, *Armaments*, ch. 6.   [48] Ritter, *Sword and the sceptre*, ii. 223.
[49] Krumeich, *Armaments*, esp. 17–18, 125.   [50] Quoted in ibid. 74.

While the Moroccan crisis hardened the Entente, and in particular France's advocacy of robustness as a means to deterrence, it alarmed Bethmann Hollweg. He did not abandon *Weltpolitik*, but he did soften it, recognizing that its pursuit should be harmonized at least with Britain. Furthermore, the chances of domestic support for a renewed attempt at an Anglo-German naval agreement seemed, on the face of it, reasonable. The naval budget had grown 134 per cent between 1904 and 1912, against an army increase of 47 per cent; naval spending now exceeded half the total military expenditure.[51] By espousing the army's case for attention Bethmann could deflect the navy's, and so play off one against the other. Furthermore, the navy itself was divided by Tirpitz's building programme: Henning von Holtzendorff, the commander of the High Seas Fleet, wanted to improve training and efficiency rather than to have more ships. On the political front, the composition of the Reichstag did not augur well for the navy's chances of further funds: the January 1912 elections had been a triumph for the left and, in March 1912, introduction of a new inheritance tax undermined any residual support from the right. The Treasury and the Bundesrat—for similar financial reasons—backed Bethmann against Tirpitz. Finally, German hopes that the British Liberal government would be more amenable than it had been in 1909 and 1910 were buoyed by the anxiety of its more radical members at the heightened Anglo-German tension; Herbert Asquith's cabinet (Asquith succeeded Campbell-Bannerman as prime minister in 1908) had to show its supporters that it had at least tried to reach an understanding with Germany.

In practice, the prospects of success were remote. Tirpitz was now openly set on a rate of construction that would proceed independently of Britain, and would give Germany a ratio of 2 : 3 in capital ships. He proposed a supplementary naval law, that would prevent a return to a building rate of two vessels per year as planned, and would instead commit Germany to three ships in each of 1912, 1914, and 1916. Domestically his cards were stronger than first appearances suggested. To those supportive of détente he could argue that Britain would never negotiate if Germany embarked on reductions unilaterally. The case for firmness was of course equally attractive to those who identified Britain as the primary author of Gemany's humiliation at Agadir. And for Tirpitz himself, conscious of the domestic political pressures now mounting against the naval programme, an international agreement fixing rates of shipbuilding would at least secure the programme's independence of the Reichstag. The Kaiser, listening to the naval attaché in London rather than to the German ambassador, backed Tirpitz and not Bethmann Hollweg. Bethmann's domestic position was further weakened on 9 February 1912 when Churchill sarcastically and provocatively characterized the German navy as a 'luxury fleet'.

[51] Herwig, *Luxury fleet*, 75.

Therefore, when the British emissary Haldane, the secretary of state for war and a student of German philosophy, arrived in Berlin, his expectations were not great. The Kaiser, it is true, was as usual using bluster and declamation as a substitute for diplomacy, and at bottom hoped and even believed that a strong line would bring Britain to terms more readily than overt conciliation. But Bethmann Hollweg still wished for a general undertaking of neutrality on Britain's part, and his hopes were raised by Haldane's apparent inclination to discuss political issues rather than naval matters. Even more encouraging was Churchill's suggestion on 18 March of a 'naval holiday'. For most Germans this suggested that their strong line had triumphed; however, Tirpitz was moment-arily nonplussed, since Churchill's suggested ratio of sixteen British Dread-noughts for ten German implied a break in the building tempo. Four days later the 1912 German supplementary naval law was published. Churchill calculated that it would compel Britain to build five ships in one year and then four the next year over a six-year period, at a cost of an extra 3 million pounds a year.[52] Whatever the financial burden, Britain was not prepared to be neutralized, to leave France to German domination, and so undermine its own strategic position. The talks reached an impasse. The Anglo-French naval agreement of 1912 was therefore in part a gesture of solidarity towards France after the flirtation with Germany. It was also profoundly pragmatic: to control naval building Britain had—given the 1912 German law—to ask France to take on responsibility for the Mediterranean in the name of the Entente.

The naval balance in the Mediterranean highlighted the fact that by the summer of 1912 both sides, and particularly Britain, were pursuing policies that were increasingly driven by factors in addition to those that determined their relationship with each other. Britain maintained a one-power standard in the Mediterranean, so that it would be equivalent to the next largest local navy after that of France. Thus the decision by Austria-Hungary to lay down two Dreadnoughts in 1910 and a further two in 1912 (so matching Italy's pro-gramme) was both a driving force in the Anglo-French naval agreement and a factor in the abandonment of the idea of a 'naval holiday'.[53] Similarly Australia, New Zealand, and to a lesser extent Canada showed an interest in contributing to the Dreadnought programme, not so much because of the German threat in the North Sea as because of their worries about Japan in the Pacific. The equivalent German pressure was the Russian decision to replace the Baltic fleet lost at Tsushima. The effect of these secondary naval arms races was to compound the principal one, each side aggregating the forces of its opponent, although elements of its own building were a response to other pressures. In May 1912 Churchill declared that Britain would build two new

---

[52] Marder, *From the Dreadnought*, i. 275–6; Epkenhans, *Wilhelminische Flottenrüstung*, 114–42.
[53] Stevenson, *Armaments and the coming of war*, 174–5, 215.

ships for every additional German ship; the implication of his programme was that by 1917 Britain would have fifty-one Dreadnoughts to Germany's twenty-eight.

Nonetheless, by late 1912 the heat had gone out of the Anglo-German naval arms race. This was due primarily neither to Churchill's determined response nor to Bethmann Hollweg's pursuit of détente. The core explanation was the implosion of *Sammlungspolitik* itself. By 1912 the latter had become more of a vehicle by which to drive Germany's armaments policies than an end in itself.[54] Arms spending in 1913 accounted for only 4.7 per cent of Gemany's net social product, and it was therefore too small to have any stabilizing effect in the economy as a whole; much of it was spent on personnel rather than plant, and its consequences were to reduce the capital available for further investment while driving up interest rates. Bethmann Hollweg's response was contradictory. On the one hand he publicly rejected international competition over arms, while on the other he espoused the army's case against that of the navy.[55] The latter was the ultimate loser. Crucially, the Kaiser withdrew his support for Tirpitz, and at the same time elements within the navy itself demanded that manning and training should take priority over matériel. On 6 February 1913 Tirpitz announced to the Reichstag's budget committee that he now found Churchill's proposed 16 : 10 Dreadnought ratio acceptable. Germany's renunciation of the Anglo-German naval arms race was effectively unilateral.[56]

The other bridge to détente open to Bethmann Hollweg was through colonial policy. Here Bethmann enjoyed greater success. Neither France nor Britain was opposed to German colonialism per se, provided it did not clash with their own interests. In the Moroccan agreement France accepted German ambitions in Central Africa; so did Britain in its negotiations with Germany over the Portuguese colonies, and specifically Angola. Between 1912 and 1914 Britain and Germany found that their interests in the Baghdad railway could, by dividing the line at Basra, be rendered complementary rather than contradictory: simultaneously Germany—short of capital because of the demands of its own rapid industrialization—welcomed French finance and involvement in the project. Within France the formation of the radical–socialist bloc in October 1913 forced Poincaré to appoint a radical, Doumergue, as prime minister, and Doumergue brought back Caillaux as his finance minister. By late 1913 both Poincaré's orientation of French foreign policy and even his status as president looked less secure, and when in January 1914 Germany and Russia argued over their respective interests in Turkey, French support for Russia was more cautious than Russia might have expected. Furthermore, the question of the three-year law was reopened for debate. Bethmann's hope, that

[54] Geyer, *Deutsche Rüstungspolitik*, 89.
[55] Kroboth, *Finanzpolitik des Deutschen Reiches*, 306, 312.
[56] Epkenhans, *Wilhelminische Flottenrüstungspolitik*, 312–24, 343, 396.

extra-European interests carefully played would show more points of contact between France and Germany and would reveal the underlying tensions between the imperial ambitions of the Entente powers, seemed to be well founded. Certainly it provided the basis for much of the optimism with which many Europeans greeted 1914. But Bethmann's policy worked because it was limited. It was effective in certain geographical areas where tensions were already low; it did not push any of the Entente powers into breaking with its allies. And it came too late. Colonial antagonisms had already shaped European alliances; it would take a long time and considerable patience before colonial agreements could loosen those alliances.

Bethmann Hollweg had come to share Bülow's position, to recognize that Germany's economic strength and great-power status made expansionist pretensions legitimate. To that extent détente was his version of *Weltpolitik*. Furthermore, it was clear that in Bethmann's hands, even more than in Bülow's, *Weltpolitik* could be accommodated in international politics. The events of 1905–14 showed that Franco-German and Anglo-German disputes could be settled without war. Even the naval rivalry had become institutionalized to the point where Churchill could claim, admittedly after the event, that it was increasingly irrelevant to Anglo-German controversies.[57] Bethmann's confidant the youthful Kurt Riezler, in his pseudonymous work of 1913, *Grundzüge der Weltpolitik* (the fundamentals of world policy), concluded that the dangers of defeat were such that war had lost its utility and that, although it might occur through irrationality or dire necessity, it would not occur through calculation. In particular, he saw the alliance system as a restraint, since in no one crisis would all allies simultaneously view their interests as so threatened that they would support each other to the point of war.[58]

Riezler's analysis, however, also revealed exactly how destructive *Weltpolitik* had been to the tenor of west European relations. All nations, he thought, conceived of coexistence 'as a preparation for hostility, as a postponement of hostility'; armaments were therefore a form of that postponement and were an essential component of the bluff necessary in diplomacy. *Weltpolitik* had militarized international relations. The naval arms race had assumed a momentum of its own, with ship construction planned up to a decade ahead, and with national budgets and patterns of employment shaped round it. The alliances had been given substance and direction by staff talks and war plans. Despite the very great level of economic interdependence between France, Britain, and Germany in 1914, and the genuine need of most businessmen and industrialists for peace, economic rivalry was increasingly expressed in national terms. Most important of all, the effect of the two Moroccan crises

---

[57] Churchill, *Unknown war*, 49.   [58] Thompson, *In the eye of the storm*, 60–5.

was to subordinate colonial questions to European. They had shown that, geographically, the division between Europe and the rest of the world was not as neat as the populations of north-west Europe sometimes seemed to imagine. The problems of the North African coastline, the balance of power in the Mediterranean, could not but affect the other powers on the Mediterranean littoral—Turkey, which was simultaneously of Europe and Asia, and Italy and Austria-Hungary. Nor had *Weltpolitik* succeeded in resolving Germany's domestic tensions: at best it had postponed them. Germany did not in the end go to war in pursuit of its *Weltpolitik*. But the conduct of *Weltpolitik*, and the setbacks which it entailed, contributed to its sense of humiliation, beleaguerment, and fatalism in 1914. And, once war was declared, the continuity of *Weltpolitik*—both in terms of Germany's war aims and in terms of Germany's domestic political and social pressures—was to become all too evident.

AUSTRIA-HUNGARY AND THE BALKANS

In both the major crises triggered by Germany in the pursuit of *Weltpolitik*, the two Moroccan confrontations of 1905 and 1911, Germany enjoyed less than fulsome support from its major ally, Austria-Hungary.[59] During the war German generals were apt to cite Nibelung loyalty when referring to the Austro-German alliance, but they did so between clenched teeth. The shared Germanic traditions to which such comparisons appealed suggested a common identity that was in practice largely superficial—or, if real, was subscribed to only by a minority (since in 1910 Germans constituted a quarter of the total) of the Austro-Hungarian population. The more recent history of the two countries suggested division rather than fusion. In 1866 Prussia had summarily ended Austria's leadership of the Germanic states on the battlefield, and although the memory of that war seems to have rankled remarkably little, the subsequent thrust of Germany's development highlighted differences as much as points of contact. German unification elevated the idea of nationalism, but Austria-Hungary—as a multinational empire—had perforce relied for its continued

[59] In addition to the works cited in n. 1 above, the following books and articles have been of general assistance in the writing of this section: Beztuzhev, *Journal of Contemporary History*, I (1966), 93–112; Bridge, *From Sadowa to Sarajevo*; Dedijer, *Road to Sarajevo*; Lieven, *Russia and the origins*; Leslie, *Wiener Beiträge*, XX (1993), 307–94; Linke, *Miltärgeschichtliche Mitteilungen*, 32 (1982), 9–34; May, *Passing of the Hapsburg monarchy*; Mommsen, *Central European History*, VI (1973), 3–43; Mommsen, 'Topos of inevitable war in Germany in the decade before 1914', in Berghahn and Kitchen (eds.), *Germany in the age of total war*; Pares, *Fall of the Russian monarchy*; Renouvin, *Crise Européenne*; Röhl, *Historical Journal*, XII (1969), 651–73; C. J. Smith, *Russia's struggle for power*; Stone, *Past and Present*, 33 (1966), 95–111; Turner, *Origins*; Valiani, *End of Austria-Hungary*; Williamson, *Austria-Hungary*; Zeman, *Break-up of the Habsburg Empire*.

integrity throughout the nineteenth century on supra-nationalism. In order to
consolidate its legitimacy as a government, Austria-Hungary had used the
networks of international relations, the authority of treaties, to buttress the
domestic status quo; the creation of Germany, the cuckoo in the European
nest, had upset the Concert system and the balance of power. Most important
of all, economic development had transformed these otherwise implicit distinctions into direct and overt competition. Although the growth rate in
industry in Austria-Hungary was impressive between 1890 and 1914, it started
from a low point and its effect was patchy. Over that period railway construction in the empire all but matched that of Germany, but by 1913 the density of
track per square kilometre of territory was only a third that of its ally. In
Hungary the number of industrial workers rose by 76 per cent between 1898
and 1913, but industrial workers only constituted 17 per cent of the working
population. In Austria industrial productivity increased 50 per cent between
1900 and 1910, but in that latter year 56.5 per cent of the workforce of Austria-
Hungary were still in agriculture. Agricultural productivity had risen, but
remained low relative to other states and, even in those years when yields
were sufficient, protectionism acted as a block to food exports.[60] The dual
monarchy was therefore in no position to compete with Germany, which used
its productive capacity as an arm of its foreign policy. Throughout the decade
before the First World War Austria-Hungary saw its Balkan markets fall to its
ally. In 1901–5 Romania drew 28.5 per cent of its imports from Austria-Hungary
and 27.1 per cent from Germany; by 1913 these figures were 23.4 and 40.3 per
cent.[61] Most galling of all was the outcome of Austria-Hungary's decision to
impose economic sanctions on Serbia in 1906. In retaliation for Serbia's
decision not to order arms from the Skoda works in Bohemia but from the
French, Austria-Hungary refused to import Serbian livestock, in particular
pigs. Serbia's response was to find alternative markets, including Germany: by
1910, when Austro-Serb commercial relations were resumed, Germany had
replaced Austria-Hungary as one of Serbia's principal trading partners.[62]

It was therefore necessity rather than affection which fuelled the Nibelung
compact. For Germany, Austria-Hungary was better than no ally at all. The
dual monarchy broke the ring of encircling and seemingly hostile powers;
more positively, and increasingly more importantly, Austria-Hungary was the
land bridge not merely to the Balkans but to Asia Minor. For the Habsburg
monarchy the Austro-German alliance replaced the Concert of Europe as the
bulwark behind its fragile identity. For Germans within Austria the alliance
removed any possible conflict of loyalty: 1866 had seemingly sundered them

---

[60] Macartney, *Habsburg Empire*, 755–6; Trebilcock, *Industrialization*, 443–4; Valiani, *End of Austria-Hungary*, 4.
[61] Fischer, 'World policy, world power and German war aims', in Koch (ed.), *Origins*, 150–1.
[62] Bridge, *From Sadowa*, 277–80; see also 268–9; Dedijer, *Road to Sarajevo*, 368–9.

from Germany proper, but the alliance and its potentialities had reunited them. Moreover, Germany's support also extended to the Magyars, whose landowning aristocracy dominated Hungary in power if not in numbers, and whom the Kaiser portrayed as honorary Teutons in their battle against the Slav. The alliance therefore provided the *Ausgleich* of 1867 with an external validation which its parlous domestic condition made indispensable.[63]

Although in 1815 and again in 1848 the Habsburgs had evaded the threat of nationalism, in 1867 they had struck a compromise with Hungary. Franz Joseph became simultaneously emperor of Austria and king of Hungary. Each state had its own assembly, the Austrian Reichsrat and the Hungarian Diet. Delegations of the two convened once a year, albeit in separate buildings, to approve common expenditure. Ministers for the two nations were answerable to the emperor. The two national ministers president, plus the three joint ministers—the foreign minister, the minister of war, and the common minister of finance—together constituted the common ministerial council. The foreign minister set the agenda for the common council and thus became the de facto chancellor of the dual monarchy. The army itself was also common to both parts of the empire, and in many ways the most effective embodiment of its supra-national and multinational status, although in addition Austria and Hungary each had a separate territorial army. The *Ausgleich* was a pragmatic and sensible response which lasted until 1918. Its strength rested on its application of internal imperialism: the Germans, albeit in a somewhat more liberal and enlightened clothing, were left free to dominate Austria, while Hungary was consigned—by virtue of a very restrictive franchise—to the Magyars. Its weaknesses were twofold. First, the *Ausgleich* was renewable every ten years: Austria-Hungary was therefore on perpetual notice as to its future. Secondly, it was a compromise that commended itself to only one group, the Magyars. For everybody else it was a halfway house. A few wanted a return to centralism. More saw the relative independence achieved by the Magyars as an indication that comparable devolution might be possible for the other ethnic groups. Of the 20 million inhabitants of Hungary, less than half were Magyars and the remainder included Romanians (nearly 3 million), Slovaks and Croats (nearly 2 million of each), and Serbs (less than a million). Austria was even more variegated: 10 million Germans formed the largest group in the total population of 28 million, but 4.9 million Poles and 3.2 million Ruthenes lived in Galicia, 6.5 million Czechs in Bohemia, and there were smaller groupings of Slovenes, Italians, Serbs, and Croats. For many of these the *Ausgleich* became not a stopping point, but an intermediate stage to trialism (a third, Slav, component in the empire) or even federalism.[64]

[63] Shanafelt, *The secret enemy,* 4–6.
[64] Williamson, *Austria-Hungary,* 14–30; Renouvin, *Crise européene,* 94; Leslie, *Wiener Beiträge,* XX (1993), 367–8.

The major block to change, and indeed the key element in domestic politics in the decade before the First World War, was the intransigence of the Magyars. Either trialism or federalism would diminish Hungary; the Magyar solution was one of repression and of Magyarization, particularly in relation to the use of the Hungarian language. In 1903 the Hungarian Diet declined to increase the recruit contingent for the army in line with the growth in population without the effective formation of a separate Hungarian army. Franz Joseph refused, a challenge to the unity of the army being a challenge to Habsburg authority itself. The Diet was twice dissolved in an effort to form a fresh government, and even the possibility of a military occupation mooted. However, the solution to the impasse most attractive to the monarchy was to widen the Hungarian franchise: the power of the Magyar aristocracy would be broken and at the same time sufficient national divisions created to allow the possibility of enhanced Habsburg influence. By the same token the major Magyar parties, and in particular Count Istvan Tisza, Hungary's minister president in 1903–5 and again from 1913, were determined to block suffrage reform. Magyar compliance with Franz Joseph's instructions was so minimal that in 1914 only 6 per cent of Hungary's population enjoyed the vote and only fifty of the 453 deputies in the Diet were not Magyars.[65] On the other hand, the threat of universal suffrage contributed to the renewal of the *Ausgleich* (albeit on terms which left the Austrians paying 63.6 per cent of the common expenses). Furthermore, Tisza forced through the army bill in 1912 and reformed the Diet so as to make its proceedings more workable. He also moderated policy towards the Croats, second only to the Romanians as the largest and most independent of the non-Magyar groupings in Hungary. Tisza was shrewd enough to realize that Magyar bloody-mindedness must not go so far as to make the *Ausgleich* unworkable: that would only hasten its demise. Hungary would maximize its power, he calculated, if it established itself as the key element in a continuing empire, and indeed if that empire remained a member of a major international alliance. The by-products of such policies—effective government and the enhancement of the army—pleased Franz Joseph, and were sufficient to persuade him to abandon the pursuit of real political reform.

But the Magyars knew that the confrontation was only deferred. Franz Joseph had come to the throne in 1848, and his succession could not be long postponed. His heir, Franz Ferdinand, was notorious for his anti-Magyar views. Both trialism and federalism had been canvassed within Franz Ferdi-nand's circle, although the heir apparent ultimately embraced centralism through the idea of a greater German Austria.[66] Whatever the means, the Magyars could expect a renewed challenge to their position in the not too

[65] May, *Hapsburg monarchy*, 394.   [66] Dedijer, *Road to Sarajevo*, ch. 7.

MAP 2. THE BALKAN PENINSULA IN 1914

distant future and this alone was sufficient to confirm the precarious state of the *Ausgleich*.

Franz Joseph's espousal of a moderate liberalism did not proceed from any love of liberalism per se but from its attraction as a device to soften national opposition and thus indirectly to buttress Habsburg power. Within Austria liberalism of this sort was progressively applied, but without achieving the expected effects. South Slav and Czech culture and education received a considerable boost from ordinances in 1880 and 1881 which allowed official languages other than German. The suffrage of 1882 progressively enfranchised the lower middle class, the shopkeeper and the artisan. The Poles in Galicia became effectively self-governing. The final step, that of universal suffrage introduced in 1907, was in part the corollary of Franz Joseph's attempt to carry through the same reform in Hungary. It was also prompted by an exaggerated fear of socialism, the 1905 Russian revolution having stimulated disturbances in Vienna and Prague. Socialism, if brought within the Reichsrat, might be channelled towards reformism, not revolution; it might—as a supra-national movement, committed to the benefits of large economic units— buttress the larger forum of the empire as a whole; and it was hoped that the clerical parties would react and organize a more conservatively inclined lower-class vote. In the 1907 elections the socialists duly increased their representation sixfold, to eighty-six seats out of 516. But socialism in Austria was not the threat or the force it was in western Europe: nationalism splintered it too, and the Czechs broke away from the Austrian socialists to form their own party. The 1907 franchise had been calculated on the basis of national groupings, and indeed had had to rest on the existence of the divisions which nationalism would create in order to prevent a Slav coalition outnumbering the German representation within the Reichsrat. Therefore, although party loyalties reflect-ing class and occupational factors were formed, ethnic division was pre-eminent. Czech obstruction was particularly vociferous. Only the Poles, driven into loyalty by their fear of the Russians and of the latter's support for the Ruthenes in Galicia, could be counted on. Parliamentary government, even parliamentary debate, was rendered impossible, and in March 1914 Count Karl Sturgkh, Austria's minister president since 1910, adjourned the Reichstag altogether. It was not to reconvene until 1917. The trappings of constitution-alism thus proved more resilient and more continuous in Hungary, where they were buttressed by a form of domestic colonialism, than they did in the more liberal conditions of Austria.

Because one of the most important political changes to emerge from the First World War was the fragmentation of the Austro-Hungarian empire into a number of new nation states, it is tempting to conclude that the disintegration was well in train before the war broke out. It is true that major change, presumably on Franz Joseph's death, was generally expected, and that the vulnerabilities of the *Ausgleich* and hence of Austria-Hungary as a whole were acknowledged. But most national groups derived benefits as well as disadvantages from membership of the empire, and therefore the majority before 1914 looked to federalism, not independence.

The cultural diversity of Vienna, home before 1914 to Freud and the philosopher Wittgenstein, the writers Rilke and Karl Kraus, the painter Gustav Klimt, and the composers Mahler, Richard Strauss, and Schoenberg, and the relative liberalism of the Habsburg empire compared with the autocracy of its Slav neighbour, Russia—all these were plus points for the inhabitants of Austria-Hungary. The strength and size of the bureaucracy, consciously expanded to embrace the nationalities of the empire, meant that effective administration continued regardless of parliamentary paralysis. Ministers were drawn from the civil service and were enabled to govern by virtue of paragraph 14 of the Austrian constitution, which conferred emergency powers when the Reichsrat was not in session.

What was, however, true was that if any state manifested a close connection between domestic policy and foreign policy, if in any country the former directed the latter, it was not so much Germany as Austria-Hungary. Generally speaking, and with notable exceptions, Austria-Hungary was neither a bellicose nor expansionist actor in international relations after 1866. The defence budget declined from the 1890s until 1912, and the war of 1866 ought to have been sufficient reminder that fighting did not necessarily resolve problems in a satisfactory manner. But in the debate on the *Ausgleich* and its future the funding and the recruitment of the army were pivotal; for some, its employment in war would be the best way to cut through the debate and the procrastination. Furthermore, the dual monarchy's ethnic groups prevented the empire from lapsing into any form of isolation. With the exception of the Magyars, each of them could look to a national homeland that lay outside the frontiers of the empire—to Serbia, to Romania, to Italy, to Russia, and even to Germany. Domestic and foreign policy were therefore inextricably linked. In 1815 Metternich had used the Concert of Europe to give this racial pot-pourri external validation and support; by 1914 the relative decline of the Concert system could only enhance Austria-Hungary's dependence on the Austro-German alliance as a substitute.

However unstable the dual monarchy might appear, however much it might seem a relic of the eighteenth century, its survival was much less remarkable than that of its immediate eastern neighbour, the Ottoman empire. The origins of the tensions in the Balkans which became the immediate cause of the First World War lie not so much in Austrian aggression (although in time this came to play its part) as in Ottoman senescence. In July 1908 the Young Turks, a group of Turkish patriots, backed by the III army corps at Salonika (the army being an agent of modernization), staged a revolution against the oriental despotism of Sultan Abdul Hamid II. Abdul Hamid granted the constitution which the Young Turks demanded, but then in April 1909 staged a counter-revolution. The Young Turks rallied, ousted Abdul Hamid, and installed his brother, Mohammed V, as the new Sultan.

The Young Turks' revolution threatened to transform the situation in European Turkey. Over the last half of the nineteenth century the great powers of Europe had endeavoured to manage Turkey's decline, and in particular its withdrawal from the Balkans, in as gradual a manner as possible. In 1878 they had stepped in after the Russian defeat of Turkey, and at the Congress of Berlin had acknowledged the independence of Serbia, Romania, Montenegro, and Bulgaria, the latter albeit under Ottoman suzerainty, and had entrusted to Austria-Hungary the administration of Bosnia-Herzogovina while leaving it technically in Turkish possession. Turkey's lingering status as a European power was confirmed by its continued direct rule over Rumelia and Macedonia. Russia, although understandably peeved at not reaping any return from its success on the battlefield, had come to accept that it must collaborate with Austria-Hungary in the management of Ottoman decline. Neither power, least of all Russia after the Manchurian defeat and the subsequent revolution, could afford disturbance on its frontiers. By July 1908, however, both had acknowledged an interest in revising the Congress of Berlin—Russia, thwarted in its Far Eastern ambitions, had turned south-west and wanted the use of the Black Sea straits for its warships, and Austria-Hungary was anxious to regularize its position in Bosnia-Herzogovina.

Austrian urgency derived from its relationship with Serbia: the latter, rather than be content with its position as a client of the dual monarchy, was touting itself as the 'Piedmont' of the South Slavs—the nation that would lead the way to the formation of a large independent South Slav state. A greater Serbia would not only draw in Bosnia-Herzogovina but also the Serbs and possibly Croats resident within the empire proper: external problems would be projected back into the domestic arrangements of the dual monarchy. In 1907 Austria-Hungary had planned a railway line to link the Austrian and Turkish networks south of Serbia, so as to consolidate the empire's stabilizing influence in the Balkans and at the same time outflank Serbia. Britain (which wrongly saw the proposal as an extension of German ambitions, and part of a Berlin-to-Baghdad railway) and Russia opposed, and by 1908 Austria-Hungary was confronted with a loss of prestige in the Balkans. Then in July the Young Turks' revolution put all the assumptions underpinning Austrian and even Russian policy into reverse. The Young Turks might apply the principles of democracy and nationalism to the Balkans, in which case Austro-Russian abilities to manage the situation would be considerably dented. Similar effects would follow on any precipitate completion of Turkish withdrawal from

Europe. Alternatively, a reinvigorated Ottoman empire might try to reassert its crumbling position in the Balkans. However, that was likely only to provoke the insurrectionary talents of Turkey's Slav subjects.

On 16 and 17 September 1908 the foreign ministers of Austria-Hungary and Russia, Aehrenthal and Izvolsky, met at Buchlau to discuss the position.[67] Both were acting independently of their alliance partners. Aehrenthal brought to the meeting a self-confidence unwarranted by the overall situation in the Balkans but no doubt buttressed by his awareness of Russia's relative weakness. In this he was right: when confrontation loomed in March 1909 the Russian minister of war said that the Russian army was not fit even for defensive operations. But Aehrenthal's aim was not aggression. Like Izvolsky, he intended to improve, not worsen, Austro-Russian relations, albeit at Serbia's expense. More specifically, he wanted a clear demarcation between Austrian interests in the Balkans and Turkish. He therefore proposed the annexation of Bosnia-Herzogovina. What he had in mind was a foreign policy success sufficient to rally the Habsburg loyalties of the national groupings and especially of the Magyars. In this he picked up the schemes of Stephan Count Burian, who felt that the incorporation of Bosnia within the empire would divide South Slav nationalism between Zagreb and Belgrade, and so weaken its impact that the threat of trialism would be removed. Moreover, if Bosnia-Herzogovina were attached to Hungary rather than to Austria, the expansion of the former would enhance the *Ausgleich* by making it more truly a marriage of equals. For Aehrenthal, the domestic benefits of putting the dual monarchy's Balkan policy back on track went further: by focusing the army's attention elsewhere, it would still the efforts of the general staff to resolve the military budget by demands for preventive war against the empire's ostensible ally, Italy.[68]

The lure for Izvolsky was the prospect of getting something for nothing. By his reckoning Austria-Hungary already exercised control over Bosnia-Herzogovina: formalizing the arrangement would leave Russia no worse off and would further Russia's wider foreign policy objectives after the defeat by Japan. The Balkan settlement imposed by the powers in the Treaty of Berlin, which still rankled in St Petersburg, would have been reopened, but through unilateral action by Austria, not Russia. Izvolsky would then be able to call for an international conference to review the treaty, and could appear as the protector of the Balkan Slavs. Most important, he could use the opportunity to ask that the straits be opened to Russian warships. Aehrenthal had indicated

---

[67] Bridge, *From Sadowa*, 297–324, provides much detail on the Bosnian crisis; for the Russian perspective, see Lieven, *Russia and the origins*, 33–7; McDonald, *Union government and foreign policy*, 102, 130–51.

[68] Leslie, *Wiener Beiträge*, XX (1993), 314, 326–8; Stevenson, *Armaments and the coming of war*, 85, 114, 141–2; Hermann, *Arming of Europe*, 108–10.

that he would support such a request, and Izvolsky reasoned that Russia's new-found ally, Britain, might also be expected to back the proposal.

Izvolsky's strategy began to unravel almost immediately. In Sofia Bulgaria declared its independence from Turkey without waiting for Russia's support. In Vienna, on 6 October, Aehrenthal announced the Austrian annexation of Bosnia-Herzogovina earlier than anticipated, and presented Russian accept-ance of it as unconditional. And in St Petersburg Stolypin was outraged to discover that the foreign minister had been developing a policy which had not been concerted in the Council of Ministers and was more ambitious than Russia's weakened state would allow. Technically, Stolypin had no cause for complaint: neither the Council of Minsters nor the Duma had responsibility for foreign affairs, which remained a fiefdom of the Tsar, and in this case the Tsar was both informed about and supportive of his foreign minister's policy.[69] But Stolypin and, ironically, Izvolsky himself had promoted the idea that Russia's domestic strength and international status were linked, and that foreign affairs should be subject to wider accountability. This line had been easier to advance after the Tsar's humiliation in the Far East and the rejection of the Björkö agreement. The publication of the details of the Buchlau agree-ment produced widespread outrage in Russia. Izvolsky received no credit for ingenuity in relation to the straits or the Treaty of Berlin, and earned equal opprobrium for having handled the interests of the Balkan Slavs with so much cynicism. His only hope of salvaging either his domestic position or Russia's external authority resided in his plan that the whole question should go to a European congress.

In this too he was disappointed. Germany had no intention of promoting another conference, with its attendant danger of diplomatic defeat. This is not to say it was particularly pleased by Austria-Hungary's independent line, since it endangered Germany's wooing of Turkey, but by December it had come round to the idea of backing its ally. Bülow recognized that, if Austria-Hungary was to be an effective support in the event of a war in Europe, it must relieve Germany of some of the burden on its eastern front. At the time Austria-Hungary seemed more likely—if it were to make war at all—to do so on Italy rather than Russia, and antagonism towards Italy weakened the Triple Alli-ance. On 14 December Bülow gave Austria-Hungary Germany's support.[70] In January 1909 Conrad von Hötzendorff, the Austrian chief of the general staff, made contact with Helmuth von Moltke the younger, his German counterpart and Schlieffen's successor, in an effort to establish German operational plans in the event of war with Russia. Moltke warned that Germany's initial concentra-tion would be against France, but assured Conrad of German support against

[69] Fuller, *Strategy and power in Russia*, 419–20; Neilson, *Britain and the last Tsar*, 289, 296–302.
[70] Lambi, *Navy and German power politics*, 304.

Russia if Russia acted with Serbia. Neither Bülow nor Moltke expected the Bosnian crisis to result in war, but their attitudes were decisive in stiffening Austrian resolve. They had simultaneously strengthened the Triple Alliance, relieved Germany's own sense of encirclement, and exposed the weaknesses of the Triple Entente.

Russia, by contrast, was not able to elicit similar backing from its allies. France made it clear that no support against Austria-Hungary would be forthcoming. Britain reverted to a more traditional policy than the 1907 Anglo-Russian Entente had suggested likely. Long-established concerns about Russian naval penetration into the Mediterranean, and the defence of the route to India, manifested themselves in a reluctance to underwrite Russia's claim to use of the Black Sea straits. What 1908 offered Britain was a renewed opportunity for a role in Turkey: anxiety not to affront the Young Turks overrode any obligations to Izvolsky.

Thus, the most important consequence of the Bosnian crisis was Russian humiliation. The withdrawal of Turkey from Europe removed any buffer between the Habsburg and Romanov empires. The Russians could only interpret the annexation of Bosnia-Herzogovina as evidence of Austrian expansionism in the Balkans, an expansionism which might eventually take the dual monarchy to the gates of Constantinople and to a landward domination of the straits. Arguably Russo-Austrian collaboration in the Balkans could not have been long sustained independently of the Bosnian crisis. But now latent hostility was unavoidable if Russia was not to forfeit its great power status in the west as well as in the east. The Duma happily approved arms appropriations. Henceforth Russia's policy was to revolve around the creation of an anti-Austrian bloc in south-east Europe.

Nor was Austria-Hungary's own position much improved, despite the apparent gains. Russian involvement in the Balkans, particularly in Bulgaria and Serbia, was not consonant with Austrian objectives in the region. Aehrenthal had hoped to compensate Serbia for Austria's annexation of Bosnia by economic concessions sufficient to draw Serbia back into Austria-Hungary's orbit. Serbia rejected Austria-Hungary's proposals. Aehrenthal's response was to invoke the threat of military action. On 29 March 1909 the mobilization of the Austro-Hungarian army was approved. Two days later Serbia climbed down, promising to be a good neighbour. Aehrenthal had not entered the crisis with any intention of applying coercion, and not until December had he been willing to countenance the Conrad–Moltke exchange of views. But now he was convinced of the value of military pressure in Balkan diplomacy. At one level this change of heart reflected the views of Conrad, who had transferred his advocacy of preventive war from Italy to Serbia, arguing that Russia's weakness gave the dual monarchy a unique opportunity to settle with Serbia. But Conrad wanted war, not the threat of war. He was furious that the opportunity for the former had been forfeited in favour of the latter. Next time, he warned, Russia would not be so compliant.[71]

Nor did long-term relations with Serbia look much more auspicious. Serb sentiment, both in the population as a whole and in the army specifically, was not in sympathy with its government's actions. When *Narodna Odbrana* (National Defence), a Serb society committed to revolutionary activity in Bosnia, was forced by the government in the light of its undertaking to Austria to modify its position and concentrate on cultural activities, its place was promptly taken by a secret organization, *Ujedinjenje ili Smrt* ('Unification or Death' but known to its enemies as 'Black Hand'), committed to Serbia's fulfilment of its self-appointed role as the Piedmont of the South Slavs, and to fighting beyond Serbia's frontiers for the achievement of that goal.[72]

Therefore Austria's relations with Serbia showed little hope of improvement. Furthermore, at home the acquisition of Bosnia-Herzogovina failed to resolve the conflicts generated by the *Ausgleich*. The new province was not incorporated into either Austria or Hungary, but administered jointly. The difficulties of concerting a wider Balkan policy were compounded: the case for a South Slav component within the empire, for trialism, was strengthened by the annexation, and thus Hungary's fears that it would lose its control over Croatia heightened. And finally, the crisis which Austria-Hungary had initiated independently of Germany had had the effect of confirming Austrian subordination to its northern partner. Although Austria-Hungary would try to pursue an independent policy on other occasions before 1914, in the eyes of the Triple Entente—and especially of Britain—Austria was now no more than Germany's stalking-horse in south-eastern Europe.

This analysis was right in so far as the Bosnian crisis did mark the beginnings of a reorientation in German foreign policy. By 1909 the domestic repercussions of *Weltpolitik*—the budgetary consequences of Tirpitz's fleet and the associated problems of managing the Reichstag—had begun to make that particular form of imperialism unsustainable, at least at such a high tempo. The process of disillusionment was completed with what was perceived as humiliation over Morocco in 1911: not only were ships expensive but they did not even guarantee diplomatic success. In place of *Weltpolitik*, the idea of Germany as the dominant continental power gained strength. Blocked by Britain at its western maritime exits, Germany should instead turn east, to central Europe and even, via Austria-Hungary, to south-east Europe and to Turkey. In 1912 Walther Rathenau of the *Allgemeine Elektrizitatsgesellschaft* sketched out to the Kaiser and Bethmann Hollweg a plan for a central European customs union. Germany's volume of trade was the highest in the

---

[71] Tunstall, *Planning for war*, 60–8; Hermann, *Arming of Europe*, 128–30; Stevenson, *Armaments and the coming of war*, 114–22.
[72] Dedijer, *Road to Sarajevo*, 371–8.

world, but it was unbalanced: between 1887 and 1912 imports rose 243.8 per cent but exports increased by only 185.4 per cent. Each of its major economic rivals, the United States and Britain, had carved out an area of effective domination, in the Americas and in the British empire respectively; Russia had the potential to do the same in Asia. Germany, not least in order to balance its trade, should become the pivot of a European economic bloc, an enclosed free-trade area, a *Mitteleuropa*.[73]

It is too simplistic to see a direct switch from *Weltpolitik* to *Mitteleuropa* occurring between 1909 and 1912. The German fleet and the now-flourishing expectation of 'a place in the sun' could not simply be put to one side. *Weltpolitik* would continue as a theme of German policy. Nor had *Mitteleuropa* arisen *de novo*. German economic penetration into south-east Europe was, as we have seen, already generating friction with Austria-Hungary. Rathenau's idea was to reinvigorate and give direction to an existing element in Germany's activities. Furthermore, *Weltpolitik* and *Mitteleuropa* were not mutually exclusive. 'Germany', Bethmann Hollweg told the Reichstag in 1911, 'can conduct a strong policy in the sense of *Weltpolitik* only if she maintains her power on the Continent.'[74] Part of *Mitteleuropa*'s attraction was that it provided a land route into Turkey and Asia: it showed once again how European and colonial concerns could no longer be neatly compartmentalized. The nature of Germany's imperialism had received a new emphasis, economic and diplomatic rather than naval and maritime, but in the long run and in its furthest reach it was just as likely to upset the interests of the existing imperial powers, particularly Britain and France, but also Russia.

Mitteleuropa in its proper sense, relating to central Europe, had a strategic justification as well as an economic one. *Weltpolitik* was a German policy; it did not in any way accord with the interests of the Triple Alliance as a whole. Italy as a Mediterranean power was dependent on Anglo-French good will for commercial freedom, and in particular derived almost all its coal (which met 87.6 per cent of its energy needs) from Britain.[75] Nor did Austria-Hungary, as it showed through its lack of support in 1905 and 1911, identify with Germany's Moroccan ventures. By pursuing *Mitteleuropa*, Germany might bring its alliance commitments and its economic imperialism into line, thus integrating its strategy. To give expression to this, the army—which had seen the navy's budget grow to 55 per cent of its own between 1897 and 1911—now began to make up for lost time, and to have increases of 29,000 men in 1912 and 136,000 in 1913. By switching the spotlight back to their land forces many Germans felt—with good reason—that they were affirming their natural strengths

---

[73] Fritz Fischer's writings are the main source for these points; see *Germany's aims*, 9–11, 28–9; *War of Illusions*, 6–11, 139–40; Fischer, in Koch (ed.), *Origins*.

[74] Herwig, 'Imperial Germany', in E. May (ed.), *Knowing one's enemies*, 82.

[75] Bosworth, *Italy and the approach*, 17.

rather than—as they had been doing with the navy—trying to build from weakness.

If all this had amounted to a consistent policy the events of 1912 to 1914 in the Balkans might not have been as confused as they became, or at least might not have had such wide repercussions. To Austria-Hungary in particular Germany seemed unable to follow a steady course. Partly this was because Germany continued both to affirm the alliance and yet at the same time to undercut Austria-Hungary's economic position in the Balkans. Furthermore, Germany's efforts could as often reflect dynastic sympathies (there were Hohenzollerns on the thrones of Greece and Romania) as Austrian interests. Not least because of its doubts about Romania's loyalty, Austria-Hungary saw Bulgaria, a power without ethnic interests in the population of the empire, as its natural ally in the Balkans: Germany did not. Ironically, too, the very pace of German industrialization confused and weakened Germany's policies in south-east Europe. By 1913 over half Germany's foreign investment in Europe and almost 40 per cent in the world was concentrated in the area between Vienna and Baghdad.[76] But, despite such figures, Germany was disconsolate. German capital was so absorbed by domestic production that the aggregate left over for foreign investment was small; France—as a power that was industrializing more slowly and where capital therefore remained uncommitted—proved a much more attractive money market for the emergent Balkan states. In Serbia, Greece, and Bulgaria French capital won out over German, and even in Romania—where Germany made special efforts—Germany's share of state loans and in the oil market fell after 1911. But this was a competition from which Austria-Hungary itself could not derive benefit. Twenty-five per cent of all German foreign loans went to the dual monarchy; the latter imported more from the former than it exported; and yet Austria-Hungary could not diminish its dependence by raising loans on the French Bourse, as the French (with Russian support) would not allow them to do so. Thus Austria-Hungary's dependence on Germany increased, but its ability to influence German policy declined.[77]

Austria-Hungary's loss of control in the Balkans was not simply the result of German activities. The substitution in the region of Austro-Russian antagonism for their erstwhile détente created opportunities for the newly emergent Balkan states. The latter could exploit great-power rivalry for their own ends in a way that great-power collaborative action had in the past made impossible. Thus, while superficially the Balkans appeared to be the focus of Austro-Russian hostility, the inner dynamism of the situation was provided by the opposition of the Balkan states to Turkey. This put Austria-Hungary at a yet

[76] Herwig, in May (ed.), *Knowing one's enemies*, 86.
[77] Fischer, *War of Illusions*, 291–8; Fischer, in Koch (ed.), *Origins*, 141–8.

greater disadvantage, for the dual monarchy had strapped itself to a losing policy, the maintenance of a Turkish presence in Europe. It hoped thereby to keep the Slav states on its frontiers, and particularly Serbia, in a state of dependence.

The next stage in Ottoman decline was not, however, initiated by the Balkan states themselves, but by the third member of the Triple Alliance, Italy. Despite its humiliation at Abyssinian hands at Adowa in 1896, Italy had not abandoned its colonial aspirations. Growing French strength in the Mediterranean and in Morocco fuelled Italian jealousy, born of the conviction that Italy too was a Mediterranean power. Floated by the patriotic rhetoric celebrating the fiftieth anniversary of the Risorgimento, and anxious to exploit a favourable constellation on the international scene, Italy declared war on Turkey on 29 September 1911 and launched an expedition to seize Libya. Proof was once again to be provided that colonial interests could not be pursued without European consequences.

The threat to Turkey increased Russian sensitivities over the future of the Black Sea straits. Between 1903 and 1912 37 per cent of Russian exports and three-quarters of Russia's grain shipments passed through the straits.[78] Russia's anxiety that no other state should control such a vital waterway was second only to its desire to control the straits itself. The presence of the Italian navy in the Dodecanese and its bombardment of the Dardanelles in April 1912 gave as concrete expressions to Russian fears as had Austria-Hungary's behaviour in the Bosnian crisis. Good relations with Bulgaria seemed to be the first step in neutralizing the landward approaches to the straits. Russia's task was made more easy by Austria-Hungary's support of Turkey, a policy with little appeal in Sofia. But, alongside this defensive motivation on Russia's part, there flourished in some quarters a more virulently pan-Slav and anti-Austrian sentiment. N. V. Hartwig, the Romanovs' representative in Belgrade, was fired by such considerations and played a key role in effecting, on 13 March 1912, a most unlikely rapprochement, an alliance between Serbia and Bulgaria.

Hartwig's policy was not necessarily the same as that of Sazonov, Izvolsky's successor as foreign minister. In 1910 and 1911 Russo-German relations improved. The Kaiser and the Tsar met; Sazonov's visit to Berlin produced an agreement over the Baghdad railway in exchange for German willingness to restrain Austria-Hungary in the Balkans; and the following year Russia—in revenge for its allies' failure to support it in 1909—stood aloof over Morocco. Even a thawing in Austro-Russian relations was not beyond the bounds of possibility: Franz Ferdinand, somewhat far-fetchedly, found his enthusiasm for the monarchical principle favouring a resuscitation of Bismarck's *Dreikaiserbund*, an alliance of Germany, Russia, and Austria-Hungary. In 1910 Russia

---

[78] Lieven, *Russia and the origins*, 45–6.

began a redeployment of its forces to the east, so threatening a weakening of its commitment to France and a reawakening of its antagonism for Japan.[79]

Therefore Poincaré's visit to Russia in August 1912 had a dual aim: he wished to restrain Russia in the Balkans, but he also had to reaffirm the Triple Entente.[80] However, Poincaré's efforts to achieve the latter could only undermine the former: France's repeated affirmation of the Entente in 1912 encouraged Russia to feel confident that, if its Balkan manoeuvres led to a clash with Austria-Hungary and then Germany, France would back it up. Such expectations, once formed, were not undermined by other signals from Paris. In a memorandum prepared for Poincaré on 2 September 1912 the French general staff welcomed war in the Balkans as likely to weaken Austria-Hungary, so freeing Russia to take on Germany: 'Under these conditions, the Triple Entente ... could achieve a victory permitting it to remake the map of Europe.'[81] Delcassé, appointed as France's ambassador to St Petersburg in 1913, affirmed France's support of Russia's grievances against the Austrians. With France standing by Russia just as surely as Germany stood by Austria-Hungary, the alliance blocs of the great powers were ranged against each other in the Balkans. Their problem was that none of them was a prime mover in Balkan politics.

Russia's policy, whether embodied by Sazonov or Hartwig, was not at bottom that of Serbia and Bulgaria. The aim of the Serb–Bulgar treaty was to complete the Ottoman ejection from Europe by the conquest and partition of the one surviving piece of Balkan Turkey, Macedonia; the terms contained a secret clause concerning possible attack against Austria-Hungary only if the dual monarchy itself intervened. The policy of Turkey in Macedonia was zealously repressive. In the course of 1912 Greece and Montenegro fell in behind Serbia and Bulgaria. While Germany, Russia, and Austria-Hungary spoke piously of restraint, the Balkan League—conscious of the opportunity created by the Italian attack on Libya—prepared for hostilities. On 8 October Montenegro declared war on Turkey. On 15 October Turkey came to terms with Italy, forfeiting Libya in its bid to concentrate on the danger closer to home. On 17 October Serbia, Bulgaria, and Greece joined Montenegro. The rapidity and scale of the Balkan League's success took the great powers by surprise. A high growth rate in the population, without any accompanying industrialization to soak up the available labour, had permitted the Balkan states to form huge peasant armies.[82] The Turks, outnumbered by almost two to one, spurned the counsel of their German military advisers and opted for

[79] Fuller, *Strategy and power in Russia*, 396, 427–30, 433.
[80] See p. 29.
[81] Hermann, *Arming of Europe*, 178.
[82] Zeman, 'The Balkans and the coming of war', in Evans and Pogge von Strandmann (eds.), *The coming*, 31.

encounter battles rather than defensive ones. By mid-November the Turks had been driven out of Thrace and Macedonia, and stood with their backs to Constantinople.

Turkey's defeat was a major setback for Germany and for Austria-Hungary. A strong Turkey, putting pressure on Russia in the Black Sea and the Caucasus, and on Britain in Egypt and Persia, relieved the burden on Germany.[83] For Austria-Hungary such stunning Slav triumphs could only foster irridentism within the empire. In the immediate term, Serbia's expansion—and claim to head a South Slav state outside Austria-Hungary—continued. To baulk Serbia, to continue its dependence on other powers, Berchtold, Aehrenthal's successor as Austria's foreign minister, insisted on the creation of Albania. His purpose was to prevent Serbia acquiring a Mediterranean port, but on 15 November the Serbs reached the Adriatic. The Austrian army, which had increased its annual intake of conscripts by 42,000 men in October, called up 200,000 reservists in Bosnia-Herzogovina. In Russia the Council of Ministers was divided. Both its chairman, Kokovtsov, and Sazonov feared another humiliation to put alongside the Bosnian crisis, and privately urged Serbia to compromise. Publicly Russia sprang to Serbia's support. The victories of the Balkan states boosted pan-Slav sentiment, and this found expression in a more bellicose grouping headed by the minister of agriculture, Krivoshein. Russia conducted a trial mobilization in Poland during October and November, and on 22 November (although the order was cancelled the following day) the Tsar succumbed to the war party's advocacy of a partial mobilization in response to Austrian concentrations in Galicia.[84] On 12 December Conrad von Hötzendorff, the advocate of a preventive war against Serbia in 1909, who had been dismissed for his continued espousal of a similar line against Italy, was recalled as chief of the general staff. As in 1909 Austria was using military signals to beef up its diplomacy. Germany had so far seen its task as restraining its ally: neither Wilhelm nor Moltke felt war with Russia could be justified by a dispute over Albania. But alliance obligations could not be totally denied. On 2 December 1912 Bethmann Hollweg declared in the Reichstag that, if Austria-Hungary was attacked by a third party while pursuing its interests, Germany would support Austria-Hungary and would fight to maintain its own position in Europe.[85] On 5 December the Triple Alliance was renewed: the danger of Serbia, a possible proxy for a great power, having possession of an Adriatic port alarmed Italy as much as Austria-Hungary. Meanwhile, on 3 December Britain threatened to abandon its erstwhile policy of restraining Russia and France. Haldane

[83] Schulte, *Europäische Krise*, 295–6; also *Vor dem Kriegsausbruch*, 14–15, 39–46.
[84] Bridge, *From Sadowa*, 348; Williamson, *Journal of Interdisciplinary History*, XVIII (1988), 800; L. C. F. Turner, 'The Russian mobilisation in 1914', in Kennedy (ed.), *War plans*, 252–6; McDonald, *United government*, 180–6.
[85] Jarausch, *Enigmatic chancellor*, 133–4.

warned the German ambassador in London that Britain would not accept a French defeat if a Russo-Austrian war led to a German attack on France. For both powers alliance loyalties outweighed the Concert of Europe.

Wilhelm was outraged by Haldane's statement. He had been persuaded that the First Balkan War was a war that Russia had fought by proxy, and that presented real dangers for the dual monarchy. Austria-Hungary was therefore in the right and the British reaction revealed the futility of Bethmann Hollweg's efforts to neutralize them. On 8 December he summoned a meeting at his palace. In attendance were Moltke, Tirpitz, August von Heeringen (the chief of the naval staff), and Georg Alexander von Müller (chief of the Kaiser's naval cabinet). Austria-Hungary, the Kaiser said, should be encouraged to persist in a strong line with the Serbs. If Russia came to Serbia's aid, Germany would fight. Wilhelm assumed that, in such a war, Bulgaria, Romania, Albania, and Turkey would stand with the Triple Alliance. Therefore Austria-Hungary would be freed from its Balkan commitments to concentrate against Russia, and Germany in turn could face west, with its full strength against France. Moltke greeted this scenario by saying that war was inevitable, and that the sooner it came the better for Germany. Tirpitz, on the other hand, reported that the fleet could not be ready for another twelve to eighteen months, by which time the Heligoland fortifications and the widening of the Kaiser Wilhelm canal to allow the passage of Dreadnoughts between the Baltic and the North Sea would be completed. Moltke remarked, not without justice, that the navy would never be ready.

Fritz Fischer has dubbed the meeting of 8 December 1912 a war council, and has seen a direct link between it and the outbreak of war in 1914.[86] The meeting ended with only one resolution, that a press campaign should prepare the German public for war with Russia. There is no evidence that the press chief of the Foreign Ministry attempted to orchestrate such a campaign, or that the newspapers could have been so manipulated if he had.[87] Fischer reckons two further conclusions were implied—that the army should be increased and that food stocks should be amassed. The 1913 law did give the army an increase of 136,000 men. In itself, however, the law does not prove Fischer's point. The navy was over-represented at the meeting, naturally enough as its immediate cause was the attitude of Britain. The minister for war, the man charged with implementing any increase to the army, was not present. In reality the new army law was already in preparation before the meeting of 8 December and its target was an additional three corps, to enter the order of battle in 1916 (and not 1914). Moreover, the bill was less a bid for strategic supremacy than a reflection of military weakness. Turkey's defeat cast doubts on the wisdom of

---

[86] Fischer, *War of illusions*, 160–203; Röhl, *Historical Journal*, XII (1969), 651–73; Röhl, *Kaiser and his court*, 162–89. A constructive critique is Lambi, *Navy and German power politics*, 382–4.

[87] Rosenberger, *Zeitungen als Kriegstreiber?*, 213.

German tactical doctrine and simultaneously removed an Asiatic counter-weight to the Russian army. Both the latter and the French army, by the virtue of the three-year service law, were being increased.

What is more supportive of Fischer's position is the change in the law's priorities and the tempo of its implementation. The general staff's worries about manpower in relation to Germany's external threats had had to compete with the Ministry of War's concerns for the army's internal order. At one level these were a demand for quality rather than quantity: ideally, growth should have been gradual, to allow first for the expansion of the army's training cadres, its officers and NCOs, and secondly to provide for the army's infra-structure, its equipment and accommodation. In the event, however, the measured growth towards 1916 was discarded in favour of an immediate increase in numbers. The army's field training, already compromised in part by its role as an agent of domestic order, was put second to its size. Heinz Pothoff, writing in the *Berliner Tageblatt* on 3 April 1913, thought such meas-ures could only be justified if war occurred within a year: it 'is no longer a peacetime measure, but simply a mobilization'.[88]

On the second point, that of food stocks, nothing was done in relation to the population as a whole—although preparations were put in hand for feeding the army. Germany's high tariffs limited its ability to stockpile grain. This omission did not indicate that Germany was not planning a war from Decem-ber 1912 if it assumed that such a war would be short: but it did not follow that it definitely was preparing for war (albeit a short one), and such discussion as did occur on the food question suggests a distinct lack of urgency.

In addition to countering Fischer's claims for the so-called 'war council', two further points need to be made. First, the meeting's most logical consequence would have been a large navy bill. The Kaiser's ire was directed at Britain, and it was the navy that said it was not ready for war. But, although the Kaiser endorsed the three ships-a-year tempo which Tirpitz had been advocating, Bethmann Hollweg was able to head off a new naval law. An increase in the navy would have cut across the needs of the army, and it was to those that the enthusiasms of the Reichstag could now be directed. The High Seas Fleet continued to plan for war against France and Russia, despite Wilhelm's injunction that it concentrate on Britain. Moltke's expectation was proved right: the navy was not ready in July 1914 and probably would not have been in 1920. Tirpitz's fleet was a weapon forged for cold war only. Secondly, Bethmann Hollweg was not present at the meeting and did not endorse its conclusions. The close relationship between the Kaiser and his service chiefs would prob-ably permit a gathering that excluded the political leadership nonetheless

---

[88] Quoted in Hecker, *Rathenau*, 148. The fullest discussion of the needs of training and civil order is in the writings of Schulte, *Die Deutsche Armee*; *Vor dem Kriegsausbruch*; *Europäische Krise*. See also Stevenson, *Armaments and the coming of war*, 295–6.

being called a 'war council'. But Bethmann Hollweg, not the service chiefs, took centre stage in the crisis that did lead to war. The policy which he—and Germany—followed between December 1912 and July 1914 is not marked by the consistency which would endorse Fischer's argument. It is even hard to sustain the case for an increase in anti-Russian propaganda in 1913.

What remains striking about the meeting on 8 December is that the decision for peace or war was made conditional not on the objectives of policy but on the state of military readiness.[89] The shift in attitudes to which this points was not confined to Germany, although it is probably true to say that the land arms race which it reflects was primarily a consequence of the 1912 German army law. Until 1910 the high-profile arms races had been between navies; in armies the modernization of equipment, and in particular the acquisition of quick-firing artillery, had acted as a brake on expansion. But after the second Moroccan crisis quantity not quality stoked the competition in land armaments. Very often the targets which the general staffs set were long term: in 1914 none of the current programmes of Germany, France, or Russia had been fully implemented. But the arguments which ministers of war used in order to secure the necessary appropriations revolved around present crises. Thus the Balkan wars sustained the momentum which Agadir had initiated. The trial mobilizations which became a feature of the diplomacy of those wars confirmed the emphasis on immediate readiness. Two independent but convergent consequences followed. First, external threats played key roles in parliamentary debates on finance, and the linking of public rhetoric to diplomacy narrowed the options open to foreign minstries. Secondly, foreign policy itself became militarized. This in turn gave general staffs greater political leverage in the formation of state strategy. As windows of opportunity seemed to close, so the idea of preventive war gained a hold.

This, then, is the real significance of the 'war council' meeting—the fact that Moltke advocated a preventive war. Nor was this the first time: he had done so in his exchanges with Conrad during the 1909 Bosnian crisis. For Moltke and the German general staff, war was endemic in international relations. Such a view was not the personal property of the Prussian soldiery: social Darwinism, the belief that states were rising and declining and would fight for position, was a prevailing orthodoxy that was just as capable of being embraced by liberal circles in more democratic states. The soldier's duty was to prepare for that war, and so fight it on the best possible terms. Preventive war was therefore the acceptance of an inevitable war at the right time. Moltke's predecessors in office had canvassed the idea—Alfred Graf von Waldersee against Russia in the 1880s,[90] and on some interpretations Schlieffen

---

[89] Geyer, *Deutsche Rüstungspolitik*, 88; the discussion which follows rests on Hermann, *Arming of Europe*, and Stevenson, *Armaments and the coming of war*.
[90] Kitchen, *German officer corps*, 65–6, 72.

in 1905[91]—and it is to be found incorporated in the popular military literature of the day, most notoriously in Friedrich von Bernhardi's *Deutschland und der nächste Krieg* (*Germany and the next war*) (1912). But none of these advocates of preventive war saw it as Fritz Fischer sees it, as a deliberate step to resolve an impending domestic crisis. Nor did Moltke approach the subject with the same calculation that previous chiefs of the general staff had brought to its consideration. Moltke talked in general terms of a coming struggle between Slav and Teuton: he was both pessimistic and fatalistic. He did not then combine these world views with the more specific military picture. As chief of the general staff he concentrated on operational plans for war against France, but did little to co-ordinate those plans with those of Conrad, and he did not attempt to formulate what we would now call a grand strategy, integrating operations with the overall picture in a specific way. Moltke's attitude accustomed both Bethmann Hollweg and the Kaiser to the possibility of war, but it did not affect policy in any immediate sense.[92]

At its most negative, the December 1912 meeting made clear what Germany did not want—a European war at that juncture. Thus Germany resumed its original policy, that of an alliance leader co-operating with the British in managing the situation. Superficially at any rate, the Concert of Europe was resuscitated. A conference of ambassadors in London rapidly agreed that an independent Albania stretching from Montenegro to Greece should be created. However, it then proceeded to emasculate the new state by allocating large chunks of its interior to Serbia and Montenegro, so depriving it of its original *raison d'être*, to be an effective barrier against the Serbs. Berchtold, caught between Conrad advocating war with Serbia and a finance minister predicting that war would entail economic collapse, gave in to his German ally and accepted the enlargement of Serbia. In February 1913 Turkey renewed hostilities against the Balkan states, and Conrad again pressed the opportunity for pre-emptive action. But Bulgaria's rapid success against the Turks, bringing it to Adrianople, led Russia to fear that Bulgaria would control the Black Sea straits: for the moment Russia tried to restrain the bellicosity of the Balkan states. Thus, when Montenegro seized Scutari, the port which the powers had allocated to Albania, Austria-Hungary's renewed threat of military action was backed up by an international naval demonstration, and Montenegro withdrew.

By May 1913 Conrad's demands for preventive war seemed to have been as ineffectual as those of Moltke. In reality the civilian front against military action was cracking. Aehrenthal's death removed its cement. Although expansionist in his policies, the former foreign minister rejected war as an option

---

[91] Ritter, *Sword and the sceptre*, ii. 106–7, 194, denies this; but see Lambi, *Navy and German power politics*, 242–4, 259–60.

[92] Hull, *Wilhelm II*, 239–42, 255–9, 262–5; see also Groener, *Lebenserinnerungen*, 136.

and curbed Conrad. His successors were less resolute in their brinkmanship. Repeated mobilization was expensive: the December 1912 crisis had cost almost 200 million crowns. The common finance minister, Bilinski, argued that war might be cheaper than recurrent mobilizations. Bilinski was a Pole, and for him the fact that the case for war, which had hitherto assumed Russian neutrality, might now embrace Russia enhanced its attractions.[93] The competition between the two states for influence in Galicia made Poland and the Ukraine almost as inflammatory elements in their relationship as Serbia. At the same time those civilians who favoured rapprochement with Russia—Magyars, like Tisza and Burian—did not therefore oppose a forward policy. They argued that two large, dynastic, multinational states should not allow themselves to be the puppets of the Balkan powers. For them the corollary of détente in the north was assertiveness in the south-east, building on Bulgaria and forcing Romania to declare its hand.[94]

For the time being the new foreign minister, Berchtold, who favoured better relations with Russia, held the line against war, but he was as aware as anyone of the dividends that Austria had reaped by its threat. Furthermore he headed a ministry that drew three further major and interrelated lessons from the events of the preceding six months. First, the Concert system was no longer the external buttress to Austro-Hungarian integrity that it had been in the past. Secondly, unilateral action, not conferences, had achieved Austrian objectives. Thirdly, the Austro-German alliance, although vital to both parties, was none-theless not supported with consistency by Germany: it paid Austria-Hungary to lead the way.

Austrian distrust of its northern partner was only confirmed by the events of the summer of 1913. In May the Serbs and Bulgars fell out over the division of Macedonia. On 1 June the Serbs and Greeks formed a defensive alliance, partitioning Macedonia and limiting Bulgaria to the line of the River Vardar. The Bulgarians, seething with indignation since they claimed that they had borne the burden of the fighting, declared war on the Serbs. The Russians were unable to check the Bulgarians, and saw their Balkan policy—and the Balkan League—disintegrate as the Second Balkan War took hold. The Greeks came to Serbia's support, and the Romanians—fearful of Bulgarian preponderance in the region and covetous of Silistria (which the Bulgarians were willing to let them have) and the southern Dobrudja (which they were not)—entered the war on 10 July. The Turks seized the moment to retake Adrianople. Further Serb victories were unacceptable to Austria-Hungary, and once again the dual monarchy prepared for war in the Balkans, this time to support Bulgaria. But

[93] März, *Austrian banking*, 103.
[94] Leslie, *Wiener Beiträge*, XX (1993), 315–17, 333–40, 360–9, 377–9; Leslie, 'Österreich-Ungarn vor dem Kriegsausbruch', 667–70; Stevenson, *Armaments and the coming of war*, 253–5, 267–75; Rauchensteiner, *Tod des Doppeladlers*, 20–1.

Germany aligned itself with the opposition. Wilhelm backed Romania and Greece, and hence also Serbia. Italy pointed out to the Austrians that any action they might take in the Balkans would be offensive, not defensive, and consequently the Triple Alliance could not be invoked. Therefore Bulgaria stood alone, and on 10 August 1913 signed the Treaty of Bucharest. Greece got southern Macedonia, Serbia northern Macedonia, and Romania southern Dobrudja. Bulgaria and Austria-Hungary had hoped that the great powers would subsequently revise these concessions. But Germany, anxious to curry favour with the victorious Balkan states, blocked any such proposal. Therefore Austria-Hungary's conclusions from May were reinforced in August—any passivity on its part was exploited; German support was capricious and therefore to be utilized when it was available; and the Concert system had irretrievably broken down. Four minor Balkan nations had flagrantly breached the Treaty of London and had not been called to order. As a result, Serbia had virtually doubled its territory and increased its population from 2.9 million to 4.4 million, to the point where its claim to head a South Slav state outside the empire had gained validity as well as shrillness. Romania, fired by its easy success in the Dobrudja, now fostered irridentism among its fellow-nationals in Hungarian Transylvania. And, even more significantly, Russia had learned that restraint in the Balkans simply resulted in the loss of influence. With Bulgaria a broken reed, Russia transferred its attentions to the waxing power of Serbia.

Those, like Fischer, who seek to trace a straight line from the December 1912 meeting to the events of July 1914 argue that Gemany's support for Austria-Hungary never wavered in 1913.[95] Furthermore, its desire to restrain the dual monarchy in the Balkans derived not from any rejection of war per se, but from the fear that it might break out prematurely. Part of the problem with the pursuit of such consistency is that its fountainhead must be the Kaiser. In that case the consistency lies in the respect for dynastic loyalties, whether in his support for the Hohenzollerns of Romania and Greece in the summer of 1913, or his affirmation of the Habsburgs that same autumn.

Both Germany and Austria-Hungary were sufficiently aware of the fractured state of their relations to make efforts to mend the bridges in October 1913. Serbia, continuing its forward policy, and justifying its actions by the revolts against Serb rule, occupied towns in northern Albania, thus clearly contravening the peace settlement. Austria-Hungary, anxious to use any opportunity to reverse the Treaty of Bucharest and even more anxious to curb Serbia, determined on a hard line. This time Germany stood by its ally: there was little risk in doing so since neither Russia nor France was prepared to condone Serb

---

[95] Fischer, 'Kaiser Wilhelm II und der deutschen Politik vor 1914', in Röhl (ed.), *Der Ort Kaiser Wilhelms II*, 264–8.

behaviour. Berchtold dispatched an ultimatum to Serbia, and Serbia gave way. In late October Wilhelm followed up Germany's affirmation of the alliance by a visit to Franz Ferdinand. The Kaiser charmed the archduke by his courteous treatment of the latter's wife Sophie, who as a Czech countess was treated as a commoner at the Austrian court. Most importantly, Wilhelm insisted that Serbia should be a client of Austria-Hungary; if Austria-Hungary had to fight to achieve this, then Germany would back the empire.[96] The centenary of the battle of Leipzig, when Habsburg and Hohenzollern had combined to over-throw Napoleon, helped bathe the Austro-German alliance—at least for the moment—in a warm light.

Neither power saw fit to remember that a third dynasty, that of the Roma-novs, had also participated in the victory of 1813. In practice the Romanovs' attention was focused on another anniversary that fell in the same year. The tercentenary of Romanov rule persuaded Tsar Nicholas II that a revival of his autocracy could be rooted in popular sentiment. In due course a stronger foreign policy would emerge as a means for the achievement of that end.[97] What marked the winter of 1913–14 and the following spring was an end to the ambivalence which had characterized Russo-German relations for so long (despite their membership of opposing alliances) and its replacement with categorical hostility.

Antagonistic commercial relations between the two countries meant that the Russian right, many of whom were naturally inclined to favour an alliance with autocratic, monarchical Germany rather than liberal, republican France, found its position increasingly hard to sustain. East Elbian landowners, as a reward for their agreement to Tirpitz's naval appropriations, had secured a tariff that effectively excluded the import of Russian grain into Germany. The effect was not reciprocal: by 1914 German rye had found its way into Finland and Russian agriculture was threatened with the loss of Scandinavian markets. Russia responded in the summer of 1914 by imposing a heavy tariff on imported grains, and the prospects for the renewal of the Russo-German commercial agreements of 1904—due in 1917—did not look good. Thus, Russian farmers found their views on foreign policy coinciding—albeit for different reasons—with those of industry. For German commercial policy cut two ways. German heavy industry wanted the reverse of German agriculture: it was anxious to lower tariff barriers between the two countries, thus opening the Russian market to German goods. Russian industry for its part needed—in its fledgling, if burgeoning state—the protection of high tariffs. Both agriculture and industry were therefore united in identifying national interests with economic policy, and both sectors saw themselves as exploited by Germany.

---

[96] Dedijer, *Road to Sarajevo*, 155–8; Fischer, *War of Illusions*, 221–3.
[97] McDonald, *United government*, 187.

In 1910–11 sections of the Russian press were advocating rapid industrialization as a foundation for waging war.[98]

In these circumstances foreign policy could become the unifying and soothing balm which the fractured state of Russian society so urgently needed. In the wake of the 1905 revolution the Tsar had accepted the establishment of a legislative assembly, the Duma, based on a wide, if indirect, franchise. But Nicholas was unhappy with the concession which he had made. The army, the navy, and the raising of foreign loans were all excluded from the Duma's competence. Under article 87 of the constitution the government was free to legislate while the Duma was not sitting provided the law was confirmed by the Duma within two months of its next sitting. Thus the Tsar had available the means to re-establish his authority, to assert that Russia's ministers were his servants and were not answerable to the Duma. In 1906 he dissolved the first Duma, an assembly that contained the flower of the Russian intelligentsia. The leaders of the Kadets—a liberal party representing the professional middle classes—decamped to Viborg in Finland, where they issued a manifesto rejecting the dissolution and called for civil disobedience until the Duma was restored. The Viborg manifesto produced little response: its effect was to divide and weaken the Kadets, since those who signed the appeal were disqualified from re-election to the Duma. The Tsar's efforts to limit the Duma were carried forward a stage further with the appointment of Stolypin as prime minister. He got the weakened second Duma to accept a revised electoral law, which favoured the countryside in preference to the towns and boosted Russian representation at the expense of the other nationalities. After 1907 the cycle of revolution and terrorism abated. Good harvests aided Stolypin's efforts to re-establish domestic order. However, the Duma—although more compliant than in 1905—was still a legislative forum where open and uncensored debate was permitted. Nationalism expressed within Russia was potentially almost as domestically divisive as it was within Austria-Hungary. But used externally, cloaked in pan-Slavism and embracing state support for the Orthodox church, it became a means to rally and manage the Duma. Liberal imperialism found powerful advocates among some of the Kadets: P. B. Struve argued that such a policy could reconcile the people and the state, and V. A. Maklakov supported Serb unification at Austria-Hungary's expense. Within the administration this sort of thinking found expression with the appointment in 1912 of the Slavophil liberal, Prince G. N. Trubetskoy, as head of the foreign ministry department concerned with the Balkans and Turkey. For Trubetskoy, and for many Russians before 1914, Austro-Hungarian policy in the Balkans was only rendered effective by virtue of German support.

---

[98] Siegelbaum, *Politics of industrial mobilization*, 13–14; also Linke, *Militärgeschichtliche Mitteilungen*, 32 (1982), 11; D. Geyer, *Russian imperialism*, 307–9.

Furthermore, Trubetskoy—like other liberals—derived strength and encouragement from the alliance with France and Britain.[99]

Thus anti-Germanism had, by the end of 1913, come to characterize the views of Russian farmers and industrialists, had the support of many of the intelligentsia, and had become a means by which domestic politics seemed capable of regulation and management. The penetration of German influence through the Balkans and into Turkey, the presence of German commercial interests in the Ottoman empire, symbolized most clearly by the Baghdad railway, triggered Russian anxiety with regard to the future control of the Black Sea straits. In 1912 the Turks had briefly to close the straits during the Italian war, and the Russian grain trade had lost 30 million roubles a month, with the adverse effects on the Russian balance of trade causing the state bank to raise its discount rate half a per cent in 1913.[100]

In October 1913 all these currents found their focus with the appointment of a German general, Liman von Sanders, to command I Corps of the Ottoman army at Constantinople. A German military mission, designed to train and upgrade the Turkish army, was not in itself a legitimate cause for objection. Liman was not the first German officer to undertake such a task in Turkey, and the British were performing a similar function in relation to the Turkish navy. But the Turks appointed Liman to a command, not to an advisory post. Furthermore, Wilhelm—in his usual bombastic way, and far exceeding the brief favoured by the German foreign ministry—had instructed Liman to Germanize the Turkish army and to make Turkey an instrument of German foreign policy and a counterweight to Russia.[101] Given the strength of Russia's reaction, the diplomats' more cautious approach prevailed over Wilhelm's instructions, military objectives were subordinated to political, and Liman von Sanders became inspector-general of the Turkish army instead. But the consequences of the affair stretched beyond its apparent solution. It consolidated Sazonov's desire that Russia control the straits, and by February 1914 he was clear that this would be a Russian war aim if war came. Even more importantly, it confirmed his fears of German ambitions, and revealed his preference for war rather than to have the Triple Alliance regard Russian interests as of no consequence. A conference convened by Sazonov in the middle of the crisis, and attended by the ministers for the services as well as by the chief of the general staff, revoked the renunciation of war that had guided Russian policy since 1905. Instead, war was deemed to be 'fully permissible', and the conference set out a series of escalatory steps designed to get Germany to comply with Russia's wishes. Sazonov was not so foolhardy as to

---

[99] Lieven, *Russia and the origins*, 90–100, 126–32; on Russia generally in this period, see Pares, *Fall of the Russian monarchy*.

[100] C. Jay Smith, *Russian struggle for power*, 63–5.

[101] Fischer, *War of illusions*, 330–54.

imagine that Russia was suddenly able to take on Germany and Austria-Hungary unaided. Thus, a necessary corollary of this shift was a much firmer allegiance to the Entente, and a determination to convert it into a fully-fledged alliance. Indeed, Sazonov had overreacted to Liman's appointment not least to test the Entente.[102]

France, through Poincaré, duly expressed to Izvolsky—now the Russian ambassador in France and working tirelessly for the promotion of the Triple Entente—its support for Russia. Such expressions were seen as inadequate by Sazonov, but they were more than sufficient to reveal the limitations of Bethmann's foreign policy. By emphasizing joint Franco-German interests in the Middle East, Bethmann had in 1913 achieved a measure of détente. Caillaux's return to office as minister of finance, the acrimony generated by the debate on the three-year service law, and the apparent waning of Poincaré's influence had all been good omens for Germany. But the Liman affair showed that, when driven to make a choice, the first priority in French foreign policy remained the Franco-Russian alliance. And, to add insult to injury, in 1914 once again French capital won out over German, with Turkey increasing its borrowings so that the level of French investment was three times greater than that of Germany.

By early 1914, therefore, the sole remaining plank in Bethmann Hollweg's foreign policy was the hope that Britain might yet be neutralized. In playing the Turkish card, Bethmann Hollweg had at least exploited the underlying and traditional weakness in Anglo-Russian relations. If Russia was unhappy about Germany's involvement with the Turkish army, it could hardly be ecstatic about the Royal Navy's comparable role with the Turkish navy—especially as the imminent arrival of two British-built Dreadnoughts would give the Turks supremacy in the Black Sea. Furthermore, other British Asian interests, particularly in Persia but also in Afghanistan, Tibet, and China, helped foster tension between the two powers. Bethmann Hollweg could console himself with the thought that, given time, the Anglo-Russian alliance showed every likelihood of collapsing from within.

Bethmann Hollweg's hopes were the stuff of Entente nightmares. Although Grey remained determined that Britain should retain a free hand, France could only endorse Sazonov's appeal in February 1914 that the Entente become a formal defensive alliance designed to deter Germany and Austria-Hungary. In April 1914 Grey agreed to the French suggestion that Russo-British naval conversations should take place, a proposal to which the cabinet gave remarkably ready approval. The naval talks were of course secret, but a German agent in the Russian embassy in London passed on their details to Berlin. On 22 May the *Berliner Tageblatt* published the details, and on 11 June questions were

---

[102] McDonald, *United government*, 190–5.

asked in the House of Commons. Grey denied that Britain was under any obligations and denied that any negotiations were in progress—a technical truth in terms of treaty commitments, but a strategic fiction.[103]

Grey had feared that, if known, the naval conversations would confirm German fears of Russia and strengthen the hand of what he saw as the war party in Germany against that of Bethmann Hollweg. His worries were realized. Grey saw the German ambassador on 6 and 9 July, and insisted that, although staff talks had taken place, the governments of the Entente were not politically committed to one another. But such artfulness, 'seeking a compromise between isolationism and a policy of alliance in order to gain the advantage of both at the same time',[104] smacked of deceit. Grey hoped to appeal to liberalism in Germany and yet betrayed his own sense of democratic accountability by misleading parliament—or at least so it seemed to Beth-mann Hollweg. For Bethmann the possibility of a German–British rapproche-ment as a basis for German overseas expansion was now gone; threatened too was the idea that each could manage its own alliance in the event of a crisis, as it had in November–December 1912.

Far more important, however, than these diplomatic setbacks was Ger-many's conviction that its encirclement was now complete. The fear which had accompanied German assertiveness gained the upper hand: the bull in the china-shop of European diplomacy began to see itself as a resigned sacrificial victim. For the Anglo-Russian naval talks gave the cue to the latent but pervasive Russophobia that gripped not only Bethmann Hollweg but also Moltke. The press and popular feeling played on the inevitability of a clash between Teuton and Slav. This emotive vocabulary did not seem inappropriate given the reality of the position. The Russian army's budget—independently of extraordinary capital grants—had grown from 406 million roubles in 1907/8 to 581 million in 1913/14. Spending on the navy nearly tripled over the same period, and in 1914 exceeded that of Germany. In 1913 the Russians introduced the 'grand programme', enacted in 1914, which aimed to increase the annual contingent of recruits for the army from 455,000 to 585,000, and to expand the total number of divisions from 114.5 to 122.5.[105] The Russian war minister accompanied these enlargements with statements calculated to stoke German anxieties. The German and Austro-Hungarian armies were already inferior to those of France and Russia by over a million men in the summer of 1914;[106] by 1917 the Russian army alone would be three times the size of Germany's. The

[103] Williamson, *Politics of grand strategy*, 335–8.
[104] Egmont Zechlin, 'Cabinet versus economic warfare in Germany' in Koch (ed.), *Origins*, 199.
[105] David Jones, 'Imperial Russia's forces at war', in Millett and Murray, *Military effectiveness*, i. 265–6; Stone, *European society*, 334–5; Knox, *With the Russian army*, vol. i. p. xviii; D. Geyer, *Russian imperialism*, 200–1.
[106] Schmidt-Richberg, *Der Regierungszeit Wilhelms II*, 38.

argument that, objectively, there was no chance of a Russian challenge in economic terms did not figure in the calculations on the military balance. By 1914 French loans had enabled the construction of strategic railways so that Russia's mobilization could be accelerated, and the first troops be into battle within fifteen days. German plans drawn up in 1905 rested on the then-valid assumption that Germany would have six weeks in which to deal with France before turning east: the very existence of that planning assumption, which by 1913 was demonstrably wrong, added to Germany's sense of panic. In May 1914, therefore, Moltke's advocacy of preventive war took on greater urgency, if no more precision: 'we must wage a preventive war', he told Gottlieb von Jagow, the foreign minister, 'to conquer our opponents as long as we still have a reasonable chance in this struggle.'[107]

Both Jagow and Bethmann Hollweg resisted Moltke's suggestion.[108] But the case for doing so seemed, in the self-absorbed atmosphere of Wilhelmine politics, to be growing weaker. As early as December 1912 Bethmann—who had visited Russia in that year—confessed: 'One must have a good deal of trust in God and count on the Russian revolution as an ally in order to be able to sleep at all.'[109] The increases in the army necessary to meet the Russian threat exposed the delicacy of his own ability to manage the Reichstag. In 1913 90 per cent of central government spending was devoted to the armed forces, and the national debt had increased 125 per cent in 1898.[110] The conservatives still opposed property taxes, and the introduction of direct Reich taxation threatened the balance between Prussia and Germany as well as increasing Bethmann's reliance on liberal support. In addition, it was not clear that spending at such levels could be maintained. By the end of 1913, the German economy was in recession, 5 per cent of the labour force was out of work, and fears of depression followed.[111] Bethmann's ability to manage the domestic situation seemed as doubtful as his competence to overcome Germany's succession of diplomatic setbacks. Bethmann himself increasingly gave way to fatalism: the death of his wife on 11 May 1914 can only have confirmed his sense of resignation.

Optimists in 1914 took comfort from the fact that the great powers had successfully surmounted a succession of crises since 1905. On the surface, it seemed that the international system could regulate itself. But none of those crises had resolved the underlying problems which had given them birth. Above all, nobody saw the Treaty of Bucharest and the end of the Second

---

[107] Jarausch, *Central European History*, II (1969), 59.

[108] Mommsen, 'The topos of inevitable war in Germany in the decade before 1914', in Berghahn and Kitchen (eds.), *Germany in the age of total war*, 40; also Jarausch, *Enigmatic chancellor*, 146–7.

[109] Jarausch, *Enigmatic chancellor*, 96.

[110] Herwig, *Luxury fleet*, 78; Kennedy, *Anglo-German antagonism*, 357–8, gives slightly different figures.

[111] Berghahn, *Germany and the approach of war*, 156–60; Fischer, *War of illusions*, 355–68.

Balkan War as more than an armistice. Austro-Serb relations remained locked in rivalry. Germany's own ability to manage another confrontation was diminished by its need to support its ally, a dependence made more pressing by Russia's military and economic growth. The fact of direct Russo-German antagonism would change the dimensions of the next Balkan crisis. And the remoteness of Balkan politics, the fratricidal nature of their warfare, did not diminish their importance for Europe as a whole. In the Balkans imperial rivalries intersected and overlapped with the cold war of the alliances. The Balkans were also the point where three empires—the Russian, the Ottoman, and the Austro-Hungarian—came face to face with the imminent prospect of their own decline as great powers.

THE JULY CRISIS

In 1914 the annual summer manoeuvres of the Austro-Hungarian army were centred on XV and XVI corps in Bosnia.[112] In March it was announced that the Archduke Franz Ferdinand would attend the manoeuvres and would visit Sarajevo. Franz Ferdinand himself was somewhat apprehensive about the trip. On one level the Austrian occupation of Bosnia-Herzogovina had been enlightened: the road mileage of the province had increased over seven times since 1878, the railways had arrived, and new coal- and iron mines had been opened. But the administration of the crown-lands smacked of colonialism. Divide and rule was the Austrian path, retaining Moslem feudal landlords and so setting them against the Christian population. The army, increasingly frustrated by what it saw as lax government in Austria and Hungary, determined that its administration of Bosnia-Herzegovina should be a model of effectiveness. Franz Ferdinand himself advocated repression and active Germanization. He was also a staunch Catholic: in Bosnia Catholics were the minority (18 per cent) and 42 per cent of the population were Orthodox. Many Bosnians looked wistfully to Serbia. They were impressed not only by Serbia's growth in 1912 and 1913 but also by its schooling: young Bosnians crossed the border to Belgrade for further education. Franz Ferdinand's apprehension had good grounds. Five assassination attempts had been made against representatives of the Habsburg administration in the previous four years. In the circum-

---

[112] In addition to the works listed in nn. 1 and 59 above, the following have been of general assistance throughout this section: Evans and Pogge von Strandmann (eds.), *Coming of the first world war*; Geiss, *July 1914*; id., *Journal of Contemporary History*, I (1966), 75–91; Jarausch, *Central European History*, II (1969), 48–76; Kennedy (ed.), *War plans*; Stone, *Journal of Contemporary History*, I (1966), 153–70; Langdon, *July 1914*; Thompson, *In the eye of the storm*; Trumpener, *Central European History*, IX (1976), 58–85; Williamson, 'Vienna and July 1914', in Williamson and Pastor (eds.), *War and Society in East Central Europe*, v. 9–36; K. Wilson, *Policy of the Entente*; id. (ed.), *Decisions for war*.

stances, and even without the benefit of hindsight, the early announcement of the visit of the heir-apparent, and the extraordinarily lax security associated with it, were inexcusable.

On Sunday, 28 June, the archduke and his wife were driven from the station at Sarajevo to the town hall, along the Appel quay. No soldiers lined the route. Nedeljko Cabrinovic, a Bosnian youth, threw a bomb, which bounced off the archduke's car, and then exploded, wounding two officers in the following car and a number of bystanders. The archduke went on to the town hall. He then decided to visit the wounded officers. At the junction of Franzjosefstrasse and the Appel quay confusion arose as to the route to be followed. The driver began to back the car. An associate of Cabrinovic, Gavrilo Princip, was at the corner, having failed earlier in the day to take his opportunity on the Appel quay. He stepped forward and shot both the archduke and his consort. Franz Ferdinand, whose unattractive character was at least redeemed by his affection for his family, called on his wife to live for the sake of their children. But by the time the car had conveyed their bodies to the governor's residence both husband and consort were dead. It was their wedding anniversary. It was also the day of the battle of Kosovo: in 1389 a single Serb, after defeat at the hands of the Turks, had penetrated the Ottoman ranks and killed the Sultan. For the Serbs and the Bosnians tyrannicide had retained a pedigree which no longer seemed so appropriate to the revolutionaries of industrialized societies.

The assassination led directly to the outbreak of the First World War. And yet, for all the subsequent efforts to trace its authorship to one of the great powers, it remains true that the prime responsibility rested with none of the major belligerents but with an amateurish student revolutionary body, Young Bosnia, whose success owed far more to luck than to a sophisticated conspiracy.

Princip—'a character from a Chekhov play except that when he fired he did not miss'[113]—was born in 1894, the son of a Bosnian Christian peasant family, had received his early education in Sarajevo but had completed it in Serbia, and had aspirations to being a poet. His brief life therefore embraced not only the Bosnian tradition of resistance to foreign, and specifically Ottoman, rule, which had been so easily transferred into opposition to Austria-Hungary, but also the fusion of romanticism and revolution characteristic of his hero Mazzini. Young Bosnia did not reflect a broad current of opinion but was one of a number of small student groups. The aims of these groups were diverse, but certainly Princip and his colleagues embraced the idea of a Yugoslavia, of a South Slav independent state, and rejected gradualism and reformism as means to achieve that end. Violence, they reckoned, would

---

[113] Taylor, *Politics in wartime*, 68; for a full account of the circumstances of the assassination, see Dedijer, *Road to Sarajevo*. Also, on Young Bosnia, see Wayne S. Vucinich, 'Mlada Bosna and the First World War', in Kann *et al.* (eds.), *The Habsburg empire*.

provoke Austro-Hungarian repression and so increase South Slav hatred of Habsburg government. Terrorism, tyrannicide, direct action, the decisive role of the individual in history—all these themes appealed to the Young Bosnians.

It is therefore hard to see how an assassination attempt would not have taken place even without support from outside. But the assassins did not operate alone. Two members of *Ujedinjenje ili Smrt*, acting under the cover of *Narodna Odbrana* and so eluding the detection of Austrian intelligence, played key roles. Major Vojin Tankosic of the Serb army provided the four revolvers and six bombs with which the conspirators were equipped; Captain Rade Popovic commanded the Serb guards on the Bosnian frontier and had seen Princip and his associates safely into Bosnia from Serbia some four weeks before. The key figure behind both officers, and the driving force in *Ujedinjenje ili Smrt*, was Colonel Dragutin Dimitrijovic, known as Apis. Apis was chief of intelligence in the Serb general staff: he had used his position to help *Ujedinjenje ili Smrt* penetrate the army, and also to create the frontier organization which Popovic represented and which allowed *Ujedinjenje ili Smrt* to carry its activities into Austria-Hungary. His objective, and that of his organization, was not the federal Yugoslavia favoured by the Young Bosnians but a Greater Serbia, with the implication that the Serbs would dominate the Croats and Slovenes in the new state. Apis was in contact with Artamanov, the Russian military attaché in Belgrade, but it does not follow that Russia was privy to the assassination. Apis's stock in trade, regicide, was not congenial to the Romanovs. Apis, for his part, wanted the achievement of a Greater Serbia to be that of Serbia itself, not that of Russia.[114]

Serb subjects were therefore implicated in Franz Ferdinand's assassination. Austria-Hungary's assumption, and indeed determination, that this was so was shared by most of the other great powers. But the involvement of the Serb government specifically remains a moot point. Although the tariff war of 1906 with Austria-Hungary (the so called 'Pig War', because the border was closed to Serbian livestock) had given Serbia a sharp push towards independent industrialization, this was a recent development and Serbia was predominantly a society of self-sufficient peasants.[115] In such circumstances the army, with its provision of professional education and its possession of sophisticated equipment and weaponry, enjoyed considerable political influence. In 1903 a group of officers, Apis among them, had effected a particularly brutal coup in which King Alexander and his wife had been murdered and the pro-Russian, albeit westernizing and liberal, Petar Karageorgevich, installed in his stead. Petar translated J. S. Mill into Serbo-Croat, and the constitution of 1903 contained all the trappings of democracy, including equality before the law, a free press, and

---

[114] In addition to the works already cited, see Zeman, *Break-up*, 24–34.
[115] Petrovich, *Modern Serbia*.

an independent judiciary. But the cabinets which followed the coup were short-lived, and the conspirators themselves continued in the army, their authority and influence increased by their king's indebtedness to them. The army was frustrated by the realistic stand taken by Serbia's ministers during the Bosnian crisis, but it was the aftermath of that affair which gave status and reality to the army's pretensions for Serbia as the Piedmont of the South Slavs. The gains of the Balkan wars hallowed the Serb army with the aura of victory. Re-equipped with French artillery (the cause and the fruit of the 'Pig War'), its peacetime strength standing at 200,000 men, it saw Serbia as an independent political actor.

Pasic, the prime minister, was more cautious, using the backing of Russia to hold the army in check, and seeking a modus vivendi with Austria-Hungary. Although he too was supportive of Serbia's expansion and of its inclusion of Serbs currently within the dual monarchy, he accepted that the achievement of that aim would be more gradual and piecemeal than did *Ujedinjenje ili Smrt*. The administration of the newly acquired areas of Macedonia brought the clash between Pasic and Apis, between the civilian government and the army, into the open. In December 1913 civilians were given priority over soldiers at public functions in Macedonia. Pasic's response to the outrage of Serb officers was to oust the minister of war. Apis and the opposition parties then rallied to oppose Pasic, and through Putnik, the chief of the general staff, put pressure on the king to dismiss Pasic's government. On 2 June 1914 Pasic resigned, and on 24 June elections were announced for 1 August. However, Apis's position was weak. King Petar abdicated, and his son Alexander backed Pasic against Apis. Both Alexander and Pasic looked to Russia for support; Apis turned to the army, but when he ordered a coup on 7 June it would not follow him. It has been suggested that so desperate had Apis's position become within Serbia that his motivation in backing Princip and his accomplices was to try to force a confrontation between Austria-Hungary and Serbia, in which the latter would be humiliated and the overthrow of the government thus become possible.[116]

In the circumstances of June 1914, therefore, Pasic could gain little from the assassination of Franz Ferdinand. But his responses were inevitably dilatory. It seems that he was informed that students armed with bombs and revolvers had crossed into Bosnia: it required little imagination to guess their likely target. Pasic therefore ordered an inquiry into the arrangements at the border, into the illegal traffic of weapons, and into Apis himself. But he did not dispatch a specific warning to the government of Austria-Hungary. An attempt does appear to have been made to halt the conspirators, but its author was probably Apis himself after the central committee of *Ujedinjenje ili Smrt* had belatedly been informed and had opposed his and Tankosic's actions. Although Pasic

[116] Geiss, in Koch (ed.), *Origins*, 83.

may not have approved of the assassination, domestically he was not in a sufficiently strong position to check it. He could not overtly antagonize the army any further, and anti-Austrian feeling and Greater Serb sentiment were genuinely popular in Belgrade. When the news of the assassination broke, his policy was to treat the matter as an incident internal to Austria-Hungary: it had occurred within the empire and had been carried out by its own subjects. But neither Serbia's ambassadors nor Serbia's press reacted with the same restraint; the enthusiasm of their responses to Franz Ferdinand's death did much to confirm Vienna's presumption of Serbia's guilt. Whatever Pasic's more sensible reflections suggested, the Serbian government after the assassination was not in a position forcefully to condemn it.

Whether an unequivocal and early response by Serbia to the assassination would have made any difference to Austria-Hungary's behaviour must be doubtful. Franz Ferdinand was not the sort of personality who commanded popularity, and his demise in itself did not cast the empire into deepest mourning: indeed, in Vienna the Prater continued its jollifications without interruption. But as the Serb press crowed, so the Austrian and even Hungarian newspapers retaliated, and indignation that the heir-apparent should have been eliminated—apparently—by a foreign power took on a totally justifiable note of grievance.

Well before this mood was common the minds of all but one of Franz Joseph's ministers were firmly set. In the preceding Balkan crises the strongest voice for restraint had been that of Franz Ferdinand himself. He had appreciated that, for all his advocacy of Germanization, the majority of the empire's population was Slav and that war against the Slavs outside the empire was not a sensible way to cement the loyalty of those within it. Furthermore, he recognized that such a war could not be restricted to Austria-Hungary and Serbia, but would draw in Russia. Not only would Austria-Hungary find a two-front war difficult to sustain, it would also automatically sacrifice his own foreign-policy objective of a renewed *Dreikaiserbund*. By his own death the archduke had made war possible in more ways than one.

The opinion that the archduke's moderation had had most frequently to counter in the previous eight years was that of his own nominee as chief of the general staff, Conrad von Hötzendorff. Conrad was a social Darwinist. He believed that a recognition that the struggle for existence was 'the basic principle behind all the events on this earth' was 'the only real and rational basis for policy making'.[117] Conrad regarded it as self-evident that Austria-Hungary would at some stage have to fight to preserve its status as a great power. For much of the early part of his tenure of office his focus had been on a preventive war against Italy, but from 1909 he came to see Serbia as the more

----

[117] Peball (ed.), *Conrad*, 148.

important issue. The irridentism of both powers threatened the southern belt of the empire, and war against one could provoke the other. Two cardinal points therefore followed. First, Serbia and Italy were both as much domestic as foreign problems, and their resolution was an essential preliminary to greater Austrian strength at home as well as abroad. Secondly, it was important to fight each power separately and independently rather than to face both simultaneously. War should therefore be undertaken logically or preventively: 'politics', he averred, 'consists precisely of applying war as a method.'[118] Conrad first advocated preventive war against Serbia in 1906, and he did so again in 1908–9, in 1912–13, in October 1913, and May 1914: between 1 January 1913 and 1 January 1914 he proposed a Serbian war twenty-five times.[119]

Ironically, by the summer of 1914, although his enthusiasm for war had not diminished, it resided less on the calculation of previous years and more on the resigned fatalism which characterized so much of German thought at the same time. The Hungarian parliament's opposition to the army's reforms had delayed the new service law's introduction until 1912, and the consequent reorganization would not be complete until 1915.[120] In conjunction, the Balkan states (without Russian support) could outnumber the Austro-Hungarian army, and the Serbs alone—Conrad was wont to reckon—could field 500,000 men (although only 200,000 would be available on mobilization, the balance being made up of reserves). Conrad saw the Balkan League as an Entente-sponsored organization which threatened the dual monarchy with encirclement.

Thus he added to his frustration with the Magyars the expectation of a life-and-death struggle between Teuton and Slav. But in so revealing his own Austro-Germanism, he placed himself at odds with the multinationalism of the army's Hapsburg loyalties. During the course of 1913 he had become increasingly distant from Franz Ferdinand, and in September, stung by the latter's acerbic (if warranted) criticisms of the army and its general staff, he had sought permission to retire. Cut off from his royal patron and distant from the key government ministers, he was becoming politically isolated once more.[121] Then the assassination and its consequences put him back at the fulcrum. His pessimism caught the apocalyptic mood prevalent in Vienna, suggesting that Austria-Hungary was already the victim of Conrad's Darwinian contest. War, he said on 29 June, would be 'a hopeless struggle, but even so, it must be because such an ancient monarchy and such an ancient army cannot perish ingloriously'.[122]

[118] Ritter, Sword and the sceptre, ii. 229; see also Peball (ed.), Conrad, 128, 148, 152.
[119] Dedijer, Road to Sarajevo, 145.
[120] Stone, Past and Present, 33 (1966), 103–11.
[121] Jerabek, Potiorek, 76–9; Leslie, 'Antecedents of Austria-Hungary's war aims', 310–13; Deak, Beyond nationalism, 72–4.
[122] Rothenberg, 'Habsburg army in the first world war', in Kann et al. (eds.), The Habsburg empire, 75.

He was determined, too, that this time the outcome would not just be more sabre-rattling: a repetition of the mobilizations used in earlier crises without actual fighting would, he warned, be bad for the army's morale. Nobody in Vienna on 29 and 30 June could misinterpret his resolve, even if its basis was no longer rational calculation but, in his own words, 'va banque'.[123] And the fact that he was listened to was itself in part a result of that previous enthusiasm for preventive war. By that enthusiasm, he had won Moltke's undertaking in 1909 that, if Russia mobilized to support Serbia against Austria, Germany too would mobilize: in other words, he was confident that he could turn against Serbia, with Germany either deterring or fighting Russia. He seems to have been remarkably slow to consider what France would do. That enthusiasm, too, had enabled him to accustom Franz Joseph's ministers to the idea and expectation of war. The domination of the chief of the general staff over the minister of war had been accomplished by 1900. Conrad's efforts to achieve comparable sway over the foreign minister had been thwarted by Aehrenthal, and indeed it was Aehrenthal's pacific line which had headed Conrad off in 1909.[124] But Berchtold was made of weaker stuff.

The foreign minister was not under pressure just from Conrad. His ministry was staffed by a group of younger diplomats, protégés of Aehrenthal, who were committed to the fulfilment of Aehrenthal's programme for an Austrian domination of the Balkans. Berchtold's conciliar style meant that he listened to their views. Each day during the July crisis he held meetings with his principal subordinates, and mapped his tactics on the basis of their advice. It was these men who shaped Berchtold's Balkan strategy before the assassination, and kept the foreign minister to his resolve as the crisis unfolded.[125]

Like Conrad, Berchtold was keen to frustrate an Entente-sponsored Balkan League. Late in June his ministry was considering a diplomatic offensive designed to create an alternative Balkan structure. Ideally its pivot would be Romania. This would please the Germans and it would give Conrad sixteen extra divisions and a secure flank in Hungary. But Austrian negotiations begun in November 1913 had foundered, in part on the Hungarians' refusal to make concessions over Transylvania. Realistically, therefore, Austria's hopes were pinned on Bulgaria, and possibly Turkey. The aim was to isolate Serbia and to block Russia. In a memorandum of 24 June Franz von Matscheko portrayed Belgrade as manipulating Russian aggressiveness in the Balkans for its own ends. Matscheko's tone was deliberately alarmist: he hoped thereby to rally both the Germans and the Magyars in support of Austrian diplomacy.

---

[123] Herrmann, *Arming of Europe*, 218.
[124] Rothenberg, *Army of Francis Joseph*, 125; Regele, *Conrad*, 60–4.
[125] Leslie, 'Österreich-Ungarn vor dem Kriegsaubruch', 662–6; id. *Wiener Beiträge*, XX (1993), 378–81; Fritz Fellner, 'Austria-Hungary', in Wilson (ed.), *Decisions for war*, 11–12.

The Sarajevo assassination presented this long-term policy with an immediate crisis. Matscheko's memorandum became the blueprint, not for forceful negotiation but for the negotiation of force. It seemed that Serb terrorism would lead to a Balkan League sponsored not by the Triple Alliance but by Russia. Swift military action—and it should be emphasized that Berchtold envisaged a war without the issue of an ultimatum and without the mobilization of Austrian resources—should eliminate Serbia's power in the Balkans, and so pre-empt a new league and destroy Russian influence. Potiorek, the governor of Bosnia-Herzogovina, no doubt anxious to cover over his inadequate security arrangements, exaggerated the unrest in Bosnia and pressed on Vienna the need for decisive and early steps against Belgrade. Berchtold and his colleagues were convinced of Serbia's culpability, and that inaction would be tantamount to diplomatic humiliation and would lead to a further decline in Austria-Hungary's status in the Balkans. By 30 June Berchtold was already proposing a 'final and fundamental reckoning' with Serbia. He told the royal household that the Entente heads of state should not be invited to Franz Ferdinand's funeral.[126] Franz Joseph did not demur, and on 2 July he reworked the Matscheko memorandum in a letter to Kaiser Wilhelm seeking his support. Count Alexander Hoyos, Berchtold's *chef de cabinet*, a protégé of Aehrenthal and a noted hawk, was chosen to bear the imperial letter to Berlin.[127]

Austria-Hungary had received no formal expression of Germany's views before Hoyos boarded his train. Hoyos had met the German journalist Victor Naumannn on 1 July, and Naumann, an acquaintance of Bethmann Hollweg and of Jagow, had assured him that the Kaiser would support the dual monarchy, even to the point of war.[128] But Germany's ambassador in Vienna, Heinrich von Tschirschky, had kept silent. Austria-Hungary's decision to fight Serbia was its own.

Firmness had worked in 1908 and 1913; on other occasions a willingness to negotiate had led the empire into restraint and loss of face. The interaction between domestic and foreign policy was not simply a contrivance, as has to be argued in the German case, but an iron law. As Conrad had remarked to Franz Ferdinand in December 1912, South Slav unification was inevitable. It could be achieved within Austria-Hungary or at Austria-Hungary's expense. If the former, given the power and strength Serbia had acquired, a showdown with Serbia could not be avoided. It was the Austrian general staff, not the German, for whom war was a strategic necessity.

---

[126] Herwig, *First World War*, 12; Rauchensteiner, *Tod des Doppeladlers*, 68.
[127] Bridge, *From Sadowa*, 368–74, 448–9; Williamson, *Austria-Hungary*, 165–89; id., in Williamson and Pastor (eds.), *War and society*, v. 9–36; id., *Journal of Interdisciplinary History*, XVIII (1988), 806–8; A. J. May, *Hapsburg monarchy*, 22–50, 55–8.
[128] Rauchensteiner, *Tod des Doppeladlers*, 70.

Franz Joseph's letter to Wilhelm was delivered by Hoyos to Count Szögeny, Austria-Hungary's aged and somewhat ineffectual ambassador in Berlin. The Kaiser had visited Franz Ferdinand and Sophie at their home as recently as 2 June, and his sense of personal loss gave him uncharacteristic decisiveness. He invited Szögeny to Potsdam on Sunday, 5 July, and over lunch—while stressing that he had yet to consult Bethmann Hollweg—expressed his conviction that Austria-Hungary should deal rapidly and firmly with Serbia, and that such action would have Germany's support. This typical display of apparent determination and swift resolve was effectively endorsed by the Kaiser's advisers. That same afternoon Wilhelm held a crown council at which Bethmann Hollweg, Zimmermann (standing in for Jagow, the foreign secretary being away on his honeymoon), Erich von Falkenhayn (the minister of war), Moritz von Lyncker (the chief of the military cabinet), and Hans von Plessen (the adjutant-general) were present; significantly neither Moltke, who was taking the waters at Karlsbad, nor any naval representative was in attendance. The meeting agreed to support the Austro-Hungarian desire to reconstruct a Bulgaria-centred Balkan League favourable to the Triple Alliance; as for Serbia, the dual monarchy's action was its own affair, but it was assured of German support in the event of Russian intervention. The following morning, 6 July, Bethmann Hollweg conveyed the council's views to Szögeny and Hoyos. Equipped with this 'blank cheque', Hoyos returned to Vienna.

What is striking about the 'blank cheque' is not that it was issued but that it was indeed blank. The council had made little effort to discuss the implications of what it was doing. Its decisions followed from previous events rather than from a projection as to the future. Falkenhayn wrote to Moltke expressing the view that neither he nor Bethmann Hollweg believed that Austria-Hungary would follow through the forceful language which it had so far employed.[129] But Bethmann Hollweg had done little to inform himself on precisely this point. When on 9 July he told the minister of the interior, Clemens von Delbrück, of the impending Austrian ultimatum he confessed that he had no idea of its contents; furthermore, so little was he disturbed by his own ignorance that he used it as a device to still Delbrück's alarm.[130] The fatalism which had increasingly gripped the chancellor had become a device to ease him of responsibility for his actions. Later in the same month he was to express the view that 'a fate greater than human power hangs over the situation in Europe and over the German people'.[131] The Kaiser too felt that the affairs of nations were beyond individual control and were subject to the inscrutable will of

[129] Quoted in Fay, *Origins*, ii. 212–13.
[130] Delbrück, *Der wirtschaftliche Mobilmachung*, 96.
[131] Diary entry for 27 July 1914, Riezler, *Tagebücher*, 192.

God.[132] Thus, nobody in Germany attempted to guide and manage events in July 1914.

Such an extraordinary abdication of responsibility is all the more remarkable in view of the fact that Bethmann Hollweg's calculations did not exclude the possibility of a major European war. The key question was the Russian response to an Austro-Hungarian invasion of Serbia. Assuming that Russia would intervene, Zimmermann told Hoyos that there was a 90 per-cent probability of a European war. But such realism—or pessimism—does not seem to have been widespread. By 11 July Zimmermann—whose reputation rested on his forthright but not necessarily consistent views—was confident that there would not be war because Austria and Serbia would come to terms. More widespread was the expectation that there would be war, but that it would be localized because Russia would stay out. That had been Plessen's view at the meeting of 5 July, and it was the line taken by Zimmermann's superior, Jagow.[133] Germany's ambassador in Russia, Pourtalès, continued to insist that the dangers of domestic revolution in the event of a major war would inhibit Russia. After all, Russia had backed down during the Bosnian crisis, and as recently as 1913 had endeavoured to restrain the Balkan states. Furthermore, its rearmament programme was not completed. If such calculations proved ill-founded, a second line of argument suggested that Britain and France would hold their eastern ally back from precipitate action. The Kaiser took comfort in the notion that his imperial cousin could not afford to condone the assassination of royalty. Outrage at the murders of the archduke and his wife seemed to have created a mood in Europe sympathetic to the Habsburgs. Bethmann Hollweg did not, therefore, embrace the probability of general war, but he was indubitably using its threat as an instrument in foreign policy, to isolate Russia both from its Entente partners and from its Balkan friends. His intentions were to strengthen the Triple Alliance by endorsing the Austro-German pact, and then, assuming the Austrians moved fast enough, to repeat the moderating role of 1912–13. The culmination of this process, according to Kurt Riezler, who was as close to Bethmann Hollweg as anyone in the July crisis, would be both a satisfied Austria and, eventually, a Russo-German agreement.[134] However, alongside the ideas of deterrence Bethmann Hollweg, and also Jagow, placed the calculations of preventive war. Serbia would be a good test as to how justified German Russophobia was: if Bethmann's bluff was called, and Russia did want war, then it was better for the two powers to fight it out in 1914, before Russia completed its rearmament programme in 1917. Furthermore, a war

[132] Moses, *War & Society*, V (1987), 31.
[133] Pogge von Strandmann, 'Germany and the coming of the war', in Evans and Pogge von Strandmann (eds.), *The Coming*, 115; Johannes Hürter, 'Die Staatssekretäre des Auswartigen Amtes im Ersten Weltkrieg', in Michalka (ed.), *Erste Weltkrieg*, 223–4; Epkenhans, *Wilhelminische Flottenrüstung*, 404.
[134] Röhl, *1914*, 22.

triggered by Serbia would ensure Austro-Hungarian support for Germany, and the fact that imperial Russia would have to initiate hostilities promised that within Germany the socialists would rally to the defence of the Reich. If European war was genuinely inevitable, the circumstances of July 1914 seemed as propitious for Germany as could be reasonably expected.

Bethmann Hollweg was playing fast and loose with the possibility, however remote he thought it, of a European war. He could only do so because his image of such a war—although widely held—was confused. The victories of 1866 and 1870 had achieved in short order and with minimal complications the political objectives for which they had been fought: Bethmann Hollweg's mental image of war in July 1914—at least as it related to an Austrian attack on Serbia—was of Königgrätz and Sedan, not of Verdun and the Somme. But also present in his mind was the idea of a long war with its concomitants, economic strain and social and political disruption. He saw a Russo-German war in such terms, for the possibility of war leading to revolution was a consequence he could envisage for Germany as well as Russia, and such a picture had to be present if he imagined that Russia might be deterred from intervention. Bethmann's policy in July was therefore made even more obscure by its ambivalence as to what war would be like—simultaneously it was a reasonable way to achieve policy objectives and the agent of total upheaval. The former implied that war could be an appropriate means to conduct policy, the latter that only its threat could so operate.

The chancellor himself made no attempt to resolve this dilemma, although his actions suggest that his hopes continued to be shaped by the prospect of a Bismarckian campaign. No preparations for a long war were made in July, and even on the 24th the Treasury rebuffed the general staff's suggestion that Germany build up its food stocks with wheat purchases in Rotterdam. Falkenhayn had assured the crown council on 5 July that the army was ready, but the authority with which he spoke was that of the minister of war, not of the chief of the general staff. He may have been buoyed up by the comparative success with which the 1913 army law had been rushed into effect, especially compared with the disruption which the three-year law was reported as having created in France. But the argument that the army was using this window of opportunity to exploit the idea of preventive war is hard to sustain. Falkenhayn thought that any conflict would remain localized, and promptly went on leave; he did not return until 27 July. Moltke, who was actually responsible for war plans, was not recalled until 25 July. Four days later the chief of the general staff was predicting 'a war which will annihilate the civilisation of almost the whole of Europe for decades to come'.[135] Bethmann had made no attempt to consult

---

[135] Quoted in Turner, *Origins*, 105; see also Afflerbach, *Falkenhayn*, 149–53; for an opposing view, see Stevenson, *Armaments and the coming of war*, 298, 303, 407.

the service chiefs earlier in July, in the first half of the month, when Germany might still have been able to fashion the progress of events. Not the least of the ambiguities that such a discussion could have clarified was Germany's support of Austrian operations against Serbia when Germany's war plans required the Austrians to turn against Russia. If, as has been claimed,[136] the 'blank cheque' was designed to get Austria-Hungary to pin down Russia, so leaving Germany free to knock out Belgium and France, then its strategic and operational assumptions were remarkably ill-thought-out.

The focus of much recent historiography with regard to the 'blank cheque' has been on Berlin. But although Berlin issued the cheque, it was Vienna that had requested it and it was Vienna that cashed it. After 6 July, and until 23 July, decisions were taken not by Germany but by Austria-Hungary. The Kaiser departed on a cruise. Jagow returned to the foreign office, but Nicolai, the head of espionage and counter-intelligence on the general staff, only came back to work on the same day as Moltke, 25 July, and Groener, the head of the railway department, not until the following day.[137] On 11 July Berlin informed its ambassadors of the possibility of Austrian action against Serbia, and in Rome the German ambassador inadvisedly told San Giuliano, the Italian foreign minister. Habsburg distrust of Italy, and in particular fears that Italy could exercise its claim to compensation in the Balkans (embodied in article 8 of the Triple Alliance), caused Berchtold to look on his northern ally with almost as much suspicion as a result of this leak as he did on his Mediterranean ally. Communications from Vienna to Berlin were therefore kept to a minimum.[138] The Germans had no direct share in drafting the ultimatum which Austria-Hungary planned to send to Serbia, although they were aware of its main points and knew that its contents were designed to be unacceptable to the Serbs. Germany's immediate purpose remained relatively consistent: an Austrian coup against Serbia, while Germany worked to localize and limit the repercussions.

On 7 July Hoyos, having returned to Vienna, attended a ministerial council summoned by Berchtold. It was the third time in twenty months that the common council had confronted the issue of war: diplomacy which carried the threat of war came naturally to it. The task which confronted Hoyos was the corollary of that which he had already fulfilled in Potsdam: having displayed Austria's resolve in order to be sure of German backing, he now had to emphasize Geman determination to forestall any backsliding in Vienna. He presented Germany's support in unequivocal terms, and as a result the Austrian prime minister, Sturgkh, shuffled off his customary ineffectiveness with a

[136] Pogge von Strandmann, in Evans and Pogge von Strandmann, *The Coming*, 116.
[137] Trumpener, *Central European History*, IX (1976), 62–6; Groener, *Lebenserinnerungen*, 141.
[138] Williamson, *Journal of Interdisciplinary History*, XVIII (1988), 809.

'firm intention of concluding the whole affair with war'.[139] Sturgkh knew how fickle Germany's support for Austria-Hungary had been in the last couple of years: it was necessary to seize the moment before Berlin changed direction, rely on Germany to deter Russia, and so shore up the empire by resolving the Balkan question once and for all. Speed was as essential to the calculations of Berchtold as to those of Bethmann Hollweg: any debate should follow a *fait accompli*, not precede it. He used Germany's support to shelve any worries about Russia and to narrow the council's focus on to Serbia alone. Self-deception led to simplification. That same day instructions went out to the Austrian ambassador in Belgrade which were unequivocal: 'However the Serbs react to the ultimatum, you must break off relations and it must come to war.'[140] But from 7 July delay set in, and with delay came loss of control.

Part of the delay was attributable to diplomatic calculation. Poincaré and the French prime minister, Viviani, were due to visit Russia from 20 to 23 July. Given the Austrian desire to limit the crisis, it made sense to postpone delivering the Austrian ultimatum to Serbia until the French leaders had quitted St Petersburg, and so avoid a co-ordinated Franco-Russian response which—on the evidence of 1912—would egg on the Russians. Much attention has been devoted to the other factors explaining Vienna's slowness in mid-July. But in the event the Austrian ultimatum was delivered as early as this reckoning would allow.

It also made sense to accompany the ultimatum with evidence of Serb complicity in the assassination. Many in Europe saw the Serbs as brigands, and were predisposed, given the 1903 regicides, to accept Austrian accusations on the basis of circumstantial evidence alone. In the event that was as much as they got. The Young Bosnians themselves were at pains to insist that the assassination was all their own work. Furthermore, even if they had Belgrade links, they—like the authors of the earlier assassination attempts—were Habsburg subjects. On 13 July the foreign ministry's investigator reported that he could find no evidence that the Serbian government had played a direct role, and by October, and the trial of Princip and his associates, the Austrian case against Serbia rested on the argument that the Young Bosnians had been the dupes of Serb propaganda. The Austrian investigation was not helped by its continuing ignorance of *Ujedinjenje ili Smrt*, and its consequent determination to pin the blame on the relatively innocent *Narodna Odbrana*.

However, the efforts to establish Serbia's guilt may not have been entirely fruitless, for Tisza, the Hungarian prime minister, maintained that they convinced him of the need to support the Austrian ultimatum. Franz Ferdinand's death had left Tisza as the single most important figure in the politics of the

---

[139] Leslie, 'Österreich-Ungarn vor dem Kriegsausbruch', 666; Stone, *Journal of Contemporary History*, I (1966), 164.
[140] Fellner, 'Austria-Hungary', in Wilson (ed.), *Decisions for war*, 15.

empire. He had been the only minister to oppose the strong line advocated at the ministerial meeting of 7 July. Indeed, his position was clear from 30 June. He saw Russia's entry in the event of an Austrian attack on Serbia as inevitable, and argued that Austria-Hungary should first engage in a diplomatic offensive to restructure a Balkan League embracing Bulgaria, Romania, and Turkey, which would support the Triple Alliance and leave Serbia isolated. Fundamental to Tisza's opposition was the issue of Magyar supremacy in Hungary. If Austria-Hungary successfully overran Serbia and then tried to digest it within the empire, the consequences would be a trialist restructuring of the empire, and a reduction in status and size for Hungary. Far more worrying to Tisza than the threat of Serbia was that of Romania. Romania, in the ascendant after its gains in 1913, was fostering irridentism among its fellow-nationals in Hungarian Transylvania. Magyar satisfaction with the *Ausgleich* as it currently stood combined with awareness of its vulnerability to produce caution. Furthermore, Tisza was well aware of the economic strains which war would impose on the empire, and which the 1912 mobilization had made manifest.

In the event, Tisza's opposition did no more than put down a marker for some of the dual monarchy's future problems. By 14 July he had been convinced by his fellow Magyar, Stephan Burian, who was effectively deputy foreign minister, that he should change his position. He was now prepared to accept an ultimatum designed for Serbia to reject. Politically, his earlier stance had become unsustainable. Popular passions against the Serbs had been roused in Budapest as well as in Vienna. The corollary of not crushing Serbia was a recognition of South Slav demands whose ramifications would impinge on Magyar interests in Croatia and southern Hungary no less than on other interests within the empire. In the shorter term Romania clearly intended to remain neutral, but its loss, Burian contended, could be compensated for by the acquisition of Bulgaria as an ally. In the longer term Romanian aspirations in Transylvania might well be influenced by the success of Serb irridentism if the latter was not crushed.[141] Finally, Tisza was fearful of forfeiting German support, not so much for the empire as a whole but for the *Ausgleich* specifically, and therefore for Magyar predominance. Berchtold was able to use the blank cheque to reinforce that fear. Tisza's earlier objections now found expression, not in opposition to going to war but in the aims of that war: on 19 July, the day on which the empire's ministers finalized the ultimatum to Serbia, they agreed in deference to Magyar concerns that Austria-Hungary would not annex any part of Serbia, but that chunks would be allocated to Bulgaria, Greece, and Albania, and the rump would be treated as a Habsburg client.

---

[141] Leslie, *Wiener Beiträge*, XX (1993), 341–7, 381.

Therefore, it was not Hungary that produced the major domestic hiccough in the dual monarchy's timetable for war; surprisingly, that was a role reserved for Conrad von Hötzendorff. On previous occasions Conrad had demanded mobilization with an initial urgency that had then given way to calls for delay. In July 1914 he repeated the pattern. Much of the army was on leave to help bring in the harvest. Conrad argued that to cancel the leave would alert other powers to Austrian intentions. Most soldiers were due to return from leave on 21 and 22 July, and therefore 23 July—in addition to being the earliest date compatible with Poincaré's and Viviani's departure from Russia—was also the first that would suit the Austro-Hungarian army. Conrad dragged his feet even beyond 23 July. He reckoned that 12 August was the first day by which he could attack Serbia, and so was opposed to any declaration of war before then. Conrad's fatalism of 1914 was a product not simply of the realities of Austria-Hungary's position, but also of an inner mood. A shrewd observer, Josef Redlich, commented at the end of August: Conrad 'lacks greater inner verve. Inwardly, he does not believe in his historical calling as Austrian commander-in-chief.'[142] Preoccupied with his long-standing love for Gina von Reiningh-aus, the wife of an industrialist, his thoughts were of a married life with her rather than of Austria-Hungary.

Conrad's fantasies were not very different from the reality for many in Europe in mid-July. Llewellyn Woodward, the British historian, heard the news of the archduke's murder while staying in a hotel in the Black Forest, but considered it 'nothing more than another political assassination in the Balkans'.[143] Some saw its implications, but for the majority in western Europe Bosnia and Serbia were too remote and too primitive to be of direct consequence in their lives. Previous Balkan crises had been surmounted without a general war. It was a hot summer. July was a month of relaxation. The affluent, reflecting the increasingly cosmopolitan atmosphere of the continent's capitals, were taking their holidays abroad. General Brusilov and his wife were among a group of Russians undergoing cures at Kissingen in Germany. The Serb chief of the general staff, Putnik, was in Budapest (where he was interned, but on 28 July released). Wilhelm Groener, head of the railways section of the German general staff, was in Switzerland. Such international contacts made the danger of war seem particularly inappropriate. Commerce, education, and culture were drawing the nations together, not driving them apart. Five of the seven honorary graduands of Oxford University in June 1914 had been German;[144] Tirpitz's daughters had an English governess and were educated at Cheltenham Ladies' College. For those who had stayed at home, domestic crises grabbed the

---

[142] Wank, *Austrian History Yearbook*, I (1965), 86; also 82–3.
[143] L. Woodward, *Great Britain and the war*, p. xiii.
[144] Michael Howard, 'Europe on the eve of the first world war', in Evans and Pogge von Strandmann (eds.), *The coming*, 1.

headlines. In Britain, Grey and Lloyd George emphasized the calm of the international scene: the real issue was Irish home rule and the possibility of Ulster loyalist opposition. French readers were engrossed in much more salacious fare. On 20 July the trial began of the wife of Joseph Caillaux. Madame Caillaux had shot the editor of *Le Figaro* in his office after he had published her love-letters to Caillaux. The affair did have serious diplomatic consequences, since *Le Figaro* was said to be in possession of deciphered German telegrams, and foreign embassies in Paris therefore changed their codes in July, thus shutting French cryptographers out from a most important intelligence source. But the Caillaux trial's popular appeal was of course as a *crime passionelle*.

The silence which Vienna had sought was thus relatively easily won. It was broken at 6 p.m. on 23 July with the delivery of the ultimatum to Serbia. Austria-Hungary cited Serbia's failure to suppress the terrorism emanating from within its borders as evidence that Serbia had failed to honour its undertaking of 31 March 1909 to sustain good relations with Austria-Hungary. It asked the Serbian government to condemn anti-Austrian propaganda, to dissolve *Narodna Odbrana*, to take action against those Serbians implicated in the plot, and to include Austro-Hungarian representation in the suppression of anti-Austrian activities within Serbia. Serbia was granted forty-eight hours within which to reply. In the capitals of the great powers German ambassadors had been instructed on 21 July to be ready to give full support to the ultimatum on 24 July and to work to keep the efforts of the Austro-Serb quarrel localized. On the face of it the ultimatum, though severe, was not unreasonable, and the initial reactions received by the Germans were reassuring.

The ultimatum was hardly a surprise to Serbia. Probably alerted to Habsburg machinations by the Rome leak as early as 7 July, Pasic had confirmation of Austro-Hungarian troop movements by 18 July.[145] Outwardly Serbia seemed self-confident and cocky. The tensions with the army and the imminence of elections meant that nobody could afford not to be nationalist, especially in a domestic context. Hartwig, Russia's ambassador to Belgrade, who had died on 10 July had been accorded a state funeral, which Pasic had turned into a paean for pan-Slavism. But militarily there was every reason for caution. The Balkan wars had left the army exhausted. Austria-Hungary's military attaché in Belgrade was of the opinion that it would take four years to recover (in itself an argument in favour of a quick Austrian strike while the opportunity offered), and the Serb ministry of war was planning a ten-year programme of reconstruction. In June Pasic had rejected a Greek request for an alliance against Turkey on the grounds that the army was not fit for another war. The assimilation of the new territories was far from complete, their

---

[145] For what follows, see esp. Mark Cornwall, 'Serbia', in Wilson (ed.), *Decisions for war*. This revises the earlier literature which gives a more bellicose twist to Belgrade's position.

populations proving resistant to military service. Revolt had resulted in the army being deployed overwhelmingly in the south, away from the axes of its mobilization in the event of war in the north.[146] Moreover, there were few obvious signs of support from Serbia's possible military allies. Above all, Russia—although it had promised military aid—had counselled restraint on 3 July, and had given no reassurances by 23 July.

On the evening of 23 July Pasic was electioneering in the south of the country. Prince Alexander immediately contacted the Tsar, expressing Serb willingness to go as far in meeting the Austro-Hungarian demands as was 'in keeping with the position of an independent country'.[147] This became the essence of the Serb reply to Vienna. Pasic returned to Belgrade on the following day. Despite his awareness of Serbia's vulnerability, he could not cave in to the Austrians without forfeiting his political position—in relation to both the electorate and the army. His aim, therefore, was to moderate the reactions of his colleagues, while playing for time in the hope that international responses, and particularly Russia's position, would become more emphatic. In the circumstances, the Serb reply was brilliant. By accepting most of the terms but not all—Pasic refused to allow Austro-Hungarian representation in Serbia's internal investigations—Serbia appeared the injured party and won widespread support. The European climate, so apparently favourable to Austria-Hungary up to 23 July, turned distinctly frosty after 25 July.

By then the Serb cabinet had given the order for mobilization. This can be seen as a show of bravado, an indication that Belgrade was confident of Russian support, and a response to the fear that its reply to Vienna would otherwise be seen as too weak by the Serb army. In practice, it was an act of desperation. Although the decision was taken on the afternoon of 25 July, before the Serb note was in Austrian hands, it was not put into effect until midnight. Even then Serbia had received only vague indications as to Russia's position: at least for the moment Serbia seemed to be on its own. It mobilized because it reckoned that Austria-Hungary would resort to military action the moment the ultimatum expired.

Its judgement was sound. The diplomatic solution, to which Belgrade had at least technically opened the path, was of no interest in Vienna. Within fifteen minutes of receiving the Serb reply the Austrian ambassador in Belgrade announced that it was unsatisfactory and that diplomatic relations between the two states were at an end. On the following day the Austro-Hungarian army began to mobilize against Serbia, and on 28 July Berchtold—still trying to push Conrad into a speedier response—secured Austria-Hungary's declaration of war on Serbia.

[146] Stevenson, *Armaments and the coming of war*, 276–7, 353–5; Lyon, *Journal of Military History*, LXI (1997), 481–502.
[147] Petrovich, *Modern Serbia*, 615.

Sazonov received the news of the Austrian démarche in the morning of 24 July. The Tsar summoned a meeting of the Council of Ministers that afternoon. Bethmann Hollweg and Berchtold rested any hopes they entertained that Russia would stand back on three assumptions: that the Austro-Serb quarrel could be isolated, that the Tsar's fear that war would lead to revolution would keep Russia out, and that—with Poincaré and Viviani at sea on their return to France—French support for Russia would not be forthcoming. On all three counts they were proved wrong.

Austro-Hungarian action against Serbia could not be localized because nobody in the Triple Entente, and certainly neither Sazonov nor Grey, saw Austria-Hungary as an independent actor. The irony of Vienna's position was that uncertainty about the strength of German support had prompted a firm line, when to the opposition that very firmness seemed indicative of Austro-German solidarity. Austria-Hungary was therefore saddled with the bellicose image of Germany. By July 1914 Germany, in the light of the 1911 Moroccan crisis and, for Russia in particular, of the Liman von Sanders affair, was judged as moving progressively towards war. Neither crisis was interpreted as a self-contained attempt to use the threat of war as a diplomatic instrument. The German attitude to preventive war, the German fear that by 1917 Russia would be too strong and would be able to mobilize too fast, had been faithfully reported by the Russian military attaché in Berlin. 'Germany', he opined in 1912, 'is strenuously preparing for war in the immediate future.'[148] Although contact between the Foreign Ministry and the War Ministry was minimal, Sazonov's immediate reaction on 24 July was to link the Austrian ultimatum to this wider, preconceived view. Germany, he was convinced, was behind Austria-Hungary; he was also sure that Germany wished to use the crisis to launch a preventive war.

Tsar Nicholas was more cautious, not least because—as Bethmann Hollweg rightly judged—he did fear that war would lead to revolution. In February 1914 P. N. Durnovo, the minister of the interior responsible for suppressing the 1905 revolution, had written a memorandum for Nicholas in which he anticipated that a future European war would be long, that it would therefore generate great economic and domestic political strain, and that the efforts to compensate for Russian industrial backwardness would lead to a social crisis and to revolution.[149] Nicholas brought this insight to his deliberations on 24 July: 'war', he said, 'would be disastrous for the world and once it had broken out it would be difficult to stop.'[150]

In 1910 it might have been possible to argue that Durnovo's prognostications owed too much to the past, to the memory of 1905; in 1914 they looked more

[148] William C. Fuller, 'Russian empire', in E. May (ed.), *Knowing one's enemies*, 109–10; also 122–3.
[149] Lieven, *Russia and the origins*, 77–80.
[150] Ibid. 66.

far-seeing. Russia suffered only 222 strikes in 1910, and the police reckoned all but eight of these were prompted by economic rather than political factors. In 1913 2,404 strikes took place, and 1,034 were classified as political; in 1914, of 3,534 strikes fully 2,565 were deemed political. Furthermore, workers' discontent had reached a peak during the French state visit in July.[151] However, a year previously the police, looking back over a decade of domestic strife, had been confident that the position was improving: they reported that the general mood of the population was calm, expressing the view that there was no danger of revolution in the near future, and that they could control such problems as did arise without the aid of the army.[152] Since the bulk of the population still worked on the land the police were probably justified in these opinions: urban strikes were not representative of society as a whole; the situation was not revolutionary in the sense that 1905 had been. In July 1914 N. A. Maklakov, the minister of the interior, reflected the police view. War, he thought, would rally the nation, and mobilization specifically would pre-empt industrial disturbance.

In discounting the fears of revolution, in seeing war as a unifying, not a divisive, agent in Russian society, ministers were also embracing the liberal imperialists' support for the Entente. Much of the weakness of Durnovo's case resided not in the arguments themselves, which were not simply perspicacious but also accurate reflections of recent Russian experience, but in his conviction that Russia's main concerns were Asiatic, that its principal rival was therefore Britain, and that by engaging in a European war against Germany Russia would be fighting as Britain's proxy. Such arguments were *passé* in St Petersburg in July 1914. Crucially, they were not ones which the Tsar was prepared to endorse. The naval talks with France and Britain had convinced Sazonov that the Entente was close to becoming a formal alliance. Poincaré's and Viviani's visit had brought Franco-Russian relations to a new high. More specifically, there are grounds for believing that during the French visit—despite Vienna's precautions—the Russians and French did know of Austria-Hungary's intentions with regard to Serbia. Again the German leak in Rome was the culprit, as the Russians had broken the Italian codes.[153] Even without this specific opportunity to concert their responses to the ultimatum, the Franco-Russian alliance was in little danger of fracturing under German pressure in late July. Izvolsky, as Russia's ambassador in Paris, and Paléologue, his French counterpart in St Petersburg, were firmly committed to the Entente and were not loath to exploit, or even exceed, the powers vouchsafed them.

[151] Siegelbaum, *Politics of industrial mobilization*, 17–18; Linke, *Militärgeschichtliche Mitteilungen*, 32 (1982), 15.

[152] William C. Fuller, *Civil–military conflict in Imperial Russia*, 256–7.

[153] Williamson, *Journal of Interdisciplinary History*, XVIII (1988), 811–12; Keiger, *France and the origins*, 150.

Therefore, given that all three Austro-German assumptions about the Russian response proved to be wishful thinking, the conclusions of the Council of Ministers at their meeting on 24 July become less surprising.[154] Its chairman, I. L. Goremykin, was a nonentity by comparison with his predecessor V. N. Kokovtsov, who had acted as a restraining influence in both the November 1912 and January 1914 crises. The important voices were those of Sazonov, whose views have already been outlined, A. V. Krivoshein, the minister of agriculture, and the two ministers for the armed forces, V. A. Sukhomlinov for the army and I. K. Grigorovich for the navy. Krivoshein, like Sazonov, was a man of more liberal disposition than many in the council, and recognized the need to co-operate with the Duma in order to achieve some measure of popular participation in government. The key factor for Krivoshein was not just, as it was for many Russians in the wake of the Bosnian crisis, Russia's status as a great power. It was the relationship between humiliation abroad and the loss of governmental authority at home. In Krivoshein's hands the fear of revolution, which had constrained Russia since 1905, was no longer a justification for international inaction, but a reason for assertiveness and an answer to the increasing manifestations of workers' discontent.[155] War was not a prospect to be relished, given Russia's relative backwardness, but a threat sufficiently strong to suggest its use was the only way out of Russia's dilemma. Neither Sukhomlinov nor Grigorovich was prepared to say that such a policy was mistaken. The rearmament programme of neither the army nor the navy was complete, but both armed forces were in better shape than they had been for a decade. It is easy, and perhaps right, to see Sukhomlinov's assertion that the army was ready as a braggart's self-defence, a reluctance to be deemed cowardly. However, the army was no longer so weak that it was unable to support Russia's foreign policy, as had happened in 1909, and Germany's fears of its potential were mirrored by the high estimates formed by French and British observers. The council concluded by agreeing to ask Vienna to postpone its deadline by forty-eight hours, by urging Belgrade to be conciliatory, and by giving permission for four military districts, Kiev, Odessa, Moscow, and Kazan, to prepare for mobilization. The Tsar ratified these decisions at a further meeting of the council on 25 July. Thus, from the very outset Russia included a military element in its response to the crisis. On 26 July Russia began to recall its reservists, in a phase preliminary to mobilization itself. On 28 July, in response to Austria-Hungary's mobilization against Serbia, the four districts already alerted were ordered to mobilize.

Sazonov saw the steps taken up to 28 July as a buttress to his diplomacy, not as an inevitable progression to war itself. Partial mobilization had not, in

[154] D. W. Spring, 'Russia and the coming of the war', in Evans and Pogge von Strandmann (eds.), The Coming, 57–86, provides a full and instructive account.
[155] McDonald, United government, 204–6, 218; Leslie, Wiener Beiträge, XX (1993), 341–7, 381.

November 1912, led to hostilities. The delay between the order for the Russian army's mobilization and its ability to commence hostilities would be a minimum of fifteen days at the very best, and full Russian mobilization would take nearer a month. Thus, there was ample opportunity for further negotiation. But such calculations were naive. First, the Russian decision preceded the Serb reply to Austria-Hungary: it had the effect of giving Serbia a 'blank cheque' of its own, and it generated a pressure for acceleration comparable to that for which Austria-Hungary and Germany were striving from the other side. To be effective in aiding Serbia, and to seize the advantage of operating against the Austrians' rear while they were embroiled to the south-east, Russia had to mobilize fast. But Germany's own war plan, aiming first to concentrate against France and then turn against Russia, rested on that very delay in Russian mobilization which the decisions of 24 and 25 July were calculated to eliminate. If the Germans allowed the Russians time to mobilize without themselves doing so, and without actually beginning operations against France, they would risk defeat in the east before they had won in the west.

Sazonov was sufficiently sensitive to this last consideration to insist on partial, not general, Russian mobilization. In particular, the Council of Ministers' decision did not include the pivotal military district in Russia's western defences, whether the enemy was Austria-Hungary or Germany or both—that of Warsaw. The Russian chief of the general staff, Yanushkevitch, was a weak character, both newly appointed and unfamiliar with the details of Russia's military plans. But Dobrovsky, the head of the mobilization division, immediately objected, and on 26 July received strong support from the quartermaster-general, Yuri Danilov, on his return from manoeuvres in the Caucasus. Danilov was convinced that the main threat to Russia came from Germany, not Austria-Hungary. In any case, from a technical point of view partial mobilization was a nonsense. Active units were stationed in peacetime in the regions from where they drew their reserves, not in their concentration areas, so as to minimize the number of train movements. Thus, each corps area drew on resources and reserves from adjacent districts, and the railway movements which mobilization involved embraced all Russia. Partial mobilization would throw the army into chaos. Operationally, the exclusion of Warsaw meant that Russia would forfeit the opportunity to envelop Austria-Hungary—should that power indeed fight alone—and would fight with unnecessarily limited forces.[156] Danilov's concerns over partial mobilization were shared by the French. Sufficiently aware of the German plan to know that they would be the initial target, the French had been pressing the Russians to increase the speed of their mobilization so that the latter could commence operations in

---

[156] L. C. F. Turner, 'Russian mobilisation in 1914', in Kennedy (ed.), *War plans*, 252–68, takes a different view; Lieven, *Russia and the origins*, 148–50, has some effective criticisms of Turner. See also Danilov, *Russie dans la guerre mondiale*, 30–8.

East Prussia within fifteen days and thus provide indirect support in the crucial opening stages of the battle in the west. Neither partial mobilization nor operations against Austria-Hungary would assist the French cause: what the alliance required was a rapid Russian advance on East Prussia—a point which Joseph Joffre, the French chief of the general staff, did not hesitate to make to the Russians on 27 July.

Thus the step taken on 28 July, to mobilize four districts only, was of a piece with the mobilizations in earlier Balkan crises—it was designed as an instrument of diplomatic utility. Militarily it was unsustainable. The idea that mobilization was not a peaceful act but 'the most decisive act of war' had been present in the thought of Russian officers since 1892. In 1912 the European military districts were told to regard mobilization as the opening of hostilities.[157] On the morning of 29 July Sazonov responded to military advice and pressed the Tsar into approving general mobilization. The Russian decision for general mobilization therefore preceded any reaction from Germany. Indeed, the developments of that day—the opening of Austrian hostilities against Serbia with the bombardment of Belgrade, and a warning from Bethmann Hollweg that Russian mobilization would force German mobilization and that for Germany mobilization meant war—although they confirmed Sazonov in his decision, produced an apparent weakening, rather than a strengthening, of Russian resolve. The Tsar, prompted by a cousinly telegram from the Kaiser, reverted to partial mobilization at midnight on 29 July. The Russian general staff was appalled, and by 30 July knew that Germany had begun its military preparations. Sazonov believed that a secret German mobilization was possible; he was also aware of German pressure for preventive action. Therefore he renewed his advocacy of general mobilization. On the afternoon of 30 July the Tsar capitulated. On 31 July Russia began general mobilization. The German ultimatum arrived the same day.

In retrospect Russian prevarication over the pattern of its mobilization had little effect on the outcome of the July crisis. The crucial decisions, given the nature of Germany's war plan, were taken on 24 July. Any military preparations by Russia, even if designed to counter Austria-Hungary alone, would have been sufficient to prompt German mobilization. This is obviously true if Germany is seen as an aggressive power, already committed to European war, and certainly not disposed to pass up the opportunity of having its eastern frontier protected by Austrian operations against the Russians and so being freed to concentrate in the west. But it is also applicable in the context of a more reactive interpretation, of Germany's self-imposed image as the tragic victim: the sense of being in a corner, the preoccupation with time which not only the mobilization timetable but also the political management of the crisis

---

[157] Fuller, *Strategy and power*, 355; Suchomlinow, *Erinnerungen*, 343; Tunstall, *Planning for war*, 113.

generated, combined with the fear of Russia and the obligation to Austria-Hungary to make Russia's partial mobilization as intolerable to Germany as general mobilization.

Bethmann Hollweg was nonetheless slow to realize the gravity of the crisis which confronted him. On 25 July Germany's ambassador in St Petersburg had reported that Russia was not likely to be held back by fear of domestic disorder. Despite this clear indication that the strategy of a short, sharp Austro-Serbian war would misfire, the German chancellor continued to pursue that objective. His policy up until 28 July was guided, as it had been before the Austrian ultimatum, by the desire to limit and to localize. On 26 July Grey, buoyed up by the apparent success of the conference system in 1913, proposed an international conference, again casting Britain and Germany as the restraining influences within their respective alliance systems. But Germany's experience of such conferences, after the two Moroccan crises, was—as it had been for its ally—one of humiliation. On 27 July the Germans rejected the British proposal, on the grounds that the affair was Austria-Hungary's alone. And by the time that Bethmann Hollweg had apprised Austria-Hungary of Britain's view (which he took pains to point out he did not share)—that the Serb reply was acceptable—Vienna had already rebuffed the Serbs and was preparing for war. From 24 July onwards Grey warned Germany's ambassador in London that war, if it came, would not be localized. But for Bethmann, politically isolated at home and with his foreign policy apparently bankrupt abroad, the lure of a quick Balkan coup was not yet gainsaid. Sazonov's policy up until 28 July could be seen as conciliatory; France—with Poincaré and Viviani not returned until 29 July—was in no position to give clear signals; even Grey's conference proposal betokened a preference for negotiation rather than belligerence. The determination to stick by the policy of 5 and 6 July put blinkers on Bethmann Hollweg and at the same time hardened the reactions of the other participants in the crisis. By the time he was alerted to the certainty of Russian involvement, and to the implications for German policy of Russian mobilization, he had lost the opportunity to manage events. Before 28 July the message from Britain above all, but also from France and Russia, was clear: the local war must be avoided in order to prevent a major war. Bethmann Hollweg did not attempt to avoid a major war until after the local war had been initiated.

The first indication of a change of tack came on 28 July. Wilhelm had returned from his cruise the preceding day. When he read the Serb reply to the Austrian ultimatum, its moderation convinced him that war was now no longer required; instead, the Austrians should halt in Belgrade and occupy it until terms were agreed. Bethmann Hollweg passed the proposal on to Vienna, but specifically disavowed any wish to hold Austria-Hungary back from the task of achieving its aims in relation to Serbia. Berchtold postponed replying. The messages being received from Berlin were contradictory; only the day before British proposals of mediation had been passed on without German endorsement, and by the night of 28/9 July Berchtold might reasonably argue that Austria's dwindling prestige in the Balkans would not survive any retraction from the military solution now under way. Speed and decisiveness were still Berchtold's objectives, as they had hitherto been those of Bethmann Hollweg.

On 29 July the alteration in Bethmann's approach became more evident. Grey must be held responsible for completing the change. Fritz Fischer, Imanuel Geiss, and others have seen Germany's policy in July as the denouement and continuation of its previous foreign policy.[158] Both Fischer and Geiss contend that the German chancellor accepted the possibility of a European war from the outset of the crisis but hoped that Britain would remain neutral. Therefore, for them, the Anglo-German naval negotiations of 1912 had had as their objective not détente per se, but the neutralization of Britain in the event of war. Undeniably Bethmann Hollweg worked for the maintenance of Anglo-German diplomatic links during July. But this, rather than evidence of continuity, is yet again an indication of Bethmann's wishful thinking and self-delusion in the three weeks up until 28 July. Over the previous decade the German general staff had entertained little doubt that, in the event of war in the west, the British would stand by the French. Clear statements to that effect had been made to Germany by Haldane in 1911 and by Grey in 1912: the implications were there in the Anglo-French staff talks and in Lloyd George's Mansion House speech. Bethmann had not shared the Anglophobia of Tirpitz, but the British naval talks with the Russians had convinced him of the rightness of the assumption that Britain would not be neutral in the event of a European war. Bethmann's hopes for Britain in July 1914 were therefore a reflection of his desire for a localized war. Obviously, if the local war became a general war it would serve Germany's interests if Britain espoused neutrality, but Bethmann Hollweg appreciated that in reality such an outcome was improbable. Where realism failed Bethmann was in his slowness to interpret Grey's warnings that an Austro-Serb war could not be localized as evidence that Britain would not long sustain the position of international arbitrator. On the afternoon of 29 July Grey made clear to the German ambassador that Britain would not remain neutral in the event of a continental war. Talk of mediation had given way to an explicit threat. Bethmann Hollweg's despair arose from the final realization that the policy of localization had failed.

By 30 July, therefore, the change in the chancellor's policy was complete. At 2.55 in the morning he dispatched an urgent telegram to the German ambassador in Vienna, calling on the Austrians to attempt mediation on the basis of

---

[158] Geiss, *Journal of Contemporary History*, I (1966), 82; see also Geiss, *July 1914*.

'the halt in Belgrade'. Faced with the immediate prospect of European war, neither the Kaiser nor Bethmann Hollweg wanted it.

The Austrian reaction was, predictably, one of confusion and frustration. The withdrawal of German support, feared and anticipated from the outset, had now come to pass. However, hostilities with Serbia had already commenced. The advice of Conrad von Hötzendorff from the beginning was that war could not be fought with limited means and limited objectives: given the size of the Serb army by 1914, Austria-Hungary would have to undergo a general mobilization to commence hostilities. A quick *coup de main* against Belgrade was therefore impossible, as well as being inappropriate. When Austria-Hungary's ministers discussed Bethmann's proposal on 31 July they could only endorse on political grounds the position adopted by Conrad on military: the last London conference was described as 'a frightful memory', and it made little sense for Vienna now to desist without a guarantee from Russia.[159]

The desire in Austria-Hungary to settle the Serb problem once and for all was supported by the attitude of Moltke. By 30/1 July the pressure from Berlin for swift Austrian action had not diminished; it simply came from a different quarter. Although Jagow had indicated to the Russians that partial mobilization would not trigger German mobilization, Moltke was of a different view. If the Austro-Hungarian army was fully committed to the war with Serbia, it would be unable to take an active role in operations against Russia, and yet this was the premiss upon which the German war plan rested. Unless a reasonable proportion of Franz Joseph's army tied down comparable Russian forces, Germany would not be able to deal with the dangers of a two-front war by concentrating the bulk of its divisions first against France. Time therefore pressed on Moltke in two ways. First, he could not afford to let the German mobilization fall behind that of Russia. But secondly, and more immediately, he could not allow the general war to follow so long after the outset of Austro-Serb hostilities that the Habsburg army could not concentrate against Russia rather than Serbia. Thus, on the afternoon of 30 July Moltke bypassed Bethmann Hollweg and urged Conrad to mobilize against Russia, not Serbia, and assured him that Germany would follow suit. Berchtold's response to Moltke's intervention was to ask, rhetorically, who ruled in Berlin: Moltke's message in itself did little more than confirm to Vienna the wisdom of its own continuing resolve.

The pressure Moltke put on Vienna, although seemingly fraught in its implications for civil–military relations, was no more than a response—and a somewhat belated one at that—to the circumstances in which Germany now found itself. German military intelligence had picked up an exchange of signals

---

[159] Regele, *Conrad*, 242–5, also 122.

between Russia and France concerning mobilization on 24 and 25 July, but as late as 26 July was still anticipating a crisis that would carry on for several weeks.[160] Not until Falkenhayn's return to work on the 27th had the army's somewhat dilatory approach been challenged. Falkenhayn was appalled by the lack of resolution displayed by both the Kaiser and by Moltke. He was clear that the responsibility for policy was Bethmann Hollweg's, but argued that the chancellor's obligation to put to one side military advice for political reasons no longer held good when 'a crucial military interest was at stake'. On 29 July Falkenhayn felt that that point had been reached. He called for the declaration, *Zustandes drohender Kriegsgefahr*, the preliminary steps to mobilization. Moltke, aware that for Germany mobilization meant war, and fearful of its implications for Europe as a whole, would not endorse the minister of war's request, and Bethmann Hollweg took his cue from the chief of the general staff.[161] The chancellor emphasized his wish to leave the initiation of hostilities to Russia. But at the same time his acknowledgement that, if European war came it would include a German attack on Belgium and France, was contained in his request for British neutrality in exchange for German respect for Belgian and French territorial integrity, and confirmed by the preparation of an ultimatum to Belgium demanding its acceptance of the transit of German troops through its territory: the former in particular was a diplomatic gaffe that made the possibility of restraint yet more remote, but which reflected the pressure that Bethmann Hollweg was now under from the army. On 30 July Moltke's respect for Bethmann's wish to await the Russian response had—as his message to Conrad testified—evaporated. That evening he got the chancellor to agree that a decision on general mobilization would be made by noon on 31 July. Moltke was quite clear that the Tsar's equivocation over general or partial mobilization could make no difference to the German decision. Five minutes before their self-imposed deadline, Moltke and Bethmann Hollweg heard that the Russians had finally decided on general mobilization. Germany issued the declaration of *Kriegsgefahr* that day, and ordered general mobilization on 1 August. Ultimatums were dispatched to St Petersburg and Paris on the night of 31 July; on the following morning Germany declared war on Russia.

The lack of either continuity or clarity in German policy was in itself a reflection of the absence of a guiding authority. Supreme command was in name vested in the Kaiser, but by 1914 Wilhelm no longer commanded the respect which his titles demanded: the monarchy was venerated as an institution rather than in the personality of its incumbent. Technically, the reconciliation of the views of the chancellor and of the chief of the general staff in late

---

[160] Showalter, *Tannenberg*, 95; Stevenson, *Armaments and the coming of war*, 400.
[161] Afflerbach, *Falkenhayn*, 153–9; see more generally Trachtenberg, *History and strategy*, 88–92.

July was Wilhelm's responsibility. In practice, the management of the crisis reflected the dominance of first one personality, Bethmann Hollweg, and then another, Moltke. Bethmann had guided events up until 28 July by acting in isolation: he had encouraged the Kaiser to put to sea and Moltke to continue his cure. When the Kaiser returned, the belligerence he had expressed to Hoyos on 5 July had softened. Wilhelm, however, was caught by his own self-image, that of the steely warrior, and thus his reluctance to fight was compromised by his relationship with his military entourage and, above all, with Moltke. Wilhelm saw himself as the victim of an Entente conspiracy, initiated by his despised English uncle Edward VII, and the latter's Francophile ways. His capacity so to reduce the crisis of late July 1914 to the level of his own personal animosities cut across any possibility of drawing out the full implications of each step which Germany took.

The most striking illustration of the consequent absence of any German grand design was the confusion between German diplomacy, which aimed to limit war as far as possible, and German war plans, which rested on a worst-case analysis, that of a two-front war against France and Russia simultaneously. After the December 1912 Balkan crisis Moltke had concluded that the Franco-Russian alliance was sufficiently strong to mean that Germany could not fight one without having to reckon with the other. Therefore the plans for war against Russia alone, which in the normal course of events were updated by the general staff each year, were abandoned in April 1913. The army thus committed itself to a two-front war. However, the timing of the Austrian ultimatum in July 1914 was dictated by the wish to minimize the chances of a two-front war, to increase the possibility that if Russia acted in support of Serbia it would do so without France's aid. Of course, neither Bethmann Hollweg nor the Kaiser was blind to the realization that war with Russia would probably lead to war with the Entente as a whole: hence Bethmann's crassly provocative communication to Britain on 29 July. But they had not appreciated that in the general staff's view war in the east had inevitably to be preceded by war in the west. On the afternoon of 1 August Germany's ambassador in London reported that Grey had guaranteed that France would not fight Germany if Germany did not attack France. The report was false, and the elation which it produced in the Kaiser and in Bethmann Hollweg short-lived. But their jubilation was in marked contrast to the despair the report engendered in Moltke. 'If His Majesty', the latter recounted himself as saying, 'were to insist on directing the whole army to the east, he would not have an army prepared for the attack but a barren heap of armed men disorganised and without supplies.'[162]

The confusion in Germany as to how France would react was in considerable measure a self-inflicted wound. On 27 and 28 July the Germans jammed

---

[162] Quoted in Barnett, *Swordbearers*, 18.

wireless transmissions between France and Russia, and between both places and the presidential cruiser. Thereafter the two allies routed their signals traffic through Scandinavia, so generating further delays in communication. Poincaré and Viviani did not return to Paris until 29 July. By deliberately trying to silence France's leaders, the Central Powers were left free to project on to France their own hopes. In practice French policy was remarkably consistent and predictable: more than that of any other great power, it reflected the developments of 1911–14 rather than the pressures and confusion of the July crisis itself.[163]

The doggedness of Poincaré's efforts to cement the Triple Entente had by 1914 achieved a momentum of their own. The original objective of his visit to St Petersburg was to promote better relations between Russia and Britain, and the crisis in the Balkans did not in itself bulk large. This was in part a reflection of ignorance: the French ambassador in Belgrade was ill, and the Quai d'Orsay received no information from Serbia between 14 and 25 July. Intelligence from Berlin was not much better, not least because Jules Cambon was home on leave until 23 July. But the comparative neglect of the Balkans in the St Petersburg talks was also an indication that, once the situation did become clear, the French would not be disposed to see the crisis in isolation. In Paris only the caretaker foreign minister, Bienvenu-Martin, sustained the hope that an Austro-Serb war could be localized. He was rapidly disabused of this notion by the ministry's senior officials, convinced that behind Austria-Hungary stood Germany, and determined that the preservation of the Entente was a more important objective in French foreign policy than the avoidance of war.

The principal problem confronting Poincaré was how to achieve the former without appearing so uncaring about the latter that France prejudiced either its international credibility or its domestic unity. The memory of France's entry to the war of 1870, when it had forfeited both, loomed large in his calculations. Military considerations were therefore consistently subordinated to diplomatic in order that France's defensive posture should be unmistakable. The war minister, Messimy, was kept in ignorance for much of July; the distinction between mobilization and a declaration of war was emphasized; and as late as 1 August the order for the army to keep 10 kilometres back from the Franco-Belgian frontier—thus making clear France's respect for Belgian neutrality—was reaffirmed. But Poincaré knew as well as Messimy and Joffre that France's security was bound to that of Russia, and that if Russia mobilized so would Germany. Thus, the tension created by affirming the Entente while asserting French defensiveness was played out in the relationship with Russia.

---

[163] The discussion that follows draws on John Keiger, 'France', in Wilson (ed.), *Decisions for war*, esp. 121–30, and Hayne, *French foreign office*, esp. 269–301.

Pivotal to this dialogue, particularly during the periods of enforced silence and delayed communication, was France's ambassador in St Petersburg, Maurice Paléologue. Paléologue's early career had left him well versed in the Franco-Russian relationship, and particularly in its military dimensions. Furthermore, he had been at school with Poincaré, and shared the president's belief in the centrality of the Entente. Lunching with Sazonov on 24 July, he responded to Sazonov's conviction that the Austrian ultimatum required a robust response by averring that the Entente should stand up to the Central Powers. As a result of this exchange and, more explicitly, of delays in his reporting the steps taken by Russia on its route to general mobilization, Paléologue has been accused of deliberately stoking Russian aggression while at the same time endorsing Paris's conviction that Sazonov's policy was essentially pacific. Consequently Paris saw Germany's decision to mobilize as unprovoked, and felt its task to be the stiffening of Russian resolve. This interpretation, quite apart from its discounting of the practical difficulties in St Petersburg–Paris communications, elevates Paléologue's role while downgrading those of Sazonov and Poincaré. It overlooks the striking fact that Russian decision-making was remarkably little influenced by France. It also neglects the similarity between the policy which Paléologue pursued and that which Poincaré would have espoused had he been free to do so. To that extent Paléologue was a more than adequate stopgap when communications were broken. Once they were restored the delays in transmission on 30 and 31 July, whether contrived or not, buttressed Poincaré's position by stilling any suggestion that Russia had initiated hostilities and had thus invalidated the defensive basis of the alliance.

As a result, even if obscured from Germany, and overshadowed in the French press by Madame Caillaux's trial (the all-male jury gallantly acquitted her on 28 July), Poincaré's affirmation of the alliance continued unimpeded by its author's enforced silence. Indeed, it is worth remembering that on board ship with Poincaré was Viviani, who as a radical prime minister was much more disposed to soften France's support for Russia. By the time that he was able to do so, advising the Russians not to offer Germany a pretext for general mobilization, it was effectively too late.

Viviani's views, and the need to muzzle them, were a reflection of the domestic imperatives under which Poincaré increasingly felt himself to be operating. The elections of April/May 1914, and the shift to the left which they had produced, although in practice no block to nationalist sentiment, did point to a continuing threat to the three-year military service law. During July itself Messimy was working on a revision of the law, and Poincaré expected its amendment in autumn 1914. The military strength of the Franco-Russian alliance was thus likely to be challenged from within France, as well as by Austro-Germany policy without. The improvements in the French army since

1911, combined with growing evidence of Russian military strength, contributed by 1914 to greater optimism within the French general staff about its prospects in a war with Germany. As in the latter, therefore, so in the former: there was a sense that if war was to come to Europe, better now, with the French army profiting from the three-year law, and with Russian support guaranteed by a Balkan crisis, than later.[164]

The French president's resolve was heightened by the ecstatic welcome which he and Viviani were accorded on their arrival in Paris on 29 July. Four days previously the *Echo de Paris* had published an account of the visit of Germany's ambassador to the Quai d'Orsay: he had been seeking France's cooperation in localizing the conflict, but the version leaked by the foreign ministry to the French press carried a somewhat different spin. The call confirmed that Germany was prodding Austria-Hungary, and that its purpose was to carry on the policy of the second Moroccan crisis and split the Entente. Furthermore, the implications of such a policy were not simply diplomatic. The three-year-law agitation, and its centrality to recent domestic politics, had accustomed the French public to the idea of a surprise German attack. The fact that among the cries of 'Vive la France' Poincaré could also hear 'Vive l'armée' left him in no doubt of the prevailing mood.[165]

France's sense of now or never was contributed to by an inflated expectation of the likely British response. Paul Cambon, France's ambassador in London, had listened to those British friendly to the Entente rather than those who were not: his dispatches reflected the expectation generated by the Anglo-French naval agreement of 1912, that in the event of war with Germany the Entente would become a definitive alliance. On 1 August the mobilization orders to the French fleet assumed that the joint Anglo-French operational plans would be put into effect: in practice Britain had neither committed itself on this point nor yet sent an ultimatum to Germany.

It is tempting to see Britain's strategic imperative, the need to prevent any great power dominating the further coast of the English Channel and so providing a direct threat to Britain's sea-power, as creating an inevitability about Britain's entry to the First World War. Grey's foreign policy, combined with both naval and military staff talks, had established—so this argument would add—a continental commitment. A minority of the cabinet, as well as general-staff officers like Henry Wilson, did think like this in July 1914. But they did not represent the sort of widespread consensus which would justify hostilities. Britain was the only great power to debate its entry to the war in parliament; it was also the only state that did not see its own territorial integrity under direct threat. The decision to fight, therefore, had to be

[164] Krumeich, *Armaments*, 214–29; also C. M. Andrew, 'France and the German menace', in E. May (ed.), *Knowing one's enemies*, 146–8.
[165] Raithel, *Das 'Wunder' der inneren Einheit*, 192–9, 252–5.

justified to more people than was the case in other countries, but itself rested on a more indirect danger. The reluctance of the Foreign Office to treat foreign policy in an open way, Grey's own tendency to keep diplomacy from the cabinet—both these factors meant that British opinion had to be educated, coaxed, given time to develop, in late July.[166]

Indeed, as has already been seen, until 29 July Grey's approach to the crisis was one of caution. Liberalism's affection for the rights of small nations did not extend to Serbia. The *Manchester Guardian* was of the view that, 'if it were physically possible for Serbia to be towed out to sea and sunk there, the air of Europe would at once seem cleaner'.[167] Grey told the Austro-Hungarian ambassador that, if his country could fight Serbia without provoking Russia, he could 'take a holiday tomorrow'.[168] On 24 July Asquith, the prime minister, recognized the implications of the Austrian ultimatum for European relations and the possibility of a 'real Armageddon', but still reckoned that the British could be 'spectators'.[169] He could not at first see why a German victory would upset the balance of power in Europe, on the grounds that it had not done so in 1871, and as much as a week later he told the archbishop of Canterbury that the Serbs deserved a 'thorough thrashing'.[170] His major concern in July was Irish home rule. If his government did not carry a bill it would lose the support of the Irish members of parliament on whom it depended for an overall majority; if it did, Ulster loyalists threatened civil war. In the event the problems of yet a third small nation, Belgium, subsumed those of Serbia and allowed the Liberals to shelve those of Ireland.

Grey's self-appointed role as mediator between 24 and 29 July was not, therefore, adopted for the benefit of Germany. Domestically, he both had to create time for a public awareness of the crisis to grow and had to have tried a diplomatic solution before he could hope to argue for the commencement of hostilities. Abroad, his purpose was to restrain Russia and France: he feared that by openly affirming the solidarity of the Entente he would encourage both powers to precipitate action. His allies, on the other hand, contended that a united front could have deterred Germany. Certainly the consequence of Grey's ambivalence was apparent failure: his efforts at negotiation did not moderate Austro-German behaviour, but they did alarm the Russians and the French. Grey could not afford to follow an independent line indefinitely. He had recognized in 1911 that Britain's own interests were too closely intertwined with those of the Entente for neutrality to be a genuinely viable option. By

---

[166] On Britain in the July crisis, see Michael Brock, 'Britain enters the war', in Evans and Pogge von Strandmann (eds.), *The coming*, 145–78; Hazlehurst, *Politicians at war*, 1–116; Wilson, *Policy of the entente*, esp. 135–47.
[167] A. May, *Hapsburg monarchy*, 52.
[168] Bridge, *From Sadowa*, 381.
[169] Brock and Brock (eds.), *Asquith*, 124–5.
[170] Cassar, *Asquith*, 13–15, 18–19.

allying with France, Britain was better able to manage its own relationship with Germany, and to give itself the sort of continental military clout which its diminutive army could not. Even more important was the link with Russia: Russia's membership of the Entente committed it to rivalry with Germany, gave its policy a European twist, and so relieved the British of the challenge of its main rival in Central Asia. If Britain had failed to support France and Russia in 1914, its links with them would have been forfeit, and the reopening and deepening of those old and more traditional rivalries would have driven Britain into the only alternative, an Anglo-German alliance. For all Asquith's hope, isolation from Europe was no longer possible, not least because of its imperial consequences.

The events of late July went faster than Grey's diplomatic machinations. For some sections of the press, notably *The Times*, the Foreign Office's reactions were dilatory. But this did not mean that it had lost its sense of direction. As early as 26 July Grey used the decision of the First Sea Lord, Prince Louis of Battenberg, to keep the naval reserve at its stations as a signal to Germany. On 27 July the army and the navy were put on precautionary alert. The cabinet approved these steps on 29 July. On 31 July Eyre Crowe, head of the eastern and western departments at the Foreign Office and a well-established harbinger of the German menace, wrote that 'if England cannot engage in a big war [it] means her abdication as an independent State'.[171]

But the British government was still not in a situation where it could adopt an unequivocal position. Grey made his commitment to the Entente clear to Germany, and was justified in doing so by Germany's own confirmation that it intended to march through France and Belgium. Yet at the same time he had to tell Paul Cambon that a clash between Austria-Hungary and Serbia did not constitute a direct threat to France, and that Britain was therefore free from any engagement. He had no other choice: on 31 July the cabinet continued to emphasize Britain's free hand, and as late as 1 August two of its members wanted a declaration that Britain would in no circumstances fight Germany.

The possibility of a split within the cabinet was the single most compelling argument for not forcing the pace of Britain's internal debate. In 1911 the radicals within British Liberalism had been weakened by the willingness of Lloyd George and Churchill to support Grey. But in 1914 Lloyd George wavered, responding to the anti-war sentiments of the Liberal press more than to the blandishments of Churchill.[172] The chancellor of the exchequer could be confident that a principled stand against entry to the war would be assured of major backbench support. Even on 2 August Asquith thought three-quarters of the Liberal party's members were opposed to war. If Asquith's

[171] Neilson, *Britian and the last Tsar*, 35.
[172] Keith Wilson, 'Britain', in Wilson (ed.), *Decisions for war*, 176–8; David (ed.), *Inside Asquith's cabinet*, 179.

cabinet did split over entry to the war, the Conservatives would gain power. The dread of such an outcome was a force for Liberal unity, even for the radicals. But its importance did not lie only in its ramifications for a single political party: a united Liberal government would be able to lead a united Britain into war, a divided party would betoken a divided country. The Labour party had discussed the possibility of a general strike in the event of war. Such a danger was real enough for a nation where the railwaymen, the dockers, and the seamen had all staged national strikes since 1911, and where trade-union membership had almost doubled since 1909. The possibility of social upheaval as a result of the economic strains of war was as threatening to Grey, who referred to the 1848 revolutions, as to other European leaders. In the City of London commercial opinion warned that war would lead to the collapse of credit. In such circumstances a Conservative-led entry to war would make the war itself a party issue; the Liberals, on the other hand, not least by virtue of the electoral pact which they had struck with the Labour party in 1903, had a greater claim to represent the national interest.

Such arguments were not lost on the Conservatives themselves. The fear of Grey's replacement as foreign secretary by somebody of a more radical disposition was their corollary to the radicals' fear of a Conservative government. Although no nearer consensus on the issue than the rest of the country in late July, on 2 August the Conservatives' leader, Bonar Law, was able to write to Asquith pledging his party's support for the war. The issues for which the Conservatives were prepared to fight were Britain's status as a great power and the balance of power in Europe: Law was affirming Grey's commitment to the Entente.

Henceforth the attentions of Asquith and Grey could be focused firmly on the need to convince the radicals, and they could back up their blandishments with the implicit threat of being able to form a coalition government with the Conservatives should the radicals not follow Grey in his determination that Britain must support France. Nonetheless, the outcome of the cabinet held on the morning of 2 August was ambiguous. Grey informed the meeting of the French naval mobilization the previous day, and of France's dependence on Britain for the defence of its northern coast. The direct danger to British maritime interests posed by a German naval presence in the Channel and the North Sea was not a divisive issue. For some in the cabinet the decision to affirm Britain's naval obligations was therefore a step to deter Germany, not a step towards war itself. Their interpretation was confirmed when Germany promptly offered to remain out of the Channel.

Nonetheless, the cabinet's decision affirmed the 1912 Anglo-French naval talks. It had, at least in small degree, recognized that Britain could not enjoy a 'free hand' *sine die*. Furthermore, Germany's willingness to limit its naval activity was not matched in regard to its army. During the course of Sunday

2 August the key question became less Britain's support for France and more Britain's commitment to the maintenance of Belgian neutrality. Although the German threat to Belgium was not a new element in British calculations, it had been assumed that the Germans would advance south of the River Meuse, and might thus avoid a major irruption through Belgium, so encouraging the Belgian army itself to stand aside. In these circumstances Britain, although a guarantor of Belgium under the terms of the 1839 treaty, might reasonably regard itself as freed of any obligation to act. However, on 1 August the Belgian government stated its intention to defend its neutrality. Indications of German violation of that neutrality were evident the following day, and on the evening of 2 August the Germans delivered to Britain an ultimatum, demanding unimpeded passage through all Belgium. In reality the obligation to defend Belgian neutrality was incumbent on all the signatories to the 1839 treaty acting collectively, and this had been the view adopted by the cabinet only a few days previously. But now Britain presented itself as Belgium's sole guarantor. Its neutrality became the symbol around which Asquith could rally the majority of his cabinet, including Lloyd George. Gladstonian liberalism might abhor the instincts of Grey and Haldane, but it was committed to the defence of small nations: that commitment became the bridge which allowed *Realpolitik* and liberalism to join forces.

By the morning of 3 August the cabinet and the country were at last effectively united. The cabinet approved the mobilization of the army and the navy. On the same day Germany declared war on France, and on 4 August Britain—its ultimatum to Germany having expired—declared war on Germany. In the event only two ministers resigned: Britain's wavering may have muddied the European scene, but it clarified the domestic position. In the afternoon of 3 August Grey spoke in the House of Commons. It was a long speech, delivered in a conversational style, but its effect was extraordinarily powerful. Its appeal was to Britain's moral obligation; its attention was to the left; it eschewed specifically strategic arguments.

The war in which Britain thought it was about to engage was above all a war for British interests. Grey argued that, as a sea-power and as a trading nation, Britain would be almost as directly affected by the war if it remained neutral. The fact that Britain was a sea-power meant that the war would be limited because it would be naval; he told the House of Commons on 4 August that, by engaging in war, 'we shall suffer but little more than we shall suffer if we stand aside'.[173] If any pre-war commitments had effected British entry to the war, it had been the 1912 Anglo-French naval talks. The staff conversations, and the 1911 resolution of the Committee of Imperial Defence to send an expeditionary force to the continent, formed no part of Britain's decision to fight. One of the

[173] Steiner, *Britain and the origins*, 210.

reasons why the cabinet had been able to accept British belligerence had been its implicit assumption that the country was engaging in a naval war. Neither it nor the House of Commons made a specific decision in favour of a continental strategy; on 2 August the prime minister himself saw the dispatch of an expeditionary force to France as serving no purpose.

Thus, Britain's thinking on the sort of war in which it was embarking was as muddled as that of the other belligerents. Naval pressure on Germany would be of value only over the long term. The needs of France and Belgium were more immediate; there was a danger that Germany would be master of both long before British sea-power would be effective. Furthermore, the navy's strategy would itself become vulnerable if the European coastline was dominated by a hostile power. The 'moral' obligation therefore carried with it a continental commitment. In addition, Grey's public presentation of the war as limited did not conform to his gloomier prognostications with regard to the economic and social consequences; this contradiction was present even if the war did remain purely maritime, because the application of sea-power and of commercial pressure implied a war that would achieve its objects slowly and by directing its efforts against the German nation as a whole, rather than exclusively against its armed forces.

Insufficient clarity about the nature of the war on which they were embarking is a feature common to all the belligerents in 1914. Such a criticism, moreover, is not simply the product of hindsight. Between 1871 and 1914 the serious study of war was transformed; the success of the German general staff in the planning and execution of the wars of unification, and the need to respond tactically to the technological transformation wrought on the battlefield by quick-firing, long-range weaponry, prompted four decades of reform and analysis. Many professional soldiers recognized, in their plans for future war, individual elements which would prove characteristic of the battlefield of 1914–18. But, perhaps partly because of the increasingly demanding nature of their own specialist concerns, their overall outlook was narrowed. Specialist and technical concerns could prompt political lobbying in order to advance specifically military interests. Generals, however, were not on the whole involved in politics per se. The army may have been the focus of much attention from the radical right in France before 1914; soldiers themselves, however, identified with the nation as a whole and tended to accept republicanism as a general concept. The Dreyfus affair was a product, not of a politicized army, but of a professional army, over-zealous in the protection of its own identity from outside intervention. In Germany, Schlieffen might advise whether or not the opportunity was right for war in 1905, but he did not see it as his task to direct foreign policy by actively and vociferously advocating preventive war; in 1914 Moltke had no role at all in the management of the bulk of the July crisis. Ironically, therefore, for all the suspicions harboured by the left, soldiers were in some respects insufficiently political. Many of them did anticipate tactical conditions in which stalemate and attrition would come to dominate warfare. But they too readily accepted, because it was the received wisdom in an area outside their specialist knowledge, that such conditions could not be long sustained because domestic economic and social collapse would follow.

The soldiers' narrow political vision was matched by the remarkable military ignorance of the civilian leaders. A century previously the tasks of military and political leadership were only just ceasing to be combined in a single individual; the First World War itself would prompt the creation of collective bodies designed to fuse the wisdom of soldiers, sailors, and politicians. But in July 1914 either there were no such committees, or where they did exist, as in Britain and France, they were not consulted. Thus, statesmen like Bethmann Hollweg and Berchtold could evoke an image of war that implied quick and decisive battlefield success, when even a limited acquaintance with the changes in warfare since 1870 might have suggested a somewhat different scenario. Furthermore, the notion of war as a major catastrophe for Europe was a common one in July 1914, and yet it was not one which was necessarily related to military conditions in themselves, but was derived from assumptions about economic factors. The year 1870 once again provided a historical but superficial analogy. The Franco-Prussian War had prompted revolution in France; yet the revolution was seen as a phenomenon separate from the conditions of the war itself.

Military factors did, therefore, play a role in the origins of the war, but more in the shaping of general assumptions than in the mechanics of the crisis of late July. This is not to deny that the war plans of the powers affected the tempo of events in late July. Mobilization for Germany did mean war; less directly it probably also meant war for France—at least that was what General Boisdeffre had told the Russians on behalf of France in 1892.[174] But the staff plans were not called into operation until events had already made the implementation of military measures probable. In the Bosnian and Balkan crises mobilizations had been effected without war. At a much earlier stage in the July crisis images of war were being employed in the manipulation of events. Bethmann Hollweg relied on an apocalyptic view of European war and on the assumption (which was widely shared) that war would bring domestic political change, and even revolution, to persuade the powers not to fight. He saw the possibility of a limited war between Austria-Hungary and Serbia, reckoning that the other states would (in the language of contemporary strategic studies) be self-deterred. He was wrong: war was preferable to diplomatic defeat. The popular image of war proved insufficiently awful for deterrence to operate.

[174] D. Jones, *Military–naval encyclopaedia*, i. 3.

Furthermore, other powers applied deterrence in different ways. Poincaré reckoned that strong alliance blocs, backed up by military preparations and firm agreements, would keep the peace. The plans which the general staffs prepared, therefore, confirmed the alliances rather than ran counter to them. Poincaré and Sazonov both argued that, if Grey had been able to pledge British support earlier, the threat of a united Entente would have forced Germany to climb down. If they were right, theirs is an argument for clarity of intention— not uncertainty—as a keynote in deterrence. However, Britain, whose uncertainty was prompted not by the needs of foreign policy, nor by the argument that the creation of doubt as to its intentions in the mind of its opponent made for more effective deterrence, but by genuine domestic division, could defend its position by replying that the likelihood of its intervention was at least sufficient to have deterred Germany if Germany had had a mind to be deterred. Germany and Austria-Hungary calculated that the alliances would encourage the Entente powers to restrain each other from intervention, but for some reason would not have the same effect on the Triple Alliance.

The accusation levelled against the alliance system before 1914 is, however, more serious than that it failed to prevent war; it is that it actually provoked war. Kurt Riezler, writing before the outbreak of war, reckoned that one ally would restrain another; a vital interest for one would not be a vital interest for another. The military context was in part responsible for transforming a system of great-power management that was designed to be defensive into one of offence. The emphasis on speed of mobilization, the interaction of war plans, and Germany's central geographical position meant that a chain reaction became possible. But the interlocking sequence of mobilizations can be exaggerated; Serbia decided to mobilize ahead of Austria-Hungary; Austria-Hungary settled for general mobilization before Russia's position was known; Russia's move to mobilization preceded Germany's and yet Germany's decision was made before it was aware of the Russian position; Britain responded to Germany before it had decided to honour any commitment to France. The imperative of the alliance system was not one of altruism, but of brutal self-interest: Germany needed Austria-Hungary; France's military position was dependent on Russian support; British diplomacy was unsustainable if it allowed the Entente to shatter.

By 1914, therefore, the alliances had become a major vehicle for the expression of a great power's status. This was the context into which Germany's *Weltpolitik* fitted. By 1914 Germany simultaneously sought affirmation as a world power and as a continental power. Furthermore, it did so in a way calculated to infuriate. Bethmann Hollweg put a large share of the blame for the war on his own country: 'the earlier errors of a Turkish policy against Russia, a Moroccan against France, fleet against England, irritating everyone, blocking everybody's way and yet not really weakening anyone.'[175] By July 1914 each power, conscious in a self-absorbed way of its own potential weaknesses, felt it was on its mettle, that its status as a great power would be forfeit if it failed to act.

Such a view, however nebulous and unsatisfactory, helps to explain why the July crisis cannot stand in isolation. To a certain extent, and particularly in the final week of that month, the crisis did generate its own momentum. The speed of events outstripped the speed of communications. Insufficient time elapsed for reflection and calculation. But the postures which the powers adopted in that week were themselves reflections of the previous crises, and the decisions taken earlier narrowed the options available later. Russia had to support Serbia because it had not done so in 1909; Germany had to support Austria-Hungary because it had backed down in 1913; France had to honour the commitments to Russia Poincaré had repeated since 1912; Britain's apparent success in mediation in 1913 encouraged a renewed effort in 1914. Thus, too, the fluidity which had characterized the international scene in the first of the major crises, that over Morocco in 1905, and which had particularly revolved around the attitudes of Britain, Russia, and Italy, had given way to considerable rigidity.

Such explanations are unfashionably political and diplomatic. Economic and imperial rivalries, the longer-range factors, help explain the growth of international tension in the decade before 1914. Economic depression encouraged the promotion of economic competition in nationalist terms. But trade was international in its orientation; economic interpenetration was a potent commercial argument against war. Imperialism, as Bethmann Hollweg tried to show in his pursuit of détente, could be made to cut across the alliance blocs. Furthermore, even if economic factors are helpful in explaining the long-range causes, it is hard to see how they fit into the precise mechanics of the July crisis itself. Commercial circles in July were appalled at the prospect of war and anticipated the collapse of credit; Bethmann Hollweg, the Tsar, and Grey envisaged economic dislocation and social collapse. In the short term, the Leninist interpretation of the war as a final stage in the decline of capitalism and imperialism, of war as a way of regulating external economic imbalance and of resolving internal crises, cannot be appropriate as an explanation of the causes of the First World War.

Indeed, what remains striking about those hot July weeks is the role, not of collective forces nor of long-range factors, but of the individual. Negatively put, such an argument concludes that the statesmen of 1914 were pygmies, that Bethmann Hollweg was no Bismarck. Nobody, with the possible exception— and for a few days only—of Grey, was prepared to fight wholeheartedly for peace as an end in itself. Domestically Berchtold, Sazonov, and Bethmann

---

[175] Herwig, 'Imperial Germany', in E. May (ed.), *Knowing one's enemies*, 93.

Hollweg had acquired reputations for diplomatic weakness, which they now felt the need to counter by appearing strong. But even this interpretation fuses the individual with wider national pressures. More bizarre is the conjunction of the individual with accident—the wrong turn of Archduke Franz Ferdinand's driver, and the fortuitous positioning of Princip who had already assumed that his assassination attempt had failed. If Bethmann Hollweg's wife had not died in May would he—it seems reasonable to ask—have been less fatalistic, less resigned in his mood in July? And Conrad von Hötzendorff, whose advocacy of preventive war proved so important to Austrian calculations at the beginning of July—were his motives patriotic or personal? He calculated that, as a war hero, he would be free to marry his beloved Gina von Reininghaus, already the wife of another.[176] Conrad's infatuation cannot, obviously, explain the outbreak of the First World War. But it remains a reminder that the most banal and maudlin emotions, as well as the most deeply felt, interacted with the wider context.

[176] Williamson, *Journal of Interdisciplinary History*, XVIII (1988), 816.

2

WILLINGLY
TO WAR

WAR ENTHUSIASM

'My darling One & beautiful—', Winston Churchill wrote to his wife on 28 July 1914, 'Everything tends towards catastrophe, & collapse. I am interested, geared-up & happy.'[1] The intensity of the July crisis released the adrenalin of the cabinets of Europe. But the statesmen knew that, if war was its outcome, the emotion which fired them would need also to be shared by their electorates. Bülow in 1909 and Bethmann Hollweg in 1912 each expressed the view that wars were caused not by the ambitions of princes and politicians, but by the action of the press on public opinion.[2] The evidence to support their belief was sparse. Public opinion had certainly played its part in railroading the British cabinet into war in the Crimea in 1854. However, in Germany's case Bismarck's wars had been cabinet wars, at least in their causation. What was true was that the outbreak of hostilities had in turn prompted public demonstrations, both in Prussia and France.[3] Popular enthusiasm might not cause war, but it certainly needed to condone it.

The distinction between the feelings of the masses in the lead-up to war and their reactions when the war broke out was particularly important in 1914. It is one which recent historiography has done much to explore. But the historian's knowledge of what is to come, not only in the war itself but also in the rest of the twentieth century, can make any analysis of the sentiments of 1914 mawkish and maudlin. The contrast, however metaphorical, between a sun-dappled

---

[1] Soames, *Speaking for themselves*, 96.
[2] Rosenberger, *Zeitungen als Kriegstreiber?*, 33.
[3] Rohkrämer, *Militarismus der kleinen Leute*, 89–92, moderates this view; for a comparison between 1870 and 1914, see Meinecke, *Strassburg/Freiburg/Berlin*, 138.

and cultured civilization and a mud-streaked and brutish battlefield can too easily suggest that, if the peoples of Europe were enthusiastic about the war, then they were, at least momentarily but also collectively, mad. It is perhaps more comforting, but equally simplistic, to conclude that war enthusiasm was a 'myth', that the cameramen caught images that were unrepresentative or were posed, fulfilling briefs that were themselves directed from on high.

The outbreak of the war has become one of the most unassailable divisions in the compartmentalization of the past. It marks the end of the 'long' nineteenth century, which began with the French Revolution in 1789, and it inaugurated the 'short' twentieth century, which closed with the end of the Cold War. This sense that 1914 was a break in continuity is not simply a product of hindsight, a manipulation of historians. It was one frequently expressed at the time. Adolf Hitler later recalled that 'I sank to my knees and thanked heaven from an overflowing heart that it had granted me the good fortune to be alive at such a time'.[4] Many people joined the crowds precisely because they felt that history was being made. Indeed, the historians of the day told them that this was the case. Friedrich Meinecke, then in Freiburg, described 1 August 1914 as 'a new historical epoch for the world'.[5] Writing thirty years later, in 1944, and aware not only of what the First World War, but also the Second had meant for Germany, he could still affirm that 3 August 1914 was 'one of the most beautiful moments of my life, which even now pours into my soul with a surprising suddenness the deepest trust in our nation and the highest joy'.[6]

What had so moved Meinecke was not the war in the Balkans but the news that all the Reichstag parties would approve war credits. Max Weber too, although hostile to the war in a political sense, welcomed the national effusion which it generated, and which gave the war meaning regardless of its outcome.[7] Popular demand may not have caused the war, but once it came, the sublimation of distinctions of class, of politics, and of profession which were the people's response to it generated its own euphoria. The Austrian writer Stefan Zweig, who was a Jew and would become an exile from Nazism, but who, like Hitler, joined the crowds, albeit in Vienna rather than Munich, wrote of 'a rushing feeling of fraternity'.

Strangers spoke to one another in the streets, people who had avoided each other for years shook hands, everywhere one saw excited faces. Each individual experienced an exaltation of his ego, he was no longer the isolated person of former times, he had been incorporated into the mass, he was part of the people, and his person, his hitherto unnoticed person, had been given meaning.[8]

---

[4] Eksteins, *Rites of spring*, 306.   [5] Kruse, 'Kriegsbegeisterung', 85.
[6] Meinecke, *Strassburg/Freiburg/Berlin*, 137.   [7] Mommsen, *Weber*, 190–1.
[8] Zweig, *World of yesterday*, 173–4.

Zweig was a middle-class intellectual and Vienna a capital city. But the sensations which he experienced were not confined to such orbits. Louis Barthas, a cooper in Peyriac-Minervois, a socialist and a non-practising Catholic, a father and a reservist, described the response of his village to France's general mobilization in very similar terms. Brothers who had fallen out were reconciled; mothers-in-law and sons and daughters-in-law, who only the evening before had been at blows, exchanged kisses; neighbours who had ceased all neighbourly relations became the best of friends. Barthas espoused the anti-militarism of his political convictions. But he acknowledged that party divisions were forgotten. The first effect of the war was, paradoxically, to bring peace.[9]

Nor was hatred of the enemy a primary element in this bonding. The crowds passed by the embassies of enemy powers. While personal encounters remained recent and therefore vivid, the foe could still be an individual. Britons caught in Leipzig at the outbreak of hostilities experienced no personal unpleasantness.[10] The first French prisoners of war to arrive in Germany were warmly received by German women, and plied with wine and chocolate.[11] The *East London Observer* on 8 August praised the local German community and reminded its readers that, 'in the indignation of the moment one must not forget to behave oneself justly, and like a gentleman and a friend'.[12] The general feeling in Paris was that the Germans were mad, not bad.[13] And in some instances official policy endorsed this restraint. In Berlin films which might arouse violence against foreign residents were censored.[14] In Vienna the Entente monarchs even retained their colonelcies of Austro-Hungarian regiments.[15]

This is not to say that xenophobia did not play its part in the popular response to the war. Indeed, at a passive level it was a powerful force for national integration. Rumour was 'the oldest means of mass communication in the world'. In the absence of news, gossip was preferable to silence; it was both a cause of communal feeling and its consequence.[16] In the towns the press could feed off such chatter and then propagate it. In the countryside things were quieter, and the press less evident and less influential. Traditionally, the peasant's distrust of ousiders embraced his fellow nationals from other districts. On the outbreak of war such suspicions could be readily subsumed

[9] Barthas, *Carnets de guerre*, 14.
[10] Cooper, *Behind the lines*, 22; see also Plaut, 'Psychologie des Kriegers', 11–15.
[11] Daniel, *War from within*, 23.
[12] Panayi, *Enemy in our midst*, 275; see also D. Winter, *Death's men*, 23–4.
[13] Raithel, *Das 'Wunder' der inneren Einheit*, 444–5.
[14] Gary Stark, 'All quiet on the home front: popular entertainment, censorship and civilian morale in Germany, 1914–1918', in Coetzee and Shevin-Coetzee (eds.), *Authority, identity*, 75.
[15] Rauchensteiner, *Tod des Doppeladlers*, 189.
[16] Geinitz, *Kriegsfurcht und Kampfbereitschaft*, 161–3; also 167–8.

within the hatred of foreigners whipped up by the chauvinism of the urban press.

Widespread migration and European cosmopolitanism meant that the opportunities for active, and frequently misdirected, enmity were numerous. In France Alsatians and Lorrainers were assaulted because of their accents. In Germany a Bavarian woman found herself under suspicion in Cologne, and in Nuremberg Prussian officers were attacked on the presumption that they were Russian.[17]

The search was not so much for the enemy without as the enemy within: this was the obverse of the solidarity which the war generated. Spies were everywhere. In Germany the scare was officially promoted. On 2 August 1914 the public was asked to assist in the detection of the large numbers of Russian agents alleged to be active in the rear, and especially in the vicinity of railway lines. By the following day sixty-four 'spies' had been exposed in the railway stations of Berlin alone. All were entirely innocent and the suspects included two army officers. Any form of uniform was deemed to be a disguise, a presumption which proved particularly vexatious for priests and nuns. The report that Frenchmen were driving cars through Germany to deliver gold to Russia stoked the enthusiasm of local governments, which set up their own patrols and roadblocks: a total of twenty-eight people were killed as a consequence.[18] The Stuttgart police became more exasperated than most. Clouds were being mistaken for aeroplanes, stars for airships, and bicycle handlebars for bombs. Their director complained that: 'Our streets are filled with old women of both sexes in pursuit of unworthy activities. Everyone sees in his neighbour a Russian or a French spy and believes himself duty-bound to beat him up—and also to beat up the policeman who comes to his rescue.'[19]

The German general staff asked the public to scale down its efforts on 7 August. But spy hysteria was not simply a response to official promptings. The suggestibility of the British public had already been primed by the novels of Erskine Childers and William Le Queux. These fictions received apparently authoritative corroboration from the British army's last commander-in-chief and most famous living icon, Lord Roberts, who had said that there were 80,000 trained German soldiers in the country, many of them working in station hotels. By the beginning of September the Metropolitan Police alone had received between 8,000 and 9,000 reports of suspected espionage. Although they deemed ninety of these worthy of further investigation, none was proved to have any foundation.[20]

[17] Gerd Krumeich, 'L'Entrée en guerre en Allemagne', in Becker and Audoin-Rouzeau (eds.), *Sociétés européennes*, 69.
[18] Verhey, 'Spirit of 1914', 175–81; Raithel, *Das 'Wunder' der inneren Einheit*, 447–54.
[19] Ulrich und Ziemann, *Frontalltag im ersten Weltkrieg*, 29; Liang, *Rise of modern police*, 190.
[20] Panayi, *Enemy in our midst*, 33–8, 153–4.

In France, where spy mania also developed without government promotion, xenophobia became fused with economic self-interest. As in Britain, the pre-war press had carried stories of German espionage. Léon Daudet of the *Action française* had accused Maggi, an international dairy-products firm with its headquarters in Switzerland, of being a front for a German spy network. Maggi was also a major competitor for smaller French businesses. Maggi's outlets were pillaged on 2 August, while the police stood by: the action was legitimated on the grounds that the firm was German.[21] Such a speedy conversion of enthusiasm into hostility, and of hostility into economic self-interest, required press manipulation. In Britain, although there were isolated attacks on shops owned by enemy aliens in August, there was no major outbreak of violence until 17 October, when it was directly provoked by the arrival of Belgian refugees. Within two days 400 police had to be deployed to keep order in Deptford, and the following weekend comparable demonstrations broke out in Crewe.[22]

An example of economic opportunism masquerading as war enthusiasm is provided by the small businesses competing in the international market for ladies' underwear. A Leipzig firm declared in its advertising that Paris corsets were un-German and a danger to the health of German women. Any lady who felt truly German, and in particular those concerned for future generations of Germans, would use only the 'Thalysia-Büstenhalter' and the 'Thalysia-Edelformer'. Wolsey, a British manufacturer, warned the country's womenfolk that there was 'a great deal of "unmarked" German made underwear about', and J.-B. Side Spring Corsets thanked them 'for their hearty response to an appeal to support the All-British corset movement'.[23]

With her hygienic German foundation garments in place, the German woman had still to resist the temptation to don the latest Paris fashions. She was warned that shameless French dresses rendered their wearer 'a caricature of human nature'. By appealing to women to resist what was implicitly a male interest in sexual exploitation, the advertisers were fusing feminism with nationalism. They were also incorporating women in a fight in which they were unlikely to participate directly, but to which their spending power could nonetheless contribute. As the Sunlight Seifenfabrik announced in its promotion of soap in the *Neukölner Tageblatt* on 4 September 1914, the transfer of its British capital to German ownership was 'not an insignificant victory in the realm of German economic life'.[24]

Etymology, so often abused by advertisers, became part of the campaign. The Leipzig corset-makers reminded their readers that clothes were no longer

---

[21] Weber, *Action française*, 89–90.   [22] Panayi, *Enemy in our midst*, 72–3, 224–8, 283.
[23] Ibid. 135–7; Hirschfeld und Gaspar, *Sittengeschichte des Weltkrieges*, i. 76–7.
[24] Berliner Geschichtswerkstatt, *August 1914*, 248, 274.

chic but *pfiff*. In a climate in which German shoppers rejected marmalade as being English and camembert as French, it made business sense to replace cosmopolitanism with nationalism. In Hamburg the Cafe Belvedere was retitled the Kaffehaus Vaterland and the Moulin Rouge the Jungmühle. Customers ate *Hühnerragu* rather than fricassée, even if they were unsure about its ingredients.[25]

The changing of names could be more than a pragmatic response to market conditions; it might also be prudent. By the autumn 500 German residents in Britain had discarded their Teutonic surnames for something more Anglicized.[26] They included the royal family, who in 1917 became Windsors rather than Saxe-Coburgs, and the First Sea Lord, who in due course ceased to be Battenberg in favour of Mountbatten, and Santa Claus, who was dubbed Father Christmas. Even the capital of Russia was no longer St Petersburg but Petrograd.

Those contemporaries who were able to stand back from such reactions turned to psychology for explanations and rationalizations. Some found it in crowd theory. Gustav Le Bon, who had postulated the existence of a hysterical mass mind in the 1890s, found proof for his arguments in the outbreak of the war. 'The mentality of men in crowds', he argued in 1916, 'is absolutely unlike that which they possess when isolated.' Beliefs 'derived from collective, affective, and mystic sources' swamped the critical faculties of even the most intelligent men. They shaped what Le Bon called the 'unconscious will', which, partly because it was inherited and partly because it was common to the nation as a whole, generated illusions which had the force of truth. Some found much of this reasoning persuasive. In 1921 Freud traced the 'coercive character of group formation' back to his theory of the primal horde, first developed in 1913.[27]

Others looked to sex for an answer. War made permissible acts which were in peace considered immoral. Sadism and brutality were part of the individual's unconscious, now legitimated and given free rein. Herein was the sense of liberation to which the crowds gave vent. The processes of mobilization and recruitment carried the implication that women were only available to soldiers, when in reality they were not available to anyone because the soldiers had to depart for the front. Thus, the lack of sublimation heightened the sexual potency of the situation. The attractions of uniform played their part. Into this mix of fetishism and sexual exploitation the psychologists also injected romance. Wives fell 'in love with their partner all over again in his new personality, the personality he assumes with his smart uniform, and this pride

---

[25] Berliner Geschichtswerkstatt, *August 1914*, 275; Ullrich, *Kriegsalltag*, 16, 23.
[26] Panayi, *Enemy in our midst*, 53–4.
[27] Le Bon, *Psychology of the Great War*, esp. 31–46, 169–73, 266–8; Pick, *War machine*, 96, 224.

and love communicate themselves to the man, who departs for the carnage with a light heart'.[28]

The employment of private emotions for state purposes was exposed by an Austrian, Andreas Latzko, in his collection of short stories *Menschen im Krieg* (*Men in battle*), published in 1918. In 'Off to war' a shell-shocked officer, a composer in civilian life, refuses to respond to the solicitude of his visiting wife. After she has left he tells the other convalescents of a fellow officer's young wife, commended by the colonel for her pluckiness, her patriotism, and above all her restraint when the regiment departed for the front. 'My wife was in the fashion too, you know,' the composer fulminates. 'Not a tear! I kept waiting and waiting for her to begin to scream and beg me at least to get out of the train, and not go with the others—beg me to be a coward for her sake. Not one of them had the courage to. They just wanted to be in the fashion.' Thus the greatest disillusionment of the war was not the war itself but the discovery 'that the women are horrible'. They sent men to war 'because every one of them would have been ashamed to stand there without a hero... No general could have made us go if the women hadn't allowed us to be stacked on the trains, if they had screamed out they would never look at us again if we turned into murderers.'

Latzko's sarcasm is vented on a major's wife who has become a nurse, a role which has given her the opportunity to flirt with lightly wounded officers while raising 'her high above herself'.[29] The ambivalence of the nurse's position is central in understanding this interpretation of the role of women in promoting war enthusiasm. She was urged to be patriotic rather than compassionate, disciplined rather than emotional. Her task was to return men to the firing line, fit to fight; to harden their resolve, not to undermine it. *Das Rote Kreuz*, the journal of the German nursing movement, told its readers in March 1914 that the most important attribute of mothers in war was the willingness to sacrifice their sons for their country, while that of Red Cross sisters was obedience. The largest German nursing movement, the *Vaterlandische Frauenverein*, known as 'the Kaiserin's army', had 3,000 branches and 800,000 members in 1914, and in all there were over 6,300 bodies of nurses with 1.1 million members. Even in Britain the Voluntary Aid Detachments, formed under the auspices of the Territorial Army, had 50,000 members by 1914. Many women were being 'militarized' before the war: the distinction between the private and the public spheres was already eroded.[30]

[28] Fischer and Dubois, *Sexual life during the World War*, 64; also Hirschfeld und Gaspar, *Sittengeschichte des Weltkrieges*, esp. x, 31–5, 48–9, 53–69. Fischer and Dubois seem to have used Hirschfeld and Gaspar, which is much fuller.
[29] Latzko, *Men in battle*, 20–1, 36–7.
[30] Henrick Stahr, 'Liebesgaben für den Ernstfall. Das Rote Kreuz in Deutschland zu Beginn des Ersten Weltkriegs', in Berliner Geschichtswerkstatt, *August 1914*, 83–9; Summers, *Angels and citizens*, 237, 247–8, 253–60, 272–3, 278.

The ability of all the belligerents to interpret the war defensively covered over the contradictions which were implicit in the nurse's vocation and of which Latzko complained. Women as a whole may have been much more dubious about the war than men, and certainly more so than allowed for by Latzko. But the soldier sallied forth to protect his wife and children. Thus a primitive and basic response could be rolled into the patriotism demanded of the modern state. Those women who could rationalized their readiness to let their husbands go as a sacrifice for 'God and fatherland'; those who could not saw it as an act of self-protection and of maternal responsibility. 'It is a thousand times better', wrote a contributor to a German magazine on pastoral theology, 'to [fight for home and hearth] on the frontier and in enemy territory, than to have the enemy enter the homeland and take everything.'[31]

Most contemporary explanations for war enthusiasm tended to rest on the rationalization of emotions rather than on logic itself. What they reflected above all was surprise—on two counts. The first was surprise that the war had broken out at all. Freud expressed this with his customary clarity in the spring of 1915:

We were prepared to find that wars between the primitive and civilized peoples, between the races who are divided by the colour of their skin—wars, even, against and among the nationalities of Europe whose civilization is little developed or has been lost—would occupy mankind for some time to come. But we permitted ourselves other hopes. We had expected the great world-dominating nations of white race upon whom the leadership of the human species has fallen, who were known to have world-wide interests as their concern, to whose creative powers were due not only our technical advances towards the control of nature but the artistic and scientific standards of civilization—we had expected these peoples to succeed in discovering another way of settling misunderstandings and conflicts of interest.[32]

The second source of surprise was that the populations of Europe embraced the war as they did. The picture of widespread enthusiasm does stand in need of modification and of amplification. But its fundamental message remains unequivocal. The belligerent peoples of Europe accepted the onset of war; they did not reject it. And yet the anticipation that there could be opposition, that mobilization could be sabotaged, that the workers in key war industries would strike, that reservists would not report for duty, was widely held. Part of the apocalyptic vision of war entertained by Bethmann Hollweg, by the Tsar, and by Grey rested on the assumption that war would not be accepted by the working class.

[31] Geinitz, *Kriegsfurcht und Kampfbereitschaft*, 157.   [32] Freud, 'Thoughts for the times', 276.

SOCIALISM AND THE INTERNATIONAL

The strength of socialism provided good grounds for their fears. After 1912 the German socialists, the SPD, constituted the largest single party in the Reichstag; the 1914 French elections gave the socialists almost thirty more seats than they had held in 1910, and their gains represented an increase of half a million votes since 1906. The rate of growth outstripped the pace of the economic and social change which underpinned it. In 1910, the socialist parties of the world claimed 2.4 million party members; by 1914 this figure had swollen to 4.2 million.[33]

A major plank of socialism for many, but not all, of its adherents was pacifism. In 1889, to mark the centenary of the French Revolution, the Second International was formed to link the socialist parties of the world. But the first Moroccan crisis revealed how little had been done by 1905 to co-ordinate the responses of its members in the face of war. The German trade unions, asked by the French syndicalist organization the Confédération Générale du Travail (CGT) to co-operate in anti-war demonstrations, responded that such an initiative should come not from them but from the SPD, as it was the German workers' political organization. The SPD was of the view that the French socialist party should take the lead, and the latter consequently accused the former of interfering in France's domestic arrangements.[34] Prompted by this fiasco, the International debated its response to war at its 1907 conference in Stuttgart. The French socialists Jean Jaurès and Edouard Vaillant proposed that war should be hindered by measures ranging from parliamentary intervention through mass strikes to revolution. But others feared that strikes and revolutions, particularly at times of national danger, were calculated to invite governmental repression and so threaten rather than advance the cause of socialism. August Bebel, the leader of the German socialists, proposed a formula that was less precise and consequently less provocative: workers and their parliamentary representatives should hinder the outbreak of war by the most effective means available; if war broke out nonetheless, they should work for its rapid conclusion. Although Bebel's resolution was adopted, it was given a revolutionary rider by three more-radical figures, Rosa Luxemburg, V. I. Lenin, and Y. O. Martov: in the event of war socialists were to use the opportunity to hasten the demise of class rule.[35]

Thus, the Stuttgart resolution was a compromise, long on strategy and short on tactics. In 1910, at Copenhagen, Vaillant, this time in conjunction with a

---

[33] Haupt, *Socialism and the Great War*, 132. For what follows, see Haupt; Joll, *Second International*; Kirby, *War, peace and revolution*, 1–40.
[34] Milner, *Dilemmas of Internationalism*, 134–8.
[35] Miller, *Burgfrieden und Klassenkampf*, 34–5.

Briton, Keir Hardie, tried to give it precision. They proposed a general strike as the means to avert war. The German socialists opposed, and rather than split over the issue the congress agreed that further consideration should be postponed until its next meeting, due to be held in Vienna in 1913. In the event, however, the outbreak of the first Balkan war disrupted the timings. An emergency meeting was held in Basle at the end of 1912. Rather than debate the Vaillant–Hardie proposal, the Basle meeting opted for a more general appeal to all pacifist elements, including the middle class. Convening in Basle cathedral, the Second International clothed its pacifism with a moral and even religious fervour which still lacked precision but now seemed to be effective. Anti-war demonstrations coincided with the conference, and the pressure for restraint put on governments was apparently reflected in their pursuit of peaceful solutions in 1913. The congress due to be held that year was postponed until September 1914, when a definitive decision on whether or not socialists would counter war with a general strike would be taken.

Governmental fears of socialist strength, and specifically of the International's pursuit of pacifism, were reflected in the optimism which overtook socialists themselves in 1913. The fact that the principal European crises of the previous decade had been settled without a major war confirmed their belief in the effectiveness of their own influence and in the argument, espoused especially by the German socialists, that premature alarm in the event of a crisis would only bring discredit on the International. Even Jean Jaurès, the great French socialist, whose primary goal became the pursuit of peace and who urged the International into a more active and interventionist policy, succumbed to the general euphoria. In July 1914, therefore, socialists everywhere were slow to respond. Their ignorance of secret diplomatic exchanges ensured that they could do no more than follow events, until—like everybody else—they were overtaken by the speed of developments in the last few days.

On 29 July 1914 the committee of the International Socialist Bureau, the permanent secretariat of the International, convened in Brussels to discuss the timing and location of the congress scheduled to be held in Vienna that autumn. First to speak was the leader of the Austrian socialists, Viktor Adler. His mood was despondent. He saw war between Austria-Hungary and Serbia as unavoidable, and regarded his most important task as the preservation of his party and its institutions: he told his international colleagues that 'the ideas of a strike and so on are only fantasies'.[36] Adler's defeatism was roundly criticized by Hugo Haase, Bebel's successor as leader of the SPD in the Reichstag. Haase called for action to uphold the peace, and was supported by the two other Germans present, Karl Kautsky (the party's principal Marxist theoretician) and Rosa Luxemburg (who represented Poland). But Haase himself was

---

[36] Miller, *Burgfrieden und Klassenkampf*, 44.

labouring under an illusion. He thought that one of the principal upholders of European peace was the German government. Misled, the mood of the meeting recovered its optimism. On Jaurès's suggestion the committee decided that the best approach would be for the national parties not to approve war credits; it did not, however, regard the situation as sufficiently urgent for it to pre-empt the deliberations of the congress itself, which were to be brought forward to 9 August and held in Paris. 'It will be like Agadir,' Jaurès remarked, to Vandervelde, the Belgian socialist, on 30 July. 'There will be ups and downs. But it is impossible that things won't turn out all right.'[37] On the same day Jaurès found time to visit the Flemish primitives at the Musée des Beaux Arts before he returned to France. The following evening he was dead, the victim of an assassin's bullet.

There is no reason to believe that, even had the International been made aware of the implications of the July crisis, it could have mounted a more effective response to the danger which confronted it. Its view of war was conditioned by its view of imperialism: its stock image was a war of territorial acquisitiveness generated by economic competition, not a war of self-defence. By concentrating on the abstract, by treating peacetime militarism as the immediate danger, and by construing the threat of war within Europe itself as remote, it avoided exposing latent splits in its own body.

Within the International the revolutionary left did not share the majority's abhorrence of war. They argued that imperialism was the last stage of capitalism, that the arms race which colonial rivalry generated increased the exploitation and consequently the class-consciousness of the workers, and that the result of war would be the opportunity to create class revolution. Some rigid theorists contended that, far from moderating militarism and imperialism, and their accompanying threat of war, true revolutionaries should be fostering them. The rhetoric of Internationalism continued to give expression to at least some of these ideas. But the success in averting war shown by capitalist society led many German socialists, including Bebel, Haase, and Kautsky, to reckon that capitalism recognized the dangers attendant on war for itself and would moderate its behaviour accordingly. Such thinking acted as a bridge to the majority of socialists, who were increasingly of a reformist rather than a revolutionary disposition. The pre-war expansion of socialism owed much to its fusion with the trades-union movement, whose objectives were less theoretical and political, more pragmatic and economic. Rosa Luxemburg's conviction in January 1913 that capitalism was breaking down, that imperialism was in its last stages, and that the moment was ripe for a socialist offensive did not reflect the dominant view. Co-operation and collaboration with capitalism at home went hand in hand with moderation in Internationalism,

[37] Joll, *Second International*, 168.

an emphasis on arbitration, and a call for arms reductions. Even if the 1914 International congress had debated the Vaillant–Hardie proposal, the majority would have rejected the use of a general strike to counter war, and the only outcome would have been a bitter split.

Not the least of the difficulties that would have confronted the International if it had embraced the idea of a general strike was its uneasy relationship with trade unionism. The International was an organization of socialist parties. Anxious in its early days to exclude anarchists, it had focused on the primacy of political action and rejected the weaponry of mass strikes. Such an approach made life uncomfortable for trade unionism, but found its rationalization in a division of labour. The economic problems of the working class were taken up internationally by the International Secretariat of Trade Unions, formally established in 1901. Dominated by the German Free Trade Unions, in the hands of Carl Legien, its focus was practical and its priority to support the development of strong national organizations rather than to promote inter-national activity per se. French syndicalists were unhappy with this approach: they were at once both more international and more anarchist, but they found that none of abstention, confrontation, or co-operation could make the Ger-mans change their position. France was far from being alone in its stance, but Geman trades unions had their way by dint of superior organization and superior numbers. In 1909 the entry of the United States to the International Secretariat of Trade Unions consolidated its approach. By 1913, when the International Secretariat changed its name to the International Federation and elected Legien its president, revolutionary syndicalism was on the defens-ive and the division between German and French trade unionism even more evident than that between German and French socialism. When, at the Belgian national congress of trades unions in Brussels on 27 July 1914, Léon Jouhaux, the general secretary of the CGT, asked Legien for a meeting, he was reluctantly accorded a five-minute conversation over a cup of coffee on the afternoon of the final session.[38]

Legien's pragmatism was realistic. Trade unionism had to be stronger nationally before it could exercise international influence. In France only 9 per cent of workers were members of trades unions in 1914. Even in Germany, as Haase pointed out in 1912, the two industrial sectors most vital to the conduct of the war, the railway and munitions workers, were not unionized. The country with a well-organized proletariat, where the trades unions could call an effective general strike, would be overrun by the country that was less well-developed in socialist terms. In the latter nascent trades unionism, if the workers opposed war, would be crushed by a state rendered more powerful by its need to respond to the onset of hostilities.

---

[38] Milner, *Dilemmas of Internationalism*, esp. 48–59, 71–83, 193–9.

The solution which Haase therefore advocated in 1912 was for each country to follow its own course. Thus the International showed itself to be no more than a federation of national bodies, within which the idea of Internationalism itself retreated as socialism within individual states advanced. In particular, the pacifist impetus in 1913 itself came not from the International but from joint Franco-German collaboration. It was left to the initiative of the socialist parties of each of these countries, and particularly of France, to fill the gap left by the inability of the International to agree on the means with which it would oppose war. And yet, although putting itself in the hands of national forces, socialism's view of nationalism remained too ambivalent for it to be able to harness its appeal to the ends of internationalism. Rosa Luxemburg saw the class struggle as an international undertaking which national self-determination could only undermine; Marx and Engels had been more pragmatic, recognizing that nationalism might be a means to the revolutionary end, but confining their support of it to the so-called 'historic' nations, and thus excluding many of the ethnic groups within the Austrian and Russian empires. In 1912 the Balkan socialists were amazed to discover that Jaurès's enthusiasm for peace extended to support for Turkey rather than his accepting the justice of a war of national liberation. Thus, by 1914 socialist theory remained undecided about the role of nationalism, while socialist practice was determined by national circum-stances.

An additional paradox was that the success of socialism in each country increased its adaptation to national circumstances, and so weakened its inter-nationalism. Thus, in those countries where internationalism remained stron-gest in the face of war, socialism as a whole was weak and the protest therefore relatively ineffectual. Both socialist members of parliament in Serbia opposed the approval of war credits. In Russia on 8 August all three socialist groupings in the Duma, the Bolsheviks, Mensheviks, and Trudoviks, proved sufficiently loyal to principles of the Second International to abstain from the approval of war credits. But the Russian socialists had no effective organizations at the local level. In Moscow there were neither Social Democrat nor Socialist Revolutionary committees functioning. In St Petersburg the socialist under-ground networks had been smashed by the secret police, and control of the legal organizations was the subject of fierce competition between Mensheviks and Bolsheviks. Furthermore, the parties of the left were divided not only against each other, but also internally, those in exile tending to be more *dirigiste* and less pragmatic than those still in Russia.[39]

Responses to the war did not resolve the differences of Russian socialism. At both the Stuttgart and the Copenhagen congresses the Socialist Revolution-aries had been amongst the foremost supporters of resolutions against war. But

[39] McKean, *St Petersburg*, 126–9; Melancon, *Socialist Revolutionaries*, 67.

the imprecision of the Stuttgart resolution—as revolutionary leaders found out when they tried to implement it at the end of July in Vyborg[40]—made it an inadequate guide. Arguably Lenin remained truest to the fundamental principles of the International, even if in practice he rejected its authority. In the 'seven theses', written at the end of August 1914, he described the war as a consequence of a crisis in capitalism, and concluded that 'the correct slogan is the conversion of the present imperialist war into a civil war'.

If Germany won, the Russian people would be handed over to the exploitation of a foreign ruling class; if Germany was defeated, Russia could help activate a revolution within Germany itself. These arguments meant that the appeal made to the Russian socialists by Vandervelde, that they support the Entente, had some unlikely supporters, including the exiled anarchist Kropotkin, and Georgii Plekhanov, Russian social democracy's leading theorist.

Lenin's fiercely independent line from abroad was moderated by the Bolsheviks still in St Petersburg. In the Duma they joined with the Mensheviks to declare that 'the proletariat . . . will at all times defend the cultural wealth of the nation against any attack from whatever quarter', and their reply to Vandervelde—although it rejected defencism per se—accepted the possibility of their defending a new democratic Russia.[41] Kerensky, the Trudovik leader, revealed how very similar considerations, especially when conditioned by pragmatism, could produce a radically different outcome. He declared that the war would not have happened if the governments of Russia and of the other belligerents had been democratic. But now that it had begun, the threat to the people of Russia—as opposed to their rulers—required that they be defended: 'Peasants and workers, all who desire the happiness and welfare of Russia . . . harden your spirits, collect all forces, and when you have defended the country, liberate it.'[42] Here was a statement that was at once both defencist and revolutionary—a paradoxical realism which left open the path to inter-socialist party co-operation within Russia but which could only undermine the immediate effectiveness of its wider appeal. Thus, to equate 'defencism' with reformism does not do justice to the revolutionary ambitions of many, if not most, of its advocates. Whereas the 'defeatists' saw the war as the opportunity for revolution, the 'defencists' saw it as the precursor to revolution: the former stood for action as soon as possible, the latter for preparation for action later.

Even if the socialists within Russia were more united than Lenin's rhetoric suggested, and even if they were collectively more loyal to the spirit of the International than socialists elsewhere, the fact remains that they lacked the power to influence their country's policies. The strongest and most successful

[40] McKean, *St Petersburg*, 356–7.
[41] Longley, *English Historical Review*, CII (1987), 599–621; McKean, *St Petersburg*, 358–61, also 350–4.
[42] Melancon, *Socialist Revolutionaries*, 65–6, also 22–6.

socialist party in the world was that of Germany. Its ability to moderate the behaviour of its government promised not merely domestic repercussions but also direct benefits to Internationalism. The argument voiced by Kerensky and others—that the Russian people had to defend themselves—would cease to operate if Germany was not, or did not appear to be, the aggressor.

Socialists in France and Russia looked to Germany for a lead, but it was in Austria above all that the SPD could have exercised a direct effect. Austrian social democracy was reconstituted in 1897 in six autonomous national group-ings. In 1910 the Czechs broke away completely, and in 1912 they were prepared to reject the war service law which made every citizen liable for war-related service and suspended the rights of workers' organizations. The Austro-German socialists, on the other hand, accepted the primacy of national defence. Viktor Adler, the leader of the Austrian party, had been virtually alone in his pessimism about the prospects for Internationalism both at Basle in 1912 and in Brussels on 29 July 1914. When war came he embodied his decision to support his country's actions with a statement of the dilemma: 'An incomprehensible German to have done anything else. An incomprehen-sible Social Democrat to have done it without being racked with pain.'[43] He then resigned his party responsibilities. If Germany's socialists had been able to take a strong stand against the war those of Austria might well have followed their lead. In the event the socialist party of neither of the Central Powers opposed the war: thus was Internationalism forfeit to national priorities.

The decision of the German socialists to support the war was both more confused and more hectic than the development of the SPD in the previous decade suggested would be likely. However, the success of the party made it revisionist rather than revolutionary, and to that extent its decision in 1914 was of a piece with its earlier development. Between 1878 and 1890 socialist activity in Germany was banned, except within the Reichstag. The ending of the anti-socialist law was marked in 1891 by the adoption at Erfurt of a party pro-gramme whose objectives, while ultimately Marxist, were in the short term compatible with liberalism and were to be achieved by parliamentary means and not by revolution. This confusion between ideals and reality was confirmed in 1903: formally speaking, the party rejected the notion that working-class conditions were improving under capitalism and that therefore the socialist objective should be to work with the existing state so as to trans-form it from within. The rejection of this argument threw up two problems: first, it denied the truth, which was that the material position of workers in Germany was improving; and secondly, it was not accompanied by a credible alternative policy, since revolution was seen as the consequence of an inevitable collapse of capitalism, not something to be actively sought. The bulk of the

---

[43] Joll, *Second International*, 181; also, Rauchensteiner, *Tod des Doppeladlers*, 35, 139.

socialists' votes came from urban workers. The trades union influence within the party was strong: at least forty-five of the 110 socialist deputies in the Reichstag in 1914 had arrived there by way of the trades unions.[44] Therefore, although the party's leaders showed their desire in 1891 and in 1903 to reflect Marxist nostrums, the practical need to attend to the economic position of its constituents, and the obvious growth and success of the party while it did so, made it more collaborationist than its overt stance allowed. Indeed, the appearance in the years after the 1905 Russian revolution of an activist left wing, whose most vociferous campaigner was Rosa Luxemburg, was evidence of the revisionist trend of the majority of the party. As the party grew in size and success, so its bureaucracy grew too: the executive authorities of the party tried to follow a position which was neutral in terms of policy but which, in practice, acknowledged the party's reliance on the trades unions, at least as a counterweight to the left. The party's declaratory status, isolating itself from the activities of the state and awaiting its opportunity to succeed when Kaiserism collapsed, was impossible to sustain after its success in the 1912 elections. The Reichstag socialist delegation had perforce to take a part in the Reichstag's (admittedly limited) role in Germany's government. Although the socialists did not form a link with the Progressives or the Centre in 1912, the possibility of such a bloc within the Reichstag was beginning to enter the realm of practical politics.

Symptomatic of the SPD's reformism was its attitude to the army. In 1904 Bebel declared that the party was a determined defender of the principle of universal military service, which it saw as an honourable obligation for all men of military age.[45] But implicit within this apparent acceptance of the principal embodiment of the state's power was a challenge to the army's function as an instrument of monarchical authority, and to its possible role in suppressing the workers. Bebel wanted a fuller form of conscription in order to create a true nation in arms, defensive in its capabilities and, more importantly, democratic in its organization. The party was anti-militarist but not anti-military; its goals were domestic and its interest in international relations peripheral. Pacifism was not integral to its identity.

But by 1907 the SPD's neglect of overseas affairs was unsustainable. Bülow's espousal of *Weltpolitik* exploited international issues for domestic ends. German expansion promised full employment and better standards of living, so luring workers from socialism to his centre-right coalition. The SPD, therefore, chose to fight the 1907 elections on German policy in South West Africa. The

---

[44] Snell, *American Historical Review*, LIX (1953), 66–7. On German socialism generally in this period, see Nettl, *Past and Present*, 30 (1965); Schorske, *German social democracy*; Ryder, *German revolution*, chs. 1 and 2; Calkins, *Haase*, chs. 3 and 4; Groh, *Journal of Contemporary History*, I (1966), 4, 151–77; Miller, *Burgfrieden und Klassenkampf*; Kruse, *Krieg und nationale Integration*.

[45] Vogel, *Nationenen im Gleichschritt*, 223.

Herero rebellion had been crushed with brutality, but its horrors failed to move German workers. The SPD lost thirty-six seats. If there was a case for continuity from Bülow's *Weltpolitik* to the origins of the war and from there to the development of German war aims, then there is also a case for saying that the workers, having embraced *Weltpolitik* in 1907 out of economic self-interest, had to support the war in 1914 for the same reason.[46]

The case against such a continuity is that, at one level, the result of the 1907 election galvanized the SPD into finding a foreign policy that was both more coherent and more distinctively socialist. To that extent the Stuttgart resolution, also of 1907, was well timed. In 1911, during the second Moroccan crisis, the party organized demonstrations in favour of peace: 100,000 people attended a rally in Berlin on 20 August, and 250,000 on 3 September. But at another level the so-called 'Hottentot' election was also a reminder of the unwisdom of challenging nationalism. Even at Stuttgart Bebel stressed that the International should be concentrating on the conditions of the working class, not on the issues of war and peace. Foreign policy was the prerogative of the Kaiser: to trespass into such territory might invite a setback comparable with the earlier anti-socialist laws, and so undermine the obvious achievements of German socialism. The SPD fought to keep foreign policy out of the 1912 election, and thereafter the pacifism of German socialism waned. The Balkan wars suggested both that détente and limitation were possible, and that capitalism itself recognized the dangers inherent in anything else. In 1913 the SPD's handling of the Zabern affair revolved once again around the domestic implications of militarism, not the external security of the Reich.

Indications that German socialists would not resort to strike action to disrupt mobilization multiplied. For the SPD mass strikes were a way to respond to repression from above, not to avert hostilities between states. Even in the midst of the pacifist euphoria of 1911 Karl Kautsky described the policy of the Vaillant–Hardie proposal as 'heroic folly', more likely to shatter the party than to prevent war. In December 1913 the general commission of trades unions rejected the Vaillant–Hardie recommendation, and in May 1914 Haase, entrusted with the formulation of the German response, urged its authors to withdraw it.[47]

The split which the SPD feared the issue of war might generate was not simply one between the socialist party and the German state but also (and perhaps inevitably, given the first danger) one within the party itself. Pacifism in 1911–12 revealed a first set of fissures; it attracted middle-class supporters

---

[46] Gunther Mai, ' "Verteidigungskrieg" und "Volksgemeinschaft". Staatliche Selbstbehauptung, nationale Solidarität und social Befreiung in Deutschland in der Zeit des Ersten Weltkrieges (1900–1925)', in Michalka (ed.), *Erste Weltkrieg*, 585–6.

[47] Stargardt, *German idea of militarism*, 93, 128–37, 140, 155; Verhey, 'Spirit of 1914', 27–30; Milner, *Dilemmas of internationalism*, 199.

who were not necessarily socialists, while at the same time antagonizing those on the left of the party who saw war as the final crisis of capitalism. The decline of pacifism in 1913 produced another set. In June a majority of the party (fifty-two members) voted for the increases in the German army: it justified its policy on the grounds that the army's growth was to be funded by a progressive tax on property, and on the promise therein of a fundamental restructuring of Germany's taxation system. But thirty-seven party members opposed, and seven abstained.

For the protagonists of the International, buoyed up by the prevalent optimism of 1913, the significance of the vote on the army law lay not in its result, an indication that most German socialists rated the defence of the nation more highly than the advancement of peace, but rather in the division, which suggested that radicalism was re-emergent within the German party following the death of Bebel in August. This uncertainty about the future direction of the German socialist party was reflected within its leadership. Friedrich Ebert, Bebel's successor as party leader, had been the party's secretary and put the priority on party unity; Haase, the new leader within the Reichstag, found himself torn between party loyalty and his own personal opposition to the growth of the regular army.

These problems were compounded by the French socialists. In emphasizing the problems of war and peace rather than the condition of the working class, they shifted the International's focus from the area of their own weakness to that of the Germans, and so were able to challenge the Germans for primacy in world socialism. A joint meeting of French and German parliamentary delegations at Berne in May 1913 illustrated the Germans' confusion. It resolved to call for limits in arms spending and the enforcement of international arbitration. At the time Jaurès and his fellow internationalists might have been encouraged by such indications. But in hindsight the message seemed different: the French provided 121 delegates, of whom only thirty-eight were socialists, while the Germans could muster a mere thirty-four, all but six of whom were socialists.

In the event, the dilemma between radical pacifism and revisionist nationalism was sufficiently genuine for both currents to find expression in the response of German socialism to the July crisis itself. The radical phase lasted from 25 July to 30 July. Ebert was on his honeymoon, and did not return to Berlin till 28 July. Of the party's parliamentary leaders, Hermann Molkenbuhr and Philipp Schiedemann were also on holiday, one at Cuxhaven and the other in the Dolomites. Haase's authority was thus unchallenged. He was unequivocal: on 25 July he issued a proclamation on behalf of the party, condemning Austria-Hungary's actions, opposing German support for its ally, and declaring the working class's resistance to war. The party's newspaper, *Vorwärts*, took a similar line.

Over the next four days mass demonstrations against war occurred all over Germany. Although none individually was on the scale of the largest held in 1911, that in Berlin on 28 July attracted 100,000 people and prompted the police, who at first had underestimated attendance at the rallies, to ban further meetings in the interests of traffic control. By 31 July 288 anti-war demonstrations had taken place in 163 cities and communes, involving up to three-quarters of a million people.[48]

These protests were designed to uphold the peace: in that sense they were not directed against the German government, nor necessarily against any ultimate decision to go to war which it might take. Haase was convinced that Austria-Hungary was at fault and that Germany was working to restrain its ally. The government itself did not feel threatened. As early as 25 July the Prussian minister of war, Falkenhayn, told the deputy commanding generals in each corps area that there was no need to take action against the SPD. On the following day Haase saw Clemens von Delbrück, the Prussian minister of the interior, who reassured him that the SPD's demonstrations would be tolerated. Thus did Bethmann Hollweg's policy of the 'diagonal' reap the reward prefigured by the 1913 army law debate. In its anxiety to avoid a clash with the government over foreign policy, the SPD put the best possible interpretation on the chancellor's actions. On 30 July Vorwärts praised even the Kaiser 'as a sincere friend of the people's peace'.[49] By then the immediate objectives of both the SPD and Wilhelm were the same, to localize a Balkan war. To all intents and purposes Haase and Bethmann Hollweg were working together, the actions of the former confirming the irenic public image pursued by the latter.

The replacement of pacifism with nationalism was more the product of external events than of machinations on the part of the SPD's revisionists. Socialists could remain united in their opposition to an Austrian war of aggression and to a local crisis that did not appear as an immediate danger to Germany itself. But as the crisis developed Russia's mobilization presented a direct threat, not only to Germany but also to socialism both within Germany and throughout the world. By 30 July the socialist leaders accepted that a war was inevitable, and that defence against Russia was its justification.

The possibility that the SPD would embrace war against Tsarism was ingrained long before 1914.[50] The socialist press was able to tap a vein of xenophobic rhetoric that was not only spiteful but also spontaneous. 'We do not want our wives and children to be sacrificed to the bestialities of the

---

[48] Kruse, *Krieg und nationale Integration*, 30–41; recent historians have played up the scale of these demonstrations, in contrast to earlier interpretations. See also Raithel, *Das 'Wunder' der inneren Einheit*, 244–7; Stargardt, *German idea of militarism*, 142.

[49] Quoted in Raithel, *Das 'Wunder' der inneren Einheit*, 186.

[50] Stargardt, *German idea of militarism*, 138–9, 147.

Cossacks', wrote Friedrich Stampfer at the end of July.[51] He was not the dupe of Bethmann Hollweg but a spokesman for German workers. In the following weeks the SPD leadership would continue to link defencism with Russophobia. Reports of atrocities from East Prussia not only justified the SPD's rationalization of the war, but also cemented the links between it and the rest of Germany. Distant from the industrial heartlands of German socialism, the peasants of the rural marchlands were portrayed as pastoralists defending order and progress against the nomads of the Asiatic steppe. This was an interpretation with which the right could be as content as the left.[52]

If the party's leaders had been slow to grasp the gravity of the crisis in early July, they were under no illusions as to what confronted them by the end of the month. But their very sense of urgency helped exacerbate the weaknesses in party leadership already consequent on Bebel's death. On 28 July Haase, Kautsky, and Luxemburg left for the meeting of the International's executive in Brussels: at a stroke the most forceful exponents of radicalism were removed from centre-stage. On the following day Bethmann Hollweg asked to see Haase. In his stead, the party was represented by Albert Südekum. Südekum was not a member of the party's committee nor of the parliamentary party's committee, but he nonetheless assured the chancellor that the SPD had no plans for strike action. On the same day Ludwig Frank, a Reichstag deputy who believed that the moment for protest was past, said that socialist soldiers must do their duty for Germany: it is possible that he went further, and began to organize a group on the right wing of the party ready to vote in favour of war credits.[53] On 30 July the rump leadership present in Berlin convened. It anticipated the resumption of the persecution endured by socialism under Bismarck, and sent Ebert to Switzerland with the party funds; he did not get back until 3 August.

Haase returned to Berlin on 31 July, and at a meeting of the party commitee held on the same day called for the rejection of war credits. The choice which the committee debated was essentially that between Haase's line and abstention: only Eduard David was ready to put the case for the approval of war credits. Thus far, therefore, German socialism seemed likely to follow the policy proposed in Brussels by Jaurès. Hermann Müller was dispatched to France to convey this message.

Formally speaking, both now and later, the SPD took little account of the trades unions. But on 1 August the free trades unions and the government struck a bargain whereby the former agreed not to strike in the event of war in exchange for a government undertaking not to ban them. Next day the trades

[51] Miller, *Burgfrieden und Klassenkampf*, 54.
[52] Peter Jahn, ' "Zarendreck, Barabarendreck—peitscht sie." Die russische Besetzung Ostpreussens 1914 in der deutschen Öffentlichkeit', in Berliner Geschichtswerkstatt, *August 1914*, 150.
[53] Miller, *Burgfrieden und Klassenkampf*, 42–3, 46–8; Kruse, *Krieg und nationale Integration*, 49–52.

unions endorsed the deal. Following Legien's emphasis on the economic functions of the trades unions, they put their priority on protecting the interests of their members against the ravages of the unemployment which it was expected war would bring—a task they could not fulfil if they were prevented from functioning. Technically the trades unions had steered clear of politics; in practice they had restricted the range of options open to the SPD.

Even more important, however, than the decision of the trades unions was the fact that Germany was now at war. Pacifism and nationalism were no longer compatible. When the parliamentary party met on 3 August to concert its position before the Reichstag session of the following day, the choice which it confronted was no longer that debated on 31 July; it was whether or not the SPD would accord the German people the means with which to defend themselves. In the circumstances the previously preferred position of the majority—abstention—was no longer a serious option. Four out of six on the parliamentary committee were in favour of approving war credits, and seem to have been better organized than the two who were opposed, Haase and Lebedour. Seventy-eight members of the parliamentary party wanted to vote in favour of war credits, and only fourteen against. The majority argued that opposition invited defeat, and with defeat would come the extinction of the party, either at the hands of the enemy or at those of disillusioned German workers. On 4 August the socialist party, reflecting its inner discipline and led by Haase, voted as a bloc in favour of war credits. Its vote was unconditional. The party's position was unaffected either by the growing awareness of Germany's possible guilt in causing the war or by the realization that Germany's intended strategy was not defensive.

The SPD would later argue that its ultimate decision was pre-empted by the will of the people. The decision of the trades unions provided backing for that view. So too did some of the evidence of party feeling at the local level. But working-class sentiment more generally was much more equivocal, and to that extent the SPD's claim was disingenuous.[54] The leadership was not as passive a victim of events as it liked to pretend. When Wilhelm II declared on 4 August, 'I no longer recognize parties; I recognize only Germans', he was expressing a sentiment with which most socialists agreed. Their relief at no longer having to maintain the effort to isolate themselves, at having to set at odds their own nationality and their political convictions, was genuine. But they did not feel that, in accepting the *Burgfrieden*, the expression of German unity, they were abandoning the class struggle. Those socialists who embraced the war did so because they saw it as a means by which to achieve their political objectives. The reward for collaboration, they believed, would be constitutional and social

---

[54] Verhey, 'Spirit of 1914', 238–40, 246–7; Mai, *Ende des Kaiserreichs*, 19; Kruse, *Krieg und nationale Integration*, 54–61.

reform. At its meeting of 3 August the parliamentary party specified as one quid pro quo the democratization of the Prussian suffrage. But it also saw on the horizon economic change, as war industry compelled the state to intervene in the management of the processes of production.

Thus, those who in 1914 wanted, by denying war credits, to obey the letter of the party's 1903 decision to reject revisionism found themselves isolated, at loggerheads not only with Germany as a whole but also with the party specifically. On the other hand, those who overturned the 1903 decision, and in doing so reflected the trends implicit in German socialism over the previous decade, found that their position was little better. In practice *Burgfrieden* did not inaugurate reform but confirmed the status quo. The price which the socialists paid for ending their battle with the German state was the transference of that division into the party itself.

In some ways French working-class politics before 1914 were a mirror image of the Germans'. The split between the socialist party and the trades-union movement, the Confédération Générale du Travail (CGT), was open; the differences between the workers and the state, a republic and the heir of the French Revolution, had less practical justification than in Germany; and Internationalism, rather than widen these two divisions, had the effect of narrowing them. It was this last point, the vitality of French support for Internationalism, expressed above all in the rhetoric and personal commitment of Jean Jaurès, which gave French socialism a significance in July 1914 that its other weaknesses might have appeared to have denied it.

From its formation in 1895 the CGT rejected parliamentary methods and political parties as means by which to free the working class. Instead, the latter was to liberate itself through strike action. This faith in revolutionary syndicalism was reaffirmed at the CGT conference in Amiens in 1906. But in repelling the more intellectual, theoretical, and bourgeois approaches of political socialism, the CGT increased its dependence on its own resources which were— both in money and in members—slender. Its dilemmas were compounded by its faith in Internationalism. Working-class solidarity across national frontiers might have provided revolutionary syndicalism with the strength that it lacked in any one country. In practice, the CGT had to reckon with the domination of the German trades unions, committed to reformism and to an economic rather than a political programme. Furthermore, in one respect at least France grew more like Germany. Although the CGT did not forget the international aspects of armed force, its anti-militarism focused increasingly on the use of the army to break strikes. These threads—revolutionary action, internationalism, and anti-militarism—were pulled together by the resolution at the CGT congress in Marseilles in 1908: 'it is necesary, on an international level, to educate workers so that in the event of war between nations the workers will respond to the declaration of war with a declaration of the revolutionary general strike.' Léon Jouhaux, appointed general secretary of the CGT in the following year, used the occasion of the peace demonstration on 28 July 1911 to affirm this policy.[55]

As the rhetoric waxed, effectiveness waned. The call of the 1908 resolution was for education. The 1911 demonstrations encouraged the CGT to believe the working class had indeed been alerted to the dangers of war. Thus, the task of the CGT was to continue its proselytism so that the workers would react spontaneously to the threat of war. Responsibility for the signal for the general strike was passed from the CGT itself to its local branches and to the workers in general. Its own statements on tactics became vague. Instead, it aimed to create a broad front in favour of peace, designed to inhibit the actions of government. On 16 December 1912 it called a general strike as a warning to the state: it claimed 600,000 supporters, but in practice only 30,000 responded in Paris, and a further 50,000 in the rest of France. Furthermore, its continuing international isolation made a mockery of its strategy, as well as tempting it into the sort of attacks on German socialists and trades unionists which were not suggestive of transnational solidarity.

Its anti-militarism meant that the CGT loomed large in the demonology of the right. The growth in military absenteeism, which accounted for the equivalent of two army corps between 1902 and 1912, was attributed to its influence.[56] In 1913 it was blamed for what were largely spontaneous demonstrations within the army against the three-year service law. Its response to these attacks was not greater militancy, but moderation. Revisionism and reformism, already gaining ground from 1908–9, grew in strength as CGT membership fell—by more than half between 1911 and 1914. In the latter year it embraced only about 6 per cent of all employees, and no more than 14 per cent of industrial workers.[57] Even those unions still committed to revolution were divided over tactics: Merrheim, the leader of the militant metalworkers' federation, felt that the CGT's anti-militarism was weakening it, and that it should focus on economic issues—views which prompted a clash with the hard-line Seine syndicate. The CGT in 1914 might still maintain the semblance of revolutionary anti-militarism, not least thanks to the attacks of its opponents, but beneath that veneer genuine anti-patriotism had declined.

The retreat of the CGT did not betoken a setback for French working-class politics as a whole. The gradual replacement of anti-patriotic pacifism by anti-militarist defencism opened the way to greater co-operation between it and the French socialist party. The leaders of both organizations, Jouhaux and Jaurès, were anxious to mark out common ground, and the former recognized full well the greater European influence exercised by the latter through the

[55] Milner, *Dilemmas of Internationalism*, 146–7, 176–80; see also 8–11, 60–3, 116–19.
[56] Porch, *March to the Marne*, 111.   [57] Renouvin, *La Crise européenne*, 73.

International. The two staged a joint demonstration against war on 24 September 1911. Thereafter, the campaign against the three-year law gave them a common domestic platform. The possibility of collaboration was already evident before July 1914.[58]

From 14 to 16 July 1914 the socialist party held an extraordinary meeting in Paris to decide on its attitude to the Vaillant–Hardie proposal. Jules Guesde wished to defuse the issue of pacifism, seeing it as an obstruction to, and distraction from, the broader tasks of socialism in France, and recognizing the practical impossibility of effecting a general strike in the event of war. Opposed to him was Jean Jaurès. Jaurès's anti-militarism did not constitute anti-patriotism. His objection to the three-year law was the specific one of opposition to a regular, professional army: in *L'Armée nouvelle* (1911) he presented the classic case for a citizen militia committed to the defence of its own territorial integrity. Jaurès, for all his fervent Internationalism, was a French patriot, fired by an idealized interpretation of the legacy of the French Revolution, and convinced that in 1793 and again in 1871 citizen soldiers had rallied to save republican France from foreign invasion. His support of the Vaillant–Hardie proposal at the Paris congress was not, therefore, a reflection of the CGT's 1908 resolution: the purpose of a general strike would not be to disrupt mobilization, to sabotage France's defence. Jaurès wanted a preventive strike, called before the crisis turned to war, internationally organized so that the workers would pressurize their governments into arbitration and away from hostilities. The fact that his support of a general strike as an instrument against war bore a superficial relationship to CGT policy was also not without its attractions. Because such a strike depended on being international, Jaurès believed that a clear decision by the French patriots in Paris would send a signal to socialists elsewhere, and above all in Germany, whose Internationalism he thought to be waxing. Jaurès's policy was visionary rather than pragmatic: he was seeking a target for the International, not dictating immediate tactics for socialism in France. However, Jaurès's calculations were not without an element of realism: it found its expression in his conviction that if the strike failed, if arbitration did not lead to conciliation and war was declared, then the proletariat must defend its nation's independence. The Paris conference approved Jaurès's motion by the convincing, but significantly not overwhelming, majority of 1,690 to 1,174.[59]

Both the CGT and the socialists in France had, therefore, provided sufficient grounds to justify the belief that they would encourage opposition to the war. Their public declarations obscured the fact that they lacked any tactics for

---

[58] Milner, *Dilemmas of Internationalism*, 179–80, 204–5.

[59] On Jaurès specifically, see Kriegel, *Le Pain et les roses*, 81, and 107–24. On French socialism generally in this period, see Becker, *1914: comment les français sont entrés dans la guerre*, pt. 1, ch. 3 and pt 2, ch. 3; Kriegel and Becker, *1914: la guerre et le mouvement ouvrier français*.

immediate implementation—that the CGT would not itself call a strike, and that the socialists needed the CGT's co-operation to be able to carry a strike through—and also that for neither body did anti-militarism constitute anti-patriotism. Both groups shared the widespread failure to appreciate the gravity of the July crisis. On 26 July, when *La Bataille syndicaliste*, the CGT's newspaper, announced that the workers must respond to the declaration of war by striking, Jouhaux was away in Brussels; the summons was that of the paper's editors rather than of the CGT itself. When the CGT committee did meet, on 28 July, and Jouhaux reported on his disappointing conversation with Legien, it rapidly became clear that most syndicalists were fearful of arrest and of being seen as traitors to France. On 29 July the CGT abandoned first the call for a strike and then Internationalism, blaming Austria-Hungary rather than capitalism for the crisis. In the areas outside Paris a total of ninety-four meetings and demonstrations against the coming war were arranged by both syndicalists and socialists; seventy-nine of them took place, and they peaked between 28 and 31 July. In Paris, a big demonstration was held by the syndicalists on the evening of 27 July, but the majority of protests thereafter (of the total of sixty-seven) were organized by the socialists and, as in the provinces, intensified at the end of the month. In general the protests were calm, and the government's response—although firmer with syndicalists than socialists—restrained. Indeed, the greater danger of violence could be from neither socialists nor gendarmes but from patriotic crowds incensed by anti-militarism and bent on taking matters into their own hands.[60]

Socialist behaviour in late July reflected the lack of urgency felt by Jaurès. His attention was on the efforts of the International; his belief was that the crisis would be protracted. Furthermore, when he met Viviani on 30 July he was convinced that the French government was doing everything possible to maintain peace, and that in the circumstances strike action was not appropriate. Jaurès's greatest achievement in these last hours of his life was to convince the CGT of his point of view, and so manage the fusion between the two major working-class political groups. A joint socialist and syndicalist demonstration in favour of peace was planned for 9 August. Jouhaux was persuaded by Jaurès that the date should not be brought forward to 2 August, that the emphasis on calm and deliberation should be maintained. So the CGT was persuaded to put a higher premium on the unity of French socialism than on its opposition to war. Thus, while socialism in Germany—despite its apparent unity—began to fragment under the threat of war, in France it coalesced.

However, the CGT's abandonment of a revolutionary strike in the event of mobilization, and its espousal of pacifist demonstrations preceding war, was also the product of necessity. On 30 July *La Bataille syndicaliste* reported the

[60] Becker, *1914*, 149–88; Pourcher, *Les Jours de guerre*, 21.

remark to the Council of Ministers of Adolphe Messimy, the minister of war: 'Laissez-moi la guillotine, et je garantis la victoire.'[61] In the following days working-class leaders were to sound the tocsin of 1793, 'la patrie en danger': they therefore needed little reminding that the defence of revolutionary France had been accompanied by the drastic domestic measures of the Terror.

The consequent fear, that outright opposition to mobilization—which the syndicalist press had openly discussed in the past—would invite such government measures as would threaten the survival of the CGT itself, was totally justified. The Ministry of War's preparatory measures for mobilization included provision for the arrest of spies and, increasingly before 1914, anti-militarists. About 2,500 names figured on the list, *carnet B*, of whom 710 were associated with anti-militarism and 1,500 were French: thus, the majority of those listed were representative figures of the French working class associated with anti-militarism. The implementation of the arrests was in the hands of the minister of the interior Louis Malvy, a radical. On 30 July Malvy told the departmental prefects that they should act firmly against any syndicalist or anarchist summons to a general strike, but that otherwise they could tolerate socialist meetings in support of peace provided they were well ordered and posed no threat to mobilization. On the following day Malvy suggested to the council of ministers that he need not arrest the militant syndicalists named in *carnet B*, and the council, on the advice of the director of the Sûreté Générale, agreed. However, before Malvy acted on the council's decision he was visited by Miguel Almereyda, the editor of *Le Bonnet rouge*, a newspaper of the militant left, who was himself listed in *carnet B*. Almereyda, it was subsequently argued, appealed to Malvy's desire for political support from the left, and urged him to exempt anarchists from arrest. On the evening of 1 August Malvy instructed the prefects of departments that no arrests at all should be made under the provisions of *carnet B*. In practice a few individuals had already been arrested in response to the earlier order to mobilize. Particularly in the departments of the Nord and Pas-de-Calais the detention of suspected anarchists and anti-militarists was more frequent and more extended. The police, the prefects, and the army, admittedly in a region conscious of its immediate vulnerability to invasion, combined to thwart the government's wishes. Malvy's interpretation of his fellow ministers' views was perhaps more relaxed than they intended. But in the circumstances of 1914, given the position adopted by the CGT, the use of conciliation rather than coercion was totally justified. The threat of the implementation of *carnet B* had been sufficient to support the syndicalist conversion to the Jaurèsian approach.[62]

---

[61] Kriegel and Becker, *1914*, 99.

[62] On *carnet B*, see Becker, *1914*, 379–400; Kriegel, *Le Pain et les roses*, 96–104; Pourcher, *Les Jours de guerre*, 24–6; in English, Watt, *Dare call it treason*, 42–7; Liang, *Rise of modern police*, 205–6.

The realization that the government was not disposed to use repressive measures helped give the CGT committee greater confidence when it met on the evening of 31 July. It resolved to take all possible steps to prevent war, albeit now limited to pacifist demonstrations and short of a general strike. It was too late. Jaurès, the pivot of the French peace movement and hence of the now-united working-class parties, was reported dead as they deliberated. Mobilization was declared a few hours later. On 2 August the CGT could do no more than appeal to the workers of France for co-operation with the government. Revolutionary syndicalism rejected its traditional hostility to the state. On 4 August Jouhaux, standing in front of Jaurès's coffin, affirmed his faith in the justice of the French cause.

Thus, when later the same day Poincaré called on the chamber of deputies for a *union sacrée*, he was formalizing what was already a *fait accompli*. Indeed, Poincaré's speech was simply read out on his behalf, as the constitution forbade the president from directly addressing the chamber. All ninety-eight socialist deputies supported the vote for war credits. The decision not to implement *carnet B* had sent the first signal for fusion, and it had been reciprocated in the CGT's acceptance of collaboration rather than segregation. But the really potent symbol of national unity was the death of Jaurès.

In mid-July, after the socialists' meeting in Paris, journalists on the right had threatened to shoot Jaurès: Jaurès, 'C'est l'Allemagne', wrote Charles Maurras in *Action française*.[63] The left could therefore easily have held the right responsible for Jaurès's death, and so made it the flashpoint for the divisions of the Third Republic. Instead, the man who had symbolized internationalism and pacifism before the war became the focus for defencism and patriotism at its outbreak. The betrayal of his hopes of socialist solidarity by the vote of the SDP in Germany consolidated and deepened this mood, but did not initiate it. Gustav Hervé, who had initially favoured revolution as the proper response to war, had already begun to moderate his position by 1912. On 1 August 1914 he wrote in *La Guerre sociale*: 'They have assasinated Jaurès; we shall not assassinate France.'[64] He enlisted the next day. More importantly, the grief of the left was affirmed by the outrage of the right: recognition of the man's worth embraced the entire political spectrum. Therefore the *union sacrée* reflected not a nationalism that suppressed political divergences, but one that embraced the full range of a liberal society. Many Frenchmen went to war specifically for Jaurès's ideals: they were fighting a war of defence, the successful conclusion to which would lay the foundation for truly lasting Internationalism and even for a republican Germany. On the right the war was a vindication of their virulent nationalism and of the three-year law. The *union sacrée* was thus an entirely utilitarian formulation, with the single objective of defending France. Only as

[63] Becker, *La France et la guerre*, 11.   [64] Duroselle, *La Grande Guerre des français*, 54–5.

the war lengthened would the ideological differences underpinning it become evident.[65]

Efforts to give immediate political expression to the *union sacrée* showed that in practice, as in Germany, the war gave strength to the political status quo rather than to change. However, in France, as opposed to Germany, the existing government rested on the radicals and on the centre-right, and thus represented a wider cross-section of opinion. On the most vital issue before the war, the three-year law, the 1914 elections had produced no clear mandate. Viviani's cabinet contained only five ministers opposed to the law and ten who favoured it. When Viviani reshuffled his ministry on 26 August he continued to exclude the clerical and nationalist right, and the two socialists who now entered the government (Guesde and Sembat) were balanced by the inclusion of Delcassé (foreign office), Millerand (war ministry), Briand, and Ribot. These four appointments were justified—and generally accepted—by the wartime need for energy and expertise, but they also signified a consolidation of the centre and of the influence of the president, Poincaré, rather than that of the prime minister, Viviani. Even radical socialism, which provided four ministers, and which in 1913 had threatened to form a left-wing bloc with the socialists in opposition to the three-year law, was subsumed by this drift to the right. Its leader, Caillaux, his credit forfeit to his pursuit of détente in 1911, found no place. Clemenceau, the maverick but Germanophobe spokesman of radicalism, refused to serve.[66] Political opposition was recognized, not by the formation of a true coalition, but by the creation of innumerable committees, which gave parliamentary figures a role in the war effort without entrusting them with ministerial responsibility. Viviani's governmental reshuffle was, therefore, among the most tardy and incomplete reflections of the *union sacrée*. More symbolic was the committee of national security, formed on 6 August to undertake relief work, and which included a cardinal, a Protestant pastor, the chief rabbi, a freethinker, a royalist, a bourgeois, a socialist, and a syndicalist.

The hopes of Jaurès and his fellow Internationalists on 29 July rested in large measure on Grey's offer of arbitration. The fact that the British government had so obviously agonized over its decision for war, and had in the process made the only significant bid for peace, is perhaps a major contribution in understanding what is otherwise a somewhat bizarre phenomenon. In both France and Germany the left justified its eventual support of the war by the need for national defence against a reactionary enemy. Britain faced no direct danger to its territorial integrity or to its domestic political institutions; and

---

[65] On the meaning of *union sacrée*, see Becker in *Revue historique* CCLXIV (1980), 65–74; *Vingtième siècle revue d'histoire*, 5 (1985), 111–21; *La France en guerre*, 11–38.

[66] On the fate of the radical socialists, see S. Bernstein in Fridenson, *1914–1918*, 65–77.

yet not only was the left effectively unanimous in its support of the war, it also gave that support with barely a whimper.

British society was openly fragmented in 1914. The activities of the suffragettes, the succession of major strikes between 1911 and 1914 (40 million working days were lost in 1912), the opposition of the Ulster Unionists to Irish home rule, were all challenges not only to the Liberal government but to liberalism. Extra-parliamentary agitation had become a major means of political expression. Even more worrying were the efforts on the right to undermine parliamentary sovereignty: in 1909–10 the Conservatives used the House of Lords to block a Commons-approved budget, and in 1914 they condoned Ulster loyalism to the point of backing the para-military Ulster Volunteer Force and supporting the so-called 'Curragh mutiny', the refusal of the officers of the 3rd cavalry brigade to enforce Irish home rule in Ulster.

Yet, despite these manifestations of class and regional division, the emotion generated by the war in Britain did not contain that element of relief at newfound unanimity across the classes which so characterized the fusion of left and right in France and Germany. The nation was united when it voted for war credits, and yet it did not give that moment of unity a title—the English language coined no equivalent to the *union sacrée* or the *Burgfrieden*. The acceptance of the war without the agonizing to be found across the Channel is perhaps the best negative indicator of how little either liberalism or parliamentary sovereignty was genuinely under threat—despite all the overt divisions—in 1914. An elected Liberal government had genuinely and conscientiously grappled with the issues that confronted it, and had then decided that war was the only possible step: both the Conservative and Labour parties supported that decision.

To the underlying faith in parliament and the constitution must be added another element—in itself a product of the first—in explaining the weakness of anti-war sentiment in Britain. Intellectual socialism lacked the strength that it had acquired in France and Germany. Indications of this were already evident in 1911, during the second Moroccan crisis, when Lloyd George managed to settle the railway strike by an appeal to the national interest. On 2 August 1914 the British section of the International staged a major demonstration against the war, and in particular against a war on behalf of tsarist Russia. Ramsay MacDonald, the Labour party's chairman, distinguished between the behaviour of the German government and his sympathy for the German people. That the war was a product of the arms race and of covert diplomacy was a theme expressed by him and, on 5 August, by a majority of the national executive of the party. But the themes in all this were not the revolutionary ones of international working-class solidarity or of an absolute opposition to war in itself. Indeed, although MacDonald resigned the party chairmanship when it became clear that the party as a whole was more enthusiastic about the war than he was, his views were not very different from those of his successor, Arthur Henderson, and both were agreed that the war should be fought until Germany was defeated. MacDonald's resignation led to his rapprochement with the more Marxist and pacifist Independent Labour Party. The Labour party itself was dominated by the trades unions: it followed that its concerns were revisionist and economic, its priorities domestic, and its general sentiment patriotic. The Trades Union Congress had withdrawn from the Second International after 1896, and resisted Legien's suggestions that it become involved in the work of the International Secretariat.[67] Working-class culture, at least in London, was determined less by socialism and more by recreation, by football, by the music hall. Middle-class intellectuals had little influence, and the Labour party itself was shown, during the pre-war strikes, to be lacking in a clear, alternative political programme. On 29 August the party executive decided to support the army's recruiting campaign.[68]

Part of the explanation for the weakness of Internationalism within the Labour party was that pacifism was not its exclusive prerogative, but was shared with elements of the Liberal party. The Gladstonian and nonconformist heritage of nineteenth-century Liberalism, plus the addition of social reforming elements in the 1890s, meant that Grey's major worry in the domestic accounting for his foreign policy was over the reactions of radicals within his own party. Their principal journal, the *Manchester Guardian*, was particularly vociferous: 'Englishmen', it fulminated on 30 July 1914, 'are not the guardians of Servian well-being, or even of the peace of Europe. Their first duty is to England and to the peace of England.' On that same day the parliamentary Liberal party resolved that 'on no account will this country be dragged into the conflict'.[69] But the strength of their case resided in their emphasis on Serbia and on their rejection of such constructions as the balance of power. When France was threatened, so was the security of Britain. Moreover, the demands of self-preservation and of anti-war instincts were no longer incompatible, but were rationalized by the claim that Britain fought to defend Belgian neutrality and to uphold international law. Not fighting in 1914 could, therefore, be interpreted as as great an affront to Liberal ideals as fighting. Thus, no immediately effective opposition to the declaration of war emerged from this quarter either. The two ministers who resigned from Asquith's cabinet retired from politics. Charles Trevelyan, a backbench MP, abandoned junior office to oppose the war, and organized a group of about thirty Liberal MPs committed to securing peace as soon as possible. On 17 November Trevelyan's

[67] Milner, *Dilemmas of internationalism*, 7, 76–8.
[68] On Labour's response to the war, see McKibbin, *Evolution of the Labour party*, ch. 5; Marquand, *Ramsay MacDonald*, ch. 9; also Stedman Jones, *Journal of Social History*, VII (1974), 460–508.
[69] J. F. V. Keiger, 'Britain's "union sacrée" in 1914', in Becker and Audoin-Rouzeau, *Les Sociétés européennes et la guerre*, 42, 44.

initiative resulted in the creation—with the support of the Independent Labour Party—of the Union of Democratic Control: the four major objectives of the union embraced a more open conduct of diplomacy, greater parliament-ary accountability, national self-determination, and measures for disarma-ment. Implicit within it was an acceptance of the current war.

The argument that the outbreak of the First World War somehow consti-tuted a failure on the part of socialism is a point of view that only a minority of socialists in 1914 would have accepted. 'War', the British socialist historian R. H. Tawney, wrote on 28 November 1914, 'is not the reversal of the habits and ideals we cultivate in peace. It is their concentration by a whole nation with all the resources on an end as to which a whole nation can agree.'[70] The emphasis of Jaurèsian Internationalism was on the better management of foreign policy, on the use of arbitration in the event of a crisis, rather than on outright pacifism. *In extremis* war could be justified. And most socialists in Europe, presented with the imminence of war, and enamoured of doctrinal debate and intellec-tual clarity as ends in themselves, found little difficulty in producing a cogent case for involving themselves in the events which overtook them. The will-ingness to defend carried with it the expectation that the nation itself could become a better society, and that the war might be the means to achieve that. The *union sacrée* and the *Burgfrieden* could be interpreted as expressions of socialist fraternity; the war—it was widely believed—would be an agent for domestic social reform. But, on the plane of Internationalism, this was also the last war, the war to end wars, the vehicle for establishing a lasting international order. Through the war, French socialists argued, republicanism would be introduced to the Central Powers; through the war, Kurt Renner of the Austrian social democrats contended, imperialism and monopoly capitalism, which were embodied in Britain, would be overcome. The First World War was therefore not the sort of war against which socialism had aligned itself: it was a war for justice and liberty, not of imperial aggrandizement.

THE IMAGININGS OF INTELLECTUALS

Furthermore, some socialists at least shared the view, common elsewhere across the political spectrum, that war between nations was inevitable. Noth-ing in Marx suggested that this was not true; a similar determination led the Italian philosopher Benedetto Croce to respond to war as part of the historical process. Many of the leading statesmen in 1914, as the previous chapter has shown, were led to comparable conclusions by their acceptance of social

---

[70] J. M. Winter, *Socialism and the challenge of war*, 155.

Darwinism. Thus, Bülow considered that: 'In the struggle between nationalities, one nation is the hammer and the other the anvil; one is the victor and the
other vanquished ... it is a law of life and development in history that where
two national civilizations meet they fight for ascendancy.'[71]

The difference between the Marxists' approach and Bülow's was one of
outcomes: socialist determinism posited a better and war-less world as an
ultimate conclusion. Present in Bülow's picture was a double pessimism: first,
that one of two nations would be forced into irretrievable decline by the
outcome of war; and second, that war was part of a recurrent and eternal
process.

Such negativity was not a necessary response to Darwinism.[72] True, Darwin
had used an emotive and Hobbesian vocabulary to describe evolution. He had
observed that tribes with superior martial qualities prevailed. But he would not
conclude that society was becoming more military as time passed. Instead, he
saw war as an evolutionary phase: culture and education, liberalism and
industrialization would in due course moderate the genetic inheritance of
struggle and violence. This positivist strain was explored by Darwin's contemporaries and successors, notably Herbert Spencer and T. H. Huxley. By 1914
many biologists were using their discipline to predict the evolution of a war-
less world.

The impact of this optimistic version of social Darwinism was muted. First,
the pacifist movement, under the influence of Norman Angell's *The great
illusion* (1910), was in the thrall more of economics than of biology: states
would not fight because war did not pay. Even reformist socialists, for all the
continuing conviction of those on the left that the crisis of capitalism could
only be resolved through war, found Angell's arguments persuasive. The
problem was that these very themes—the triumph of capitalism and of
economic self-interest—fed fears which were deemed to have biological
implications. Prosperity was not merely softening people, rendering them
decadent and ultimately unfit; it was also—through social reform—keeping
alive the weak who in harsher times would have died. Therefore a world in
which military competition was replaced by economic rivalry was likely to be
racially degenerate.

Thus, the popular and fashionable impact of biology before the outbreak of
the First World War was less in social Darwinism per se and more in the field of
eugenics. Some students of heredity contended that humanity could only
advance by improving its genetic endowment, and that future generations
should therefore be fathered not by the weak, propped up by the nascent
welfare state, but by the strong. The latter would be forged in war, itself a

---

[71] Quoted in Stephen van Evera, 'The cult of the offensive', in Steven Miller, *Military strategy*, 63.
[72] The discussion which follows is heavily dependent on Crook, *Darwinism, war and history*.

parent to innovation as well as to the advancement of the great civilizing empires. Those who opposed this line of thought did so because they disagreed not with its basic assumptions, but with its belief that the effects of war were eugenic. The unfit were exempted from military service: consequently war eliminated the strong while protecting the weak. Pessimism was inherent in both camps. Those who saw war as eugenically favourable had to accept war as a biological necessity; those who concluded that war was dysgenic reckoned that war would be biologically disastrous.

Any solutions to this dilemma were long term and fanciful rather than immediate. The American philosopher William James called in 1910 for 'the moral equivalent of war'. He wanted to hone military ideals, but in a more constructive and pacific environment than combat. Graham Wallas of the London School of Economics was influenced by James and worried about the 'baulked disposition' of young men endowed with warlike qualities but unable to find alternative outlets for them. His solution, a change in the quality of life interspersed with challenges, was vague. His conclusion was pessimistic. Fear of 'the blind forces to which we used so willingly to surrender ourselves' had replaced the liberals' faith in progress. 'An internecine European war', Wallas wrote in *The great society*, which appeared in the spring of 1914, 'is the one enormous disaster which over-hangs our time.'[73]

Therefore the debates surrounding Darwinism by 1914, for all the positivism of many of their proponents, were couched in apocalyptic terms. In this they reflected what was perhaps a general trend: the subordination of science to art, the triumph of Romanticism over the Enlightenment. From physics to psychology, science was being moulded less by the dictates of its own empirical reasoning amd more by a total conception in which art, and the emotional experience which it conveyed, as well as history were central to the overall vision.[74]

Pre-1914 art—using the word in its broadest sense— abounds with images of the apocalypse, of the world's end and of Christ's second coming. For the religious, like Vasily Kandinsky, the message of the Resurrection was ultimately optimistic, devastation and despair were the path to renewal and regeneration. Kandinsky's less abstract imagery used mounted figures, knightly riders with military overtones. But many artists portrayed the apocalypse in terms that were not exclusively associated with the inevitability of destructive war. Thomas Mann's novella *Death in Venice*, published in 1913, employs the metaphor of plague, not war. The series of paintings executed by Ludwig Meidner in 1912 and 1913, with their bombed cities, storm-laden skies, and piles of corpses, undeniably gave forceful and visual expression to the anticipated terrors of modern war; in conception, however, they were as much a

---

[73] Wallace, *War and the image of Germany*, 16–19.   [74] Eksteins, *Rites of spring*, 31–2.

response to the frenzied pace of industrialization and urbanization (and particularly, in this case, of Berlin).[75] Where the references to war are more direct, as in Franz von Stuck's allegorical painting of war completed in 1894 or Arnold Böcklin's rendering of the four horsemen of the apocalypse painted two years later, they may be as much a reflection of the *fin de siècle* as anticipations of imminent European conflict.

Stuck's picture portrays war as a handsome young man, his head crowned with the laurels of victory, while corpses are piled at his feet. But with the new century these associations of beauty and heroism gave way to decadence and decay: the painters Walter Sickert and Egon Schiele may have explored murder, prostitution, and disease rather than war, but the apocalyptic undertow is still present. War became part of the vocabulary of fatalism.[76] Oswald Spengler started writing his book *Decline of the West* in 1911; Andrei Belyi's novel *Petersburg*, published in 1914, used the somewhat hackneyed metaphor of a time-bomb to illustrate the condition of Europe; Gustav Holst spent the summer of 1914 composing the *Planets*, beginning with Mars. Such prefigurings were not uncommon.

The apocalyptic view of war was not primarily concerned with the causes of war in the same way as either Marxism or social Darwinism. Many artists, for all their anticipations of war, were still surprised by its outbreak. Much of the intellectual and artistic attention to war before 1914 was devoted to war as a phenomenon in itself, with battle not as a means but as an end. For a generation younger than that directly influenced by social Darwinism,[77] war was a test of the individual rather than of the nation. It was Friedrich Nietzsche who appealed to the student, to the radical, and to the romantic. 'You say it is the good cause that hallows war?', he had written in *Thus spake Zarathustra*; 'I tell you: it is the good war that hallows every cause.' Nietzsche's metaphors, the superman, the will to power, were replete with martial images. Marking what would have been the philosopher's seventieth birthday on 15 October 1914 in the *Strassburger Post*, Theodor Kappstein celebrated his summons to 'a life-endangering honesty, towards a contempt for death ... to a sacrifice on the altar of the whole, towards heroism and quiet, joyful greatness'.[78] For the Kaiserreich Nietzsche's influence was subversive. Only after the war broke out was he appropriated as a patriotic icon, a process in which the radical right and enemy propaganda colluded. After all, Nietzsche himself was a self-confessed European, scathing about the nationalist preoccupations of Bis-

---

[75] Cork, *A bitter truth*, 13–14.
[76] Klaus Vondung, 'Visions de mort et de fin de monde: attente et désir de la guerre dans la litterature allemande avant 1914', in Vandenrath *et al.* (eds.), *1914*, 221–8.
[77] Stromberg, *Redemption by war*, 78–9.
[78] Aschheim, *Nietzsche legacy*, 143; see also Joll, '1914: the unspoken assumptions', in Koch (ed.), *Origins*, 1972 edn., 323.

marckian Germany. Intellectuals influenced by him did not reflect the national limitations of politicians: in 1910 Rupert Brooke, to be seen in 1914 as representing something essentially English in British letters, found his inspiration abroad, writing: 'Nietzsche is our Bible, Van Gogh our idol.'[79] What Brooke and his contemporaries expected to find in war was, therefore, more immediate and more personal than the serving of patriotism. Indeed, if they had viewed the war primarily as one fought for national objectives they might have found it far harder to accept. Another British poet, Charles Sorley, recognized the irony in his fighting for England, which embodied 'that deliberate hypocrisy, that terrible middle-class sloth of outlook', against Germany, which was doing 'what every brave man ought to do and making experiments in morality'.[80]

Brooke has been castigated as the embodiment of British public-school idealism, gulled into enthusiasm for the war by false ideals and vain hopes. This misses the point. Brooke was scared. The war was therefore a test of his courage, a personal challenge to which he had to respond or think less of himself: 'Now God be thanked,' he wrote, 'who has matched us with this hour.' By embracing the war in spite of his fears the individual became a hero. He also gained the means to live life more intensely: soldiers, a Hungarian, Aladar Schöpflin, said in late August 1914, 'are going into the totality of life',[81] and Walter Bloem, a novelist and German reserve officer, felt that war service had made his novels 'my own living present'.[82]

The notion that modern society was too safe, that boredom and enervation were the consequences, was propagated by popular British writers like John Buchan and H. Rider Haggard. In France Charles Péguy and Ernest Psichari, both killed in the opening weeks of the war, had written successful books venerating the glory of war and the asceticism of military service. In Germany A. W. Heymel penned a poem in 1911 that longed for war as an end to the 'opulence of peace', and in the winter of 1912–13 Johannes R. Becker portrayed his generation as rotting, seated at their desks, as they waited for the trumpet call to a 'great world war'.[83]

Much of this was self-consciously an attack on rationalism. The development of psychoanalysis in the years before the war had emphasized that balancing man's intellect were his subconscious and his emotions. Sigmund Freud above all had criticized the intellectual tendency to suppress or ignore feelings. But even Freud was unprepared for the emotional force of the war's outbreak. To his surprise he found that his 'libido' was mobilized

[79] Stromberg, *Redemption by war*, 38.
[80] Jay Luvaas, 'A unique army', in Kann *et al.* (eds.), *Habsburg empire*, 100–1.
[81] Eva Balogh, 'The turning of the world' in Kann *et al.* (eds.), *Habsburg empire*, 188.
[82] Bloem, *Advance from Mons*, 21.
[83] Vondung, 'Visions de mort', in Vandenrath (ed.), *1914*, 231–2.

for Austria-Hungary. The war revealed to him how thin was the veneer of culture: he was appalled to discover that civilized states committed horrors and barbarities against each other which they would never have condoned in their own citizens. He could only conclude that many men observed social norms in defiance of their true natures: 'we are misled', he wrote in the spring of 1915, 'into regarding men as "better" than they actually are.'[84]

In emphasizing the need to integrate both intellect and emotion by being more aware of the latter, psychoanalysis legitimized a preoccupation with the mystic, the inexplicable. Something of what psychoanalysis was saying had been anticipated by Romanticism, by its emphasis on the worth of the individual and his own creativity, and Nietzsche could be employed as a link between the two. By forsaking his desk for action, the writer gathered those experiences which were essential to his creativity. Thus, the seemingly irrational search for danger was rendered rational as a means for emotional and intellectual self-discovery.

Although the willingness to wage war for many was, therefore, a personal test rather than a national one, the response of the intellectuals went on to emphasize the collective social good which would follow from war's conduct. Indeed, for men whose inclinations and callings tended to render them solitary, not the least of war's attractions was its effect in integrating their individual aspirations with those of society as a whole. The idea that the destructive effects of war were beneficial, that war cleansed and renewed society, was one familiar to social Darwinists. Both they and the younger generation of intellectuals were ready to welcome war as driving out decadence: 'Today's man', Dezso Kosztolanyi wrote on 4 October 1914,'—grown up in a hothouse, pale and sipping tea—greets this healthy brutality enthusiastically. Let the storm come and sweep out our salons.'[85] Jettisoned were the bourgeois values of the commercial classes: war trampled on their financial calculations, and in clothing their sons in uniform rendered null the niceties of social rank. The individual found fulfilment, not in pursuit of personal profit, but in the altruism and hardness of military service. The causes of war lay, at least indirectly, in the softness and self-indulgence of pre-1914 Europe. 'This is not a war against an external enemy' opined the painter Franz Marc, 'it is a *European civil war*, a war against the inner invisible enemy of the European spirit.'[86] Brooke's famous description of recruits remains remarkably evocative of the mood—

---

[84] Freud, 'Thoughts for the times', 283; see also Falzeder and Brabant (eds.), *Correspondence of Freud and Ferenczi*, 13.

[85] Balogh, in Kann *et al.* (eds.), *Habsburg empire*, 187.

[86] Quoted in Ecksteins, *Rites of spring*, 94; see also Hynes, *A war imagined*, 3–4, 19.

'as swimmers with cleanness leaping, glad from a world grown old and cold and weary'.

Less pleasing to the elder statesmen of social Darwinism was the reversal of the traditional hierarchy implicit in this rejection of bourgeois society. Front-line service was a young man's activity; the middle-aged struggled to be accepted by the army, and in doing so denied the seniority and maturity of their years in pursuit of the fashion for youth. War enthusiasm was an assertion of the values of the younger generation against those of the older. Max Scheler, the German philosopher, declared that the war had rendered the nostrums of the older generation *passé*, while for their successors it was neither a nightmare nor a burden but 'an almost metapysical awakening from the empty existence of a leaden sleep'.[87] In France in 1913 Henri Massis and Alfred de Tarde, under the pseudonym of 'Agathon', had published a study of the student generation of 1912: they had depicted their calling to action, to absolutes, to things of the spirit, to order and hierarchy, and their turning away from introspection and relativism.[88] The French generation of 1914 was thus given an identity that was specifically opposed to that of their republican and anticlerical fathers.

However, the conflict of ideas was not one simply between generations but also one between different views of the values which wartime society would elevate. For some the liberation from materialism and from bourgeois nostrums was to be accomplished by a return to a pastoral idyll. Western Europe had still not come to terms with its increasingly urban existence; G. D. H. Cole, Maurice Barrès, Émile Durkheim, Max Weber—all saw city life, with its destruction of community and its erosion of family, as under-mining social cohesion. The war, by calling men to a life that demanded physical fitness, to a career spent outside, that tested the individual against the natural elements as much as against the enemy, was consonant with a return to nature. It is striking that writers from Britain, the country that had been most industrialized for longer, were the most expressive of this aspect of war enthusiasm. Officers in autumn 1914 proved acute observers of the coun-tryside through which they were passing, and readily fell back on the termino-logy and analogies of field sports. B. F. Cummings, whose multiple sclerosis prevented any such escape, used more turbulent imagery in his diary on 30 June 1914: 'Civilization and top hats bore me. My own life is like a tame rabbit's. If only I had a long tail to lash it in feline rage! I would return to Nature—I could almost return to Chaos.'[89]

---

[87] Scheler, *Genius des Krieges*, 12.
[88] Wohl, *The generation of 1914*, 5–10; also Cruickshank, *Variations on catastrophe*, 18–23.
[89] W. N. P. Barbellion [B. F. Cummings], *Journal of a disappointed man*, 129.

Cummings's threat of violence provides a bridge to a very different vision of society, and one embraced particularly by artists. The avant-garde had already declared war on the existing order before July 1914. The opening manifesto of the Futurists, published in 1909, began with the lines: 'There is no more beauty except in strife.' In this and subsequent declamations the Futurists replaced romanticism with industrialism. 'Let's kill the moonlight,' F. T. Marinetti announced; 'the first lines of the great Futurist aesthetic' lay in the locomotive, the factory, the products of heavy industry; 'a roaring motor car, which seems to run on shrapnel, is more beautiful than the Victory of Samothrace'.[90] Marinetti lived out his elevation of violence by going to Tripoli in 1911, to the Balkans in 1912, and joining the Italian army in 1915. Although Marinetti claimed that Futurism was an Italian movement, he had published the first manifesto in Paris, and its appeals were to find echoes in German Expressionism and in British Vorticism.

The Vorticists' publication *Blast*, the first number of which was published on 20 June 1914, and whose prime movers were Wyndham Lewis and Ezra Pound, emphasized the unconscious, the 'crude energy' of the primitive world, but derived from Futurism its use of machines for subject-matter, and its belief that war's violence and destruction would be liberating influences. 'Killing somebody', Wyndham Lewis wrote, 'must be the greatest pleasure in existence: either like killing yourself without being interfered with by the instinct of self-preservation—or exterminating the instinct of self-preservation itself.'[91]

The paradox was that war, with its bringing of death, was the end of dead life: for Rilke war was 'a deadly enlivening'.[92] It meant the end of art for art's sake. 'The fight over words and programmes is over,' declared Julius Meier-Graefe in the opening issue of an avant-garde publication *Kriegszeit*, on 31 August 1914; 'What we were missing was meaning—and that brothers, the times now give us . . . The war has given us unity. All parties are agreed on the goal. May art follow!'[93] Thomas Mann had struggled to come to terms with the war; for all his anticipations of catastrophe, he had not reckoned with his imaginings becoming reality. But by September he had identified with the German nation and its people, and in October his 'Thoughts on the war' likened the artist to the soldier: both live life with intensity and thrive on danger. The artist—the soldier in the artist—should, he declared, thank God

[90] Northern Arts and Scottish Arts Council, *Futurismo 1909–1919: exhibition of Italian Futurism*, 25–6, 33.

[91] Quoted by Hynes, *A war imagined*, 9–10.

[92] Bernhard Boschert, ' "Eine Utopie des Unglückes stieg auf". Zum literarischen und publizistichen Engagement deutscher Schriftsteller für den Ersten Weltkrieg', in Berliner Geschichtswerkstatt, *August 1914*, 130–1.

[93] Cork, *A bitter truth*, 46.

for the collapse of a peaceful world; victory was immaterial; war was a moral necessity, both 'a purging and a liberation'.[94] Nor was this determination to put the war to the service of art simply a manifestation of German *Kultur*. Across the Channel the elder statesmen of literature, painting, and music, including Edmund Gosse and Charles Stanford, made similar points.[95]

Too often conscious of their isolation, intellectuals welcomed the opportunity for incorporation. 'We were no longer what we had been for so long: alone!', wrote Max Scheler. 'The gaps which had opened up, breaking contacts between life's elements—individual, people, nation, world, God—were closed again in an instant.'[96] For Scheler, as for his fellow sociologist Georg Simmel, the war united the demands of the day with the direction of ideas. Poetry, philosophy, prayers, and culture were fused. A new form of society was forged.[97] Friedrich Meinecke wrote: 'Every immeasurable division of labour and distinction of talents and interests, which hitherto had threatened to tear apart our common life and to contract our lives as individuals, brought forth in us benedictions.'[98]

The Expressionist painter Max Beckmann, who in 1909 anticipated that war would be a force for regeneration and social reunification, found what he was looking for in the opening stages of the campaign in the east (where he was a medical orderly). Exhilarated by the mood of universal enthusiasm, he concluded on 24 September 1914 that 'I have in this short time lived more than I have done for years'.[99]

Most writers, intellectuals, and artists therefore not only embraced the popular enthusiasm for war but actively promoted it. Stefan Zweig revealed that 'poems poured forth that rhymed *Krieg* [war] with *Sieg* [victory] and *Not* [necessity] with *Tod* [death]'.[100] The satirist Frank Wedekind, the immorality of whose plays (including *Pandora's Box*) had roused official disapproval, delivered a speech in the Munich playhouse on 18 September 1914 vaunting 'the loyal brotherhood of arms', the unity of Germany, social democracy, and the imperial high command.[101] Those who opposed the war, who resisted the nationalization of culture, the German condemnation of Shakespeare, or the British rejection of Goethe, were few, and most even of them were temporarily carried away by the exuberance of the moment.

---

[94] Mann, 'Gedanken im Kriege', 9–11; see also Wysling (ed.), *Letters of Heinrich and Thomas Mann*, 120–3.

[95] Hynes, *A war imagined*, 10–19.

[96] Scheler, *Genius des Krieges*, 11.

[97] Michael Reiter, 'Deutschlands innere Wandlung: Georg Simmel zum Krieg', in Berliner Geschichtswerkstatt, *August 1914*, 215–16; see also 132–3.

[98] Raithel, *Das 'Wunder' der inneren Einheit*, 478–9.

[99] Beckmann, *Briefe im Kriege*, 10; see also Cork, *A bitter truth*, 37.

[100] Zweig, *World of yesterday*, 178.

[101] Sackett, *Popular entertainment*, 70.

POPULAR RESPONSES

Historians can too easily fall victim to the testimony of their own kind. The written word, particularly when conveyed with power and elegance, provides accessible and seductive evidence. The temptation is all the greater in relation to 1914, when intellectuals themselves wished to imagine that their ideas shaped the popular mood. Because the young, the students, the educated, the articulate—in sum, Agathon's subject-matter—staged demonstrations supporting the war, the phenomenon of war enthusiasm can become over-blown, with the result that the high-falutin ideas of a minority are projected on to the majority.

This caveat is important. Genuine enthusiasm was more frequent in towns and among white-collar workers. The largest single occupational group in most armies was the peasantry, and the reactions of agricultural communities to mobilization were less positive. These differences can be exaggerated. Compulsory primary education meant that the populations of at least Britain, France, and Germany, rural as much as urban, were broadly speaking literate. Words were a way of giving the emotions of the individual a common currency. The 'over-production' (to use the description of one contemporary commentator) of diaries, letters, and poetry in 1914 is characterized by a shared vocabulary, an approved style, which is itself evidence of the ability of language to pervade, externalize, and universalize the emotions which war generated.[102]

Education was also a potent means of creating national identity. Germany's victory in the Franco-Prussian War was widely interpreted as a triumph of more than battlefield prowess. It was also seen as a reward for modernization, in which educational excellence had played a major part. The effect was not only to promote reform in schools but also to nationalize the curriculum. 'I seek soldiers,' the Kaiser told the Berlin schools conference in 1890; 'we should educate young Germans, and not young Greeks and Romans.'[103] Between 1870 and 1914 the pedagogues of Europe began to give instruction in their own national histories as well as in those of the ancient world.

For France, its recent past—a mixture of revolutions and defeats—was the stuff of continuing political debate. In 1880 the Third Republic signalled its determination to inculcate patriotism through the conceptual legacy of the Revolution. Unable to identify a recent French victory that was the product of a politically safe regime, it settled on 14 July and the storming of the Bastille as an annual celebration of nationhood. An example of domestic strife, in which the army had turned against the government, was not the happiest of precedents. Furthermore, the use of the classroom for the dissemination of the same

---

[102] Plaut, 'Psychographie des Kriegers', 2–3, 8.   [103] Schubert-Weller, *Kein schönrer Tod*, 54–5.

message aroused the ire of the monarchical and clerical right. But with the passage of time the Bastille Day parade became a vehicle for the integration of the army with the republic. Soldiers found that their values of discipline, order, and devotion to duty were trumpeted as models for emulation by the citizens of the republic. In 1912 the veterans of the Franco-Prussian War, hitherto neglected as the servants of an imperial regime and the victims of defeat, were invited by Poincaré to take part in the 14 July festivities. Ernest Lavisse set about defusing the divisiveness of France's recent past by constructing a national history which integrated the legacies of both royal and republican regimes. On 28 June 1914 France celebrated the 700th anniversary of the battle of Bouvines.[104]

Other states had less difficulty in finding victories which could become the focus of national commemoration. In 1912 Russia honoured the centenary of Napoleon's defeat with éclat.[105] In Germany the anniversary of Sedan could combine the army's homage to the veterans of 1870 with its celebration of the Reich's foundation. But after the twenty-fifth anniversary in 1895, Sedan Day declined in significance, and in 1913 was superseded by the unveiling of the massive memorial on the battlefield of Leipzig, significant less for the defeat of Napoleon and more for its part in the evolution of a populist German nationalism. War, argued the most politicized figure in German historical writing, Heinrich von Treitschke, was the key to the creation of the state, and the state was what gave society its shape.[106]

Songs, speeches, sermons, parades, and public festivals—these were the means by which words, and the ideas behind them, permeated the consciousness of the illiterate. But it was the printed word which in 1914 possessed a power which it had never had before, and of which the cinema, the radio, and the television would deprive it in the future. The proliferation of schools, which created a market, and the advent of the railway, with its ease of delivery, stimulated the growth of a national press. In Britain Lord Northcliffe's *Daily Mail*, which anticipated the war and stoked fears of German militarism, claimed a circulation in 1910 of 900,000.[107] *The Times*, bought by Northcliffe in 1909, followed a similar editorial line, and by reducing its price tripled its circulation early in 1914, and then doubled it again with the outbreak of war.[108] In France the leading Paris dailies had national distribution networks. *Le Petit Parisien* enjoyed a circulation of 1.5 million, and *Le Matin* and *Le Journal* 1 million each. Although about 3,000 daily newspapers were published in

[104] Hanna, *Mobilization of the intellect*, 5–6, 28–35; Raithel, *Das 'Wunder' der inneren Einheit*, 19; Mitchell *Victors and vanquished*, 143–57; Becker, *France en guerre*, 19–20; Vogel, *Nationen im Gleichschritt*, 39, 98–9, 125–6, 178–88, 196–9, 208–9, 228.
[105] Suchomlinow, *Erinnerungen*, 349.
[106] Pick, *War machine*, 90–2; Vogel, *Nationen im Gleichschritt*, 144–5, 170–8.
[107] McEwen, *Journal of Contemporary History*, XVII (1982), 466.
[108] Morris, *The scaremongers*, 346.

France, the mass-circulation papers, with their headlines, photographs, and sensationalism, accounted for about 40 per cent of the market. In Germany, by contrast, readerships remained regional or, at best, clearly defined in party and religious terms. Thus, *Vorwärts*, the SPD's paper, spoke for the party as a whole, but was only one of ninety-one socialist dailies with a combined readership of 1.5 million. About eighty newspapers were published in greater Berlin, and 4,221—as well as 6,421 periodicals—throughout Germany.[109] Russia in 1900 had 125 daily papers; in 1913 it had 856, and those that flourished were overtly nationalistic in tone.[110] By 1912 Serbia had 199 newspapers and magazines, and they claimed a total circulation of 50 million copies.[111]

In the case of the German press a symptomatic change occurred between the first Moroccan crisis and the events of July 1914. It became increasingly self-referential, with newspapers reporting as news opinions voiced by other publications. Those views were themselves more often the comments of other journalists than of the principal political actors. The press was therefore creating its own reality. The mediation of the newspapers and the gloss which they gave to events themselves helped shape outcomes.

Although more German papers opposed war than advocated it between 1905 and 1914, significant shifts occurred within that pattern. Less often was war portrayed as an extreme and unique solution to a foreign crisis; hostility to the Entente meant that the nature of the anticipated conflict moved from being a bilateral engagement to a multilateral *Weltkrieg*. In 1905–6 four major German papers from across the political spectrum advocated peace. In 1911 they had split, both collectively and individually, with the SPD's *Vorwärts* opposing war most consistently but even then not continually. By July 1914 the dominant mood was fatalism, a belief that the peaceful conduct of international relations had failed and that war was the sole untested solution. Only 25 per cent of articles published by the four advocated war, but roughly 66 per cent expected that war would be the outcome of the crisis; and although 46 per cent reckoned that the war would be a local Austro-Serb clash, 30 per cent anticipated a major war. Furthermore, these were opinions derived more from the experience of the previous international crises than from the events of July 1914. In the last week, between 26 July and 2 August, an unsurprising 44 per cent of articles regarded war as probable; exactly the same percentage had taken a similar stance from the outset of the crisis, in the week beginning 5 July.[112]

[109] Kriegel and Becker, *1914*, 22; Raithel, *Das 'Wunder' der inneren Einheit*, 11, 35–7; Verhey, 'The spirit of 1914', 55–7. Rosenberger, *Zeitungen als Kriegstreiber?*, 71, is the source for German newspaper totals; Verhey says there were 3,600 and Raithel over 2,000.
[110] Lieven, *Russia and the origins*, 119, 130–2.
[111] Petrovich, *Modern Serbia*, 585–7.
[112] Rosenberger, *Zeitungen als Kriegstreiber?*, esp. 163–4, 200–5, 263–72, 283–300, 325–6.

At least indirectly, therefore, the societies of Europe imbibed some of the more rarefied thinking about war and nationalism. Furthermore, the campaign for military preparedness was not conducted by the press alone. The significance of the leading German extra-parliamentary groups rose steadily before 1914, and in the latter year the Navy League boasted 331,000 members and 776,000 affiliated members. The claim that these organizations were new in two senses—in that they appealed to the petty bourgeois and that they signalled a form of radical nationalism which ultimately would lead to the Nazis—has been disputed. The combined membership of all these groups, about 1 million in 1914, undoubtedly includes a large measure of double-counting. The Pan-German League, which acted as a sort of holding organization for the others, peaked at 22,000 members in 1901. Moreover, the leadership of the Army League was not petty bourgeois but solidly professional—as well as middle-aged. Its membership rose in step with the agitation for the 1912 and 1913 army bills, and declined thereafter. Nonetheless, such efforts to downplay the significance of the nationalist organizations in Germany neglect the fact that their primary purpose was to mould opinion beyond their own memberships through the instrument of propaganda. *Die Flotte*, the Navy League's monthly magazine, had 360,000 readers in 1912, and *Die Wehr*, the Army League's equivalent publication, 90,000 in 1913. Furthermore, the message of these journals was deeply uncomfortable for traditional conservatism. Increased armaments carried as their corollary tax reform and genuinely universal service. If the membership of the veterans' organizations, many of whose values stood comparison with those of the extra-parliamentary pressure groups, is added, perhaps 15 per cent of voters were involved, including a large proportion of industrial workers, peasants, and smallholders.[113]

The weaknesses in party politics made pressure groups a more significant feature of debate in Germany than elsewhere. Nonetheless, Britain established its own Navy League in 1893, and it had 100,000 members in 1914. The National Service League was formed in 1902 to lobby for conscription and claimed 270,000 members, including associate members, in 1914.[114] Much of the effectiveness of the British groups rested on the fears of a German invasion, preceded by a swarm of German spies and fifth-columnists. Erskine Childers's *Riddle of the sands* (1903) has been one of the few lasting works of this genre, but more famous at the time was William Le Queux's *The Invasion of 1910*, serialized by the *Daily Mail* in 1911. The best-known of the French nationalist

[113] Shevin-Coetzee, *German Army League*, esp. 4–12, 17, 59–60, 78–97, 122; Thomas Rohrkämer, 'Der Gesinnungs-militarismus der "kleinen Leute" im Deutschen Kaiserreich', in Wette (ed.), *Krieg des kleinen Mannes*, 95–6; Rohrkämer, 'August 1914—Kriegsmentalität und ihre Voraussetzungen', in Michalka (ed.), *Erste Weltkrieg*, 762.
[114] Kennedy, *Anglo-German antagonism*, 370–3. Membership figures given for the British National Service League fluctuate; these are from Adams and Poirier, *Conscription controversy*, 17.

organizations, *Action française*, indicates the perils of judging influence in terms of circulation. *Action française*'s eponymous newspaper, characterized by *Vorwärts* as offering 'the most bizarre mixture of intelligence, vulgarity, science, and stupidity', increased its circulation immediately before the war, but still sold only 31,000 copies in 1914.[115] *Action française* and the others were not without significance, but in explaining war enthusiasm their importance resides in their being part of a much greater whole.

Alongside them must be placed the youth organizations, frequently para-military in nature, which cultivated physical fitness and group loyalty, and so prepared their members for military service. Baden Powell, the founder of the Boy Scouts, declared that every boy 'ought to learn how to shoot and obey orders, else he is no more good when war breaks out than an old woman'.[116] Formally speaking, the features that are most striking about these youth movements are the opposite of those of the extra-parliamentary organiza-tions—those of the liberal societies were founded first and even tended to be more openly military.

In this respect Britain's principal contribution in international terms, the Boy Scouts, was somewhat misleading. First, they were founded comparatively late, in 1908. Secondly, Baden Powell, himself the hero of the siege of Mafeking in the Boer War, averred that their aims were imperial, to be 'the frontiersmen of our Empire', and not military. Plenty of the precepts promulgated in *Scouting for boys* had warlike applications, but the core activity was what the founder called 'wood craft', essentially survival skills for life in the wild. The scouts themselves were organized into small patrols and encouraged to be self-reliant; they were not formed into large groups and drilled in the execution of the tactics of fire and movement.

Much more overtly militarist, with drum and bugle bands and pill-box hats, were the members of an evangelical organization dating from the 1880s, the Boys' Brigade. William Smith, its founder, was not only a member of the Free Church of Scotland but also an officer in the Volunteers. The Volunteers were part-time soldiers, organized for home defence, and in 1903 about 8 per cent of British males—including an increasing number of the working class—had gained military experience through service with them.[117] When in 1907 Hal-dane set about the reorganization of the Volunteers to form the Territorial Army, he included provision for the establishment of an Officers Training Corps in schools and universities: accused of fostering militarism in British educational establishments, he replied by saying that militarism already ran high. The evidence generated by the Boer War, both nationally in the demon-strations after the relief of Mafeking, and specifically in the willingness of the

[115] Becker, *1914*, 24–7.   [116] De Groot, *Blighty*, 38.
[117] Anne Summers, *History Workshop*, 2 (1976), 104–23.

Volunteers to serve overseas, suggests that this was fair comment. The recreational appeal of part-time service became the means by which a Nietzschean anxiety to test one's courage was transmitted into action. On the outbreak of hostilities Herbert Read, a member of Leeds University Officers Training Corps, applied for a Territorial Army commission despite his pacifism; and John Reith, who had joined a Territorial infantry battalion from Glasgow University Officers Training Corps, excitedly greeted the war as 'an entirely personal affair'.[118] By 1914 possibly 41 per cent of all male adolescents in Britain belonged to a youth organization, one in three Oxford undergraduates was a member of the Officers Training Corps, and Cambridge was debating whether service in the corps should be a condition of graduation.

Increasingly, therefore, concerns about the lack of compulsory military service in Britain came to underpin public support for the more militant youth movements. Unlike Britain, France had conscription, but still feared that it did not have enough men to hold the line against Germany. Therefore, alone of the major powers, it developed its 5,500 societies for the promotion of gymnastics and shooting among the young specifically as a preparation for military service. The army supported the groups from 1895, and in 1905 the government accorded them formal approval as a corollary of two-year service. In 1912 the minister for war, Alexandre Millerand, told France's schools that, 'You prepare their minds as well as their bodies with the patriotic duty to love France, to place it above all else, to be ready to sacrifice even their lives'.[119] In that year the scheme claimed 650,000 members, but in doing so exaggerated its influence: at best only about 14 per cent of all conscripts underwent pre-service training, and in some areas the figure dropped as low as 1 per cent.

By contrast, Germany's initial reasons for embracing comparable schemes were domestic. The worries about urbanization, that it was corrupting the young, undermining their health, and drawing them into a world of alcohol, tobacco, and pulp fiction, were ones shared in Britain. But significantly, the first fruits of this fear of decadence and degeneration, a movement to promote gymnastics, were manifest in 1889, the year in which the Second International was founded. The real danger was socialism. In the following year the rehabilitation of the SPD created direct competition for the hearts and minds of Germany's working-class youth. Karl Liebknecht reckoned that socialism's window of opportunity was the gap between leaving school at 14 and being called up for military service at 18. The German gymnastics association set out to counter socialism, claiming 400,000 members in 1889, 625,000 in 1899, and 945,000 in 1910. However, some of the members went further, seeing in it a

[118] Stryker, 'Languages of sacrifice', 149; Reith, Wearing spurs, 13.
[119] Farrar, Principled pragmatist, 147. Farrar says there were 8,500 clubs; the figure of 5,500 is from Storz, Kriegsbild und Rüstung, 314. See also Jules Maurin and Jean-Charles Jauffret, 'L'Appel aux armes 1872–1914', in Pedroncini (ed.), Histoire militaire de la France, iii. 93.

device by which to prepare for and maximize the benefits from military service.

The military imperative did not assume parity with, let alone primacy over, the political until 1911. The scouting movement, propagated through a bastardized translation of Baden Powell's book in 1909, emphasized health and hygiene, and had only 14,000 members by the end of 1911. It was more overtly military than its British equivalent, concentrating on marching and group activities rather than the individual and his return to nature, but the indirect effect was to promote these attributes in its rival organization, the *Wandervogel*. In January 1911 the Prussian minister of public worship and instruction allocated a million marks from the state budget to fund the youth movements. His aims were still domestic, but the response he elicited linked *Volkskraft* to *Wehrkraft*. General Colmar von der Goltz established an umbrella organization, the *Jungdeutschlandbund*. It built on regional intitiatives, particularly in Bavaria, where officers had already begun to involve themselves in the training of Germany's adolescents. The *Jungdeutschlandbund* had access to the army's barracks and exercise areas. Unlike the Boy Scouts, it made clear to parents that their offspring were being prepared to serve Germany in the next war. The movement took its members away most weekends, so rupturing the bonds of family and community (and upsetting the churches). Its marching songs spoke of combat and death on the battlefield. By 1914 the *Jungdeutschlandbund* claimed 700,000 members. In reality, the active membership may have been as little as 10 per cent of that. Falkenhayn, as Prussian minister of war, was worried that the organization was not getting to those German male youths particularly at risk from anti-militarism. Prompted by the French three-year service law, he proposed to Bethmann Hollweg that, if voluntary enlistment failed, compulsion should follow.[120]

Falkenhayn's desire to extend conscription to Germany's teenagers in 1913–14 coincided with his ministry's increasing acceptance that conscription for adults should be truly universal rather than selective. The manpower needs of its war plans had caused the general staff to lobby for a true nation in arms since Schlieffen. The Ministry of War feared the radicalizing effects both for the army, not least in the composition of its officer corps, and for society. After all, the classic corollary of military obligations was civic rights. In 1904 it was the SPD's leader, August Bebel, who declared that his party favoured the full enforcement of universal military service.[121] But by 1913 Falkenhayn, smarting

---

[120] Schubert-Weller, *Kein schönrer Tod*, is full; see also Stargardt, *German idea of militarism*, 98–103, 130; Storz, *Kriegsbild und Rüstung*, 314; Shevin-Coetzee, *German Army League*, 53–4; Thomas Rohrkrämer, 'August 1914—Kriegsmentalität und ihre Voraussetzungen', in Michalka (ed.), *Erste Weltkrieg*, 769–70.
[121] Vogel, *Nationen im Gleichschritt*, 222–3.

from the Zabern affair, saw that conscription could enable the army to strike back; it could militarize society.

The success of the German armies in 1870 had hallowed a form of conscription which emphasized the principle of universal military service, not as part of a defensive citizen army but within the context of a professional regular army. Military service aimed to internalize values which linked the government, the people, and the nation, and which made the army the school for the nation. Furthermore, the preferred recruit remained the peasant. Thus, that very occupational group least likely to be affected by the other nationalist currents was directly involved in this, the most pronounced form of the subordination of the individual to the state.

The call-up was a rite of passage, the moment when, probably for the first time, the young man left his family and village to step into the wider world. He departed an adolescent and returned an adult. The sphere which he entered contained comradeship and sexual opportunity; but in forsaking the constraints of parental authority the soldier submitted to the state in its most obvious manifestations. Many remained within the army's thrall for the rest of their lives. The veterans' organizations established in Germany to commemorate the dead and to honour the victors of 1870 in due course also accepted those who had completed their service after the Franco-Prussian War and had never seen combat. By 1914 these organizations claimed 2.83 million members. They kept alive the virtues of crown and nation originally inculcated by military service itself. They were opposed to membership of the SPD or of trades unions. They also promoted tension between the generations. First as sons and then as soldiers, those too young to have served in 1870 heard the stories of the heroes of Sedan. They saw the medals on their chests and paid homage at the memorials to their fallen comrades. On the one hand the experience created a social Darwinian fear, that Germany had reached its apogee in 1871 and was therefore in decline. On the other, it fostered rivalry—a need for the young men to prove themselves as valiant in battle as their fathers. Both responses could only, it seemed, be resolved by the next war.[122]

The widespread experience of military service already possessed by those mobilized in 1914 is perhaps the single best explanation for the mood of acceptance which predominated throughout Europe. Those passing through the countryside of Germany, France, or Russia in late July 1914 commented not on the enthusiasm of the population but on its calm and quietness. Hysterical crowds, anxious to fight, were phenomena of Berlin, Paris, and Moscow, not of the hinterlands. They were responses to events rather than their precipitants. The very first assemblies in Germany and France, on 24 July,

[122] Rohkrämer, *Militarismus der kleinen Leute*, esp. 27, 34–41, 49–50, 56, 72–3, 148–9, 182–3, 258, 270.

were in Strasbourg and Nancy, both border towns liable to be invaded at the outset of hostilities. Panic buying of food generated long queues; anxiety about savings produced runs on the banks. The time of year helped. Although the weather became cooler after 22 July, the long summer evenings encouraged people seeking mutual reassurance to congregate outside. Above all, crowds were formed by the appetite for news as the crisis unfolded. In Berlin people assembled along the Unter den Linden and the Potsdamer Platz, close to government buildings; in Paris they congregated in the northern boulevards, especially between the Madeleine and the Place de la République, where the main press offices were situated. Another focus were the cafés and bars in which newspapers could be scanned and information exchanged and dissected. The press and the people formed a symbiotic relationship, the latter gathering to buy the latest editions and the former reporting those gatherings and interpreting them as evidence of enthusiasm.[123] The reports of the metropolitan papers were then propagated by the local press, so encouraging smaller towns to emulate what was believed to be the example of the capital.[124]

Domestically, governments were aware that if the crisis ended in war they needed to be able to command the consent of their populations. Internationally, they were using the responses of the public in their management of the crisis. At the very least, therefore, the crowds were tolerated rather than dispersed. Suggestions that governments went even further and orchestrated them have been made in relation to Russia and Germany, but have not been corroborated by firm evidence.[125] That there was manipulation by other bodies is not in doubt. In Vienna its promoters were army officers and in Berlin youth groups, student societies, and the media themselves.[126]

The first patriotic demonstrations in Berlin occurred on the evening of 25 July, as the Serb response to the Austro-Hungarian ultimatum brought extra editions of the newspapers on to the streets. Crowds of between 2,000 and 10,000 people formed, making perhaps 30,000 demonstrators in all. Many of them were drunk. They gathered at sites of national commemoration and moved between the embassies of the major powers, singing patriotic songs. Two aspects of this phenomenon were new. In the past street demonstrations were the method of political protest preferred by the urban working class; workers were absent from these crowds, which were made up of students and

[123] The fullest comparison of the July 1914 crowds is that for France and Germany in Raithel, *Das 'Wunder' der inneren Einheit*, esp. 222–64. For Germany alone, see Verhey, 'The spirit of 1914', 85–157, and more briefly Fritsche, *Germans into Nazis*, 13–36.

[124] Geinitz, *Kriegsfurcht und Kampfbereitschaft*, 70–8, 132.

[125] Dittmar Dahlmann, 'Russia at the outbreak of the First World War', in Becker and Audoin-Rouzeau (eds.), *Les Sociétés européennes*, 59; Röhl, 'Germany', in Wilson (ed.), *Decisions for war*, 32—but see Wolff, *Tagebücher*, i. 65–6.

[126] Michel, *Guerres mondiales et conflits contemporains*, 179 (1995), 7.

young members of the middle classes. Secondly, the police, instead of breaking them up, let the demonstrations run their course, the last not dispersing until 3.45 a.m.

The next day was a Sunday, and as such provided the freedom from work which allowed fresh crowds to form. The other major cities of Germany, some of which witnessed demonstrations on a much smaller scale than those of Berlin on the 25th, saw larger assemblies on the 26th. But most consisted of no more than 200 people, and there was still little feeling evident in the towns and countryside. The crowds were airing their support for Austria-Hungary in its struggle with Serbia rather than seriously contemplating the imminent advent of European war. In France, on the other hand, an awareness of the implications of what was happening was evident from the outset. In 1900 the cry of 'vive l'armée' had been deemed anti-Dreyfusard, anti-republican, and indeed—in the view of one newspaper—positively Jesuitical.[127] As major crowds formed in Paris for the first time on the night of the 26th, the shout that came up was not 'vive la République' but 'vive l'armée'.

Although demonstrations persisted throughout the week, the resumption of work and the hope that the conflict would be localized at first diminished their scale and promoted their orderliness. On 27 July the *Berliner Tageblatt* said that it was now time for the rowdy young men who had been on the streets for the past two days to go to bed.[128] On Wednesday 29 July Poincaré and Viviani returned to Paris, proceeding in state from the Gare du Nord surrounded by crowds shouting 'vive la France'. On the same day the report of Russia's partial mobilization alerted the German people to the dangers of war. The crowds which assembled on the following day were very different from those of 25/6 July. They were drawn from all classes; they were older and less noisy. Although *Vorwärts* called the idea of war enthusiasm an 'absurd fraud',[129] enthusiasm was not entirely absent from the major assemblies of 31 July. The Kaiser returned to Berlin to a welcome comparable with that vouchsafed Poincaré two days before. Nonetheless, the mood was no longer buoyed up by the elements of student frivolity that had characterized the first demonstrations. Seriousness was now the keynote. Hoarding was evidence of anxiety, not enthusiasm. In Hamburg, according to Wilhelm Heberlein of the SPD, 'most people were depressed, as if they were to be beheaded the next day'.[130]

The following day, 1 August, crowds assembled throughout Germany, not out of enthusiasm but in nervous anticipation of general mobilization. Indeed, Theodor Wolff, looking back on the anniversary of 1 August in 1919, was persuaded that when the order came what followed was not 'what one calls

[127] Vogel, *Nationen im Gleichschritt*, 240.
[128] Berliner Geschichtswerkstatt, *August 1914*, 16.
[129] Kruse, 'Kriegsbegeisterung', 174.
[130] Quoted by Verhey, 'The spirit of 1914', 153; also by Kruse, *Krieg und nationale integration*, 59.

mass enthusiasm' but 'the release of an enormous inner tension'.[131] Some got drunk to dull their pain; others sang hymns; almost all bowed to the inevitable and accepted their patriotic duty. When Hans Peter Hanssen, an SPD deputy, travelled from Schleswig to Hamburg and thence to Berlin on 2 August, the mood of resignation had deepened. Class distinctions evaporated as people went out of their way to be kind to one another, but he was emphatic that there was no rejoicing and no enthusiasm: 'over all hung that same heavy, sad, and depressed atmosphere.'[132]

In Germany those units that departed first did so in subdued spirits. Many were worried about the economic implications of their absence. Would their jobs remain open? How would their families survive? Would the withdrawal of so much labour from the workforce result in the collapse of businesses and widespread unemployment for those who stayed behind? By late August many of these fears would seem warranted, as urban unemployment rose from 2.8 per cent in June to 23 per cent.[133] In rural areas the economic problems were even more immediate. The harvest was still not complete, and the problems of gathering it were compounded by the army's requisitioning of horses. Regions close to frontiers anticipated invasion, with further depredations likely to be the least of its consequences. The defensive nature of the war seemed all too obvious in south-west Germany, where the sounds of fighting in Alsace were soon followed by the visible evidence of wounded and prisoners of war. Fears in Freiburg, fed by the memory of fighting in the region in 1870–1, dwelt on the atrocities likely to be committed by French African troops. In southern Bavaria some wives committed suicide rather than confront these problems on their own.[134]

The most striking evidence of an alternative picture, indeed of genuine enthusiasm, was the rush of volunteers to the German colours. Propaganda spoke of at least 1.3 million voluntary enlistments by mid-August: in reality 260,672 men had attempted to join up by 11 August, and 143,922 had been accepted. By the beginning of 1915 308,000 Germans had enlisted voluntarily. The response was most sluggish in Bavaria and Württemberg. Although the real figure for enlistments was significantly lower than was claimed, it remains high for a country with conscription. Germany did, of course, exempt nearly half of its elegible male population from service in peacetime, and it was in part these men on whom voluntary enlistment depended. Not to go was to court social rejection; to go might be the only alternative to short-term

---

[131] Verhey, 'The spirit of 1914', 162; see also Ullrich, *Kriegsalltag*, 13; Gerd Krumeich, 'L'Entrée en guerre en Allemagne', in Becker and Audoin-Rouzeau (eds), *Les Sociétés européennes*, 67–71.

[132] Hanssen, *Diary of a dying empire*, 11–14.

[133] Kruse, *Krieg und nationale Integration*, 160–1; Raithel, *Das 'Wunder' der inneren Einheit*, 420–1.

[134] Geinitz, *Kriegsfurcht und Kampfbereitschaft*, 104, 135, 314–29, 330–4; Ziemann, *Front und Heimat*, 44–6.

unemployment.[135] But many were under-age, the youthful students celebrated in wartime propaganda and post-war literature. The schools returned from their holidays between 3 and 12 August. Teachers were amazed by the 'self-sacrificing love of the fatherland' shown by pupils they had come to see as materialistic and peace-loving. In all three Berlin schools subject to one annual report the entire top forms, those aged 17 or over, volunteered. The *Wander-vogel* produced disproportionate numbers, and for those rejected on account of their age special 'youth companies' were formed.[136] Others were of their fathers' generation, too old to be liable for immediate call-up and too young to have served in 1870. Many of the latter confronted what Paul Plaut, an applied psychologist who gathered evidence at the time, reckoned to be a 'psychic crisis': the war shattered the normal tenor of their lives and created a new focus. The positive reaction was to embrace the war. Many of his respondents cited the importance of patriotism, but all of them discounted the phenomenon of war enthusiasm. The most common thread was a sense of duty.[137]

War enthusiasm in Germany developed during the course of August: it followed the war's outbreak rather than preceded it. As the enemy took shape, the idea of pure defence on which the war's immediate acceptance was grounded was moderated. The aims of the war gained in definition, and included objectives which could be defined as offensive and even annexationist.

The sense that the war was a new departure for Germany internally now became common currency for both right and left. Johann Plenge, writing in 1915, said that if there were to be a public festival to commemorate the war, it should be the celebration of mobilization of 2 August—'the celebration of inner victory'. Thomas Mann described this triumph in paradoxes in November 1914, speaking of 'the brotherly co-operation of social democracy and military authority', and citing a radical writer to the effect that 'under the military dictatorship Germany has become free'.[138]

The SPD was less cynical with regard to such contrivances than might have been expected. Ludwig Frank, who had lobbied for his party's support for war credits, wrote to a lady friend on 23 August, 'I am happy: it is not difficult to let blood flow for the fatherland, and to surround it with romanticism and heroism.'[139] Frank, a Jew as well as a socialist, was killed in action on 3 September, one of only two Reichstag deputies to fall in the war.

---

[135] Bernd Ulrich, 'Des Desillusionierung der Kriegsfreiwilligen von 1914', in Wette (ed.), *Krieg des kleinen Mannes*, 114; Ulrich, 'Kriegsfreiwillige. Motivationen-Erfahrungen-Wirkungen', in Berliner Geschichtswerkstatt, *August 1914*, 233–7; Verhey, 'The spirit of 1914', 206–10.

[136] Ingeborg Rürup, ' "Es entspricht nicht dem Ernste der Zeit, dass die Jugend müssig gehe". Kriegsbegeisterung, Schulalltag und Bürokratie in den höheren Lehranstalten Preussens 1914', in Berliner Geschichtswerkstatt, *August 1914*, 181–2; Schubert-Weller, *Kein schönrer Tod*, 214, 229.

[137] Plaut, 'Psychographie des Kriegers', 4–16.

[138] Rürup, 'Der "Geist von 1914"', 17; Mann, 'Gedanken im Kriege', 9.

[139] Kruse, *Krieg und nationale Integration*, 101.

Socialists of middle-class backgrounds may have been more responsive to the opportunity which the war presented for reintegration in German society. But during August the working classes became increasingly proud of their own reaction to the hostilities. Reports of victories began with the (premature) news of the fall of Liège on 7 August; the battles of the frontiers after 20 August produced a sequence of celebrations that climaxed on 2 September, the anniversary of Sedan. Flags, hitherto rarely flown in Germany, and associated in any case with the monarchy, appeared in growing profusion in working-class areas. *Deutschland über alles* gained in popularity, as did evangelical hymns linking Protestantism with nationality.[140] By late August the police in Berlin reported that, despite the worries about unemployment, the mood of the workers was good.[141]

Feelings in France evolved in not dissimilar ways. Boarding a train in St Étienne on 28 July, Daniel Halévy had watched a young officer taking leave of his parents: he had seen expressions such as theirs only in cemeteries, at gravesides. Regular soldiers were being deployed on the frontiers, but Halévy's own hopes of peace only evaporated on 30 and 31 July, the days of waiting, which he described as 'like one endless evening'.[142] He called 1 August the end of hope. On the same day *Le Temps* said the mood in Paris was serious but not sad. Patriotic crowds, mostly of young men and numbered in hundreds rather than thousands, formed in the city's streets that evening.[143] Halévy arrived in the capital on the following day. He observed a man in tears, supported by his friend, a sergeant, on the Pont-Neuf. He described Paris as a scene from the Bible, but of a superhuman Bible which had never been committed to paper: 'this city of three million inhabitants had received a death blow.' He acknowledged the mood of resignation, but saw also despair.[144] Monsignor Alfred Baudrillart, the rector of the Institut Catholique in Paris, who arrived in the city on the same day, noticed the role that drink had in evoking overt enthusiasm. His verdict on the underlying mood reflected a more fixed resolve: an acceptance of the inevitable and a determination not to give in.[145]

France differed from Germany in being less industrialized, with fewer large regional cities. Thus, small rural communities were even less touched by the speculation of the press. In the Languedoc under half the population read the newspapers, and much of what it did read was concerned with local reporting.[146] When the church bells rang out late on the afternoon of 1 August

---

[140]   Raithel, *Das 'Wunder' der inneren Einheit*, 460–6; also 428–34, 440; Berliner Geschichtswerkstatt, *Aug. 1914*, 69, 124.

[141]   Materna and Schreckenbach, *Dokumente aus geheimen Archiven*, 22 Aug. 1914.

[142]   Halévy, *L'Europe brisée*, 25–7, 39.

[143]   Raithel, *Das 'Wunder' der inneren Einheit*, 268–74.

[144]   Halévy, *L'Europe brisée*, 31.

[145]   *Carnets du Cardinal Baudrillart*, 26–7.

[146]   Maurin, *Armée-guerre-société*, 566–7, 572.

the peasants were working in the fields, bringing in the harvest. Many assumed that there was a fire. They were put right by the local gendarme or the notice which he had posted—not by the press. As the realization broke, the strongest emotions were shock and consternation. In the villages of the Isère, according to the reports of the local authorities, only 5 per cent of people greeted the war with enthusiasm. This figure rose to 31 per cent in the towns of Grenoble and Vienne. But the key point was that, as in Paris, the general mood was one of resolution.[147] An analysis of six different rural departments suggests that 16 per cent of people received the news of mobilization with favour, 23 per cent with *sang froid*, and 61 per cent with reserve.[148] This may not have been the enthusiasm of legend, but nor was it rejection.

The French army had anticipated that 13 per cent of those mobilized would fail to appear. In the event 1.5 per cent were classed as deserters, and many of those proved to be vagrants, mentally deficient, or Bretons who could not read French. The numbers of genuine defaulters—perhaps 1,600 in all—were so few as to make generalizations fraught. Anti-militarism was not a significant factor; religion may have been, as Catholics in particular were alienated by the anticlericalism of the Third Republic, several to the point of seeking out missions overseas.[149]

Many reservists left for the front immediately. But for others there was more time to come to terms with what was happening. Women were vital in helping men accept their obligations. The search for mutual reassurance drew communities together.[150] Even more important was the mood in the barracks themselves. Soldiers had been more aware of the preceding tension, and greeted the war with both relief and optimism: they found the sadness of civilians somewhat embarrassing. It was their positive outlook which swept up the more reluctant reservists.[151] By the time of departure enthusiasm was more in evidence: only 20 per cent now manifested reserve, whereas 30 per cent showed *sang froid*, and 50 per cent favour.[152] Étienne Tanty's company marched off in the early evening of 8 August, and most of his comrades used the afternoon to get drunk. By the time they fell in, two-thirds of them did not know where they were; they could not stand up straight and threw everything into chaos as they struggled to find their equipment. Maurice Maréchal, the cellist, left Rouen at 7 a.m. on the following morning, too early to satiate his

[147] Flood, *France 1914–18*, 7–15.
[148] Becker, *1914*, 294, also generally 270–357; for a briefer survey see Becker, in Fridenson (ed.), *1914–1918*.
[149] Jules Maurin and Jean-Charles Jauffret, 'Sous les drapeaux', 113–15, and 'Les Combattants face à l'épreuve de 1914 à 1918', 272–5, in Pedroncini (ed.), *L'Histoire militaire de la France*, iii; Maurin, *Armée-guerre-société*, 383–5.
[150] Flood, *France 1914–18*, 7–15.
[151] Maurin, *Armée-guerre-société*, 573, 679.
[152] Becker, *1914*, 319.

anxiety with alcohol. His inner fear competed with the pride generated by the popular acclaim.[153] As units marched off to the strains of the *Marseillaise* and the *Chant du départ*, tricolours waving over their heads and flowers falling at their feet, public and private feeelings were fused. Families who said farewell to their fathers, husbands, and sons were sustained by the sharing of the experience and by a sense of fellowship.

These public displays gave substance to the *union sacrée*, helping to transform what was initially a formula for national defence, a response to a temporary crisis and a term little used by newspapers, into a more sustained effort to put national divisions to one side. The *union sacrée* could not draw on France's immediate past: deeply divided by the Dreyfus affair, it nurtured at least two different conceptions of society, one libertarian and egalitarian, and the other hierarchical and authoritarian, the most potent manifestation of this division being the clash between republicanism and clericalism. Baudrillart was abused at the Gare St Lazare and in the street on 2 and 3 August. As August wore on he encountered more tolerance. The government itself, through its prefects and mayors, deliberately promoted the *union sacrée* at the local level. On public occasions teacher and priest—the representatives of the republic and of Rome—joined together on the same platform for the sake of France. The underlying tensions were not removed, but all sides recognized that the corollary of a war of national defence was a sustained effort to generate national unity: 'it is vital', wrote Baudrillart in his diary on 29 September, 'not to do anything to destroy a union which is so precarious.'[154]

In Austria-Hungary the army expected one in ten of those called up not to appear.[155] On the whole its fears proved unfounded. Some inducement was provided by the fact that mobilization orders were issued in the native tongues of the reservists. In the Austrian lands problems were greatest in Croatia and Slovenia, where between 600 and 700 men deserted. But figures were lower in the Italian-speaking areas of Tyrol and the Adriatic, and in Bohemia fell to only nine. Foreigners proved anxious to demonstrate their loyalty and enlisted voluntarily in large numbers. In Hungary the Magyars used the excuse of mobilization to arrest large numbers of non-Magyars on the basis of a secret list and on the grounds of suspicion alone.[156] The immediate effects were less damaging than might have been expected. Romanian peasants in Hungary responded without enthusiasm, but they

---

[153] Guéno and Laplume (eds), *Paroles de poilus*, 13, 37.

[154] Baudrillart, *Carnets du Cardinal Baudrillart*, 27–8, 31, 80, 85; also Flood, *France 1914–18*, 17–23; Robert Vandenbussche, 'Psychose de guerre dans le nord? 1910–14', in Vandenrath *et al.* (eds.), *1914*, 128–9, 138, 160–4; Jean-Jacques Becker, 'La Genèse de l'union sacrée', in ibid. 208–9, 214–15; Becker, *La France en guerre*, 13–15, 30–8.

[155] Glaise von Horstenau, *Ein General im Zwielicht*, i. 285.

[156] Herwig, *First World War*, 79, 127.

nonetheless arrived at the depots earlier and in greater numbers than anti-cipated.[157] In Bosnia anti-Serb excesses in the aftermath of the Sarajevo assassinations cowed dissidents.

However, the opportunity to stress the solidarity of the state was not seized. The Reichsrat was not recalled, and the political parties thus evaded any pressure to commit themselves to the defence of the empire in formal terms.[158] Much of the evidence of real exuberance in late July derives solely from Vienna. As in other countries, it did not anticipate the war's outbreak but was a response to it. It therefore rested on the idea of a short, sharp war against Serbia alone, in the hope that it would resolve Austria-Hungary's internal problems. As the Balkan conflict gave way to a general European war, and as Austria-Hungary confronted conflict with Russia, the enthusiasm of its people ebbed. In Germany and France popular determination deepened during the course of August; in Austria-Hungary it declined. Freud, having joined in the earlier euphoria, found that 'gradually a feeling of discomfort set in, as the strictures of the censorship and the exaggeration of the smallest successes' reminded him of the empire's underlying weaknesses. 'The only thing that remains real', he concluded on 23 August, 'is the hope that the high ally will hack us out.'[159]

But a war for Germany was not what the Czechs wanted. Many were at least passive supporters of Russia. The mood in Prague was more reserved than that in Vienna from the outset. Both the 1908 and 1912 mobilizations had triggered mutinies in Czech units. On 22 September two Czech Landwehr battalions left the city displaying their national colours and a red flag with the words 'we are marching against the Russians and we do not know why'. One of the battalions was disbanded in April 1915 after large-scale desertions to the enemy.[160] In Bohemia itself a railway strike and popular demonstrations meant that 121 Czech radicals were arrested within a few months, and eighteen of them condemned to death; by the year's end almost a thousand would be impri-soned.[161]

In Russia itself the belief that the war could be popular was an important element in sustaining the resolve both of the Tsar and of the council of ministers. The latter had convinced itself from the outset of the crisis, on 24 July, that a failure to support Serbia would foment the prevailing disorder rather than assuage it. When Nicholas II approved general mobilization his own determination, which—particularly in the light of Durnovo's telling memorandum—was shaky at best, was sustained by the thought that what

[157] Taslauanu, *With the Austrian army*, 6, 11.
[158] Michel, *Guerres mondiales et conflits contemporains*, 179 (1995), 7.
[159] Falzeder and Brabant (eds.), *Correspondence of Freud and Ferenczi*, 13.
[160] Deak, *Beyond nationalism*, 197; Zeman, *Break-up of the Habsburg empire*, 50–2, 55–7.
[161] Rauchensteiner, *Tod des Doppeladlers*, 178–80.

he was doing commanded popular support.[162] Certainly the press across a wide political spectrum commended his actions, and called for national unity.

Superficially the incidence of strikes during July might have suggested that any opposition to mobilization would be focused in the cities. Workers and reservists in Riga paraded with banners saying 'Down with the war!' But in some senses socialist activity had exhausted itself by the time mobilization was declared. The responses among the workers of St Petersburg were resigned, if not enthusiastic. This was the mood caught by Marc Chagall in a series of drawings depicting the troops' departure for the front.[163] Overt opposition was a rural more than an urban phenomenon. Surprise, the initial response as elsewhere, generated first stunned silence and then lamentation. But as the news was assimilated, communities were divided more than united by their reactions. In the wake of the 1905 defeat, military reformers had argued that effectiveness in modern war relied on a sense of nationalism. Two-thirds of pre-war conscripts were literate, and their period in uniform became an opportunity to inculcate a loyalty to Russia. On the other hand, an appeal to national unity, even if endorsed in varying degrees and for divergent reasons by the Duma, meant little to a population whose lives were regulated by regional loyalties. Although long used to the state's conscription of manpower, the peasants were particularly concerned by the economic dimensions of mobilization. On the one hand were their worries for the provision and sustenance of their families; on the other were the shortages of food and accommodation at the collection and redistribution centres for the troops themselves. Calculations as to the scale of the subsequent disorders vary: thirty-one districts in seventeen provinces were affected on mobilization, and a month later the police reckoned that forty-nine out of 101 provinces and oblasts in European and Asiatic Russia had suffered riots. In Barnaul, the authorities lost control of the city for a time, and over 100 died. In four provinces tens of thousands of reservists were involved, and one report put the numbers of dead and wounded at 505 in European Russia alone. On 13 August Maklakov, the minister of the interior, authorized the provincial governors to suppress any disturbances without mercy.[164]

In the circumstances, the fact that 96 per cent of those mobilized reported for duty represented a successful outcome. Provincial officials orchestrated patrotic demonstrations as units left for the front. And the mood, even if not as resilient as that of France or Germany, hardened as the weeks passed. The

[162] Lieven, *Nicholas II*, 197, 204.

[163] McKean, *St Petersburg*, 357–8; Lobanov-Rostovsky, *Grinding mill*, 20; Cork, *A bitter truth*, 40–1.

[164] Dittmar Dahlmann, 'Russia at the outbreak of the First World War', in Becker and Audoin-Rouzeau (eds.), *Les Sociétés européennes*, 53–61; Wildman, *End of the Russian imperial army*, 77–9; Rogger, *Journal of Contemporary History*, I (1966) 105–6; Sanborn, *Slavic Review*,LIX (2000), 267–89 . See also Andolenko, *Histoire de l'armée russe*, 306, and Danilov, *Le Russie dans la grande guerre*, 155–6.

Duma's resolution to support war credits, however much it embraced even more divergent motives than did the comparable votes in Germany and France, at least betokened a political armistice for the time being. Victories against the Austrians, despite the dire reports from East Prussia, fed these different interpretations of Russianness. Major patriotic demonstrations were reported by the police in October, and in the same month popular culture reflected national feeling through circuses, films, and puppet shows.[165]

Because of its comparatively underdeveloped economy Russia was less exposed to the currents of pre-war nationalism, but its people went to war nonetheless. Belgium was its mirror image; possessed of an advanced economy, its neutrality prevented it being subject to the full force of pre-war militancy. If surprise was a common response to the outbreak of war, then it reached its greatest intensity in Brussels. As late as 28 July the Catholic press supported Austria-Hungary's handling of Serbia as though the crisis was still localized. The German ultimatum to Belgium and its rejection produced a reaction whose spontaneity and scale amazed the gratified government. Belgians were outraged by the Germans' implication that their honour could be bought in return for financial compensation. Thus, it was the ultimatum rather than the invasion which produced integration. The king became its focus, appealing to a sense of nationhood and history in terms which were effectively novel in Belgian discourse. Belgium's socialists cleaved to these notions rather than to the International, and Albert reacted by appointing Emil Vandervelde a minister of state on 4 August. Up to 20,000 volunteers joined the army, most for reasons of patriotism rather than economic necessity, and mostly (as elsewhere) from urban rather than rural areas. As Belgium lost its territory it found an identity.[166]

It is Britain, however, that provides by far the best illustration of the development from war enthusiasm into fighting power. Britain saw its navy as its prime defence; it had no tradition of conscription, and its small army was drawn to a disproportionate extent from the lower end of the working class. Popular militarism embraced many forms before 1914, but they did not include that of being a regular soldier. The army needed 35,000 recruits each year, and yet only once between 1908 and 1913 did it get more than 30,000. Nor was the Territorial Army, which Haldane had grandly portrayed as the nation in arms, committed to home defence, any more popular: in 1913 it was almost 67,000 men below its establishment of 300,000, and it had a 12.5 per-cent annual wastage rate.[167]

[165] Jahn, *Patriotic culture in Russia*, esp. 8–9, and n. 13.
[166] Jean Stengers, 'Belgium', in Wilson (ed), *Decisions for war*, 152, 157, 161–4; Stengers, *Guerres mondiales et conflits contemporains*, 179 (1995), 17–20; Stengers, 'La Belgique', in Becker and Audoin-Rouzeau (eds.), *Les Sociétés européennes*, 79–85.
[167] Simkins, *Kitchener's army*, 17–19.

On 6 August 1914 the newly appointed secretary of state for war, Lord Kitchener, received parliamentary approval for an increase in the army of 500,000 men. This was the first of his 'New Armies'; by mid-August he was aiming for four such armies, giving him twenty-four divisions in addition to the six formed by the existing regular army. Between 4 and 8 August a total of 8,193 men enlisted; in the second week of the month 43,354 came forward, and in the third 49,982. With the news of the battle of Mons and the retreat to the Marne, and press reports of the exhaustion and disarray of the exiguous British Expeditionary Force, recruiting in the final week of August reached 63,000, and in the first week of September 174,901. By 12 September 478,893 men had joined the army since the war's outbreak, and 301,971 since 30 August. Of a total of 5.7 million who served with the British forces in the First World War, 2.46 million were to enlist voluntarily by the end of 1915.[168]

Two features are immediately striking in these figures. First, popular enthusiasm was clearly transformed into active service; secondly, the process by which it did so was delayed in its operation. All classes responded positively to Kitchener's appeal. However, the professional and commercial classes did so disproportionately: over 40 per cent of those eligible in both categories joined the army, thus suggesting that their exposure to the influences of the press, to the appeal to escape the office routine of bourgeois life, was not without its effect. By contrast, only 22 per cent of those in agriculture enlisted, and they constituted 8.4 per cent of all recruits. The agricultural workforce was older than many other occupations, and its contribution to the war effort was direct, but in addition it was cut off from many of the influences of popular nationalism. The methods of recruiting employed in rural areas were traditional and paternalist, relying on a sense of deference and obligation rather than on regional links and bonds of friendship. In Sussex such techniques were insufficient.[169] In the Highlands of Scotland the sparseness of the population underlined the impossibility of adhering to strictly territorial recruiting. Cameron of Lochiel recalled emigrants to Scotland. Macdonald of Clanranald appealed to the memory of the 1745 rebellion, citing the Hanoverian (i.e. British) army's treatment of the Jacobites as evidence of German brutality.[170] Just under 30 per cent of those employed in manufacturing industry enlisted. It is possible that high working-class enlistment in August and September was related to unemployment. The immediate effect of the war's declaration was an increase in unemployment by 10 per cent: 78 per cent of Birmingham recruits in August came from the same social classes as before the war, and by September nine out of ten unemployed were reported as having enlisted. As

---

[168] Simkins, *Kitchener's army*, xiii–xv, 39–40, 49–75.

[169] Grieves, *Rural History*, IV (1993), 55–75.

[170] Ewen Cameron and Iain Robertson, 'Fighting and bleeding for the land: the Scottish Highlands and the Great War', in C. M. M. Macdonald and E. Macfarland (eds.), *Scotland and the Great War*.

a general pattern, therefore, industrial and urban areas produced more recruits than rural areas. By 4 November 1914 237 per 10,000 of the population had volunteered from southern Scotland, 196 from the Midlands, and 198 from Lancashire; by contrast the west of England had mustered only eighty-eight per 10,000, the eastern counties eighty, and southern Ireland thirty-two. Urban civic pride became a powerful factor and was embodied in the idea of 'Pals' battalions, units made of up friends, linked by professional, recreational, or educational ties: 145 service battalions and seventy-nine reserve battalions were raised locally. The 'Pals' movement was particularly strong on Merseyside, and comparatively weak in Scotland. The big exception, Glasgow, raised three battalions for the Highland Light Infantry, the 15th battalion from the corporation's tram service, the 16th from the Boy's Brigade, and the 17th from the city's chamber of commerce. Typical of a community cut off from such collective influences, from the excitement generated by the press and the parades, was Gwynedd in north-west Wales. Perplexity at the war, the lack of military traditions, the separateness from England, all combined to produce low rates of recruiting.[171]

Some of the factors experienced in Gwynedd were common to Britain as a whole, and help explain the slowness with which recruiting boomed in August. Ernest Jones wrote to his friend Sigmund Freud on 3 August that, 'London is absolutely quiet and indistinguishable from other times except for the newspapers'.[172] The Liberal press concluded, once war was declared, that it had no option but to support the national effort. With no immediate danger to Britain, the prevailing mood was one of obligation. Reservists reported for duty almost without exception. But others had to put their affairs in order; there were delays in sorting out separation allowances for their families; and their employers were reluctant to lose them.

Within a month many of these factors were operating in the other direction. Women distributed white feathers to those not yet in uniform; employers promised to keep jobs open for men on their return. Britain's delay was evidence of a general European phenomenon. The speed of the crisis had changed war from a remote contingency to an immediate actuality: people took time to adjust. The attempt by international socialism to prevent the war and the obvious manifestations of bellicosity were more sequential than they were simultaneous: the failure of the first created the opportunity for the second.

The enthusiasm with which Europe went to war was therefore composed of a wide range of differing responses. Its universality lay in their convergence

---

[171] Parry, *Welsh History Review*, XIV (1988), 78–92; on voluntary recruiting in general, see Simkins, *Kitchener's army*; Beckett and Simpson, *Nation in arms*, 7–12; Winter, *The Great War and the British people*, 25–35; Douglas, *Journal of Modern History*, XLII (1970), 570–4; Dewey, *Historical Journal*, XXVII (1984), 199–223.
[172] Paskauskas (ed.), *Correspondence of Freud and Jones*, 298.

and not in their component parts. Intellectuals welcomed war as an instrument with which to change pre-war society; many of those who joined up did so to defend it. For the latter, the foundations were as much psychological as ideological: community and conformity gave shape to lives disordered by the upheavals which the war caused.[173] The common denominator may more accurately be described as passive acceptance, a willingness to do one's duty; enthusiasm was the conspicuous froth, the surface element only.

The mood relied in large part on an ignorance of the conditions of modern war. The bulk of popular literature continued to portray war as a matter of individual courage and resource, to use imagery more appropriate to knights-errant and the days of chivalry. 'Where then are horse and rider? Where is my sword?', Wilhelm Lamszus had asked ironically in *Das Menschenschlachthaus* (the slaughterhouse of mankind), published in 1912. Like H. G. Wells in Britain, Lamszus had recognized that the next war would represent the triumph of the machine over human flesh.[174] But the inherent optimism of the human condition, the belief that the best will occur rather than the worst, the intimations of immortality to which youth is subject, persuaded many that technical progress would make war less lethal, not more so. The *Breisgauer Zeitung* assured its readers on 1 August that their chances of coming back in one piece from this war were greater than in previous wars. The modern battlefield was much less bloody because of the extended distances at which fighting occurred. Moreover, high-velocity bullets were of smaller calibre and therefore passed through the body with less damage. Such wounds as were inflicted could be rapidly treated thanks to the advances of modern medicine.[175] British regular soldiers who had served in South Africa did not share the general exuberance; recent knowledge of war—in their case that with Japan in 1904—may also have contributed to the reluctance of Russian reservists.[176] But in France, Germany, and Austria-Hungary no such experience of combat could clutter their idealized views.

Popular enthusiasm played no part in causing the First World War. And yet without a popular willingness to go to war the world war could not have taken place. The statesmen had projected internal collapse as a consequence of prolonged fighting. Instead, the societies of all the belligerents remained integrated until at least 1917, and in large part into 1918. The underlying conviction of the war's necessity, of the duty of patriotic defence, established in 1914 remained the bedrock of that continuing commitment.

---

[173] Geinitz, *Kriegsfurcht und Kampfbereitschaft*, 178–9.
[174] Boschert, 'Eine Utopie des Unglücks stieg auf', in Berliner Geschichtswerkstatt, *August 1914*, 134.
[175] Geinitz, *Kriegsfurcht und Kampfbereitschaft*, 285–6.
[176] Meinertzhagen, *Army diary*, 78; Gordon-Duff, *With the Gordon Highlanders*, 343; Terraine (ed.), *General Jack's diary*, 22; Dunn, *The war the infantry knew*, 1, Wildman, *End of the Russian imperial army*, 82.

3

THE
WESTERN FRONT
IN 1914

WAR PLANS

Probably no single episode in the military history of the First World War attracted so much controversy in the inter-war years as the events of the first six weeks on the western front. The Germans had come—or so it seemed—within a hair's breadth of defeating France. For the French it had been a pyrrhic victory. Defeat was averted, but the Germans had overrun France's industrial heartlands and had conquered sufficient territory to be able to determine much of the strategy of the rest of the war. Nonetheless, France's officers squabbled as to whom among their commanders, Joffre or Gallieni, best deserved the title of victor. What dogged the German generals was not comparative success but ultimate failure. The first objective of their memoirs was to disown responsibility for Germany's inability to achieve a quick victory; the second, to deny that they had been defeated at all.

After the armistice in 1918 the German army was anxious to consolidate its argument that it was not responsible for Germany's final collapse. Its case rested not simply on its interpretation of the events of the war's last year but also on those of 1914 itself: the fact that the war in the west had not been won in short order, as had allegedly been promised, was the fault—it was argued—of a handful of individuals, and not that of the army as a whole. In 1930 General Wilhelm Groener, the head of the railway section of the German general staff in 1914, stated that the legacy of Schlieffen as chief of the German general staff was to 'point his successor on the path to victory in the battle of Germany against an enormous superiority in numbers'.[1] Groener and others, notably Hermann von Kuhl and Wolfgang Förster, characterized the war plan drawn up by Schlieffen as containing the perfect operational solution to Germany's dilemma of a war on two fronts. By electing to concentrate first against France in the west, and by achieving victory in six weeks, Germany would be ready to turn east against Russia before the latter could be sufficiently mobilized to bring its strength to bear. The initial campaign in the west was the nub of this strategy. The German army was to pivot on its weaker left wing in Alsace-Lorraine, sending its stronger right wing swinging through Belgium to envelop Paris, cut the communications of the French, and then roll their armies up against the frontier. Groener's argument that Schlieffen's genius for operations had correctly divined the solution to a seemingly intractable problem was embraced by writers outside Germany. Liddell Hart used all his considerable powers of metaphor—likening the balance between the two wings to 'a revolving door'[2]—to conjure up what was a totally false image of the problems of manoeuvring a mass army. For Groener and Liddell Hart, what went wrong was that Schlieffen retired in 1905. The plan that was implemented in 1914 was one weakened by the emendations of his successor in office, Helmuth von Moltke the younger.

Liddell Hart, who probably did not know better, and Groener, who certainly did, grossly distorted the methods by which the German general staff evolved its war plan. By 1913 up to 650 officers were employed on the 'great general staff', making it one of the major institutions of the Wilhelmine state. Theirs was a continuous task of analysis and revision: for this there was an annual cycle incorporating staff rides and war games. Whatever was planned for 1905 was specific to that year; it was an incremental evolution from the plans of previous years, and it was not a definitive statement, intended to remain unchanged over subsequent years. It contained at least two different options, one for application only in the west against France, and another for use in the event of having to fight on both fronts simultaneously. The interaction between these two possibilities was contingent on the diplomatic situation, and on the strengths and mobilization schedules of Germany itself and of Germany's two potential enemies. Consequently, the initial phases of a war, those of mobilization, concentration, and deployment, attracted the bulk of the planners' attentions. The propositions which the process threw up were contingent and conditional. There was no single solution, no one plan.

The 'Schlieffen plan' acquired its status for two reasons. The first was historiographical: the desire of the German army in the 1920s to persuade itself that it had had the means to win the war. The second was Schlieffen's own influence as a teacher and guru, which survived both his death in 1913 and the

---

[1] Groener, *Der Feldherr wider Willen*, p. vii; on the general issue of Germany's publicization of the Marne, see Lange, *Marneschlacht und deutsche Öffentlichkeit*.
[2] Liddell Hart, *World war*, 68, and *Through the fog*, 19.

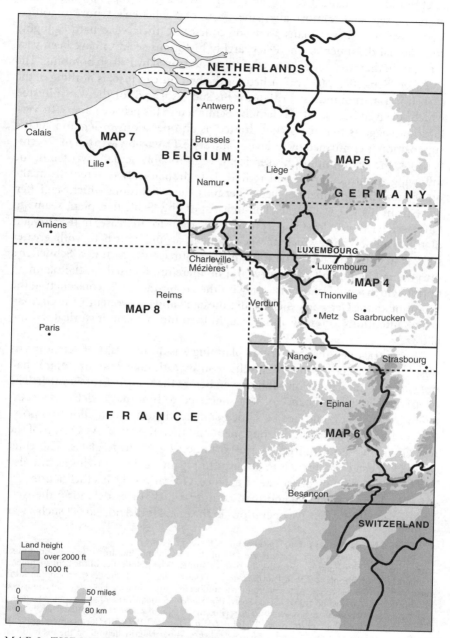

NETHERLANDS

Calais

MAP 7

BELGIUM

Antwerp

Brussels

Lille

Namur

Liège

MAP 5

GERMANY

Amiens

LUXEMBOURG

Charleville-
Mézières

Luxembourg

MAP 4

Reims

Verdun

Thionville

MAP 8

Metz

Saarbrucken

Paris

Nancy

Strasbourg

FRANCE

Epinal

MAP 6

Besançon

SWITZERLAND

Land height
■ over 2000 ft
□ 1000 ft

0   50 miles
0   80 km

MAP 3. THE WESTERN FRONT

First World War. In practice, however, we know less about the planning process
of 1905 itself than almost any other year of Schlieffen's tenure of office.
Germany's actual war plans were, of course, by their very nature, highly
confidential documents. The Reichsarchiv historians seem to have been very
cautious in their use,[3] and in 1945 they were destroyed by British bombing. The
so-called 'Schlieffen plan', published for the first time in 1956, is nothing of the
sort. It is a memorandum written for his successor and for the war minister,
which survived because it was kept by Schlieffen in his private papers. Its very
location suggests that it was not drafted as an operations order, and such a
supposition is confirmed by its layout and style. Ostensibly written in December 1905, the last month of his service, it was probably actually written in the
following month, after he had retired. It is dramatically different from the
other surviving document of December 1905, the conclusions which Schlieffen
drew from his last war game. The first paper, the 'Schlieffen plan', seems to
have been written at least in part in order to argue for increases in the strength
of the army, a cause which the general staff would return to with greater
success in 1912 and 1913. The pursuit of resources was as much Schlieffen's
purpose as the pursuit of victory, and he therefore focused on the planning
option which would make his case with the greatest force. Reconstructing the
evolution of the German general staff's thought, and consequently the German
army's intentions in 1914, is more fraught than much recent historical writing
allows.[4]

The central dilemma for German planning was the difficulty of defending its
western and eastern frontiers simultaneously. Although acute in 1914, it had
preoccupied the senior von Moltke even before the Franco-Prussian War. The
protracted French resistance of 1871 suggested to him that a victorious campaign in the west could not be settled sufficiently quickly to allow the possibility of dealing with first one opponent and then the other. As a result of the
war Germany had acquired Alsace-Lorraine as a strategic glacis. The elder
Moltke expected the French to attempt to regain the lost provinces, but also
saw them as Germany's best line of defence. Operationally, his inclination was
to ride a French offensive and then counter-attack, or to defend in the west
while conducting offensive operations in the east. He did not expect such a war

---

[3] Zuber, *War in History*, VI (1999), *passim*, but esp. 270–1, 284–5.
[4] Ritter, *The Schlieffen plan*, presents the text of the 1905 memorandum, with some additional
documents and commentary; it provides the basis of Turner, 'The significance of the Schlieffen plan',
in Kennedy (ed.), *War plans*. Zuber, *War in History*, VI (1999), 262–305, challenges the memorandum's
status, and shows how Schlieffen still entertained a number of options in 1905. This is a point confirmed
by Schlieffen's last war game, for which see Foley, *War Studies Journal*, III (1998), 117–33, and IV (1999),
97–115. All the older literature now needs to be revised in the light of Zuber, although Wallach, *Dogma*,
identifies the key historiographical issues. T. Holmes, *War in history*, VIII (2001) (forthcoming) presents
an effective critique of Zuber. Bucholz, *Moltke, Schlieffen*, is particularly helpful on the institutional
background. The inter-war German literature includes Kuhl, *Grand état-major allemand*; Foerster,
Schlieffen; Elze, *Tannenberg*. Groener, *Lebenserinnerungen*, provides an insider's view.

to produce a complete German victory, and he ominously referred to the historical analogies of a war lasting seven or even thirty years.

Moltke's immediate successor, Alfred von Waldersee, moved away from these cautious responses in favour of offensives on both fronts, to the west as well as to the east. Two factors shaped this shift. First was the German army's conviction, established in 1870, that man for man, and corps for corps, it was better than the French army. This remained a fundamental assumption up to—and beyond—1914.[5] It suggested to Waldersee that, if the French attacked in order to regain Lorraine, they would create opportunities for Germany to stage a counter-offensive. Second was the growing importance of railways to the making of strategy. The possibility of mounting simultaneous or nearly simultaneous offensives on two fronts emerged from the flexibility conferred by an increasingly sophisticated railway network. By using interior lines, Germany could switch troops from east to west and vice versa, so transforming its central European position from a liability to an advantage. The benefits were primarily defensive, but they were shoehorned into an offensive framework conditioned by the determination to seek battle and therefore to concentrate mass on the decisive spot. The greater railway densities of western Europe acted as a pull in establishing the priority of that front over the east. Furthermore, the centrality of railways conferred an additional advantage for staff officers anxious to manage and limit the uncertainties of war: the military travel plan created standard operating procedures, so making strategy the servant of technology.

Thus, when Schlieffen, who had been Waldersee's deputy, succeeded him as chief of the general staff in 1891 a reorientation in planning assumptions was already under way. The conclusion of the Franco-Russian military convention in 1892 confirmed Schlieffen in his decision that Germany should concentrate against France first. His initial plan, that for 1893–4, allocated forty-eight divisions to the west and fifteen to the east. Schlieffen never abandoned planning for war against Russia, but in his western variants he increasingly left the eastern front to the attentions of Austria-Hungary. His difficulty was how to give his scheme operational expression.

Three factors conditioned both his calculations and those of his successor. The first was numerical inferiority: although Germany had pioneered the application of the short-service conscript army in peacetime, France went further in its application and acquired in Russia the European power with the largest manpower potential as its ally. The second was the speed of mobilization and concentration. France had done so much to improve on its lamentable performance in 1870 that it was clear it could achieve both ahead of Germany. And the third was the impact of the firepower revolution in offensive operations.

[5] Holger Afflerbach, 'Die militärische Planung des Deutschen Reiches im Ersten Weltkrieg', in Michalka (ed.), Erste Weltkrieg, 282–3; Showalter, Tannenberg, 32.

Schlieffen saw clearly enough the tactical nature of modern war: the development of firepower would force infantry to entrench and to use cover, and frontal attacks would degenerate into protracted battles that would produce only limited victories. The erection of fortifications by both France and Russia on their German frontiers seemed to make the prospect of a rapid campaign against one and then the other even more remote. A general staff study of 1895 concluded that a German attack in the direction of Nancy had no prospect of achieving a quick, decisive victory. Schlieffen's answer was not to confront France's fixed defences, but to go round them: he began to explore the idea of an offensive directed against the enemy's flank and rear. His aim was to achieve both a local superiority in manpower and a decisive victory in short order. The plan of 1897 pushed elements of the German army north of Verdun. The 1899 plan, in the variant which assumed an attack in the west only, proposed to turn the French by pushing through the Ardennes. Schlieffen was nervous about the implications. If the French army mobilized faster, his right could be isolated and crushed. One solution was to be ready to respond to the French redeployment to the north with his left in the south. Both elements in such a riposte—the emphasis on the counter-offensive and the readiness to switch from an attack on the right to one on the left—remained present in his considerations up until 1905. The alternative approach was to strengthen his right. This was the line advocated by General Hans Beseler in January 1900. The deployment plan for the west in 1900–1 increased the right flank to three armies, while the centre armies south-east of Metz were given the task of fixing the French in Lorraine. Metz itself was not the hub of a great wheel to the north and west, but the base for German thrusts designed to tie the French down and to split them between north and south. In the 1904 staff ride Schlieffen divided his attack—the right wing advancing between Trier and Aachen, and the left between Metz and Strasbourg. The key battles were in the centre, and the task of the right was therefore to march south—not west—in order to support the German centre and left by entering the battle on the frontiers from the French rear. The result of the exercise was indecisive: the left encountered the French who pushed forward from their defensive positions, while the right was insufficiently strong to avoid becoming embroiled in frontal battles.

In his conclusions to the 1904 staff ride Schlieffen for the first time considered the possibility of breaching Belgian neutrality. His readiness to do so was predicated on the belief that the French would already have infringed it. His assumption at this stage was that the Belgians would join the French, but in the conclusions to his last war game in 1905 he was to argue—perhaps in response to his manpower worries—that the effect of France's violation of Belgian neutrality would bring Belgium in on Germany's side.[6] Railway

---

[6] Foley, *War Studies Journal*, III (1998), 119.

densities were a basic precondition for a strong German right wing, and Belgium's network was indeed a lure. The head of the railway section of the general staff, Heinrich von Staabs, had encouraged increasing deployments north of the Moselle from 1903.[7]

Undoubtedly Schlieffen recognized the benefits of greater radicalism in the use of the right wing. The results of a second staff ride of 1904 were not vastly different from the first, but on this occasion Schlieffen criticized his commanders for not persisting with their advance against the line Lille–Verdun. He was now of the view that by moving into open space and ignoring developments on their left, the armies of the German right wing would threaten Paris, while the French armies crossing the Rhine into southern Germany would have put themselves out of the battle. Thus, the assumptions of the December 1905 memorandum are apparent in Schlieffen's conclusions. But they themselves had never been tested in any war game or staff ride—and significantly, the outcome of the second staff ride of 1904 was a French victory, in which the German 1st army was isolated and the bulk of the 2nd and 3rd armies encircled as they moved to respond to the invasion of southern Germany. What we know of the 1905 staff ride for the western front illustrates similar themes. Schlieffen said that the right wing would pass through Belgium, leaving Liège and Namur to its left and Antwerp to its right, and would then move on Paris from the north. But as the exercise progressed the battle was, as before, fought out around the frontiers and Metz, with the Germans responding to the opportunities created by French initiatives.

Nothing in these exercises suggested that Schlieffen had devised a solution to Germany's two-front dilemma. He had allocated sixty-five divisions for the 1903/4 deployment plan in the west, leaving only ten in the east, and yet had still not produced a decisive victory in short order. He recognized that in the event of an active eastern front he would have far fewer troops to play with in the west. The plans for the second deployment option, that which required simultaneous operations in the east, tended to divide the German forces in the ratio two-thirds for the west to one-third for the east. They effectively eliminated any chances of early success in the west. For all the pull of a deployment exclusively in the west, Schlieffen never ceased to update the two-front scenario. Moreover, his very last war game, conducted in November–December 1905, focused on a possible initial victory over Russia rather than France. Given his numerical inferiority, particularly when split over both fronts, his solution was to let both his enemies take the initiative and to rely on a counter-stroke for success. He deemed the chances of this to be greater in East Prussia, where the Masurian lakes provided a screen behind which the Germans could

[7] Zuber, *War in History*, VI (1999), 275–96; Bucholz, *Moltke, Schlieffen*, 103, 107, 125, 145, 196–200; Stig Förster, *Militärgeschichtliche Mitteilungen*, 54, (1995), 74–8.

manoeuvre and where Königsberg could become an entrenched camp for the collection of an army to strike against the Russian flank from the north. Thus, in this exercise only ten corps and ten reserve divisions were directed west-wards, but thirteen corps and twelve reserve divisions eastwards. These were the most the railway network could support. They were not sufficient to annihilate the Russians, but the exercise showed that they would enable a victory big enough to allow the Germans to disengage and redeploy to the west by the thirty-fifth day after mobilization. Schlieffen assumed that in the interim the French would themselves have broken Belgian neutrality by advan-cing along both banks of the Meuse. His aim was to move outside the French left. Resting his calculations on the assumption that Belgium would be Ger-many's ally, not France's, he planned to get three corps into Antwerp by the thirty-third day and a further three by the thirty-seventh. 'The further west this [German] attack fell the more effective it would be, as it would threaten not only the enemy's flank, but also his rear.'[8] He argued that the French would be so preoccupied with their own plans that they would not realize the danger from the north until the thirty-sixth day, too late to prevent their being enveloped in the Ardennes.

Schlieffen's final memorandum, his so-called 'war plan', therefore takes to an extreme trajectory one aspect of the thinking he had already developed. Undoubtedly, the idea of a massive envelopment through Belgium had become stronger between 1892 and 1905, but it was predicated on an increasing readi-ness to make major assumptions and to take massive risks. In his conclusions to the 1905 staff ride Schlieffen bore testimony to his own recklessness. Because the German army in the west would be smaller than the French, even after the redeployment from the east, its own flanks and rear were more at risk from envelopment than were those of the French: 'Such an action requires a focused leader, who has an iron character and who possesses a determined will to win.'[9] While he was in post, this side of his thinking was held in check by the tests to which war games and staff rides had exposed it. In retirement, such balances were removed. Schlieffen's refusal to modify his plans in the light of the resources available to Germany became more fixed. His more excessive state-ments about the decisive nature of envelopment and the strength of the right wing date from this period. And, unlike his war plans, they were published. Schlieffen's main tenets—the immediate adoption of the offensive as the means to defend Germany, the decision to put the weight in the west, and the conviction that the war could be short—now became fixed. The feasibility of all three came to rest on the decisiveness of envelopment. Much of his energy

---

[8] Foley, *War Studies Journal*, IV (1999), 103; see also III (1998), 117–33; Zuber, *War in History*, VI (1999), 117–33.
[9] Foley, *War Studies Journal*, IV (1999), 113.

leading up to retirement and after it was devoted to the acquisition of evidence to support these assumptions.

Schlieffen saw himself as an intellectual, just as Moltke the elder had done, but he used ideas in a very different way. While he was in office the academic syllabus of the general staff was narrowed, while the span of military history which it studied broadened. This focus on concrete examples seemed to imply a more rigorous and ongoing approach to the study of war than was possible through the simple acceptance of abstract and generalized principles. But military history, initially Frederick the Great's conduct of the Seven Years War, and especially the battle of Leuthen, and latterly Hannibal's victory over the Romans at Cannae, was exploited to justify Schlieffen's central propositions. In both battles inferior numbers had triumphed by bringing their weight against the flank of the enemy. But the thinking was very selective. The military historian Hans Delbrück engaged in a long-running exchange with the German general staff, contending that Frederick had fought a war of attrition, and had settled for only limited success. The failure of the two to agree arose in part because they were not comparing like with like. Delbrück was considering an entire war; Schlieffen—reflecting the whole bias of his planning activity as chief of the general staff—focused on a single campaign. In rejecting Delbrück's interpretation, Schlieffen also limited his own under-standing of future war. He saw war as a professional soldier's activity, suscept-ible to rational management and fine calculation. His decision to elevate Cannae rather than Leuthen to the status of a prototype perhaps reflected his inability to come to terms with Delbrück's more sophisticated analysis of Frederickian strategy. At Cannae Hannibal had left his centre weak, so that the Romans had broken in only to be crushed by the two strong Carthaginian wings. But there were methodological problems here too. Hannibal's success lay in the realm of battlefield tactics; the fire-effect of modern armies might prevent the closing on the centre and front which had characterized Cannae. Furthermore, Schlieffen was endeavouring to apply precepts derived from tactics to operational strategy. Not only was the analogy incomplete, it also failed to acknowledge that, despite his victory, Hannibal had lost the war. In the context of the Carthaginian wars as a whole, Cannae was not a decisive battle but an incident in a long war of exhaustion. The same could be said of Leuthen. The battle of Königgrätz in 1866, in which Schlieffen himself had served, was the real—if less frequently expressed—prop to his thinking. Thus, Schlieffen's use of history was a bogus intellectualism. On staff rides, junior officers worked through possible alternatives in their annual revisions of Germany's war plans. In doing so, they gained a thorough training as well as an unbounded admiration for Schlieffen. But Schlieffen's central propositions were never seriously challenged. The function of analysis was not to revise but to confirm the leading features of his thought.

By 1905 Schlieffen had developed a view of operations where mobilization, deployment, and manoeuvre all flowed into each other. The focus of the general staff on these aspects of war elbowed out tactics, and the decline in the rotation of staff officers between general staff appointments and appointments with troops helped to widen an emerging gap between the two levels of war. Field service regulations and tactical manuals were drawn up by commissions answerable to the war minister, and training was in the hands of the commanding generals of corps areas. The day-to-day thinking of the bulk of the army on the basic grammar of warfare lay outside the competence of the chief of the general staff.[10] It seemed as though what Schlieffen envisaged was a succession of engagements rather than a climactic battle. The right wing of the German army was to envelop the French left, successively forcing it back from the river lines of the Meuse, the Aisne, the Somme, the Oise, the Marne, and the Seine, preventing it from withdrawing into central France, and pushing it eastward. The purpose was the annihilation and surrender of the French army. But of this final destructive act—how, where, and when it was to take place— Schlieffen said remarkably little. 'No order', one officer recalled of his days at the war academy, 'that would have been given *in* combat was ever discussed, hardly even a real order *for* combat.'[11]

Some attributed Schlieffen's departure in 1905 to his advocacy of a preventive war in the first Moroccan crisis. But he was now aged 74 and his retirement was already planned in 1904. His successor as chief of the general staff was Helmuth von Moltke the younger. Despite his pedigree, Moltke was not the obvious selection. His experience of staff-work was limited, he had been a guards officer, and his career had been at court. The choice, therefore, was very much the Kaiser's own. Most professional observers expected Moltke to be replaced in the event of war. At times Moltke himself seemed to share this low estimation of his own abilities, and initially resisted the idea of his appointment. He combined two qualities—fatalism and intelligence—which not only stood uneasily with each other, but also were ill-adapted to the exercise of decisive leadership. His fatalism, manifested in his response to the so-called 'war-council' of 8 December 1912, reflected both his personal philosophy and his wider sense of the general decline of his own social order.[12] His intelligence meant that he could see alternative interpretations more clearly than Schlieffen, but then, all-too conscious of their relative merits, he could not make a choice between them. 'In my opinion,' he told the Kaiser before assuming office,

---

[10] Foley, *War Studies Journal*, IV (1999), 99 (n. 4).
[11] General Marx, quoted in Samuels, *Command or control?*, 23; see also Bucholz, *Moltke, Schlieffen*, 189–91.
[12] Hull, *The Kaiser and his entourage*, 232–5, 239–42.

it is in any case very difficult, if not impossible, to picture now what form a modern war in Europe would take. We have at present a period of over thirty years of peace behind us and I believe that in our outlook we have become very unwarlike in many ways. How, if at all, it will be possible to lead as a unit the immense armies we shall create, no man, I think, can know in advance.[13]

Thus, if military history played a role in shaping Moltke's thought, its effects were more pragmatic and less idealized than in the case of Schlieffen. Increasingly, Schlieffen's thinking was politically unrealistic in its neglect of the implications of breaching Belgian and Dutch neutrality, and militarily suspect in its attempt to plot a self-contained war right through to its final victory. After the Franco-Prussian War the older Moltke had a staff of 154 men to mobilize an army of 700,000, a railroad network of 45,000 kilometres for its concentration, and reckoned on a war that might last a year. By 1913 his nephew's staff numbered 650 men to mobilize an army up to five times the size, with double the railway network, and yet there was talk of Germany completing a campaign in six weeks. Numbers and space were expanding, while time was contracting. Schlieffen recognized the difficulty of command in such circumstances, but his solutions—the dissemination of a common doctrine and the emphasis on prior planning—downgraded the flexibility to deal with the unexpected. The younger Moltke, on the other hand, appreciated even better than Schlieffen that no plan was likely to survive its first contact with the enemy. However, his greater realism merely confirmed his pessimism. He anticipated a long and arduous struggle. He recognized that the French could not be relied on to conform to the expectations of Schlieffen's more grandiose propositions: in May 1914 he disarmingly told Conrad that in a war with France 'I will do what I can. We are not superior to the French.' Schlieffen had seen the fruit of his labours as a formula for victory; for Moltke it was a last resort.

Symptomatic of Schlieffen's optimism and fundamental to Moltke's pessimism were their differing attitudes to manpower. The plan which Schlieffen outlined for the minister of war in 1905 required ninety-four divisions for its execution: Germany had barely sixty. Schlieffen squared his aspirations with reality by proposing to incorporate reservists in the order of battle from the very outset of the campaign. For Moltke such a solution was a measure of how desperate were the expedients of the 1905 memorandum. Logically, reservists required more fire-support than active troops; in practice, the reserve corps had no heavy artillery and half the divisional allocation of field artillery. When the Landwehr went off to war in 1914 it still wore the old blue uniforms and not the field grey adopted by the active army in 1910. Admittedly, even Schlieffen embraced the reservists with reluctance. It was an arrangement that affronted

---

[13] Quoted in Barnett, *The swordbearers*, 33–4.

professional sensibilities about training and fitness; it also left the commander with no general reserve to deploy in the course of the battle, nor any fall-back in the event of a long war. Thus did Schlieffen's preconceptions about the nature of the war interact with his planning. On mobilization in 1914 the German field army's strength rose from 800,675 men to 2,100,000. Reservists, in addition to increasing regular battalions from 663 to 1,090 men, made up fourteen-and-a-half corps in 1914 (as against twenty-five active corps). The older categories of men (those aged 28 to 45), who formed the Landwehr, Landstürm, and Ersatz units, constituted a separate army of occupation, even less well-equipped than the reserve corps but numbering a further 1,700,000 men.

Schlieffen would have preferred to increase the active army, but he had been opposed by von Einem, the minister of war. Some have seen this clash as the real source of the pressure for Schlieffen's retirement at the end of 1905. Certainly the resolution of the manpower issue points to the danger of exaggerating the powers of the chief of the German general staff in peacetime. The central debate over the size of the army in peace revolved less around operational needs and more around funding, and it was the minister of war, at the interface between the army and the Reichstag, who had the major role in framing policy.

One argument used by Einem in his opposition to the expansion of the army rested on its role as an agent of domestic order. The smaller the army, the more it could confine its recruiting disproportionately to rural areas. In 1914 only 5.84 per cent of reservists came from big cities. Thus, the army was kept comparatively free of socialism, making it a reliable tool of the established order in the event of revolution. Furthermore, a small army required a small officer corps, and it was therefore easier to sustain the latter's aristocratic ethos. But although he played on the army's domestic functions, Einem was not claiming that these were its principal mission. If the argument in relation to the social order had force, it was only in the context of the pace at which change was effected, not of the implementation of change per se. Headlong expansion would do more than erode the army as an instrument of counter-revolution, it would also diminish its fighting effectiveness; gradual growth, on the other hand, would allow training and equipment levels to keep step with numerical expansion.

The prime professional issue, therefore, was the need to balance quality against quantity. When forced to express a preference in 1888, Moltke the elder had opted for the former.[14] By 1899 Einem was the spokesman for this view: greater mass, he told Schlieffen, was not decisive in itself but depended on the quality of its commanders. What worried him about a larger army was that the funds would not be forthcoming to ensure that it had equipment levels commensurate with its size. He would rather have more machine-guns than

---

[14] Bucholz, *Moltke, Schlieffen*, 93–5.

more men. In part, therefore, the debate was about whether the goal in the army's expansion should be more men, or whether more armament would be a better subsititute.[15]

Einem also wished to establish a steady pace in growth for parliamentary reasons. Like Tirpitz in his management of the navy's finances, Einem viewed a fixed cycle—in the army's case one of five years—as the best way to curtail the Reichstag's powers of intervention. A request for supplementary credits out-with the five-year cycle might lead to annual reviews, and thus make the army's manning and equipment levels much more volatile and much less amenable to long-term planning.[16]

At first the younger Moltke embraced Einem's position, which was of course also the one favoured by his uncle. The army's budget increased between 1905 and 1909, but the number of men rose by only 10,000 against a possible ceiling of 80,000. Up to and including the 1911 army bill arms took priority over manpower. Thus, the chief of the general staff and the minister of war marched in step once more. But from 1911 Moltke began to call for more men, and in doing so reflected the needs of operational planning more wholeheartedly than he had hitherto. Intellectually, the position of the War Ministry was unchanged; in practice, Einem's successor, Heeringen, prompted by Bethmann Hollweg's anxiety to outflank the navy, was now prepared to bring the War Ministry into line with the general staff. Therefore, the 1912 Army bill increased the infantry of the active army, acknowledging the general staff's premiss that the opening battles could be decisive.[17] In the process it abandoned the evenness of the five-year cycle. Even more importantly, it subordinated financial policy to military policy. The theoretical brake on the army's expansion—that (like the navy) it had hit the buffers imposed by the Reich's system of taxation—was not applied; the army's targets in 1912 and 1913 were approved before their financing had been fully resolved.[18]

The net result was that the German peacetime army doubled in size between 1880 and 1913, from 434,000 to 864,000. Furthermore, the pressure for expansion overrode social conservatism. The numbers of aristocrats in the officer corps fell from 65 per cent in 1865 to 30 per cent in 1913. The general staff conformed to the main trend: by 1914 only 40 per cent of its officers were titled. Its bourgeois members included such rising stars as Groener and Erich Ludendorff, the chief of operations. Their ethos was careerist, and their allegiance to Hohenzollern dynasticism proportionately weaker. Arguably,

---

[15] Storz, *Kriegsbild und Rüstung*, 295–7, 323–7.

[16] Herrmann, *Arming of Europe*, 66–7.

[17] Ibid. 162–71; Stevenson, *Armaments and the coming of war*, 97, 179, 210–11, 292–6; Kroboth, *Finanzpolitik des Deutschen Reiches*, 136.

[18] Kroboth, *Finanzpolitik des Deutschen Reiches*, 192, 210–11; Geyer, *Deutsche Rüstungspolitik*, 84–5; for the argument that domestic politics did set the size of the army, see Ferguson, *Historical Journal*, XXXV (1992), 725–52.

the effects were divisive. The overall shift was offset by the concentration of nobles in certain prestigious regiments, notably the cavalry and those from Prussia, and it was these whose company the Kaiser found more congenial.[19]

Moltke was not necessarily any happier. Although he was successful in getting an increase of 136,000 men in 1912 and 1913, he had asked for 300,000. The 1912 army estimates calculated that 540,000 adult males received no form of military training. Moltke and, to a greater extent, Ludendorff aspired to the creation of a true nation in arms. The worries of the ministry of war about training and equipment levels now resurfaced. In the summer of 1914 Heeringen's successor, Erich von Falkenhayn, was prepared to accept the training of all able-bodied German males as a long-term objective, but to begin in 1916, and not to be fully implemented until 1926. He regarded heavy artillery, fortification, and enhanced levels of training as more immediate needs.[20] Therefore, when war broke out, although the German army had expanded its hope of ultimate superiority still resided in its qualitative edge. Germany and Austria-Hungary could mobilize 136 divisions to 182 of the three Entente powers.

By 1914, therefore, Moltke was no nearer the solution of the dilemma that had preoccupied his predecessor and his uncle. Although he had more men, he still did not have enough to resolve the conundrum of a threat on both fronts. His central dilemma was where to deploy the additional troops. In 1905 Russia was weakened by war and revolution. Throughout his tenure of office Moltke had to reckon on the increasing speed of Russian mobilization, and finally to come to terms with the fact that, however fast his victory in the west, the Russian army could be operational before he could turn to face it. The solution to this problem was not to jettison Schlieffen's preference for an attack in the west first. The eastern railway network was too poor for rapid operations, and the Russians could retreat, so trading space for time. Instead, the December 1912 crisis forced Moltke to follow through the logic implicit in Schlieffen's thinking: the Germans ceased even to update their plan for operations in the east. Increasingly, their response to Russia's opening moves was to rely on their Austro-Hungarian allies.

Moltke's development of Schlieffen's planning assumptions rested on the exercises of 1904 and 1905, and not on the December 1905 memorandum. The latter had expected the French army's movements to conform to those of the German. It tended to assume that the French would obligingly sit in defence of their eastern frontier while the Germans bore down on their rear. Indeed, both the need for, and the rationale of, the great flank march only made sense if they did do this. Nor in the particular context of December 1905, with the Russian army disabled and thus unlikely to mount a reciprocal action in the

---

[19] Schulte, *Die deutsche Armee*, pp. xxxv–xxxviii; Bucholz, *Moltke, Schlieffen*, 133–4.

[20] Stevenson, *Armaments and the coming of war*, 361; Afflerbach, *Falkenhayn*, 133–5; Herrmann, *Arming of Europe*, 184–91.

east, was this presumption unreasonable. Schlieffen had fortified Metz and Strasbourg in order to render a French attack into Lorraine an unpromising proposition. But his staff rides had never made the same assumptions of the French as did the memorandum for the war minister. Moltke was even more persuaded that the French would not conform to a German agenda.

He devoted more attention than had his predecessor to the collection of intelligence, and became increasingly persuaded that the French might try to seek battle in the open field and might therefore advance either from Verdun into Luxembourg or from a front between Metz and the Vosges into Lorraine. Faster mobilization and improved railway construction gave them the choice as to which it was to be. Since the planned envelopment was no more than a means to bring Germany's greatest possible strength against the French army, and was not an end in itself, it followed that Germany's plans must recognize and incorporate possible French intentions. If the German plan did not do this, operationally it would fail to fix the French from the front while the envelopment was effected, and it would also expose south Germany and the Ruhr to invasion.

Evidence as to the evolution of Moltke's exact thinking is fragmentary up until 1911–12 and virtually absent thereafter. In the 1906 staff ride he did direct his main attack in the west through Belgium, but he was unhappy with the outcome. As he believed that the French would attack in Lorraine, he reckoned that the decisive encounter would take place there before any envelopment would take effect. The main purpose of the right wing, therefore, was to counter-attack through Metz in order to take advantage of the fact that the French would have abandoned the security of their fortifications. By 1908 his expectation that the British would support the French, but that neither would be the first to infringe Belgian neutrality, pulled the possible direction of the French offensive into the Ardennes. He continued to plan on a major envelopment of the French between the Meuse and Verdun, not to push south in the direction of Paris.[21] In 1909–10 Moltke provided for a new army (the 7th) of eight divisions to cover upper Alsace and so support the 6th army in Lorraine. The possibility of the 7th army transferring to the right wing was studied, but gradually became less important as the idea of a decisive battle in Lorraine gained ground. On a staff ride in 1912 Moltke planned, in the event of a French attack between Metz and the Vosges, to defend on the left until all the troops not required for the right wing could be brought south-west through Metz and on to the French flank. Moltke was thus working a number of options into the German plan, including both a possible thrust from the centre and, more significantly, a true 'Cannae', an envelopment from both wings, the left as well as the right.

[21] Zuber, *War in History*, VI (1999), 297–304.

The fact that Moltke had added eight divisions to the German left wing and not to the right became, after the war, the key criticism of Groener and Liddell Hart. The balance between the two wings was changed from 7:1 in the 1905 memorandum to 3:1 in the plan put into effect in 1914. Liddell Hart's argument assumed that an army deployed the length of the German western frontier would behave as a united mass, gaining impetus on its right specifically from the weakness of its left. An army, however, is a combination of individuals, and not a weight obeying the laws of physics. None of the criticisms of Moltke's changes voiced after 1918 were vented before 1914. The right wing itself was not quite as strong as envisaged in the 1905 memorandum, but its tasks were lighter since Moltke did not expect it to deal with Holland nor to march as far as Antwerp before it turned south-west. Ludendorff, who was responsible for much of the detail, was happy with the 1909 version. Schlieffen recognized the wisdom of what his successor had done. In 1912 he accepted that the French were more likely to mount an offensive than had been the case in 1905, and he conceded that therefore the Germans must be ready to attack and to exploit a possible breakthrough at any point along the front. The strength of the army on the right wing should be effectively double that of any other army, but its role now was to lead the whole line forward. Thus, if the 1st army was checked, the adjacent armies would be able to exploit the opportunities created by the enemy's own move to counteract it.

The real difference between Schlieffen and Moltke did not, therefore, lie in any differences in operational thought. The crux was Schlieffen's inner certainty about the correctness of his own prescriptions; Moltke, on the other hand, was reluctant to be dogmatic. By trying to anticipate the options open to the French, Moltke had created a number of possibilities but no categorical plan. Schlieffen's thinking, for all his acceptance in 1912 of the wisdom of Moltke's emendations, still at bottom anticipated victory through the use of a strong right wing. Moltke's plan had at least two different options—the one adumbrated by Schlieffen, and the other in which an advance through Belgium could create the conditions for success elsewhere, probably in Lorraine. Moltke was intelligent enough to see the limitations of what could be achieved. But the consequence was that he lacked convictions of his own and could not, therefore, stamp his doctrine on the minds of the general staff. Schlieffen had lived by his belief in envelopment, and his certainty that only through that could a decisive and annihilating victory be achieved. Schlieffen's critics, and especially Schlichting and the popular military writer Bernhardi, argued that breakthrough battles would also have to be fought, that breakthrough and flank attacks should often be combined, and that therefore command should be more pragmatic and less mechanistic. Moltke recognized the force of all this. But the result was near-anarchy. The 1910 instructions for higher command sensibly recognized the fire-effect of modern weaponry in enforcing dispersion on the one hand and in favouring envelopment on the other. They therefore observed that 'too broad a front entails the danger of a break-through, a too narrow one of becoming encircled and out-flanked'.[22] By having it both ways, such efforts to define doctrine provided little indication as to how an individual army commander would respond in particular circumstances. Yet the same publication accepted that a campaign would be made up of a succession of independent corps and army battles which would combine to produce an outcome. It therefore presumed that a common approach would characterize those battles, not least to permit the supreme command to be able to co-ordinate them.

Even had he wished to do so, Moltke could not have added any additional manpower to the German right wing. His chosen deployment area was too small to admit of any greater initial concentration. Schlieffen's intention to infringe Dutch neutrality by crossing the so-called Maastricht appendix, the part of Holland which projects south between Belgium and Germany, was not acceptable to Moltke. Recognizing the possibility of a long war and the dangers of a British blockade of German commerce, Moltke appreciated the need for a friendly neutral adjacent to Germany through which overseas trade could be maintained. He therefore narrowed the point across which the right wing would advance so that it came south of Dutch territory. Directly in its path, and mastering the principal railway lines, lay the Belgian fortress of Liège. The corollary, therefore, of Moltke's decision to respect Holland's neutrality was the need to seize Liège before it could delay the German advance. Much of the urgency with which Moltke pressed mobilization by 30 July derived from the necessity, dictated by his own war plan, to attack Liège by the third day of mobilization.

German self-interest, not an enlightened approach to international rights, determined Moltke's decision to revoke Schlieffen's intention to invade Holland. Similar considerations prevailed in regard to Belgium. Schlieffen's conviction, that if the Germans did not violate Belgian neutrality the French would, was widely shared in Germany. The general staff was genuinely surprised that its invasion of Belgium should have become a *casus belli* for Britain. Moltke recognized how important Belgian neutrality was to British interests, but had assumed that what would determine Britain's behaviour was not Belgium but its commitment to France. The stronger the Entente seemed— and the 1911 crisis confirmed its resilience—the more the breach of Belgian neutrality became militarily necessary but diplomatically unimportant. It would be the act of war between France and Germany which would bring in the British, not the passage of the German army through the Low Countries.

---

[22] Cited in Wallach, *Dogma*, 78; see also Borgert, 'Grundzüge', 474–6; Hughes, *Journal of Military History*, LIX (1995), 272–3.

Therefore, although they both hoped that the British Expeditionary Force might be depleted by the needs of imperial security, neither Schlieffen nor Moltke was in much doubt about its commitment to European land operations. In the main, they correctly assumed that it would be deployed alongside the French in Belgium and northern France, but they also considered the possibility of its use in support of maritime operations by landings either in Jutland or on the Scheldt and Rhine estuaries. Indeed, the latter eventuality would confirm what for them would be the more serious consequence of Britain's entry to the war, the superiority of the Royal Navy over the German. Uncertainty with regard to even local maritime supremacy was itself one rationalization for mastering the Low Countries. In its presumptions as to Britain's intentions the German general staff showed how it projected its own strategic outlook, its cavalier approach to the question of neutrality, on to its opponents.

German war plans, therefore, went through a progression, from Schlieffen's allegedly taking little account of French intentions to Moltke's taking too much. Both chiefs of the general staff have consequently been criticized, albeit on diametrically opposed grounds. French planning moved through a similar sequence, but in reverse order. France's military inferiority in the 1870s placed its army's calculations as to German intentions at the heart of its planning effort. However, with increasing confidence, and particularly with the national revival after 1911, the French general staff argued that by taking the initiative it could force conformity to France's will. Thus, as in the German case, the mood for a defensive strategy transformed itself into an operational offensive. But, even in the context of relative optimism, France's generals never completely lost sight of the fact that, if war came, its purpose would be to defend their nation against Germany. Therefore, gaining assertiveness did not blind French planners to the need to take account of Germany's intentions. Even so, the French got it wrong. They failed to realize the extent of Germany's proposed swing through Belgium. In part this was a product of their own assumptions. However, just as importantly, it was also a natural result of any objective consideration of intelligence on the German army. The significance of the German right wing is clear in hindsight. But in the decade immediately before the war the Germans debated the strength and the roles of both wings; and it was on the left wing that reinforcements were placed. The fact that the French themselves planned with more attention to Lorraine than to Belgium was both a product of their own proclivities and a fair reflection of the state of the German railways, the disposition of the German army, and the politics surrounding Belgian neutrality.

The development of French war plans between 1871 and 1914 is an excellent illustration of how long-term capital investment can determine the direction of strategy. The possession of plant forces any shift in policy to be incremental and gradual rather than fundamental and revolutionary. The defence of France planned by General Séré de Rivières in the 1870s rested on the creation of a series of forts between Verdun and Toul. Gaps north and south of these points were designed to channel any German attack, where it would be met by mobile forces able to strike against the German flanks. Major railway construction, begun in 1877, was to enable the concentration of fifteen army corps on the German border by the twelfth to fourteenth day of mobilization. A total of 166 forts, forty-three secondary works, and 250 batteries had been completed by 1884, at a cost of 660 million francs. But within a year the development of the high-explosive shell, which with a delayed-action fuse could penetrate before it detonated, challenged the construction principles on which Séré de Rivières's system rested. The response to the new artillery, including the use of reinforced concrete and armoured cupolas for the guns, added considerably to the cost of fortification. Conveniently and simultaneously, French strategic thought shifted, Georges Gilbert criticizing forts on France's frontiers as equally useless whether to the conduct of major battles or as havens in the event of defeat. After 1888, therefore, the French narrowed their efforts to the improvement of the forts of Verdun, Toul, Épinal, and Belfort: by 1914 not even a quarter of the defensive perimeters of these four had been fully modernized. But, both in 1914 itself and in 1916, France would derive considerable benefit from the forts and from the railway communications linking them to Paris. And, in the immediate term, by the mid-1890s a system of defence had been created that was sufficient to convince Schlieffen that a German attack from Lorraine across France's eastern frontier would be an unprofitable business.[23]

The operational basis of Séré de Rivières's assumptions proved more resilient than the technical. Influenced by their own defeat in 1870 and by *Sadowa*, H. Bonnal's study of Prussia's defeat of Austria in 1866, published in 1894, the French reckoned that the Germans would seek an early offensive, manoeuvring independently with a view to converging on the battlefield. The French answer was to adopt a flexible defence, keeping their forces concentrated so as to be able to counter-attack and defeat the dispersed elements of the German advance. As on the other side of the Rhine, doctrine was hammered out through the use of historical examples—in France's case Napoleon's campaign in 1813–14. The key element in this defensive strategy was the use of advance guards. Their first task was to identify the direction of the enemy thrust; but they had to have an offensive capability to reconnoitre effectively, to force the enemy to reveal his strength, and—most important of all—to fix him so as to limit his subsequent freedom of movement. Embodied in the use of advance guards, therefore, was the idea of the encounter battle. The main force

[23] Mitchell, *Victors and vanquished*, 49–70, 111–15; J.-C. Jauffret, 'Le Bouclier', in Pedroncini (ed.), *Histoire militaire de la France*, iii. 30–6; P. Rocolle, *2000 ans de fortification française*, i. 265–94.

MAP 4. ALSACE AND LORRAINE

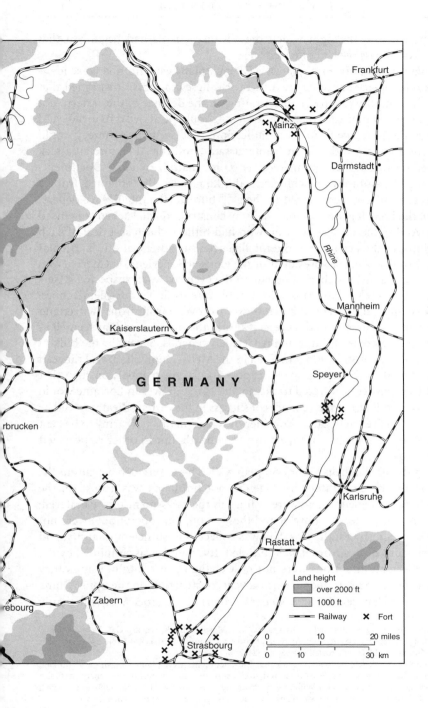

Frankfurt

✕
✕ ✕
✕ Mainz

Darmstadt

Rhine

Mannheim

Kaiserslautern

G E R M A N Y

Speyer

✕✕✕
✕✕
✕✕

rbrucken

✕

Karlsruhe

Rastatt

Zabern

Land height

over 2000 ft
1000 ft

Railway   ✕ Fort

ebourg

✕✕ ✕
✕   ✕
✕ Strasbourg
✕

0   10   20 miles
0   10   30 km

would be fed into the fight which the advance guards had begun, so that defence would pass over to offence.[24]

The plan finalized in 1903, plan XV (French plans were numbered sequentially as one replaced another), worked with these concepts. It assumed that Belgium's neutrality justified concentrating on the defence of the eastern, not the northern, frontier, and that the Germans should be allowed to invade and then be counter-attacked. However, indications that Germany's strategy would favour envelopment rather than frontal assault, and that therefore an attack would come through Belgium, received confirmation in 1904. Documents containing the outlines of Schlieffen's thinking, allegedly obtained from a German staff officer, were passed to the $2^{\text{ème}}$ bureau (the intelligence department) of the French general staff.[25] Railway construction at Aachen convinced General André, the minister of war, who had hitherto been sceptical of such suggestions, of the accuracy of the intelligence. But others, and in particular General Brugère, the vice-president of the Conseil Supérieur de Guerre (who was the commander-in-chief designate in the event of war), suspected a German ruse. Brugère's main reasons for doubt were to find subsequent echoes. First, Germany did not have the manpower to cover a front from Switzerland to the Channel unless it used its reserves from the outset, and that seemed as unlikely to Brugère as it did to many German generals. Secondly, the bulk of German railway construction remained in the Metz–Thionville area. France, if it concentrated to the north, would expose its eastern frontier; on the other hand, if Germany concentrated to the north, its manpower in Lorraine would be so weakened that France's chances of success in the eastern theatre would be enhanced. The French began to consider the creation of a new army to be kept in reserve to meet a German thrust from the north, but in other respects left plan XV alone.

In 1907 the French began work on plan XVI. There were deficiencies in the collection of French military intelligence; not until 1913 was a post on the Belgian border opened. There were failings in the assessment of the material: relations between the $2^{\text{ème}}$ bureau and the $3^{\text{ème}}$ bureau (operations) were not intimate. But in general the raw data was collected in sufficient quantity, and the conclusions drawn from it well founded. Its analysis was simplified by the fact that German intentions were not now changing as continuously as they had in the period 1897 to 1905. Their railway construction on the upper Rhine had continued apace. By 1908 General Henri de Lacroix was sufficiently

---

[24] Much of the above is informed by discussions with Matthew Buck. See also Gat, *Development of military thought*, 128–30, 138, 169–72; Akavia, *Decisive victory and correct doctrine*, 25–6; of older literature, Gascouin, *Le Triomphe de l'idée*, 20–2, 126.

[25] Contamine, *La Révanche*, 96–7, argues that the documents were planted by the $2^{\text{ème}}$ bureau, themselves convinced of German intentions and anxious to persuade the rest of the general staff. On French war plans generally, see also Williamson, *Politics of grand strategy*; J. K. Tannenbaum, 'French estimates of Germany's operational war plans', in E. R. May (ed.), *Knowing one's enemies*, 150–71.

convinced of Germany's operational attachment to envelopment to conclude that Germany would invade Belgium. Plan XVI, which was approved in 1909, therefore shifted France's putative deployment more to the north-west, and made provision for an army to cover the frontier with Belgium and Luxembourg. On the whole it was assumed that the Germans would come south of Liège, east of the Meuse, and through the Ardennes on to Verdun and Sedan. Thus, the plan added to the provisions of its predecessor rather than replaced it: by not taking on board the possibility of an advance north and west of the Meuse the French avoided the dilemma of whether or not to leave their forces in Lorraine weakened and their eastern frontier exposed.

In 1910–11, however, a radical reappraisal of plan XVI was proposed by General Victor Michel, the new vice-president of the Conseil Supérieur de Guerre. Michel was persuaded that the Germans would cross the Meuse. Reports that the Germans were increasingly using automobiles suggested that they planned to advance over flat, well-roaded terrain. The Belgian plain was a far better avenue for an invasion of France than either the hills of the Ardennes or the fortified area of Lorraine. Secondly, Michel appreciated that, by integrating their reserves, the Germans could extend their front to the north and west. He therefore reckoned on creating a French army of 1.3 million men, with 500,000 of them grouped around Lille and facing north. Michel's plan rested on France, like Germany, using its reserves from the outset of the war. He felt that the restraining factor in France's use of its reserves was the lack of qualified staff officers. He therefore proposed that each reserve regiment should be brigaded with a regular regiment: thus, the existing higher formations—brigades, divisions, and corps—would be effectively doubled in size with no increase in staff.[26]

This issue, the employment of reserves, whether by Germany or by France, became the focus of Michel's proposals. Their cause was not advanced by Michel's personal unpopularity within the army, which saw him as politically too malleable and consequently inconsistent, 'in turn *boulangiste, antidreyfusard, dreyfusard*'.[27] The 3ème bureau rejected the tentative suggestion of the 2ème bureau that the Germans would use their reserves in the front line. The Conseil Supérieur de Guerre accepted the view of the 3ème bureau, and was thus able to turn down Michel's proposed reorganization of France's reserves. The strategic implications of Michel's plan, that the Germans would come north of the Meuse, became peripheral. Michel resigned.

Although their conclusions were related, the judgement of the 3ème bureau was wrong, that of the Conseil Supérieur de Guerre was not. The failure to appreciate the extent to which German planning rested on the use of reserves

[26] Ministère de la Guerre, *Les Armées françaises*, Tome I, 1er volume, 13–15, and annexes, 7–17.
[27] Michel, *Gallieni*, 258; see also Messimy, *Mes souvenirs*, 74–5.

was the single biggest mistake in French calculations. Because the French had a low opinion of the quality of their own reserves, they were reluctant to accept that the Germans could form a better estimate of theirs. But it does not necessarily follow that the reason that the French could not convince themselves that the Germans would use their reservists in the front line, and would therefore swing west of the Meuse, was because they themselves were determined not to admit their own reservists into their initial order of battle.[28] Indeed, all the indications suggested the opposite.

In 1911, when the Conseil Supérieur de Guerre rejected Michel's proposals, France's reservists were at a nadir of inefficiency. Because France took a larger proportion of its available manpower, the standard of fitness of France's reservists was much lower than that of Germany. The 1905 law, which had established two-year service in France, had reduced the size of the active army but had created a larger French reserve. However, the training areas and the money required to make the reservists efficient were not forthcoming. In 1907 36 per cent of reservists, excluding those excused because of the needs of agriculture, had failed to report for service.[29] Even more serious was the lack of officers. The impact of the Dreyfus affair, the efforts by André positively to republicanize the officer corps through the management of promotions, and the use of the army to suppress domestic disorder had all contributed to declining morale. Applications to the military academy at St Cyr had fallen from 1,895 in 1900 to 871 in 1911, and re-enlistment by NCOs from 72,000 to 41,000.[30] Measures to boost the number of reserve officers, including a requirement that all pupils at the grandes écoles should receive military training, were part of the 1905 law. But supply still could not match the demands of plan XVI, which assumed the employment of 463 reserve battalions. (Plan XV had not only rejected the initial use of reserves but had also reckoned on ultimately using only 320 reserve battalions.) The reduction in the number of reserve battalions to 401 for employment in plan XVI's successor was a deliberate attempt to improve the ratio of officers to men so as to enhance the ability to integrate the reserves with the regulars. It was a measure adopted, not because reservists were not to take their place in the line, but because they were.[31]

The specific issue over which Michel fell was yet another aspect of this quality-versus-quantity argument. He planned to double the numbers of front-line infantry without any increase in artillery. Dubail, the chief of the general staff, called for 216 additional guns, both light field howitzers and

---

[28] This is the argument of Snyder, *Ideology of the offensive*, chs. 2 and 3.

[29] Jauffret, *Revue historique des armées*, (1989), 35.

[30] Watt, *Dare call it treason*, 31; on the French army generally in this period, Porch, *March to the Marne*; on Michel's proposal, Rocolle, *L'Hécatombe des generaux*, 173–6.

[31] J.-C. Jauffret, 'L'Appel aux armes 1872–1914', in Pedroncini (ed.), *Histoire militaire de la France*, iii. 75–9; Gat, *Development of military doctrine*, 154–9. I have followed Gat's figures for reserve battalions, which are significantly higher than—although proportionally similar to—Jauffret's.

heavy artillery.[32] In 1911, in the middle of the second Moroccan crisis, with war an imminent prospect, the preoccupation of the Conseil Supérieur de Guerre was with immediate combat-readiness. On this particular count Michel displayed little decisiveness and less urgency.

In the aftermath of 1914 the correctness of Michel's diagnosis would be used to castigate his opponents. In particular, Michel's plan became associated with the defensive—not so much because it advocated the defensive (it actually spoke of French attacks both in Belgium and in Lorraine), but because the delays in mobilization and concentration which his proposed organization would impose would lose France the initiative and force it to fight defensively. His advocates therefore contended that his fall was the work of the proponents of the offensive. French military thought—and action—in 1914 was presented as the victim of a semi-mystical belief that the will to win was sufficient to achieve victory. Ferdinand Foch, in his lectures at the École Supérieure de Guerre, had declared: 'A battle won is a battle in which one will not confess oneself beaten.' Thus, the argument ran, in August 1914 the French armies rushed forward, drums beating, with cries of 'à la baionette', only for their red-trousered infantry to fall, casualties of twentieth-century firepower.

Foch was one of two inspirational professors at the École Supérieure de Guerre in the late 1890s and early 1900s. The other was Charles Lanrezac. Stung by the surprise and speed of the defeat in 1870, their operational watchword was security and their solution the doctrine of advance guards. They were not the metaphysical advocates of superior morale suggested by selective use of Foch's more tub-thumping and inspirational dicta. Instead, they presided over a rational analysis of warfare that produced a generation of professionally competent officers, immersed in the pursuit of practical solutions, and exposed to a high level of military debate.[33] Much of this was, inevitably, concerned with the most problematic area of warfare, the tactical offensive.[34] To win, an army had eventually to attack. And yet the development of breech-loading magazine rifles, the addition of machine-guns and quick-firing field artillery, gave the advantage to the defence. The broad solutions were for the attack to approach under cover, to close by breaking into small groups, advancing in bounds, and then to build up fire superiority. Once the attackers had gained fire superiority the final rush forward could follow. But both the last two stages were fraught with difficulties. The acquisition of fire superiority required troops which had dispersed in order to advance to concentrate again:

[32] Stevenson, *Armaments and the coming of war*, 217–18.

[33] Gascouin, *Le Triomphe de l'idée*, 20–2, 126; Brécard, *En Belgique*, 14–15, on Lanrezac; Cailleteau, *Guerres mondiales et conflits contemporains*, 155, (juillet 1989), 17–18; 156, (octobre 1989), 14.

[34] On the French 'spirit of the offensive', see Porch, *March to the Marne*, ch. 11; Snyder, *Ideology of the offensive*, ch. 3; House, *Military affairs*, XL (1976), 164–9; Arnold, *Military Affairs*, XLII (1978), 61–7; Contamine, *Révanche*, ch. 14; *Victoire de la Marne*, 122–36; Michael Howard, 'Men against fire', in Paret (ed.), *Makers of modern strategy*.

in so doing they themselves provided fresh targets for the defence. But if they did not do this and did not gain fire superiority, the final rush forward would end in bloody disaster.

French tactical thought, therefore, became a blend of realism and unavoidable wishful thinking. In a booklet published in 1906 Colonel Loyzeaux de Grandmaison emphasized the role that artillery support would play in giving attacking infantry fire superiority, and stated categorically that a frontal attack across open ground was impossible. On the other hand, infantry had to believe that they could succeed if they were to attack at all. The conquest of fear through discipline and morale became central to tactical possibilities. In the days of close-order drill command and cohesion had prevented troops running away. But dispersion put a premium on individual training and courage. Professionalism was, therefore, increasingly important.

In all this, French tactical thinking was little different, and no less perplexed by the problems of firepower, than that of most other European armies on the eve of the First World War. Like other armies, that of France possessed many officers who were respectful of firepower, recognized the inherent superiority of the defensive, but were trying to integrate fire and movement in order to be able to sustain the attack. Thus, like other armies, its tactical thinking in 1914 was in a state of flux. Yet the uncertainty with regard to tactical doctrine was not in any direct sense the debate which Michel had entered. To be sure, his use of ill-trained reservists would make the prolonged skirmish and firefight stages of the attack harder to manage, and would therefore predispose the French army to the defence. However, Michel's real concerns were not tactical but strategic. His task, like that of his predecessors, was how best to defend France. The debate about reservists therefore spanned two different levels of warfare. The principal accusation to be levelled at the French army before 1914 was its failure to distinguish between these two levels: generalized rhetoric about how to cross the last few hundred yards of a fire-swept battlefield became confused with the specific operational problem of how to respond to war with Germany.

The confusion was exacerbated by the $3^{\text{ème}}$ bureau, a main centre of opposition to Michel's ideas, whose head in 1911 was the same Grandmaison who in 1906 had so presciently recognized the tactical difficulties of the attack. In February 1911 Grandmaison gave two conferences for the general staff derived from his observation of Germany's manoeuvres and the latter's preference for envelopment. He was concerned that the emphasis on envelopment, itself the reflection of the problems of a frontal attack, had percolated so far into operational thought that security, and broad and deep deployment, had become ends in themselves. If French and German forces actually came into contact, the Germans would immediately attack. The French, therefore had, to remember the need to upset the enemy's plans, to press home their own attack on the decisive sector. They should echelon their reserves for that purpose, and not in order to secure or to seek the flanks: taking the initiative would provide its own security. Grandmaison's lectures were designed to inject impetuosity and boldness into French operational thought, to challenge the caution and defensiveness which had characterized it from Séré de Rivières onwards. He was enormously influential. The 1913 edition of the instructions for the conduct of large formations was his work. At a tactical level, these echoed the themes he had voiced in 1906: the need for method and preparation in the attack, and the impossibility of attacking over open ground. But the regulations specifically failed to distinguish between the strategic offensive–defensive and the tactical. Grandmaison failed to provide clarification in the one area where it was most needed.[35]

Michel's resignation became the cue for a major reorganization of France's military administration. Its effect was to unite the general staff and the Conseil Supérieur de Guerre, and so fuse the tactical and operational considerations of the former with the planning activities of the latter. Thus was the position of the 3ème bureau and of Grandmaison elevated. Thus too was confirmed the confusion between strategic and tactical thought.

The Third Republic's anxiety to subordinate its army to civilian control had made it reluctant to embrace the idea of a centralized general staff. The general staff itself was but one of fourteen *services* and *directions* answerable to the minister of war. Its chief was responsible for peacetime training, but in war not he but the vice-president of the Conseil Supérieur de Guerre would be supreme commander. The chances of the minister of war uniting the efforts of these two offices were limited not only by the bureaucratic demarcations within the ministry itself but also by the instability of the republic's governments. In 1911, however, the army's argument, that its purpose in life was professional efficiency, not political intervention, found—in the context of Agadir—a more sympathetic audience. Messimy, the war minister, recognized the need to avoid the sort of internal divisions to which Michel's proposal had given rise. He therefore abolished the post of vice-president of the Conseil Supérieur de Guerre, and the chief of the general staff became the professional head of the army in peace and its potential commander-in-chief in war.

The man appointed to the new post was not Messimy's first choice, Joseph-Simon Gallieni, nor even the second, Paul-Marie Pau. The former considered himself too old and too directly associated with Michel's fall, and the latter was disqualified by virtue of his active Catholicism and his association with General André's use of freemasons' reports on the political attitudes of officers to regulate promotions between 1900 and 1904, the *affaire des fiches*. The new chief of the general staff was Joseph Joffre. Like Gallieni, he had made his

[35] Rocolle, *L'Hécatombe*, 25–9; Snyder, *Ideology*, 91–3; Laloy, *Military Historian and Economist*, II (1917), 282–3; Akavia, *Decisive victory and correct doctrine*, 44–62.

reputation in the colonies; unlike Pau, his republican credentials were not in doubt. Assessments of Joffre remain sharply divided. Part of the problem is that, while physically Joffre loomed large, intellectually he remained elusive. Indeed, he was not an intellectual. He was a technician and an administrator, an engineer who had excelled in the construction of railways. He had not been at the École Supérieure de Guerre and he had no pretensions to knowledge of staff work. Unlike Grandmaison or Foch, he made no contributions to military thought, even his memoirs being written by other hands. Lyautey, the conqueror of Morocco, said Joffre was no strategist, and yet Joffre was to accomplish the most obviously 'strategic' victory of the First World War. Joffre, then, must be judged by his achievements. Between 1911 and 1914 these were considerable. Professional qualities, not political attachments, played an increasing role in appointments. Joffre was a good listener, and grouped round him, in his *cabinet*, those who were to form his staff when war came. By 1914 the French army enjoyed a greater fitness for war than at any period since 1870; many problems remained, but it had recovered its self-confidence and found an inner unity.

Joffre's most important task was to revise France's war plan. The increases to Germany's active army of 1912 and 1913 confirmed the $3^{\text{ème}}$ bureau in its belief that Germany did not intend to use its reservists from the outset of the campaign. Furthermore, France's response, the three-year service law of 1913, helped ease its own manpower problems. A total of twenty-eight annual classes were embraced by the new law, three years of active service, eleven in the reserve, and fourteen in the territorials. In 1914 the active army had three classes in service, 1911, 1912, and 1913, and was thus stronger by 200,000 men. In addition, with the prospect of a better-trained army and a proportionately larger regular component, the army's officers felt happier about the incorporation of reservists. In 1914, of a total of 3.6 million men mobilized, 2.9 million were reservists and territorials aged between 24 and 48. The 1913 law provided for the maximum strength of an infantry company to rise to 250 men. In addition, Joffre made arrangements for the surplus reserve manpower of one region to be made available to other regions with deficiencies. Thus, in December 1913 a total of 367,500 of the younger reserve classes was available for inclusion in the active army. Joffre's war plans incorporated a reserve regiment in each active division for duties in the rear, and increased the number of reserve divisions to be deployed from twenty-two to twenty-five. The latter, formed into groups, were positioned so as to guard the flanks and rear of the active armies.[36]

Although Joffre was anxious not to forfeit quality in his pursuit of quantity, the three-year law reflected France's bias towards a manpower-intensive

---

[36] Jauffret, *Revue historique des armées*, 174, (1989), 27–37.

solution to the problems of its security. Despite—or perhaps because of—the fact that its falling population in relation to that of Germany generated a sense of vulnerability, it sought to raise proportionately larger armies than its neighbour rather than invest in more firepower. In 1911 it conscripted 83 per cent of its available manpower compared to Germany's 53 per cent. Certainly, equipment rose as a proportion of the Ministry of War's expenditure between 1874 and 1913—from 3.5 per cent in 1874–84 to 4.5 per cent in 1905–13 (and 5.53 per cent between 1909 and 1913). Nonetheless, the French calculated that the Germans had spent twice as much as they had on artillery between 1898 and 1912. In 1913 the French had 4.8 field guns per thousand men to the Germans 5.76, and 4.93 field howitzers to the Germans 6.6.[37]

The three-year law was undoubtedly a boost to professional self-confidence, and helped convince the French army that it could also execute a tactical offensive. Nonetheless, it is only in the light of the confusion between tactics and strategy generated by Grandmaison and others that the three-year law can be blamed for the more offensive bias of France's new plan, plan XVII.

The shape of the plan was determined primarily by strategic considerations. Its tendency to move away from the idea of defence and then counter-attack was no doubt a reflection of the prevailing mentality in the 3ème bureau. But, more importantly, it was the consequence, first of the Franco-Russian military convention and second of French uncertainties with regard to German intentions. By 1913 French pressure on Russia to begin operations against Germany as soon as possible, so as to divide the attentions of the German army, had won Russia's agreement to do so by the fifteenth day of mobilization. It behoved France to reciprocate. Logically, given the uncertainty as to whether Germany's main thrust would come through Belgium or through Lorraine, the case for a delay before an attack remained strong. Joffre's plan did not dispute that: but in the interests both of protecting French territory from invasion and of disrupting the Germans' own plan, that delay could not be long.

Joffre's own inclination, as Schlieffen had expected, was to consider the possibility of attacking Germany through Belgium. The difficulties of operating in the Ardennes and in Lorraine contrasted with the suitability of Belgium's terrain. In addition, operations in this quarter would capitalize on British support because of their proximity to the Channel ports. But such a plan assumed that France, not Germany, would be the first to breach Belgian neutrality. Belgium itself, having looked more sympathetically on the Entente in the winter of 1911–12, then rebuffed efforts by the British and the French to involve it more closely in their military operations. In February 1912 Poincaré,

[37] J.-C. Jauffret, 'Les Forces de la révanche', in Pedroncini (ed.), *Histoire militaire de la France*, iii. 17–18; Dieter Storz, 'Die Schlacht der Zukunft: die Vorbereitungen der Armeen Deutschlands und Frankreich auf dem Landkrieg des 20. Jahrhunderts', in Michalka (ed.), *Erste Weltkrieg*, 267–8; Storz, *Kriegsbild und Rüstung*, 299.

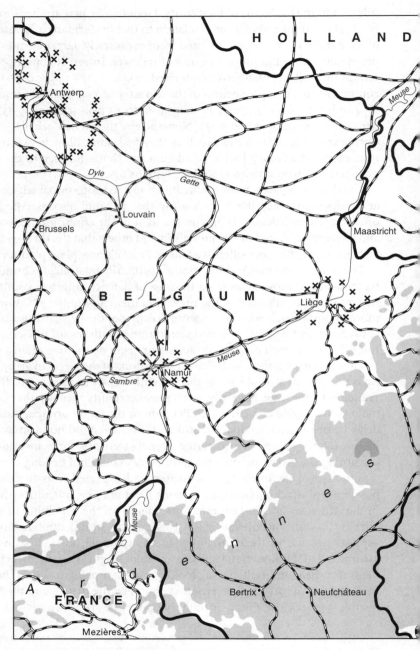

MAP 5. BRUSSELS TO THE RHINE

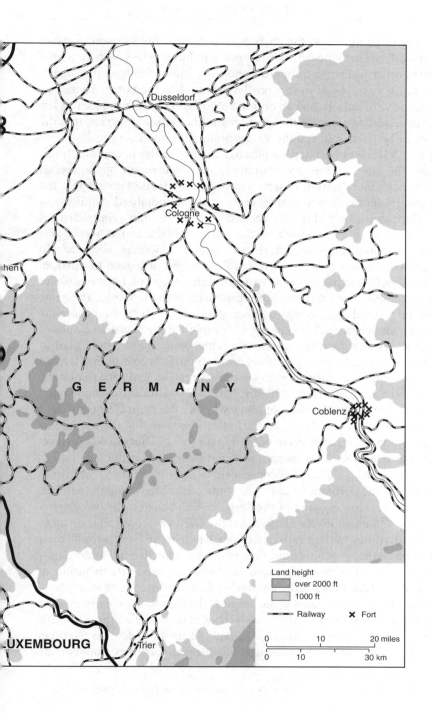

Dusseldorf

X X X X X
X X
Cologne
X X X

hen

G E R M A N Y

Coblenz
XX XX
X X X

Land height
over 2000 ft
1000 ft

━ ━ ━ Railway   ✕ Fort

0   10   20 miles
0   10   30 km

LUXEMBOURG   •Trier

anxious not to compromise the chances of a British commitment, forbade further consideration of the Belgian option. On 30 July 1914 he was to underline the point by ordering French troops to withdraw 10 kilometres from the Belgian border. France was obliged to stay on the defensive in the north. Therefore, Joffre's offensive intentions had no option but to focus on the two passages left clear on the eastern frontier—either north of the line Verdun–Metz and into the Ardennes, or between Toul and the Vosges mountains into Lorraine.[38]

But plan XVII was not primarily a plan to launch offensive operations. It was a plan for the mobilization, concentration, and deployment of the French armies. France's mobilization in 1870 had been chaotic. By January 1912 the French general staff reckoned that its army could be mobilized as quickly as that of Germany. Partly this was because France was not constricted, as Germany was, by the bottleneck of the Rhine bridges; but it was also a reflection of railway building, which had turned a German advantage in strategic lines of nine to four in 1870 to a French lead of sixteen to thirteen. France's failure to maximize the potential of technology as a force multiplier at the tactical level was therefore not reproduced at the strategic. The same troops could be used successively in different locations. The railways gave the French army an operational flexibility which exploited the doctrinal emphasis on security, advance guards, and the encounter battle: Joffre could plan to deploy to east or north, leaving the final decision until the axis of the German advance was manifest.[39] Schlieffen, at least in retirement, had tried to plot the course of Germany's advance right through to its victorious denouement; Joffre was more realistic. He did not know whether the main German weight would come in Belgium or Lorraine: the indications were that there would be significant troop concentrations in both. By 1914 the $2^{\text{ème}}$ bureau was predicting that Germany would use its reserves from the outset of the war. Joffre's neglect of this conclusion, and his consequent acceptance of the $3^{\text{ème}}$ bureau's assessment that the Germans would come south of the Meuse and the Sambre, was only in part a consequence of the deep division between the two departments. The $2^{\text{ème}}$ bureau itself reckoned that the Germans would allocate up to twenty-two divisions to their eastern frontier, when in the event—for all their fears of Russia—they sent only nine: therefore French intelligence underestimated the number of German divisions in the west, despite its inclusion of reservists in the reckoning. Joffre's views on German intentions were also a consequence of his calculations about Liège. If the Germans were determined to avoid the fortifications of Lorraine, why should they take on those of Liège and Namur, both recently modernized and likely to delay the German advance? If they passed north and south of the Belgian forts they would divide

---

[38] Pedroncini, *Revue d'histoire diplomatique*, XCI (1977), 143–58.
[39] Stevenson, *Armaments and the coming of war*, 220, 296; Stevenson, *Past and Present*, 162, (1999), 175–6.

their armies. The French had gained possession of a map exercise conducted by the German general staff early in 1905: in it the German right wing had not extended north of Namur, and so the French could construe German plans to besiege the Belgian forts as a means to contain the Belgian army rather than to extend the depth of the envelopment.[40] Joffre concluded that the probability was that the Germans would breach Belgian neutrality but would do so south of Namur, in the direction of Mézières. They would also attack in Lorraine, possibly with Verdun, Nancy, and St Dié as objectives.

Further fortification was one possible response to this scenario. Although out of fashion, it was not an option which Joffre dismissed. He was, after all, an engineer, and while director of his service between 1904 and 1906 had exploited the first Moroccan crisis and the example of the siege of Port Arthur to secure further funds for upgrading the defences of Lorraine. After 1911 Joffre planned field fortifications for all the points of vulnerability which the general staff's operational calculations revealed—the Trouée de Charmes north of Épinal, the Grand Couronné de Nancy, the heights of the Meuse screening Toul and Verdun, and the possible bridgeheads of Sedan and Mézières. But finance and politics, as much as doctrine, militated against the adoption of the defensive as operational method. The 1914 army law included provision for 231.3 million francs to be spent over seven years on fortification, but it was not approved until 15 July, and only the works at the Grand Couronné de Nancy had been taken in hand by the outbreak of war. As significant was the continuing focus in these plans on France's eastern frontier. To the north, the obsolescence of the works at Maubeuge and Lille meant that the intention in 1914 was to declassify the former and abandon the latter. France's inability to plan for its northern defences imposed a requirement for flexibility and manoeuvrability.

This, then, was the task of plan XVII, which became effective in May 1914. It represented a bigger shift to counteracting any threat from Belgium than had plan XVI. However, like plan XVI it remained incremental rather than revisionist, and thus still failed to appreciate the extent of the German manoeuvre. In the circumstances, given the conflicting intelligence and the available manpower, Joffre distributed France's forces as sensibly as was possible. Ten corps (the 1st, 2nd, and 3rd armies) were posted on the frontier of Alsace-Lorraine, between Épinal and Verdun. Five corps (the 5th army) covered the Belgian frontier from Montmedy through Sedan to Mézières. Six corps (the 4th army) were concentrated behind Verdun, ready to go east or north as circumstances demanded. Joffre reckoned that if he attacked from this quarter, in a direction between Thionville and Metz, he could threaten the southern flank (and the lines of communication) of a German attack in Belgium or the northern flank of a German attack in Lorraine. The extent of the front, especially assuming the

---

[40] Gamelin, *Manoeuvre et victoire de la Marne*, 34–5, 42–4.

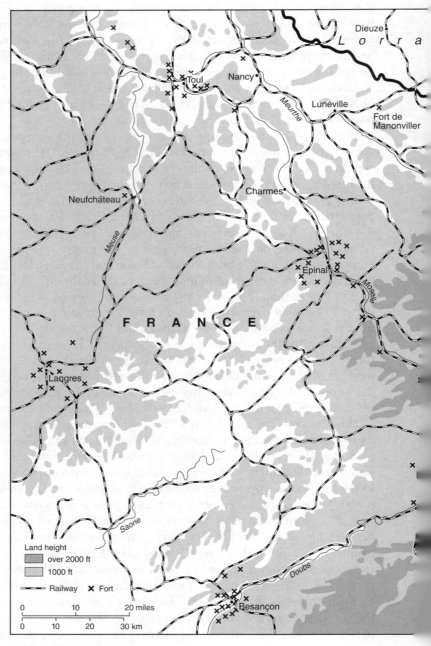

Dieuze

L o r r a

Toul
Nancy
Meurthe
Lunéville
Fort de Manonviller

Neufchâteau
Charmes

Meuse

Epinal
Moselle

F R A N C E

Langres

Saone

Doubs

Besançon

Land height
over 2000 ft
1000 ft
Railway   ✕ Fort

0   10   20 miles
0   10   20   30 km

MAP 6. THE VOSGES

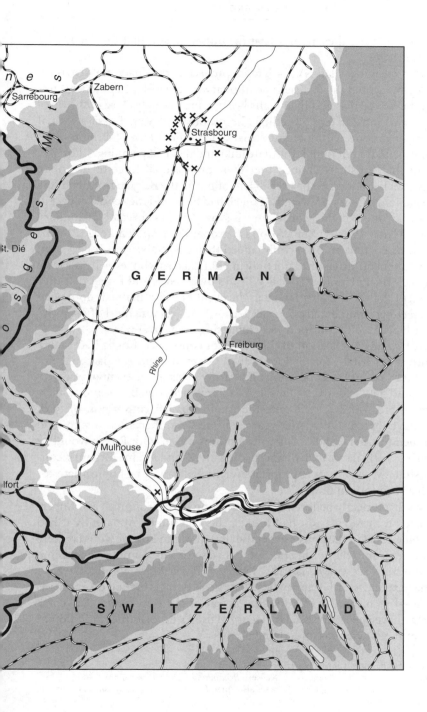

Germans did not use their reservists at the outset, meant that they had to be weak somewhere.

Formally speaking, plan XVII—like its predecessors—made no provision for the deployment of the British Expeditionary Force (BEF). In practice, links between the two armies and their staffs became increasingly close in the three or four years immediately preceding the outbreak of war. Russia's formal commitment produced annual but remarkably limited talks;[41] Britain's lack of commitment did not inhibit intimate links and detailed planning. Joffre was open with the British. He hoped that their professional force of up to six divisions could be added to the French left, opposite the Belgian frontier in the area of Maubeuge. This was what the French had been told they could expect in the middle of the second Moroccan crisis by Britain's director of military operations Henry Wilson. But Wilson's personal Francophilia, forged by his contacts with Foch when both commanded their respective staff colleges, led him into statements unjustified not only in political terms but even by the state of the army's own planning. For all Wilson's own views, and for all that they were in fact fulfilled, British strategy in the event of war remained more open than its creeping continentalism suggested. On 2 August 1914 most of Asquith's cabinet still believed that Britain was embarking on a naval war.

In part this was a reflection of the power of continuity. Russia had been a major threat to Britain for far longer than Germany, and Russia could not easily be hit by major land operations. The army's task in the event of war with Russia would be defensive. Central Asia remained the BEF's most likely deployment area until 1911, despite the Anglo-Russian convention of 1907. The scheme adopted in the latter year, and unrevised thereafter, was to send 100,000 men to defend India. Offensive options in war with Russia would be exercised through naval and financial pressure. This became Britain's continental strategy: what was appropriate for Russia would be appropriate for war with any European power.[42]

Henry Wilson clearly believed that the meeting of the Committee of Imperial Defence on 23 August 1911 had broken this continuity. Apparently it had endorsed the belief of the army's general staff that war in Europe would require it to put troops onto the continent. But that was not a unanimous conclusion. The committee's secretary Maurice Hankey, a Royal Marine and a navalist, wrote the next day to Fisher to say that: 'The great point is that no decision was arrived at—this means, in my opinion, defeat of our opponents.' The committee may have been impressed by Henry Wilson's exposition, but it did not follow that it endorsed his underlying premiss.[43]

[41] Douglas Porch, *Journal of Military History*, LIII (1989), 372–5.

[42] Williams, *Defending the empire*, 196–7; Neilson, *Britain and the last Tsar*, 136, 141.

[43] Keith Wilson, *War in History*, I (1994), 87; see also Offer, *First World War*, 242–3, 291–309; Johnson, *Defence by committee*, 97–100.

What Wilson did get out of the 1911 meeting was a firm rejection of amphibious warfare. The idea that Germany could be attacked through raids on its colonies, scouted in 1902, had gone by 1905–6. Fisher's navy was not interested in devoting its energies to servicing the army in far-flung corners of the world. But it was keen on schemes for landings on the Baltic coast, on Heligoland, and at the estuaries of the Ems and Elbe rivers. The army's opposition to such proposals was already clear by 1908–9, but they still figured in the navy's strategy on 23 August 1911. The general staff argued—persuasively—that operations against the German coastline would bring pressure to bear too late and too slowly to be of much influence in the event of a German invasion of France.[44]

What the navy's ill-developed Baltic schemes highlighted for the Committee of Imperial Defence was the poverty of the navy's argument when compared with that of the army. Hence, the principal conclusion on 23 August 1911 was the need to establish a naval war staff. Pending the latter's evolution, the Committee of Imperial Defence itself partly filled the gap. Between 1911 and 1914—largely through Hankey's efforts—it became the focus for thinking on economic warfare and blockade. Its strategy by 1914 was that these were the long-term means to ultimate victory in the event of war in Europe.

In these circumstances, the dispatch of the BEF to the continent could not constitute the adoption of what would later be described as a continental strategy. The immediate job of the army was to provide aid to France, to stave off the possibility of the latter's defeat before economic warfare could take its toll of Germany. This was the strategy endorsed on 23 August 1911, as Henry Wilson himself was very well aware. Privately he was not optimistic that the French and British forces would fare well against the Germans in their opening encounters. 'But', he wrote, 'the longer the war lasted the greater the strain would be on Germany.' Britain's job was to prevent a quick German victory, for 'if we once allow Germany to defeat France an expeditionary force would be valueless and the duration of our naval predominance could be measured in years'.[45] Wilson's strategy was an integrated strategy. So too, by 1 August 1914, was that of the naval war staff, which, for all the rivalry between the two services, endorsed the dispatch of the BEF to the continent.[46]

If Wilson's relative success had genuinely been the triumph of full-fledged continentalism, its logical immediate outcome would have been, not the creation of a naval war staff, but the restructuring of the British army on lines adapted to European war. This did not happen.

---

[44] Paul Hayes, 'Britain, Germany, and the Admiralty's plans for attacking German territory 1906–1915', in Freedman, Hayes, and O'Neill (eds.), *War, strategy and international politics*, 96–9.
[45] Herrmann, *Arming of Europe*, 156–7.
[46] Keith Wilson, 'Britain', in Wilson (ed.), *Decisions for war*, 176.

The overall size of the BEF, six divisions and a cavalry division, reflected the largest force that could be created from those troops left at home: half the infantry of the regular army was overseas. The French and German armies were organized in corps, a corps having in peacetime a geographical location, and being made up of two divisions, each of two brigades. The British in 1906 decided to organize their army not around the corps (although corps commands were created on mobilization in 1914) but around a division of three brigades, rather than two. Total divisional strengths were comparable, as the European brigade consisted of six battalions, the British of four. One argument for carrying more divisional and brigade commands was that, although the army was small, it had the staff to enable a modest expansion. But the determining factor in 1906 was the need to have a form similar to that of the Indian army so that the organizations would be compatible in the field.[47]

Mobilization in France and Germany resulted in the creation of mass armies for European war. Britain also expanded its army on mobilization: the expeditionary force incorporated about 60 per cent reservists in its total strength, which in proportional terms bore comparison with the growth in the armies of Europe. But it started from a much lower base-point. What had driven Britain's arrangements for expansion and replacement was its experience of colonial warfare, and specifically the Boer War, not its expectations of European conflict. When, by 1913, it had confronted the latter possibility, it had also calculated—on the basis of the Russo-Japanese War—that it would suffer 75 per-cent losses in the first six months of fighting. Moreover, if the entire BEF went to Europe immediately on the outbreak of war, it would leave behind no cadres as the basis for subsequent expansion, no forces for home defence, and no contingency in the event of crisis in the empire. The army's roles had outstripped its size. The British general staff had entered on a continental commitment without a continental army.[48]

Henry Wilson recognized this point, privately reckoning that six divisions were probably 'fifty too few'.[49] Wilson was therefore an ardent conscriptionist. But, although conscription had its supporters, both within the army and without, they were not united on its strategic justification. Wilson's view, that conscription was required to create a sufficiently large army for Britain to implement a continental strategy, was not the rationale for conscription that the National Service League embraced. It argued for conscription for the purposes of national defence; and that, after all, was the basis for conscription

[47] Spiers, *Haldane*, 81–3. On British plans in general, see Williamson, *Politics of grand strategy*; Gooch, *Plans of war*; Gooch, *Prospect of war*; J. McDermott, 'The revolution in British military thinking from the Boer War to the Moroccan crisis', in Kennedy (ed.), *War plans*; Howard, *Continental commitment*, chs. 1 and 2.

[48] Williams, *Defending the empire*, 9, 102–3, 215–19.

[49] Quoted in K. M. Wilson, *Policy of the Entente*, 63.

in the rest of Europe. Haldane, however, reckoned that the Territorial Force, part-time volunteers whose reorganization he had carried through in 1908, would be sufficient for that task. In the event, doubts about the Territorials' efficiency and their failure to recruit to establishment, combined with the reactivation in 1913 of the fear of German invasion, led to pressure for two out of the BEF's six divisions to be retained in Britain for home defence. Pragmatism meant that if the general staff wanted to send its full complement of six divisions to France, it had to endorse the Territorial Force. Thus, not only was the maximum size of the BEF paltry by European standards, but by 1914 it was still not clear that its full complement would be dispatched overseas. Each time the possibility of invasion had been seriously studied it had been discounted; indeed, it was this that had allowed the army to embrace continentalism at all. And yet conscriptionists within the army, although in many cases at heart continentalists also, needed the invasion fear to popularize their advocacy of national service.

The army was also uncertain about where the BEF would operate. As in the French case, this was at least in part a product of intelligence about German strength and German intentions. Sir James Grierson, the director of military operations in 1905, had been persuaded that the Germans would attack through Belgium. The attractions of dispatching the BEF to Belgium were threefold. First, Antwerp would provide a secure base of operations, enabling direct maritime links with Britain. Secondly, by operating against the Germans' right flank the BEF might have greater effect than its small numbers would otherwise achieve. Thirdly, the British command would be independent of that of France. By 1908, however, the general staff had begun to move in favour of supporting the French left. Belgium's own desire to remain unequivocally neutral made the development of the Belgian option not only complex but possibly even (if the Germans respected Belgian neutrality) redundant. Nonetheless, direct support to France, although adumbrated before 1910, was not fully developed until Wilson's appointment in that year. Wilson's overriding object was to ensure that Britain, although not formally committed to France, in practice found that it was. His method of achieving this aim was to present detailed proposals, to narrow the discussion to their implications, and so avoid debate on the general policy. Acceptance of the detail created acceptance of the policy.

The meeting of the Committee of Imperial Defence on 23 August 1911 is illustrative both of Wilson's approach and of much of the spuriousness which it cloaked. Wilson argued that the Germans would enter France between Verdun and Maubeuge, and that the thirteen roads available in this sector would allow the Germans to commit there forty of the seventy divisions which they would deploy in the west. Reckoning France's contribution to the defence of the area at thirty-seven to thirty-nine divisions, he concluded that the swift commitment of the BEF's six divisions could save France. To present a neat argument, Wilson begged two questions—the size of the German army and the direction of its advance. Privately, Wilson reckoned the Germans would use their reservists from the outset, would denude their eastern frontier, and would therefore commit to the west a total of eighty-four divisions, not seventy. It followed, not only that the British contribution would not swing the balance so neatly, but also that the Germans were likely to come north of Maubeuge and the Meuse. Wilson was convinced of this latter point in 1910, but from April 1911 brought his thinking into line with France's 3ème bureau, and rebutted suggestions by Winston Churchill, Lloyd George, and General Sir John French which did no more than reflect his own earlier convictions. The intelligence and operational conclusions on which Wilson was relying were, to all intents and purposes, French.[50] Thus, a congruity emerged which subordinated Britain's strategy to France's.

Although it would be foolish to pretend that Wilson's was not the most effective and decisive voice in British strategic counsels before 1914, it is important to recognize that it was not the only one. Wilson did not enjoy a status comparable with that of Moltke or Joffre; he was not, as they were, the chief of the general staff and the putative commander-in-chief. That office was held, from 1912, by Sir John French.[51] French was a short, white-haired cavalryman, who had made one reputation in South Africa and another in ladies' bedrooms. It is not irrelevant to his strategic thinking to note that he had commenced an abortive career in the Royal Navy, and that he had never been to the Staff College. The status of the general staff within the army, given its novelty as an institution (it was formed in 1906), deprived it of the commanding influence it enjoyed in Germany. The new policies with which it was associated had to compete with the weight of the army's established experience and long-received wisdom. The application of a general staff to a bewildering variety of unpredictable colonial campaigns, and the relevance of continentalism to a tradition of imperial service or European amphibious operations, were moot points. French himself was not of the general staff or particularly appreciative of it. Admittedly, his views moderated after 1912. He even warmed to Wilson, a man he had hitherto distrusted as a protégé of Lord Roberts. But he never came completely to terms with the subordination of the British army to French planning and French strategy. The Belgian option favoured in 1906 lived on in French. His was the initiative to renew approaches to Belgium in 1912, and to consider the possibility of landings at Zeebrugge, Ostend, and Antwerp. The attractions of a Belgian strategy were not simply the desire to

[50] On the inadequacies of British intelligence, see Hiley, *Historical Journal*, XXVI (1983), 867–89, and XXVIII (1985), 835–62.
[51] Recent biographies of French are Holmes, *The little field marshal*, and Cassar, *The tragedy of Sir John French*.

pursue a role independent of the French, but also its conformity to more traditional British strategic assumptions. By placing itself athwart the Belgian coast, the BEF would be both contributing to the defence of Britain against invasion and creating the possibility of joint operations with the Royal Navy. Although French's thinking did not appeal to Wilson, it did attract Asquith. The commitment to France was not a foregone conclusion by 1914.[52]

Therefore, although Wilson's advocacy of swift support for France did determine the nature of British strategy for 1914, and consequently for the war as a whole, it did not do so until after war itself had been declared. The cabinet and the government did not address the issue, and the army was in no state to speak coherently. The Curragh 'mutiny' in March 1914 had led to the resignations both of the secretary of state for war, J. E. B. Seely, and of French. In July the position of the former was temporarily held by Asquith, that of the latter by Sir Charles Douglas. Wilson, himself an Ulsterman and a key, if shadowy, figure in the Curragh incident, embraced the prospect of war as a way of shelving the Irish home rule issue and of mending the divisions in the army. But his advocacy of direct support for France, conveyed to the Unionists and indirectly to *The Times*, still did not constitute policy. When, on 3 August 1914, the army received its mobilization orders, they made no mention of how it was to be employed. Only the previous day the cabinet had emphasized that the tasks of the BEF were home and imperial defence.

Asquith's decision, taken late in the evening of 4 August, to appoint Lord Kitchener to the War Office had the merit of éclat, but did not clarify the situation. Kitchener was a serving soldier, not a politician; his reputation had been made in the Sudan, in South Africa, and in India, and he was already en route for Egypt when he was recalled to London. He thus laboured under a double disqualification for the office which he now entered—an office which he did not wish to occupy, and which his cabinet colleagues had little desire to bestow on him. But Haldane, Asquith's natural choice, did not enjoy popular approval, being seen as a Germanophile, whereas Kitchener did. Whatever the constitutional improprieties of a soldier holding cabinet office, the appointment gave the Liberal administration an aura of professional military competence which earned widespread public approval. Much of what Kitchener did in his two years at the War Office was disfigured by his mistrust of his colleagues, his doubts about their ability to keep confidences, his reluctance to work with the idea of collective responsibility, and his undermining of the War Office's procedures through his own imperial and proconsular habits. But failures in administrative methods are not the same as defective policy. Some of what he did in the latter area was bad, but not half as bad as the memoirs of

<hr>

[52] K. M. Wilson, *Policy of the Entente*, 121–34; d'Ombrain, *War machinery and high policy*, 145–7; W. J. Philpott, *Journal of Strategic Studies*, XII (1989), 458–78; Philpott, *Anglo-French relations and strategy*, 3–6.

those politicians who survived the war, especially Lloyd George, suggested. Above all, Kitchener realized from the outset that a European war would be a long one, perhaps lasting three years, and that as the exiguous BEF was Britain's only combat-ready army its immediate use to support the French should be balanced by its need to underwrite the formation of a truly continental-sized British army.

Kitchener's views on the use of the BEF were not so unorthodox as Wilson's single-minded advocacy of French strategy suggested. On 4 August Haldane, imagining that he would return to the War Office, considered holding the BEF back to allow it to become the nucleus of a larger army. Douglas Haig, who when director of military training in 1906–7 had worked closely with Haldane and had come to admire the Swiss nation in arms, was of a similar opinion: he felt that the war might last for several years, and that the army should reckon on being expanded to a million men.[53]

On 5 August a war council was held to decide the issue of the BEF's employment. Kitchener, Haldane, and Haig were all present. But so too was Wilson. Although he did not speak, his conviction that the war would be short, and that, if British aid to France was delayed, it would be too late, forced them to compromise on their long-term views. Sir John French, now named as the BEF's commander, revived the Belgian option, suggesting that Antwerp be used as a base and that the BEF operate on the German flank. Both banks of the Scheldt downstream of Antwerp were Dutch. But the fact that the Royal Navy could not have defended Antwerp without breaching Dutch neutrality as surely as the German army had breached Belgium's worried nobody—least of all Churchill. The First Lord of the Admiralty quashed French's proposal on the grounds of practicality, not international law: he announced that the navy could not support operations based on a port so far north. French earned a double penalty: he had thoroughly alarmed both Wilson and Haig, who would be subordinate to him in the field, and he found himself responsible for the execution of a strategy which was not his own. The war council agreed that the BEF should go to France. The most significant single strategic decision taken by Britain in the war was thus in the first instance reached not by the cabinet, but by an ad hoc committee convened by the prime minister and dominated by the army.

Churchill had said that the navy could protect Britain from invasion, and that therefore all six divisions were free to go to the continent. Others were less sure. Offers of service from Canada, New Zealand, and Australia were accepted; India was asked to send a division to Egypt and to hold another in readiness; but none of these troops was immediately available. Kitchener,

---

[53] Cassar, *Kitchener*, is the most obvious reinstatement of its subject's reputation; but see also Simkins, *Kitchener's armies*, and Neilson, *Strategy and supply*. Cassar provides an account of the events of early August; see also Terraine, *Mons*, chs. 1 and 2; Hankey, *Supreme Command*, 169–73, 187–8.

despite Churchill's assurance, remained concerned about home defence, and was also, of course, anxious to retain the nucleus for a greatly expanded army. Asquith was worried about public order: the fears that the loss of overseas trade would cause both large-scale unemployment and a fall in food stocks combined with recent experience of trades-union militancy to make a case for keeping back two divisions. At a second meeting of the war council on 6 August Kitchener announced the cabinet's decision that only four divisions and the cavalry division would go immediately; the fifth might follow in the near future, but the sixth would stay at home. The withdrawal of troops from South Africa was designed to offset in some measure the outflow.

The pre-war staff talks had concluded that the BEF would concentrate in the area Le Cateau–Maubeuge–Hirson, thus extending the French left-wing opposite the Belgian frontier. From the outset Kitchener was unhappy with the choice. He favoured a concentration much further back, at Amiens. This would not disrupt the shipment of the BEF to Rouen, Le Havre, and Boulogne, or the arrangements for its transport in France, but it would preserve its freedom of action and leave it less exposed. Kitchener had seen the collapse of the French armies in 1870; he had no desire for the BEF to be swept up in comparable disasters. Furthermore, he early on developed a sense of the true direction of the German advance. The Germans, he felt, could only have decided to attack Liège and to accept the involvement of Britain in the war if a sweep north of the Meuse was integral to their war plan.

Sir John French too favoured Amiens. Henry Wilson did not, and set about working on French. He was supported by Victor Huguet, France's liaison officer, who reflected Joffre's worry that if the BEF concentrated as far back as Amiens it would upset the forward deployment of the entire allied left wing. On 12 August one of Kitchener's acolytes, the military correspondent Charles Repington, argued in *The Times* that the main weight of the German advance lay in Belgium. But at a meeting on the very same day the BEF's concentration was once again brought forward to Maubeuge. Kitchener waived his reservations for the sake of alliance solidarity. British strategy was being subordinated to alliance politics, while British policy was being overborne by French strategy. Britain's entry to the war had been determined by Belgium and the balance of power in Europe; the disposition of its army was being settled by the French general staff.[54]

It was not just Britain's deployment area that worried Joffre; it was also the three days lost in Britain's mobilization schedule because of the cabinet's procrastination in entering the war. The BEF might not be ready to fight until 26 August, when Joffre planned to commence operations on the 20th.

---

[54] Philpott, *Anglo-French relations and strategy*, 9–14; Prete, *Canadian Journal of History*, XXIV (1989), 55–60; Huguet, *Britain and the war*, 40–1.

In the event, the dispatch of a smaller force than Wilson had anticipated enabled time to be made up. Reservists were speedily incorporated: the 1st Somerset Light Infantry absorbed 400 men in four days. Despite the congestion to civilian traffic caused by the August bank holiday, railway movements were accomplished without major disruption. Over five days 1,800 special trains ran, and they arrived at Southampton every three minutes for sixteen hours a day. With no intelligence as to crossing dates and with its destroyers operating at their maximum range, the German High Seas Fleet could not realistically hope to disrupt the BEF's passage.[55] The embarkation began on 9 August, and was accomplished by 17 August. On 20 August the concentration at Maubeuge was complete. On the same day the cabinet offered the release of the fifth division; the sixth followed in early September, and a seventh—formed from the troops from South Africa—in the middle of the same month.

French mobilization and concentration were carried out with similar slickness: herein was the triumph of plan XVII. Beginning on 2 August, the 800,000 men of the peacetime home army absorbed 621,000 reservists into its forty-five divisions, a further 655,000 formed the twenty-five reserve divisions, and 184,000 were put into twelve territorial divisions. A further 1 million men remained at their depots. Using fourteen railway lines, each carrying on average fifty-six trains a day, the concentration was completed by 18 August. Of a total of 4,278 trains, only about twenty were late.[56]

Across the Rhine, German mobilization was ordered on 1 August, and as in France began on the 2nd. Some had anticipated the order. Baden had called up its reservists early, on 14 July, and for a longer period of training than usual; in Prussia, on the other hand, Walter Bloem, a reserve officer in the 12th Brandenburg Grenadiers, left his regiment on the same day, having finished his annual training commitment. Most reservists were recalled on 29 and 30 July. Only the two youngest (and therefore most recently trained) classes were needed by active units to reach their war strength. The older reserve and some of the younger Landwehr classes (up to age 31), with a cadre of professional officers, formed a total of 353 reserve battalions, giving thirty-one reserve divisions; the remainder of the younger Landwehr classes were formed into eighty-seven Ersatz battalions. The older Landwehr classes (aged under 39) contributed 314 battalions, and the Landsturm embraced those aged between 39 and 45.[57]

The first two days of mobilization were devoted to the mobilization of the railways themselves. Groener had worked hard to incorporate Germany's civilian railway administration into the military and so make it an effective

[55] Halpern, *Naval history*, 29; Hörich, *Deutsche Seekriegführung*, 27.
[56] Duroselle, *La France et les français*, 82–5.
[57] Camena d'Almeida, *L'Armée allemande*, 85–124.

tool of the general staff. Although his planned construction programme was not complete, Groener's administrative arrangements functioned superbly: all the railways in Germany came under his command, and his major struggles were not with civilians but with corps commanders. Each corps required 6,010 wagons, organized in 140 trains, to complete its movement. Between 2 and 18 August one train crossed the Rhine over the Hohenzollern Bridge at Cologne every ten minutes. The active corps were in position by 12 August, the reserve by the 14th, and the Ersatz divisions on the 18th.[58] The 1st army (von Kluck, 164 battalions) and the 2nd (von Bülow, 159 battalions) were grouped on the Belgian frontier opposite Liège. The 3rd (Hausen, 104 battalions) and 4th (Albrecht, Grand Duke of Württemberg, 123 battalions) faced the Ardennes, down as far as Luxembourg. The 5th army (Crown Prince Wilhelm of Prussia, 147 battalions) was in the Thionville–Metz area of Lorraine, north of the 6th (Crown Prince Rupprecht of Bavaria, 131 battalions). The 7th army (von Heeringen), the weakest of all at 108 battalions, was echeloned back and to the south, from Strasbourg down east of the Rhine.

Calculations as to the actual balance of forces in the west vary—partly according to the numbers of garrison and line of communication units included, and partly because, although the concentrations were virtually complete by 18 August, additional formations (notably two French divisions from North Africa) were still to arrive. The mobilized strengths of France and Germany were roughly comparable, just short of 4 million men each, and in the west numbering 1,108 French battalions to 1,077 German. Germany had incorporated rather more reservists, but the quality and training of Germany's reservists were at a higher level than those of France. On the other hand, France could count on the BEF (at the outset a further forty-eight battalions) and 120 Belgian battalions. The French and the British had the benefit of more recent battle experience than the Germans, who—the Herero War in South-West Africa apart—had not fought since 1871. Both in the quality of their field artillery and the quantity of their cavalry (thirteen divisions against ten) the Entente powers could claim a superiority. The Germans, on the other hand, enjoyed better and more heavy artillery. Aggregate figures, 2 million French troops against 1.7 million German, gave a sufficiently close balance in the west to mean that manoeuvre and concentration, operational and tactical nous, might well be decisive.[59]

[58] Groener, *Lebenserinnerungen*, 131–4, 143–4, 154; Westwood, *Railways at war*, 133.
[59] Contamine, *Révanche*, 200; *Victoire de la Marne*, ch. 3; see also Tyng, *The Campaign of the Marne*, 355, for somewhat different calculations, and Koeltz, *La Guerre de 1914–1918*, 557–60.

THE BATTLE OF THE FRONTIERS

The war plans of both France and Britain were vitiated by Belgium's vigorous affirmation of its neutrality.[60] The second Moroccan crisis in 1911 had made clear to Brussels not only the danger of war, but also the probability of German invasion. A meeting in the foreign ministry on 16 September 1911 recognized that Belgium must be ready to defend itself against the German army or stand accused by Britain and France of complicity with Berlin.[61] But Belgium continued to treat all its neighbours, even the Dutch, as possible enemies.

Before 1911 Belgium had taken solace in the memory of 1870, arguing that it was far more sensible for the German army to drive into France with its left wing, so trapping the French armies against the Belgian border, than to use its right to push them south where the French could trade space for time. But in 1870 the British had been the defenders of Belgium's neutrality. By 1912 the Belgians reckoned that Britain saw Belgium's neutrality as a protectorate established in Britain's interests, not their own. The Entente with France undermined Britain's impartiality, and the operational importance of Belgium to the British army's calculations was made clear by Britain's military attaché in Brussels. The possibility of a British landing to seize Antwerp was scouted both in 1906 and in 1911.[62]

Grey reiterated his country's guarantee to Belgium in 1913, just as Poincaré had done three times in the course of the previous year. By contrast, the Germans gave several indications in 1913 and 1914 that any Belgian hopes that a European war would bypass the Low Countries were misplaced. The Belgian military attaché in Berlin reported that Moltke had been enquiring about what Belgium would do if a large foreign army crossed its territory. On 6 November 1913 the Kaiser and Moltke warned King Albert that Belgium should throw in its lot with that of Germany in the coming war. Thus, scrupulous neutrality boxed Belgium into a position of international political purity but strategic and military absurdity. If invaded by the Germans, it would ultimately depend on the other powers to eject them. But it was not prepared to see those powers as allies; it was not even willing, in the event of war, to subscribe to objectives that went beyond the defence of its own independence. The fact that in 1914 Belgium felt itself to have been abandoned by France

---

[60] The best synthesis of the extensive literature of the 1920s and 1930s, and still probably the best account of all, is Tyng, *Campaign of the Marne*. Helpful later perspectives are provided by Contamine, *Victoire de la Marne*; Jaschke, *Historische Zeitschrift*, CXC (1960), 311–48; Rocolle, *L'Hécatombe*. Good popular accounts—Isselin, *The battle of the Marne*; Terraine, *Mons*; Tuchman, *August 1914*; Barnett, *The swordbearers*, pt. I. Spears, *Liaison 1914*, is a graphic mixture of personal observation and historical commentary, and Gamelin, *Manoeuvre et victoire de la Marne*, does the same for France.

[61] Bitsch, *La Belgique*, 423–39.

[62] Ibid. 452–4, 472.

and—to a lesser extent—Britain was in large part the necessary military consequence of its own pre-war policy. The logical corollary of its strict neutrality in peacetime was preparation for a self-sufficient defence in war.[63]

King Albert had been impressed but not intimidated by what Wilhelm and Moltke had said to him. A member of his household and a contemporary at the École Militaire in Brussels, Émile Joseph Galet, argued that the Belgian army should be ready to mobilize at the first sign of impending war, and that once mobilization was complete the units of the Belgian army should concentrate on the frontier facing its enemy (who would by then have declared his hand). What in essence Albert and Galet wanted was a defence on the Meuse, its flanks resting on the fortresses of Namur and Liège. This had been the basis of the army's autumn manoeuvres in 1913, and it was the planning task assigned to General de Ryckel when he was appointed deputy chief of the general staff in December.[64]

However, the effect of their intervention in planning was to deepen the discord within Belgian military counsels. Albert had been responsible for the formation of a Belgian general staff in 1910. Its chief, Jungbluth, fell out with the minister of war and was retired in 1912. Not until May 1914 was his successor appointed, de Selliers de Moranville, a compromise candidate and an officer of the gendarmerie. Only in July 1914 itself did the general staff take in hand plans for concentrating the army: its first contact with the railway authorities was on the 29th of that month. Many on the staff remained wedded to an all-round defence that reflected Belgium's espousal of neutrality. Its pivot was Antwerp, and the task of the field army was to delay an invader's advance but not to sacrifice itself uselessly. On this basis the defensive powers of Namur and Liège alone would be enough to secure the frontiers, and the field army should be massed in central Belgium. The implications were that units would begin their concentration while still mobilizing, that the concentration itself would be completed 60 kilometres back from the frontier, and that the border strongholds would be held only by over-age garrison troops. As late as 1 August 1914 de Selliers de Moranville was pushing for a concentration in central Belgium that was compatible with a war against France as well as against Germany.[65]

Belgium's strategy was not the only aspect of the defence of its neutrality that was in disarray. Although universal conscription was adopted in 1909, it had been accompanied by a reduction of the period of service in the infantry to only fifteen months. The 1911 Moroccan crisis moved army reform up the agenda, but only in 1913 was the army's size fixed as a proportion of the population. The aim was to have a force marginally superior to the numerical difference between the German and French armies (deemed to be three corps),

---

[63] Jean Stengers, 'Belgium', in Wilson (ed.), *Decisons for war*, 151–5.
[64] Bitsch, *La Belgique*, 492, 496.
[65] Galet, *Albert King of the Belgians*, is fundamental to the discussion that follows.

and therefore sufficient to give the Germans pause for thought before invading France by way of Belgium. The case for neutrality was preserved by observing that such a force, if added to the German army, would give it such a preponderance as to persuade the French not to go to war in the first place.[66] The annual contingent of recruits was increased from 13,300 to 33,000, so enabling the six youngest classes to form a field army of 180,000, while the older classes were incorporated as garrison troops. This scheme would be fully effective in 1926, when it would give Belgium a maximum strength of 340,000 men. The view of the French military attaché on 1 May 1914 was that 'the Belgian army could not be mobilized in 1914, neither in its new form which lacks men, cadres, staffs, material, nor its old form which has been smashed; it will have to improvise a temporary organization'.[67] Three months later, confronted with crisis, de Brocqueville, the minister of war, resolved to split the existing regiments in two and to incorporate eight (not five) of the current classes into the field army, so as to give it an immediate total of 117,000 men. This left 200,000 to man Belgium's fortifications; the remaining male population was liable for service in the Garde Civique. But the consequence of instant expansion was a loss in tactical effectiveness. The cohesion of units was sacrificed, and the already inadequate supply of trained officers was further diluted by their being spread over too many formations. On mobilization the 6th division had only two officers per company. The experience of most officers for most of the year had been to command, in Galet's words, 'phantom battalions and skeleton companies':[68] thus, their knowledge was theoretical and their experience of actual leadership minimal. Manoeuvres in the 3rd division in May 1914 revealed that only a third of the troops understood the principles of fire control or movement. Moreover, the rapid expansion of the field army deepened the imbalance between manpower and equipment levels. Organized in six large divisions, the field army possessed only 102 machine-guns and had no heavy artillery.

On mobilization the king, not the chief of the general staff, became commander-in-chief. The first decision which confronted him was the choice of the army's concentration area. On the one hand its lack of cohesion and low level of training favoured the central position, so delaying contact with the Germans for as long as possible. On the other, an army as improvised as Belgium's would clearly need all the help it could get from fixed positions, and these were forward on the frontier. To confuse matters further, the advocates of a forward deployment at the beginning of August were not now Albert and Galet, but a young guard of staff officers swayed by the French advocates of the offensive. Albert himself was more pragmatic. He realized that not to work with the grain of existing general staff planning would cause

[66] Bitsch, *La Belgique*, 474.   [67] Ibid. 481.   [68] Galet, *Albert*, 73.

further chaos, and so recognized that he had no choice but to implement a strategy of which he did not approve, albeit with modifications. The main Belgian forces concentrated on the River Gette, but two divisions of the field army were pushed forward to cover Liège and Namur respectively. Indicative of the confusion were the hopes of Max Deauville, a medical officer with the Belgian army: he looked forward to the arrival of the French and 'a new Waterloo', despite the fact that in 1815 the French had been on the other side and it was the advent of the Prussians that had saved the Belgians.[69]

In the event the Belgian army acquitted itself with much more distinction in the opening days of the war than it had a right to expect. The German envelopment depended on the swift capture of Liège. Erich Ludendorff, who in 1913 had forfeited his post as chief of operations on the general staff, allegedly as a penalty for his outspoken demands for increases in manpower, had planned that Liège would fall within forty-eight hours. He had visited the city, ostensibly as a tourist, in 1909. It was protected by a ring of twelve forts, all of recent construction, but designed for frontal rather than all-round defence. The intervals between the forts were meant to be filled with field fortifications, and Liège therefore required a stronger force than its garrison of 40,000 men and 400 guns. Leman, the garrison commander, was not sure what forces he would have available. The differences between the king and the general staff as to the field army's concentration area meant that the possibility of the entire army advancing to the Meuse continued to be canvassed until 6 August. Galet would later argue that if the whole field army had been concentrated on the Meuse from the beginning of the war the Germans would have been stopped in their tracks. As it was, the Liège garrison, reinforced by the 3rd division, forestalled the Germans' hopes of achieving surprise and a quick victory: the initial assaults on the morning of 5 August were repulsed with heavy losses. On 6 August Liège had the dubious distinction of being the first city in European warfare to suffer an aerial attack: bombs from a Zeppelin killed nine civilians. Leman now realized that elements of five German corps confronted him, and that German cavalry threatened to encircle him from the north, so he returned the 3rd division to the field army, and decided to put his efforts into the defence of the individual forts and not into the whole perimeter. Thus, during the night of 6/7 August, German brigades were able to infiltrate between the forts, and early on the morning of 7 August—in a typical piece of theatricality which earned him Germany's highest decoration, the *pour le mérite*—Ludendorff himself took possession of the undefended citadel.

However, the position of the Germans, both in general and specifically of those within the city, who were now effectively cut off from outside, was still precarious. The forts had been constructed to resist artillery calibres of up to

---

[69] Deauville, *Jusqu'à l'Yser*, 20.

210 mm. In anticipation of this problem, in 1906–7 the German general staff—bypassing the War Ministry—had commissioned Krupp to develop a 420 mm mortar. But by 1914 only five were complete. The Germans therefore had to bring up four batteries of Austrian Skoda 305 mm howitzers, and not until 12 August could these guns open fire. The forts on the right bank of the Meuse were cleared by 13 August, and on the left by the 16th. The siege of Liège had lasted eleven days, not two. In practice, the delay to the German advance was at most a couple of days, as the concentration of the active corps was not completed until 13 August. But already operations were not going according to plan.

At the southern end of his line Moltke's fears of an early French offensive in Alsace and Lorraine proved well founded. The difficulty for the Germans of defending upper Alsace had resulted in the logical conclusion not to do so. With a speed that surprised the Germans and anticipated his own concentration, Joffre pushed VII corps from Belfort, south of the Vosges, into the southernmost lost province. He had told the commanders of 1st and 2nd armies on 3 August that their task was to fix as many German corps as possible, so freeing the French forces to the north. He also aimed to provide quick support for Russia. On 8 August French popular enthusiasm was fuelled by the news that the tricolour once again flew over Mulhouse. Dubail, commanding 1st army, now wanted to consolidate and complete his concentration; Joffre was determined to push on. However, the the advance of VII corps was dilatory and its reconnaissance inadequate. Two corps of the 7th German army retook Mulhouse and drove the French back across the frontier to Belfort.[70]

The Germans had created a strong defensive network between Metz and Thionville, the *Moselstellung*. Its task was to secure the pivot of the right wing from any French thrust across the German lines of communication. But Joffre assumed that it also screened the main German concentration. He therefore decided to mask this sector, and to mount major thrusts across the frontier into Lorraine in the south and into the Ardennes in the north. His assumptions about German dispositions were wrong. Only five German divisions and a Landwehr corps held the Thionville–Metz sector, and the French therefore had a three-to-one superiority in mobile troops. In Lorraine, on the other hand, not six corps, as Joffre imagined, but eight, giving a total of over twenty-four divisions, opposed the twenty divisions of the 1st and 2nd French armies earmarked for the attack. Furthermore, the Germans were fighting in an area whose terrain was familiar, and whose defence had been long planned. Dubail's 1st army was set the main objectives, Sarrebourg, and then Strasbourg. Its right was to be supported by the army of Alsace, newly created by combining VII corps with four other divisions and commanded by General Pau. On Dubail's

---

[70] Dubail, *Quatre années*, i. 12–28.

left was Castelnau's 2nd army. Even before the war Castelnau had advised against an early offensive into Lorraine, preferring to take up a strong defensive position in front of Nancy. Joffre overruled him, insisting that there were no significant forces in front of the 2nd army.[71]

Thus the second French invasion of Alsace, mounted on 14 August, was this time subordinate to the more major thrust north of the Vosges into Lorraine. The bulk of the 7th German army was therefore drawn north, and only four Landwehr brigades faced the army of Alsace. By 19 August Mulhouse was once again in French hands. Thereafter, however, Pau, distrustful of the reserve divisions that made up a large part of his command, restricted his activities to threatening the German flank from the security of the Vosges mountains.

Pau's caution left the 1st army with less support than it needed. Heeringen's 7th German army was free to threaten Dubail's flank, and forced him to extend southwards. Castelnau's right had been instructed to support Dubail's left, but on 18 August Joffre ordered the 2nd army to face north, rather than north-east. His intention was to hold the Germans in Lorraine and so enable the French 3rd and 4th armies to manoeuvre. The effect was to pull Castelnau's command in two different directions. Bowed as it faced north and east, it lost contact with Dubail's army. The German 6th and 7th armies, the latter subordinated to the command of the former, fell back on to prepared positions on the heights of Morhange and on Sarrebourg.

Joffre continued to press the offensive. Castelnau intended that his attack should be echeloned from the right, but in fact XX corps on the left, commanded by Ferdinand Foch, had made better progress. Castelnau instructed Foch to halt while the rest of the army pivoted on its left. Foch's corps— whether deliberately or not—disregarded these orders, and pushed on to the heights of Morhange. Although the 2nd army had been stripped of its cavalry, its aircraft had until now provided valuable intelligence, and indeed had warned Castelnau of the strength of the German positions on the 18th. But on 20 August early morning mist prevented any aerial reconnaissance. The Germans enjoyed an overall superiority of 328 battalions to 268, and of 1,614 field guns to 1,080. The French 1st and 2nd armies advanced into devastating fire. By the afternoon its victims included Castelnau's own son. The advance of Foch's corps had exposed the left flank of 2nd army's two centre corps, and it was against these that the 6th German army directed its counter-attack. Thus the main defeat was inflicted not on Dubail but on Castelnau's three corps on the Morhange heights. That night he ordered his army to fall back to the River Meurthe and the Grand Couronné de Nancy. Both Dubail and, further to the south, Pau were forced to conform. Castelnau's priority was to recover his links with Dubail's army, and he was ready to fall back yet further, to the Meuse or

---

[71] For this phase of the battle, see Gras, *Castelnau*, 149–74; also Dubail, *Quatre années*, i. 40–64.

MAP 7. BELGIUM AND NORTHERN FRANCE

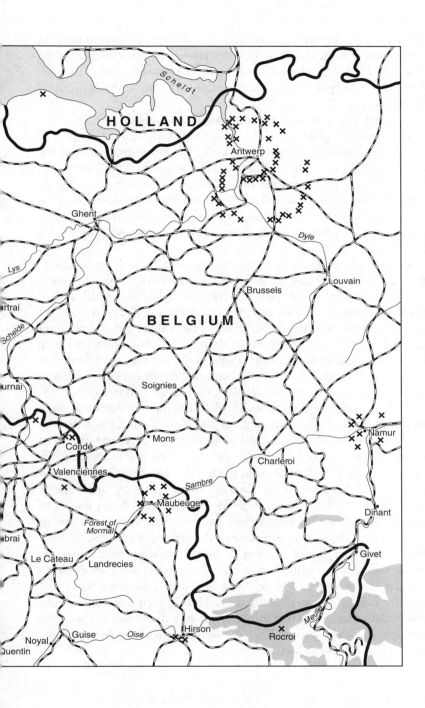

towards Épinal, to accomplish that objective. In the event the force of his own attack on the 20th, plus the resistance of Fort Manonviller (sustained until the 27th), proved to have been enough to slow the German 6th army's pursuit, enabling Castelnau to break contact and establish the 2nd army in front of Nancy on the 23rd.

Joffre's original plan for his advance north of the line Verdun–Metz embraced the possibility of using three armies, the 3rd, 4th, and 5th. However, as early as 31 July Lanrezac, the commander of the 5th army, expected the Germans to cross the Meuse, and was increasingly anxious that he face north, towards Belgium, and not north-east. But, whatever his supporters said later, Lanrezac had not anticipated the full scale of the German envelopment. If he had, he would not—presumably—have been rash enough to advance into its jaws. He thought the Germans would come between Givet and Namur, and south of the Sambre.

The problem for both Joffre and Lanrezac was what weight to attach to events in Belgium. For Joffre, persuaded that the main battle would be fought in the centre, the value of the Belgian army—if it had any—was that it extended his left flank as he advanced into Luxembourg. Thus, on 7 August the French thought the Belgians could do one of two things: either they could push their field army up to the Meuse, so aiding the French offensive in the Ardennes, or they could be ready to strike against the German right flank as it moved south of the Meuse. Joffre therefore saw the Belgian army as an adjunct to a grand allied conception orchestrated by himself and embracing north-western Europe as its deployment zone. The Belgians, on the other hand, were convinced that they faced the main weight of the German army, knew that the Meuse positions had already been turned to the north of Liège, and were bent on protecting Belgian territory. Their plan was to hold on the line of the River Gette and wait for the French to come to them. Whereas the French expected the Belgians to fall back south on Namur, towards France, the Belgians intended to retreat north to the stronghold of Antwerp. Albert's efforts to impress upon Joffre and his headquarters both Belgian plans and German designs were frustrated by the intermediaries through whom he had to communicate: the French military mission at Belgian headquarters appeared, according to Galet, 'less inclined to accept our reports than to question them'.[72] So persuasive were the convictions of Joffre's emissaries that by 16 August even the Belgians began to doubt the wisdom of their own conclusions. Albert's and Galet's plans for a staged withdrawal were challenged by their own intelligence section, which played down the significance of the German concentrations on and across the Meuse.

---

[72] Galet, *Albert*, 106; for a French account, Brécard, *En Belgique*, esp. 16–21.

It was argued that the German attack on Liège did not necessarily confirm the direction of the main German advance. The city's railway communications gave it a logistical importance independent of its position as a gateway to the Belgian plain, and its fortresses would have presented a threat to the German right flank for an advance south of the Meuse. But in the latter case it would have been sufficient for the Germans to mask Liège rather than attack it. Moreover, from 8 August onwards intelligence of German concentrations between Thionville and Liège multiplied. On 15 August the Germans attacked Dinant, on the Meuse and midway between Givet and Namur. That evening Joffre gave way to Lanrezac's pressure and ordered the 5th army to advance north and northwest, to Namur and the junction of the Sambre and Meuse rivers.

Neither Joffre nor Lanrezac imagined that the 5th army's advance would be in isolation: it would be extended to the left by the BEF and by the Belgians, and it would be sheltered by Namur. But French plans did not conform with the expectations of either of their allies. Lanrezac's push to the north overthrew the planning assumption of the British war council of 12 August, that the BEF was to guard the left flank of a French offensive into Luxembourg. Safely shipped across in 240 requisitioned vessels, the BEF was about to be chivvied into a counter-offensive against the main German envelopment, while its supply columns were still struggling to keep up. At least the British did their best to meet French wishes; by contrast, the Belgians expected the French to conform to theirs. On 18 August, knowing that the German 1st army was north of Liège and the 2nd army facing it, the Belgians finally concluded that the French would not get to them in time, and began to pull their field army back to Antwerp. Only the 4th division remained forward, committed to the defence of Namur which, although now isolated, became a possible pivot for the Belgian, British, and French armies. It failed to fulfil such grandiose conceptions, falling on 23 August.

The results of the pressures on Joffre's headquarters from Lanrezac and from King Albert were a change in deployment, more than a change in strategy. Only the French 3rd and 4th armies now faced the Ardennes. Joffre began to create a new army, the army of Lorraine, found from reserve divisions and commanded by Maunoury, to form up behind them and to guard their southern flank. But his intention to advance into the Ardennes remained unswerving, confirmed rather than undermined by the knowledge that the Germans were moving across the face of the French armies to their right. The intelligence which he acquired after 15 August, in particular the capture of the order of battle of the 2nd German army on 17 August and the conclusion reached on 18 August that the Germans would advance north of the Meuse between Namur and Brussels, further buttressed this decision. The strength of the Germans on both their wings suggested—given the French underestimate of the total German strength in the west—that they would be weak in the centre. Moreover, a

French thrust through the Ardennes into Neufchâteau and Arlon would outflank the German right wing on its own left and so frustrate the German
manoeuvre. But Joffre's picture of the German deployment was still only
partial. He failed to realize that the thrust of the 3rd and 4th French armies
would be directed into the hub of the German wheel. The German advance
into the Ardennes was slow, as the 4th and 5th German armies had to mark
time while the 1st and 2nd swung through Belgium. But, as the wheel took
effect, so the Ardennes would fill. Thus, two key assumptions were valid only
for a short period. First, the German weakness in the centre—Joffre imagined
that six German corps would face his eight—would not last. Secondly, Joffre
was wrong to conclude that the Germans would not fight in the wooded and
broken ground of the Ardennes but would be found on the further side. On 21
August Joffre ordered the 3rd and 4th armies to attack through the Ardennes,
and the 5th to do so on the Sambre. The latter would hold the Germans while
the attack of the former took effect.

In the subordinate formations of the 3rd and 4th armies 21 August was a
confusing and exhausting day. At its outset the 87th infantry brigade of II
corps, on the right of 4th army, was charged with a defensive battle facing east;
it was then told to turn north, albeit still with a defensive mission; by the
evening its task was offensive. As a result it had three or four hours extra
marching and was still not in its allocated start positions on the following
morning. In common with the rest of 3rd and 4th armies, it did not halt until it
was too late to establish its command links. In particular, II corps was not in
contact with its right-hand neighbour IV corps, on the left of 3rd army. The
reorientation of the 3rd and 4th French armies, from facing north-east to
north, meant that their deployment was in echelon, each formation constituting a step in a staircase falling away to the south and east. The danger to each
unit's right flank was meant to be warded off by the support of the unit below it
and to the east. But the lack of liaison meant that on the following day II corps
attacked to the north, while IV corps was engaged by superior numbers to the
east. The vulnerability of the French alignment was exacerbated by the south-
westerly direction of the advance of the 4th and 5th German armies, which hit
the French obliquely. Although on 21 August the 3rd French army had indications that it would encounter the German 5th, French reconnaissance was bad.
The cavalry division attached to the 3rd army was poorly commanded and
inadequately trained. The infantry divisions and brigades had been deprived of
their integral cavalry in order to enable the formation of independent cavalry
corps, and consequently each division had only three troops of reservists
mounted on requisitioned horses. Aircraft had done good work so far, but
on the 22nd they were grounded by early morning mist. The French began
their advance in columns of march, with their 75 mms to the rear. As the guns
came up they were deployed well forward for direct fire, and thus, when the

mist lifted, were exposed to immediate German observation. The hilly terrain favoured the high-angle fire of howitzers, each German division having six 105 mms and each corps sixteen 150 mms. The 3rd army battle broke into a series of independent, ill co-ordinated engagements. V corps in the centre turned east to face the German line of advance and so opened a gap between it and its left-hand neighbour. On the 3rd's left, the 4th army had a two-to-one superiority at the beginning of the day, although this was whittled away as the German redeployment took effect. More importantly, however, its centre and right were badly mauled before its left—with which it led and which could therefore have lapped around the German columns—was engaged. XVII corps' right flank was exposed by the slowness of XII corps to advance in support, and suffered heavy losses at Bertrix. The 3rd colonial division on the left of 4th army's II corps advanced furthest, but was not alerted to the cavalry's reports that Germans were in the neighbourhood and so advanced in columns of four. As elsewhere on the front, it was not supported on its right. Thus it was caught in a devastating fire from its front and flank, and lost 228 officers and 10,275 other ranks killed, wounded, or captured in the course of the day. To the division's south-east, at Virton, 3rd army's IV corps was almost as battered. In the 130th Régiment d' Infanterie the colonel was dead, all three of its battalion commanders killed or wounded, and only one of its twelve company commanders unscathed. Its neighbour, the 124th, had almost no officers, and had lost 770 men, or about a third of its strength. Nonetheless, both armies reckoned the day's outcome had been indecisive. The German infantry had come on in dense formations, with their supports closed up, and where the 75 mms had been able to take effect had suffered horribly. The French planned to renew the attack the next day: the 4th army did so. But the losses, particularly of officers in battalions with a high proportion of reservists, were unsustainable without consolidation. The French retreat began on the 24th.[73]

An integral part of Joffre's plan for the defence of the northern frontiers was his expectation that the 5th army would attack on the Sambre at the same time as the 3rd and 4th armies to the 5th's south advanced into the Ardennes. On 21 August, still underestimating by about half the German strength in Belgium, Joffre imagined that an attack by Lanrezac, with the BEF coming up from Maubeuge on his left, would link with the Belgians in Namur and so create an effective barrier to the north. Lanrezac, however, was less certain. His army's change of direction had been accompanied by a reshuffle of divisions which—although it reinforced it—disrupted its internal workings. His view of fortifications was that common among the pre-1914 students of mobile warfare: they were traps. Therefore, he was reluctant to hinge his operations on Namur

[73] Grasset's two studies, Ethe and Virton, provide operational narratives; see also the account of 87th brigade's commander, Cordonnier, Une brigade au feu, 237–303.

or commit part of his army to support its defence. The Sambre itself was not a good defensive line: its valley was overlooked and filled with factories and pit-heads which would inhibit manoeuvre and prevent the acquisition of clear fields of fire. Most compelling of all, his $2^{\text{ème}}$ bureau was beginning to form an accurate picture of the German strength in Belgium. On the afternoon of 21 August Lanrezac finally recognized the scale of the threat in front of him and wisely decided to fall back south of the Sambre to fight a defensive battle. But he had dithered too long. That evening Bülow's 2nd army secured crossings on the Sambre between Namur and Charleroi. The 5th army was now in contact with the enemy. Furthermore, von Hausen's 3rd army was marching west-wards, towards the Meuse south of Namur, and therefore threatening Lan-rezac's right flank. Whether he liked it or not, Lanrezac was committed to fighting a defensive battle in the Sambre valley—and not out of it—on the following day. His inability to decide earlier whether to attack or to defend meant that his troops were not entrenched and that he had not reinforced the Namur garrison.

His own uncertainty as to his operational intentions was mirrored by the secrecy of his $3^{\text{ème}}$ bureau and their failure to communicate openly with either Joffre or the BEF. Consequently, both the latter continued to assume that Lanrezac's overall objective remained offensive. Joffre therefore asked the BEF to advance northwards, in conformity with Lanrezac. The BEF's own com-mand decisions were caught in the thrall of those of the French. On 22 August both General Macdonogh, the BEF's director of military intelligence, through aerial reconnaissance, and the British liaison officer with the 5th French army warned Sir John French that a massive German envelopment seemed to be taking place: rather than turning in behind each other as they reached the Sambre, the German units were pushing out to the west. Nonetheless, Sir John ordered the BEF to march on Soignies, a move which imperilled his command on both its left, to the German envelopment, and its right, as it opened the gap between the BEF and the 5th army now behind and to the east on the Sambre.

Although French counter-attacks on the 22nd proved unsuccessful, the position of the 5th army was stable. Bülow was temporarily checked, and the gap between the French and the BEF was bridged by Sordet's cavalry corps. Sir John French wisely refused Lanrezac's request that he swing right to attack Bülow's flank, since he would thus have exposed his own army to Kluck's 1st German army, but he did agree to halt on the Mons–Condé canal. By fighting frontally, the BEF would help guard the French left from the German en-velopment.

The potentially dangerous position in which the BEF found itself—forward of its allies and directly in the path of the main weight of the German army—was rendered null by the Germans' own ignorance of the BEF's whereabouts. The German naval staff had expected the shipment of the BEF to begin on 16

August, a full week later than was the case.[74] The German advance through Belgium began on 18 August. Kluck, commanding the 1st army on the German right wing, believed that the British had landed, not at Le Havre and Boulogne but at Ostend, Dunkirk, and Calais. His inclination was to protect his outer flank by pushing towards the Channel coast. However, the effect of doing this would have been to stretch the German armies too thinly and to have opened gaps in their line. Kluck was therefore subordinated to Bülow, commanding the 2nd and inner army, so that the movements of the two armies would conform to those of the latter. The effect was to bring the line of Kluck's march through Belgium south, and not south-west, and to direct Kluck against the BEF's front and not towards its flank. But Bülow's alignment only increased Kluck's worries about the possibility of the BEF lying outside his right wing. The German cavalry failed to clarify the fears and suspicions of either army commander. The 2nd cavalry corps was brought under Bülow's command on 21 August and directed south towards Charleroi, but was then drawn north-west in the direction of the Scheldt and reallocated to Kluck. A false report that British troops were arriving at Tournai, 48 kilometres to the west of where they really were, caused Kluck to halt for two hours while the report was investigated. The effect was to redirect the march of II cavalry corps on to Tournai from the north. Exhausted by its peregrinations, the German cavalry played no effective part in the fighting of the 24th. At noon on the 23rd, 3 kilometres north of Mons, one battalion of Kluck's infantry was told by cavalry scouts—who had presumably reconnoitred to the south-west and not to the south—that there was no enemy within 80 kilometres.[75]

Sir John French's optimism about his strategic position—he was persuaded that at most only two German corps opposed him, when Macdonogh told him there were three—was thus somewhat vindicated by the nature of the battle the BEF was now to fight. Kluck's initial attacks against the British were inevitably little more than part of his continued advance: they were not co-ordinated and were delivered in dense formations. The BEF had the advantage of prepared positions where it could develop the firepower of its infantry. But its corps commanders were uncertain whether French intended the action on which they were embarking to be the jumping-off point for a further advance or the preliminary to a general retreat. Tactically, the line of the Mons canal was no better for sustained defence than that of the Sambre: the canal itself did not constitute a major obstacle, and the buildings and pit-heads of the area obstructed fields of fire. On the right of the British position a bend in the canal created a salient which became exposed to German artillery as Kluck's attack developed purpose and effort. The Germans broke into smaller groups

[74] Goldrick, *King's ships*, 71–2.
[75] Edmonds, *France and Belgium 1914*, i. 68–70; Bloem, *Advance from Mons*, 53; Poseck, *Deutsche Kavallerie*, 209; Anglesey, *History of British cavalry*, vii. 143–4.

and advanced by rushes, finding as they closed that the British were having to fire high because of the canal embankment and that once within 500 yards they were less exposed to its effects.[76] The salient was abandoned in mid-afternoon. However, the BEF anticipated renewing the fight from its second line on the 24th.

The salvation of the BEF was the sharp disillusionment of its commander. Sir John French's reluctance to listen to Macdonogh's accurate assessments of the German strength can only be explained by the dominance of Wilson and the consequent reliance on the conclusions of the French. Thus, it was the change in French intentions, not the efforts of his own intelligence services, that persuaded Sir John on the evening of the 23rd to order the BEF to retreat. Joffre was at last beginning to recognize the true nature of the German movement. The French commander therefore suggested that the BEF and the 5th army pull back to the line Maubeuge–Valenciennes. More immediately for the position of the BEF, Lanrezac had—independently, and in advance of Joffre's orders—already ordered the 5th army to retreat. During the course of the afternoon of the 23rd the pressure of Hausen's 3rd army on the right flank of the 5th army had begun to swing the balance against the latter. Without consulting the BEF, fighting—as Sir John saw it—on his behalf, Lanrezac began to pull back. From unrealistic optimism the British commander-in-chief switched to unjustified despondency. His erstwhile excessive faith in French assessments now contrasted with a deep distrust of Lanrezac.

The two British corps spent the night of 23/4 August in positions 5 kilometres south of Mons, preparing to renew the battle the following day. Not until 1 a.m. were their chiefs of staff told that their orders now were to retreat, and even then no general plan for the withdrawal was issued. Sir John's intentions fluctuated wildly. At one moment he spoke of falling back to Amiens and thus away from the 5th army; both it and the BEF would have been liable to defeat in detail. At another, he favoured placing the BEF within Maubeuge; most of its fortifications were out of date and trees obstructed its fields of fire. Ultimately, French did follow Joffre's suggestions, but he still left the two corps commanders—Haig (I corps) and Smith-Dorrien (II corps) to make their own arrangements. The 24th was well advanced before they could meet to do this. The opportunity to break contact with the enemy, if it had ever existed, was thus lost. II corps in particular, lying on the extreme left of the allied line, merited Kluck's continuous attention as the Germans sought to envelop the BEF. On the night of 25/6 August the two corps were obliged to separate from each other by the forest of Mormal, II corps passing to the west and I corps to the east. In the course of the evening German advance guards clashed with a brigade of Haig's corps at Landrecies. Haig, who, whatever his

[76] Bloem, *Advance from Mons*, 59–64.

other failings was not a man prone to panic, seems—probably because he was also ill—to have done so on this occasion. French therefore concluded that the greater danger lay on his right than on his left, and that I corps, not II corps, needed nursing.

In reality, Smith-Dorrien's corps was scattered and exhausted, and had been fighting continuously for three days. By the time it was fully assembled around Le Cateau in the early hours of the 26th, daylight made it impossible for it to extricate itself. Smith-Dorrien decided he must turn and fight the Germans, the better to secure his retreat. Anxious to stiffen the infantry, the artillery of 5th division placed its guns well forward to give direct support. The effect was to ensure that the Germans' counter-battery fire hit both elements simultaneously. Le Cateau cost II corps 7,812 casualties. The morale of some, regular soldiers though they were, snapped. On the following day the commanding officers of two exhausted battalions, now at St Quentin, agreed to surrender rather than carry on. The conclusion of Sir John French—that Smith-Dorrien should not have fought at Le Cateau and that the action had effectively broken II corps—seemed well founded. Smith-Dorrien did not agree. In the event his corps, though sorely tried, did not lose its cohesion.

He was extraordinarily lucky. He had assumed that I corps would close up, having passed the forest of Mormal, and so secure his right: in reality, the effect of Landrecies had been to widen the gap between the two corps. However, Kluck still imagined that the British line of retreat lay to the south-west, not the south, and the Germans had therefore failed to appreciate the British alignment, and—as at Mons—had thus found their attack deprived of co-ordination. Once again poor German intelligence allowed inferior British forces to fight a successful delaying battle against Kluck's army. During the battle von der Marwitz's cavalry corps fought dismounted, and therefore did not push towards II corps' flanks; after it, it failed to pursue. On the afternoon of the 26th Smith-Dorrien's corps left the battlefield. By 28 August it was 56 kilometres to the south, and the gap between Kluck and itself had been widened as the former persevered with the south-westerly direction of his advance.

From Alsace, through Lorraine and the Ardennes to Mons and Charleroi, the allied armies had been forced to retreat. By the evening of 23 August the battle of the frontiers was over. At 9.35 the following morning Joffre reported to Messimy that his armies would be passing from the offensive to the defensive: 'Our object must be to last out as long as possible, trying to wear the enemy out, and to resume the offensive when the time comes.'[77]

Joffre's critics suggest that these initial defeats were self-inflicted, and harp on the slowness with which he realized the full scale of the German

[77] Quoted in Spears, *Liaison 1914*, 195.

envelopment through Belgium. This is only partly justified. The German advance did not begin until 18 August. Thus, little could be clear before then: between 6 and 15 August Sordet's cavalry corps conducted a long-range reconnaissance into Belgium but found nothing, as the Germans had not yet begun to move. However, after 18 August preconception played powerfully on Joffre: as late as 23 August he was underestimating the German strength in Belgium by 300,000 men. Not until 25 August was the veil truly pulled to one side.

PROBLEMS, AND SOME SOLUTIONS

What followed looked far worse. Companies, battalions passed in indescribable disorder. Mixed in with the soldiers were women carrying children on their arms or pushing little carts in front of them, girls in their Sunday best, old people, carrying or dragging a bizarre mixture of objects. Entire regiments were falling back in disorder. One had the impression that discipline had completely collapsed. Nonetheless all these units had regular cadres and belonged to the active army.[78]

This was how *Le Matin* on 24 August 1914 reported the retreat of Castelnau's XV corps, shattered by the German 6th army at Morhange. It was not an isolated account. As the wounded were conveyed to the rear they propagated rumours and bore evidence on their bodies of realities which both shattered popular illusions and jeopardized the army's morale. With them came others whose departure from the front was less honourable. In Caen, at 8 p.m. on 27 August, 120 men of the 27th Territorial Infantry alighted. Under the command of two officers, and bearing the regimental colours, they had panicked at Valenciennes, boarded a train for the capital without a travel order, and then been directed westwards.[79] As the French and British armies fell back from the frontiers retreat threatened to become rout.

Joffre was alive to the danger. On 10 August the French military authorities had been accorded the right to use the death sentence whenever immediate repression was essential. On 1 September the ministry of war instructed officers to carry out death sentences within twenty-four hours unless there were good grounds for clemency. This became the norm. Soldiers were executed without trial.[80] By October rumours had reached Britain that those who had abandoned Namur were punished by being drilled under heavy shellfire, and that a

---

[78] Cited by Rocolle, *L'Hécatombe*, 98–9.
[79] Pourcher, *Les Jours de guerre*, 91; also 87.
[80] Pedroncini, *Les Mutineries de 1917*, 13–14, 21–3.

unit of Niçois who had run away in Lorraine had been stood with their backs to the enemy in front of their own trenches—again under shellfire.[81]

Retreat did not turn into rout. The resilience of the French army's morale, despite the heavy casualties and tactical defeats of August, argues for the positive functions of punitive and repressive discipline. But this was not the only reason why the army did not collapse. The retreat generated its own determination. After Le Cateau a British unit, the 2nd battalion, the Cameronians, marched 91 kilometres in thirty-six hours, and the BEF as a whole covered 320 kilometres in thirteen days.[82] On its right, the French 5th division, in Lanrezac's 5th army, averaged 22 kilometres a day in the week before 6 September. Exhausted by continuous marching in late summer, the soldiers longed to halt. When the order to attack finally came it seemed to Joffre's men that he had done no more than reflect their own mood: 'the idea of the Marne', wrote one junior officer, 'surged up from the army itself.'[83]

Joffre's own resolution never wavered. Outwardly he appeared imperturbable. He ate regularly and well; he insisted on undisturbed sleep. His calm conveyed itself to his staff, and from it to his armies. His claim to be a great commander rests on his conduct on 25 August and the days immediately succeeding it. During that time the competing interpretations of the unfolding situation could so easily have resulted in the implosion of French general headquarters, Grand Quartier Général (GQG). That it did not do so was a reflection of Joffre's moral authority.

The dominant personality at GQG, after Joffre himself, was the energetic but corpulent deputy chief of staff, Berthelot. So modest and self-effacing was Berthelot's direct superior, Belin, that this inversion of the hierarchy was not itself productive of tension. The trouble was that Berthelot embraced operational concepts that did not always accord with reality or with realism. Thus, the pre-war division between the 3ème bureau (operations) and the 2ème bureau (intelligence) persisted, and it was compounded by disagreements within the 3ème bureau itself. Joffre's *chef de cabinet*, Maurice Gamelin, although as persuaded of the merits of the offensive as Berthelot, could not but recall Foch's pre-war conviction that the German right wing would extend across the Meuse and up to the Channel coast. From 16 August others at GQG woke up to the reach of the German envelopment, but Berthelot was not one of them. Even as late as 29 August, according to Huguet, the French liaison officer with the BEF, 'he did not appreciate fully the importance of the German threat to our left flank'.[84] Joffre's reluctance to listen to the Belgians needs little further explanation.

[81] David (ed.), *Inside Asquith's cabinet*, 199.
[82] Terraine (ed.), *General Jack's diary*, 43, 48.
[83] L. V. Smith, 'Command authority in the French army', 159–60.
[84] Huguet, *Britain and the war*, 75–6; see also Gamelin, *Manoeuvre et victoire de la Marne*, 63–6, 91–4.

No generals in the history of warfare had commanded such large armies on such a broad front as did Joffre and Moltke. The problems of communication and control were enormous. However, by placing GQG close behind the front at Vitry-le-François, Joffre positioned himself so as to be able to maintain regular contact with his armies. He strove for ubiquity. On 26 August he drove 340 kilometres, on the 28th 390, and on the 29th 240.[85] When he could not see the situation for himself, he listened to the reports of his liaison officers. These men, relatively junior but frequently brilliant, were Joffre's eyes and ears. They picked up the mood of the generals, and compared their own impressions of the situation with the reports GQG was receiving. In so far as was possible, Joffre's views became grounded in reality.

The opening defeats were the sanction which Joffre needed in order to reconstitute the French army. The apprehension, and even distrust, felt by the generals towards GQG's liaison officers were well-founded. The average age of French generals on mobilization was 64.2. The mobilization of reserve divisions had resulted in the recall of retired officers, and their commanders were on the whole almost three years older than those of active divisions. General Brugère, who had been vice-president of the Conseil Supérieur de Guerre in 1900–6, assumed the command of a territorial division aged 73. Pau and Maunoury, both summoned to command armies, were aged 67. Some of these older men performed distinguished service; others lacked the fitness to cope with the physical strains. However, age was not the only problem of the French high command; German generals were no younger. In 1900, in the aftermath of the Dreyfus affair, promotions had become subject to ministerial approval. Between 1900 and 1904 General André had promoted officers of proven republicanism. During this period 290 brigadiers had been appointed and 125 divisional generals: many of them were among those recalled in 1914. Professional qualities were at a discount. Even more important than those who were promoted were those who were not. The average period spent as a lieutenant-colonel in the pre-1914 French army was 3.5 years. Sarrail, whose republican credentials were impeccable, held the rank for 1.5 years. By contrast, Foch and Fayolle, both to become marshals of France but both educated by Jesuits, were lieutenant-colonels for five and eight years respectively. In 1911 Joffre, with Messimy's support, had begun the process of restoring professional qualifications as the prime claim to rank. More importantly, his *cabinet* had set about informing itself of the qualities of France's officer corps. On mobiliza- tion the bulk of this *cabinet* became the staff of GQG. Messimy, on 10 August 1914, with his fondness for the memory of 1793, authorized Joffre to conduct a purge of the higher command. The biggest single factor uniting those who were *limogés* was age, and what united those who were not was professional

---

[85] Contamine, *Victoire*, 187.

competence. Many of those who suffered did so because they had been given in wartime the corps or divisional commands that had eluded them in peace. Of the ten commanders of territorial divisions eight were removed, and their average age was 62. By 6 September 1914 Joffre had dismissed three army commanders, seven corps commanders, thirty-four divisional commanders, and fourteen brigadiers. When casualties are included, almost one-third of the French high command had changed. By the end of the year 162 commanders of higher formations had been sacked; only three army commanders, six corps commanders, and twenty-one divisional commanders had remained in post since mobilization. Furthermore, the changes which Joffre effected determined the senior command of the French army for the rest of the war. Foch, commanding XX corps on mobilization, became an army commander on 30 August, and took over an army group, as Joffre's deputy, on 5 October. Philippe Pétain, about to retire as a colonel when mobilization came, was a temporary general by the end of August, and an army commander by June 1915.[86]

Pétain was exceptional. He was one of only three officers aged 56 or over in 1914 who were not already generals but who rose to become army commanders in the course of the war (the others were Nivelle and de Mitry). Of the remaining thirty-six who claimed this accolade, the vast majority were therefore pursuing an upward trajectory already set in peacetime and determined by professional competence rather than by republican loyalties. Pétain had been held back by his views on tactics, not on politics. Thus, Joffre's purge was dependent on his knowledge of, and belief in, the qualities of the officer corps as a whole. It reflected his conviction that the battle of the frontiers was a series of tactical defeats.

Lackadaisical leadership had characterized the battles in Alsace, in the Ardennes, and on the Sambre. But the defeats were not entirely the fault of the generals. The tactical instructions issued both by GQG on 16 and 18 August and also by individual army commanders reflected pre-war precepts about the difficulties of the offensive. Stress was put on artillery support, on the need to develop fire superiority, on the combination of artillery with infantry, and on immediately entrenching once ground was gained. In the event the infantry did not wait, did not prepare their attacks with method. This was less a consequence of the 'spirit of the offensive' and more of a lack of training. The three-year law had not only come too late, it had also been implemented by taking in two classes in 1913 rather than retain the 1911 class for a further year. Therefore, in July 1914 two-thirds of the conscripts then serving had been in uniform for less than a year, and none of them had been on manoeuvres; the 1912 class was still under arms but had only attended divisional or corps

[86] Rocolle, *L'Hécatombe*, *passim*, but esp. 40–74, 158–91, 212–18, 262–362; Cailletau, *Guerres mondiales et conflits contemporains*, 156, (octobre 1989), 4–9, 20. The precise totals of those dismissed varies according to the nature of the calculation: the three army commanders were Ruffey, Lanrezac, and Pau.

manoeuvres, as army manoeuvres were held only once every four years. Nor was this inexperience confined to the most junior ranks. A French infantry company had on average less than half the number of non-commissioned officers enjoyed by a German company. In 1913 the French army was short of 6,000 sergeants and 23,000 corporals. Thus, only one problem addressed by the three-year law, that of manpower, had been resolved; the other, that of tactical competence, would take longer to put right than the July crisis had allowed. In August 1914 the excitement of action overtook professional wisdom. The influence of rhetoric proved greater than that of common sense.[87]

Matters were not helped by the manner in which the French used their 75 mm field guns when on the attack. In 1897 France had led the world in the introduction of quick-firing field artillery, and in 1914 the 75 mm was still arguably the best of its type. Although the Germans had upgraded their 77 mm gun, first introduced in 1896, in 1905, they had concluded from the Russo-Japanese War that long-range fire with field guns was useless: its fall could not be adequately observed and its shrapnel shells in particular were ineffective against field fortifications and enemy gun-pits. These tasks were transferred to heavier artillery, and in particular the 105 mm light howitzer and the 150 mm heavy howitzer. The key attribute of the 77 mm became its mobility, and the facility with which it could accompany infantry over broken ground.[88] By contrast, French artillery doctrine was built around the light field gun rather than a blend of such guns with heavier artillery. The French had no howitzers at any level up to that of the corps; they argued that the German 105 mm and 210 mm howitzers were slow to come into action, tended to fire high, and did more moral than material damage. Speed of deployment and rate of fire—it was claimed a 75 mm could fire twenty rounds a minute—were rated over weight of metal. Neutralizing the enemy was more important than destroying him. French field guns were therefore organized in four-gun batteries, not the six-gun batteries favoured by the Germans, and so a French corps could field thirty batteries, although armed with only 120 field guns, to a German corps' twenty-four batteries made up of 144 field guns. In all, France could equip 999 batteries to Germany's 812.

To support this approach to the use of artillery, its command was delegated down to subordinate formations. Percin, the inspector-general of artillery between 1907 and 1911, wanted to establish direct liaison between the artillery battery and the infantry company, his idea being that the infantry would use the support of the guns as it encountered resistance to its advance. Therefore,

[87] Spears, *Liaison 1914*, app. VII; Contamine, *Révanche*, 237–47; id., *Victoire*, 122–36; Foch, *Memoirs*, 15–20; L. V. Smith, 'Command authority in the French army', 66–81; Stevenson, *Armaments and the coming of war*, 303; Herrmann, *Arming of Europe*, 202–3.

[88] Benary, *Ehrenbuch des deutschen Feldartillerie*, 38; Müller, *Militärgeschichtliche Mitteilungen*, 57, (1998), 398, 423.

the French artillery did not prepare the attack, did not exploit its maximum range, and did not counter the enemy's artillery. No range tables for the 75 mm firing high-explosive shell had been drawn up before the war, and its normal maximum range with shrapnel had become set at 4,000 metres. The guns' task began when the infantry entered the danger zone from enemy small-arms fire, at say 800 metres, and lasted until it was within 350 metres. They could not perform this task from a distance or indirectly, as the army had insufficient telephone line to link the forward observers to the batteries: the guns had either to use direct fire or to be controlled by an observer on an adjacent hill. Although the 75 mm was technically capable of high-angle, indirect fire, using the 'plaquette Malandrin' to curve the shell's trajectory, such tactics required the gun to be dug in and therefore militated against the mobility and speed which had become the artillery's watchwords. Without such preparation the 75 mm's maximum elevation was 18 degrees.[89]

The fighting on the frontiers had been in broken and wooded ground, demanding indirect fire and high-angle elevations. The French infantry had suffered from the attentions of the German heavy artillery, often dug in, in prepared and covered positions, and capable of inflicting damage at long ranges. But trials even at this early stage of the war showed the maximum range of the 75 mm with high-explosive shell was 6,800 metres to the 5,500 of the 77 mm, and at Mortagne, with a delayed-action fuse and its trail dug in to increase its elevation, it had ranged 9,000 metres and provided a match for the German howitzers.[90] Ballistically the 75 mm was far superior to the 77 mm. Its cone of fire was long, deep, and dense compared with the more perpendicular cone of fire characteristic of the German gun, and its long carriage enabled it to sweep fire to left and right. Its shrapnel shell was slightly heavier, and its high-explosive charge was 650 grams compared to the 77 mm's 190 grams. Using delayed-action fuses for ricochet fire, a 75 mm battery was able to sweep an area of 4 hectares, 400 metres deep, in forty to fifty seconds, and three batteries could cover 12 hectares in a minute in the so-called *rafale*. Although the fire was not accurate, it was precise in the height at which it burst: between one and three metres. A 75 mm battery firing shrapnel, even if it only fired ten rounds per gun, discharged 10,000 balls a minute. Thus it was far more effective against advancing infantry than any small-arms or machine-gun fire.[91]

Therefore, the disadvantages in French artillery doctrine when on the offensive were neutralized on the defensive. Able to choose their ground, the French presented their 75 mms with good fields of fire. The comparative

---

[89] Contamine, *Victoire*, 187; Gascouin, *L'Évolution de l'artillerie*, 22–5, 39, 58–9; Storz, *Kriegsbild und Rüstung*, 207–13, 260–4; Ripperger, *Journal of Military History*, LIX (1995), 599–618; Linnenkohl, *Vom Einzelschuss*, 65–80. I have also learnt much from Matthew Buck on these points.

[90] Dubail, *Quatres années*, i. 22–4; also Gascouin, *Le Triomphe de l'idée*, 195–6, 234–5.

[91] Gascouin, *Le Triomphe de l'idée*, 176–8, 211–12.

immobility of the heavy artillery worked against the Germans if they were the attackers; its shell supply could not keep up with the advance, and it could not choose prepared or concealed positions.

The change from the offensive to the defensive is the best explanation for the transformation in tactical performance. Joffre's tactical instructions of 24 August, so often cited as the cause of the transformation in the French army's performance, were little different from those of 16 and 18 August. He reiterated the need not to launch the infantry prematurely or from too great a distance. Above all, he emphasized that the role of the artillery was not only to support but also to prepare the attack.

Part of Joffre's purpose was moral rather than tactical—to shore up the shattered French infantry. Nonetheless, it is remarkable how quickly French fighting methods improved. One gunner subsequently described the battle in the Trouée de Charmes between 24 and 26 August, as 'une petite victoire de la Marne, précédant la grande',[92] in its tactical and moral effects. Otto von Moser, commanding a Württemberg infantry brigade, found as the German 4th army cleared the Ardennes that the French infantry was already using trenches on 26 August, spurning an open fight in favour of the protection of buildings and folds in the ground. To his left, in Lorraine, the command of Ernst Röhm, a lieutenant in the Bavarian infantry, was overwhelmed by French firepower—rifle, machine-gun, and artillery—directed from behind impenetrable cover. In the fighting that followed the 75 mm gun became the hub of the French battle, and the Germans developed a respect for French field artillery fire which was to last throughout the war.[93]

Despite the tactical defeats which they had borne, the French armies were intact. True, some units in the battle of the frontiers suffered horrific casualties. Between 20 and 23 August 40,000 French soldiers died, 27,000 of them on the 22nd. By 29 August total French losses reached 260,000, including 75,000 dead. But the impact varied considerably according to regiment, division, and even army. The 1st and 2nd armies in Lorraine, and the 5th in the north, had suffered less than the 3rd and 4th in the Ardennes: the 3rd had 13,000 killed or wounded out of 80,000 infantry engaged. Furthermore, only forty-eight out of a total ninety-six allied divisions (or their equivalent) were involved in the fighting between 18 and 23 August. In the same period fifty-four of eighty-six German divisions were in action, including seventeen reserve divisions to only four French. France was able to make up its losses. By not having used all its reserves from the outset, and by falling back on to its lines of communications, it could bring over 100,000 men from the depots to fill its depleted ranks. By 6

[92] Ibid. 63.
[93] Moser, *Feldzugsaufzeichnungen*, 20; Röhm, quoted in Storz, 'Die Schlacht der Zukunft', in Michalka (ed.), *Erste Weltkrieg*, 252; Rommel, *Attacks*, 17–18, 37–46; Schulte, *Europäische Krise*, 182; Wild von Hohenborn, *Briefe und Tagebuchaufzeichnungen*, 16, 22–3.

September most French units were up to 80 or 85 per cent of their establishment. Moreover, Italy's prompt declaration of neutrality enabled the dissolution of the army guarding the Alps, and the reallocation elsewhere of its five
regular divisions and one territorial. Two more divisions arrived from North
Africa. On 31 August a third British corps, albeit only of one division initially,
was formed. The Entente armies grew stronger, not weaker, after the battle of
the frontiers.[94]

Finally, although a series of defeats, the battle of the frontiers had conveyed a
number of strategic advantages. To the east the engagements of Morhange and
Sarrebourg had committed the German left wing and prevented it being used
to reinforce the right. To the north Mons and Charleroi had pulled the Germans south, away from the Channel ports and the Belgian army, now
ensconced in Antwerp. The fact that plan XVII had been a plan for the
concentration of France's armies, not a plan of campaign, gave Joffre a flexibility denied the Germans. Previous French war plans had emphasized the
need to identify the direction of the enemy thrust, the role of manoeuvre
before the counter-attack. This was the basic philosophy to which Joffre now
returned. The battle of the frontiers had given Joffre an understanding of the
general situation, which—although delayed—was now complete and wholly
realistic. He had managed to break contact with the enemy: nowhere had the
Germans fixed him and robbed him of his freedom of manoeuvre. On this
basis a fresh plan of operations was possible.

By contrast, the mood in the German general headquarters on 25 August,
although jubilant, was not grounded in reality. Tappen, Ludendorff's successor as head of operations, was convinced that the major battles had now been
fought, and that the campaign in the west was effectively over. But the
information on which he based this conclusion was partial in both senses of
the word. Army commanders, vying with each other for the laurels of victory,
were sending back reports that exaggerated their own achievements. In truth,
neither their headquarters nor that of Moltke had the means to gather sufficient intelligence to confirm or deny the claims.

In 1914 cavalry remained the most numerous and still the most effective
means of gaining information, as well as of denying it to the enemy. The major
obstacle to its effectiveness on the western front at this stage of the war was less
firepower and more the intensively cultivated and semi-urbanized nature of
the terrain, broken up by canals, fences, walls, slag-heaps, and railway lines. To
these obstacles were added those of fortification: detours around Liège,
Namur, and Maubeuge, and tracing paths between Brussels and Antwerp,
and Lille and Condé, increased the distances that the advancing cavalry had
to cover and lost time.

---

[94] Contamine, *Révanche*, 234, 246–7, 276; Contamine, *Victoire*, 120, 285–7.

Man for man, as well as horse for horse, the best cavalry in 1914 were the British. The Boer War had dinned into them the need for effective horse management to avoid sore backs, colic, and other equine complaints. It had also caused them to accept with better grace than either the French or Germans that cavalry was as likely to fight dismounted as mounted. Of the three, they were the ones equipped with rifles rather than carbines, with the result that their musketry emulated that of the infantry.[95] Nonetheless, the German cavalry division, because it contained its own integral infantry, could collectively match the British in terms of firepower. The inability of the French I cavalry corps to penetrate the protective screen of the German right wing was a tribute to the German cavalry's defensive capabilities. But its qualities were less pronounced when its roles shifted from protection to tactical and strategic reconnaissance. Its bridging equipment proved unsuitable for the canalized and deep-banked rivers of north-western Europe, and the cyclist companies of its infantry battalions encourged it to follow the lines of the roads. The hard surfaces quickly wore out the horses' shoes. Because of the nature of its line of march, it opted to advance in small, narrow, deep formations rather than in broad, strong ones. When it encountered the enemy's cavalry, probably dismounted and using the defensive advantages vouchsafed by urbanization and agricultural development, it was forced to deploy to right and left, and also to wait for—or fall back to—its own infantry. Its tactical timidity was compounded by its lack of a body of trained senior cavalry commanders. Not until the 1913 manoeuvres was the cavalry exercised in divisions, and only one cavalry division had existed before mobilization.[96]

Schlieffen and Moltke had laid great store on the encounter battle: that depended on the cavalry. If they had been entirely confident of it occurring on their right flank, then the bulk of their cavalry should have been here, and Schlieffen had indeed allocated eight cavalry divisions to the right wing and three to Lorraine in his 1905 memorandum. In the event, however, although ten of the German army's eleven cavalry divisions were assigned to the west, they were distributed evenly along the front—so confirming the evidence that suggests there was no predisposition to see the right wing as decisive in itself. As a result the right wing was woefully deficient in cavalry, and Kluck's army in particular was unable to reconnoitre effectively. Kluck had failed to locate in advance the true positions of the BEF at Mons and Le Cateau: he was now to conclude—wrongly—that the BEF was out of the battle. The BEF itself had already shown the contribution which aircraft could make to intelligence.

[95] Richard Holmes, 'The last hurrah: cavalry on the western front, August–September 1914', in Cecil and Liddle (eds.), *Facing Armageddon*; also Holmes, *Riding the retreat*.
[96] Poseck, *Deutsche Kavallerie*, esp. 210–18; Marwitz, *Weltkriegsbriefe*, 12–13, 20, 22; Storz, *Kriegsbild und Rüstung*, 276–8; Rittmeister von Ammon, 'Kavallerie', in Schwarte (ed.), *Militärischen Lehren*, 1st edn., 74–9.

However, the German organization of its flying arm—one field flying section of six aircraft for each army headquarters and each active corps—left no aircraft directly subordinate to general headquarters and none to the reserve corps. Thus, detailed reports were presented to army and corps commanders who were not necessarily aware of the overall picture, while Moltke himself was not in a position to order his own reconnaissance. Again, Kluck in particular was the loser; his right flank was guarded by a reserve corps and so was deprived of the benefits of aerial observation.[97] The Germans were guilty of seeing things as they wanted them to be, not as they were: it was the memory of 1870, the conviction of German military superiority, which buoyed their sense of victory. And yet this too was proving an illusion: the strain of the advance was revealing the imperfections of Germany's military organization.

The failure in intelligence collection was associated, at least in part, with the problems of communication. The elder Moltke had offset the problems of co-ordinating mass armies on the move by making a virtue of self-reliance among his subordinate commanders. But the nature of Schlieffen's planning, with its search for a complete solution to a single campaign, created a tension in German doctrine. Schlieffen's opponents continued to preach the virtues of initiative and of commanding well forward.[98] Schlieffen himself looked to new technology to confer on the desk-bound commander a degree of ubiquity. But the equipment available was still at an intermediate stage of development. The field telegraph, which could not keep pace with rapidly moving forces, was obsolescent. Its replacement by the telephone, begun in 1905, was incomplete by 1914. In any case, land lines were hard to set up and maintain in mobile warfare. Radios, recognized by both Schlieffen and the younger Moltke to be the optimum solution, were cumbersome and still at an early stage of development. Trials with light field radios were begun in the two years before the war.[99] Von der Marwitz, commanding II cavalry corps in August 1914, used them to communicate with Bülow's headquarters, and forward to his own reconnaissance squadrons. He was impressed, although frustrated by what they meant for traditional interpretations of cavalry generalship.[100] Probably more representative of the responses of German generals was that of Erich von Falkenhayn. In 1912 he organized a corps exercise involving the whole range of the new technologies—telephones, wirelesses, motor cars: 'When these inventions of the devil work, then what they achieve is more than amazing; when they do not work, then they achieve less than nothing.' Falkenhayn concluded that for the moment all the old methods of communication had still to be

---

[97] von Matuschka, 'Organisationsgeschichte des Heeres', 294–5, 301–2.
[98] Hughes, *Journal of Military History*, LIX (1995), 274; Storz, *Kriegsbild und Rüstung*, 321.
[99] Bucholz, *Moltke, Schlieffen*, 183–4, 240–1.
[100] Marwitz, *Weltkriegsbriefe*, 22, 31.

retained as back-up.[101] Most senior commanders in 1914 preferred to use dispatch riders and motor cars.

None of these factors is a wholly satisfactory explanation for the general staff's neglect of communications in its pre-war planning. Neither intelligence nor signals specialists were part of the deployment plans.[102] An exercise, fought out on the map with telephones in 1906, had shown some of the problems of communication within a single army command; what it had not attended to were the difficulties of communicating at a higher level, between the army and general headquarters, nor of employing radios, the only technology with the range and flexibility which the German war plan required. By 1914 wireless stations, equipped for cross-border signalling up to a range of 280 kilometres, had been established at Metz, Strasbourg, and Cologne in the west, but they were subordinated to local unit commanders with other priorities.[103] On 16 August, with his headquarters at Coblenz, Moltke was already 219 kilometres from the frontier and 330 kilometres from Kluck. His move to Luxembourg on 29 August still meant that the distances were too great for road links to be sufficient. The French were not slow to profit from German transmissions. Able themselves to use the civilian telephone and telegraph links, they could observe radio silence, while intercepting the messages of the Germans. Some of these were sent in clear and others in codes which the French had broken. Moreover, Moltke's headquarters had only one receiving set, and the relay stations at Luxembourg and Metz soon became overloaded. Transmissions were disrupted by summer storms and by French interference directed from the Eiffel Tower; the Kaiser did not help, taking up valuable air time with unnecessary messages. The result was that the information which Moltke did receive was frequently twenty-four hours old.[104]

Deprived of effective intelligence and efficient communications, Moltke was thus left to exercise command without its basic tools. But his problems did not end there. In 1870 the King and Bismarck had accompanied Moltke's uncle into the field; the term 'general headquarters' denoted the fusion of political and military direction and referred to the location of Wilhelm, the supreme commander, not of Moltke. Moltke's headquarters, Die oberste Heeresleitung (OHL), were thus a part, albeit the most important part, of a much larger imperial entourage. When he had become chief of the general staff, Moltke had shown that he—unlike Schlieffen—would not pander to Wilhelm's military pretensions: in order to give greater reality to manoeuvres he had asked the Kaiser to cease taking an active role in them. But he did not

[101] Afflerbach, *Falkenhayn*, 82.
[102] Storz, *Kriegsbild und Rüstung*, 321.
[103] Bucholz, *Moltke, Schlieffen*, 281.
[104] von Matuschka, 'Organisationsgeschichte des Heeres', 183–4; Groener, *Lebenserinnerungen*, 75; Barnett, *Swordbearers*, 76; Gamelin, *Manoeuvre et victoire de la Marne*, 139.

enjoy in war the freedom which this independence deserved. Schlieffen had tried to minimize the potential problems consequent on imperial intervention by making command a matter of regulation and management. Moltke's approach could ultimately have restored real responsibility to the centre. But the Kaiser, with war just declared, had suddenly abandoned his passivity when he had proposed on 1 August mobilization and concentration against the east alone. Although Wilhelm's intervention had proved abortive, and ultimately—in the context of the war as a whole—isolated, its effect on Moltke was salutary. The management of his royal master became a major preoccupation, and a constant reminder of the limits of his own responsibility. Each day he reported to the Kaiser on the military situation; until 11 September he refused to leave Coblenz, and then Luxembourg, for fear that Wilhelm would take it into his head to exercise more than just the title of supreme command. Furthermore, with the Kaiser came the intrigues and jealousies of court. Moltke knew that his replacement as chief of the general staff, in the event of war, had been widely canvassed. Indeed, his own indifferent health (he had a heart complaint) made sense of such rumours. The chief of the Kaiser's military cabinet, von Lyncker, on 10 August asked Falkenhayn, the minister of war, whether he was ready to succeed Moltke should the need arise. Falkenhayn was indeed ready: he was openly critical of Moltke's command. In Luxembourg one hotel, the Kölner Hof, housed the general staff, and another, the Hotel Brasseur, the military cabinet and the war minister. The division was indicative of more than the conveniences of accommodation. Well might Moltke envy Joffre: Messimy gave the latter full support, and the political direction was far removed from GQG—first in Paris and then (from 2 September) in Bordeaux.[105]

The structure of OHL, the interpretation of its responsibilities, and its style of command could only deepen these problems. The choice of Coblenz and Luxembourg was determined not least by the need to maintain communications with the eastern front as well as the west; in criticizing Moltke's performance in the west, it is as well to remember how much his attention was also taken up with the defence of East Prussia. However, given that his responsibilities embraced two fronts, he should perhaps have created an intermediate level of command between himself and the army commanders—what would later be called an army group. He tried to achieve something of the same effect by temporarily subordinating, on the right, Kluck to Bülow, and on the left, Heeringen (the 7th army) to Crown Prince Rupprecht of Bavaria (the 6th). But, in the former case in particular, this arrangement simply served to exacerbate rivalries. Three of Moltke's army commanders, Duke Albrecht of Württemburg (the 4th army), Crown Prince Wilhelm of Prussia (the 5th), and

---

[105] Schulte, *Europäische Krise*, 175–9; Wrisberg, *Heer und Heimat*, 11.

Crown Prince Rupprecht, were of royal blood and inherently difficult to dismiss; control was exercised through their chiefs of staff. In any case, Moltke's chosen means of command reflected his reluctance to be dogmatic, leaving his army commanders a scope for individual initiative which ill-accorded with the tight control and determinism of his predecessor. 'The plan of the supreme command', Crown Prince Wilhelm later complained, 'was simply to overrun the enemy's country on as broad a front as possible. No definite detailed plan was held in view.'[106] Aping what he construed to be his uncle's style, but in the process distorting it, Moltke conveyed his wishes by directives rather than by orders. Victory would be the fruit of a series of independent actions which would ultimately give the result. Thus each army, and in particular at various points Kluck's, Bülow's, and Crown Prince Rupprecht's, was left free to act in a way that did not conform with the general situation or with Moltke's own intentions.

The German emphasis on independent leadership only made sense in the context of a common body of accepted operational doctrine. Thus, generals would be likely to take individual decisions whose effects would converge and support each other. The general staff was the agent for the transmission of doctrine, but the expansion of the army had diluted its presence to the point where there were only three trained officers in each corps and one in each division.[107] Even more serious was the fact that Schlieffen's operational thought, his emphasis on seeking the flank and rear of the enemy, had not been fully assimilated. A number of independent critics, and most influentially Friedrich von Bernhardi in his book of 1912 *Vom heutigen Kriege*, had rejected Schlieffen's insistence on envelopment and argued that in some circumstances frontal attacks and breakthrough battles would be more appropriate. Moltke's own more sceptical approach acknowledged the wisdom of considering alternatives, and the possibility of tactical breakthrough battles was addressed in the 1912 and 1913 manoeuvres. If an enemy, threatened by a strategic movement to the flank, turned to meet that threat, the frontal battle that followed would in tactical terms aim for a breakthrough. Germany's generals in 1914 had at best been battalion commanders in 1870: tactical immediacy outweighed strategic concepts in their priorities. Another of Schlieffen's critics, Sigismund von Schlichting, concluded from his close study of infantry tactics that the increased ranges at which battles could now be fought extended fronts to the point where tactical envelopment would be very hard to achieve.[108] The problems of mounting a frontal assault, the reinforcement of the firing line in order to achieve fire superiority, was the focus of the generals' pre-war attention. Thus, operational thought grew from tactics. In late August 1914

---

[106] Naveh, *In pursuit of military excellence*, 76.
[107] Samuels, *War in History*, II (1995), 28–9.
[108] Hughes, *Journal of Military History*, LIX (1995), 263–4, 272–3.

army commanders followed their noses. Opportunities for envelopment went begging. Tappen emphasized the frontal attack. Bülow, also an advocate of breakthrough battles, insisted on keeping the right wing tightly dressed to eliminate any gap. Moreover, those who did think in Schlieffen's terms, who did seek the flanks, tended to do exactly what the French hoped they might. They neglected frontal strength to such an extent that they failed to fix their opponent, and thus left the latter free to break contact and to address the threat from the flank.

Although the distinction between tactics and operations, therefore, proved as difficult for the Germans to sustain as for the French, it does not—as it does for the French—provide such a convincing explanation as to why German tactics were so confused in 1914. Some reports of the fighting in the first six weeks show the German excellence in the use of ground, the rapidity with which they built up fire superiority, and the small, dispersed formations in which they delivered the final assault. But in other cases the Germans came on in dense formations, without adequate preparation and with insufficient artillery support. A couple of reasons for this contrast reside in the immediate circumstances of the German advance.

First, much of the fighting in the advance was the product of encounter battles: troops moved from the line of march to combat. Fully to deploy for the attack could take a corps, which occupied 24 kilometres of road space, as much as twenty-four hours.[109] In some cases they did not have the time, or they deemed it unnecessary to await the artillery to prepare the assault. Given the needs of the siege operations in their rear, and the supply problems for artillery horses, the German front-line advantage in heavy artillery—their best counter to French superiority in field artillery—was not as great as their established strength would suggest. German 77 mm batteries, in their anxiety to give moral support to the infantry, rushed forward, frequently siting their guns on forward slopes and thus rendering themselves vulnerable to the French 75 mms.

Secondly, poor tactical performance may have been the pay-off for including reserve formations at the outset of the campaign. The tendency to rush forward prematurely, to clump together and not to disperse, to become over-excited in the heat of battle, was exactly what the professionals had expected of reservists. Furthermore, German reserve corps did not have the sixteen heavy field howitzers possessed by the active corps, and reserve infantry divisions had only thirty-six field guns, half the allocation of an active division. Nor did all reserve infantry regiments have machine-gun companies.[110] With inadequate firepower, careful instructions about artillery preparation and establishing fire superiority before the assault could prove impossible to effect.

[109] Bucholz, *Moltke, Schlieffen*, 302.
[110] von Matuschka, 'Organisationsgeschichte des Heeres', 226–7.

However, Germany's tactical inadequacies stretched beyond its reserve formations and lasted longer than the first six weeks of the war. The 1888 infantry regulations, with which incidentally the name of the young Wilhelm was associated, had spoken much good sense. They instructed the infantry to deploy in swarms, not in closed formations. They had distinguished between an encounter battle and an attack against an enemy in a prepared position; in this latter case fire preparation would be a lengthy process and the attack would not be delivered until fire superiority had been gained. The infantry regulations of 1906 represented little advance on those of 1888, and in some respects were distinctly retrograde. The big issue in the decade before the war was whether the priority in infantry tactics should be the use of ground, which implied dispersion, or the acquisition of fire superiority, which implied concentration. Both were versions of modernization: the compromise was a skirmish line capable of fire effect. But what followed, and was embodied in the 1906 infantry regulations, was a skirmish line so thick that it forfeited the security of looser formations or small groups. The 1906 regulations were modified in 1909 to allow for thin lines at the outset of the advance, thickening prior to the final assault. But what they did not contain was any recognition that fire superiority could be achieved by supporting units or even by machine-gun fire, rather than by the attacking infantry itself. The infantry regulations treated the infantry as the main arm, capable of attacking independently. The artillery regulations talked of co-operation between the two arms, but no regulations for combined tactics were published. Furthermore, in Germany as elsewhere, it was recognized that the fire-swept battlefield would increase the demands made of man's morale. Thus, in coming to grips with the modern battlefield the 1906 regulations fell back on vocabulary that was traditionalist. Prudent recommendations about field fortification were lost in the general tenor, which highlighted the attack regardless of casualties, and put the weight on morale and not material. The principal lesson the Germans derived from the Boer War was that effective tactical exploitation of the new firepower in itself only produced defensive successes: in the end the Boers had lost the war. The offensive spirit was cultivated no less assiduously in Germany than in France. The emptiness of the modern battlefield, the strength of the tactical defensive, the importance of field fortifications—all were reflected in official publications, but were then categorized as 'uncanny', atypical, or one-sided, and so not placed at the heart of tactical thought.

Even if tactical theory was grounded in reality, and much of it—including parts of the 1906 infantry regulations—was, training and practice were very different. Most officers were technologically unsophisticated: the domestically conservative role of the army, its function as a counterweight to urban influences, and its potential use in suppressing revolution militated against tactical innovation.[111] Parade standards were appropriate in aiding the civil power, but were also applied in manoeuvres. Commanders liked to have their units well in hand, and therefore regarded close formations as normal and dispersal as exceptional. The regulations for the field artillery assumed, even with guns not firing at their maximum ranges, that the fire-zone would be 6 to 7 kilometres deep; yet the infantry were still instructed to approach the battlefield in marching columns and to deploy into shallower columns, both good targets for artillery. In October 1911 the military correspondent of *The Times*, Colonel Repington, attended the German manoeuvres: 'No other modern army', he concluded, 'displays such profound contempt for the effect of modern fire.'[112]

The popular estimate of German military superiority, held abroad as firmly as in Germany itself, and sustained as much after the First World War as before it, obscured its remarkably traditional, even Napoleonic, nature. What is striking about the German general staff in 1914 is not its political hamfistedness, its advocacy of preventive war, and its brutal invasion of Belgium. It is the contradictions and gaps in the areas of its own professional competence. In 1866 and 1870 the Germans had led the way in the use of railways in warfare. And yet in 1914 their practice in this regard had changed little. Trains brought the troops to their concentration areas; thereafter soldiers moved as they had always done—on foot or on horseback. Kluck's 1st army, in its massive wheel, marched on average 23 kilometres a day every day for three weeks. Even Hausen's 3rd army had to sustain a comparable rate, albeit over two weeks.

Schlieffen's approach to logistics had been to think through an operational solution and then to expect the railways to conform. He used the argument that the Belgian network provided the best link between France and Germany to justify his decision. Moltke disagreed. From the outset he recognized the vulnerability of the German plan to the destruction by the Belgians and the French of their railway systems.[113] His fears proved justified. Groener did a magnificent job in managing the railways. He had a line open to Cambrai by 3 September, and to Noyon by the 8th and Compiègne by the 9th. But the total number of railway troops available to him was small given that Germany was fighting a two-front war, and peacetime service had not practised them in repairing wartime damage. Furthermore, although the railway department

---

[111] Schulte, *Die deutsche Armee, passim*; Schulte, *Europäische Krise*, 299–322. An important corrective to Schulte is Storz, *Kriegsbild und Rüstung*, esp. 175–9; also his essay, 'Der Schlacht der Zukunft', in Michalka (ed.), *Erste Weltkrieg*.

[112] Quoted in Luvaas, *The education of an army*, 315; earlier in the same year Repington formed a much more favourable assessment, see his *Essays and criticism*, 202–38. On German tactics generally, see von Matuschka, 'Organisationsgeschichte des Heeres', 152, 159, 162; Borgert, 'Grundzüge', 427–32, 474–89; Elze, *Tannenberg*, 45–51; Müller, *Militärgeschichtliche Mitteilungen*, 57, (1998), 385–442.

[113] Wallach, *Dogma of the battle of annihilation*, 89–90.

was directly responsible to the chief of the general staff, the main supply departments were not; the quartermaster-general—who was charged with the oversight of the supply trains—was not kept fully informed as to the operational picture. Thus, inevitably, the full functioning of the railways lagged behind the armies' advance. When the battle of the Marne began on 6 September the key railheads for the 1st, 2nd, and 3rd armies were 136 to 168 kilometres behind their front.[114]

The army recognized the utility of the lorry to cover the gap between the railhead and the front. Subventions to encourage civilian ownership, introduced in 1907, resulted by 1912 in an increase in Germany's lorries which was more than twice that of vehicles in general. By 1913 3,744 lorries were available for military use. In peace almost half of them were employed in the haulage of beer, but in war their task was munitions supply: the 1st and 2nd armies each had 198 on their establishment. However, the roads were so congested that their speed was of limited value. Schlieffen's deployment frequently required two corps to use a single line of communications. By the time of the Marne 60 per cent of lorries had broken down.[115]

Horse-drawn transport, therefore, remained fundamental to forward supply. Kluck's 1st army had 84,000 horses. Nearly 2 million pounds of fodder a day was needed to feed them. Thus, the greater the distance from the railhead, the more transport was devoted to servicing itself rather than the front-line soldier. A single infantry regiment of three battalions, with 233 horses and seventy-two wagons, took up 2 kilometres of road. Most of the transport formations were newly formed on mobilization, their men predominantly reservists who had not served in transport when originally conscripted, and the horses recently requisitioned and not used to military harness. Often fed on green fodder, horses succumbed at a high rate (hence another reason for the cavalry's deficiencies and for poor reconnaissance). For those that were sick and exhausted, veterinary surgeons were in short supply: an infantry brigade with 480 horses had none.

Logistically, therefore, Schlieffen's plan was a nonsense. But there is a danger in exaggerating the significance of Germany's problems with transport. Most serious were the problems of ammunition supply. The 6th army was told to restrict its consumption of heavy artillery shells on 6 September, but sufficient got through for the other armies. Although there was never enough bread, each regiment was equipped with a field kitchen and its members managed to feed themselves by requisitioning. Three days before the Marne von der Marwitz,

---

[114] Groener, *Lebenserinnerungen*, 154–6; see also Addington, *Blitzkrieg era and the German general staff*, 15–21; van Creveld, *Supplying war*, ch. 4; Herwig, *Journal of Strategic Studies*, IX (1986), 53–63.

[115] von Matuschka, 'Organisationsgeschichte des Heeres', 262; also 195, 231, 264; Laux, *Journal of Transport History*, 3rd series, VI (1965), 64–70; Storz, *Kriegsbild und Rüstung*, 352–3; Afflerbach, *Falkenhayn*, 62–3.

whose cavalry was as far ahead as anyone, recorded that the supply arrangements were still well regulated.[116] As forward troops, the horsemen were of
course first into new areas in which to requisition, but the German army was
not about to be defeated because of the logistic weaknesses in its war plan.
What remains true, however, is that it performed well in 1914 in spite of its
supply arrangements, not because of them. Moltke's post-war critics blamed
him, above all, for not hearkening to the words of the dying Schlieffen, that the
right wing be kept strong. In 1914 the right wing was as strong as the logistics of
the Schlieffen plan permitted it to be. By the beginning of September those
soldiers who marched with it were totally exhausted; many were reservists and
had necessarily been unfit at the start of the campaign; all, their day's march
completed, had then to begin foraging for food.

The biggest drain on the German army's manpower, and cause of the
eventual weakness of the right wing, was the consequence of the advance itself.
Constant fighting, particularly in the light of ill-conceived tactics, wore
down the strength of regiments. On the right of the line many units had
suffered 40 per-cent losses. On the left, the 1st Bavarian infantry regiment lost
fifteen officers and 1,000 men, over a third of its strength, on 28 August alone.
Each battalion of one regiment of foot guards was down to company strength by
29 August. The fact that so many reservists had been used from the outset, and
the fact that what transport there was was needed for supply, meant that these
gaps could not be made good. By 6 September the German army's field strength
had fallen by about 265,000 men, the total of killed, wounded, and missing.[117]

Relatively, therefore, even the loss of five corps—which was what the right
wing bore by 6 September—was less important in the manpower balance.
After the fall of Liège the Belgian army had pulled back to the fortified camp of
Antwerp: two German corps had therefore been detached to cover Belgium.
The investment of Maubeuge was completed by 27 August, but the town,
despite the inadequacies of its defences, held out until 7 September, so pinning
a further corps and also blocking the main Cologne–Paris railway line. But the
decision for which Moltke has been most severely censured was his reaction to
the alarm of the 8th German army in East Prussia, faced by a Russian advance
of considerable strength. Moltke's initial inclination was to send up to six
corps, and he considered drawing them from his left wing. However, it was felt
that the Bavarians, who constituted the 6th army, were unlikely to be ardent
defenders of Prussia, not least because their army wished to be kept as an intact
unit. Nor was it clear in operational terms that the 6th army had corps to spare.
Bülow, on the other hand, declared that the two corps besieging Namur were
available when their task was completed. On 25 August, the day of apparent

---

[116] Marwitz, Weltkriegsbriefe, 34.
[117] Contamine, Victoire, 288; on regimental losses, see Schulte, Europäische Krise, 181–2; Camena
d'Almeida, L'Armée allemande, 160.

victory, Moltke ordered these two corps to the aid of the 8th army. At the time neither Bülow nor Tappen, both convinced that the campaign in the west was settled, deemed the decision unwise. The two corps mattered less in themselves than as part of a gradual erosion of German strength. Moltke's lines of communications were lengthening by the day; his front broadened as the movement through France developed—by 30 August it would be 50 kilometres longer than it had been a week previously. The combination of the detached corps, the heavy losses through tactical ineptitude, and exhaustion through the march and its attendant supply problems meant that a stage would be reached when the Germans had too few men.

Thus, in almost every key index of military strength—in command, in communications, in manpower, in tactics—the balance was swinging from Germany to France. Much of the swing was inherent in the advance itself and in the plan which had given rise to it. But the Germans did not defeat themselves. All too much attention has been devoted to what the Germans did or did not do, to asking why the Schlieffen plan failed. The Marne was a French victory. The French had to manoeuvre in order to win; they had to fight in order to check the Germans; and to do this the morale of the army and its commanders had to be sustained despite punishing retreats.

THE BATTLE OF THE MARNE

Up until 25 August Joffre's attention to his left wing had been grudging. The conventional wisdom is that what little he did was no more than the product of Lanrezac's importunities and unanticipated German advances. But the idea of manoeuvring in the space on the left and defending in the wooded hills on the right had been present in his calculations in 1911–12, and had re-emerged once more on 2 and 3 August 1914. On both occasions what had held him back was uncertainty about Britain—whether it would condone a French breach of Belgian neutrality, whether it would deploy the BEF on the continent, and, if it did, whether the latter would be in time.[118] On this interpretation the battles in Alsace and Lorraine were fought because British strategy meant that an offensive in the east was the only option available to Joffre if he was to support the Russians and to fix the Germans. Even if such an analysis is overstated, its relevance is endorsed by two further observations. The first is the alacrity with which Joffre responded to the threat of the German right wing after 25 August, and the second is his refusal then to adopt the more cautious and conservative

---

[118] Pedroncini, *Revue d'histoire diplomatique*, XCI (1977), 145–58; Prete, *Canadian Journal of History*, XXIV (1989), 51, 53–4.

strategy advocated by Berthelot.[119] The latter proposed an offensive directed against the inner flank of the German right wing, opposite the BEF. Joffre, however, ordered the centre of gravity of French operations to be switched from Lorraine to Amiens. His object was to create a fresh army to be outside the German enveloping wing, and to strike it from west to east as it passed on its march south.

Military orthodoxy in 1914 regarded redeployment by rail during the course of operations as excessively dangerous. Troops in trains were necessarily out of the fighting line. But Joffre's own experience with railways, and the fact that he had already—before the war—studied the possibility of just the operation which he now proposed, encouraged him to try it. The legacy of his predecessors gave him the means to do so. The multiplication of track between central France and the eastern frontier, designed to hasten the concentration which had just taken place, was now used to bring the troops back again. Maunoury's army of Lorraine and part of Pau's army of Alsace were brought west to form a new 6th army, under Maunoury and formed of nine infantry divisions and two cavalry. A total of 163 trains were required, and between 27 August and 2 September an average of thirty-two trains sped westwards every twenty-four hours. By 10 September a total of twenty infantry divisions and three cavalry divisions had been moved by rail from the French right to the centre or left.[120] On 23 August the three armies constituting the German right wing could muster 24.5 divisions against 17.5 allied divisions: on 6 September they confronted forty-one allied divisions.[121]

Such a manoeuvre would not have been possible without the defences of the Meuse and of Lorraine. The French redeployment meant that the German left wing was now stronger than the troops which opposed it. Because of the overall manpower superiority which France was now beginning to enjoy, the margin was not as great as that gained by the French in the west. But the corollary of the manoeuvre which Joffre initiated on 25 August was a successful defence in the east, one in which the fortifications of Séré de Rivières, and even of Vauban, helped compensate for local manpower inferiority.

The possibility of the French withdrawing troops from the east to the west was one regularly reviewed in German general staff studies between 1905 and 1914.[122] It meant that the task of the German 6th and 7th armies was always much more ambivalent than that of the right wing. Even Schlieffen himself never saw it as that of a 'revolving door': he assumed the French would defend, not attack, and therefore the German left wing was itself to attack, in order to fix the French and prevent their redeployment in the path of the German right.

[119] Gamelin, *Manoeuvre et victoire*, 105–6.
[120] Miquel, *Grand guerre*, 151; Contamine, *Victoire*, 393–4.
[121] Tyng, *Marne*, 189.
[122] Förster, *Militärgeschichtliche Mitteilungen*, 54, (1995), 85–6.

Moltke, recognizing the likelihood of a French attack into Lorraine, had favoured pulling back so that the French advance would enter a sack and be enveloped from either wing. In the event, the battles of Morhange and Sarrebourg had been partial engagements from which the 1st and 2nd French armies had been able to extricate themselves. The chief of staff of 6th army itself had, at the start of the war, seen the principal role of the left wing as being that of the protector of the flank of the right. Its defensive roles accomplished, the German left could—he reckoned—either attack so as to fix the French or, if the French proved weaker than the Germans, it could carry the offensive across the Moselle.

This last idea, an attack with decisive rather than limited objectives, appealed to the *amour propre* of Crown Prince Rupprecht and his Bavarians. Even before Morhange and Sarrebourg, 6th army had broached the idea of an attack on Nancy. Moltke's response, though indecisive, was not negative: lurking at the back of his mind was the possibility of a 'super-Cannae', a breakthrough on the left enabling the envelopment of the French army on both wings. The decision to follow up the victories at Morhange and Sarrebourg was thus quickly taken. A pause would allow the French time to regroup and redeploy. The fall of Liège suggested that Schlieffen had exaggerated the effectiveness of fortifications in delaying an attack. Moreover, the victories of the right wing made the case for disengaging Heeringen's 7th army, and rerouting it via Metz to Belgium—never strong, given the available railway lines—yet weaker. Indeed, the reverse happened: the left wing was reinforced at the expense of the right. Six-and-a-half Ersatz divisions, intended to guard the lines of communication through Belgium, were directed instead to Lorraine. The strengthening of the German left wing fed the ire of post-war critics: at the time Moltke's decision was welcomed.[123]

After Morhange, Castelnau had fallen back west of the River Meurthe, his left flank covered by the positions on the Grand Couronné de Nancy. Moltke therefore instructed the 6th and 7th armies to pass south, aiming for the gap at Charmes, between Toul and Épinal. A breakthrough here would allow the Germans to envelop Nancy. The effect of the German move was to place Castelnau's 2nd French army on their flank as they marched south against Dubail's 1st army. The weather, which had been poor on the 22nd and 23rd, cleared on the 24th, revealing the German movements to French aerial reconnaissance. On 25 August Castelnau took his opportunity and counter-attacked. His gains were limited, but the Germans were stopped. The weather broke again on the 26th. Already weakened in the Morhange and (particularly) Sarrebourg fighting, the 6th and 7th armies were not able to exploit their earlier victories. The ground over which they were attacking was well suited to

[123] Schulte, *Europäische Krise*, 183–90, 217, 224, 226–7, 231–2, 235–7.

the defence, and well fortified. Their line of communications between Dieuze and Lunéville came under fire from French batteries. The 7th was the weakest of the German armies, and the Ersatz divisions—although appropriate for their original task—were not ideal formations for the offensive. The Germans made some gains to the south, but were checked by 28 August. For ten days the front south of Verdun was stable: France's redeployment to the west could proceed uninterrupted.

That Moltke was no longer thinking simply of an envelopment by the right wing is confirmed in his directive of 27 August. The line of march which he gave the 1st, 2nd, 3rd, 4th, and 5th armies remained south-west, with Kluck pointed south-west of Paris and Bülow on Paris itself. But at the same time the 6th and 7th were instructed to attack along the Moselle, and to break through between Toul and Épinal. The tough fighting in which the 6th and 7th armies were engaged generated the need for the 4th and 5th to relieve the pressure by attacking on the western side of France's eastern fortifications. Moltke was therefore advancing on all points. The effect of this in practice would not be to maintain his thrust south-west, but to bring it south, and even south-east. If each army was to support the other in order to achieve a reciprocating effect in the advance, the overall alignment would be set by the left and by the centre, and not by the right.

This change in the alignment of the German advance was confirmed by the effects of the fighting in late August. Joffre set his retreating armies, the 3rd, 4th, and 5th, the task of limited counter-attacks so as to delay the German advance while his new concentration could be effected. On 27 August he instructed Lanrezac to turn and drive in a north-westerly direction towards St Quentin and the right wing of Bülow's army, which was still bearing south-west. The manoeuvre the French 5th army had to execute was not easy: it had simultaneously to face north, towards Guise, in order to hold Bülow's centre. Furthermore, Sir John French refused the co-operation of the BEF despite the fact that his I corps was ideally placed to join in by striking against Kluck's left flank. Lanrezac prevaricated: Joffre was furious. Events justified both of them. The battle on 29 August did not go as Joffre anticipated, but Lanrezac fought it well: although effectively defeated at St Quentin, at Guise he used his artillery to good account and pushed Bülow back 5 kilometres on a 25-kilometre front. Bülow's army was fought to a standstill, and its losses were high. Pausing for a thirty-six hour respite, on 30 August Bülow summoned Kluck to his support. If Kluck had continued on his original, south-westerly line of march he could have disrupted the formation of the French 6th army and enveloped the BEF. But the gap between the two German right-wing armies would have widened. By changing direction from south-west to south-east, Kluck's army threatened the rear of Lanrezac's 5th.

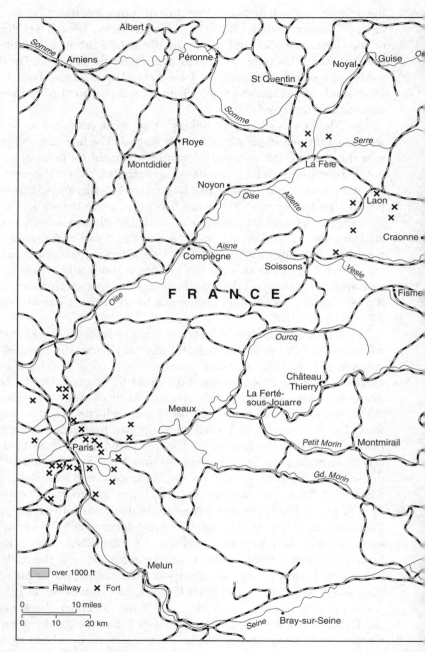

Albert

Somme

Amiens

Péronne

Noyal

Guise

St Quentin

Somme

Roye

Serre

Montdidier

La Fère

Noyon

Oise

Aillette

Laon

Craonne

Aisne

Compiègne

Soissons

Vesle

Fisme

F R A N C E

Oise

Ourcq

Château
Thierry

La Ferté-
sous-Jouarre

Meaux

Petit Morin

Montmirail

Paris

Gd. Morin

over 1000 ft

Railway   ✕ Fort

0   10 miles

0   10   20 km

Melun

Seine   Bray-sur-Seine

MAP 8. PARIS TO VERDUN

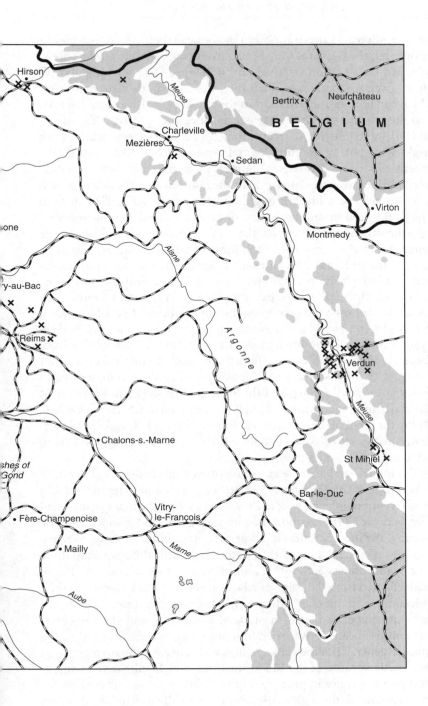

Rather than allowing gaps to appear in their line in their efforts to achieve a full envelopment, the Germans were opting to close up. Moltke's orders of the 29th embodied the situation that had now developed. The 2nd, 4th, and 5th armies were given southern axes of advance, the 1st south-eastern. The 3rd army, which had not been able to support the 2nd at Guise because of the need to rally to the 4th and 5th on the Meuse, now became the pivot. The atmosphere at OHL was confused. Many anticipated a decisive victory, achieved not by the right wing but by the three central armies on the Aisne, and by the encirclement of Verdun. Moltke's moodiness interpreted the same situation negatively: his right wing was too weak for the tasks that confronted it, his left was unable to achieve a breakthrough, and his centre was pulled in both directions by the need to support in first one direction and then the other.

At GQG the situation was reversed: the staff was becoming desperate, while the commander-in-chief remained cool. Joffre's plan of 25 August was awry. The retreat of the BEF, and the gap which it left to allow Kluck's turn to the south-east, made a general counter-attack on the line Amiens–Reims impossible. Joffre's principal task was to extricate the 5th army from its immediate danger, and to give time for a new army, the 9th (entrusted to Foch), to form on the 5th's right, so as to fill the growing gap between it and the 4th. In these circumstances Berthelot, continuing to look away from the French left, advocated a breakthrough in the centre. Technically, such a conception was not incompatible with Joffre's orders of 1 September. They allowed for a possible retreat as far as the southern bank of the Seine, so that the French line would form a great arc running south-east from Paris, and then north-east to Verdun. But for Joffre the pivot of the manoeuvre remained on the left, and round Paris rather than Amiens. He reckoned that the allied armies would not pass over to the attack until after 8 September.

The major imponderable in the execution of even this design was the role of the BEF. Was it, after Landrecies and Le Cateau, in a state fit to fight? And, if it was, would its commander allow it to do so? In practice, the first question had only arisen because of the second. The physical strains under which the BEF was labouring, the incorporation of 60 per-cent reservists, the long marches, and the losses suffered by II corps at Le Cateau were little different from those undergone by the soldiers of the other armies in August 1914. True, their line of retreat had deviated from their line of advance, and so pulled away from their communications and supplies. Moreover, administrative responsibility for supply was not integrated with the task of command, and the inspector-general of communications was therefore not formally subordinated to the quartermaster-general. But the consequences were not as serious as they might have been, partly because of the BEF's small size, which enhanced its adaptibility, and partly because in practice responsibility was concentrated on the quartermaster-general, the highly competent and totally unflappable William

Robertson.[124] Nonetheless, in the mind of Sir John French the problems of the BEF were grievous. Kitchener, in his instructions to Sir John, had stressed the BEF's small size, the limited reinforcements available, and the resulting need to minimize casualties. French's sense of this responsibility deepened into despondency and despair. His GHQ seemed unable to form a balanced view of the state of the troops under its command. The original intention had been for the BEF to have no corps commands, so that GHQ would have direct control of the divisions. The available wirelesses were used to link GHQ with its cavalry division. Effective communications between GHQ and its corps broke down in the retreat. French sited his headquarters too far from his corps; he moved without notice. At Mons and Le Cateau Smith-Dorrien was left to take his own decisions. French bore a long-standing grievance against Smith-Dorrien, foisted on him as II corps's commander at the last moment after the sudden death of Sir James Grierson, and this may have led him to exaggerate the weaknesses of II corps. Haig, commanding I corps, had determined even before the fighting started that French was an 'old woman' and 'quite unfit for this great command at a time of crisis in our Nation's history'.[125] GHQ itself spent more time listening to the French than to either Smith-Dorrien or Haig. This gave Henry Wilson, although only deputy chief of staff, a key role—increased when Sir Archibald Murray, the chief of staff, suffered a temporary nervous collapse after Landrecies. Wilson had a low opinion of both French's and Haig's abilities, but proved in the retreat just as liable as the former to exaggerate the dangerous situation of the BEF.[126]

Sir John's attitude towards his ally was soured by Lanrezac's lack of co-operation, and by his conviction that the latter had left him in the lurch at Mons. Kitchener had told him that, if the French armies were defeated, he was to retreat along his own lines of communication to the coast. British strategic independence, which had been subordinated to the needs of the alliance in the lead-up to Mons, now reasserted itself. When even Wilson believed that the BEF should go 'to Havre and home' the Anglo-French alliance lost its principal advocate at British headquarters.[127] French refused to support the 5th French army in the St Quentin/Guise battle, and on 30 August announced that he planned to pull the BEF out of the line for ten days, to refit west of Paris and behind the Seine. If this had happened Maunoury's 6th army would have had to close up to cover Lanrezac's flank, and Joffre's chance of envelopment would have gone. The French commander-in-chief, who had never been fully apprised of Kitchener's instructions to French, and who persisted in behaving

---

[124] Brown, *British logistics*, 46–53.
[125] Blake, *Haig*, 70, 72.
[126] On the pre-war army, and its problems in 1914, see Bidwell and Graham, *Fire-power*, esp. ch. 3; also Miller, *Military Affairs*, XLIII (1979), 133–8; Bourne, *Britain and the Great War*, 27–8.
[127] Philpott, *Anglo-French relations*, 23.

as though his powers were those of an allied generalissimo, was perplexed. He appealed via Poincaré to the British government.

The French message reached a cabinet that was already exchanging one approach to British strategy for another. If France were defeated by Germany, Britain would be left without a major striking force on the continent, and its hopes of neutralizing the Channel ports and Belgium would be dashed for the foreseeable future. Britain had already discovered that its security needs meant that it could not abandon the Entente in July; now the same imperative meant that it had to stick by it in the field. Asquith and his ministers decided to support the French counter-attack. Furthermore, alarmed by the depressed tone of Sir John French's missives, they sent Kitchener to France. Donning his field marshal's uniform, the secretary of state met French on 1 September and told him that he must conform with Joffre's desires. French might with justice have observed that his fault thus far had been to adhere too faithfully to Kitchener's wishes, but his reaction was more petulant, and revolved round matters of etiquette rather than of strategy. Two days later Joffre poured oil on these wounds by replacing Lanrezac with the ebullient Franchet d'Esperey, whose corps had distinguished itself both on the Sambre and at Guise. Although Joffre still did not count on it, the conditions for the BEF's co-operation were set.[128]

Ironically, the longer-term strategic effects of the BEF's withdrawal rebounded to the allies' advantage. On 31 August the 3rd and 4th French armies west of Verdun launched limited counter-attacks to enable themselves to face north rather than north-east, and so secure the right flank of Foch's 9th army as it entered the line. Thus, Foch could concentrate on securing the right of the 5th army, potentially exposed to Kluck's advance by the withdrawal of the BEF on its left. Moltke interpreted this manoeuvre as a general counter-attack and concluded—when it failed to go further—that it had been success-fully checked. He therefore focused his attentions on his centre and on Verdun, rather than on his right and Paris.[129] On 2 September his orders expressed the intention to drive the French in a south-easterly direction. Without pause or preparation, Moltke was shifting the conceptual base of the German advance from envelopment to breakthrough. Not only did he expect his army com-manders to grasp what he now proposed, he also hoped that they would implement it despite the fact that the French grip on Verdun and the heights of the Meuse would splinter their efforts. Aerial reconnaissance had indicated to OHL troop movements in the area of Paris. Kluck's role, therefore, was no longer to lead the advance, but to turn westwards, following Bülow in echelon, to guard the German right flank. Kluck was understandably confused. He was

[128] Philpott, *Guerres mondiales et conflits contemporains*, 180, (1995), 48–52.
[129] Gamelin, *Manoeuvre et victoire*, 144–6, 159–60, 175.

already one day's march ahead of Bülow. He was convinced that the BEF was out of the fight. To turn back would be to abandon the possible destruction of the French 5th army. He decided to go on. On 3 September his advanced units began to cross the River Marne.

The fact that Kluck's 1st army was passing east of Paris was known to Joffre from 31 August. Intercepted German signals, some of them transmitted in clear, were confirmed by aerial observation.[130] The manoeuvre, planned on 25 August to take place at Amiens, could now be resurrected round Paris. GQG was preoccupied with extracting the 5th army from Kluck's clutches, and only slowly did it realize how immediate was the opportunity for an offensive. On 2 September Berthelot still favoured a withdrawal behind the Seine, but Belin and the rest of the 3ème bureau advocated consolidation on a more northerly line and then a general offensive, including an attack against Kluck's flank using Maunoury's 6th army. As yet, however, Gallieni, who had replaced the hapless Michel (the author of the 1911 proposals) as governor of Paris on 26 August, was more concerned for the direct protection of the capital. Although he had set about improving the defences of the city with considerable energy, he was pessimistic about his chances of success. Joffre's argument—that the mobile army's campaign in the field would prove Paris's best shield—was at this stage still lost on him.

Late on 3 September Gallieni personally briefed the pilot who was to observe and report on the position of Kluck's army early the following morning. The results of that observation confirmed him in the view that he had begun to form on the 3rd—that Maunoury's 6th army should debouch from Paris eastwards, towards Meaux, and along the south bank of the Marne. Independently but simultaneously, Joffre at GQG had come to the same conclusion. The subsequent polemics, claiming Gallieni as the author of the manoeuvre on the Marne, do more than neglect Joffre's development of the plan from 25 August onwards. They fail to take into account the fact that Gallieni's conception was local, concerning itself with the situation around Paris and with Kluck's 1st army; Joffre's plan embraced the whole front and depended as much on the situation in the centre and on the right as on the left.

Common to both of them was the question of the BEF's co-operation. On the afternoon of 3 September GHQ had been told that there appeared to be no Germans in front of them, and French agreed that the BEF would move eastwards, to close the breach between it and the 5th army against Kluck's threatened envelopment. However, French was not yet fully briefed on the developments in GQG's thinking. Murray believed that Joffre's intention was to fall back south of the Seine—a move still favoured by Berthelot and not finally quashed by Joffre until the morning of 4 September. Therefore, if the

---

[130] Bréguet and Bréguet, *Revue historique des armées*, 166, (mars 1987), 92–100.

BEF moved east to support the 5th army while the French armies fell back, it would uncover its left flank.[131] Stung by the memory of Mons, French changed his mind once more and reverted to the idea of pulling the BEF back behind the Seine. If this had happened Kluck would have been free to parry any blow by Maunoury's 6th army. Both Joffre and Gallieni, therefore, planned the 6th army's movement not simply to drive into Kluck's flank, since a thrust north of the Marne, not south, would do this to much greater effect, but to rally to the BEF. By closing the 6th army up with the BEF south of the Marne, the BEF would be supported on both its flanks and the two armies would be in a position to support the 5th by striking Kluck's outer flank.[132] This was the nub of an agreement reached between Gallieni and Sir Archibald Murray on the afternoon of the 4th.

While Gallieni and Murray were meeting at Melun, Franchet d'Esperey and Henry Wilson were consorting at Bray-sur-Seine. At 12.45 p.m. Joffre had asked the 5th army commander whether he would be ready to co-operate in the attack. Given the pressure on the 5th army over the previous few days the reply might well have been negative. However, Franchet d'Esperey reckoned that, if the BEF could pivot quickly and if Foch's 9th army could support on the right, the 5th army could play its role. The Gallieni–Murray plan required the BEF to continue its retreat for a further day to create room for the 6th army south of the Seine. The Franchet d'Esperey–Wilson plan assumed that the BEF would halt to complete its alignment with the 5th army, and that the 6th army would attack north of the Marne, at right-angles to the main line, on the River Ourcq. Fortunately the coolest head at GHQ, Macdonogh's, was at Bray. His clear exposition of the BEF's position combined with Franchet d'Esperey's fierce energy—'seen from the back', one witness recalled, 'his head reminded one of a howitzer shell'[133]—to clinch the plan that would become the Marne battle. At 10 p.m. that evening Joffre issued his orders. The 6th army was to cross the Ourcq in the direction of Château Thierry, the BEF was to advance east towards Montmirail, the 5th army was to turn north—although its first task would be to hold until the BEF's advance told on the Germans—and the 9th army was to cover the 5th's right flank along the marshes of St Gond. The attack was to begin on the morning of the 6th.

Joffre's order did not specify the task of the 1st, 2nd, 3rd, and 4th armies. That was clear enough. They must hold, or there would be no overall success. For, while the drama of the Marne lies to the west, the German hopes of

[131] Huguet, *Britain and the war*, 88–93; Philpott, *Anglo-French relations*, 27–8; Gamelin, *Manoeuvre et victoire*, 181–94.

[132] The controversy over the relative contributions of Gallieni and Joffre continues. The interpretation given here is pro-Joffre, and follows Tyng and Contamine. For an account that is consistently hostile to Joffre, see Liddell Hart, *World war* and *Reputations*. A recent discussion of 4 September, and the crucial position of the BEF, is Seince, *Revue historique des armées*, 172, (septembre 1988), 9–15.

[133] Spears, *Liaison*, 397.

winning the battle now lay to the east. The 5th German army was struggling to break through between Verdun and Toul, and to envelop the French defences south of Nancy from the north. The 6th and 7th armies, whose dilatoriness was irking Moltke by the end of August, were reinforced with nearly seventy heavy batteries, many of them drawn from the fortifications at Metz. On 4 September they renewed their attack along the Moselle.

Moltke's directive of 2 September, bringing the right wing away from Paris, had aroused criticism within German general headquarters. Most recognized that the French had withdrawn troops from the Toul–Épinal front—the Germans now had a superiority of seven divisions there—but could not identify whither they had gone. Falkenhayn thought they were west of Verdun, opposite the 4th and 5th German armies. He advocated a wholly new operation, effectively splitting the German advance in two. The 1st, 2nd, 3rd, and 4th armies should aim for Paris. The 5th should incline towards its left in the direction of the Vosges, and should co-operate with the attack of the 6th and 7th.[134] Some of this thinking is evident in Moltke's directive, dispatched at 6.30 p.m. on 4 September. By now aware of Kluck's disobedience and of the consequent danger to the right flank from Paris, Moltke detailed not only the 1st army (between the Marne and the Oise) but also the 2nd (between the Marne and the Seine) to act as flank guards. The 3rd was to continue facing south, but in sustaining its link with the 2nd army was in danger of overstretching itself. The 4th and 5th were to attack to the south-east, and the 6th and 7th to the south-west. Moltke's directive embraced, although to a lesser degree, the divergent objectives set by Falkenhayn, and its targets were distant rather than immediate. But, if it had a focus it was on the German left flank, on the Argonne, on the Meuse, and at Nancy. These were the very areas whose fortifications the original plan had been designed to avoid.

Kluck did not receive Moltke's order until 7.00 a.m. the following morning. By then the 1st army had begun its day's march. Moreover, the order's contents made little sense to an army commander unaware of the overall situation. Kluck had won a succession of victories, engaged in a rapid advance without check, and yet was being asked to fall back. Furthermore, his doctrine was envelopment: a directive whose philosophy was breakthrough was inherently unsympathetic. Not until the afternoon, when Hentsch, OHL's head of intelligence, visited 1st army headquarters, did Kluck grasp what was intended. But even then neither he nor Hentsch imagined a general French offensive to be imminent. Hentsch's concern was to secure the Germans' line of communications on their open flank. Kluck still assumed that the French and the BEF were defeated. The main reconnaissance effort of II corps was to the front, and its aeroplanes reported the roads between the Marne and the Seine clogged with

<hr />

[134] Schulte, *Europäische Krise*, 253.

troops marching south; Kluck's flank guard, IV reserve corps, had no integral airpower and was therefore ignorant of the situation to the west. Kluck could see no need for urgency in the execution of the order.

Contact on the Ourcq between Kluck's flanking force, IV reserve corps, and some French units was made at dusk on 4 September. During the course of the 5th Maunoury's pressure on the Ourcq built up, and by midnight Kluck was aware that IV reserve corps was heavily outnumbered. Joffre's order of the day, marking the beginning of the French attack, was known to OHL and distributed to the individual armies, before it was read by front-line French soldiers. Kluck was, therefore, able to see the significance of the Ourcq battle to the overall French design, and concluded that a rapid victory by the 1st German army over the French 6th would unhinge the French plan. On 7 September he belatedly executed his orders to protect the German flank. The weight of 1st army, two corps, which had been on Bülow's right flank, were marched 100 kilometres on to the northern flank of IV reserve corps in an effort to outflank Maunoury. Maunoury's position was desperate. Reinforcements, including some (but fewer than legend suggests) borne in commandeered taxis, were pushed into the battle from Paris. The effect of Kluck's move was to open a gap between the 1st and 2nd German armies.

Kluck was not unduly perturbed about the position to his front. It was screened by two cavalry corps, von der Marwitz's and Richthofen's from 2nd army. Von der Marwitz's corps had just had two days' rest to reshoe their horses and refurbish their weapons in anticipation of heavy fighting on the Seine. It seemed sufficient to contain any threat the BEF might present. The latter had continued its retreat on 5 September, and did not begin its advance until the morning of the 6th. Its line of march, therefore, was not to the east as intended, but to the north-east and then north, as it entered the gap created by Kluck's turn towards Paris. This had two effects. First, any ongoing concerns on the part of Sir John French about his flanks were rendered redundant by the fact that the BEF began 16 kilometres south of its designated start line, and so behind—not ahead of—the adjacent French armies. Secondly, Joffre's line was echeloned back from the left, so that if need be its components could turn in to the right to provide mutual support.

The German efforts to win the battle in the east began quickly to disintegrate. From 31 August Moltke had considered weakening the left wing, not in order to reinforce the right (something which did not seem particularly necessary until 6 September itself), but to guard his lines of communication, especially in Belgium. Reports of British landings in Ostend and of the dispatch of a Russian corps, transported by the Royal Navy, preyed on Moltke's fears. Since the task of 6th and 7th armies was now to hold the French, while the 4th and 5th broke through, the left wing could be seen as having disposable forces. Moltke began to prepare to shift the 7th army to Belgium, and so weakened the Moselle attack. Castelnau, having threatened withdrawal on the 6th, was still solid in his position on the 8th.

Joffre became more worried about the situation around Verdun and to its west. Sarrail, who had taken over command of the French 3rd army, made great play of maintaining the city and its fortifications within the French line. This worked to the extent that the German 5th army increasingly committed itself to its assault, so weakening its efforts on its flanks. But it worried Joffre, who saw the defence of the town as secondary to the need to ensure the integrity of the line itself. A German attack south of Verdun did get across the Meuse, but was checked by the French forts along the river. The 3rd army's concentration on Verdun opened a gap between it and Langle de Cary's 4th. However, the German 4th army did not exploit it. Foch's 9th army was caught in a dangerous position. Its right flank was exposed by the 4th's need to maintain contact with Sarrail. Therefore, while Foch's left faced the obstacle of the marshes of St Gond and was supported by the 5th's advance, his right extended over undulating ground and then ended at Mailly with a 20-kilometre gap covered by a single cavalry division. XXI corps, ordered to close the gap, did not come up until the evening of the 8th. Fortunately for the French, the hole in their line was matched by one in the Germans', Hausen's 3rd army being stretched too wide. But it was with Hausen and opposite Foch's right that German hopes of victory now resided. In the grey light of the morning of 8 September, to avoid the devastating effects of the French 75 mms, Hausen's army attacked without artillery preparation and with the bayonet, routing Foch's XI corps. Foch, denied assistance by Langle de Cary, appealed to Franchet d'Esperey. The 5th army generously released its right-hand corps, allowing Foch to move a division behind his line from left to right and so stabilize the position. Foch's army had been beaten, but Foch himself had doggedly refused to admit it. Although the ground provided little shelter, it optimized the ricochet fire of the 75 mm. Some of Foch's guns fired a thousand rounds each per day. His repeated calls to counter-attack had elicited scepticism from his troops but not disobedience. The line held.[135]

By 7 September Bülow was worried about the position of the 2nd army. Its front engaged by the French 5th army, its left by Foch's left, its right and rear were completely exposed to the advance of the BEF. The focus of Kluck's battle—his desire for envelopment and his protection of his right wing—was not Bülow's. Kluck had not told Bülow of his intentions, nor of the withdrawal of the two corps from Bulow's flank. On 8 September Bülow pulled back his exposed right wing, so that 2nd army was deployed on a north–south line and more to the east. The gap between 1st and 2nd armies was thus increased. Neither Kluck nor Bülow thought to keep either each other or OHL informed

[135] Tardieu, *Avec Foch*, 51; Gascouin, *Le Triomphe de l'idée*, 129.

of what was happening. Deprived of information, Moltke ceased to issue directives. Co-ordination of the German armies had collapsed.

However, on the morning of the 8th Moltke learned of the BEF's advance through wireless intercepts. Still without effective communications—wireless links between OHL and the army commanders were ordered on 6 September but were not established until 2.30 p.m. on the 9th—Moltke decided to send Hentsch on a mission to establish the situation along the entire front. Moltke was not convinced that any retreat on the part of the right wing was necessary, but Hentsch was authorized to allow it if that was the only way to close the gap between the 1st and 2nd armies. Hentsch first visited the 5th, 4th, and 3rd armies, and found all in satisfactory positions. Not until 7.45 p.m. did he reach Bülow. Bülow had already decided that a retreat, on converging lines to close the gap, was necessary. Hentsch did not oppose Bülow, not least because he did not know Kluck's position. But if Bülow did fall back, Kluck would have no option but to conform.

Hentsch's drive the following morning to Kluck's headquarters, although only 90 kilometres distant, took five hours on the crowded roads. Kluck was not there when Hentsch arrived. Instead, he saw the chief of staff, von Kuhl. Kluck's absence has allowed his defenders to argue that the 1st army was on the verge of defeating Maunoury's 6th, and that it could then have turned against the BEF and won the battle of the Marne. Given the exhausted state of the 1st army and the fact that it was outnumbered, this case is hard to sustain. The BEF's advance had begun to threaten the 1st army as well as the 2nd, causing Kluck to pull back his left wing on the Ourcq on 8 September, and so releasing some of the German pressure on Maunoury. It is just as possible to contend, therefore, that Kluck had already acknowledged the need to retreat before Hentsch arrived at his headquarters. Hentsch's own demeanour may have been somewhat flustered: it was he who was feeding Moltke's worries about the Belgian lines of communication, and any inherent pessimism would have found confirmation from Bülow. He told von Kuhl that the 2nd army was defeated and being driven back.[136] He therefore ordered the 1st army to retreat. The 1st army's line of march had to be due north, not north-east towards the 2nd army, in order to avoid passing across the front of the BEF. Hentsch's hope that the 1st and 2nd armies would converge on the Vesle was thus disappointed. Kluck was once again subordinated to Bülow on 10 September, in order to aid the conjunction of the two armies. But it required the insertion of fresh troops definitively to close the gap.

Moltke's hopes of limiting the extent of the retreat had not entirely dissipated. On his return to OHL Hentsch was relatively buoyant, and saw the

[136] Nobécourt, *Fantassins*, 44; the best overall treatment of this phase of the battle is Jaschke, *Historische Zeitschrift*, CXC (1960); Lange, *Marneschlacht*, discuss the subsequent apportionment of blame within Germany.

withdrawal as confined to the 1st and 2nd armies. The prospect of the 4th and 5th armies capturing Verdun would help cover the movement on the right. On 11 September Moltke himself left Luxembourg to visit the armies' headquarters. The key to restricting the retreat was the state of the hard-pressed 3rd army—in the centre and thus pulled back on its right and forward on its left. But Hausen was sick and his army exhausted. Moltke spoke to Bülow on the telephone while he was at Hausen's headquarters: the French advance, Bülow reported, pushing in a north-easterly direction, was about to strike the centre of the 3rd army, so as to threaten the communications of the 4th and 5th. Moltke decided to order a general retreat along the whole front. The German armies would both contract and fall back to the Aisne. In Lorraine, Moltke's worries about Belgium—reinforced by a sortie from Antwerp begun on 9 September and sustained until the 12th—led to the withdrawal of ten divisions, and a separate retreat in front of Nancy and to the south.

During the German advance Moltke had resisted the premature celebration of victory: where, he wondered, were the prisoners and the guns of a defeated army? As the allies advanced they asked themselves the same question. Its chief of staff described the 1st German army as completely disorganized and its individual corps no longer in being. But, if that was the case, it is proof of the German army's powers of regeneration. Order was restored, by divisions, by 12 September. Within the 1st army, Bloem's company of Brandenburg grenadiers had no sense of defeat and had time to drink ninety bottles of claret on its march.[137] Indeed, empty bottles were the most obvious and frequent signs of the Germans' recent departure. The pioneers, who in the German army were treated very much as combat troops, and at least one company of whom was attached to each division and one battalion to each corps, were sent ahead to prepare defensive positions on the Aisne. The line the Germans had chosen followed the steep ridge on the north bank of the river. It covered all the main river crossings, and spurs projected into the valley to break up attacks. The position was flanked on its north-west by the forests around Compiègne, and to the south-east it ran along the hills of Reims and then into the woods of the Argonne. To its north was a possible second line of defence on the Aillette. By 13 September Kluck's and Bülow's armies were both safely across the Aisne. VII reserve corps, released by the fall of Maubeuge, was thrown into the gap between the two armies, and on the 14th was joined by Heeringen's 7th army head-quarters and XV corps, both originally withdrawn from Alsace to go to Belgium. By the evening of the 13th the major crisis for the Germans was already passing.

The advance of the BEF into the gap was particularly slow. Only on the left, where the Germans destroyed the bridges and defended the crossings against the newly formed III corps, was there serious resistance. I corps on the right

[137] Kuhl, *Grand état-major*, 141–2; Bloem, *Advance from Mons*, 171.

was checked by a single cavalry division and II corps by a brigade and von der Marwitz's corps. The latter's horses were now beginning to succumb to lack of fodder.[138] The Germans had not even secured the Marne crossings. Total British casualties in the Marne battle were 1,701. And yet between 6 and 9 September the average progress of the BEF's own cavalry was only 14.5 kilometres a day.[139]

Joffre's orders on 11 September directed the 3rd, 4th, and 9th French armies against the Germans' eastern group, and the left of the 5th, the BEF, and the 6th against the western. His hope was to exploit the gap in order to effect a breakthrough, and so separate and destroy Kluck's and Bülow's armies. By 12 September both Franchet d'Esperey and Sir John French had recognized the need for energetic and rapid pursuit, seeking objectives beyond the Chemin des Dames, the road running along the northern ridge of the Aisne valley. But their subordinate commanders were more cautious. Fears of an encounter battle were not dispelled. The weather on the 12th was wet, hampering the advance and, as importantly, aerial reconnaissance. The allies knew that the Germans were adapting their order of battle, but found it hard rapidly to impose order on the information available. On 14 September GQG's 2ème bureau received 487 dispatches: it appreciated that the Germans had withdrawn XV corps from Alsace, but then placed it simultaneously on the Russian front, at Metz, and in Belgium.[140] By the 13th the 5th French army was athwart Reims and the British were across the Aisne on the Chemin des Dames. XVIII corps, on the 5th's left, was well forward at Craonne. The Aisne bridges near Berry-au-Bac, between Craonne and Reims, were clear. At midday one French cavalry division was operating at Sissone, 20 kilometres beyond the Aisne, deep into the breach between Kluck and Bülow. But as the 7th German army began to form these forward units fell back, and the Berry-au-Bac position was abandoned without a fight. The British renewed their attack on 14 September but found the going tough and their positions overlooked by the Germans. By the evening even Franchet d'Esperey had recognized the strength of the German position. Joffre's directive that night, reflecting the tactical difference between all-out pursuit and a methodical attack against a prepared position, announced the switch from the first to the second: 'that means that every position, as soon as it is occupied, must be fortified.'[141] On the 15th the 5th army was fighting a defensive battle between Craonne and Reims. It was to continue to do so well into October.

---

[138] Marwitz, *Weltkriegsbriefe*, 41.
[139] Jaschke, *Historische Zeitschrift*, CXC (1960), 335, 342; Edmonds, *France and Belgium 1914*, i. 332–40; Terraine (ed.), *General Jack's diary*, 49–51; Bourne, *Britain and the Great War*, 23.
[140] Ratinaud, *La Course à la mer*, 27.
[141] Wallach, *Dogma*, 160. On this phase of the fighting, see Nobécourt, *Fantassins*, ch. 2; Rocolle, *L'Hécatombe*, 206–8; Miquel, *La Grand Guerre*, 188–93.

Critics of the allied failure to exploit the victory on the Marne argue that two strategic options presented themselves. The first, which is what the allies attempted, was to drive into the gap between Kluck and Bülow. But they moved too slowly and too cautiously. That they did so, given the experience of the earlier German victories, and given the break in the weather after 10 September, is not surprising. Indeed, the fact that the allied armies were able to turn, to fight, and then to push forward at all was itself a major achievement. Both the French and British armies (like the Germans) had marched off the maps with which they had been issued. Even more importantly, the soldiers themselves were exhausted. On the thirteen days of the retreat the BEF's cavalry had had an average of three hours' rest in every twenty-four and the infantry four hours.[142] One division in the French 5th army calculated that in the eight days preceding the battle it had marched 22 kilometres a day.[143] The thrust of Joffre's orders from 7 September, to close the line up, and to direct the line of march to the north-east, was a reflection both of his justified hope that the German centre would break (as Bülow feared it would on the 11th) and of the physical resources of the men under his command.

The second option at least theoretically available to Joffre was to exploit the Germans' open flank to the north. The territory bounded in the west by the line Paris to Antwerp, through which the German communications ran, was effectively untenanted. Two forces seemed to be available to take this opportunity. The first was the 6th army. Joffre had been urging Maunoury to gain ground on the right bank of the Ourcq ever since 7 September, and his orders of the 11th directed it even further north, to the right bank of the Oise. But Maunoury's army was short of cavalry and had no bridging equipment. Furthermore, it was committed to the BEF's left flank: when Kluck turned his main weight against the 6th army Joffre could not simultaneously exploit the gap in the German front and seek to envelop the German right. The evenly balanced situation around Verdun and Nancy meant that he could not easily or rapidly effect a further major concentration in the west. On 12 September he reinforced the 6th army with two more divisions, hoping that Maunoury would outflank the German line and keep Kluck so engaged that he would be unable to close the gap with Bülow. But the 6th army's passage of the Aisne was no faster than that of the others, and by the 13th Maunoury found himself facing Kluck frontally and in strong positions.

The only other force available was Sordet's cavalry corps. Theoretically the open flank to the north was exactly the strategic opportunity which justified the maintenance of large formations of horsemen in modern war. But France's cavalry was deficient in a number of respects. As in Germany, the corps

---

[142] Terraine, *Mons*, 211.   [143] L. V. Smith, 'Command authority', 149.

organization was improvised on mobilization. French cavalry corps had no artillery, and their divisions lacked firepower and efficient radios. Because pre-war remount policy had been driven by the commercial needs of the ministry of agriculture, rather than by the likely demands of the army in war, Anglo-Norman breeds designed for traction were preferred to hardier saddle horses. Accustomed to exercising on soft soils in peacetime, they had been worn out by the constant road-work in August. In the opening month of the war Sordet's cavalry had covered 1,000 kilometres, and by 10 August the corps had already needed 15,000 new shoes. In the retreat pauses to water were proscribed for fear of lengthening the columns of march. Nor did French cavalrymen—unlike the British—see the need to dismount to save their horses. Too many of them, Foch fulminated, have 'their brains in their legs'.[144] Sore backs devastated the cavalry's fighting power: 90 per cent of French horse losses in 1914 were due to sickness rather than combat, and by the end of 1914 a quarter of France's total horse strength on mobilization had died.

The substantive criticism against cavalry in 1914, therefore, was that the horse could not sustain continuous operations characteristic of modern war. France's other cavalry corps, commanded by Conneau, had been shifted from Lorraine to support the 5th army at the beginning of September. Although it had done far less than Sordet's corps, by 8 September it was already incapable of sustaining the advance. Sordet's corps was moved by rail to the left of the 6th army on 7 September, but it could only deploy one out of three divisions, a total of 1,300 horsemen. This raided in the direction of Soissons, between the Ourcq and the Oise, and returned exhausted on 13 September.

The British cavalry was entirely out of the equation. In front of it were six river lines and thick woods. It had been divided into two divisions on 5 September and given tasks that were defensive. Collectively both were to guard the front and flanks of the infantry, but in addition the 1st cavalry division under Allenby was to maintain contact with the French 5th army on the right and the 2nd under Gough with Maunoury's 6th army on the left. Given their own losses (their regiments averaged 250 men each) and the assumption of the German cavalry's numerical superiority, more aggressive tactics were ruled out.[145]

The Marne is remembered as a great manoeuvre battle—rightly, as it was the manoeuvres which made it decisive. Moreover, both sides were on the attack. But in reality most of the battle was characterized by fighting that was static. On 6 September 280 kilometres of the line, from Switzerland to Verdun, were already stable. By the 9th a further 100 kilometres, from Verdun to Mailly,

[144] Tardieu, *Avec Foch*, 62. The discussion that follows relies largely on Gazin, *La Cavalerie française*, esp. 70, 87–90, 102–3, 114, 308–19; see also Bogros, *Guerres mondiales et conflits contemporains*, 185, (1997), 7–12.
[145] Anglesey, *History of British Cavalry*, vii. 179–80.

was also fixed. The movement on that day was confined to 105 kilometres between Mailly and La Ferté-sous-Jouarre.[146]

On the Aisne this process was taken one stage further. Moltke had ordered the positions of the 3rd, 4th, and 5th armies from Reims to north of Verdun to be built 'as fortresses'. The allied commanders renounced the resumption of an immediate general offensive. Orders were for local attacks only; positions were to be consolidated. The ease with which the soil was worked hastened the construction of positions, despite the relative lack of tools. The trenches themselves were narrow and rarely continuous. They were not yet ends in themselves, but means to an end. Tactically, they were sited to provide protection from artillery fire. Operationally, they enabled ground to be defended with fewer troops, so allowing tired men a chance to recuperate and—above all—permitting the creation of new formations for mobile operations elsewhere. Bitterest of ironies, trench warfare was adopted to enable mobile warfare to take place.[147]

Much of the combat on the Marne was, therefore, tactically indecisive. The soldiers who took part in it only knew its outcome from the direction in which they marched when they had ceased fighting. And yet strategically and operationally the Marne was a truly decisive battle in the Napoleonic sense. It was exactly the sort of battle which generals in 1914 had been educated to expect. The French had 'fixed' the Germans in the east and manoeuvred to strike against them in the west; the Germans' initial victories had been valueless because they had neither fixed nor destroyed their opponents, but left them free to manoeuvre and to fight again. The immediate consequences were political. France and the French army were saved: without that the Entente would have had no base for continuing operations in western Europe. Italy was confirmed in its decision to be neutral, in the unwisdom of honouring its commitment to the Triple Alliance. The longer-term effects were strategic. Germany had failed to secure the quick victory on which its war plan rested. From now on it was committed to a war on two fronts. With hindsight, some would say that Germany had already lost the war.

In Germany, however, the truth about the Marne was never fully divulged. The press releases between 6 and 16 September presented the withdrawal around Paris as tactical, a regrouping preliminary to a fresh attack on the French capital, and set it in the context of victories elsewhere, especially on the eastern front. Thus, an essentially false picture of the military prospects was allowed to develop, one which was embraced not only by the press but also by many of the main power groups in Germany. Above all, the army could not recognize that it had been defeated, that its position at the heart of German

[146] Contamine, *Victoire*, 289–90.
[147] Edmonds, *France and Belgium 1914*, i. 430–4; Fayolle, *Cahiers secrets*, 40–1; Reichsarchiv, *Welt-krieg*, vi. 394–400.

society had been implicitly challenged by its failure to succeed in its prime role. Thirty-three generals were dismissed after the battle,[148] but rather than acknowledge a collective responsibility, the army blamed Kluck for having disobeyed orders and created the gap, Bülow for having been the first to decide to retreat, Hentsch for having ordered the 1st army to conform, Hausen and Crown Prince Rupprecht for not having achieved the breakthroughs that would have retrieved the situation, and Moltke for having failed to prove himself a true *Feldherr*. By seeking explanations in the shortcomings of individuals, and by arguing that a particular error was decisive, the German army could conclude that the Marne was really a battle which it had effectively won. Thus, the Marne did not form the basis for a strategic reassessment of Germany's objectives in the war, or for self-appraisal by the German army as an institution. Because the truth was never simultaneously and wholeheartedly grasped, what followed was muddle and compromise. In the immediate aftermath of the Marne some at general headquarters accused Moltke of following the prescriptions of Schlieffen too closely;[149] by 1919 it would be widely held that Moltke's failure was not to follow Schlieffen closely enough. Thus, the debate was about operational ideas, not about grand strategy; it continued to reflect the belief that ideal intellectual solutions could be imposed on the conduct of war; and it showed that even at this most basic level of generalship the German army had not found consensus.

FROM THE AISNE TO THE YSER

On the evening of 14 September von Lyncker called on Moltke and conveyed to him the Kaiser's command that he report himself sick. The confidence between the emperor and his chief of the general staff had never recovered from the interview on 1 August. But Moltke himself—although genuinely ailing—was anxious to continue. Because he was not formally relieved until 3 November, he remained at general headquarters, a sad if still occasionally perceptive man.

Wilhelm's choice as Moltke's successor was the Prussian minister of war, Erich von Falkenhayn. The decision was a personal one, albeit adumbrated by von Lyncker and the Kaiser's military entourage for some time past. Falkenhayn—tall, good-looking, relatively youthful by the standards of the German generals (he was now 53, and younger than all the army commanders)—was a Prussian junker who had commanded a guards regiment. To these

---

[148] Herwig, *First World War*, 105.
[149] Falkenhayn and Wenninger especially: see Schulte, *Europäische Krise*, 190–1, 279. Much of this paragraph reflects the themes of Lange, *Marneschlacht*.

qualifications for imperial favour he added his record as war minister, having proved a doughty defender in the Reichstag of the army and of its more questionable practices. Over the long term Wilhelm's support was to prove a major factor in Falkenhayn's survival in office. In the short term the appointment, although not perhaps the one which either the chancellor or the army itself might have made, seemed sensible enough. Falkenhayn was cold and aloof, not good at getting alongside his new colleagues at OHL. But he had a political breadth and flexibility, attributed to his decade of service as a military adviser in China and German chief of staff in the Boxer rebellion, which his Germany-bound professional colleagues could not match. His reputation was for energy, shrewdness, and decision. Above all, he was on the spot. By employing somebody already at general headquarters to hold two offices, not one, Moltke's supercession could be concealed and the fiction of military invincibility sustained.[150]

Falkenhayn's appointment confirmed the idea that if any accusation was to be levelled at Moltke it was that of following Schlieffen too closely, not of departing from his prescriptions. For Falkenhayn himself seemed to represent not a reassertion of Schlieffen's influence but a further shift away from it. The period of the latter's domination of the general staff coincided with Falkenhayn's Far Eastern service. The new chief of the general staff described himself as an 'autodidact'.[151] Furthermore, the pivot of operational decision-making in the Marne battle was Tappen, a strong advocate of the breakthrough, not of envelopment. Yet Tappen was retained as head of operations. Indeed, his role—for the moment, at any rate—waxed stronger. Falkenhayn had been able, by virtue of his post as war minister and his presence in general headquarters, to keep abreast of the general situation. From 12 September he was actively involved in operations. But inevitably he was dependent on Tappen to help guide him in his new office. The qualities which Falkenhayn was expected to bring to OHL were administrative—to centralize command, to move OHL forward to Charleville–Mézières, to bring the army commanders to heel; the ideas would be Tappen's, and even Moltke's.

For ten days past Moltke had been anxiously looking to Belgium and had been preparing to move thither the 7th and then the 6th armies from Alsace-Lorraine. Others, including Falkenhayn, had wanted to employ the 6th and 7th armies alongside the 4th and 5th, either as part of the attempt to break through or as a counter to an anticipated French attack northwards on the front Verdun–Toul. By 14 September, the opposing lines on France's eastern frontier were up to a kilometre apart and the French were showing no indication that

[150] On Falkenhayn, see Afflerbach, *Falkenhayn*, and Janssen, *Der Kanzler und der General*; for contemporary comments, Riezler in Jarausch, *Enigmatic Chancellor*, 267, and Groener, *Lebenserinnerungen*, 187–8.
[151] Reichsarchiv, *Weltkrieg*, v. 9.

they would attack. The stabilization of the line in Champagne and the Argonne lessened the fear of a French thrust northwards from Verdun and also argued against the idea of trying to push the French 3rd and the 4th armies to the south-east. The 7th army had been used to plug the gap between the 1st and 2nd. But the 6th army was still available as a strategic reserve.

During the night of 14/15 September Falkenhayn weighed a number of options. The Germans' overall frontier in the west was stabilizing, but the open flank of the 1st army, guarded by a single reserve corps, and the latent threat from Antwerp meant that this next move must be at least in part defensive. And this was the heart of the dilemma. The Germans had to secure their position in France, but simultaneously they had to regain the moral ascendancy they had enjoyed before the Marne and go on to achieve a quick victory in the west. The pressure of time, particularly given the insistent appeals to reinforce the eastern front, was no less than it had been at the start of the war.[152] Falkenhayn's inclination, therefore, already evident in late August before he became chief of the general staff,[153] was now no longer to use the 6th army to achieve a breakthrough round Verdun but to resurrect Schlieffen's plan for envelopment by pushing it wide, to the right wing.

However, Falkenhayn had not resolved Schlieffen's original dilemma, that of numbers in relation to space. The right wing ran from Compiègne to Antwerp, and he had a single army to cover the entire area. He could use it cautiously, to thicken the 1st army and secure the flank. He could push it wide, to help mop up Antwerp, and then to secure the Channel coast and its ports as far as the mouth of the Somme. Thirdly, he could allocate less substantial reinforcements to both the 1st army and the Antwerp besiegers, and give the 6th army a more independent role between the two geographical extremes of Compiègne and Antwerp.

The third option was the one which Falkenhayn favoured. In an operation which would both defend the open flank and resume the offensive, he planned to concentrate the 6th army around Maubeuge and then use it to envelop the Entente's left wing. The movement of the 6th army could not be completed until 21 September, and to cover the intervening days Falkenhayn intended to authorize the 1st, 7th, and 2nd armies to fall back to the line La Fère–Laon—Reims. The 3rd, 4th, and 5th armies were to hold if they were attacked, and if they were not, were to attack—beginning on the left with the 5th on 18 September, and moving in a south-westerly direction.

The 'autodidact', for all his criticism of Moltke's dependence on Schlieffen, had embraced the idea of strategic envelopment. However, while Falkenhayn

[152] The tone of Falkenhayn's memoirs suggests that he saw his position as essentially defensive: Falkenhayn, *General headquarters*, 9–10, 12–15; the German official history is much more positive, saying that Falkenhayn expected a decision in the west within a month: Reichsarchiv, *Weltkrieg*, v. 3–4.
[153] Rupprecht von Bayern, *Mein Kriegstagebuch*, i. 121; Afflerbach, *Falkenhayn*, 181.

was forming his plan the two key exponents of breakthrough—Tappen and Bülow—had devised a totally different scheme. They wanted to use the left wing of the 1st army, the 7th army, and three corps which had been drawn off from each of the 3rd, 4th, and 5th armies to attack on the front Soissons–Fismes–Reims. Tappen's criticism of Falkenhayns's plan was comprehensive. Three points proved particularly telling. First, Falkenhayn's proposal involved a delay in which the French would be given the chance to regain the operational freedom which they seemed to be losing by 14 September. They had the advantage in the use of railways (a point reinforced by Groener), and could regroup faster than could the Germans. Secondly, stretching the line to the right might reopen the gap between the 1st and 2nd armies. Finally, and most importantly for the new chief of the general staff, his first manoeuvre involved a retreat, which, however sound strategically, was not sensible in the immediate aftermath of defeat. The effect on Germany's putative allies, Italy and Romania, would be no less than the further damage to the morale of the German soldier.

Falkenhayn was convinced, at least in part. He determined that there would be no further retreat on the right wing or in the centre. But he did not think a decision could be reached between Noyon and Verdun. He therefore persevered with the idea of moving the 6th army, ostensibly to protect the 1st army's flank in the area of St Quentin, although privately nursing the hope of envelopment. And on the left he decided to renew the attack on the Meuse forts, just south of Verdun, reckoning that the French forces in this sector were now weak, and hoping to be able to encircle the city itself. The purpose of the Soissons/Reims attack was therefore to fix the French in the centre and prevent the reinforcement of their wings. Once again, however, the overall effect was to create a plan with too many options, and that was too ambitious, given the resources available.[154]

Germany's hopes of a decisive victory between September and November 1914 came to rest on the right wing. But never did its army regain the initiative which it had enjoyed in August. Falkenhayn has taken the brunt of the criticism for this: he has been blamed for a reluctance to strip the rest of his line and to lose ground in order to create a strong right wing.[155] But in truth the causes were in large part outside Falkenhayn's immediate control. Troops were fed into the right wing in penny packets and were never in sufficient depth. This was as much a product of the transport problems as of the needs of the rest of the front. Much of the railway line in German-occupied Belgium and northern France was still not fully operational. Until the fall of Maubeuge only one line, that from Trier to Liège, Brussels, Valenciennes, and Cambrai

[154] Reichsarchiv, Weltkrieg, v. 16–25; also Ratinaud, La course, 44–9.
[155] Groener, Lebenserinnerungen, 179–81, 193–8.

linked Germany to Belgium and northern France. This single line had simultaneously to carry supplies for the right-wing armies in one direction and
enable the regrouping of the 6th army in the other. At the most forty trains per
day could run, and thus the movement of a single corps took four days. Even
after Maubeuge fell, the second line—that from Diedenhofen to Luxembourg—
was disrupted until the bridge over the Meuse at Namur was restored. In late
October the German corps operating round Ypres went days without food,
and were reduced to taking the turnips from the fields where they fought. Joffre
knew this, and made the harassing of German communications around
Péronne and St Quentin a focus of his operations.[156] His flow of intelligence,
through wireless intercepts, was sufficient to enable him to anticipate German
movements. The Germans, on the other hand, had to rely much more on
agents' reports, and were often remarkably vague and even far-fetched in their
estimates of Entente movements and intentions. Tactically the German inferiority persisted, the French proving far more canny in their use of ground and
far more economical in their expenditure of men.[157] And, finally, for all the
expectations vested in him, Falkenhayn did not manage to bring his army
commanders to heel. His approval of Bülow's attack on the Soissons–Reims
front on 16 September—against his own judgement—was a dangerous concession to Moltkean precedent. Bülow asked Kluck for his support but did not
get it, and the attack made little progress. The consequence of their continuing
problems—of command, tactics, communications, transport, and manpower—was that Falkenhayn's defensive needs, the protection of his exposed
flank and his lines of communication, could never be entirely subordinated to
his need to regain the initiative.

The French army's conduct of the campaign was not necessarily more
distinguished. But it was not burdened with the continuous pressure for a
decisive victory in short order. After the Aisne, Joffre could view protracted
operations—and therefore more cautious tactics—with equanimity. The preservation of the army in the field was quite sufficient as an immediate objective. Indeed, in the light of this the strategy which Joffre adopted seems almost
rash. From 15 September Joffre had planned two levels of operation against the
exposed German flank. In the first place, he wanted Maunoury's 6th army to
advance up the right bank of the Oise. Secondly, he envisaged a much larger
turning movement between the Oise and the Somme. The caution of Maunoury's advance, his decision to go up the left bank of the Oise, and therefore
his failure fully to threaten Kluck's right flank meant that he was slow to
execute Joffre's wishes. When, on 17 September, he threw XIII corps onto the
right bank of the Oise it hit Kluck's right wing proper, and the whole French

[156] Miquel, *La Grande Guerre*, 195–7; Fayolle, *Cahiers secrets*, 44; on supply problems at Ypres, see
Unruh, *Langemarck*, 58–9, 109–10.
[157] Schulte, *Europäische Krise*, 182; Genevoix, '*Neath Verdun*, 193–4.

6th army was checked. But simultaneously the blocking of Bülow's attack increased Joffre's confidence in once again stripping his left to feed his right. The 2nd army at Nancy was dissolved, and a new 2nd army, still commanded by Castelnau, was formed south of Amiens. Four territorial divisions, covering the French line of communications in the Amiens area, extended Castelnau's left. Thus, shorn of cavalry, France's marching wing was entrusted to over-age and under-trained troops, commanded by a recalled 74-year-old. The hope that they could envelop the Germans by way of Arras and Bapaume was doomed to disappointment.[158]

The opportunity presented in the east by this further French move to the west was not neglected by the Germans: the planned attack on the Meuse forts was met in somewhat dilatory fashion by Sarrail's 3rd army, and by 25 September the Germans had formed a salient south of Verdun round St Mihiel. Furthermore, with the failure of Bülow's attack, Falkenhayn felt able to resume his own conception, and on 18 September ordered the movement of the 6th army from Lorraine to the area around St Quentin. The moves of each army mirrored those of the other.

The task which Crown Prince Rupprecht was set was poorly defined. His army, Falkenhayn told him, was to seek a decision on the northern wing and to secure the right flank. Falkenhayn had therefore failed to resolve his ambivalence between recognizing the defensive needs of his army and the pressure for quick victory in the west; furthermore, he gave Rupprecht no indications as to how he should execute his open-ended mission. Falkenhayn's inclinations were to stress speed, to forestall the French advance between Roye and Montdidier, and so emphasized the defensive. Rupprecht overruled him, recognizing that the railway problem would delay the concentration of the 6th army, but anxious to postpone operations until he had sufficient strength mustered for a decisive effort.[159]

Not until the evening of 23 September did the 6th army begin its advance, moving up the Oise to the left of Compiègne. Bad weather had impeded aerial reconnaissance and the French cavalry was exhausted. Lack of intelligence buttressed Joffre's belief that a decisive victory was in Castelnau's grasp if only he would push northwards with enough energy. But Castelnau had acquired enough information during the course of 22 and 23 September to realize that the Germans were pre-empting him and were in strength. He proceeded with caution. By the 24th the limited encounters of the previous few days had given way to fierce fighting along the front from Noyon to Albert. The Germans struck Castelnau's right flank as he pushed across the Somme. Their efforts were bent on breaking IV corps at Roye, so as to isolate the French to the north.

[158] Gras, *Castelnau*, 177; Ratinaud, *La Course*, is the best single source for this and for what follows, until the end of the year.
[159] Rupprecht, *Mein Kriegstagebuch*, i. 127; Reichsarchiv, *Weltkrieg*, v. 58, 61–2.

The French 2nd army hoped to neutralize this danger by continuing to out-flank the Germans, but the latter were already at Bapaume on the 26th. The attack at Roye, although held, forced Castelnau onto the defensive. Falken-hayn, encouraged by the limited success at St Mihiel to believe that the French must be weakening their line elsewhere, responded to their lateral moves by resuming the attack in the centre. Launched on 26 September in heavy columns against prepared positions, this advance was repulsed with heavy losses. By the 27th it was clear that Falkenhayn had succeeded neither in destroying the French 2nd army on Rupprecht's flank, nor in breaking through in the centre.

While Falkenhayn's attention was being pulled away from his right to his centre and left, Joffre's purpose remained fixed. On the 25th itself he shifted XI corps from the 9th army to Amiens: by 1 October, using road as well as rail, two more corps, plus three infantry and two cavalry divisions, had set off for Amiens, Arras, Lens, and Lille.[160] Castelnau's army now embraced eight corps and extended along a 100-kilometre front. Its task was no longer to outflank but to hold, while a detachment under Maud'huy of two of its corps and a cavalry corps manoeuvred on Arras. Maud'huy was drawn to the untenanted north-east, to Vimy and the Scarpe valley. The line south of Arras, between Maud'huy's force and the 2nd army proper, was held by the territorials.

Falkenhayn too continued to manoeuvre on his wing. But although he pushed all his disposable forces towards Rupprecht, and on 28 September directed the 6th army to attack Arras, he did not forsake the possibility of a breakthrough in the centre. Thus, unlike Joffre, either by inclination or as a consequence of the logistical constraints he was not prepared to weaken the centre to reinforce the wing. Given the balance of forces, Rupprecht's plans seem ambitious. He hoped to hold Maud'huy frontally at Arras and, wheeling north round the city, to envelop the French left wing. To do this, on 3 October he reinforced the reserve corps operating north of Arras, and sent IV cavalry corps from Valenciennes, north of Lens, towards Lille. However, chances of success also beckoned south of Arras, on Maud'huy's right, where the resist-ance of the territorials was weakening.

By the evening of the 4th Maud'huy's position at Arras was threatened with encirclement. The Germans were north-west of Vimy, at Givenchy, and Maud'huy's left-hand division had lost contact with the cavalry corps to its north. To the south a breach was opening between the territorials and X corps. Maud'huy said he must retreat to avoid 'a new Sedan', and Castelnau asked whether Maud'huy should go in the direction of St Pol or Doullens. Joffre's belief that Castelnau was given to pessimism, formed in the light of the battles

[160] Joffre, *Mémoires*, i. 438–9.

round Nancy, found corroboration in his conduct of the battles of Artois and Picardy.[161] He feared that the 2nd army would withdraw south of the Somme, so abandoning not only Maud'huy but all northern France. His response was threefold. First, he confirmed Maud'huy's independence of Castelnau by making his command the 10th army. Secondly, he reiterated to Castelnau that the pressure on the 2nd army would be relieved as the allied strength accumulated in the north: he was on no account to fall back. Thirdly, he acknowledged that the northern armies now constituted a separate area of operations in need of more direct control than he personally could give it. He therefore appointed Foch as his deputy, making him responsible for co-ordinating the operations of the 2nd and 10th armies and the territorials. Foch's own army, the 9th, was suppressed.

Castelnau now had the indignity of being under the command of his erstwhile subordinate—the man whom he could with reason see as responsible for the disaster at Morhange. To personal pique was added a difference of temperament. Both were devout Catholics, but Castelnau, André Tardieu recorded, had 'a taste for nuances', while Foch had 'a passion for unities'. Castelnau believed the conception of operations entertained by Foch and by GQG—that the decisive battle of the war had been won and that they were embarked on the exploitation of France's victory—to be fundamentally mis-conceived. He was concerned about his right, under heavy attack at Roye, and saw plans for retreat as a sensible precaution.[162] Foch continued to look to the left and told Castelnau that withdrawal was out of the question. Maud'huy too was instructed to hold Arras. Energy and determination, not operational or strategic insight, constituted Foch's contribution in 1914. While this spirit could not easily percolate through to the soldiers of the front line, it was most certainly conveyed to their commanders. Furthermore, he succeeded in projecting his doggedness onto the British and the Belgians. Within fifty-seven hours of his appointment on 4 October Foch had motored 850 kilometres.[163] By 6 October the allied line from the Oise to north of Arras was secure. That evening Falkenhayn decided to cease all further attacks in Picardy; his atten-tion—and that of Foch—was now moving north of Lens, to Flanders and the area between the River Lys and the sea.

The engagement of, first, Heeringen's 7th army and then Rupprecht's 6th in the battle on the German right wing had underpinned the original purpose in their withdrawal from Alsace-Lorraine. In the midst of the Marne battle Moltke and Hentsch had plotted their redeployment to quell their fears for the slender line of communications through Belgium. Both in the retreat from

---

[161] Most accounts are shaped by the memoirs of Joffre and Foch, both inimical to Castelnau. Gras, *Castelnau*, is an important corrective.

[162] Ibid. 191–2; Tardieu, *Avec Foch*, 88.

[163] Foch, *Memoirs*, 138.

Mons and again during the battle of the Marne the Belgian army had sallied forth from its Antwerp base and mounted raids in the direction of Brussels. Later in August a brief appearance by some British marines at Ostend had been seen as a portent of the operational flexibility which seapower vouchsafed the Entente. The fear of a major landing, combined with a Belgian operation from Antwerp, was fed by some of the wilder intelligence received at OHL. The capture of Antwerp and the destruction of the Belgian army therefore promised to remove any invitation to the British, to safeguard German communications, and to release the German troops masking the city for operations on the main front.

Falkenhayn was later to claim in his memoirs that he was anxious to secure the Channel ports as a base for operations against Britain. The very title so often given to the operations consequent on the Marne and continuing until November—'the race to the sea'—supports the idea that the armies were battling for comparative coastal advantage. If the German army secured Calais and Boulogne, then Britain's Channel fleet would be outflanked and Germany would have opened the southern exit from the North Sea. Britain's sensitivities to exactly this threat have made its historians ready to impute to OHL the strategy which they themselves would have followed. But there is no evidence that Falkenhayn was thinking on these lines in September and October 1914. The withdrawal of the Grand Fleet to Scapa Flow meant that the German High Seas Fleet was closer to the Belgian coast than were the principal formations of the Royal Navy. Moreover, as the fighting developed along the coast, and specifically on the Yser, the guns of Germany's battleships could have made a significant tactical contribution. But the fleet—partly out of ignorance as to the Grand Fleet's position as well as of its own army's situation—did not push its cause, and Falkenhayn did not ask for its aid. He decided to finish with Antwerp because of the needs and security of the right wing, in the pursuit of a quick victory in France, not because of a belated recognition of the tactical or strategic desirability of securing the Channel ports for the conduct of a long war.[164]

On 28 September von Beseler's III reserve corps, made up of five inferior divisions but reinforced with 173 heavy guns, began the siege of the great port. The Belgian perimeter was 96 kilometres in length, but its main defences were concentrated in an outer ring of forts. These provided concentrated targets for the German artillery attack, and because they had not been modernized since 1900 were not proof against the plunging fire of calibres in excess of 210 mm or 220 mm. A dispersed defence, less reliant on armour and concrete, would have

---

[164] Hörich, *Deutsche Seekriegsführung*, 36–7, 65–84. Falkenhayn, *General headquarters*, 13, 28–9, stresses his desire to secure the Channel ports as a base for operations against Britain. Farrar-Hockley, *Death of an army*, 28–9, follows him. But this seems to be hindsight; in late September 1914 Falkenhayn's preoccupation was with a swift victory in France.

stretched the Germans' heavy artillery and ammunition supply to far greater effect. The city's physical vulnerabilities were compounded by the divided counsels of those charged with its defence. The general staff, whose chief was responsible for the army when it was in the field, favoured operations that were independent of the city. This line of thought tied in with the hopes of the French mission, who wished to see the Belgian army co-operating in Joffre's great alllied envelopment developing from the south. But while the field army was within the fortifications its command was in the hands of Antwerp's governor. His problem was that he had insufficient men to hold the perimeter and to keep open a line of retreat to the west. His need was to pull the British and French to the Belgians, rather than to have the Belgians pulled to the British and French. In this respect Belgium's priorities reflected those of Britain, anxious for the security of the Channel coast. The problem for both the Belgians and the British was that Joffre's envelopment, even if successful, could not get to Antwerp in time. On 30 September the Belgian government appealed to France and Britain for direct support. On the following day the German infantry began to advance.[165]

Joffre's response to Belgium's appeal was half-hearted. He refused to release anything more than a scratch force of territorials, Zouaves, and marines. Furthermore, their task as he saw it was to cover the Belgian army's retreat into France, so that it could join the main operations and extend his left wing. While the British were urging the Belgians to prolong Antwerp's defence, Joffre was simultaneously using his emissaries to persuade them to abandon it.

The British reaction to Belgium's request was altogether more urgent, if somewhat more muddled. Anglo-French co-operation in the field had produced victory on the Marne, but once more lost its appeal on the exposed slopes of the Aisne valley. On 24 September Henry Wilson suggested that the BEF move back to the allies' left, so bringing it nearer to its bases and simplifying its lines of communication. Wilson's proposal was of a piece with Joffre's grand envelopment, but French was hesitant for that very reason: having nearly lost the BEF in August, he did not want to find himself isolated once more. What swung the commander-in-chief in favour of the idea was the promise of the First Sea Lord, Winston Churchill, that the navy would provide support from the coast. This scheme smacked less of Anglo-French co-operation and more of British independence, a return to the options adumbrated at the beginning and end of August. By early October French was, on the one hand, suggesting to Kitchener that the entire BEF would come to Antwerp's rescue, while on the other, continuing to give priority to Joffre's operations. The irony in French's enthusiasm for Churchill's plan was that, if effected, it would have exposed the BEF far more than had the French at Mons. Churchill

[165] Galet, *Albert*, 166, 200–41; Deauville, *Jusqu'a l'Yser*, 32; Labbeke, *Stand To!*, 28, (1990), 22.

hoped that Antwerp would lock the allied left wing, and that the line would then run through Ghent to Lille. The BEF would have been the occupants of an exposed salient, vulnerable to artillery attack from the south, and its line of communications continuously exposed to flanking fire. Antwerp itself could only have been directly supplied by sea if the allies had been prepared to breach Dutch neutrality in the Scheldt estuary. Joffre agreed to the BEF's redeployment, but managed the situation by arguing that it could only be effected in stages because the troops were in such close contact with the enemy. The withdrawal from the Aisne began on the night of 1–2 October.

Britain's real problem was that it had not the men to pursue two strategic options simultaneously. Its decision to send the newly formed 7th division to Belgium did not stop the Belgians concluding on 2 October that the government should leave Antwerp the next day. This was widely interpreted as a resolve to abandon the city entirely, a confusion compounded by Churchill, who thought that what was intended was the evacuation of the field army. On 3 October the Belgians made clear that they would hold Antwerp for a further ten days provided the British and the French could dispatch a relief force in three days. On 4 October Kitchener promised 53,000 men—a force whose main components would be Joffre's territorials and marines, which the latter was meanwhile directing on Poperinghe and Lille, and the British 7th division, which Joffre wanted landed at Boulogne so that it could extend his left flank.[166]

In the event, Britain's direct contribution to Antwerp's defence was limited. Winston Churchill had himself appointed the British plenipotentiary, and together with the Royal Naval Division undertook to revitalize the city's defence. The First Lord's actions generated severe doubts as to his judgement. It was not appropriate for a cabinet minister to leave his post in the middle of a war in order to undertake a de facto field command. Nor was the division which he brought of much use: alongside a brigade of marines it contained two barely trained and inadequately organized naval brigades. Churchill justified his unconventional behaviour by arguing that he had prolonged the defence of Antwerp until 10 October, and that in doing so he gave sufficient time for the allies to secure the Channel ports.[167] In reality, Belgium's decision-making was determined not by Churchill but by the continuing power struggle between its senior commanders. By the 10th only one section of the outer forts had been destroyed, and both the second line and the city's enceinte were intact; furthermore, von Beseler's guns were running short of ammunition.[168] Arguably Churchill failed to get the Belgians to hold out as long as they might have done. Britain's main role was not to sustain Antwerp's powers of defence, but,

[166] Philpott, *Anglo-French relations*, 32–48; Philpott, *Guerres mondiales et conflits contemporains*, 180, (1995), 53–60.
[167] Prior, *Churchill's 'World Crisis' as history*, 30–5.
[168] Galet, *Albert*, 216–17, 237–8.

through the arrival at Zeebrugge and Ostend of the 7th division—reinforced by a cavalry division, and somewhat grandly called IV corps (commanded by Henry Rawlinson)—to expedite the Belgian withdrawal.

As IV corps fell back it was brought into line with the BEF proper, being directed to the area north of Ypres. It took up its positions on 14 October, and was joined by I corps on 19 October. Cavalry covered the gap south of Ypres, while by 12 October II and III corps were advancing to the front La Bassée-Armentières. French had suggested to Joffre that the Belgian plain would give freedom of action for his cavalry,[169] while Joffre had hoped that the BEF would be in time to secure the industrial centre of Lille. But the strength of German cavalry now concentrated in the area (eight divisions) forced the BEF to detrain so far to the west—at Abbeville, St Omer, and Hazebrouck—that it was too slow coming up. No serious attempt was made to defend Lille, and on 12 October it was occupied by the Germans.

Joffre failed to grasp how disorganized the retreating Belgian army had become. He assumed that it could return to the fray within forty-eight hours, intending it to swing inward towards Ypres, and so extend once more his left wing. King Albert had different ideas: his priority was to preserve his army and even, if possible, a bit of Belgium. He wanted to move south-west, not south-east. Moreover, by 14 October Beseler's III reserve corps had entered Bruges and was reaching towards Ostend and Roulers, thus threatening the Belgian wings. Rawlinson's IV corps was pushed out from Ypres to Roulers as part of the more general move to the east. It was checked almost immediately, but its effect was to draw the Germans away from the Belgians. The latter wanted a defensive position behind which they could consolidate, absorbing Antwerp's fortress troops into a reorganized field army and restoring their shattered morale. The line of the Yser, its flanks resting on Dixmude and Nieuport, had been identified as just such a position in 1913, and it was thither that the Belgian army moved on 15 and 16 October. The French marines were told by Foch to hold Dixmude at all costs.

On the same day Sir John French, now experiencing one of his periodic bouts of optimism, and buoyed by the fighting talk of Foch, planned that the BEF should stage a general advance eastwards. The line between his left and Dixmude was held by two French territorial divisions, reinforced by a French cavalry corps on 17 October. French reckoned that the right wing of the main German army terminated at Courtrai. On the evening of the 19th he told Haig that only one German corps lay between Menin and Ostend. I corps's orders were to capture Bruges and advance on Ghent, so simultaneously relieving the Belgians on the Yser and pushing north-eastwards round the German right wing. However, Rawlinson, responsible for the British left until

---

[169] T. Wilson, *Myriad faces of war*, 147; also Cassar, *French*, 154–5; Holmes, *Little field marshal*, 242–4.

Haig's arrival, lacked his chief's conviction that a rapid advance on Menin would at last place the allied line round the German flank. He was right. By the evening of the 19th, but ignored by French, British intelligence calculated that there were three-and-a-half German corps north of the Lys. In reality there were in excess of five.[170]

On 4 October, while the battle round Arras was at its zenith, Falkenhayn had decided to push a cavalry corps well to the north, towards Ypres, with a view to its falling onto the French rear. However, the cavalry did not proceed as fast as Falkenhayn hoped. By 8 October, when its advance guards were at Bailleul and Hazebrouck, it was encountering thickening resistance and its hesitation was increased by its loss of contact with the 6th army. Falkenhayn concluded that he needed, not a cavalry corps, but a whole new army to place on the Flanders section of the front. The new army, the 4th, was commanded, like the old 4th (which was suppressed), by the Duke of Württemberg. It embraced von Beseler's III reserve corps and four of six new reserve corps forming in Germany. The measure of Falkenhayn's urgency, his anxiety to clinch the campaign in the west, can be gauged by his decision to use these four corps. The popular image, exploited by German propaganda, was that they were composed of young students, volunteers fired with patriotic enthusiasm. In reality most battalions had only one volunteer in ten; the majority of the soldiers were older men who had either completed their military service or who had never been called up at all. Their equipment was incomplete and only recently delivered: a month before they entered the line some battalions had received only half their complement of rifles. They were short of maps and entrenching tools. The lack of sufficient junior officers and NCOs did nothing to compensate for the inadequacies of their training. The senior officers were old, brought out of retirement, advocates of the tactical ideas of the 1870s: many were unfit, the 208th reserve regiment losing its commanding officer and all three battalion commanders to sickness in five days in October. And all these problems were even worse when related to the more demanding technical and tactical tasks of the artillery: practised only in direct fire and lacking the telephones to link the batteries to their forward observers, the field guns were to prove woefully inaccurate.[171] Britain's new armies were no better. But Kitchener, anticipating a long war, did not permit their use until a whole year later. Falkenhayn needed victory in 1914: there was no virtue in preserving these corps for a contingency which he could not afford to entertain.

Falkenhayn's plan was for the 4th army to form to the left of Beseler's corps on the coast, supported by the heavy artillery from Antwerp. It would move from Belgium southwards, outflanking the allied left around St Omer. The 6th

---

[170] Edmonds, *France and Belgium 1914*, ii. 136–7. General accounts of the Flanders fighting are Foch, *Memoirs*; Ratinaud, *La Course*; Farrar-Hockley, *Death of an army.*

[171] Unruh, *Langemarck*, chs. 2–6.

army, holding the line from La Bassée to Menin, was to attack and hold the French and British from the front. If the allies turned to meet the 4th army, the 6th would be able to break through north of Arras. The extension of the BEF into Flanders did not change the basic intention. Either the 4th army would strike the BEF in the flank as it tried to envelop the 6th, or the BEF would attack the 4th and so create the opportunity for the 6th to separate the French and British. If the BEF fell back, it would simply be enveloped by the 4th army from the north.

The free manoeuvre of the 4th army required that the Belgians be dislodged from their line on the Yser. The battle which developed around Ypres, therefore, depended for its outcome on the dogged determination of King Albert's 53,000 men and Ronarc'h's marines between Dixmude and Nieuport. Albert's order of the day to the Belgian army on 16 October was uncompromising: those who fled the battlefield would be shot by marksmen posted to the rear, officers claiming to be sick would be court-martialled, and general staff officers were to be posted to the front line.[172] The Yser itself was not a major obstacle, and the waterlogged ground meant that trenches could only be one or two feet deep. The Belgians' 75 mm field guns were becoming unserviceable through incessant firing, and ammunition was low. The 4th army was supported on its right by the heavy guns from Antwerp, but they were countered by the gunnery of the Royal Navy's Dover Patrol stationed off the coast. The Germans' attack opened on 18 October, and by the 22nd they had gained a foothold across the river at Tervaete, in the centre of the line. With the flanks at Dixmude and Nieuport thrown back, the centre formed an exposed salient which the Belgians were now desperate to reinforce. The French had sent the 42nd infantry division to Nieuport, but Foch's plan was for it to thrust along the coast in the direction of Lombartzyde, while in the centre Ronarc'h's marines pushed on Thourout and on the right elements of IX corps attacked towards Roulers. He argued that a French offensive north of Ypres would disengage the Belgians, and that all they had to do was to hold their ground. The Belgians said they could not do so, and indeed were already not doing so; the aid from France needed to be direct, not indirect. By the evening of 23 October the Belgians had been driven out of the salient, and were planning a general withdrawal. The 42nd division had already begun its attack, and the French would only release one brigade so that the ground the division had already gained would not be forfeit.

During the course of 24 October the Germans launched fifteen assaults and by dark were established beyond the Yser on a 5-kilometre front. The French now agreed that the remainder of the 42nd division should reinforce the Belgian centre. The division seemed to be too late. The Belgians had been fighting continuously for seven days, without relief, and had no reserves. They

---

[172] Deauville, *Jusqu'à l'Yser*, 86; Galet, *Albert*, 265.

had already fallen back to the railway embankment, which was parallel to the river and was raised 1 to 2 metres above sea level because of the waterlogged state of the ground. On the 26th their commander, Wielmans, and his staff resolved to retreat once more. The head of the French military mission, Brécard, warned the Belgians that in that case they would leave the French isolated, as they had received no instructions to fall back. The situation was saved by the intervention of King Albert, who forbade any further withdrawal.[173] On 27 October, the lock gates at Nieuport were opened at high tide, so that the sea flooded the area between the Yser and the embankment. As the tide fell the gates were closed, and thus gradually the depth of the inundation rose. On the 30th the Germans made a last attack, getting across the embankment at Ramscapelle, but being driven out again at nightfall on the 31st. Thereafter the floodwater blocked the Germans' path; the allied left flank was secure.

The crisis on the Yser was part of a larger encounter battle, pivoting on the city of Ypres. On 19 October the advance of the 6th and 4th German armies began. Simultaneously Sir John French directed the BEF's left wing in the direction of Menin and Roulers. On 21 October the 4th army's reserve corps suffered heavy losses in a series of ill-prepared and ill-supported attacks. By 23 and 24 October Falkenhayn's efforts were concentrated on the army's right, on the Yser, and on the 6th army's battle south of Ypres. Foch, on the other hand, continued to push in the direction of Roulers and Thourout, north-east of Ypres. The burden of the attack was now taken over by French units, forming the 8th army under d'Urbal, and so allowing Haig's I corps to drop down, to the east of Ypres. Dixmude, tenaciously held by the French marines, became the key to the movements of both sides. Foch's persistent attacks, although making no gains, contained the Germans and shamed both the Belgians and the British into abandoning thoughts of withdrawal. But the BEF was getting very tired: by the end of the month it had been in continuous action along its entire front for ten days.

Falkenhayn, checked on both the 6th army's front and on the 4th's, and with the chances of breakthrough on the Yser disappearing, planned a fresh attack. The task of the 6th and 4th armies would be to tie down the allied reserves. A new formation, renamed after its commander, von Fabeck, and composed of six additional divisions and over 250 heavy guns, was inserted between the 6th and 4th armies. It had a local superiority of two to one, and was to attack south of Ypres, driving north-westwards between Messines and Gheluvelt, on the Menin road. Haig's I corps lay in front of Ypres, astride the Menin road. The line to the south was held by Allenby's dismounted cavalry corps. On 29 October the Germans made initial gains along the Menin road, and on the 30th Allenby's cavalry was driven back from Zandvoorde and Hollebeke to

[173] Brécard, *En Belgique*, esp. 55–87.

within 3 kilometres of Ypres. D'Urbal, his left relieved by the Yser inundations, sent three battalions in support of I corps. But on the following day a German shell struck the staffs of two of I corps' divisions while they were conferring at Hooge. By now the British position at Gheluvelt was collapsing and the path to Ypres lay open. The situation was restored by the 2nd battalion of the Worcestershire Regiment, in reserve north of the Menin road, who advanced at the double for a mile, driving the Germans off the crossroads to the south and east. South of the road further cracks in the line appeared, but on the left of the German attack the British hold on the Messines ridge was consolidated, the first territorial unit into action, the London Scottish, coming into the line at Wytschaete.

By 1 November Sir John French's anxiety for the state of the BEF had good grounds. Of eighty-four infantry battalions, seventy-five mustered less than 300 men, a third of their strength in August: eighteen battalions had fewer than 100 men of all ranks.[174] To Foch, French appeared gloomy and anxious. At an allied conference held that day Kitchener offered to replace the BEF's commander with Sir Ian Hamilton, but the French decided they preferred the devil they knew. Moreover, as Foch and Haig realized, the crisis was now waning. D'Urbal's XVI corps, moved onto the St Eloi–Wytschaete front, propped up Allenby, and his IX corps attacked the German right from the north against Becelaere. Thus, pressure on Haig's corps was relieved on both its flanks. Falkenhayn pondered the wisdom of continuing the assault. By 3 November Fabeck's group had lost 17,250 men in five days, and the vigour of the German assaults was fading.

Foch now planned attacks—although he had never admitted that the fighting of the previous fortnight had been anything other than a continuous allied offensive—towards Messines and Langemarck, timed for 6 November, and designed to widen and consolidate the allied salient around Ypres. Falkenhayn, however, pre-empted him. Recognizing the failure of the attempt to break through at Ypres itself, the German chief of the general staff resolved to attack at the pivots south and north of the salient. Even limited gains here would—as Foch had recognized in his attention to the same areas—allow the German artillery to overlook the city and its network of roads. A local victory would help cover the absence of a decisive breakthrough. The German attacks began on 5 November, waned on the 9th, but resumed with great fury on the 10th and 11th. The assault was intended to embrace the whole front to the south of the Menin road, but on 10 November was mounted principally by the 4th army on the front between Langemarck and Dixmude. Dixmude itself was taken. The following day, on the other half of the front, the Germans staged the heaviest artillery bombardment the British had yet experienced and attacked

[174] Farrar-Hockley, *Death of an army*, 169.

between Messines and Polygon Wood. Again a breach was made on the Menin road, the mist and the gunfire covering the advance of the Prussian guards. But they were not well supported by the reserve division to their right, and the situation was restored. By now both sides were exhausted. Total German losses at Ypres were in the region of 80,000, and most of the newly formed reserve regiments had suffered at least 60 per-cent casualties. The BEF's losses for the war up to 30 November, 89,964, exceeded the establishment of the original seven divisions, and 54,105 of them had fallen around Ypres. The combat strength of the Belgian army had halved. Total French dead for 1914 were 265,000, but casualties of all types were already 385,000 by 10 September.[175] On 13 November the first battle of Ypres—although formally it continued until 22 November—was effectively over.

The casualties of 1914 were the highest of the war in relation to the establishments of the participating armies. Such a rate of loss was unsustainable over the long run. So too were the pace and intensity of the first four months' fighting. Digging trenches in October and November was as exhausting—albeit physical exercise of a different form—as the sustained marches of August and September. But trenches also gave protection; they minimized casualties and they stabilized the line. The first battle of Ypres highlighted the fact that the conduct of war was on a cusp.

Tactically, the battle seemed to its participants confirmation of a new form of warfare. But with the wisdom of hindsight some of the features appear remarkably old fashioned. A junior officer of the German 46th Reserve Field Artillery Regiment, who came into action in the sector Langemarck—Bixschoote on 23 October, recorded that his battery fired as many as 960 rounds during the course of that night alone, and that during the pauses between British infantry attacks it had directly engaged the enemy's artillery. But the latter was only 1,400 to 1,800 metres distant, most of the battery's fire had been at ranges between 400 and 800 metres, and its crews could hear the enemy's rifle bullets as they struck their gun shields. Using direct fire, the guns were deployed as though for mobile warfare, but found themselves confronting the tactical realities of more static formations. The horses of the regiment's munition column panicked under shrapnel fire and fresh shell supplies had to be lugged up by hand.[176] Elsewhere on the battlefield horses were still in evidence. On 26 October the Royal Horse Guards, on I corps' right flank, covered the retreat of a brigade of the 7th division, two squadrons galloping for a quarter of a mile, parallel to and only 200 metres from the Germans; they then dismounted and engaged the enemy with their rifles; the regiment's total losses were only eight men and twenty-five horses.[177] True, most of the cavalry on both sides spent

[175] Unruh, *Langemarck*, 182–5; Edmonds, *France and Belgium 1914*, ii. 466–7; Contamine, *Révanche*, 276–7.
[176] Foerster and Greiner (eds.), *Wir kämpfer in Weltkrieg*, 95–7.   [177] J. Williams, *Byng*, 74–5.

the battle dismounted. But the surprising fact is that cavalry could hold such important stretches of the line for so long. The French cuirassiers went into the line still attired in helmets and breastplates, and clutching their lances and carbines. British cavalry at least had rifles rather than carbines, but their divisional artillery consisted only of 13-pounders (the infantry field gun was an 18-pounder): thus it was deficient in the conventional index of First World War firepower. And yet by the standards of what was to come, this—the German heavy artillery and field howitzers apart—was not really a gunners' battle. Much of the German field artillery was ill served. Both sides were short of ammunition, and what they fired tended, as the weather worsened, to bury in the mud rather than explode on contact. Rifle fire, not shellfire, predominated, particularly for the British. One soldier fired 600 rounds in a single day.[178]

But all this was what contemporaries expected. What they did not anticipate was a battle of such intensity, over effectively three weeks, with so little movement. 'I am getting awfully bored by the trenches,' wrote a British officer on 5 November, 'and am feeling fearfully tired. I hope we won't be in them much longer. I wish they would order the advance.'[179]

Those who did well were those who recognized that they must change their thinking. A British cabinet member reported on 20 October that Foch and Castelnau had originally imagined that the course of this war, like previous wars, would be shaped by big battles punctuated by quiet intervals. They had not appreciated the continuous powers of resistance conferred by trenches; now they did.[180] On the same day Wilhlem Groener, despite being in the rear, recorded his appreciation that progress would be slow: 'The whole war has taken on the character of a battle of fortifications. Fresh, joyful open warfare is not, in the current circumstances, the order of the day.'[181] The capture of Dixmude on 10 November is an index of how quickly the skills of position warfare could be learnt, particularly by the Germans. A German reserve division, which three weeks previously attacked without sufficient artillery preparation and with inadequate reconnaissance, was put under the command of officers from the active list: they ordered the fortification of the ground gained, built up the heavy artillery, and gradually pushed forward the line until it was within 200 metres of the Franco-Belgian positions. Only then, with artillery superiority and proper preparation, did the attack go in.[182]

Although the character of the fighting—after the initial contact was made— was static, its commanders continued to see the battle as mobile. Falkenhayn and Foch ordered attack and counter-attack. But the movement effected in response to these orders was limited. Indeed, most of the battle was outside

[178] Farrar-Hockley, *Death of an army*, 101.   [179] Dunn, *The war the infantry knew*, 90.
[180] David (ed.), *Inside Asquith's cabinet*, 199.   [181] Groener, *Lebenserinnerungen*, 527.
[182] Unruh, *Langemarck*, 123–7.

their control. The landscape around Ypres was still closed, the roads converging on the city dividing it into self-contained compartments, and its woods and houses providing cover. British infantry, trained to regard 500 yards as a minimum field of fire, found 200 to 400 yards to be the norm.[183] Tactical command was therefore exercised at a much lower level. The decisions which closed the gaps on the Menin road on 31 October and 11 November were taken by a brigadier. The corps commanders, and Haig especially, had responsibility for the management of the battle, and acted accordingly within the fighting zone. The quality most urgently required of a general in such circumstances, devoid of information for long periods and too often unable to resolve his tension with activity, was an inner certainty, a belief in ultimate success, a bloody-minded obstinacy. These the first battle of Ypres had shown that both Haig and Foch possessed in abundance.

Foch did not fight the sort of battle which he imagined he fought. After all, the Entente success was defensive, not offensive. Furthermore, the ground on which the lines eventually rested reflected this attacking intent, not the needs of protracted defence: too often they were sited on forward slopes, observable by German artillery, or were indented by local German gains. But the hand-to-mouth nature of such expedients had a wider benefit. When the battle closed, British and French units stood intermingled along the perimeter: adversity under fire had forced co-operation and trust.

Falkenhayn had, for all his independence of the Schlieffen school, fought Schlieffen's battle. He had continued, despite the Marne, to seek a rapid victory in the west. He had done so by moving towards the right flank, in the hope primarily of envelopment, but secondly of breakthrough should the enemy line weaken elsewhere. However, the Entente had constructed a solid and continuous line from Switzerland to the sea. Envelopment was no longer possible. Neither the shells nor the men were available to attempt a breakthrough. On 25 November he ordered the German armies in the west to form defensive positions, and to hold the ground which they had already conquered. His instructions gave method to position warfare, and anticipated its adoption for some months. But its purpose remained that of enabling the creation of fresh forces for mobile and decisive operations.[184] For both sides, trench warfare continued to be a matter of expedience, not a foundation for strategy.

---

[183] Terraine, *General Jack's diary*, 70.   [184] Reichsarchiv, *Weltkrieg*, vi. 372, 398–404.

4

THE
EASTERN FRONT
IN 1914

WAR PLANS

The reputation of the Austro-Hungarian army was honourable but ambiguous. 'Although, of course, the Austrians had been victorious in all the wars in their history,' wrote Robert Musil, himself a former officer of the Habsburg army, 'after most of these wars they had had to surrender something.'[1] Distinguished conduct on the battlefield had been accompanied by narrow defeats. In 1866 victory over Italy had been negated by Königgrätz. And in the subsequent half-century the imperial army had not seen action. Its chief of staff from 1906, Conrad von Hötzendorff, had never been under fire. His career was founded on his abilities as a teacher and theorist. The Germans after the war were wont to say of their allies that peacetime training had elevated knowledge over leadership.[2]

Like many peacetime armies, appearances seemed to outweigh substance. And yet bands and uniforms, the impression of military strength, constituted their own substance. A major role of the army since the late eighteenth century had been domestic. Its high profile constituted a source of unity in the polyglot empire. Conrad shared with his mentor, Franz Ferdinand, a firm conviction that a solution to Austria-Hungary's internal problems should precede any attempts to deal with those that were external, and that the army should lead the way in

---

[1] Robert Musil, *The man without qualities*, i. 15. The major English-language work is Rothenberg, *Army of Francis Joseph*; see also Regele, *Conrad*; Deak, *Beyond nationalism*; Wandruszka and Urbanitsch (eds.), *Die bewaffnete Macht*.
[2] Ludendorff, *My war memories*, i. 75; Balck, *Development of tactics—World War*, 29.

this process. Hungary's prolonged resistance, from 1903 to 1912, to the new army law made the inconveniences of the dual monarchy a threat to military efficiency as well as to imperial unity. Magyar intransigence jeopardized the integrity of the army in ethnic terms and its size in manpower terms. Thus, for Conrad, political reform could not be divorced from professional considerations.

Although a German, Conrad was also—at least occasionally—a federalist. The army of which he was the professional head was made up of 25 per cent Germans, 20 per cent Magyars, 13 per cent Czechs, 4 per cent Slovaks, 9 per cent Serbo-Croats, 8 per cent Poles, 8 per cent Ukrainians, 7 per cent Romanians, 2 per cent Slovenes, and 1 per cent Italians. Over three-quarters of its regular officers, and a comparable number of NCOs, were Germans. And yet, once officers, non-Germans found their nationality little bar to their advancement. Officers perforce owed their primary loyalty to the empire as a whole. Although German was the language of command, *Regimentsprache* embraced the native tongues of the soldiers, and officers had three years in which to master them. Most battalions had at least two recognized languages, and some had three or four. Of the 142 units that were monoglot in 1914, German was the recognized language of only thirty-one. Conrad himself spoke seven languages. But such multiculturalism aroused distrust when fashion favoured nationalism. The officer corps was pilloried as German by the Magyars, as insufficiently German by the Austro-Germans, and as anti-Slav by the Slavs.[3]

Particularly worrying for the army were the concessions made to Magyar military identity. Hungarian insistence on an independent military status and on the use of Magyar as the language of command in Hungarian units threatened to replace unity through a German-dominated federalism with duality. After 1907 the Honved, the Hungarian territorial forces, and the Landwehr, Austria's counterpart to the Honved, had their own artillery and support units. Thus, the effect of the Honved's increasing independence of the common regular army was to create a three-part division in the empire's land forces—the common army, the Landwehr, and the Honved—with neither of the last two constituting the true reserve for the first which their titles suggested. The confusion that followed on mobilization in 1914 was predictable. In one territorial reserve battalion of the Honved, composed of Romanians, none of the three regular officers spoke Romanian, and some soldiers (having done their service in the common army) regarded German as the language of command while others (having been in the Honved) were accustomed to orders in Magyar.[4]

[3] Deak, *Beyond nationalism*, 99, 129; see also James Lucas, *Fighting troops of the Austro-Hungarian army*, 32. Most of this paragraph is derived from Stone, *Past and Present*, 33 (Apr. 1966), 95–111.
[4] Taslauanu, *With the Austrian army*, 13, 19, 21–2.

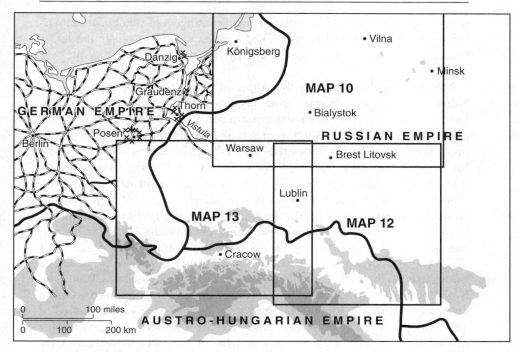

MAP 9. THE EASTERN FRONT

Even more damaging were the consequences of Budapest's postponement of the new army law until 1912. The law of 1889 had fixed the total annual recruit contingent at 135,670 men,[5] who served for three years in the regulars (although in reality they were given leave for the third) or two in the Landwehr or Honved. A proportion of those not conscripted received ten weeks' training in the Ersatz reserves. Thus, the army's size kept pace neither with the growth in population nor with the expansion of other armies. By 1900 Austria-Hungary was training 0.29 per cent of its population, compared with 0.35 per cent in Russia, 0.37 per cent in Italy, 0.47 per cent in Germany, and 0.75 per cent in France. Nor did quality compensate for quantity: the military budget remained low, 14.6 per cent of the total in 1906. In 1912 the annual recruit contingent rose by 42,000 men a year and the period of three years' service was reduced to two for the infantry. The fact that the army was prepared to accept that it therefore had less time to inculcate Habsburg loyalty shows the urgency it attached to the manpower problem. But the decade lost could not be made up by 1914. Those untrained before 1912 could not now be trained; a new bill planned in June 1914

[5] These are Stone's figures; Regele, *Conrad*, 181, gives 10,000 fewer in the Landwehr.

would not reach its full effect, with an annual contingent of 252,000, until 1918.[6]
When war came, Austria-Hungary had simultaneously to repair the losses
incurred in combat and make up for the relative neglect of the pre-war
years.

The combined strength of the common army, the Landwehr, and the
Honved rose on mobilization from 415,000 men to about 2 million. The
Landwehr and the Honved were not complements to the common army but
alternatives. Put positively, this meant that Austria-Hungary's principal reserve
units were unequivocally integrated into its front-line forces: thus the pay-off
for the Magyars' enthusiasm for their own army was that the dual monarchy
was spared the debate on the operational role of reserve formations which so
dominated France and Germany. Put negatively, it meant that Austria-
Hungary had no reserve organization comparable with that of Germany. The
sixteen corps each absorbed one or two Landwehr divisions (except in Bosnia-
Herzogovina), but there was no provision for the creation of reserve corps or
divisions. And, even if there had been, there would have been no adequate
troops to form them. Virtually the entire stock of trained reservists, kept small
by the 1889 army law's survival, was absorbed by the initial expansion. Only a
quarter or a fifth of an infantry company on mobilization was composed of
active troops; units had only one regular NCO for seventeen men.[7] A further 1
million men, in the Ersatz reserves and in the Landsturm (former active
soldiers now aged between 33 and 42), had either little or no recent training.
In one Landsturm brigade, its platoons were commanded by rural policemen
and its men were equipped with five different types of rifle.[8] Thus the field
strength of the Austro-Hungarian army in 1914—forty-eight infantry divisions,
two Landsturm divisions, eleven cavalry divisions, and thirty-six independent
brigades—was approximately half the size of that of France or Germany; and
not only was it smaller, it was also qualitatively inferior.

The officer corps had not rejected the professionalizing trends evident
throughout European armies between 1871 and 1914, but in doing so it had
jeopardized its social status, its numbers, and even its political homogeneity.
Friedrich Beck established the general staff on Prussian lines in the 1880s.
Aristocratic domination was dented by the incorporation of men from business and bourgeois backgrounds: Beck's own father was a university professor
of surgery. But the shift was in part involuntary—an indication of the growing
nationalism of the empire's nobility and of a distancing between the officer
corps and its emperor. The combination of a declining social cachet with

[6] Bridge, *From Sadowa to Sarajevo*, 367.   [7] Regele, *Conrad*, 181.
[8] J. Stone and Schmidl, *The Boer War and military reforms*, 203–4.

continuing low pay and high indebtedness deprived an army career of many of its attractions. In 1897 3,333 potential officers had enrolled in the dual monarchy's nineteen cadet schools, but by 1911 this figure had dwindled to 1,864. A combined officer corps of 60,000 in 1914 proved inadequate for forces that mobilization soon pushed close to a total of 3 million.[9]

The other armies, in coping with the rustiness of their reserves' training, with their lack of field-craft, their tendency to bunch in the attack, relied on artillery as a substitute and as a cover. But the Austro-Hungarian army was the most under-gunned in relation to its (already inferior) strength of any army in Europe. A common army division had forty-two field guns compared with fifty-four in a German division, and the Landwehr and Honved divisions only twenty-four (including no field howitzers in the case of the Honved). Technically Austrian guns could match their rivals': the 30.5 cm Skoda heavy mortar, designed to tackle Italian forts, was outstanding. However, only in the case of the 1905/8-model 76.5 mm field gun had good design been transformed into mass production. This was a by-product of the failure to increase the recruit contingent, which had left a surplus for the acquisition of quick-firing artillery. After 1912 the growth in the army's manpower was achieved at the expense of its armament.[10] The field howitzer was still the outdated 1899 model, without a recoil mechanism, and possessed of a bronze barrel and a fixed carriage; the guns of the heavy artillery (two batteries per corps) had similar characteristics. The excellent new mountain guns—the 70 mm and the 100 mm howitzer— had by 1914 only been issued to four out of fifty-two batteries. The artillery regiments themselves were below strength, even on their peacetime establishments: they were short of 110 officers and 10 to 15 per cent of their gunners.[11] Finally, a better-prepared artillery arm in 1914 would not necessarily have profited the Austro-Hungarian army, which still lacked the doctrine to exploit it. The 1911 regulations emphasized that infantry could act independently of other arms; the foot-soldier's principal resource was his own determination.

The emphasis on the offensive, and the centrality of morale to its achievement, found in Conrad one of its most vociferous advocates. As a social Darwinist, Conrad believed that victory would fall to him who seized the initiative, even if his forces were inferior. As a realist, however, Conrad had to acknowledge that the Habsburg army was of a size suitable only for a Balkan war. His advocacy of preventive wars against Italy and Serbia was a reflection of

[9] Deak, *Beyond nationalism*, 72–6, 159–64.
[10] Stevenson, *Armaments and the coming of war*, 86, 137–40.
[11] Storz, *Kriegsbild und Rüstung*, 244; Stone and Schmidl, *Boer war and military reforms*, 287–9, 299, 61; Matuschka, *Organisationsgeschichte des Heeres 1890–1918*, 213–15; Regele, *Conrad*, 210–12.

both traits. Austria-Hungary would have to fight to preserve its great power status, to protect itself from irridentism within the empire; on the other hand, it could only win a local, limited war. It should, therefore, choose its ground and its time. Implicit in all this was the realization that Austria-Hungary could only undertake war with Russia in conjunction with Germany. Least of all did Conrad—any more than had Beck before him—entertain the prospect of simultaneously fighting all three putative opponents—Russia, Serbia, and Italy.

Nature had provided Austria's Galician frontier with excellent defences. The major barrier to invasion, the Carpathians, lay to the west of the river lines of the San and the Dniester. However, both cost and doctrine limited the enhancement of these natural obstacles with man-made additions. Beck was anxious not to leave all the spoils of victory in Russian Poland to Germany. He therefore fortified Cracow and Przemysl in the late 1880s, but as concentration points for an Austrian advance, not as the hubs of Galicia's defence. Lemberg was not completed, and fortification—like artillery—became a casualty of the competing demands of the defence budget. His analysis of the Boer War led him to reject the use of defence at the operational level, and instead to apply to strategy his tactical thinking on the offensive.[12]

In 1908, reckoning on a slow and staggered Russian mobilization, Conrad planned to push two armies north, between the Vistula and the Bug. By mobilizing faster and concentrating first, he would be able to meet portions of the Russian army with locally superior forces. Having created space to the north, the Austrians would direct two more armies to the north-east, towards Rowno and Ostrow. The 1911 version of the Austrian plan, which united the two prongs in one north-eastern thrust towards the line Kowel–Dubno, extended the major Austrian thrust more to the east. But by 1913 and 1914 Conrad reckoned, in the light of France's pressure for immediate Russian aid, that Russia's concentration would be as far to the west as possible, and that the line of the middle Vistula would therefore be pivotal to the defence of the Central Powers' eastern front. Beginning, therefore, with the 1908 plan, Austria-Hungary had, for the better defence of Galicia and the Vistula river line, and for the further frustration of the Russians' concentration, planned an initial northward thrust. In its most ambitious forms, the plan envisaged the envelopment of the Russian forces facing Galicia; it did not have at its core nor as its first phase the possibility of a massive Austro-German envelopment combining the whole of the eastern front.[13]

    [12] Lackey, *Rebirth of the Habsburg army*, 114–17, 161–2; Stone and Schmidl, *Boer war and military reforms*, 305–7.
    [13] Pitreich, *1914*, ch. 1.

It was nonetheless true that German co-operation was fundamental to Austro-Hungarian thinking. The staff talks opened with Germany in 1882 clearly indicated the elder Moltke's intention to adopt the defensive in the west and to mount limited offensives in the east. The Germans said that 100,000 men would be sufficient to hold the western fortifications and that 400,000 men could be allocated to the east. Although in 1887 the eastern figure had been cut by 200,000, Beck was still able to reckon that Germany would divide its forces equally between east and west. Thus, the possibility of Austria and Germany jointly enveloping at least a portion of the Russian army was present from the outset of the two powers' staff discussions. By 1890 the southern and Austrian prong of this manoeuvre was planned to contain eighteen divisions on a front of 40 to 50 kilometres, thrusting towards Krasnik and Lublin. Although the ultimate objective was convergnce east of Warsaw, none of Beck, Moltke the elder, or Waldersee (Moltke's successor) saw the plan as aiming for anything more than a victory limited to Russian Poland. It was not a scheme for the annihilation of Russia itself.

Beck's principal worry was less the intentions of his ally and more the security of his eastern flank. In driving northwards, the Austro-Hungarian army would be exposed to its right to a Russian thrust from eastern Galicia. By securing Romania as a secret signatory to the Triple Alliance in 1883, Austria-Hungary diminished this danger: it was able not only to redistribute the forces allocated to its Romanian frontier, but also to rely on the Romanians to tie down the Russians. With his right flank now secure, Beck was free to develop his plans for a possible Russian war. He moved the direction of the putative Austrian attack further to the east, towards Dubno and Rowno, and so into the Russian areas of concentration and preparation, before turning north. Schlieffen's intention in 1892, to attack from Posen into western Poland, not from East Prussia, confirmed the possibility of close operational interaction between the two allies.

In the 1880s the biggest block to Austro-German collaboration against Russia had been diplomatic. Bismarck took exception to planning for war against an ally in the east, when the obvious enemy lay in the west. Bismarck's fall and Russia's alliance with France eliminated these considerations. But in their stead the operational preoccupations of the new chief of the general staff bulked increasingly large. The elder Moltke had feared the slowness of Austrian mobilization, but did not let it shape his strategy. Schlieffen did. Furthermore, by 1895 he was increasingly attracted by the opportunities for defensive manoeuvre which the Masurian lakes presented the Germans in East Prussia. He therefore wanted Austria-Hungary to assume responsibility for operations on the middle Vistula, opposite Poland. The Austrians refused to split their forces. By 1896 contacts between the two staffs had

fizzled out. Their legacy, at least in Vienna, was the idea of a joint envelopment.[14]

Schlieffen's subordination of strategy to operations was even more evident
than in his plans for the west, and it was of course these that were the prime
factor in prompting and sustaining the breakdown in communications
between the two allies. His thinking created a contradictory expectation of
the Austrians, that they should draw the Russians off the Germans' backs, and
so assume the major burden in the east. Schlieffen's pursuit of an early decisive
victory as an end in itself led him to plan to face France first. The Russians, with
their ability to trade space for time, with a succession of river lines and fortified
bridgeheads to protect their concentration, promised the Germans protracted
operations with only partial outcomes. The lack of good rail and road communications on Germany's eastern frontier favoured its use for defence but
limited its value as a base for offence. In 1905, when Schlieffen retired, the
decision to concentrate in the west was justified by the slowness of any
prospective Russian mobilization and by Russia's defeats at the hands of the
Japanese. Russia would not be able to put its entire weight in the west, and
what it did put there would take time to arrive. Thus, the basic premiss of
Austrian thinking on a possible war with Russia, that of active German co-
operation, was wrong. And yet Schlieffen was loath to confront his ally with the
truth: Beck and Conrad continued to labour under a misapprehension. Without either side explicitly saying so, each was expecting the other to take the
major burden against the Russians.

Contacts between the two general staffs were resumed, on Conrad's initiative, during the Bosnian crisis. Moltke revealed to Conrad Germany's intention
to concentrate against France first, but the context and manner in which he did
so did not challenge the assumptions within which Conrad was planning.
Conrad's specific worry in January 1909 was that if Austria-Hungary attacked
Serbia, Russia would come to Serbia's aid. Moltke was able to reassure him that
in these circumstances Germany would support Austria-Hungary. Thus, the
major conclusion which Conrad drew from the 1909 exchange was that if an
Austro-Serb clash led to a European war, Austria-Hungary would be supported
by Germany and therefore could continue to concentrate a major part of its
forces against Serbia. Moltke promised that the German 8th army in East
Prussia would draw in the Russians because the Russians would be committed
by their alliance with France to attack Germany. He reckoned that it would
then take three weeks to defeat the French if they obliged Germany by attacking
and four weeks if they cleaved to the security of their fortifications. Ten days
would be required to shift the German forces to the east. Since, at the outset,

[14] Tunstall, *Planning for war*, 16–48; this is the fullest English-language account of Austro-Hungarian
planning.

Conrad had promised an Austrian attack into Russian territory by the twenty-second day of mobilization, Moltke's proposed timetable was perfectly acceptable. Both chiefs of staff recognized the danger that Austrian troops might be embroiled in Serbia before the war had been declared against Russia or France, but Conrad still assured Moltke that he would be able to push twenty-eight divisions into Poland.

Conrad had not secured German backing without paying a price, but the price was one which appealed to his strategic imagination. Moltke was increasingly anxious about the security of East Prussia. Schlieffen had argued that the Masurian lakes would divide a Russian advance into two eccentric directions. By operating offensively on interior lines, and so exploiting their railways, the Germans could—despite an absolute inferiority—achieve local successes. However, the 8th army would be made up of a maximum of thirteen (and perhaps only nine) divisions, and its prospects for continued use of the offensive-defence were not good. Schlieffen conceded that it might eventually have to fall back behind the Vistula, and even the Oder, until it was reinforced from the west. Militarily this plan, advanced by Schlieffen and embraced by Moltke, made sense; politically its implications were horrific. In order to accomplish its offensive in the west, the German general staff was prepared to abandon a large slice of its own country to Russian invasion.[15] Thus Moltke's quid pro quo in 1909 was a request that Austria-Hungary draw the Russians away from East Prussia by launching an attack into Poland from the south, between the Bug and the Vistula. To get Conrad's agreement, Moltke promised that the Germans—once reinforced from the west—would also drive into Poland, from the north and the River Narew. This prospect—the confirmation of a massive Austro-German envelopment designed to destroy the bulk of the Russian army, a 'super-Cannae' in the east—was irresistible to Conrad. The 1909 exchanges therefore managed to keep both sides' illusions intact. Conrad made an Austrian offensive against Russia conditional on the promise of German support, and Moltke, desperate to be relieved of his worries about East Prussia, could only agree. The proposed envelopment in Poland, the apparent evidence of unity, was not subject to detailed operational planning.[16]

In reality, German thinking about the eastern front underwent a complete revolution between 1905 and 1914. In 1905 Germany's emphasis on the west reflected Russian weakness; Moltke's 1914 plan, which gave even less attention to the east, did so not because of Russia's weakness but because of its strength. Moltke's Russophobia was in large part self-induced: his response to a worsen-

---

[15] Showalter, *East European Quarterly*, XV (1981), 163–80; Groener, *Lebenserinnerungen*, 101–2.

[16] On the 1909 exchanges, see N. Stone 'Moltke and Conrad: relations between the Austro-Hungarian and German general staffs 1909–1914', in Kennedy (ed.), *War plans*; Ritter, *Sword and the Sceptre*, ii. 240–6.

ing balance of forces in the east was finally to abandon (in April 1913) any plans for attacking the Russians first and to reduce yet further the forces allocated to the east's initial defence. The outcome of the Balkan wars was to lessen the likelihood of Romanian support for the Triple Alliance, and to remove Turkey's value as a counterweight to Russia. The Russian decision to concentrate its western armies not in Poland, but further to the east, on the line Kowno–Grodno–Bialystok–Brest-Litovsk, was known to the Germans in 1913 and made nonsense of the proposed Austro-German envelopment.[17] In any case, Moltke's recognition of the likely complexities of the war in the west included the realization that Schlieffen's intention of having twenty-two divisions moving east by the 27th day of mobilization was absurdly optimistic.[18] Therefore, on 10 February 1913, with that mixture of realism and desperation typical of him, he told Conrad that the struggle between Germany and France would be 'the centre of gravity of the whole European war, and consequently the fate of Austria will not be decided on the Bug, but definitely on the Seine'.[19] The relative strengths of the two alliances in the east meant that he could not afford to believe anything else. In May 1914 he calculated that German troops would not begin a switch from the French front until seven weeks after the start of operations, or, in other words, up to ten weeks after the opening of hostilities.[20] Although Moltke expected war to be the result of a crisis in the east, his plans focused on the west.

But Conrad elected not to hear him. After the war Conrad repeatedly emphasized that his allies had failed him, that he was led to expect German support within six weeks and an envelopment battle as the opening (and probably concluding round) of fighting in the east. In reality, Moltke's concession of 1909 was palpably the direct product of Conrad's own demands. Thereafter Moltke's own needs meant that he could only modify, but never overturn his promise. Significantly, its strongest subsequent endorsement came in November 1912, when Conrad had been replaced as Austrian chief of the general staff by the more cautious Schemua. Moltke's vulnerability in the east meant that he could not risk the danger that there would be no Austrian offensive at all. He therefore emphasized Germany's support for its ally in the event of a Russian threat, and said that its own attack would not be 'hesitant' but 'a powerful one' in parallel with Austria-Hungary's.[21] In contrast, two months later, on 24 January 1913, by which time Conrad had been restored to office, Count von Waldersee, a close associate of Moltke and the putative chief of staff to the 8th army in East Prussia, was more ambiguous. Conrad claimed that Waldersee had strengthened the impression that the Germans would attack in the east, and that their right wing would be directed on Warsaw

---

[17] Foerster, *Schlieffen*, 40; Kuhl, *Grand état-major*, 113–14. [18] Contamine, *Révanche*, 81.
[19] Wallach, *Dogma*, 116, n. 28. [20] Tunstall, *Planning for war*, 138.
[21] Tunstall, *Planning for war*, 93.

and would extend to Siedlitz. Waldersee insisted that he had outlined this attack, not as the first phase of operations in the east, but as a subsequent one. Moltke's own words to Conrad of 10 February 1913, only just over a fortnight later, serve to confirm Waldersee's account.[22]

Conrad's real problem was that the offensive interpretation of his defensive task, given the rising strength of the Serbian and Russian armies, and the acceleration in Russian mobilization times, looked increasingly impossible to fulfil. The deployment plans of the Austrian army by 1914 suggested that if there was talk of a joint envelopment, it was a manifestation of weakness not strength—a lure for the German southward thrust on which the Austrians were becoming increasingly dependent.

Conrad calculated that he would need twenty divisions to defeat Serbia, leaving a minimum of twenty-eight to go to Galicia. He therefore organized his army in three parts. Eight divisions, forming the 5th and 6th armies were to go to Serbia, this being sufficient to hold the empire's south-eastern frontier. The 1st, 3rd, and 4th armies, a total of twenty-eight divisions, were to go to Galicia. The balance of twelve divisions, the 2nd army, was to constitute a reserve, to go to Serbia if Russia did not support its Balkan ally and to go to Galicia if it did. The main Galician group would be concentrated between the fifteenth and nineteenth days of mobilization. However, the 2nd army's mobilization and concentration would be both separate and later. In the event of war with Russia, it would not arrive in Galicia until between the twenty-first and twenty-fifth day. Austria-Hungary could not begin active operations in Galicia until after then. Moltke warned Conrad that Russia's mobilization was becoming faster, and in February 1914 correctly calculated that two-thirds of the Russian army would be mobilized by the eighteenth day, not the thirtieth as in the past. To this information was added intelligence suggesting that the Russians now planned to concentrate their forces further forward, west of the Vistula, so as to give more direct support to France and possibly also to prepare for the opening of a central front in Poland.

The major danger now facing Conrad was a rapid Russian advance to the Vistula and the envelopment of his armies on their western flank. He, therefore, knowingly forfeited his ambition to anticipate the Russian concentration. Rather than take the initiative, and hope to deal with Russian units piecemeal, he elected to stand back.

By March 1914 his intention was to place up to thirty divisions on his left wing, on the San, ready to push north; his right, reduced to only ten divisions, had to conform and bring its concentration back to the line of the Dniester. A number of arguments supported this move. Most pressing, but particularly embarrassing, was the probability that the details of the previous deployment

---

[22] Elze, *Tannenberg*, 79.

plan had been betrayed by Colonel Alfred Redl, a homosexual general staff officer who had shot himself in 1913. Treason of a different sort also confronted Austria-Hungary in Galicia: there were growing indications that Romania would not declare common cause with Vienna, and might even join the Entente. By refocusing the plans towards the north and west, the Austrian right flank was less exposed to the south and east. The Russians would now have further to advance, and so would exhaust their strength before making contact. The Austrians themselves would be holding a front of 340 kilometres rather than 440, and so would require fewer infantry divisions. Moreover, a decision about whether the 2nd army should be deployed against Russia or Serbia could now be left until the fifteenth day of mobilization.

But balancing the advantages were a range of potential penalties. The Russians would have more time and space in which to complete their mobilization, deployment, and concentration. For the Austrians all three phases faced considerable challenges. First, the new plan, drawn up in March, was due to be tested in manoeuvres in the autumn, and was therefore still relatively unfamiliar in August 1914; secondly, the railway effort had been geared to achieving a greater concentration to the east and not to the west, and thus the 2nd army, as and when it arrived, would be—according to the ratios planned by Conrad—in the wrong place, on the right wing not the left; and, finally, there remained the danger that the Austrian thrust would be a blow in the air, with the major Russian formations advancing from the east. More positively, the new orientation brought the Austrians closer to the Germans. Implicit here, however, was the contradictory nature of the expected shape of allied co-operation—on the one hand an increasing Austrian reliance on the idea of a German supporting thrust across the Narew, and on the other, a blunted Austrian attack in Galicia, making even more remote the likelihood of prompt German aid.[23]

Conrad was, to a considerable extent, in the hands of his railway department. Railway construction in the empire had reflected economic considerations rather than strategic. The track into Bosnia-Herzogovina was no more than a branch line, and yet the annexed provinces constituted the principal deployment area against Serbia's flank. Beck's efforts in the Carpathians in the 1880s had considerably accelerated deployment in Galicia, raising the maximum number of trains per day from thirty-three to 132. But by 1914 the Russian effort could outstrip the Austrian. Russia could direct 260 trains a day against Austria-Hungary, whereas the Austrians could only manage 153 in reply: it would take Russia twenty days but Austria thirty to run 4,000 trains to Galicia. Although the decision to pull the Austrian deployment back

[23] N. Stone, 'Austria-Hungary', in E. R. May (ed.), *Knowing one's enemies*; Pitreich, *1914*, 115–36; Tunstall, *Planning for war*, 96–116; Maurer, *Outbreak of the First World War*, 27.

helped mitigate this inferiority, it also required stations that had not been prepared for the task to cope with massive troop movements.

The Bosnian crisis had revealed the difficulty of redeploying troops from Serbia to Galicia, not least because four lines ran to Serbia while seven ran to Galicia. Local railway interests frustrated any effort to improve the links between the two fronts, neither Austria nor Hungary being prepared to accept responsibility for the cost of new track. In 1912–13 both the operations and the railway departments assured Conrad that a decision to mobilize against Serbia could be replaced by a full mobilization against Russia without disturbance to the overall deployment scheme. The significant expectation in this note of comparative optimism was that one option would replace another; no consideration was given to the two operating in tandem. What followed was the decision—in itself a reflection of railway capacity—to mobilize and concentrate the 2nd army separately.[24]

In most other respects the Austro-Hungarian railway timetable was based on realism to the point of pessimism. Straub, the head of the railway department, preferred to think in terms of the worst possible performance by goods trucks, when his staff—perhaps equally unrealistically—urged him to calculate on the basis of fast passenger trains.[25] Thus, Austro-Hungarian train speeds were calculated at 11 kilometres per hour on single-tracked lines, and 18 on double-tracked, compared with German estimates of 30 kilometres per hour. Halts to water and coal were allowed for at the rate of six hours in every twenty-four. And the capacity of the trains themselves was deliberately constrained, with a standard military train being fixed to conform to the size of an infantry battalion (fifty carriages), rather than scaled up to its maximum peacetime size of twice that. Even locomotives made available by the rearward deployment in Galicia were not re-employed in Straub's scenarios. In the event, therefore, mobilization and concentration against Russia were achieved ahead of the Austrians' unnecessarily pessimistic schedule.[26]

In July 1914 the two Central Powers were still remarkably ignorant of each other's plans. Each had formed a mental picture of the other which conformed to its own wishes rather than to the other's intentions. 'It is high time', the German military attaché in Vienna wrote to Moltke's deputy on 1 August 1914, 'that the two general staffs consult now with absolute frankness with respect to mobilization, jump-off times, areas of assembly, and precise troop strength.'[27] It was too late. On 25 July Conrad had taken the decision to mobilize against Serbia alone. Not until 30 July was there any direct communication between

[24] Regele, *Conrad*, 215–17, 246, 318; Tunstall, *Planning for war*, 60, 95, 165–7.
[25] Glaise von Horstenau, *Ein General im Zwielicht*, 343.
[26] Tunstall, *Planning for war*, 184–7.
[27] Quoted by Herwig, *Journal of Strategic Studies*, IX (1984), 56–7; on relations between the two, see Kronenbitter, *Militärgeschichtliche Mitteilungen*, 57 (1998), 519–50.

the two chiefs of staff, when Moltke, thoroughly alarmed by the fact that the Austro-Hungarian army was still ponderously preparing for a Balkan coup and not for the European war which was now imminent, pressed for mobilization against Russia. On 1 August Conrad finally absorbed the German message: a German attack in East Prussia was most unlikely, there would be no offensive in Poland, and thus Austria-Hungary was the mainstay of the Triple Alliance in the east.

Conrad's decision to mobilize against Serbia alone had been made before Russia's position was clear. But a quick victory over Serbia, not a European war on unequal terms with Russia, was both what he wanted and what his army was capable of. Moreover, there seemed a chance that speedy success on the battlefield might determine the political situation. The point at issue was Austria-Hungary's status as a Balkan power, not as a great power. The defeat of Serbia could secure relations with Bulgaria, Romania, Italy, and Turkey. A defensive campaign against Serbia, although an easy military task, was therefore not an option in political terms. Indeed, Berchtold, reflecting the diplomatic priorities, wanted even more troops to be sent to the Balkan front.[28]

Redl's treason made it likely that the Serbs had been apprised by the Russians of Austria-Hungary's war plans. It prompted the fear that the Serbs would fall back into the interior, so prolonging the campaign. Conrad, there-fore, proposed to direct his main forces into Serbia from Bosnia and the west, not from the north, so as to cut the Serbs' line of retreat. But to do this he needed to pin the Serbs in the north, and for that the 2nd army was vital. Hence the determination that mobilization against Serbia and mobil-ization against Russia should be separate and distinct steps followed opera-tional logic and manpower availability as well as the railway constraints. On 23 July, the day that the Austrian ultimatum was delivered to Serbia, Edmund Glaise von Horstenau, a divisional staff officer from Lemberg, was encouraged to go on leave, having been assured by a railway department officer that the implementation of the Balkan mobilization meant that that against Russia could not possibly occur in under three weeks.[29]

Mobilization against Serbia was scheduled to take sixteen days, and Conrad needed to know by the fifth day—and therefore still eleven days before actual operations had begun—whether to redeploy the 2nd army against Russia. In practice, however, the delays in the implementation of mobilization against Serbia meant that the military options did not close as rapidly as Conrad had hoped. The railway department deemed that little could be done on the first day—26 July—as it was a Sunday and the post offices would be closed. The first

---

[28] Regele, *Conrad*, 302–4.
[29] Glaise von Horstenau, *Ein General im Zwielicht*, 281–2; more generally, Jerabek, *Potiorek*, 102–3.

day of mobilization proper, 27 July, was planned as a free day to enable those called up to put their domestic affairs in order. On 28 July, when Austria-Hungary declared war on Serbia, Conrad reckoned that the option of mobilization against Russia would be open until 1 August. Both Russia's decision for general mobilization and Moltke's pressure on Conrad to concentrate against the threat to his north were abundantly clear before that deadline. But Conrad defied his own schedule. On 1 August he explained his position to Moltke: 'We could, and must, hold fast to the offensive against Serbia, the more so since we had to bear in mind that Russia might merely intend to restrain us from action by a threat, without proceeding to war against us.'[30]

The confused tenses testify to Conrad's self-exculpating purpose. But the point remains that for Austria-Hungary, unlike Germany, mobilization, at least against Russia, did not mean war. The mobilization of the three armies in Galicia was, Conrad explained to Moltke on 31 July, a response to Russia's mobilization, a defensive step designed to discourage Russia from itself moving from mobilization to war. The revised deployment in Galicia was compatible with such a defensive posture. Austria-Hungary did not declare war on Russia until 6 August. For Conrad, the dangers of exaggerating the Russian threat—of allowing the worst-case analysis to become a self-fulfilling prophecy—had less to do with any norm that war planning should not overtake diplomacy and rather more to do with the fear that armed diplomacy might prevent war fulfilling its political objectives. If Austria-Hungary responded to Russia's mobilization by abandoning its concentration against Serbia for fear of a war in Galicia that might not happen, its army would have no chance of delivering the speedy victory in the Balkans which was Vienna's prime purpose.[31]

Thus, on 30 July Conrad's first reaction to Germany's pleas that he look to Russia was to abide by his original decision. Since the first day of actual mobilization had been 28 July and major movements were not due to begin until the following day, 31 July, it was still possible for the 2nd army to be redirected towards Galicia. But Conrad asked the railway department to find a way to continue the movement of the 2nd army to Serbia and simultaneously begin the mobilization of the 1st, 3rd, and 4th armies against Russia. The implementation of partial mobilization against Serbia had been sufficiently lackadaisical thus far to suggest that, even at this late stage, Conrad's request might have been met without undue chaos. That, however, was not the view of the railway department. Although told to prepare such a plan in November 1913, it had done nothing, nor had it made any approaches to the Germans with regard to the possible exploitation of their underused south-eastern railways. It concluded that simultaneous mobilization could only be achieved by delay-

---

[30] Tunstall, *Planning for war*, 221; also 141, 148–57, 172–3; Stevenson, *Armaments and the coming of war*, 370, 378; Bussy (ed.), *Tisza: Letters*, 10; Williamson, *Austria-Hungary and the origins*, 206–8.

[31] Tunstall, *Planning for war*, 157; Maurer, *Outbreak of the First World War*, 25, 80–3; Tisza, *Letters*, 12.

ing the first day of mobilization against Russia until 4 August. Conrad accepted this arrangement. On 31 July he issued the order for the mobilization of the Galician front, specifying 4 August as the first day. But that evening the persistent pressure from Germany—and also Hungary (Tisza was worried about Romania coming in on the Russian side)—caused Conrad to change his mind about the 2nd army: he now asked the railway department to send it north. He was told it was too late. The railway system could not cope with yet another simultaneous movement in two different directions. Its head, Johann Straub, argued that units would be split up, unless those already in the Balkans were brought back to their home garrisons and then re-embarked for Galicia. This was morally unacceptable: the anticlimax, after the ceremonial and excitement of their recent departure, would shake the confidence of the civil population as well as of the soldiers themselves. The 2nd army would therefore have to continue on its journey to the Balkan front, and then turn round and go back to Galicia. Even after 31 July, trains bound for the Balkans continued to take priority over those destined for Galicia.

Cumulatively, the outnumbered armies of the dual monarchy had forfeited the immediate advantages over the Russians which a speedier mobilization and concentration might have conferred. This loss did not originate with the delayed arrival in Galicia of the 2nd army. At bottom, it reflected the decision for partial mobilization against Serbia alone. It had been compounded by Conrad's earlier decisions with regard to the Galician front— to concentrate further west, to postpone the commencement of mobilization against Russia until 4 August. These meant that the 2nd army would still get to the north-eastern front within twenty-four days of the commencement of mobilization, on 28 August. The disruption of Austro-Hungarian operations in Galicia—for which Conrad blamed the lack of German support in Poland on the one hand, and his own railway department's inflexibility on the other—was entirely of his own making.[32]

Given their failure to confront each other's intentions, it is perhaps not surprising that the two allies remained vague about Russia's. The intelligence services of both powers were small and underfunded, lacking sufficient agents and, in the Austrian case, dependent on the co-operation of the foreign ministry.[33] The attention to Russia's railway capacity rather than to its operational planning reflected a natural preference for facts rather than speculation. But it produced remarkable confusion as to Russian intentions. The basis to the 1905 Schlieffen plan, the reluctance to consider an offensive in the east, rested on the assumption that the Russians would fall back, trading space for

[32] N. Stone, in May, *Knowing one's enemies*, 54–60; N. Stone, *Eastern front*, 70–80; Tunstall, *Planning for war*, 179–83, 198–9, 208; Rauchensteiner, *Tod des Doppeladlers*, 118. On the efforts by Austrian historians to cover up for Conrad, see Tunstall, *Austrian History Yearbook*, XXVII (1996), 181–98.

[33] Hoffmann, *War of lost opportunities*, ii. 13–14; Regele, *Conrad*, 218–22.

time and so denying the Germans the chance of an early decisive battle. This line of thought was still present in the 1914 edition of the German general staff's handbook: it stressed that Russia's tactical strengths were defensive, and that operationally it would eschew the chance of an encounter battle for a more passive role.[34]

And yet Schlieffen had also anticipated operations around a two-pronged Russian offensive into East Prussia. By 1914 this expectation was reflected in Moltke's orders to Prittwitz, the commander of the 8th army, that he fall back behind the Vistula rather than risk the destruction of his force. Thus, at the broadest level, the Germans saw that Russia's strength lay in retreat, while operationally they accepted the fact that Russia would support France by an early thrust into Prussia. And there was a second unresolved ambiguity to add to the first. Assuming that the Russians did attack in East Prussia, would it be the major thrust, or would that be reserved for the attack in Galicia? The Germans did not know on which front the Russians intended to employ the main weight of their forces. Because Germany needed Austria-Hungary to draw off the bulk of the Russian army, its military attaché in St Petersburg could easily fall prey to the expectation that that was what would happen. Others were less sure.[35]

The information which shaped the calculations of the Central Powers was, like most intelligence pictures, selectively accurate. All the indications which they had picked up were present. The broad conclusion—that Russia's military strength was rapidly growing, but that its likely operational application remained uncertain (although not so neatly formulated by the general staffs of Germany and Austria-Hungary)—was a fair reflection of the situation. Furthermore, the rapidity and scale of Russia's military growth in the years immediately before the war inevitably meant that the bases for the Central Powers' conclusions were constantly shifting. Despite continuing pressure from the finance minister to balance the budget, especially given Russian dependence on foreign loans, Russia's armed services claimed about a quarter of state expenditure between 1900 and 1909 and about a third thereafter. With 1.4 million men, and a total of 114.5 infantry divisions, Russia's army in 1914 had become, on paper at least, the strongest in Europe, and was still growing. The capacity to mobilize improved at a rate that not only enabled it to encompass this expansion, but to outstrip it. Between 1910 and 1914 the number of trains that Russia could send westwards rose from 250 a day to 360, and a target of 560 had been set for 1917.

Russia's mobilization schedule improved as a result, but it still could not compete in international terms. Although Russia led the world in the rate at

---

[34] von Matuschka, 'Organisationsgeschichte des Heeres', 216.

[35] Herwig, 'Imperial Germany', in E. R. May (ed.), *Knowing one's enemies*, 69; but see Hoffmann, *War of lost opportunities*, ii. 13–14, 18–19.

which it constructed railway line between 1890 and 1913, it nonetheless trailed far behind western Europe in the length of open track in relation to size of territory: by 1913 Germany had 12 kilometres of track per 100 square kilometres, France 10, Austria-Hungary 7, and Russia 1. Nor was the explanation for this continuing inferiority exclusively Russia's enormous extent. Important after 1909 were the opportunity costs consequent on increased spending on the armed services. The rate of annual growth in railway construction fell after 1909 to one-third of that which Russia had sustained at the turn of the century, and orders for rolling stock were cut so that in 1914 the system was short of 2,000 locomotives and 80,000 wagons. Standardization was forfeit and three-quarters of the entire network was still single track.[36]

Russia's greatest resource was manpower, and it was this crude quantitative assessment which gave immediate support to the exaggerated expectations of Russia's military might, entertained in France and Britain as much as in Germany and Austria-Hungary. But Russia's ability to tap its manpower was constrained by its own backwardness: any expansion to its army set back its ability to enhance its timetable for mobilization. The western powers, as nations in advanced states of industrialization, possessed of much of the infrastructure for waging modern war, enjoyed greater incremental effects on their immediate military strength from small additions to their defence budgets than did Russia from major expenditure. In Russia a large proportion of military spending had to go into basic investment, into research and development, into plant rather than production. It also had to make good the material losses of the Russo-Japanese War, especially in the fleet after the crippling blow at Tsushima. By 1911 more was being spent on the navy's re-equipment than the army's, but in 1914 the navy still had not commisioned a single Dreadnought; the money had been spent on shipyards as much as on ships.[37]

The Russian army was not unmindful of the trade-off between manpower and machinery. Its numerical expansion was tempered by the rate of its re-equipment. Artillery was put at the centre of each of the major pre-war army programmes. The 76 mm quick-firing field gun, approved in 1902, was finally issued to all units in 1910–11, and at the same time 122 mm and 152 mm howitzers were adopted. One hundred and eighty-one million roubles, of 225 million allocated to the army in March 1913, were earmarked for artillery, and when these appropriations were overtaken by the so-called 'great programme' of 1913, a target of 8,358 guns in all was set.

Again, the improvement was more impressive relative to Russia's own immediate past rather than to its international comparators. For every gun in 1914, Russia had 200 men to Germany's and Austria-Hungary's 135.[38] Men

[36] Gatrell, *Government, industry and rearmament*, 148, 197–8, 305.
[37] Stevenson, *Armaments and the coming of war*, 80, 149–50 .
[38] Gatrell, *Government, industry and rearmament*, 299.

were easier and quicker to raise than guns were to produce. The 1913 programme, approved in June 1914, increased the recruit contingent from 450,000
to 580,000 for that year, whereas the armaments contracts had until 1917 for
final completion.[39]

Furthermore, low levels of educational achievement meant that manpower
in quantity did not necessarily translate into manpower in quality. Although
having an exceptionally low ratio of officers to men (1 : 27, as against 1 : 21 in
Germany), the Russian army was over 4,000 officers below establishment in
1909.[40] The German army could keep its officer corps small by dint of its
excellent NCOs, mostly drawn from the wealthier peasantry or the lower
middle class, and reflecting high levels of national education. In Russia such
men were commissioned. Consequently, the Russian army was as short of
NCOs as it was of officers. In 1903 it had two re-enlisted NCOs per company, as
against twelve in Germany and six in France.[41] Russian backwardness, therefore, demanded that more resources be devoted to military education, but also
dictated that, because so much attention had to be given to basics, the overall
level of professional competence would nonetheless remain low. The scale of
these structural problems meant that, despite the high levels of military
expenditure, Russia was constantly trading off manpower against equipment,
or one of them against training: in the desire to improve the first two, the third
suffered.

Effectively, army reform was delayed until 1910, and proceeded rapidly
thereafter. The loss of time before 1910 was not necessarily the product of
military complacency. The Franco-Russian military convention of 1892 had
provided the Russian army with a westward orientation and a European
yardstick. Russia had the highest growth rate in terms of financial appropriations of any European army in the 1890s. But the Russo-Japanese War had cut
across the geographical orientation of its thinking. Shattered in Manchuria, it
had then had little time to recover in the years immediately following. To
battles with the minister of finance, Rediger—the minister of war—had now to
add those with Stolypin, the minister of the interior. Rapid economic growth
after 1905, based in part on government spending, helped ease the former
tension. But for the latter the army's task was, in the light of the 1905 revolution
and its aftermath, internal order not external defence. The deployment into
small units necessitated by its policing role undermined the army's own
discipline: between May and July 1906 alone there may have been more than
134 mutinies. Not until 1908 was the revolution, technically at any rate, brought

[39] Ibid. 132–4; Menning, *Bayonets before bullets*, 231–4; Stevenson, *Armaments and the coming of war*,
322; Suchomlinow, *Erinnerungen*, 327–9, 339, 341 .

[40] Kenez, *California Slavic Studies*, VII (1973), 129.

[41] David Jones, 'Imperial Russia's forces at war', in Millett and Murray (eds.), *Military effectiveness*, i.
281–2.

to an end. In 1909 Rediger was able to increase the training budget by 2 million roubles, to 4.5 million.[42]

The period 1905–10 was also one of administrative confusion. Before 1905 the so-called general staff was not an effective planning staff but a section of the main staff of the war minister. Bureaucratic functions prevailed over operational. After the defeat in Manchuria the case for reform was highlighted, in the Tsar's eyes, by the summoning of the Duma and the latter's aspirations to control the war minister. Therefore, the general staff was hived off from the main staff, and its chief made responsible directly to the Tsar and not to the ministry. At the same time a Council for State Defence was formed, embodying as its permanent members the inspectors-general of the various arms, the war minister, the navy minister, the chiefs of the main staffs of both services, the chief of the general staff, and the chairman of the council of ministers; others were appointed as standing members. Technically, the role of the council was consultative; in practice, its chairman, Grand Duke Nicholas, as the Tsar's nominee, became a sort of joint defence minister independent of the Duma's control.

It looked as though the new arrangement embraced the best of two systems: it had the supreme strategic advisory council comparable with Britain's Committee of Imperial Defence, and it had, as Germany did, an independent chief of the general staff answerable only to the monarch. In reality, it did not work. The Tsar had originally been proposed as the council's chairman: this would have given it authority and even executive powers. As it was, its relationship to the Council of Ministers, which the Tsar did chair and which was revived in 1905, remained unclear. The Council of Ministers had no formal authority over war and foreign policy, but it did support the plans for new battle fleets in the Baltic, the Black Sea, and the Pacific, which the Tsar also favoured. The Council for State Defence did not: with six army members to four naval, and charged with developing an overall plan for national defence, it wanted a land strategy, not a naval one. Frustrated in its pursuit of co-ordination and prioritization in defence planning, the council became as interested in senior promotions and appointments as strategy. The former task had been given it in an effort to promote professional standards, but the main staff of the war ministry remained formally responsible for personnel matters, and so the council found itself also at odds with the ministry of war.

The factionalism was compounded by the Duma. In November 1907 A. I. Guchkov and the Octobrists, committed nationalists, and seeing narrowly conceived tsarism as a block to Russia's full development, set up their own commission for national defence. Rediger, casting about for allies against the finance ministry, and also anxious to reinvigorate the status of his own office,

---

[42] Fuller, *Civil–military conflict in Imperial Russia*, 130–68; also 52–3, 220.

established links with the new commission, using his deputy, A. A. Polivanov, as go-between. The Duma was supportive of naval and military spending, and to that extent buttressed the minister of war. But Guchkov's attack on court influence in military affairs—and particularly on the Grand Dukes Nicholas and Sergei (the inspector-general of artillery)—were an assault on the royal prerogative which the Tsar was bound to counter. In 1908, announcing that he proposed to take matters more into his own hands, he ousted Grand Duke Nicholas as chairman of the Council for State Defence, so simultaneously asserting his navalist enthusiasms while curbing the Duma's complaints. In August 1909 the Council for State Defence was itself dissolved.

The Tsar's solution to the problems of the services was to strengthen both the army and the navy ministries, and to appoint to them heads whose loyalty was to him and not to the Duma. The general staff, which had proved just as secretive and obstructive as the other agencies, especially in its dealings with the War Ministry and the Council for State Defence, was reincorporated with the War Ministry in 1908, and V. A. Sukhomlinov was appointed its chief. In March 1909 Sukhomlinov became minister of war, with instructions from the Tsar not to attend the Duma. Between 1909 and 1910 his powers as war minister were progressively reinforced. Thus, just as the army was able to begin focusing on the external threat to the west, so at last it began to gain centralization and direction in its administration.[43]

Sukhomlinov has had a bad press. He was extravagant, adulterous, and corrupt. His self-appointed image was that of the swashbuckling hussar, the upholder of the honour of the officer corps, however dubious the conduct of those officers. Much of the criticism has derived from his political opponents—from the Duma, who saw him as the Tsar's representative; from the circle of the Grand Duke Nicholas, whom he had effectively replaced. Until the 1970s these men had a major role in shaping western historical writing on the run-up to the revolution, and their frustration at tsarism's failure to liberalize gained much of its bite from the army's performance in the war. But their attacks on Sukhomlinov obscured the fact that, whatever his deficiencies, both personal and professional, by 1914 he had the Russian army in a state far fitter for war than it had been in 1910. What he had not overcome, as the personal vendettas reveal, were the deep internal divisions within the army.

One corollary of the enhancement of the War Ministry was the subordination of the general staff. When the former took over responsibility for the latter once more, in 1909, Polivanov was appointed its chief. But Sukhomlinov was convinced that Polivanov was still intriguing with Guchkov and so promoting

[43] Fuller, Civil–military conflict in Imperial Russia, 202–3, 219–36; David Jones (ed.), Military-naval encyclopaedia, ii. 128–42; Stone, Eastern front, 19–24; Perrins, Slavonic and East European Review, LVIII (1980), 370–98; Lieven, Nicholas II, 169, 174–6; Stevenson, Armaments and the coming of war, 77, 150; Suchomlinow, Erinnerungen, 268, 278–9, 283–94; Menning, Bayonets before bullets, 218–21.

the Duma's authority over the army at the expense of the Tsar's. Polivanov was removed in 1912; and by 1914 there had been six chiefs of staff since 1905.

Despite its vulnerability as a 'capital' organization, the progress of the general staff at troop level seemed more promising. In 1904 there were eighty vacancies a year at the Nicholas Staff Academy, and its graduates held 45 per cent of staff appointments. After the defeat in Manchuria 4,307 officers, including 337 generals, were retired over two years. At the same time the number of places at the staff academy was increased to 150, and between 1906 and 1914 80 per cent of all staff jobs went to the academy's products. By the outbreak of the First World War eighty-two out of the 100 generals of the army had received general staff training. But the results were more limited than appearances and statistics suggested. The syllabus of the Nicholas Staff Academy was narrow, focusing on administration rather than command, and emphasizing tactics rather than operations. In 1907 Colonel Alexander Gerua called for the study of what he called 'applied strategy', 'to afford a series of firm rules for moving armies along contemporary routes of communication… manoeuvring large armies towards the field of engagement'. Gerua was not heeded. Nor did practical instruction compensate for the deficiencies in theory. The officer's task, according to General M. I. Dragomirov, was to turn peasants into soldiers. Although Dragomirov died in 1905, his influence persisted: district manoeuvres practised tactical drills but did little to promote initiative or imagination. Exercises involving large bodies of troops tended to be entrusted to the command of members of the royal family, so those who would hold higher command in war did not do so in peace.[44]

The infighting which followed institutional weakness was provoked as much by professional as by political arguments. Fierce doctrinal debate was a natural corollary of the defeat at the hands of the Japanese. The 'Young Turks', a group of reformist officers at the Nicholas Staff Academy, identified with western European tactical thought. N. N. Golovin had sat at the feet of Foch at the École de Guerre, and favoured his applied method of teaching; he also rated the importance of technology over morale. Sukhomlinov, on the other hand, had been raised in the Russian national tradition, which venerated the moral rather than the physical elements, and which saw foreign influences as inappropriate. The professor of strategy at the Nicholas Staff Academy, A. A. Neznamov, called for a debate on the virtues of a unified military doctrine, but his opponents warned of the dangers of rigidity, and in 1912 the Tsar told him to stop writing on the subject. In the same year rumours that the Young Turks were hatching a conspiracy prompted Sukhomlinov to return them to regimental and district duty. The effect was not to establish the primacy of the

---

[44] Menning, *Bayonets before bullets*, 101–3, 205, 236, 250–1; John W. Steinberg, 'Russian general staff training and the approach of war', in Coetzee and Shevin-Coetzee (eds.), *Authority, identity*, 278–80, 289.

national school but to disseminate the views of the Young Turks throughout the army.[45] Rather than embrace a general staff view, the operational thought of the Russian army broke into competing groups. Each military district contrived a measure of autonomy that set it at variance with its neighbouring district and with the general staff itself. Even the individual districts were prey to disunity: if Sukhomlinov secured the appointment of a district commander, then Grand Duke Nicholas or the Young Turks endeavoured to appoint his chief of staff. Common doctrine was forfeit. And, without either a common doctrine or a dominant general staff, Russia's war plans lacked foundation. Sukhomlinov's achievements lay in peacetime consolidation, not in preparation for war.

The fundamental doctrinal issue for Russia was whether it should operate offensively or defensively. Like Neznamov, N. P. Miknevich, who was chief of the main staff of the war ministry from 1911 until 1917, sought to fuse the nationalists and the Young Turks in a common solution, which used historical examples but recognized change over time. His treatise on strategy, first published in 1899 and thrice revised, became the dominant text in late imperial Russia. In the edition of 1911 Miknevich argued that the next war would be long because nations would commit to it all their resources. He thought this would work to Russia's advantage: the authoritarianism of a strong monarchy, the hardiness of its peasantry, and the backwardness of its economy all rendered it less dependent on a quick victory. Because 'time is the best ally of our armed forces', Russia should fight defensively from the outset, avoiding combat while exhausting its enemies' offensive powers.[46]

The case for the defensive was strongest at the strategic level. Russia's military commitments lay on every point of the compass except the north: to the west lay Germany and Austria-Hungary, and to the east Japan; competition with Turkey in the Caucasus and with Britain in Persia demanded vigilance to the south. To sustain the strategic offensive, Russia would have to be able to strike a quick blow in one direction and rapidly reconcentrate in another. Even if the density of rail track had permitted such a Schlieffenesque solution (and it did not), the distances between the fronts would not.

A combination of geography, industrial backwardness, and common sense suggested Miknevich was right. But Russia could not simply abandon its border territories, trading space for time. It still needed some system of forward defence. One alternative was to station its active and mobile formations close to the frontier, leaving its reservists in the rear; but the consequence of that would be the separation of mobilization and concentration into two

[45] Fuller, *Civil–military conflict*, 201–2; Wildman, *End of the Russian imperial army*, 69; Menning, *Bayonets before bullets*, 215–16.
[46] Menning, *Bayonets before bullets*, 132–4, 208–10.

phases, distinct in space and time. The second was to create a barrier of forts to hold off the invading armies. Fortification, however, was particularly susceptible to technological change, and—as the French and Belgians had discovered—its modernization generated an unrelenting and ultimately unsustainable pressure on the defence budget. Furthermore, to rely on fortification was to make strategy dependent on the tactical defensive.

The difficulty of accepting the tactical defensive proved more divisive than any debate over strategy. What Miknevich had proposed on the strategic or operational level was entirely in accordance with the precepts of the historically minded national school. It was what had happened in 1812; it reflected the legacy of A. V. Suvorov—that Russia should fight in accordance with its own nature, terrain, and capabilities. But Suvorov had also famously praised the bayonet at the expense of the bullet. His advocacy of the tactical offensive enabled the nationalists in at least this respect to march to the same beat as the Young Turks, the latter being persuaded of the modernity of the offensive by what they had learnt of French and German thinking. When Moltke studied the reports of Russian manoeuvres in 1913 he saw the repeated rejection of retreat and the persistent requirement that all tactical solutions incorporate the offensive as evidence of Russian improvement.[47]

In practice, the war in Manchuria meant that the Russians had no cause to look to any other European army for tactical wisdom: their own experience of the battlefield was both recent and extensive. The war provided plenty of evidence of the lethality of modern firepower. Nevertheless, its precepts could not definitively resolve the debate over the respective merits of defence and attack. On the one hand, Miknevich's ideas were reinforced by the fact that the war showed how hard it was to defeat modern armies, and by the way in which victory was achieved through a series of engagements rather than in a single decisive battle. But the artillery, which went on to argue in tactical terms that a future war would therefore be won by forts and heavy guns, was accused of neglecting the baleful influence of Port Arthur on Russian strategy. Too much reliance had been placed on its incomplete defences at the outset of the war, and too much attention given to its relief during its course. The infantry looked to a more aggressive solution, with field fortifications as pivots for manoeuvre and howitzers to prepare the attack. The 1912 field service regulations contained considerable evidence of lessons well heeded from the battlefields of 1904–5: they emphasized security in breadth and depth, and urged the infantry to use cover and to establish firepower dominance. But the point remained that the Russians had displayed tactical caution against the Japanese and lost; the Japanese themselves had attacked with determination on the one

[47] Showalter, *Tannenberg*, 82.

hand, and without regard for casualties on the other. The tactical offensive was explicit in the 1912 regulations; doubts about the operational functions of fortification were implicit.[48]

The war in Manchuria fuelled strategic as well as tactical change. When Russia entered into its alliance with France in 1890 it reckoned—quite rightly at that juncture—that Germany would strike east first, before it turned west. The alliance, therefore, conferred immense benefits on Russia. First, France's ability to draw off Germany enabled it to face Austria-Hungary, to the south-west. Secondly, it provided compensation for Russia's slowness in the opening phases of the war: N. N. Obruchev, the chief of the main staff, believed that mobilization was not just a political signal but 'the most decisive act of war'.[49] But Russia's attention to the Far East drew its forces from both its western fronts, and so increased its dependence on the French alliance. Moreover, with the commencement of annual Franco-Russian staff talks in 1900, France became more conscious of Russia's preference for an attack against Austria-Hungary at precisely the stage when Germany was switching its own planning priority from Russia to France. Russia succumbed to French pressure, and from 1901 planned an offensive into Germany. But it could not simply abandon its Galician front, and so it continued simultaneously to sustain the idea of an attack into Austria-Hungary.[50]

Poland was the salient which conferred on Russia the option of attacking either Germany or Austria-Hungary: it outflanked Austria-Hungary in Galicia and Germany in East Prussia. But Poland itself was not well adapted for the conduct of operations. Its farms generated insufficient produce to feed even its own indigenous population, and its railway systems were incapable of supplying an army from Russia's interior. Furthermore, if Germany and Austria-Hungary launched a joint attack on Russia, and Russia was the defender, Poland would be liable itself to envelopment. The choice which Poland presented was stark. A headlong offensive would enable Russian troops to feed on enemy territory and could forestall the manoeuvres of the Triple Alliance. The alternative was its abandonment. This would minimize any trade-off between Russia's north-west and south-west fronts, would shorten its armies' lines of communications, and would create the potential to fuse the phases of mobilization and concentration.

When the Tsar proposed just such a strategy in 1902 the main staff rejected the option on political rather than military grounds: Russia would forfeit its status in the Balkans and would renege on its alliance with France. But the combination of defeat at the hands of Japan and revolution at home made

[48] Menning, *Bayonets before bullets*, 171–91, 198–9, 257–9.
[49] Fuller, *Strategy and power*, 355–61; Fuller is both fundamental and revisionist on Russian war planning.
[50] Ibid. 386–93.

the idea politically viable, and it drew on military arguments for its support. The Grand Duke Nicholas, as chairman of the Council for State Defence, favoured a concentration in the Volga Basin, in the heart of Russia, so that the army could be deployed either to the west or to the east. F. F. Palitsyn, the chief of the general staff, was no Francophile and was fearful of renewed hostilities with Japan: he endorsed Grand Duke Nicholas. Supporting both of them was a general staff study prepared by Y. N. Danilov which demonstrated that Russia could not expect to conduct a successful defence of western Poland.[51] Thus, for all the bureaucratic bickering, planning assumptions at the strategic level began to converge after 1907. Furthermore, they were underpinned, rather than undermined, by Sukhomlinov's determination to make the army readier for mobilization.

In 1909 Russia's active army was concentrated to the west in recognition of the frailties of its railway system. Thus, on mobilization 220,000 reservists would have to travel to other districts just to join their units, and 87 per cent of recruits were stationed far from their homes, even in peacetime. This geographical separation between the units and their sources of men not only clogged the mobilization timetable, it also limited the Russian army's capacity for expansion. Sukhomlinov's solution was to redistribute the active army throughout Russia, withdrawing ninety-one battalions from the Warsaw district and thirty-seven from the Vilna district. Before 1910 47 per cent of the army's strength would have been deployed between the western frontier and the Dvina–Dnieper line; after 1910 only 10 per cent remained in the same area. As a result, corps drew their manpower from the districts in which they were stationed, and 97 per cent of recruits joined units quartered in their own districts.[52]

Danilov embodied the new deployment in plan 19, which was approved in June 1910. Poland was to be abandoned, and the army was to be concentrated as well as mobilized further to the east. It would then direct fifty-three divisions against Germany, but only nineteen against Austria-Hungary. In this respect it reflected the experience of the Bosnian crisis: that suggested that Russia could not rely on France, but Austria-Hungary could depend on Germany. Therefore, in the event of war with the Triple Alliance, Russia must be ready to take on Germany.

What Sukhomlinov had not done was adopt the defensive in the terms advocated by Miknevich. Sukhomlinov had imbibed Suvorov's teaching on the virtues of the attack by way of Dragomirov. His premiss was tactical: Manchuria showed that victory was won by the bayonet. But his conclusion was

[51] Ibid. 385, 424–7; also Spring, *Slavonic and East European Review*, LXVI (1988), 577–8; Cimbala, *Journal of Slavic Military Studies*, IX (1996), 379.
[52] Fuller, *Strategy and power*, 426–7; Menning, *Bayonets before bullets*, 222–7; Hermann, *Arming of Europe*, 131–4; Stevenson, *Armaments and the coming of war*, 153–4.

strategic: Russia, he later wrote, had to break with the Tartars' principle of withdrawing back into the steppe.[53] Sukhomlinov therefore shifted Russia's deployment to the centre, not to defend Russia as an end in itself but the better to counter-attack. When the Russian armies advanced they would do so with their concentration complete, and they could strike with equal facility to the east as well as to the west.

Sukhomlinov's determination to imbue the army with the offensive was nowhere more evident than in his decision not to upgrade the fortifications on the Narew, on the Vistula, and round Warsaw. They would consume vast sums of money, and tie both men and guns to fixed positions rather than enable their employment in the field. His decision, though representative of current western European thought, aroused the ire of the Grand Duke's circle. Like Sukhomlinov, Palitsyn had planned to mobilize in the centre but, unlike Sukhomlinov, to concentrate forward, and so he needed the fortifications of western Poland as a screen. Territorial mobilization focused attention on the line of forts which lay further east, running from Kowno through Grodno and Brest-Litovsk. In the controversy which followed a compromise was struck: in addition to Kowno, Grodno, and Brest-Litovsk, the fort at Osovets (on a tributary of the Narew, to cover any deployment into East Prussia) and at Novo Georgievsk (on the confluence of the Vistula and the Bug, north-west of Warsaw) were scheduled for reconstruction. Those at Ivangorod, the bridgehead on the Vistula south of Warsaw, were not. Thus, resources were dissipated over more objectives. By 1914 Russia had neither one thing nor the other: many of the old fortifications had been demolished, much of the new was still incomplete.[54]

The basic orientation of plan 19 was, at least in its initial phases, defensive. But when Russia went to war in 1914 it adopted the offensive from the outset. Some observers, then and since, were determined that the shift was not homegrown. They argued that the faith in the tactical offensive which underpinned Sukhomlinov's thinking had not percolated through to replace the defensive orientation of Russian operational thought.[55] They therefore attributed the change to French pressure. At the 1911 staff talks the French, already anxious because of what they knew of plan 19, told I. G. Zhilinskii, the newly appointed chief of the general staff, that they would attack the Germans by the twelfth day of mobilization. They demanded that the Russians do the same by the fifteenth day. A year later, at the 1912 meeting, Zhilinskii gave this undertaking. Furthermore, in 1913 France used the loans raised on the Paris money market for Russian railway construction to gain additional leverage: in the past Russia had diverted most of this money towards commercial track, but the 1913 loan was

---

[53] Suchomlinow, *Erinnerungen*, 330–1.
[54] Danilov, *Russie*, 69–75; Gourko, *War and revolution*, 13–14; Stone, *Eastern front*, 30–3.
[55] Frantz, *Russland auf dem Wege*, 32–40.

made conditional on a third of it being used for military railways. Joffre demanded that the lines to the frontier be double-tracked.

France was undeniably worried by Russia's plans, but Russia acceded to the pressure as much to suit its own needs as to assuage French anxieties. By 1912 the Japanese threat had receded. In its stead loomed war in the Balkans and the dangers of an Austro-Hungarian bid to reassert its suzerainty over the region. If Russia persisted with the 1910 version of plan 19, ceding the initiative on its south-west front to the dual monarchy, it courted revolution in Poland. But Vienna would not act without Berlin's support, and the indications that the Germans would first concentrate against the French and only later turn east were multiplying. Once again the attraction of the French alliance was its ability to confer an offensive option on the Austrian front, but its corollary— not only because of Russia's alliance with France, but also because of Austria-Hungary's alliance with Germany—was a simultaneous operation on the German front.[56]

The renunciation of an early attack on Austria-Hungary was the other principal domestic criticism—alongside the fortifications dispute—of plan 19. The Russians received a steady flow of accurate intelligence on Austro-Hungarian intentions, culminating in the revelations of Colonel Redl. They saw the Austro-Hungarians, in contradistinction to the Germans, as beatable. Galicia's position athwart the flank and rear of any Russian army facing Germany to the north meant that it could not be neglected; more positively, its ground favoured offensive operations. The focus of this train of thought was M. V. Alekseev, chief of staff first of the Warsaw military district and then of Kiev, the two commands closest to Austria-Hungary. At a conference in February 1912 the district staffs, dominated by Alekseev, prevailed over Danilov and the general staff. They favoured a concentration in Poland and an attack across the Vistula so as to threaten simultaneously the flanks and rear of the Austrians in Galicia and the Germans in East Prussia.[57]

Danilov was not completely routed. As quartermaster-general on the general staff, his continuity in office ensured his influence at a time when chiefs of the general staff rotated fast and Sukhomlinov himself showed little interest in war plans. He believed that French pressure for a Russian offensive did not take sufficient account of the difficulties of the East Prussian theatre, which was divided in two by the Masurian lakes. He favoured a northerly concentration, at least partly because he was worried that Sweden would side with Germany, so threatening Finland and St Petersburg. Thus, his defensive preoccupations were reinforced by a deep pessimism. The intelligence which he received— which was not integrated with that of the Kiev district and was also less

[56] Fuller, *Strategy and power*, 433–6, 439–41; Spring, *Slavonic and East European Review*, LVI (1988), 580–1.
[57] Menning, *Bayonets before bullets*, 241.

accurate—concentrated on the German army and its strengths. He was in possession of a German war game suggesting that they would not attack in the east. But his calculations continued to include the possibility of a German offensive by up to twenty-five divisions within ten days of mobilization, and in the spring of 1914 he was still allowing for a joint Austro-German offensive against Russia alone.

The upshot was compromise: a revised plan 19, adopted in June 1912. It possessed two variants, A and G. Case A rested on Alekseev's assumption, a major offensive against Austria-Hungary. The 1st and 2nd Russian armies would face Germany; the 3rd, 4th, and 5th would go south-west to Galicia. Case G assumed a major concentration against Germany, directing the 1st, 2nd, and 4th armies towards East Prussia, and leaving the 3rd and 5th to face Austria-Hungary. In both cases the 6th and 7th armies were to be kept in reserve. The decision as to which variant was to be adopted could be left until the seventh day of mobilization.[58] The assumption was that Case A would be implemented unless orders to the contrary were issued.

The competing pressures of cases A and G produced fluctuations between 1912 and 1914. In 1912 Alekseev argued that the Germans would not achieve the early success in the west for which they were striving. But the chance of Russia being able to exploit this opportunity by an easy victory in East Prussia was limited by the terrain and by the probability that the Germans would fall back behind the Vistula. Therefore, Russia should go over to the defensive in East Prussia, and seize the opportunity to crush Austria-Hungary. Alekseev talked of crossing the Dniester, pushing west to Cracow, and so creating the conditions for an advance on Budapest and Belgrade. But, even with case A dominant, Russian planning restricted the chances of a rapid and decisive victory. The natural defences of north-west Russia, the river lines of the Niemen, Narew, and Bug, suggested that the barest minimum of troops needed to be left to face Germany. In fact case A still kept twenty-nine divisions on the German front. Thus, only just over half the available Russian divisions would implement case A. In particular, the forces in southern Poland, which could have been designed to envelop the Austro-Hungarian left in Galicia, were kept weak. Therefore, the practical implications of case A were not as dangerous for France as Alekseev's ambitions suggested—particularly since victory in Galicia would still threaten Germany, albeit by way of Silesia rather than East Prussia.

In 1913 Zhilinskii's agreement with the French took the planning initiative away from the military districts and gave it back to Danilov and the general staff. Danilov's pessimism now took the form of an increasing worry that

[58] Snyder, *Ideology of the offensive*, chs. 6 and 7, has a full discussion of Russian war planning; see also Ironside, *Tannenberg*, 31–7; William Fuller, 'The Russian empire', in E. R. May (ed.), *Knowing one's enemies*.

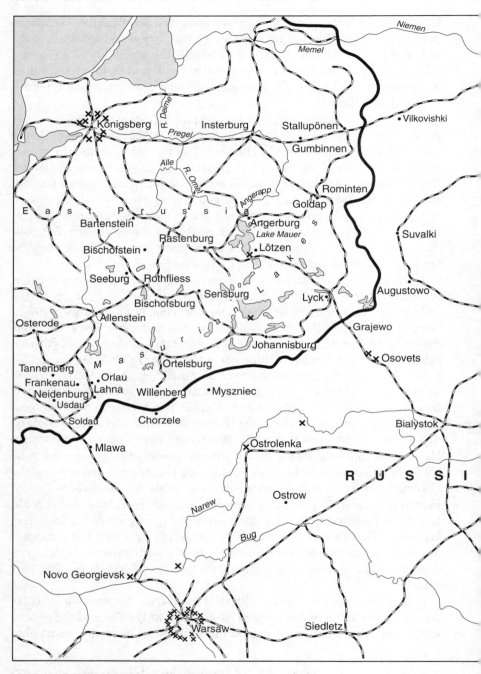

MAP 10. RUSSIA AND EAST PRUSSIA

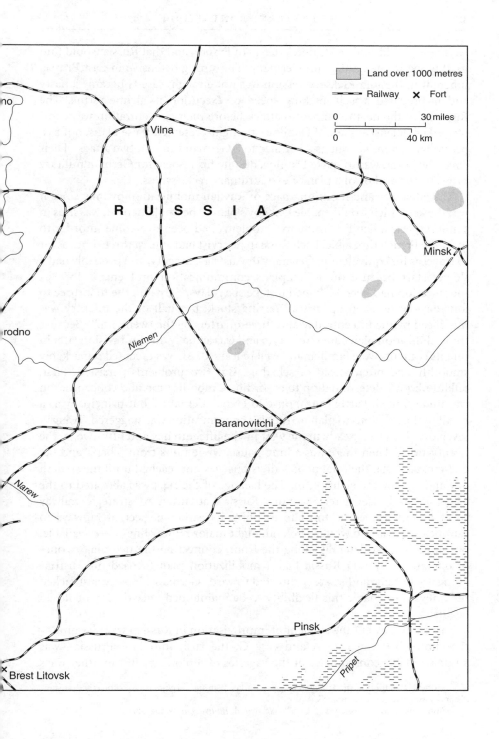

Germany would achieve its quick defeat of France, and that Russia would find itself alone in the battle with Germany. The strong defensive in East Prussia inherent in the 1912 Alekseev version was not enough; case G became a hasty and ill-prepared attack, making speed of execution its prime virtue. The Russians in the north planned to attack before their concentration was complete. The defensive slant of Danilov's thought presented these plans, not as a precipitate offensive, but as a counter to a German pre-emptive attack. Their effect, however, was to make Danilov, despite his respect for German military prowess, the author of a plan of extraordinary recklessness.

The efficiency and mounting pace of Russian mobilization by 1914, since it was the key which would enable Danilov's plan to be implemented, was thus in some respects a liability. Immense problems had been overcome in order to meet the French timetable. Each Russian reservist had at least three times as far to travel as his equivalent in Germany or Austria-Hungary, and probably had a slower start because of the empire's communication problems.[59] In 1892 mobilization had been reckoned to take sixty days.[60] By 1914 the first three to four days were taken up in transferring stock, but half of the infantry was mobilised by the fifteenth day and three-quarters by the twentieth.[61] Because the mobilization plan dated from 1910 and was actually due for revision later in 1914 its contents were familiar and well rehearsed. All was executed remarkably smoothly and often ahead of schedule. But two problems persisted. First, Sukhomlinov's determination to co-ordinate mobilization and concentration was undermined. Partly in response to French demands, but principally as a result of the revisions to plan 19, Russia's concentration was staggered. Twenty-seven divisions were ready in the west by the fifteenth day and fifty-two by the twenty-third. Then there was a long pause, while units from Siberia and the east crossed Asia: the total of 90.5 divisions was not reached until the sixtieth day and 94.5 by the eighty-fifth. The balance of the 114.5 was allocated to the Caucasus and elsewhere. Secondly, Russia's attention to strategic railway construction had come too late to offset its earlier neglect of railways in European Russia and western Poland. Eight major railway lines were available, but none that ran laterally along the front, connecting the two major zones of operation. By 1914 Russia had a mobilization plan focused on Austria-Hungary, but a grand strategy directed towards Germany. However, it lacked the railways to enable this flexibility to be maintained once deployment had begun.

To a certain extent the element of improvisation in Russian war planning—the choice between case A and case G, the rush into East Prussia—was an unavoidable consequence of the vagaries of diplomacy. But in other ways

[59] Lincoln, *Passage through Armageddon*, 25; Gourko, *War and revolution*, 4, reckons the transport distances were five times Germany's.
[60] Andolenko, *Armée russe*, 322.   [61] Westwood, *Railways at war*, 125–8.

much that could and should have been resolved before the July crisis was not.

Still open when war was declared was the question of who would be commander-in-chief. The Tsar clearly had himself in mind. Only the argument that it was a colonial conflict had restrained him from taking command in the Russo-Japanese War; it was implicit in his handling—and in the failure—of the Council for State Defence; he was to have acted as referee in the war games proposed for 1911. The regulations for the field administration of the army in wartime, still in draft in July 1914 and hurriedly approved, implied that the Tsar would act as commander-in-chief, if not in the operational sense at least as a supreme political and military co-ordinator. All Russia west of the line from St Petersburg to Smolensk, and along the Dnieper to the Black Sea, was placed under the direct authority of Stavka, the field headquarters. The commander-in-chief was thus vested with absolute powers, including direction of the navy. However, at their meeting of 31 July 1914 the Council of Ministers vigorously opposed the suggestion that Nicholas assume the command, arguing that defeat would threaten his personal position. The following day the post was offered to Sukhomlinov, who refused on two grounds. First, he was mindful of the legacy of Kuropatkin in the Russo-Japanese War, who had made just such a shift with disastrous consequences. Secondly, he was anxious to minimize the disruption to existing arrangements in a time of crisis. Finally, on 2 August, Grand Duke Nicholas accepted the command, albeit with the implication that he was no more than the Tsar's proxy.[62]

The appointment at least had the merit of popularity. The Grand Duke was seen as sympathetic to reform, a reputation based on little more than his opposition to Sukhomlinov, and his consequent following in the Duma. Physically, his height evoked the idea of leadership. But, as inspector-general of cavalry, he had had no direct experience of the war in Manchuria. Since 1908 he had been on the sidelines, and was not conversant with plan 19 and its variants. In 1910–11 he had successfully thwarted the only major command exercise planned before April 1914, a war game devised by Sukhomlinov.[63] 'He appeared', Polivanov recorded, 'to be a man entirely unequipped for the task, and in accordance with his own statement, on the receipt of the Imperial order, he spent much of his time crying because he did not know how to approach his new duties.'[64]

The Grand Duke is variously regarded as wanting either Alekseev or Palitsyn (chief of the general staff from 1905 to 1908) as his chief of staff.[65] He got

[62] D. Jones, *Sbornik*, XI (1985), 55–6; id. *Military-naval encyclopaedia*, i. 167–8, and ii. 143–9; Danilov, *Russie*, 148–53, 166–77; Suchomlinow, *Erinnerungen*, 368–71.
[63] Frantz, *Russland auf dem Wege*, 43–4; Suchomlinow, *Erinnerungen*, 294–7.
[64] Florinsky, *End of the Russian empire*, 208.
[65] Pares, *Fall of the Russian monarchy*, 193; Lincoln, *Passage*, 54.

neither. On the insistence of the Tsar, N. Yanuskevitch, a youthful general who owed his rise to service at court but had never commanded a formation larger than a company, became chief of staff. Yanuskevitch, like the Grand Duke, knew his own limitations: his solution, understandable but hardly appropriate, was not to interfere. Thus Danilov, who as quartermaster-general was head of operations, became the key figure at Stavka. He, furthermore, was a protégé of Sukhomlinov.

Although the Grand Duke was then saddled with the pre-war split between himself and Sukhomlinov, he did not let it interfere with the internal workings of Stavka. However, it was institutionalized in another way. Stavka possessed no section to administer supply. The regulations for field administration had assumed that the minister of war would be subordinated to the commander-in-chief by virtue of that office being held by the Tsar. The effect of the Tsar not assuming the command was therefore to divorce supply from operations. An army group organization was established, the North-West Front for East Prussia and the South-West for Galicia. With regard to supply, the Fronts dealt directly with the ministry of war, bypassing Stavka. Thus Stavka could plan operations while remaining totally oblivious to logistic considerations. Already, in his pre-war planning for East Prussia, Danilov had shown scant regard for the question of supply. This tendency was now confirmed by the command structure. Palitsyn commented of Stavka in May 1915:

They devote themselves mostly to operational matters, to strategy, to drawing maps. Believe you me, all this strategy is playing in comparison with the problems with which they should occupy themselves before all other things: with the Etappen, the supply and provisioning of the army. This is the fundamental in the war.[66]

And when Stavka's designs were confounded by supply problems, it could blame the minister of war. Thus, even during the war itself the animosity between the Grand Duke and Sukhomlinov continued to cut across the search for constructive solutions.

Stavka's weaknesses—in personnel and in structure—created the opportunity for the Fronts to develop as autonomous commands. Rather than an overall scheme with variants, plan 19 spawned two separate theatres, the north-west and the south-west. Each became independent in the disposition of the resources under its command, and in the objectives which it pursued. Grand Duke Nicholas established his headquarters at Baranovitchi, too removed to exercise any direct influence had he cared to do so. His staff possessed a train, but usually it remained in a siding, the commander-in-chief being anxious not to clog the railway lines. Danilov's communications were restricted to one Hughes telegraph.[67]

[66] Frantz, *Russland auf dem Wege*, 154, also 152.   [67] Danilov, *Russie*, 249.

The independence vouchsafed to the Front commanders was reproduced down the chain of command. This could have been a strength, had the Russian army been spared the clashes of personality and the deep divisions on doctrine characteristic of the pre-war years. But, with differing ideas as to how to fight, independence in command spelt loss of co-ordination. Moreover, training in the exercise of command had been virtually non-existent. Peacetime needs had meant that promotion had gone to the bureaucrats in offices rather than those in regimental command: Zhilinskii and Yanuskevitch were typical of the results. A map exercise in the Kiev district in April 1914 had been Sukhomlinov's only success in his effort to institute war games, and even that had been undermined by its neglect of the supply question and by the tendency of officers to see it, not as a testing ground, but as a direct challenge to their professional competence. When the army did mobilize the peacetime command structure was disrupted. Staffs were immediately needed for Stavka, for the chief commands (the two Fronts and the Caucasus), and for eleven armies. The existing district staffs were due to supervise the mobilization and to stay with their corps. Thus, front-line units lost their senior officers to the new staff appointments. Men were appointed to posts for which peacetime training (manoeuvres centred on the division, not any higher formation) had not prepared them. And even those designated for a particular command frequently found themselves unable to take it up: A. A. Brusilov was due to command the 2nd army on the North-West Front, but his peacetime command (a corps) was in the Kiev region and he therefore took over the newly designated 8th army on the South-West Front.[68]

The Russo-French discussions and plan 19 concerned themselves with initial preparations; they were not, as the German plan tried to be, a complete war plan. Danilov had recognized this deficiency. Therefore, for him, plan 19 derived its unity not from its attention to case A and case G, both of which were conceived as preliminaries, but from the second stage of operations. The purpose of the campaigns in both East Prussia and Galicia was to secure Russia's flanks, so that the army could then go on to exploit the geographical advantage of the Polish salient. A decisive victory in East Prussia would, for example, shorten the Russian front by 300 kilometres, and would open the path—once Austria-Hungary had also been defeated—to Posen and Silesia. Beyond them lay Berlin.

This unifying concept, which had remained shadowy before the war, gained substance during August itself. Reassured by the fact that Germany was concentrating against France, on 6 August the Grand Duke allocated the 4th army to the South-West Front. But then, reflecting Danilov's attention to the second

[68] Ibid. 142–3; Gourko, *War and revolution*, 5–6; Brusilov, *Soldier's notebook*, 13; Kenez, *California Slavic Studies*, VII (1973), 133–4, 139.

stage of the war, and responding to French pressure for direct and immediate aid, he set about the creation of two further armies, drawn from troops from the Finnish and East Asiatic frontiers, first the 9th around Ivangorod, and then the 10th around Warsaw, to operate on the line Thorn–Posen–Breslau. The Grand Duke saw the armies in Poland as the follow-up to victories on the flanks. But those victories had yet to be won. Alekseev, now chief of staff to the South-West Front, protested bitterly at the division of resources. The Grand Duke, insufficiently intimate with recent staff developments and too anxious to please the French, had not welded case A and case G into a whole but had added a third variant. The effect was to dissipate Russia's absolute supremacy in manpower, and to divide yet again its direction of the war.

EAST PRUSSIA

For the general staffs of both Russia and Germany East Prussia in 1914 was a secondary theatre.[69] The Germans allocated to it eleven infantry divisions and one cavalry division, or just over a tenth of their total strength. Therefore, the Russians, although by 1914 their alliance commitments had made Germany their major enemy, were free to follow their underlying preference for a war with Austria-Hungary. To all intents and purposes Stavka's decision on 6 August, the seventh day of the Russian mobilization, was to implement case A. For the time being only the 1st and 2nd armies were to face Germany. But that was still sufficient to enable offensive operations in support of France. Between them the two armies mustered thirty infantry divisions and eight cavalry divisions. Since a Russian division comprised sixteen battalions (not twelve, as in a German division), the manpower superiority of the Russians in the northern theatre was even more marked than the divisional balance suggested.

The command of the North-West Front was vested in Zhilinskii, the former chief of the general staff, unpopular and 'an official of the cut-and-dried type'.[70] Zhilinskii had the merit of being familiar both with recent staff thinking and with France's needs. There was logic too in the appointment of Paul Rennenkampf, commander of the 1st army, who had spent seven years as a

---

[69] For the Eastern front throughout the war see Stone, *Eastern front*; of the older literature Churchill, *Unknown War*, is a reasonable narrative. On Tannenberg specifically, the best and most recent account is Showalter, *Tannenberg*; of the older literature, most helpful is Elze, *Tannenberg*; Ironside, *Tannenberg*, is a clear if somewhat didactic analysis; Golovine, *Russian campaign of 1914*, sets out to attack Sukhomlinov and Zhilinskii, while praising the Grand Duke and Rennenkampf. Of the German memoirs, Hoffmann, *War of lost opportunities*, is best; Goodspeed's *Ludendorff* is superior to Ludendorff's own version.

[70] Knox, *With the Russian army*, i. 46.

corps commander on the potential German front, and since 1913 had been in charge of the Vilna district. Less appropriate was the recent experience of Alexander Samsonov, to whom the 2nd army was entrusted. Like Rennen-kampf, he had acquired his reputation in the Russo-Japanese War. The story that the two had come to blows on Mukden Station in 1904 was probably apocryphal; but the differences between them were real enough. Rennenkampf was a protégé of the Grand Duke Nicholas, Samsonov of Sukhomlinov. By 1914 Samsonov was physically unfit and professionally out of touch. He had spent the preceding seven years as governor of Turkestan. His return to active duty was not eased by Zhilinskii: the 2nd army's best staff officers were purloined by Front headquarters, and P. I. Postovskii, appointed 2nd army's chief of staff, was sufficiently highly strung to be nicknamed the 'Mad Mullah'.[71]

The operational possibilities open to the Russians in East Prussia were rendered relatively predictable by its geography. To the north, Königsberg was a heavily fortified zone, capable of supply from the Baltic, and a potential threat to the flank of any advance from east to west. The Insterburg gap extended 69 kilometres south and east from the Königsberg perimeter to Angerburg, at the top of the northernmost of the Masurian lakes, Lake Mauer. The gap was screened by the River Angerapp, whose west bank commanded its eastern. Along the south-eastern frontier the Masurian lakes presented a formidable barrier. In the south, the front from Johannisburg to Soldau had been deliberately neglected by the Russians, so as not to facilitate any German invasion. On the Russian side no major road or railway approached the frontier; both were available on the German.

A war game, devised by Zhilinskii and played in May, had rehearsed the permutations which the theatre offered. Because the German mobilization was anticipated to be thirteen days ahead of the Russian, and the Austrian ten days, nothing would be gained by haste. Instead, both concentration and deploy-ment were to be completed before any advance. Zhilinskii put great stress on logistic order—although ironically the rear services did not constitute part of the exercise. It was assumed that the Germans would fall back on the Anger-app. The fact that the 2nd army was to use the unroaded Johannisburg–Soldau sector not for defence but as the base for an advance meant that its pace would be slower than that of the 1st army. Thus, when the offensive began Rennen-kampf's responsibility, as the war game made clear only months before the event, was restraint.[72]

At the war's outbreak Zhilinskii's emphasis on the completion of the Front's concentration and on its methodical advance was immediately put under pressure by Stavka. This was a relationship which the May 1914 war game had not rehearsed. Stavka's instructions on 6 August had the North-West Front

[71] Harrison, 'Samsonov', 17.   [72] Menning, *Bayonets before bullets*, 252–5.

mount an energetic offensive as soon as possible in order to ease the position of the French in the west. Accordingly, Zhilinskii now proposed that the 1st army should begin its advance towards the River Angerapp on 13 August. It was to march in echelon, so that its refused left wing would not cross the frontier until 17 August. On the same day the 2nd army was to advance from the south, west of the Masurian lakes but close in behind them, aiming north in the direction of Rothfliess and Rastenburg. Zhilinskii's aims were both local in conception and limited in geographical scope. He was preoccupied with the German attention to envelopment, so much emphasized in their published manuals and in their manoeuvres before 1914. His plan aimed to answer the Germans in kind, by enveloping them from north and south to the west of the Masurian lakes. It met the spirit of Russia's commitment to France by beginning operations as soon as possible, but it accepted the subordinate nature of the northern front by not aiming deep into East Prussia. Above all, it treated the theatre as self-contained.

However, Stavka's conception of the East Prussian operations was not so restricted. The balance of forces in the north encouraged hopes of a major victory rather than just a raid; furthermore, success would be defined not in terms of East Prussia alone but in terms of a Russian invasion into the heart of Germany. Although it had effectively opted for case A, Stavka's attention in August was not only to the defeat of Austria-Hungary but also to the improvisation of a campaign against Germany. Therefore, for Grand Duke Nicholas and Yanuskevitch, the centre of gravity of the North-West Front lay to the south; its operations were to link with those of the new 9th army forming round Warsaw. In fresh instructions to Zhilinskii, on 10 August, Yanuskevitch directed the 1st army to draw the bulk of the German forces onto itself, while the 2nd army was to aim more to the west, so as to cut off the Germans falling back on the Vistula. Once the 1st and 2nd armies had cleared the area east of the Vistula, and were level with Warsaw, the 9th army would lengthen their line to the south, preparatory to the advance into Germany. To meet these instructions Zhilinskii extended Samsonov's left to the west. Moreover, the 2nd army's advance was no longer to be simultaneous with that of the 1st, but was to begin two days afterwards, on 19 August, to ensure that Prittwitz's 8th German army was drawn towards Rennenkampf, so leaving its rear and communications exposed to Samsonov's advance.

The plan was a compromise between the Front's concentration on its initial objectives and Stavka's concern with the second stage of operations. The consequence was the sacrifice of the Russians' numerical advantage. At one extreme was Zhilinskii's concern for Germany's own proclivity for envelopment. He dissipated his strength to protect his flank and rear, particularly the areas of concentration around Kowno and Grodno. Second-line forces taken for these tasks weakened front-line strengths: up to a third of its infantry and cavalry, and two-fifths of its artillery was lost to the 2nd army.[73] At the other end of the spectrum was a plan of envelopment so vast that contact between the 1st and 2nd armies could not be sustained either in space or in time. The cavalry on Rennenkampf's left now linked up with that on Samsonov's right. The 2nd army, with further to go, fewer roads, and a start delayed by two days, ended up five to six days behind the 1st army. Thus, the German 8th army was able to meet first Rennenkampf and then Samsonov, and to have a local superiority in manpower on both occasions. And behind it all was an abandonment of any realism inherent in plan 19: Stavka was effectively stretching its resources to implement both case A and case G, not one or the other.

The problem of conflicting priorities was not confined to one side only. Moltke's capacity for simultaneously retaining all the options while confusing the lines of responsibility was visited as surely on the eastern front as on the western. OHL's pre-war instructions were for the 8th army's commander 'to conduct operations according to his own judgement'.[74] The trouble was that Moltke, with good reason, did not trust Prittwitz's judgement; he had therefore appointed Waldersee, who was familiar with pre-war planning and with the talks with Conrad, as Prittwitz's chief of staff. Prittwitz himself had been privy to neither. Moreover, his responsibilities were contradictory. He had to defend East Prussia; at the same time he had to do his best, with insufficient forces, to support the Austrians. Waldersee, who had been serving with the general staff in Berlin in July, knew that it might be some time before the bulk of the German forces could be freed from the west. He was also only too aware that Vienna's focus was on Serbia rather than Russia. Germany had to encourage the Habsburg army to re-orientate itself. In the first three weeeks of August Conrad's enthusiasm for converging Austrian and German thrusts grew more pronounced.[75] OHL could have interpreted this as a sign of desperation, of the Austrians' need for the Germans to take the Russians off their backs; it could equally have been the basis for optimism, suggesting that a German attack might be sufficient to switch the Austrians off Serbia and onto Russia. On 14 August Moltke signalled to Waldersee: 'When the Russians come, not defence only, but offensive, offensive, offensive.'[76] The trouble was that by 1914 the balance of forces was even less favourable to the execution of an envelopment than it had been in 1909.

Moltke knew that. Between the Bosnian crisis and the assassination at Sarajevo more resources were allocated to the defence of West Prussia than

---

[73] Lincoln, *Passage*, 63–4.   [74] Elze, *Tannenberg*, 83; see also 83–5, 93–6.
[75] Pitreich, *1914*, 140–5.
[76] Showalter, *Tannenberg*, 143; see also John C. G. Röhl, 'Germany', in Wilson (ed.), *Decisions for war*, 44–5; Mombauer, 'Moltke', 175–6, 214. It is worth pointing out that the German *wenn*, rendered by Showalter as 'when', could also be translated as a conditional 'if'.

to making East Prussia the base for an offensive. In 1912 he requested 320 million marks in order to modernize the fortifications of Posen and Graudenz, on the Vistula; he only got 200 million, but in 1913 a further 210 million (or 21.5 per cent of the total allocated to the army for that year) was also earmarked for defensive works in the east.[77] The trouble was that, operationally, as general staff studies had shown in 1885, a defence on the line of the Vistula could require more men than a concentrated and directed thrust into Poland.[78] Moreover, the adoption of the tactical and operational defensive was incompatible with the strategic defensive which underpinned the war's justification in 1914: it hardly behoved the German army to begin hostilities by abandoning all Germans east of the Vistula to the Russians.

Prittwitz's combination of apparently condoning the independence and offensiveness of his corps commanders, while choosing the Vistula as his defensive base, was thus an ineffective compromise of two fundamentally irreconcilable positions. He had not the slightest intention of being drawn too far east by Rennenkampf. He assumed that Rennenkampf's would be the main thrust, and that the Russian 1st army—because it had the easier and more direct route—would be on him before Samsonov's. Therefore, although he had underestimated the Russian advance from the Narew, his dispositions were sensible enough. He left a single corps, XX corps, around Ortelsburg facing south. His three remaining corps he prepared for a defensive battle on the position of the Angerapp, well back from the Russian frontier and so placed as to allow rapid redeployment to the south or retreat to the west. At the same time his dispositions did not entirely abandon the offensive, giving him the opportunity to strike Rennenkampf's right flank from the north.

Prittwitz had correctly calculated that lengthening the Russian 1st army's advance would diminish its fighting power. By 19 August, although Rennenkampf had only just crossed the frontier, his troops had been on the move for a week, and their rear services and supply organization were in complete disorder. Despite their considerable strength, the Russian cavalry failed to push ahead of the main body, to establish contact with the Germans or to feel round the German left flank. It had become too heedful of the virtues of defensive firepower: trained as mounted infantry, its inclinations were to dismount when opposed rather than to press forward. With Rennenkampf's six divisions spread over a 56-kilometre front, it saw its task as closing the gaps between them. On the morning of the 19 August Rennenkampf instructed his army to rest on the 20th. The message, like many others sent by both sides in this early stage of the war, was transmitted in clear, and was intercepted by the Germans.

---

[77] Stevenson, *Armaments and the coming of war*, 10, 212.   [78] Showalter, *Tannenberg*, 21 .

Prittwitz was increasingly worried by the rapidity of Samsonov's advance. Rennenkampf's halt would postpone the planned battle on the Angerapp, and might leave the Germans with insufficient time to cover the threat to the south. He therefore resolved to turn the headstrong actions of one of his corps commanders, von François, to good account. François commanded I corps, whose district in peacetime was East Prussia. Loath to abandon his 'own' territory, he had been encouraged by the general staff before the war in the idea of mounting local spoiling attacks across the frontier. By 13 August most of his corps was on the line Goldap–Stallupönen, well to the east of the Angerapp and therefore in danger of being isolated from the rest of 8th army. Prittwitz ordered XVII corps and I reserve corps to close up on the Angerapp, while I corps was to fall back on Gumbinnen: his hope was that I corps would thus be able to strike the Russians on their northern flank as they approached the main German positions on the river. François disregarded his instructions. On 17 August I corps engaged the Russians at Stallupönen. Although instructed to break off the action, François was still in contact with the enemy on 19 August. He reported the carelessness of the Russian advance and urged Prittwitz to allow him to attack. Prittwitz agreed. The 8th army was ordered to concentrate in line with I corps, east of Gumbinnen, and thus well forward of its planned defensive line, the Angerapp and the Masurian lakes.[79]

The battle of Gumbinnen reflected credit on neither side. However, it was not the flank attack planned by Prittwitz for the Angerapp position, but an operation to support I corps forced on 8th army by François' headstrong independence. The latter's corps began its attack at 3.30 a.m. on 20 August. It took the Russians by surprise, but given the strength of the enemy its own flanks were vulnerable. Therefore, the 2nd division switched from François' right wing to his left, marching 16 kilometres through a forest during the night, and so pushing against the Russian right flank from 4 a.m. The Russian cavalry standing on François's wing took no part in the action, and each Russian division was left to fight its own action against an enemy superior in numbers and in artillery. But the German attack was too hurried and too uncontrolled. On François's right Mackensen's XVII corps, to the south of I corps, marched forward from the Angerapp throughout the night of 19/20 August, on roads crowded with refugees, and did not enter the fight until 8 a.m. As in the battles in the west, the infantry came straight off the line of march into action without artillery preparation. The Russians had entrenched, and their artillery and infantry, linked by telephone, co-ordinated their firepower to telling effect. One Russian regiment fired 800,000 rounds from its 3,000 rifles and eight

---

[79] Showalter, *Tannenberg*, 155–8; on this phase of the battle, see also Showalter, *War & Society*, II (1984), 60–86.

machine-guns, and its supporting field artillery discharged over 10,000 shells. The Germans, still in close order, suffered heavy losses: unable to see their enemy, they became demoralized and by 5 p.m. were in full flight; they had suffered 8,000 casualties out of a strength of 30,000.[80] On Mackensen's right, I reserve corps also had a trying night and did not make contact until 11 a.m. Its task was to strike the Russian III corps, which was facing Mackensen, in the flank. But instead it ran into the Russians' IV corps, on the edge of the Rominten forest. Made up of recruits, and undergunned in comparison with the formations of the field army, I reserve corps closed with the enemy. The two sides were so intermingled that the Russians could not exploit their artillery and their infantry tended to fire high. But, while a tactical success, I reserve corps' attack failed to distract the Russian III corps and so did not support Mackensen as intended.

From the German viewpoint the fighting on 20 August could not be counted a success. Three separate corps battles had resulted in incomplete victories on the flanks and defeat in the centre. However, the prospects for 21 August seemed good. Their concentration was now complete and they enjoyed a superiority of nine divisions to six-and-a-half. I corps had taken 6,000 prisoners in the course of the day, XVII corps had been allowed to withdraw and reorganize unhindered by Russian intervention, I reserve corps stood victorious on the battlefield, and III reserve corps would enter the battle to envelop the Russians the following day. Both François and Hoffman, the 8th army's head of operations, were keen to finish with the Russian 1st army, the former saying that he could roll up the Russians and relieve XVII corps. Furthermore, XX corps insisted that it could hold off the 2nd army for the time being. With Rennenkampf crushed, the 8th army could with confidence face Samsonov.

But Prittwitz's mood on the evening of 20 August was jittery. The battle of Gumbinnen was not his conception. Both XVII corps and I reserve corps had suffered heavy casualties. The fact that circumstances now presented the opportunity for a classic envelopment victory was hard to discern when the origins of the battle had been so different. Prittwitz's inclination to break off the battle therefore developed independently of the broader situation to the south.[81] But an aerial reconnaissance report that Samsonov's army was now in Mlawa, and was therefore extending westwards and threatening 8th army's lines of communication, confirmed its wisdom. Defence triumphed over offence in Prittwitz's mind. His sense of caution was increased by 8th army's exaggerated idea of Samsonov's strength. At 7 p.m. Prittwitz ordered the action at Gumbinnen to be broken off, and the 8th army to fall back to the Vistula.

[80] Golovine, *Russian campaign of 1914*, 27–8, 134–47.   [81] Elze, *Tannenberg*, 106–9.

Prittwitz was doing no more than what Moltke had told him to do—to preserve his army, and to do so by falling back westwards, not by tying it up in the fortress of Königsberg. But, as Hoffman was at pains to point out, it was now too late to retreat to the Vistula. Samsonov would get there first—and would do so having effected an unimpeded concentration with Rennenkampf. If Prittwitz was to secure his line of communications, he must deal with the Russian 2nd army east of the Vistula. Hoffmann therefore proposed that François's I corps be switched by rail to the right wing of XX corps facing Samsonov, so attacking the 2nd army's left wing. Its entrainment would be covered by reserve units from Königsberg. I reserve corps and XVII corps should march westwards, if Rennenkampf allowed them to break contact, with a view to supporting XX corps on its left and on the Russian 2nd army's right. But the effectiveness of this second move would depend on Rennenkampf. Osterode should be the 8th army's area of concentration so that, screened by the Masurian lakes on one side, it could face Rennenkampf rather than Samsonov if the latter resumed his advance.

In Hoffman's advice, given and adopted on the evening of 20 August, lay the manoeuvre which enabled the victory at Tannenberg. Hoffmann was a pre-war student of the Russian army; he had been an observer in Manchuria; he knew of the differences between Rennenkampf and Samsonov; and he was in possession of intercepted Russian messages. But, as Hoffmann himself acknowledged, the battle developed 'entirely by itself', not as a result of a master plan.[82] Indeed, this was its strength, and perhaps even Schlieffen's real legacy. In the west the temptation to plan the campaign through to its denouement had worked against the grain of the general staff's resources as an institution. It had made insufficient allowance for France's reactions and, in turn, denied scope for the German army's powers of improvisation and flexibility. In the east these very qualities were made central by the assumption of the defensive-offensive, and the consequent need for the Germans to respond to the manoeuvres of the Russians. Decisions flowed not from pre-scription but from intelligence and from the experience of war games and staff rides. East Prussia was the exercise area for the German army: its geography and its potential were well known to its officers. Schlieffen had recognized that the Masurian lakes created the opportunity for operations on interior lines, and that that possibility was supported by the availability of adequate road and rail links, in particular the line from Insterburg to Allenstein and Osterode. In manoeuvres in 1910 I corps and XVII corps had actually used the same communications network that they employed in August 1914. The authorship of the Tannenberg manoeuvre was therefore not confined to

[82] Hoffmann, War diaries, 18; see also Pogge von Strandmann, Rathenau, 202–3; Ludendorff, Memoirs, i. 47.

Hoffmann; it was institutional. At 8th army headquarters Waldersee and Grünert, the army's quartermaster, worked to convert Prittwitz; at OHL Moltke and, at XX corps' headquarters, Scholtz came independently to similar conclusions.[83]

The resolve of these officers grew on 21 August and was consolidated on the 22nd by the reports from aerial reconnaissance. Rennenkampf did not intend to pursue. This was entirely in accordance with the conclusions of the Russians' May 1914 war game: the danger that had been revealed then was not that the advance of 1st army would be too slow but that it would be too fast. Rennenkampf's army had expended a great deal of ammunition at Gumbinnen; it needed time to consolidate and to make good its supply position. By 23 August all the Germans facing 1st army, with the exception of a single cavalry division, had gone.[84]

Nonetheless, the mood at OHL was far from confident. Prittwitz's decision to fall back to the Vistula, relayed on a bad line via Berlin, had evoked in Moltke that characteristic sense of resignation. The Vistula itself was not much of a defensive line: the water was low and it would need more men to hold it against the combined armies of the North-West Front than were available to Prittwitz. Moreover, the abandonment of East Prussia would expose Silesia to invasion and the Austro-Hungarian army to the full weight of the Russians. The messages coming through to OHL were admittedly contradictory. François had used his corps commander's right of direct access to report to the Kaiser via his deputy in Königsberg. He claimed a great victory at Gumbinnen. This intelligence only confirmed Moltke's increasing loss of faith in the command of the 8th army. Prittwitz, although now convinced of the wisdom of what Hoffmann proposed, and although the latter's suggestions began to be put into effect on the night of the 20th, did not inform OHL or do anything to correct the impression of weakness which he had created. Equally, Moltke, despite seeing what was required—as in the west—failed to assert himself. He reckoned that only the local commander could assess the situation. He did not tell Prittwitz he was not to retreat.

The initiative to recall Prittwitz and his chief of staff, Waldersee, did not originate with Moltke but arose from within the operations section of OHL. Max Bauer telephoned each of the 8th army's corps commanders. All were agreed that the retreat to the Vistula was premature.[85] The upshot was that Erich Ludendorff, freshly adorned with the laurels of Liège, and himself of course a former head of the operations section, was asked to report to Moltke at Coblenz at 6 p.m. on 22 August. Ludendorff was named chief of staff to the

---

[83] Reichsarchiv, *Der Weltkrieg*, ii. 103–13; Bucholz, *Moltke, Schlieffen*, 104–6, 209, 248, 250–1; Showalter, *Tannenberg*, 33, 193–4.

[84] Hoeppner, *L'Allemagne et la guerre de l'air*, 43; Showalter, *Tannenberg*, 207, 210.

[85] Goodspeed, *Ludendorff*, 51.

8th army; the appointment of the new army commander, Paul von Hindenburg, was confirmed that night. The two men met for the first time on the
platform at Hannover station at 4 a.m. on the morning of the 23rd. Hindenburg, square-headed and big, a veteran of Königgrätz as well as of East Prussian
manoeuvres, had been retired in 1911 at the age of 64. Although sounded out by
Moltke on 3 August as to his availability, he had spent the first three weeks of
the war chafing in anticipation of the Kaiser's call.

Because the outline of the Tannenberg manoeuvre was already in place, it is
easy to diminish the role played in the battle by Hindenburg and Ludendorff.
The victory established their joint reputation, and yet they were not its
authors. But they were its executors, and each made a vital personal contribution. Ludendorff had already issued his first orders on the evening of 22
August. Dismissing any intermediate contact via 8th army headquarters, he
had dealt directly with the corps commanders. He confirmed the movement of
I corps to XX corps' right flank. He told XVII corps and I reserve corps to rest
on the 23rd. Hoffmann complained that Ludendorff thereby lost a day and
increased the already considerable demands which would be made on the foot-
soldiers of those two corps. But that was with the wisdom of hindsight. What
Hindenburg and Ludendorff inherited was defensive and reactive in conception; it made possible a more extensive manoeuvre, but it did not anticipate it.
Furthermore, if any German formation had the potential for envelopment at
this juncture it was I corps bearing down on Samsonov's left, not XVII corps
and I reserve corps, whose immediate task was to support XX corps in its
frontal battle. By holding these two corps back for a day Ludendorff hoped
to be clearer about Rennenkampf's intentions. If Rennenkampf followed up,
the two eastern corps should march south; if not, their movement could be to
the south-west.[86] On 24 August I reserve corps was instructed to advance
in the direction of Bischofstein and XVII corps to Bartenstein. Whereas
Hoffmann on the 20th had had to allow for a possible battle with Rennenkampf, Ludendorff on the 24th could be clear that his objective was Samsonov.
Hindenburg's task was less evident, but nonetheless vital: it was to steady
the nerves of his chief of staff. Hindenburg's personality has remained elusive;
he had been favoured by Schlieffen as his successor as chief of the general staff,
but his memoirs suggest a simple and somewhat unimaginative man. If these
were his qualities, they were the ideal foil to Ludendorff. The latter, having
adopted a plan, would then be seized with self-doubt. Even as he closed in on
Samsonov, Ludendorff's worries about Rennenkampf threatened to rob his
actions of decisiveness. Hindenburg's contribution, too easily underestimated—not least by the vainglorious Ludendorff—was to convey imperturb-
ability.

---

[86] Reichsarchiv, *Der Weltkrieg*, ii. 113; Hoffmann, *War of lost opportunities*, 331.

The speed of Samsonov's advance, which had so alarmed Prittwitz, had been achieved at the expense of sufficient preparations for the march. And even then the 2nd army was not fast enough. The penalty of the pre-war neglect of supply was far heavier for Samsonov than for Rennenkampf. Samsonov had only one lateral railway line available to him, and that ran from Vilna through Grodno and Bialystok to Warsaw—in other words, well behind his front. The lines running at right angles, which crossed the frontier, lay outside the army's initial frontage, to Mlawa on the left and Grajewo on the right, and were single-tracked. That directly behind the concentration area ended at Ostrolenka, 50 kilometres from the German border. The roads north of Ostrolenka were sandy and unmetalled. As a result units began their march still incomplete. The four corps of which the army was comprised came from four different districts, and therefore the army as a whole lacked homogeneity. They shared lines of communication, meaning that one corps tended to receive too much and another too little. The push to the west, encouraged by Stavka but opposed by Zhilinskii, became a necessity in order to be able to exploit the Mlawa line. However, the effect of the reorientation was to send the army first in one direction and then in another, and to confuse its deployment and communications yet further. By 22 August all units had marched for ten to twelve hours each day for the past week, and yet had only just crossed the frontier. Their daily distances were extended by the need to requisition. But the local hay and oats had not been cut, and much of the terrain was in any case a sandy desert. Samsonov's army had still to make contact with the enemy; it was already close to collapse.

As alarming was the absence of effective communications. The army had two field radio stations. Most of their messages were in clear, in part because each corps had different ciphers, but principally in the interests of speed and accuracy; in this respect the Russians were little different from the other armies of 1914. There were twenty-five telephones and only 130 kilometres of wire for the entire force. While within Russia the army used the three government telegraph lines which ran as far as the frontier, to Myszyniec, Chorzele, and Mlawa. Each corps then extended the line as far as it could with its own stock of cable, but it had nothing spare with which to establish links between its own headquarters and those of its component divisions. A lateral line laid behind the frontier was then taken down to conform with the army's advance. Thus, the army's internal communications had collapsed by 20 August. Nor was its liaison with other bodies any better. Samsonov left his administrative staff in Ostrolenka and was accompanied by a field headquarters only. By the time he had established his command in East Prussia, at Neidenburg, messages between the two components of his staff were relayed through five stations. He had no direct contact with Rennenkampf, and little with Zhilinskii. Telegrams from the Front headquarters, whose main purpose was to hasten his progress, were forwarded from Warsaw by car. Therefore, the dispersion of Samsonov's army and its separation from the 1st army were not offset by efficient communication. Loss of command and control was the inevitable consequence.[87]

Samsonov's advance was predicated on two totally false assumptions: first, that Rennenkampf was still pushing from east to west; and second, that the Germans were fleeing back to the Vistula and must be cut off before they got there. Pre-war thinking in Russia had praised the German practice of not having an independent advance guard to establish the enemy's position and intentions, but of instead directing independent columns to converge on the battlefield. This practice led to German deployment straight from the line of march and to heavy losses in 1914. The Russians followed them, a 1911 manual dispensing with a vanguard for long-range security and leaving each column responsible for its own protection.[88] Samsonov's army, therefore, had no advance guard; each corps moved independently and was responsible for its own reconnaissance. But in this latter task the Russian cavalry, although three divisions strong, failed miserably: many mounted units stuck to the flanks, fearful of German envelopment, rather than pushed forward, and those that pushed forward lacked the means of communication with corps head-quarters.[89] Once into East Prussia the Russians were on unfamiliar ground, referring to maps marked in the Latin alphabet, not in Cyrillic, and confronted with a population that (if it had not fled) was adamantly hostile. Captured German documents were rendered valueless for the lack of a German linguist. Aerial reconnaissance, of much value on other fronts in 1914, was largely denied Samsonov, since the bulk of the available Russian aeroplanes had been directed to Galicia. The reports of the 2nd army's staff 'were framed in the form of abstract statements and presentiments, but gave no assistance by means of clear and concrete appreciations'. Such specific intelligence as was gained thus lacked a context into which it could fit.[90] Even as late as 27 August Samsonov could continue to underestimate the forces opposing him.[91] Stavka's preoccupation with Poland had taken full hold after Gumbinnen; Samsonov's intelligence failures did nothing to correct the belief that the Germans were intent on the abandonment of East Prussia.

On 23 August Samsonov asked Zhilinskii for permission to advance onto the line Allenstein–Osterode, in order to cut off the German retreat after Gumbinnen, rather than the line Rastenburg–Seeburg. Zhilinskii gave in to the prevailing optimism, setting Samsonov the compromise target of Sensburg–

---

[87] Ironside, *Tannenberg*, 61–7, 144–5; also Stone, *Eastern front*, 63; Goodspeed, *Ludendorff*, 69.
[88] David Jones, *Military-naval encyclopaedia*, iv. 111–42, esp. 123, 127.
[89] Gourko, *War and revolution*, 24–5.
[90] Golovine, *Journal of the United Service Institution of India* (Jan. 1933), 498–500.
[91] Knox, *With the Russian army*, i. 65–6, 70–1.

Allenstein by 26 August. To achieve this move to the north-west, Samsonov shed II corps on his right, now caught up in the Masurian lakes and transferred to Rennenkampf's command. He was also instructed to leave I corps at Soldau, to guard his left. Thus, while Samsonov's front widened to 96 kilometres, his strength fell to just over three corps.

On the same day XV corps, in his centre, ran into the Germans' XX corps on the line Orlau–Frankenau. A fierce frontal battle developed on 24 August, with Hindenburg and Ludendorff telling Scholtz to hold well forward in order to give I and XVII corps the space in which to deploy. If they had intended to envelop Samsonov at this stage they would have lured him into a sack by pulling XX corps back; instead, they opted to run the risk that Scholtz would himself be enveloped.[92] The men of XX corps responded to the challenge: their peacetime headquarters lay only a few kilometres away at Allenstein, and at one stage their chief of staff, Emil Hell, was directing artillery fire onto his own house.[93] Not until 25 August did XIII Russian corps, on XV corps' right, begin to pressurize the Germans' flank. Poor inter-corps communications and inadequate reconnaissance was costing the Russians the opportunity to accomplish their own envelopment. Scholtz now pulled his corps back, ready to align with François's I corps, which was due to enter the line on his right on the morning of the 26th. However, Samsonov interpreted Scholtz's move as fresh evidence of the supposed general German retreat, and secured Zhilinskii's permission to advance on the line Allenstein–Osterode. The effect of yet another move to the west was to separate XIII Russian corps from VI corps, now on Samsonov's extreme right and still directed northwards to Sensburg and Bischofsburg. During the course of the 25th Samsonov began to realize his mistake, and his doubts were fuelled by reports of the movements of the Germans' I and VI corps.[94] But Zhilinskii encouraged Samsonov to continue his advance, the Russians construing the threat as one from inferior German forces concentrating on the 2nd army's left, where it had the support of I Russian corps at Soldau. Samsonov therefore reckoned on enveloping them with his right. The Germans were now threatened on both their flanks, and by 26 August the atmosphere at 8th army headquarters was strained. But what Samsonov did not appreciate, principally because of his misapprehension about Rennenkampf's movements, was the perilous position in which his right now found itself. On 26 August Mackensen's XVII corps and I reserve corps, by dint of a prodigious effort on the 24th and 25th, after their halt on the 23rd, came up to strike VI corps at Bischofsburg. Russian pilots had reported troops moving south-west, but had concluded that they were Rennenkampf's. VI corps had failed to use its cavalry to reconnoitre and was preparing to swing

---

[92] Showalter, *Tannenberg*, 228–9.   [93] Uhle-Wettler, *Ludendorff*, 126.
[94] Harrison, 'Samsonov', 22.

to its left, onto Allenstein, to support Samsonov's centre. It was totally surprised. Only the Germans' exhaustion enabled its escape. Driven back in disorder, the Russians did not stop until they had reached Ortelsburg. Now Samsonov had no protection on his right and no reinforcements for the two corps, XIII and XV, in his centre.

Ludendorff's tetchiness on the 26th was fed by I corps' slow approach to the battlefield. What he had in mind was a comparatively limited victory. The task of XX corps was to fight and fix the Russians, not to lead them on; the task of I corps was to extend XX corps' front to the right and at right angles. He was becoming anxious about Rennenkampf and the threat to XVII corps' flank; he was not privy to the intercepts of Samsonov's orders, which made it clear that the Russians would not attack Scholtz's corps on the 25th. He told François to attack XV Russian corps' left flank at 10 a.m. on the 26th. François disobeyed. Despite the prodigious efforts of the railway departments, only twenty out of thirty batteries were at his disposal, and his corps was therefore not ready to attack the Russians in prepared positions; in any case, he preferred envelopment to a frontal attack. The effect of the delay was to allow Samsonov to continue to focus his attention on XX corps, and so draw in his two centre corps. François's attack on the principal Russian position between XV corps and I corps, at Usdau, began on the morning of 27 August. The Russian trenches were continuous, without traverses or overhead protection, and thickly manned. I German corps' artillery, now up, inflicted heavy casualties. Usdau fell by 11 a.m. François then turned south to push I Russian corps back to Soldau. The burden of the Russian attack therefore fell on XX corps. By the morning of the 28th François realized that the threat from Soldau was diminishing and that he could resume the attack on the Russian centre. Ludendorff ordered him to do so by a direct advance at Lahna. For the second time François disobeyed. He opted to direct his march on Neidenburg, so aiming to the east and achieving a fuller encirclement. By nightfall he was at Neidenburg, and his advance units were moving eastwards to Will-enberg.

If any German created the opportunity for the envelopment of Samsonov's left between 26 and 28 August, it was François. But its principal author was not a German but Samsonov himself. The delay in I German corps' attack until 27 August encouraged him to focus on his centre. On his right XIII corps was advancing on the railway junction of Allenstein, both to secure food and to converge with VI corps. Unable to establish radio contact with VI corps, and unaware that the latter was falling back to the south-east, XIII corps entered Allenstein on the afternoon of the 27th. It was now poised to break through to Rennenkampf (indeed, 8th army headquarters feared it might belong to Rennenkampf's army), or to cut across the communications of the German corps to left or right. Hindenburg's and Ludendorff's priority, therefore, was to drive XIII corps out of Allenstein. I reserve corps was instructed to abandon its advance south, across the Russians' line of retreat, and to turn west to Allenstein; XVII corps was told to conform. But Samsonov responded less to the movements of XIII corps and more to François's attack. On the evening of 27 August he told XIII corps to move south from Allenstein to combine with XV corps in an attack on the flank and rear of Scholtz's XX corps. The weary soldiers of XIII corps assumed that I reserve corps, now approaching it from the west, was VI Russian corps, which would therefore protect their right; at dawn on 28 August they set off on their 32-kilometre march to the south-west. It was these Russian movements which delivered the 2nd army into the jaws of a German envelopment.[95]

On the morning of the 28th Samsonov learned of the defeat of both his flanking corps, I corps on the left and VI corps on the right. The precariousness of his position at last became clear. But even now his situation could be construed as serious rather than hopeless. The Germans, although enjoying a superiority of 155 batteries to 132, had only been strong enough to envelop a part of Samsonov's army, XIII corps and XV corps, leaving both I corps and VI corps outside the net. François had had to spread twenty-five batteries over a distance of 50 kilometres in order to form a thin cordon to the south. The Germans had communication problems of their own, and only I corps was in regular contact with Ludendorff. Below's I reserve corps was slow to start its march on the morning of the 28th, and it was 10.30 a.m. before it realized that Allenstein was only lightly held. Below switched his route back to the south, but Mackensen was not told of this until 12 noon. Although XVII corps had reported that VI Russian corps was in full retreat to the south at 1.20 a.m., its movements remained subordinate to those of I reserve corps until 2.35 p.m. By the time Mackensen received definitive instructions to push south as fast as he could, the day was hot; moreover, the roads before him were poor. Even now Hindenburg and Ludendorff continued to think defensively. Fearful of an intervention by Rennenkampf, they were inclined to leave both their left-flanking corps in the vicinity of Allenstein. Furthermore, the fact that XIII corps had evaded the clutches of I reserve corps increased the possibility of it helping XV corps to escape east. Thus, their orders of 10 p.m. on 28 August told I reserve corps to attack south and east on the next day, while XVII corps was to be ready to face either Samsonov or Rennenkampf. But the order never reached Mackensen. At 6.30 a.m. on the 28th Ludendorff learnt that XVII corps was approaching Ortelsburg. It was now too far south to protect 8th army against Rennenkampf, and so Ludendorff authorized it to proceed. Closing the gap with François was a protracted process.[96]

On the morning of 28 August, Samsonov went forward from his army headquarters at Neidenburg to join XV corps: he was therefore unable to direct the operations of I corps and VI corps. I corps fell back to Mlawa, thus drawing away yet further from the remnants of the 2nd army. XV corps tried to break out to the south, but found German artillery and machine-guns posted at the exits to the forest. Turning east, on the night of the 29th, it blundered in the dark into XIII corps, in the process of falling back to the south-east. The Russians' problems of command, communications, and supply, multiplied by the forests in which they found themselves fighting, broke XIII corps and XV corps into isolated groups of exhausted and hungry men. Samsonov went off into the woods, and killed himself. Russian attempts to fight their way out on 30 August were ill co-ordinated and demoralized. By the 31st the Germans could claim the capture of 92,000 prisoners and nearly 400 guns.

Rennenkampf, meanwhile, had barely moved, advancing with excessive deliberation, and doing so in the wrong direction. His losses had been heavy. For three days after Gumbinnen his cavalry, still preoccupied with their flanks, failed to push forward to establish the direction of the German retreat. Confident that the 8th army was falling back to the Vistula, Rennenkampf could argue that an energetic pursuit would only push it out of the clutches of the 2nd army, toiling northwards from the Narew. His concern was not with events to the south but with his northern flank, where Königsberg's fortifications presented a continued threat. Zhilinskii did nothing to suggest that greater urgency was required; his aim was still to hold the 1st army back, while the 2nd army pushed the Germans north. Nor was this particularly surprising, when even Samsonov himself continued to regard the situation as favourable until the morning of 28 August. Thereafter, it was too late for Rennenkampf to save the 2nd army. However, it was not too late to exploit the vulnerability of the German 8th army, exhausted by battle and concentrated to the south. But the actions of the 1st army and the responses of the North-West Front remained dilatory. On the 30th Zhilinskii told Rennenkampf that Samsonov had been completely defeated. Zhilinskii's preference for security, only reluctantly suppressed in the previous few days, resurrected itself. The position of the 1st army was now seen as one of acute danger, as the Germans were free to concentrate against it. Therefore, rather than seize the opportunity to achieve a victory before the 8th army could redeploy, Zhilinskii approved Rennenkampf's adoption of a strong defensive position along the rivers Alle and Omet and down to the Masurian lakes. When, on 4 September, he did consider the possibilities of an offensive he was not only too late, he was also the victim of fantasy. The activities of German reserve units round Mlawa led him to believe that the Germans were ignoring Rennenkampf and were already turning against Poland. He therefore instructed the 1st army to attack into East Prussia on 14 September. He somehow assumed that the shattered remnants of the 2nd army would be able to play a supportive role.

Despite Samsonov's defeat, Zhilinskii did in fact have sufficient troops available to mean that an effective plan could give him a numerical superiority on the battlefield. Rennenkampf's army had been reinforced; in addition, the two corps of the 10th army, forming in Poland, were now being brought up to the area around Johannisburg in order to cover the gap between the 1st and 2nd armies. But this strength was dissipated. Faulty Russian dispositions were partly a consequence of the ambivalence over whether Rennenkampf was attacking or defending. They were also a reflection of Zhilinskii's preoccupation in either case with the flanks, with Königsberg to the north and Mlawa to the south. If the North-West Front had attacked on 14 September it would have done so concentrically. In defence, Zhilinskii assumed the German weight, if not on the Polish wing, would be on the Baltic. The Germans sent messages in clear to encourage this fear of a thrust from Königsberg. Twelve divisions of Rennenkampf's army were concentrated on a 30-kilometre front on the river Deime, east of the city; only seven were allocated for the 64 kilometres between the River Pregel and Angerburg; little attention was given to the Lötzen gap, which formed a narrow bridgehead through the Masurian lakes and was held by the Germans.

The units around Mlawa that had so changed Zhilinskii's appreciation of the situation were no more than a flank guard. OHL's directive to Hindenburg of 31 August had made the 8th army's priority the security of East Prussia; operations in Poland would follow once that was guaranteed. The plan which the 8th army adopted to deal with Rennenkampf was in large part a product of Russian dispositions. Although reinforced by the two corps from the west, the 8th army lacked the strength for a successful frontal attack on Rennenkampf's line north of Lake Mauer. Four corps, therefore, were to hold the Russians in the Insterburg gap from the front, while two corps and two cavalry divisions were to wheel to the south, XVII corps breaking through the Lötzen gap, and I corps passing south of the Masurian lakes and so rolling Rennenkampf up to the north. On 8 September the Russians north of Lake Mauer held the frontal attack, and even counter-attacked; for Mackensen's corps the Lötzen gap proved a bottleneck, and three attacks on 8 September failed to produce a breakthrough. Once again François's energy came to Ludendorff's rescue. I corps marched 123 kilometres in four days, fighting some of the way, and on the morning of 9 September came in on the right flank of Mackensen's attack. In the early hours of the 10th Francois's right-flanking division took Lyck. Zhilinskii responded by pulling back the Russian 10th army to the area south of the Augustowo forest. Thus, Rennenkampf's left was unsupported. On the night of the 9th Rennenkampf, despite the success of the frontal battle, responded to the weakness of his southern flank and ordered his army to retreat. By the evening of 10 September the 1st army had fallen back 48 kilometres. Within fifty hours most units had covered 88 kilometres, and were back inside Russia. Rennenkampf, breaking contact both with the Front and with his corps, changed his headquarters four times in twenty-four hours, and by 13 September was as far back as Kowno.

Ludendorff and his post-war defenders liked to present the battle of the Masurian lakes as a great envelopment operation, whose results could have matched those at Tannenberg, but whose achievement was limited by factors outside of his control. The argument was justified in that Rennenkampf's precipitate retreat most certainly avoided any danger of his succumbing to the same fate as Samsonov. But, as at Tannenberg, the signs are that Ludendorff's expectations of the envelopment operation were not as great as subsequent claims came to suggest. His task, after all, was to clear German territory of an enemy army entrenched in good positions with superior forces. The weight of the 8th army lay in the frontal attack, not in the turning movement. A determined counter-attack by II Russian corps on 10 September stopped XX German corps in its tracks. Thus, Russian actions rather than German intentions increased the importance of the right wing. The dominant mood in the staff of the 8th army was caution. Mackensen's and François's corps were themselves vulnerable to envelopment by the greater strength of the 1st and 10th Russian armies, as the 8th army's staff had recognized from the outset. Even after Lyck, François and Mackensen were directed to the north, towards Insterburg and Gumbinnen, to relieve the pressure which Rennenkampf was exerting on the German centre and left. Direct support for XI corps, one of two corps recently transferred from the west and struggling on the left, was deemed a greater priority than deep envelopment; only a single division was pushed eastwards. Not until the night of 11 September did Ludendorff realize the opportunity for a great victory, which in any case had by then eluded him, and push the German pursuit. Here, as later in the war, Ludendorff's focus was not on broad strategic conceptions, of the sort so favoured by Schlieffen, but on immediate tactical circumstances; it was from the latter, not the former, that he hoped to fashion operational success.

Hindenburg described the battle of Tannenberg as 'a series of scenes'.[97] Ludendorff told Walther Rathenau in November 1915 that victory was not due to a fixed plan, 'but rather to decisions made instinctively at the time'.[98] But neither could wholly resist the widespread German wish to mistake effect for cause. The super-Cannae that had eluded Schlieffen's pupils in the west had been achieved in the east. Furthermore, it had been planned that way by a great combination of commander and chief of staff. In practice, Ludendorff's objectives had been much more limited and sensible: his aim had been

[97] Hindenburg, *Out of my life*, 94; but see 87–8.   [98] Pogge von Strandmann, *Rathenau*, 202.

to defend East Prussia, his concentration had been as much on the centre—on XX corps' position at Tannenberg, on the frontal battle at the Masurian lakes—as on the flanks, and he had expected no more than 30,000 prisoners from the defeat of Samsonov. The doctrinaire advocate of envelopment had been François. The fact that envelopment had been achieved, largely through Russian mismanagement, at Tannenberg, and had apparently been missed only narrowly at the Masurian lakes, created a totally false expectation both of Hindenburg and Ludendorff as strategists and of possible operational outcomes as a whole.

Tannenberg's strategic significance was at best indirect. Germany's success was defensive; the Russian army, despite the loss of 310,000 men in the opening six weeks, had not suffered a crippling blow. In the wider context of the war, what both powers had done was to provide aid to their allies engaged in the main theatres of the war. The speed of the Russian advance had prompted OHL to withdraw two corps from France: they were thus lost to Germany on the Marne, although they did contribute to the victory of the Masurian lakes. The Germans themselves, despite the accusations of perfidy from Austria-Hungary, claimed that thirty-four Russian divisions (including, somewhat tendentiously, the Russian 9th army in Poland) were directed against them, leaving only just over forty-six divisions in Galicia.[99] Thus, although the fighting in East Prussia did not, in the broadest sense, matter in itself, it did contribute to the outcomes elsewhere.

Above all, Tannenberg mattered because of its propaganda effect, its effect on perceptions. Hindenburg requested the battle be so named in revenge for the defeat of the Teutonic Knights at the hands of the Poles at Tannenberg 500 years previously: as Georg von Müller commented: 'very gallant but not very politic as regards the Poles whom we now need.'[100] Such symbols were important to the Prussian mentality. Furthermore, the idea that it created, of a decisive and historic success, helped obscure the absence of such a victory where it was actually wanted, in the west. The illusion of German military invincibility was fostered, not simply in the minds of the press-reading public but also in those responsible for the direction of policy itself.

By the same token, Tannenberg confirmed the Russian army in its own sense of inferiority. Germany had won the campaign not only with forces that were inferior in overall numbers, but were also inferior in alleged quality. Landwehr units and garrison troops had been pressed into the field; they had screened Rennenkampf's army during the concentration against Samsonov, and had guarded the Polish flank in the battle of the Masurian lakes. François's right-hand division, which had moved so quickly in its swing south and fought so

[99] Reichsarchiv, *Weltkrieg*, ii. 36.   [100] Görlitz, *The Kaiser and his Court*, 25.

well at Lyck, was a reserve division. Comparable Russian troops were not regarded as fit for active operations. The cavalry, in which the Russians had enjoyed an eight-to-one superiority, had—despite the favourable and open terrain—contributed little. Industrial backwardness could not be offset by such traditional strengths. German artillery had dominated. Speed of concentration had been the decisive German advantage, and that had rested on the railway line. Never, throughout the war, would the Russians acquire the conviction that they could beat the Germans.

But the quality of the men, the relative value of cavalry, the use of artillery, the availability of railway lines—these were but tools. They became excuses to avoid confronting the main issue. Much more worrying for Russia than any of them was the problem of command. Hindenburg, Ludendorff, Hoffmann, François, and even Prittwitz had independently contributed to the German victory. Their actions had coalesced because the principles underpinning their decisions were, broadly speaking, similar. The Grand Duke Nicholas, Zhilinskii, Rennenkampf, and Samsonov had all pulled in different and contradictory directions. The man held immediately responsible was Zhilinskii, replaced as Front commander by Nicholas Ruszkii on 17 September. But many felt Rennenkampf was to blame, for the defeat of the Masurian lakes as well as for Tannenberg. The panic which had overtaken the 1st army in defeat, its failure on 12 September to hold the Germans frontally while driving south against the weak German right, suggested major deficiencies in the army's command. Rennenkampf's detractors pointed to his German name, muttered about corruption and court favour.[101] Russia's ally had responded to defeat with a major restructuring of its higher command. Stavka attempted nothing comparable. The pre-war clique and the overlapping responsibilities in command were institutionalized rather than resolved.

SERBIA

On 28 July 1914 the Serbs destroyed the bridges across the Save and the Danube.[102] The following day Austro-Hungarian artillery opened fire across the river, in order to bombard Belgrade. These, the opening shots of the First World War, did at least reflect the war's immediate origins. Furthermore, at

[101] Frantz, *Russland auf dem Wege*, 125, 129; for a defence of Rennenkampf, see Gourko, *War and revolution*, 10–11, 62.

[102] Recent general accounts of the 1914 Serbian fighting are Jerabek, *Potiorek*; Dimitrije Djordjevic, 'Vojvoda Putnik, the Serbian high command, and strategy in 1914', in Kiraly *et al.* (eds.), *East Central European Society in World War I*; G. Rothenberg, *Journal of Military History*, LIII, (1989), 127–46; K. Peball, *Österreichische militärische Zeitschrift*, Sonderheft 1 (1965), 18–31; Schindler, *War in History*, VIII, (2001) (forthcoming); of the older literature, Pitreich, *1914*, is most helpful.

this stage the complaint of Austria's allies was not that the dual monarchy was concentrating against Serbia rather than Russia, but that it was doing so too slowly.

Within three days, however, Conrad had been persuaded that the major enemy lay to the north-east, not the south-west. In 1909 he had argued that the defeat of Serbia would take three months.[103] In August 1914 he could not sustain the concentration of forces which had underpinned this calculation. The 2nd army would have to turn back towards Galicia almost the moment its deployment on Serbia's northern frontier was complete. The 5th and 6th armies which would remain were intended to be sufficient for defence alone. Their three corps were brought up to a strength of 140,000 men only by the addition of Landsturm brigades; they lacked recent military experience, and 40 per cent of the total themselves belonged to south Slav ethnic groups.

Furthermore, Conrad now argued that a pro-Habsburg Balkan alliance should be the precondition of a campaign against Serbia, not its consequence. As in his youth, it was Italy that worried him. On 8 August he argued that an attack on Serbia only made sense if Bulgaria simultaneously launched four divisions across the Serbs' eastern frontier, so allowing the Austrians to maintain their guard against the Italians.[104] The cold-war warrior had got cold feet. In fact, of course, delay against Serbia did make sense—not, however, because of the Balkan position but because of the situation in Galicia. Following the logic of their own war plans, the Austro-Hungarian high command should have remained on the defensive in the south-east.

They did not. Conrad could only envisage the conduct of war in terms of grandiose offensives. Up to and including the 1909 Bosnian crisis, an ambitious scheme for the envelopment and defeat of Serbia—its army relatively unproven and its support from Russia unsure—could be justified. The legacy had not been shed in July 1914. Conrad's temperamental resistance to half-measures had led him to oppose plans for a limited operation against Serbia, designed to seize Belgrade, vulnerably situated on the Austro-Hungarian frontier.[105]

But Conrad was only in part to blame. The political pressure for an early attack on Serbia was considerable. Domestically, victory would quash irredentism; diplomatically, it would provide the foundations for a Balkan alliance. Strategically, pure defence, with inferior forces stretched along a frontier totalling 600 kilometres, their lateral communications so poor that rapid concentration would be impossible, had little to recommend it. Targets sensitive to Serb thrusts abounded, and if exploited would undermine the army's efforts against the Russians. To the north, Tisza was anxious lest Serbia advance

[103] Regele, *Conrad*, 266.   [104] Wank, *Austrian History Yearbook*, I (1968), 82–3.
[105] Regele, *Conrad*, 242–4.

into Hungary. To the west, Montenegro had thrown in its lot with Serbia, and a Serb sally in the direction of Sarajevo might rouse Bosnia. Thus, within the Balkans themselves the politico-strategic situation of 1914 conformed with the operational premisses of 1909 and before to argue for an offensive.[106]

Austria-Hungary, like Germany, had no properly developed machinery for the co-ordination of the political and military direction of the war. As in Germany, this was the task of the emperor. Supreme command was a royal prerogative. On 25 July Archduke Friedrich was appointed commander-in-chief for the operations in the Balkans. If Franz Ferdinand had been alive in all probability he would have exercised these functions. The new aspirant to the throne, Archduke Karl, was deemed too young and inexperienced for the task. Friedrich was chosen because he would let Conrad have his head, but would complement the chief of the general staff by moderating his more impulsive side and conveying royal gravitas in dealings with Germany. On 31 July, when the rest of the army was mobilized, Friedrich became commander-in-chief of the armed forces as a whole. With the elevation of Galicia over Serbia, Przemysl was chosen as his headquarters, and it now became necessary to appoint a separate theatre commander for the Balkans.[107]

Oskar Potiorek, the military governor of Bosnia, had been named commander of the 6th army. On 6 August he was also entrusted with responsibility for the Serbian front as a whole. He now had three jobs to do. He also had a new chief of staff, as his previous one, Erik von Merizzi, had been wounded at Sarajevo in the first assassination attempt on 28 June. Potiorek was blamed for the lax security arrangements on that day, and some have attributed his desire for a prompt offensive to personal reasons. But his involvement with plans for war with Serbia stretched back to the late 1880s. He was imbued with their long-term assumptions, and his scheme of operations was already well developed by 4 August. Conrad might automatically disown Potiorek's plan, but its political objectives and its excessive ambition both bore a Conradian stamp.

Potiorek had been passed over for the post of chief of the general staff in Conrad's favour. Thus, the most important difference between them was professional jealousy. Its symbol was the control and use of the 2nd army on Serbia's northern frontier: at an operational level its command was Potiorek's responsibility, at a strategic its deployment was Conrad's. Not until his formal appointment on 6 August did Potiorek know he was not to have full use of the 2nd army. It was a decision he never accepted. From 14 August he began to agitate for a measure of relative independence in relation to the army's supreme command, *Armee Oberkommando* (hereafter AOK). On 21 August he was formally placed under the direct authority of the emperor. Thus, Conrad lost control of the conduct of operations in the Balkans after late

---

[106] Ibid. 305–6; also Pitreich, *1914*, 73–83.   [107] Rauchensteiner, *Tod des Doppeladlers*, 110–11.

August. Conrad's defenders have projected back from this to argue that the chief of the general staff's better judgement was thwarted by Potiorek from the outset. In reality the position was even worse: two minds, not one, were shaping operations against Serbia.[108]

An offensive from the north, crossing the Danube and attacking Belgrade, would confer the quickest success. This was the conclusion of a study at the war school in May 1913, and it was one strongly advocated by many in 1914, including Alfred Krauss, formerly the war school's commandant and then chief of staff of the 5th army.[109] Such a plan kept the lines of communication short, and it exploited three potential routes into Serbia's interior. To the east of Belgrade a thrust on Semendria might open up the line of the Morava valley to Nis. To the west and south of the city the Kolubara river led towards Valjevo. Another offensive in Serbia's north-west corner, across the Save at Sabac, could converge on Valjevo from the opposite direction.

The danger was that the Serbs would not be drawn in to the defence of Belgrade. They might concentrate in the south or, even if they did not, they might fall back to Nis, so prolonging the campaign and extending the Austrians' lines of communication. During the Bosnian crisis, therefore, Conrad put the weight on the west, planning to support the thrust across the Save with another across the River Drina, and up the course of the Jadar to Valjevo. Between 1909 and 1914 this drift from north to west intensified. If the Serbs attacked the empire their most likely line of advance was into Bosnia-Herzogovina. Conrad stressed the difficulties of crossing the Danube, and removed from the command of the 5th army those (including Krauss) who disagreed with him. Potiorek, who had at first favoured the attack on Belgrade, went even further than Conrad. As commander of the 6th army, his responsibility was for the defence and security of Bosnia. He was anxious to encounter the Serbs as far east of Sarajevo as possible. He therefore planned to advance directly on Uzice, via Visegrad and crossing the upper Drina. The area was mountainous, it lacked road or rail communications, and a war game conducted in April 1914 revealed that independent attacks on the upper and lower Drina would be too far removed from each other to have reciprocal effects. The 6th army's advance would therefore be slow, hampered—in all probability— by unrest to its rear, as well as by stubborn Serb defence to its front.

The immediate strategic purpose of the offensive from the west was defence. It failed to meet any of the required political objectives of 1914. Vienna could not 'halt at Belgrade' as the Kaiser requested because it had no plan for such an operation; nor could the army deliver the quick victory the diplomats wanted

---

[108] Regele, *Conrad*, 302–4; also Rothenberg, 'Habsburg army in the First World War', in Kann *et al.* (eds.), *Habsburg empire in World War I*, 77; Österreichischer Bundesministerium für Heerwesen, *Österreich-Ungarns letzter Krieg*, i. 146–7.
[109] Rauchensteiner, *Tod des Doppeladlers*, 78, 114.

MAP 11. SERBIA

in order to shore up the empire's position in the Balkans. The offensive's
wider military purpose was to cut the Serbs' line of retreat from the south.
But the Austrians could not be sure of having accomplished this objective
until they had crossed the width of Serbia and reached Nis. In the interim the
Serb army would need to be held in the north, not left free to manoeuvre. Thus,
in practice the western offensive could not proceed without some form of attack
in the north, and vice versa. Operational demands meant that the success of a
thrust along any one axis would depend on some activity along the others.[110]

Accordingly, the plan for war with Serbia finalized in November 1913 contained both elements. The 5th and 6th armies would cross the lower and upper

[110] Jerabek, *Potiorek*, 94–5, 99–105.

Drina respectively, the 2nd army would attack on the Save, and a reinforced corps, the 'Gruppe Banat', would traverse the Danube east of Belgrade and push up the Morava valley. Throughout the July crisis Potiorek developed this plan, assuming that the Balkans would be the principal theatre of operations and that he would have full use of the 2nd army in its implementation. The decision to switch the 2nd army to Galicia ought, in terms of strict military logic, to have resulted in a move from offence to defence. The strength of the Austrian forces in the theatre was clipped from 370,000 men to a maximum of 290,000, including a large proportion of garrison troops; the Serbs swelled to 350,000 as they incorporated their reservists.[111] Potiorek was told that his minimum task was to prevent a Serb invasion of Austria-Hungary. But the maximum was not specified. Operationally, Conrad's acceptance of the offensive orthodoxy meant that he would not oppose an attack; diplomatically, Berchtold remained desperate for a Balkan victory. Potiorek was nothing loath. His administrative responsibilities in Bosnia-Herzogovina and the constant threat of Serb irridentism swelled him in his conviction that attack was the best form of defence and that the approach across the upper Drina should be the main avenue for such an operation. The fact that the 2nd army was only temporarily available confirmed him in his wisdom. It meant that he should act now while he still had the manpower advantage, and it confirmed that the main thrust would have to come from the west and not from the north.

On 6 August AOK gave Potiorek the use of the 2nd army until 18 August, when it would begin its move to Galicia; it was not to cross the Danube or the Save. Potiorek decided to centre his operations on the efforts of the 6th army, although lack of transport meant that it would not be able to concentrate near Sarajevo before 13 August. It would then have to march for five days before it could deploy on the River Drina. The pressure on the Serbs to the north would be lifted as that to the south began to take effect. The logical conclusion would have been to leave the 2nd army on the Serb frontier and to move the 5th, the army due to mount the thrust from the north-west along the Jadar river towards Valjevo, to Galicia. The fact that this option was not considered was not simply because there were too few railway lines to effect a switch sufficiently rapidly; it was also the product of the differing conceptions of Serbian operations entertained by Potiorek and Conrad. Potiorek saw the task of the 5th army as support for the movements of the 6th. The terrain which confronted it was less mountainous, and he wanted the 5th to push on Valjevo as fast as possible, weakening the flank of any Serb thrust from Uzice to Sarajevo, while itself inclining to the right so as to ease the path of the 6th. The Serbs would be drawn onto the 5th army and then hit in the flank by the 6th. Conrad

[111] Rauchensteiner, *Tod des Doppeladlers*, 128.

attached less importance to the 6th army. For him, the major offensive was to be mounted by the 5th, the focus therefore lay along the Save and the Danube, and the 2nd army could thus provide real diversionary aid to facilitate the 5th's opening moves. Potiorek protested that the 5th army was untrained for warfare in the mountains. He harked back to the plan concerted by Beck in 1882 and still preferred by Conrad in 1909, to encircle Serbia's army in its north-west corner, between the Save and the lower Drina. Massive envelopment would become impossible if the 5th army's offensive proved successful in fulfilling Conrad's aim, 'to defeat the enemy and to prevent him breaking into the empire through a thrust into his heartland'.[112]

Both plans egged on the 5th army and minimized the obstacles in its path. Conrad wanted it to exploit the availability of the 2nd army, and so was more concerned to achieve reciprocal action on the 5th's left than he was worried by the six days' gap between the attacks of the 5th and 6th armies on the right. Potiorek did not object because this separation in time was exactly what he hoped to achieve. He believed that the Serbs had only light forces on the lower Drina. Accumulating indications that this might not be true did no more than serve the hopes of both commanders that Serbia's forces would be pulled into its north-west corner and enveloped.

Conrad's growing respect for the Serbian army before the war had much justification. It had transformed itself from a poorly trained militia, relying on a spontaneous peasant uprising, into a modern conscript force, possessed of a professional officer corps and a body of trained reserves. All men aged between 20 and 27 were called up for two years' regular service. On reaching the age of 31 soldiers transferred first to a second and then to a third levy, finally completing their military liability when they were 50. Therefore, the first-levy strength of 180,000 men rose on mobilization to 350,000. Between 1898 and 1901 the closure of half the gymnasiums in Serbia and the increased availability of scholarships to the military academy had attracted to the army the bright and the ambitious. The officer corps saw itself as democratic, nationalist, and professional. In 1912 the army had mobilized ten infantry divisions and one cavalry division, and had beaten first the Turks and second, in 1913, the Bulgarians. Thus, unlike the Austro-Hungarians, the Serbs had recent battle experience. They had learnt the value of heavy artillery and the importance of entrenchment. The experience of guerrilla operations in Macedonia against the Turks had modified the formal tactics of European models.[113]

---

[112] Pitreich, *1914*, 98; in general, 88–98; also Peball, *Österreichische militärische Zeitschrift*, Sonderheft 1 (1965), 22.

[113] Gale Stokes, 'Milan Obrenovic and the Serbian army', in Kiraly *et al.* (ed.), *East Central European Society*, 555–67.

But the Balkan wars had also weakened the Serb army. The newly acquired territories had not been fully assimilated for military purposes, and parts were in near revolt. Total losses may have risen as high as 91,000. More serious for a country of such economic backwardness was the loss of equipment and the expenditure of ammunition. On 31 May 1914 the minister of war, having embarked on a ten-year programme to rebuild the army, declared that Serbia was not yet fit to fight.[114] The rifles in use were of a variety of types (ironically, the best and most widely used, Mausers, had been supplied by Germany), and there were only enough modern patterns for the peacetime complement of 180,000. In some units up to 30 per cent of infantrymen had no rifles at all. There was less than one machine-gun for each infantry battalion. The Serbs had acquired 272 75 mm field guns from the French, and had better field howitzers than the Austrians. But after they had given 100 guns to Montenegro, their total complement of field guns was 528, of which only 381 were quick-firers. Each first levy division had twenty to twenty-four guns as well as up to twelve howitzers, and each second levy division had half that, many of them not horsed. The recent fighting had depleted shell stocks. Serbia itself could produce 250 to 260 shells per day, but only enough powder for eighty to 100. It had about 700 rounds per gun in stock, and looked to France and Russia to make up the deficit.[115] The Serbs' reliance on the Entente powers for equipment created a dependence that robbed them of strategic freedom, and a vulnerability which their land-locked isolation did nothing to mitigate. The Russians sent 150,000 rifles, the French sent artillery; in exchange, both powers demanded that the Serbs attack.

The bulk of the Serbian army on the war's outbreak was concentrated in Macedonia, in anticipation of war with Bulgaria. This threat to the east could never be totally discounted. Furthermore, the value of the ally to the west, Montenegro, was limited. The 35,000 men of its national militia had only sixty-five guns and thirty machine-guns; it possessed no real headquarters, and there were no plans for joint operations with the Serbs. The nominal commander-in-chief of the Serb army was Crown Prince Alexander, whose reputation (and political ambition) had been reinforced by the success of the Balkan wars. But the real direction of war rested with the chief of staff, Radomir Putnik. Putnik, the son of a teacher, a gunner and former lecturer at the military academy, had stood at the apex of the Serbian army since 1903—as chief of the general staff for most of the time, and minister of war for the rest. He was 67 and he was suffering from emphysema, but he had two great strengths: he commanded the

[114] Ibid. 567; Mark Cornwall, 'Serbia', in Wilson (ed.), *Decisions for war*, 58.
[115] Djordjevic, in Wilson (ed.), *Decisions for war*, 569–70; also Renouvin, *La Crise Européenne*, 219–20; Larcher, *La grande guerre dans les Balkans*, 30; Österreichischer Bundesministerium, *Österreich-Ungarns letzter Krieg*, i. 97–101; Lyon, *Journal of Military History*, LXI (1997), 481–502.

respect of the competing political groups in Serbia, and he was thoroughly familiar with the plans for his country's defence.

Putnik's return from taking the waters at Gleichenberg was followed by a bout of pneumonia. He did not, therefore, arrive at his headquarters until 5 August. Extraordinarily, he had taken with him the keys to the safe in which Serbia's war plans were locked, and his staff had to blow it open before they could begin the process of mobilization and concentration.[116] The Serbs had expected their mobilization to be slow—not because of this haphazard start to the war but because the railway lines for moving their forces from south to north were inadequate. The country was divided into five divisional regions, each being responsible for raising one first levy division and one second levy. But the result of Serbia's enlargement and of the problems in the south was that seventeen infantry regiments were outside their mobilization areas. Furthermore, the deplacement to the south meant that, whereas in 1912 half the army had been able to march to the front, in 1914 only 30 per cent could do so. The rest had to go by train. Of the 2,023 carriages required, 1,597 were available. The deployment plan had been drawn up in 1908, and it may subsequently have been updated in the light of information derived from Colonel Redl and passed on by the Russians.[117] Its preparation had been ordered on 11 July. The Serbs, as the Austrians appreciated, had at least had plenty of practice in the drills of mobilization. Furthermore, Putnik had an able deputy in the shape of Zivojin Misic. By 10 August the Serbs' concentration was complete.

Putnik's preferred modus operandi was offensive defence: he deployed defensively and in depth, but only as a preliminary to the counter-attack. He reckoned that, on balance, the Austrians would attack from the north. However, he concentrated his three armies in such a way that they could, if necessary, face a threat from the west. They were placed in a central position in north Serbia, along the east–west railway line from Palanka to Valjevo. A separate group in Uzice guarded their rear from an attack and linked with the Montenegrins. The 2nd Serb army was reinforced and given the principal operational task—either to counter-attack against the right flank of an invasion from the north or the left flank of one from the west. The 3rd army, on the 2nd's left, was poised to counter any thrust from the Drina–Save triangle. Frontier guards had the task of identifying the main direction of the enemy's attack.

Potiorek began his advance on 12 August. His forces had not had time to complete their concentration, their supply services in particular still struggling to catch up. The 5th army lacked sufficient bridging equipment, and its

[116] Djordjevic ' "Vojvoda" Radomir Putnik', in Kiraly et al. (eds.), East Central European War Leaders, 234.

[117] Lyon, Journal of Military History, LXI (1997), 488, 494–5; Jerabek, Potiorek, 106; Cornwall, 'Serbia', in Wilson (ed.), Decisions for war, 74; Williamson, Austria-Hungary, 102.

commander had wanted to postpone the attack for two days. The Drina was a formidable obstacle—broad, deep, fast-flowing, with steep, wooded banks. The 5th army did not get across until 15 August. AOK allowed the 2nd army to establish bridgeheads at Mitrovica and Sabac. By the 14th Putnik had concluded that the 5th Austro-Hungarian army's thrust on Valjevo was the main attack, and the 2nd's on Sabac was secondary. He began warily—for he was still anxious about the position in the north—to move his armies westward, with the 2nd army to the north, the 3rd in the centre, and the 1st to the south. On 15 August the 5th Austro-Hungarian army, supported on its left by elements of the 2nd, ran into the 2nd and 3rd Serb armies on a front shielded by the Dobrava and Jadar rivers. The Austrians, sniped at by guerrillas, toiled uphill in soaring temperatures. They had outstripped their supplies and they were not equipped for mountain warfare. Frank, the 5th army's commander, was preoccupied with the threat of envelopment by the 2nd Serbian army on his left; Potiorek continued to stress the right. The latter's orders on 16 August treated the Serbs as beaten troops and set distant objectives on the Kolubara river. But Putnik, focusing on the centre rather than on the flanks, fought a stubborn battle on the Cer plateau. With the 2nd Serb army holding to its front, the 3rd Serb army was able to restore the situation on Putnik's left. Potiorek now shifted his attention to the Austrian left. But it was stuck at the Sabac bridgehead.

On the Austro-Hungarian left Potiorek demanded to be allowed to commit all the 2nd army against the Serb right. Conrad, however, was anxious to move the 2nd army to Galicia on 18 August as planned, and would only agree to the temporary release of one corps to the 5th army. This, Tersztyansky's IV corps, attacked on 19 August, but then, just as the 2nd Serb army was about to give way, broke off on the orders of AOK. VIII corps of the 5th army, elements of which had been hit hard in a Serb attack on the Cer plateau on the night of 16 August, was ordered to withdraw across the Drina; at least one division had lost a third of its rifle strength. By 20 August the 5th army's other corps, XIII, was unsupported: Frank told IV corps to fall back across the Save, an order reiterated by AOK. But Potiorek instructed IV corps to hold the Sabac bridgehead, so as to enable the 5th army to stay east of the Drina. The Austrians were shaken by the ferocity of the Serb attacks and by the way in which the entire population rallied to the country's defence. The 2nd army began its move to Galicia on 20 August, although IV corps stayed behind until the 24th as it continued to hold the Sabac bridgehead. The 2nd army had been denied a decisive role in Serbia. It could have achieved a major success at Sabac only if it had put its entire strength across the Save. Furthermore, by acting so close to the 5th army, it failed to mount any major threat along the Danube, opposite Belgrade. Thus, Putnik was able to leave weak forces in the north and east and concentrate to the west.

In practice, therefore, the 6th army had to support the 5th army, not vice versa as Potiorek had planned. Under Potiorek's personal command it completed its approach and deployment on schedule. On 20 and 21 August it won local successes at Visegrad and Priboj. But their effect was too late and too distant from the main battlefield. The Serbs were able to fight a series of separate battles on interior lines. The 6th army fell back. Potiorek had failed to combine in time or space, Putnik had not.[118]

With its own territory clear, at least for the moment, Serbia began to pay the price of its dependence on its allies. Russia, which had entered the war in Serbia's defence, now demanded that Serbia launch an attack into Austria-Hungary in order to draw Austrian troops away from Galicia and so support the South-West Front's advance. Potiorek's offensive suggested that there were few Austro-Hungarian forces to the north and that Herzogovina and south-east Bosnia were only weakly held. On 6 September the 1st Serb army crossed the Save in the direction of Srem, just north of Belgrade, while the 2nd army launched a feint against Mitrovica to the left. The remainder of the 2nd and all the 3rd army faced the Austrian 5th and 6th armies on the Drina. To the south, the Uzice group and the Montenegrins moved behind the 6th Austrian army, towards Sarajevo, hoping to trigger a popular rising in Bosnia.

Potiorek attributed his first defeat to the interventions of AOK and the loss of the 2nd army, rather than to his own failings. He began immediately, on 24 August, to plan a second attack, and AOK, sensitive to the possibility of Serb offensive, approved its commencement on 3 or 4 September. But Frank dragged his feet: the 5th army had lost more than a quarter of its strength of 80,000 men, and needed to re-equip and re-form. Potiorek, therefore, brought the 6th army further north, to the middle Drina, so closing the gap with the 5th army. Rain postponed his attack, and then came news of the Serbs' advance across the Save. XV corps, the formation linking the 6th army's left to the 5th's right, was not yet ready, but Potiorek ordered the reluctant Frank to attack, together with XVI corps from the 6th army's right. The 5th army's attack on 8 September, unsupported by artillery and with its pontoons swirling in the river, failed. But to the south XVI corps, striking north-east across the front of XV corps and to the south of Loznica, got across the middle Drina with light losses and hit the flank of the 3rd Serb army. The Serbs had to bring elements of the Uzice group up to support their 3rd army, so weakening their advance on Visegrad. The Serb invasion of Bosnia failed to produce any popular response, despite the use of bands of guerrillas dubbed Cetniks, and the Serbs and Montenegrins fell out.

The success of the 6th army enabled Frank's 5th army to renew its efforts to cross the Drina on 13 September. Heavy rain continued to hamper bridging

---

[118] Jerabek, *Potiorek*, 119–31.

operations, and once on the far bank both armies found their mountain guns outmoded when confronted with the Serbs' quick-firing field artillery. Potiorek's struggles to break out of the bridgeheads which had been established by the 15th peaked in the mountainous areas south of Loznica on 21 and 22 September: control of Jagodnja changed four times on the 22nd alone. By then the 5th and 6th armies were held, but their efforts had been enough to neutralize the Serb offensives to their north and south. The Serbs, having penetrated sufficiently deeply into Hungary to force the evacuation of Semlin, broke off the attack in response to the advance of Frank's 5th army, and were back across the Save by the morning of 14 September. On 23 September the Uzice group and the Montengrins broke into south-east Bosnia, followed a few days later by the first of the snow. Rallying fortress troops to the support of his field formations, Potiorek took the Serbs in their northern flank and by 30 October had driven them back across the upper Drina.

Krauss had once again urged Potiorek to follow up the retreating 1st Serb army with a direct attack on Belgrade. But Potiorek had too few men to sustain operations simultaneously on the northern and western fronts. His complaints, that Conrad was starving him of troops and, above all, of munitions to feed the Galician front, at first found a sympathetic hearing. The invasion of Hungary, even if checked, had alarmed Tisza, and Berchtold remained dependent on smashing Serbia to carry through his Balkan diplomacy. By October, however, Potiorek's refrain reflected the consequences of the positional warfare which now prevailed on the Drina front, as on others. Potiorek's operational solutions were not adapted to the new circumstances, or to the resources available to him, but continued to be derived from textbooks. In military, if not political, circles his efforts to undermine Conrad began to lose him face. Whereas in August he had yet to secure his independence of AOK, by October he had, and the fact that he failed to deliver according to the grandiose expectations he generated reflected badly on him rather than on AOK. He had a ready-made scapegoat in Frank, characterized by one officer as senile, pedantic, and obstinate. But Potiorek protected the 5th army's commander because he was also malleable. Caught in the crossfire between Potiorek and Conrad, Arthur von Bolfras, the chief of the emperor's military chancellery, became sufficiently frustrated by the end of September to consider installing Franz Joseph as commander-in-chief, with himself as chief of staff.[119]

Strategically, if not tactically, Serbia had won a major victory. Austria-Hungary's bid to use military might to re-establish its Balkan pre-eminence had been thwarted. And yet its need for prestige prevented the dual monarchy from simply abandoning operations on its southern front. Conrad advocated the adoption of a defensive position against Serbia. He reckoned that a victory

[119] Jerabek, *Potiorek*, 150–61; Rauchensteiner, *Tod des Doppeladlers*, 133–6.

against Russia in Galicia, not the conquest of Serbia, would settle the Balkan aspirations of the empire. Potiorek disagreed. The tug of war between the two for troops kept the Austrian forces on the Drina stronger than they needed to be for true defence, but still too weak for a major offensive. The same applied in Galicia. Thus, in neither theatre was a decisive concentration achieved.

GALICIA

The embroilment of the Austro-Hungarian army in offensive operations in Serbia, and its inability to bring them to a speedy conclusion, was the third in a succession of blows knocking away the props of Conrad's plans for operations in Galicia. The first, evident by January 1914, had been his realization that Austria-Hungary could not rely on the support of Romania, a covert adherent to the Triple Alliance. The second was the German decision to concentrate on the defence of East Prussia rather than on the drive into Poland.

The manpower implications of these losses demanded a fundamental change in operational planning. Romania's support would have secured Conrad's southern flank and contributed up to 600,000 men; German operations in Poland would have reinforced the north. Of the four corps in the 2nd army, only two were released on 18 August, a third was retained until the 24th, and the fourth never left the Serb front. The first two corps did not reach Galicia until 28 August, and the third until 4 September. The total Austro-Hungarian strength in Galicia was thirty-seven divisions, and until 28 August only thirty-one divisions. The slowness of this concentration, in part the product of the mobilization against Serbia, but much more the result of Conrad's decision to delay the mobilization against Russia until 4 August, meant that Austria-Hungary abandoned its attempt to gain any compensating advantage in time.

Thus, from an anticipation of relative superiority, Conrad had to adjust his expectations to one of inferiority. At first it seemed that he would do so. The decision to deploy further west, on the San and the Dniester, implied a defensive intention. But Conrad was never good at modifying his grandiose strategic objectives in the light of reality. Franz Joseph was later to say of him: 'We cannot find any suitable sphere of activity for a chief of staff with such soaring plans. We would be far better off with a man who doesn't want to bridge the ocean.'[120] The great envelopment operation, the convergence of the Austrians and the Germans on Siedlitz, east of Warsaw, increasingly played on Conrad's imagination. The thrust northwards into Galicia began to lose its

---

[120] Silberstein, *Troubled alliance*, 278.

preliminary, precautionary intention; conceived as a move to clear the line of the Vistula before turning east, it had by 15 August become an operation in its own right, the southern pincer of a joint envelopment of the Russians in Poland. Having deployed to defend, the Austro-Hungarian army advanced to the attack. The long marches with which the Austrians had intended to weaken the Russians were instead imposed on themselves.

When Conrad's plans miscarried he blamed anybody but himself. His principal targets were his allies, for their failure to support the invasion of Poland. He argued that OHL had only told him of their abandonment of the Siedlitz manoeuvre when it was already too late to change his intentions. This was untrue. Moltke told him that the Germans would fight defensively in East Prussia on 3 August; on 20 August Conrad responded that he would advance on Lublin and Cholm nonetheless.[121] He blamed his intelligence services. The conduct of long-range cavalry reconnaissance by both sides in Galicia, particularly given the suitability of the terrain, was of extraordinary incompetence. On 15 August the full strength of the Austro-Hungarian cavalry crossed the frontier to establish the whereabouts of the enemy. But by then, because of Conrad's decision to deploy back from the frontier, many regiments had already been on the move for a week. They now had only four days in which to gather information over an area 144 kilometres deep on a 400-kilometre front. They had outstripped their divisional infantry and artillery, and were themselves trained for dismounted action. They therefore lacked the firepower to penetrate the Russian screen. As in East Prussia, the Russian cavalry filled the gaps between corps rather than pushing forward to scout, and so the two bodies failed to encounter each other. The Austro-Hungarian cavalry came back with little information of value. The combination of these demands with a new but ill-fitting saddle halved the horse strength of Conrad's mounted formations virtually from the outset of the campaign.[122]

Conrad expected about fifty Russian divisions to be concentrated on Galicia. Despite the defects in information collection, this was a good enough calculation. His difficulty was in the accurate plotting of their deployment. Early indications suggested that their main force was to the north, in the area Brest-Litovsk–Ivangorod–Cholm, and that any forces on the eastern Galician frontier were falling back rather than coming forward. Aerial reconnaissance reported that there were no major Russian formations on the roads between the line Proskurov–Tarnopol to the north and the River Dniester to the south. This was what Conrad wanted to hear; it compensated for the absence of the 2nd army in Serbia and it confirmed his own wish to strike north. Contra-

[121] Herwig, *First World War*, 89.
[122] Rauchensteiner, *Tod des Doppeladlers*, 126–7; Stone, *Eastern front*, 78–82; Pitreich, *1914*, 145–8; a general account in English of the Galician campaign, based on the Austrian official history, is in *Army Quarterly*, XXII (1931), 23–40, 261–80.

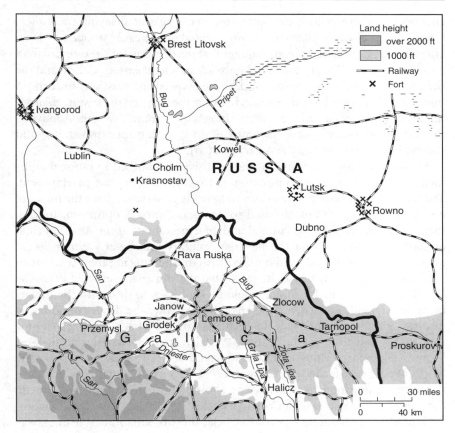

MAP 12. GALICIA

dictory information was suppressed. From 18 August Hermann Kövess's group, containing elements of two corps and responsible for screening eastern Galicia until the arrival of the 2nd army, reported encounters with Russians. On 23 August a captured Russian officer revealed that the whole of the Russian 8th army was deployed around Proskurov; Conrad still refused to believe it. In fact, not one but two Russian armies were advancing from the east, marching by night but protected by the woods from overhead observation by day.[123]

Thus, neither the actions of his German allies nor those of his Russian opponents could deflect Conrad from his set intentions. As long before as 1878 he had stressed the need to seize the initiative in any war with Russia in Galicia. This emphasis was reinforced rather than moderated by the prospect of numerical inferiority. The possibility that weakness would increase, that the

[123] Tunstall, *Planning for war*, 228–34.

enemy's strength would grow, were arguments against delaying the attack. Once into the Galician plains the Russians could not be easily stopped.[124] Even after the war, Conrad remained adamant that the decision for the offensive had been the right one. He argued that the abandonment of eastern Galicia and the occupation of the Carpathians would have allowed the Russians to turn on Berlin. Furthermore, he had to attack between the Bug and the Vistula in order to protect both Silesia and the Austro-Hungarian communications. A move to the east would not only leave the centre of the eastern front exposed, it would also pull the Germans and the Austrians apart.[125]

Although Conrad's espousal of the offensive was clothed in rational argument, its basis lay in wishful thinking, in the hope of the great envelopment. The Germans, for their part, anxious to have the Austrians relieve the pressure on East Prussia, were not disposed to dampen Conrad's optimism. Indeed, they themselves could be as fanciful in their expectations as the Austrian chief of staff. On 1 August 1914 the Bavarian military attaché at German headquarters managed to reduce the likely Russian forces facing the Austrians to two armies of five corps each: he calculated that three armies would face the Germans, and that major forces would be kept back to deal with the threats posed by Finland, Sweden, and Japan, and to counter the danger of domestic disorder. He also assumed that the Russians would fall back, trading space for time as they had done in 1812. Thus, an Austrian attack against the South-West Front would be victorious, and Conrad would be free to press on to strike the North-West Front facing the Germans.[126] This sort of scenario, which gave the Austro-Hungarian army so decisive a role on the eastern front, was exactly the sort of thinking to which Conrad's weaker side could so easily fall victim.

Conrad's main concentration in Galicia, the 3rd, 4th, and 1st armies, was completed between 19 and 23 August. The 3rd, on the right, was drawn up round Lemberg, facing east. Its task, together with that of the 2nd when eventually it arrived, was to guard the flank of the 4th and 1st armies. These latter two, the 4th round Przemysl and the 1st at the confluence of the San and the Vistula, were to strike north-east. Dankl, commanding the 1st army on the left, was ordered on 22 August to advance in the direction of Lublin, and Auffenberg with the 4th was told to follow a day later in the direction of Cholm. If the Russians, against expectation, attacked further south, moving from east to west, they would be held by the 3rd army while the 4th and 1st described a great arc to the north and fell on their rear. The front covered by these three armies was enormous, about 280 kilometres. It would be extended as the attack to the north developed. Furthermore, the left wing did not enjoy the preponderance of strength over the right envisaged by Conrad in his March 1914 plan. The 1st army was intended to be twelve divisions strong, and the 4th

[124] Regele, *Conrad*, 317–18, 444–9; Tunstall, *Planning for war*, 218.
[125] Peball, *Conrad*, 105–8.   [126] Schulte, *Europäische Krise*, 208.

was to begin with eight and then be increased to ten or twelve by elements of the 2nd army. In fact, both the 1st and 4th armies contained nine divisions each. Thus, Conrad's operational bias in favour of the thrust to the north was not reflected in his deployment. Nor was the eventual arrival of the 2nd army calculated to improve the situation. To fulfil his initial intentions, the 2nd army should have moved to the left, to western Galicia; the railways were available for it to do so. In fact it went to the right, to eastern Galicia, a victim of poor liaison between the operations department and the railway department. Conrad's response to the situation was increasingly divorced from reality. Rather than reflect concern about his poor force-to-space ratio, he made a virtue of the fact that the 2nd army would arrive both late and in the wrong place, giving the right wing a more offensive role and allowing Brudermann's 3rd army to push eastwards. Thus, Conrad's convex line was pushed further outwards, its component parts pursuing divergent objectives, not massing for a decisive attack.[127]

Whereas Austro-Hungarian planning lacked coherence despite unity of command, Russian objectives differed precisely because direction was not centralized. Ultimately, however, Russia's numbers meant that its problems proved less grievous. By the thirtieth day of mobilization the Russians had forty-five infantry divisions and over eighteen cavalry divisions in the Galician theatre. The 9th army forming in Poland added another eight-and-a-half infantry divisions. Against thirty-seven Austro-Hungarian divisions, and two ill-equipped German Landwehr divisions under von Woyrsch screening Silesia, the Russians had a considerable margin for error.

As in East Prussia, Russian intentions represented two sets of plans superimposed on each other—one drawn up by the South-West Front and one by Stavka. Both assumed that the Austrians would concentrate close to their eastern frontier, round Lemberg. The Front chief of staff was Alekseev. His plan, reflecting his pre-war emphasis on the priority and relative independence of the war against Austria-Hungary, saw Cracow as the key to Austrian control of eastern Galicia. The railway lines running west to east through Cracow were superior in capacity to those crossing the Carpathians. Thus, a Russian attack, launched from the line Ivangorod–Lublin–Cholm towards Cracow, would have the effect of cutting the main Austro-Hungarian line of communications, pushing the Austrians south, and pinning them against the wall of the Carpathians. Stavka, and specifically Danilov, envisaged an operation that was much more cautious in its intentions. Rather than descend from the north, they proposed to advance from the east. However, Danilov recognized the value of Alekseev's proposal to the development of the second phase of operations, the attack from Poland. The attack on Cracow would drive the

---

[127] Pitreich, *1914*, 126–38, 152–9.

forces of the two Central Powers apart and would expose Silesia. Therefore both attacks, that from the north and that from the east, were approved, and were clothed as a masterful scheme for double envelopment.[128]

The differing conceptions underpinning this apparent unity were evident as soon as the concentration and deployment of the South-West Front began. The Russian armies, the 4th, 5th, 3rd, and 8th, were drawn up along the Galician frontier from Ivangorod to Romania. Alekseev's plan suggested that the 4th army, on the right, should be strongest; Stavka's favoured the newly formed 8th army on the left. In reality the two central armies claimed twenty-two of the then-available thirty-eight divisions. The strength in the centre conformed with the Russians' continuing expectation, based on their acquisition of pre-war Austrian plans, that the enemy would concentrate round Lemberg. They proved very reluctant to modify this supposition, despite intelligence reports to the contrary. The 4th and 5th armies on the right were in conjunction stronger than the 3rd and 8th on the left. The latter, according to Alekseev's plan, should have advanced first, to pin the Austrians in eastern Galicia. In practice, the Grand Duke's anxiety to respond to the urgent promptings of his French allies now—as in East Prussia—led him to push his armies forward before their concentrations were complete. Still convinced that the Austrians were around Lemberg and about to advance to the east, the Grand Duke cut across the intentions of the Front command and prematurely pressed the 4th army across the San and west of Przemysl. The poverty of communications on the southern wing soon slowed the advance of the 3rd and 8th armies. Thus, the 4th and 5th armies, moving from north to south, encountered the main weight of the Austro-Hungarian army, the 4th and 1st armies, advancing from south to north and not as yet distracted by any major threat to the east.

On 23 August the 4th Russian army and the 1st Austro-Hungarian army ran into each other east of the San, and on the 24th Dankl was pushing the Russians back towards Krasnik. The Russians still refused to modify their expectations of Conrad, and, despite its superior numbers, saw Dankl's 1st army as independent from the 4th, which was construed in its turn as the flank guard for the anticipated Lemberg concentration. Therefore they interpreted the Krasnik operations, not as the major Austro-Hungarian thrust but as an opportunity for isolating and enveloping Dankl. The commander of the 4th Russian army was blamed for the tactical setback at Krasnik—once again, troops on the advance had attacked semi-fortified positions with insufficient preparation [129] —and was replaced by Alexei Evert. The 9th army, forming in Poland, detached a corps to reinforce Evert's right, and the 5th army (commanded by

---

[128] Stone, *Eastern front*, 82–4; Golovine, *Revue militaire française*, 158 (1934), 220–50, and 159 (1934), 281–301.
[129] Knox, *With the Russian army*, i. 101; Churchill, *Unknown war*, 150.

Plehve) moved to its right to threaten Dankl's rear. Dankl had, for the time being, relieved any Russian pressure on Silesia by way of Poland.

Conrad still underestimated the threat to the east, and therefore he too pivoted round Dankl. But the moment for an Austro-Hungarian victory on the left was already passing. The apparent success of the 1st army had to be weighed against the slow arrival of Auffenberg's 4th army, whose concentration was still not complete when its advance began. Dankl was pulled in two directions, first to his outer flank and the possibilities of lapping round the Russians, and second to closing the gap to his right. The latter prevailed. Thus, the 1st army was drawn into a frontal battle, and its movements made to conform to those of the 4th army, not the 4th's to the 1st's. Furthermore, the 4th was due to be reinforced on its right with three divisions drawn from Brudermann's army. By the evening of 25 August, when Auffenberg's 4th army was coming up on Dankl's right, Conrad's focus was not on the 1st army and its thrust towards Lublin, but further east, on the 4th and Krasnostav. Auffenberg's army therefore hit Plehve's left flank as Plehve hit Dankl's right. Auffenberg, his audacity fed by his gross underestimate of the strength of Plehve's force (he imagined that only three divisions confronted him), pushed his flank forward hoping to envelop the Russians. His prospects of doing so were facilitated by Plehve's attention to Dankl and by the imminence of the three divisions from Brudermann. By 29 August, after three days of confused and desperate combat, Auffenberg's forces had not only pushed in Plehve on his left but had also separated him from Evert on his right. The three corps of the 5th Russian army were in immediate danger of envelopment. On the 30th Plehve decided to fall back on Krasnostav. By doing so he would expose Evert's left flank. Simultaneously, the news of Samsonov's defeat and the apparent imminence of German victory in the west suggested the possibility of a German attack into Poland, and thus danger to the rears of the 5th and 4th armies. Conrad's northern thrust between the Bug and the Vistula seemed on the verge of success.

However, Conrad's mood was not so confident. On the evening of the 25th Brudermann's 3rd army and Kövess's group, securing the Dniester before the arrival of the 2nd army (commanded by Böhm-Ermolli) from Serbia, were being pulled north-east, not east, to conform with the movements of the 4th and 1st armies. However, the Russian 3rd army detached only a cavalry division to the north, and kept its main weight moving steadily—but slowly—westwards towards Lemberg. Ivanov, the Front commander, and Dragomirov, the 3rd army's chief of staff, were still convinced that the main Austrian concentration lay directly in the 3rd army's path. On 26 August, Brudermann's weakened 3rd Austro-Hungarian army, mistaking Russian deliberation for Russian weakness, attacked Ruzskii's 3rd army at Zlocow and on the River Zlota Lipa. Brudermann's task was to halt the Russians before they took Lemberg, but his attacks were poorly co-ordinated, and pushed in too quickly for effective artillery support. The Austrians' losses were heavy, and the Russians—turning from defence to counter-attack—drove them back. Brudermann reckoned that he was threatened on both wings as well as to his front. Conrad's policy of pushing to the northern flank had weakened his centre, and opened gaps between his armies. One hundred kilometres separated the 3rd army from the 4th, but if he brought the 4th army south-east he would open the distance between it and the 1st. Caught between the prospects of Auffenberg and the threat to Lemberg, Conrad twice recalled the three divisions released from the 3rd army to the 4th and twice gave them back again. Force-to-space ratios also restricted his options to the south: although tempted to bring the 2nd army up from the south to strike the Russian flank, he had to acknowledge that for the moment—with IV corps still extracting itself from Serbia—it lacked the strength to be effective.[130]

In the event the Austrians had time to take up defensive positions on the next river line, the Gnila Lipa. Ruszki's pursuit remained cautious. He argued that his units were still dispersed as a result of their precipitate advance, their supply columns trailing in the rear. Ivanov's deployment was complete by 30 August. He enjoyed a two-to-one superiority, with little more than two corps facing the four corps of Brusilov's 8th army on the 3rd's southern flank. Brusilov used his two central corps to pin the Austrians while his VII corps, on the right, crossed the river and outflanked Kövess's group, driving it south and away from Brudermann's 3rd. By the evening of the 30th the latter was routed, its troops falling back to Lemberg in disorder. Conrad, though on the verge of at least a local victory in the north, was being overtaken by defeat in the south. On 2 September the 3rd army gave up Lemberg without a fight and fell back 32 kilometres.

Stavka's new priority was to recover the situation in the north, and above all to ensure that neither the 5th army nor the 4th suffered the same fate as Rennenkampf's 2nd. On the 30th itself the immediate danger to Plehve was lifted. False reports that Russian troops were advancing to his aid caused the Austrian pincers to look to the safety of their own flanks and rears long enough to open a 32-kilometre gap through which the 5th army could escape. The 9th army in Poland was brought in against Dankl's left, so supporting the 4th's right. The gap between the 3rd and the 5th armies, which had opened to three or four days' march, began to be closed by Stavka's repeated insistence that Ivanov and Ruzskii put their preoccupation with Lemberg to one side, and push the 3rd army north of the city to Plehve's aid. The task of occupying Lemberg and covering the Russian left was allocated to Brusilov's 8th army.

[130] Tunstall, *Planning for war*, 238–43.

While the Russians inclined to the north on 1 September, the Austrians moved to the south. Thus, at the very stage, after Tannenberg, when the Germans might have been free to push south-westwards into Poland, Conrad himself moved away from a joint envelopment in the centre of the eastern front to another independent Austro-Hungarian undertaking; although Conrad called on OHL to implement the Siedlitz operation four times between 23 August and 1 September, it was far from being AOK's only and constant preoccupation. Auffenberg was told to abandon his pursuit of Plehve, and to turn on the 3rd Russian army. His immediate task was to save Brudermann's army and, with it, to forestall the loss of Lemberg. But from the evening of 2 September, as the collapse of the 3rd Austro-Hungarian army became clear, a more ambitious conception gripped Conrad. He noted the slowness and deliberation of the Russian advance. He also, mistakenly, concluded that Plehve's army was defeated. His cavalry was too broken to lift the veil over the Russian movements. What Conrad now aspired to was nothing less than the envelopment of the Russian 3rd and 8th armies. The entry of his 2nd army from Serbia, the continued resistance of Halicz on Brusilov's left flank (it did not fall till 3 September), created the opportunity to attack the Russian rear from the south. Auffenberg was to take the rear of the 3rd Russian army from the north. As before, and as would happen again, Conrad's imagination out-stripped the dictates of common sense: the task of envelopment which he now set his troops took no account of their numbers or of the punishing schedule of battles and marches which they had already undergone. The 4th army could only engage its divisions *seriatim*. The 2nd army, its attacks uncoordinated and unsupported, made little impact on Brusilov; the 3rd—the body around which the movements of the 2nd and 4th armies pivoted—was already broken. The Russians in the south, although no longer enjoying a numerical superiority, were not advancing into a sack, as Conrad might hope, but into a paper bag with the bottom blown out.

Brusilov's 8th army, on the line of lakes at Grodek, west of Lemberg, and the 3rd army to the north at Rava Ruska accomplished the tasks which they had been set. Attacking despite their numerical inferiority, they fixed the Austrian 2nd and 3rd armies from 6 September. Auffenberg's 4th army, going south, met Ruzskii's 3rd going north. The latter, aided by two corps of Plehve's undefeated army, outflanked the former to the north-east. On 8 September Conrad ordered Auffenberg to hold on the front Rava Ruska–Janow, while attacking with the 2nd and 3rd armies at and to the south of Lemberg. But the 3rd army was now being pulled into the 4th's battle on its left. Conrad hoped that the 2nd army could redeem the situation, relying on his greater strength in the south to roll the Russians up to the north. But the Russian 8th army held. On 9 September Dankl's 1st army to the north, left isolated against stronger Russian forces, and with a large gap between its right and the main Austrian forces, was already falling back to the San. Plehve's 5th army exploited the widening gap between Auffenberg and Dankl. As the Austrians fought to stabilize their position west of Lemberg, their weakness to the north exposed the 4th army's rear. On 11 September Auffenberg, the full dimensions of the Russian manoeuvre revealed to him by wireless intercepts, pulled back to the south-east. Conrad had no choice but to order a retreat to the Dniester, and then to the San.

The defeat suffered by the Austro-Hungarian army in Galicia ought to have been shattering. Its total losses were about 350,000 men; some divisions were reduced to a third of their combatant strength. Particularly grievous in the long run were the disproportionately high casualties among junior officers and professional NCOs. Those that remained were exhausted: Auffenberg's 4th army had been in the front line for twenty-one days and had been engaged in combat for eighteen of them. When, on 10 September, AOK drafted its by-now customary appeal to the Germans, its request was not that they manoeuvre on Siedlitz, but that they send troops straight from France to Galicia.[131]

The message was never sent. Pride intervened, but so too did the realization that the army was still intact. Its retreat was chaotic. After the surrender of Lemberg supply dumps were set on fire so that nothing but charred rubbish remained for the remants of the 3rd army. Its transport collapsed. One thousand locomotives and 15,000 wagons were abandoned.[132] The roads, turned to mud by heavy rain, were crowded with refugees. Older reservists succumbed to their lack of fitness. But Conrad asserted himself. Brudermann, sacked on 5 September, was only the most distinguished of those purged. The 3rd army's chief of staff also went, as did the corps commanders of the 4th army. Franz Joseph endeavoured to protect the reputations of his generals, demanding a careful inquiry into each case. His efforts, a vain attempt to reflect the monarch's authority over his army, were fruitless: by the year's end four of the original six Austro-Hungarian army commanders were dismissed. Conrad may have been covering his own back; he acknowledged to his staff that Franz Ferdinand, had he been alive, would have had him shot.[133] However, his justification was that, in the succeeding days, both tactically and operationally the Austrians responded with good sense. They were reading Russian wireless traffic with a maximum delay of three days, and so could offset Russian numbers with Austrian anticipation.[134] The Russian use of the defensive and of field fortifications, learnt in Manchuria and applied at the Zlota Lipa and on the Gnila Lipa, was emulated by the Habsburg army.[135] From mid-September the Austrians too began to entrench. And, as at Mau-

[131] Rauchensteiner, *Tod des Doppeladlers*, 161–3.
[132] Herwig, *First World War*, 92.
[133] Ibid. 94–5; Rauchensteiner, *Tod des Doppeladlers*, 163, 187–8.
[134] Glaise von Horstenau, *Ein General im Zwielicht*, 343.
[135] Taslauanu, *With the Austrian army*, 84, 102–3.

beuge in the west, so at Przemysl in the east major fortifications were proved to have greater worth than the pre-war advocates of manoeuvre warfare had allowed. As the Russians advanced, so the line of the Carpathians, running south-east to north-west, shouldered their 8th and 3rd armies in the same direction. Due west of Lemberg, guarding the north-eastern approaches to the Carpathians and shielding Cracow to the west and Hungary to the south, was the railway centre and fortified city of Przemysl, on the River San. Conrad resisted the suggestion, made especially by Boroevic, Brudermann's successor in command of the 3rd army, that it be abandoned. Its defences had not been fully modernized before the war, and its resistance had been planned to last a maximum of three months. But with its selection as AOK's headquarters at the outset of the campaign, 27,000 workers had been brought in to create seven new defensive belts with twenty-four strong-points, to dig 50 kilometres of trenches, and to install 1,000 kilometres of barbed wire. Fields of fire for 1,000 guns were cleared by the felling of 1,000 hectares of woodland and the razing of twenty-one villages. From 21 September Przemysl was under Russian siege, and was to remain so, except for the period 3 October to 8 November, until 22 March 1915.[136] Its defence sucked in the Russians and covered the Austrian recovery.

Brusilov, impatient with his neighbour, argued that if the 3rd army had advanced with unwonted rapidity it could have seized Przemysl. That it did not do so may have been a failure of command, but it was also a product of the very logistic constraints which now made it essential that Przemysl be stormed rather than screened. The Russians had deliberately not developed the railways and roads out of Poland into Galicia; the assumptions underpinning strategic communications, in Galicia as in East Prussia, proved to have been too defensive. Thus, the South-West Front now had more troops in Galicia than it could feed or move. By October the roads were at times waist-deep in mud.[137] The problem was exacerbated by the change in railway gauge, that of Austria-Hungary being narrower than that of Russia, and by the destruction effected by the retreating Austrians. The Russian armies were being stopped by their own weight. They paused to consolidate their conquests. The dual monarchy could enjoy a brief respite.

POLAND

By mid-September 1914 the military prestige of Austria-Hungary had reached its nadir. The attempt to restore its authority in the Balkans by battle had

---

[136] Regele, *Conrad*, 357–9; Rauchensteiner, *Tod des Doppeladlers*, 123–4, 162.
[137] Knox, *With the Russian army*, i. 139–40; Lobanov-Rostovsky, *Grinding mill*, 76, 79.

failed; instead, Serbia had cocked a snook at its mighty neighbour, and Russia stood poised at the gates to Hungary. Conrad blamed his ally for his defeats. He claimed that the Germans had reneged on a written agreement that the two powers would mount the Siedlitz operation; in reality no such document existed. OHL responded by suggesting that Austria-Hungary make territorial concessions to Romania; an active ally to the south could transform the outlook on the Galician front. Conrad's riposte was to attribute Romania's neutrality to Britain's entry to the war, itself the result of Germany's provocation. Thus, a squabble over operational matters assumed a political complexion. Indirectly the dual monarchy threatened to conclude a separate peace.[138]

On 31 August OHL had already accepted that a thrust into Poland would follow the clearing of East Prussia. At this stage operations in Galicia still seemed evenly balanced. By mid-September, when the defeat of the Austro-Hungarians was patent, East Prussia was secure. Now it was Silesia, its Galician flank-guard in Russian hands, that was confronted with the prospect of invasion. As was the case further north, an attack seemed to be the best defence: by taking the initiative the Germans in the east could compensate for their lack of numbers and buy time for their armies in the west.[139] Self-interest, as much as alliance obligations, directed Germany's immediate attention to Poland and the aid of Austria-Hungary.

Hindenburg's intention was to cross the Narew and march in the direction of Siedlitz. In mid-September, therefore, it was the Germans, not the Austrians, that were lured by the prospect of a great envelopment battle in Poland. Freed from worries for the security of East Prussia by the victory of the Masurian lakes, Hindenburg spoke to OHL on 13 September about an advance in 'a decisive direction';[140] not simply aid to Austria-Hungary, but a wider success became his objective. However, Conrad argued that it was now too late to implement the Siedlitz manoeuvre. His army was no longer advancing to the north-east but was being driven back on Cracow. His talk was not of attack but of further retreat. By the time a German thrust in Poland took effect against the Russian South-West Front the latter might already have completed its demolition of the Austro-Hungarian army. OHL was convinced by Conrad. It told Hindenburg that direct support for Conrad was politically essential, whatever Hindenburg imagined might be militarily desirable. What the Austrians wanted was German troops in Upper Silesia and around Cracow in order to meet the Russian advance, which Conrad (correctly at this stage) imagined would be directed westwards, rather than southwards towards Hungary. Conrad hoped in this way to give his army the

---

[138] Silberstein, *Troubled alliance*, 255; Bussy, *Tisza: letters*, 47; Rauchensteiner, *Tod des Doppeladlers*, 164–5.
[139] Uhle-Wettler, *Ludendorff*, 153.   [140] Reichsarchiv, *Weltkrieg*, v. 405.

opportunity to recuperate. When that was done, it might then resume the offensive.

Two totally distinct concepts for operations in Poland were thus being formed. Moltke, confronted with a strong-willed army commander, and pre-occupied with the German recovery from the Marne, lacked the authority to impose unity. Hindenburg argued that the railway movements to effect the redeployment desired by the Austrians would take twenty days. Given that the Austrian need was for speed, the Germans should push from a position north of the Austrians, due east towards the Vistula. The proposal, whose origin reflected the need to compromise on the Siedlitz operation, counterbalanced by a refusal to meet Conrad's demands, was easy to rationalize. If Ivanov continued to push Conrad westwards towards Cracow, the Germans would fall on his flank and rear. If he did not, the Germans would protect the Austrians on their unprotected flank, on the north or left bank of the Vistula. The Germans would then push north and east towards the line Warsaw–Ivangorod, and so fall on the South-West Front's flank and rear. The proposal, in the hands of Hindenburg and Ludendorff, was not for the Germans to extend to meet the Austrians, but for the Austrians to reach out towards the Germans. Ludendorff told Conrad that the Austrians were in danger of being boxed in, wedged in a narrow space along the Visloka, the Vistula on their left and the Carpathians on their right. To avoid this, AOK should put Dankl's 1st army across the Vistula to link up with the Germans. Thus, a limited man-oeuvre designed to relieve the pressure on Austria-Hungary was becoming a grandiose scheme. By 22 September Hindenburg could tell the Austrians that 'a greater success could be achieved against the Russians through envelop-ment'.[141] Once again, a refusal by two independent commands to compromise was being dressed up as an envelopment operation. Not one plan but two were to be implemented. The Germans' basic notion was still guided by the Siedlitz idea, and emphasized speed in the attack; the Austrians' concern was to keep their army intact, and saw offence as a later stage. Neither command formed its plans with any accurate information as to Russian intentions. Conrad ima-gined that their main weight faced his armies. Ludendorff placed at least some forces further north on the middle Vistula, but still concentrated in southern Poland and not above Ivangorod.

The need to develop a German operation independently of the Austro-Hungarian was a product, not only of personal pride but also of national prestige. If, instead of a German attack from the west and an Austrian from the south, a combined operation had been maintained in the Cracow area, the case for a joint command would have been irrefutable. The balance of forces was

---

[141] Ibid. 415; for the ad hoc development of the plan, see 402–16; also Österreichischer Bundesmi-nisterium, *Österreich-Ungarns letzter Krieg*, i. 341–7.

Austrian; moreover, although Hindenburg was the victor of Tannenberg and Conrad the loser of Lemberg, the former had been in retirement only a month previously. Therefore, such a command would have had to be held by Conrad. But the subordination of Hindenburg to Conrad was not only unacceptable to Germany's de facto leadership of the alliance, it was also incompatible with Hindenburg's and (particularly) Ludendorff's self-image.

OHL's first attempt to create a German army for Poland had planned an allocation of two corps under the command of Schubert, with Ludendorff as his chief of staff. Ludendorff was thoroughly alarmed. Perhaps he recognized the contribution of Hindenburg's calm to his own success. In any event he refused to be separated from the commander of the 8th army. He went to Silesia, argued that two corps were insufficient for operations there, and convinced OHL that an enlarged 9th army should be formed, with Breslau as its base, Hindenburg as its commander, and himself as its chief of staff.[142] Ludendorff's ability to get his own way—in the organization of the command, the distribution of forces, and the operational plan—has to be set in the context of the disarray at OHL. All these issues reached their climax on 14 September, the very day that Falkenhayn replaced Moltke. Although the arrangements that resulted were initiated by his predecessor, it was Falkenhayn who would have to bear the burden of their implications. The clash between Hindenburg and Conrad, Conrad's growing Germanophobia, Ludendorff's independence of OHL—for all these Falkenhayn had, by the circumstances of his appointment, already become the butt.

To create a 9th army sufficiently strong to meet Ludendorff's wishes and Hindenburg's newly won prestige the 8th army in East Prussia was reduced to two corps, supplemented by Landwehr and garrison troops. In addition to the positions on the Masurian lakes and the Angerapp, a line beyond the East Prussian frontier, between Vilkovishki and Suvalki, was ordered to be built. Falkenhayn asked the navy to mount a demonstration in the Baltic, off the coast of Courland, in order to aid the weakened forces in East Prussia and to prevent the Russians shifting troops to the south.[143] However, the navy had concentrated its main forces in the North Sea, and so was insufficiently strong to sustain offensive action against the Russians in the Baltic. The demonstration, begun on 19 September, was broken off on the 25th. Nor was the Vilkovishki–Suvalki line constructed. At the end of September the 10th Russian army began to push the Germans out of the Augustowo forest and Suvalki, back towards the frontier. By mid-October the 1st and 10th armies had re-established a Russian foothold in East Prussia.

---

[142] Janssen, *Der Kanzler*, 25; Hoffman, *War of lost opportunities*, ii. 48–9.
[143] Reichsarchiv, *Weltkrieg*, v. 11.

The 8th army's loss was the 9th army's gain. Hindenburg deployed four corps, a reserve division, and a cavalry division, with his main weight on the line Kattowitz–Kreuzburg. On 28 September the 9th army began its advance towards the Vistula. The weather was bad, the roads muddy, the railways of the broad Russian gauge. The Germans' handling of these problems was exemplary. Locally requisitioned Polish carts coped better with the conditions than the heavy German transport. A marching rate of 30 kilometres a day was maintained. On 4 October the 4th, 3rd, and 1st Austro-Hungarian armies took up the line to the south, crossing the Visloka on the 5th and relieving Przemysl on the 9th. Dankl's 1st army followed the course of the Vistula as it moved north-east, crossing to the left bank and aiming for Sandomir. The major objective of the advance—relief for the Austro-Hungarian army, the security of Przemysl—had thus been achieved.

Conrad's confidence grew with the lack of serious Russian resistance south of the Vistula. But neither he nor Ludendorff seems to have thought too deeply about what the Russians were doing. The Austrians had cracked the Russian codes, and between 28 and 30 September intercepted Russian signals suggested to Conrad that a redeployment was in train; by the 30th AOK knew that the Russians planned to hold on the San and the Vistula, and to mount a thrust from Warsaw in the north.[144] But Ludendorff still reckoned on the main Russian forces lying to the right of the 9th army's advance, and still—despite his recognition that Ivangorod was strongly held—relied on seizing the Vistula bridgeheads up as far as Warsaw before the Russians could regroup. German surprise was virtually complete when on 9 October, the day that Przemysl was reached, details of the Russian order of battle were found on the body of a dead Russian officer. Corroborated by signals intelligence, they revealed that three Russian armies were massing behind the Vistula. The 9th German army was advancing straight into the mouth of the enemy's principal striking force. With the main weight of the Central Powers' forces—the Austro-Hungarians—still on the San, the Russians had brought weight against weakness.

The proposal for a Russian attack in Poland had, of course, been formulated by Stavka at the war's outset. Although the conditions for its fulfilment— security on the flanks—had not been met on the North-West Front, they had been on the South-West. Furthermore, the prospect of continued retreat on the North-West Front threatened not only the Russian interior but also the rear of the successful South-West Front. Therefore the consolidation of the Galician victory could only be achieved by a success in Poland; a simple advance southwards into Hungary—even if possible in logistic terms— would eventually become exposed to German intervention. Although the operations in Galicia had gradually sucked in the 9th army, drawing it across

---

[144] Österreichischer Bundesministerium, *Österreich-Ungarns letzter Krieg*, i. 349.

Land height
▓ over 2000 ft
▒ 1000 ft
┅ Railway   ✕ Fort

0   10   20   30 miles
0   20   40 km

MAP 13. POLAND

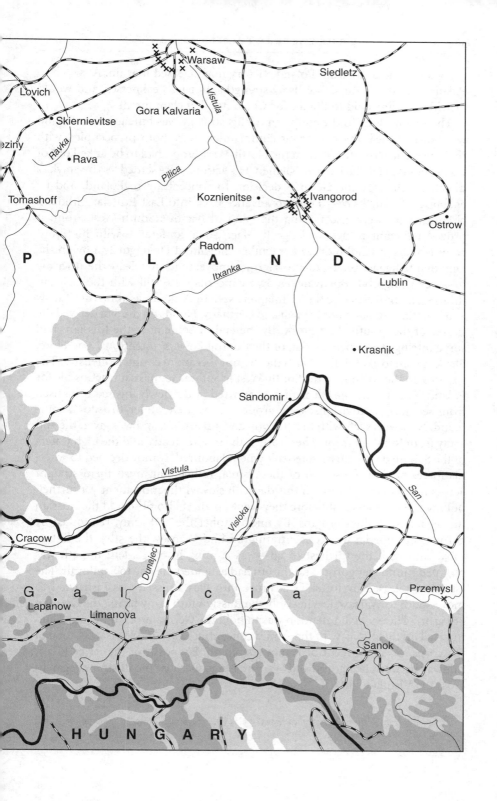

the Vistula and away from Poland, victory now released it again. A switch to Poland would use Russia's railway strengths, not its weaknesses, and would provide the direct aid to France for which its allies clamoured.

The major block to the adoption of this strategy was bureaucratic. Poland was Stavka's idea; the two Front commanders were both preoccupied with their own concerns, Ruzskii, on the North-West Front, had to be talked out of his proposal to fall back to the Niemen. His actions were settled less by Stavka's directions than by the German decision to concentrate in Poland, and by enabling the North-West Front to advance back into East Prussia. Although circumstances were also forcing the hand of Ivanov's South-West Front, it proved reluctant to acknowledge the fact. At a conference with his Front commanders at Cholm on 22 September the Grand Duke got Ivanov, in the light of intelligence on the Austro-German movements, to release the 4th army to cover Ivangorod. But Ivanov's own concerns were still with the Galician theatre, and moves across the Vistula were seen by Alekseev as aimed at Cracow and Austria-Hungary, not Breslau and Germany. Floods on the San delayed the moves of the South-West Front. By the end of September the Russians had some intelligence, albeit partial, of the Central Powers' intentions. Therefore, Stavka's plan to exploit the Polish theatre now became a counter-offensive. The solution to the attitude of the South-West Front was to make it responsible for Poland. The 3rd and the 8th armies, supported by the newly formed 11th raised from second-line divisions, were grouped separately under Brusilov's command. Ivanov was left with the 4th, 9th, and 5th armies, and was given the 2nd army from Ruzskii's front. The weather, the muddy roads, and the high waters of the San made the Russian redeployment laboured. Ivanov decided to wheel his forces behind the screen of the Vistula, rather than push them straight across into Poland. Although this decision slowed the movement yet further, pulling the Russians east before they went north, it also obscured the Russian intentions from the Germans. By mid-October the 2nd army, reinforced by corps from Siberia, was concentrating around Warsaw, the 5th—the last to move and with the furthest to go—was coming in on its left, the 4th was grouped round Ivangorod, and the 9th had extended the line to Sandomir. The 1st army, released by Ruzskii's advance into East Prussia, was instructed to move south to Warsaw, leaving only the Russian 10th army facing the German 8th army. The Russian intention was to hold the Germans on the Vistula, and then fall on their flank with the armies concentrated around Warsaw. A total of ten corps, or 40 per cent of Ivanov's strength, lay north of the River Pilica, midway between Ivangorod and Warsaw. On 10 October the Russians began to cross the Vistula to attack.[145]

[145] Inostrantzeff, *Revue militaire française*, 143 (mai 1933), 274–98; also Stone, *Eastern front*, 95–8, and Danilov, *La Russie*, 259–78.

By 9 October the Germans had accomplished their original aim, the relief of the Austro-Hungarian army. But it had been achieved largely by dint of the Russians' pause and redeployment rather than through the efforts of Hindenburg and Ludendorff. The command of the 9th army, still now buoyed by its own talk of a major decision, sought more. Rather than reshape their operations in the light of the balance of forces deployed in Poland, Hindenburg and Ludendorff persisted. Their object now was to defeat the Russians south of Warsaw before Ivanov's Front could complete its final concentration. To muster sufficient strength for such an undertaking, they demanded that Conrad's armies extend their line northwards to Ivangorod, so releasing the 9th army from responsibility for south Poland. The Germans would then be able to hold the main Russian formations south of Warsaw, while the Austrians manoeuvred on the San and the Vistula.

Ludendorff's illusions were nurtured by the Russians' slowness in completing their concentration. Although individual corps effected crossings of the Vistula around Ivangorod and Gora Kolvaria, nearer Warsaw, between 10 and 12 October, the main body remained east of the Vistula. On 12 October Mackensen's corps, on the 9th army's left, drew the 2nd Russian army back towards Warsaw. Ivanov was alarmed by the Germans' movements and was anxious not to come to grips at Ivangorod before his concentration at Warsaw was complete. Grand Duke Nicholas urged speed. Unable to contact his Front commander, he resorted to deviousness: in a bid to weaken Ivanov's authority in the Warsaw area, he suggested Alekseev as commander of the 2nd Army. Ivanov countered by asking that Stavka hand over Danilov as Alekseev's replacement as chief of staff to the South-West Front. The Grand Duke then tried a different tack. Both the 2nd and 5th armies, although under Ivanov's command, were dependent on the North-West Front for their supply. On 13 October he put both of them under Ruzskii's command. The Polish operation thereby became a joint manoeuvre involving both Fronts and requiring Stavka to co-ordinate it. But, although west of Ivangorod the III Caucasian corps was battling at Koznienitse, across the Vistula, both Fronts continued to counsel delay. Thus, the general offensive, originally ordered by Ivanov on 10 October, was postponed until 18 October and then 21 October. It was too late. On the night of 20 October the Germans began to fall back. Stavka's object had perforce to be pursuit rather than a blow to the German flank.[146]

Entirely overlooking the original object of the exercise, Hindenburg and Ludendorff blamed the failure to achieve a decisive victory in Poland on their allies. The Austro-Hungarian army was exhausted; it was ravaged by cholera, which had gained a foothold in Galicia; its movements were clogged by the

---

[146] Stone, *Eastern front*, 98–9, gives the version followed here, that Stavka urged speed and Ivanov delay. Danilov, *La Russie*, 278–84, has it the other way round.

rains and muddy roads. Furthermore, its main body was engaged in heavy fighting with Brusilov's group along the San and south of Przemysl in the Carpathian foothills. On the night of 17/18 October the Russians crossed the San. Przemysl, whose resistance had become as important a symbol to the Austrians as Verdun was to the French in 1914, was threatened once more. As the Russians again lapped round the city, supply trains steamed into its station every fourteen minutes for six days, delivering the supplies for a six-month siege. But AOK had calculated the garrison to be 85,000 when in reality it had swelled to 130,000, and had left its 30,000 civilians entirely out of account. Furthermore, the retreating 3rd Austro-Hungarian army plundered the garrison's food stocks. Encircled once more, Przemysl's position was worse than it had been before its relief on 9 October.[147]

In the by-now customary tit-for-tat, Conrad attributed these fresh ills on the Germans' hunger to seize Warsaw. Looking north, not south, Hindenburg and Ludendorff wanted Dankl's 1st Austro-Hungarian army to give direct support to Mackensen on their left wing. Conrad, reasonably enough in the circumstances, refused. He said that the 1st army could not go further than the mouth of the River Pilica. This concession was sufficient to relieve the German right, around Ivangorod, so allowing the Germans themselves to sidestep northwards. However, Conrad warned that he would not be in a position to act until 20 October. But Hindenburg's and Ludendorff's consequent complaints about the immediate security of their right conveniently obscured the major danger, which was inevitably—given the Russians' intentions—to their left. Mackensen had already had to pull back from Warsaw on 16 October, and on the 17th Ludendorff decided he would have to refuse his left flank, bidding Mackensen to hold on the line Rava–Lovich. Excessive German ambition in relation to numerical strength, rather than Austro-Hungarian failings, explain the unravelling of the Hindenburg–Ludendorff master-plan.[148]

Ninth army's new proposal was to withdraw their left, hoping to hold the Russians debouching from Warsaw in the direction of Lodz. Dankl's army was now to be the main striking force. Given the delay in its arrival, and the existence of Russian bridgeheads around Ivangorod, Conrad did not propose that Dankl should try to defend the Vistula crossings. Instead, the 1st army was to mass on the River Itxanka, which flowed into the Vistula south of Ivangorod, and fall on the Russians as they moved westwards. Russian movements wrong-footed this plan from its inception. Ruzskii and Ivanov advanced their armies in echelon refused to the right, each corps crossing the Vistula successively and so supporting its neighbour to the north. Thus, Dankl's army was not able to attack as it had planned, while the Russians reinforced and

---

[147] Rauchensteiner, *Tod des Doppeladlers*, 167–8.
[148] Kiszling, *Österreich-Ungarns Anteil*, 18; Brusilov, *Soldier's note-book*, 83–93; Matthes, *Die 9 Armee im Weichselfeldzuge.*

expanded the bridgehead so stubbornly held at Koznienitse. On 27 October Dankl ordered his army to fall back on Radom. The Germans made much of the fact that this order was not immediately communicated to their right-hand corps, Dankl's neighbours. Mutual suspicion between the allies, and the provision of such grounds for its reinforcement, helped the argument that the retreat was the product of Austrian weakness. In reality, Mackensen had been hard hit on 25 and 26 October and the German left had already pulled back to Lodz.

The Germans' retreat was, in technical terms, as well-conducted as their advance. The communications they had prepared for the latter now aided the former. Although Ludendorff fell prey to his customary nervousness, Hoffmann remained confident. Roads, railways, and bridges were destroyed by the Germans as they fell back. Hoffman reckoned that the Russians' supply arrangements were such that they could not advance more than 120 kilometres from their railheads. The lack of railways west of the Vistula meant, he wrote in his diary on 18 October, that 'nothing can go wrong. If we have to retreat, the Russians can follow us only for three days.'[149] Signals intelligence confirmed his optimism. By 1 November the Russian pursuit was exhausted.

However, Hoffmann's operational self-confidence could not deny that in strategic terms Ludendorff's apprehensions had some justification. German troops had proved consistently capable of defeating the Russians in battle. But there were not enough of them. The Russians had re-entered East Prussia, regained most of western Poland up to the line of the Varta, had pushed along the Vistula towards Cracow, and were across the San. The relief brought by the sally towards the Vistula promised to be brief.

At the end of October Ludendorff travelled to Berlin to discuss the situation with Falkenhayn. The latter's attentions were concentrated on Ypres; his loyalty was with Germany's original strategy, a decisive victory in the west which would, in its turn, resolve the situation in the east. Although Conrad wanted thirty German divisions for the east, Falkenhayn insisted that the six new corps, forming in Germany, were needed for Ypres. Only when the battle was over would the 8th and 9th armies be reinforced. Ludendorff, at this stage, seems to have been prepared to accept these arrangements. As a former chief of operations on the general staff he could not but agree with OHL's continuing efforts to achieve success in the west. Moreover, the danger to Silesia, given Russian supply problems, was not pressing. Stavka's immediate efforts seemed likely to be concentrated on their flanks, the advance in Poland having once again created an exposed Russian salient. Two thrusts were likely, the first along the Vistula towards Cracow, and the second into East Prussia by way of Mlawa. The former was Conrad's responsibility. The second Ludendorff felt

[149] Hoffman, *War diaries*, i. 46.

capable of countering himself. Falkenhayn, for his part, was clearly happy to leave affairs in the east in Hindenburg's and Ludendorff's care. On 1 November Hindenburg was appointed commander-in-chief of all German troops in the east, with Ludendorff as his chief of staff and Hoffmann as chief of operations. The command of the 9th army was given to Mackensen.

However, *Ober Ost*, as the new command was called, once again set about transforming its limited tasks into grandiose ideas that far exceeded the resources available to it. Ludendorff argued that the available railways would allow the 9th army to be rapidly concentrated at Thorn, where it could link with the 8th army and whence it could thrust south-east to Lodz. The movement would threaten the right flank of the Russian armies in Poland and the left of those in East Prussia. By its very nature the aim of the operation could only be limited, to disrupt the Russians and to gain time for the Ypres battle to be completed. Ludendorff did not have the men to hope for more. As it was, his plan demanded that the hapless Austrians cover the German concentration by extending north along the Silesian frontier. And even then, Mackensen's army only mustered just over five corps for its advance on Lodz.

The failure of OHL to grasp the growth in *Ober Ost*'s objectives was in part the product of the speed with which the Lodz operation was mounted. Ludendorff's ambitions developed as events around Lodz developed. He began planning for what was seen by Falkenhayn as a local counter-attack on 3 November. On 4 November Falkenhayn renewed his attack on Ypres and thus postponed further the transfer of the six corps from the west. Russian efforts were put into the South-West Front and the advance against the Austro-Hungarians. The direction of the Russian attack, Stavka's and the North-West Front's belief that the Germans were protecting Silesia to their front, and the consequent neglect of their right flank in Poland all added to the pressure in favour of a major German blow towards Lodz. By 10 November 800 trains had carried out the redeployment of the 9th army. On 11 November it began its advance. By now Ludendorff was convinced that the chances of a major success were greater in the east than in the west. The case was doubtful. A total of 135 Russian divisions faced seventy-five of the Central Powers: the six corps which Ludendorff coveted could have done little more than strengthen the defensive. And, even had Falkenhayn been swayed by the factors that convinced Ludendorff, these corps could never have been extricated from around Ypres and transported eastwards in time to have the decisive effect which *Ober Ost* claimed was achievable. Ludendorff needed to act fast if he was to effect surprise; he needed to wait if he wanted to be reinforced.[150]

The Russians were slow to realize what was afoot. Ruzskii emphasized the non-existent danger in East Prussia. The 10th army was therefore supported on

---

[150] Janssen, *Der Kanzler*, 35–8; Kraft, *Staatsräson und Kriegführung*, 27–9.

its left, around Mlawa and north of Warsaw, by the 1st, under Rennenkampf. The 2nd and 5th armies in Poland were delayed by Ruzskii's caution and by their ongoing supply problems. Stavka endorsed the South-West Front's priority, that of defeating the Austro-Hungarians, but without consistency. The 4th army, advancing in southern Poland, was allocated to Ruzskii's front, so that the latter might have overall co-ordination of the invasion of Germany. The effect was to weaken Ivanov's Front in its battle with the Austrians. Reports of a German concentration around Thorn, received from 10 November, were disregarded both by the North-West Front and by Stavka. The Grand Duke's attention remained focused on his own planned advance, timed to begin on 14 November and aimed at the railway, running southwards from Ostrovo inside the length of the German frontier. Not until the night of the 16th did the North-West Front halt its attack and begin to regroup to meet Mackensen.

Thus, the 9th army made good progress. Frost hardened the ground. The Vistula acted as a flank guard for the German left. Rennenkampf had detached only one corps to the south or left bank of the Vistula; the 2nd army contributed another. But communications between the two armies were not firmly established and, by striking at their hinge, Mackensen exploited their lack of co-ordination. The Germans broke through, detached a single corps to observe Rennenkampf, and pressed on towards Lodz with their remaining four, covering 80 kilometres in four days. On 14 November Scheidemann, commanding the 2nd Russian army, began to redeploy, changing front to his right and so facing north, flanking Mackensen's advance up the left bank of the Vistula. But Plehve's 5th army continued with its westward advance until the 16th. Although Rennenkampf had thrown an additional corps across the Vistula on 12 November, the remainder of the 1st army stayed out to the north. Scheidemann's army faced defeat in detail.[151] By the 18th Mackensen had encircled Lodz and with it four Russian corps. That morning the Germans intercepted a message ordering the Russians to retreat from Lodz. Another German victory seemed imminent.

Blame for what had happened so far, and credit for what followed, was hotly disputed by the Russian generals. Stavka, the North-West Front, and the army commanders each rejected the former and claimed the latter. The dispute is itself indicative of the continuing divisions and rivalries within the Russian command. What happened was what ought to have happened. The 2nd army held fast and its southern neighbour, the 5th, by dint of determined marching, regrouped around it. The South-West Front continued to attack, so pinning the Central Powers and preventing any further deployment in support of Mackensen. On the night of 18 November Plehve's 5th army struck the right wing of the German envelopment, so buttressing Scheidemann's left. Thus the Germans were no longer pursuing a retreating and defeated enemy, as Luden-

---

[151] Knox, *With the Russian army*, i. 202–4.

dorff imagined, but were facing a position of considerable strength. Lodz was base to both the 2nd and the 5th armies; the Russians, close to their supplies, mustered twice the numbers possessed by Mackensen.

Rennenkampf's 1st army, however, could not move as fast as Plehve's. Blooded by Mackensen's initial breakthrough, it was kept back from the German left. The latter was therefore free to move east and then south of Lodz, in order to cut off the Russian retreat and so complete the German victory. The battle that followed was immensely confused, almost continuous, and conducted in freezing temperatures and limited visibility. On a 40-kilometre front there were eight separate fighting lines, back to back or face to face.[152] By 21 November Scheffer's XXV reserve corps, the left wing of the German envelopment, had stuck fast, deep in the Russian defences to the south-east of Lodz, and still 32 kilometres from the German right.

Ober Ost had sent orders to Scheffer not to go so far, but to halt north-east of Lodz and hold Skiernievitse and Lovich, thus blocking any Russian relief from Warsaw. The orders never reached their destination.[153] Therefore the route from the north-east into Lodz remained open. Rennenkampf, jockeyed into activity by Ruzskii, directed one group from Lovich on 20 November and another from Skiernievitse on the 21st, to cut off Scheffer's retreat. A major Russian victory seemed to be in the offing: the envelopers would themselves be enveloped. Danilov ordered up the transport for 50,000 prisoners. But the Skiernievitse force was too weak to make any progress. The advance of the Lovich group was limited to between 10 and 15 kilometres a day. Freezing conditions and heavy snow did not help. Once again, however, the real problem was the Russian command. At 6 p.m. on 20 November Rennenkampf, dismayed at the Lovich group's slow start, replaced its commander. The new man was insufficiently briefed on the overall situation; communications with 1st army headquarters were poor. On the 21st the commander of the Lovich group was changed once again, this time by Ruzskii. The force was divided, half to reinforce the 2nd army and half to move south-east against Scheffer. Finally, on 2 December, the Lovich group took possession of Brezeziny and Strykoff, east of Lodz. Scheffer's corps and its attendant formations were cut off. That evening they were ordered to retreat.

After the action was over, Ruzskii blamed Rennenkampf for the Russian failure to secure the victory which now seemed theirs. 'In the army commanded by General Rennenkampf chaos reigned,' he claimed, not without justification. 'The troops marched without specific objectives; the direction of march was constantly changed; the troops were driven hither and thither and never received orders.'[154] When considered in conjunction with Rennen-

---

[152] Churchill, *The unknown war*, 247.
[153] Hoffmann, *War of lost opportunities*, ii. 77.   [154] Frantz, *Russland auf dem Wege*, 124.

kampf's conduct of the East Prussian campaign, much of the mud thrown at the commander of the 1st army was bound to stick. But in doing so it obscured Ruzskii's own failings. The initial weakness at the hinge of the 1st and 2nd armies had been his. Now it was his task to co-ordinate the manoeuvres around Lodz. The Lovich group, which barred Scheffer's escape, was weak, the 5th Siberian division having suffered 70 per-cent losses and the 6th being exhausted by its efforts. However, units of the 5th army were fast approaching the Lovich group's right flank. If the Front command had relayed this information via the 1st army, as it could have done, perhaps the Lovich group would have held. As it was, Scheffer broke through the 6th Siberian division on 23 and 24 November, and escaped north-westwards to be reunited with the main body of Mackensen's army. The achievement of Scheffer's men—who took with them 10,000 prisoners—was immense; it was indicative of the psychological superiority which German troops (even, in this case, reservists) had established over Russian. But it also confirmed a sense of inferiority higher up. Despite the crushing numerical superiority which his Front enjoyed, on 22 November Ruzskii planned to withdraw the 1st, 2nd, and 5th armies to a line running from Mlawa to Lovich and Tomashoff.[155] The belief in German superiority was clearly flowing in two directions, not only from front to rear, but from rear to front.

Danilov checked Ruzskii from immediate action. Thus, the battle of Lodz could be seen as a draw. But ultimately Ruzskii's view prevailed. Lodz had proved the validity of Russian pre-war planning: no advance from Poland into Germany was possible unless the East Prussian flank was first secure. Danilov argued at the end of November that the Russians were strong enough to set about doing this. Ruzskii disagreed. Russian superiority in numbers was not matched by Russian munitions. Shell shortage, reported as acute even before the advance into Poland, although probably exaggerated then, was real enough by late November. The opportunity for a Russian advance after Lodz was, in any case, fleeting. The Ypres battle over, the German strength in Poland was gradually built up. On 6 December the Russians abandoned Lodz to the Germans. Ruzskii took up positions along the rivers Bzura and Ravka, 56 kilometres west of Warsaw. The shorter line allowed the creation of a compact defensive position: the three divisions of Gourko's VI corps, which had embraced a 40-kilometre front at the end of November, were now reduced to one of 15 kilometres.[156] The North-West Front could re-equip and recuperate.

Ruzskii's decision to fall back and consolidate raised once again the danger to the South-West Front's northern flank if it continued its offensive westwards

[155] Danilov, *La Russie*, 300–15; also Knox, *With the Russian army*, i. 204–15.
[156] Gourko, *War and revolution*, 87–9.

towards Cracow. Conrad's decision to pull Böhm-Ermolli's 2nd army out of the Carpathians and north to the Silesian frontier, so as to allow the 9th German army's advance on Lodz, only increased the apparent validity of Ivanov's worries. But Brusilov urged his Front commander to attend to his southern flank, not his northern. The release of Böhm-Ermolli's army was facilitated by the defensive strength of the line of the Carpathians. As the 3rd Russian army, on the right flank of Brusilov's 8th, once again pushed towards Cracow in November, its southern flank lay exposed to the remaining Austrian troops occupying the Carpathians, Pflanzer-Baltin's group and Boroevic's 3rd army. The lack of material felt on Ruzskii's Front began to worry the armies of Ivanov. On 10 November one corps of Brusilov's army, together with the 11th army, resumed the siege of Przemysl. Two further corps were pulled west and north to support the 3rd army before Cracow. Only a single corps, in the first instance, and the besiegers of Przemysl in the second guarded the southern flank of the over-extended advance of the South-West Front.[157]

Conrad was beleaguered. The renewed threat to Hungary provoked Tisza to echo criticisms already prevalent among some army commanders. The incorporation of the 1st Austro-Hungarian army in Germany's Polish operations had resulted first in a request for its transfer to Hindenburg, and then, at the beginning of November, in a suggestion that a joint Austro-Hungarian/German command be established for Poland and Galicia. Conrad's defence—that Austro-German relations on the eastern front were bedevilled by the fact that the 9th German army had to route its communications via OHL at Mézières—was rendered less strong by the creation of Ober Ost. In September a joint command had been likely to see the elevation of Conrad at Hindenburg's expense; by November the reverse applied. Archduke Friedrich would be the nominal head, with Ludendorff as his chief of staff. Franz Joseph was both keen on the proposal and ready to see Conrad as the casualty of its implementation. Only the continued support of Archduke Friedrich saved the chief of the general staff, and in keeping Conrad Austria-Hungary rejected its military subordination to its ally.[158]

Ivanov's belief that the South-West Front was about to achieve a breakthrough gave Conrad the opportunity both to refurbish his reputation and to carry off the sort of envelopment operation which so tickled his fancy. At the beginning of December the 4th Austro-Hungarian army attacked south of Cracow, and the 3rd struck towards Sanok, south-west of Przemysl on the San. Brusilov's 8th army regrouped to cover its flank, and the 3rd Russian army fell back from Cracow in conformity. Although it was the thrust of Boroevic's 3rd army which had checked the Russians, the attack by elements of the 4th on

[157] Brusilov, Soldier's note-book, 95–113.
[158] Rauchensteiner, Tod des Doppeladlers, 167–71; Janssen, Der Kanzler, 34.

the rear of the Russian 3rd army south-east of Cracow, and driving south to north from Limanova-Laponow, was what Conrad himself highlighted. AOK, desperate to claim an Austrian victory, trumpeted its success south of Cracow, and claimed that Austria-Hungary itself was now secure. In practice, the Austrians were not able to exploit their success. At the year's end Ivanov counter-attacked and Boroevic's army and the right-wing of the 4th army fell back to the high ground of the Carpathians.

Thus, 1914 closed with the eastern front in a condition as static as that of the west. The line rested for much of its length on natural obstacles—on the Carpathians, on the Dunajec, on the Vistula. But the trenches themselves lacked great sophistication. The hard weather made excavation difficult. The length of the front, double that of the western front, meant that it lacked the density of troops characteristic of France and Belgium. Firepower encouraged dispersion and breadth, and so in operational terms troops lacked the concentration and mass needed to effect a decision. In the east 1.5 German divisions occupied a front that would have been held by five divisions in the west.[159] Moreover, the poverty of communications rendered rapid reinforcement harder to achieve, and so counters to enemy penetrations were slower to take effect. The lack of movement in the east was therefore less the product of defensive strength, as it was in the west, than of exhaustion. The battles of the eastern front in 1914 had been characterized by all the mobility and decisiveness which pre-war thinking had led generals to expect. That these battles had not produced a strategic outcome was not so much the product of operational problems as of broader considerations—of Germany's prior commitment to another front, of Austria-Hungary's efforts in Serbia, of French pressures on Russia. Mobile warfare in the tactical conditions of 1914 was enormously costly. In the first two years of the war the Russians captured more Germans than did the British and French combined. Therefore the stagnation that gripped both fronts in December 1914 was similar only at a superficial level. All the armies needed to retrench and rethink. All saw the lack of movement as temporary. However, the conditions which made this assumption incorrect in the west did not apply in the east. The battles of 1915 on the eastern front were to be as full of incident and fluidity as those of 1914; those on the western front were not.

[159] Jay Luvaas, 'A unique army', in Kann *et al.* (eds.), *Habsburg empire in World War I*, 99; also Stone, *Eastern front*, 92–3, 133–5; Pitreich, *1914*, 228–9.

5

THE WAR IN NORTHERN WATERS
1914–1915

PREPARING FOR WAR

The development of the British Expeditionary Force from 1906, its orientation towards Europe rather than the empire from 1910, the apparent triumph of Henry Wilson's continentalism at the Committee of Imperial Defence in 1911—all these generate a sense of creeping inevitability about British military support for France, of the primacy of land operations over sea, that is doubly distorting.

In the first place, it gives undue emphasis to hindsight. That a continental commitment was one option open to Britain in 1914 was not in dispute; that it was the obvious one was much less clear. Hankey, the secretary of the Committee of Imperial Defence, wrote to Lord Esher on 31 July 1914: 'The great question as to whether we shall do what our War Office friends want or not is, I believe, quite undecided, and it must be settled at the Cabinet and not here.'[1] Indeed, the cabinet in the following days opted for what it thought was a naval war. For many, including Grey, the antithesis was in any case a false one: the commitment of Britain's regular army to France did not mean that the nation's major contribution would not be at sea. Naval and military strategies could be complementary in their effects, even if independent in their execution.

Secondly, land operations in Europe presented a choice only to 'strategic man'. For the British people as a whole, for those not intimately versed in the diplomatic machinations of the previous decade, the navy was both

---

[1] Quoted in Offer, *First World War*, 308; see also Asquith, *Letters to Venetia Stanley*, 142–3.

historically and currently Britain's pre-eminent fighting arm. It impinged directly on their lives in a way which a small professional army, committed to imperial policing, could not. Naval spending, having more than doubled between 1884 and the end of the century, doubled again by 1914. The rise in naval costs levelled off after 1906, but began again in 1909 thanks to the threat of fresh German building (in the event, a crisis manufactured out of faulty intelligence), worries about Austro-Hungarian construction in the Adriatic, and an end to economic recession; by 1914 annual naval spending stood at £48.7 million, and was due to rise to £51.5 million in 1914–15. The navy was paid for out of taxation, and by 1914 consumed a quarter of the total tax yield. Thus British sea-power was a means by which fixed capital was brought into circulation, and wealth redistributed; thus too, by 1914 Britain, unlike France or Germany, already had the machinery to pay for war out of income.[2] The cost of the navy had a second, albeit more indirect, democratizing effect. The commitment to cheap food and the refusal to protect British agriculture, the symbols of liberalism's attachment to free trade, made Britain dispropor- tionately dependent on grain imports from overseas. Expenditure on the navy, as the protector of the nation's trade routes, was thus an indirect subsidy for the population's food supply.[3] The disproportionate increase in naval spend- ing up until 1905–6 and again after 1909 might have called both policies into question—the basic rate of income tax rose from 5d. in the pound in 1884 to 1s. 3d. in 1903, and the trade-off between food imports and naval costs became a bad bargain. But a growing navy had other beneficial effects on the economy. Its need to remain at the forefront of new technology made it a force for innovation and investment in British engineering and British heavy industry. By 1913 one-sixth of the total British workforce—according to one presumably exaggerated but still significant calculation—was dependent on naval con- tracts.[4] These links between the navy and the nation were kept active by a flair for publicity and propaganda that made nonsense of the idea of a 'silent service'. The scare of 1909 was nurtured by the patriotic press and the Navy League to fuel appropriations for capital ship construction up until war itself.[5] The fleet, not the army, was vital to both the perception and the reality of Britain's status as a great power.

Throughout the century since Waterloo the Royal Navy had measured its capabilities by European yardsticks. Lord Roberts, the last ever commander- in-chief of the British army, and an advocate of the army's primacy in con- tinental strategy, argued in 1912 that the navy's reach was global, and that particularly if Britain were free from the danger of invasion its ships should be

[2] Sumida, *In defence of naval supremacy*, 18–21, 24–6, 186–90.
[3] Offer, *First World War*, 218–20.
[4] McNeill, *Pursuit of power*, 285.
[5] On the Royal Navy's management of the press, see Morris, *Scaremongers*.

so deployed. But, as Fisher recognized, Roberts missed the point. The with-drawal of the fleet to home waters rested on the premiss that its putative opponents were other industrialized nations. Similarly, the introduction of the Dreadnought, a step which for many was absurd since it rendered obsolescent all the navy's existing ships, was mandatory for a power which aspired to dominate the oceans: British battleships had to lead the way in design and in technology. Neither pressure—the need to concentrate nor the need to innov-ate—was as great for the army, at least while its combat roles were confined to the imperial periphery. When the navy set itself the two-power standard in 1889 its targets were France and Russia; the army's preoccupations were with Afghans and Dervishes.

In this broad context, the redirection in naval policy achieved by Fisher in 1904–5 did not represent a change in grand strategy. That, the need to be able to defeat the navies of other industrialized powers, remained constant. Nor, more specifically, was the shift in the first instance the product of Anglo-German naval rivalry. Fisher's primary task was to curb the mounting costs of the previous two decades, while improving efficiency. Simultaneously, however, Tsushima removed the Russian fleet as a threat for the foreseeable future and indicated the potentially decisive importance of apparently marginal technical superiority. The rapid orientation of British naval strategy and British naval construction towards Germany did not require any change in these funda-mentals. In October 1906 an Admiralty memorandum declared, 'our only potential foe now being Germany, the common-sense conclusion is that the outlying Fleets no longer require to be maintained at the strength which was admittedly necessary a year ago'.[6] By 1909 Britain was effectively on a one-power standard, setting itself the target of a fleet equal to Germany's plus 60 per cent. In terms of international relations the navy was far more contin-entalist than was the army.

The single-minded attention to Germany was made possible by the Entente with France. The maintenance of the two-power standard against France and Russia had placed a potential naval war as much in the Mediterranean as in the North Sea or the Channel. By creating an Atlantic Fleet in 1904 Fisher had—in theory at any rate—allowed the six battleships at Gibraltar (which were part of the Atlantic Fleet) the option to go north to join the Channel Fleet or east to join the Mediterranean Fleet at Malta. He was thus able to halve the Mediter-ranean Fleet to six battleships by 1907. By 1908 Fisher was planning to leave the Mediterranean to the French in the event of war.

Independently, the French elected in 1906 to concentrate their efforts in the Mediterranean. They did not do so because of the Entente with Britain but because their fleet was not strong enough to face the Germans in the North Sea.

---

[6] Quoted in Marder, *From the Dreadnought*, i. 71.

The success of the *jeune école* in challenging the primacy of the battleship left its legacy in French warship construction. At the close of the nineteenth century the torpedo boat, with its ability to sink capital ships, especially in coastal waters and at close ranges, promised to revitalize the potential of *guerre de course*. Camille Pelletan, the naval minister between 1902 and 1905, championed such arguments until Tsushima put the battleship back at the intellectual heart of the French navy. But the result, the six capital ships of the *Danton* class ordered in 1907–8, espoused rapid fire with medium guns rather than long-range fire with big guns.

Under-armed for the North Sea, France's battleships soon proved to be of doubtful utility for the Mediterranean as well. In 1905 Italy embarked on a programme of Dreadnought construction, providing for four in 1909 and six by 1915. Its main rival was, formally speaking, its ally, Austria-Hungary. The dual monarchy responded in kind, laying down two Dreadnoughts for its Adriatic fleet in 1910, and two more in 1912 and four in 1914. The navy's share of the total Austro-Hungarian defence budget rose from 10 per cent to 20 per cent between 1900 and 1914.

Although Italy and Austria-Hungary were building against each other, France had to reckon on the possibility that the two allies would act in conjunction. In late 1912 Germany established a Mediterranean division of two cruisers precisely to promote such co-operation. France ordered its first Dreadnought, the *Courbet*, with twelve 305 mm guns, in 1910, and in 1912 Delcassé, now minister of marine, broke the tyranny of annual parliamentary negotiations over the naval budget by setting a programme of twenty-eight battleships for completion by 1920.[7] The dynamic and unstable arms race of 1912–14 was in the Mediterranean, not in the North Sea.

The inability of either Britain or France alone to compete in this race gave purpose to their naval agreement. Qualitatively the Royal Navy could no longer treat the Mediterranean as a secondary theatre of operations, in which it could deploy its pre-Dreadnoughts. Quantitatively it had to give priority to the North Sea, as Germany's 1912 naval law made clear. Churchill, as First Lord of the Admiralty, wanted to pull the Mediterranean Fleet back to Gibraltar. He did not achieve that; but nor did the Committee of Imperial Defence see its wishes of 4 July 1912 implemented. The committee proposed a battle fleet at Malta of eight capital ships, in other words a one-power Mediterranean standard excluding France. At the opening of hostilities in 1914 Malta was home to four battle cruisers but no battleships. Their task was to guard the eastern basin against Austria-Hungary; the French at Toulon

---

[7] Philippe Masson, 'La Marine française de 1871 à 1914', in Pedroncini (ed.), *Histoire militaire de la France*, iii. 125–49; Stevenson, *Armaments and the coming of war*, 30–1, 85–7, 135–6; Halpern, *Naval history*, 6–15.

took on the management of Italy and the western basin. Anglo-French tactical co-operation, made possible by the preparation of a joint naval code in 1911 and by the naval talks authorized in November 1912, was in practice more fully developed for operations in the Channel than in the Mediterranean. But it was the very real strategic dependence on the other power, the broad division of areas in the Mediterranean, and the French reliance on Britain in the Atlantic approaches that made the naval commitment far less equivocal than the military.[8]

In terms of grand strategy, therefore, the Royal Navy was committed to Europe, and was geared to fight one power only, Germany. But the navy's clear strategic thrust was not carried through into operational planning.

Since the mid-nineteenth century the Admiralty had been a model for the army in its ability to fuse civil and service authority without friction. The naval minister, the First Lord of the Admiralty, presided over a board of Sea Lords, the first of whom was responsible for the fighting and sea-going efficiency of the fleet. The Admiralty, therefore, had to function as a unit, the individual board members relying ultimately for their authority on their colleagues' support. The Board's operational functions were restricted to the distribution of the fleet and an indication as to the general lines of policy through war orders. It was the task of fleet and station commanders to draw up specific plans.

Fisher upset this balance. He managed to elevate his status as the First Sea Lord from that of a *primus inter pares* to that of commander-in-chief of the navy, and he enjoyed the backing of the First Lord (especially, from 1908, of Reginald McKenna) in doing so. But the authority of Fisher as First Sea Lord attached to him as an individual, and a formidable one, not to his office. Furthermore, its exercise made issues that should have been resolved in more objective ways a matter of personality.

In 1906 Fisher created the Home Fleet, and in the process began the suppression of the other two home-water commands, the Atlantic and Channel Fleets. In 1907 the latter was entrusted to an admiral as dogmatic and as volatile as Fisher himself, Lord Charles Beresford. Between 1907 and 1909, when Beresford finally hauled down his flag, the clash between the two extended to most aspects of naval change, from gunnery to submarines, from fighting instructions to neutral rights. It was fuelled by Fisher's determination that the navy was a 'democratic' service, especially in comparison with the army: a belief challenged by Beresford's pedigree as well as by his enjoyment of royal patronage. Beresford became the lightning-conductor for those opposed to Fisher's reforms, whether within the navy or within the

---

[8] Marder, *From the Dreadnought*, i. 288–309; Williamson, *Politics of grand strategy*, chs. 9, 11, and 12; Halpern, *Naval war in the Mediterranean*, 2–8.

Conservative party (which in due course Beresford served as an MP). The Conservative leader, Arthur Balfour, sided with Fisher and so struggled to maintain a cross-party consensus on naval matters, but by March 1909 the navy was at the centre of parliamentary politics. Ultimately the dispute made Fisher's own position as First Sea Lord unsustainable, forcing him into early retirement in January 1910.

The feud split the navy into warring factions, becoming an end in itself rather than a vehicle for addressing Beresford's original and quite proper concerns, the need for a naval staff, for war planning, and for clarity over the likely operational roles of the fleet.[9]

Fisher's obstinate refusal to further war planning or to foster a staff to whom he could delegate it still lacks a coherent explanation. Most leaders in the First World War rationalized their failings after the event: in this respect Fisher's *Memories* are remarkably deficient. Navies encouraged authoritarianism. Captains enjoyed absolute and independent power over their crews; admirals were less caught up in logistics, in the management of war, so integral to command on land, and continued to exercise direct control under fire. Fisher may, therefore, have interpreted the giving of advice by others as a trammel on his own authority. But there is also a more subtle explanation. Since the Napoleonic Wars (and even in the course of the Crimean War) the might of the Royal Navy had been exercised by its existence rather than by battle. The navy had become a player in diplomacy, not in war. Thus, for Fisher, the navy's ultimate justification was as a deterrent. It is significant that he interpreted the debates about continentalism not as an argument about strategy, not about how the next war would be fought, but about whether the army or the navy was to have priority in defence budgets. Fisher's bottom line was that a strong navy would keep the peace, and therefore his efforts should be devoted to technical and quantitative superiority rather than to how that superiority should be applied.

External pressure, principally from the Committee of Imperial Defence, made it impossible for Fisher entirely to evade the demands for planning. But his responses were a mixture of postponement and ad hoccery. In 1907 he set up a committee at the War College to consider plans for a war with Germany, but gave it a brief with conflicting objectives and in 1908 decreed that its proposals should not be discussed with any admiral afloat. Possible breaches of confidentiality, as well as the danger that the actual circumstances of war would be different, became standard excuses for inaction.[10]

---

[9] Williams, *Defending the empire*, 68–9, 86–8, 121–35, 163–76; Marder, *From the Dreadnought*, i. 90–103, and in *Fear God and dread nought*, ii. 39–44, is very critical of Beresford; for the legitimacy of Beresford's case, see his own letter to Fisher, 2 May 1907, in *Fear God and dread nought*, ii. 123, and P. Haggie 'Royal Navy and war planning in the Fisher era', in Kennedy (ed.), *War plans*, 129.

[10] John Gooch, 'Adversarial atitudes: servicemen, politicians and strategic policy in Edwardian England, 1899–1914', in Smith (ed.), *Government and the armed forces*, 60–1, 67–8, 71.

The performance of Sir Arthur Wilson at the Committee of Imperial Defence on 23 August 1911 showed the deficiencies of Fisher's personal rule. Wilson was abrasive, inarticulate, and autocratic. He was selected as Fisher's successor because he was the potential protector of his legacy: Wilson's seniority would enable him to control the twelve full admirals on the active list, at least five of whom belonged to the 'syndicate of discontent' committed to dismantling Fisher's reforms if given the opportunity. But by 1910 Wilson had been retired three years. Furthermore, although his reputation had been gained at sea rather than in the corridors of the Admiralty, he had never commanded Dreadnoughts. Wilson survived for even less time than was intended by the stopgap nature of his appointment. His successor in November 1911, Sir Francis Bridgeman, also got the job by default. From a thin list, Bridgeman had one unusual quality in the pre-1914 navy: a willingness to delegate. But he was also subject to ill-health, and in barely a year this had provided the excuse for his replacement in December 1912 by Prince Louis of Battenberg. Battenberg was a Fisherite, both in his support for the material changes in the navy and in his fluency. However, he lacked Fisher's dogmatism. Not the least of his attractions to Churchill was his malleability. The combination of frequent change and weak appointees ensured that the professional leadership of the Royal Navy lost its direction in the four years preceding the war.[11]

Power now lay with the service's civilian head, and from 24 October 1911 specifically with Winston Churchill, appointed in McKenna's stead with the ostensible mission of establishing a naval general staff. Herein was justification for the navy's belief that the verdict on continentalism was still open. The navy was to be asked to formulate coherent plans for the contingency of European war; as importantly, the creation of a staff would prevent the service's operational roles being so subject to the personal vagaries of its First Sea Lords.

Until 1909 the Naval Intelligence Department had functioned as a prototype staff, using the information it gathered as a basis for operational advice. The enquiry of that year into Beresford's criticisms of Fisher had recognized the need for a fully fledged naval staff: but the committee's main preoccupation was with the issue of personality, of the 'Fishpond' (as Fisher's followers became known) against the Beresfordians, and the proposed naval staff was therefore as much a palliative for the immediate crisis as an end in itself. The upshot of the committee's recommendations, the creation of the Navy War Council, did little to advance the cause of a naval staff. The council was given an advisory role on strategy, but it met only on the initiative of the First Sea

---

[11] See the essays by Nicholas A. Lambert on Wilson and Bridgeman, and by John B. Hattendorf on Battenberg, in Murfett (ed.), *First Sea Lords*.

Lord and it had no executive powers. The main effect was to emasculate the Naval Intelligence Department, alleged to be rife with Beresfordians, in order to strengthen the position of Wilson, as Fisher's prospective successor. In October 1909 the Naval Intelligence Department lost its trade division (which had been responsible for blockade planning) and its mobilization division, leaving its functions restricted to intelligence only. Arthur Wilson castigated general staffs as appropriate to armies but not to navies.

Nonetheless, it was the Navy War Council which Churchill used as the basis for the Admiralty War Staff, set up in January 1912. The War Staff had three divisions—operations, intelligence, and mobilization—but it ran in parallel with the Board of Admiralty rather than converged with it. It had no direct representation on the board, and it lacked executive authority, not least because the opportunity to combine the post of chief of the war staff with that of First Sea Lord was not taken. Formally the former was meant to advise the latter. In practice, he counselled the First Lord. As First Sea Lord, Sir Francis Bridgeman was given no role in the shaping of the war staff or in the appointment of its first chief. The division between the war staff and the Board of Admiralty became a means whereby the First Lord could bypass the Sea Lords, and so enhance his own profile in strictly operational and professional matters.[12] Furthermore, there was no naval staff college. The naval war course, set up in 1900, was for commanders and above, and lasted only four months. A staff course for junior officers, devised in 1912, emphasized staff duties in the narrowest sense. Even if it had been more broadly conceived, it would have been too late to shape the thinking of the senior naval officers in post in 1914.[13] Their preoccupation was with technology, not with doctrine.

When war began, the Admiralty, Britain's naval ministry, was also the navy's operational headquarters. The scene in the 'war room' on 1 August 1914 was 'wild, thousands of telegrams littered about & no-one keeping a proper record of them'. With only thirty-three officers on the war staff, twenty-eight more had to be drafted in—three of them from half pay and fourteen from retirement. The room became overcrowded, and the intelligence section was moved out and so divided from operations. The movements of British and foreign ships were handled by different sections, even if they were potential enemies in the same waters.[14]

The growth of the fleet and the expansion of its complement in the late 1890s had not been accompanied by a commensurate growth in the navy's bureaucracy. Tight Treasury control had inculcated a painstaking and laborious

[12] Ibid., esp. Lambert, 'Bridgeman', 57–9.
[13] Marder, *From the Dreadnought*, i. 247–50, 265–7; v. 313–14, 317–19; James Goldrick, 'The irresistible force and the immovable object: *The Naval Review*, the Young Turks, and the Royal Navy, 1911–1931', in Goldrick and Hattendorf (eds.), *Mahan is not enough*, 84–90.
[14] Miller, *Superior force*, 64–5.

approach to paperwork among senior officers.[15] The chief of the War Staff, Sir Frederick Doveton Sturdee, gained operational authority by default, far too much administrative responsibility being centralized on his superior, Battenberg. But Sturdee was not a natural chief of staff: he failed to involve his subordinates, preferring instead to go 'about looking very important & mysterious'.[16] An informal 'war staff group' emerged, consisting of Churchill, Battenberg, and Sturdee, but it had no staff of its own, and each of its members was preoccupied with other duties. The departmental responsibilities of the junior Sea Lords, whose co-ordination was the duty of the First Lord, were neglected.

Churchill had not resolved the naval cult of the personality; indeed, he did his best to become that personality himself. His energy and high profile were matched by an assumption of technical and professional competence which was not warranted. He used the advice of juniors against their seniors. The Sea Lords became disgruntled, and in November 1913 came close to resignation en masse: Sir John Jellicoe, a Second Sea Lord before the war, likened the board to a volcano.[17] In August 1914 Churchill brought back the twice-retired Sir Arthur Wilson as a strategic adviser, and by November Wilson was part of the 'war staff group'; the First Lord's pugnacity was tickled by Wilson's enthusiasm for seizing Heligoland, a scheme which appalled Wilson's service colleagues.[18] Churchill's high profile made him the obvious butt for any deficiencies in the navy, whether warranted or not; he was distrusted by the Conservatives, and his Antwerp escapade in September 1914 reinforced doubts about his judgement. By late October 1914 Churchill's projection of himself was beginning to rebound. Fortuitously, however, Battenberg was neither fully fit nor fully British (at least in the popular view). Battenberg's departure deflected the opprobrium from the First Lord to the First Sea Lord, and the recall of Fisher in Battenberg's stead was calculated to redound to Churchill's political credit. But within the service the reshuffle reopened Fisher's vendetta with those whom he construed to be Beresford's supporters, including Sturdee. Furthermore, Churchill, who had maintained a correspondence with Fisher in the latter's retirement, had overestimated his ability to manage the First Sea Lord. Fisher back in an executive role was different from Fisher as conspiratorial adviser. Now the Royal Navy had two strong personalities at the helm, each equally convinced of the correctness of his own judgements. The fact that Fisher rose early in the morning, whereas Churchill's creative period was late at

---

[15] Sumida, *Journal of Military History,* LIV (1990), 9–10, 19–21.
[16] Goldrick, *King's ships were at sea,* 19 and generally 15–20.
[17] Ibid. 16.
[18] Lambert, 'Wilson', in Murfett (ed.), *First Sea Lords,* 49; Paul Hayes, 'Britain, Germany, and the Admiralty's plans for attacking German territory 1906–1915', in Freedman *et al.* (eds.), *War, strategy and international politics,* 104–5.

night, may have served to avoid direct confrontation, but it did not aid the already difficult problem of co-ordination. Sir David Beatty, commanding the battle cruiser squadron, was not sanguine: 'Two very strong and clever men, one old, wily and of vast experience, one young, self-assertive with great self-satisfaction but unstable. They cannot work together; they cannot both run the show.'[19]

Beatty was writing in December 1914: by then the operational inconveniences of Admiralty control and of the lack of a fully fledged naval staff were already clear. Not yet so evident were the technical deficiencies in the Royal Navy, and in Fisher's great construction programme, which the presence of a naval staff might have obviated.[20]

In August 1914 Britain could deploy twenty Dreadnoughts (with twelve more building) to the Germans' thirteen (with seven building), and nine battle cruisers (with one building) to the Germans' five (with three building). In addition, the Royal Navy enjoyed a twofold advantage in pre-Dreadnoughts and a threefold lead in cruisers; although many of these vessels were obsolescent in the context of the North Sea and of the Mediterranean, they were the workhorses that enabled Britain to maintain a presence in more distant waters and to sustain the blockade. This quantitative superiority stood the Royal Navy in good stead throughout the war. But Fisher's aim had been to outbuild the Germans qualitatively, to save costs by reducing the number of units. Ironically, the margin of technical superiority was much more open to doubt.

When Fisher arrived at the Admiralty as First Sea Lord in 1904 he did so on the back of a reputation enhanced by the command of the Mediterranean Fleet between 1899 and 1902. Then his putative opponents were France and Russia. In terms of battleships, the French, with their enthusiasm for the torpedo and the changeability of their governments, could not compete. But, stung by the Fashoda incident in 1898, they set about the creation of a commerce-raiding fleet of armoured cruisers: by 1904 thirty-five had been ordered. The Admiralty responded in kind, itself ordering twelve large armoured cruisers for trade defence between 1902 and 1906. In doing so it generated the crisis in the navy's finances which Fisher was summoned to address. The estimates for 1904–5 were fixed at £36.8 million, in contrast with estimates of £19.6 million in 1895–6. The First Lord, Selborne, conscious of German building, had set a margin over and above the two-power standard: he reckoned on having six battleships more than the joint totals of France and Russia, and twice as many armoured cruisers. The size of the merchant navy—9 million tons to the 1.5 million tons of the next two naval powers combined—made the two-power

[19] Roskill, *Beatty*, 98.
[20] Fundamental here is the work of Sumida, *In defence of naval supremacy*; also his article, *Journal of Modern History*, LI (1979), 205–30, and his edition of *The Pollen papers*. See also Fairbanks, *International History Review*, XIII (1991), 246–72.

standard a totally inadequate yardstick for the protection of commerce against a *guerre de course*.[21]

The formative experience of the French threat and the ongoing nature of the Russian (even after 1907) meant that British naval construction remained geared to achieving a global capability, for all the pressures generated by Germany in the North Sea. The adoption of steam made vessels dependent on the supply of coal and so reduced their endurance; oil-fired turbines exacerbated the problem. But Britain's worldwide network of sovereign bases rendered it less vulnerable on this score than any other power. After 1905 the Admiralty enlarged its docks in Auckland, Bombay, Fremantle, Hong Kong, Simonstown, Singapore, and Sydney.[22] Moreover, steel alloys allowed armoured vessels to have high freeboards without creating instability through excessive topweight. Warships, which had hitherto had to fight their battles in calm coastal waters because their gunports, close to the water-line, had to be closed in choppy conditions, could now engage on the high seas.[23] The effect was to negate the danger posed to the warship by torpedoes. Lacking in sea-keeping qualities, torpedo boats were largely restricted to the coast, and the extra sea space allowed the battleship to use her guns while staying out of torpedo range. Maritime strategy and warship design, therefore, supported the creation of a fleet of global and oceanic capabilities.

In Britain the major objection to this line of argument in 1904 was the fear of invasion from the continent. But it was precisely in the North Sea and the Channel that the torpedo retained its efficacy. Fisher therefore planned to liberate his major units for worldwide deployment by building up a coastal-protection force of submarines and smaller vessels. This flotilla defence would constitute a second-line navy whose task would be to target the troop transports of an invading force. Spending on flotilla craft doubled under Fisher's direction, and against the background of a falling construction budget moved from 10 per cent to 20 per cent of the whole between 1904 and 1909.[24]

In the long run, the most striking element in this strategy is its reliance on the submarine. The first practicable ocean-going submarine (as opposed to French battery-powered submarines with only limited cruising ranges) was developed from the design of J. P. Holland and had entered service with the United States Navy as recently as 1900. Submarines played only a minor role in

[21] Fairbanks, *International History Review*, XIII (1991), 265–72; Nicholas A. Lambert, 'The opportunities of technology: British and French naval strategies in the Pacific, 1905–1909', in Rodger (ed.), *Naval power*, 43–4; Williams, *Defending the empire*, 30, 59–67, 72–5; Bryan Ranft, 'Parliamentary debate, economic vulnerability and British naval expansion 1860–1905', in Freedman *et al.* (eds.), *War, strategy and international politics*.

[22] Lambert, 'The opportunities of technology', in Rodger, *Naval power*, 50.

[23] Lautenschläger, *International Security*, VII (1983), 13–14, 17–18.

[24] Lambert, *Journal of Military History*, LIX (1995), 639–60, is vital on this point; see also Sumida, ibid. 620; Hadley and Sarty, *Tin-pots and pirate ships*, 20–1.

the Russo-Japanese War. Holland's submarine was powered by internal combustion engines on the surface and by electrical motors when submerged. Making good speed on the surface and having a reasonable radius of action were considered essential in order to enable the submarine to act in conjunction with conventional warships. But the reliance on petrol restricted the range of the submarine and created dangers in an airtight vessel. Most significant, therefore, in naval attitudes to the submarine before 1914 is not the neglect of new technology, nor a purblind adherence to the capital ship in preference to its challenger, but rather an enthusiasm for the potentialities of something hitherto untried.

Scepticism with regard to the battleship was also evident in Fisher's original conception of the Royal Navy's striking force. Its key component was to be the armoured cruiser. Capital-ship construction required the reconciliation of three not necessarily convergent objectives—firepower, armour, and speed. For Fisher, the last of these three was pre-eminent. 'Sea fighting', he later instructed Churchill, 'is pure common sense. The first of all necessities is SPEED, so as to be able to fight *When* you like *Where* you like and *How* you like.'[25] The speed of the armoured cruiser was both strategic and tactical. It enabled a navy with global reponsibilities to achieve a rapid local concentration. Once in contact with the enemy, it ensured the ability to catch him; Fisher was assuming that the navy's most likely operational task was the overhauling of fleeing French cruisers.

Implicit in Fisher's twin conception of 1904—flotilla defence by submarines and a striking force of fast armoured cruisers—was an abandonment of the conventions of the two-power standard. Naval supremacy was no longer to be measured in numbers of battleships. But two factors militated against such radicalism. The first was political: prestige overseas and expectations at home were attuned to battleship supremacy. The second was technical: smokeless powder gave naval ordnance higher muzzle velocities, and therefore greater ranges and greater striking power. Guns were the capital ship's answer to the torpedo. They constituted a case for the retention of the battleship. Fisher himself preferred to give the guns to the armoured cruiser. 'The armoured cruiser of the first class', he wrote in 1902, 'is a swift Battleship in disguise.'[26] What he had in mind came to be dubbed the battle cruiser, a ship which, in addition to the traditional role of the cruiser, would also have the ability to operate in the battle-line, scouting for the main force and then forming its fast wing. Fisher's ideas were referred to a committee on designs in 1905; its answer, although, innovative, did not go quite so far. It proposed a new sort of battleship, the Dreadnought.

[25] Marder, *Fear God and dread nought*, ii. 426; see also Sumida, *In defence of naval supremacy*, 159.
[26] Jon Tetsuro Sumida, 'The historian as contemporary analyst: Sir Julian Corbett and Admiral Sir John Fisher', in Godrick and Hattendorf (eds.), *Mahan is not enough*, 127.

In the interim the Russo-Japanese War had confirmed the direction of British naval thought in tactical terms while undermining its strategic context. The removal of the Russian navy as an immediate threat meant that the security of the Pacific trade routes no longer depended on the presence of major units. At the same time the profile of the German threat became more pronounced. Both armament and armour were likely to be more important in the North Sea. Furthermore, the injection of the battle cruiser into the Anglo-German naval arms race could have deleterious consequences for the Royal Navy. As long as the Germans concentrated their efforts on battleships they confined their capabilities to the North Sea. If they responded to British battle cruisers by creating a comparable force of their own, they could penetrate into the northern Atlantic and wreak havoc along merchant-shipping lanes. By emphasizing Dreadnoughts rather than battle cruisers, the Admiralty ensured greater stability in Britain's projection of maritime power, while suggesting greater comparability between the two navies in practice than existed in theory. Both of Fisher's successors, Wilson and Bridgeman, endorsed this policy. The price was the construction of eighteen capital ships in the three years after 1909 compared with eight in the three previous years.[27]

The fact that *Dreadnought* was the first of the new constructions to be completed, that it was built so quickly, and that its main armament was ten 12-inch guns, therefore obscured the point that *Invincible*—the battle cruiser rather than the battleship—was for Fisher the truly innovatory design. *Invincible* also had 12-inch guns (eight of them), but could achieve a speed of 25 knots (as opposed to the *Dreadnought*'s 21). H.M.S. *Lion*, the next class of battle cruiser, built in 1909, had 13.5-inch guns and a speed of 27 knots. And in 1912 Fisher was urging on Churchill battle cruisers with 15-inch and even 16-inch guns, and speeds of up to 30 knots. In the event Churchill stuck to battleships, at least in name, for the 1912–13 programme. The oil-burning *Queen Elizabeth* was nonetheless capable of 25 knots, while possessing a main armament of 15-inch guns. The focus on the North Sea and on the arms race with Germany had resulted in a preponderance of battleships over battle cruisers, but in Fisher's eyes the two were similar, and in practice each had some of the qualities of the other.

Fisher's ultimate objective, therefore, was to fuse in one vessel the firepower of the battleship with the manoeuvrability of the cruiser. The single type would meet three key objectives. First, it would fulfil Fisher's fervour for rationalization as an end in itself. Secondly, and relatedly, it would obviate duplication and so cut costs. And thirdly, its capacity for rapid redeployment would give it

---

[27] Stevenson, *Armaments and the coming of war*, 165, 174–5; Epkenhans, *Die wilhelminische Flotten-rüstung*, 123–4; Lambert, 'Bridgeman', in Murfett (ed.), *First Sea Lords*, 59–60; Lambert, *Journal of Modern History*, LXVII (1995), 599.

strategic significance as well as tactical: it would maintain Britain's global reach even while the navy concentrated in home waters.

Fisher achieved celerity by sacrificing armour. In 1904 a 12-inch high-explosive armour-piercing shell could penetrate the main armour of any vessel, battleship or cruiser, at ranges up to 10,000 yards. His designs, therefore, concentrated armour around the ship's vital parts, rather than around the vessel overall. Some additional protection was provided by increasing the watertight subdivisions of the hull. But the vessel's main security was its speed and its ability to engage the enemy at long ranges. Its task was to hit before it itself was hit. Firing at high elevations, as long-range combat required, would result in shells striking ships either at oblique angles or vertically rather than horizontally. In theory, therefore, the battle cruisers needed armoured decks as well as armoured hulls. But shooting at extreme ranges seemed unlikely to be so accurate or so effective. In the battles of 1904–5 the fuses of the Japanese armour-piercing shells had proved too sensitive, and they had therefore detonated too soon for maximum effectiveness. British trials in 1909 corroborated these doubts: 12-inch armour-piercing shells fired at ranges beyond 9,000 yards, and so striking plate at oblique angles, broke up rather than penetrated. Jellicoe, as director of naval ordnance, proposed that a new fuse be developed, but the decision of Sir Arthur Wilson as First Sea Lord in 1911 was that high-explosive shell should be used at long ranges (and therefore be aimed against unarmoured parts of the ship only), and armour-piercing shell at close ranges. High-explosive shell might detonate above the deck rather than into it, and in any case by the time it struck its velocity would be largely spent, and its effect minimized by the angle of impact.

These calculations lost their force if the enemy possessed comparable vessels, and if armour-piercing shells gained in effectiveness. By 1914 the British battle cruiser, with armour plate 3 to 6 inches thinner than on a battleship, was vulnerable to a 12-inch gun at 16,000 yards.[28] Furthermore, the lack of armour on the gun turrets increased the dangers of flash down the ammunition hoists to the magazines.

Long-range gunnery was the attribute which squared the circle of Fisher's designs: it was the complement to speed, and guns and speed in conjunction were the theoretical antidote to lack of armour. Of the quality of British naval armament, and its superiority to that of the Germans, there is no doubt. In the 1880s the emphasis had been on quick-firing guns and close ranges. Ranges had then been increased by the danger of torpedoes, and by the concomitant development of destroyers (and in due course battle cruisers) to provide a forward defensive screen. At long ranges the variation in types—and multi-plication in numbers—of guns had made accurate fire control difficult.

---

[28] Lambert, *Journal of Military History*, LXII (1998), 54.

Fisher's answer, embodied in the Dreadnought, was a concentration on big guns, on the neglect of secondary armament, and on slower rates of fire. His ships would use their speed to bring a fleeing enemy to action. They would then keep the ranges long, so that their salvoes would be easier to spot and correct. The calibre of the big guns meant that fewer could achieve a heavier broadside than a larger number of smaller-calibre guns. The ten guns of the *Dreadnought* were placed so that eight could fire on each broadside, or six ahead or astern. The broadside of the super-Dreadnought, *Queen Elizabeth*, with eight 15-inch guns, amounted to 15,600 pounds; that of the German battleship *Kronprinz Wilhelm*, also laid down in 1912 but with ten 12-inch guns, was 8,600 pounds.[29] In July 1914 Germany had only four vessels building with 15-inch guns compared with Britain's ten, and the dominant calibre in service in Germany was 12-inch to Britain's 13.5-inch.

The maximum ranges of the guns of the Dreadnought generation were enormous: 20,000 yards was normal (the Russians had opened accurate fire at 18,000 yards in the Russo-Japanese War), and *Queen Elizabeth*'s 15-inch guns could range 35,000 yards. However, Britain's long-range gunnery performance remained theoretical. A stationary ship firing at a stationary target could achieve one hit per gun per minute. Pre-war tactical orthodoxy assumed that a naval battle would in most cases imitate the conditions of stationary combat, and the ships would engage in one long line on parallel courses. In reality, a firing ship and its target would normally manoeuvre at varying ranges at different speeds and on convergent or divergent courses. The calculation of the rate of change had to predict the relative positions of the two ships and to make allowance for the flight times of the shells themselves. Gunnery's problems were compounded by the fact that a ship was not a stable gun platform. Pitching and rolling, particularly in a heavy sea, meant that the guns were only fleetingly covering their targets. Poor weather conditions, spray, smoke, and even darkness itself could hamper observation and had to be taken into account in controlling fire.

Fisher, although he—like many others in the Royal Navy—grossly underestimated the scale of the difficulty, did not totally neglect it. When he became First Sea Lord he appointed an inspector of target practice, Percy Scott. In 1907 Scott managed to have stationary targets replaced by towed ones, and increased to 7,000 or 8,000 yards the ranges at which firing was undertaken. But by 1914 practice was still performed at half the guns' maximum range, conducted in good, clear weather, and divorced from tactical manoeuvre. Scott's principal achievement was the system of director firing, the placing of a centralized sight for all a ship's guns on the foremast: the sight would then be as clear of spray and smoke as possible, and the guns would fire simultaneously, allowing the fall of

---

[29] Marder, *From the Dreadnought*, i. 414.

shot to be more easily observed and corrected. However, the advocates of individual gun-laying were sufficiently vociferous to ensure that Scott's proposal had to wait until 1912 for formal adoption.

Fisher also showed some interest in the work of Arthur Hungerford Pollen, a civilian, trained in the law but interested in naval matters, who produced a mechanical solution to the problems of long-range fire control. Pollen's system plotted the course and bearing of the enemy ship, related them to those of the firing ship, corrected for movements by both ships and for the flight times of the projectiles, and performed all this at speed. Pollen's system would have enabled the navy to break the tactical tyranny of formations in line-ahead, that is of ships following each other in single file, so that a fleet could concentrate their fire in broadsides to port or starboard. Greater flexibility, which had been promised by the advent of rams and torpedoes, seemed to have been put in abeyance by the revival of gunnery. But Pollen's system was never universally adopted. Instead, Captain F. C. Dreyer, with the backing of Sir Arthur Wilson, pirated Pollen's Argo clock (effectively the computer of the system) to mechanize the plotting of bearings but retained the manual plotting of ranges, so producing a fire-control system which was cheaper than Pollen's, and which performed well enough on the straight courses and limited ranges of pre-war battle practice. Despite all Pollen's promotion of his inventions, the Admiralty bought only five clocks, for installation on the King George V class battleships.

The frustration of Scott, and in particular the virtual rejection of Pollen, meant that despite the primacy for Fisher of effective long-range gunnery no reconciliation of its problems had been achieved. Engine speed, as Pollen emphasized in 1911, was not the same as tactical speed: high engine speed was only valuable if the knowledge could be acquired to enable its use in combat. But Pollen was an outsider, not a naval man, and he was taking on the elite of the Royal Navy, its gunnery experts. Pollen had produced a mechanical solution to problems whose resolution had hitherto relied on the training and skill of naval gun crews: he was arguing that professional, human qualities, which had marked off British naval superiority in the age of sail, should be abandoned in favour of the machine. Dreyer, as a naval officer, had powerful backers—first Reginald Bacon, director of naval ordnance from 1907 to 1909, and then Arthur Wilson. Pollen, on the other hand, had lost the support of Fisher because the latter reckoned him a Beresfordian. His chances looked up again when he enlisted the enthusiastic aid of Captain Frederick Ogilvy, commanding HMS *Natal* and responsible for the 1909 trials of Pollen's system. But Ogilvy succumbed to typhoid, ironically the product of some oysters presented to him by Pollen. Battenberg was also sympathetically inclined to Pollen, but was probably reluctant to reactivate an issue whose nature was calculated to invite Churchill's interference in technical matters. The objective assessment of the Pollen system was thus prey to individual favour, to accident, to prejudice.

All this is not to say that the qualitative balance was actually weighted against the British in 1914. The Germans too practised firing at no more than 10,000 yards, albeit at speed and in poor visibility. They did not have director firing or, for all its deficiencies, the equivalent of the Dreyer range table: in the matter of fire control their only advantage lay in their stereoscopic sights. The first German Dreadnoughts, the Nassau class completed in 1909–10, had reciprocating engines rather than turbines and thus—unlike their British equivalents—lacked the space to mount twin-turrets. But the fact that they were therefore relatively under-gunned in more ways than one was not to prove decisive. Being built in more modern dockyards, the German ships were up to ten feet broader in the beam than British Dreadnoughts. Their limited operating radius, since they were intended for the North Sea only, allowed a larger number of watertight compartments. And, as a general principle, the Germans used armour of a thickness equivalent to their guns' calibre: thus, the Nassaus had plate 300 mm thick compared to 279 mm on the Dreadnoughts, and it extended (unlike the British armour belt) from bow to stern.

The capital ship of 1914 had become, by virtue of its construction, its armour, its watertight compartments, and its speed, stronger in relation to defence than to offence. However great their own offensive capacities, the British were going to find it hard to sink the robustly built and more stable German ships. The Royal Navy's difficulties in this respect were increased through self-inflicted and largely avoidable deficiencies. In July 1914 fifteen out of twenty-eight British capital ships did not have the optimum fire-control gear, and in only eight had Scott's director firing been installed. The theoretical capabilities of firepower could not be realized in practice. The possibility of a decisive fleet action was more remote than the massive 15-inch guns of the super-Dreadnoughts suggested.[30]

What had sunk ships in the Russo-Japanese War was fire and water: as crews shipped water to fight fires they added to that already entering through holes in the hull and so rendered vessels unstable. Neither problem was inherently incapable of management, but the efforts of the crews of stricken ships were impeded by a hail of close-range high-explosive shell discharged from lighter, quick-firing secondary armament. Wilson's belief that 8,000 yards was an extreme range for battleships did more, therefore, than mirror his own pre-Dreadnought fleet-handling experience in 1904; it also reflected the most recent (albeit also pre-Dreadnought) lessons of war.

[30] Sumida, *In defence of Naval Supermercy*, 207; Herwig, *Luxury Fleet*, 59–60; Marder, *From the Dreadnought*, i. 417–18.

Intellectually, this was the Royal Navy's greatest problem. The service radically revised its capabilities in the decade before 1914, but in doing so it had rendered its continued maritime pre-eminence dependent on equipment untested in combat. The fear that theory had outstripped performance was reinforced by its increasing focus on the North Sea. Sturdee, calculating that on twenty-five out of thirty days visibility there was restricted to a maximum of 10,000 yards, concluded that battle was likely to open at 6,000 yards. At such a range the deficiencies of armour-piercing shell were not relevant, and, because in close action torpedo-boats would once again constitute a threat, the values of quick-firing guns were enhanced. Furthermore, line-ahead would remain essential, and the Pollen system would be redundant.[31]

Fisher's critics were therefore worried that technological innovation had become, in the words of a future First Sea Lord, Ernle Chatfield, 'a master rather than a servant'.[32] In their youths first the ram and then the torpedo had meant that speed of decision and rapid executive action would be essential command qualities in a fleet action if it had occurred. The advent of long-range gunnery decelerated the pace of combat at sea, while reimposing order through its insistence on line-ahead to enable concentrated and accurate fire. Fisher himself neglected naval tactics, and so was slow to see that the consequences of his own radicalism at this level were, paradoxically, in some respects conservative.

New equipment did not have to create a tactical straitjacket: materialism could be a servant. Pollen's fire-control system would have permitted battle squadrons to assimilate frequent changes in ranges and bearings. Wireless, which the Royal Navy tested in 1899, could in theory confer flexibility through real-time intelligence and reporting. Scouting cruisers were now able to relay information over distances of 70 miles, from points far over the horizon. Leading units could take the initiative in closing with the enemy, confident that their actions would not go unsupported. But practice did not match these expectations. Ships had been designed without wireless offices close to their bridges, and so the information wireless conveyed was not readily incorporated with command. The messages themselves had to be encoded before transmission and then deciphered on receipt. Thus, as ranges closed, wireless became less and less efficient at providing real-time intelligence. By contrast, wireless enabled excessive control at long ranges. Manoeuvres in 1906 condemned the wireless as inefficient, not so much on technical grounds as because it invited the transmission of far too many useless messages.[33] In

---

[31] David Brown, *Warship* (1996), 68–72, 76; Lambert, 'Wilson', in Murfett (ed.), *First Sea Lords*, 403; Gordon, *Rules of the game*, 351, 369; Semmel, *Liberalism and naval strategy*, 139–40; Lambert, *Journal of Military History*, LXI (1998), 32–9.

[32] Gordon, *Rules of the game*, 349; for what follows see also 318–19, 325, 340–7, 349–56.

[33] Ibid. 584.

March 1910 Sir Arthur Wilson directed the manoeuvres of the 2nd battle squadron off Portugal from the Admiralty.[34] Thus the wireless's initial impact was not to promote tactical flexibility through the delegation of command but to further tactical restraint through its centralization.

The navy, after all, was a hierarchical profession, in which seniority prevailed over selective promotion. The advent of steam, with its ability to equalize the speeds of ships, provided the opportunity for further regulation. 'The chief aim of the naval tactician', according to Philip Colomb in 1874, was 'to work a fleet at speed, in the closest order.'[35] The arrival of the wireless did not change the fact that tactical control was exercised primarily through flag signals. In the 1880s a fleet required a minimum of 14,000 different signals, and despite efforts to reduce this number little had changed by 1914. Signalling promoted the cult of fleet control, although steam ensured that there were fewer masts on which to fly the flags and more smoke with which to obsure them.

By 1891 Sir George Tryon, appointed commander-in-chief of the Mediterranean Fleet in that year, feared that fleet manoeuvres orchestrated by flags had become an end in themselves, usurping effectiveness in battle. Recognizing that in close action an excessive dependence on flag signals could rob commanders of initiative and the fleet of tactical flexibility, he experimented with the delegation of command through signal-free manoeuvring. But his efforts to reinject the reality of war into the navy's peacetime training were confounded in 1893 when his flagship, HMS *Victoria*, was rammed by HMS *Camperdown*. Although not the consequence of signal-free manoeuvring, the disaster discredited Tryon's principles, as well as drowning their author. Signalling became a naval specialism, as self-important and self-promoting as gunnery. The dangers did not go unrecognized, but responses tended to be defeatist. In 1908 E. J. W. Slade, the director of naval intelligence, wrote: 'The tendency for signalling methods to be based on peace conditions and to become increasingly complicated has been apparent for some time: it is an almost inevitable corollary of such conditions.'[36]

The navy liked to think that its view of battle was Nelsonic. Its belief was justified in so far as fleet action remained the operational focus for every right-thinking officer. Nor was the stress put on decisive battle as ill-conceived as subsequent experience might suggest. The evidence of Tsushima just as much as Trafalgar supported such a stance. What was not Nelsonic was the centralization of command which steam propulsion and flag signalling fostered. The fleet would approach the enemy in column, deploy into line, and would engage in a gunnery duel on a parallel course to the enemy's. The ultimate objective was to outdistance the enemy line and so be able to cut across his van, to cross

---

[34] Lambert, 'Wilson', in Murfett (ed.), *First Sea Lords*, 40.
[35] Gordon, *Rules of the game*, 189; for what follows see also 193–213, 243–92, 300–7.   [36] Ibid. 361.

the 'T' in the naval parlance of the day, bringing the fire of the line's broadside against the reduced weight of the enemy's fire ahead. But the speed of the line would, for the sake of the formation, be restricted to that of the slowest ship. Ships would fight, not as independent units but as part of a larger formation.[37]

A decisive victory over the German fleet would fulfil the objectives of British strategy: it would secure Britain's maritime approaches and resolve most of the other responsibilities of admiralty. But the pursuit of such an action was in no sense obligatory. The navy's overriding task was defensive: to maintain Britain's supremacy at sea and to rebuff the challenges of others. In their so-called 'green pamphlet', Slade, in his previous incarnation as director of the navy's war college, and the civilian maritime strategist Julian Corbett told the war course at Portsmouth in November 1906 that defensive action could well prove both stronger and sufficient. According to Corbett, dominance of the sea rested on the control of its lines of communication. The impulse to battle, he argued in *Some principles of maritime strategy* in 1911, should not, 'for all its moral exhilaration', become 'a substitute for judgement'. As the power in possession, Britain should only seek battle when it commanded overwhelming force and when the circumstances were exactly right.[38]

And there was a further factor militating against fleet action: the Germans might not come out to fight. In the immediate aftermath of Tsushima, with the Russian threat eliminated, Britain's margin of maritime superiority was so massive as to make fleet action both unnecessary and improbable. The German navy in the North Sea was growing but still manageable, and the Admiralty's pursuit of plans for blockade and for amphibious operations between 1906 and 1908 reflected the fact that it was very unlikely to seek a decisive engagement of its own volition. Indeed, Asquith was so confident in Britain's mastery of the seas that in March 1908 he embraced a two-power standard, plus 10 per cent.[39] This confidence was of course shaken by the 1909 scare, but its legacy persisted in two forms. First, the aim of Britain's pre-1914 naval programme was to intimidate the Germans. Throughout the period 1905 to 1918 the British never lost a clear quantitative lead in capital ships; deterrence was therefore as likely to operate during the war, to keep the German fleet in harbour, as it had done in peacetime. Secondly, if the German fleet was so neutralized, the navy would be free to pursue options other than fleet action.

At one level, therefore, the intellectual origins of close blockade lay in the idea that the German fleet would not sally forth; moreover, close blockade would serve both of Britain's pre-eminent defensive objectives, resistance to invasion and protection of its trade routes. But at another level close blockade

[37] Marder, *From the Dreadnought*, i. 344, 367–8, 395–400.
[38] Corbett, *Some principles*, pp. xvii–xxvii, 167, 171; see also Semmel, *Liberalism and naval strategy*, 141–2; Dirks, *Militärgeschichtliche Mitteilungen*, 37 (1985), 40; Gray, *Leverage of Sea Power*, 17–18.
[39] O'Brien, *British and American naval power*, 30–1, 36, 39.

fed the offensive instincts of the Royal Navy. By stopping up Germany's main waterways, it would force the German fleet into action, despite its inferiority, in a bid to reopen navigation.

The dangers of close blockade were, however, evident as early as 1904; the advent of the submarine, the mine, and the torpedo, in addition to the threat of coastal batteries, suggested that the maintenance of an immediate watch on the estuaries of the Jade and the Elbe would result in the steady erosion of British capital ships, with no comparable loss to Germany. Fisher's war orders of 1908, therefore, compromised by ordering the blockading fleet to pull back at night to a point at least 170 miles from the nearest enemy destroyer base. Confusion ensued. The commander responsible for the operational execution of the First Sea Lord's war orders was Beresford: thus, the conversion of concept into detailed plan fell foul of the two admirals' personal animosities. Nor did their joint retirements clarify the situation. Wilson had been responsible for some of the more hare-brained thinking of 1905–6, including a scheme (endorsed by Fisher) to destroy the forts at Cuxhaven, sink the German fleet at anchor, and master the Kiel canal in order to threaten Hamburg.[40] As First Sea Lord, therefore, Wilson reverted to close blockade, arguing on the basis of his experience in 1904 that submarines could not manoeuvre in shallow waters and would not attack destroyers. (In fact, in the manoeuvres to which he was referring the submarines had been evading escorts in a bid to get at battle-ships.) Wilson concluded that destroyers could enforce a blockade close to the coast, and that the Grand Fleet should be at hand in the event of the High Seas Fleet coming out to break it up. Wilson's plan rested on an overestimation of the destroyer and an underestimation of the submarine. It would be criticized on both counts.

Destroyers were built to 'destroy' torpedo boats; they had been designed both for attack with torpedoes and as a defence against them. The combination of reciprocating engines and a limited displacement restricted their endurance at sea. Thus—in a further reflection of its global remit as a maritime power—Britain had fewer destroyers than did Germany: forty-two to eighty-eight in 1914. Moreover, as the possessor of a network of sovereign bases, the Royal Navy had only one collier: the Grand Fleet alone reckoned it needed in excess of 200 on mobilization. The blockading destroyers would have to return to coal every three to four days. As the nearest British port was 280 miles from the German coast, the blockading force would require three reliefs—one on station, one in port, and one en route—or twice as many destroyers as Britain possessed. Wilson's response to these difficulties was to suggest the seizure of Heligoland, so as to create a forward base. Both Bridgeman, the Second Sea Lord, and Sir George Callaghan, who became commander-in-chief, Home

---

[40] Gooch, 'Adversarial attitudes', in Smith (ed.), *Government and the armed forces*, 65.

Fleet, in November 1911, were appalled. The confusion was compounded by the Declaration of London, which in bolstering the maritime rights of neutrals, threatened the use of blockade as a weapon of war. The navy's confusion at the Committee of Imperial Defence on 23 August 1911 was an accurate and direct reflection of the confusion in its war planning.[41]

At first Callaghan's own solution was an observational blockade. During the course of 1912 the naval war staff examined the idea of deploying cruisers and destroyers in a line 300 miles long, from the Norwegian shore to the east coast of England. Again the navy had too few ships to match its operational objectives. Battenberg dubbed such thinking 'plain suicide'; Callaghan himself rejected the idea, and by November was advocating the adoption of a distant blockade.[42] Its logic was geographical, exploiting Britain's land mass athwart Germany's exits to the oceans, and dividing its warships into two components, one from Orkney to Norway, across the northern exits from the North Sea, and the other in the Channel, at its southern exit.[43] The fact that the North Sea was thus rendered a no-man's land was not seen necessarily as a disadvantage. Flotilla defence could guard the eastern coast of Great Britain against German raids, while the temptation of German capital ships to sally forth would be thereby increased, and the opportunity for fleet action created.

By 1913–14, therefore, distant blockade had begun, at least formally speaking, to give the Royal Navy a coherent operational plan, which integrated the possibility of fleet action with Britain's wider strategic objectives. But the issue was far from settled. Wilson's low opinion of the submarine was not shared by Fisher, who had promoted it for the purposes of coastal defence. By 1909 the combination of Fisher's enthusiasm and Vickers' nose for easy profits (submarine construction did not require expensive plant)[44] meant that Britain led the world in the development of ocean-going submarines. But Wilson's appointment as First Sea Lord and the cabinet's acceptance of the need to surpass German Dreadnought construction rates left the submarine programme in disarray. Not until Churchill took up the reins at the Admiralty did Fisher's voice again find a hearing.

Churchill was receptive to the submarine for reasons that were strategic, political, and operational. By February 1912 Fisher's solution to the naval arms race in the Mediterranean was flotilla defence. The objections to such a strategy were political: not only the public but also the Committee of Imperial Defence

[41] Halpern, *Naval history of World War I*, 21–2, 26; Lautenschläger, *International Security*, VIII (1983), 18–19; Sumida, *Journal of Military History*, LVII (1993), 465–7; Lambert, 'Wilson', in Murfett (ed.), *First Sea Lords*, 44–7.
[42] Miller, *Superior force*, 146; Lambert, 'Bridgeman', in Murfett (ed.), *First Sea Lords*, 63–4.
[43] Marder, *From the Dreadnought*, i. 369–77.
[44] Trebilcock, *Vickers*, 105–8; what follows relies overwhelmingly on Lambert, *Journal of Modern History*, LXVII (1995), 595–626.

measured naval strength in terms of Dreadnoughts. Churchill, therefore, wavered. However, submarines were cheaper than battleships, and by the end of 1913 he was able to promise the prime minister that he could substitute the latter with the former and so meet the Treasury's determination to cut the naval estimates from 1915–16. But Churchill's conversion to the submarine was not simply the product of political expedience or the needs of the Mediterranean; it was also a manifestation of his pugnacity. The submarine might enable a reversion to close blockade in the North Sea.

By 1908 the Royal Navy possessed in the *D1* a submarine capable of sustaining itself in the North Sea for up to a week, and with the range to operate off the German coast. The D-class's successor was the E-type, a long-range patrol submarine. So impressive, however, was the *D1*'s performance that it also fostered experiments with other types, and particularly with a much larger vessel, capable of 24 knots on the surface and therefore of operating with the Grand Fleet. By 1915 this line of development would result in the K-class. But in the short term the consequence of experimentation and proliferation was loss of momentum. In 1913 Britain lacked the plant to develop and produce three different types of submarine at the same time. To allow room for the fleet submarine, E-type production was retarded in favour of the F-class, which had been designed for coastal protection and which the fleet submarine advocates argued was as fit for close-blockade work as the E-class. By late 1913 it was clear that the F-class lacked the endurance to operate off the German shore.[45]

Fisher wrote to Churchill in November casting doubts on the fleet submarine, and pushing the E-class. Typically, his advocacy almost did as much to damage his case as advance it. Churchill, Battenberg, and the commodore of the submarine service, Roger Keyes, were scandalized by Fisher's suggestion that submarines might sink unarmed merchant vessels. Furthermore, his belief that the submarine challenged the hegemony of the battleship was at least superficially a case for proceeding with fleet submarines rather than patrol craft. Certainly, one consequence of the secret conference held at the Admiralty on 9 December 1913 to discuss Fisher's views was an acceptance that if the K-class was to enter service it should do so at the expense of battleships and not of patrol submarines.

Britain's increasing insouciance concerning its inability to sustain the two-power standard, therefore, derived from an impending change in naval strategy. However, the abandonment of the battleship as the yardstick of naval power could not be public. Domestically, Dreadnoughts had too high a profile to be rapidly abandoned; internationally, Britain's rivals had to be encouraged

[45] See, in addition to Lambert, Halpern, *Keyes papers*, vol. i. pp. xx–xxiv; Marder, *Fear God and dread nought*, iii. 33–4.

to persist with expensive technologies whose impending obsolescence the Admiralty now began to recognize.[46]

The long-term consequence of the December 1913 conference would be to throw the strategy of distant blockade into disarray once more. It endorsed a submarine blockade of Germany's ports and the procurement of E-class submarines to effect it. However, the fact that war broke out in the following summer meant that the navy still had too few submarines—and was still too Dreadnought-dependent—for such a policy. Distant blockade was endorsed by default.

The fluctuations in war planning were compounded by their implications for the navy's bases. Portsmouth and Plymouth on the south coast, developed when France and Russia were the likely enemies, were replaced by Harwich, Rosyth, and Cromarty on the east coast after 1905. But the emphasis on additional ship construction and the need to repay the loans contracted for the southern bases left insufficient funds for new shore facilities: Harwich was suitable only for light craft, in 1914 development at Rosyth was just beginning, and both it and Cromarty were open to submarine attack. A possible altern-ative, the Humber, was also vulnerable to submarines, and in any case drew insufficient water. In the event, Cromarty and then Rosyth were to play host only to the battle cruisers. Neither was big enough for the Grand Fleet whose major base was established at Scapa Flow. The choice of Scapa was consonant with the decision for distant blockade but with little else. No more than an anchorage, without defences, and exposed to severe weather conditions, it lacked good internal communications to the south of England and lay at the furthest possible extremity from Britain's traditional naval orientation.

The decision for distant blockade, and the subsequent selection of bases, gave the fleet a less offensive and provocative stance. But in most minds blockade remained a defensive means to an offensive end, to bring the German fleet to battle; it was not primarily an end in itself. Blockade as it subsequently came to be understood and applied, as the conduct of economic warfare, was not totally neglected by the pre-war navy, but—once again—it was the victim of divided counsel rather than the fruit of sustained analysis.

The trade division of the Naval Intelligence Department, recognizing British dependence on overseas imports of food, came also to appreciate Germany's comparable vulnerability. In 1906 Germany reckoned to import 20 per cent of its annual grain consumption.[47] The opportunity for offensive action there-fore existed, and was confirmed by Britain's geographical position athwart Germany's sea lanes and by British naval supremacy. Between 1905 and 1908 the

---

[46] See, in addition to Lambert, Epkenhans, *Die wilhelminische Flottenrüstung*, 135.

[47] Offer, *First World War*, 230; for what follows see principally ibid. 218–43, 271–98, but also Bell, *History of the blockade*, 8–31; Offer, *Journal of Contemporary History*, XXIII (1988), 99–119; Offer, *Past and Present*, CVII (1985), 204–26.

MAP 14. THE NORTH SEA AND THE BALTIC

Gulf of
Bothnia

St Petersburg
(Petrograd) •

Gulf of
Finland

Reval •

Gulf
of
Riga

Riga •

SWEDEN

Courland

Memel •

Kiel •
ıburg

Elbe

POMERANIA

N Y

| 0 | 100 | 200 miles |
| 0 | 100 | 200 | 300 km |

Naval Intelligence Department gave sustained attention to a war on German trade: it concluded, in the words of its director Sir Charles Ottley, that 'the mills of our sea-power (though they would grind the German industrial population slowly perhaps) would grind them "exceedingly small"—grass would sooner or later grow in the streets of Hamburg and wide-spread death and ruin would be inflicted'.[48]

Such talk was totally in keeping with Fisher's espousal of deterrence, and indeed the First Sea Lord was attracted to the notion of economic warfare for that very reason. But his enthusiasm lacked consistency. In 1909 he presided over the disbandment of the trade division, the navy's 'think-tank' on blockade, and in 1910 he engineered his succession by Wilson, who thought economic warfare could not work because Germany would be able to compensate by trading through the neutral powers on its borders.

Even more confusing was Fisher's attitude to the declaratory aspect of deterrence, the need to make threats clear to a potential opponent for the deterrent to be effective. The Declaration of Paris of 1856 had applied a narrow definition of contraband designed to encourage neutral trade in wartime. Thus, enemy goods carried on neutral ships were not liable to capture; furthermore, the definition of conditional contraband, that is to say, goods that were not munitions of war but which could have indirect military applications (such as food for belligerents), was unclear. One of the upshots of the Hague Conference of 1906–7 was an effort to clean up this area of maritime law, and in 1909 the Declaration of London extended neutral rights by giving contraband a narrow definition, establishing a long free list, and by keeping food as conditional contraband (to qualify it had to be consigned to soldiers, not civilians). The Declaration of London reflected British interests as a commercial maritime power, as the home of 48 per cent of the world's merchant shipping; it did not reflect British interests as a belligerent. The latter consideration provoked sufficient outcry, in the context of the 1909 naval panic, to cause the House of Lords to block Britain's ratification of the declaration. But most extraordinary was the behaviour of the Admiralty. Ottley and his colleagues, having advocated economic warfare in a strategic context, supported the Declaration of London and its encouragement to neutral trade. The argument that Germany could circumvent a blockade by trading through its border neutrals thus received indirect confirmation from those best qualified to oppose it, and most interested in doing so. For the army, seeing blockade as the alternative to continentalism, and the Foreign Office, persuaded that Germany could continue to trade through border neutrals, the Admiralty's confusion was an extraordinary opportunity. Moreover, it militated against the deterrent impact of the threat of economic war on Germany,

---

[48] Offer, *First World War*, 232.

since it publicly suggested that commercial blockade was not part of Britain's armoury. The only rationalization of the Admiralty's, and of Fisher's, position is hard-headed cynicism: that in the event of Britain being at war the declaration would be neglected, in the event of neutrality it would be enforced. Whatever the situation, in the last five years before the war's outbreak naval thinking on economic war went cold.

The fact that Britain was not totally unprepared to begin economic war against Germany in August 1914 was the achievement of Maurice Hankey, a former member of the Naval Intelligence Department, and from 1908 assistant secretary and then secretary of the Committee of Imperial Defence. Hankey had the full confidence of Fisher (although the latter had less faith in the body which Hankey served). The trust was certainly justified in so far as Hankey saw strength in naval terms: 'my belief in sea-power', he wrote after the war, 'amounted almost to a religion. The Germans, like Napoleon, might overrun the Continent; this might prolong the war, but could not affect the final issue, which would be determined by economic pressure.'[49] Hankey's pre-war work took two complementary directions. First, in 1910 he began the preparation of the 'War Book', a document designed to set out in detail every step to be taken by the government and its departments in the period preparatory to and on the outbreak of war. The first version of the 'War Book' appeared in 1912, and it was revised annually. One of its major aims—despite the procrastination of the Treasury on insurance—was to set out the legal and financial measures to be taken in the initiation of economic warfare. Secondly, Hankey steered the inquiry of 1911–12 on trading with the enemy to a position which put to one side the commercial interests of British business and declared that on the outbreak of war all trade with Germany should cease, and even that the major neutral ports serving Germany—Antwerp and Rotterdam—should be blockaded. All this was partial and incomplete; the Committee of Imperial Defence lacked the executive powers or the central authority to give its proposals bite; the 'War Book' was far from being a war plan; but Hankey kept the idea of economic warfare alive, and in some areas and in some respects the implementation of blockade in August 1914 was both immediate and effective.

However, as even Hankey realized, the full impact of blockade on Germany itself would be progressive and slow. France and Russia might be defeated on the battlefield long before the grass was growing in the streets of Hamburg. Nor would an early and annihilating victory over the German fleet in the North Sea postpone the advance of Germany's armies. Maritime strategists, therefore, cast around for a strategic option that would have immediate consequences on the European mainland. The development of amphibious operations, the idea that the army was a bolt fired by the navy, had by 1910 a

---

[49] Hankey, *Supreme command*, i. 166; see also Roskill, *Hankey*.

distinguished body of historical and intellectual support. Until at least 1905
the army imagined that, if it went to war in Europe, it would do so as the
cutting edge of sea-power. Sir Charles Callwell, who was recalled to be
director of military operations at the War Office in 1914, had cited the
Peninsular and Crimean Wars as examples of the correct application of sea-
power, allowing British armies to strike a continental enemy at points of
Britain's own choosing. Julian Corbett, an eighteenth-century historian by
vocation, was the navy's chief exponent of this method of limited involvement
in continental warfare. Corbett influenced both Hankey and Fisher. Hankey
himself, as an officer in the Royal Marines, was by profession predisposed to
think in terms of amphibious warfare. Fisher in 1905 supported a suggestion
made by Ottley that the Committee of Imperial Defence should establish a
committee on combined operations. The timing was wrong, the army's
attention was just beginning to turn to independent operations on the continent, and no committee was created. Fisher nonetheless continued to
canvass amphibious options for the Baltic—the seizure of a naval base in
Schleswig-Holstein or a landing in Pomerania to threaten Berlin, the latter
possibly in conjunction with the Russians. The directorate of military operations reviewed the possibilities in 1907 but condemned them in 1908, and the
general staff's opposition was relayed to the Committee of Imperial Defence
in December 1908 and again in March 1909. The army itself was too weak to
fight German troops unaided, and the decisive land battles would be fought
on France's frontiers irrespective of whether the British Expeditionary Force
was dispatched. As pertinently, Fisher's proposals made no sense in terms of
the navy's structure. By scrapping large numbers of old vessels and concentrating on fewer capital ships of high quality, Fisher had ceased to possess an
armada of ships appropriate to troop transport. He lacked the minesweepers
and escort vessels to cope with the naval defences of the Baltic. And the loss of
a single Dreadnought to torpedo or mine would be relatively far more costly
(and more likely) than that of a lighter but better-adapted craft.

  Without the army, the navy switched its attention from the Baltic to the
North Sea. Most developed were plans relating to the estuaries of the Ems and
the Elbe. But the navigational problems were immense, and the ineffectiveness
of naval gunfire against shore batteries eliminated several possible options.
Wilson's enthusiasm for the seizure of Heligoland as a destroyer base, in
addition to its other objectionable features, presumed the availability of an
army division. The scheme did not find favour within the navy, but Wilson was
of course his service's spokesman at the Committee of Imperial Defence. It was
singular perversity to persist with an option on 23 August 1911 which the army
had been rubbishing for at least the previous three years.[50]

_____
[50] Paul Hayes, 'Britain, Germany and the Admiralty's plans for attacking German territory 1906–
1915', in Freedman *et al.* (eds.), *War, strategy and international politics*.

Wilson's humiliation did not mean that the navy abandoned its consideration of combined operations. It did, however, recognize that it needed sustained staff-work to make them a viable option. In 1913 Hankey advocated the
exchange of officers between the navy's and army's staffs with the intention of
promoting a greater awareness within the army of the needs of maritime
strategy. The assistant director of naval operations, Captain Herbert Richmond, went further: with Churchill's and Battenberg's support he called for
the re-creation of the Committee of Imperial Defence's subcommittee on
combined operations. The war broke out without anything having been
achieved, but with amphibious warfare still on the navy's agenda.[51]

In 1914, in none of its three possible areas of operations—fleet action,
blockade, amphibious landings—did the Royal Navy have a viable war plan.
This fact, extraordinary enough in itself, is amplified by the observation that
Britain—although perhaps the most culpable—was not unique in this regard.
The obvious manifestation of pre-war rivalries, the naval arms race, was not
accompanied by much thought as to what those navies would do with themselves in the event of war. Russian naval construction is a case in point.

In 1904 lack of sea control had proved strategically decisive: it had allowed
the Japanese to get ashore in the first place. Fortuitously, the Russian navy's
losses at Tsushima were of a generation of vessels outdated by the Dreadnought. Russia was therefore under pressure to initiate a major construction
programme on a number of counts. But it did not follow that the new fleet had
to be of ocean-going Dreadnoughts. In geopolitical terms Russia was a land
power, whose military efficiency could be undermined if resources were
diverted from the army to the navy. In the shallow and enclosed waters of
the Baltic in particular, capital ships were highly vulnerable and coastal defence
promised to be sufficient: mines had sunk two out of seven Japanese capital
ships at Port Arthur and could be just as effective against the Germans in the
Gulf of Finland. When, in 1906, the naval minister Admiral Birilev favoured
this approach, he enjoyed the support not only of the war minister and the
chief of the general staff but also of Stolypin.[52]

But Birilev was dismissed. The naval general staff, formed in 1906, wanted
Dreadnoughts, and so did the Tsar. Moreover, the treasury was anxious to
make the state yards financially independent,[53] and was therefore susceptible
to the argument that they needed a minimum order of two Dreadnoughts at a
time to be viable. Birilev's successor, Admiral Dikov, duly drew up a programme envisaging four squadrons each of eight battleships, four heavy and
light cruisers, and thirty-six torpedo boats and smaller units. The Council for

---

[51] John B. Hattendorf, 'Battenberg', in Murfett (ed.), *First Sea Lords*, 81.
[52] Menning, *Bayonets before bullets*, 154, 159, 197; Perrins, *Slavonic and East European Review*, LVIII
(1980), 385–90.
[53] Gatrell, *Government, industry and rearmament*, 199–206.

State Defence threw it out, in the process forfeiting the Tsar's confidence and sealing its own demise. The Council of Ministers approved a revised programme, phased over ten years, beginning with the laying down of four Dreadnoughts in 1909. The financial prudence of Kokovstov was circumvented by I. K. Grigorovich, the minister of the navy from 1911: he ended the chief of the naval staff's direct access to the Tsar, so making himself the navy's sole intermediary with the head of state, while at the same time managing to win the support of the Duma.[54] Between 1907 and 1913 Russian naval spending rose 178.4 per cent, outstripping that of Germany.[55]

The Duma's enthusiasm for the navy was prompted by the closure of the straits in 1911 and 1912. Their vital commercial importance meant that the rhetoric of Russian navalism, and the grand designs of the Russian naval staff, were increasingly focused on Turkey and the route to the Mediterranean. But not until 1910, with its order for the next three Dreadnoughts, did Russia set about creating a naval presence in the theatre where it might have had influence. Its declared objective was a Black Sea fleet at least half as strong again as those of the other states which maintained navies in the area. Immediately this meant Romania and Bulgaria as well as Turkey; but from 1912 the Black Sea arms race had the potential to interact with that of the Mediterranean, and so Germany and Austria-Hungary might also come into play.[56]

In the event, none of Russia's Black Sea Dreadnoughts was completed for use in the war. The money allocated to the navy had to go into the creation of plant before it could go into the building of ships. There were no yards big enough for the construction of Dreadnoughts on the Black Sea, but the neutralization of the straits meant that they had to be built there and not on the Baltic.[57] Moreover, in one respect Dikov's 1907 programme was sensible: if Russia espoused navalism, it had to create three separate battle squadrons—one each for the Black Sea, the Pacific, and the Baltic. By the time awareness of the first had been heightened, it had to compete with the pre-existing claims of the latter. But the outcome was unrealistic: the distribution of inadequate resources over too many theatres. The first Dreadnoughts, the four laid down in 1909, were intended for the Baltic. Germany, not Japan or Turkey, took priority in the plans of the Russian navy. Grigorovich believed that a major fleet in the Baltic would cement the Entente. He argued that, if the Russian navy forsook coastal defence for forward defence in the Baltic, it could hold the

[54] Stevenson, *Armaments and the coming of war*, 146–8.

[55] Geyer, *Russian imperialism*, 260; for what follows see also D. Jones, *Military-naval encyclopaedia of Russia*, iii. 159–66; Alan Bodger, 'Russia and the end of the Ottoman empire', in Kent (ed.), *Great powers*; Mitchell, *Russian and Soviet sea power*, ch. 13; Gatrell, *Economic History Review*, 2nd series, XLIII (1990), 255–70; Pavlovich (ed.), *Fleet in the First World War*, i. 1–67.

[56] Gatrell, *Government, industry and rearmament*, 137–8; Halpern, *Naval history*, 17; Allen and Muratoff, *Caucasian battlefields*, 232.

[57] Nekrasov, *North of Gallipoli*, 11.

balance between the British and German fleets.[58] But, in spite of the convergence of Grigorovich's arguments with Fisher's designs for amphibious operations, Anglo-Russian naval planning never developed. In 1912 the Russians decided to block the entrance to the Gulf of Finland with mines, and to cover them with coastal batteries. The Baltic fleet was to manoeuvre behind this barrier, using Reval as a forward base. It was a plan which made Dreadnoughts redundant; one proposal advanced in 1913 was for them to be sent to the Mediterranean so that eventually they could find an excuse to force the straits and so be based where they could be used, at Sevastopol. As it was, when war broke out the docks at Reval had not been developed, the coastal batteries were incomplete, and not a single Dreadnought was ready.[59] The operational role of the navy in the Baltic became that which common sense directed, coastal defence. The islands across the gulfs of Finland and Bothnia, linked with mines, screened St Petersburg and the land operations of the North-West Front. In 1914 such naval clout as Russia had was in a sea where it could not use it rather than in the Black Sea, where it was likely to want to use it. No more graphic illustration is needed of the difference between arms races and war plans.

Germany proved no more of an exception to this general rule. Its navy began its life as a Baltic fleet, the Kaiser aspiring in 1892 to being able to defeat Russia and Denmark. The subsequent primacy of the North Sea was in itself a reflection of the Russian Baltic fleet's obliteration at Tsushima. By the same token, Russia's recovery as a Baltic power meant that by 1913 the tempo of German battleship building was not set solely by the higher-profile rivalry with the Royal Navy. The original rationale of the latter was, after all, to browbeat Britain into some sort of naval alliance; thus, the corollary of Tirpitz's 'risk' strategy was the likelihood of Russian and French hostility. Every realistic German naval plan before 1914 concentrated on a clash with Russia and France rather than Britain.[60]

The logic of Germany's military planning also suggested that the Baltic, not the North Sea, should have been the main deployment area of Germany's High Seas Fleet. Free navigation in the Baltic was an important means to trade through the neutral powers of Scandinavia, and in particular gave direct access to Swedish iron ore. The weakness of the German 8th army in East Prussia, plus the recurrent fear (however far-fetched) of Russian landings on Germany's Baltic coast, meant that for both Schlieffen and Moltke the navy

---

[58] Stevenson, *Armaments and the coming of war*, 149.
[59] Nekrasov, *North of Gallipoli*, 12–14; Halpern, *Naval history*, 181.
[60] Peter Winzen, 'Zur Genesis von Weltmachtkonzept und Weltpolitik', in Röhl (ed.), *Der Ort Kaiser Wilhelms*, 191, 196, 198, 215–17; Epkenhans, *Die wilhelminische Flottenrüstung*, 359; id., 'Die kaiserliche Marine im Ersten Weltkrieg: Weltmacht oder Untergang?', in Michalka (ed.), *Der Erste Weltkrieg*, 323.

could play an important ancillary role in diverting and pinning Russian troops. Russian naval weakness after Tsushima removed the threat but reinforced the opportunity. In 1911 consideration was given to mounting a feint landing at Riga to tie down a Russian corps.

Operations against Russia remained a feature of German naval war planning in 1912–13 and 1913–14. But the mounting pace of Russian rearmament made the German approach increasingly defensive, an orientation confirmed in 1913 by Moltke's decision not to continue planning for war against Russia alone.[61] In August 1914 Germany enjoyed a naval superiority in the Baltic which it elected not to use. Its commander, Prince Heinrich of Prussia, the Kaiser's brother, was happy to subordinate his role to that of the High Seas Fleet in the North Sea, an arrangement which was formalized at his own request on 9 October. The Germans, like the Russians, emphasized coastal defence. The suitability of the Baltic for extensive minelaying made a mutual stand-off technically realistic, if militarily disappointing. In mid-August the German army felt that the fleet should be bombarding St Petersburg; in September Falkenhayn requested a naval demonstration off Courland.[62]

The case for the German navy's concentration in the Baltic, even if not supported by either the Kaiser or Tirpitz, was reinforced by the defensive strength of Germany's North Sea bases. In 1889 the opening of the Kaiser Wilhelm canal linked Kiel, Germany's main Baltic base, to the North Sea, and by 1914 the canal had been widened to accommodate the passage of Dreadnoughts. (This had been Tirpitz's precondition for naval readiness at the so-called war council of 8 December 1912.) Thus, concentration in one sea did not prevent a rapid redeployment in the other; thus too, Denmark's position, dividing Germany's fleet and Germany's maritime interests in two, became proportionately less threatening and less significant. Germany's North Sea naval bases, Wilhelmshaven and Cuxhaven, on the Jade and Elbe estuaries respectively, and also its principal commercial ports, Bremen and Hamburg, were naturally well protected. Shallow water made a submarine approach difficult. In 1890 Germany acquired from Britain (in exchange for Zanzibar) the island of Heligoland, guarding the Jade and the Elbe approaches; to the south-west the Borkum islands screened the mouth of the Ems. Even if the High Seas Fleet had been drawn east to the gulfs of Riga or of Finland, it is hard to see how Britain could have established a local naval supremacy for a period sufficiently long to exploit the opportunity in the west.

But the defensive strength of Germany's North Sea bases also implied offensive weakness. The High Seas Fleet could not pass the shoals and

[61] Lambi, *Navy and German power politics*, 395–9, 406–7. In addition to Lambi on German plans, see also Kennedy, 'Development of German naval operations plans against England,' in Kennedy (ed.), *War plans*. Fundamental on the German navy are the works of Herwig, especially '*Luxury*' fleet.
[62] Schulte, *Europäischer Krise*, 225; Ironside, *Tannenberg*, 259–65; Halpern, *Naval history*, 26, 180, 182.

sandbanks on the Jade or the Elbe at low water, and two high waters were required for the entire fleet to put to sea. Therefore, if the normal state of the fleet were to be in harbour, it automatically sacrificed operational flexibility. Secondly, when it entered the North Sea, it did so from its south-eastern corner only—what one German commentator was later to describe as 'a dead angle in a dead sea'.[63] Its other route, through the Belts, past Denmark, and out to Skaggerak, would have increased Germany's offensive possibilities and brought it closer to the northern exits to the Atlantic; but Denmark, in the interests of its own neutrality and with German support, mined this waterway at the war's outset. Therefore, if the Germans were drawn too far to the north of the North Sea or too far to the west they laid themselves open to being outflanked or to being cut off from their line of retreat.

Tirpitz's acceptance of the Dreadnought challenge, coinciding with the first Moroccan crisis and Russian naval weakness after Tsushima, put the focus of Germany's navy firmly in the North Sea. German naval building was centred on battleships designed to fight the Royal Navy in a fleet action. But in terms of grand strategy such a thrust was contradictory. Tirpitz's navy was not the arm of a policy concerned with regional authority, with the European balance of power; that was the army's task. The navy was intended to further *Weltpolitik*. In the pursuit of colonies it was not exclusively or even necessarily Britain's opposition with which Germany had to contend; its potential challengers were as often other powers with commercial or imperial interests. German–American naval rivalry was fanned in the Pacific over competition for Samoa in 1889 and over the Philippines in 1898; German naval planning thereafter embraced first an invasion of the United States and then, with marginally greater realism, looked to the establishment of bases in the West Indies.[64] The arms race with Britain, therefore, produced a fleet that was not constructed to fulfil the ultimate purposes and more distant objectives of German navalism.

But nor did it create a fleet that was capable of accomplishing its more immediate operational purposes. Tirpitz's fleet was 'not large enough to seek a decision, but too large to be squandered in offensive operations'.[65] In 1894 he had reckoned a 30 per-cent superiority was required before Germany could take the strategic offensive against France and Russia.[66] Against Britain his building programme did not even aim for parity, let alone superiority. And yet, paradoxically, the number of hulls was its determining factor. Tirpitz's tight

---

[63] Wegener, *Die Seestrategie*, 8.

[64] Herwig and D. F. Trask, 'Naval operations plans between Germany and the U.S.A.', in Kennedy (ed.), *War Plans*; also Gemzell, *Organization, conflict and innovation*, 70–4; Hadley and Sarty, *Tin-pots and pirate ships*, 31–47.

[65] Herwig, *International History Review*, X (1988), 82; see also ibid., XIII (1991), 273–83.

[66] Werner Rahn, 'Strategische Probleme der deutschen Seekriegführung 1914–1918', in Michalka (ed.), *Der Erste Weltkrieg*, 342.

management of the naval budget was designed to prevent the cost per unit jeopardizing the overall number of units under construction. Quality could suffer as a consequence. Tirpitz was prepared for Germany to lag behind Britain in turbine development rather than risk the Imperial Naval Office taking an undue share of its research costs. Partly as a result of turbine problems, private German yards were lucky if the navy's contracts covered their outgoings after 1908, and in the six years before the war Germaniawerft, Blohm and Voss, and Stettiner Vulcan were all building major ships at a loss. Similarly, Tirpitz screwed down the prices of armour plate and ordnance, endeavouring to break Krupp's hold on the market to do so. In 1913 he was prepared to set the calibre of his new battle cruisers' guns at 35 cm (i.e. 13.5-inch), not 38 cm (or 15-inch), rather than jeopardize the overall building tempo of the naval laws.[67] Deficiencies relative to the Royal Navy were more important as domestic pressure for continued building than in terms of their implications for battle.

The justification for such apparent perversity was deterrence. As a result, Tirpitz's strategic thought, when assessed in war-fighting terms, seemed unresolved and contradictory. This was particularly the case after 1911, when gunboat diplomacy failed at Agadir. The German navy now found itself forced to assess its capabilities in relation to Britain in terms of defence rather than of negotiation. Tirpitz had to argue that a 2 : 3 ratio in capital ships had military utility.[68] He suggested that, as the Royal Navy was already large, more of its new building represented replacement rather than incremental growth than was the case for Germany. Somewhat less speciously, he also pointed to the problems which Britain would have in manning a larger fleet, when—unlike Germany—it did not have conscription.[69] But these were still answers that pivoted on building rates rather than on operational solutions. Despite the setback of 1911, Tirpitz did not recast his thinking. In May 1914 he reckoned that the German navy would still need another six to eight years before it was ready;[70] in reality—by Tirpitz's standards—it would never be complete.

The confusion thus generated in the objectives of German naval policy was compounded by the divisions within German naval administration. Tirpitz was head of only one part of the navy, of the Imperial Naval Office, the *Reichsmarineamt*; his responsibilities were political and financial, to oversee the construction of ships and to lobby both in the Reichstag and in the press. Tirpitz enjoyed pre-eminence in German naval matters up until 1914, not least because these were the major policy objectives of the peacetime navy, as well as

[67] Epkenhans, *Die wilhelminische Flottenrüstung*, esp. 188–92, 202–11, 234–44, 257–60, 322–3.

[68] Ibid. 93, 98; Stevenson, *Armaments and the coming of war*, 197.

[69] Volker Berghahn, 'Des Kaisers Flotte und die Revolutionierung des Mächtesystem vor 1914', in Röhl (ed.), *Der Ort Kaiser Wilhelms*, 176; Halpern, *Naval history*, 4.

[70] Röhl, *Historical Journal*, XII (1969), 667.

being those with the highest profile. However, in reality Tirpitz's office was that of a *primus inter pares*.

The second arm of the navy's administration, the Admiralty Staff, was established as a subordinate department in 1889, and gained independent status a decade later. Theoretically its functions, planning in peace and directing operations in war, were the same as those of the army's general staff. But the chief of the Admiralty Staff did not command the High Seas Fleet: this was a separate appointment, with its own staff and consequently its own plans. With only brief exceptions, relations between the two departments, in peace and war, verged on the fratricidal. Between 1899 and 1914 the Admiralty Staff had seven chiefs and did not, therefore, enjoy the continuity of direction vouchsafed the Imperial Naval Office or the naval cabinet. Tirpitz worked hard to neutralize yet further the staff's potential importance. Many of those who served on it were his protégés, men who had first established their careers in the Imperial Naval Office and whose skills were honed as intriguers and dealers rather than as naval planners. In 1907–8 Tirpitz scored a succession of major triumphs over the Admiralty Staff. He wrested from it responsibility for naval education; he blocked a proposal that half the naval academy's graduates should serve on the staff for three years; and he ensured that the special status of staff officers, with dual allegiance to their immediate appointment and to their staff background, was terminated. Thus, it was possible for Franz von Hipper, who had neither been to the naval academy nor served on the staff, and whose professional education was almost entirely technical, to end the war as commander of the High Seas Fleet. Tirpitz therefore blocked the Admiralty Staff's development as the intellectual core of the service.

The third major department was the Kaiser's naval cabinet, responsible for promotions and appointments, and headed from 1906 until 1918 by Georg von Müller. The Kaiser continued to exercise supreme command in naval matters when he had increasingly relinquished it in military affairs; Müller's position therefore grew in significance as his own seagoing experience receded. But this did not make the naval cabinet the decisive body in naval affairs. The heads of each of the three major departments, in addition to five others, including each of the operational commands, had the right of direct access to the Kaiser. Tirpitz exploited the Kaiser's weakness, encouraging infighting and fragmentation so as to establish his own indirect supremacy. In particular, by establishing close links between the Imperial Naval Office and the fleet commands, the 'front', he aimed to isolate the Admiralty Staff.

Tirpitz's blocks to the development of the German naval staff impeded the possible reconciliation of the navy's divergent objectives. Tirpitz set an overall policy of deterrence and of operational caution in order to preserve the fleet; thus strategy, for want of a better word, emanated from the Imperial Naval Office. Tactics, the task of thinking how actually to fight the Royal Navy, was the domain of the Admiralty Staff. Preoccupied in part with its own survival, it used a less conservative approach to the employment of the fleet as a means to counter Tirpitz's attacks on it as an institution. Its tactical instructions, which were less dependent than those of the British on flag signals, emphasized the exercise of initiative at lower levels of command; they spoke of the need to annihilate enemy forces regardless of cost in terms more familiar in the manuals of land forces. Doctrinally, tactics and strategy were being prised apart: the former sought battle without using the latter to say what the purpose of the battle might be. Institutionally, the Admiralty Staff was sufficiently successful to ensure that the foundations of Tirpitz's authority, although outwardly intact, in reality were progressively eroded, even before August 1914.[71]

The preliminaries of the second Hague Conference forced on Tirpitz a recognition of Germany's vulnerability to British blockade, the attendant dangers of a protracted war, and the internal economic strains which would thereby be generated for Germany.[72] Furthermore, between 1906 and 1908, with German naval construction in relative confusion and the fleet in absolute inferiority after the launching of the Dreadnought, naval war plans were cautious and defensive. But such thought, while likely to keep the German fleet intact, was totally inappropriate as a challenge to the power that enjoyed maritime supremacy: it would allow Britain to hold what it had, to tighten the blockade, and to win the long war that would result. In 1908 Friedrich von Baudissin, the chief of the Admiralty Staff, argued that time would work against Germany and that it must therefore adopt the offensive to force the British to fight. He canvassed the possibility of action between the German light forces and the British blockading line, which could lead to a major battle; he appreciated the possibility that the British blockade might be distant, but concluded that this would expose Britain's eastern coastline, and open attacking possibilities, including a battle in the northern half of the North Sea for access to the Atlantic. Baudissin and his successor, Max Fischel, therefore challenged the caution of Tirpitz and his acolytes.

In 1909 a change in command enabled Tirpitz to counter Baudissin with the support of the High Seas Fleet. But in 1911–12 Tirpitz's new building programme alienated the fleet: the 'front' now wanted a pause to assimilate the vessels it had already received, to bring the quality of training into line with the quality of technology. Tirpitz was correct in assuming that conscription conferred on the German navy at least one clear advantage over the British. By 1912 the Royal Navy feared that it would lack the crews to keep sufficient ships in

[71] Gemzell, *Organization, conflict and innovation*, ch. 2; Gordon, *Rules of the game*, 395–6; Rahn, 'Strategische Probleme', in Michalka (ed.), *Der Erste Weltkrieg*, 343–4.

[72] Dülffer, *War & Society*, III (1985), 23–43; Offer, *First World War*, 340–1; Pearton, *Knowledgeable state*, 130–1; Lambi, *Navy and German power politics*, 254–5; Baer, 'Anglo-German antagonism and trade with Holland', 25–6.

commission, but significantly the shortage it anticipated was less in the overall manpower base and more in the technical skills acquired by long service.[73] Tirpitz's equation of quantity with quality was revealing. Nor was it just a question of manpower; shore establishments had been neglected in favour of ships, and new vessels preferred to repair facilities for those already in commission.[74] The question of battle-fitness which preoccupied the High Seas Fleet accorded with the diplomatic objectives of Bethmann Hollweg, anxious to use naval arms limitation to neutralize Britain; the Kaiser and the naval cabinet also turned against Tirpitz.

But the alliance emerging within the navy, although it weakened Tirpitz, did not resolve the conundrums of German naval operations. In 1911 Fischel was succeeded as chief of the Admiralty Staff by August von Heeringen, who took Tirpitz's side against the High Seas Fleet. A war game in that year showed that thrusts across the North Sea would not allow the Germans to engage and defeat fractions of the Royal Navy; the latter would be able to concentrate to meet the High Seas Fleet. Therefore any action against the British would have to be confined to German waters, and to ensure sufficient strength would have to rely on the light forces and the High Seas Fleet operating in conjunction with each other. However, such a strategy would only reap rewards if the Royal Navy posted itself in German waters. Both Tirpitz in 1906–7 and Baudissin in 1908 had appreciated that this might not be the case. Thereafter, the mixed messages from Britain resulted in confused responses—and ultimately wishful thinking—in Germany.

The Declaration of London, the result of the London Conference in 1908–9, suggested a triumph for German naval strategy. By adopting a tight definition of contraband, by prohibiting the blockade of neutral harbours, and by removing the belligerent right to seize conditional contraband under the doctrine of continuous voyage, the declaration eased the threat of the British blockade for Germany. More immediately, it required a blockade to be effective to be legal; in other words, it demanded a close blockade, not a distant one. The Admiralty Staff was now torn between planning on the basis of international law, which would require the British to approach the German coast, or of strategic sense, which suggested that they would not. Heeringen appreciated the difficulties which Britain would create for Germany if it adopted a distant blockade. Nonetheless, the operational orders to the fleet of November 1912 assumed a close blockade and a battle in the Heligoland Bight. In 1913 British naval manoeuvres persuaded the Admiralty Staff to veer towards the likelihood of a distant blockade. But it still reckoned on a residual British presence in German waters. A war game of its own suggested that even in the case of a

---

[73] Nicholas Lambert, 'Economy or empire? The fleet unit concept and the quest for collective security in the Pacific, 1909–14', in Kennedy and Neilson (eds.), Far-flung lines, 72–3.
[74] Epkenhans, Die wilhelminische Flottenrüstung, 205–6, 326, 393.

distant blockade the British would post sufficient ships in the Bight to ward off a German strike against the British coast or against the BEF's troop transports in the Channel. By 1914 German naval planning was not only defensive, but was even more so than it had been in 1908–9. There were no plans for sweeping aside the anticipated British blockade, whether close or distant. Its destroyers lacked the range to accompany the High Seas Fleet or sustain operations on the British east coast. Its hope that a skirmish in German waters would draw in more British vessels, and that their numbers would then be steadily reduced by submarines and mines failed to reflect the material constraints: Germany had only two minelayers fit for warlike operations, and only eighteen submarines adapted for coastal defence.[75]

When war broke out Tirpitz's hold on the navy seemed outwardly strong. Two of his protégés occupied key posts, Hugo von Pohl as chief of the Admiralty Staff, and Friedrich von Ingenohl as commander-in-chief of the High Seas Fleet. In reality both his personal position and his policies were bankrupt. On 29 July he tried to complete the pattern of his pre-war intrigues by proposing the formation of a naval high command with himself at its head. But he had already forfeited Wilhelm's confidence. The Kaiser's compromise, to instruct the chief of the Admiralty Staff to consult Tirpitz and the Imperial Naval Office when appropriate, seemed to boost Tirpitz's position. In reality it weakened the authority of the Admiralty Staff without giving Tirpitz the supreme authority which he craved. Furthermore, the actual conduct of war meant that his power base, the Imperial Naval Office, lost primacy to the Admiralty Staff. The policy established for the High Seas Fleet, and endorsed on 6 August by the Kaiser, Bethmann Hollweg, Pohl, and Müller, was Tirpit-zian in its ultimate objectives, to maintain the fleet intact as a bargaining counter in the peace negotiations. However, its means contradicted the rhet-oric of fleet action with which Tirpitz had justified his pre-war building. The Admiralty Staff's thinking had suggested that U-boats would steadily erode British strength, but at least until 1910 Tirpitz had taken a strong line against U-boat construction, and in 1914, like other naval leaders, he saw the submarine as an adjunct to the operations of surface warships, not as an arm in its own right.[76] The orders to the fleet on 30 July, although allowing it to take on the enemy's full fleet, preferred it to engage only portions. Tirpitz came to embrace this limited strategy, hoping thereby for at least some naval action which would ensure his own credibility and establish the navy's continued claims in post-war budgets. But his advocacy lacked consistency or conviction. Pohl and Müller disagreed with him, and as these three made up the naval

---

[75] Baer, 'Anglo-German antagonism and trade with Holland', 51–71; Coogan, *End of neutrality*; Halpern, *Naval history*, 23; Hörich, *Deutsche Seekriegführung*, 8–17, 21–2.

[76] Weir, *International History Review*, VI (1984), 174–90; Gemzell, *Organization, conflict and innova-tion*, 59–62, 96–7.

representation at general headquarters the navy's voice was discordant as well as muffled. Both the Kaiser and Bethmann Hollweg (the latter, in the view of some historians, still hoping to minimize British involvement in the war and therefore reluctant to encourage action at sea) avoided Tirpitz. The grand admiral became isolated and marginal. As August turned to September, the army's triumphs were accompanied by naval quiescence.[77]

Much ink has been spilt on the so-called 'spirit of the offensive'. At times the armies' discussions of the issue are put into the context of a general mood in the Europe of 1914, a melting-pot of social Darwinism and proto-fascism. Consideration of the navies is a powerful corrective to some of the more absurd propositions. The navies had proved less adept than the armies at developing staff organizations; their consideration of operational issues was partial; debates were dominated by issues of personality; these blocks to rational analysis might suggest a predisposition to rash attacks. And yet the broad parameters within which the British and German navies elected to operate in 1914 were defensive. Sea captains were no less anxious to prove their worth in battle than were infantry officers. But the pre-war function of the navies, as manifested by the arms races in both the North Sea and the Mediterranean, was deterrence: war plans were relatively neglected.

Furthermore, if considered on a purely maritime level, deterrence succeeded. The mobilization of the British and German fleets was potentially far more provocative than that of the armies. On 26 July 1914 Battenberg, without cabinet approval, prevented the dispersal of the fleet, assembled for exercises in July, and the Royal Navy was put on a war footing on 29 July. The German navy, although mobilization was not ordered until 1 August, put its ships on alert on 7 July and moved its High Seas Fleet into the North Sea on 31 July. But although the navies therefore anticipated the actions of the armies, neither those steps nor the longer-running arms races themselves generated the war. Tirpitz thought Britain's naval mobilization on 29 July was a bluff, and the deputy chief of the Admiralty Staff agreed with him. Even on 3 August the sailing orders of German auxiliary cruisers emphasized that they should do nothing to jeopardize the possibility of British neutrality.[78] To the very end the German navy persisted in seeing the Anglo-German naval competition in terms short of war. Moreover, deterrence and defence persisted as themes for the next four years. The preservation of what each side had, the security of coasts and of commerce, the importance of ships as bargaining counters not as agents of war, prevailed over the conduct of offensive operations.

[77] Schulte, *Europäische Krise*, 196–7, 224–6, 281–4.
[78] Epkenhans, *Die wilhelminische Flottenrüstung*, 404–7.

THE NORTH SEA, 1914–1915

On the evening of 1 August 1914 Sir John Jellicoe, having accomplished the long train journey to Scotland's northern extremity, found his progress from Wick to Scapa Flow blocked by fog. At 10 p.m. he took the opportunity to dispatch a telegram to the First Lord of the Admiralty: 'Am firmly convinced that the step you mentioned to me is fraught with gravest danger.'[79]

Jellicoe carried with him orders to assume command of the most powerful fleet in the world. He showed no enthusiasm for the job. Sir George Callaghan, whom he was to replace, and who had just completed the task of bringing the Grand Fleet through the Dover straits and up to its battle station at Scapa Flow, was well-respected in the navy. Callaghan was aged 62, eight years older than Jellicoe, and was due to retire in two months' time. Jellicoe enjoyed the imprimatur of Fisher; and nobody could cavil at his elevation on professional grounds. But Jellicoe's protests continued. He was no doubt loath to hurt Callaghan; he was conscious of the vulnerability of the fleet while its command was disrupted as he eased himself into his new responsibilities; most important of all, he feared becoming the conductor for the professional disapprobation of Churchill's interventionism.

Jellicoe's attitude, however, was also indicative of his temperament. Intelligent and analytical, he lacked the thrust and daredevil approach considered characteristic of British naval commanders: Fisher's description of him as 'the future Nelson' could hardly be more inappropriate.[80] He was reluctant to delegate, he was a worrier, and he was a hypochondriac. Like his mentor and like Corbett, he believed in the central importance of the preservation of British naval supremacy, of the fleet in being. This, and not the lust for battle, would determine his actions.

The offensive spirit, therefore, received a powerful corrective with Jellicoe's appointment. But Jellicoe's task—in Churchill's words, 'to secure the safety of the British Fleet during the long and indefinite period of waiting for a general action'[81]—was not an easy one to sustain. The First Lord himself, while recognizing the wisdom of the policy, found it temperamentally uncongenial. The public, whose consciousness of British naval supremacy had been heightened by the pre-war arms race and its attendant propaganda, became impatient for battle. Most important, the fleet itself chafed at its enforced inactivity.

---

[79] Gilbert, *Churchill*, vol. III, Companion pt. 1, p. 9; see also 7–17.

[80] Marder, *Fear God and dread nought*, ii. 399; see also 419, 421, 424, 439, 443, 479. German sources argue that Callaghan's replacement by Jellicoe represented a deliberate decision for prudence over offensive-mindedness, but this is not an argument found in the English sources; see Güth, 'Die organisation der deutschen Marine', 298, and Assmann, *Deutsche Seestrategie*, 48.

[81] Gilbert, *Churchill*, vol. III, Companion pt. 1, p. 180.

Three officers in particular, each holding quasi-independent commands, came to represent a more adventurous style than that of Jellicoe. The best known was Sir David Beatty, still only 43, his uniform worn with a jauntiness that owed much to his tailor's reinterpretation of the dress regulations, and until 1913 Churchill's naval secretary. Beatty's reputation for dash was earned in operations ashore, in the Sudan in 1896 and in the Boxer rebellion, and was confirmed by the appointment he now held, the command of the battle cruiser squadron. Beatty was to make much of Jellicoe's caution, his determination to centralize, and his fear of independent-minded subordinates. In reality, he himself was in due course to prove as prudent in the exercise of command as his superior. Beatty was subordinate to Jellicoe, but because he was based at Rosyth personal meetings between the two were rare. Distance also played its part in encouraging Jellicoe to forego authority over the second of the three, Commodore Reginald Tyrwhitt, who commanded a flotilla of light cruisers and destroyers at Harwich; Tyrwhitt's command formed part of the Southern Force under the direct authority of the Admiralty. Associated with Tyrwhitt in the Southern Force was Commodore Roger Keyes, commanding a submarine flotilla. Tyrwhitt and Keyes represented a younger generation of officers, frustrated by the more plodding approach of their seniors, most of whom had never seen active service, and many of whom had been promoted beyond their real abilities by the rapid expansion of the fleet in the 1880s and 1890s; it was to men like them, and to Keyes in particular, that Churchill would turn for ideas with which to goad his admirals.

The opening task of the war for the Southern Force was to blockade the northern approaches of the Channel in order to ensure the safe passage of the BEF. Herein was an opportunity, which Ingenohl recognized, to deal with a fraction of the Royal Navy. But the waters of the Channel were ideal for British submarine attacks, and the limitations of coal supply would curtail the presence of German torpedo boats, especially since the Germans lacked precise intelligence as to the timings of the BEF's movements. While the Grand Fleet stood by in case the High Seas Fleet did come out, the Southern Force blocked the Channel, and the transports crossed independently and without impediment.

This task completed, Keyes and Tyrwhitt cast around for more positive undertakings. Together they hatched a plan for the Harwich Force to attack the German destroyers in the Heligoland Bight at dawn, when both the day and the night patrols would be out, and then to drive them towards the open sea. Keyes's submarines were to be poised to deal with any larger German ships that came out. When Keyes took his plan to the War Staff its members were too busy to consider it. However, on 23 August Churchill, stung by a couple of recent German sorties and anxious to cover the operations at Ostend, adopted Keyes's proposal. It was then referred back to Sturdee: the chief of the naval war staff retimed the raid so that only the German day patrols would be out, and then limited the involvement of the Grand Fleet (despite Jellicoe's wish to take out his whole force) to Beatty's battle cruisers and Commander W. E. Good-enough's 1st light cruiser squadron. By the time the involvement of Beatty and Goodenough was settled Keyes and Tyrwhitt had already sailed, all their ships having been told that Tyrwhitt's two light cruisers would be the only British vessels bigger than destroyers in the Bight on the morning of 28 August. The other large units expected in the vicinity were two battle cruisers from the Humber, accompanying on the Harwich Force's starboard quarter, to the west, as it ran south past Heligoland. Beatty himself was only marginally better informed—at 8 a.m. on 27 August he signalled to his squadron: 'Know very little. Shall hope to learn more as we go along.'[82]

The German patrols on the morning of the 28th were weak, only four light cruisers were out, and the state of the tide meant that no capital ships would be able to pass the bar until noon. Shortly before Tyrwhitt began his sweep past Heligoland he encountered Goodenough and learnt also of Beatty's presence. At 8 a.m. his two light cruisers were engaged by two German cruisers, which screened the retreat of the German torpedo boats to the cover of the Heligo-land batteries. A single German torpedo boat was isolated, driven out to sea, and sunk. However, HMS *Arethusa*, the light cruiser in which Tyrwhitt was flying his pennant, suffered engine damage and, more significantly, had her wireless shot away. Thus, when Keyes spotted Goodenough's light cruisers through the morning mist his signal to *Arethusa* for clarification received no reply. Keyes concluded that he had four enemy light cruisers in tow, and reckoned he was leading them north-west onto the guns of the Humber-based battle cruisers *Invincible* and *New Zealand*. Goodenough, having picked up Keyes's signal, responded, effectively giving chase to himself, and Tyrwhitt also conformed. At 9.30 a.m. one of Keyes's submarines attacked HMS *South-ampton*, Goodenough's flagship, and the latter responded by trying to ram the submarine: fortunately both were unsuccessful. Twenty minutes later Keyes had finally identified the *Southampton*.

This tale of British confusion and misadventure was in part redeemed by the second half of the action. Within the Jade both *Moltke* and *Von der Tann*, two German battle cruisers, were getting up steam to pass the bar at 12 p.m. In addition, a number of German light cruisers had put to sea; their actions were not co-ordinated, their wireless reporting was poor, and they were converging on the Harwich Force oblivious of Beatty's or Goodenough's presence. For an hour-and-a-half, between 11 a.m. and 12.30 p.m., Tyrwhitt's force engaged the

[82] Goldrick, *The King's ships*, 86; this is the fullest recent account of the action, and indeed of the war in the North Sea 1914–15. In addition, see Corbett, *Naval operations*, i. 99–120; Bennett, *Naval battles*, 145–51.

German light cruisers, but was faced with odds which were progressively becoming more uneven. At 11.35 Beatty responded to Tyrwhitt's signals (sufficient repairs now having been done to *Arethusa*), and changed course to the east, increasing his speed to 27 knots. Shortly after noon Goodenough's light cruisers came to Tyrwhitt's support, and then half-an-hour later Beatty's flagship HMS *Lion* led the battle cruisers into the fray. Admiral Franz von Hipper, commanding the German cruiser squadron, ordered his light cruisers to fall back on *Moltke* and *Von der Tann*. But SMS *Mainz*, which had come up from the Ems to the south-west, was caught between the 1st light cruiser squadron and the Harwich Force; she was hit between 200 and 300 times, and finally sank shortly after 1 p.m. *Lion's* gunnery accounted for another light cruiser, SMS *Köln*, at 1.35 p.m., and left a third, *Ariadne*, so damaged that she too also went down. At 2.25 *Moltke* and *Von der Tann* came into sight, but Ingenohl had already ordered that they should not engage the British battle cruisers, and Hipper himself was anxious not to risk battle without his full squadron. Beatty in any case was turning away; the dangers to his command were multiplying.

The victory of the Heligoland Bight, three German light cruisers and one torpedo boat sunk with no British loss, was a timely fillip both to the navy and to the Entente. It provided a welcome contrast to the steady retreat of the armies in France. Moreover, it established a moral superiority at sea that remained to the British advantage for the rest of the war. The relative inferiority and vulnerability of the German torpedo boats and light cruisers was a powerful disincentive even to German attritional operations in the North Sea. But the euphoria of victory helped to render less urgent the rectification of the Royal Navy's faults. Most palpable, and perhaps predictable, were the failures of command and staff-work: the confusion of authority did not deserve the success which was achieved. Jellicoe's response was to emphasize tighter tactical control, but the difficulties in signalling encountered on 28 August were not addressed. Nor had the British, thanks to the performance of the *Lion*, detected what the Germans had noticed—that many British shells had failed to explode and that others, although they detonated, did not penetrate. Heligoland Bight was no test of Fisher's ideas on long-range gunnery. When Beatty's battle cruisers arrived the contest became entirely one-sided, the Germans having no capital ships with which to reply. Beatty therefore used his speed to close the ranges, not keep his distance, and the German light cruisers were hit at between 3,000 and 6,000 yards.

Beatty's decision to enter the battle was, of course, the key to the Royal Navy's victory. The consequent British dominance suggests that his choice was more self-evident than was actually the case. The waters into which he advanced contained not only British submarines which might not know of his presence, but possibly also German submarines which would welcome it if they did. The underwater threat therefore counselled caution, whatever

Tyrwhitt's plight. The long-term significance of the action of the Heligoland Bight, therefore, lies as much in what did not happen as in what did. Both sides had planned on their submarines playing a major role, the British positioning theirs to catch German surface vessels as they came out into the open sea, the Germans hoping to use theirs in attritional actions on the occasions when the Royal Navy ventured too close to their coasts. In the event, neither hope was fulfilled.

Fisher's pre-war enthusiasm for the submarine seemed to have been endorsed in the 1913 manoeuvres, in which British submarine officers claimed to have accounted for 40 per cent of the surface vessels present.[83] What is remarkable is not how few submarines the Entente powers possessed in 1914 but how many—Britain had fifty-five, France seventy-seven, Russia thirty-three. Although the Central Powers had fewer—Austria-Hungary six and Germany twenty-eight—the latter were technically better.[84] Initially Tirpitz had opposed submarines, through prejudice certainly, but on grounds of performance too. However, in entering the field late the Germans were able to benefit from the experiments and failures of those who had gone before. In 1910 German allocations for submarine construction doubled over the previous year (and quadrupled compared with 1907); by 1913 they doubled again. They focused on diesel propulsion; the first were completed in 1913, and had a cruising range of 5,000 nautical miles. The fact that by early 1914 Germany, after a late start, was building superior submarines at a faster rate than Britain was a point Fisher did not hesitate to make to Jellicoe.[85]

The respect accorded the submarine was due less to the vessel itself, whose warlike applications still remained uncertain, than to the torpedo. The torpedo boat had been the main plank in the *jeune école*'s advocacy of a *guerre de course* in the 1870s and 1880s. The riposte was long-range gunnery. At Tsushima the torpedo was only effective at the closest ranges and against vessels that were already disabled. But in the intervening decade its range and speed had doubled, to about 11,000 yards and 45 knots. Whereas in the Royal Navy gunnery was the specialist branch which attracted elite status, in the German navy torpedoes had a comparable claim. Müller, Pohl, and Hipper were all torpedo experts. Tirpitz himself had played a major part in the development of the torpedo, and torpedo boats had a high profile in his fleet (they outnumbered the Grand Fleet's destroyers two to one). The Germans, therefore, reckoned to compensate for their relative lack of firepower by attention to the torpedo: the U-boat was thus primarily a torpedo-firing platform.

---

[83] Hough, *Great War at sea*, 29.
[84] Brodie, *Sea power*, ch. 15; Watts, *Imperial Russian Navy*; Gemzell, *Organization, conflict and innovation*, 59–62.
[85] Marder, *Fear God and dread nought*, ii. 497, 498.

Therefore, the criticism to be levelled at the navies of 1914 is not that they failed to respond to a new weapons system, but that they integrated it with existing operational thought rather than recognized that it would create its own operational environment. Fleet action was the dominant concern of naval officers: the submarine threat was assessed in relation to that. What only a few anticipated was that the submarine would operate independently of other warships and would become the principal adjunct of economic warfare. The relative lack of attention to blockade removed the context into which the submarine would subsequently come to fit. Moreover, the state of international law, which assumed that an attacking ship would take over a merchantman as a prize, made the submarine a poor means by which to harass commercial traffic.

The opening months of the war in the North Sea appeared to confirm the worst fears of Fisher and of the man to whom he had relayed them, Jellicoe. On 6 August ten U-boats set off northwards in a sweep through the North Sea to locate the Grand Fleet and the line of the British blockade. During the course of August the Germans lost two submarines and their sustained cruising exposed defects in the others; in return, they had encountered only fractions of the Grand Fleet and had not established the pattern of the British blockade. But their activity fuelled Jellicoe's worries, particularly given the lack of submarine defences at Scapa and Rosyth. On 5 September a U-boat sank a cruiser in the Forth. On 22 September three old cruisers, *Aboukir*, *Hogue*, and *Cressy*, were sunk by a single U-boat, U9, with the loss of 1,459 lives, including a large proportion of middle-aged reservists and 15-year-old cadets. The cruisers had been patrolling the 'Broad Fourteens' off Holland against the possibility of a German raid into the Channel. Tyrwhitt, Keyes, and ultimately Churchill had all recognized their vulnerability, but the threat seemed to be more from single vessels than submarines, given the expectation that the effectiveness of the U-boat would be in confined waters, not on the open sea. The three cruisers had no destroyer escort (as the weather had been too heavy when they put out), they were not zigzagging, and their speed was only 10 knots. When *Aboukir* was struck she was first assumed to have hit a mine, and, even when the true danger was identified, *Hogue* and then *Cressy* stopped to pick up survivors. The lessons were clear: ships in submarine-infested waters were to steer a zigzag course, to maintain a speed of at least 13 knots, and were to refrain from stopping. Nonetheless, on 15 October another cruiser, HMS *Hawke*, was sunk off Aberdeen. In the course of 1914 warship losses to U-boats totalled 120,000 tons.[86]

In September and October the U-boat gave the Germans effective control of the North Sea. The loss of the *Hawke* and the vulnerability of Scapa Flow

---

[86] Goldrick, *The King's ships*, 122–33, 138; Brodie, *Sea power*, 358.

persuaded Jellicoe to pull the Grand Fleet back to Lough Swilly. Even here he was not safe. *U20* observed the Grand Fleet's move, and on the night of 22/3 October the *Berlin*, a German liner re-equipped as a minelayer, having made an extraordinary voyage around the north of Scotland and rendezvoused with *U20*, laid its mines north-west of Lough Swilly. On 27 October HMS *Audacious*, a super-Dreadnought battleship, struck one of the *Berlin's* mines; conscious of the submarine danger, the adjacent ships were slow to close and take her in tow; in full view of her sister ships and of the White Star liner SS *Olympic*, the *Audacious* went down.

Now Jellicoe's anxieties were multiplied. The Germans' superiority in mine numbers had been recognized at the war's outbreak, but their lack of mine-layers and the British superiority in surface vessels had restrained German minelaying activity. Jellicoe anticipated the German use of mines and submarines in conjunction; the Grand Fleet would have to be preceded by mine-sweepers (of which it had only six), and its speed would therefore be cut to 10 knots, thus rendering its units more vulnerable to U-boat attack. On 30 October he outlined his conclusions to the Admiralty. He should aim to fight the Germans only in the northern part of the North Sea, where the Grand Fleet would be closer to its own bases and the German mines and submarines would be fewer. The Grand Fleet should only operate in conjunction with a destroyer screen. Above all, it should beware of being lured by the High Seas Fleet onto U-boats and mines: if the German fleet turned away Jellicoe would refuse to be drawn. He concluded that the only way to conduct an attack was to move at high speed to the flank, so ensuring that the battle was not fought in waters of the enemy's choosing, and so also forcing submarines to surface if they wished to follow. The key question was whether the Germans would conform. Jellicoe was prepared to risk losing the chance of battle rather than risk his fleet.[87]

In reality the U-boat threat to British warships had already peaked. For all their faith in the torpedo, the Germans had begun the war with only 60 per cent of their established stocks,[88] and with a weapon whose calibre was 50 centimetres to the British 21 inches. The defensive steps adopted after the sinking of the three cruisers on 22 September were, broadly speaking, sufficient. Moreover, the torpedo was not the danger to warships which the Germans had imagined. Manoeuvring at speed, and particularly confronted ahead or astern, the warship was a difficult target to hit. The Germans themselves never fully appreciated the extent of their success or the longevity of the subsequent British fears. They regarded their U-boat operations in 1914 with disappointment: as scouts, the submarines had failed to identify the major

---

[87] Marder, *From the Dreadnought*, ii. 70–7; Halpern, *Naval history*, 37–8.
[88] Philbin, *Hipper*, 22.

British formations or to keep track of them; as offensive weapons, they would take a long time to reduce the Grand Fleet to numbers equal with those of the High Seas Fleet.

Britain's ability to regain the initiative in the North Sea was derived in large measure from another unanticipated application of sea-power. Before 1914 the world's communications relied principally on underwater cables, the majority of them in British hands and lying along the major shipping lanes. From 1898 Britain reckoned, in the event of war, on cutting the underwater cables of its opponents, so isolating them from the rest of the world. Therefore, within hours of Britain's ultimatum expiring, Germany's cable communications were effectively restricted to Europe only. Germany had, however, recognized the danger, and in the decade preceding the war had made considerable strides in the development of an alternative global communications network, using wireless. Throughout the war, therefore, Germany's communications with its ships and its embassies had to be broadcast; consequently they could be intercepted by their enemies, and to offset this danger messages were sent in cipher.[89]

The German navy used three principal codes in 1914. That for communication between German warships and merchant vessels was captured by an Australian boarding party off Melbourne on 11 August and reached London late in October; the main naval signal book was taken by the Russians from SMS *Magdeburg*, which went aground in the Baltic, and was passed over to the British on 13 October; the third code, used by flag officers and for diplomatic purposes, was contained in a box brought to the surface in the nets of a trawler off Texel on 30 November. The majority of German signals were encoded and then reciphered, and the cipher itself was changed at frequent intervals. The Royal Navy's ability to read German messages was, therefore, not instantaneous or absolutely constant, but it was relatively continuous from December 1914 onwards. The changes in cipher perhaps in part explain the remarkably lackadaisical attitude of the Germans to the possibility of a breach in their signals' security. In May 1915 one of their cruisers, SMS *Königsberg*, gave a specific warning to that effect. The Germans can hardly have been surprised: as early as November 1914 they knew that the British were in possession of their commercial code, and they were also aware of the possibility that the *Magdeburg*'s codebooks had not been destroyed. But not until 1916 was the commercial code replaced, and not until May 1917 was the navy given a new code. Even then the British advantage was not lost. The introduction of the new codes overlapped with the use of the old, and thus was their solution facilitated. Moreover, the very sophistication and long range of the German wireless

---

[89] Paul Kennedy, 'Imperial cable communications and strategy 1870–1914', in Kennedy (ed.), *War plans.*

systems encouraged their excessive use, providing plenty of raw material for the cryptographers. Even ships in port spoke to each other through the medium of the wireless. When at sea the High Seas Fleet was free of the operational control of the Admiralty Staff—unlike the Grand Fleet and the Admiralty—but its commander still employed wireless to communicate with his subordinate units. By contrast, the Royal Navy when at sea maintained much stricter radio silence and used visual signals as far as possible. The Germans felt that it was worth sacrificing signals security in order to be able to convey information correctly and speedily.[90]

Cryptography was not established as an arm of British intelligence in 1914. Rear-Admiral Henry Oliver, the director of the intelligence division, therefore established a new and secret department to decipher the intercepted German signals. From early November the section was dubbed 'Room 40', after its location in the Admiralty Old Building. Its head was a Scottish engineer and the director of naval education, Sir Alfred Ewing. Ewing recruited an able team of cryptographers, but their backgrounds were academic and not seagoing: they did not, therefore, enjoy the professional approbation of the other Admiralty departments, and they also—at least initially—lacked the expertise required for the comprehension and evaluation of the intercepts which they were decoding. The initial mistakes which ensued were enough to ensure the continued mistrust of Rear-Admiral Thomas Jackson, the director of the operations department. The appointment of Commander H. W. W. Hope to inject a little naval knowledge into Room 40 remedied the worst defects, and Hope gradually established himself as the de facto head of the department. Thus Ewing's role diminished, Hope himself looking to Captain W. R. Hall, Oliver's success as director of the intelligence division, for leadership. 'Blinker' Hall—'half Machiavelli and half schoolboy'[91]—proved a master of intelligence and covert operations. But although he enjoyed access to Room 40, he was not to gain full control of it until May 1917. Instead, Oliver, who succeeded Sturdee as chief of the naval war staff on 14 October 1914, continued to regard Room 40 as his personal fiefdom. The informal war group—Oliver, Churchill, Fisher, and Sir Arthur Wilson (now recalled as an unpaid assistant)—received the decrypts but lacked the time or powers of delegation to make best use of them. The failure to establish a full naval staff thus prejudiced the proper use of a major resource.

The operational value of Room 40's labour lay in two principal directions. Every night each German squadron or unit reported its position by radio. Hall established a series of listening-posts along Britain's east coast, whose

---

[90] Beesly, *Room 40*, is the major work on British naval intelligence. See also Santorini, *Revue internationale d'histoire militaire*, 63 (1985), 95–110; Andrew, *Secret service*, ch. 3; on Germany, Philbin, *Hipper*, 45–9.

[91] Beesly, *Room 40*, 37.

configuration aided the taking of cross-bearings to locate vessels using wireless. This vast bulk of routine information enabled the Admiralty to form a full and up-to-date picture of the Germans' order of battle and deployment. Offensively, herein lay the basis for operational planning: in practice, the lack of a fully fledged war staff and the poor integration of intelligence with operations meant that the opportunity was not exploited, or at least not until 1917–18. Defensively, Room 40's value was more specific: it gave warning of any likely German attack. From late autumn 1914 it relieved the Grand Fleet of the constant chores of patrolling or of sweeps through the North Sea, and allowed time for training and refits. It enabled fuel economy. But when intelligence of German offensive movements was received, it was both immediate and urgent. Oliver's reluctance to delegate and his determination not to pass on all Room 40 decrypts as a matter of course meant that Jellicoe and the other operational commanders were told no more than the Admiralty thought they should know. Jellicoe's request that he be equipped to decode intercepts at sea was refused for reasons of security. The intelligence from Room 40 which reached the Grand Fleet was therefore in danger of being late, partial, or incorrectly interpreted.

Britain established its decisive lead in naval intelligence just in time. The first German responses to the Heligoland Bight battle had been defensive. The action had not enabled the German coastal artillery to engage, and Hipper therefore instructed his cruisers to fall back in any future encounter. Minefields were laid to the west of Heligoland itself. The Kaiser insisted that the High Seas Fleet should not engage without his express permission.[92] But the battle also demonstrated the weakness of a German strategy that relied exclusively on the defensive: the British had done what the Germans hoped they would do, attack close in to the German coast. In the process it was the Germans who had lost ships, and it was the British who, by choosing when and where to attack, had achieved surprise and enjoyed a local superiority. Ingenohl therefore argued that the High Seas Fleet be allowed greater freedom to manoeuvre and to attack. The vulnerability of the torpedo boats had been demonstrated in the action of 28 August, and their range was limited to forty-eight hours' cruising; the toll which both they and the U-boats would take of the Grand Fleet would be minor and slow. Therefore the attrition of the Royal Navy, in preparation for the eventual decisive battle on relatively equal terms, could only be achieved by the full German fleet engaging fractions of the British fleet. Since the British would not oblige by approaching the Heligoland Bight in a weakened state—or perhaps in any state, given the improvements to the Bight's defences—the Germans should aim to imitate the Royal Navy and sally forth towards the British coast. The shortest distance from the German

---

[92] Halpern, *Naval history*, 32.

bases to the nearest points on Britain's eastern shores was considerably less than the distance from Scapa Flow to those same points. If kept in harbour indefinitely the fleet and its crews would lose their fitness for sea. On the other hand, by choosing when and where to fight the High Seas Fleet would ensure that it was not weakened because units were under repair or in the Baltic, and it would have the benefits of surprise and concentration.[93]

Ingenohl's case for committing the High Seas Fleet rested on sound strategic premisses. Britain, and through Britain the Entente as a whole, enjoyed a maritime preponderance which relieved it of the need for offensive action; as Jellicoe's thinking recognized full well, the Grand Fleet fulfilled its purpose by holding, not by fighting. Germany, on the other hand, was the challenger. If it wished to gain the Atlantic approaches it would have to fight for them: the onus to seek battle lay on the High Seas Fleet. In August 1914 it had forsaken this option, not only for political reasons but also for naval ones. The relative rate of completion in the construction of capital ships meant that the gap between the two competing forces would narrow in three months' time: for the fleet, if not for the Kaiser or Bethmann Hollweg, the instructions of 30 July and 6 August represented a temporary postponement, not a long-term deferment. Indeed, over the long term the comparative position would worsen again as the Royal Navy's orders of 1914–15, let alone any subsequent construction, entered service.

But all this assumed that the function of the German fleet was to fight, and even by October 1914 this was still not necessarily self-evident. Indeed, battle seemed to be receding as an option: the first fleet instructions of 30 July had ordered that, even before the fleets were on an equal footing, if 'favourable opportunities for battle are offered, they must be taken'.[94] The subsequent indecisiveness of the situation on land was itself a powerful argument for indecision at sea: a defeat at sea could adversely affect the situation on land when the latter was still in the balance; the navy as a defensive force at least secured Germany's 'northern frontier', its coastal approaches, and so freed the army to fight on its western and eastern boundaries. The need to break the British blockade was not compelling: its economic effects would be long term, and there was as yet no reason to believe that the decision on land would not precede the impact of the blockade. Thus, the short-term arguments for offensive action were not so powerful as to overcome the long-term political benefits of a 'fleet in being'. On 1 October 1914 Albert Ballin, the German shipowner, confided to Tirpitz, 'The fleet in my eyes has become nothing other, and will never be anything other, than the irreplaceable resource of a healthy

[93] What follows is largely based on the discussion in Marine-Archiv, *Der Krieg zur See: Der Krieg in der Nordsee*, ii. 83–108; Assmann, *Deutsche Seestrategie*, 38–68; see also Castex, *Théories stratégiques*, ii. 208–13; Hörich, *Deutsche Seekriegführung*.
[94] Gemzell, *Orgnization, conflict, innovation*, 138.

economy'.[95] Its existence at the end of the war would be a vital component in settling with Britain, whose European interests would be restricted to ensuring the maintenance of a balance of power. The Kaiser and Bethmann Hollweg took a not dissimilar view.

However, the decision as to the tasks of the High Seas Fleet was not a simple matter of weighing immediate operational aims versus post-war political objectives, or even of the question as to whether the immediate situation might not be so urgent as to outweigh consideration of the latter. Ingenohl's efforts to have his operational orders revised raised in acute form the question of command authority. In order to exploit any opportunity to commit the whole High Seas Fleet to action against fractions of the Grand Fleet, its commander-in-chief needed the freedom to act with speed and decision, and on his own initiative. Ingenohl was formally asking the Kaiser to delegate authority; informally, he was urging clarification of his status in relation to that of Pohl, Tirpitz, and Müller.

In open debate, Pohl was Ingenohl's most clear-cut opponent; the pre-war bureaucratic division between the staff and the fleet continued, both, as before, using strategy as a means to express their institutional differences. In 1913 Pohl had been attracted to the use of submarines and mining as the first stage of an attritional campaign to wear down the British superiority in capital ships. The idea had been tested in an Admiralty Staff war game that winter, and the following summer, in May 1914, U-boat commanders claimed that they had achieved hits on every large surface ship within range on the first day.[96] Pohl therefore rejected Ingenohl's interpretation of the strategic position; he argued that the British would come into the Heligoland Bight once more, and that the next time they would suffer heavy losses; as a pre-war Tirpitzian, he assessed naval power in numbers of intact capital ships; the recklessness of the attack by the German light cruisers on 28 August reinforced his inclination towards caution. But the Admiralty Staff did not speak with one voice. Pohl's need to dance attendance on the Kaiser at general headquarters meant that his deputy, Paul Behncke, had the major influence in Berlin, and Behncke supported Ingenohl.

Tirpitz too backed the commander of the High Seas Fleet, at least in formal terms. By mid-September he was advocating fleet action and complete operational freedom for the fleet commander. Indeed, he had no option, as he recognized that if the fleet remained unblooded in war it would have no budgetary leverage in peace. But at the same time he was intriguing for Ingenohl's replacement by Pohl so that he himself could become chief of the Admiralty Staff.[97] He blamed Ingenohl for not exploiting the very offensive

[95] Marine-Archiv, *Krieg in der Nordsee*, ii. 106.
[96] Philbin, *Hipper*, 38; Gemzell, *Organization, conflict, and innovation*, 139.
[97] Müller, *The Kaiser and his court*, 39, 42–5.

opportunities which Ingenohl himself was now anxious to create. Further-more, he was still hedging his bets, still reflecting his pre-war assumptions: he wanted the battle sooner rather than later, but—or so he said at first—not until Turkey had entered the war on Germany's side and there had been a decision in the west; and the battle, when it came, should be contrived to be fought within 100 nautical miles of the Bight. By now, however, Tirpitz had lost the ear of the Kaiser. Müller, who had gained it, played an even more devious game than Tirpitz. He managed variously to present himself as the ally of Pohl and Ingenohl. In reality he backed the former, whose operational views were at least in accordance with the Kaiser's political wishes.

On 3 October Pohl visited Ingenohl at Wilhelmshaven; it was the only time that the chief of the Admiralty Staff and the fleet commander met while Ingenohl held office. Pohl outlined his views but, Ingenohl reported, told him that they were only adopted in deference to the Kaiser. Ingenohl repeated his own position, but did so in such a low key that the others present failed to appreciate the depth of the difference. Ingenohl argued that a battle close to the German coast would by definition be one the British had sought, and therefore would be on their terms; he wanted the High Seas Fleet to be able to seek battle, even against superior forces. Pohl believed that such an encounter would never occur, as the Grand Fleet was based so far from the German coast. Three days later the Kaiser issued revised operational instructions. Their keynotes were ambiguity and confusion. The possibility that the High Seas Fleet might be allowed to operate outside the Bight, say towards Skaggerak, was not totally excluded. But it could only do so when there was no risk of loss, when political and military conditions were right, and when the Kaiser himself decided. The only real flexibility given Ingenohl related to Hipper's battle cruisers, which could be used to inflict losses on British forces. But this concession revealed how little had been achieved in squaring operational needs with political purposes. It was already axiomatic that Germany's relative inferiority in numbers of capital ships meant that the battle cruisers should not operate independently of the High Seas Fleet. A similar ambiguity was more directly expressed in relation to torpedo boats: Ingenohl should use these in his war of attrition against the Grand Fleet, but he should remember that (given the German belief in the efficiency of the torpedo) enough should be left over for the decisive battle. In sum, portions of the German fleet could engage in battle provided they did not suffer losses thereby. Ingenohl's subsequent indecisive-ness had clear roots.

However, during the course of October and November British redeploy-ment helped support Ingenohl's case for offensive action, and gave a fitful clarity to Germany's maritime strategy.

By the beginning of October 1914 there were, in addition to the Territorial Force, only four regular battalions left in the United Kingdom. British security from invasion was fundamental to the maritime strategy of the Entente; defensively, its land mass provided the basis of the blockade; and offensively, it was the logistic base for the armies on the continent, supporting through sea-power the trench lines of the western front. The navy before the war had insisted, at a meeting of the Committee of Imperial Defence in 1908, that it could stop any German invasion mounted by upwards of 70,000 troops. The army's responsibility was to deal with raids by smaller bodies, the detection of whose preparations would be harder, and whose advent could be swifter. Between 1908 and 1913 the fear of invasion had shaped much of the rhetoric, if little of the substance, of Britain's defence debates. The navy, having announced that Britain would not be invaded, modified its position in 1913 in order to tie the regular army to home defence and so block its continent-alism; the War Office used the invasion threat to popularize the Territorial Army, and it also became an important tool of the advocates of conscription; in addition it formed the stuff of popular novels. Thus, in autumn 1914 the exposure of Britain's east coast, with the withdrawal of the Grand Fleet to Irish waters and the abandonment of cruiser patrols in the face of U-boat threats, locked into a set of existing anxieties. Kitchener was the most affected. Germany's establishment of defensive positions on its western front created a disposable land force which could be directed as well against Britain as to its eastern front. The Committee of Imperial Defence in April 1914 had stipulated that two regular divisions and the Territorial Force would be enough to check a German invasion; Kitchener no longer had two regular divisions, and he did not trust the Territorials. The Admiralty was therefore constrained to cover the east coast. On 12 November it ordered a battle squadron and a cruiser squad-ron to Rosyth; ships were stationed on the Tyne, the Humber, and the Wash; a squadron of pre-Dreadnoughts was established at Sheerness; the fleet was therefore scattered from the Pentland Firth to the Thames. The price of home defence (and indeed of the army's continentalism) was the navy's dispersion.[98] Ingenohl now had the opportunity to engage fractions of the Grand Fleet.

German naval intelligence was poor. The pre-war network of German naval spies in Britain was very small, a total of twenty-two, and they were successfully identified by the secret service bureau of the British War Office (established in 1909 and the predecessor of MI5). The ring was smashed beyond repair immediately on the war's outbreak.[99] Since the British were far more restrained in their use of wireless than the Germans, signals traffic did not provide the lucrative source it proved for the Admiralty. Increased traffic did, of course, indicate probable movements by the Grand Fleet, but not until March 1916 was

[98] Corbett, *Naval operations*, ii, 4–10.
[99] Hiley, *Historical Journal*, XXVIII (1985), 856–60; Andrew, *Secret Service*, 59–61.

the German intercept station at Neumunster regularly receiving and decipher-ing British messages.[100] Ingenohl therefore did not, apparently, realize the opportunity thus afforded him. However, he did know that the defeat of Rear-Admiral Sir Christopher Cradock's squadron at Coronel, in the Pacific, on 1 November 1914 had prompted the Admiralty to dispatch three battle cruisers from home waters to reinforce the efforts to seek Cradock's conqueror, Graf von Spee. Never again could the balance of forces be so favourable to the Germans. For a brief period the Grand Fleet's margin of superiority in the North Sea rested on seventeen Dreadnoughts to Germany's fifteen, and an equal number of battle cruisers (four each). However exaggerated the fear of mines and U-boats, the consequences for the Royal Navy of a single miscalcu-lation seemed likely to be grave.

On 3 November Ingenohl mounted a raid on Yarmouth with Hipper's battle cruisers as a cover for minelaying operations off Lowestoft. The Admiralty was slow to respond, and the local patrols were hampered by the weather. The lack of accident reinforced Hipper's pressure for further raids, and in mid-Novem-ber Ingenohl settled on the bombardment of Hartlepool and Scarborough. As before, the raid would cover minelaying in the hope that the Grand Fleet might be stung by the raid back into the North Sea and so be drawn across the new field. In defiance of the Kaiser's orders, Ingenohl decided he would take out the High Seas Fleet in support. The news that von Spee's squadron had been destroyed at the Falklands on 8 December promised the return of the detached British battle cruisers before long, but Ingenohl was anxious to wait until mid-December when the repairs to *Von der Tann* would be completed.

Thus, the night of 8 December, when there was no moon and the tides were right, passed—to Jellicoe's surprise—without incident. But on 14 December Room 40 warned that Hipper's battle cruisers were coming out the following day. Since the High Seas Fleet observed radio silence, the intelligence said nothing about German battleships and its collectors were not consulted on the point; given an incomplete picture, Oliver assumed that the High Seas Fleet would stay in harbour. Jellicoe wanted the whole Grand Fleet at sea, but he was overruled by the Admiralty. The latter's plan was to use Beatty's battle cruisers, Goodenough's 1st light cruiser squadron, and the 2nd battle squadron under Sir George Warrender, to cut off Hipper after he had completed his raid; the whole force was to rendezvous at a position only 30 miles south of the station taken up by the High Seas Fleet. The Harwich Force was to shadow Hipper.

At 5.15 a.m. on 16 December Warrender's destroyers made contact with escorts of the High Seas Fleet. Ingenohl was worried: he could only reckon that the destroyers were the van of a larger formation, in all probability the Grand Fleet, and in addition their torpedoes represented an immediate danger

[100] Philbin, *Hipper*, 50–1.

to his capital ships, particularly in the dark. Given the Kaiser's orders of 6 October he had no option but to turn away to the south-east, a move he executed at 5.42. In doing so he forfeited Germany's only major opportunity for a decisive naval victory in the entire war.

The reporting of Warrender's destroyers was patchy, incomplete, and on occasion inaccurate. Thus, fortunately for the British, Beatty's pursuit of Ingenohl was delayed and ill-directed. At 9.03 a.m. he abandoned the chase. Reports of Hipper's action, which had begun at 8 a.m., had been reaching him, and it was to deal with the German battle cruisers that Beatty now turned. When Hipper withdrew homewards at 9.30 a.m. his prospects were poor. He knew from a signals intercept the previous day that the British had been alerted to his sortie. He therefore expected action, but he did not know that four British battle cruisers and six Dreadnoughts lay between him and safety. Nor did he know that Ingenohl, who had been due to stay on his station until the operation was completed, was no longer in support. Tyrwhitt's Harwich Force began to move northwards at 8.40 a.m. At 10 a.m. the 3rd battle squadron was under way from Rosyth in case Hipper should follow the coast northwards in order to skirt the mines off the coast, and by noon most of the Grand Fleet had left Scapa Flow. The British concentration, although delayed, still seemed sufficient.

Hipper's possible route back across the North Sea was complicated by minefields and the shallows round the Dogger Bank. Jellicoe correctly anticipated that he would aim for a gap in the mines due east of Whitby, and warned Beatty and Warrender accordingly. By 11 a.m. the weather, and with it the visibility, were worsening, but at 11.25 a.m. Goodenough in *Southampton* reported contact with an enemy light cruiser and some destroyers. In fact Goodenough's engagement was with the three light cruisers of the 2nd German scouting group, and concentration on the *Southampton* would have brought Beatty onto the 2nd scouting group of Hipper's main force, astern and to the west. Instead, *Southampton* broke contact. Beatty's ill-phrased signal, 'Light cruisers—resume your position for look-out', was intended for two only of Goodenough's four light cruisers, to get them to spread out in the search for the rest of Hipper's force. It was not meant for *Southampton* or *Birmingham*, but with no indication to the contrary Goodenough assumed it applied to his entire squadron. Hipper, having been alerted to Goodenough's presence, turned south-east at 11.39, hoping to draw the British away from the light cruisers of the 1st scouting group. At 12.15 Warrender's battleships also saw the German light cruisers, but did not open fire as Warrender himself did not issue an order to that effect. At 12.32 the German light cruisers signalled that they could see no British forces and that they were out of danger. Hipper then turned north, with the purpose this time of drawing off Warrender's battle squadron. A mixture of chance, poor visibility, and bad signalling had enabled

Hipper to wend his way through the British screen. Not even Keyes's flotilla off Terschelling was able to intercept the Germans; wireless communications between his destroyer and the Admiralty were delayed by their operating on different wavelengths, and thus he was not in position off Heligoland until too late.

Both sides berated themselves for the missed opportunities of the Scarborough raid. The Germans had least cause; they had effected their purpose, conducting the first successful attack on English shores since 1667 and doing so without loss. Ingenohl was unfairly blamed for missing an opportunity that was only created thanks to his own attacking spirit. British recriminations were somewhat better founded. The navy—apparently surprised but in reality forewarned—had allowed the raids to go ahead, with the loss of 122 killed and 443 wounded (most of them civilians), on the grounds that it would finish with Hipper's scouting groups on the latter's return journey. It had failed. The official historian's conclusions were swingeing:

Two of the most efficient and powerful British squadrons, with an adequate force of scouting vessels, knowing approximately what to expect, and operating in an area strictly limited by the possibilities of the situation, had failed to bring to action an enemy who was acting in close conformity with our appreciation and with whose advanced screen contact had been established.[101]

What was culpable in the Royal Navy's behaviour was less the failure per se; after all, it was lucky to have escaped major defeat in the early hours of the morning, and the result of any engagement between Beatty and Hipper (given Hipper's ability to outdistance Warrender's battleships) would not have been a foregone conclusion. The major omission was the inability to learn for next time. Room 40's intelligence, which had proved vital in creating the opportunity, had been poorly integrated with the battle's operational direction; its intercepts in the course of the action had been passed to Jellicoe with a delay of up to two hours, by which time the information it contained was out of date or even potentially misleading. The news that the German fleet was out was relayed so late that Jellicoe and Beatty assumed Ingenohl was advancing when in fact he was already retreating. On the high seas themselves, Beatty's signals had been ambiguous and individual commanders—both Goodenough and the captains of Warrender's squadron—had failed to use their initiative. The staff and command failings were manifest. On 30 December Jellicoe decided that officers in contact with the enemy were to treat orders from those ignorant of the immediate conditions as instructions only: but at the same time both he and Beatty opposed the Admiralty's suggestion that they loosen their battle formations, so ensuring that tight control remained the order of the

---

[101] Corbett, *Naval operations*, ii. 43.

day. The only real response was to address the problem of concentration at a strategic level: on 20 December Beatty's battle cruisers were moved down to Rosyth.

The outcome of the Scarborough raid did nothing to diminish Ingenohl's case for more offensive operations. Furthermore, the frustrations of simply waiting for the British to come into the Bight were multiplied on Christmas Day, when a small force under Tyrwhitt penetrated far enough in to launch a seaplane attack against the Zeppelin base at Cuxhaven. Four of the seven seaplanes were lost, but not a single British serviceman was killed; one of the seaplane carriers successfully eluded the attentions of a Zeppelin, and in the ensuing stramash *Von der Tann* ran into another German cruiser. Two days later a report by Pohl's own chief of staff, Hans Zenker, commissioned as a result of a suggestion made to the Kaiser by Müller, convinced the chief of the Admiralty Staff that he could no longer oppose Ingenohl's arguments. Zenker said that the current strategy, *Kleinkrieg*, was not working; the British were not attacking and the blockade was still holding. The High Seas Fleet must be prepared to go to sea and to stay there for longer periods; its aim should still be to seek fractions of the enemy force, and to this end both U-boats and Zeppelins should be employed as scouts, but the fleet should not shun the possibility of confrontation with the entire Grand Fleet.

The substance of Zenker's proposals was discussed at an audience with the Kaiser on 9 January 1915. Significantly, Tirpitz was not present, but nor was Ingenohl. Pohl took Ingenohl's part, asking, albeit 'with more pathos than skill',[102] that Ingenohl be allowed greater operational freedom. The Kaiser conceded to the extent that the High Seas Fleet was authorized to make thrusts into the North Sea, but it was still to recoil in the face of superior forces. In the balance between the political value of the fleet and its operational functions, the weight still lay with the former.

Early January was a poor time for the German navy to decide to go on the attack: the weather was unfavourable, and the repair problems of the fleet were accumulating. However, worries about the activities of British fishing boats— which were not used so much for intelligence purposes, as the Germans imagined, as for patrols to protect the east coast—provided the basis for a fresh thrust by Hipper's battle cruisers. Hipper suggested another minelaying raid, this time on the Forth, combined with an attack on the fishing boats on the Dogger Bank, fortuitously both a favourite fishing ground and on the direct route between the German bases and the British coast. Hipper hoped for the High Seas Fleet's support, but Ingenohl refused. The repair needs of the fleet had reduced its strength, and he could see little prospect of it being

---

[102] Müller, *The Kaiser and his court*, 54; on Zenker's proposals, see Marine-Archiv, *Krieg in der Nordsee*, iii. 155–9; Hörich, *Deutsche Seekriegführung*, 95–8.

required. He wrongly assumed that Beatty's battle cruisers were at Scapa Flow, and that therefore Hipper was likely to meet only light forces, or at worst battleships from Rosyth which he could outdistance. At 5.45 p.m. on 23 January the two scouting groups, a combined force of four battle cruisers, four light cruisers, and eighteen torpedo boats, put out to sea.

However, a signal from Ingenohl's chief of staff, aboard SMS *Deutschland*, to Hipper's flagship *Seydlitz* while both vessels were still in the Jade, alerted Room 40. The intelligence led Oliver to make two assumptions—one right (this time), that the High Seas Fleet was not coming out, and one wrong, that Hipper's purpose was to raid the east coast again. His subsequent orders were therefore better adapted to screening the coast than they were to cutting Hipper off from his base. Beatty and Tyrwhitt were to rendezvous at daylight near the Dogger Bank, which meant that the former's course was almost due east towards Hipper and not behind him. The 3rd battle squadron and 3rd cruiser squadron were to block escape to the north. The Grand Fleet set out from Scapa through the North Sea on a sweep which could have placed it beyond Hipper, but it did not sail until 9 p.m. and proceeded without urgency; Keyes's submarines were once again posted off the German estuaries. None of the Admiralty's instructions revealed to the commanders at sea the assumptions on which they rested. Their implications were that the Grand Fleet would take no part in the action, and that Hipper's escape to the east would not be closed.

The thrust of the Admiralty's orders was confirmed by the course steered by Hipper. In order to ease the progress of his torpedo boats in the heavy seas, he proceeded more to the north and less to the west than he had intended. Therefore at 7.05 a.m. on 24 January, when HMS *Aurora* began the action by encountering SMS *Kolberg*, Hipper was not so far to the west as to be isolated. Once again the reporting of the British destroyers proved unhelpful: *Aurora* signalled to Beatty, 'Am in action with German Fleet'.[103] Beatty, rightly, ignored this report. The High Seas Fleet took no part in the action. Although Hipper informed Ingenohl of the situation at 7.47 a.m., and reported at regular intervals thereafter, he did not specifically request the Fleet's support until 9.23. Ingenohl argued that it would take three hours for the High Seas Fleet to assemble, and that Hipper's escape to the south-east was clear. Hipper assumed from the British call-signs that his opponents were the 2nd battle squadron, and that his battle cruisers would have the legs to outdistance the battleships. Not only was the assumption false, but also his ships—deprived of sustained sea trials—developed problems with their condensers and steam turbines: the maximum speed they could maintain was 23 knots.

---

[103] Goldrick, *King's ships*, 255. Goldrick's is the most recent account of the battle; see also Marder, *From the Dreadnought*, ii. 156–68; a German perspective, and especially on *Blücher*, Philbin, *Hipper*, 104–12; the fullest account is Marine-Archiv, *Krieg in der Nordsee*, iii. 189–249.

Beatty enjoyed two initial advantages; the sun, as it rose, silhouetted the German ships to the east, and the wind, a north-easterly, blew the smoke clear of his line of sight. By 8.23 he had built up his speed to 26 knots, and at 8.34, just after the chase changed course from south to south-east, he ordered 27 knots. In the next twenty minutes the speed was raised again to 29 knots. Despite the furious efforts of his stokers, none of Beatty's five battle cruisers actually attained this speed, and two of them, *New Zealand* and *Indomitable*, were now lagging. Shortly after 9.00 a.m. fire was opened at 20,000 yards. It would be another forty-three minutes before *New Zealand* was in the fight, and nearly two hours before *Indomitable* was. The German shooting was reserved until the range was 18,000 yards and was then concentrated on the leading British vessel, Beatty's flagship *Lion*. Their aim was obstructed by their own thick smoke belching out astern. But both sides had to deal with the problems of spray. To the breaking of waves were added waterspouts a hundred feet high caused by near misses. The Germans' practice of finding their targets by increasing the range probably did more to upset Beatty's view than the British practice of straddling their targets disrupted Hipper's. The harassing attacks of the German torpedo boats and the misplaced fear that the German cruisers would lay mines in their wake also prevented the British battle cruisers from steering too straight a course.

However, the principal British problem was self-inflicted. At 9.35 a.m. *Lion* signalled, 'Engage the corresponding ship in the enemy's line'. With *Indomitable* not yet in the battle, the two battle cruiser squadrons were equal in number. But HMS *Tiger*, immediately behind *Lion*, assumed that there were five British ships to the German four, and that therefore both *Lion* and *Tiger* should engage the leading German ship, SMS *Seydlitz*. Thus *Moltke*, the second ship in the German line, was able to fire without impediment, and joined *Seydlitz* in concentrating her attentions on *Lion*.[104] At 9.50 a shell from the *Lion* penetrated the deck of the *Seydlitz* and set alight the charges in one of the after gun-turrets. The fire spread into the adjacent turret and downwards into the magazines, thus threatening the whole ship; she was saved by the prompt flooding of the magazines, and although her after guns were now silenced, her steering gear was only temporarily disrupted and her speed and stability continued unimpaired. Two minutes later Beatty reduced speed to 24 knots to allow his squadron to close up. *Tiger* now shifted her fire to *Blücher*, the last ship in the German line; the first three, *Seydlitz*, *Moltke*, and *Derfflinger*, concentrated their attentions on *Lion*. Beatty's flagship was struck by two shells from the *Derfflinger* at 10.18; by 10.50 the *Lion* had taken fifteen hits,

---

[104] Corbett, *Naval operations*, ii. 91, says *Derfflinger* was left undisturbed, and this would accord with *Derfflinger*'s good practice on *Lion*. But Marine-Archiv, *Krieg in der Nordsee*, iii. 210, says *Moltke* was spared, and Marder, *From the Dreadnought*, ii. 160, agrees.

had lost electric power, was listing 10 degrees, and was reduced to a speed of 15 knots.

Throughout this period Beatty's signals created confusion; the wind pulled his flags dead astern and were hard to read—particularly given the smoke—by vessels also dead astern. At 10.54 Beatty himself was sure he saw the wash of a periscope on his starboard bow; the correct Grand Fleet procedure for dealing with torpedoes was to turn away; without giving any explanation as to the reason Beatty ordered the entire squadron—not just the *Lion*—to turn eight points to port. The other ships, already perplexed, could not understand their commander's apparent wish to break off the action. Hipper, equally bemused, called off an attack by his torpedo boats which he had just ordered. Beatty attempted to recover the situation by bringing his three effective battle cruisers, *Tiger*, *Princess Royal*, and *New Zealand*, back into the battle between the *Blücher* and Hipper's main force. He signalled 'Course North-East', and then added 'Attack the rear of the enemy'. The expression of Beatty's wishes was limited by the choice available in the signal book; there was no order to attack the enemy main body, which was the intention Beatty wished to convey. The two signals were read together to mean 'attack the rear of the enemy, bearing north east'. *Blücher*, brought out as a replacement for the damaged *Von der Tann*, was the only enemy ship to the north-east. Her armour was thinner than that of the fully fledged German battle cruisers, and she had a central ammunition supply placed amidships; these vulnerabilities meant that a salvo down near her water-line disrupted the shell supply to her guns, and her speed—which, though marginally lower, had at first enabled her to keep pace with the group—was steadily clipped by the ensuing fire. By the time of Beatty's order *Blücher* had already swung out of the German line and most of her main armament had been rendered useless. In any case her 8.2-inch guns were no match for those of the British. In an absurdly one-sided contest the battle cruisers circled the stricken vessel, pouring in fire, until she went down. Hipper's remaining ships were free to pull away.

The Dogger Bank was the first battle between Dreadnoughts; it was the second frustration for Beatty's battle cruisers in just over a month. Naturally the Royal Navy's attention focused on the errors which had repeated themselves. The division between intelligence and operations persisted: Room 40 knew that there were no U-boats within the area, but Beatty did not. Subordinate commanders had again failed to exercise their initiative: Admiral Archibald Moore, to whom the command of the battle cruisers fell when *Lion* was disabled, was shunted off to the Canary Islands, and Captain Henry Pelly of the *Tiger* was blamed for not taking up the attack when *Lion* left off. But the real problem of tactical control was that British naval command was having it both ways. The advent of wireless allowed tight and centralized direction, the Admiralty at Whitehall being able to determine the operations of individual ships at sea, and so frustrated the exercise of independence. But signals between ships in contact with the enemy were made by flag, and with this Nelsonic means of communication came a false expectation of Nelsonic styles of command. 'Engage the enemy more closely' was restored to the signal book, but there was no overall revision of the book and too little effort to dent its underlying assumptions. As Beatty's signals officer wrote to his mother: 'Signals went through like clockwork...when I say they went like clockwork I mean until the clock stopped.' Without electricity and reduced to two pairs of halliards, *Lion* had been unable to communicate, so as to break the logjam of excessive dependence. Beatty was anxious that the battle cruisers at any rate should realize that doctrine was more robust than reliance on the mechanisms for the transmission of orders: 'The Admiral', he instructed in the immediate aftermath of the battle, 'will rely on Captains to use all the information at their disposal to grasp the situation quickly and anticipate his wishes.'[105]

The fact that the prospect of a major victory had been denied by the problems of command and communication meant that insufficient attention was paid to gunnery. After all, in one sense a torpedo that was not there had proved more decisive than all the big guns that were. This was the first true test of Fisher's theories about long-range gunnery and speed. The battle had been fought at distances of between 16,000 and 20,000 yards; apparently the virtues of the British heavy gun had been proven, *Lion* scoring a hit with one of its opening rounds at 20,000 yards, *Blücher* having been sunk, and *Seydlitz* being badly damaged. The rate of range change had been sufficiently low not to expose the deficiencies of the Dreyer tables. But of 1,150 heavy shells fired by Beatty's cruisers, only six (excluding a further seventy poured into the hapless *Blücher*) had found their targets, and only one out of 355 fired by *Tiger*. *Tiger's* deficiencies were attributed to her scratch crew, and for the rest the speeding up of the installation of directors and the increase in range of practice firing to 16,000 yards were deemed sufficient. The inadequacy of the armour-piercing shells, particularly against the German side-armour, was neither recognized nor corrected.

In this, there was bitter irony. Beatty reported after the action that 'German shell, for incendiary effect and damage to personnel are far inferior to ours'.[106] He was right, in so far as the German 12–inch shells too lacked penetrative power, and included a good proportion that failed to explode on impact. But the concentration on this German deficiency relieved the British of the need to attend to their own corresponding vulnerability. The consequences of Fisher's neglect of armour had been exposed by the gunnery of *Derfflinger*. In particular, the *Lion's* experience had shown the need to limit access to the guns' magazines and so prevent flash passing from the turrets. But, although the

[105] Gordon, *Rules of the game*, 383, 591.   [106] Philbin, *Hipper,* 52.

structural problems were attended to on the *Lion*, they were not dealt with on her sister ships.

Moreover, rapidity of fire now became more important than accuracy. Even before the war, in 1913, Sir George Callaghan had demanded more ammunition for the Home Fleet, anticipating that, if rapid fire was to be opened at long ranges, it must be done without fear of compromising shell stocks. In 1915 Jellicoe pointed out that a quick-firing ship was itself a hard target to hit. Partly as a result of the limited opportunities at Rosyth, the battle cruisers spent more time practising their rate of loading than in live firing. Ready-use cartridges were kept in the gun turrets and stowed close to the magazine doors. Neglect of safety procedures compounded the lack of armour in highlighting the vulnerability of the British battle cruiser when confronted by her own kind.[107]

For their part, the Germans were totally taken aback both by the range at which the battle had been fought and by the number and weight of shells fired. A major reason why they did not venture out for over a year after Dogger Bank were the implications for ship construction consequent upon the battle. The loss of the *Blücher* persuaded them that quality was all, and that pre-Dreadnoughts—'five-minute ships', in reference to their anticipated survival time—had no place on the open seas. The Germans increased the elevation of their major armament, revised their fire-control arrangements, and expedited the introduction of heavier guns. More crucially, the damage to *Seydlitz* showed the importance of protection against the plunging fire of long-range gunnery. Deck, turret, and magazine armour were all thickened. Anti-flash precautions included the removal of ventilation ducts from the magazines, and the adoption of topside vents to channel flames upwards rather than downwards. The amount of 'ready-use' ammunition in each gun turret was limited.

For British observers, what is striking is the systematic way in which the Germans analysed the tactical and constructional implications of the battle for the whole fleet. No comparable programme followed in Britain; the improvements to the *Lion* were not universally applied. This failure of operational analysis has rightly been used in criticism of the Royal Navy and of Fisher's Luddite opposition to the development of a proper naval staff.[108] But strategically the battle of Dogger Bank was a major setback for Germany.

Hipper had lost an armoured cruiser that arguably should never have been taken out; that was the sole margin of British victory. Moreover, his guns, excluding *Blücher*, had scored twenty-two hits out of 976 rounds. If, as Hipper subsequently advised, U-boats had been in position, the *Lion* at least might have gone down. And yet the essence of the action on 24 January, as it had been

---

[107] Lambert, *Journal of Military History*, LXII (1998), 32–42.
[108] e.g. Goldrick, *King's ships*, 306–9, 311–15; Roskill, *Beatty*, 117–20; Sumida, *In defence of naval supremacy*, 298–9. On gunnery, see also Hough, *Great war at sea*, 140–1.

on 16 December, was Germany's flight, the escape of Hipper's scouting groups. Rather than seek action the Germans were shunning it. The effect of such a policy was to consolidate British sea-power, not threaten it.

German defensiveness suited Fisher admirably. The day after the battle he wrote to Churchill: 'Being already in possession of all that a powerful fleet can give a country, we should continue quietly to enjoy the advantage.'[109] In December 1914 he secured approval for a new design of oil-fired battle cruisers, with a speed of 32 knots and six 15-inch guns. Already by 1 May 1915, with his three battle cruisers returned from the Atlantic, Jellicoe could count on thirty-two Dreadnoughts to the Germans' twenty-one. But, as one member of the cabinet, Charles Hobhouse, noted on 27 November 1914, 'One thing is certain and that is that "command of the sea" can no longer be assured by number, speed or size of your battle fleet'.[110] Fisher's determination not to deploy Dreadnoughts in the North Sea, and the renewed fear of invasion that was its consequence, revitalized his ideas on flotilla defence. More important in the long run in his 1915 programme than its five battle cruisers and two light cruisers were its fifty-six destroyers and sixty-five submarines; perhaps more revealing in the short term were its 260 landing craft. Fisher was set on a lengthy war, and a long-term programme to accompany it: in October 1914 he spoke of an armada of 600 smaller vessels.[111]

German construction, by comparison, fell into disarray. The army's need for manpower challenged the building programme. What labour there was had to divide its energies over new building and refits and repairs; the tactical lessons of Dogger Bank had to be incorporated into this schedule. The Imperial Naval Office continued in its old ways, although now at least aiming for parity with Britain: in January 1915 its target was a doubling of the naval budget to produce a fleet of eighty-one capital ships by 1934.[112] But Tirpitz's own strategic confusion, as well as his loss of influence, meant also a lack of continuity as to priorities. Battle cruisers capable of independent action, of great speed and heavy armament, and similar in conception to Fisher's found advocates in the Kaiser and Hipper; U-boats were supported by Pohl. The opportunity for a decisive fleet action had presented itself in the winter of 1914–15. The Germans, for all their talk, had failed to take it; by the following winter the chances of a battle which would create a sufficient dent in British capital ship numbers to represent a real challenge to the Entente's naval mastery were virtually nil. Although in a tactical sense it was possible for the Royal Navy to lose a battle in 1916, it had become strategically impossible for Germany to win one.

[109] Gilbert, *Churchill*, vol. III, Companion, pt. 2, p. 454.
[110] David (ed.), *Inside Asquith's cabinet*, 207.
[111] Halpern, *Naval history*, 36; Barry Gough, 'Fisher', in Murfett (ed.), *First Sea Lords*, 25.
[112] Epkenhans, 'Die kaiserliche Marine im Ersten Weltkrieg', in Michalka (ed.), *Der Erste Weltkrieg*, 332–3; Herwig, *First World War*, 304.

The battle of the Dogger Bank was therefore more decisive than was apparent to Jellicoe or Beatty. It gave full rein to the already fissiparous tendencies in the German navy. Tirpitz's plot to oust Ingenohl now received fresh momentum from within the fleet itself. The battle cruiser captains of Hipper's scouting groups (who increasingly saw themselves as yet another naval staff) felt that the commander of the High Seas Fleet had twice let them down, and they wanted Reinhard Scheer, commanding the 2nd battle squadron, to have the job. On 2 February 1915, when Ingenohl struck his flag, he was replaced by Pohl. 'A more unlikely choice could not have been made', was Hipper's reaction.[113] Tirpitz appeared to have got his way, but his success was illusory. Not he, but Admiral Gustav Bachmann was the new chief of the Admiralty Staff. Tirpitz could console himself with the thought that he got on well with Bachmann, but Bachmann was not a strong man and from the outset Pohl asserted the High Seas Fleet's independence of the Admiralty Staff. Pohl himself had become increasingly critical of Tirpitz.[114] Neither Bachmann nor Pohl, Müller concluded, 'was entirely welcome ... At the time there were no better alternatives'.[115]

With Ingenohl's departure the advocates of an offensive use of the fleet in the North Sea were reduced to relative silence. Tirpitz, of course, continued to advocate action, but still within reasonable range of Germany's bases; Pohl himself argued that eventually the British would appear once again off the Bight; and Hipper, who by now was the most battle-hardened admiral in the navy, was opposed to a fight in British waters.

Those who chafed at the inactivity which this implied looked to the Baltic. Admiral Wilhelm von Lens, commanding the 1st battle squadron, wanted the High Seas Fleet concentrated against Russia. The navy could cut the Entente's links with its ally, secure Germany's trade with Scandinavia, and check any British amphibious landings on the north German coast.[116] Pohl was prepared to go along with this, at least in so far as planning amphibious operations against Memel were concerned. Tirpitz and Bachmann were opposed: the perversity of a battle in the Baltic was that here Germany reigned supreme, as Britain did in the North Sea; there was no need to fight; the maintenance of an intact fleet was the most effective, as well as the least costly, way of proceeding. Lens, in any case, had been bypassed for the fleet command, allegedly through ill-health, and in due course lost the 1st battle squadron as well.

A more offensive, if somewhat ambitious, slant to his thinking was developed by one of his staff in the 1st battle squadron, Wolfgang Wegener. Wegener

---

[113] Philbin, *Hipper*, 117.
[114] Hörich, *Deutsche Seekriegführung*, 57, 63.
[115] Müller, *Kaiser and his court*, 61.
[116] Werner Rahn, 'Strategische Probleme der deutschen Seekriegführung', in Michalka (ed.), *Der Erste Weltkrieg*, 351–2.

had served on the Admiralty Staff between 1908 and 1912, and had imbibed the thinking of Baudissin, Fischel, and Holtzendorff. He was the author of a memorandum designed to promote the Baltic option for 1915, and counter-signed by Lens on 1 February. But by June and July Wegener's pursuit of the offensive had swung his focus back to the west. He argued that Tirpitz's pre-war construction policy had been founded on a sense of implied German naval inferiority, that the object had been to match Britain, not to be superior to her; thus, although the fleet's units looked the part of a major sea-power, in reality the fleet's philosophy was still wedded to coastal defence. The military and continental traditions of Bismarckian Germany had only endorsed this defensiveness. But with Britain as Germany's major opponent a continental strategy had proved insufficient; indeed, it had markedly failed to meet Germany's needs as a world power and as a sea-power because, by virtue of the defeat on the Marne, it had not secured for the fleet the Atlantic bases of Brest or Cherbourg. And access to the Atlantic and to the world's sea routes, not battle per se, was for Wegener the essence of the offensive application of sea-power. Nothing could be achieved in the North Sea while Britain's geographical position enabled the Royal Navy to control its exits. Geography, not numbers of ships, was the nub of naval strategy. The task of the navy, therefore, given the fact that the French and British armies barred the way to the Atlantic ports in the south, was to open the route through Skagerrak, 'the gate to the Atlantic'. But the Danes' mining of the Belts, encouraged by Germany in order to secure the defences of the Baltic, had closed off its most obvious offensive exit into the North Sea. The neutralization of the Belts freed the Royal Navy from itself guarding Skagerrak, while further confining Germany.[117]

Wegener's ideas embraced the fundamental challenge to German naval strategy: as the power without maritime supremacy it had to attack the power in possession. They circulated through the fleet in 1915. But they suffered from three major limitations: they were bitterly opposed by Tirpitz, their implications for Danish neutrality were horrific for a foreign ministry searching for allies and for an army already heavily committed on two fronts, and—most immediate of all—Wegener remained vague on their operational application.

Pohl's own response to the pressure for an offensive option was the U-boat. It is hard to resist the argument that this was a decision grounded, not on strategy but on bureaucratic necessity. Pohl needed to mark out a policy that

---

[117] The argument as developed is that presented by Wegener in 1929 in *Seestrategie des Weltkrieges*; it was originally formulated in spring and summer 1915 and had a wide circulation: see Gemzell, *Organization, conflict, and innovation*, 215–25, 228–33; Herwig, '*Luxury' fleet*, 191. Its evolution can be traced in the English edition edited by Herwig, which publishes the original memoranda of February, June, and July 1915.

was different from that of Tirpitz.[118] He agreed with the rejection of major operations in the North Sea; although he considered the Baltic options, their limited versions seemed redundant and their expansive versions far fetched. But in February 1915 the U-boats too had little to recommend them. In 1914 they had lost a quarter of their strength, sinking only ten of sixty-one vessels accounted for by German action.[119] Most German naval thought still saw the submarine in ancillary terms, not as a major new way of exercising sea-power.

Thus, just as Germany's naval administration remained divided by faction and function, so did its strategy get pulled in divergent directions. The net consequence was the neglect and incipient decline of Germany's High Seas Fleet. By the end of 1914 two marine divisions were fighting in Flanders, their numbers being made up with reservists, and in February 1915 the 6th battle squadron was taken out of commission and the 5th reduced. After the demise of the *Blücher* only the most modern capital ships were kept operational. On 23 March 1915 Pohl wrote to the Kaiser,

I do not know the positions of the enemy naval forces. My scouting forces are too weak for me to be able to know when meeting weak enemy forces if the main body is in the vicinity. I can therefore find myself—in spite of myself—engaged in a naval battle that I must avoid. In the current military situation, I think therefore that the offensive opportunity must be very brief, and limited to showing that we dominate the Heligo-land Bight.[120]

The Kaiser agreed. By the spring of 1915 the Royal Navy had to all intents and purposes won the battle which it had set out to win; the German surface fleet was crushed, even if its units were intact. Tirpitz's pre-war policies were in ruins. But, as Wegener had observed, neither the fleet nor battle was an end in itself; there were other ways of exercising sea-power.

---

[118] Gemzell, *Organization conflict, and innovation*, 142–4, 184–6.
[119] Philbin, *Hipper*, 96.
[120] Castex, *Théories stratégiques*, ii. 224.

6

WAR IN THE PACIFIC, 1914–1917

OCEANIC SECURITY AND THE CRUISER THREAT

On 21 July 1914 Sir F. C. D. Sturdee wrote a minute for the two First Lords of the Admiralty: 'it is very evident', he remarked, 'that our next maritime war will be world-wide, more so even than former wars.'[1] The concentration of the British fleet in home waters and the high profile accorded the Anglo-German naval arms race had not gainsaid the continuity of the navy's task in British grand strategy. The British empire was bonded by maritime communications; the homeland was dependent on a vastly increased oceanic trade; the Royal Navy's global responsibilities, even if somewhat humdrum, remained indivisible from its mission in the North Sea.

Therefore, the fleet which Fisher built was not designed, as much of the German was, exclusively for North Sea operations. The features of his battle cruisers which excited criticism in that context became assets when placed alongside the demands of global service. The relative lack of armour and of subdivision in watertight compartments, so problematic in fleet action in narrow seas, allowed speeds and cruising ranges which were fundamental on the oceans. Fisher's designs, and indeed his very preference for the battle cruiser over the battleship, betrayed his broad interpretation of the nature of British sea-power. His willingness to embrace the notion of blockade, his deep-seated revulsion at the army's continentalism, suggested an Atlantic and imperial orientation that he shared with Hankey and Esher.

---

[1] Public Record Office, ADM/8386/213. I am grateful to Dr Maurice Pearton for this reference.

Navalism, which when expressed by any other power sent British strategists into flurries of self-induced panic, provoked little response when taken up by the United States. Co-operation not confrontation was the keynote, even if not formalized, of pre-war Anglo-American relations. Britain's economic dependence on the world's producers of primary materials left it no choice.

Before the war 58 per cent of the calories consumed in Britain arrived by sea—grain from the prairies of North America, meat from Australia, New Zealand, and Argentina; cheap food kept British wages down and therefore made the prices of its finished goods competitive; in return the dominions of South Africa, Australia, and New Zealand took 60 per cent of their imports from Britain. Moreover, exports by themselves were insufficient to cover Britain's trade deficit. London paid for its imports by its overseas investment, by the world dominance of its shipping, banking, and insurance. Britain's livelihood was therefore global, oceanic, and imperial.[2] Thus, the concentration of the fleet on home waters was not, in its ultimate purposes, designed to bring about a fleet action; it was—as the policy of distant blockade abundantly testified—to prevent German cruisers breaking out into the oceans and trade-routes of the world.

But, as with so many other aspects of Britain's pre-war naval policy, its global perspective remained ill-developed. There was little effort either publicly or in the Committee of Imperial Defence to reconcile the immediate focus on Germany with the underlying continuities of British sea-power. Fisher's critics pointed out that the scrapping of obsolescent vessels on economic grounds removed from service those very ships most suitable for trade protection. The First Sea Lord replied that the threat to merchant shipping would come from enemy cruisers operating in squadrons, not in isolation. The Royal Navy could therefore best serve the interests of commerce by seeking out and attacking those enemy cruiser squadrons.[3] But his argument was self-serving. It put a premium on all his own personal predilections—on modernization, on concentration, on the offensive, and on the battle cruiser. Its failure to convince was hardly surprising when the Admiralty simultaneously reduced the Mediterranean and China squadrons, and terminated that in the South Atlantic.

In reality, economic necessity combined with the German challenge to give the Admiralty little room for manoeuvre. The British navy could not independently sustain a global presence. The solution to its far-flung problems was, of course, the establishment of local proxies and regional balances—informally the United States in the Pacific and western Atlantic, formally France in the Mediterranean and Japan in the Far East.

---

[2] For a fuller development of these themes, see Offer, *First World War*, esp. 81–90, 244–69.
[3] Marder, *From the Dreadnought*, i. 54–6.

After 1907 Russia, if it posed any threat to Britain, did so in Persia, not in China or India. The strategic buttress of the Anglo-Japanese alliance, fear of Russia as an east Asian power, was therefore removed. The renewal of the alliance in 1911 consequently came to rest on somewhat different foundations. Japan, which had derived both status and great-power backing from the alliance, saw it as a means for Anglo-Japanese co-operation in the exploitation of China. In this it was not as totally deceived as Britain's defence of the status quo in the Far East and of the open door in China might seem to suggest. Grey recognized the legitimacy of Japanese expansionism, albeit within limits. The alliance was therefore the means by which Britain could—and before 1914 did—moderate Japanese foreign policy. But such a justification for the alliance was insufficient from the British perspective, particularly when Japanese economic ambitions in the areas of British influence, on the Yangtze and in South China, were creating unease in British commercial circles. For Britain, the fundamental purpose of the alliance was naval. By the end of the nineteenth century the Pacific had become a hub of naval competition, attracting significant French, Russian, and Japanese fleets. In 1901 the Admiralty had maintained thirty-eight battleships and cruisers in Far Eastern waters, but by 1910 that number was halved.[4] The French fleet had been withdrawn, the Russian eliminated, and the Japanese neutralized. By calling in the Japanese navy as reinforcement, Britain could rest easy with regard to its defensive obligations, both coastal and commercial, in the Pacific.

However, this solution to its naval requirements, while attractive to London and consonant with its reconciliation of global and European concerns, was less satisfactory to those Anglophone countries whose shores were washed by Pacific waters. A corollary of Britain's close trading links with the Americas and the Dominions was the continuing identification of the emigrant communities and settler societies of those lands with the mother country. They were white and determined to remain so. The emigration of Japanese to British Columbia and to California agitated both Canadian and United States opinion; racism found its most virulent expression in Australia, and its most forceful exponent in that country's future Labour leader Billy Hughes. The policy of exclusion, although populist and protective in markets where labour was scarce and jobs plenty, was not, therefore, economically motivated in the first instance.[5] It was rather a statement of emergent national identity. Australia's popular fiction portrayed the Japanese as its invaders, not its defenders. Moreover, many Australians could not see any long-term advantage to Tokyo in the Anglo-Japanese alliance. Britain needed Japan to protect its possessions in the Far East; Japan, on the other hand, had no comparable need

[4] Lowe, *Great Britain and Japan*, 17–18; also Nish, *Alliance in decline*.
[5] Lowe, *Great Britain and Japan*, 267–93; Nish, *Alliance in decline*, 62–3; Offer, *First World War*, 164–209.

of Britain in Europe, and could not rely on Britain to face its most likely Asian or Pacific opponents, Russia and the United States.

But the Japanese threat did not pre-empt the German threat: the latter also had resonances in the Antipodes. If Germany defeated Britain in Europe the Dominions might find themselves reallocated as colonies of Germany. Less extreme but more immediately, Germany's acquisition of Pacific islands pointed menacingly at the coastal trade of Australia and New Zealand; the German consular service in Australia worked hard to ensure that the sizeable German immigrant population retained its cultural identity.[6]

Ultimately the Dominions' long-term security lay in the co-ordinated efforts of the empire as a whole: the defensive capability of the sum was greater than that of the parts. In 1909 Sir Joseph Ward—prime minister of the most British, if also the most far-flung, Dominion New Zealand—told the Imperial Conference: 'Our country is very anxious and willing to assist the Old Land in the event of trouble arising to do so voluntarily by men or money, and... always would be ready to do its share in fighting for the defence of the Motherland in any portion of the world.'[7] Ward recognized that an investment in defence equipment sufficient to sustain viable independent forces would cripple the New Zealand economy: thus, his loyalty to London was not at the expense of the needs of New Zealand but was their corollary. Nascent nationalisms were compatible with a continuing imperial identity.

Grey exploited these convergences. When meeting the dominion prime ministers in 1911 he took care to put the case for the alliance's renewal in its global and naval context. He preferred to see Japanese ambitions and Japanese emigration as directed towards China rather than into the Pacific. In revealing his sensitivity to opinion in the Antipodes and North America, and by consulting the Dominions (if not deferring to them), he did much to appease them.

Australia's response to its fears of invasion, whether Japanese or German, was to create its own fleet. In 1906 it planned a force of eight coastal destroyers and four torpedo boats; by 1908 it had developed this into a putative navy of twenty-four destroyers. The Admiralty could see no value in such proposals. For the orthodox, A. T. Mahan's advocacy of battle fleets and the advent of the Dreadnought made gunboat defence an even more inadequate expedient against a first-class power. For the unorthodox, like Fisher, submarines were a more promising means of coastal defence—a point which both Australians and New Zealanders appeared to take on board at the Imperial Conference in 1907, but did nothing to implement.[8] Fisher did not push it: he saw the

---

[6] Moses, *War & Society*, VII (1989), 56–76; Overlack, ibid., X (1992), 37–51; Overlack, 'Australasia and Germany'.

[7] McGibbon, *Path to Gallipoli*, 167; for Australia, see Wilcox, *Australian Journal of History and Politics*, XL (1994), 52–4.

[8] McGibbon, *Path to Gallipoli*, 174–5.

Australians' fears of invasion as preposterous. Since Tsushima, the only significant navy in the Pacific, apart from that of the United States, belonged to Britain's ally Japan. Even if the alliance lapsed, Japan could hardly mount a realistic challenge to antipodean security, since it lacked the bases to render it logistic support, and the advent of wireless telegraphy was likely to give timely intelligence of its advance. Such views did not mean that Fisher was averse to a revived Pacific fleet. Its task, however, should not be defence against invasion but the protection of oceanic trade. For such a mission cruisers, not destroyers, were required.

Fisher's cause was boosted by New Zealand's vision of imperial defence. Ward was worried by the possibility of an Australian navy; its effect could be a further reduction in the Royal Navy's presence in the south Pacific, with New Zealand's defence dependent on Australia as it could not afford its own. On 22 March 1909 he responded to the German naval scare in London by announcing that New Zealand would fund at least one Dreadnought, and possibly a second, as its contribution to the imperial fleet. Such controversy in Wellington as his initiative caused was generated more by his failure to secure prior parliamentary approval than by a desire to follow the Australian route. Across the Tasman Sea both New South Wales and Victoria responded to New Zealand's gesture, and put pressure on the Commonwealth of Australia also to offer a Dreadnought.[9] It duly did so.

At the Imperial Conference held in July 1909 Fisher responded enthusiastically to both these initiatives, while trying to channel them in different directions. His aim was inter-operability, and his preferred tool was his beloved battle cruiser. McKenna duly told the Dominions that a navy needed to be at least 2,000 men strong and to be formed of one battle cruiser, three light cruisers, six destroyers, and three submarines in order to present a viable fleet unit both in terms of career structure and of operational utility. Individually such units would not create the logistic, manning, or fiscal demands of a fully fledged oceanic battle fleet. But by operating in conjunction with each other they would be the building blocks for an imperial Pacific fleet. Fisher imagined that Canada and Australia would each provide one fleet unit, and Britain two (to be based at Hong Kong and Singapore). New Zealand would help subsidize the Hong Kong unit, and South Africa and India might contribute in due course.[10] The political merit of the fleet unit idea was its ability to appease Australian nationalism; to that extent Ward was disappointed by the dilution of his conception of an overarching imperial navy. Its operational utility was both logistic and tactical. The line of battle, vulnerable in any case to long-range torpedoes, was hard to support across the expanse of the Pacific; its

[9] Ibid. 175–9; Gordon, *Dominion partnership*, 223.
[10] Nicholas Lambert, 'Economy or empire? The fleet unit concept and the quest for collective security in the Pacific, 1909–14', in Kennedy and Neilson (eds.), *Far-flung lines*, 55–76.

replacement by the battle unit, in which each capital ship would fight in conjunction with smaller, supporting vessels, but independently of other Dreadnoughts, eased the constraints of fuel supply.[11]

The policy unravelled almost as soon as it was created. Fisher's retirement removed its prime advocate in Whitehall. Canada saw the scheme, not as a concession to dominion nationalism but as a reassertion of imperialism.[12] But its principal challenger was Churchill. The conclusions of the Imperial Naval Conference overlapped with the 1909 naval estimates crisis. Its focus was Germany, and Churchill agreed that true economy rested in concentration against the main enemy in the potentially decisive theatre. As First Lord he was delighted to accept the naval units of the Dominions, but on condition that they were incorporated into the Royal Navy, and he was bent on bringing that navy home at an even more resolute pace than Fisher had been.

In 1911 Sir Robert Borden's Conservative party won the Canadian election. It had campaigned on a policy of imperial unity. Borden therefore rejected the proposals of Sir Wilfred Laurier's Liberal party for a Canadian navy of four cruisers and six destroyers for coastal protection. In 1912 Churchill persuaded Borden that Canada should allocate $35 million for the construction of three Dreadnoughts, not for the Pacific or even for the Atlantic but for the Mediterranean. Borden's bill was thrown out by the Liberal-dominated Canadian Senate. In 1914 the Royal Canadian Navy possessed two ageing cruisers, one for either coast. In two years its strength had fallen from 800 men to 350, sufficient to provide half a crew for one vessel.[13]

Churchill's policy ought to have proved as disastrous with the Australians and New Zealanders. He insulted them in 1913 by suggesting that they would be sufficiently protected by a quick-reaction force based as far away as Gibraltar. The First Lord argued that there were only two battleships in the Pacific, one Chilean and one American: the Japanese did not count as they were allies. But in this case events rebounded to Churchill's advantage. The New Zealand naval defence bill of November 1913 commenced the training of a New Zealand navy, while still promising that its men would be transferred to the Admiralty in time of war. Australia's response was to look to embark on a twenty-two-year programme of naval construction, and its annual naval spending approached £2 million. By the outbreak of war the Australian navy comprised one battle cruiser, four light cruisers, and three destroyers.[14]

The Australian brand of navalism was a fruit of Pacific rivalries and of fears of Japan. The deployment of the Australian navy was from the outset the affair

---

[11] Nicholas Lambert, 'Economy or empire? The fleet unit concept and the quest for collective security in the Pacific, 1909–14', in Kennedy and Neilson (eds.), *Far-flung lines*, 62–3.

[12] Gordon, *Dominion partnership*, 248.

[13] Hadley and Sarty, *Tin-pots and pirate ships*, 1–29, 55–74.

[14] Meaney, *Search for security*, 159–92, 208–60.

of the Commonwealth of Australia. But in the minds of the Admiralty, *Australia* and *New Zealand*, the eponymous battle cruisers provided by each of those Dominions, improved the naval balance against Germany. The Admiralty had been able to play off the Japanese against the Dominions and so secure the contributions of both. The building blocks of a Pacific fleet existed, even if its design was not in place.

Therefore, in the Pacific as much as, if not more than, in the North Sea, ships were symbols of power rather than executors of strategy. Churchill's case rested on the Anglo-Japanese alliance as the 'bond that is the true and effective protection for the safety of Australia and New Zealand'.[15] But the service of which he was the political head resolutely refused to develop this conceptual framework, this grand strategy, into operational reality. The Japanese suggested that the two navies conduct joint exercises and establish a common signal book. The Admiralty refused. The concept of security to which the Japanese alliance subscribed was a generalized one; the specific threat of Germany was not addressed. Indeed, the Admiralty assumed that Japan would not become involved in the event of war with Germany in Europe. This was reasonable in so far as the Anglo-Japanese alliance was designed as a settlement and stabilizer of Far Eastern issues. It was militarily naive in view of the fact that Germany's major overseas naval base was at Tsingtao in the Shantung peninsula. The forces stationed there, the East Asiatic Squadron, constituted the principal grouping of German cruisers overseas. Indeed, the German vessels, two armoured cruisers and three light cruisers, were numerically comparable with those of the British Chinese station (two armoured cruisers, two light cruisers, and eight destroyers), and—being all of the latest construction—were qualitatively superior. Sir Thomas Jerram, who took up the command of the China station in 1913, was very worried. The Admiralty's sop to his concerns, HMS *Triumph*, was a pre-Dreadnought battleship capable of only 20 knots, and was in dry dock in Hong Kong when war broke out. Jerram recognized that real security lay with the addition of the Japanese navy, and cultivated Anglo-Japanese relations accordingly. But Japan itself was no better disposed than the Admiralty to resolve his difficulties: the army was worried by Russia's resurgence and feared a renewed threat to its position in Manchuria; the navy saw its putative enemy as the United States.

The waters of the Far East, not those of the North Sea, were therefore the most obvious area of British maritime vulnerability. The Germans had acquired Tsingtao in 1898. Tirpitz, who himself had vacated the command of the Far Eastern squadron shortly before, saw the port as the first of a series which would girdle the globe, and so provide the means to integrate navalism with *Weltpolitik*. In the event, Germany's colonies by 1914 fell into two groups,

---

[15] Nish, *Alliance in decline*, 97.

the islands of the Pacific—the Marianas, the Marshalls, the Carolines, New Guinea, and Samoa—and the territorially more sizeable acquisitions in sub-Saharan Africa—Togoland, the Cameroons, South-West Africa, and German East Africa. None of these possessed a major naval base. Tsingtao, therefore, stood alone in its capacity to service modern warships. But the Pacific archipelagos did at least provide a network of supporting points and hiding places for the conduct of cruiser warfare.

Germany's operational possibilities were therefore at odds with strategic sense. The greatest concentration of British shipping was to be found in the eastern Atlantic, as it converged on its home ports. It was, however, precisely here that the Royal Navy's defences were strongest and the German cruisers would have the shortest life-expectancy. Moreover, the Atlantic lacked both the German bases and the island networks possessed by the Pacific. A possible intermediate solution, attacks in the Red Sea and Indian Ocean on the traffic approaching the Suez Canal, offered only limited opportunities. East Africa, the obvious home for such operations, did not have the coal stocks for regular bunkers. The Germans consoled themselves with the thought that raids further east would at least indirectly challenge the traffic bound for Suez and the Mediterranean.[16] But their cruisers would therefore have to operate on the periphery of Britain's maritime trade, not at its heart.

Cruiser warfare, having been popularized by the *jeune école* in France, had become a less fashionable aspect of naval strategy by 1900. Mahan had concluded from his analysis of naval warfare in the late-eighteenth and early-nineteenth centuries that cruiser operations were an option exercised only by the weaker power and that their effect, though not negligible, was secondary. The subsequent arrival of steam navigation seemed to have conferred more disadvantages than advantages on *guerre de course*. The main routes of world trade became set, not varied according to the direction of the wind, and could therefore be more easily defended. The sophistication of the twentieth-century warship, with its need for fuel and munitions, made cruisers more dependent on regular supply, and therefore on bases, than their sail-powered predecessors. A German armoured cruiser carried enough coal to last a week at moderate speeds and only five days of sailing at 20 knots.[17] Furthermore, Britain's defence of neutral rights, which seemed so absurd in the context of its plans for economic warfare, made abundant sense when related to the protection of its own trade. The 1907 Hague Conference had ruled that a belligerent could berth a maximum of three ships in a neutral port at any one time, that they could stay there for no more than twenty-four hours, and that they could take on sufficient supplies only to allow them to complete their homeward

---

[16] Marine-Archiv, *Der Krieg zur See. Das Kreuzergeschwader*, i. 25–6; 1–34 for the basis of German cruiser operations in general; also Overlack, *War & Society*, XVII (1999), 1–23.

[17] Ganz, *Militärgeschichtliches Mitteilungen*, 21 (1977), 39–40.

journey. Thus, to all intents and purposes neutral ports could not sustain cruiser warfare: Mahan's weaker option was weakened yet further.

Early German naval thought had embraced the ideas of the *jeune école*, of fighting a *guerre de course* against major fleets, and the initial emphasis was therefore on the construction of cruisers and torpedo boats. In 1896 the Kaiser favoured cruisers to support Germany's world role, and in 1903 and 1905 he advocated the adoption of battle cruisers built on lines similar to those suggested by Fisher. But after 1897 Wilhelm lost control of naval construction to Tirpitz. Battleships, not cruisers, dominated German naval orders. Tirpitz argued that cruisers would not be able to break out from the North Sea without the aid of battleships, and that once on the world's oceans their operational capabilities would be restricted for lack of bases. Although both were valid points, his use of war-fighting propositions was self-serving. His emphasis on battleships reflected the fact that the purposes of his fleet were ultimately peaceful—to use naval power as a deterrent and as a means to a new diplomatic order. When his building policies hit the buffers of the 1912 naval law in 1913 and 1914, he was prepared to support the construction of cruisers. The Imperial Naval Office discussed with MAN (Maschinenfabrik Augsburg-Nürnberg) the use of diesel engines in surface ships, so as to reduce the problems of fuel supply by enhancing the ships' range. Tirpitz himself was attracted to cruisers largely because their numbers were not so subject to Reichstag scrutiny.[18]

In the circumstances, Germany was more prepared for cruiser warfare than might have been expected. The last pure armoured cruisers, *Scharnhorst* and *Gneisenau*, launched in 1906, were the key units of the East Asiatic Squadron. But even Tirpitz was prepared to concede that their successors, the battle cruisers, though based at Wilhelmshaven, might have an independent role outside the North Sea. And by 1914 Germany had thirty-four light cruisers.[19] Contingency plans were made to requisition as auxiliary cruisers modern merchant vessels, equipped with wireless, their decks strengthened to take guns, and with sufficient watertight compartments and speeds of at least 17 knots. Recognizing both the inadequacy of most of Germany's colonial harbours and their obvious focus for enemy attack, the navy rejected any proposal to defend Germany's peacetime bases, Tsingtao apart. Instead, their war instructions directed the cruisers to neutral harbours and isolated anchorages.[20] To minimize the supply problem, a series of *Etappen* were established in Asia and along the east and west coasts of South America,

[18] Epkenhans, *Wilhelminische Flottenrüstung*, 396–8, 414; id., 'Germany 1880–1914', in Phillips O'Brien (ed.), *Preparing for the next war at sea*; Stevenson, *Armaments and the coming of war*, 290.

[19] Güth 'Organisation der deutschen Marine', 276–8.

[20] Overlack, *War & Society*, X (1992), 44; Ganz, *Militärgeschichtliches Mitteilungen*, 21 (1977), 46–7.

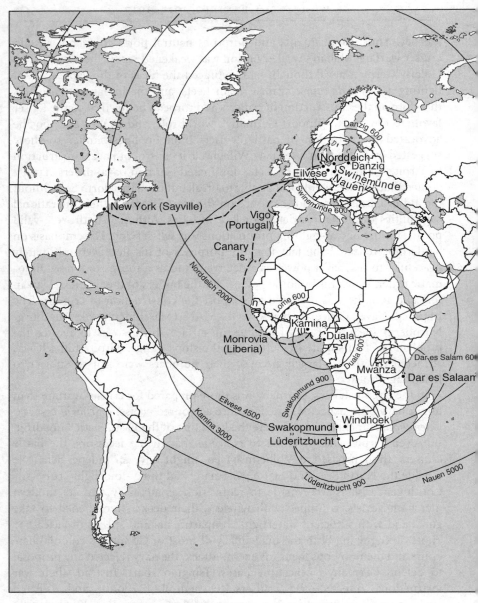

MAP 15. GERMAN CABLE AND WIRELESS COMMUNICATIONS

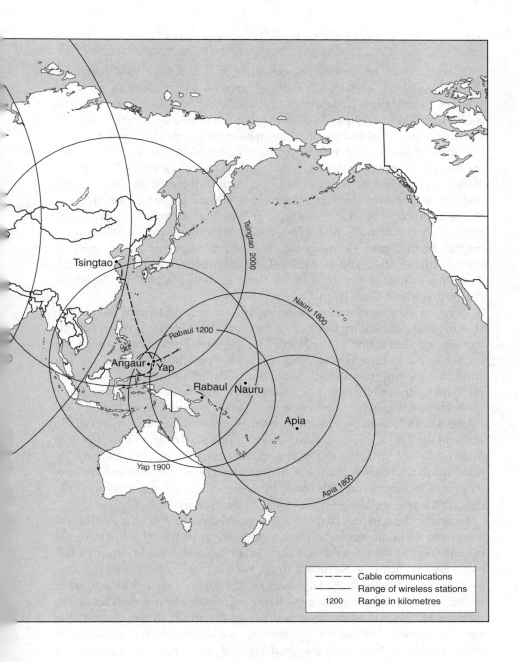

Tsingtao

Tsingtao 2000

Nauru 1800

Rabaul 1200

Angaur• •Yap

Rabaul• Nauru•

Apia•

Yap 1900

Apia 1800

----- Cable communications
——— Range of wireless stations
1200 Range in kilometres

each with a staff responsible for collecting fuel and food locally and for dispatching them on supply vessels to prearranged rendezvous with the cruisers. In 1900 the commander of the East Asiatic Squadron had 5.5 million marks in letters of credit and access to other funds held by German agents in order to acquire coal and supplies throughout the Pacific. Most striking of all was the development of a global wireless network. In Germany the Nauen station could transmit signals 5,000 nautical miles, as far as Peking and Bangkok in the east, to the Cape of Good Hope in the south, and to Chicago and Rio de Janeiro in the west. Intermediate stations in the German colonies, the most powerful of which were those at Windhoek (whose range was 2,000 nautical miles) in South-West Africa and at Yap (1,900 nautical miles) in the central Pacific, gave Germany effective communications across most of the Atlantic, all Africa and the Middle East, and the Far East and South Pacific. The obvious hole in the network lay along the entire American side of the Pacific and round Cape Horn.[21]

Germany's preparations for cruiser warfare rested in part on the recognition that in reality the choice between cruisers and battleships, between oceanic warfare and fleet action in the North Sea, was a false one. The two were not exclusive, but complementary. The Germans appreciated that the cruisers would account for only a small proportion of British tonnage. But by driving up freight rates and insurance premiums they might stop up shipping, block the trade in raw materials, and cause widespread unemployment. In 1912 Vice-Admiral Curt Freiherr von Maltzahn even argued that the panic which would ensue in the City of London, as well as the effects of starvation in the north of England, would bring the war to an even more rapid conclusion than operations on land. What was essentially an instrument for a long war would achieve its effects in short order. This was, of course, a self-serving argument: the quicker the war, the less grievous would be the cruisers' lack of bases.[22]

Secondly, the activities of the cruisers would serve to draw the Royal Navy away from the home waters, whither it had concentrated, and back to the more distant areas of the world. If the East Asiatic Squadron could divert British battle cruisers from the North Sea to the Pacific, then it would have rendered appreciable assistance to the High Seas Fleet. Equally, if the British refused to be drawn for fear of the more immediate danger posed by the High Seas Fleet, then the East Asiatic Squadron would be free to damage British trade. Either way, the addition of cruiser war to Germany's naval options was disproportionately valuable to the inferior power: it brought comparative strength against Britain's most vulnerable point, its import routes. In the narrow confines of the

---

[21] Marine-Archiv, *Kreuzergeschwader*, app. II, provides a graphic illustration of the belligerents' global wireless networks.
[22] Overlack, *Journal of Military History*, LX (1996), 657–9; id. *Journal of Strategic Studies*, XX (1997), 94–114.

North Sea one warship balanced another; in the wide spaces of the Pacific one warship would draw out many more. Thus, the true prop to Germany's conduct of the cruiser war was the High Seas Fleet itself. The greatest strategic criticism of Pohl's advocacy of defensiveness and inactivity in 1914 was that it left Germany's major maritime striking arm unsupported.[23]

Although such thinking had its advocates in 1914, it was not elevated to the status of policy. The potential of cruisers in the event of war had to compete with the fact that the navy overseas had a highly active role in peace. Much of what was effected in the way of wireless stations and cruiser construction was determined more by Germany's need for a naval presence to buttress its colonial and global policies. In the first half of 1914 two battleships and a light cruiser sailed the Atlantic from West Africa to South and Central America. The deployment of ships to meet the navy's peacetime functions was necessarily different from its active preparation for war.

The dichotomy also had its institutional manifestations. Formally speaking, the German Colonial Office was charged with colonial defence. It saw Germany's possessions as administrative burdens and as vehicles for economic expansion, not as the pivots of maritime warfare. Its more forward-thinking officials focused their attentions on their African colonies, which by 1914 were moving—in the case of East Africa in particular—along more civilized and enlightened paths than the early history of German colonialism had rendered imaginable. The vulnerabilities of all Germany's sub-Saharan African colonies in the event of European war were evident, and the common verdict—one in which the army's general staff was happy to collude in order to avoid imperial demands on its manpower—was that their fate would be decided by the outcome of events in Europe. This somewhat fatalistic position was buttressed by an optimistic reading of the Berlin act of 1885 (to which Britain, France, Belgium, and Germany were signatories), stating that if all the powers were agreed the Congo basin was to be considered neutral territory. The garrison of each of the African colonies therefore numbered in the region of 2,000 men. But, while the Colonial Office orientated itself on Africa and hoped for at most a limited impact from war in Europe, the navy focused on the Pacific.[24] Tsingtao was the fiefdom of Tirpitz's Imperial Naval Office, not of the Colonial Office. The expanse of the Pacific and the availability of isolated atolls as bases bestowed opportunities for harrying trade in the south Pacific. With a well-organized intelligence network centred on Sydney, the offensive instincts of German cruiser captains were buoyed by the slow progress of the Pacific fleet idea and of the Royal Australian Navy.[25] The only threat to an otherwise

[23] Marine-Archiv, *Kreuzergeschwader*, i. 7; Wegener, *Seestrategie*, 65–7; Assmann, *Deutsche Seestrategie*, 70–2.
[24] Lambi, *Navy and German power politics*, 409–11.
[25] Overlack, *Australian Journal of Politics and History*, XL (1994), 36–51.

favourable regional balance of naval forces was the possibility of Japan adding its fleet to that of Britain. So German plans for cruiser warfare in the south Pacific rested ultimately on a division of the globe as arbitrary as that embraced by the Colonial Office. Neutrality in the China Sea was necessary in order to avoid triggering the Anglo-Japanese alliance. In practice, hopes for sustaining neutrality in one quarter of the globe were undermined by the determination to attack in another.

The outbreak of war, therefore, found neither Germany's colonies nor its cruisers with an integrated operational plan. Germany's main assets, in addition to the East Asiatic Squadron, were two light cruisers in the West Indies, *Dresden* and *Karlsruhe*, and one, *Königsberg*, off East Africa. Little use was made of the July crisis to pre-position ships. Full naval mobilization was ordered too late, on 1 August, to enable the converted merchant ships to get out of the North Sea. Of the four auxiliary cruisers requisitioned on the war's outbreak, one developed problems with its boilers, and one was already overseas and could not be armed. Thus, only two became operational. *Kronprinz Wilhelm* was equipped at sea by the *Karlsruhe*, and *Kaiser Wilhelm der Grosse* broke out into the Atlantic on 4 August but was sunk just over three weeks later. The only subsequent addition to this number was *Berlin*, responsible for the sinking of *Audacious*. The instructions to the cruiser captains, in origin those issued by Wilhelm I in 1885, were specific as to types of target but short on overall strategy. Their burden was 'to carry on cruiser warfare against enemy merchant vessels and against contraband carried in neutral vessels, raid the enemy's coasts, bombard military establishments, and destroy cable and wireless stations'.[26] However, what they lacked in the way of plan, they made up for in common sense. Recognizing its inability to exercise effective control, the Admiralty Staff made a virtue of the independence and initiative of its subordinate commanders.

Britain was no better prepared. At the time of the Anglo-French staff talks of 1906, the army had given some thought to the capture of German colonies, but had seen them as potential bargaining-counters in the peace negotiations, not as important in the conduct of the war itself.[27] Britain's major desire, as the positioning of the bulk of its fleet testified, was to restrict the global consequences of events in Europe. For Britain, as for Germany, colonies produced an inhibiting effect, and imperialism, at least in the specific sense of lust for annexation, was neither a trigger for war nor a response to its outbreak.

However, colonies were indivisible from seapower, and it was both the exercise and the defence of this that made a rigid demarcation between Europe and empire impossible. Hankey had rated the defence of maritime trade as a

---

[26] Bennett, *Naval battles*, 50; for the full instructions, see Marine-Archiv, *Kreuzergeschwader*, i. 33–6.
[27] Ekoko, *Journal of Strategic Studies*, VII (1984), 443–8.

priority second only to the defence of Britain itself; moreover, his advocacy of amphibious operations could be taken to include landings outside Europe.[28] But his agency, the Committee of Imperial Defence, had made little headway in planning this sort of undertaking. Its subcommittee on combined operations of 1905 had gone into abeyance. Talks about its reactivation in the summer of 1914 were concerned rather more with amphibious operations on the continent than outside Europe, and so were seen as marginal, a diversion from the army's commitment to France. Not until 5 August was a subcommittee convened to consider overseas operations. The navy's was the leading voice: its demand, urgent and strident, was for the defence of British maritime communications by depriving Germany of its bunkers, wireless stations, and cable communications, the essential props of cruiser warfare. But the army's fear of diversion from the continent was also heard. Two cardinal principles were established as pre-eminent. First, the object was not the conquest of territory. Second, any land operations had to be undertaken by local forces only. From the outset, therefore, Britain's conduct of the war overseas was determined by tenets that were supportive of the effort in the main theatre and not diversionary.[29]

JAPAN ENTERS THE WAR

On 1 August, in conformity with its pre-war expectations, the British Foreign Office told the Japanese government that it was unlikely to invoke Japanese aid. Under the terms of the alliance, Japan was obliged to help Britain defend its Asiatic possessions against an unprovoked attack by another power. Grey thought only an assault on Hong Kong or Weihaiwei, both of them improbable eventualities, would produce a British summons. On 4 August Japan affirmed its neutrality.[30]

Germany was no danger to Japan. But in 1895 Japan had acquired Taiwan and had secured treaty rights in China. In 1905 the defeat of Russia rendered Korea first a Japanese dependency, and then—in 1910—a colony. In the decade before the First World War Japan behaved in China as did the great powers of Europe, promoting informal empire through exports and advocating the sort of modernization from which their own development had so recently

[28] Roskill, *Hankey*, i. 79.
[29] D'Ombrain, *War machinery*, 111–14; Corbett, *Naval operations*, i. 128–30; Louis, *Great Britain and Germany's lost colonies*, 36–7.
[30] On Japan's entry to the war, see esp. Chi, *China diplomacy*, ch. 1; La Fargue, *China*, ch. 1; Lowe, *Great Britain and Japan*, ch. 6; Nish, *Alliance in decline*, ch. 7; id., *Japanese foreign policy*, 93–6; id., 'Japan', in Wilson (ed.), *Decisions for war*; Ikuhiko Hata, 'Continental expansion 1905–1941', in Peter Duus (ed.), *Cambridge History of Japan*, vol. vi.

benefited. War in Europe therefore presented a double challenge to the Far East. First, Japan itself had twice recently used war to advance its own interests in the region with considerable success. Second, the nations' spheres of influence in China, guarded by their own troops, provided the opportunity for European rivalries to spread.

China itself badly needed stability. It had undergone revolution in 1911, and the Manchu dynasty had abdicated in 1912. In 1913 the president of the new republic, Yuan Shih-kai, had accepted a loan, funded by a consortium of five powers, to enable him to reorganize the country and consolidate his rule. The revolutionary republican party (the Kuomintang), whose strength lay in the south, was disgusted on two counts. It saw the loan as an affront to China's nationhood and as a form of western imperialism, and it feared that Yuan would use the money to advance his own despotic aspirations. In February and March 1913 Sun Yat-sen, the Kuomintang leader, had visited Japan and had been encouraged in his visions of a pan-Asian community by the outgoing prime minister, General Katsura Taro, as well as by Japanese nationalists and businessmen. But the rebellion which Sun staged in July ended in defeat. Japan, as one of the subscribers to the reorganization loan, had effectively backed both sides. Yuan's financial muscle ensured the loyalty of the armed forces and the support of the commercial classes. Sun went into exile in Japan, and the Kuomintang lost cohesion and direction. With Japan's policy over China divided, Yuan's hopes for order were raised. To the British he appeared to be the representative of constitutionalism and efficient government. His response to war in Europe was to maintain the status quo throughout east Asia, and to neutralize the foreign concessions in China.[31]

He was encouraged in this policy by the British ambassador in Peking Sir John Jackson, who shared Yuan's fear of Japan's ambitions on the Chinese mainland. In America too, the State Department was ill disposed towards Japan and was supportive of China's republic, which it saw as an agency for Christianity and democracy. On 1 August China called on the United States to neutralize China and the Pacific, a plea to which the Dutch added their voice on 3 August. William Jennings Bryan, the secretary of state, was optimistic, believing that the maintenance of neutrality throughout the Far East might be possible. But on 6 August Woodrow Wilson's wife died, and with the president in seclusion American foreign policy drifted until his return.[32]

On the very day on which Japan affirmed its neutrality, British policy began to shift. The Royal Navy's worries for the defence of British trade, coupled with the rough equivalence of German forces in Far Eastern waters, prompted a mood of near panic in the Admiralty—a mood which was to find endorsement

[31] Jansen, *The Japanese and Sun Yat-sen*, 154–73.

[32] Duus, Myers, and Peattie (eds.), *Japanese informal empire*, pp. xi–xxv; Dignan, *Indian revolutionary problem*, 76–7; May, *Mississippi Valley Historical Review*, XL (1953–4), 279–90.

at the meeting of the Committee of Imperial Defence subcommittee the following day. Although the seizure of Tsingtao was the most obvious immediate action in the Pacific theatre, it was rendered impossible first by the CID's requirement that Britain itself should use only local forces, and second by the need to restrict Japanese expansionism. But, if Tsingtao was unassailable, the German cruiser threat remained proportionately greater. What the Admiralty, therefore, wanted was the Japanese navy—fourteen battleships (four of them Dreadnoughts), a battle cruiser, fifteen cruisers, eighteen light cruisers, fifty-one destroyers, and thirteen submarines.[33] Only with this addition could the Royal Navy hope simultaneously to blockade Tsingtao, protect the Pacific's shipping lanes, and hunt down German ships. On 6 August, therefore, Grey found himself changing tack. He now sought Japanese assistance, but of a particularly limited variety. He was conscious of the United States's desire that the Pacific remain a neutral zone; he was aware of the fears of the Dutch East Indies and of the British Dominions that Japan as an active belligerent would soon convert to Japan as a south Pacific power. Therefore, all that he asked of Japan was that it seek out Germany's armed merchantmen: the Royal Navy would take on the task of dealing with German warships. Grey's diplomatic hand was not an easy one to play.

Britain's request was a lifeline to the Japanese navy. The victory over Russia had brought it from under the army's shadow, and its dominant Satsuma clan had established close connections with the Seiyukai party in the Diet. By 1910 the Japanese navy was twice as big as it had been in 1904, and in 1911, with a Seiyukai prime minister, the cabinet approved the construction of one battleship, *Kongo*, and four battle cruisers. The former, laid down in 1912, had twelve 14-inch guns and a displacement of 29,330 tons, making it at the time the most powerfully armed and largest battleship in the world. The battle cruisers, developed in emulation of the Royal Navy's, had eight 14-inch guns and a speed of 27.5 knots. Naval spending approached that of the army. Although the army toppled the Seiyukai-controlled government in December 1912, the navy and the Seiyukai prevented the formation of a pro-army cabinet. In 1913 Admiral Yamamoto Gombei became prime minister. Naval spending now outstripped that of the army. Three more battleships were approved, and the navy's ambition of a programme of eight battleships and eight battle cruisers looked closer to fulfilment. Then, in January 1914, its grip on politics was shattered by the revelation that admirals had accepted bribes in the allocation of shipbuilding contracts. Public demonstrations in February and an attack on the naval estimates in the House of Peers in March forced Yamamoto to resign. The navy needed the opportunity to restate its case which war would present.[34]

---

[33] Meaney, *Search for security*, 261–3.
[34] Schenking, *War in History*, V (1998), 308–11, 318–20; Evans and Peattie, *Kaigun*, 160–6.

The navy's building standards were set by the United States. Its leading strategic theorist, Sato Tetsutaro, argued that Japan's maritime security was contingent on its ability to strike a decisive blow against the enemy in the latter's home waters. He concluded that the Japanese navy therefore required a capability equivalent to 70 per cent of that of the United States. This was a figure which reflected the global consequences of regional naval arms races: Theodore Roosevelt's battleship programme, which found part of its justification through Tirpitz's expansion of the German fleet, increased the American 'threat' to Japan, but at the same time the American navy's division over two oceans diminished it.

The navy had selected the United States as its yardstick for the convenience of its building programme. But the rivalry was given an edge by anti-Japanese racism in California, and derived geopolitical reality from America's westward extension across the Pacific, to Hawaii, Samoa, the Philippines, and Guam. The Japanese fleet's manoeuvres of 1908 assumed that its enemy was the United States, and in 1910 the Japanese navy studied the problems of attacking the Philippines.

The United States did not figure on the army's list of potential enemies. Its focus was not maritime but continentalist; its expansionism was directed not into the Pacific but to the mainland of Asia. Thus, the rivalry between the two services had a strategic spine. The navy saw the army's continentalism as risky and expensive. Japan in Asia should emulate Britain in Europe: it should seek an ally, in this case China, in order to create a protective buffer against Russia. But in 1910 rebellion in Korea gave the army its opportunity to further its continental interests. It suppressed the rising with considerable ferocity, and the formal annexation which followed brought Japan's frontier adjacent to that of Russia. In 1912 the minister of war accordingly demanded an additional two divisions, and when he was thwarted brought down the government. Dominated by the Choshu clan, and close to the emperor, the army exploited constitutional division between civil and military authority to plough a politically independent furrow. Katsura Taro, a product of the general staff, was prime minister in 1901–6, 1908–9, and 1912–13.[35]

The army was particularly influential among the *genro* (or elder statesmen, a group without formal standing but which linked the government to the emperor). Their uncertainties concerning the government formed in April 1914 ensured that its dominant personality, Kato Takaaki, was offered not the premiership but the foreign ministry. As a former ambassador in London, Kato was a supporter of the Anglo-Japanese alliance. But he also saw in the war an opportunity to further Japan's interests in China. From the beginning of

---

[35] Peattie, *Nanyo*, 36–7; Myers and Peattie, *Japanese colonial empire*, 17–18; Evans and Peattie, *Kaigun*, 134–51; Humphreys, *Way of the heavenly sword*, 8–13, 19–20.

August his response to the British was both warmer and more bellicose than the state of the alliance or Japan's indifference to German aggression in Europe would have led the Foreign Office to expect. In January 1913 Grey, in a conversation with Kato shortly before he left London, had conveyed to the latter his recognition of the reasonableness of at least limited Japanese expansion in mainland Asia. Thus the war provided Kato with the opportunity to use the alliance in the way which made best sense to Japan, as a vehicle for the joint Anglo-Japanese exploitation of China.

Domestically, the decision to enter the war required of Kato some adroit political footwork. On 7 August the cabinet convened to consider Britain's request. Kato persuaded it to support him. But cabinet government in Japan, still largely shaped and staffed by the bureaucracy, was not powerful enough to proceed without the backing of the *genro*, the navy, or the army. On 8 August the cabinet reconvened with the *genro* in attendance. The latter were cautious, given Germany's military prowess and Japan's relative economic weakness. The services, on the other hand, saw in war the opportunity for the implementation of both their spending programmes. Kato emerged triumphant. Japan told Britain that it would declare war on Germany, arguing that the latter was threatening peace in the Far East and that the alliance had therefore been called into operation. The claim was doubtful. Formally speaking, Germany had done nothing to trigger the terms of the alliance, but, by insisting that this was the banner under which Japan fought, Kato gave himself the maximum freedom of movement within the Far East while eschewing any wider obligations to Europe—or specifically to France and Russia—which would have followed from cleaving to the Entente.[36] Japan's purpose was to eliminate German influence in China.

Kato wanted to capture Tsingtao. China, and those Britons involved with China, were alarmed. Grey replied that he would rather Japan did not enter the war than that it should do so on such terms. The alliance was committed to the maintenance of China's integrity, not to its partition. Kato now argued, somewhat spuriously, that public opinion in Japan was sufficiently agitated to make it impossible for him to reverse his policy. It was true that the Tokyo crowd played an active role in Japanese politics after 1905, and that by 1918 the violence of its demonstrations on four occasions led to cabinet changes;[37] it was also true that party politics were playing a growing role in the Diet, in the press, and even in cabinet formation (Kato himself derived part of his authority in the ministry from his leadership of the Doshikai party). Entry to the war was calculated to appeal to Japanese nationalism, and to the demands for an aggressive foreign policy manifested by populists. But in fact the

[36] Dua, *Anglo-Japanese relations*, 139–43, 152, 166–7, 175.
[37] Gordon, *Past and Present*, 121 (Nov. 1988), 141–70.

outbreak of the First World War was not marked by crowd demonstrations; anti-Germanism was both tardy and somewhat contrived. However, once again Kato's tactics succeeded. The danger that Kato's appeal to Japanese domestic feeling opened up before Grey was far more awful than that of Japanese entry on the side of the Entente—it was that of Japan's abandonment of the alliance and even of its siding with Germany if that served the interests of its China policy. Britain therefore accepted Japan's involvement in the war. Its statement, that Japanese action would be restricted to the China Seas, to the 'Asiatic waters westward of the China Seas', and to 'territory in German occupation on the continent of eastern Asia', was designed to appease the United States and the Dominions. Japan neither approved it nor honoured it. Kato's policy after 11 August was entirely self-interested. The ultimatum issued to Germany on 15 August was framed without reference to Britain; the alliance had become no more than a legitimizing cloak for the prosecution of Japanese aims, but a cloak under which—by virtue of its own weakness in the Pacific— Britain too was forced to shelter.[38]

In ten days Kato had effectively played off against themselves and against each other Japan's ally, Japanese domestic opinion, and the Japanese bureau- cracy. The only remaining hurdle was Germany.

Without Japan in the war, and with Britain concentrated on Europe, Germany's prospects for a successful defence of Tsingtao—at least in the short to medium term—were reasonable. Japan's entry, on the other hand, promised Tsingtao's fall with a speed and certainty that were ineluctable. The voluntary abandonment of the colony therefore had merits likely to commend themselves to the German general staff. Tsingtao's return to China would permit German reservists in the Far East to make their way back to the fatherland. Its surrender to Japan in exchange for some sort of alliance would have more far-reaching strategic implications, forcing Russia to leave troops in Siberia rather than concentrate them in the west. Germany's diplo- mats in Peking and Tokyo, operating in isolation from Berlin, tried a third tack. They exploited the desire of many of those in the region—particularly China itself—for neutrality. But their intermediary in this process was the United States, and although America favoured neutrality for the Pacific, it was not prepared to make its prestige in the area contingent on such a policy. The German proposal for neutrality was both overambitious and late. It embraced the entire Pacific Ocean, from east of India to Cape Horn, an extension that was likely to be unacceptable to Britain, and that was unrealistic given the simultaneous machinations of the German navy. For, while Germany's diplo- mats looked for peace in the region, Germany's sailors made ready for war. Tsingtao's governor, Meyer-Waldeck, was drawing in men and supplies in

[38] Chi, *China diplomacy*, 16–18.

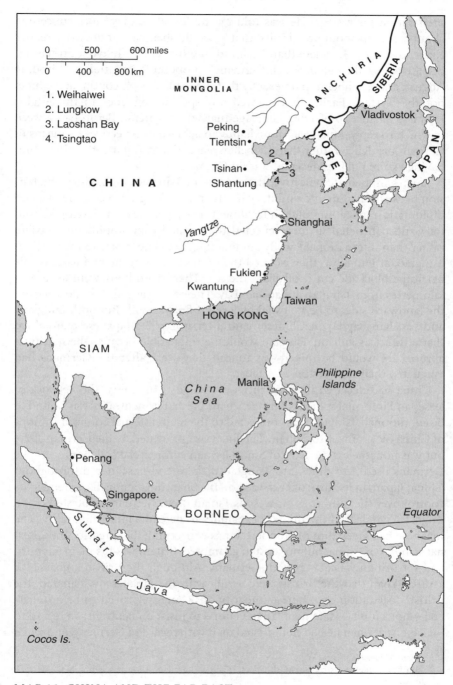

0   500   600 miles

0   400   800 km

INNER
MONGOLIA

1. Weihaiwei
2. Lungkow
3. Laoshan Bay
4. Tsingtao

MANCHURIA

SIBERIA

Vladivostok

Peking

Tientsin

KOREA

JAPAN

C H I N A

Tsinan

2 1

Shantung

3

4

Yangtze

Shanghai

Fukien

Kwantung

Taiwan

HONG KONG

SIAM

China
Sea

Manila

Philippine
Islands

Penang

Singapore

BORNEO

Equator

Sumatra

Java

Cocos Is.

MAP 16. CHINA AND THE FAR EAST

preparation for a siege. He was told by the Kaiser, always more concerned about face than about practicality, that 'it would shame me more to surrender Kiaochow to the Japanese than Berlin to the Russians'.[39] Tokyo's ultimatum, dispatched on the day in which Germany's proposal for neutrality arrived, 15 August, asked Wilhelm to do exactly that. Its focus was on continental China, not the western Pacific; it eschewed any specific reference to the Anglo-Japanese alliance, preferring language that was unilateral. Berlin had a week in which to reply. Japan was quite happy to achieve its objectives by means of German prudence rather than by belligerence. On 23 August, the ultimatum having expired, Japan declared war on Germany.

Japan's immediate objective, the capture of Tsingtao, highlighted the tension between the Entente's military needs and the long-term commercial and diplomatic implications of their fulfilment. The Japanese plan, developed from 1907 and concocted in 1913, reflected their practice in amphibious warfare rather than international law. By landing forces 130 kilometres to the north of Tsingtao, at Lungkow, they isolated their objective from the mainland, while maritime blockade cut it off from the sea. Their main body went ashore 24 kilometres from Tsingtao at Laoshan Bay. Their aim was a slow build-up from the landward side, to be followed by a rapid final assault. But both Lungkow and Laoshan Bay lay in Chinese neutral territory. The Japanese maintained that a direct assault on Tsingtao would be impossible because the maritime approaches would be mined—as indeed they were after the Germans had evacuated their families on 22 August.[40]

China had declared its neutrality on 6 August. In reality, the network of leases and informal spheres of influence meant that its neutrality was bound to be conditional. Tsingtao was connected to the main internal communications of China by a railway to Tsinan. The line was not owned by the German state, but was nonetheless the fruit of Sino-German commercial collaboration. The Germans used it to draw into Tsingtao their reservists scattered throughout China; Japan, in its turn, once landed on the Shantung peninsula, extended its control over the railway as far west as Tsinan itself. Germany protested on 20 August. Yuan lacked the military capability to defend China's neutrality. The Japanese had given him oral undertakings concerning the integrity and internal stability of China, but no written guarantee. Britain was his main support, and yet Britain was at war with Germany. Although the British ambassador assured Yuan that the British were acting with the Japanese at Tsingtao, the British declaration on Chinese integrity of 18 August proved to be a unilateral—not a joint—statement. Yuan's efforts to insist on neutrality in regard to the Japanese when he had not insisted on it with regard to Germany, and when

[39] Nish, *Alliance in decline*, 135.
[40] Burdick, *Tsingtau*, 65, 79–80; Mark Grove, 'The development of Japanese amphibious warfare, 1874 to 1942', 30.

the Japanese could cite the precedent of their attack across Chinese territory on Port Arthur in 1905, were doomed to failure. His only option, short of war with Japan, was to isolate Shantung by declaring it a war zone.[41]

The principal defence of Tsingtao in the event of war was intended to be maritime, the East Asiatic Squadron. Meyer-Waldeck's peacetime garrison amounted to a battalion of naval infantry, a field artillery battery, and some naval guns. In the light of the Boxer rebellion, its task was to deal with an attack by the Chinese. Therefore the main defences were landward and were adapted to a technology inferior to that possessed by the Japanese. By drawing in the units based at Peking and Tientsin, and by incorporating the reservists working in China, Meyer-Waldeck swelled his complement to 184 officers and 4,390 men. He also mustered ninety land-based guns, although most of them were of small calibre and the larger pieces had no more than twenty rounds each.

The slowness of the subsequent assault was as much the product of the weather and of Japanese caution as it was of Meyer-Waldeck's energetic efforts to protract Tsingtao's resistance. Japan's forces totalled 60,000 men; this included, to the detriment of allied relations, a British and an Indian army battalion. Heavy rain for the first two weeks of September washed away roads and railways. Thus, although the first Japanese landed at Lungkow on 2 September, there was no contact with the Germans until 18 September, and the advance on the main German positions did not begin until the 25th. The Japanese superiority in artillery was crushing—100 siege guns with sufficient shells to fire eighty rounds a day for fifteen days, plus the offshore support of the guns of the Japanese fleet. The broken nature of the ground in the German centre, with ravines to break up the defences and so aid the Japanese advance, led the Germans to expect the Japanese to exploit their superiority in a rapid assault. The Japanese preferred instead the gradual methods of siege warfare. Unlike the Germans, they had experienced—in 1904–5—positional warfare under the conditions created by modern firepower. The capture of Prince Heinrich Hill in a desperately fought night attack on 17 October gave the Japanese gunners observation over the whole position. The subsequent use of their artillery was instructive; they forebore from preliminary registration to avoid revealing the guns' positions or their fire plan; when the artillery attack opened, on 31 October, it included the use of counter-battery fire; by night the Japanese continued with shrapnel to prevent the Germans repairing the damage done by high explosives during the day. The Japanese infantry consolidated the ground they gained by pushing forward their trenches under cover of dark. Equally innovatory was the Japanese employment of airpower, not only for the purposes of reconnaissance but also for bombing. By

[41] Chi, *China diplomacy*, 21–4; Jones, *Britain's search for Chinese co-operation*, 18–22; Craft, *International History Review*, XVI (1994), 4–5.

2 November the German artillery was running out of shells. On 7 November Meyer-Waldeck sought an armistice.[42]

In curbing Japanese expansionism in 1914 the gaze of the powers was focused on China. Their aim was to minimize the impact of the Japanese army on the Asiatic mainland. The result was that even powers with interests in the Pacific, and particularly the United States, temporarily neglected the naval dimension to Japan's ambitions. Japan's ultimatum to Germany made specific reference only to Shantung, but in failing to mention Germany's Pacific colonies Kato had not foreclosed on the possibility of action to the south as well as to the north. Britain's hope that the Japanese fleet could be confined to the China Sea was operationally nonsensical if the target was the German East Asiatic Squadron: its commander, Graf von Spee, would not feel obliged so to confine his movements, particularly when the German islands of Micronesia provided him with a supporting network across the length of the western Pacific. In fact Spee had already left the Marshall Islands by 14 September, when Japan's 1st South Seas Squadron sailed, and when it first occupied Jaluit on 30 September the counsel of those anxious to appease Britain (and particularly Kato) prevailed, and the island was abandoned.

But the naval general staff and the naval affairs division of the naval ministry were convinced of the strategic importance of Micronesia as an advanced base in any future war with the United States. Nationalist groups provided support, stressing the islands' economic value. Phosphates could give the navy commercial leverage, while the possession of colonies in the southern seas would justify the expansion of the fleet. Between them the naval staff and the naval affairs division set about the subversion of the instructions of Yashiro, the naval minister, and of Kato. When the 2nd South Seas Squadron put to sea, nominally in response to Britain's request for escorts for Australian and New Zealand troop ships, its commander was told by the naval affairs division not to pay too much attention to the instructions of the naval minister. By 3 October Yashiro had been won over to his subordinates' view, and by 14 October Japan's occupation of Micronesia was accomplished.[43]

Japan's actions were furtive, but the British could hardly protest. Both Australia and New Zealand harboured their own imperialist ambitions. The former deeply resented France's presence in New Caledonia and the New Hebrides, and the latter was readied by the commander of its defence forces, Alexander Godley, for the seizure of the German possessions in Samoa and New Guinea. The Committee of Imperial Defence subcommittee of 5 August, when requesting the assistance of both Dominions in seizing the wireless stations of Yap and Nauru, mentioned New Guinea only in passing and the

[42] Burdick, *Tsingtau*, chs. 4, 5, 6.
[43] Schenking, *War in History*, V (1998), 321–3; Peattie, *Nanyo*, 40–4.

other territories not at all; it stressed, moreover, that any territory occupied as a consequence would remain at London's disposal. But by the time the Colonial Office, responding to the Committee of Imperial Defence, invited the two governments to assist in the conquest of the German possessions in the south Pacific, they had already agreed a division of the spoils: those to the east of the line of longitude 170° were to fall to New Zealand, those to the west to Australia. Preparations for the plan's implementation began immediately. Screened by the Australian squadron, a force of 1,383 New Zealanders proceeded by way of Noumea and Suva to Samoa, which it occupied without fighting on 30 August. Australia's ships were now free to escort their own troops to New Guinea. Landings at Rabaul on 11 September encountered some opposition. The Germans' aim was to defend their wireless station, inland at Bitapaka and intended as an intelligence-gathering centre for their cruisers. Although the Australians did not know its precise location, a combination of bluff and good luck was rewarded with success on the 12th. The Germans were commanded by a reserve captain of artillery without guns and a police inspector qualified as a riding master but without horses. On 15 September their governor surrendered the entire area of German New Guinea and the Solomon Islands.[44] Isolated resistance continued on Papua, orchestrated by the leader of a German surveying expedition, Detzner. Having established good relations with the local tribes, and supported by German missionaries, Detzner remained active until the end of the war.[45]

Despite the ease of their conquests, and despite the promptings of the Colonial Office in London, the two Dominions were slow to extend their movements further north. The navy was reluctant to proceed with territorial occupation until the seas were safe from German cruisers; the land forces of Australia and New Zealand were more concerned with readying themselves for Europe. By late November, when Australia began to consider pushing across the equator into the northern Pacific, Japan had already reached south, having taken the Marshall and Caroline Islands in early October. Thus, the equator became the de facto division between the two occupying powers.

[44] Jose, *Royal Australian Navy,* 47–99, and Mackenzie, *Australians at Rabaul,* give an account of the operations while glossing over their sub-imperialist thrust; see also Klein-Arendt, *Kamina ruft Nauen,* 257–60.
[45] Hiery, *Neglected war,* 12–14, 18–25.

THE CRUISE OF THE GERMAN EAST ASIATIC SQUADRON

Neither the siege of Tsingtao nor the occupation of the German South Pacific islands was disrupted by the activities of German cruisers. Graf von Spee, commanding the East Asiatic Squadron, had deliberately kept his ships out of Tsingtao in order to be able to retain the power of manoeuvre. He had argued before the war that, by harassing commerce, he would force his opponents to lift their blockade of the port in order to deal with him and thus would keep the entrance to Tsingtao open. It was on this basis that Meyer-Waldeck had reckoned on a lengthy defence. All von Spee's early movements conformed to this intention. When the news of European developments reached him on 17 July, he and the major units of his squadron, *Scharnhorst* and *Gneisenau*, were at Ponape in the Caroline Islands. Of the three light cruisers, *Nürnberg* was en route from her station off California, *Leipzig* was proceeding to take over from *Nürnberg*, and only *Emden* was at Tsingtao. Spee ordered *Emden* to leave Tsingtao together with the squadron's supply ships, and for all his command, less *Leipzig*, to rendezvous at Pagan Island in the Marianas. Spee had chosen Pagan before the war; it lay away from the main shipping routes and yet enjoyed a sufficiently central position in the western Pacific to enable him to draw supplies from northern Japan, Tsingtao, Shanghai, and Manila. It also left his subsequent options open.

The decision which confronted Spee on 12 August, the day on which the assembly of his squadron at Pagan Island was effected, was not easy. The basic propositions of *guerre de course* argued that cruisers should be kept at sea as long as possible (an objective Spee had ensured, albeit by forsaking Tsingtao), that they should operate individually in order to force a superior enemy to disperse, and that their targets should consequently be merchant vessels and shore installations. What they should not do was seek out enemy warships. However tempting battle might be, its effect would be to allow the enemy to concentrate, enabling him to bring strength against weakness; the consequent danger would lessen, or possibly even eliminate, the sea-keeping capacities of the cruisers. Spee's quandary arose because in the immediate area of the China Sea his squadron was not an inferior force. With Jerram's sole battleship, *Triumph*, out of commission in Hong Kong, and with the Japanese entry to the war not yet confirmed, the only ship capable of challenging the 8.2-inch guns of *Scharnhorst* and *Gneisenau* was the battle cruiser *Australia* with 12-inch guns, but it was far to the south. Both Spee and the Admiralty Staff had therefore recognized before the war that in the Pacific the Germans might have the opportunities for tactical success and for establishing at least temporary domination of the ocean. Ultimately such a strategy would serve to paralyse commerce as effectively as would a pure *guerre de course*. It might even draw British cruisers away from German trade. Spee, as befitted a professional seaman anxious for action, was temperamentally drawn to this second option. It meant that his forces should be kept concentrated.[46]

Individual ships were easier to resupply and refuel. Spee had acknowledged at the beginning of July that the case against concentration was the problem of coal. At Pagan Island he had collected eight colliers and storeships. For the moment *Scharnhorst* and *Gneisenau* were stocked with good quality Shantung coal, but once those supplies were exhausted they would have to rely on brown coal, if they could get it. Spee's ships carried enough coal for eighteen days' continuous cruising at an economical speed; if forced to increase speed they would exhaust their stocks much faster. Prudence therefore suggested coaling every eight or nine days so that the bunkers were always at least half full. Ships were particularly vulnerable while coaling at sea, unable to manoeuvre or to have full use of their guns. British ships, by contrast, had access to a network of secure bases, and to Welsh anthracite and bituminous black coal from New South Wales, both of which burnt more slowly and with greater heat, so giving increased cruising ranges.

The opportunity for Spee to reconsider his decision to remain concentrated came on 12 August, with a report from Tsingtao that Japan was likely to enter the war. Spee no longer enjoyed the margin of superiority sufficient to justify keeping his squadron assembled, and yet he could not bring himself to accept a reconsideration of his original intentions. Japan was about to make the north-east Pacific too dangerous; British forces, it seemed, were moving south and west to Hong Kong; yet further south lay the *Australia*. Spee discounted breaking through to the Indian Ocean, despite the lucrative pickings on offer there, because of the lack of neutral coal and because Britain's strength would be reinforced by the Royal Navy's East Indies Squadron. The only remaining option was to go south-east, towards South America. He had already canvassed this idea on 5–6 August; in other words, it was less the product of Japan's imminent belligerence and more the result of the supply needs consequent on keeping his squadron united. Chile, though neutral, was reported to be well disposed and could provide coal. The proximity of the United States might deter the Japanese from chasing him across the Pacific, and radio intercepts suggested that the British were focusing on the capture of Tsingtao; only a light

---

[46] On Spee's strategy, see esp. Castex, *Théories stratégiques*, ii. 139–92; Marine-Archiv, *Kreuzergesch-wader*, i. 30–4; Corbett, *Naval operations*, vol. I, is an important corrective to Castex's eulogy of Spee. Overlack, *Journal of Military History*, LX (1996), 657–68, reviews Spee's decisions. Good recent accounts are Yates, *Graf Spee's raiders*, and Bennett, *Coronel and Falklands*; Hough, *Pursuit of Admiral von Spee*, adds little; Pochhammer, *Before Jutland*, is the testimony of the senior surviving German officer of Spee's squadron; Halpern, *Naval history*, adds important detail.

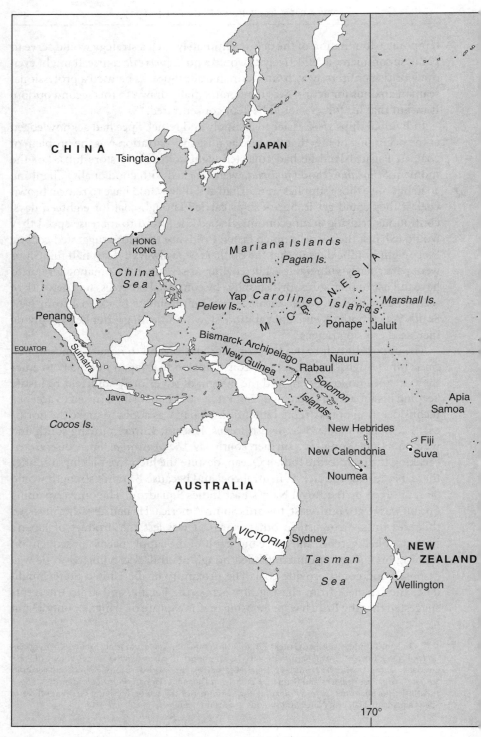

MAP 17. THE CRUISE OF VON SPEE'S EAST ASIATIC SQUADRON

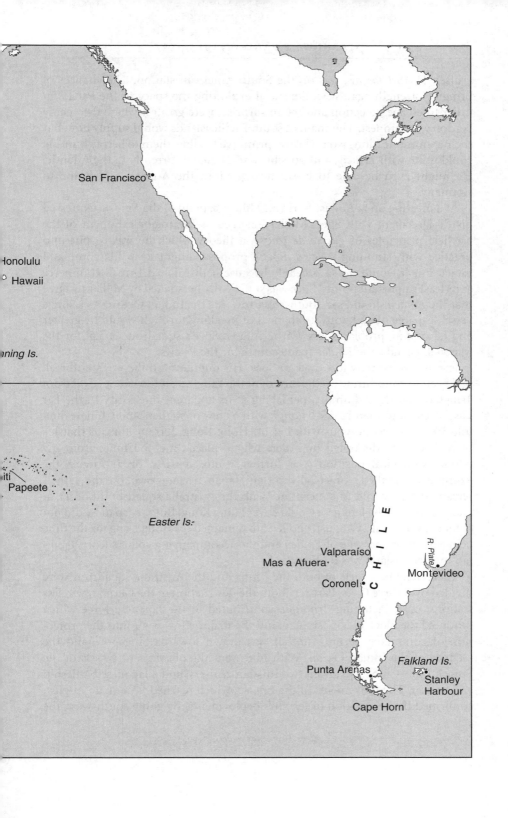

San Francisco

Honolulu
Hawaii

...ning Is.

...iti
Papeete

Easter Is.

C H I L E

Valparaíso
Mas a Afuera
Coronel

R. Plate
Montevideo

Falkland Is.
Punta Arenas
Stanley
Harbour

Cape Horn

cruiser, HMS *Glasgow*, was on the South American station. The chances of bringing strength against weakness, of exploiting the space of the Pacific in order to escape detection and retain surprise, were greatest where the enemy cordon was thinnest. The chain of south Pacific islands would supply him, but their communications would be too primitive to allow them to betray him. He could unite with *Leipzig*, and possibly also *Dresden*, currently in the Atlantic. He might even be able to break through into the Atlantic and home to Germany.

At a meeting on 13 August Karl von Müller, captain of the *Emden*, expressed his disagreement with Spee. Müller emerged as the major exponent of the classical principles of *guerre de course*, a theory which he was to put into practice with stunning success. Spee's proposal might keep his command intact, but it would do so precisely because it threatened British commerce at its least important points. Spee was sufficiently persuaded by Müller to agree that the *Emden* should sail south-west, towards the Indian Ocean. As a single vessel, capable of 24 knots, its chances of breaking through would be greater and its coaling problems less. On 14 August Spee's squadron set sail for the Marshall Islands; the *Emden* made course for the Pelews.

Jerram had entirely lost track of Spee. His intention on the war's outbreak had been to concentrate off the mouth of the Yangtze, and so cut Spee off from Tsingtao. But the Admiralty, panicking at its apparent inferiority in the Far East, decided to man HMS *Triumph* with a crew of soldiers and Chinese, and told Jerram to rendezvous with her off Hong Kong. Jerram, furious that his plans had been disrupted by orders which 'placed me 900 miles from my correct strategical position', was further confused when on 11 August the Admiralty signalled, 'practically certain Japan declares war on the 12th'.[47] Jerram was now told to concentrate with the Australia squadron in order to take on Spee, as the Japanese would cover Hong Kong. But the Japanese did not enter the war until 23 August, and Jerram remained off Hong Kong for the time being. Thus the passage of *Emden* and the accompanying colliers from Tsingtao to Pagan Island was undisturbed.

Thereafter the efforts of both the China and the Australia squadrons were divided over three tasks. Part set about the destruction of the German wireless stations; part, including *Triumph*, contributed to the Japanese force which mounted the blockade of Tsingtao; but the major effort went into the protection of commerce. Jerram himself was drawn towards Singapore and the security of the Indian Ocean. With him went the obsolescent vessels of the French Indo-China squadron, two Russian cruisers, and a Japanese battleship and cruiser. The movements of the *Emden*, which reached Java on 29 August, confirmed the orientation of Jerram's deployments. By going south-west, the

---

[47] Yates, *Graf Spee's raiders*, 33, 40.

China squadron could not team up with the Australia squadron, and in particular with the big guns of *Australia* herself. The Australia squadron's commander, Rear-Admiral Sir George Patey, was clear that his first mission should be to seek out and destroy *Scharnhorst* and *Gneisenau*, but wireless intercepts at the outbreak of the war had placed Spee in the Bismarck Archipelago, and the fear of the Germans' proximity persisted.[48] Even after the capture of New Guinea, the most powerful ship at Britain's disposal in the Pacific remained tied by the imperatives of local defence and the need to convoy Australian troops. The Japanese navy, its entry delayed by Japan's leisurely ultimatum, took on responsibility for the northern Pacific trade routes, along the Chinese coast and towards Hawaii. In mid-September it established a squadron in the Marianas, Carolines, and Marshalls, but it did not push across the equator. Thus the Admiralty's preoccupation with the importance of commerce produced a defensive response geared to the protection of the main lines of communication rather than to taking the offensive to the German cruisers. It was hardly consonant with Fisher's pre-war thought on the matter. Moreover, it gave Spee several opportunities in August to defeat the Entente's forces in detail—albeit opportunities which, largely through lack of intelligence, he did not take.

The destruction of German wireless stations was two-edged in its effect. It served to isolate Spee: all his decisions were taken on the basis of inadequate information. But he was simultaneously spared the sort of intervention from afar which dogged Jerram. Moreover, he was muffled. Spee's own insistence on wireless silence was reinforced by the fact that increasingly he had nobody to speak to. Consequently the British were as deprived of up-to-date and accurate information as the Germans.

On 9 August Spee's squadron was placed in the Solomon Islands when it was still at Pagan; the following day three of his light cruisers were reported at Tsingtao. The bulk of the subsequent intelligence suggested that Spee was operating in the south-western Pacific, around New Guinea. The preconceptions and fears of the Admiralty were therefore confirmed. After 8 September Spee's own information was somewhat better. He had detached *Nürnberg* to go to Honolulu, with the task of relaying to Germany via the neutral networks of the United States news of his movements; signals were sent to *Leipzig* and *Dresden* to join him at Easter Island, and to the German *Etappen* in South America to buy in coal. *Nürnberg* returned with a supply of American newspapers. From these Spee learnt of the fall of Samoa, and of the probability that some allied vessels, and possibly even *Australia*, could be caught at anchor there. His offensive instinct overcame the discretion appropriate to a cruiser commander. *Scharnhorst* and *Gneisenau* appeared off Apia on the morning of

---

[48] Jose, *Royal Australian Navy*, 5, 10–11, 18–19.

14 September. Spee was disappointed: no major targets presented themselves. He then made course for the north-west, only doubling back towards Tahiti when it became dark. Thus, the British, although at last they had a definite sighting of Spee, continued to assume that he was operating in the western Pacific.

Spee's luck finally deserted him on 22 September. Knowing that Tahiti possessed no wireless, and concerned that his lengthy and actionless cruise would undermine the morale of his crews, he bombarded Papeete. However, a French steamer was able to report the German attack, and this sighting—together with the Apia report—confirmed Patey in the belief which he had held since mid-August, that the German East Asiatic Squadron was on course for South America.[49] The Admiralty remained fearful that Spee might double back, that he would attack Samoa, Fiji, or even New Zealand, and that he would threaten the Anzac convoys. But in the western Atlantic *Dresden* was stopping British merchantmen and then releasing them when they were shown not to be carrying contraband: in so doing she revealed her southward course. And on 4 October two wireless intercepts indicated that *Scharnhorst* was en route for Easter Island and that *Leipzig* was waiting to meet her off the South American coast.

The officer commanding the Royal Navy's Western Atlantic Squadron off South America, Admiral Sir Christopher Cradock, had guessed Spee's likely course in early September. The first weeks of Cradock's war had been frustrating. A man of considerable courage but little reflective capacity, he was of the view that 'a naval officer should never let his boat go faster than his brain'.[50] He had been pursuing *Karlsruhe* and *Dresden* without success. The prospects of his being able to continue this hunt and simultaneously to track the much more powerful combination of the East Asiatic Squadron should it round the Horn seemed remote. The Admiralty, however, had little choice. Its defensive interpretation of its oceanic task meant that Jerram, Patey, and the Japanese should all stay in the western Pacific. Cradock was to divide his command, leaving part to deal with the German light cruisers in the Caribbean, and taking four ships through the Magellan Strait to meet Spee. Of the four, only HMS *Glasgow*, a fast modern light cruiser, inspired confidence. Cradock flew his flag in an old armoured cruiser, *Good Hope*, largely crewed by reservists and boys; *Monmouth*, a cruiser also with an inexperienced crew, had only 6-inch guns, and *Otranto* was a converted passenger liner possessed of light armament and a maximum speed of 16 knots in a head sea. Cradock was not happy. On 14 September the Admiralty responded with the promise of HMS *Defence*, a new armoured cruiser and the equal of Spee's major units, and of *Canopus*, an

[49] Ibid. 22, 122–8.
[50] Gordon, *Rules of the game*, 391.

ageing pre-Dreadnought but at least equipped with 12-inch guns.[51] Then came news of the *Emden*, now off Calcutta, and of Spee's attack on Apia and his subsequent course for the north-west. London concluded that Cradock had been wrong: Spee was not bound for South America. On 16 September the Admiralty revised its instructions. Cradock was to harass German trade off the west coast of South America, and to do this he need not keep his squadron concentrated. It also decided that *Defence* should be retained in the western Atlantic, north of Montevideo, to deal with *Karlsruhe* and *Dresden*; however, it omitted to tell Cradock this.

Cradock's own views about Spee's intentions had not changed. The wireless intercepts of 4 October, relayed by the Admiralty to Cradock on the 7th, confirmed he was right. In signals on 8 and 11 October Cradock reported that he would concentrate on the Falklands and that he would patrol round Cape Horn up as far as Valparaiso. Perhaps the Admiralty assumed that Cradock did not intend to bring the Germans to action—or at least not in the Pacific. If Cradock shadowed them into the Atlantic, his forces and those now concentrating under Rear-Admiral Archibald Stoddart north of Montevideo could unite to overwhelm Spee. But the Admiralty did not clarify this point with Cradock, and its own orders were ambiguous—Cradock was to harass German trade and to seek out the enemy. On one reading Cradock was to regard his force as the equal of Spee's. The arrival of *Canopus* at the Falklands, a week late, only served to heighten the uncertainty of what was intended. If Cradock was to find Spee he would need all the speed he could get. The senior engineer on *Canopus* reported that her maximum speed was 12 knots and that she needed four days' overhaul. Therefore, if Cradock acted in formation with *Canopus* Spee would escape; but if he acted without *Canopus* he lacked the firepower to deal with *Scharnhorst* or *Gneisenau*. Cradock consoled himself with the mistaken thought that *Defence* was imminent. On 22 October he sailed from the Falklands without *Canopus*. Only after he had done so was it revealed that her engineer was suffering from psychological problems, and that her engines were capable of over 16 knots. With hindsight, Cradock should have used *Glasgow* to find Spee and then drawn him onto *Canopus*'s guns, but as *Glasgow*'s captain, John Luce, said, 'I had the feeling that Cradock had no clear plan or doctrine in his head but was always inclined to act on the impulse of the moment'.[52]

As he rounded the Horn Cradock's thirst for action was spiced by the increasingly strong wireless signals from *Leipzig*. Cradock assumed that he was about to catch the German light cruiser on its own. In fact Spee had

---

[51] In addition to the works cited above, see also Jack Sweetman, 'Coronel: anatomy of a disaster', in Jordan (ed.), *Naval warfare*.
[52] Hough, *Pursuit*, 87.

rendezvoused with *Leipzig* and *Dresden* at Easter Island by 14 October, and had then restricted the use of wireless to one vessel in order to obscure the presence of the others. Cradock's ability to fall for this ruse was extraordinary, in view not only of his own earlier prescience as to Spee's movements but also of the fact that he used *Glasgow* in exactly the same way. Spee too, as offensive-minded and potentially rash as his opponent, was led on in the belief that a single enemy vessel was in the offing.

On 1 November the Germans moved south to cut off *Glasgow*, emerging from Coronel Bay. At about 4.30 p.m. they found her, but not for another hour were they to appreciate the proximity of the remainder of Cradock's force. Cradock could have escaped. He knew from *Glasgow*'s reporting that he was now approaching Spee's entire squadron, but his decision was to concentrate on the *Glasgow*, the ship nearest to the enemy. He did not fall back on *Canopus*, although he did summon her assistance, or on *Defence*, as he still imagined her to be approaching. If he thought beyond his own impulse for battle, his justification was twofold; first, he had finally tracked Spee down, and he could not afford to lose him again in the expanses of the Pacific or the Atlantic, and secondly, he had a faint prospect of success. While the western sun was above the horizon it shone in the eyes of the German gun crews and gave the British a temporary advantage. Once the sun had set, the light, as long as it lasted, would be to Spee's benefit, silhouetting the British ships against a reddening sky. Spee's moment would be brief, and the sea was rough and would upset his aim.

But Cradock lacked the pace to close while the light was right. *Otranto* kept the maximum speed of the British ships to 15 knots; Spee worked his cruisers up from 14 to 20 knots, and so maintained his distance. Then, at 7 p.m., when the light had turned to his favour, he closed. The Germans' broadside weighed 4,442 pounds to the British 2,875;[53] their gunnery was faster and more accurate. The heavy seas meant that up to half the British guns, which were mounted low, could not be used without water flooding the casemates. The appalling weather round the Horn and up the Chilean coast, which had made *Glasgow* 'practically a submarine',[54] had covered the range finders with salt spray. Cradock's flagship was hit before she had been able to open fire. The range came down from 13,000 yards to 5,100. By 7.30, when the German armoured cruisers ceased firing, *Good Hope* was ablaze and sinking; *Monmouth*, badly damaged, went down two hours later. Only *Glasgow* and *Otranto* escaped.

The news of Coronel did not reach the Admiralty until 4 November. Churchill was quick to blame Cradock; only later would the admiral's quixotic courage be compared with that of Sir Richard Grenville and the *Revenge*.

---

[53] Marder, *From the Dreadnought*, ii. 109–10.   [54] Yates, *Graf Spee's raiders*, 139–40.

Fisher, on the other hand, newly restored to the Admiralty, sought responsibility closer at home. The dispositions of the Royal Navy's oceanic resources had been diffuse and defensive. As the governor-general of Australia complained, 'The maxim of seeking out the enemy's ships and destroying them has been ignored'.[55] Cradock's demise was the product of a lack of concentration that was not entirely his own fault. *Defence* had been kept north of Montevideo until too late; neither Patey nor the Japanese had extended eastwards to converge on Spee from the west. The Australians blamed these strategic faults on 'the remoteness of Admiralty control'. The fact that they might also be the consequence of the lack of a proper war staff—a point reinforced by the confusion and ambiguity in the Admiralty's instructions—was of course not an interpretation to which Fisher's mind was open. His criticism was more personal, and directed at the chief of the war staff which did exist, Sir F. C. D. Sturdee. Crucial to the First Sea Lord was the fact that, in his eyes, Sturdee was a Beresfordian. Coronel seemed the ideal excuse for his removal. Churchill demurred. The Admiralty could ill-afford yet more upheavals and bad publicity. The First Lord's solution, to promote Sturdee and give him the task of making good Cradock's defeat, had an irony that appealed to Fisher.

To accomplish the task Sturdee was given two battle cruisers, *Inflexible* and *Invincible*, and a third, *Princess Royal*, was allocated to Stoddart. Sturdee and Battenberg had wanted to send battle cruisers from the outset, but they had given in to Jellicoe's objections. Now Jellicoe's protests at a further weakening of the North Sea balance were ignored, and on 11 November Sturdee sailed from Devonport. The Japanese were encouraged to cross the Pacific towards the equator and Fiji, while Patey's Australian squadron pushed eastwards to Fanning Island. A total of almost thirty British ships, excluding those of Japan or France, were bearing down on the East Asiatic Squadron.

The detachment of the battle cruisers was soon known in Germany, and the news signalled to South America. But it never reached Spee. The German admiral called at Valparaiso on 3 November, and then sailed south, his bunkers full. He was now, as far as the German wireless network was concerned, in the dead corner of the world. Even in peace the relay stations had not conveyed the signals of the Nauen transmitter beyond the Andes to the south-west coast of South America; in November 1914 storms and radio silence confirmed Spee's ignorance.

But inadequate intelligence is insufficient explanation for Spee's subsequent moves. At Valparaiso, for the first time, he had received specific advice from Berlin—to break for home. He also learned that his route was compromised, and that he would struggle to get sufficient coal for his five ships. Already fatalist, Spee now became indecisive. Ten days were lost, allowing the British

---

[55] Jose, *Royal Australian Navy*, 55.

time to react, before on 15 November he left Mas a Fuera for Cape Horn. *Prinz Eitel Friedrich* remained behind, sending wireless transmissions to persuade the Royal Navy that the entire squadron remained off the Chilean coast. The sensible course to pursue, and the one favoured by all but one of his ships' captains, was to pass Cape Horn and continue east, giving the Falkland Islands a wide berth, before heading northwards. If he wished to resume a *guerre de course* he could do so off the River Plate; little trade would be disrupted by his staying in the further reaches of the south Atlantic. Whether he harassed merchant shipping or not, he needed to be wary of his ammunition stocks, for after Papeete and Coronel only 878 8.2-inch shells remained, and he would need all of those to force his way into the North Sea.

Spee's decision to raid the Falkland Islands was therefore the antithesis of good tactics, irrespective of the presence of the battle cruisers. Possibly he was the victim of a British deception, a report circulated in Valparaiso that the Falklands was empty of warships.[56] If so, it hardly constitutes a great coup for counter-intelligence, as the story was essentially true, and remained so on 6 December when a German agent at Punta Arenas again told Spee that there were no warships in the Falklands. Both pieces of information did no more than confirm Spee in his own inclinations, which were to destroy the British communications centre for the south-west Atlantic. Once again his proclivity for action, as at Apia and at Tahiti, would reveal his presence, consume his shells, but achieve little in real terms.

On 8 December 1914 the East Asiatic Squadron approached the Falkland Islands. Spee had not even pushed his light cruisers forward to reconnoitre; with sufficient warning from them his squadron could have made good its escape. Oblivious of the battle cruisers' presence, he no doubt reckoned that all of his units had the legs of any British warships in the vicinity. As the *Gneisenau* neared Cape Pembroke its senior gunnery officer spotted many more masts beyond Sapper Hill than he had anticipated; eventually he made out the three-legged tripod masts characteristic of Dreadnoughts. His fear that there might be battle cruisers in Port Stanley was pooh-poohed by the *Gneisenau*'s captain: the latter reported to Spee the presence of several cruisers and possibly two battleships. By 10.30 a.m. Spee's squadron was bearing away from the Falklands on a south-easterly course. Its speed, Spee reckoned, would enable it to escape the guns of the battleships.

Indeed, the Germans did have major initial advantages in the subsequent chase. From the outset Sturdee's approach had been surprisingly lackadaisical. An intercepted telegram from the German consulate at Valparaiso, relayed via

---

[56] Beesly, *Room 40*, 76–7, suggests that Spee might have been led on by a deliberately placed false report that the Falklands were abandoned. Occleshaw, *Armour against fate*, 115–16, is much less cautious in accepting this story.

San Francisco to Berlin, had requested that supplies be prepared for the East Asiatic Squadron at Buenos Aires.[57] But Sturdee acted as through oblivious of this intelligence. Only Luce's sense of urgency had persuaded the squadron commander so far south so soon. A surprise attack by Spee a little earlier in the morning might have had a devastating effect. At 7.30 a.m., when the Germans were first spotted, the British ships were coaling. The dust hampered subsequent communications, the work needed completion, and steam had to be raised. Luce's ship *Glasgow*, having finished its coaling, was one of the first away, shortly before 10 a.m.; the last did not clear harbour until nearly 11.00. However, Sturdee was relaxed and calm. The weather, after almost continuous rain and cloud, was clear; he still had most of the day in which to catch Spee, and he had the speed and the guns with which to do it. Two battle cruisers, four armoured cruisers, two light cruisers, and one armed merchant cruiser constituted a crushing superiority. Aboard the *Gneisenau*, as the truth dawned, 'We choked a little at the neck, the throat contracted and stiffened, for that meant a life and death grapple, or rather a fight ending in honourable death'.[58]

The initial speeds of *Inflexible* and *Invincible* were 26 knots. The German armoured cruisers, their bottoms fouled by their long journey, made 18 knots, although *Gneisenau* at one stage reached 21.[59] Sturdee slowed down to allow his force to regroup, but then at 12.20 ordered the battle cruisers and *Glasgow* back up to 26 knots. At 16,500 yards *Inflexible* opened fire. Its guns were calibrated for ranges of 12,000 yards, and its shooting was slow and falling short. The wind direction meant that the ships' own smoke obscured their observation; furthermore, the British, being dead astern of the Germans, could only bring half their guns to bear.

Spee looked anxiously to the south, willing a break in the weather. But none came. At 1.25 he split his force, dispatching the light cruisers to the south, hoping that their speed would enable them to stay clear until cloud or night protected them. *Scharnhorst* and *Gneisenau* he brought round to the east, to engage *Invincible* and *Inflexible*. The two sides could now open with their broadsides, 3,500 pounds to 10,000 pounds. The Germans' fire was concentrated on *Invincible*, which suffered twenty-two hits, leaving *Inflexible* undisturbed. At lower elevations the British shells had greater penetration. Spee needed either to close, in order to be able to employ his secondary armament, or to break away. Twice the British need to turn to clear their own smoke gave him a respite. But the intervals were only temporary, and, with the range never falling below 12,000 yards, his 5.9-inch secondary guns had little effect. Sturdee

[57] Santorini, *Revue internationale d'histoire militaire*, 63 (1985), 103.
[58] Pochhammer, *Before Jutland*, 202–3.
[59] Ibid. 205; Pochhammer noted how relatively clean *Gneisenau*'s hull was as she went down: p. 217.

was mindful of the fact that his battle cruisers, with this action over, would be recalled post-haste by Jellicoe. Ideally, he had a margin of 2,500 yards within which to work, 14,000 being the maximum for the Germans' 8.2-inch main armament and 16,500 for his. By keeping the fight at about this range he avoided damage to his Dreadnoughts and to their crews (only one seaman was killed). At 4.17 p.m. *Scharnhorst* was sunk; at 6.02 *Gneisenau*, now out of ammunition, followed. One of Spee's sons, Heinrich, went down with her.

The other, Otto, was on the *Nürnberg*, to which HMS *Kent* gave frantic pursuit. By feeding her boilers with all available fuel, including the chaplain's lectern, *Kent* raised her speed to 25 knots, 5,000 horse-power above her designated maximum, and by 5 p.m. had closed to within 12,000 yards of *Nürnberg*. The latter turned to port to bring her broadside to bear, and by 5.30 p.m. the action was being fought at 3,000 yards. At 6.30 p.m. two of *Nürnberg*'s overstrained boilers blew up. *Leipzig* was also overhauled, by *Glasgow* and *Cornwall*. The lyddite shells of the latter 'would burst in the middle of a group and strip them of their arms and legs—men would rush about with exposed bones, crazy from the effects of the shell'.[60] Those who ended up in the sea soon died from exposure, their bodies attacked—even while still living—by skuas and albatrosses. Of Spee's light cruisers, only *Dresden* escaped.

The battle of the Falkland Islands was the most decisive naval engagement, whether interpreted tactically or strategically, of the war. Its conduct vindicated Fisher's advocacy of the battle cruiser: the combination of speed and long-range gunnery had proved lethal. Fisher's new designs, to become *Renown* and *Repulse*, capable of 32 knots, equipped with 15-inch guns but with less armour, were approved the same month. By March 1915 Fisher was projecting schemes for battle cruisers with speeds of 35 knots and with 20-inch guns.

In reality the Falkland action was less a pointer to the future of naval warfare than an exception. Because it was fought on the oceans and not the narrow seas, its conduct was free of the intervention of the new technology—of mines, submarines, and aeroplanes, all still at an intermediate stage of development. Surface ships would never enjoy such a freedom again. Furthermore, the fact that it had occurred at all was the product of bad judgement on Spee's part. It proved, as Tsushima had done, how conclusive—in the right weather conditions—a marginal technical superiority could be. The consequence was that a prudent and well-informed commander would shun combat, not seek it as Spee had done.

Furthermore, victory had overshadowed the two major tactical deficiencies of the battle cruisers. Their lack of armour had not become an issue. The Germans had never closed to 10,000 yards in order to be able to use

---

[60] Yates, *Graf Spee's raiders*, 214.

their 5.9-inch shells; some of the 8.2-inch shells had not burst, and those that had had little incendiary effect. More palpable were the deficiencies in British gunnery. It had taken five hours' shooting and 1,174 12-inch shells—or one hit per gun every seventy-five minutes—to sink two German armoured cruisers. The lack of director firing on the two battle cruisers engaged was only a partial explanation. The long ranges had exceeded those of battle practice. More importantly they, the changes of course, and the rate of change had exceeded the capacities of the mechanical aids available to the gunnery officers. Most of the range-finding in the battle was done by spotting the fall of shot. Even when the British shooting did find its target, the long ranges may well have caused the fuses of the armour-piercing shells to fail because of the oblique angle at which they struck the German armour.[61]

Strategically, the annihilation of the East Asiatic Squadron marked the end of the cruiser war. Lack of coal forced *Kronprinz Wilhelm* and *Prinz Eitel Friedrich* into internment in the spring of 1915. *Glasgow* ran down the cautious *Dresden* thanks to a signals intercept on 14 March 1915. *Karlsruhe*, which indirectly had so much influence on the outcome of Coronel, captured eighteen ships by 24 October 1914, sinking sixteen of them and keeping two as supply ships. By putting two auxiliary ships abreast of her, she could extend her search to a range of 80 miles, while at the same time ensuring greater warning of approaching danger. She continued to exercise the minds of the Admiralty for some weeks after she had ceased to exist. On 4 November she was blown in half off Barbados by an internal explosion, probably caused by unstable ammunition. *Königsberg* sank a merchantman in August 1914 and a British destroyer in September, but was blockaded in the Rufiji delta in East Africa from November.

However, it was the exploits of the *Emden* that captured the imagination of the public, almost as much in Britain as in Germany. Müller began his operations in the Bay of Bengal on 10 September; on the evening of 22 September he bombarded Madras; and on 4 October his tender coaled at Diego Garcia, the British inhabitants not having heard of the declaration of war. On 28 October he torpedoed a Russian cruiser and a French destroyer in a raid on Penang. The Russians had no lookouts posted and only twelve rounds on deck ready for the guns; but there were sixty Chinese prostitutes below. The ship's captain, who was engaged in similar dalliance ashore, was stripped of his commission and his title, and spent three-and-a-half years in prison. Four times the *Emden* escaped the attentions of HMS *Hampshire*, albeit by the narrowest of margins. But on 9 November she was sunk, after raiding the wireless station on the Cocos Islands, by *Sydney*, an Australian light cruiser

---

[61] Sumida, *In defence*, 297–9; id. (ed.), *Pollen papers*, 334–5; Roskill, *Beatty*, 100–1; appendix by H. E. Dannreuther in Hough, *Pursuit*, 171–5.

detached from convoy escort. *Emden* used a dummy funnel with which to disguise herself, but in this case the funnel was so poorly rigged that a message expressing suspicion was dispatched before the Germans could jam the wireless. *Sydney*'s gunnery was poor at first but, using her speed to keep her distance from *Emden*, she eventually hit the German vessel about a hundred times: in the word of one of *Sydney*'s officers, 'everybody on board was demented—that's all you could call it, just fairly demented—by shock, fumes and the roar of shells bursting among them'.[62] In seventy days *Emden* had captured twenty-three vessels, and had disrupted trade over a wide area. On five out of the ten occasions when she had had to coal she had been able to do so from her own prizes.

Both Müller and Spee had earned the respect and admiration of their foes; but Müller was a prisoner of war by 11 November 1914, and Spee was dead a month later. Ultimately, neither of the differing interpretations of cruiser warfare that each had embodied was vindicated. By January 1915 the Germans had sunk seventy-five merchant vessels or a total of 273,000 tons; of this the largest proportion, 215,000 tons, was accounted for by surface vessels. But these losses represented a mere 2 per cent of British commercial tonnage.[63] It would require a great many Müllers (and no other German cruiser captain displayed his flair for the conduct of *guerre de course*) and a great many *Emden*s before such action would be more than disruptive. Spee, on the other hand, did not sink a single merchant ship. But his effect had been felt in a different and— to Mahanites—more direct way. British warships had been thrown onto the defensive and their effects dissipated. It is tempting to argue that if the East Asiatic Squadron had been broken up and had fought independently, as *Emden* did, even more would have been achieved. But then there would have been no Coronel. Jellicoe would not have been forced to disgorge his battle cruisers without the effect of that defeat. Spee's policy did, therefore, directly weaken the Grand Fleet, albeit temporarily. But, although this had been a major aim of German pre-war cruiser policy, Pohl did not take the opportunity thereby offered him. Instead, the loss of *Scharnhorst* and *Gneisenau* confirmed in the cautious minds of the German naval leaders the unwisdom of *Kleinkrieg*. Spee's own offensive spirit turned, ironically enough, into an argument for increasing defensiveness. Such a policy, questionable enough in 1914, became mandatory in 1915, now that the Royal Navy was free to concentrate in home waters.

[62] Yates, *Graf Spee's raiders*, 214.
[63] Marder, *From the Dreadnought*, ii. 127.

EMPIRE IN THE PACIFIC

On 12 August 1914 the Japanese military attaché in Washington declared that 'Japan now had a free hand in the Far East'.[64] The occupation of Micronesia was the first manifestation of Tokyo's intent. The 2nd South Seas squadron became the 'Provisional South Seas Islands Defence Force', and readied itself for a possible engagement with the United States. By the end of 1914 the naval ministry had dispatched teams of scientists to survey the islands and assess their resources. Occupation became settlement: cut off from the outside world, the local population was accorded 'brotherly racial equality' while being taught Japanese and Japanese ways. To their existing exports of phosphates and copra were added sugar and coconuts. But even economic development had a strategic end: the profits accrued to the navy as the islands' administrators. And with its consolidation of Japan's outermost possessions, the navy's claim on the defence budget multiplied faster than that of the army: between 1914 and 1918 the army's share rose from 87.7 million yen to 152 million, whereas the navy's soared from 83 million to 216 million. By the war's end it had secured approval for its programme of eight battleships and eight battle cruisers.[65]

Even after the battle of the Falkland Islands the British Admiralty remained far too dependent on the continuance of Japanese naval assistance for the pursuit of anything other than conciliation. In November 1914 Grey suggested to Kato that the occupation of the German Pacific territories should be temporary pending the final peace settlement. If Germany was then still in a dominant position on the continent of Europe, the islands would be bargaining-chips for the restoration of Belgium. Kato accepted the principle, but concluded that 'the Japanese nation would naturally insist on the permanent retention of all German Islands north of the equator'.[66]

Thus, the removal of the German threat in the Pacific had been achieved by the activation of that from Japan. For Australians and New Zealanders the exchange was a poor one. The Dominions contended that the surrender to them of New Guinea, the administrative centre for all the German Pacific islands, implied Australian control of the entire network. But, though an explanation for the antipodeans' slowness to act themselves, their argument carried little weight when compared with possession.[67] Lewis Harcourt, the colonial secretary in London, switched from being the spokesman of

---

[64] May, *Mississippi Valley Historical Review*, XL (1953–4), 286–7.

[65] Hiery, *Neglected war*, 130–49; Schenking, *War in History*, V (1998), 324–5; Evans and Peattie, *Kaigun*, 167

[66] Peattie, *Nanyo*, 45.

[67] On this clash, see Louis, *Great Britain and Germany's lost colonies*, 38–49; Lowe, *Great Britain and Japan*, 201–7.

Dominion concerns in Britain to being the emissary of the Anglo-Japanese alliance in Australia. Nor were his efforts without success. Australia's complaints tended to obscure its recognition that the alliance had actually worked to defend it from attack. Even more importantly, Australia moaned about what it had not got rather than what it had. With considerable ease and minimal expense the German south Pacific islands had been added to the bounds of the British empire and formed a fresh defensive buffer to the north.

All this made nonsense of the CID subcommittee's renunciation of annexationism at its meeting on 5 August 1914. London's efforts to contain Japan or to argue that the occupation of Germany's Pacific colonies was temporary were vitiated by the determination of its Dominion partners to turn conquest into commercial exploitation. Furthermore, the colonization of New Guinea was not moderated, as it was in Micronesia, by attention to the welfare and education of the indigenous population.

In New Guinea, Australia handed the firm of Burns Philp and Co. a virtual monopoly of imports and exports. The company's turnover and profits all but doubled between 1914 and 1918. Copra production was the key. The German planters were not expropriated until after the end of the war. Instead, they were encouraged to continue trading, and palm tree plantings were doubled. The value of New Guinea's trade rose from £225,416 in 1915–16 to £1.2 million in 1919–20, almost all of it copra exports carried through Australian ports. This achievement was built on the backs of the Melanesian population, forcibly recruited and then kept in check with corporal punishment. British observers were appalled as Australian entrepreneurs and German planters drove forward a policy determined primarily by racism and profit-making.[68]

Outwardly, affairs were better managed in Samoa, where the indigenous population welcomed the New Zealanders' discrimination against the Chinese, even when it entailed the forcible separation of mixed families, as well as the closure of all German businesses by April 1916. As in New Guinea, Burns Philp was granted a virtual monopoly, and copra production was emphasized to the detriment of other produce: by 1916 copra accounted for 66.5 per cent of all Samoa's exports, and by 1918 80.4 per cent. But, unlike New Guinea, military administration remained in place. Determined 'to procure for the men absolutely the best quality beer that is on the market, at the lowest possible price',[69] the New Zealand military government pursued a populist policy that was ultimately self-defeating. Its costs were covered by an export tax on agricultural products which reduced the profits paid to Samoan producers, while the price of imports rose. Many Samoans withdrew from the market. Furthermore,

---

[68] Hiery, *Neglected war*, 46–115; Newbury, *Journal of Imperial and Commonwealth History*, XVI (1988), 90–1.

[69] Hiery, *Neglected war*, 158, and generally 154–72.

what trade remained was increasingly carried in American ships owing to the lack of British tonnage: by 1918 only 14.5 per cent of Samoa's trade was with New Zealand, but 59.5 per cent was with the United States.

The perceived benefits of sub-imperialism eased the Dominions' sense of loss. Australia and New Zealand accepted the de facto division of power at the equator. In 1916 British war aims policy included the retention by Australia and New Zealand of their south Pacific acquisitions and by Japan of theirs in the north Pacific. Therefore, although the secret Anglo-Japanese agreement of February 1917 continued to embody a caveat allowing for the outcome of the peace negotiations, each of the contracting parties—Britain with Australia's and New Zealand's concurrence—recognized the permanence of the other's possessions. What had begun as the defence of trade had been transformed into colonial annexationism.[70]

However, Britain, for all its double-standards in the matter, was at bottom a satiated power, committed to maintaining the status quo in the Pacific, and only responding to the allocation of the German colonies because the circumstances of war forced it to. Japan, on the other hand, was an emergent empire, which had entered the war in pursuit of its Pacific policy, not shaped its policy around the fact of its being at war. In August 1914 it faced no threat to its territory or to its vital interests. But some thought it to have reached the zenith of its powers. Short of capital at home and having difficulties in raising loans abroad, it struggled to make the investment necessary for modernization. Britain boxed in Japanese commercial expansion in the Yangtze valley; Russia looked set to recover its status as a Far Eastern power; and to the east the United States disputed hegemony of the north Pacific. Then the First World War, by emptying the Far East of Europe's exports and by making the European powers dependent on Japanese support, provided Japan with opportunities for penetration and expansion. The only problem was that Japan's attentions were not focused primarily on Germany: the north Pacific islands were an incidental bonus. Japan's aims lay in China, a neutral state whose integrity was a declared objective of the Anglo-Japanese alliance.

On 18 January 1915 the Japanese ambassador in Peking presented Yuan with Japan's Chinese shopping list, the so-called twenty-one demands.[71] The demands were organized in five groups. The first required that China accept Japan's right to settle the future of the Shantung lease with Germany; the second aimed to consolidate Japan's hold in southern Manchuria and eastern Inner Mongolia, and in particular to extend the Japanese lease of Kwantung for

[70] On the evolution of British war-aims' thought on colonial questions, see also Rothwell, British war aims, 67–74; Galbraith, Journal of Imperial and Commonwealth History, XIII (1984), 26.

[71] What follows rests on Chi, China diplomacy, ch. 2; La Fargue, China and the World War, chs. 2 and 3; Lowe, Great Britain and Japan, ch. 7; Craft, International History Review, XVI (1994), 1–24. Brief discussions are Renouvin, Crise européene, 404–6, 459–63, and Stevenson, First World War, 133–4.

a further ninety-nine years; the third asked China to admit Japan to joint ownership of the Hanyehping iron and coal company; the fourth reflected Japan's worries about the possibility of an American installation at Fukien, opposite Taiwan, and obliged China not to give or lease any harbour to foreign powers; the fifth group were dubbed 'wishes' rather than 'demands', and became the focus of most of the subsequent debate. Japan's 'wishes' were that China should accept Japanese political and military advisers, that Japanese should have the right to own land in China, that Japan should—in short—exercise indirect control over those portions of China over which it did not already have direct control.

The timing of the delivery of the twenty-one demands, soon after the fall of Tsingtao and in the immediate context of a debate with China over the extent of the Shantung war zone, suggested that Japan was doing little more than tidy up after its defeat of the Germans. China cancelled the war zone on 7 January 1915. Although it did not ask Japan to withdraw from Tsingtao for fear of creating the impression that it had used Japan to defeat Germany for its own ends, it argued that Japan's occupation of Tsingtao was temporary, pending the reversion of the German lease to China. Japan, of course, believed that the German lease should be bestowed on Japan, and feared that reversion to China would not preclude the re-emergence of Germany in China after the war. The dispute over Tsingtao provided the immediate context for the formulation of the twenty-one demands. However, their origins were of a piece with the development of Japanese foreign policy since 1905.

The conclusion to the Russo-Japanese War, the Treaty of Portsmouth, had not been generous in its handling of Japan, although the latter was the victorious power. The basis of Japan's foothold in China, the lease on Kwantung, was due to expire in 1923; defeated Russia had consolidated its hold in Outer Mongolia, while victorious Japan had not achieved the same in Inner Mongolia. Japan's economic weakness meant that in the scramble for railway concessions and for capital investment in mainland Asia the European powers consistently came out on top. And yet China's proximity made it proportionately more important to Japan than to any of the other treaty powers: in 1914 it took a fifth of all its exports, 92 per cent of its exported yarn, and 70 per cent of its exports of cotton piece goods.[72] Nor was China simply a market. Ethnic kinship stoked a sense of Asian nationalism to which Chinese such as Sun Yat-sen responded. In this form, a common cultural identity imposed on Japan an obligation to aid in the modernization and reinvigoration of its larger continental neighbour in order to save China from the exploitation of western imperialism. On 29 November 1914 Uchida Ryohei, the far-right leader of the nationalist Black Dragon society, submitted to Okuma and Kato a

---

[72] Duus, Myers, and Peattie (eds.), *Japanese informal empire*, 71–3.

memorandum 'for a solution of the China problem': it was, to all intents and purposes, a first draft of the twenty-one demands.[73]

A precondition of Uchida's programme was the replacement of the Yuan government. In 1913 the Hanyehping company had agreed to repay a Japanese loan with deliveries of 17 million tons of iron ore and 8 million tons of crude iron over a forty-year period; the effect would be to foster Japan's industrialization while retarding China's. On 22 November 1914 the Chinese government nationalized China's iron ores. Both in this and in the dealings over Shantung Yuan demonstrated a healthy suspicion of Japan. Given time, he might even establish a secure government for China, thus further restricting Japan's opportunities. His external strength lay in the network of treaties which bound the commercial interests of the great powers to the stability and integrity of China. The war, by weakening the leverage of the treaty powers, gave Japan the opportunity to try to establish by a diplomatic coup what it had failed to do by largely economic means.

Whether or not Japan's attempt was successful largely depends on the interpretation given to its aims. Japan's industrialization was reliant on foreign capital. By establishing an enclave of its own in China, it hoped ultimately to end that dependence. Between 1902 and 1914 Japan's share of the total foreign investment in China rose from 0.1 per cent to 13.6 per cent. But in the short term it had to balance its economic imperialism with its own domestic need for overseas investment. Thus, compromise was implicit in its foreign policy.[74] The twenty-one demands were a maximum programme. Kato had incorporated the views of all interested parties, including the army, the navy, big business, and the pan-Asiatic nationalists. But Kato himself reckoned to do no more than consolidate Japan in Shantung, southern Manchuria, and eastern Inner Mongolia. This, after all, was what he had gone to war for, and what he had concluded—from various statements by Grey—that Japan's ally would support. The fifth group was therefore redundant. By including it he appeased Japanese nationalists, but at the same time—by calling its contents 'wishes', not 'demands'—he earmarked it as clearly negotiable. The fact that the Diet had been dissolved in December 1914, and that no new assembly convened until May, gave the government a free hand in the conduct of what Kato hoped would be secret diplomacy. By the time the apparent crisis was reached in the Sino-Japanese negotiations, at the end of April, China had actually conceded to Kato most of what he had set out to achieve. The dispute was over the residue, not over the twenty-one demands as a whole.

On 26 April Kato presented the outstanding issues, and in particular the fifth group of objectives, in a revised and moderated form. China responded by

[73] Jansen, *Japanese and Sun Yat-sen*, 180–2.
[74] Hayashima, *Illusion des Sonderfriedens*, 18–26.

persisting in defence of its sovereignty. At a cabinet meeting on 6 May the Japanese decided to drop group five in its entirety. Yuan has been given the credit for persuading the *genro* to force Kato to this step. However, more important to the cabinet's decision must have been Britain's protest that group five contravened the terms of the alliance treaty. Kato, as a defender of the alliance, was too shrewd not to have predicted such an outcome. Therefore the demands contained in the ultimatum served on China by Japan on 7 May, although far milder than those contained in the original draft, can have been no more mild than Kato himself originally anticipated. China duly accepted their terms two days later. The Sino-Japanese treaty of 25 May secured Japan's hold on southern Manchuria and eastern Inner Mongolia, ceded Germany's economic rights in Shantung to Japan and left the settlement of the leasehold to the final peace settlement, established the Hanyehping company as a Sino-Japanese concern, and embodied the non-alienation of Fukien.

The only legitimate Japanese objection to Kato's diplomacy was that he might have achieved as much with greater stealth if he had proceeded gradually and waited until 1919 for confirmation of what he had gained. But that argument assumed a knowledge that the war would not end sooner, and that when it did the European powers—in particular Russia and Germany—would not be in a position to press their Asiatic claims with greater strength.

If Kato failed, therefore, it was not as a diplomat but as a domestic politician. The nationalists, led on by the inclusion of their aspirations in group five, were frustrated by the length of the negotiations and their final outcome. The *genro*, already alarmed by Kato's bellicosity in August 1914, were annoyed at their exclusion from the processes of diplomacy; they saw Yuan's appeal as evidence of the damage done to relations with China and Britain's protests as a blow to Japanese prestige. By sidelining the *genro* Kato ran the risk of empowering the army, which the *genro* had hitherto held in check and which saw force as a solution to the crisis. Caught between competing pressures that even the most successful foreign policy could never truly reconcile, the government weakened, and in August Kato was removed, ultimately to be replaced as foreign minister by Ishii Kikujiro.

Kato's handling of the twenty-one demands, and in particular of group five, came to be seen as a diplomatic blunder in part through these domestic divisions but also in part through Yuan's self-advertisement. Yuan liked to believe that his conduct of the negotiations had been outstandingly successful. Committed to secrecy, particularly in relation to group five, he spun out the talks sufficiently long to enable Britain and the United States to become conversant with the terms of the twenty-one demands. He then, so his defence runs, forced Japan to the ultimatum, and thus made it evident that China's submission was the product of *force majeure*. Finally, what he gave away were chunks of China which he had never fully controlled. In reality, Yuan lost all down the line. The initial secrecy over the twenty-one demands proved enormously hard to rupture. Not until 10 February did the British Foreign Office know the demands in full, and even then incredulity over group five's existence persisted. In the United States William Jennings Bryan, the secretary of state, initially welcomed group five as extending to Japan the 'open door' in China already enjoyed by the United States and Europe. His department, anxious not to reawaken the issue of Japanese immigration to California, looked to Britain to restrain its ally. But Grey, given the military situation, felt 'our proper course is to lie low'.[75] The response of both powers slowly grew as the crisis developed, but neither made up for this initial delay. If Kato had always recognized group five as negotiable, its inclusion thus became a stroke of genius. British and American attentions focused on it rather than on the substance of the demands; the abandonment of group five gave Yuan the opportunity to save face at home while at the same time conceding the essence of what Kato wanted. Britain, having been instrumental in the Japanese decision to drop group five, then advised China to submit to the Japanese ultimatum. The United States, when it made a belated attempt to rally the Entente powers behind China, got no support. At bottom, the United States seemed as ready to allow limited Japanese expansion into China as was Britain. Thus, Yuan's delaying tactics could not gainsay the fundamental weakness of his position. The day on which the Japanese issued their ultimatum, 7 May 1915, was dubbed 'national humiliation day', evoking in the Chinese people a genuine sense of nationalism. But popular sentiments were a threat to Yuan's regime, not a springboard to reform and regeneration. The net effect of Yuan's so-called successful diplomacy was to weaken the fragile links between the leader and his people, while not fully awakening him to the pusillanimity of the powers on whom his policy resided.

The extent of his self-deception, and the reality of Japan's hold on China, became evident over the course of the following year. The twenty-one demands had further weakened the Kuomintang. Torn between competing interpretations of Chinese nationalism, over 150 revolutionaries had accepted pardons from Yuan and returned from exile. The few that stayed, pre-eminently Sun Yat-sen, advocated such a level of subordination to Japan that they forfeited political credibility in their homeland and so deprived them-selves of any value to their hosts.[76] With the revolutionaries weakened, Yuan concluded that the next step to stability and order would be the fulfilment of his ambition to become emperor. He imagined that Japan, satiated by the treaty of 25 May, would support him in this desire: privately his Japanese advisers egged him on, publicly the Japanese government quite properly stated

[75] Chi, *China diplomacy*, 38.
[76] Jansen, *Japanese and Sun Yat-sen*, 188–97.

that the constitution of China was China's own affair. Yuan had also to reckon with the frustration of Japan's nationalists and of its army, smarting at the outcome of the 1915 negotiations. His apparent diplomatic success had thwarted Japan; an accretion to his power might threaten Japanese interests yet further. He had faced the consistent opposition of the intelligence bureau of the Japanese general staff since 1911. Kato's fall gave the army an opening in the making of foreign policy. With the prime minister, Okuma Shigenobe, as an interim foreign secretary until October 1915, and then with the appointment of Ishii, who had been ambassador in Paris, the civilians' grasp of Chinese affairs declined. The army was prepared to support the restoration of the monarchy in China, but the emperor it had in mind was a Manchu puppet.[77]

In November 1915 Yuan suggested that the Entente powers support his candidature in return for China's entry to the war. He now recognized that belligerence might be the price of entry to the peace negotiations. China could then press directly for the return of Tsingtao. In June China tried to curry the support of the Entente by offering infantry and arms: the former were to provide labour for the western front and the latter were German-made rifles, many of which had still not been paid for. In London the Foreign Office had been cautious, not least because its Far Eastern policy was predicated on the existing alliance with Japan rather than on a putative arrangement with a weaker power. But within China itself some Britons, including Yuan's political adviser George Morrison, encouraged the president. The British military attaché was attracted by the offer of men; British business interests saw the opportunity to eliminate German competition in China; and Indian intelligence was fearful of propaganda and subversion emanating from Germany's embassy in Peking.[78]

Grey's solution to Yuan's initiative was to propose that the Entente approach Japan for its reactions. However, the Japanese had been reading British ciphers and knew perfectly well that the idea of China's entry to the war was Peking's, not London's. It was one which put the danger which Yuan posed for Japan in its starkest terms. China would create an army, ostensibly for the war, in reality to counter Japan; it would do so under the umbrella of Britain, the ally around whom Japan's foreign policy was constructed. Japan's path became clear. On 6 December 1915 it blocked China's entry to the war; by the end of the month its army was covertly sponsoring revolution in Yunnan.

Britain, France, and Russia saw Yuan's monarchy as a means to stability; Japan said that it could not support the idea while it self-evidently did not command consent in China. Deprived of money and munitions, and

---

[77] Kitaoka Shin'ichi, 'China experts in the army', in Duus, Myers, and Peattie (eds.), *Japanese informal empire*, 351–4.
[78] Jones, *Britain's search for Chinese co-operation*, 50–73.

geographically isolated, the revolutionary warlords made slow progress at first. In February Yuan postponed his plans for monarchy, and in March abandoned them. But by that stage the military governors of south China had deserted Yuan and the Japanese army had increased its support for his opponents. Warlordism increased the leverage of military advice. The revolutionaries in the south accepted it in the name of republicanism, those in the north in the hope of a Manchu restoration. Once again Japanese policy was caught between competing attractions—the establishment of a separate enclave in Manchuria now or the exercise of indirect control throughout China in the future. The dilemma was resolved on 6 June 1916, when Yuan died just as he was about to flee into exile.

Japan acknowledged his successor as president, Li Yuen-kung, who became the advocate of parliamentary government, the representative of the south and of the revived Kuomintang. Opposed to him was Tuan Chi-jui, the prime minister and the spokesman of the military governors. To describe Chinese politics from June 1916 in terms of two distinct divisions is to disguise the factionalism and self-interestedness manifest within each. In its weakness each grouping looked outside China for support. China's discord therefore strengthened Japan's hand, while Japan itself could protest its respect for Chinese integrity.

Outwardly, Japan moderated its policy towards China. It could afford to do so. The settlement of 25 May 1915 had met its principal diplomatic objectives. By 1916 its tack could be different. Japan was in the midst of an economic boom. Exports, which had totalled 526,581,000 yen in 1912, rose to 1,127,468,000 yen.[79] Commerce could therefore consolidate Japan's holdings and become the agent of expansion without ruffling relations with other powers. The boom was fuelled by the removal of European competition, by the low level of economic commitment to the war, and by a rise in cotton exports. Japan's sales soared all round the Pacific littoral, to Peru and Chile, to the United States, to Russia, and to Australia. Japanese exports to China grew four times between 1913 and 1916. This increase was not the largest in absolute terms or in rate of growth; more significant was the change in the structure of the relationship. China's importance as a market declined after 1915, while its attractiveness as a home for Japanese investment increased. Between 1914 and 1919, while wages in Japan itself more than doubled on the back of the wartime boom, those in China remained low; in 1915 legislation limited the length of the working day in Japan, while China's labour force enjoyed no such protection. Japanese industrialists therefore used their wartime profits to establish production in China. In 1914 Japanese owned 111,936 cotton spindles in China; by 1918 this figure had risen to 240,904, and by 1924 to 1,218,544. As a result,

---

[79] Nish, *Alliance in decline*, 196.

Chinese yarn production doubled in volume between 1913 and 1918. At the same time Chinese raw materials enabled Japan to become a major producer of capital goods. The Hanyehping iron and coal company's average loss of 1.2 million Mexican dollars a year before 1915 turned in Japanese hands to a profit of 2.8 million. New iron production in Manchuria, rather than becoming the foundation-stone for China's industrialization, was integrated into Japan's heavy industry. Cut off from European imports by the war and financed by the boom in cotton exports, Japan's iron and steel industries thrived. Between 1914 and 1919 the gross value of Japan's industrial production rose from 1.4 million yen to 6.7 million.[80]

The possibility of China upsetting the consolidation by Japan of its 1915 gains became increasingly remote. In economic terms China was at least an indirect beneficiary of Japan's success. But with the war's conclusion Japan could expect a renaissance of European economic competition in the Far East; Germany, if victorious, might reclaim Tsingtao; Russia would resume its push into Mongolia and Manchuria. Kato's preferred method of managing this scenario, the maintenance of the Anglo-Japanese alliance, had begun to look less secure over the long term. However late and however weak its response, Britain had not been impressed by group five of the twenty-one demands. During the course of 1916 it came to believe that the flight of Indian revolutionaries to Japan enjoyed the support of that country's government. The India Office, its anxieties for Russia and the north-west frontier temporarily stilled, worried instead about Japanese penetration into southern China and its implications for the north-east frontier.[81] In Japan itself, anti-British feeling enjoyed a currency in the press and among the pan-Asian nationalists. Britain's policy over group five and over Yuan's bid to join the war was interpreted as directed against Japan. The army, its conviction in Germany's military invincibility strengthened by its contacts with British troops at Tsingtao, argued that Britain would lose the war.

In reality the strains in the alliance, although more evident than its underlying strengths, were manageable. Japanese policy became more, not less, wedded to the Entente. In January 1915 the Germans made two approaches for a separate peace with Japan—through Paul von Hintze, their minister in Peking, and through Uchida, the Japanese ambassador in Stockholm. The Stockholm talks were renewed in March 1916. The aim of Germany's policy was relief for its eastern front: the neutralization of Japan would remove one of Russia's major arms suppliers and reopen Russia's fears for its Asiatic frontiers. It might even lever Russia out of the war. In the longer run commercial

---

[80] Hardach, *First World War*, 258–66; Renouvin, *Crise européenne*, 676–7; Duus, Myers, and Peattie (eds.), *Japanese informal empire*, 77–84.

[81] T. G. Fraser, *History*, LXIII (1978), 366–82.

interests suggested that Japan's need for finance could make Germany a more obvious Far Eastern partner than Russia or Britain. But in 1915 Germany's approach was ambivalent. The Foreign Office confessed itself ignorant about Japan. The navy was directly affected by, and directly involved in, the negotiations. Hintze was an admiral; the need to keep Tokyo sweet argued that the U-boat campaign should be eased to allow Swedish iron ore to be exported to Japan, despite the fact that it might be transformed into weapons for Russia. Most sensitive of all, the navy was being asked to cede to Japan both Tsingtao and the islands in the north Pacific. The problem was that Germany could only offer Japan areas of which Japan was already in possession. Furthermore, if it did renounce its territory in the Far East, Germany still had no guarantee that it would secure an alliance with Japan. In 1915 Germany was not, in the final analysis, prepared to forfeit a possible foothold in China for a possible treaty with Japan. By 1916 it had steeled itself to such a trade-off. But the tokens with which it was playing had no bargaining value.[82]

For Japan, the attractions of the German offers were their usefulness in underlining to the Entente powers the continuing value of Japan as an ally despite the elimination of Germany as a Pacific power. Uchida was punctilious in keeping Britain informed. In 1916, while Germany pursued in Stockholm a policy that had specific wartime and post-war objectives, Uchida thought the talks were aimed at the achievement of a general peace.

Russia's dependence on Japanese good will, even more than Britain's, was highlighted by the German approaches. In 1914 Russia, together with France, favoured the formation of a quadruple alliance (the three Entente powers plus Japan), but ran foul of the opposition of Kato and of Grey, both reckoning that such an alliance would complicate the settlement of China. However, Japan's ambassador in St Petersburg, Motono Ichiro, was a strong supporter of the Entente; moreover, the Russians were able to read the signals passing between Stockholm and Tokyo, and so were forcefully reminded of the value of good Russo-Japanese relations. Kato's fall opened the path for Russia's persistence to bear fruit. The first step, taken on 19 October 1915, was Japan's adherence to the Declaration of London—the undertaking originally made on 5 September 1914 that Britain, France, and Russia would not seek a separate peace with Germany. Japan's motivation in making a move which Kato had resisted was not the conduct of the war but the pursuit of war aims: Ishii thus ensured Japan a seat at the peace conference. Russia's war needs prompted Sazonov to persist in pursuing closer links. On 3 July 1916 the two countries negotiated an alliance committed to the exclusion of a third party from China. Again, Japan's regional gain was the most evident outcome. The treaty ensured Russia's

[82] Hayashima, Illusion des Sonderfriedens, 31–118; Iklé, American Historical Review, LXXI (1965), 62–76; Fischer, Germany's war aims, 228.

acceptance of Japan's position in China and constituted provision for the possible collapse of the Anglo-Japanese alliance. But its very existence made the latter contingency less likely as it rendered the Anglo-Japanese alliance the only effective diplomatic check on resurgent Russian ambitions in Asia. While both alliances ran concurrently Japan would be the arbiter of affairs in the Far East.[83]

The treaty made no mention of China's independence or of the rights of other states in China. For Peking the virtues of neutrality were being wrung dry. Racked by inflation, its government needed fresh loans to survive. In June 1916 the Entente powers agreed in principle to a new loan consortium, but the close working relationship established before the war between the Hongkong and Shanghai Bank and the Deutsch-Asiastische Bank created problems dissolving the old one. German indebtedness meant that Anglo-German loans could not be wound up without damage to British investors and to the standing of British financial institutions. At the same time, Britain's policy in China was increasingly in thrall to Japan, and Japan's aim was now to get China to participate in the war.

In October 1916 General Terauchi Seiki, a former war minister and an old Manchuria hand, formed a new coalition government in Japan, with Motono Ichiro as foreign minister. Motono's policy was one of moderation; Japan's industrial investments on the mainland now required stability, not military adventurism and civil war. If China joined the Entente its dependence on Japan would increase. Japan could secure for Peking the funds it needed to ensure its domestic political stability, while at the same time legitimizing a purge of German interests in the Far East. Britain had moaned so often about these, but even more about the threat to India from revolutionaries in China and Japan itself, that it could not admit that it now believed that its fears, in the latter regard in particular, had been exaggerated. Moreover, Britain's pursuit of Chinese labour throughout 1916 came to fruition in January 1917. The arrangements made to transport its recruits centred on Japanese-occupied Tsingtsao. On 14 January 1917 Motono agreed to accord Britain further naval assistance in exchange for a settlement of the two powers' colonial ambitions in the Pacific and Britain's recognition of Japan's claim to Shantung. Motono's moderation of Japan's policy in China and his support for the Entente had found its final pay-off. Essentially, Britain saw concessions to Japan in China as a reasonable return for Japan's contribution to the war effort and for security in India. For many in China, the only way forward now seemed to be belligerence and an even closer relationship with Japan, in the hope that once it had stability it could then eject its unwelcome partner.[84]

[83] G. D. Malone, 'War aims towards Germany', in Dallin *et al.* (eds.) *Russian diplomacy*, 150–3.

[84] Craft, *International History Review*, XVI (1994), 14–15; Dignan, *Indian revolutionary problem*, 100, 154–8, 162–3, 183–5; Jones, *Britain's search for Chinese co-operation*, 33, 93–6, 127–30, 133–4.

Japan's identification of its policy objectives with the Entente, therefore, remained entirely self-serving. Japanese resistance to being drawn into the war outside Asia and the Pacific was obdurate. France and Russia in particular hoped for the dispatch of Japanese ground forces to Europe. Britain, more conscious of its status as an imperial power in Asia than of its need for men, was ambivalent: 'I confess I am not very much enamoured of the idea that the war shd. be decided by the importation of these Yellow men,' confided Asquith on 31 December 1914.[85] He need not have worried. The Japanese, both in 1914 and thereafter, consistently rebutted the Europeans' proposals. They needed their army intact for the achievement of their Chinese objectives, and for the latter's possible defence should European rivalries reopen in the Far East after the war. The army conveniently reckoned that its minimum realistic contribution to the Great War would be 400,000 men, a number so large that it would denude Japan. Privately, Japan's soldiers may also have been concerned by the growing backwardness of their tactics and technology; having been trained by Germans, they had faith in Germany's military superiority.

Nonetheless, the military value of Japan's contribution to the Entente should not be underrated just because it remained limited by Japanese policy objectives. Japan entered the war as Britain's ally, not as a member of the Entente, and it did so as an Asian empire, not a European one. Therefore it was within the confines of the navy and of the Pacific that it elected to operate, and it is within these confines that its military value should be judged. Its initial assistance to the Royal Navy, which enabled the Chinese trade to resume within three weeks of the war's outbreak,[86] was sustained throughout the war. In 1916 it was extended to the Indian Ocean, and in January 1917—a step for which the Anglo-Japanese secret agreement became a quid pro quo—to the Mediterranean. In 1918 the Japanese flotilla was the most efficient of the Entente naval units in that theatre.[87] Russia too derived direct military benefit from its relationship with Japan; in addition to security on its eastern frontier, its arms purchases from Japan totalled 430,000 rifles and 500 heavy guns by the end of the first year of the war. Japan's military contribution can be even better appreciated if stated negatively rather than positively. Without it, the ability of Britain and Russia, both major Asiatic powers, to concentrate on Europe would have been considerably diminished.

Britain's readiness to concede to Japan can only be interpreted as weakness if strategy is interpreted in terms of war aims and their achievement. Britain's global priority between 1914 and 1918 was a victorious conclusion to the war with Germany. The Anglo-Japanese alliance was so managed by the Foreign

---

[85] Asquith, *Letters to Venetia Stanley*, 349; more generally, Rothwell, *History*, LVI (1971), 35–45; Nish, 'Japan 1914–18', in Millett and Murray (eds.), *Military effectiveness*, vol. I.
[86] La Fargue, *China and the world war*, 4–5, 18.
[87] Marder, *From the Dreadnought*, iv. 36.

Office (and by the Admiralty) that it made a significant contribution to that objective. Japan's principal purpose was somewhat different—the use of the war to fulfil its war aims in the Pacific region. Alone of the belligerent powers, Japan made sure that—for all the war's inbuilt pressures to the contrary—conflict served the purposes of its policy. For the political theorist, what is extraordinary about this outstandingly successful use of war for the achievement of political objectives was that it was effected by a government that was weak and divided. In Japan cabinet government was hesitant, the party system ill-developed, the emperor a cipher, and the army disproportionately influential in politics. And yet Japan's foreign policy attained a consistency and direction that eluded (admittedly under far greater pressures) the more developed political systems of western Europe.

7

THE DARK CONTINENT: COLONIAL CONFLICT IN SUB-SAHARAN AFRICA

WAR IN AFRICA

On 12 August 1914, in Togoland, Regimental Sergeant-Major Alhaji Grunshi of the West African Frontier Force became the first soldier in British service to fire a round in the Great War. On 25 November 1918, two weeks after the signature of the armistice in Europe, at Abercorn in Northern Rhodesia Colonel Paul von Lettow-Vorbeck surrendered, the last German commander of the war to do so.

As much from its outset as beyond its formal conclusion, therefore, the First World War was far more than just a European conflict. In August 1914 British, French, Belgian, and German belligerence embraced the entire continent of Africa with the exception of Liberia, Ethiopia, and the relatively smaller colonies of Spain, Italy, and Portugal. Not even these would remain exempt from the war, at least in its indirect forms.

In the eighteenth century Britain and France had fought in North America and India for the possession of empire. Conflict between the great powers had as often originated in the colonies as in Europe itself. But in the course of the nineteenth century overseas expansion was conducted without such clashes: mercantilism gave way to free trade, and governments did not see territorial possession as the key to exclusive commercial rights. In 1898 Marchand and Kitchener, soldiers both, staked rival claims at Fashoda, on the upper reaches of the Nile, but neither France nor Britain resorted to arms in pursuit of those ambitions. Wars were plenty, but they were conducted against the native populations, and their purposes were local and limited.

In 1914 none of the central governments of the belligerent powers was harbouring notions of imperial aggrandizement at the expense of its European neighbours through the use of battle. The Anglo-German antagonism had scant relevance to Africa. Britain encouraged the Germans to expand, possibly at the expense of Belgium and Portugal; Germany respected rather than reviled British rule. Thus, in 1914 the flow of major war was the reverse of that in the eighteenth century—from Europe to the colonies, rather than vice versa.

Moreover, when the news of the crisis of late July 1914 reached the white settlers of Africa it rarely provoked the popular manifestations of enthusiasm exhibited in the capitals of their parent countries. The duty of Europeans, opined the *East Africa Standard* of Mombasa on 22 August 1914, was not to fight each other but to keep control of the Africans.[1] The objective of colonial government was pacification. The advent of war was against the common interests of all whites, whatever their nationalities; their numbers were exiguous; their hold on the recently conquered African interior was precarious, and in many areas incomplete. The nominal title of government did not necessarily conform to the actual exercise of power, which often still lay with local chiefs and headmen. Economic penetration through the construction of ports and railways, through plantations and mining, had only just begun. Where mass meetings in support of the war did take place, for example in Salisbury in Southern Rhodesia, they emphasized the exceptional nature of such settlements—their urbanization and, in this case, their Englishness. But even in Rhodesia, German and Austrian reservists were able to leave for Europe in late August,[2] and in South Africa not until May 1915, after the sinking of the *Lusitania*, were there riots against German firms operating within the Union.[3]

The fear of the white settler was a dual one. First, the spectacle of white fighting white would reduce the status of the European. Secondly, war would either rekindle the warrior traditions of those tribes in whom they had only recently been crushed or train in the use of arms those to whom they were unfamiliar. Blacks would kill whites, and the forfeit would be white racial supremacy. In the event, the notion that the European hold on sub-Saharan Africa would be destabilized by the re-emergence of traditional forces proved misplaced; the impact of the war deepened collaboration, and its contribution to colonial decline was much longer-term—through the erosion of tribal loyalties and the broadening of new black elites that were urbanized, westernized, and politically aware.

[1] Savage and Munro, *Journal of African History*, VII (1966), 314.
[2] McLaughlin, *Ragtime soldiers*, 2, 5–7.
[3] Ticktin, *South African Historical Journal*, (Nov. 1969), 69–70.

For the Great War in Africa, although the product of European devices and desires, was fought principally by the Africans themselves. In all, somewhere over 2 million Africans served in the First World War as soldiers or labourers, and upwards of 200,000 of them died or were killed in action.[4] By comparison with Europe such figures are low—the first represents between 1 and 2 per cent of the total population of Africa. But in a local context a comparison with twentieth-century industrialized nation states is inappropriate; never before in the history of Africa had manpower been mobilized on such a scale.

Both during the war and after it, British and French propaganda accused the Germans of militarizing Africa: they had, said Lloyd George on 24 January 1919, 'raised native troops and encouraged these troops to behave in a manner that would even disgrace the Bolsheviks'.[5] Such rhetoric was fed by the ferocity with which the Germans suppressed the wave of resistance that struck their colonies with simultaneous force between 1904 and 1906. Genocide and famine were both deployed against the Herero in South-West Africa and the Maji-Maji in East Africa. Thereafter, however, German colonial administration became more liberal. Military responsibilities were circumscribed, commercial development promoted, and settlement doubled. As a result, the German colonial forces, the *Schütztruppen*, could draw in more whites: from 1913 conscripts were allowed to complete their reserve service overseas rather than remain liable for recall to Germany. But the settlers themselves became increasingly reluctant to meet the costs of an inflated military establishment, and order on a daily basis was handed over to an expanded police force. Admittedly their armament was similar to that of the *Schütztruppen*, and they could be and were, incorporated with it.[6] Nonetheless, the point remains that it was not so much Germany as the Entente which was responsible for arming the African.

The idea that the immense manpower pool of the African colonies might be harnessed for military purposes was given its most coherent and ambitious pre-war expression in France, by Charles Mangin in his book *La Force noire*, published in 1910. Mangin predicted that French West Africa could raise 40,000 men, or 4 per cent of the total population of 10.65 million, and that enlistment in some areas could rise to 8 or 10 per cent. At the time such projections looked far-fetched, but by the end of the war France had enlisted 200,000 soldiers in West Africa.[7] When Britain declared war, the Africans

---

[4] These approximations are derived from M. E. Page, 'Black men in a white men's war', in Page (ed.) *Africa and the First World War*, 14; M. Crowder, 'First World War and its consequences', 283, 293.

[5] S. C. Davis, *Reservoirs of men*, 160.

[6] Wolfgang Petter, 'Der Kampf um die deutschen Kolonien', in Michalka (ed.), *De Erste Weltkrieg*, 397–9

[7] Michel, *L'Appel à l'Afrique*, 21–4, 404; Echenberg, *Colonial conscripts*, 25–32.

involved, directly or indirectly, in hostilities totalled 50 million.[8] The actual burden of service was unevenly distributed. In West Africa Britain recruited about 25,000 soldiers[9]—a relatively large figure, but small by comparison with French efforts in the adjacent areas. Southern Rhodesia, influenced by the South African opposition to using blacks as soldiers in a white man's war, enlisted no Africans until 1916. But by then 40 per cent of the white adult male population was on active service, and sufficient fresh drafts for the Rhodesia Regiment could not be procured. The Rhodesia Native Regiment, formed in 1916, had embodied only 2,360 men by 1918, less than 1 per cent of the total African male population, and 75 per cent of them originated from outside the colony.[10]

The majority of those Africans enlisted during the war were not soldiers, or not primarily so. They were carriers.[11] The major problem of conducting operations in Africa, as it had been in all the small wars of European conquest in the nineteenth century, lay 'not in defeating, but in reaching the enemy'.[12] Lettow-Vorbeck likened the march and supply of a single company in East Africa to the movement of a division in Europe.[13] Railway construction had only just begun to open up the hinterland; roads were few, and motorized vehicles fewer. Draught or pack animals, although usable in the highlands and savannah of some parts of Central Africa and in South Africa, fell prey to the tsetse fly in many tropical areas. For the campaigns in the Cameroons and East Africa, therefore, a human chain linked troops to their bases, and without it they could not move, feed, or fight.

None of the major belligerents had anticipated the numbers of carriers which major operations would demand. The pre-war colonial units of all three powers, Britain, France, and Germany, had been designed primarily for internal policing, employing limited numbers in each column, and projecting themselves over short distances. For these purposes some units, but not all, had their own enlisted carriers. However, in 1914–15 Britain and France launched offensive operations deep into German territory. In the Cameroons both the British and the Germans reckoned they needed between two and three porters for each soldier; the French tried to make do with less, but continually

---

[8] Osuntokun, *Nigeria in the First World War*, viii.

[9] Roger Thomas, *Cahiers d'études africaines*, XV (1975), 57.

[10] Peter McLaughlin, 'The legacy of conquest: African military manpower in Southern Rhodesia during the First World War', in Page (ed.), *Africa*, 121, 132; McLaughlin, *Ragtime soldiers*, 75; id., *Small Wars and Insurgencies*, II (1991), 249–57.

[11] On carriers, see esp. Geoffrey Hodges, *Carrier corps*; Hodges, 'Military labour in East Africa and its impact on Kenya', in Page (ed.), *Africa*; D. Killingray and J. Matthews, *Canadian Journal of African Studies*, XIII (1979), 5–23; D. Killingray, *Journal of Contemporary History*, XXIV, (1989), 483–501; D. C. Savage and J. F. Munro, *Journal of African History*, VII (1966), 313–42.

[12] *East African Standard*, 6 Apr. 1917, quoted by Savage and Munro, *Journal of African History*, VII (1966), 314.

[13] Lettow-Vorbeck, *Reminiscences*, 30.

found their communications close to collapse.[14] Thus, in West Africa the forces of Britain and Germany in the Cameroons each employed a force of about 40,000 carriers.[15] In East Africa the distances were greater, and the numbers grew accordingly. The British recruited over a million labourers for the campaign.[16] They were drawn from a vast area, from the eastern Belgian Congo, Ruanda, Uganda, Kenya, German East Africa, Northern Rhodesia, Nyasaland, and the northern areas of Mozambique. The district commissioner of Tanganyika, an area where both sides had recruited labour, reported that a third of the taxable male population had been taken.[17] For the East African and other theatres, the British West African colonies provided over 57,500 carriers, twice as many as they did soldiers, and in 1917 Nigeria specifically had to procure 4,000 carriers a month.[18] British East Africa and Nyasaland each raised over 200,000 men (83 per cent of the total available manpower in the latter case), and Uganda 190,000. The Belgian Congo drew in 260,000 porters during the war, both for domestic and external needs; Portuguese East Africa contributed 30,000 porters to the British and 90,000 to its own forces.[19]

Such numbers could not be raised voluntarily. Most were impressed, either directly or indirectly. Chiefs would undertake to provide quotas. In British East Africa settler pressure to maximize the available labour supply led in 1915 to conscription. Desertion was therefore endemic. A convoy dispatched from Bangui in French Equatorial Africa in September 1914 had only forty-nine of its original complement of 298 porters left when it arrived at Boda.[20] One solution, adopted on this particular route but practicable only where the lines of communication were clear and local manpower abundant, was to fix the stages between villages so that the porters could return home each night. The alternative and more frequently applied check to desertion was to remove the porter from his native locality, and thus eliminate the temptation to abscond. But, once away from his own area, the carrier became prey to disease, the second major cause of high losses.

The carriers chosen by headmen were frequently those who were locally dispensable, and probably the less fit. Distant from their own homelands, they were often issued with rations with which they were unfamiliar. Many Europeans thought that mealie meal, made up of maize flour and cobs, was the standard African diet. In reality, maize was only just being introduced in

[14] Gorges, *Great War in West Africa*, 203; Purschel, *Kaiserliche Schütztruppe*, 28; Ministère de la guerre, *Armées françaises*, IX, 2ᵉ vol., 540–4.

[15] Mentzel, *Kämpfe in Kamerun*, 45; Gorges, *Great War in West Africa*, 203.

[16] Hodges in Page (ed.), *Africa*, 148.

[17] Killingray, *Journal of Contemporary History*, XXIV (1989), 489.

[18] Killingray and Matthews, *Canadian Journal of African Studies*, XIII (1979), 10; Osuntokun, *Nigeria*, 252.

[19] Hodges, *Journal of African History*, XIX (1978), 101–16; Belgique, Ministère de la Défense Nationale, *Campagnes coloniales belges*, i. 34; Pélissier, *Mozambique*, ii. 684–5.

[20] Ministère de la Guerre, *Armées françaises*, IX, 2ᵉ vol., 141.

inland areas. Ugandans subsisted on bananas, sweet potatoes, and beans. Fed on grain, they developed intestinal diseases and 40 per cent of the contingent raised in August 1914 were invalided within three months. In March 1917 Uganda focused its recruiting efforts on grain-eating tribes, but could pass only 5,763 of 41,706 called up as fit for service. Rice-eating tribes given maize fell victim to beri-beri. Even for those accustomed to mealie meal, the problems of its preparation undermined its nutritional value. In the porters' villages food was prepared by women. The men, therefore, lacked culinary skills. However, on the march they were expected to cook their own food. Mealie meal had to be boiled for one and a half hours, and the largest size of pot required six hours. The halts at night were too brief to allow sufficient wood to be collected for the fire, and for the food to be dried and properly cooked. Dysentery was the consequence: it was responsible for half the porters' hospital admissions, and intestinal diseases of all sorts for half the fatalities.[21] Finally, the nutritional content of the porters' diet was often inadequate. Porters in British pay in the Cameroons received daily rations on two scales, either 2,702 or 1,741 calories: neither was sufficient for a man expected to carry up to 60 pounds for 24 kilometres a day. In East Africa in 1917 porters were getting less than 1,000 calories a day.[22]

Wastage levels were enormous. Among East and West Africans employed as carriers in the war the death rate (including those reported as missing) was—at about 20 per cent—similar to that of an army on a so-called major front.[23] Belgian porters succumbed in comparable numbers, which were five times those suffered by the native soldiers—or askaris—in Belgian service.[24] Many more were invalided, victims of ulcerated feet, malaria, and chest infections. Of 20,000 porters sent to the Cameroons by the British, 574 died and 8,219 were invalided.[25] The West African carriers in East Africa, after nine months service, could muster only 37 per cent effectives in the case of southern Nigerians and 8.3 per cent in that of northern Nigerians.[26]

Thus, a series of interlocking problems kept the lines of communication constantly on the verge of breakdown. Better provision for the care of carriers reduced death and disease, and so eased the demands for fresh recruitment. But it also threatened to place the personal needs of the porter ahead of those of the fighting troops. The longer the line of march, the more likely would the porters be to consume larger loads than they carried. Assuming an average ration of 3 pounds per day and a load of 60 pounds, a line of communication of

[21] Hodges, *Carrier corps*, 119–30; Lucas, *Empire at war*, iv. 236–8.
[22] Killingray and Matthews, *Canadian Journal of African Studies*, XIII (1979), 17–18.
[23] Hodges in Page (ed.), *Africa*, 143–4; Killingray, *Journal of Contemporary History*, XXIV (1979), 493; Lucas, *Empire at war*, iv. 214–15.
[24] Belgique, *Campagnes coloniales belges*, iii. 268.
[25] Moberly, *Togoland and Cameroons*, 427.
[26] Killingray and Matthews, *Canadian Journal of African Studies*, XIII (1979), 18.

ten daily marches needed as many porters as there were soldiers in the front line. A march of three weeks and the porter consumed his entire load himself.[27] Thus, there was a trade-off between the porter's own nutrition and the needs of the soldier, both in food and munitions.

Compromise had also to be sought in determining the European component of the forces engaged. Both sides were firmly convinced that the morale of their troops depended on the presence of white officers who were known to their men. But each British officer in East Africa needed between seven and nine porters. Such a ratio was not unusual: a Belgian officer had eight porters, and a German officer in West Africa had four to six porters, a servant, and a cook. The French scoffed at what they saw as luxurious over-provision. In the Cameroons two Frenchmen were reckoned to require three porters.[28] In reality such proportions were a reflection of the cavalier French approach to supply problems, not an indication of French immunity to the hazards of war in the tropics. Even in the final stages of their epic march through Portuguese East Africa, the Europeans in Lettow-Vorbeck's force were allowed three porters each.[29]

Disease, not battle, disabled armies in Africa. Thanks to the elimination of typhus and cholera, the armies fighting the war in Europe were the first to suffer more casualties through combat than through sickness. Outside Europe the old order prevailed. In East Africa 3,156 whites in British service died; 2,225 of these were victims of disease.[30] But the true scale of the problem is revealed by reference to non-fatalities: men fell sick rather than died. In West Africa the allied forces lost a total of 4,600 men through death or wounding in action or through death by disease; by contrast, over 35,000 cases were admitted to hospital.[31] Casualty evacuation was therefore another load for the hard-pressed carrier.

The conventional wisdom argued that not only was the European more reliant on the maintenance of the lines of communication, he was also less immune to local diseases. Of the vulnerability of whites, particularly in East Africa, there is abundant evidence. On 31 October 1915 one British battalion had 836 of its strength in hospital and only 278 in the field. By the end of 1916 12,000 out of 20,000 South Africans had been invalided home.[32] The 2nd Rhodesia Regiment, whose effective strength was 800 men, was often reduced to 100, and had a wastage rate of 20 per cent per month.[33] Malaria was the

---

[27] Lucas, *Empire at war*, iv. 269–70, 292–3; Fendall, *East African Force*, 206–7.
[28] Charbonneau, *Revue militaire française*, 129 (mars 1932), 412–15; Student, *Kameruns Kampf*, 171; Belgique, *Campagnes coloniales belges*, i. 33.
[29] Deppe, *Mit Lettow-Vorbeck*, 108.
[30] War Office, *Statistics of the military effort*, 302.
[31] Gorges, *Great War in West Africa*, 261–2.
[32] Charles Miller, *Battle for the Bundu*, 139, 233.
[33] McLaughlin, *Ragtime soldiers*, 41, 46.

principal cause of sickness: it resulted in 50,768 hospital admissions among the British forces in East Africa between June and December 1916. But it was not the most fatal of illnesses: only 263 deaths resulted, whereas 3,795 of the 8,902 admitted with dysentery succumbed.[34]

The argument that therefore campaigns in Africa should be fought by those native to the continent was not the straightforward solution it seemed. The health problems of the porters provide abundant evidence to the contrary. In the Cameroons, of the British forces 151 out of 864 white soldiers were invalided through sickness, and 434 out of 5,927 Africans; the French figures similarly showed only a marginal health advantage in favour of the native.[35] In East Africa African soldiers in British service suffered 1,377 deaths through combat as against 2,923 from disease.[36] In some respects the medical problems of the African were different from those of the European. His bare feet were vulnerable to jiggers, and 40 per cent of the West African Frontier Force were lame by the end of the Cameroons campaign.[37] One German doctor thought typhus, smallpox, meningitis, and sleeping sickness were all more dangerous to blacks than to whites.[38] The Europeans were convinced that the Africans enjoyed a relative immunity from malaria, or that they suffered it less acutely. But an African from a malaria-free region was no less vulnerable than a European if moved to an area where the illness was endemic. The migration of so many Africans out of their native localities exposed them to fresh infections, and the physical and psychological demands lowered their resistance to disease. By the same token, those fighting in or close to their own homelands proved more hardy. The health of the German forces in the Cameroons, most of them native to the area, held up remarkably well through eighteen months of campaigning. They were lucky, in that they had just taken delivery of a year's worth of medical supplies when war broke out. But the efforts to treat the sick as far as possible within their own companies showed the Germans' recognition of the value of familiarity in the morale of the patient.[39]

In aggregate, the fitness of the soldiers in Africa bore a direct relationship to the efficiency of the supply system and to the provision of satisfactory medical arrangements. The French were negligent in both respects, and paid the penalty. In the Cameroons expeditionary force, the French contingent had four medical officers; the comparably sized British contingent had twenty-seven. The French sickness rate was just over double that of the British.[40] The Germans were not slow to attribute their relatively good health in the West

[34] Mitchell and Smith, *Medical services: casualties*, 259.
[35] Moberly, *Togoland and Cameroons*, 427.
[36] War Office, *Statistics of the military effort*, 302.
[37] Lucas, *Empire at war*, iv. 66, 118.
[38] Deppe, *Mit Lettow-Vorbeck*, 154.
[39] Purschel, *Kaiserliche Schütztruppe*, 81–3.
[40] Moberly, *Togoland and Cameroons*; Charbonneau, *Revue militaire française*, 129 (mars 1932), 419–20.

African campaign to their having sufficient doctors, allowing them to allocate one per company. To do less was false economy. A sick soldier undermined the efforts of the porters to supply that soldier; a sick porter starved the soldier and rendered him less robust; casualty evacuation consumed more labour; and manpower losses through preventable causes increased the demands on a fast-diminishing pool of available men.

The difficulties of supply, rather than the experiences of battle, did most to disseminate the impact of the Great War throughout the African continent. The numbers who experienced combat were few. The war in Africa was an affair not of 'big battalions' but of individual companies. A unit any larger than 100 to 120 men could not be readily supplied. Moreover, a company with its attendant porters mustered about 300 men and on the tracks of the equatorial rain forests of Central Africa constituted a column 1,500 to 2,000 yards long; a formation any bigger was, too large for effective, tactical control. The force-to-space ratio was, therefore, totally different from that of the western front. Small-scale actions in Africa settled the balance of power in territories as big as a whole theatre of operations in Europe.

One of the most striking differences was the almost total absence of artillery. Individually, heavy guns proved of value in the open grasslands of the northern Cameroons or northern Tanganyika. But collectively, guns had little opportunity. Even where draught animals were more readily available, in South-West Africa, the Germans were not able to turn a relative strength to advantage. Oxen moved slowly, and not at all in the midday heat. Mules were used for the transport of pack guns, but the lack of clear paths through the bush meant that they could take twice as long to cover the same distance as did the foot-soldier. Thus, the guns tended to arrive too late. In theatres where the tsetse fly ruled out animal draught, 300 porters could be required for a single field gun,[41] without considering its likely shell consumption. In the jungle, even a small-calibre mountain gun firing at a high trajectory needed a clearing of 100 yards, as well as good telephone communications with forward observers, for indirect fire.[42] Because none of the European powers had planned to fight each other, the guns possessed by each colony tended to be of varying calibres, obsolescent, and short of ammunition. In the Cameroons the Germans had fourteen guns of different types and 3,000 rounds.[43] When used, their moral impact, particularly on black troops unaccustomed to artillery fire however light, outstripped their destructive effect. Fighting in Africa was therefore predominantly an infantry affair, the machine-gun being the heaviest and most significant weapon regularly deployed.

[41] Charbonneau, *Revue militaire française*, 129 (mars 1932), 404–5; Beadon, *Royal Army Service Corps*, ii. 296; Deppe, *Mit Lettow-Vorbeck*, 250–4.
[42] Haywood and Clarke, *Royal West African Frontier Force*, 272–3.
[43] Mentzel, *Kämpfe im Kamerun*, 18.

Thus, the individual was not tyrannized, as he was on the western front, by the industrialization of warfare. The division between war and exploration, between the dangers of the bullet and the snakebite, was unclear in many of the pre-1914 imaginings of the war: both were antidotes to bourgeois decadence. In Africa, unlike Europe, the distinction could remain obscure. A single cruiser, SMS *Königsberg*, whose contribution to the balance of forces in the North Sea would have been negligible, acquired in East Africa a significance out of all proportion to her firepower. Her lair in the Rufiji delta was discovered by Pieter Pretorius, a big-game hunter whose skills and courage would have been, relatively speaking, nugatory in the trenches of Ypres or the Somme. Another big-game hunter, F. C. Selous, joined the 25th battalion, the Royal Fusiliers, the so-called Legion of Frontiersmen. His reputation as a naturalist and explorer was embroidered with stories that extended back to his schooldays at Rugby. His death in action in East Africa on 4 January 1917, at the age of 65, was of a piece with his entire life, not at odds with it; few other subalterns were as lucky.

The experience of Pretorius or of Selous was directly relevant. The major problems of the opposing sides were geographically determined. The Royal Navy knew that the *Königsberg* was at Salale from signals intercepts, but Salale was not marked on the navy's charts; eleven days elapsed in late October 1914 before it was identified as being on the Rufiji.[44] Cursed with inadequate maps, intelligence efforts were devoted as much to establishing the nature of the country and its resources as to learning the enemy's whereabouts and strength. Both the climate, with its switch from dry to rainy seasons, and the insect life, with its impact on the health of livestock and humans, were strategically decisive. East Africa was home to the anopheles mosquito, the tsetse fly, the jigger flea, the spirillum tick, the white ant, the scorpion, the poisonous spider, the wild bee, and the warrior ant. The range of larger fauna provided more than an exotic backdrop to the fighting. Soldiers, if sick or sleeping, were liable to be eaten by lions or hyenas; both elephants and rhinoceroses were known to attack patrols, with fatal consequences. On the other hand, game provided an important supplement to the diet, hippopotamuses and elephants in particular being shot for their fat.

Although fought between European powers for objectives that were also European, the African campaigns of the First World War bore more relationship to the nineteenth-century campaigns of colonial conquest than they did to the Great War itself. In relation to the outcome of the war they were, as is too often remarked, sideshows. But neither observation should be allowed to trivialize their importance. The first demonstrates the danger of characterizing the war in terms appropriate to only one theatre, even one not fitted to the entire geographical span of the war. The second judges Africa in terms of that

---

[44] Yates, *Graf Spee's raiders*, 249–59.

one theatre, instead of recognizing that relatively the impact of the war on the dark continent was as great as that on Europe, that few black families were unaffected, and that at the end the transfer of territory completed the partition of Africa commenced four decades earlier.

TOGOLAND

The first Entente victory of the war was the fruit, not of central staff planning, but of improvised action at the local level. The seizure of German Togoland was in perfect consonance with the objectives set out by the subcommittee of the Committee of Imperial Defence at its meeting in London on 5 August 1914—it employed only local forces, and it eliminated Germany's single most important overseas wireless station, that at Kamina, linking Nauen with Germany's other African colonies, with shipping in the South Atlantic, and with South America. However, both the initiation of the British attack and the rapidity of its execution were due primarily to Captain F. C. Bryant, temporarily commanding the Gold Coast Regiment in the absence on leave of both its senior officers.[45]

The main focus of the defensive plan for the Gold Coast was the protection of its north-eastern frontier, and of the navigation of the Lower Volta. Its offensive options included the possibility of pushing across the Volta into Togoland, isolating the north, and then swinging south, meeting a second and subsidiary thrust moving eastwards along the coast from Ada to Lome. The plan had been last revised in May 1913. It made no provision for French co-operation from Dahomey, to the east of Togoland, and, more importantly, it antedated the completion in June 1914 of the Kamina wireless station. That its basic thrust, the defence of the Gold Coast, should be abandoned in 1914 in favour of an attack on Kamina was not in dispute. Brigadier-General C. M. Dobell, inspector-general of the West African Frontier Force, and fortuitously in London on leave, told the subcommittee of the Committee of Imperial Defence that Lome and Kamina were the only worthwhile objectives in Togoland. But Dobell was disposed to caution. Although Lome was just over a kilometre from Togoland's frontier with the Gold Coast, Dobell regarded that as a sufficient advance for the time being, and even made it conditional on the presence of a naval escort.

---

[45] The best narratives of operations are Lucas, *Empire at war*, iv. 3; Moberly, *Togoland and Cameroons*, ch. 1; Sebald, *Togo 1884–1914*, 593–605; Haywood and Clarke, *Royal West African Frontier Force*, 97–104. On Bryant's role and plans, see Grove, *Army Quarterly*, CVI (1976), 308–23; Ekoko, *Journal of Strategic Studies*, VII (1984), 440–56.

Events on the ground outstripped such calculations. The Gold Coast Regiment mobilized on 31 July, three days ahead of Britain's general mobilization. Bryant shifted the axis of its deployment from the north-eastern frontier to the south, concentrating three companies at Kumasi and two at Ada. On 4 August the French, on Togoland's other flank, prepared to implement their plan, also drawn up in ignorance both of their ally's intentions and of Kamina's existence, for a westward advance along the coast to Lome, beginning in the evening of 6 August. Bryant's energy was attributable as much to his desire to forestall any independent French initiatives as to a lust for battle.

The prospects confronting the Germans in Togoland were not encouraging. Their colony, a thin strip stretching inland from a coastline only 51 kilometres long, was bounded on all its frontiers by enemy territory. No regular soldiers were available for its defence; the garrison consisted of 152 paramilitary police, supplemented by 416 local police and 125 border guards; they had four machine-guns, only fourteen of the 1898-pattern rifles, and otherwise relied on the 1871-pattern *Jäger* carbine.[46] The governor was on leave. The first step, therefore, of his deputy, Major von Doering, was to propose neutrality to his British and French neighbours.

The Congo act, ratified by the Treaty of Berlin in 1885, allowed any power within the Congo basin to declare itself neutral. However, its provisions did not extend so far from the Congo itself. The basis for Doering's suggestion was not international law, but the self-interest of the white colonial powers of West Africa. The economic interdependence of the three belligerents was obvious. For the British colonies, Germany was the major purchaser of their palm kernels, and was strongly represented in the trading houses and shipping arrangements of Nigeria and of the Gold Coast; for French West Africa, Germany had become between 1910 and 1914 its fastest-growing export market, and was particularly strong in Togoland's neighbour, Dahomey.[47] But von Doering's bid rested less on common commercial grounds than on German worries about the loyalty of their black subjects. Thus, instead of playing to the Entente's weakness, he highlighted its strength. Britain's local reputation as a benevolent colonial administration was a powerful incentive to Entente belligerence, not to neutrality. Bryant, although restrained by W. C. F. Robertson, the acting governor of the Gold Coast (another whose superior was on leave), even wanted to arm the Ashanti and foment insurrection on the Gold Coast—Togoland border. Thus, appeals on the basis of white

---

[46] Reichsarchiv, *Weltkrieg*, ix. 466. German strengths are variously given; Schwarte, *Weltkampf*, iv. 360, has 400 effectives; Sebald, *Togo*, has 500, rising to 1,000 on mobilization; Haywood and Clarke, *Royal West African Frontier Force*, 98, manage to find 1,500.

[47] Killingray, *Journal of African History*, XIX (1978), 43, 54; Osuntokun, *Nigeria*, 22–4; Crowder, 'The 1914–1918 European war and West Africa', 503; Lucas, *Empire at war*, iv. 21; Michel, *L'Appel à l'Afrique*, 147–8.

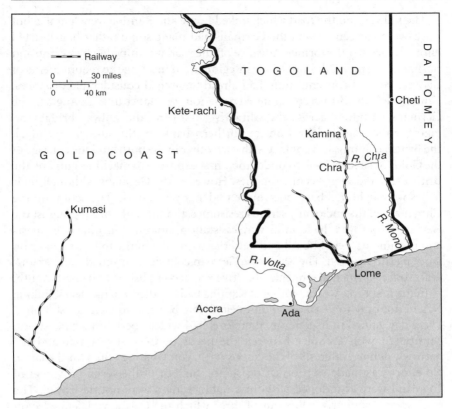

MAP 18. TOGOLAND

supremacy were not calculated to restrain the British or the French. Von Doering's bid for neutrality was seen for what it was—a reflection of German weakness.

Bryant's response to the French initiatives and to the German plea was unequivocal. Without consulting Robertson, let alone London, he sent an emissary to Lome on 6 August to demand the surrender of Togoland. Von Doering signalled to Berlin that he planned to abandon the defenceless Lome and the territory 110 kilometres to its north, and to fall back inland to Kamina. Dispatched by wireless in clear, the intercepted German message justified Bryant's impetuosity. On 9 August the Colonial Office, assured of French co-operation, allowed Bryant to attack Kamina. On 12 August two companies of the Gold Coast Regiment took possession of Lome. It was the decisive step of the campaign. The harbour at Lome enabled Bryant to concentrate fourteen days sooner than if he had been confined to land routes.

The railway and the road which linked Lome and Kamina were 'parallel but not always adjacent',[48] and the Germans had made some rather half-hearted efforts to destroy the former. Advance off the road was impeded by swamp and bush. Furthermore, the Gold Coast Regiment, in meeting the requirements of Bryant's revised concentration, had already marched considerable distances. Nonetheless, the British encountered no serious resistance until 22 August. The Germans withdrew across the Chra river, blowing the railway bridge and taking up strong positions on its northern bank. In the subsequent attack the British columns lost contact with each other in the bush, and the courage of the Gold Coast forces wilted under their first exposure to machine-gun fire: the British suffered 17 per-cent casualties. However, the Germans, although their losses were light, fell back once more under cover of dark. The action on the Chra marked the end of any serious resistance. On the night of 24/5 August the Germans destroyed the Kamina wireless station, smashing its nine huge masts and burning its switchboard and batteries with oil. On the following day von Doering surrendered. The war in the German colonies continued for over four years, but its principal strategic objective was accomplished in its first month.

In the first three weeks of August Kamina had handled 229 messages, linking Nauen not only to German colonies elsewhere but also to German shipping. Every day gained in its defence, therefore, had wider operational effects. But, confronted with a choice between the needs of Germany at war and the narrowly defined interests of the colony itself, von Doering opted for the latter. No effort was made to protract resistance. Six out of the seven provinces of Togoland were abandoned without a fight. Bridges were not destroyed. The Chra was the only river line out of three which the Germans defended. Von Doering interpreted the instructions to protect Kamina in the most literal terms: he held its perimeter, not its outworks. And even then the British captured there three machine-guns, 1,000 rifles, and 320,000 rounds, enough for several days' continued resistance.[49]

Manpower was a problem. The wireless operators, newly arrived and quartered inland, constituted an enclave with which the settler population did not identify. Over the three weeks of hostilities von Doering's strength had probably doubled from its peacetime establishment; he had 300 German residents available, including 200 who were reservists, and he had compulsorily recruited native levies during the course of his retreat from Lome. However, the Kamina position was still too extensive for the number of troops available. Furthermore, the Germans' military commander, Captain Georg Pfähler, had been killed in action on 16 August. Von Doering took counsel of his fears. He almost certainly exaggerated the strength of Bryant's force, whose only marked advantage in relation to his own lay in its possession of three 2.95-inch mountain guns. But,

---

[48] Lucas, *Empire at war*, iv. 29.   [49] Klein-Arendt, *Kamina ruft Nauen*, 265–74.

having failed to strike Bryant early, von Doering was confronted with converging forces of greater numbers. To the west a British force was moving on Kamina from Kete-Krachi, and to the east a French column from Cheti. Further Entente forces, mostly French irregulars, were pushing into northern Togoland. Thus, the defence of Kamina could only have been protracted for a matter of days. The maintenance of resistance in the bush, the primary objective having been lost, held no appeal for the deputy- governor; he could not be sure of native support, and its effects would be likely to set back the economic benefits of colonialism. Von Doering's less-than-vigorous defence and his expeditious surrender were thus of a piece with initial hopes for neutrality.

THE CAMEROONS

Germany's second West African colony, the Cameroons, was, like Togoland, bounded by the possessions of its enemies. Along the length of its north-western border, from the Atlantic to Lake Chad, lay British Nigeria. From Chad southward to the Congo, and then back westwards to the ocean, stretched the expanses of French Equatorial Africa. Only the rectangular slab of Muni or Spanish Guinea, stuck like a postage stamp in the bottom left-hand corner of German territory, and the offshore island of Fernando Po, also a Spanish possession, broke the German sense of isolation. Spanish neutrality was to prove a major boon to German defences.

The bulk of German development lay in the west, on the Atlantic littoral, with the hill-station of Buea, and the ports and wireless masts of Victoria and, above all, Duala. In 1914 two major railway lines were under construction; one to the north-east, destined for Lake Chad, had reached Nkongsamba, and the other south and east, bound for Jaunde, was complete as far as Eseka. But if the bulk of European infrastructure lay on the coast, the heart of the Cameroons itself was inland. In the north a line of mountains, parallel with the Nigerian frontier, formed a plateau, covered in tall elephant grass, free of the tsetse fly, and favourable to livestock; its major feature, Mount Cameroon, lay some 5,000 metres above sea level as a symbolic barrier to the west. To the south the highlands fell away to the central rivers, the Sanga and the Njong. Below them, and as far as the French border, lay jungle and swamp, an area whose rivers, notably the Sanaga, fed the Congo. In 1911 French concessions after the second Moroccan crisis had extended Germany's frontiers to the south-east, at one point to the Ubangi, at Singa, and at another to the Congo itself, at Bonga. Thus, of the 480,000 square kilometres of German territory, the coastal strip was but a small fraction, and effectively as isolated from the interior to its east as it itself was by the sea to its west.

Germany's pre-war thinking about the defence of its colony had shifted focus in accordance with its own advance. The recent settlement of its inland frontiers—1911 with France, and (in matters of detail) 1913 with Britain—had been accompanied by the problems of pacification (barely completed in some areas) and incorporation (still under way in the Congo territory in 1914). The navy, although happy to have Duala as a base for cruiser operations in the South Atlantic, was prepared neither to produce the funds to fortify it nor provide the ships to protect it. The general view in the Colonial Office was that international agreement would provide no better defence. The Congo act embraced the eastern and south-eastern Cameroons, but for the French and British to remain neutral on one front, so allowing the Germans to concentrate on the north, seemed improbable. The logical conclusion, to rest the defence of the colony on its own forces, the *Schütztruppen*, and to conduct it from the interior of the country, was not, however, an easy step. The governor, Ebermaier, was averse to using black troops in a white man's war; his military commander thought that, given the vulnerability of the Cameroons' extended frontiers, sustained resistance would be impossible if the colony's link with Germany through Duala was not kept open. Therefore, only reluctantly, with a renewal in 1913 of the decision not to spend money fortifying Duala, did the local authorities begin to reckon on defending the colony from the interior.[50]

The plan, drawn up on 24 November 1913, and to provide the basis of German operations until mid-1915, chose as its focus not Duala but Ngaundere, in the centre of the northern highlands. The south, however impenetrable to the invader, was not considered because its climate was poor and it lacked the agricultural resources of the northern plateau. Four of the twelve companies of *Schütztruppen* were to be based on Ngaundere, three at Bertua to the east of Jaunde, two (plus the police training company) at Jaunde, and three at Bamenda in the north-west. Thus the central and northern plateau of the Cameroons, naturally defended by mountains to the north, by jungle and swamp to the south, was to become an inner bastion. The loss of the coastal

---

[50] The basic premisses of German strategy, which have almost entirely eluded English-language authors, are spelt out by Mentzel, *Die Kämpfe in Kamerun* (1936), 25–34, and are also to be found in Reichsarchiv, *Weltkrieg*, ix. 470–2. Mentzel's is the most sensible overview of the campaign in any language; his earlier survey (1932) is also suggestive, but brief. The fullest (as well as most critical) operational account is the French official history, Ministère de la Guerre, *Les Armées françaises*, IX, 2ᵉ vol.; the British official history, Moberly, *Togoland and Cameroons*, focuses on British operations but fails to provide a wider context; Student, *Kameruns Kampf*, the most detailed German account, has the same defect. On the tactics of bush war, see Purschel, *Kaiserliche Schütztruppe für Kamerun*, and Charbonneau, *Revue militaire française*, 129 (mars 1932), 397–420, and 130 (avril 1932), 80–99. Memoirs, helpful but posing as more objective accounts, include Aymérich, *Conquête du Cameroun*, and Gorges, *Great War in West Africa*. Haywood and Clarke, *Royal West African Frontier Force*, ch. 4, and Osuntokun, *Nigeria*, ch. 6, are both valuable. The only recent English-language survey, Farwell, *Great War in Africa*, is bounded by the Anglocentric concerns of Moberly and Gorges. Michel, *Guerres mondiales et conflits contemporains*, 168 (1992), 13–29, is helpful; Nouzille, *Revue internationale d'histoire militaire*, 63 (1985), 9–20, is disappointing.

strip or France's reconquest of the territories forfeited in 1911 would not represent setbacks of strategic significance. The Germans in the Cameroons intended to conduct a defence sufficiently protracted to ensure that when the hostilities in Europe came to an end Germany's claim to the colony would, at the peace talks, still be bolstered by possession. Thus, the stubborn resistance of the Cameroons was motivated not by any German desire to draw Entente troops from Europe, not by a wish to use a sideshow for a wider strategic purpose, but by the fact that colonization mattered as an end in itself.

The major implication of the 1913 plan was that the *Schütztruppen* were to defend the Cameroons against an external enemy. This was not a task for which they were either equipped or trained. The stated role of the *Schütztruppen* was to protect the white settlers, to maintain order, and to suppress slavery. Their total establishment was 205 white officers and NCOs and 1,650 blacks. When first formed, they had recruited from outside the Cameroons and from the coastal areas; by 1914, although 13 per cent of the askaris were still drawn from outside, the major recruiting area had become the central Cameroons, and in particular the district of Jaunde. Enlistment was voluntary, and the minimum term of service fixed at three years. In reality, most served for an average of five years, and some for much longer; the Germans feared that if warriors trained in the arts of war returned to their tribes when they were still militarily effective, any insurrection would benefit from their skills. The consequence of this concern was a body of men that, by the standards of its potential foes, was homogeneous and well-trained. The askari was accustomed to fighting superior numbers and winning by virtue of his discipline and his firepower. But the *Schütztruppen* also suffered from the weaknesses of regular, professional armies. The families of the men became part of the military establishment and accompanied those of more than two years' service on campaign. Morale was closely identified with the leadership of individual officers, bonds forged over time and not easy to replace in the event of casualties. And although the mobilization of reservists was allowed for in 1913, no reserve organization was in place in 1914.

Indeed, little had been done by 1914 to follow through the implications of the 1913 plan. Quality sustained the *Schütztruppen* in their domestic tasks; quantity would be at issue when facing the comparable forces of their European neighbours. France had 20,000 black troops in its West African and Equatorial colonies in August 1914;[51] Britain's West African Frontier Force (which encompassed Nigeria, the Gold Coast, Sierra Leone, and the Gambia) mustered 7,552 of all ranks.[52] Many of these formations were, like the Germans', committed to peacetime tasks, and would not be available for an

[51] Michel, *L'Appel à l'Afrique*, 42–3.
[52] War Office, *Statistics of the military effort*, 383.

expeditionary force to the Cameroons. Nonetheless, the most urgent need of the German government was to procure more men. The idea of the nation in arms became reality far sooner for the 2,000 white settlers than it did for their fellow-nationals at home; the incorporation of the police immediately doubled the Germans' strength to 3,200 black troops; the reservists were under arms by January 1915; and the maximum force achieved at any one time was 1,460 whites and 6,550 blacks, a total of thirty-four companies.

Two strains were generated by this quintupling of the armed forces. The first was persistent, but not ultimately decisive. Fully sixty-five of the *Schutztruppe's* German officers and NCOs were at home on leave in August 1914. The deficit was never made good. The addition of the police worsened it; for a peacetime strength comparable with that of the *Schütztruppen*, they had only thirty Germans. The European reservists did little to improve it. On mobilization they were formed into separate companies. The supply problems of purely European units robbed these companies of mobility, and thus of any utility after the loss of the coastal areas, and they were disbanded in 1915. But the dispersion of their members to other formations did not ease the demand for trained German officers. Most field companies in 1915 had only one or two European officers each, plus a medical officer and a couple more Europeans for each of the machine-guns (of which each company had three to four). Combat experience suggested an optimum would have been twelve to fifteen Germans per company.[53] In these circumstances the loss of a single German officer could have considerable repercussions.

The second strain was both persistent and decisive. Some effort was made to increase the firepower of the *Schütztruppen* in the light of the 1913 plan. The number of machine-guns, forty-three initially, rising to sixty, was probably sufficient given the limited fields of fire available in the enclosed territory of the equatorial rain forests. The issue of the 1898-pattern rifle, to replace the 1871 *Jäger* carbine, was expedited. But the process was not complete in 1914. The colony possessed 3,861 1898-pattern rifles and carbines, and 2,920 of the older patterns; there were 2.25 million rounds available for the former and for the machine-guns, and 500,000 rounds for the latter.[54] Therefore, only nine-tenths of the available men could be armed. By 1915 supplies of the 1898-pattern ammunition were having to be restricted to the use of machine-guns. The colony put in hand the manufacture of its own rifles and ammunition, but the performance of the latter served to undermine the askaris' faith in the former. The munitions factories established at Jaunde and Ebolowa were a tribute to German ingenuity, not least in view of the fact that all but one of the five munitions artificers in the colony had been captured by the

---

[53] Purschel, *Kaiserliche Schütztruppe*, 118–19; also 54–60.
[54] Ibid. 60–2; Mentzel, *Kämpfe in Kamerun* (1936), 18–19, and Student, *Kameruns Kampf*, 23, adopt these figures but Mentzel, *Kämpfe in Kamerun* (1932), 44, has different totals.

end of September 1914.[55] Spent cases were collected from the battlefield; percussion caps were manufactured from the brass plates worn by the inhabitants of the grasslands; black powder was made from sulphur, saltpetre, and charcoal, and when the saltpetre was exhausted nitroglycerine was extracted from stocks of dynamite: 800,000 rounds were produced in this way. But such ammunition could not be stored for long periods; frequently it would not enter the breech or got stuck in the barrel; when fired, the smoke identified the position of the firer, and the bullet itself rarely ranged more than twenty yards.[56]

Limited in men and munitions, restricted in objective to protracted defence, the Germans were constrained to adopt manners of fighting very different from those used either by the *Schütztruppen* in the past or by the armies of Europe on the western front. In essence, the askari now had to wage war as his tribal opponents had done. Before 1914 his task had been to bring a reluctant foe to battle; after 1914 his main endeavours were to avoid intense fighting, to limit his own casualties while inflicting losses on the enemy, and to give up ground rather than hold it. Close-order tactics based on the 1906 German infantry regulations were replaced by open order, frontal attack by all-round defence. Munitions shortages put a heavy emphasis on fire discipline and short-range combat, on surprise rather than fire-effect. The terrain, the force-to-space ratio, and the extended lines of communication of the British and French forces all suited the tactics of guerrilla warfare. The opportunities for outflanking the enemy or for threatening his rear were abundant, and envelopment was the normal mode of attack. Thus the defence was active, not static. But though the style of small wars became the means of fighting, position war remained at its core. The *Schütztruppen* were still committed to the protection of specific areas and their points of entry; river crossings, jungle clearings, and—in the north—the forts guarding the highland plateau were the scenes chosen by the Germans for their encounters with the enemy.

Ebermaier, however reluctant he may in origin have been to embrace this form of operations, became the heart and soul of its effective execution. The split between purely military exploitation of the colony's resources for the purposes of war, and the civilian defence of its peacetime advances and infrastructure, evident in East Africa and implicit in Togoland, never surfaced in the Cameroons. The overall strategy, to hold as much of the Cameroons for as long as possible, was one that harnessed military priorities to the objectives of German colonialism. Ebermaier's powers were enhanced, after the destruction of Kamina, by his isolation from Berlin. He was able to impose a

---

[55] Schoen, *Deutschen Feuerwerkswesens*, 1395–6.
[56] Student, *Kameruns Kampf*, 154–6, 286–7, is particularly graphic on these difficulties.

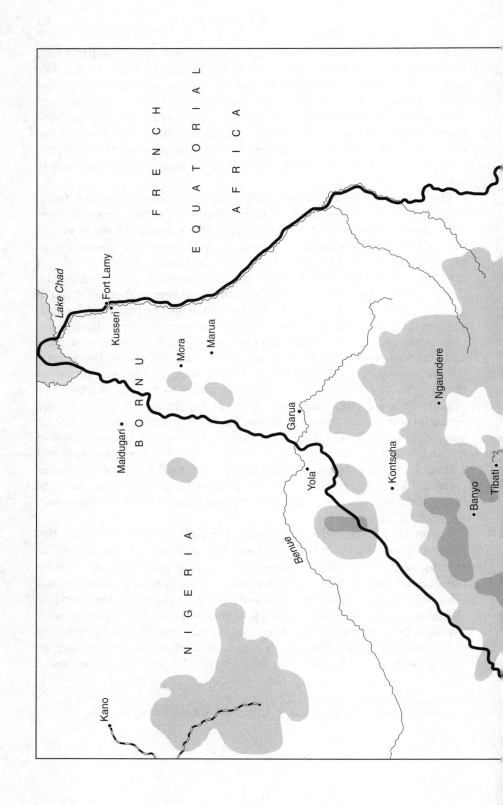

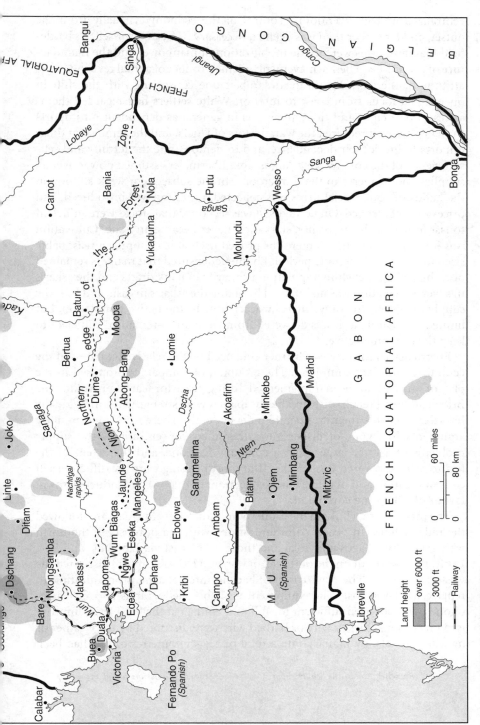

MAP 19. THE CAMEROONS

centralized and interventionist control of the economy virtually from the outset, and far earlier than was deemed necessary in Germany itself. Its battlefield manifestations were in the mobilization of manpower and the manufacture of munitions. Their achievement was the product of a total revision in the attitude of the German authorities, albeit one consonant with the shift in operational focus from coast to interior. White settlers had regarded themselves in particular and the Cameroons in general as dependent on imports from Germany. It required the war, the loss of Duala, and the removal of those imports to break their dependence, and to demonstrate the fertility and self-sufficiency of the colony. On 7 August 1914 Ebermaier assumed power over all supplies and property in the Cameroons. In the subsequent week all food in the hands of commercial firms was collected, rationing was introduced, and prices were controlled. On 14 August it was reckoned that stocks were sufficient to last four months. In reality, starvation never became an issue. Cultivation was intensified, and the Cameroons proved itself able to supply a reasonably sized force for an indefinite period. Ebermaier ensured that markets remained open by paying the white population primarily in bank drafts and the askaris in silver. Circulation was maintained by taxing the askaris in cash, and thus the supply of silver—the only currency acceptable to the native population, but limited in quantity as it was delivered from Germany—remained sufficient to keep the economy active.[57]

Ebermaier's authority was further enhanced by the relative weakness of the centralized military command. The grouping of companies proposed in the plan of 1913 had not been implemented during peace for fear of provoking the British and the French. Instead, the companies were strengthened individually in order to enable them to operate independently. There were good military arguments in favour of dispersion rather than concentration—the supply problems of a force larger than a company was one, and the extent of the territory to be covered was another. But most pressing were the difficulties of communication and of intelligence-collection, both powerful inducements in favour of delegating command.

The main internal links in the Cameroons radiated from Duala and followed the railway lines. In peace, communications with the outposts in the north were relayed via Lagos and Yola, and those in the east via Libreville and Fort Lamy. Both were cut on the outbreak of war, and Duala's capture disrupted the western network. The *Schütztruppen* had no integral signals organization to replace what was lost. The equipment available, heliographs and field telephones, was not even sufficient for full unit contact at the local level; improvised links using chicken wire or barbed wire were disrupted by the weather or by wild animals. By January 1916 a total of 2,435 kilometres of line had been

---

[57] Purschel, *Kaiserliche Schütztruppe*, 30–1, 76–80; Student, *Kameruns kampf*, 153–9.

created, and the equipment was salvaged and re-erected as the Germans withdrew.[58] But the main signals system was a series of posts communicating by flag. Messages travelled slowly—about 50 kilometres a day—and without security.

Intelligence was hard to gather, and when obtained tended to be of immediate relevance only. The terrain was too enclosed to make reconnaissance easy. The problems in assessing information provided by the local population—that they saw all bodies of troops as enemies, that they often could not count, and that they tended to say what they thought the hearer wanted them to say— applied also to reports from the askaris themselves. Therefore Europeans were used to reconnoitre, but their inability to move as discreetly as the natives meant that fighting patrols were the norm. Thus, the Germans knew if the British and French planned to attack; what they could not so easily do was form an overall idea of their purposes or of the distribution of their forces.

Without adequate communications or sufficient up-to-date intelligence command from the centre was impossible. Furthermore, the maps were poor and on too small a scale (1:300,000) to enable detailed orders to be based upon them alone. Zimmerman, who had succeeded to the command of the *Schütztruppen* in April 1914, was condemned to being a frustrated spectator. He had no chief of staff, and therefore he could not abandon his headquarters for a visit to one of the fronts. The problems diminished as the Germans were pushed inwards and their front contracted. But even then Zimmerman could not direct the operations in the north, the defence of the forts of Mora, Garua, and Banyo, which screened Ngaundere. And so a tension arose between the pivot of his strategy and the fact that his own effectiveness was greater in the centre and the east. The only easement open to him was to create an intermediate level of command, as had been intended in 1913. Six battalion-sized formations (*Abteilungsverbande*) were established—one each in the north, the west (covering the southern Nigerian frontier), the south, the south-east, and the east, and one placed centrally at Jaunde. Significantly, this distribution put the weight in the east and not in the west. However, for all his problems, Zimmerman had two major advantages over his opponents. First, he was operating on interior lines, and thus could switch companies between each *Abteilung* and, as became necessary in 1915, merge those in the north and west and those in the south and south-east. Secondly, his command structure was nationally homogeneous.

The key to understanding the course of the Cameroons campaign is to appreciate how imperfectly the British and French understood these intentions of the Germans. Neither power had anticipated offensive operations in West Africa, neither power had formed a plan for the conquest of the

[58] Klein-Arendt, *Kamina ruft Nauen*, 274.

Cameroons, and thus neither power had set about building up the intelligence necessary to the conduct of a campaign there. A major windfall for the British was the capture of a large stock of German maps of the Cameroons from a liner in the Atlantic.[59] The French in the south-east had to wait until the fall of Molundu on 22 December 1914 for a similar stroke of luck.[60] But in general the problems of acquiring intelligence during the campaign were as great as, if not greater than, they were for the Germans. The ignorance of the German strengths, dispositions, and strategy was still virtually complete when the official histories came to be written.[61] Moreover, the strategy of each of the Entente powers was determined by its own national considerations. Thus, particularly for the first year of the war, the three major belligerents in the Cameroons provided an extraordinary spectacle, the French and British pursuing divergent objectives, and neither of them striking the Germans sufficiently hard at the points where they could be hurt.

The priorities of Joseph Aymérich, the military commander of French Equatorial Africa, were defensive. But French plans had been thrown into confusion in the south-east Cameroons, where additional territory had been ceded to Germany in settlement of the second Moroccan crisis in 1911. The two prongs of the German New Cameroons, extending to Singa and Bonga, split the French colony in three, and sat on the main means of internal communication, the Ubangi and Congo rivers. At Singa the French telegraph line between Brazzaville and Bangui passed over German territory for 12 kilometres. The length of the frontier (3,000 kilometres), and the dispersed and isolated nature of the French posts put a premium on efficient communications in order to enable French concentration and an effective defence. On 6 August, therefore, the French seized Singa and Bonga. Simultaneously Aymérich set about the formation of four columns designed to take the war into German territory. From the east, Morisson's column was to follow the course of the Lobaye river from its confluence with the Ubangi at Singa; the second, Hutin's, was to move from the south-east along the Sanga; the third, Le Meillour's, with its base in Gabon, was to push up from the south; and the fourth, Miquelard's, was to do the same, cutting the Cameroons from Muni.

War, therefore, arrived in the Cameroons as a result of local French initiatives. No orders to attack had been received from Paris; the Germans, their signals intercepted by the French, had heard from neither Duala nor Berlin, and frequently had no forewarning that hostilities had begun.

The confusion was prolonged by the desire of Belgium, master of all the eastern bank of the Congo and of its estuary with the sea, to preserve the neutrality of the Congo act. The British had no intention of observing

---

[59] Gorges, *Great War in West Africa*, 136.   [60] Aymérich, *Conquête*, 63.
[61] The only German source referred to by Moberly or Gorges is Schwarte, *Weltkampf*, iv. 377–85; Entente intelligence during the war had clearly provided little.

the act,[62] the Germans had no expectation that it would be. The Belgian initiative did not reflect the local interests of colonial government but was prompted from Europe, based on a desire to enforce Belgian neutrality there rather than in the Congo.[63] The effect was to hamstring French movements, and in particular to isolate Gabon from the rest of Equatorial Africa. The French noted that the Belgian governor had a German name, Fuchs. His replacement by a 'veritable Belge', Henry, coincided with a German attack on the Belgian Congo from East Africa.[64] On 28 August the reliance of Belgium on France in Europe was at last reciprocated by France's ability to rely on Belgium in Africa. Thereafter France's use of Belgian railways, rivers, and telegraph lines, as well as 600 Belgian troops with Hutin's column, proved vital to Aymérich's movements.

French operations against the Cameroons had thus assumed a momentum before they received a direction. In Paris the general staff had no plans for an offensive in West Africa. But M. Merlin, the governor-general of Equatorial Africa, home on leave like the other senior colonial administrators of the day, took the opportunity to concert his thinking with that of Gaston Doumergue, foreign minister until 26 August 1914 and colonial minister thereafter.

Both Merlin and Doumergue were convinced of the desirability of recovering the territory ceded in 1911. The war provided the opportunity not only to do so, but to go further—to eject the Germans from West Africa with British co-operation. The instructions which Merlin, therefore, delivered to Aymérich on his return to Africa on 15 September specified two objectives—one operational, to mount an offensive in the south and east, and so give indirect support to the British who would land at Duala; and the second political, to recover the ceded territory. However, the apparent congruity of these tasks, both with each other and with what Aymérich had already done, was unsustainable. The French offensive had already been commenced as an independent operation, and the impossibility of rapid communication with the British in the west would maintain that independence. Secondly, the fulfilment of the political objective gave the French attack an aim which was not secondary but primary.

While France's concerns were territorial, Britain's were maritime. The Admiralty wanted to deny the use of Duala's wireless station and port facilities to German cruisers. The irrelevance of territorial conquest was confirmed by Dobell, who in a memorandum of 3 August advised the Committee of Imperial Defence's subcommittee that the seizure of Buea, Victoria, and Duala would be sufficient to strangle the enemy. The attractiveness of Duala as the focus for

[62] Osuntokun, *Nigeria*, 173; Moberly, *Togoland and Cameroons*, 16.
[63] Belgique, *Campaignes coloniales belges*, i. 17–23; Aymérich, *Conquête*, 26–7.
[64] Michel, *Guerres mondiales et conflits contemporains*, 168 (1992), 13, 16.

British operations was confirmed by the Colonial Office's reports of black disaffection in the Cameroons. Although exaggerated, they were not without foundation for the coastal region, where British influence had dominated until 1884 and was still far from extinguished in 1914.[65] A plan to develop Duala as a white settlement by forcibly removing the black population had aroused the ire of Rudolf Bell, the German-educated paramount chief of the Duala. Bell was charged with high treason in May. Then a message to the French from Martin-Paul Samba of Ebolowa, announcing his intention to lead a revolt, was intercepted by the Germans. Both Bell and Samba were executed on 8 August. The Germans in Duala expended as much military effort in controlling the local population as in preparing to meet a British landing.[66]

The formation of the Cameroons expeditionary force took a month. A landward thrust from Nigeria towards Duala was rendered inadvisable by the nature of the intervening country. Therefore troops had to be collected along the West African coast, and the shipping assembled for a seaborne invasion. The interval allowed the completion of Togoland's conquest, and the consequent isolation of Duala from Germany by the destruction of the Kamina wireless.

On one level the Cameroons expeditionary force met Merlin's and Doumergue's objectives. It included a French contribution of 2,000 Senegalese from Dakar under the command of Colonel Mayer. Thus, of the total of 13,000 Entente forces deployed in the Cameroons, the majority (7,000) were French. The expeditionary force, therefore, served France's political objectives by enhancing its claim to be the dominant voice in the eventual partition of the Cameroons. But it did not serve the operational purposes relayed to Aymérich. The orders given Dobell, who was to command the force, were to seize Buea, Victoria, and Duala. He had no instructions to undertake the further conquest of the colony, and thus Merlin's idea of a reciprocating effect between Dobell's advance and Aymérich's was, at this stage, complete fantasy. From the outset of the war the War Office had recognized that the Germans were likely to continue their defence from the interior,[67] but not until 29 September did the CID subcommittee ask itself how Dobell could break off his attack at the coast. It concluded that he could not: to secure Duala, the conquest of the colony must be completed and more men would be required. But its recommendation to that effect was ignored by the government, both then and thereafter.[68] The original British strategy, to secure German ports and wireless stations, and to use only minimal local ground forces, remained valid well into 1915.

[65] Osuntokun, Nigeria, 177–8.
[66] Digre, Imperialism's new clothes, 23; Andreas Eckert, '"Verdammt seien die Deutschen!"', Die Zeit, 5 Aug. 1994, 58; Stoecker, German imperialism, 275.
[67] Osuntokun, Nigeria, 176–7.
[68] Moberly, Togoland and Cameroons, 71–2, 145, 215–16.

The contribution of the West African Frontier Force to the Duala expedition was limited to 2,500 men, because the primary concern of Britain's local forces in relation to the Cameroons was, like that of France, defensive. Furthermore, again like France although for different reasons, those defensive arrangements were in disarray.

On 1 January 1914 a new administrative structure, amalgamating the emir-dominated north and the largely acephalous south, had been imposed on Nigeria. The Nigeria Regiment contributed 70 per cent of the West African Frontier Force. When war broke out, the defensive scheme for Nigeria, revised in the light of the administrative and regimental amalgamation, was still in draft. The confusion was compounded by the fact that Sir Frederick Lugard, the colony's governor-general, had taken the only available copy home on leave. Moreover, neither it nor the regiment's primary tasks had prepared the latter for what it was now expected to do. Training, on Lugard's insistence, had been kept to company level; the main attention in dealing with an external threat had been to coastal defence, and the troops were therefore more adept at entrenching than at mobile operations. Like the *Schütztruppen*, they had no indigenous staff organization or technical services. It had been assumed that operations would be conducted within Nigeria, and that consequently these would be provided by the local infrastructure.[69]

Nigeria's defensive scheme allowed for the formation of five columns on the Cameroons border, two in the north at Maidugari opposite Mora, one at Yola on the Benue river opposite Garua, one at Ikom on the River Cross facing Nsanakang, and one near the coast at Calabar. On 6 August the Colonial Office, anxious for the internal security of Nigeria, ordered the columns not to advance into the Cameroons without further instructions.[70] However, Lugard's absence and the uncertainties about the offensive-defensive implications of the new plan helped to create a vagueness about what was intended. The cause of clarity was not served by communication difficulties between Lagos and Kaduna, the headquarters of Colonel C. H. P. Carter, commanding the Nigeria Regiment. On 15 August a retired British officer told Carter that the German garrison at Garua had on 11 August known nothing about the outbreak of war. A day previously London had authorized reconnaissances by the northern and southern columns. Carter now requested permission to attack Garua, and when this was granted extended his order to include an attack on Mora. Thus in late August all five columns were advancing into enemy territory.[71]

[69] Ibid. 8–9; Haywood and Clarke, *Royal West Africa Frontier Force*, 104; Osuntokun, *Nigeria*, 169–72; Gorges, *Great War in West Africa*, 40–4, 47.
[70] Gorges, *Great War in Africa*, 79; Moberly, *Togoland and Cameroons*, 59–60.
[71] Osuntokun, *Nigeria*, 181–2; Haywood and Clarke, *Royal West Africa Frontier Force*, 106–11.

Carter's advance was of course unwittingly directed at the guts of the German defences. Both Mora and Garua were the main northern guardians of Ngaundere and the highland plateau. Garua's specific task was to support the *Schütztruppen* deployed further north in Mora and Bornu, and to provide a rallying point in the event of their retreat.[72] Its defences consisted of five self-contained circular works, positioned to give each other supporting fire, and whose approaches were broken up with barbed wire and traps; their trenches, 7 metres deep, with overhead protection and deep dugouts, represented the techniques of modern war. Those at Mora were similarly well-constructed, and rose to 500 metres, atop precipitous and intersected slopes. Both would require heavy artillery for their reduction. Carter had only 2.95-inch mountain guns. Moreover, the French garrison at Fort Lamy, under Colonel Largeau, could not assist in the attack on Mora. Its efforts were concentrated on suppressing the German post at Kusseri, whence it was repulsed in August, and which it did not take till 25 September. By the end of August the British attack on Mora had fallen back to the south, adopting a position designed to block Mora's links with Garua. At Garua itself the rebuff was more severe. Von Crailsheim, the German commander, had picked up sufficient from the unusual movements on the Nigerian frontier to increase his garrison to three companies. The British attack, undertaken with insufficient reconnaissance over open ground, was a complete failure, the Nigerians breaking under a German counter-attack, and the commanding officer being killed. The Cross river column took Nsanakang, but on 6 September was surprised by the Germans and suffered 50 per cent casualties as well as losing eight of its eleven British officers. Thus, all along the Nigerian frontier the British were forced onto the defensive. The effect on the German askaris' morale was of crucial significance; never before had they fought the enemies of other European powers, and yet in all the initial engagements in the north they had proved victorious. Almost as impressed were the tribes of the Benue valley. In September and October the ambitions of the northern *Abteilung* at Garua had grown sufficiently for it to push strong patrols into Nigeria itself, to Yola, and also northwards towards Marua and its links with Mora.

Carter's attacks, however misconceived, did at least serve one broader purpose—they confirmed the Germans in their neglect of Duala. Dobell, who left Lagos on 20 September, instructed the frontier columns in the south to remain on the defensive, and those in the north and centre to concentrate against Garua. Carter was replaced in command by Colonel F. Cunliffe. Cunliffe's task was to support the main thrust on Duala.

By early September a flotilla of small craft had clustered around the British cruiser HMS *Cumberland*, and on 5 and 6 September anchored in Ambas Bay,

[72] Suren, *Kameruns Kampf*, 109, 114.

off Victoria. The original intention was to land here and cut across Cape Cameroon to Duala. However, the rainy season rendered the intervening rivers impassable. By the time the convoy had changed plans and proceeded round the cape into the Cameroon estuary the converse pressure had begun to apply. Although the Germans had not mined the rivermouth, they had sunk mine ships across its main channel. A direct advance on Duala along the shore was impossible. Therefore, the only means of ingress was up the rivers and creeks leading off the bays of the Cameroon estuary, using the smaller boats in the shallow waters. When the rainy season ended the water would fall and further advance become impossible. Thus, the middle weeks of September were passed in a series of navigational thrusts and in running battles between British and German light craft. On 16 September the German gunboat *Nachtigal* was sunk, and by the 22nd the survey was complete and a channel 19 feet deep cleared to within 5,000 yards of Duala.

On 25 September Dobell, his command now assembled at the entrance to the channel, issued an ultimatum calling on Duala to surrender. His plan was to push his main force up the Lungasi river to Japoma, where the river was bridged by the railway to Eseka. Thus he would cut off the town and its garrison from the south and east. But the Lungasi was blocked by a boom, and on 27 September Dobell readied himself for a frontal attack on Duala. The Germans, meanwhile, had no intention of fighting for Duala. Realizing from Dobell's ultimatum that attack was imminent, they fell back inland on 26 September, taking what they could in transport and destroying what they could not. On 27 September Dobell captured Duala without a shot being fired. On 6 October the Senegalese, this time in the face of stiffer opposition, took the Japoma bridge.

The immediate British objectives, certainly in the eyes of the Admiralty, had been gained. However, the Germans had not withdrawn far. Some had followed the northern line towards Bare and Dschang; most had gone east along the Wuri river to Jabassi or south-east on the midland line to Edea. All three concentrations had to be cleared in order to render Duala safe from German attack.

While the rains lasted Jabassi was the most accessible. Using the river, and mounting a 6-pounder gun on a dredger, a British force attacked on 7 October. However, its movements lost unity in the thick bush, and once into open ground the West Africans wilted under the concentrated fire of machine-guns. The waters of the Wuri then fell, and the attackers retreated to Duala. On 13 October the water-level rose again. The attack on the following day was directed up both banks of the river, and was better co-ordinated by Gorges, the British commander, as he stayed afloat to be able to observe the progress of operations. He was rewarded with success.

The value of riverine transport was even more graphically illustrated in the capture of Edea. The obvious route followed the railway line. But the British established that the Sanaga and Njong rivers, both issuing into the bight of Biafra, the former from Edea, and the latter linked to Edea by a track from Dehane, were navigable by small craft. Using the vessels released by the fall of Jabassi, British and French columns pushed up on Edea from the south, while a third column followed the railway. Again the Germans fell back without fighting, and Edea was taken on 26 October.

The advance up the northern railway, being less dependent on water navigation, was left until December. On 2 January 1915 the British took Dschang. However, having advanced beyond the railhead they destroyed the fort of Dschang, and then fell back onto securer lines of communication at Bare and Nkongsamba. Similarly, when the Wuri fell Jabassi was abandoned for a post further downstream which could be more readily supplied.

By the end of 1914 Dobell had achieved all his immediate objectives. The obstacles he had overcome had been almost entirely navigational and logistical; at no point, except at the Japoma bridge, had the Germans mounted a sustained defence. Even Dobell himself recognized that he had encountered at best only two of the twelve regular *Schütztruppen* companies;[73] most of his opposition had been provided by the police or by European reservists, and it had not been their job to mount major operations in the coastal areas.

In part, the ease of his task was attributable to Cunliffe's columns on the Nigerian frontier. But the major contribution in 1914 was made by Aymérich's attack in the south and east. It would be wrong to say that Cunliffe and Aymérich cleared the path for Dobell at Duala, because the Germans had never proposed to block the latter's advance in the first place. But Merlin's strategy succeeded to the extent that it was defence of the New Cameroons that caused most worry for Zimmerman in 1914.

Since its acquisition in 1911 the Germans had had little opportunity to survey the new territory or to incorporate it within the original colony. They had stationed no troops on the River Sanga south of Nola. The three companies of *Schütztruppen* on the upper Sanga, both east of the river and west as far as Dume, had an area of 200,000 square kilometres and a front of 1,700 kilometres to defend. The easternmost company, having initially planned an offensive from Carnot towards Singa, was recalled by Eymael, commanding the *Ostabteilung*. Thus, throughout August the only German troops east of the Sanga and south of Nola were police detachments.

The tempo of Morisson's and Hutin's advances was therefore dictated by the constraints of supply rather than by enemy action. None of the French columns had the lines of communication or the forward stocks necessary for immediate offensive operations. The navigability of the Sanga compensated for the pre-war deficiencies as far as Hutin was concerned. His most vulnerable

---

[73] Haywood and Clarke, *Royal West Africa Frontier Force*, 125–6.

point was Wesso, on the confluence of the Sanga and the Dscha, and just inside French territory. But an attack mounted by the Germans from Yukaduma miscarried because of the swollen state of the rivers. Morisson's initial difficulties were far greater. The Lobaye was not navigable, and therefore forward movement was impossible until porters were organized.

Aymérich's intention was that both columns should converge on Nola, and he anticipated a joint attack on 16 or 17 October. But the co-ordination of the two columns was impossible. Lateral communications took eight to thirteen days. When Morisson was first apprised of the plan to take Nola (the order was received on 21 September), he reported his supply problems as so great that Aymérich revised his instructions, suggesting a defensive role on the Lobaye. This second set of orders was dispatched by Aymérich on 30 September and reached Morisson on 7 October. In the interim, however, Morisson had resolved his logistical difficulties, and on 2 October had begun his advance on the line Carnot–Bania (north of Nola) as originally instructed. On 17 October Morisson entered Carnot without opposition. Hutin, meanwhile, acting in accordance with his orders from Aymérich to take Nola in conjunction with Morisson (orders given on 29 September), arrived there the day after Morisson entered Carnot. The news of Nola's capture did not reach Morisson until 24 October, and Aymérich (who, understandably uncertain where he could best position himself, had moved to Wesso) two days later. But by now the information was out of date. Hutin became worried about the supply of so many troops so far forward, and feared that the Germans on the Dscha would try to cut his communications at Putu. Leaving a single company at Nola to link with Morisson, he withdrew his main body back to Wesso.

On 29 October Morisson, perplexed as to his next move, asked Aymérich for further guidance. However, what Morisson could not afford to do was to stay still while he awaited Aymérich's reply. For much of October the Africans had been on half rations and on the 21st the Europeans were put on two-thirds. So he advanced. By the end of the month the problems were resolved as he was into territory fertile enough to enable him to requisition. But, as his troops ate off the surrounding land, so they needed to move to find fresh sources of supply. Therefore he continued to advance. He captured Baturi on 9 December. But the further he went, the remoter became his contact with Aymérich. From Baturi to Brazzaville, telegrams took between thirty and thirty-five days, and replies a further twenty to twenty-eight days. While Morisson pushed westwards, in obedience to one scheme of operations, Aymérich developed another.[74]

The collection of porters and the co-ordination of command for Le Meillour's and the Miquelard's columns proved even more complex than it had

[74] Ministère de la Guerre, *Armées françaises*, IX, 2ᵉ vol., 206–31.

been for Morisson's. Orders from Libreville to Miquelard's base at Mitzvic took between nine and twenty-seven days, and then a further nine days elapsed before they reached Le Meillour at Mvahdi. One letter from Brazzaville to Mitzvic took fifty days, and another, from Mvahdi to Libreville, forty-four days. Aymérich's decision to go forward from Brazzaville to Wesso left the two Gabon columns to their own devices. The original intention was to put the weight on Miquelard's, directing it along the southern border to Muni, and then north to Ojem, so cutting the German links with neutral Spanish territory. However, in mid-September, at Mimbang, midway between Ojem and the border, the French column ran into the Germans; its officers suffered heavy casualties, and its three companies broke and ran. In October the Germans advanced up to and across the border. Their victory was a major one. The decision not to defend Duala heightened the value of Muni as the Germans' point of contact with Europe and the wider world: supplies, including ammunition, continued to enter the Cameroons via Muni at least until early 1915.[75]

Not until November were the Gabon columns ready for forward movement once more. Now the weight was placed on Le Meillour, not on Miquelard, and the former was given overall command. His objective was Akoafim. Facing him were eight German companies, both regular and reservist. The obvious way to ease Le Meillour's path, at least from the perspective of Merlin, now in Libreville, was to get Hutin's column to act in conjunction with Le Meillour's right flank. Zimmerman, in order to reinforce Eymael and bring the strength facing Morisson in the Bertua–Dume area to five companies, had reduced the troops holding the Molundu–Lomie–Yukaduma sector to 750 policemen and reservists.

Aymérich's orders of 1 December, therefore, reflected the movements of Le Meillour's column and not those of Morisson's. Ignoring the facts that Hutin was held up at Molundu, and that his column's advance would be slowed once it left the line of the Sanga, Aymérich instructed Hutin to take Molundu, and then to move south-west to aid Le Meillour's advance from Gabon. Hutin's and Le Meillour's columns were now to have the major role, with Lomie as a joint objective. Only when they had reached that point was Morisson to resume his advance. Morisson was indeed dealt severe blows by Eymael at Bertua on 25, 27, and 28 December 1914. But Eymael still abandoned Bertua, and soon thereafter he lost to the north the two additional companies with which he had been reinforced. Moreover, in late November Morisson's supply problems were eased once more, as the route up the River Sanga became available to him.

Hutin meanwhile had not one but two sets of orders. Those given him on 17 November told him to take Yukaduma, and clearly intended him to retain

---

[75] Aymérich, *Conquête*, 94.

contact with his detached company at Nola; they had not been cancelled by those of 1 December. Molundu fell on 22 December; thereafter, part of Hutin's column pushed north to Yukaduma and part west to aid Le Meillour.

At the close of 1914 the Germans could be reasonably satisfied with their position. In the north and south German defences still rested, broadly speaking, on the frontiers. The losses of territory to Dobell's force in the west and to Aymérich's columns in the south-east had been anticipated; the defensive core in the northern highlands remained intact; to the south-west communications with Muni were secure. German casualties had been more than compensated for by new recruitment. Zimmerman had two major worries. The first was the rapid progress of Morisson's column, which he feared would advance on Ngaundere from the south, converging with the French from Chad and the British from Nigeria. He was prepared to weaken his forces facing Le Meillour to check Morisson, thus illustrating how different from French strategy was the Germans' sense of their own vulnerability.[76] His second concern was Dobell's next step. If Dobell elected to persevere beyond the head of the northern railway and Dschang, he would enter the northern plateau. Alternatively, he might choose to reinforce the French at Edea, on the midland railway, and push on to Jaunde between the Sanaga and Njong rivers, so threatening the link between Ngaundere and the south-west coast.

The Germans mounted two attacks in January and February 1915 designed to bring relief from the threats to east and west. Zimmerman could not easily concentrate forces against the British column at Dschang, but he did have companies around Edea. On 5 January Mayer's Senegalese held Edea against a determined German assault. Tactically, French fire superiority prevailed; strategically, Zimmerman achieved his objectives—the British became alarmed for their rear and fell back from Dschang, and talk of Mayer's column co-operating with Miquelard's advance from the south was quashed.[77] In the east, von der Marwitz's *Südostabteilung*—relieved on its southern flank by Hutin's move to the west—co-operated with Eymael's *Ostabteilung* to threaten the flank and rear of Morisson's extended, and now unsupported, advance. On 24 February the Germans retook Bertua, and by the end of the month Morisson had fallen back 100 kilometres to the line of the Kadei.

Dobell was in a quandary. The ease of his initial operations, up until December 1914, had opened up the prospects of a more extensive advance than that so far authorized by the Colonial Office. He asked for more troops, and on 26 December 1914 justified his request by alluding to 'the possibility, by constant activity of effecting the surrender of the whole of the Cameroons'.[78] But the reinforcements approved, 400 men from Sierra Leone, did no more

[76] Student, *Kameruns Kampf,* 104–5.
[77] Haywood and Clarke, *Royal West African Frontier Force,* 127, 133–6.
[78] Moberly, *Togoland and Cameroons,* 216.

than make good his losses. On 5 March 1915 he reported that he had only two battalions fit, and demanded reliefs, deeming six months' campaigning in the Cameroons sufficient for any man.[79] But he had strained the resources of British West Africa to their limit. Lugard argued that the security of Nigeria was being undermined by the demands of the Cameroons campaign; a revolt in Warri province gave force to his resistance to Dobell's needs.[80] Dobell suggested that the Indian army contribute. The battalion which he was eventually given was of low quality, and in February 1915 had mutinied in Singapore. His other expedients, to recruit native levies, and to establish a local police force at Duala so as to release troops for the front, were no more than palliatives.[81] The French component of Dobell's command was in an equally poor state. Although Dobell was responsible for Mayer's orders, Dakar was responsible for his supply. But Senegal had no stocks from which it could provision an expeditionary force. Mayer was left to find most of his porters within the Cameroons. At the end of October, despite Mayer's proximity to the coast, the rice to which the Senegalese were accustomed was replaced by locally requisitioned root crops. Health declined, and the problems compounded themselves as the French had too few doctors. By mid-December only one officer and a maximum of three NCOs were fit to march in each company.[82] On 10 March 1915 London signalled to Dobell that he was to make the best defensive arrangements possible and that no further offensive was anticipated. The basic CID strategy remained unchanged.

But that strategy had never been in accord with the grand schemes, both political and operational, of Merlin. The French experience of 1914 showed that effective command was exercised by the column commanders, and that the orders issued from Brazzaville bore little relation to the situation pertaining on the ground. The consequence was a series of separate advances whose effects in combination were the result of chance rather than design. Aymérich's direct influence was restricted principally to Hutin's column, and then only by virtue of his abandoning Brazzaville for points further forward. Aymérich's absences created Merlin's opportunity. Merlin had failed to achieve the co-ordination in operations which he had anticipated in September 1914. Command was divided over three governments (including the Belgians), four governors-general, six independent commanders-in-chief, and eight column commanders.[83] Dobell had the major responsibility, but liaison between him and the French was effected via London and Paris; Cunliffe in the north was not in direct contact with Dobell; the status of Brisset's column from Chad, now

[79] Ibid. 246.
[80] Osuntokun, *Nigeria*, 110–14, 222–4.
[81] Lucas, *Empire at war*, iv. 86.
[82] Ministère de la Guerre, *Armées françaises*, IX, 2ᵉ vol., 195–205.
[83] Charbonneau, *Revue militaire française*, 130 (avril 1932), 89.

acting with Cunliffe and outside Aymérich's control, was unclear. By February 1915 Aymérich at least had begun to recognize that the solution was greater delegation. But Aymérich had lost the initiative to Merlin. Merlin's ambition, despite all the practical difficulties, was to achieve the centralization of strategy which had so far eluded him.

On 6 February 1915 Merlin convened a conference in Brazzaville to discuss the next moves. Its central idea was an advance from the south and south-east towards Lomie and Dume, with the object of cutting off Jaunde. Morisson would have to take Dume, or run the risk of being exposed and isolated. Miquelard's column should advance to the Ntem in order to complete Jaunde's separation from the south-west. To the north Brisset was to be placed under Cunliffe's command, and the two should take Barua, and possibly then link up with Morisson.

An advance on Jaunde was therefore the concept that would unite the advancing columns in reciprocating action. On 11 February Aymérich left Brazzaville in order to attend to the supply and communication problems of Hutin's column, which were worsening as it extended to the west. Merlin set off for Duala, to convince Dobell that he too should adopt Jaunde as his objective.

Dobell was in no state to fall in with Merlin's schemes. His inclination was to put the weight on attrition and on seapower. By tightening the blockade of the Spanish coast the Germans would be exhausted, and at the same time the limited Entente forces would not be overextended. Furthermore, on 4 February a captured message from Zimmerman to the Garua garrison revealed that Ngaundere, not Jaunde, was the centre of the German defensive scheme. This intelligence was relayed to the Entente commanders on 26 February, and was taken with particular seriousness by Largeau in Chad, who acquired further information to corroborate its thrust. Merlin dismissed it.[84] Dobell was sufficiently won over by Merlin to abandon his own instincts, to accept that the attack on Garua—instead of being the major thrust demanded if Ngaundere was the hub of German resistance—should be supportive, and to agree that he himself could lead a direct advance on Jaunde. Merlin's representation of the French advance in the south and east was what convinced Dobell. The line Dume–Lomie–Akoafim–the River Ntem, the objective set at Brazzaville on 6 February, would be reached, Merlin said, by the end of March. As he spoke to Dobell, Merlin—freed from the embarrassment of Aymérich's presence or intervention—placed the French columns where he imagined or desired them to be, not where they were. Furthermore, in the plan finally agreed on 12 March Merlin committed the French to a timetable and an advance of which neither Aymérich nor his column commander had cognizance, and to a degree

---

[84] Ministère de la Guerre, *Armées françaises*, IX, 2ᵉ vol., 368–9.

of co-ordination and lateral communication which experience had proved was impossible to achieve.[85]

Two routes led from Edea in the direction of Jaunde. The southern was the railway line, but it was complete only as far as Eseka. The northern was a forest track passing through Wum Biagas. Dobell formed two columns, the British under Gorges to take the track, the French under Mayer the railway; when the French reached Eseka they were to join the British at Wum Biagas, and the two would then proceed together. Forest and swamp, until just short of Jaunde, made the ground ideally suited to defence. With 300 rifles on the track and 275 on the railway,[86] the Germans forced Dobell's troops into fighting for every day's advance. The British took Wum Biagas on 4 May, and the French captured Eseka on 11 May. On 25 May Mayer's troops led the way out of Wum Biagas towards Jaunde. His command, weakened by malnutrition and disease before he started, was now taking heavy casualties. When attacked, his men were slow to deploy off the track into the bush. Twenty-five per cent of those engaged in the advance were killed or wounded. The Germans harried the French flanks and rear. The carriers, mostly local men pressed into service, disappeared as soon as shots were exchanged. By 5 June Mayer had only progressed 19 kilometres beyond Wum Biagas, a rate of a 1.5 kilometres a day. At that speed Dobell could not reach Jaunde before the rainy season halted all movement. On 11 June he approved Mayer's request for permission to retreat. The following day a German attack against Mayer's rear, scattering his carriers, wreaked havoc with his lines of communication. By 28 June Dobell was back at Ngwe. Both his Nigerian battalions were reduced to half their strength;[87] sickness and supply difficulties ruled out any immediate resumption of the offensive. The advent of the rains provided confirmation. Until October, therefore, action in the west was confined to a tightening of the blockade of Muni. Dobell used the respite to repair his shattered forces, to give leave, to let his sick recuperate.

The degree to which Dobell's first advance on Jaunde was a failure depends on the object which it was trying to fulfil. For Merlin, it was the major stroke to ensure total victory in the Cameroons. For Dobell, it was—at least initially—a supporting move to relieve pressure on Aymérich; not his own but the French advance from the south and east promised, particularly given the optimistic account of its progress from Merlin, to be the decisive blow against German resistance. Dobell had, after all, received no authorization from London to move beyond the coastal area, and France, not Britain, desired to complete the conquest of the German colony. But, whatever the views of the War Office (which on 3 April took over military responsibility for the campaign from the

[85] Ibid. 395–8.
[86] Student, *Kameruns Kampf*, 180.
[87] Haywood and Clarke, *Royal West African Frontier Force*, 150.

Colonial Office), Dobell himself began to be attracted by Merlin's ambitions. On 12 April the setbacks to the progress of their columns led the French to ask Dobell for a postponement until 1 May. Dobell could have cancelled the offensive—justifying his decision by reference to his own instructions from London, to the state of his command, to his doubts about whether Jaunde was even the right objective, and to the proximity of the rainy season. Buoyed by his own initial good progress, he did not.

Aymérich, absent from Duala in March, remained committed to the fulfilment, not of the programme conceived then but of that to which he had been privy in Brazzaville on 6 February. Like Merlin he saw Jaunde as the heart of the German defence; unlike Merlin he had few illusions about the pace of his columns' advance. He anticipated their reaching the objectives set on 6 February not in late March or early April, but in June. Finding himself committed by the Duala conference to a plan in whose formulation he had had no share, his first response had been to seek its postponement.

In April none of the French columns was in a position to give effective support to each other, let alone to Dobell. Morisson was not yet fit to move after his retreat to the Kadei. The effect of his falling back was to force Hutin to reorientate himself to the north, and thus away from Le Meillour and the lines of advance fixed at Brazzaville and Duala. Moreover, Hutin's movements remained ponderous and painful. His supply problems, although ameliorated by local resources, were still not fully resolved. On 16 April he calculated he would need 1,512 porters; Aymérich thought a figure double that would be nearer the mark. The supply officers at Brazzaville and Molundu reckoned 12,000 porters were needed to transport three months' supplies to both Morisson's and Hutin's columns. But they were uncertain how many porters were actually present with Hutin's column, given the rate at which they were deserting and falling sick. They therefore did not know how many effectives they were trying to feed. Overestimating the number of porters in line with their own expectations, they created loads that were beyond the capacity of the porterage available. Moreover, the further Hutin advanced the more reliant he became on land rather than on riverine communications, and the more porters were carrying food to feed other porters, not to feed fighting men.[88]

More serious than Hutin's problems were those of the southern offensive, adumbrated at Brazzaville and at Duala as the principal French offensive, but which had collapsed into a series of uncoordinated and feeble sallies. Le Meillour had planned to begin his advance on 1 March, but had brought it forward to late January in order to aid Hutin. He therefore set off before his supply arrangements were complete. Like Hutin, he was naively optimistic

---

[88] Ministère de la Guerre, *Armées françaises*, IX, 2ᵉ vol., 540–4.

about his needs. In December 1914 he reckoned that both his and Miquelard's columns would require 400 porters; in March 1915 he announced he would need more than double that number for his column alone; in fact he had only forty. On 13 February he learnt that Miquelard, whose line of march had been fixed as Ojem and then Akoafim in order to support Le Meillour's own advance, had encountered strong German forces. Miquelard therefore called on Le Meillour to support him by attacking Akoafim. The latter did so, but his efforts were half-hearted, publicly because of his supply problems, privately because of his own lack of drive. On 17 March Le Meillour received the results of the conference at Brazzaville on 6 February, but he was now back at Minkebe, not advancing on Lomie. Furthermore, the Brazzaville conclusions did not make clear whether his task was to act in conjunction with Miquelard on his left or Hutin on his right. Communications with either took at least twenty days. Le Meillour decided to support neither, but to push between Ojem and Akoafim. The German forces, up to 75 per cent of them at any one time racked with dysentery or blackwater fever, were able to check an attack that lacked either administrative coherence or strategic direction. Thus Aymérich, whose communications with the Gabon columns were further lengthened by his leaving Molundu on 25 April for Yukaduma, learnt on 14 May that Le Meillour was neither attacking Akoafim nor conforming to the February programme.[89]

In June the failure of the French offensive in the south began to be offset by the recovery of that in the east. On 7 May Aymérich, succumbing to Merlin's pressure for progress, instructed his columns to take such offensive opportunities as presented themselves. Their objectives were still limited, their tasks to fix the enemy, not to pursue him *au fond*. On 22 May he brought coherence to Hutin's movements by directing his column and Morisson's to aim at their eventual convergence. The pause on the Kadei, the support of the local population, and the fact that he was on the edge of more fertile territory enabled Morisson's column to rebuild. Morisson resumed his advance, reaching Moopa on 23 May, Bertua a month later, and finally entering Dume on 25 July. Hutin's supply problems were countered by weakening German resistance. Only those *Schütztruppen* companies still issued with peacetime ammunition could be used in major operations. In mid-June all but ninety men in *Südostabteilung* mutinied, a reflection of the inadequate ammunition supply, of the death of their respected commanding officer von der Marwitz, and of the fear of capture.[90] Although Hutin was not in a state to exploit the opportunity—most of the mutineers returned to the ranks in late June—he finally entered Lomie on 24 June; Hutin was now able to recruit locally, even

[89] Ibid. 323–32, 351–5, 562–70; Student, *Kameruns Kampf*, 216–17.
[90] Student, *Kameruns Kampf*, 219; Purschel, *Kaiserliche Schütztruppe*, 67–8.

drawing in former askaris.[91] In August the two columns were united under Morisson's command, and together formed a joint front facing west and running from Bertua and Dume to Abong-Bang and Lomie. At last, therefore, the French were beginning to meet the commitments entered into by Merlin. But by now Dobell's advance and retreat were done.

Nonetheless, a strategic breakthrough was achieved between March and October 1915. It came on the front where neither Merlin nor Dobell had sought it. Its significance was therefore more evident to the Germans than it was to the Entente powers.

In April 1915 the dominant concerns of both sides in the northern Cameroons were defensive. A German thrust to the Benue on 10 April caused the Emir of Yola and his native administration to flee, so threatening to undermine the British hold in northern Nigeria. Lugard, therefore, wanted Garua taken to restore British prestige in northern Nigeria, not to give Britain control of the Cameroons. The purpose, however, of the German attack was to ensure that Cunliffe's forces did not simply mask Garua in an advance into the highland plateau. Zimmerman had told von Crailsheim in January that the task of the Garua garrison was to protect Ngaundere. Provided the Germans held Ngaundere, they could exploit their interior lines in order to concentrate sufficient men against individual enemy columns scattered over all fronts. If Garua fell then Ngaundere would follow, and, in Zimmerman's words, 'the whole war plan would collapse'.[92]

Crailsheim's faith in his chief's analysis was confirmed by the capture of a letter from Morisson, saying that the French forces in the south could not advance any further until Cunliffe's column in the north had captured Garua. But Zimmerman changed his mind. In fresh orders, dated 13 April 1915, Zimmerman now warned against the dangers of locking up all available forces in a fort. He feared that Cunliffe might mask Garua, and fall on Ngaundere and Banyo. In such circumstances the defence of Garua, however heroic and protracted, would be useless. Garua's garrison was cut to one-and-a-half companies, a total of 250 rifles, so as to create a mobile force to cover the flanks of Ngaundere and Banyo. To add insult to injury, Zimmerman also took two officers and 60,000 rounds (although the Garua garrison was convinced that the total was twice that) to reinforce the *Südabteilung*. Crailsheim protested that in the rainy season the high water meant that Garua could not be bypassed; he argued in vain.[93]

Cunliffe, with fourteen companies in all, plus supporting arms, now enjoyed an overwhelming superiority. But he continued to treat Garua with the respect its fortifications deserved. He supplemented his mountain guns with two

[91] Aymérich, *Conquête*, 127.
[92] Student, *Kameruns Kampf*, 147; see also Osuntokun, *Nigeria*, 189–90.
[93] Suren, *Kampf um Kamerun*, 197–228, 326.

heavy artillery pieces, a naval 12-pounder sent up the rivers Niger and Benue when the waters were high enough, and a French 95 mm from Chad. By 9 June his infantry had worked forward to within a kilometre of the German positions, the British to the south and south-east and the French under Brisset to the east. He hoped to cut off Crailsheim's retreat, but the askaris were alarmed by their first experience of heavy artillery fire. Half the garrison escaped by swimming down the Benue, and thence to Banyo; the balance, 300 men, surrendered without an assault having taken place, on 10 June.

Cunliffe was oblivious to the enormity of the blow which he had delivered the Germans. He was convinced that Jaunde, not Ngaundere, was the centre of their defensive effort, and that his role was, as the Duala conference had specified, to support Dobell. Dobell, however, was in retreat, and could not resume his advance until the rains ceased. Therefore, Cunliffe concluded, the sensible thing for him to do was not to push south but go north, and reduce the now-isolated Mora with his heavy artillery.

Brisset, technically his subordinate, disagreed. Of all the allied commanders, both Brisset and his immediate superior, Largeau, the military governor of Chad, had been the most impressed by the intelligence pointing to the German reliance on Ngaundere. The fertility of the highland region, the support of neighbouring Chad, and the relative lack of rain made rapid movement easier in the north than in any other area of operations. On 28 June a British column took Ngaundere. Brisset then moved south-west on Tibati, and pushed a company south to Kunde to link with Morisson's right. By late July Brisset's thoughts and actions aimed at a total inversion of allied planning, placing the initiative on a general offensive with the North Cameroons force.

For the British, Brisset's independence was not a manifestation of a different strategic view but of insubordination and French bloody-mindedness. Cunliffe concluded that the rainy season would preclude immediate operations south of the line Kontscha–Banyo–Bamenda, and that those positions should therefore be consolidated, whereas the lack of rain in the north created the ideal opportunity to take Mora. Largeau's ambivalence—recognizing the military need for obedience, while being in sympathy with Brisset's objectives—gave Brisset continuing leeway. That leeway was consolidated by delays in communication with Merlin, Dobell, or Aymérich. The subordinate status of Brisset's command, in reality clear enough since February, was not reaffirmed until the end of August. However, Brisset lacked the men to achieve the objectives which he had set himself without Cunliffe's aid. Thus the Germans had time to regroup.[94]

---

[94] The British sources all see Brisset's actions as evidence of French Anglophobia and not of a different strategic appreciation. Ministère de la Guerre, *Armées françaises*, IX, 2ᵉ vol., 363–4, 387–92, 458–61, 586–98, provides a corrective.

With the fall of Garua the *Schwerpunkt* of German defences did at last shift to Jaunde. Thus, for the first time in the war German strategy and allied objectives were brought into line. Zimmerman's lifeline could no longer be the northern plateau; it had now to be the resources of neutral Spanish Muni, and therefore the axis of his operations became Jaunde and Ebolowa, both of them supply dumps and manufacturing centres. In the north he created a new *Nordabteilung* by drawing troops from Banyo and Dschang, and sending them east. Too late to hold Ngaundere, they centred their defences on Tibati and Banyo, forming an arc that ran west to Ossindinge through Dschang to the Sanaga, a front of 1,000 kilometres. Equipment was pulled back south of the Njong. Allied confusion gave Zimmerman sufficient respite to plug the gaps in the north, at least for the time being.[95]

Dobell's retreat and the coming of the rains brought a pause in the west which allowed Zimmerman to improvise an attack in the east against Morisson's communications between Bertua and Dume, the aim being to drive the French once again beyond the Kadei. The Germans' intention was to reinforce their left in order to lap round Morisson's northern flank. But the command structure was confused; the troops drawn from the west and from Banyo were still formally part of the *Nordabteilung*; and Duisberg, the officer in charge of the attack, was pulled south by his concerns for the dangers from that quarter. Thus, by 13–16 September the German offensive, their last major effort of the campaign, had stalled. Even as it did so, Zimmerman drew off two companies to the south and one to the north, thus blocking any hopes of its renewal.

Broadly speaking, therefore, the major German concentrations between July and September were pointed north and south, not east and west. The latter were, however, the points from which the British and the French proposed to press their advance. The fall of Ngaundere had convinced Dobell that Jaunde was now his proper objective in a way it had not been in March, and thus only its reduction, not the blockade of the coast, would force the Germans to surrender. Moreover, he was determined to create a force sufficiently strong to enable his columns to take Jaunde even if Aymérich could not give them effective support. The French were equally decided that Aymérich should be enabled to advance on Jaunde from the east even if British action in the west remained limited. On 25 and 26 August Merlin and Dobell, this time with Aymérich also present, conferred once again at Duala and a joint thrust on Jaunde was fixed to begin after the rains were over, on 15 October in the east and on 15 November in the west. The problems of communication with Cunliffe's command reinforced the decision that, as before, opportunities in the north should be subsidiary and supportive.

---

[95] Student, *Kameruns Kampf*, 207–9.

The second Duala conference also discussed an attack from the south. Merlin and Aymérich favoured a thrust from Campo on the coast, designed to combine with the French columns coming up from Gabon. They had been prodded in this direction by Doumergue, who, with one eye cocked towards French territorial ambitions and the other to the German line of communications to Spanish territory, wanted to give the French companies at Campo a role more significant than that of 'frontier guards and customs officers'. But Doumergue was in Paris and had to defer to Dobell in Duala. The latter was the de facto allied commander in the Cameroons, and he preferred to concentrate his forces. He was supported by Mayer, who was anxious that he, rather than the Campo contingent, should secure any available reinforcements. Britain's material superiority meant that Mayer was struggling to keep France's end up in the advance from the west; only two months previously Doumergue himself had reminded him that, although he was Dobell's military subordinate, he was also 'the representative of the Republic in the Cameroons'.[96]

Such grandiloquent language might have surprised Aymérich, whose role in the campaign now became direct. With Morisson's and Hutin's columns adjacent to each other, but with the two column commanders at loggerheads, Aymérich could assume personal control of the eastern advance. His left, under Hutin, moved along the Njong, its task being to protect the major thrust by Morisson, whose right rested on the Sanaga, feeling north in the hope of linking with Brisset. In practice, the balance in Aymérich's advance was reversed. Hutin's column encountered the heavier German resistance, while Morisson's progress on the Sanaga was comparably easier. Moreover, the link with Brisset proved elusive. Not until 6–8 December did news filter in of Brisset's position, and he was then still 150 kilometres from the Sanaga. Of Dobell's movements Aymérich knew nothing; in going forward to exercise command himself, he lost contact with the other columns. By late December his isolation and his lengthening communications forced him onwards, the choices confronting him being the rapid seizure of Jaunde or retreat. On 2 January 1916 his gamble began to pay off. He learnt that Brisset was just north of the Nachtigal rapids, above Jaunde on the Sanaga. Two days later he heard that Dobell's British column had reached Jaunde. The co-ordination of the columns, even if not their communication, had been achieved, and thus their individual movements had had reciprocating effects.

In the west Dobell's British column had retaken Wum Biagas on 9 October and his French column Eseka on 30 October. Both places were prepared as forward bases, linked by motorized transport to Edea, so that the final assault on Jaunde could proceed without a halt. A force of 9,700 men was assembled. Their advance in late November avoided the tactical failings of the first attempt: a

---

[96] Michel, *Guerres mondiales et conflits contemporains*, 168 (1992), 20, 26.

strong column on the forest road was flanked on either side by detachments on as wide a front as possible, so checking German sallies against the rear. By mid-December the British were out of the jungle and into open country. The French reached a comparable point a week later, at Mangeles. The British pressed on without waiting for the French, and entered Jaunde on New Year's Day 1916.

To the north, converging forces from Bare and Ossindinge had cleared Dschang by 6 November. Cunliffe, recalled from Mora without capturing it, directed Brisset on Tibati, and most of the rest of his force on Banyo. Banyo was a strong-point as formidable as Mora and Garua. The position rose to a height of 400 metres, and was formed of a network of 300 stone breastworks or sangars. The advance of Cunliffe's troops up its steep slopes on 4 November was protected by mist; holding the ground gained the following day, they assaulted the summit on 6 November. On 2 December the Ossindinge column took Fumban, and by 18 December Cunliffe's command was arrayed on the front Joko–Linte–Ditam. On 8 January 1916 his and Aymérich's troops linked at the Nachtigal rapids.

The allied advances from east, west, and north had encountered little sustained German resistance. In part, this was the product of superior numbers, and (at last) efficiently organized supply columns and better-protected lines of march. The Germans, as they were boxed in, should have profited from a shortening of their lines of communication to put up a more vigorous defence. In reality this was impossible. None of Zimmerman's units had sufficient ammunition to allow itself to be drawn into a sustained firefight. Most of the rounds issued to askaris were the ersatz manufactures of Jaunde and Ebolowa. One company facing Morisson's column fired eight rounds per man on 29 November; by the end of the following day each soldier had only twelve rounds, and then only four after further fighting on 1 December. An effort by Zimmerman to counter-attack against Dobell on 16 December lasted forty minutes, until his men ran out of ammunition.[97] Retreat was therefore unavoidable, and as they fell back the Germans could neither plunder the ammunition of their enemies nor, increasingly, rescue their own spent cases for recycling.

But the softness of the German defences had another cause. The sources of ammunition lay to the south of the Njong—ersatz production was based at Ebolowa, and the only route for communication from Europe lay via Spanish Muni. And yet the thrust of the allies' advance on Jaunde was directed north of the Njong. Aymérich's efforts had emphasized not his left but his right, Morisson's column and the link with Brisset. Dobell was similarly resistant to being drawn south. He was told by the War Office on 2 August of the importance of the axes between Jaunde and Muni and Jaunde and Kribi, and of

---

[97] Student, *Kameruns Kampf*, 286–7, 298

the road from Ebolowa to Ambam.[98] But in his desire to take Jaunde without having to rely on Aymérich, Dobell concentrated his forces further north, on the direct route to Jaunde, and made clear to the French that he could not support Le Meillour.

The task of cutting the Germans' line of retreat, therefore, lay with the Gabon columns. Both the Brazzaville conference in February and the second Duala conference in August had paid lip-service to the need to block the Germans off from Muni. But in the allocation of manpower this objective never received sufficient priority. In July Le Meillour's efforts to clear the eastern side of the Muni border were rewarded with the capture of Ojem and Bitam, but were halted by the Germans on the River Ntem. Merlin and Aymérich hoped to support Le Meillour by reinforcing a column landed on the coast at Campo, and intended to stop traffic on Muni's northern border. But Dobell refused to favour the Campo column at the expense of the advance on Jaunde, and even withdrew the troops which he had provisionally allocated to it. Merlin appealed to Paris for six companies from French West Africa. On 20 October 1915 two companies landed at Campo from Dakar, but without maps, interpreters, or guides. On 15 December two further companies and a proper complement of supporting arms made the Campo column a going concern. But it was too late. Le Meillour's efforts to cross the Ntem in late October and again in late November were checked, not least because for two months part of his command was diverted to Akoafim. Le Meillour finally got beyond the Ntem in mid-December. Even then his progress towards Ambam remained slow.[99]

Thus, in December the Spanish frontier still remained open for 200 kilometres. Zimmerman determined that he would take his command through this gap and into neutral territory. The German decision to retreat was therefore not prompted by the fall of Jaunde. As at Duala, the Germans preferred not to sacrifice the investments and developments of peacetime colonialism in a short-term defensive action, but instead to evacuate the town before Dobell's arrival. What proved decisive was Le Meillour's crossing of the Ntem, which made the cutting of German communications only a matter of time.[100] On 28 December, four days before the British arrival in Jaunde, Zimmerman issued orders for the retreat of the German forces to the south-west. The axis Jaunde–Ebolowa–Ambam now became the corridor whose collapsing walls must be kept open long enough to allow the evacuation of the *Schütztruppen* still in the north and west. The gap on the frontier closed to 50 kilometres, but by 15 February a great exodus had been accomplished. About 15,000 people—and possibly more—had crossed into Spanish territory, including 1,000 Germans,

[98] Moberly, *Togoland and Cameroons*, 314–15.
[99] Aymérich, *Conquête*, 103, 109–10, 158–66.
[100] Student, *Kameruns Kampf*, 318–19.

6,000 askaris, and 7,000 family and followers. The loyalty of the Beti of Jaunde to the Germans was the major factor in ensuring that, even in defeat, the *Schütztruppen* retained their integrity and their cohesion as a fighting force. Thus was the German policy of integrating the wives and children of the askaris vindicated; thus too was evidence provided that many in the Cameroons saw the German defeat as no more than temporary.[101]

The failure of the Campo and Gabon columns to cut off the German retreat was complemented by the delay in the allied pursuit from Jaunde. Dobell was slow to recognize the direction the Germans had followed. Some anticipated that the *Schütztruppen* would break into small units to continue guerrilla operations within the colony. Dobell himself reckoned that major units still lay north and west of Jaunde. When he did finally realize that his efforts should be bent to the south, he was anxious not to press the pursuit too hard for fear of driving the Germans across the frontier before the Campo and Gabon columns had been able to form a cordon to block their path.

Aymérich was put in command of the pursuit. But his eastern columns were exhausted, and their lines of communication extended. Not until 14 January was he ready to leave Jaunde. Hutin's column moved south and south-east to Sangmelima, to mop up any pockets of German resistance in that direction, and to be ready to outflank Ebolowa. Two columns, one under Haywood and another under Faucon, moved directly against Ebolowa, Faucon entering the town on 19 January. The supply problem was now acute. Hutin's column was left to live off the land. But the area between Jaunde and Ebolowa had been stripped of supplies by the retreating Germans, and the Beti had abandoned their villages in deference to German wishes. Dobell therefore argued that forces the size of Aymérich's could not be sustained in the south-western Cameroons. Moreover, for him the fall of Ebolowa marked the end of German resistance. Haywood and the British forces in the pursuit were directed towards Kribi. Not until 28 January did Dobell reverse his decision, and by then Haywood's resumption of the march to the south was too late.

Dobell's decisions, however misguided in terms of the reality of Zimmerman's movements, were justified by logistic realities. Aymérich's force was advancing too fast for its lines of communications; already extended at Jaunde, which lay 700 kilometres from its intermediate base at Nola on the Sanga, they were increased by 200 kilometres in ten days in the advance on Ebolowa. Beyond Ebolowa supply could no longer be maintained. The Germans having just been through the area, the villages were empty, and few porters could be found; those that were recruited did not stay. Faucon reduced the supplies

---

[101] Frederick Quinn, 'The impact of the First World War and its aftermath on the Beti of Cameroun', in Page (ed.), *Africa*, 175–6.

carried by his column from six days' to four, and increased the load carried by each soldier from two days' to three, so saving on porters. Switching the lines of communication from Jaunde and Nola to Eseka and Duala took time. Aymérich's columns did not finally link with Le Meillour's until 14 February.[102]

The final act of the Germans' defeat in the Cameroons was accomplished not on the Muni frontier but at the opposite extreme. The *Schütztruppen* at Mora, undefeated but apprised of the retreat into Spanish territory, surrendered on 18 February. The garrison of 155 soldiers still had 37,000 rounds of ammunition.[103]

For all their abundance at Mora, the lack of munitions became the major German explanation as to why their defence of the Cameroons had not been more protracted. The companies facing Dobell and Aymérich had been unable to sustain combat since September 1915. And without ammunition the idea of continuing operations from the jungle fastnesses of the south, or of raiding across the French border into Gabon or Equatorial Africa became absurd.

Yet, although real enough, the munitions' deficiency gained importance only in the light of von Lettow-Vorbeck's campaign in East Africa. When, after 1918, it became apparent that von Lettow-Vorbeck had fought on after German territory had been all but overrun, and had kept his forces intact until the end of the war, the question—implicit but nonetheless real—arose as to why Zimmerman had not done the same. Thus, rather than celebrate the achievement of a defence far longer and far more successful, against considerably superior forces, than had ever been anticipated, the Germans tended to ask why it had not been even better sustained.

The true answer lay less in the munitions supply than in the higher direction of the campaign. In East Africa the overall conduct of the defence was assumed by the *Schütztruppen* commander, and his objective became not the preservation of a German colony, but the use of that colony to distract the British from concentrating all their efforts in Europe. In West Africa the civilian governor, Ebermaier, became the inspiration of German defence. His objective was to maintain Germany as a colonial power in the Cameroons. At no stage was heavy fighting allowed to do damage to the principal settlements, in particular Duala and Jaunde. Moreover, despite their continuous retreat, and despite their belief that the local tribes would follow the power that exercised the greater strength, the Germans continued to have a lien on local loyalties. There were major exceptions. In the west older contacts with the British resurfaced, and the disruption of the commercial life of the coastal areas produced dissatisfaction with German rule. In the south-east the territory had been

[102] Aymérich, *Conquête*, 169–86; Ministère de la Guerre, *Armées françaises*, IX, 2ᵉ vol., 756–807.
[103] Osuntokun, *Nigeria*, 193.

too recently French for Aymérich's men not to have some leverage, even if at times they threatened to forfeit it by their own brutality. But in the central heartlands, and particularly of course among the Beti, loyalty to the Germans lasted even beyond defeat.

The retreat into Spanish Muni, although it condemned the *Schütztruppen* to military inutility, was thus of a piece with their political purposes. A German enclave persisted in West Africa. The Spanish authorities, with only 180 militiamen, had neither the inclination nor the power to intern the *Schütztruppen*. In April 1916 the Germans moved to Fernando Po. Aymérich received reports that there ammunition was reaching Ebermaier's men, that he had 500,000 rounds, and that his troops were drilling and training, awaiting the day of German victory in Europe before re-establishing themselves as a major West African power.[104]

French fears were exaggerated; the British blockade made Muni and Fernando Po poor bases for the Germans. But it remains true that the final settlement of the Cameroons was the product more of affairs in Europe than of the outcome of the campaign in the Cameroons. If Germany had won the war in 1918 it might still have re-established its authority in the Cameroons. Neither Britain nor France managed adequately to fill the administrative vacuum created by Germany's withdrawal.

As the conquest of the Cameroons proceeded, its de facto occupation developed three separate enclaves—to the west, to the north, and to the south-east. Confronted by what seemed to be the total absence of state administration, the column commanders had to assume civil, financial, and technical responsibilities, as well as military. Dobell enjoyed a staff of British colonial officers specifically trained for such functions; moreover, he had the medical equipment and logistical support to sustain at least some of them. As early as December 1914 it seemed likely that a partition which followed the lines of spheres of influence as well as the preferences of the population would divide the Cameroons centrally, along the line of the Sanaga. This was much further south than the growth of Doumergue's territorial ambitions could now countenance.[105] The French therefore proposed that the south-east, the territory that had belonged to them until 1911 and which they had conquered by dint of their own efforts, should be administered by them; the remainder, including Duala, should be a condominium pending a final partition at the end of the war.

Britain's responses to condominium were divided. The Foreign Office, anxious to concede to the French where it could in order to gain elsewhere, was happy to accommodate France's wishes. By early 1916 the Cabinets's war

---

[104] Ibid. 193–4; Aymérich, *Conquête*, 198–9.
[105] Michel, *Guerres mondiales et conflits contemporains*, 168 (1992), 24, 27.

committee too saw France's immersion in West Africa as a way of keeping it out of East Africa. But other departments were more annexationist. The Admiralty wanted Duala, and if Britain had Duala, then it held the economic key to all of the Cameroons except the south. The Colonial Office, whose campaign this was in terms both of finance and direction, came under pressure from its local officials. In Nigeria Lugard's policy of 'indirect rule' had been deepened by the outbreak of war. The withdrawal of district officers and their supporting troops increased Britain's reliance on the loyalty of the emirs. In Bussa, where administrative reorganization failed to respect traditional authority, rebellion flared in June 1915. Elsewhere the authority of the chiefs often lacked deep roots and was vitiated by corruption; the manpower and fiscal demands of the war cast them in the roles of British agents. On the Gold Coast resistance to chiefly direction was evident as soon as the troops departed for Togoland in August 1914, and in 1916 fuelled the Bongo riots.[106] Lugard therefore wanted to bolster the chiefs of northern Nigeria by the restoration of what he deemed to be their traditional lands. In doing so, he simplified the fluidities of the political relationships within the emirates, and tended to define them in terms of geographical boundaries rather than of more subtle influences. His determination to ensure the integrity of the emirates of Bornu and Yola extended to Ngaundere, Tibati, and Banyo.

At a meeting on 23 February 1916 Georges Picot for France, 'who knew nothing of the lands and peoples he was dividing', drew a line 'with a heavy pencil' which Sir Charles Strachey, the representative of the Colonial Office, was constrained to accept. As one of Strachey's colleagues later observed: 'If only you had not had a pencil in your hand at the time.'[107] The provisional partition followed the main north–south road, not the distribution of tribal affiliations. It gave the northern Cameroons to the line Garua–Ngaundere–Tibati–Joko–Nachtigal to the British and the rest to France. The Foreign Office had prevailed. The Admiralty did not get Duala. The traditional territories of the major British loyalist on the northern Nigerian frontier, the Emir of Yola, remained split. The zones of occupation created in 1916 ran across the boundaries formed by right of conquest, especially in the west.

Administratively, neither power was up to the task of resettlement and reconstruction. The British zone was incorporated as part of Nigeria, but the Nigerian administration was already weakened by the departure of its staff for military service, and was therefore not equal to an extension of its territorial responsibilities. In the French zone, the territories originally ceded in 1911 were

[106] Crowder, *Revolt in Bussa*; Thomas, *Journal of African History*, XXIV (1983), 57–75; also Afigbo, *Warrant chief*, 118–57.
[107] Yearwood, *Canadian Journal of African Studies*, XXVI (1993), 235.

reincorporated with French Equatorial Africa, and the remainder was governed by the army and answerable directly to Paris.[108]

The casualties were the tribes of the Cameroons. Where there had been fifty Germans there were now five or six Frenchmen. Education fell victim to the internment and evacuation of German Catholic pastors. German doctors left with the *Schütztruppen*. In their stead witchcraft and magic regained dominance. Feuds and thefts multiplied, evidence of the loss of order and of the violence already legitimized by the war.[109] Ultimately, the post-war settlement did confirm the French hold on three-quarters of the Cameroons, but it was a grip that reflected the realities of diplomacy more than the realities of French rule in the period 1916–18.

SOUTH-WEST AFRICA

The replacement of domestic discord by renewed national purpose, a sense of union that conquered class and even ethnic divisions—these are the themes seen as characteristic of the early months of the war for most of its belligerents. South Africa was an exception. Furthermore, the splits which sundered the newly formed Union were a direct reflection of pre-war tensions. South Africa is therefore the exception that proves the rule—not the rule that powers went to war as a flight from domestic crisis, a creation of hindsight, but the rule that the fear that war would provoke revolution inhibited the move to war while not in the end preventing it. Admittedly, the pressures to which South Africa was exposed were unusually severe. Its internal conflicts were at once social, racial, and national; it was only on the third that the Union foundered.[110]

In August 1913, and again in January 1914, troops were deployed on the Rand to suppress strikes among white miners. The effect of martial law was to boost the status and membership of the South African Labour party, to fuse the English skilled worker and the landless Afrikaner in joint action. In 1911 the party affiliated with the International. But when war broke out this link proved brittle. The party's executive committee remained loyal to its principles, and resolutions opposing war were passed at conferences in December 1914 and January 1915. However, many of the party's branches supported the war, and so did its principal organ *The Worker*, edited by F. H. R. Creswell, a major in the

---

[108] Elango, *International Journal of African Historical Studies*, XVIII (1985), 657–731; Louis, *Great Britain and Germany's lost colonies*, 57–62; Andrew and Kanya-Forstner, *France overseas*, 97–9; Osuntokun, *Nigeria*, 206–32; Aymérich, *Conquête*, 200–9; Digre, *Imperialism's new clothes*, 37–48.

[109] Quinn, in Page (ed.), *Africa*, 177–8; Quinn, *Cahiers d'études africaines*, XIII (1973), 728–30.

[110] On South Africa in the period of the First World War, see Garson, *Journal of Imperial and Commonwealth History*, VIII (1979), 68–85; Hancock, *Smuts 1870–1919*; Katzenellenbogen, 'Southern Africa and the war of 1914–18'; Meintjes, *Botha*; Walker, *History of Southern Africa*, ch. 14.

Rand Rifle Corps. In parliament the Labour party backed the Unionist party, while outside it the pacifists began to break away, setting up the War on War League in September. The popular responses to the sinking of the *Lusitania* in May 1915 made this split overt: in August the English members ensured that the party declared its loyal support for the war, while in September the leaders of the left formed the International Socialist League. The Marxists found that their fellow-travellers included at least some Afrikaners, driven by nationalism to reject a war undertaken by the British empire.[111]

One of the principal planks around which the pre-war Labour party had coalesced was its advocacy of the industrial colour bar. The dependence of the mines on the skills of white workers became a means to protect the employment of all whites against black competition. Socialism stood cheek-by-jowl with racism. Civil rights discrimination against coloureds, and particularly against Indian immigration, countered by Gandhi's tactics of passive resistance, provoked a strike by 130,000 Indians in Natal in 1913. Some amelioration of the Indians' plight was effected in June 1914, and when war broke out the colour bar was eased by shortages of skilled white labour. Both coloureds and blacks used the opportunity to stress their loyalty, at least to the British empire if not to South Africa. Persuaded by London's propaganda that this was a war for liberalism and self-determination, the less radical and more middle-class elements argued that co-operation could be the path to full citizenship. The South African Native National Congress, the future African National Congress, declared its support for Louis Botha, the prime minister, and Walter Rubusana, its leader in the Cape, offered to raise 5,000 infantry. The coloureds' association, the Africa Peoples' Organization, issued its own attestation forms in a bid to form a Cape Coloured Corps in August: by September it had mustered 10,000 volunteers, and in 1915 the unit was approved by the government.

Thus the war quietened agitation in two of the major areas of domestic division. But for Afrikaner nationalism war provided fuel to flames only recently rekindled. In 1907 the Treaty of Vereeniging had promised unity for Boer and Briton within South Africa, and in 1910 the creation of the Union gave Afrikaners an effective measure of self-government. But the Boers themselves were divided. In 1902 some had left South Africa for German South-West Africa or for Portuguese Mozambique rather than be subject to British rule. Many more, then or later, effected a compromise—to live within the empire for the time being while still harbouring as ultimate goals both independence and republicanism. Thus, the collaboration of Louis Botha, the Boer general and the Union's prime minister, could be deemed temporarily expedient. But Botha's policy of conciliation was shattered by the speeches and actions of

---

[111] Ticktin, *South African Historical Journal*, I (1969), 59–80, on the Labour party; on popular responses in general, see Nasson, *Journal of Imperial and Commonwealth History*, XXII (1995), 248–76; also Nasson, *War & Society*, XII (1994), 47–64.

J. B. M. Hertzog of the Orange Free State. Hertzog accepted English and Dutch equality within South Africa, but argued that equality should be expressed through separation, both linguistic and cultural; fusion would be a cloak for Anglicization. Botha's first efforts to meet Hertzog's challenges included his incorporation within the Union cabinet. But in 1912 Hertzog's criticisms were too overt for any fiction of unity to be sustainable. Following his exclusion from the cabinet, Hertzog seceded from Botha's South Africa party, and in January 1914 formed the Nationalist party. Thus Botha had already lost a large section of Afrikaner support when war broke out.

In August 1914 Hertzog did not disagree with Botha's assumption that British entry to the war automatically involved South Africa. Botha's immediate release of imperial troops from South Africa for Europe was therefore uncontroversial. It was the move from passive participation to active involvement that made specific the doubts of Afrikaner nationalists.

On 7 August, in pursuit of the objectives laid down by the CID subcommittee, London asked Pretoria whether it could seize the harbours and wireless stations of German South-West Africa. In this case, however, the immediate naval priorities chimed with echoes of pre-war annexationism. The German presence in southern Africa had provided a haven for diehard Boer rebels; it had also, in its ruthless suppression of the Herero rebellion in 1904, triggered fears of a native uprising within the Union. Thus, for London, the conquest of South-West Africa would ease the long-term security considerations of South Africa, and would tie the Union more closely to the empire.[112] For Botha himself it opened even grander visions—the incorporation of all southern Africa, including Bechuanaland, Rhodesia, and Nyasaland, within the Union.[113] He was therefore anxious that South Africa itself, and specifically its troops and not those from elsewhere in the empire, should respond to London's request.

Botha's cabinet was less convinced. At its meeting on 7 August four members supported him and four opposed. Much of the discussion focused on the practical difficulties of mounting the campaign. But the fundamental concern was Afrikaner reaction. The Boers of the Union could well end up fighting the Boers of South-West Africa. Principle was also at issue: Britain justified its engagement in the war by reference to the rights of small nations, and yet such scruples had not restrained it from crushing the Boer republics fourteen years earlier. For Boers to become the agents of British imperialism, particularly when the empire itself might be forfeit if Germany proved victorious in Europe, was to the Nationalists both morally unacceptable and politically inexpedient.

[112] Louis, *Great Britain and Germany's lost colonies*, 31.
[113] Meintjes, *Botha*, 205–6; M. W. Swanson, 'South West Africa in Trust 1915–1939', in Gifford and Louis (eds.), *Britain and Germany in Africa*, 632; Hyam, *Failure of South African Expansion*, 26.

Nonetheless, by 10 August the cabinet had convinced itself that, rather than become a source of increasing division among Afrikaners, the conquest of German South-West Africa could be a means for a newfound unity between English and Dutch. London had renewed its request on 9 August. The cabinet agreed to meet it on two conditions, both designed to ensure domestic unity. Parliament was to be asked to approve the campaign, and only volunteers were to be called upon to serve. Botha mentioned neither condition in his reply to London.[114] Nor was the prime minister alone in his underestimation of Boer opposition. J. C. Smuts, the minister of defence, reckoned that, 'when all is over and German South-West Africa again forms a part of our Afrikaaner heritage, feeling will quickly swing round and our action be generally approved'.[115] His inner conviction overrode his acceptance of mounting evidence to the contrary; it generated a mishandling of South Africa's mobilization that fell only just short of disaster.

A month elapsed before the South African parliament was called. On 10 September the assembly dutifully approved Botha's policy by ninety-one votes to ten, and on the 12th the Senate followed suit by twenty-four votes to five. On 14 September parliament was prorogued, and did not reconvene until 26 February 1915. Formally, the decision to invade South-West Africa was hallowed by popular approval. In reality, the inauguration of military preparations had preceded their ratification; the commencement of operations was postponed until late September, not because of constitutional nicety but because of the problem of naval co-operation. Most telling of all, the public justification for the campaign was no longer conquest but defence. The theme on which Botha and Smuts harped in their parliamentary speeches was the possibility of a German takeover of South Africa. Such improbabilities were buttressed by reference to border incidents, duly dressed up as a German invasion. The annexation of German territory and the cabinet's hope that this would fuel domestic conciliation were never mentioned.

The parliamentary session was the first open acknowledgement of South Africa's plan to invade South-West Africa. But speculation had begun on 11 August, when Smuts published the government's intention to organize adequate forces 'to provide for contingencies'.[116] Smuts specifically mentioned four volunteer regiments, thus reflecting the cabinet's condition of the previous day. But the 1912 Defence act, which created an army for South Africa, made all European males aged 17 to 60 liable for military service in time of war, and committed all those aged 17 to 25 to compulsory training. South Africa's forces had four main elements: a small body of permanent troops, either mounted rifles or artillery; an 'active citizen force', largely English in composition, based

---

[114] Spies, *South African Historical Journal*, I (1969), 47–57.
[115] Hancock and Poel, *Smuts papers*, iii. 201.
[116] Hancock, *Smuts 1870–1919*, 379.

on pre-1912 volunteer regiments, but completed to a strength of 25,000 if insufficient volunteers were forthcoming; rifle associations for older men, predominantly Boer burghers liable to be commandeered as they had been in the war with the British; and a cadet corps for those aged 13 to 17. The declared aim was Anglo-Boer integration but for many Boers the effects smacked of British imperialism. Khaki uniforms, clean-shaven faces and hierarchical rather than patriarchal and elective command structures were the military tools of the Boers' enemies not of the former Boer republics. The establishment of a cadet corps confirmed that the ultimate objective was Anglicization.

Moreover, the dualities of the Defence act carried a further threat. The act embodied both voluntarism and conscription. The intention to rely on the former could not be effected without providing expectations as to the latter. Botha declared in 1912 that he wanted 'a real Army, not only capable of coping with a little Kaffir war, but also able to defend South Africa against any odds, wherever they came from'.[117] His readiness in 1914 to dispense with the imperial troops stationed in South Africa displayed his resolve—an ambition which suggested that Smuts's four volunteer regiments would not be enough.

The ambiguity in Smuts's actions may have been the product of genuine confusion. The South African forces had no central staff and no command organization; Smuts and the civilian officials in the ministry of defence did everything. The minister's own command experience in the Boer War, although distinguished, was restricted: he had handled only small bodies of troops, with limited logistical needs. Furthermore, the outbreak of war found him without contingency plans, either for the defence of the Union or for the seizure of German territory.

On 14 August Smuts held a meeting of senior officers to make good some of these deficiencies. He endeavoured not to reveal the objective of the proposed arrangements, a manoeuvre that displayed his naivety about military planning as much as his sensitivity as to what he intended. However, C. F. Beyers, the commandant-general of the defence forces, having elicited that an invasion of South-West Africa was proposed, expressed his opposition. Beyers was not alone; many of the commandants had been appointed on his recommendation, not Smuts's, and two in particular, J. C. G. Kemp (the district staff officer of Western Transvaal) and S. G. Maritz (the district staff officer of the northern Cape, adjacent to the German frontier) made no secret of their sympathy for Beyers. Nobody resigned; nobody was dismissed. Smuts reasoned that to have such men in the service, and under oath, was better than to have them out.

Without an effective planning organization, and with what there was split as to what to do, the weakness of Pretoria's initial proposals for offensive action is

---

[117] Swart, *Journal of South African Studies*, XXIV (1998), 746; for what follows see also Collyer, *Campaign in German South West Africa*, 15–20.

unsurprising. But the major cause of confusion in fact arose from the difficulties of co-ordination with the Royal Navy.

The spine of German South-West Africa, running through the relatively fertile tableland in the north and centre of the colony, was the main railway. Beginning in the north, with spurs from Tsumeb and Grootfontein, it ran south-west to Karibib, and then south to the capital and main wireless station at Windhoek. From Windhoek it progressed through Keetmanshoop as far as Kalkfontein, about 95 kilometres short of the Orange river. Two lines ran to the coast, one in the north from Karibib to Swakopmund, and the other in the south from Keetmanshoop to Lüderitz. These two breaches apart, the perimeter of the colony was well-endowed with natural defensive barriers. The Atlantic coastline was bordered by a waterless strip, between 65 and 95 kilometres wide. The eastern frontier was bounded by the Kalahari desert. The obvious landward route for invasion, therefore, lay to the south, from the Cape across the Orange river. But the supply problems presented by this approach were considerable. The South African railhead at Prieska was about 225 kilometres from Upington, the base for offensive operations across the frontier. The territory north of the Orange river was arid. Furthermore, any advance from this direction would simply push the Germans back up their railway line, onto their own resources and lines of communication. It would not strike directly at the maritime objectives so important to the CID subcommittee.

By contrast, control of Swakopmund promised to bring decisive results in short order. Britain owned a small slab of territory alongside it, at Walvis Bay. It gave onto the most direct route to Windhoek, and seizure of these points would cut off any German troops facing south. Swakopmund was therefore Smuts's initial preference for a landing. But it was abandoned for lack of sufficient shipping to transport and escort expeditionary forces to both Swakopmund and Lüderitz. The fact that, given the choice, Lüderitz was selected over Swakopmund reveals how muddled the thinking had become. An offensive from Lüderitz carried many of the disadvantages present in the advance across the Cape frontier. The idea that it could be co-ordinated with the latter was far-fetched: the forces so deployed would describe an arc of up to 950 kilometres, without lateral communications, and would be attacking an enemy that would enjoy the advantage of the central position and the use of the railways in order to effect local concentrations.[118]

This, nonetheless, was the scheme adopted by Smuts on 21 August. Naval bombardment was to account for the wireless station and jetty at Swakopmund. The land forces were divided into three groups: Force A at Port Nolloth, on the Atlantic coast south of the Orange river; Force B at Upington; and Force

---

[118] Collyer, *Campaign in German South West Africa,* 28; Corbett, *Naval operations,* i. 316; Hancock and Poel, *Smuts papers,* iii. 201–2.

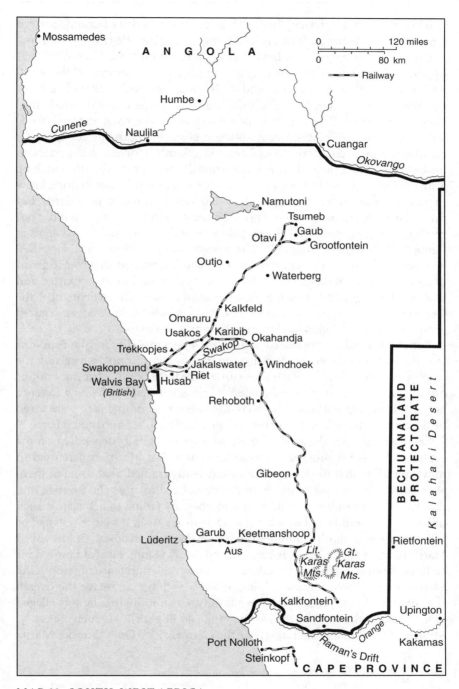

MAP 20. SOUTH-WEST AFRICA

C at Lüderitz. The total strength of all three groups was 5,000 rifles and fourteen guns, and in isolation each was insufficiently strong for offensive operations.

On 19 September Force C landed at Lüderitz. With three aircraft to their opponents' none, the Germans were able to track the movements of the South Africans. They decided not to defend the harbour, concluding that the guns of the Royal Navy would give the British artillery superiority. Instead, they concentrated their defensive efforts on the Orange. The river, although fordable in a number of places, was a sufficient obstacle to provide good opportunities for local counter-attacks before the South Africans could establish bridgeheads. Force A pushed north-eastwards from Port Nolloth, reaching Raman's Drift on the Orange by 14 September. On 24 September Pretoria knew that the Germans were moving south to Kalkfontein, not west to Lüderitz, but they relayed this information to Force A by post, with the result that it did not reach the force commander, Henry Lukin, till 7 October. Lukin's problems at Raman's Drift were considerable. The strength of his column was 1,800 rifles; he reckoned he had sufficient transport for 800. He pushed an advance guard of about 300 men and two guns forward of the Orange, but unsupported and without the wagons to carry their reserve ammunition. On 26 September the Germans, with 1,200 men and three batteries, encircled Lukin's advance guard at Sandfontein and killed or captured the entire command.

Both Lukin and Smuts shared a measure of responsibility for the Sandfontein disaster. Moreover, neither the conduct of the reconnaissance nor the resilience of the fighting (when they surrendered, the South Africans' ammunition stocks were far from exhausted)[119] reflected well on the new Defence Force. But the reputations of both commanders and commanded were saved by the action—or lack of it—on the part of S. G. Maritz, commanding Force B.

Lukin argued that the success of his advance was vitally dependent on the support of Force B progressing from Upington. But Maritz had refused to move, pleading that his forces were insufficiently trained, that some of them were conscripts and therefore could not be obliged to cross the frontier, and that many of his officers would refuse to obey. By failing to act against such dissent earlier, Smuts had now left it too late to act at all. If Maritz resigned or was dismissed, Lukin's column would be even more exposed. Smuts asked Maritz to come to Pretoria. He refused, and on 2/3 October instead moved his command out of Upington to Kakamas. Smuts, under pretence of reinforcing Maritz, moved fresh units to Upington on 4 October and gave the overall command to Coen Brits. The latter's loyalty was unthinking: he was alleged to have told Botha (in Afrikans, for he spoke no English), 'My men are ready; who[m] do we fight—the English or the Germans?'[120] On 7 October Maritz

---

[119] Hennig, *Deutsch-Südwest im Weltkriege*, 98.
[120] L'Ange, *Urgent imperial service*, 4; this is the most recent account of the campaign.

made contact with the Germans along the border, and on the 9th went into open rebellion, promoting himself to general and declaring South Africa's independence and war on Britain. He threatened to attack Upington unless he could speak to Christiaan De Wet, Beyers, Kemp, and Hertzog.[121]

Maritz's summons to the Afrikaner nationalists for support confirm that, from his perspective, the rebellion was a planned coup against Botha's government and not a spontaneous uprising by diehard Boers still carrying on the war of 1899–1902. After the commandants' meeting with Smuts on 14 August Maritz had initiated a plot to install Beyers as president of a provisional government, J. H. De La Rey as commandant-general of the defence force, Christiaan De Wet as head of the Orange Free State, and himself as head of the Cape. The rebellion was timed for 15 September. But in reality the uprising collapsed into a series of ill-co-ordinated movements, with diverse objectives, its execution characterized by compromise and indecisiveness.

Maritz himself was relatively junior, an unpleasant personality, and—in his station at Upington—remote from the centres of power within the Union. Potentially far more influential was De La Rey, a venerable hero of the Boer War and a close friend of both Botha and Smuts. De La Rey, fired by the apocalyptic visions of a crazed seer, was convinced that the return of the republic was imminent and that the outbreak of the war provided the opportunity to act; he also seems to have believed that Botha remained wedded to a declaration of Afrikaner independence if the opportunity arose. At any rate, De La Rey was persuaded by Botha and Smuts not to go into open rebellion on 13 August, and at a meeting on 15 August told his followers to disperse. At the Nationalists' first congress, held in Pretoria on 26 August, De La Rey's public position was akin to that of Hertzog: his loyalty was to South Africa, not to Britain or Germany. For Hertzog, neutrality promised success for South Africa whoever won in Europe; commitment to one side could prove fatal if the other proved victorious.

On 15 September, the day appointed for the rebellion and the day after parliament had been prorogued, Beyers, Kemp, and others resigned their commissions, protesting their opposition to the proposed invasion of South-West Africa. But Maritz was not ready. Moreover, that same afternoon Beyers and De La Rey failed to stop at a police roadblock, and the latter, mistaken for a member of a murderous gang, was shot dead. Beyers and Kemp felt that the opportunity to rebel had passed. At a meeting following De La Rey's funeral they confined themselves to protests against the invasion of South-West Africa, and to the organization of further meetings. When Botha, who had replaced Beyers as commandant-general, asked the comman-

---

[121] Davenport, *English Historical Review*, LXXVIII (1963), 73–94, is the major scholarly account of the rebellion; both Hancock, *Smuts*, 379–91, and Meintjes, *Botha*, chs. 14 and 15, are helpful; Lucas, *Empire at war*, 377–432, is full but partisan.

dants to volunteer for service in South-West Africa they did so without exception.[122]

But for Maritz's move to open defiance, therefore, Boer discontent might have fizzled and crackled without explosion. Maritz's declaration prompted Beyers, De Wet, and Kemp to renew contact with each other on 13 October. Even now they tried to cajole Botha rather than to topple him. Botha refused to listen. Moreover, on 11 October, in response to Maritz's rebellion, Smuts declared martial law, thus definitively moving from voluntarism to conscription for the recruitment of the defence force and so forcing Boers to decide where they stood. On 22 October the rebel leaders took a rather lukewarm decision to act, leaving the initiative to Beyers in the Transvaal and to De Wet in the Orange Free State. The fact that they did so hardened Maritz's resolve as he began to consider surrender after suffering defeat at Brits's hands at Kakamas on 24 October. Thus a series of ill-co-ordinated risings gained an outward appearance of cohesion and conspiracy. Thus too, 'strong speech and rash action went hand in hand with compromise'.[123]

Most rebels saw their action in a Boer tradition of 'armed protest' against a government policy of which they disapproved. Their motivations embraced opposition to conscription, resistance to the invasion of South-West Africa, and a sense of betrayal by Botha and Smuts. But they tapped into other grievances as well. Their strength was greatest in the regions which drought had ravaged and where indebtedness had increased, and among the landless, ousted by the farmers' preference for cheaper black labour. Landless Afrikaners were confronted by 'encroaching urban proletarianization'.[124] It was a process which threatened the familial and familiar values engendered by a society of pastoralists; their political values were egalitarian and republican. Into these they injected millenarianism, foretelling not only the end of British rule but also of capitalism. The Dutch Reformed Church, which at the outset supported the war, refused to decide whether the rebellion was treasonable or not. The fact that Hertzog, though appealed to by Maritz, stayed silent throughout—neither condoning nor repudiating the rebellion—increased the ambiguity as to the rebels' main aims. But it also ensured that, although Hertzog was its major beneficiary, the rebellion never assumed an exclusively national character. Opposition to the British, although present, took second place to the domestic dispute among the Boers.

To avoid Boer killing Boer in South-West Africa, Boer proposed to kill Boer within the Union. For Botha this was a better outcome than for either British or (as was offered by London) Australian troops to suppress the rebellion. By using Afrikaners rather than Englishmen, Botha hoped to preserve his policy

---

[122] Meintjes, *Botha*, 230.   [123] Lucas, *Empire at war*, iv. 396.

[124] Nasson, *Journal of Imperial and Commonwealth History*, XXIII (1995), 264. See also Swart, *Journal of South African Studies* XXIV (1998), 738–43.

of conciliation between the white races. Manoeuvre and negotiation, not battle and bloodletting, were the key features of the conduct of the rebellion on both sides. The total government casualties were 101 killed and wounded for 30,000 engaged. The rebels, whose maximum numbers may have reached 10,000, had 124 killed and 229 wounded.[125]

De Wet's personal dominance of the Orange Free State, allied to the central position of the province, gave his rising the greatest significance. Furthermore, his son's death in action envenomed his motives more than those of the others. With a following of about 5,000 men, he was attacked by Botha in Mushroom Valley, south of Winburg, on 12 November. Botha's plan miscarried: he hoped to have Lukin's and Brits's forces from the west in position to encircle De Wet. Nonetheless, the rebel force was broken and De Wet himself forced to flee into the desert, where he was captured on 2 December.

Botha's influence in Eastern Transvaal limited the dangers in that quarter. In Western Transvaal Beyers's efforts to negotiate with the government while still resisting it were an open confession of the weakness of his following and of his own uncertainty as to the correct course of action. Efforts to link with De Wet came to nought after Mushroom Valley, and on 16 November Beyers's own force was broken in an attack near Bultfontein. Beyers fled, first east, then west, and finally north. On 8 December he was drowned in the Vaal river while trying to escape capture by government forces.

Only Kemp was still in the field, and he—together with 500 men—had been dispatched by Beyers across the Kalahari to link with Maritz. After an epic trek, that defied the elements as well as the government, Kemp entered German territory to effect a junction with Maritz on 2 December. Kemp's report on the state of the rebellion within the Union was optimistic. But the exhausted condition of his men and horses prevented immediate offensive action. He himself was sick. Maritz did not inspire the confidence of the Germans. Conflicts between Maritz and the commander of the 'free corps' formed by the Germans from Boers within South-West Africa deepened the distrust. A thrust across the Orange river on 22 December that achieved both surprise and envelopment failed owing to the problems of Boer command. Kemp refused to subordinate himself to Maritz, and wanted to cut back to the Transvaal. Maritz in his turn felt he could not be seen to attack in direct co-operation with the Germans. When the Boers crossed the frontier once again, on 13 January 1915, with 1,000 men, they were only accompanied by four German guns; the main German thrust was intended to be over a 160 kilometres away to the west, on Steinkopf via Raman's Drift. Maritz's attack was directed at Upington but was not delivered until 24 January, and even then scattered its efforts over an

[125] Hancock, *Smuts 1870–1919*, 391; Lucas, *Empire at war*, iv. 425–6, gives much higher losses, totalling about 1,000 for both sides; Meintjes, *Botha*, 249, says 374 government troops were killed and wounded, and 190 rebels were killed and 350 wounded.

8-kilometre front. Reports of the rebellion's defeat increased the bickering. In a bid to revive the rebellion, the Germans abandoned their attack on Steinkopf for one closer to Upington, at Kakamas, on 31 January. But the attack miscarried, and they were in any case too late. The Boer rebels, including Kemp, had surrendered on the previous day. Only Maritz, the 'free corps', and the artillery which the Germans had allocated to the rebels returned across the frontier.[126]

Botha's policy of conciliation, begun during the course of the rebellion with an amnesty, continued after its conclusion with clemency. Only one rebel was executed: an officer who had not taken the precaution of resigning his commission before turning against the government. Of the leaders, 281 were put on trial, but by 24 March 1916 only fifty were still serving sentences and by the end of that year all had been released. Nonetheless, Botha had failed. The split between his South Africa party and Hertzog's Nationalists, between self-government within the empire and republicanism without, was confirmed. The threat of Boer rebellion persisted throughout the war. In the elections of October 1915 the Nationalists made a net gain of twenty seats, pulling in Afrikaner support from the South Africa party and the Labour party. Botha's power rested on the votes of English Unionists.

What had not prompted the rebellion was a pre-war German conspiracy to destabilize the British empire. Superficially the connections existed to confirm such a theory. The Kaiser had rattled his sabre in support of the Boers in 1896; Hertzog had been educated in Europe and not in Britain; Beyers had visited Germany just before the outbreak of war; Maritz had served in the campaign against the Hereros and was alleged to have been negotiating with the Germans since 1912. But not until the outbreak of war itself, and Britain's entry to it, did the Germans see the exploitation of British vulnerabilities at the Cape as an appropriate means of warfare. Furthermore, even then the perspective in Windhoek differed from that in Berlin. On 2 August Moltke included a Boer rebellion in a catalogue of indirect means by which Britain might be distracted from Europe.[127] But Dr Theodor Seitz, the governor of South-West Africa, realized that his support for rebellion must be measured and limited if its effects were not to backfire on Germany. Anything that smacked of a German-sponsored invasion of the Union from South-West Africa was in danger of reuniting South Africa's fractured peoples in a war of national defence. Contacts with the rebels were initiated on 26 August 1914, but because of the practical difficulties of communication could only be sustained with Maritz. On 17 October the Germans were prepared to recognize the formation of an independent South African republic in exchange for Walvis Bay, but left its

---

[126] Hennig, *Deutsch-Südwest in Weltkriege*, 102–5, 123–4, 129–32, 155–9; Oelhafen, *Feldzug in Südwest*, 98.

[127] Kautsky (ed.), *Die deutschen Dokumente zum Kriegsausbruch*, iii. 133.

achievement in the hands of the Boers themselves. Seitz was therefore punctilious in limiting German aid to the Boers to food and equipment. In this he was supported by the commander of the *Schütztruppen*, von Heydebreck, who shied away from the problems of direct co-operation in the field.[128]

At no stage, therefore, did the Germans mount a major attack across the Orange into South African territory. Pre-war instructions from the Colonial Office in Berlin, to remain on the defensive, were reiterated by Heydebreck on 4 August. The Germans were unable to exploit Botha's moment of maximum weakness, in November 1914, for fear that offensive action on their part would undermine the bases of rebel support. When in late January they did plan an attack, it miscarried owing to the Boers' failure at Upington and their subsequent surrender. By February 1915, when the rebellion was over, the Germans' moment to launch limited attacks against weak and scattered South African forces had passed. The only real advantage which the rebellion brought the Germans was a stay of execution. Botha was forced to postpone his invasion of the German colony, and thus was boosted the German hope that victory in Europe would come in time to settle Germany's position in South-West Africa.

The delay was not, however, a period in which the Germans' capacity for protracted defence waxed noticeably stronger. Seitz's consciousness of his vulnerability was accentuated by the fact that the forces available to him were considerably less than they had been a decade earlier. In August 1905, during the Herero rebellion, the Germans had 21,000 troops in South-West Africa. In August 1914 they numbered 2,000. Of the German population of 15,000, about 3,000 were mobilizable reservists. Thus, the Germans' total strength hovered around 5,000 men. The South Africans consistently exaggerated it, and even after the war put it at 7,000. Such a figure could not have been reached except by including auxiliaries of little military value. The major manpower resource, the native population of 80,000, was deliberately neglected, in the firm expectation that war with an external enemy would provoke at least the Hereros, and perhaps other tribes, to insurrection. The same argument kept the police force, in any case only 482 men, tied to its peacetime role except in the frontier areas. The Boer 'free corps' raised just over 100 men from a population of 1,600, and was disbanded after the fiasco before Upington at the end of January 1915.

In addition to numerical weakness, the Germans suffered from a lack of tactical and operational cohesion. This was not, as it was in the Cameroons, the product of inadequate communications. The completion of the railway in 1910 had been used to justify the reduction of the colony's garrison. So efficient were the internal wireless links that the Germans used them to excess, feeding the

[128] Seitz, *Südafrika in Weltkriege*, 29–32, 35–9; Hennig, *Deutsch-Südwest*, 74–5; Oelhafen, *Feldzug in Südwest*, 8–9, 31–2; Zirkel, 'Military power in German Colonial Policy', 104–7.

South Africans a flow of valuable intelligence in the form of intercepts. But the *Schütztruppen* had not, as a consequence, been grouped in larger formations. Instead, they were scattered in squads throughout the country, so as to provide local protection to the German settlers. As late as 10 February 1915, 132 separate units could still be counted. Thus, the senior officers had no experience of higher command. Moreover, in a war of low casualties it was ironic that those with staff training proved particularly vulnerable. Von Heydebreck fell victim to a premature explosion from a rifle grenade on 12 November 1914; his obvious successor had been killed at Sandfontein; and on 31 March 1915 the chief of staff to Viktor Franke, the new commander, died as a result of a fall from his horse. For the major stages of the campaign the Germans had as their chief of staff a reservist without staff training, and they had no officer to run the railway on military lines. They did organize three, and later four, battalions, each of three to four companies. They gave these the title of regiment in a bid to deceive the South Africans, not to reflect their actual strength, which at 450 men was equivalent to about half of a normal battalion.

The German forces in South-West Africa were therefore small both in aggregate and in their component parts. But South-West Africa could not have sustained forces of any larger size on a war footing. The colony had about 7 million marks in circulation; Seitz reckoned a further 5 million were needed to cover the costs of mobilization and defensive preparations. On 8 August, disregarding the colonial office's instructions to the contrary, Seitz printed his own note issue, and then introduced a savings scheme to keep gold in circulation.[129] With this cover he was able to accumulate sufficient food stocks to provide for the *Schütztruppen*'s peacetime strength in men and horses for fourteen months. But Seitz reckoned that, for the population as a whole, there was food for five months, and in some areas, including Windhoek, barely enough for three. In October the private purchase of food was forbidden. Only the Ovambo in the north cultivated enough to produce a surplus, and that only in years of heavy rain. The 1915 harvest was bad, and the Ovambo themselves starved. The Herero and Hottentot to the south had been hunters until the arrival of the Germans, and had become dependent on imports of maize and rice. The German farmers concentrated on cattle farming rather than on arable. On one level, therefore, the postponement of the South Africans' attack worked against the Germans. Oxen and mules were requisitioned to meet the *Schütztruppen*'s transport needs. Consequently, the livestock normally available for cultivation consumed existing stocks of fodder without contributing to its replacement.[130]

---

[129] Solff, the colonial minister, said he had authorized governors to issue promissory notes, or 'weissen Schuldscheine', as wages for employees, 10 August 1914; see Wolff, *Tagebücher*, i. 69.

[130] Reichsarchiv, *Weltkrieg*, ix. 475; Seitz, *Südafrika in Weltkrieg*, 15–17; Oelhafen, *Feldzug in Südwest*, 15–16 takes a more positive line on food.

The military impact of virtual famine in 1915 was considerable. Units could not remain either concentrated or stationary for long, as they had to disperse to forage and to water. Apart from a camel-mounted company for service in the Kalahari desert, the regular *Schütztruppen* were organized as mounted infantry with Cape ponies. The loads which they carried were heavier than those borne by the South African commandos; the latter, by riding lighter, put less strain on their mounts and proved far more mobile than their opponents. Moreover, the lack of fodder deprived the Germans of their ability to exploit their one area of real military strength. The *Schütztruppen* had forty-six guns, in addition to eleven machine cannons and nine light mountain guns; furthermore, they possessed, in dumps at Windhoek and Keetmanshoop, sufficient shells.[131] But the guns went short of ammunition for want of food for the oxen to draw the wagons.

The obvious route by which the Germans could relieve their economic plight lay to the north, through Portuguese Angola and its main southern port Mossamedes. German officials had already prospected across the frontier before the war. Ideas for linking the Portuguese and German railways had been adumbrated. But such talk was not congenial to the Portuguese. Their hold on Angola was incomplete, about a fifth of the colony enjoying effective independence in 1914, and was sustained only by continuous and brutal campaigning. Indeed, so notorious was Portuguese colonialism, so damaging to the cause of European civilization, that Britain and Germany had considered the partition of Portugal's African colonies in 1913.[132]

Anglo-German hostility in Africa both deepened and eased Portuguese fears for their colonies. German rhetoric about a central African empire gained credibility, and threatened Portugal's two major possessions, Angola and Mozambique. On the other hand, worries about British designs were abated by virtue of the Anglo-Portuguese alliance. The alliance, which dated back to 1386, did not require Portugal to become a belligerent. Indeed, the disorganized state of the armed services, the volatile political position after the fall of the monarchy in 1910, and the lack of any immediate war aim determined the contrary. Nor was there pressure from Britain. Portugal seemed likely to be a liability, not an asset; on 3 August Sir Edward Grey asked it to be neither neutral nor belligerent. But such an undignified stand, with Portugal obliged to Britain but not equal with it, rankled. Little by little, the belief that Portuguese self-respect demanded active belligerence, and that Portugal's

---

[131] Reichsarchiv, *Weltkrieg*, ix. 475; Seitz, *Südafrika in Weltkrieg*, 11–12, gives 70 in all; Hennig, *Deutsch-Südwest*, 30, says 30 guns, but he may be referring to field guns only. Oelhafen, *Feldzug in Südwest*, 13, gives 12 mountain guns, 8 field guns, and 50 antiquated pieces of eight different calibres. Seitz and Hennig are the two principal sources used to describe the German aspects of the campaign. Oelhafen is less analytical than either, and often differs from Hennig on numbers and even dates.
[132] Langhorne, *Historical Journal*, XVI (1973), 361–87.

African colonies would thereby be assured of British guarantees, gained credibility.[133]

The combined effect of these responses was to move Angola onto a war footing. On 11 September 1,500 troops left Lisbon for Portugal's West African colony, with a similar contingent bound for Mozambique. In Angola itself the governor-general ordered a state of siege on 8 September. His public intention was to check the banditry of the Ovambo in southern Angola; his true purpose was to stop the Germans' traffic from Mossamedes, via Humbe, and across the frontier. The troops from Europe, which boosted the total Portuguese strength in southern Angola to between 6,000 and 7,000 men, were to make this barrier effective. On 19 October 1914 a German patrol (according to the Portuguese) or mission (according to the Germans), fifteen strong, was arrested at the Portuguese border fort of Naulila. The Germans' interpreter, a Dane, deepened the confusion rather than elucidated it. In the ensuing mêlée the German administrator from Outjo and two reservist lieutenants were killed, apparently while making their escape.

When the news of Naulila reached Seitz he was uncertain whether or not Germany and Portugal were at war. The destruction of the Kamina wireless station precluded regular and direct contact with Germany; transmissions from Windhoek were interrupted by electric storms, and reception (Windhoek could listen to messages between Nauen and the United States) did not necessarily answer specific questions. In reality, as Seitz discovered in July 1915, Germany and Portugal were not at war. But the evidence on the ground— the build-up of Portuguese troops in southern Angola, the closing of the frontier to commerce, and now the murders of German officials—suggested the contrary. Seitz could not afford to have large bodies posted on his northern frontier. But the Boer rebellion gave him sufficient respite to organize punitive actions with a view to negating any Portuguese threat at the outset.

On 31 October a Portuguese post at Cuangar, its garrison oblivious of the events at Naulila, was surprised and massacred by a small German detachment operating out of Grootfontein. Four adjacent posts were then abandoned by their men rather than face the Germans. Meanwhile a much larger force, about 500 Germans, aided (as the Grootfontein force had been) by local Africans, and commanded by Franke, temporarily quitted the south for an attack on Naulila itself. Franke's advance beyond the railhead was slow, his column needed 2,000 oxen to move, and the Portuguese were alerted to his approach by mid-November. Franke attacked Naulila on 18 December. The two sides were approximately equal in strength, but the Naulila fortifications had been designed to deal with native insurrection, not the Germans' six artillery pieces. A lucky shell detonated the Portuguese munitions dump. The Portuguese,

[133] Vincent-Smith, *European Studies Review*, IV (1974), 207–14.

poorly commanded and not acclimatized to African service, broke and fled; their losses totalled 182.

The defeat, though severe, was local. But Alves Roçadas, the Portuguese commander, fell victim to exaggerated notions of German military brilliance. Anticipating a German envelopment, he fell back to Humbe, abandoning all the Ovambo region between the Cunene river and the Rhodesian frontier. Equipped with the arms (including 1,000 rifles and four machine-guns) left by the Portuguese in their panic, the tribes of the entire area rose in revolt, spurred by their hatred of Roçadas, by the evident military weakness of Portugal, and by famine. The Portuguese, now commanded by Pereira d'Eça, confronted a long campaign, punctuated with major battles and conducted with fearful brutality. Pereira d'Eça was alleged to have ordered the killing of all natives aged over 10: some were hanged with barbed wire, others crucified. Franke, meanwhile, retired southwards. Throughout the rest of the South-West African campaign Germany's northern frontier would be neutralized by a buffer of insurrectionary Ovambo.[134]

Franke's reputation as a fighting soldier, evidenced by his being awarded the *pour le mérite* for his services in the Herero rebellion, was confirmed by the Naulila attack. He returned to Windhoek to find himself appointed commander of all German forces in South-West Africa. But his tenure of that command suggested that courage and initiative on the battlefield were not allied to strategic or operational resourcefulness. The conduct of the German defence, which in 1914 had not been without its rewards, was in 1915 to be marked by an almost total lack of fighting spirit.[135]

Heydebreck, Franke's predecessor, had correctly identified the main routes by which the South Africans might advance. But the lack of German fortifications at Swakopmund and Lüderitz, and the problems for an invader of crossing the coastal desert strip, had decided him to concentrate his western defences inland at Usakos and Aus. In a plan drawn up in 1911 he had identified the major danger as lying in the south, and had proposed to conduct his principal operations on the Orange river. The course of events in 1914 reinforced his pre-war thinking.[136] No landing had taken place at Swakopmund. That at Lüderitz was advancing on Aus, rebuilding the railway which the Germans had destroyed in their retreat, but its progress was slow and easily observed.

---

[134] Pélissier, *Guerres grises*, 482–8; Pélissier, *Cahiers d'études africaines*, IX (1969), 97–100; Hennig, *Deutsch-Südwest*, 108–22; Seitz, *Südafrika in Weltkrieg*, 39–41; Ribeiro de Meneses, *Journal of Contemporary History*, XXXIII (1998), 91. Oelhafen, *Feldzug in Südwest*, 76–92, gives different figures from those adopted here.

[135] Botha suggested his nerve had gone, 25 May 1915: Hancock and Poel, *Smuts papers*, iii. 283.

[136] On Heydebreck's 1911 plan, see Reichsarchiv *Weltkrieg*, ix. 476; Schwarte, *Weltkampf*, iv. 364, makes related points.

Franke's strategy followed Heydebreck's—to fall back into the interior and to the north, forcing the enemy to expend both time and effort in coping with the inhospitable border regions. While Franke was at Windhoek with two companies, two were left at Swakopmund, four were positioned at Aus, and seven were distributed in the south. Franke's intention to withdraw and Windhoek's central position in relation to the colony's railway and wireless communications made sense of his dispositions, provided he remained responsive to enemy movements. But the bulk of the *Schütztruppen* lay outside the orbit of his direct command, facing south, and not ready to guard the Germans' line of retreat to the more productive areas of the north.

On 25 December 1914 the South Africans landed at Walvis Bay. The destruction of Spee's East Asiatic Squadron on 8 December had removed the major threat to British amphibious operations in the South Atlantic, as well as German hopes of naval success. The German response was extraordinarily lackadaisical. Major Ritter, temporarily commanding in Franke's absence in Angola, and determined to mount an offensive in the south, reckoned that any advance from Walvis Bay could be pinched out round Windhoek by redeployment from Aus and by Franke's troops returning from the north. Franke took over from Ritter on 20 January, but even he, though much less optimistic, averred that the operations in the north were no more than a demonstration. The South Africans occupied Swakopmund without opposition on 13 January. The Germans fell back to defensive positions between Riet and Jakalswater. Throughout January most of their efforts were put into reinforcing Aus, and planning the abortive thrusts across the Orange. On 25 February the German command finally acknowledged that the major South African advance might develop from Swakopmund. Offensive and counter-offensive operations south of Kalkfontein were abandoned. But only one company was diverted to the north. Aus remained the largest single concentration, and the troops at Kalkfontein were given the task of protecting it from the south and east.

With hindsight, the Germans would have been better advised to abandon the south of the colony and to concentrate all their forces against Swakopmund. Such decisiveness, however, would have presumed a greater clarity and urgency in the movements of the South Africans.

By early 1915 South Africa had at least 70,000 men under arms, of which 43,000 were employed in the campaign in South-West Africa. Such abundance of manpower apparently freed Pretoria from the compulsion to concentrate. Thrusts from Swakopmund, Lüderitz, the Cape, and even across the Kalahari were all possible, and all undertaken. Botha, who on 22 February landed at Walvis Bay to take over command of the northern force, was convinced that the advance from Swakopmund on Windhoek would be the blow that proved strategically decisive. It would sever the Germans' main axis of communications at its centre and wrongfoot the German strategy of a fighting withdrawal from south to north. He was also persuaded, both by common sense and by the intercepts of German communications, that the Germans would recognize this and withdraw to the north of the colony. He wished, therefore, to co-ordinate the offensives from Lüderitz and across the Orange river in the light of this appreciation. But Botha was not able, at least at first, to give the Swakopmund landing the priority which his status suggested.

Throughout 1914 the landing at Lüderitz had assumed a primacy which could not now be easily set aside. Progress there was slow: the railway had to be restored, and horses died of thirst or sank knee-deep in the soft sand. The force commander, Sir Duncan McKenzie, proceeded with excessive deliberation. But Botha feared that if he pushed him too hard he would resign, and that his Natal commandos would take offence, thus bringing English–Afrikaner tensions into play. To the south Smuts, although nominally defence minister in Pretoria, was planning his own campaign, combining three brigades in a push on Keetmanshoop from the south, and a further column coming across the Kalahari from the east. Botha told Smuts that his advance would be redundant if McKenzie took Aus, as all points to the south and east would then fall automatically. In April he prevailed on Smuts to go to Lüderitz, to direct the southern operations both there and on the Orange river. The penalty, however, was further confusion in Pretoria, where the defence ministry was robbed of its head and therefore could not issue orders on its own responsibility.

If the manpower superiority available on paper had translated directly into fighting power these frustrations would not have mattered. But Botha's concept of operations rested on the mobility and horsemanship of the Boer commandos. Manoeuvre, envelopment, and speed were the essentials with which he planned to dislodge the Germans. To do this, the mounted brigades need their own integrated transport. The only alternative or additional means of supply was the railway line from Swakopmund inland. But this had been destroyed by the Germans and had first to be reconstructed. Moreover, the decision was taken to convert it from narrow gauge to the South African standard gauge. Although the earthworks and embankments were intact, progress was sluggish: 42 kilometres in two months, up until the end of February, and 1–5 kilometres a day thereafter. At that rate Boer mobility would be forfeit, and the Germans would have ample opportunity to fall back on their own communications, fighting a series of defensive actions in prepared positions.

Pretoria nonetheless assumed that Botha's advance would follow the pace and direction set by the railway line. Troops left the Cape assured that their transport needs would be met at Swakopmund. On arrival they found nothing. The brackish water on the coast rendered horses ill for the first few days. Inland, the Germans had poisoned the wells with sheep-dip. Fresh wells were dug, but their capacity was limited to a maximum of 8,000 gallons a day. Water was therefore shipped from the Cape. The remount position remained desperate. Wagons had teams of ten mules, when they needed twelve to cross the sandy terrain. A round trip of 95 kilometres, to the front and back, rendered the beasts unserviceable for a week. In theory each regiment's transport carried sufficient supplies for two days, and each brigade's for a further three; in practice the regiment's bore half a day's, and the brigade's one. Thus, the loss of weapons and mules under McKenzie and Smuts whittled away Botha's striking power. Eight thousand mounted troops were deployed in the south, but only 5,000 in the north.

Friction between Pretoria and Swakopmund and between Swakopmund and Lüderitz flared. Within the northern force, the engineers building the line and the remount officers allocating the mules and horses were predominantly English; the frustrations they engendered exacerbated Boer animosity. For British staff officers, Boer independence—manifested tactically by a failure to report back progress or to co-ordinate actions—proved equally infuriating.[137]

Botha's advance on Windhoek was therefore a staccato affair. Unusually heavy rain flooded the bed of the Swakop river, and reports of sufficient grazing inland decided Botha to abandon the railway route to Usakos in favour of the more direct approach along the Swakop. On 19 March he struck out from Husab towards Riet and Jakalswater. The Germans had rested their defences on an arc of hills west of Jakalswater and Riet and curving round to the south. The whole position extended over 48 kilometres and was held by four under-strength companies, with minimal artillery support and only thirty rifles in reserve at Jakalswater. On 20 March the South Africans enveloped the Germans with mounted brigades to north and south. The infantry in the centre engaged the Germans frontally at a range of 1,000 yards. The Germans on the right were pulled northwards towards the Swakopmund–Jakalswater light railway, opening the gaps in the centre; their retreat to the east lay across open ground now flanked by enemy cavalry. Virtually the entire German command on the central heights, about 200 men, was captured. But Botha's hopes of sufficient grass for his horses proved misplaced. On 24 March he had no choice but to pull them back to Swakopmund. Riet was established as a forward base for the accumulation of supplies. Deprived of transport, Botha could not move on either Usakos or Windhoek. Thus, during late March and early April, as the southern offensives developed, the Germans' line of retreat to the north lay open.

[137] Collyer, *German South West Africa*, 58–61, 73, 77, 85–6, 156–7, is blunt on most of these issues; Collyer was Botha's chief of staff and his account is incisive, if didactic. See also Botha's letters to Smuts, Hancock, and Poel, *Smuts papers*, iii. 242–70. Other English-language accounts: Lucas, *Empire at war*, iv. 433–58; Farwell, *Great War in Africa*, 72–104. Reitz, *Trekking on*, is the memoir of a participant.

Jakalswater–Riet proved to be the only major defensive action fought by the Germans in the entire campaign; it finally convinced Franke of the seriousness of the threat from Swakopmund. Furthermore, an intercepted message from Botha to McKenzie revealed that a major advance from Lüderitz was also in hand. Aus was directly threatened from the west, but also increasingly from the south and east. All the river crossings on the Orange were in South African hands by the end of March, and with the capture of Kalkfontein on 5 April Jacob van Deventer's southern force gained a foothold on the German railway: the South Africans' own railhead was pushed forward from Prieska with the aim of linking the two networks. On 31 March 3,000 men under Berrangé breached South-West Africa's eastern frontier near Rietfontein. By pushing motor vehicles carrying water ahead of the main column, they had traversed 400 kilometres of the Kalahari desert in two weeks. With Deventer's and Berrange's columns converging on Keetmanshoop from south and east, the potentially strong defensive postion of the Karas mountains was enveloped from both sides.

McKenzie had halted at Garub to muster sufficient supplies to sustain the large forces which he calculated would be required to take Aus. But when he entered the town on 30 March he was unopposed. Despite its strong defences, Aus was evacuated on 27 March and most of its garrison directed north.

The German withdrawal from the south was conducted by Hauptmann von Kleist, a strong-willed officer of fighting temperament and outdated tactical views. Franke was too distant or too confused to impose his will. Kleist's principal task was to get his command and as much livestock as possible intact to the north. But, like many of the Germans whose only direct experience of Afrikaners had been Maritz's rebels or the diehard Boer émigrés, he under-estimated the military qualities—and above all the speed of manoeuvre—of his opponents. He concluded that McKenzie's force would halt at Aus, and that the southern columns would aim to converge on Keetmanshoop, not encircle his own units. Kleist therefore allowed small fractions of his forces to become engaged in minor actions, and failed to press his retreat with sufficient expedition. He abandoned Keetmanshoop on 19 April, but then halted at Gibeon, concluding that he had sufficient distance between himself and his opponents. However, on 14 April McKenzie's horsemen had quitted Aus and the line of the railway, striking north-east towards Gibeon. The South Africans covered 335 kilometres in eleven days, and on the night of 25/6 April hit the railway line just north of Gibeon. Kleist's command, 800 men and two field guns, was completely unprepared. McKenzie's men blew the line north of Gibeon during the night, but the enveloping force was deployed too close to the site of the explosion, in exposed positions, and the bright moonlight enabled the Germans to counter-attack and drive the South Africans back. When daylight came, McKenzie's handling of the main assault from the south did much to recover the situation, but the Germans were able to escape to the north in the direction of Rehoboth, albeit at the cost of 241 casualties.

So far, much to the Germans' surprise and relief, the native population had remained quiet. But Kleist's defeat at Gibeon, combined with the German evacuation of the south, spurred the Bastards to rise in revolt. The Germans felt aggrieved. The Bastards, or Basters, émigrés of mixed blood from the Cape, had been treated with relative generosity, granted their own lands and the formation of their own police company. But the company, intended for use within the Bastards' own territory, was employed first on German lines of communications and then in guarding white prisoners of war. In performing these duties it released Germans for the front line. Furthermore, the Bastards did not escape the requisitioning of oxen and wagons. On 1 April Neels van Wyck, a Bastard chief, contacted Botha, offering to co-operate against the Germans. Although himself reliant on at least 30,000 blacks and coloureds as labourers and drivers, Botha remained keen that this should be a white man's war and told van Wyck not to get involved. But ten days later the Bastards began seizing weapons and oxen from German settlers, killing three who opposed them. On 18 April Bastard police attacked Rehoboth. By 25 April three German companies were engaged in a punitive expedition into Bastard territory, west of the railway line and south of Rehoboth. But the collapse of the Germans' hold on the south forced them to break off their action on 8 May, and to carve out a line of retreat to the north, skirting Windhoek to its east.

The combination of Kleist's slow withdrawal and then the Bastard rebellion prevented the rapid formation of a large German concentration to face Botha. On 25/6 April the Germans tried to use their control of the main Swakopmund–Usakos railway line to attack the South African infantry at Trekkopjes. The aim was to blow the railway to the South Africans' rear so that the forward formations could be isolated and defeated in detail. German pilots had revealed that the South Africans had withdrawn their artillery but had mistaken a dozen armoured cars for water trucks. The Germans lost their way in the dark, failed to destroy the railway, and so allowed the South Africans to be reinforced.

Until now Botha's supply problems had prevented him taking advantage of the Germans' dispersion; the chance of cutting off the forces to the south by mastering the railway line at Karibib evaporated, as his men slaughtered and ate the draught oxen for his artillery and the goats intended to trigger the mines which the Germans had laid in his path. On 18 April he had only 125 of the 400 wagons he reckoned he needed to maintain two to three days' supply with his troops. However, at the end of the month Pretoria promised 300 wagons and sufficient mules. Confident he would soon be able to sustain his advance, Botha now felt able to exploit the five days' supplies which the light railway to Jakalswater had allowed him to accumulate. He concentrated four mounted brigades at Riet, and directed two under Brits northwards to Karibib and the other two under M. W. Myburgh eastwards up the Swakop to Oko-handja, so cutting off Franke to the north and forcing Kleist to the east as he retreated on Waterberg. On 3 May the Germans abandoned Karibib and its wells. Two days later the South Africans, their horses desperate for water, and confronting disaster if they did not get it, entered the town. Despite the broken terrain, they had encountered no German resistance.

Karibib was the railway junction which linked the north of the colony with the centre and the south. Its possession consolidated Botha's hold on all the objectives set by London. On 13 May he was able formally to take possession of Windhoek. At the start of the war Windhoek's wireless station had been out of commission, as it was undergoing repairs. But after Kamina's fall it had become the new pivot of communication between Africa and Nauen. Its signals were liable to daily interruption because of atmospheric conditions, and were entirely suspended in November. But full links were restored by January. Without Windhoek, the Germans depended on the wireless at Tsu-meb in the north. Constructed from materials taken from the station at Swakopmund, it had begun operation on 24 November 1914. It provided good links throughout the colony and into Angola, but it could not commun-icate with Mwanza and Bukoba in German East Africa, as had been hoped, nor could it signal Nauen.[138] Thus the campaign's principal strategic objectives, the wireless stations and the ports, had been secured. Smuts's southern force was dispersed, most of it returning to South Africa and only part reinforcing Botha.

Botha calculated that a field force of 8,000 mounted men, giving a total of four brigades would be enough for the final stage of the campaign. What dictated the size of his command was his wish to have sufficient supplies and transport to be able to sustain continuous marches for three to four weeks. Getting the ratio between men and wagons right imposed a halt of six weeks. Karibib was virtually without food when it was occupied. On 15 May the railway from Karibib to Usakos and Swakopmund was reopened, thus allowing Botha to shift his line of communications from the Swakop and to begin the accumulation of stocks. The process was slow: on one day seven out of twelve engines broke down. The railways gave priority to the needs of humans rather than of horses. There was little grazing around Windhoek, and in desperation animals were reduced to eating their own dung. When Botha resumed his advance, 10,000 horses and mules had to be left behind. But their fitness, given their privations, was more striking than their sickness. At the outbreak of the war the Union Defence Force had one veterinary officer, who was on the sick list, one veterinary NCO, and one civilian storeman. Its complement of

[138] Klein-Arendt, *Kamina ruft Nauen*, 276–89.

veterinary officers and NCOs swelled to forty-seven and 450 respectively. Annual equine mortality on the campaign was only 9.09 per cent. Such disease as occurred was principally a product of starvation rather than other causes.[139] By 11 June Botha had collected sufficient wagons to carry two to three weeks' supplies, giving him a total of 100 for each mounted brigade. The fact that the north was more fertile than the territory he had so far traversed also enabled him to reckon on feeding off the land.

German strategy remained unaltered: its objective was to retain sufficient territory to uphold Germany's claim to South-West Africa at the final peace negotiations. Seitz therefore proposed, on 21 May, that the two sides agree an armistice on the basis of the territorial status quo, to be valid for the duration of the war. He gave his efforts bite by threatening the involvement of the black population in the campaign. But the negotiations failed. Botha's aims were now patently South African rather than imperial—to complete the conquest of German South-West Africa with Union troops, so reinforcing Pretoria's claim to the colony. Seitz and Franke therefore reworked their strategy in the light of an imminent renewal of Botha's offensive. A German presence would be sustained by forces in being rather than by territorial possession: the *Schütztruppen* should give ground and should avoid battle, because in their size and cohesion rested the symbols of German authority.

Both Botha and Smuts were worried that Franke would go over to guerrilla warfare, as they themselves had done in comparable circumstances. But the *Schutztruppe*'s commander discounted the possibility. Small bush patrols would represent no real threat to the South African forces, and would be easily outnumbered and crushed; the victims would be the German settlers, caught up in the plundering and looting which guerrilla operations would license. Instead, Franke proposed to fall back up the railway line from Omaruru to Kalkfeld, regrouping with Kleist's forces retreating northwards on a more easterly line to Waterberg. The munitions dump, originally at Keetmanshoop, 1,200 kilometres distant, had been shifted to the railhead at Tsumeb, and a stiff defensive battle could be staged at Otavi. Beyond Tsumeb the battle could be continued no further than Namutoni. The Germans lacked the wagons to operate far from the railway. The famine in Ovambo territory ruled out a retreat into Angola. Botha considered that the Germans might even try to break through to East Africa, but Franke does not appear to have given the idea serious consideration.

On 18 June Botha began his advance, with a total of 13,000 men and 20,000 animals. His command was divided into four columns, two hugging the railway and two far out on either flank, the left under Coen Brits and the right under Myburgh. He now had a far better picture of the enemy's inten-

---

[139] Blenkinsop and Rainey, *Veterinary services*, 385–402.

tions; he knew from wireless intercepts that Namutoni was the terminus for the Germans' withdrawal, and since the end of May six Henri Farman reconnaissance aircraft had given him the ability to track Franke's movements over vast distances. Nonetheless, the key remained supply. The mounted brigades operated without a pause, using the open flanks to envelop the Germans and advancing with a speed that caught them unprepared. By the end of the campaign Brits's brigade had advanced 735 kilometres from its base, and had covered the last 545 kilometres in twenty days. Myburgh's moved 767 kilometres from its base. Even the infantry brigade following the railway sustained a marching rate of 22.5 kilometres a day for sixteen days.

The Germans fell back to Otavi on 26/7 June, mistakenly imagining that they had created sufficient breathing space to organize their defences, and assuming that Botha would be slowed by his supply and water problems. Franke had a total of nine regular and eight reservist *Schütztruppen* companies, three infantry companies, and eight-and-a-half artillery batteries. He placed himself at Tsumeb, and entrusted the key position at Otavifontein to seven companies and ten machine-guns under Major Ritter. Ritter's task was to buy eight to fourteen days while the Germans prepared further defences. The flank to the east and Grootfontein were protected by a line of mountains, its passes guarded by Kleist's group.[140]

On 1 July Botha's two central mounted brigades, about 3,500 men, approached Otavi. The South Africans believed that they were about to encounter the main German body, and thought that, with their strength disposed to the flanks, they would be outnumbered. In fact Ritter had about 1,000 men, and had not had time to prepare his defences. He decided to deploy in depth, reflecting the fears that the South Africans' penchant for envelopment had now generated. Thus, the low hills screening Otavi and Otavifontein, and giving fields of fire over both the railway and the road, were only thinly held, and the troops there so posted on either flank as not to give each other mutual support. Botha moved forward on his left, threatening the western flank of the hills and, further back, of Otavi. Ritter drew back to Otavifontein and to Otavi mountain behind it. But he had no artillery positions prepared, and the bush which covered the area broke up the co-ordination of his units as they retreated. By 1 p.m. Ritter was pulling back to Gaub. His total losses were three dead, eight wounded, and twenty captured. A defence of only two days would have compelled Botha to retreat for lack of water.

On 3 July Seitz and Franke met to review their position. Kleist had been ordered to fall back on Gaub the previous night, Myburgh's men having appeared before his front on the 2nd. Reports from Outjo suggested that Brits would be in Namutoni in a couple of days. An attack to retake Otavi-

---

[140] Hennig, *Deutsch-Südwest*, 272–90.

fontein was mooted, but the feebleness of its defence on the 1st suggested that the *Schutztruppe*'s morale had collapsed. Certainly there was little fight in Franke. Seitz the civilian was the most reluctant to surrender; Franke the soldier saw only needless casualties through continuing. Seitz was persuaded to ask for an armistice.

The South-West African campaign was characterized by a maximum of movement and a minimum of casualties. Its heroes were the horses and mules which had enabled the deep envelopments favoured by Botha. On occasion they had covered 64 kilometres a day. More than half of Botha's force was mounted, a ratio redolent of warfare in the sixteenth century and earlier. But it was a composition made possible by the internal combustion engine. Rapid advances across sandy wastes, the wells poisoned by the retreating Germans, relied on lorry-borne water; only in the final stages, north of Karibib, had the horses been able to draw to any great extent on local supplies.

The concomitant of mobility was a low casualty rate. The Union suffered greater losses in the rebellion than in the South-West African campaign proper: 113 had died through enemy action and 153 through disease or accident; 263 had been wounded. The determination of the Germans to keep their forces intact, and their readiness in pursuit of this policy to give ground rather than to fight, were only too evident at the final surrender: 4,740 men, with thirty-seven field guns, twenty-two machine-guns, and large stocks of ammunition (even after guns had been sunk in a deep-water lake, and 2 million rounds and 8,000 rifles at Tsumeb had been burnt[141]) had agreed terms without a climactic battle. Of the total of 1,188 German casualties, only 103 were killed and fully 890 were prisoners of war. The campaign's legacy, for all its failure to cement English–Afrikaner relations as Botha and Smuts had hoped, was a rapid reconciliation between German and South African.

On 9 July Botha agreed to terms which allowed the German reservists to return to their homes, German schools to continue to function, and the German civilian administration to remain in place. Botha's aim was white settlement. He recognized clearly the need for the ruling minorities to collaborate. The Germans could provide stability while Boer immigration got under way. On 25 June 1915 the Cape railway, extended from Prieska to Upington on 20 November, reached the German railhead at Kalkfontein. Into this local co-operation other, imperially derived considerations did not intrude. The glut of diamonds on the London market, and the freezing of diamond sales to prevent their export to Germany via Holland, put a major commercial pressure on South-West Africa into temporary abeyance. The vivid portrayal of German colonial atrocities, fed by the vicious suppression of the Herero rebellion, which had been ignored before 1914, took off after the war's outbreak. None-

---

[141] Schoen, *Deutschen Feuerwerkswesens*, 1356–7.

theless, the cause of humanitarianism did not prompt the South Africans to remove Germans from South-West Africa. In 1918 there were still about 12,000 Germans resident. Only after the deportation of half that number in the same year were the remainder outnumbered by immigrant Afrikaners.[142] By biding his time in 1915, Botha laid the foundations for South Africa's own brand of colonialism in 1918.

EAST AFRICA, 1914–1915

On 2 March 1919 the Germans who had returned from East Africa marched through the Brandenburg Gate to be received by representatives of the Weimar government. At their head rode Paul von Lettow-Vorbeck, wearing the slouch-hat of the *Schütztruppen*, his neck adorned with the *pour le mérite*. It was a victory parade. The following year, in his book *Heia Safari!*, Lettow-Vorbeck would tell German youth of his exploits, of how with inferior forces he had sustained the war in Africa until surrender in Europe had forced him to lay down his arms. The *Schütztruppen* of East Africa embodied the German army's notion of its own invincibility; leadership and determination had enabled the few to prevail against the many; morale had triumphed over matériel.

Lettow-Vorbeck was indubitably a fine commander, who led by example and drove himself as hard as he drove his men. The loyalty he inspired in his troops became a key element in the agitation of German colonialists for the return of their territories after 1919. But his reputation has rested not simply on the needs of German militarism or German imperialism, on its supporting role in the argument that Germany was stabbed in the back. Beyond his own country, the *Schütztruppen* commander came to be venerated as a master of guerrilla war. The origins of such an interpretation lay with the South Africans who had fought him in 1916. The Boers among them, mindful of their own war against the British, and perhaps sensitive about their performance when the roles were reversed, responded happily to the idea that they had influenced Lettow's strategic outlook.[143] Lettow lived on until 1964. By then the practice of communist insurgency gave the techniques of guerrilla warfare fresh fascination, providing the lens through which Lettow's achievements were reassessed, and augmenting his band of Anglophone admirers.

---

[142] M. W. Swanson, 'South West Africa in Trust 1915–1939', in Gifford and Louis (eds.), *Britain and Germany in Africa*, 635–7, 645–50; Louis, 'The origins of the "sacred trust" ', 56–8; Newbury, *Journal of Imperial and Commonwealth History*, XVI (1988), 92–4, 100–3.

[143] Deppe, *Mit Lettow-Vorbeck*, 459.

Thus, the campaign in East Africa has not met with the neglect meted out to the other sub-Saharan theatres of the First World War.[144] But its analysis has been skewed by two mistaken premisses.

First, while it is true that Lettow himself remained active in the field throughout the war, his sustained defence of German East Africa extended to only twenty months (March 1916 to November 1917). Zimmerman's battle in the Cameroons was comparable in length. Indeed, without the Cameroons and without South-West Africa British forces would have been able to concentrate against Lettow much earlier in the war and at a stage when he was much less ready. If Lettow had taken the command in the Cameroons and not in East Africa (as was originally intended in 1913), or if the Entente had elected to deal with East Africa before the Cameroons and not vice versa, Zimmerman, not Lettow, might have ridden through the Brandenburg Gate in 1919.

Secondly, Lettow was never consistently a practitioner of guerrilla warfare. The *Schütztruppen* were trained to bush fighting, and in this both they and their commander excelled. But Lettow's own operational priorities remained those of the German military doctrine in which he was trained. His memoirs contain no theory relevant to the guerrilla; instead, they again and again bear testimony to his desire for envelopment, encirclement, and the decisive battle. Wintgens's great raid into the north of British-occupied territory in 1917, a model of guerrilla practice, was criticized by Lettow as undermining the principle of concentration.[145] Most telling of all, contemporary theories of guerrilla war are grounded in ideas of national liberation; nothing could have been further from Lettow's mind.

The primary strength of the guerrilla rests not on force of arms but on his knowledge of the country and on the material support vouchsafed him by its population. Lettow's protracted resistance was sustained by both factors. And yet Lettow himself never fully recognized the political and economic foundations on which his campaign rested. His views were shaped by the circumstances of his appointment. Both Heydebreck in South-West Africa and Zimmerman in the Cameroons were creatures of the military department of the Colonial Office; hence, their priority was to protect their respective

---

[144] The best of the recent English-language accounts of the campaign, all of them 'popular' histories, include Farwell, *Great War in Africa*; Miller, *Battle for the Bundu*; Mosley, *Duel for Kilimanjaro*; Miller is the most stimulating. The fullest operational narrative is Boell, *Operationen in Ostafrika*: Boell served on Lettow's staff. The British official history, Hordern, *Military operations: East Africa*, is good, but only Volume I appeared (up to September 1916). Lucas, *Empire at war*, Volume IV, covers the whole campaign. Two of the more illuminating memoirs are British. Fendall, *East African Force*, covers the campaign to 1918 and is provocative on supply and administration. Meinertzhagen, *Army Diary*, is opinionated, runs only to 1916, but is full of insights. Of the Germans, Schnee, *Deutsch-Ostafrika im Weltkriege*, both discusses civil administration and, surprisingly, gives a clearer account of operations than does Lettow-Vorbeck, *Reminiscences*. Deppe, *Mit Lettow-Vorbeck*, is particularly full for 1917–18.

[145] Lettow-Vorbeck, *Reminiscences*, 4, 198, 205–6, 209–10, 213, on offensive-mindedness; 189 on Wintgens.

colonies. Lettow was the product of a bureaucratic takeover, an appointee of the general staff.[146] On 15 May 1914, four months after arriving in East Africa, he reported to Berlin that war in the colony should not 'be treated as a self-sufficient episode. It and the great war can react off each other.'[147] By taking the offensive, the *Schütztruppen* would draw British troops away from the main theatre and employ British warships in oceanic escort duties distant from home waters. German East Africa was therefore a means to an end. African interests were subordinate to German, local political stability and economic progress secondary to European military necessity. On 15 September 1918, as the war drew to its conclusion, Ludwig Deppe, a doctor with Lettow's force, wrote in his diary: 'Behind us we leave destroyed fields, ransacked magazines and, for the immediate future, starvation. We are no longer the agents of culture; our track is marked by death, plundering and evacuated villages, just like the progress of our own and enemy armies in the Thirty Years War.'[148] 'Lettow-Vorbeck's brilliant campaign', Tanganyika's historian has concluded, 'was the climax of Africa's exploitation: its use as a mere battlefield.'[149]

Lettow's pre-war proposals never found formal sanction. The old East African hands, military as well as civilian, anticipated disaster. The concentration of the *Schütztruppen*'s field companies for the attack would remove the main peace-keeping force at the local level. Between 1889 and 1904 Germany had conducted over seventy-five punitive expeditions in the area, some of breathtaking brutality. As recently as 1905–6 the Maji-Maji rebellion had rocked Germany's hold on the south of the colony, and in 1914 two districts, Iringa and Mahenge, were still under military administration. For every German in East Africa there were 1,000 natives. To take away the soldiers, to enlist porters, requisition food-stocks, to suspend overseas trade—all these were direct routes to the incitement of rebellion.

In Wilhelmstal a great redoubt was built, behind which the white civil population could seek refuge. But its wooden palisades became a joke. The great unspoken assumption on which Lettow's campaign in East Africa rested was the absence of rebellion. Broadly speaking, where German administration remained in place, there order and loyalty persisted. The exceptions were minor. In the north the Masai on the frontier used the power vacuum to revert to their cattle-stealing and lawless ways; during the course of 1915 some of them were won over to the British. In the south, fears of fresh rebellion—while persistent—proved greater than their actuality. The scorched-earth policies of the Germans after the Maji-Maji rising had caused famine and depopulation

---

[146] Wolfgang Petter, 'Der Kampf um die deutschen Kolonien', in Michalka (ed.), *Der Erste Weltkrieg*, 399–400.
[147] Boell, *Operationen*, 23.
[148] Deppe, *Mit Lettow-Vorbeck*, 393.
[149] Iliffe, *Tanganyika*, 241.

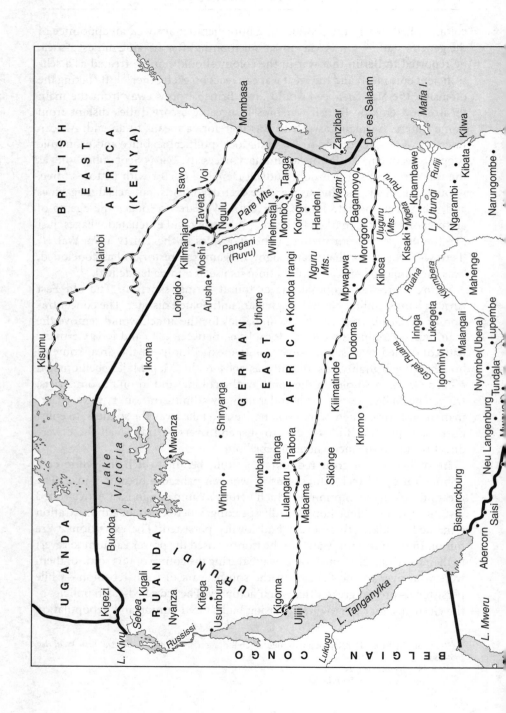

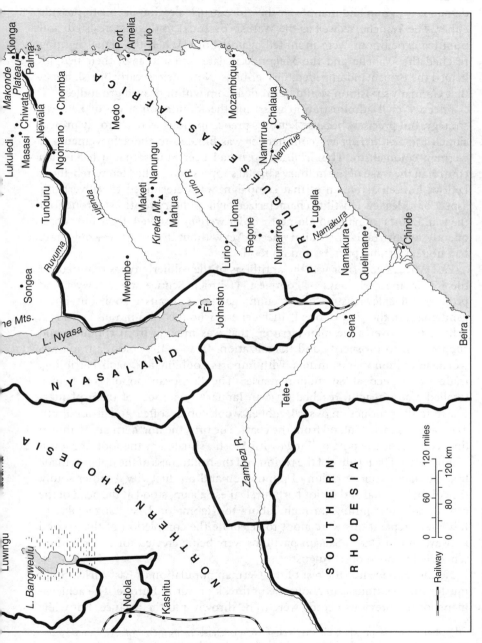

MAP 21. EAST AFRICA

around Mahenge. The rains then failed in 1913. The Germans' war-driven demands for grain and manpower therefore struck a region ill able to provide either. The Wahehe, as well as the Watusi (or Tutsi) to the east, resisted, and punitive expeditions were mounted against both. When the actual fighting reached the Wahehe and the Makonde in late 1916 and 1917, their peoples helped the British and impeded the Germans. Nonetheless, early British hopes that Germany's position would be eroded from within proved groundless.[150]

Effective civil administration was thus the foundation-stone of Lettow's strategy. But precisely because Lettow's preoccupations were narrowly professional, the *Schütztruppen*'s commander was blinded to the achievements of German colonialism. The *Schütztruppen* had been subordinated to civilian control in the wake of the military's brutal suppression of the Herero rebellion. Lettow, himself a veteran of that campaign, was determined to subvert this aspect of its legacy. Hostility characterized civil–military relations throughout the war. Efforts to maintain domestic order were interpreted, then and subsequently, as obstructive of military needs. Yet without them Lettow would have had no recruits, no porters, and no food.

East Africa's governor was the antithesis of the soldierly types required for the job in the early days of conquest. Heinrich Schnee was a lawyer and professional colonialist—'full of cunning, by no means a fool, but not a gentleman', in the view of one British general who met him in 1918.[151] In 1912 Schnee took over a German territory that was moving from conquest and suppression to prosperity and liberalization. In 1906 the colony's trade was worth 36 million marks; in 1913, with imports doubling and exports tripling, trade was valued at 89 million marks. The European population, which totalled 2,000 in 1901, reached 5,336 in January 1913, most of them planters drawn to the production of sisal, rubber, wool, copra, coffee, and groundnuts. Two railways thrust inland from the coast. The first, the northern or Usambara line, connected the port of Tanga with Moshi, situated at the foot of Mount Kilimanjaro. The fertility of the region and the healthiness of the uplands made this the major concentration of population and productivity. Further south, the colony's capital and major harbour, Dar es Salaam, stood at the head of the central railway, running through Tabora to Kigoma on Lake Tanganyika. In July 1914 preparations were afoot to celebrate the completion of this second railway, and in Dar es Salaam pavilions were being erected for an exhibition scheduled to open on 15 August.

Neither Schnee nor the rest of the German population of East Africa could muster much enthusiasm about the outbreak of war in Europe. The achievements of the previous decade were to be thrown into the balance. But while

---

[150] Ibid. 251–5; Deppe, *Mit Lettow-Vorbeck*, 100–1, 191; Schnee, *Deutsch-Ostafrika*, vi. 77, 118–25, 218–24, 270–3. I am grateful to Ross Anderson for the point about the Makonde.

[151] Fendall, *East African Force*, 129.

neutrality would serve Schnee's purposes, his hopes for its fulfilment were never unrealistic. On 2 August 1914 the colonial office in Berlin, uncertain about the likelihood of British involvement, instructed Schnee to quieten fears of war among the settler population. This, and not a naive faith in the Congo act, buoyed Schnee's hopes. On 5 August Schnee knew that Britain and Germany were at war, and told the German population to expect an attack from British East Africa. If the Congo act had really affected Schnee's calculations it would have been evident in his dealings with his western neighbours, the Belgians, who in August did pursue a policy of neutrality in Africa. But on 9 August Schnee (wrongly) concluded that Belgian belligerence embraced Africa as well as Europe, and it was an attack by a German gunboat against a Belgian on Lake Tanganyika on 22 August that precipitated Belgium's abandonment of neutrality.

Nonetheless, the neutrality question generated the first major clash between Lettow and his nominal superior, Schnee. Lettow argued in terms consonant with his European military priorities: neutrality would be to Britain's advantage, not Germany's, since Britain would be able to redeploy its assets in other theatres, whereas Germany, by dint of its naval inferiority, would not. Schnee's concern, however, was not with the grand strategy of European war but with the immediate issue of coastal defence. None of German East Africa's ports had been fortified. The only major naval unit in the region was the light cruiser *Königsberg*, based at Dar es Salaam. Dar es Salaam was a better harbour than any of those possessed by Germany on Africa's west coast. But a British colony, Zanzibar, lay athwart its entrance. The German navy, therefore, had no intention of using it in wartime. In accordance with her orders, *Königsberg* put to sea on 31 July rather than risk being blockaded in harbour. Her captain, Max Looff, was clear that he would be unable to return to Dar es Salaam. Schnee's position was most unsatisfactory: he possessed a port which he knew the British would regard as a base for cruiser warfare but which the cruiser in question had no intention of using. The Royal Navy's Cape Squadron already had *Königsberg* under surveillance; that it would bombard Dar es Salaam, killing women and children and destroying civilian installations, was highly probable; the Germans' inability to reply would dent their prestige with the native population. On 5 August Schnee declared Dar es Salaam an open town, and ordered the troops within it to positions outside. His solution to his defencelessness was therefore partial neutrality—to abandon the protection of the coast and so counter the only imminent external threat.[152]

Schnee's decision was in accord with the plan concerted with the German general staff before the war and essentially adopted by Lettow at its outset: to

[152] Marine-Archiv, *Krieg zur See. Kreuzerkrieg*, ii. 122–8; see also Ganz, *Militärgeschichtliche Mitteilungen*, 21 (1977), 40, 47.

abandon the coast and withdraw inland to where the British could not easily follow.[153] But Lettow was furious. Schnee's plan appeared to deny the use of Dar es Salaam to the *Königsberg* but permit it to her British opponents. In reality the German navy, not Schnee, had deemed Dar es Salaam superfluous. To underline the point, the commander of the survey ship *Möwe* ordered that a floating dock be sunk across the harbour entrance, and then scuttled his own command in the harbour itself. On 8 August two British cruisers bombarded the harbour, their objective being to destroy the wireless station. Under the protection of a white flag, Schnee's representatives explained their policy, blew up the wireless station, and withdrew into the interior. On 17 August the Royal Navy's Cape Squadron accepted the neutralization not only of Dar es Salaam but also of Tanga. Thus was British naval weakness in the region writ large: inferior to the *Königsberg* in speed and no more than its equal in armament, the Cape Squadron was much more concerned about threats to the Indian Ocean's trading routes than it was about the East African coastline.[154]

Lettow's bellicosity in these early days of the war seemed faintly ridiculous: among the German population he acquired the nickname the 'Mad Mullah'.[155] Schnee's policy in relation to the coast infuriated him because of its connotations of cowardice; strategically, it served Lettow's purposes extraordinarily well.

In 1912 Schnee's and Lettow's predecessors had agreed a plan that anticipated an all-round defence of the colony combined with limited offensive thrusts. By leaving the *Schütztruppen* scattered, the purposes of domestic order as well as of colonial defence would be simultaneously satisfied. The plan presumed that the defence of the coast would be abandoned at an early stage. However, on his arrival in East Africa Lettow had proposed to recast the 1912 plan in the light of his European priorities. He argued that the Germans should not scatter their forces but should unite in the north for an attack into British East Africa, thus forcing the enemy over to the defence and so relieving the Germans of their own defensive obligations. Lettow's proposal had received an ambivalent response in Berlin. In East Africa itself the fear of rebellion cautioned against concentration. When war broke out, therefore, Schnee favoured a more limited grouping at Pugu, outside Dar es Salaam. But on 15 August the Germans captured Taveta, south-east of Kiliminjaro, just across the frontier into British territory and a vital staging post for any British advance. With his northern defences more secure, Lettow's case for thrusts against the Uganda railway, running from Mombasa to Kisumu on Lake Victoria, gained in credibility. On the German side of the northern frontier

---

[153] Deppe, *Mit Lettoew-Vorbeck*, 22.
[154] Corbett, *Naval operations*, Volume I, draws a veil over these Anglo-German negotiations, and their implications.
[155] Boell, *Operationen*, 43.

were the resources—both men and food—which would permit troop concentrations to be sustained and supplied; on the British side was a waterless expanse which would inhibit any enemy counter. British agreement to Dar es Salaam's neutrality, by relieving the Germans of any residual obligations to protect the coast, confirmed Schnee in his acceptance of Lettow's proposals. Between 20 and 24 August seven field companies began their move from the central railway to the northern.[156]

The strength of the *Schütztruppen* on the outbreak of war stood at 218 Europeans and 2,542 askaris, divided into fourteen field companies. Each company numbered between 150 and 200 askaris, and had sixteen to twenty German officers and NCOs. With its complement of porters and auxiliaries, its total ration strength could rise to 400. Four further companies were raised on mobilization, although the number of fit and young reservists was—owing to the long service of the regular askaris—small. The European civilian population had formed rifle associations in the years preceding the war, primarily for self-defence in the event of rebellion, and these contributed three more companies: by the end of 1914 1,670 German reservists had been called up. Finally, the police numbered fifty-five Europeans and 2,160 blacks. Lettow was scathing about their military qualities and resented their ability to draw recruits from the *Schütztruppen*. Moreover, not until 1917 was the last of them incorporated into the military forces. But it may not be fanciful to see in their numbers and in their subordination to civil control a reason for the unexpectedly good order of the colony during the war.[157]

The *Schütztruppen* were a professional military elite, proud of their vocation and often the sons of soldiers. Originally their recruiting area had embraced the Sudan, Abyssinia, and Somalia, but by 1914 well over two-thirds came from within German East Africa itself, from Urundi, Tabora, Iringa, and Songea. Their initial period of enlistment was five years, and the combination of generous pay and enhanced status ensured frequent re-enlistment. Their officers served in the colony for a minimum of two-and-a-half years. In reality many served much longer, and six had been in East Africa since before 1908. Lettow himself, although only recently arrived, boasted experience far more relevant than most German officers could claim: he had visited the Boer republics, served in the Boxer rebellion, and had been wounded in the Herero uprising. The Germans' discipline was harsh, but clear and uncapricious: fifteen lashes with a horsewhip was the penalty for not obeying orders, and twenty-five for lying. The askaris' loyalty is a moot point. Of the 13,430 casualties which they suffered throughout the war, 4,510 were reported as

---

[156] Boell, *Operationen*, 22–4, 39–41; Reichsarchiv, *Weltkrieg*, ix. 480–2.

[157] The minor variations given in 1914 strengths deny any attempt to be definitive. On the whole, Boell, *Operationen*, 28, has been followed in preference to Lettow-Vorbeck, *Reminiscences*, 19; Reichsarchiv, *Weltkrieg*, ix. 480, 483; Matuschka, 'Organisationsgeschichte des Heeres', 204–5.

missing, 4,275 as captured, and 2,847 as deserters. Sufficient indications of poor morale are present in these figures to give the lie to German claims of an extraordinary faithfulness to the Kaiser. Those who soldiered on frequently did so because their wives accompanied them: their homes and property rested in the *Schutztruppe*. But equally, the casualty figures were disproportionately swollen in 1917–18, when the askaris were far from their native territories with inadequate supplies and with pay considerably in arrears. No question-mark stands over askari loyalty until late 1916; and equally Lettow still had—for all its diminution—an effective fighting force in November 1918.[158]

In January 1914 all bar three of the field companies were armed with the 1871-model, black-powder carbine. Its retention had been justified on the grounds that bush warfare involved fighting at close quarters, success resting on surprise rather than on musketry. Lettow was anxious to increase the firepower of his troops, and by the outbreak of the war the number of companies equipped with the 1898 smokeless magazine rifle had risen to six. In addition, each company had two to four machine-guns. The thirty-one field guns were all obsolete, of small calibres and provided with insufficient ammunition.[159]

The askaris never achieved the level of markmanship to which Lettow aspired. The key weapon proved to be the machine-gun, more mobile than the field gun and manned by Europeans.[160] But their small-unit tactics were brilliantly adapted to the terrain in which they fought. Rather than embrace the 1906 German infantry regulations, the *Schütztruppen* of East Africa had their own manual based on their experiences against local insurgents. They recognized that retreat with minimum losses could be counted success, that pursuit of an apparently vanquished foe could be the prelude to ambush. The Germans had learnt the techniques of bush warfare, how to use ground but avoid fixed positions. Herein is the source of Lettow's claim to be a guerrilla leader. In reality, these tactics were the bread and butter of the *Schütztruppen* before his arrival. His achievement was to recognize their potential application in the event of conflict with the adjacent colonial powers.[161]

The British made no such imaginative leap. For them bush warfare and operations against European powers belonged in separate and largely self-contained compartments, at least until January 1917. They had, in the King's African Rifles, a unit comparable with the *Schütztruppen*. But in August 1914 it boasted only three battalions, one each in Nyasaland, Uganda, and Kenya. A fourth, also based in Nyasaland, had just been disbanded. Many of its members

---

[158] Boell, *Operationen*, 427, for casualties; on morale, see Ranger, *Dance and society*, 53–4, 58, 66; Iliffe, *Tanganyika*, 248, is more critical; for punishments, review of Burkhard Vieweg, *Macho Porini*, in *Militärgeschichtliche Mitteilungen*, 56 (1997), 572; for problems in 1917–18, Deppe, *Mit Lettow-Vorbeck*, 385, 390, 392.

[159] Again figures vary; those given here are maximums.

[160] Reitz, *Trekking on*, 84; Young, *Marching on Tanga*, 215.

[161] Miller, *Battle for the Bundu*, 15–19.

had crossed the frontier to Neu Langenburg to enlist in the better-paid *Schütztruppen*, with the result that the company there used British bugle-calls and English words of command. Both the Uganda and the Kenya battalions were engaged in operations on their northern frontiers, in Turkana, Jubaland, and Somalia. Thus, of the King's African Rifles' total strength of 2,319 askaris, only about 150 were available in Nairobi to protect the Uganda railway. Moreover, the battalion organization, apparently so much better adapted for war against a European opponent than the field-company structure of the *Schütztruppen*, was misleading. Each battalion consisted of eight small and therefore weak companies, not four large ones as had just been adopted in the British army proper. The ratio of Europeans to blacks was much less favourable than in the German units: the numbers of officers were comparable (sixty-two British to sixty-three German), but there were only two British NCOs to sixty-seven German. Like the *Schütztruppen*, the King's African Rifles had no supporting units, no transport and supply services; unlike them, its administration was based not in East Africa but in London.[162]

Therefore, when the CID subcommittee met on 5 August 1914 it had to reckon with the problem that British East Africa had insufficient local forces for defence, let alone attack. The most recent operational plan for the area, that of 1912, recognized this: its thrust was entirely defensive, relying on the Royal Navy and developments in Europe. But the subcommittee's decision to target the port and wireless station of Dar es Salaam demanded an offensive capability. Its solution, first adumbrated in an ill-worked-out plan of 1898, was to call on the Indian army. Present at the meeting was Brigadier-General A. R. Hoskins, the inspector-general of the King's African Rifles, who was home on leave. Hoskins warned the committee of the problems of campaigning in East Africa, reminding them that the low-lying coastal strip was hot, humid, and malarial. The favoured point of invasion in the 1898 plan had been from Voi towards Moshi, via Taveta, in the much healthier uplands of the foothills of Kilimanjaro. Seaborne attacks along the coast were to prevent the Germans concentrating to the north. Thus, the immediate naval priorities in 1914 were at odds with the likely area of land operations. Moreover, the limited objectives of the former contrasted with the ambition of the latter: the 1898 plan reckoned on the conquest of all German East Africa.[163] The subcommittee's conclusion was to ask for not one but two Indian Expeditionary Forces (IEFs), B to go to Dar es Salaam and C to reinforce the King's African Rifles in British East Africa. Hoskins apart, the committee was deprived of intelligence or serious studies to support what it now proposed. The campaign and the King's African Rifles

---

[162] Moyse-Bartlett, *King's African Rifles*, 259–60, 265, 335; Hordern, *East Africa*, i. 9, 11, 15, 561–4, 575, 579; Lucas, *Empire at war*, iv. 209, 225, 229.

[163] Hodges, *Carrier Corps*, 18–19; Geoffrey Hodges, 'Military labour in East Africa', in Page (ed.), *Africa and the First World War*, 137.

were the responsibility of the Colonial Office; the Colonial Office had asked the India Office for troops; those troops were to fulfil objectives set by the Admiralty. The War Office was not directly involved and yet was the only ministry that possessed a general staff with which to work through the implications of the undertaking.[164]

By September East Africa came low in the priorities of the India Office. Its first need was for India's own security and good order, particularly on the north-west frontier; secondly, it had agreed to send two divisions to Europe; thirdly, Indian Expeditionary Force D was being readied for operations in the Persian Gulf in the event of war with Turkey. On 28 August IEF B's raid on Dar es Salaam was postponed. But, for the Admiralty, the cruiser threat, and German East Africa's position alongside the main shipping lanes through the Indian Ocean to the Red Sea and the Suez Canal, made the dispatch of IEF B increasingly urgent. *Königsberg* had, by virtue of her speed and the prevailing bad weather, eluded the Cape Squadron, and had captured a British merchantman off Aden on 6 August. Deprived of Dar es Salaam, *Königsberg* profited from the coastal survey completed in early 1914 by the *Möwe*. It revealed eight useable channels in the delta of the Rufiji river, more than the Royal Navy could blockade even if it had known about them, which it did not. It was here that *Königsberg* established her lair. On 20 September she sallied forth once more, raided Zanzibar, and sank a British light cruiser. The material damage done by *Königsberg* was sustainable. But the inability to track her, the suddenness of her incursions, and—from September—the combined effect of *Emden*'s entry on the eastern end of the scene were creating havoc with the maritime traffic of the Indian Ocean.

IEF B was resuscitated. But its objectives were now expanded to meet Admiralty needs, and far exceeded the resources allocated to them. Major-General A. E. Aitken, IEF B's commander, was instructed to take possession of all the bases on the German East African coastline, beginning not with Dar es Salaam but with Tanga. If IEF B took the more northerly port first, its operations could—so Aitken was advised—be combined with a thrust by IEF C from Tsavo towards Moshi. Having got control of both ends of the northern railway, Aitken would be in a position to advance on the central railway. The Germans would probably then seek terms. On 5 August the CID subcommittee envisaged a limited raid; on 1 October it was aiming 'to bring the whole of German East Africa under British authority'.[165]

The version of his instructions telegraphed to Aitken seemed to leave him no discretion with regard to a landing at Tanga. That at least was the view in India. The supporting document, sent by post and only received by Aitken on his

---

[164] Hordern, *East Africa*, i. 12–13, 16–18, 29–31; Callwell, *Experiences of a dug-out*, 175–7; Maxon, *Struggle for Kenya*, 79–80.
[165] Hordern, *East Africa*, 65.

arrival in Mombasa on 31 October, did leave him with a choice. But by that stage Aitken had fallen victim to the optimism prevailing in the British camp. The British ex-consul in Dar es Salaam, Norman King, was its principal author, encouraging the view that rebellion would ensue the moment the British attacked, that the German civilian population had little fight, and that Tanga itself would be virtually undefended. At the conference held in Mombasa on 31 October IEF B's intelligence officer, Richard Meinertzhagen, a man of considerable Kenyan experience, did not disagree with the last point. But he observed that the Germans were concentrated in the Moshi area, and that they could therefore move troops by train to Tanga within thirty hours; at the very least they could operate on interior lines against IEF B and C, commands too far apart to have reciprocal effect, and thus liable to defeat in detail. Meinertzhagen's views should have weighed more heavily with Aitken in view of the—for him—major revelation of the Mombasa conference, that the British would not enjoy the advantage of surprise. The navy's agreement to respect the neutrality of Dar es Salaam and Tanga had been rejected by the Admiralty on 26 August. Rear-Admiral King-Hall, commander-in-chief at the Cape, was duly informed, but decided that the two towns would not be told until 'shortly before any further offensive action', in order to avoid the Germans preparing their defences. The abrogation of the neutrality agreements was confirmed in Mombasa on 22 October. By now the East Africa station had been transferred to the East Indies command, and administrative confusion may explain the determination of Captain F. W. Caulfeild, commanding the light cruiser *Fox*, that a separate notice of intention to resume hostilities was required at Tanga. If King's appreciation of German morale was right, a peaceful approach might pay dividends. Aitken agreed, albeit reluctantly, that one hour's notice be given.

The planning of the Tanga landing was deficient in many respects, but the real stumbling-block was the shambolic state of IEF B. Originally built round a brigade subsequently purloined for the Gulf, it was composed of units that encountered each other and their commanders for the first time a week before embarkation. One brigade came from Bangalore, not one of the 'martial' areas of India, and the other was formed of the troops of the Indian princely states. Meinertzhagen thought them 'the worst in India'. Aitken, however, remained confident that 'the Indian army will make short work of a lot of niggers'.[166] With a command 8,000 strong against an anticipated 4,500, most of whom he expected either to be at Moshi or to desert, Aitken felt that he could refuse the offer of the 3rd King's African Rifles. Thus, none of his force was versed in bush warfare. Two battalions had not seen field service for a generation, and their

---

[166] Meinertzhagen, *Army Diary*, 82, 84, 105; Hordern, *East Africa*, i. 60–78, is full on the planning, if too generous to Aitken. See also Ross Anderson, *War in History*, VIII (2001) (Forthcoming).

equipment was accordingly antiquated: short-magazine Lee-Enfield rifles and machine-guns were only issued just prior to departure. Once aboard, the force remained at anchor for a week awaiting escorts before sailing. The troops were not allowed to disembark and refit at Mombasa for fear of losing surprise. Therefore, when IEF B's convoy stood off Tanga on 2 November its members had been afloat for the best part of a month, many of them seasick throughout that time, and all of them losing what little battle-fitness they had.

At 7.05 a.m. on 2 November Caulfeild took HMS *Fox* into Tanga and called on the German district officer, Dr Auracher, to surrender the town or be exposed to bombardment. Auracher procrastinated, saying he must refer to higher authority. At 10.40 a.m. Aitken received a signal from *Fox* to say that Tanga had not surrendered. The convoy carrying IEF B was 15 miles off shore in order to be over the horizon while these negotiations were conducted. Not until the afternoon did the British ships approach land. Caulfeild meanwhile was obsessed with the fear of mines across the harbour entrance, and refused to bring *Fox*'s guns to bear to cover Aitken's landing. HMS *Goliath*, a battleship with 12-inch armament, had broken down off Mombasa, and thus its firepower too was lost. Aitken therefore decided to disembark not at Tanga itself but at a beach sufficiently distant from the town to be undefended. The light was already going when the first battalions began to come ashore; the unfamiliar process of disembarkation, carried out in the dark, left the Indian states forces exhausted and bewildered on a crowded beachhead as dawn broke on 3 November. The lead units, part of M. J. Tighe's brigade, set off towards Tanga at 4.30 a.m., but they were pinned down on the eastern edge of the town by 5.30. Dense bush impeded Tighe's communications and observation, and he was outflanked on his left. By 10 a.m. his demoralized brigade was back at its start point.

When the action began Tanga was held by a single company, consisting of former policemen and charged principally with the maintenance of order. Although Lettow had received abundant intelligence from spies and wireless intercepts of IEF B's coming, his attention had remained fixed on the north. He believed that any British attack on the coast was likely to be co-ordinated with an advance on Moshi. This made an attack on Tanga more likely than one on Dar es Salaam to the south, but to meet it head on conflicted with the pre-war plan to abandon the coast. Therefore, Lettow's initial response to the threat was to want to blow up 40 kilometres of railway track inland from Tanga, so as to isolate any beachhead the British might establish.[167] Such a course of action could have made sense if the British had indeed simultaneously attacked from the north, but they did not: they did not even consider the idea until the Mombasa conference on 31 October, far too late for there to be a realistic chance of its being effected.

[167] Deppe, *Mit Lettow-Vorbeck*, 22.

Schnee stopped Lettow blowing the line. Lettow's sole response was to pre-position two further companies some kilometres to Tanga's west. Admittedly, his plans were complicated by Schnee's continuing to argue that Tanga was an open town. But by late October its population was no longer under such illusions, and on the 29th Lettow reminded Auracher that his duty as a reserve officer was to obey the military commander, not the governor. On 2 November Auracher, the moment he had finished his parley with Caulfeild, donned his uniform and placed himself under military command. Three further companies had already begun the move from Moshi to Tanga. Each company required an independent train. Between 2 and 6 November the northern railway's locomotives covered 6,443 kilometres compared with the 2,785 normal in peace for the same period, and on 3 November (the crucial day) they tripled the peacetime performance.[168]

Lettow himself arrived at Tanga on the night of 3/4 November to find that the three pre-positioned companies had been withdrawn. Mounting a bicycle, the *Schütztruppen* commander went through the deserted town on a personal and unimpeded reconnaissance of the British beachhead. He now had the equivalent of seven companies immediately available, with two more due to arrive during the course of 4 November. He decided to hold Tanga to its east, and to position his reserves behind his right wing with a view to counter-attacking the British from that quarter.

IEF B's advance began at noon on 4 November. It was very hot; units lost touch with each other in the thick bush; the fighting was mostly at ranges of 50 yards or less; the Indians were already wilting before they reached the eastern environs of Tanga. Because of the congestion on the beach, Aitken had decided not to disembark his artillery but to work the guns from the ships' decks. Caulfeild, however, remained reluctant to bring *Fox* in close, and there were no observation officers forward on land to direct the guns' fire. Thus the infantry was deprived of effective artillery support. Aitken's right, formed of the best Indian battalion and a British regular battalion, made satisfactory progress nonetheless, and got into Tanga. But the heaviness of the fighting at the town's eastern end pulled them towards the right and away from the left, which by the afternoon had disintegrated. One battalion broke and ran, causing what remained of the others on the left to bunch even further to the right. At 4.30 p.m. Lettow, his position apparently desperate, but now optimistic of accomplishing the cherished envelopment despite his inferior numbers, committed his reserve company against the British left. A further German company arrived from Moshi, but, to Lettow's chagrin, in the confusion followed and supported the first, rather than extended the German right. To regain control of their units some company commanders ordered their buglers to sound the

<hr/>

[168] Boell, *Operationen*, 74–6, 83.

recall. The call was taken up and an effort to regroup became a signal to fall back.

Thus, as darkness began to descend Aitken's position was far from irredeemable. Meinertzhagen recognized the German bugle call, but others on Aitken's staff insisted it was the charge. Aitken himself had lost confidence. He had kept no reserve in hand to exploit such an opportunity as now presented itself. At 8 p.m., rather than occupy the untenanted German positions, he ordered re-embarkation.

By 5 November Lettow had collected 1,500 troops. He awaited a fresh British onslaught, his defences far from secure, and conscious that only three companies remained to hold the area around Kilimanjaro. Tanga itself was at last under naval gunfire. At 5 p.m. Lettow concluded that the town was untenable, and prepared to fall back out of range. But IEF B was already on its way. By 3.20 p.m. the British evacuation was complete. All the heavy stores, whose rapid reshipment had not been envisaged, were abandoned on the beachhead. In the north IEF C had fallen back, its attack on 3 November too late to hold the Germans around Moshi and too lackadaisical to reach the water at Longido. Aitken had handed his adversary a major victory.

Aitken was relieved of his command. His successor, Major-General R. Wapshare, was 'a kindly old gentleman, nervous, physically unfit and devoid of military knowledge'.[169] Four months later he too had gone, replaced by Tighe, a much more pugnacious character, but given to drink. Overall responsibility for the East African theatre was shifted from India to the War Office. IEFs B and C were amalgamated, and distributed along the northern German frontier. Wapshare reckoned two further brigades were required to enable him to go over to the offensive, Tighe said one-and-a-half. Kitchener allowed them one British battalion. In addition he sent his brother to look into the expansion of the King's African Rifles. Wapshare thought two new battalions could be raised; the Colonial Office approved an increase of only 600 men, to be absorbed within the existing battalion structure; and the secretary of war's brother reported that it would require European units to do the job. Kitchener's policy was adamantly defensive.

Colonial Office concerns not only postponed the real growth of the King's African Rifles, they also blocked the exploitation of other sources of manpower. In August 1914 Gaston Doumergue, first as France's foreign minister and then as colonial minister, had suggested joint French and British operations in East Africa, hoping thereby to boost France's claims in that quarter of the continent. The Colonial Office had no wish to excite French ambitions in an area where hitherto they had been non-existent. Thus, French troops in Madagascar remained unemployed.[170]

---

[169] Meinertzhagen, *Army Diary*, 109.
[170] Andrew and Kanya-Forstner, *France Overseas*, 60, 62; Digre, *Imperialism's new clothes*, 79–80.

More serious was the question of Belgian co-operation. At the very least, Belgian gains at the expense of German East Africa might be used as bargaining counters to ensure the restoration of Belgian territory in Europe. But Belgium too had its advocates of colonial expansion; 'the country', the colonial minister, Jules Renkin, was to tell a sceptical King Albert, 'will never pardon its leaders for a peace without advantages and aggrandisements'.[171] The poor reputation of Belgian rule and Anglo-German desires for détente in Africa after 1911 had both fuelled Belgium's fears for its continued sovereignty in the Congo. The possibility that in any peace negotiations Britain and France would foster a German central African colony at Belgium's expense persisted into 1916. Therefore the seizure of Ruanda and Urundi from Germany might be traded for a more secure recognition of Belgium's status as an African power. More specifically, a slice of German East Africa might be given to the Portuguese in exchange for Portugal's allocation of northern Angola to the Belgian Congo, so lengthening the colony's exiguous 40-kilometre coastline.[172]

On 24 September 1914 the Germans confirmed their control of Lake Kivu by taking Kwijwi Island. The Belgian garrison, somewhat implausibly by this stage, said that they had not realized there was a war on. Their uncaptured compatriots behaved rather as though they subscribed to the same belief. They claimed that they were confronted by 2,000 Germans, when by October Lettow's concentration of his forces to the north had reduced the strength in the west to twenty-four Europeans and 152 askaris. The energy of the Germans' commander, Wintgens, did much to mask their numerical weakness, and the line of the Russissi river to the south of Lake Kivu impeded the offensive efforts of both sides.[173]

During 1915 the Belgians' ambitions grew with their increasing awareness of the true balance of forces. In February Charles Tombeur was appointed commander-in-chief in the Congo. His role was in part to moderate the more exaggerated notions of the colonialists. However, Tombeur inherited a plan whose military ambitions now far exceeded any political illusions. In a sketch drawn up in January 1915 and intended for execution in April, the Belgians proposed an offensive in two converging thrusts, one Belgian from the area between lakes Kivu and Tanganyika into Ruanda and Urundi, and the other Anglo-Belgian from northern Rhodesia. The Germans still dominated the waters of Lake Tanganyika itself; the Belgian columns were widely separated and out of direct communication; the supply arrangements for such a large-scale advance were nowhere in place.[174]

[171] Overstraeten, *War diaries of Albert I*, 79; also 88–91.
[172] Digre, *Imperialism's new clothes*, 105–16; Thielemans, *Albert Ier*, 252.
[173] Louis, *Ruanda-Urundi*, 209–15.
[174] Belgique, Ministère de la Défense Nationale, *Campagnes coloniales belges*, i. 173–220; Hordern, *East Africa*, i. 198–209.

In London, Lewis Harcourt, the colonial secretary, was as unenthusiastic about Belgian co-operation as he was about French, and for similar reasons. British control of German East Africa would open the link from the Cape to Cairo, and would provide a focus for Indian emigration.[175] In Nairobi, on the other hand, Wapshare was anxious to secure all the support he could get. Ignorant of the Belgian plan, he sent Brigadier-General W. Malleson to discuss with the local Belgian commander, Henry, the possibility of joint Anglo-Belgian operations between Lake Kivu and Lake Victoria. Malleson proposed an idea of his own making, an Anglo-Belgian concentration in Uganda, which would proceed to capture Mwanza and move south on Tabora. Such a scheme rested on a major British effort on the eastern side of Lake Victoria, and yet this was exactly what the War Office would not counsel, at least for the moment.

Tombeur's first response to this mixture of messages and confusion of intentions was to want to take the offensive everywhere at the same time. He argued that invasions from Uganda, British East Africa, the Indian Ocean, Portuguese East Africa, Nyasaland, Rhodesia, and the Congo would present the Germans with seven or eight attacks and leave them unable to decide which was the most important. But in due course Tombeur realized that, despite the contrary impression created by Malleson, the British did not propose an offensive for 1915. Most importantly, Northern Rhodesia, whose front was still under Colonial Office, not War Office, control, announced itself unwilling to co-operate in the Anglo-Belgian thrust adumbrated in the January 1915 Belgian plan. This, together with the situation on Lake Tanganyika itself, persuaded the Belgians to restrict their preparations to independent but limited operations against Ruanda and Urundi, renouncing all thought of converging on the axis of the central railway. Tombeur accordingly ordered the Belgian troops south of Lake Tanganyika to move to its northern end.

It would not be totally just to say that planning confusion kept 7,000–8,000 Belgian troops idle. In reality logistic constraints made the Belgian plans unrealizable in 1915. Moreover, the Congo would not be free of its commitment to the Cameroon campaign until early 1916. Belgian inactivity nonetheless conformed to the sense of increasing weakness in the British camp. Tanga caused Aitken to inflate German strengths (he claimed that the Germans had had 4,000 troops deployed against him), and to write down his own effectives. Even Meinertzhagen fell prey to the prevailing depression, reckoning in March 1915 that of the British strength of 15,000 rifles 4,000 only were reliable.[176] The Indian troops were the main source of concern, their officers proving as inefficient as their men were demoralized. Friction flourished between the Indian army and the King's African Rifles. The former saw the latter as

---

[175] Digre, *Imperialism's new clothes*, 85–6.
[176] Meinertzhagen, *Army Diary*, 120; see also Mosley, *Duel for Kilimanjaro*, 105–6.

irregulars; the latter were accustomed to look down on Indians as the traders and artisans of East Africa. Tanga supported that judgement, and the vulnerability of the Indians to malaria confirmed it. Although the War Office had assumed direction of the campaign, the administrative responsibilities for the units fighting it remained divided over their parent ministries. Thus, the complications of supply, already profound with so many racial and religious dietary preferences, compounded to dampen morale yet further.

Not only was the army divided within itself, it was also at odds with the civil administration of British East Africa. The Colonial Office's role in the region had been marginalized when it forfeited its control of operations. Harcourt, its minister until May 1915, was weakened by a heart attack in early November; he was succeeded by Bonar Law, who as leader of the Conservative party had other priorities. The balance of power therefore swung to the periphery. Sir Charles Belfield, Kenya's governor, disowned the war and its conduct, which he saw as an unwelcome intrusion on civilian priorities. He had a point: 64.6 per cent of his officials served in the army during the war, thus severely weakening his administration. He responded to the demands of headquarters with indifference or even passive resistance. To escape Tighe (and his own wife), Belfield preferred to reside in Mombasa rather than Nairobi. The deadlock was not broken until 11 August 1915, when the fear of a German thrust into Kenya prompted a joint meeting of the War and Colonial Offices in London. On 14 August Belfield was instructed to support the army and to improve civil–military relations.

The beneficiaries of the power vacuum in Kenya in 1914–15 had been the settlers. The Crown Lands ordinance of 1915 gave them effective control of all land hitherto occupied by Africans, even if that land had been reserved for native use. The value of Kenyan exports, which fell from 5.8 million rupees in 1913 to 3.35 million in 1914, recovered to 4.24 million rupees in 1915 and 5.9 million in 1916. These figures obscured the boom in exports of coffee and—above all—sisal: the value of the latter soared 2,400 per cent between 1912 and 1916. But neither was a crop produced by Africans. They grew cotton, whose price fell 25 per cent in early 1915, and a further 56 per cent in 1915–16. In 1913 settlers provided 14 per cent of Kenya's exports, in 1915 42 per cent, and by 1919 it would be 70 per cent. In part they were reaping the benefits of pre-war plantings and investment; but they were also maximizing the opportunities which the war vouchsafed them.

Belfield's response to the Colonial Office's instruction was to create a war council made up of four civil officials, two military representatives, and three Europeans who were not officials. He then accepted a demand that three 'practical farmers' be added. The balance of power in the committee swung from the government to the settlers. In September the settlers, prompted by the machinations of British military intelligence, staged a mass meeting suggestive of greater enthusiasm for the war than they had expressed hitherto. But underpinning their love for the army was the realization that it constituted a new and large domestic market. Furthermore, compulsion was applied to native labour more readily than to the settler population, which was protected by virtue of the War Office's demand for sisal. Settler dominance of the war council was evident in the passage of the Native Followers Recruitment ordinance, which created powers to mobilize labour and to control wages. Porters' pay was reduced from the prevailing 10-to-15 rupees per month to 5 rupees for the first three months of service and 6 rupees thereafter. The settlers thus brought carrier pay into line with the rates general in agriculture. In December the war council ruled that those who left employment without passes from their employers would be liable to conscription as carriers. But these powers were not utilized until 1917. Their immediate effect was the reverse—to exempt from portering those Africans working on alienated land. The war council's action represented the desire of white settlers to maximize the available labour pool for farming more than it constituted a recognition of wartime exigencies.[177]

The only apparent operational glimmer was a raid on the German town and wireless station of Bukoba on 21–3 June 1915. Launched from Kisumu across Lake Victoria (over which the British established control in March 1915), its main purpose was to counter apathy and deterioration by offensive action. Looting and rape were sanctioned—perhaps for this reason, perhaps themselves indications of the problems that the attack was designed to arrest. One German eyewitness said that not a house was untouched by the British troops' barbarity. Although successful, the attack's outcome was nonetheless disadvantageous. The destruction of the wireless deprived Tighe's intelligence services of a valuable source of intercepts. Bukoba was abandoned.[178]

British gloom, however, was in itself a good indication of how distracted and divided British strategy had become. In reality 1915 represented not setback, but the achievement of the CID subcommittee's initial objectives. The threat of cruiser war in the Indian Ocean, the prime reason for grappling with German East Africa at all, was finally removed in July 1915.

After her raid on Zanzibar *Königsberg* returned to the Rufiji delta, her operational capacities hamstrung by lack of coal and by engine problems. While her boilers were being lugged overland for repair in Dar es Salaam three British cruisers searched the East African coast. On 30 October 1914 they found her. But her berth was inaccessible except at high water, the delta being barred by mudbanks, and her position unidentifiable from the sea owing to a screen of mangrove swamps. Although blockaded, *Königsberg*'s value to the

[177] Maxon, *Struggle for Kenya*, 79–82, 98–102, 103–5; Overton, *Journal of African History*, XXVII (1986), 79–103; Savage and Munro, in ibid., VII (1966), 319–22; Meinertzhagen, *Army Diary*, 149–51, and also 103, 106, 118; Lucas, *Empire at war*, iv. 210–13.

[178] Occleshaw, *Armour against fate*, 117; Klein-Arendt, *Kamina ruft Nauen*, 312.

German naval effort was not exhausted. While she yet floated she consumed the attentions of twenty-five vessels, a significant drain when, first, von Spee remained at large, and then in the new year naval operations began in the Dardanelles. Furthermore, keeping track of the *Königsberg* was no easy matter, as she drew further up the river, her form shaded by overhanging trees. Efforts to bomb her with aircraft of the Royal Naval Air Service failed. Finally two shallow-draught monitors, their indirect fire corrected by airborne observers, sank the *Königsberg* on 11 July 1915.

This was not the outcome that had been envisaged by the Admiralty Staff in Germany. Looff's mooring was the antithesis of pre-war cruiser doctrine; it was exactly what the abandonment of Dar es Salaam had been designed to avoid.

Communications between German East Africa and its mother country remained effective—if sometimes intermittent—until at least September 1916. Despite the loss of first Kamina and then Windhoek, Nauen could be heard with reasonable regularity provided the atmospheric conditions were right. Transmission was more of a problem: all three of the existing stations in 1914, Dar es Salaam, Mwanza, and Bukoba, had only limited ranges, and the construction of a station of greater capacity at Tabora had been postponed in favour of those in West Africa. But the Dar es Salaam wireless was rebuilt after its destruction in August 1914, and this—together with *Königsberg*'s own wireless and the possibility (until autumn 1915) of communication through Portuguese East Africa—ensured sufficient two-way communication.[179] On this basis plans were laid to convey coal and ammunition from Germany so as to enable *Königsberg* to break out and make for home.

Rubens, disguised as a Danish merchantman bound for the River Plate, left Wilhelmshaven on 18 February 1915. On 3 March Looff received a signal via Windhoek telling him to communicate directly with *Rubens* on 1 April in order to arrange a rendezvous. Looff was well aware that these messages would not pass unnoticed by the British; he also came to realize that the Admiralty was reading German naval codes. To distract attention from *Rubens* he filled the air with wireless traffic designed to obscure the signals that were important and to create the impression that a second (but apocryphal) blockade-runner was imminent. Most importantly, he realized that *Königsberg* had no chances of breaking the blockade and effecting a junction with *Rubens*. By endeavouring to confirm the impression that *Königsberg* would be coming out, he drew British attention onto the *Königsberg* and away from *Rubens*. Looff therefore put the needs of the East African campaign ahead of those of cruiser warfare, his efforts being bent on saving *Rubens*'s cargo for the benefit of Lettow's troops. *Rubens* was instructed not to make for the Rufiji but for Mansa Bay,

---

[179] Marine-Archiv, *Krieg zur See. Kämpfe der Kaiserlichen Marine*, ii. 214–20; Schnee, *Deutsch-Ostafrika*, 24–5, 64, 96, 158–9, 232–3; Klein-Arendt, *Kamina ruft Nauen*, 292, 295, 299.

north of Tanga and adjacent to the front for land operations. Hotly pursued by
the British light cruiser *Hyacinth*, *Rubens* went aground in Mansa Bay. *Hyacinth* drew off, her captain made fearful of mines by further false signals from
Looff, and a boarding party having been persuaded that *Rubens* was sinking. In
reality the *Rubens* had executed a further deception on the British by setting
fire to the wood battened across her hatches. The bulk of her cargo, preserved
from total loss by being below the water-line, was brought ashore over the next
five weeks. The principal losses were the coal for the *Königsberg* and the
medical supplies and wireless equipment for the *Schütztruppen*.[180]

The voyage of the *Rubens* was of enormous significance for the course of the
campaign in East Africa, first because of Looff's acceptance of Germany's
decision that his priority was now to support Lettow's operations. The *Königsberg*'s guns, wireless, and crew proved major additions to Lettow's fighting
power. Secondly, the Royal Navy's shame at its inability to impose a blockade
formally declared on 1 March led it to hide from the army what had happened.
Not until the Germans were found using ammunition marked '1915' were the
implications of this lack of co-operation borne in on British military intelligence.[181] The failure to develop amphibious operations as a British offensive
option in 1916 may stem as much from the subsequent lack of trust as from the
Tanga debacle. Thirdly, the permeability of the British blockade suggested to
the Germans that, provided they retained possession of the coastline, fresh
munitions supplies from Germany could be forthcoming.

Nonetheless, owing to the German colonial office's exaggeration of the
outcome of *Rubens*'s voyage, almost a year elapsed before a second blockade
runner, *Marie*, reached East Africa. On Schnee's instructions *Marie* observed
strict wireless silence, and in March 1916 arrived unobserved in Sudi Bay, in the
remote south of the colony. *Marie*'s cargo had been packed into 50,000 porter-
loads, and in a sequence of carefully orchestrated marches was brought to the
central railway within three weeks with only 1 per cent loss. Plans for two more
ships to make the journey were postponed in September as Germany heard of
the British advance. In 1917 the demand for U-boats in home waters blocked a
proposal that they be used to supply the colony. The final attempt to resupply
Lettow's troops was made on 21 November 1917 by an airship from Jamboli in
Bulgaria. This time, however, British use of wireless intelligence was more
successful. Alerted by intercepts to the Zeppelin's flight and intentions, the
British sent a false signal, reporting Lettow's surrender and recalling the airship
when it had already passed over Khartoum.[182]

---

[180] Marine-Archiv, *Krieg zur See. Kreuzerkrieg*, ii. 181–6.
[181] Meinertzhagen, *Army diary*, 140–5.
[182] Occleshaw, *Armour against fate*, 115–16; Klein-Arendt, *Kamina ruft Nauen*, 319–25; on efforts to
supply East Africa in general, see Marine-Archiv, *Krieg zur See: Kampfe der Kaiserlichen Marine*, ii. 149–
51, 197–214, 234–5.

Rubens's cargo included two 6 cm ships' guns, four machine-guns, 1,800 1898-model rifles, and quantities of medical equipment and other stores. Potentially most important to Lettow was its ammunition: 5,500 shells out of 7,500 (including 1,000 rounds for the 10.5 cm guns of the *Königsberg*), and 2 million out of 4.5 million small-arms rounds were salvaged. Bullets were carefully unloaded, the powder dried, and then reloaded, the entire process being performed without the proper tools.[183] But in the process some rounds were double-loaded, and in any case up to 80 per cent of the rifle ammunition had been so long under water that 60 per cent misfired and was therefore fit only for training purposes. Small-arms ammunition consequently remained the outstanding need. *Marie* brought 4 million rounds for the 1898-model rifle and 1 million for the 1871-model. In addition, she delivered four 10.5 cm field howitzers, two 7.5 cm mountain guns, four machine-guns, 2,000 rifles, 3,500 grenades, and equipment and clothing for 12,000 soldiers.[184] The shells which she delivered were spoilt by humidity and moisture; like the small-arms ammunition from the *Rubens*, they were unloaded and black powder used instead. This work was carried out by the naval artificers from the *Königsberg*, who also salvaged shells from their own ship, washing them with water and cleaning them with sand.[185] Never, therefore, did German East Africa have to resort to producing its own munitions.[186] Furthermore, the capture of enemy munition stocks, which at Tanga netted eight machine-guns, 455 rifles, and half-a-million rounds,[187] did not thereafter play a major part in German calculations until 1917.

Thanks to the voyages of *Rubens* and *Marie*, the direct military consequences of the blockade, on which the British were tempted to pin their hopes in 1915, were by and large negated. But naval efforts were not without their economic consequences for the colony. The two railway lines ran from east to west; north–south links followed the line of the lakes in the west and of the coast in the east. Britain added to its offshore control by overrunning Mafia Island, opposite the Rufiji delta, in January 1915. Internal communications in the eastern half of the colony were restricted to the land routes, and became proportionately slower and more laborious. Most importantly, the loss of coastal navigation effectively excluded the exploitation of Portuguese neutrality for the import of supplies.

German East Africa's domestic and civilian economy therefore became largely self-sufficient. Its most spectacular achievements were the production

---

[183] Schoen, *Deutschen Feuerwerkswesens*, 1407.
[184] Boell, *Operationen*, 103, 179; Marine-Archiv, *Krieg zur See*, gives contradicting figures, *Kreuzerkrieg*, ii. 182, and *Kämpfe der Kaiserlichen Marine*, ii. 149–50, 199, as does Deppe, *Mit Lettow-Vorbeck*, 165.
[185] Schoen, *Deutschen Feuerwerkswesens*, 1452–5.
[186] Crowe, *Smuts' campaign*, 32, says the opposite, but there is no German evidence to corroborate Crowe.
[187] Boell, *Operationen*, 82; Lettow's figures, *Reminiscences*, 45, seem inflated.

of ersatz goods to replace the loss of European imports, of clothing and shoes, even of petrol and cigarettes. More fundamental was the shift in the cultivation and consumption of food.

Schnee reckoned that the colony, provided it remained intact, could produce sufficient sustenance to feed itself. What was at issue was the marketing and distribution of surpluses. Low rainfall in the south in 1913/14 and 1914/15 resulted in famine around Lindi; the European population was accustomed to a diet heavy in meat, fats, and white bread, much of it imported; the expansion of the *Schütztruppen* created a new demand for food in their area of concentration in the north. Regional imbalances had therefore to be corrected, and fresh sources of supply brought on stream. In the north European planters were given guarantees to encourage them to switch from the cultivation of export goods to that of maize. Thus, full employment was maintained in the area, political stability buttressed, and the troops fed. German diets were sustained virtually unchanged until 1916, in large part owing to the growing of wheat, concentrated in the remote south-west around Neu Langenburg. A retired Saxon major-general, Kurt Wahle, who was visiting his son on the war's outbreak, was given responsibility for *Schütztruppen* supply. Wahle established a network of purchasing points, designed to draw surplus native food production onto the market. Ninety per cent of the food brought for sale to points along the central railway was produced by Africans and only 10 per cent by Europeans. These measures tapped new sources of production but allowed patterns of consumption to remain unchanged. Not until late 1916, and the German evacuation of the major food-producing areas of the colony, did European diets follow African.[188]

Schnee was able to spurn the tools of state intervention, of rationing and requisitioning, and instead to foster the invigoration of free enterprise. It was a position that squared well with liberal colonialism. Price controls for domestic products, fixed in June 1915 at 25 per cent above the peacetime level, were a belated and largely ineffectual response to what was being done in Germany. The big European commercial houses had been driven out of business by the loss of export markets and by Wahle's direct dealing with the producers. Local trade was in the hands of small dealers and shopkeepers, and neither the market nor its prices could be adequately policed.

The fundamental difficulty confronting Schnee's faith in a demand economy was therefore financial. The economic mobilization required by the war accelerated the penetration and establishment of the cash economy as a whole. But the loss of overseas imports negated the increased purchasing power of the native producer and trader; with nothing to buy and with prices rising, his

---

[188] Schnee, *Deutsch-Ostafrika*, 141–8, 165–7; see also Deppe, *Mit Lettow-Vorbeck*, 136, 169; Monson, *Journal of African History*, XXXIX (1998), 116.

inclination was to hoard. Cash disappeared. Furthermore, it could not be readily replaced. Both the silver rupees and the notes of German East Africa were imported from Germany itself. The Deutsch-Ostafrikanischen Bank increased its rate of interest from 4 to 5 per cent in a bid to draw in cash, and outflow was sustained by paying salaries monthly rather than quarterly. The effectiveness of civilian administration meant that the tax yield of 1915 exceeded that of 1913. Nonetheless, by the second half of 1915 real shortages of cash became evident. Without it, food could not be bought nor porters paid: the German war effort would grind to a halt. The obvious solution, for the colony to print its own notes, encountered a number of practical difficulties: the paper was of poor quality, the notes became damaged in the heavy rains, and the currency did not command the confidence of its African users. Furthermore, British military intelligence forged several million 20-rupee notes and thus contributed to the discrediting of German paper currency. Schnee's riposte was to mint coins, using copper and brass for the lower denominations and gold for the 15-rupee piece. His efforts were sufficiently successful to ensure that where German rule pertained there German currency ensured exchange. Even in Portuguese East Africa in 1918 the local population was prepared to accept payment in German notes.[189]

These, then, were the economic foundations which during the course of 1915 underpinned the expansion and training of von Lettow-Vorbeck's command. Without the cargoes delivered by the *Rubens* and the *Marie* there would have been no weapons with which to equip or train an increased number of men; without a shift in food production and supply, and without the capacity to pay farmers and porters, an underdeveloped economy could not have sustained the formation and concentration of such a large force. By December 1915 the fighting power available to Lettow had grown to 2,712 Europeans, 11,367 black soldiers, and about 2,000 auxiliaries. In March 1916 the *Schütztruppen's* strength embraced 3,007 Europeans and 12,100 askaris. The number of field companies rose to thirty, and the total number of all units to sixty.[190] The European rifle associations were integrated with the African companies, so perpetuating the *Schütztruppen's* relatively high ratio of whites to blacks. Furthermore, during the course of 1915 two preconditions were fulfilled which allowed Lettow to maximize his strength even when in 1916 and 1917 he no longer enjoyed numerical equivalence.

Most significant, relative to their opponents, was the fitness of the *Schütz-truppen*. The sickness rates of the askaris never escalated as did those of the

---

[189] Schnee, *Deutsch-Ostafrika*, 124, 163–5, 280–90, 317; Deppe, *Mit Lettow-Vorbeck*, 284–8; both Franz Kempner 'Verwaltung und Verteidigung von Deutsch-Ostafrika', 63–6, in Draeger (ed.), *Gouverneur Schnee*, and Henderson, *German colonial history*, ch. 7, repeat Schnee's own points. See also Meinertzhagen, *Army Diary*, 164.

[190] Reichsarchiv, *Weltkrieg*, x. 484; Belgique, *Campagnes Coloniales Belges*, i. 138–9; Boell, *Operationen*, 28–9, 158; Lettow-Vorbeck, *Reminiscences*, 71–2.

British forces. The explanation for this that points to the German use of native troops and to the British of European and Indian is only partial. As significant was the scale and quality of German medical care. When war broke out, a research programme on sleeping-sickness meant that the colony possessed a relatively large medical establishment. The *Schütztruppen*'s complement of thirty-two medical officers immediately increased to sixty-three, without taking into account mission doctors, ships' surgeons, and others. Each company, therefore, had its own doctor, and the most prevalent illness, malaria, was treated in the field rather than in hospital. Vital to the management of malaria was the supply of quinine. The Germans used 1,000 kilograms of the drug during the war, and only half that supply represented pre-war stocks or wartime deliveries. Cultivation of the Peruvian bark from which quinine is derived had been begun in the north of the colony before the war, and from January 1915 the research stations at Amani and Mpwapwa were able to manufacture their own quinine. When the Germans were driven south of their laboratories on the central railway they could no longer take the medicine in pills, but had to boil the bark. The foul-tasting liquid which resulted became known as 'Lettow-schnapps'. The German practice, of giving quinine at lower doses but over a longer period, proved more efficacious than the British of administering it in larger doses but only during hospitalization.[191]

If a German officer died he could not be replaced. Therefore a bigger threat than malaria, whose effects were temporary rather than fatal, was dysentery. Much to their surprise, the Germans found that they were remarkably free of dysentery. Three things happened as they fell south of the central railway in late 1916. First, the shibboleths of European life in the tropics—with which in any case Lettow had little truck—were unsustainable. The idea of limited exertion in the midday heat was ditched along with pith helmets and mosquito nets. Long marches and sustained exercise made the Germans fitter. Secondly, their diet changed. It became set by local availability and local habit. Alcohol, fats, and salt became luxuries; vegetables and fruit, especially millet and mangoes, dominated; meat came in the form of game. Thirdly, even the doctors themselves—deprived of medicines and forced to create dressings from plants— came to see therapy rather than intervention as the best cure. A new system of tropical hygiene emerged, and because of it the Germans were able to sustain the high ratio of European officers and NCOs which was deemed so important to the fighting effectiveness of the *Schütztruppen*.[192]

Again, Lettow used the lull in major operations to establish a more effective network of internal communications. To compensate for the loss of the south–north coastal route, the road from Kibambawe on the Rufiji river to Mombo

[191] Taute, *Tanganyika Notes and Records*, VIII (Dec. 1939), 1–20; on quinine production, Schnee, *Deutsch-Ostafrika*, 149–50; Lettow-Vorbeck, *Reminiscences*, 70, 195.

[192] Deppe, *Mit Lettow-Vorbeck*, 149–52, 169–76, 384–5.

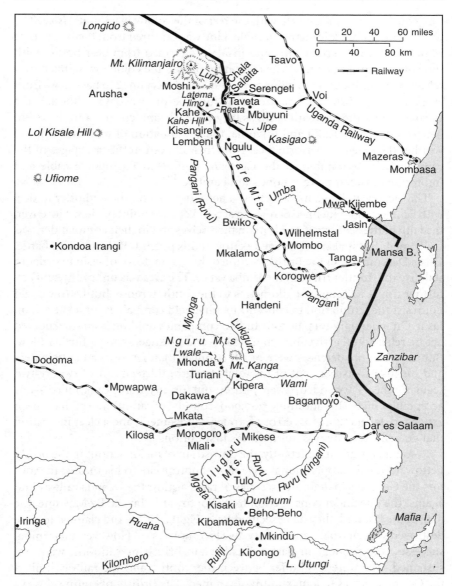

MAP 22. EAST AFRICA: NORTH EASTERN REGION

on the northern railway was divided into stages, so that porters could be locally recruited, accommodated, and provisioned. From Mombo itself a light railway, using equipment from the plantations of the north, snaked its way south at a rate of 2 kilometres a day: by March 1916 it had reached Handeni. The telegraph line was extended to Mahenge and to Neu Langenburg, which before

1914 could only communicate with the rest of the colony via South Africa. The *Möwe* brought 500 kilometres of cable. Line was captured from the Belgians or improvised from barbed wire, and insulators formed from beer bottles with the bottoms broken out. By the beginning of 1916 the colony was linked by a telegraph network of 3,000 kilometres, and Lettow reckoned to have news from even the most distant of his fronts within one or two days. Although the Germans took the line with them as they fell back, and created a fresh system between the rivers Rufiji and Ruvuma, the combination of wear and tropical weather degraded its performance. Nonetheless, even in the last stages of the campaign, in Mozambique, the Germans plundered Portuguese cable and improvised insulators from bones and bamboo.[193]

The victory at Tanga made Lettow a hero. It gave him the authority to deal with Schnee, and it inclined Schnee to accept Lettow's point of view. Moreover, the faith of the *Schütztruppen*, both in themselves and in their commander, was confirmed. But it also encouraged Lettow in his pursuit of the decisive battle. On 25 December 1914 the British occupied the coastal town of Jasin in order to stabilize the frontier tribes in the Umba valley. The area was unhealthy, and any further threat to Tanga, 64 kilometres to the south, remote. But Lettow could not resist the temptation to concentrate nine field companies for an attack on Jasin. On 19 January 1915 the four Indian companies holding Jasin surrendered before relief could arrive; British morale—and prestige—took a further blow. But in reality the defences were much stronger than Lettow had anticipated, and his losses—15 per cent of his total strength, thirteen out of twenty-two regular officers wounded, twenty-three out of 265 Europeans killed—unacceptably high. In addition, 200,000 rounds of ammunition had been expended. Jasin was a gross error of strategic judgement, and a clear indication that guerrilla warfare was not Lettow's first option.

Recognizing, albeit reluctantly, the unwisdom of major actions in the north, Lettow adopted an operational style more appropriate to his means. In April 1915 the Germans inaugurated a series of raids against the Uganda railway and against the line under construction from Voi towards Taveta. By May 1916, the date of the last raid, they had executed forty-eight attacks, and claimed to have destroyed sixteen trucks and twenty-five locomotives.[194] However, their initial successes, the product in part of inadequate British precautions, were not sustained. The waterless buffer between the frontier and the railway limited the German parties to a maximum of ten men. The British, operating close to their own bases, responded by organizing large fighting patrols of 100 men, able to defeat the Germans, or much smaller reconnaissance groups of three to four men, able to track and report the Germans' movements. By placing vans

---

[193] Deppe, *Mit Lettow-Vorbeck*, 281; Klein-Arendt, *Kamina ruft Nauen*, 314, 317.
[194] Boell, *Operationen*, 107–10, 112–15; Mosley, *Duel for Kilimanjaro*, 97, has different figures.

loaded with sand in front of the engine, and by travelling at slower speeds, the locomotives of the Uganda railway increasingly escaped serious damage.

Both more promising and more urgent as a theatre of operations in 1915 was the west of the colony. Lettow had three vital strategic interests vested in the defence of the west—the wheat production of the Neu Langenburg area, the head of the central railway at Kigoma, and the navigation of Lake Tanganyika. Reports reached him of the preparation of a Belgian flotilla at Lukugu, opposite Kigoma, and of Tombeur's plan to invade Ruanda and Urundi. Both posed a long-term threat to the flank and rear of the *Schütztruppen* in the north. In May Lettow began the build-up of a German concentration around Bismarckburg, at the southern end of Lake Tanganyika, its mission either to forestall the Belgian gunboats at Lukugu or to push south-east against the flank of any invasion of the Neu Langenburg area. On 29 May Wahle was given the command, his task—in Lettow's words—'not border protection or the pushing back of the enemy, but a decisive success'.[195]

In reality Wahle had neither the men nor the guns for such an objective. On 28 June he attacked the British post of Saisi (Jericho to the Germans), situated east-south-east of Abercorn and across the frontier in northern Rhodesia. The attack was repelled but then renewed on 25 July. Again Wahle was held, and on 2/3 August fell back on Bismarckburg. The slowness of Belgian preparations at Lukugu suggested that a switch to that quarter would be premature. Instead, a new German concentration was formed to the north, its task to thrust across the Russissi river, linking lakes Tanganyika and Kivu, with a view to capturing Belgian equipment stockpiled for the invasion of Ruanda. On 26 October Wahle was given command of the entire western area of operations, and by late November had ten companies grouped around Tabora, his headquarters. Nonetheless, on 12 December the Russissi project was abandoned, a recognition of increasing Belgian strength in the area as well as of more pressing realities in other sectors. Wahle had not achieved Lettow's more grandiloquent objectives. Instead, both he and Tombeur had successfully negated each other's offensive intentions. The attack on Saisi had been sufficient to upset the Belgians' plan to concentrate their forces north of Lake Tanganyika for the invasion of Ruanda and Urundi. Equally, by leaving two battalions on the north Rhodesian frontier until late October, Tombeur successfully distracted the Germans from concentrating all their efforts on the Russissi sector.[196]

Lettow's strategy for 1914 and 1915 lacked coherence. In the pursuit of a major victory, the operations in the west augured well: the Germans had better communications to the rear, the British and Belgian forces were weaker, more isolated, and less well trained. But to have shifted its headquarters and even more of the *Schütztruppen* to Tabora or Bismarckburg would have left the

[195] Boell, *Operationen*, 117.
[196] Ibid. 115–27; Hordern, *East Africa*, i. 183–91; Belgique, *Campagnes coloniales belges*, i. 121, 200, 211–12.

north and east exposed. As it was, the fear of another amphibious attack caused Wahle and three companies to be shifted from the west to Dar es Salaam from late August 1915 until October. The *Kleinkrieg* in the north can only be seen as the centrepiece of Lettow's strategy in the retrospective context of guerrilla warfare. In practice, the attacks on the Uganda railway were a holding operation, engaging only small bodies of German troops while freeing others either for the west or for training in the more salubrious climate of Wilhelmstal. Formally, Lettow may have rebutted the premises of the 1912 plan; in reality, its prescription, all-round defence with limited offensive thrusts, was exactly what he ended up doing.[197]

However, in October 1915 Lettow began to plan a major offensive. The British adoption of the defensive, their concentration on Europe, and their beleaguered state at Gallipoli—all of these factors suggested that no major threat was imminent. The projected thrust across the Russissi, which drew in troops from Dar es Salaam on the coast and Mwanza on Lake Victoria, reflected that confidence. On 2 November Lettow received a message dispatched from Berlin in May reporting revolution in Sudan; simultaneously, the prospect of a Turkish victory at Gallipoli opened the door to an attack by the Central Powers on Egypt. With the British assailed in north-east Africa, and tied to their defence of the Suez Canal, Lettow could unleash his *Schütztruppen*—their strength now waxing, comparable in quantity and probably superior in quality to the British forces in East Africa. His immediate objective was Mazeras, a railway station on the Uganda line 25 kilometres from Mombasa itself. A road pushing north from Karogwe had been begun in late September, and in mid-December had reached Mwakijembe, with munitions dumps established on its route. On Christmas Eve Lettow ordered three companies forward to support the Germans holding the mountain at Kasigao, hitherto a forward base in the raids on the Uganda railway and now about to be the flank guard for the thrust on Mombasa.[198] Lettow's conception was Napoleonic—to place himself athwart his enemy's main line of communications. The British would have no alternative but to turn and face him. Lettow was bent on achieving the decisive battle which had so far eluded him.

The possibility that the forces of South Africa would be dispatched to East Africa once South-West Africa had been overrun had been considered by Lettow and Schnee in June and July. A descent on Dar es Salaam or Bagamoyo, a landward thrust following the railway under construction from Voi, or a combination of the two—all contributed to Lettow's concerns for protection to the north and east. But by October he had convinced himself that the South Africans would go to the western front or to Gallipoli. His illusions were

---

[197] The only really effective criticism of Lettow, albeit slightly misconceived, is Buhrer, *L'Afrique orientale allemande*, 336–9.

[198] Boell, *Operationen*, 124–5, 134–5.

shattered on the very day he ordered the support for Kasigao. The district commissioner of Lindi reported that the press of Portuguese East Africa and of South Africa had announced that Smuts and up to 25,000 men were bound for the East African theatre in order to launch an attack early in the new year. Moreover, Portugal, German East Africa's southern neighbour, seemed bound to enter the war. A week later a letter captured at Tsavo, originating from London, confirmed the intelligence.

Lettow abandoned his offensive. He was still uncertain whether the attack would come from the sea or from Voi. But the coastal climate, and its unsuitability for white mounted troops, suggested the Kilimanjaro area as more likely. British reconnaissance activity corroborated Lettow's analysis. From mid-January the thrust of British strategy was manifest. Longido, a hill north-west of Kilimanjaro, was occupied on 15 January, Mbuyuni to the south-west was taken on the 22nd, and Serengeti on the 24th. The Germans abandoned Kasigao. On 12 February a major British attack on Salaita Hill (known to the Germans as Oldorobo), which barred the way to Taveta, was repulsed. Lettow concentrated almost half his total forces, 800 Europeans and 5,200 askaris, together with forty-seven machine-guns and ten field guns, in the Kilimanjaro area.[199] His indirect bulwark, South-West Africa, had collapsed; the fight for German East Africa was about to begin.

EAST AFRICA, 1916–1918

The conquest, rather than the neutralization, of German East Africa, had already entered the minds of the CID subcommittee when it issued its orders to Aitken in October 1914. In February 1915 Wapshare recommended the construction of the railway line from Voi to Taveta, an essential preliminary to an offensive action from British East Africa. Thus Kitchener's insistence on defence, sustained throughout 1915, smacked of procrastination. Not even his own director of military operations, Sir Charles Callwell, had much enthusiasm for the policy.[200]

Nonetheless, British soldiers in East Africa concluded—rightly—that their needs and preoccupations did not attract much attention in the War Office. The London department much more concerned by the fights at Jasin and Saisi was the Colonial Office. The German raids across the frontier into Northern Rhodesia had created a lawless strip, whence colonialism had retreated and where a scorched-earth policy to create a neutral buffer appeared to be the only viable option. In British East Africa, the tribes around Jasin had fallen back

[199] Ibid. 142. [200] Callwell, *Experiences of a dug-out*, 178–9.

northwards to escape German rule, and inland British prestige was being eroded by the attacks on the Uganda railway.

On 23 January 1915 John Chilembwe, an American-educated black mission-ary, had led an attack directed against the employment practices of white-owned estates in Nyasaland. Chilembwe's rebellion was limited and easily contained. But a number of elements gave cause for concern. Millenarianism, anticipating that the war would eliminate the colonial powers and would enable the black elect to enter the New Jerusalem, found an audience among the African educated elite. Traditional, tribal divisions had been overcome, even if only in a limited and specific way. Secondly, economic pressures, already evident before the war, had been compounded by the loss of labour through the recruitment of porters, and threatened to give a mass appeal to a minority movement. Thirdly, Chilembwe challenged the basis on which the war was being fought. In a mixture of Christian pacifism and natural law, he repudiated the notion that Africans should fight for white men's rivalries, not least when their lack of property and of civic rights should have relieved them of military obligations. Chilembwe's death did not prevent his spectre haunt-ing colonial minds thereafter. The withdrawal of white administrators for military service, the preoccupation of those that remained with wartime needs, and the progressive Africanization of Christian missions all served to reinforce the bases of Chilembwe's original appeal.[201]

The Conservative leader Bonar Law, who succeeded Harcourt at the Colo-nial Office with the formation of the coalition government in May 1915, was soon convinced that the need to restore British prestige in East Africa demanded the conquest of German East Africa 'once and for all'.[202] What he needed was a sufficiently large body of troops with which to do it. Tombeur's preparation of the Belgians' *Force publique*, far from solving that problem, added urgency to Colonial Office considerations: the brutality of the Belgian askaris had not contributed to good order in Northern Rhodesia, and a successful Belgian invasion around Lake Tanganyika, if independently con-ducted, would weaken Britain's relative status yet further.

As in the case of South-West Africa, London's short-term needs conveni-ently merged with Pretoria's long-term ambitions. The implicit agenda in South Africa's act of Union was its extension to the line of the Zambezi. The motivations were at once elevated, economic, and national. Smuts identified himself with Cecil Rhodes, and saw South Africa's task as 'the progress of European civilization on the African continent'. Commercially, the adjacent ports for the Transvaal were not Capetown and Walvis Bay but Delagoa Bay

[201] Shepperson and Price, *Independent African*; S. E. Katzenellenbogen, 'Southern Africa and the war of 1914–18', in Foot (ed.), *War and Society*, 117–19; E. J. Yorke, 'A crisis of colonial control', 20–36, 127–8, 133–4, 150–8.
[202] Yorke, 'A crisis of colonial control', 131–2.

and Beira, both in Portuguese hands. Thus, the development of Pretoria and of Afrikaner interests was stunted by the geographical configuration of the Union. The addition of South-West Africa would increase the weighting in favour of Capetown and the English population, not diminish it. The solution suggested in April and May 1915 by Harcourt and by South Africa's governor-general, Lord Buxton, was to persuade Portugal to swap Mozambique for South-West Africa. Smuts, however, recognized that the deal would be too poor to commend itself to the Portuguese. His idea was to conquer German East Africa, and then allocate its northern territory to Britain and its southern to Portugal. In exchange, Portugal would be asked to give the southern part of its existing colony, including Delagoa Bay and Beira, to South Africa. To achieve this the South Africans were prepared to provide troops for the East African campaign, initially at imperial expense, but—if the deal worked—eventually at South Africa's.[203]

The obstacle remained the War Office. The case for allocating South African troops, Europeans of proven military worth, not to East Africa but to the western front or at least to Gallipoli was supported by Kitchener's own determination that the main fronts were European. However, two political factors weighed against the strategic argument. First, the use of Boers in the conquest of South-West Africa, despite being an area of immediate South African interest, had aroused anti-imperial sentiment; thus, their deployment outwith the African continent was likely to be even more provocative. Secondly, imperial rates of remuneration were two-thirds less those paid to South African troops. To reward South Africans in Europe at South African rates promised ill-feeling between them and the British troops, and would create friction between London and Pretoria as to who should pay the difference. Sending the South Africans to East Africa, therefore, sidestepped the pay issue, albeit in part and only temporarily.[204] The War Office could console itself with the prevalent notion that East Africa was ideal country for the operations of Boer commandos. It was not; but then nor was the western front.

Even so, War Office agreement was not secured without subterfuge. Kitchener was absent from London, visiting Gallipoli, when the CID subcommittee reported to the War Council on 12 November 1915. The subcommittee recommended that 10,000 troops be sent to East Africa with a view to commencing operations before the April rains and to conquering the German colony with as little delay as possible. Kitchener was not at all happy when he returned. Both Sir Archibald Murray, the chief of the imperial general staff, and Callwell had colluded with Bonar Law to force his hand. Kitchener's

---

[203] Hyam, *Failure of South African expansion*, 23–9, 36; Hancock and Poel, *Smuts papers*, iii. 307–10; Warhurst, *South African Historical Journal*, XVI (1984), 82–8.

[204] Garson, *Journal of Imperial and Commonwealth History*, VIII (1979), 76–7; Hancock, *Smuts*, 408; Hancock and Pool, *Smuts papers*, iii. 296–7.

riposte was to ensure that no British brigade was sent as part of the 10,000 and to withhold the proper complement of supporting arms, including artillery and engineers. During December the staff of the East African force planned their campaign in daily anticipation of its cancellation.[205]

Sir Horace Smith-Dorrien, the hero of Le Cateau but subsequently Sir John French's scapegoat, was appointed to the command. Smith-Dorrien's principle was 'more haste less speed'. Having built up a staff of East African and colonial experience, he was convinced that nothing should be attempted until training was complete, lines of communication secure, and the rains over. He anticipated doing no more by March than drive the Germans in on Taveta; the main offensive would not be launched until June, but would then be sudden, complete, and inexorable. Kitchener had never formally sanctioned the campaign. Now Smith-Dorrien forfeited South African and Colonial Office approval as well: both were anxious for an attack before the rains. They got it. Smith-Dorrien became ill en route for Mombasa and was replaced by Smuts.[206]

Bonar Law had wanted Smuts for the job all along, but the latter had initially pleaded the state of the Union's domestic politics as reason against his going. In every other major British command of the war, professional experience with the regular army counted for more than the qualities of intellect and personality possessed by many amateurs. But Bonar Law was convinced by reports from France that 'we are suffering from the want of brains in the higher command'. So anxious was he not to appoint a soldier to the job that he (if nobody else) was prepared to take seriously Churchill's request to go as governor-general and commander-in-chief, equipped with a fleet of armoured cars.[207] The fact that Law got his way is indicative both of the War Office's indifference to East Africa and of the divided counsels emanating from the War Office during Kitchener's absence. Callwell, the British army's leading authority on colonial operations, supported Smuts. In reality, Smuts's military experience was almost entirely irrelevant to the task that now faced him. In the Boer War he had led a commando of 300–400 men with minimal logistical needs in a defensive campaign in a moderate climate over familiar terrain. In East Africa he was responsible for a ration strength of 73,300 men, committed to the conquest of a tropical colony, much of it barely mapped. His South African experience made him 'a remarkable soldier', often to the front and admired by his men; but it also rendered him 'a bad tactician and strategist' and 'an indifferent general'.[208]

[205] Hordern, East Africa, i. 211–13; Callwell, Experiences of a dug-out, 178–9; Fendall, East African Force, 39–49.
[206] Smith-Dorrien, Memories, 482–9
[207] Gilbert, Churchill, iii. 563–6; see also Companion, 1251–2.
[208] Meinertzhagen, Army Diary, 194; see also Fendall, East African Force, 57; Page, International Journal of African Historical Studies, XIV (1981), 467–9.

The obvious foil to such a commander was his staff. But Smuts, albeit gently, dismantled the body created by Smith-Dorrien. Thus, not one officer in Smuts's field headquarters had 'ever previously filled an appointment on the General Staff with troops'.[209] Hoskins, whose local knowledge was to have found sensible employment as chief of staff, was shunted out to a division; J. J. Collyer, his replacement, was an ex-ranker of entirely South African experience. British commanders—Tighe, Malleson, and Stewart—were, with good reason, removed, but their places were taken by South Africans of experience comparable to Smuts's own—Deventer, Brits, and Enslin. Divisions therefore fought their own battles, failing to report back to a staff that lacked the authority to exercise initiative. Smuts followed the procedure ordained in *Field Service Regulations*, but modified in practice in France, and divided his headquarters in two, with himself and a small group at his advanced headquarters, and the heads of the administrative services at base. Thus, field command and logistics were separated in a theatre of operations where their mutual dependence was paramount. Supply was initially in the hands of an Indian army colonel with a tendency to over-centralization and peacetime economies, and communications in those of a former chief of East African police, who knew the area but was highly strung and fearful of giving offence. At the end of January a veteran of the western front and a rare survivor from Smith-Dorrien's appointees, P. O. Hazelton, took charge of transport. But lack of existing records prevented him from determining what resources units already had, and lack of time forestalled his remedying any deficits. Smuts's continued, if paradoxical, reliance on the higher formations of European warfare, divisions and brigades, increased the logistical burden, and contrasted with Germans' preference for the more flexible and self-contained field company. Never resolved but constantly disputed was the chain of command— between supply, transport, and communications; between the rear and the front; and between the operational and administrative branches of Smuts's headquarters.[210]

Smuts justified his practice of placing himself well forward by reference to the difficulties of communication in the bush. But although this impressed his troops, it militated against effective command. Close liaison with the heads of his administrative services was further jeopardized. Wireless was unreliable, visual signalling impossible. Cable was therefore vital. Laying it was another job for the porters; in places it had to be raised 8 metres to avoid damage by giraffes; telephones were superimposed on a single line also operating as a telegraph circuit. The entire service was described by Collyer as composed 'of men of different nationalities—of different training—speaking different lan-

[209] Crowe, *General Smuts' campaign*, 4.
[210] Ibid. 3–4; Fendall, *East African Force*, 144–8; also 53–6; Collyer, *South Africans with Smuts*, 60; Beadon, *Royal Army Service Corps*, ii. 297, 299–301; cf. Ian Brown, *British logistics*, 44–51.

guages, with equipment of varying patterns thrown together without any co-ordinated training to carry out an important operation in unknown coun-try'.[211] None of the confusions generated by his polyglot force, logistic or linguistic, was resolved before Smuts advanced.

During the course of 1915 Meinertzhagen had taken the intelligence services in hand. By a variety of methods, including the recovery of German orders that had been used as lavatory paper, he built up a picture of Lettow's order of battle.[212] But there was still a tendency to exaggerate the Germans' strength: Smith-Dorrien put it at 2,200 whites and up to 25,000 blacks.[213] Moreover, the use of captured German maps created a false security. Plausible because they 'were presented in a form which [commanders] associated with accuracy', in reality they omitted much. Roads built since 1914 were frequently unmarked; duplications and difficulties with place-names were not resolved; marching distances proved much greater than cartographic distances. Thus, orders based on maps proved consistently over-optimistic.[214] Reconnaissance could rarely fill the gap. Thick bush obscured the ground from aerial observation and tsetse fly limited the value of mounted troops.

Smith-Dorrien's plan had been to attack around Kilimanjaro, while the Belgians thrust in from the north-west and a third attack from Northern Rhodesia entered in the south-west. When Lettow had been forced to commit his forces to the west, a brigade was to be landed at Dar es Salaam or Tanga, supported by four cruisers. The decisive thrust would thus have rested on secure and short lines of communications. Neither Smuts nor his staff was sea-minded. No landing at Dar es Salaam or Tanga was attempted. The main blow ran across rather than along the two main land lines, the northern and central railways. Smuts's invasion, therefore, played to the strengths already bestowed on the German defence by the nature of the terrain. The available axes of approach were limited by the mountain ranges, and the valleys were covered with bush. As he pushed on, his line of communications lengthened. The halts to allow his supply services to catch up gave the Germans the opportunity to regroup. Thus, his onset lacked the momentum that his dispatches suggested. Throughout 1916 Smuts's rate of advance failed to match his strategic concep-tions.

Moreover, for all his talk of battle, Smuts's aim was to manoeuvre rather than to fight. Lettow's avoidance of a decisive engagement throughout 1916 can be attributed to Smuts's supply difficulties, the consequent loss of operational flexibility, and the German desire to avoid fighting in order to preserve lives

[211] Collyer, *South Africans with Smuts*, 280.
[212] Meinertzhagen, *Army diary*, 127.
[213] Smith-Dorrien, *Memories*, 486.
[214] Hordern, *East Africa*, vol. i., pp. vi–vii; Young, *Marching on Tanga*, 195, 213.

and ammunition. But it can also be seen in the context of Smuts's political preoccupations. By the end of 1916 the conduct of the campaign would be the focus of public outcry in South Africa. Smuts was constantly reminded from Pretoria of the difficulties of raising men; he dreaded returning to the Union dubbed a butcher.[215] The fighting in South-West Africa suggested that indeed wars could be won by sweat rather than by blood, by mobility rather than by hard fighting. Neglecting or even abandoning lines of communication had been made possible by the speed of envelopments conducted by mounted troops. And so Smuts planned a sequence of envelopment battles, where success eluded him because of Lettow's refusal to fight. In reality, East Africa was—particularly thanks to the tsetse fly—not appropriate for mounted troops. His flank attacks, partly no doubt because of his supply problems, never extended sufficiently far to master German communications. Instead, he would probe towards the German wing without fixing the enemy frontally, so dispersing his troops and enabling the numerically inferior Germans to use the bush to break the battle up into a series of isolated fire-fights. Forced to deploy on ground of Lettow's choosing, Smuts would have to wait for the arrival of heavier weaponry; no attempt would be made to retain contact as night fell. Thus Lettow could escape because he had never been gripped.[216]

Plans for the initial attack east and west of Kilimanjaro had already been drawn up when Smuts arrived. The main German concentration was in the sector bounded by Salaita–Moshi–Kahe. Lettow had left only weak forces west of Kilimanjaro. His main concern was for his line of retreat down the northern railway, and he therefore watched with anxiety the Ngulu Gap through the Pare Mountains, opposite Lembeni. The original British intention was to launch their mounted troops not here but west of Kilimanjaro, past Longido, on to Moshi, in order to cut off the Germans protecting Taveta.

Smuts amended this plan. He recognized the strength of the German defences at Salaita, but calculated that Lettow had too few troops for his area of concentration. He therefore brought the major thrust east of Kilimanjaro, directed not at Salaita itself but in a flanking move to its north. On the night of 7/8 March the South African brigades under Deventer marched on Chala, north of Salaita, and on the morning of the 8th the 2nd division moved into positions in front of Salaita. Despite the British patrols sent towards the Ngulu Gap, Lettow realized the true direction of the advance only on the 8th. When the 2nd division launched its attack on Salaita on 9 March it found the German trenches untenanted.

---

[215] Hancock and Poel, *Smuts papers*, iii. 356–7, 359; Hancock, *Smuts*, 412–13; Meinertzhagen, *Army diary*, 166, 200.
[216] Meinertzhagen, *Army diary*, 191; Buhrer, *L'Afrique orientale allemande*, 352–3, 355. I have also profited from Ross Anderson's tactical analysis.

The Germans fell back west of Taveta to the hills of Reata and Latema. This position was well prepared but it was 19 kilometres long, too extensive for the troops available, and Lettow kept his main concentration to the rear at Himo. Smuts was determined to follow up as fast as possible, but owing to the need to consolidate his rear, had only three battalions available to attack. The main hills rose to 330 metres, and an attempt to seize the nek between the two during the course of 11 March was unsuccessful and costly. The bulk of the artillery was still being brought up, and the efforts of forward observation officers to direct its fire were hampered by the bush. Tighe, commanding the 2nd division, decided to use the cover of night to attack with the bayonet. Lettow, meanwhile, concluded that the major threat lay to his left, in the north, and at 5.30 p.m. sent two companies thither. But at 7.50 p.m. he received reports that Kraut's positions on the Latema side of the nek had been broken. At 9.30 p.m. he lost telephone contact with Kraut, and by 10.30 Kraut was reported as in full retreat. Lettow therefore ordered the whole position to be abandoned, and his forces to take up a new line backing onto the River Ruvu, facing north, with their left on Kahe.

In reality, although Kraut had ordered a retreat at 10 p.m., one company had not received the order and Latema could have been held. Moreover, there was comparable confusion in the British command. Smuts had never intended the frontal attack to precede Deventer's envelopment to the north. Nor did he appreciate that some of his troops had reached the summits of both Reata and Latema in the course of the night. On the morning of 12 March he ordered the 2nd division to fall back, while Deventer's outflanking move to the north— Lettow's original fear—took effect. Deventer pushed on towards Moshi to link up with the 1st division on 14 March.

Smuts had opened the door into the northern part of German East Africa. But he had not inflicted a major defeat on the *Schütztruppen*. The blame was laid on Stewart, commanding the 1st division. The advance west of Kilimanjaro, although no longer the major thrust, began from Longido on 3 March, so giving Stewart three days to get across the German line of retreat before Deventer's and Tighe's attacks took effect. Stewart's progress was slow, manifesting an undue concern about problems of supply. But the real difficulty was that Smuts's plan did not make clear in which direction he thought the Germans most likely to withdraw. Stewart's advance would have its greatest and most immediate effect if Lettow planned to fall back to the west, from Moshi to Arusha. Moreover, Deventer's move to the north of the Taveta Hills rested on a similar assumption. As Lettow planned to fall back down the northern railway, an advance on Moshi by Stewart and Deventer could only shoulder the Germans in the direction which they already planned to follow. Stewart would have had to reach Kahe by 12 March to have fulfilled Smuts's hopes of true envelopment. It must, therefore, be presumed that Smuts, given his predisposition to see Lettow as a guerrilla, imagined that the German commander would seek the interior, would show the same disinclination to use railways and harbours as Smuts did himself, and would be confirmed in that tendency by the demonstrations around Ngulu. On this basis Lettow could only be expected to fight if not threatened with envelopment; wide turning movements by mounted troops would only keep the Germans moving, and were therefore a way of avoiding battle, not of seeking it.[217]

Lettow's new position was a strong one which sustained the threat to Taveta and to the railway line from Voi, but which also gave further opportunities for a British tactical success. His right flank rested on the River Lumi and Lake Jipe, his left on the Pangani, as the Ruvu became after Kahe. Any British frontal attack would be channelled by the crocodile-infested rivers flowing north–south into the Ruvu. But Lettow had both the Ruvu and the Pare Mountains to his back. His principal line of withdrawal, the railway, lay behind his left, while his own inclinations were to concentrate for a counter-attack on his right.

Smuts's plan was to attack frontally with the 1st division while sending Deventer's mounted brigade from Moshi, west of the railway, to Kahe in order to cut off the German retreat. The difficulties confronting the 1st division in its attack caused it to move against Kahe more than against the centre. On 21 March Deventer was unable to find crossings on the Pangani. Eventually part of his command swam the river and took Kahe Hill. Deventer then pushed back north on Kahe, while sending two dismounted squadrons south to cut the railway below Kahe. The Germans had already abandoned Kahe, and were in positions south of the Pangani strong enough to check Deventer's relatively weak command from working round their southern flank to the railway. Sheppard, Stewart's successor in command of 1st division, did not know that Deventer had control of Kahe, and at 4.45 p.m. ordered his men to dig in 3 or 4 kilometres to the north. Thus the South Africans failed to push in the attack at the vital moment. To the south, Deventer's two detached squadrons were blocked by impenetrable and seemingly endless bush. However, their efforts did not go unobserved. They were reported to Lettow as threatening Kisangire. A determined German counter-attack might have regained Kahe and Kahe Hill. But the danger to Kisangire decided Lettow that he should withdraw there himself, pulling his troops south of the Ruvu during the night of 21/2 March. Thus the British gained command of the Ruvu, and so secured their communications from Voi to Moshi. But once again they had failed to trap the German troops.

The March–May rainy season came late in 1916. Smuts was therefore lucky to have got as far as he had. But when the rains did arrive they were the heaviest for some years. All operations on the northern railway were suspended. Else-

---

[217] Collyer, *South Africans with Smuts*, 68, 267–9.

where the effects were less severe. In the west the Belgians advanced into Ruanda and Urundi; in the south-west a force under Brigadier-General Northey began its push from Northern Rhodesia; and to the south Portugal declared war on Germany in March. Tombeur's plan of a year previously, that of a number of converging but independent thrusts along the circumference of the German colony, thus found practical application. Co-ordination was admittedly non-existent. Smuts had no direct line of communications to Tombeur; Northey was answerable directly to the Colonial Office, not even to the War Office; no joint commander was appointed nor planning conference held. But the momentum of the allied onset was not lost.

Smuts's transport and supply services had banked on the rainy season for a moment's pause and consolidation. However, Smuts was unhappy at the prospect of inactivity on the northern front until June. He assumed that the Germans did not intend to fall south of the central railway. Thus neither Northey's column nor any Portuguese effort promised immediate effects. The pivot of Lettow's resistance seemed to be Tabora. Schnee had transferred his capital there, given the danger to Dar es Salaam; it was the *Schütztruppen's* major recruiting centre; and its inland position on the central railway played to German strengths and British weaknesses in matters of supply and communication. Intelligence gathered by Deventer, when he took Lol Kissale on 6 April, confirmed this analysis of German intentions; it pointed to plans for the defence of Ufiome and Kondoa Irangi, in order to bar the western route to the central railway.[218] Smuts was committed to accepting Belgian co-operation in the west, but on the assumption that Tombeur's operations would be secondary, not primary. However, if Smuts did nothing during the rains, the Belgians not the British would spearhead the advance on Tabora. Britain's credit in Africa would not be fully restored; South Africa's war aims might be forfeit to Belgium's.

Smuts briefly reconsidered the amphibious option favoured by Smith-Dorrien. Given his assumptions about the significance of Tabora, Tanga seemed remote and unimportant. Dar es Salaam, by virtue of its position at the head of the central railway, gave directly onto Tabora, but heavy seas and the unhealthy coastline helped confirm Smuts in his predisposition against such a scheme. Communication difficulties precluded the formation of a major British concentration at Mwanza for a direct drive on Tabora. Instead, Smuts opted to march on Kondoa Irangi. Although supported in his decision by Meinertzhagen, the conception and execution were essentially Boer. Afrikaner settlers in the north assured Smuts that the rains to the south and west would not be as severe as those around Kilimanjaro. His forces were reorganized into three divisions, two of them exclusively South African and each

---

[218] Crowe, *General Smuts' campaign*, 113; more generally Hordern, *East Africa*, i. 263–70.

composed of an infantry brigade and a mounted brigade: mobility was emphasized over firepower. Smuts's aim was less the defeat of Lettow than the occupation of territory. The lessons of South-West Africa were being applied in circumstances that were totally different.

Success in their first campaign had made the South Africans heedless of the needs of horse management. The remounts they had employed had been shattered by the punishing marches imposed upon them. But the campaign had not collapsed; railways and motor-transport had kept some form of supply going, and disease in itself was not a major threat. In East Africa mechanical transport was not so readily available, and great areas, embracing a zone up to 400 kilometres inland or until the altitude reached 1,000 metres, were home to the tsetse fly. Ultimately all horses in East Africa would succumb to the fly. The task of the veterinary services was to keep it at bay for long enough to enable the advance to take effect. This could be achieved in two ways, prophylactically or operationally. The first was undermined by the inability of regimental veterinary officers to establish their authority over the decentralized commands of Boer units, whose squadron and troop leaders had powers of discretion. Arsenic powder could prolong the horse's life, but it was issued in pills and soldiers gave it to their mounts whole, with the result that it was left unconsumed at the bottom of the feed-bag. The second was the casualty of Smuts's staff arrangements. The veterinary staff was 'always miles away' from the commander-in-chief and his chief of staff. The British knew— as a result of maps obligingly provided by German veterinarians before the war—the locations of the worst tsetse areas, but this intelligence was not incorporated in the campaign plan. Equine wastage in 1916 ran at 100 per cent per month, when the veterinary services reckoned it could have been half that.[219]

The newly constituted 2nd division, commanded by Deventer, left Lol Kissale on 8 April. Its mounted brigade, in the van, reached Kondoa Irangi on 19 April, and the infantry brigade arrived by the end of the month. The weather contradicted the predictions: nearly 18 inches of rain fell at Moshi in the last fortnight of April. The supplies dumped at Longido and destined for Deventer's men became bogged on muddy roads. Tsetse fly annihilated the mounted brigade's mobility: of 3,894 horses issued to the brigade by 23 May, 1,639 had died since March and 718 were unfit for service.[220] Fortunately Kondoa Irangi itself was a fertile area.

However, the weather was not partial in its effects. The 'short' rains, those that fell in November, had proved light in 1915, and accordingly the harvest yields in the Kilimanjaro area had been low. Throughout February and March

[219] Blenkinsop and Rainey, *Veterinary services*, 407–18.
[220] Hordern, *East Africa*, i. 278, 284.

the German troops in the north were threatened with starvation. Food was brought from the depots on the central railway. To bridge the gap between Kilosa and the light railway at Handeni, an extra 20,000 porters were required. Then came the heavy rains of late March. Although the nine-day hike between the railways was organized in relays, both shelter and provisions proved inadequate. About 20,000 porters died, and many others fell prey to dysentery and respiratory illnesses.[221] As the intelligence captured at Lol Kissale revealed, Lettow was already planning to regroup around Kondoa Irangi in order to ease his supply problem before Deventer began his main advance.

Smuts's strategy thus conformed to Lettow's intentions. It allowed him to use his railway communications and the availability of interior lines to maximum advantage. Leaving Kraut and ten companies (2,400 men) in the Pare Mountains, Lettow brought the strength facing Deventer's 3,000 rifles to eighteen companies (4,000 rifles) and six guns (two of them heavy guns from the *Königsberg*). Deventer began to look dangerously vulnerable. For the first time in East Africa the Germans countered artillery with artillery.[222] But the ground before Kondoa Irangi was open and exposed. Furthermore, German reconnaissance was inadequate, and failed to spot British positions south of the town. Lettow's decision to attack on the night of 9/10 May, reflecting the lack of cover for a daylight advance, did not take account of his shortage of intelligence. The Germans were checked with 35 per-cent losses. Thereafter, Lettow remained unwontedly passive. Deventer's position was entrenched, and in early June was supplemented with heavy artillery.

In concentrating south of Kondoa Irangi, Lettow decided to abandon the northern railway. If Smuts wished to end the campaign quickly, he should have used the advent of dry weather to reinforce Deventer and then risked heavy casualties in a battle for the Dodoma–Kilimatinde section of the central railway. Such counsels were not lacking at his headquarters.[223] But Smuts now insisted that the northern railway was vital and that the Pare Mountains should be cleared. Given his previous assumptions about the importance of Tabora and the irrelevance of Tanga, this was perverse; it confirms the supposition that the avoidance of major battle was not Lettow's strategy but Smuts's. Deventer was to be supported indirectly, through an advance on Mombo and then Handeni: Lettow was to be outmanoeuvred, not outfought.

The rains in the north abated in the second week of May. Smuts decided to follow the line of the Pangani rather than of the railway. The east bank of the river was apparently undefended. The railway, on the other hand, marked a succession of German points of resistance, and its destruction by Kraut could delay Smuts's progress if he allowed its repair to dominate the tempo of his

[221] Schnee, *Deutsch-Ostafrika*, 143–4.
[222] Benary, *Ehrenbuch der deutschen Feldartillerie*, 642–3.
[223] Meinertzhagen, *Army diary*, 187–8.

advance. Smuts therefore organized his forces in three columns, the river column, the centre column (to follow the railway), and the eastern column (to move from Mbuyuni to the Ngulu Gap and then through the Pare Mountains). The centre column would threaten the German front, while the river and eastern columns moved to its flanks. Smuts's aim was speed, not battle. Convinced that Lettow intended to reconcentrate on the northern railway, and reckoning that it would take him fifteen days to do so, Smuts wanted to get to Handeni and its railhead as soon as possible.

Kraut's inclination was to fight. But the nature of the British flanking moves ensured that combat rarely occurred. The river column found its momentum slowed by thick bush. Thus, it threatened the Germans without ever endangering them. Kraut's offensive spirit took second place to common sense, Schnee's admonitions to prudence, and the availability of the railway line for rapid retreat. Only if the centre column had fixed the Germans in frontal assaults could Smuts's succession of enveloping moves along the Pangani have had any effect.[224]

Kraut's force was, of course, never designed to give battle. Nor did Lettow plan to reconcentrate at Handeni. Smuts's advance was therefore as fast as he could have hoped. Beginning on 21 May, in ten days his troops covered 208 kilometres and reached Bwiko. Smuts then directed the river column on Mkalomo, assuming that Kraut would hold Mombo against the centre column.

Kraut intended to do so but was manoeuvred out anew, and so fought a brief action at Mkalomo on 9 June. The same happened at Handeni. Finally, the Germans took up defensive positions on the River Lukigura, north of the Nguru Mountains. Smuts hoped to take Kraut in the rear from the west, but the poverty of the maps and the difficulty of the terrain once again betrayed the ambition of the manoeuvre. Smuts had advanced 400 kilometres in under five weeks. The major constraint on his progress was not enemy action but his line of communications. The nearest railhead was Bwiko, 144 kilometres to his rear. His men were on half rations, restricted to a diet of hard-tack and mealie flour. A halt was called.

Smuts imagined that his advance to the Lukigura had eased the pressure on Deventer at Kondoa Irangi.[225] He now envisaged the two columns advancing in tandem towards the central railway, pinning the Germans between Morogoro and Dodoma.[226] In reality, Deventer's lack of movement throughout May and June was due not to Lettow's attentions but to health and supply problems. Moreover, Lettow had no intention of being tied to the central railway. At the end of April he and Schnee had agreed to abandon their original

[224] Boell, *Operationen*, 189–95; Schnee, *Deutsch-Ostafrika*, 185.
[225] Crowe, *General Smuts's campaign*, 163–4.   [226] Hordern, *East Africa*, 294.

intention of withdrawing west to Tabora. Instead, they proposed to plunge south to Mahenge. Lettow used the veterinary surveys which Smuts had spurned, deliberately posting his men so as to draw mounted troops into fly-infested areas. Thus tsetse and extended communications would slow the British pursuit.[227] Lettow began to move his troops away from the Kondoa Irangi front on 20 June, over three weeks before Deventer was ready to advance.[228] He joined Kraut at Turiani in the Ngurus, his aim being to cover the evacuation of supplies from the central railway southwards.

On 14 July Deventer resumed his advance, directing his main column on Mpwapwa, and smaller columns on Dodoma and Kilimatinde. By the end of the month Deventer was astride the central railway and pushing eastwards on Kilosa to link up with Smuts.

Smuts spent July in the shadow of the Ngurus and the *Königsberg*'s guns. The main German positions were on Mount Kanga, facing the Lukigura. Smuts was informed that the valleys of the Mjonga and the Lwale, running north–south behind the Kanga massif, were practicable for troops. He therefore planned that one column (Sheppard's) should engage the Germans on Kanga, while two more marched first west and then south following the valleys through the hills, converging on Turiani, thus cutting off the Germans' line of retreat. Sheppard set off on 7 August, but found his progress through the bush and along the mountain slopes too slow. He therefore had to retrace his steps and skirt the mountains to the east, following the line of the Lukigura. Meanwhile, the advance of the two western columns, begun on 5 and 6 August, proved equally laborious. The 2nd mounted brigade, heading the Mhonda valley column, reached the Mjonga on 8 August. But its position was unobservable from the air owing to the thickness of the cover, and it had no wireless. Sheppard's column was at this stage back at its start position, and the main bodies of the other two were only just beginning their southward ascent into the hills. Although the 2nd mounted brigade was in the right position, in isolation it lacked the strength to cut the German communications. Lettow made good his escape through Turiani to the Wami.

On 16 August the two western columns debouched from the Ngurus and at Dakawa ran into German fire from across the Wami. Sheppard's column had already crossed the Wami at Kipera, and moving up the right bank threatened to strike the German flank on the 17th. The Germans fought a delaying action and then fell back on the night of 17 August, Lettow and the main force retiring on Morogoro and Kraut moving south-westwards towards Mahenge.

---

[227] Schnee, *Deutsch-Ostafrika*, 182–3; Lettow-Vorbeck, *Reminiscences*, 141–2; Rainey and Blenkinsop, *Veterinary services*, 419.
[228] Boell, *Operationen*, 188.

On 16 August Smuts began to realize that Lettow did not propose to oblige him by fighting it out on the central railway.[229] He nonetheless hoped to be able to pin the Germans against the Uluguru Mountains, a range rising in places to 3,000 metres, and whose northern tip extended to Morogoro and the railway. Deventer reached Kilosa on 22 August. But his division was exhausted, and he reported that he could not continue unless the Germans facing him were threatened from the rear. Smuts therefore directed Enslin's 2nd mounted brigade to the south-west, to strike the central railway at Mkata. Deventer and Enslin, with Enslin leading, were then to push south and west of the Ulugurus to Mlali, while Smuts's main body moved to the east of the range. Smuts did not know whether Lettow planned to retire to Mahenge or to the Rufiji river: his hunch in favour of the latter explained the greater weight attached to his eastern hook. But once again he ducked a frontal assault. Arguing that the hills which screened Morogoro to the north would make a direct advance from the Wami a costly and protracted operation, he put all his weight into the flanks. Enslin reached Mlali on 23 August; Mikese, 32 kilometres east of Morogoro, was gained on the 26th. Thus, when Morogoro itself was occupied on the same day, no German troops remained to contest Smuts's entry. Abandoned German supplies bore testimony to the speed of the British advance, but by now Smuts's operational style was too manifest for there to be any likelihood of Lettow waiting to fight. Lettow's orders of 26 August established the main German positions at the southern end of the Ulugurus, on the further bank of the River Mgeta. By deploying his troops in depth to the north, he hoped to render them proof against British turning movements, and also to enable them to strike blows against isolated components of Smuts's forces, scattered by design and divided by the terrain.

On 5 September Brits's 3rd division, which had taken up the western movement from Deventer's shattered 2nd division, was approaching Kisaki. Lettow had 600,000 kilos of supplies dumped here, and the poverty of the region south of the Mgeta encouraged him to fight for their protection.[230] On Brits's left, plunging through the Ulugurus themselves, was Nussey's 1st mounted brigade, detached from Deventer's division and now without its horses. Both commanders had wireless, and on 7 September, the day Brits attacked, each was within 8 kilometres of the other. But 'once off the road . . . even the sky overhead was invisible, and one could not see one's next-door neighbour three feet away'.[231] Not even the sound of Brits's rifle fire was audible to Nussey. His wireless was lost over a precipice. Lettow was able to deal with each in turn, smashing Brits on 7 September and checking Nussey on the 8th.

---

[229] Hancock and Poel, *Smuts papers*, iii. 396; Collyer, *South Africans with Smuts*, 153–4, gives indications that this would be so in late June.

[230] Lettow, *Reminiscences*, 152–3; Boell, *Operationen*, 226.

[231] Reitz, *Trekking on*, 101.

To the east the pattern was repeated. Delayed by the need to repair roads and bridges, Hoskins's 1st division did not reach Tulo until 9 September. The Germans, in entrenched positions on the Dunthumi river, could therefore be reinforced by the victors of Kisaki. The Germans fought a stubborn action from the 10th to the 12th, but in their wish to counter-attack were as hampered by the terrain as the British were in their advances. On 14 September Lettow abandoned Kisaki, withdrawing across the Mgeta and establishing a new base at Beho-Beho.

Smuts now paused. Most of his staff thought he should have done so at Morogoro. Deventer's 2nd division was 650 kilometres from its railhead, Brits's 3rd division 390 kilometres, and Hoskins's 1st division 360 kilometres. All three were on half rations; Hoskins's had no forward dumps and depended on a daily lift of 17,000 to 20,000 pounds.[232] Smuts used lorries as far as he could. But, although formally speaking the rains had not yet begun, rain was falling and within a day tracks across the black cotton soil were turned into a sea of 'sticky, black mud'.[233] Baggage animals could not make good the deficiency. Of 54,000 mules, donkeys, horses, and oxen put to work on the supply lines around and south of the central railway between June and September 1916, all but 600 fell prey to the tsetse fly.[234]

The health of the humans was little better. By May 1916, within three months of their arrival, most South African units had already lost half their strength to disease. The 9th South African Infantry mustered 1,135 all ranks on 14 February; on 25 October its parade state stood at 116. The 2nd Rhodesia Regiment deployed 1,038 all ranks between March 1915 and its departure from the theatre in January 1917. Thirty-six were killed in action, eighty-four wounded, and thirty-two died of disease. But there were 10,626 cases of sickness, including 3,127 of malaria, and 2,272 of these resulted in hospital admission.[235] Some at least were the product of the punishing rates of march, and of malnutrition caused by insufficient food or inadequate cooking. Thus, 'what Smuts saves on the battlefield he loses in hospital, for it is Africa and its climate we are really fighting not the Germans'.[236] An early battle, a frontal assault when lines of communication were short, might ultimately have proved less costly than long-range but combat-free manoeuvring.

The means by which to improve the supply position were available. At the beginning of September 1916 Smuts's base was still Mombasa. And yet Tanga was taken on 7 July. Smuts, convinced that complete victory was imminent, saw its restoration and use as of no value. The British entered Dar es Salaam on 3 September. Little energy was put into its reopening. Smuts's administrative staff remained at Tanga to the north, while his shipping was securing the ports

---

[232] Hordern, *East Africa*, i. 393–4.   [233] Fendall, *East African Force*, 194–5.
[234] Mosley, *Duel for Kilimanjaro*, 153.   [235] Hordern, *East Africa*, i. 521.
[236] Meinertzhagen, *Army diary*, 200; also 195.

of Kilwa, Lindi, Sudi, and Mikindani to the south. The damage to the central railway was not as severe as it might have been. The Germans had destroyed the bridges and removed much of the rolling stock to its western end, around Tabora. But the track was largely intact. By converting Ford cars to run on the rails, the British were able to use the permanent way almost immediately. During November locomotives once again linked Dar es Salaam and Morogoro. If Smuts had paused on the central railway, and re-established his communications through Dar es Salaam before pushing on into the Ulugurus, he might have been able to terminate the campaign north of the Mgeta, or at least of the Rufiji.

However, the advance to the central railway had inflicted at least one major blow on the *Schütztruppen*. Lettow's theatre of operations was bisected. In the west Wahle and his men were out of contact, left to conduct their own operations. The campaign which he and Tombeur waged was comparable in range and significance with that in the east. It served neither British colonial interests, nor the post-war publicity accorded to Smuts and Lettow, to acknowledge the fact. But Tabora, Wahle's headquarters, was the largest town in German East Africa, centrally positioned in the colony. According to a British estimate of 1 April 1916 as many as 373 European troops and 7,650 askaris were deployed in the square Kivu–Mwanza–Tabora–Ujiji.[237] In themselves these figures confirm how exaggerated were Meinertzhagen's estimates of Lettow's total strength. Wahle's disposable force actually numbered about 2,000. But the calculation reveals how dependent Smuts's thrusts in the east were on Tombeur's simultaneous commitment in the west. The troops concentrated under Lettow's direct command in the north only just exceeded half the *Schütztruppen's* total force.

The campaign in the west also showed how unsympathetic to guerrilla operations and how wedded to colonial stability were many Germans. Both at Bukoba and at Mwanza the principles of German peacetime administration persisted for the first two years of the war. The local economy was nurtured, porters only served within their own regions, and productivity was sustained. Loyalty to Germany enabled auxiliaries to be raised, and even prompted rebellion across the Ugandan frontier at Kigezi. The basis existed for a sustained popular defence of Ruanda and Urundi. But instead the people were prepared for the arrival of the British and told to co-operate with them. The commander of the Bukoba area's final words were that the Germans 'wished to find the country in the same condition as they left it when they returned in three months time after the approaching German victory in Europe'. A preference for German colonialism, not the prosecution of the European war, led to the rejection of revolutionary methods.[238]

[237] Belgique, *Campagnes coloniales belges*, ii. 177. This is the fullest source on the Tabora campaign.
[238] Austen, *Northwest Tanzania*, 118, also 113–18; see also Louis, *Ruanda-Urundi*, 213.

The first phase of the Entente's offensive in the west was bizarre, even in a theatre of operations dominated by larger-than-life personalities. Lieutenant-Commander G. B. Spicer-Simson was one of the Royal Navy's less distinguished officers. In command of a destroyer he had sunk a liberty boat, and he had been ashore entertaining some ladies when a gunboat anchored under his orders had been torpedoed. Nonetheless, Spicer-Simson was selected to command two gunboats that were hauled overland from Capetown via Elizabethville to Lake Tanganyika. Most of the journey was by rail, but the significant sections were not. The expedition sailed from England on 15 June 1915; on Boxing Day Spicer-Simson's two craft put out into the waters of Lake Tanganyika. By February two German gunboats were accounted for, but a third, the *Graf von Götzen*, a much bigger vessel, only recently completed and mounting one of the *Königsberg*'s 10.5 cm guns, remained at large. Spicer-Simson, who had now taken to wearing a skirt with his commander's jacket, refused Belgian pleas to engage the *Graf von Götzen*. Instead, he set off to the southern end of the lake to support the British forces on the Northern Rhodesian frontier. The Germans' control of the lake was sufficiently dented to allow the Belgians to transport goods along its western coast, but the navigation of the eastern bank remained in their hands. Thus, both sides were able to use the lake route to feed their forces in Ruanda and Urundi.[239]

For the Belgians, supply was a major headache. In August 1914 the *Force publique* concentrated 1,395 men along the Congo; in May 1916 Tombeur's strength was 719 Europeans and 11,698 blacks (a much lower ratio of Europeans to blacks than the other powers thought advisable). They were deployed in three groups: a brigade north of Lake Kivu close to the Ugandan frontier (Molitor's); a brigade on the Russissi (Olsen's); and a defensive group on the western shore of Lake Tanganyika. No food reserves had been formed before the offensive. The Belgians hoped to live off the land. But the 1916 harvest was not yet in, and the 1915 crop was either eaten or destroyed.[240] Dispersing to requisition, the Belgian askaris developed a fearsome reputation. Tombeur had stressed that the Belgians' war was with the troops of Germany, not with the inhabitants of Ruanda and Urundi;[241] in reality, the lack of sufficient European officers to ensure adequate supervision undermined the hopes of local collaboration. Each of the groups needed 7,000–8,000 porters for its own needs in addition to the porters for the lines of communication. The former were locally impressed. Tombeur tried to recruit the latter from the interior of the Congo, but eventually had to ask the British for 5,000 porters and 100 ox-wagons. The effect of this British contribution was temporarily to rob the

---

[239] Farwell, *Great War in Africa*, 217–49, tells the colourful story; Boell, *Operationen*, 131–4, emphasizes its limited outcome.
[240] Belgique, *Campagnes coloniales belges*, ii. 51–90.   [241] Ibid., i. 184–7.

troops in Uganda, Lakeforce (commanded by Sir Charles Crewe), of their offensive capacity.

Tombeur, like Smuts, was more interested in the conquest of territory than in the defeat of the *Schütztruppen*. Moreover, the examples of Tanga and Kahe convinced him that his opponents were masters of the defensive battle. Although sixteen 70 mm howitzers, originally ordered by the Mexican government, had been promised him by the French, they had yet to arrive. Therefore, the *Force publique* was instructed to shun attacks on trenches and strong-points. The Germans would thus be denied the opportunity of crushing one Belgian column before turning against the other, and so would be robbed of any advantage to be derived from operating on interior lines. Tombeur wanted to combine tactical conservatism—the holding of ground once gained, the avoidance of defeat, the keeping of casualties to a minimum—with a strategy of manoeuvre. And yet the porter problem, the lack of intelligence, and the absence of effective communications between the brigades all constrained such operations. The best that Tombeur could do was to set down his general principles and to agree a common date on which Molitor and Olsen were to advance.[242]

On 5 April Wintgens, the officer commanding the three *Schütztruppen* companies in Ruanda, received a letter from the Belgians offering an armistice. Tombeur said that the war in East Africa had been begun by Germany, not Belgium, and therefore asked Schnee for compensation. Lettow, his mind focused on the eastern theatre, was not unenthusiastic; Schnee saw it as a Belgian ruse to lower Wahle's guard, and said he would have to refer the whole matter to Berlin. In fact Tombeur was behaving with remarkable consistency. An armistice on such terms would have fulfilled Belgian objectives to the letter.[243]

On 12 April the Belgians, without replying to Schnee, opened fire on the Russissi front. Tombeur imagined that the Germans would fall back to a line flanked by Kigali in the north and Nyanza in the south. The northern brigade demonstrated against German positions on the River Sebea while directing its main body towards Kigali. Wintgens's communications with Wahle were cut on 22 April, and on 2 May he ordered the evacuation of Kigali. Further south, Olsen got across the Russissi and took Nyanza on 21 May. The Belgians had won Ruanda by manoeuvre alone.

So far Molitor's and Olsen's columns had pursued convergent lines of march. But now annexationism and operational necessity created divergent objectives. Olsen thrust south at the end of May towards Usumbura and Kitega (entered on 17 June), in order to secure Urundi. Molitor moved east towards the south-western corner of Lake Victoria in order to collaborate with Crewe's

---

[242] Ibid., ii. 186–9.
[243] Schnee, *Deutsch-Ostafrika*, 205; Boell, *Operationen*, 260; no Entente source refers to this episode.

Lakeforce. Thus the Belgians fanned out, their force-to-space ratio diminishing and their units increasingly pursuing independent objectives. The Belgian government's priority was the seizure of Ujiji and the domination of Lake Tanganyika; Olsen, therefore, had the principal role. But for the British Molitor was more important. They wanted him to combine with Crewe in the capture of Mwanza. By the end of June both objectives had been adopted. On Crewe's suggestion Mwanza, once secured, was to be the base for a thrust on Tabora. Olsen would support by moving eastwards from Ujiji along the central railway.

In practice, Olsen's progress proved more rapid than Molitor's: thus Belgian aims prevailed over British. Wintgens had reckoned that the rains would cause Tombeur to halt on the Kigali–Nyanza line. In reality, the lack of porters proved a greater impediment to pursuit. Those recruited in Ruanda were reluctant to follow Olsen into Urundi. The southern brigade overcame its immediate problems by shifting its base to Usumbura on Lake Tanganyika. It then occupied Ujiji without opposition, Wahle having decided to concentrate his forces north of Tabora. The British took Mwanza on 14 July. By 19 September 40,000 loads were accumulated at Mwanza. But its value as a base was minimized by lack of porters to carry them forward. The area south of Mwanza was waterless, its resources stripped, and its population shifted by the Germans. In the Belgian column seven out of every twelve loads were needed to feed the porters themselves. Crewe's force had 10,000 porters for 2,800 combatants.[244]

By the beginning of August Molitor reckoned Wahle's major positions were at Kahama, south of Whimo, with a supporting group opposite Crewe at Shinyanga. Crewe concluded that the Shinyanga positions were stronger. Each, therefore, saw himself as having the principal task and requested his ally to support him. For Tombeur, Molitor's job was to continue due south, so relieving the pressure on Olsen as soon as possible. If Crewe was right, then Molitor's troops would turn the Germans at Shinyanga without their having to lose time by marching to the east. Crewe, nonetheless, insisted on Molitor's direct support. He was proved wrong, but not until 17 August was Molitor able to resume the original direction of his advance.[245] On 28 August Crewe took the Shinyanga position without fighting.

In Tombeur's mind he was commanding a massive concentric attack on Tabora, with Olsen's southern brigade leading while Molitor's northern brigade fixed the Germans around Whimo. In reality, Tombeur was a spectator. By early September his forces described a quarter-circle of nearly 200 kilometres, each brigade's base 400 kilometres distant from the other. On 2

[244] Buhrer, *L'Afrique orientale allemande*, 381–3.
[245] Belgique, *Campagnes coloniales belges*, ii. 419–25.

September an intercepted German signal reported a German victory over Olsen's brigade the previous day at Mabama. This was Tombeur's first indication of Olsen's current position. The check to Olsen was minor, only one battalion having been engaged at Mabama, but Tombeur now decided that the northern brigade should take up the running while the southern held its ground. However, the supply problems of Molitor's brigade made his advance sporadic and slow. Each daily stage of his route could accommodate only two battalions, and his troops carried sufficient ammunition for a single day's fighting. On 9 September he took up defensive positions in order to reconcentrate. The southern brigade, not the northern, made the offensive efforts of the next four days. Even when direct contact between the two brigades was established on the 14th, the northern brigade remained on the defensive. Olsen's push on Lulanguru on 16 September was thus unsupported.

Wahle knew of Tombeur's intentions from radio intercepts and therefore established his main positions north of Tabora at Itanga. The proximity of Itanga and Lulanguru, particular given the railway line, enabled him to move troops from one to the other. But his force had now fallen to 1,100 rifles. He disbanded the naval unit under his command in order to redistribute its Europeans among the field companies. Nonetheless, desertions multiplied. Many of the askari came from the Tabora region and had no intention of leaving it. The Germans no longer had the men to defend the town's perimeter. On 16 September a captured letter, intended by Crewe for Molitor, revealed that the main blow from the north would be delivered on the 19th. Wahle divided his command into three components, two to go east along the central railway before turning south to Kiromo, and one to go due south from Tabora to Sikonge. The Germans abandoned their positions under cover of dark on the 18th.[246]

The pursuit of the *Schütztruppen* was half-hearted and limited. The occupation of Tabora on 19 September marked the limit of Belgian territorial ambitions. Logistic constraints as well as political directives tied Tombeur to the town. Now that the *Force publique* was reconcentrated its demands for food exceeded the capacity of the local supplies. The plight of Lakeforce, outside Tabora to the east, and 390 kilometres from its base, was even worse. On 3 October Crewe's command was dissolved. Had military priorities carried more weight than colonial rivalries in allied counsels, Olsen's advance from the west would have been held back. Crewe might then have hit the railway to the east before the attack from the west had made itself felt. As it was, Olsen's outpacing of Molitor and Crewe meant that Wahle's path to the south and east lay open. His three columns made off towards Iringa, in a bid to reunite with Lettow and the main force.

[246] Ibid., app., pp. 173, 176, 181–6; Boell, *Operationen*, 283–5; Marine-Archiv, *Kämpfe der Kaiserlichen Marine*, ii. 269; Schnee, *Deutsch-Ostafrika*, 206–13.

The Germans' retreat south of the central railway gave the British advance from Northern Rhodesia more than local significance. In origin, however, the Colonial Office's decision to switch from defence to attack related not to the East African campaign as a whole but to the increasing instability in Nyasaland and Northern Rhodesia. The colonization of the northern parts of both territories was not complete in 1914. The district staff in Northern Rhodesia fell from 102 in 1914 to seventy-six by the end of 1915. And yet the strains on the colony multiplied. The German incursion across the frontier—and the demand for labour to support the troops needed to counter it—threw the value of British protection into question and caused economic crisis. Famine was evident by late 1915. Brigadier-General Edward Northey, the only British general in East Africa for whom the Germans confessed admiration, was appointed to the command, and his force boosted to 2,500 men. Having established four posts from Karonga to Abercorn, he took the offensive on 25 May 1916.[247]

But Northey's attack exacerbated many of the colonial and economic problems it was designed to mitigate. The railhead for his force was at Ndola, 960 kilometres from Abercorn and 730 kilometres from his main base at Kasama. The road cut from Kashitu, south of Ndola, to Kisama and Abercorn in 1915 was not suitable for wheeled traffic, particularly in the rains; an experiment in the use of oxen in 1914 fell victim to tsetse fly. So porters were vital. The demands on the adult male population were enormous. In Nyasaland alone, perhaps 200,000 men, or 83 per cent of the total available, were employed as labourers in Northey's campaign. In north-east Rhodesia 92,337 carriers were engaged between April 1915 and March 1916, and 138,930 between April 1916 and March 1917. At a local level Abercorn, with a population of 8,500 taxable males, contributed 5,000 carriers and 800 road-builders by August 1916; Luwingu, with 7,000 taxable males, drew in sufficient labour from outside to account for 12,786 engagements between March 1915 and March 1916. The effect of such massive new employment was to jeopardize local cultivation. The British South Africa Company could not introduce measures to encourage African food production without threatening the preferential arrangements for white settlers, already alienated by rising labour costs generated through the army's demands and rates of pay. Food production, therefore, fell. Increasingly, the porters had to carry their own supplies as well as those of the troops. Sir C. A. Wallace, the administrator of Northern Rhodesia, reckoned that if the porters carried their own food only 1/27 of their load from Ndola would reach its destination at Kasama. To deliver 1 ton of food a day (enough for 1,000 men) from Ndola to Kasama needed 2,250 carriers if food was available en route and

---

[247] Crucial background to Northey's offensive is Yorke, 'Crisis of colonial control', 20–54, 118–65, 272–91; on Nyasaland, see Page, *Journal of African History*, XIX (1978), 87–100.

23,300 if not. The exponential effects of the lack of local produce raised these numbers to 3,000 and 71,000 respectively, if delivery was to Abercorn. At the end of 1914 about one load in twenty was actually reaching its destination. The decision to move from defence to attack increased the numbers of troops to be supplied, extended the lines of communication yet further, and took the porters away from their own territories. The major threat to Northey's advance was less the Germans than administrative collapse, and even rebellion.[248]

Northey developed two palliatives to ease his supply problem. The first was to use boats to cross the swamps in Belgian territory, between Ndola and Kasama. More than half the total food delivered in the build-up to Northey's attack came by this route, and in 1916–17 12,000 paddlers using 2,000 canoes delivered 2,500 tons. Secondly, as Northey advanced so he established bases at the head of Lake Nyasa, and was able to use the route from Beira to Chinde, thence up the Zambezi, and finally to Fort Johnston.[249]

By 4 June Northey had cleared the frontiers of Northern Rhodesia and Nyasaland, and had established his headquarters at Neu Langenburg. A thrust north towards Tabora and Kilimatinde would have taken Northey's force across barren country and extended his line of communications. Therefore, as the main German forces were pushed in on the central railway, Northey inclined north-east towards Iringa. For Lettow, Northey's attack was both a threat and an opportunity. Its impact on his plan to withdraw to the south was immediate, robbing him of the cultivated areas around Neu Langenburg and endangering Mahenge. On the other hand, Northey's command, kept small by its supply problems, and divided into separate columns spread over a broad front, created the chance of local German successes. Lettow boosted the forces around Iringa to five companies, drawing troops from Dodoma and Dar es Salaam to do so. However, on 24 July Braunschweig, the local German commander, was defeated at Malangali, south-west of Iringa, by two British columns. The British were scarcely superior in numbers, but their converging movements and Braunschweig's undue concern about his single but useless howitzer unhinged the German conduct of the battle from the outset.

Smuts now asked Northey to shun Iringa, and instead to aim south for Lupembe. He was worried that Northey's column would drive the Germans off the central railway before the main attack could trap them there. But on 27 August, with the Germans south of the central railway and concentrated around Morogoro, Smuts changed tack, telling Northey to take Iringa in order to discourage Lettow from any attempt to move in that direction. The combination of Northey's move to Iringa and of Deventer's to Kilosa kept

---

[248] Yorke, 'Crisis of colonial control', 71–102; Lucas, *Empire at war*, iv. 270–2, 290–309; Hodges, *Journal of African History*, XIX (1978), 113.
[249] Yorke, 'Crisis of colonial control', 76–8, 195; Lucas, *Empire at war*, iv. 268, 293–5.

Kraut—after the German retreat from the line of the Wami—to the south-east and Mahenge.

Northey was increasingly worried. His small command was spread over a 160-kilometre front, between Lupembe and Iringa, and his line of communications stretched back to Mwaya. Lettow's main forces were moving south and would be anxious to secure the harvest around Mahenge. Northey wanted Deventer to relieve his northern flank at Iringa, but the 2nd division was exhausted and in any case was required further east. Instead, Smuts urged Northey on, sensing the need to deny the Germans the use of the Mahenge area before the rains. By the end of September Northey's Lupembe column was 96 kilometres from its base on the Ruhuje, and a further force had been detached south to Songea. Although his total strength was raised to 3,800 men, his front was now 320 kilometres long, and his supply dependent on the 17,000 reluctant carriers north of the frontier.[250]

Facing him, Kraut had concentrated 2,450 rifles in the Mahenge area. Kraut's efforts to turn defence into local counter-attacks were hampered in part by the mountainous terrain and the extent of his front. The Germans had simultaneously to face west to the Ruhuje, between Lupembe and Mahenge, and north on the Ruaha. But Kraut's problems were not eased by the offensive instincts of his superior. Lettow's interventions, including direct communications with Kraut's subordinates, added to the difficulties of co-ordination.[251]

Onto this fragile and delicately balanced scene broke Wahle's force from Tabora. After setting a frantic pace for the first ten days in order to escape any Belgian pursuit, Wahle had found himself deep in unexplored and uninhabited terrain. Neither water nor food was readily available. A supply dump had been prepared at Malongwe, on the central railway east of Tabora. But the porters had run off, and with only 600 Indian prisoners of war as carriers Wahle had to leave most of the food, to concentrate on carrying munitions and medical supplies. After six days such food as he had was exhausted, and his men had to forage, and even harvest and thresh, as well as march. The Wahehe, whose territory he entered in November, secreted their food stocks and supported the British. An initial strength of 5,000 men was whittled away: 786 askaris were captured, 146 were reported as missing, 916 deserted, and 300 were left behind. Morale, even among the Europeans, slumped. But Wahle kept his command active. He knew from intercepts that Northey had captured Iringa and that Lettow was moving south from Morogoro. He therefore determined to attack Iringa, so threatening Northey's lines of communications and forcing the British to turn west away from Lettow. But his supply problems forced him to remain divided in three columns, and by 24 October, two days before the day appointed for the attack on Iringa, he had still not regrouped. The British,

---

[250] Hordern, *East Africa*, i. 468–508.   [251] Boell, *Operationen*, 250–8.

alerted by a German assault on Igominyi, were already turning back to cover Iringa. Wahle therefore abandoned the attack on Iringa, and instead pressed on towards Mahenge and Lupembe, believing he would effect a junction with Lettow. Northey's movements in response to Wahle's relieved Kraut, but also confused him, as he was unaware of Wahle's approach. On 9 November Wahle made contact with a patrol sent out by Kraut. On the 26th one of Wahle's columns was surrounded and surrendered, but the other two, a total of 750 men, four guns, and fifteen machine-guns, completed their junction with Kraut. At the end of November Wahle superseded Kraut in command of the Mahenge area. His force totalled 350 Europeans, 3,000 askaris, nine guns, and thirty-nine machine-guns, spread over a front of 450 kilometres. His task was to protect the area under cultivation and, if possible, extend it westwards to Ubena (or Nyombe).[252]

Thus, throughout November Northey's force was exposed to the dangers of defeat in detail, and was engaged in a series of small fights to its rear and to its front. In December Deventer took over responsibility for Iringa. Northey's sector now ran from Songea to Lupembe, his line of communications snaking across the Livingstone Mountains east of Lake Nyasa to Mwaya.

The Germans' withdrawal towards the south-east corner of their colony increased the potential significance of Portugal's entry to the war in March 1916. In practice, however, unlike Northey's advance, Portugal's impact remained local and limited. The prime reason was Portuguese incompetence; but in addition, British interests no more than German would be served by Portugal extending its claims across the Ruvuma river.

In August 1914 reports that Portugal had declared war on Germany and that Portuguese agitators were at work among the native population north of the Ruvuma led to clashes and casualties. Schnee established the truth in September, and apologized to the Portuguese. But in German eyes Portuguese neutrality seemed increasingly fictional.[253] Lisbon allowed the passage of British troops through Mozambique and it authorized its Angolan administrations to co-operate with Pretoria in mopping up after the conquest of South-West Africa. In the autumn of 1915 the postal service via Portuguese territory was disrupted and then suppressed. More significantly, an expeditionary force of 1,527 men arrived in November 1914 from Lisbon to boost the existing garrison of twelve poorly equipped native companies. It was relieved by a second, comparably sized force the following year. The immediate task of this second force was to create a network of posts along the German frontier. But the real aim of the government was the recovery of the Kionga triangle at the mouth of the Ruvuma, seized from Portugal by Germany in 1894. Portugal continued to

---

[252] Ibid. 286–98; Deppe, *Mit Lettow-Vorbeck*, 187–96.
[253] Boell, *Operationen*, 68–70; Marine-Archiv, *Kämpfe der Kaiserlichen Marine*, 275–6.

pursue its imperial ambitions against the background of European war, but until March 1916 contrived to do so without committing itself to the larger conflict: even after 1914 clashes in the colonies did not inevitably lead to belligerence in Europe. When at last it did formally enter the war against the Central Powers, its military actions remained confined to Africa for the time being. In April 1916 Portuguese forces occupied the Kionga triangle. The Germans retaliated by seizing sixteen Portuguese posts on the Ruvuma, largely without opposition.[254]

The apparent success of Smuts's campaign gave urgency to Portugal's ambitions. A British conquest of German East Africa without Portuguese participation would diminish its claims to territory. But, once south of the central railway, Smuts's own ambivalence on Portuguese co-operation became evident. If the Portuguese gained by their own efforts that which Smuts wished to give them, the case for getting them to hand over to South Africa Delagoa Bay and its adjacent territories would be considerably weakened. On the other hand, a Portuguese advance on Lindi would, militarily, be a considerable contribution. The successful voyage of the *Marie* clearly demonstrated how important to the Germans the continued possession of the coastline might be. Therefore, when a third Portuguese expeditionary force, mustering 4,642 men, arrived at Palma on 5 July, and its commander, General Jose Cesar Ferreira Gil, proposed to move up the coast, Smuts responded by saying that the British could do that. Instead, he asked Gil to move into the German food-producing areas inland around Masasi, and pointed to Liwale as an ultimate objective. No roads existed to aid such a march.[255] It was alleged that Gil himself had been appointed because of his political credentials (he was a good republican), rather than his professional aptitude. He lacked experience of Africa; his exercise of command was lackadaisical. He was reported to be far to the rear playing cards while his forward units pressed on without proper reconnaissance.[256] His men showed no interest in the rudiments of tropical hygiene; they would not take quinine; they were reluctant to drink boiled water; tuberculosis, syphilis, and malaria were rampant. By the beginning of September Gil's effective strength was 2,700 rifles. Smuts's proposed line of advance could only reduce such a force to total ineffectiveness.

Gil crossed the Ruvuma and on 26 October occupied Newala. The local population on the Makonde plateau welcomed the Portuguese. Lettow had been so anxious to concentrate all his forces in the north that in 1915 he had appealed to Berlin in a bid to override Schnee's wish to keep a company at

---

[254] Pélissier, *Naissance du Mozambique*, ii. 687–90. Pélissier is the main work on Portuguese aspects of the East African campaign. On the diplomatic background, see Texiera, *L'Entrée du Portugal dans la Grande Guerre*, esp. 205–10, 239, 247–50, 308–11, 358.

[255] Hordern, *East Africa*, i. 388–91.

[256] Ribeiro de Meneses, *Journal of Contemporary History*, XXXIII (1998), 90.

Lindi.[257] Looff, whose *Königsberg* crew formed the kernel of the German garrison in the south-east in the autumn of 1916, agreed with Schnee. Despite having inferior numbers (a total of 840 men), Looff checked Gil's advance and encircled him in Newala. On 28 November, after six days' siege, Gil abandoned Newala and retired across the Ruvuma, leaving four mountain guns, six machine-guns, and 100,000 rounds. Portuguese credit among the tribes of the Makonde withered. Looff's resolute action secured the food-producing areas of the south and made possible Lettow's continued resistance a year later.

Smuts's support for Gil was indirect, delayed, and, ultimately, thwarted by Lettow. Forced to pause on the Mgeta in September, he at last began to exploit his naval supremacy to secure the coastline. Kilwa was seized in September, and during October and November the whole of Hoskins's division was transported thither. Smuts's intention was not so much amphibious envelopment—Kilwa was too far from the Mgeta positions for such a move to have reciprocal effects. Instead, Hoskins was to advance inland on Liwale, so converging with the Portuguese and laying waste the crops on which Lettow might rely in 1917. By using a division, where originally he had intended a brigade, Smuts prevented Hoskins being ready to move until 29 November. The tracks inland were barely passable, sand alternating with black cotton soil. The rains came early and the area was thick with fly. The whole scheme proved ridiculously ambitious, making more sense on the map than it did on the ground.[258]

Moreover, Lettow was not fixed to the Mgeta position by offensive action. The South African artillery plotted the German trenches and lines of communication, and kept them under well-directed harassing fire. But Lettow was still free to divide his force, switching his *Schwerpunkt* from the river to the coast. The first British troops to move inland from Kilwa had occupied Kibata to the north-west, as a guard for their right flank. Lettow saw the opportunity to inflict a defeat on a portion of the enemy forces. Increasing his strength to ten companies, he advanced on Kibata on 5 December. The battle that developed was one of the most desperate and sustained of the campaign, fought in incessant rain between positions often only 80 yards apart, and dominated by artillery and grenades. By 21 December each side had fought the other to a standstill. The British had progressively reinforced Kibata during the battle, so leading Lettow to claim the strategic victory as he had deflected the danger to Liwale. But Lettow had not overwhelmed the British post, and protracted, attritional combat made little tactical sense. By the end of the year he could muster only 1,100 Europeans and 7,300 askaris fit for service.[259]

---

[257] Boell, *Operationen*, 122.

[258] Crowe, *General Smuts' campaign*, is the best English source for this phase of the operations; see also Haywood and Clarke, *Royal West African Frontier Force*, 182, 187; Beadon, *Royal Army Service Corps*, ii. 317.

[259] Boell, *Operationen*, 241–2, 246–9, 300; Lettow-Vorbeck, *Reminiscences*, 168–70.

Lettow's concentration at Kibata had left only 1,000 men on the Mgeta. Smuts therefore embraced the plan which earlier he had spurned. The Kilwa force was to push north-west on Ngarambi, so pinning Lettow, while his main body crossed the Mgeta and then the Rufiji. On 1 January 1917 Smuts attacked the Mgeta positions, using his main force to envelop from the west. The British were on the Rufiji by the 3rd. But the Kilwa force had not been able to hold Lettow. He had already anticipated Smuts's men and placed himself in a central position between the two attacks, at Lake Utungi. The British crossed the Rufiji on 17 January, taking Mkindu and Kipongo. But German resistance was now hardening. Smuts discounted the rains, of whose effects he had received ample warning. They had never really stopped in December, and now began in earnest. The Rufiji turned into a torrent, hundreds of yards across, its current too strong for any of the available boats. As the Germans had already discovered, the area between the Mgeta and the Rufiji, afforested and uninhabited, was devoid of food. It was becoming a swamp. The nearest railhead was at Mikese, 255 kilometres distant. Although Dar es Salaam was open and the central railway functioning, the supply services had still not recovered from their punishing marches earlier in the year. 'The transport was used up; the mechanical transport broken down, and in need of thorough overhaul and reconditioning; the animal transport mostly dead, and the porters worn out and debilitated.'[260] The British advance again ground to a halt.

This time Smuts would not be able to renew it. On 27 December 1916 he heard that he was to go to London, to represent South Africa at the Imperial War Cabinet. He left on 20 January. He had continuously anticipated a short campaign; his cables had consistently reported great successes; he had avoided mentioning the effects of the weather; now he described the war in East Africa as all but finished. At one level he was right. South African war aims were territorial. Four-fifths of the colony and nine-tenths of its infrastructure had been overrun. This was conquest, even if it was not ultimate victory. Smuts had served the cause of imperialism rather than that of the Entente's war effort. In doing so he had behaved as a politician rather than a general, boosting his own reputation and aiming to hallow the integration of the Union with battlefield triumph.

Where propaganda turned to fiction was in the depiction of a great South African feat of arms. On their arrival both Smuts and his fellow countrymen had dubbed the German askaris 'damned Kaffirs'.[261] But they had learnt that blacks could outfight and outwit whites. Privately their respect had grown; publicly they could not admit it. The deadliness of the East African climate was exaggerated rather than acknowledge the effectiveness of the *Schütztruppen*.

[260] Fendall, *East Africa Force*, 88–9; also 169–70.
[261] Meinertzhagen, *Army diary*, 165.

'Hospitals', Meinertzhagen commented on 8 October, 'are full to overflowing with strong healthy men suffering from cold feet or an excess of patriotism.'[262] South African medical officers colluded. Invalids were sent to recuperate in South Africa, and then did not return. When convalescent camps were established in Kenya, wastage rates were cut by about half.[263] Carried to its logical conclusion, the South African arguments about health had to acknowledge that the British, like the Germans, should rely on black, not white, troops. In October 1916 Smuts himself eventually concluded as much. But, by saying that after January 1917 only policing duties remained, he simultaneously protected the *amour propre* of the white South Africans.[264]

The Africanization of the campaign began with the completion of the conquest of the Cameroons. In July 1916 the Gold Coast Regiment arrived, and it bore the brunt of the fighting at Kibata. But Lugard at first opposed the use of the major component of the West African Frontier Force, the four battalions of the Nigeria Regiment. Their losses in the Cameroons had been greater than those of the Gold Coast Regiment. About 1,000 men had been discharged when the campaign ended, and the remainder were anticipating a period with their families. Lugard asked the War Office for forty-two senior officers, but was told that, in view of the demands of the western front, he could have only fifteen subalterns. The advice that he enlist from the local European population, although eventually followed, filled him with apprehension for the internal security of the colony. Over a third of his pre-war administrators were absent on army duties. A rebellion among the Oujo in November 1916, prompted by the chiefs' methods of recruiting porters, lent credence to his fears. Nonetheless, the Nigerians sailed in the same month, their establishment of 5,000 filled by voluntary re-enlistment. Not until 1917 would an indirect form of conscription be necessary. They entered the line on the Mgeta, and occupied the Rufiji valley during the rains.[265]

In April 1916 Hoskins had prevailed on Smuts to sanction a moderate increase in the King's African Rifles. Four new battalions were raised, doubling the strength to 8,000 men. Smuts remained sceptical, bound by the idea that most tribes of the British East African possessions were not warlike, and that therefore the recruiting capacity of the colonies was restricted. Nonetheless, by January 1917 the King's African Rifles had thirteen battalions, and in February a target of twenty was set. By November 1918 the establishment was twenty-two battalions, and its total strength 35,424 all ranks.[266] One regiment, the 6th,

---

[262] Ibid. 199; also 201.
[263] Fendall, *East African Force*, 153–5.
[264] See Smuts's remarks in Collyer, *South Africans under Smuts*, pp. vii–viii.
[265] Osuntokun, *Nigeria in the First World War*, 119–24, 239–250; Haywood and Clarke, *Royal West African Frontier Force*, 188–9, 245–9.
[266] Hordern, *East Africa*, i. 265, 561–75; Moyse-Bartlett, *King's African Rifles*, 301, 413.

raised its three battalions from former German askaris; elsewhere, recently pacified tribesmen enlisted in order to recover their traditional vocations. But generally the notion of 'martial races', imported from the Indian army, was abandoned, and the recruiting base accordingly broadened.[267]

The expanded King's African Rifles was designed ultimately for imperial, not simply East African, service. Smuts, after all, was predicting a rapid end to the campaign, and the conventional wisdom was that the formation and training of each new battalion would take a year. Sensing a fresh source of manpower for other theatres, and thinking particularly of Palestine, which took priority over East Africa from February 1917, the War Office took a more benevolent interest than might otherwise have been the case. In June 1916 the battalions adopted the four-company structure, thus aligning themselves with European norms. A year later the allocation of machine-guns for each battalion was increased to four. Smuts had argued that the efficiency of the *Schütztruppen* was due to their high proportion of European NCOs; the Germans agreed. From a ratio of one white for every 35.5 blacks in January, the King's African Rifles moved to one for 9.25 by the end of the war. However, not all the experienced campaigners shipped out from Britain proved valuable, some being selected because shell-shock had made them unfit for further service in France.[268] In the event, the King's African Rifles' only other service than in German East Africa was on the northern frontiers of Kenya and Uganda, against Somalis, Swazis, and Abyssinians. Their contribution to the major theatres of war was therefore indirect. Henceforth, Lettow was not tying down white troops that could be deployed in France and Flanders. A major strategic rationale for his campaign had been eroded.

The Africanization of the British effort in East Africa did not resolve its logistical problems. On 28 November 1916 715 of 980 other ranks in the Gold Coast Regiment were on the sick list; ironically, the British officers, with nineteen out of thirty-six unfit, were rather more robust.[269] The supply arrangements reached their nadir on the Rufiji in February 1917. Half rations were ordered. The daily food allocation averaged 17 ounces, predominantly of maize. Carriers ate roots and berries, and consequently died of alkaloidal poisoning.[270] Labour was at a premium: 12,000 porters were needed for every 3,000 soldiers, and the British forces on the Rufiji required 135,000, and eventually 175,000.[271] A. R. Hoskins, Smuts's successor, had taken over an army robbed of offensive capacity. Only his West African units could be deemed

---

[267] Lewis J. Greenstein, 'The Nandi experience in the First World War', in Page (ed.), *Africa*, 82–5; Savage and Munro, *Journal of African History*, VII (1966), 324.

[268] Fendall, *East African Force*, 198–9; Hordern, *East Africa*, i. 575; Moyse-Bartlett, *King's African Rifles*, 333–6.

[269] Haywood and Clarke, *Royal West African Frontier Force*, 183.

[270] Killingray and Matthews, *Canadian Journal of African Studies*, XIII (1979), 18.

[271] Miller, *Battle for the Bundu*, 256.

reliable; it would be some months before the new battalions of the King's African Rifles were sufficiently trained to face the *Schütztruppen*.

Lettow's problems were worse. The area into which he had now retreated was the focus of the Maji-Maji rebellion: to the south the Makonde had welcomed the Portuguese, to the west some of the Wangeni in Songea had joined Northey. The rains had failed in 1913/14 and 1914/15, and famine ensued. Two armies had entered a region already made destitute. Lettow had reckoned on having 450,000 kilos of corn stored between the Rufiji and the Mbemkuru. On 26 January 1917 he learned he had only 350,000. There were a further 150,000 kilos in the Lindi area, but to bring them north would have required porters, and his ration strength was already a quarter above what he had anticipated. Lettow dispensed with all useless mouths, handing over to the British those not fit to fight. Each European was reduced to five porters, each company to 150, and those on the lines of communication were sent home: a total of 8,000 carriers were thus discharged. Rations, which might otherwise have been cut to a quarter, were set at a third. The askari (including his wife or boy) got between 600 and 700 grammes of meal a day, the Europeans about 6 kilos of food for twenty-eight days. Maize was eaten before it ripened. Sickness rates reached 80 per cent among the Europeans, and dysentery ravaged the blacks.[272]

Lettow's objective was to hold the ground south of the Rufiji until the harvest ripened in March and April. Even sowing the crops was complicated, given the loss of labour and the lack of pre-existing German administrative control in the area. But the rains were heavier and more prolonged than for some years. The harvest was good, although the water flooded the fields and impeded its distribution.[273]

On the Rufiji, Hoskins's paralysis saved Lettow. To the north-west, Deventer's line of communications from Iringa to Dodoma was sundered by the flooded Ruaha, which reached a width of 26 kilometres. His push on Lukegata was reduced to three battalions and a squadron, and then halted entirely. Only Northey remained active. His forces were healthier, not so much because half of them were blacks but because they were operating on the higher ground away from the coast. In January a captured German message revealed that the detachments under Kraut and Wintgens were dependent on supplies in the area north of Songea. Northey's columns began to converge on Iringa from Lupembe and Songea.

Wahle's main concentration was now to Northey's north, threatening Hoskins's right flank while converging on Lettow. The food available to him was

[272] Boell, *Operationen*, 316–17; Lettow-Vorbeck, *Reminiscences*, 160–2, 175–80; Marine-Archiv, *Kämpfe der kaiserlichen Marine*, 253–5; Taute, *Tanganyika Notes and Records*, 8 (1939), 5–6, 14–15; Deppe, *Mit Lettow-Vorbeck*, 136–41.

[273] Schnee, *Deutsch-Ostafrika*, 141–2, 269–75.

not sufficient to support Kraut's and Wintgens's men, and on 29 January he ordered them to move south and north, to feed off the enemy lines of communication. Kraut entered the area between the Ruvuma and Lake Nyasa, marching first south-east and then north-west, before finally turning east along the Ruvuma to Tunduru.

Kraut told Wintgens to follow him. Wintgens refused and took his 524 men north-west towards Tundala, and thence along the Northern Rhodesian border towards Tabora. Wintgens fed off the land, causing mayhem on the supply routes stretched across German East Africa. The pursuit, conducted initially by Northey's Lupembe column, traversed a land already laid bare.

As the Germans approached Bismarckburg early in March, the British asked the Belgians if they could use the western end of the central railway, within the Belgian area of occupation; they also requested permission to recruit. Two months previously, anxious to limit Belgium's gains, Britain had told it that its assistance was no longer required. Only 2,000 of the *Force publique* remained in German East Africa, others had been demobilized, many of the whites had returned to Europe, and the porters had dispersed or entered British service. By handing Tabora over to the British the Belgians had left the protection of Urundi and Ruanda against any fresh German offensive to their allies. Nonetheless, they preferred to offer the British troops rather than indirect support. At the beginning of April Hoskins and Huyghé, Tombeur's successor, agreed on a Belgian contribution of 6,600 askaris, 600 Europeans, and 18,000 porters. In reality, only 456 Europeans were available, and therefore junior officers occupied senior posts; 5,000 of the 18,000 porters were already in British service and could not be released. The Hoskins–Huyghé plan, to deploy 4,000 rifles in Wintgens's path, was unrealizable.[274] Without porters, the Belgians could not move with sufficient speed.

On 1 May the British element in the pursuit was changed. Northey's column fell back south, and a new force of 1,700 men, including a King's African Rifles battalion still under training, took up the running. The Germans were approaching Tabora. On 21 May Wintgens himself, sick with typhus, surrendered. Heinrich Naumann, his successor, planned to rejoin Wahle by marching south-east, but finding his path barred he moved north-east, across the central railway, towards Mwanza and Lake Victoria. Responsibility for this area had been passed over to the Colonial Office, and friction between the army and the civilian administration now added to the problems of British and Belgian coordination. The lack of a united command meant that the pursuit was devoid of consistency or purpose. Early in July Naumann, now operating in the north around Ikoma, flirted with the idea of a raid on Nairobi. But instead he decided to thrust south in an effort to reunite his troops with Lettow's. By

---

[274] Belgique, *Campagnes coloniales belges*, iii. 11–17, 24, 33–52, 121.

August he realized that he could never get through, and divided his command into three sections, each to go in divergent directions with the aim of drawing as many British troops from the main theatre as possible. The section sent to the south-east surrendered on 2 September. But the two northerly sections held out for a further month, Naumann himself raiding Kahe on 29 August. Naumann remained a reluctant guerrilla. At the end his intention, once again, was to link with Lettow, rather than maximize the effects of dispersion. Nonetheless, he had conducted a classic guerrilla operation.[275] His men had marched almost 3,200 kilometres since February; they had found a population that was passively, if not actively, supportive; they had drawn the attention of up to 6,000 men away from the main battle.

Wintgens's and Naumann's marches served to deepen London's frustration with Hoskins's failure to complete a campaign already pronounced victorious by Smuts. Hoskins, however, was the first, and last, British commander-in-chief in East Africa who appreciated the constraints under which he was operating. His knowledge of local conditions, his awareness of the training needs of the African troops, led him to avoid the hyperbole of Smutsian advances. From February to May the British forces in East Africa were rebuilt. Their demand for porters—they needed 160,000, and a further 15,000 a month to cover wastage—so exceeded supply (Hoskins had about 40,000 when he took over) that lorries became an increasingly vital component. Hoskins reckoned that one lorry was equivalent to thirty porters, and wanted 400 of them. But lorries were unusable in the rains, and therefore necessitated a pause in operations until May.[276]

Hoskins's demands embarrassed both Smuts and his new colleagues in the War Cabinet. Warnings against the presumption of speedy or easy victory chimed ill with the South African's claim that the campaign was effectively over. If the spoils of East Africa were to go to Pretoria, Smuts had to argue that his South Africans had done the job. If they had not, then the credibility of white South African citizen soldiers would be forfeit to the subsequent achievements of blacks. 'Military training of the native' in Central Africa would thereby be endorsed, and, he warned in May 1917, would eventually present 'a danger to civilization'.[277] Personal pique coincided with the territorial needs and the racial policies of the Union.

Hoskins recognized that Lettow might well cross the Ruvuma into Portuguese East Africa. His plan, therefore, rested not on continued pushes southward to clear territory, but on a concerted effort to trap the Germans. The British agreement with the Belgians included provision for a column to join Deventer's forces south of Dodoma: their task, once they had dealt with

[275] Boell, *Operationen,* 325–32. [276] Hodges, *Carrier corps,* 51–7.
[277] McLaughlin, *Small Wars and Insurgencies,* II (1991), 248.

Naumann, was to advance on Mahenge. The Nigerians on the Rufiji would also strike towards Mahenge. Liwale would be approached from the west by Northey and from the east by the 1st division at Kilwa. The brigade at Lindi, which had been occupied on 16 September 1916, was to break free of Looff's attentions and aim for Masasi, so cutting German communications to the south.

The chances of trapping Lettow seemed good. The main German forces were deployed along the coast rather than inland, presumably in the hope that a third supply ship might break the blockade. In April Lettow concentrated south of Kilwa. On 3 June Wahle, his junction with Lettow complete, was given overall authority around Lindi. But on 29 May, before the British offensive could get under way, Hoskins was relieved of his command. Smuts's lobbying had convinced Sir William Robertson, the chief of the imperial general staff, that Hoskins was losing his grip, and that his successor should be 'Jaap' van Deventer.[278] Once again a British regular had been replaced by an Afrikaner amateur. Deventer's instructions were to end the campaign as soon as possible; with merchant tonnage losses soaring in the Atlantic, the objective was to save shipping. He was given no territorial or operational objectives.

Lettow's strengths against the British converging movements remained interior lines and deployment in depth. For neither side was the apparent front line, the Rufiji, of major concern. The key battles of the second half of 1917 were fought around Kilwa and Lindi. The foundation of Lettow's strategy was the containment of the British attempt to break out from Lindi, thus keeping open the Germans' route to the south. In June Lettow reinforced Wahle at the expense of the Kilwa front.

Like Hoskins, Deventer was aware that Lettow intended ultimately to move into Portuguese territory. He therefore remained loyal to Hoskins's plan, consolidating his position at Lindi so as to cut off the Germans' line of retreat. But Kilwa had the better harbour, and his main initial effort came from there. On 19 July the three converging British columns from Kilwa were fought to a standstill by a German force of 945 men at Narungombe. The Germans, reduced to five rounds of ammunition per man and unaware that Lettow was marching north to reinforce them the next day, fell back to Nahungu, on the Mbemkuru.[279] But Deventer's progress on the Kilwa front was halted until September. On the 19th of that month, his communications extended to enable the next advance, Deventer's Kilwa force moved on Nahungu. In the next eighteen days the Germans counted thirty-seven separate engagements, many of them battles for the control of water supplies. The thick bush impeded not only the British aerial reconnaissance but also the Germans' co-ordination on

[278] Hodges, *Carrier corps*, 51.
[279] Schwarte, *Weltkampf*, iv. 406; Boell, *Operationen*, gives dates a day later than those given in British accounts.

the ground. The British were again held on 27 September, but the Germans fell back once more. They were running low on smokeless ammunition, and by 1 October were having to rely on the 1871-model carbine, whose bullets used black powder, so providing targets for British guns.[280] Deventer now decided to put his weight on the Lindi sector. He ordered the Nigerian brigade to detach itself from the Kilwa force and march on Nyangoa, so converging with the Lindi force attacking from the east.

However, British intelligence had lost track of Lettow himself. The German commander moved between fronts, his attention during the August lull increasingly drawn south to Masasi and Tunduru, one of Northey's columns having begun operations along the Portuguese frontier. Whether the Nigerian brigade's task was to envelope Wahle as he faced the Lindi force, or to prevent a junction between Wahle and Lettow is therefore not entirely clear. Lettow himself saw the opportunity to strike a decisive blow, using his interior lines to effect a concentration in a way that had eluded him at Narungombe and Nahungu. The Nigerians' eight-day march, dogged by lack of water, halved their effective strength to 1,000 men. Rather than envelop the Germans, they themselves were encircled. Lettow had concentrated a total of eighteen out of twenty-five available companies. In a fierce four-day battle at Mahiwa, beginning on 15 October and fought at close quarters, ground was won and lost up to six times. The Lindi force found itself endeavouring to break through Wahle and so extricate the Nigerians from Lettow's clutches. British losses totalled 2,700 out of 4,900 engaged. But German casualties, though ostensibly light (about 600), were relatively more serious. By the second day the number of wounded exceeded the number of porters to carry them, and men with three or four injuries continued to fight. Wahle's command lost nearly 30 per cent of its combat strength, and two field companies were disbanded. Moreover, all their smokeless ammunition (500,000 rounds) was expended, machine-guns had to be destroyed, and only twenty-five rounds remained for each of the older-pattern rifles.[281] Mahiwa was the first sustained battle of the entire campaign. It confirmed that the avoidance of combat had been the strategy not of Lettow but of Smuts; it also demonstrated that such a strategy had served Germany's interests rather better than Britain's.[282]

The third major German group, in addition to those round Kilwa and Lindi, was the twelve companies in the Mahenge area, from 9 May under the command of Theodor Tafel. Deventer's plan was for the Belgians to advance on Mahenge from Kilosa. But the Mahenge region had been stripped bare by

[280] Deppe, *Mit Lettow-Vorbeck*, 296–305.

[281] Boell, *Operationen*, 377, gives total German losses of 580; Lettow, *Reminiscences*, says 800. See also Haywood and Clarke, *Royal West African Frontier Force*, 207–35; Schnee, *Deutsch-Ostafrika*, 255; Deppe, *Mit Lettow-Vorbeck*, 165, 260–1.

[282] Hodges, *Carrier corps*, 51.

the Germans, and consequently the Belgians could not live off the land to the extent that they had done in the Tabora campaign. Too few porters were collected in time to allow them to take part in the first stages of the July offensive. Carriers recruited from the Belgian-occupied areas of East Africa proved useless in the pursuit of Naumann; the British therefore allowed the Belgians to requisition up to 6,000 porters in their zone of occupation to replace the 5,000 previously handed to the British by the Belgians; a further 10,000 were raised in the Congo between July and November 1917. The Belgians were finally ready to move in September, and on 9 October occupied Mahenge. Tafel withdrew to the south-east. Further supply problems delayed the Belgian pursuit for eight days. Then the rains came and the road from Kilosa to Mahenge was rendered impracticable. Two Belgian battalions, the most that could be fed, were left at Mahenge, and the rest pulled back to the central railway for redeployment to Kilwa and Lindi.[283]

Tafel made good his escape to the south-east. Northey's columns, reorganized in July with bases at Lupembe, Songea, and Fort Johnston, entered Liwale on 29 October. But his force was now up to 480 kilometres from its Lake Nyasa bases and the striking powers of each component limited. Tafel broke through Northey's screen on 15 November and made for Newala, hoping to link with Lettow.

Lettow had gone. Between April and September 1917 a detachment of Kraut's force, 400 strong, had entered Portuguese territory, and reached as far south as Lurio and Fort Johnston. This preliminary reconnaissance suggested that the local population would be friendly and the country fertile. At a conference at Lukuledi on 24 October the German leaders debated their next step. Schnee, the defeat of his colony complete, advocated surrender. Lettow answered with an argument that drew its inspiration as much from Schnee's own creed, that of German colonialism, as it did from the needs of war in Europe. With German territory forfeit, Germany's claim to be an African power resided in the *Schütztruppen* themselves.[284] They must carry on the war across the Ruvuma, in Portuguese East Africa, so maintaining German presence in Africa until the peace. Schnee agreed.

Practical as well as political considerations shaped the German decision. The area between the Rufiji and the Ruvuma was on the brink of famine. The harvest was not due until March, and in the event the rains failed in November. Lettow had sufficient food for six weeks. His stocks of quinine would last a month. He could not fight in order to capture supplies because the ammunition situation made him reliant on the 1871-pattern carbines and two-thirds of his force were equipped with the 1898-models or captured British equivalents. The artillery ammunition, so painstakingly dried and reassembled in 1915–16,

---

[283] Belgique, *Campagnes coloniales belges*, iii. 121–219. [284] Mosley, *Duel for Kilimanjaro*, 174–5.

had got wet again: in 1917 the fuses in particular required refabrication. He now had only enough shells for two mountain guns, and the last of the *Königsberg*'s guns was destroyed. Lettow therefore shaped his force according to his resources. In July his rifle strength had been 800 Europeans and 5,500 askaris. On 25 November, when he crossed the Ruvuma, he took 300 Europeans and 1,700 askaris. One thousand fit askaris were left behind, as well as over 1,500 Europeans, mostly the sick and wounded, and women and children. At least 3,000 blacks—wives, porters, and boys—accompanied the *Schütztruppen*; their families' presence was a major factor in the continuing loyalty of the askari, and only a small number responded to British appeals to surrender.[285]

Mahiwa, for all its self-inflicted damage to the Germans, enabled them to break contact with the British. The Kilwa force, its line of communications now 200 kilometres long, could not open a shorter connection through Lindi until the Lindi force was ready to resume its movement. Deventer planned to round up Lettow's forces in the area of Chiwata. He asked the Portuguese to demonstrate north of the Ruvuma in the hope of blocking the Germans to the south, and so encouraging them to hold Newala. But the junction of the Kilwa and Lindi columns was not effected until 11 November. By then the major threat seemed not to be Lettow but Tafel. His command, a ration strength of 5,471, including 181 Europeans and 1,558 askaris, still had 262,000 smokeless rounds. On 20 November three out of four British columns were directed against Tafel. Uncertain of the whereabouts of the German western forces, Deventer also lost track of Lettow's lines of march, covered by the thick bush of the Makonde plateau from aerial observation. Deventer got Tafel. However, his success was the result, not of manoeuvre nor of battle, but of a loss of nerve on the part of the German commander. Tafel crossed the Ruvuma, failed to find either food or Lettow, and then returned into German East Africa, surrendering on 28 November.

Mindful of the experiences of a year previously, Deventer did not at first follow Lettow into Portuguese territory. Fear of the rains (which in practice proved far less heavy than on the Rufiji), and the need to regroup, brought the British to a halt. Deventer issued a somewhat optimistic summons to Schnee to surrender. It was ignored. He saw the move into Portuguese territory as short-lived, reckoning that the Germans would recross the Ruvuma once the harvest was ripe in the Songea region. His immediate operational objectives were consequently defensive—to stop the Germans breaking back into German East Africa and to guard Nyasaland. He reduced his forces, sending the Nigerians home and keeping only the Gold Coast Regiment and the King's African Rifles.

[285] Lettow-Vorbeck, *Reminiscences*, 216–25; Schoen, *Deutschen Feuerwerkswesens*, 1455–6.

Nor was Lettow under any pressure from the Portuguese. A fourth expeditionary force, mustering 5,277 men, had arrived from Lisbon in 1917, and a further 4,509 reinforcements were dispatched to make good the losses to the 1916 expedition. But Portuguese strength in numbers and equipment was betrayed by the poverty of command and morale. Tomas de Sousa Rosa, a cavalryman in tsetse country, who had never been to Africa before, succeeded Gil in September 1917; his tenure 'went beneath the lowest levels of insignificance'.[286]

Portugal's preoccupations in 1917 were not with the Germans but with their own internal order. The Portuguese Makonde, south of the Ruvuma, had never been properly pacified. The tasks of the 1917 expeditionary force were the systematic reduction of tribal resistance in the area, and the construction of a road from the coast inland. By the time of the German invasion the first objective was almost fulfilled but the second was not; the road did not reach Chomba until 30 July 1918.

Concentration in the north weakened Portuguese presence in the south, while at the same time increasing labour demands. The Portuguese drafted their carriers, and neither paid nor fed them. In March 1917 the Makombe rebellion broke out in Portuguese Zambezia. The Portuguese themselves were defeated and besieged in Tete. The revolt derived its strength from traditional elites, who briefly overcame ethnic divisions in the rejection of Portuguese colonialism. The Portuguese held Sena, but their strategy for reconquering an area 800 kilometres broad, and embracing up to 20,000 rebels, was confused. The army and the Mozambique Company found themselves at loggerheads over how best to proceed. The British, aware that the Makombe saw their rule in Rhodesia in a favourable light, refused their allies troops, Nyasaland instead presenting 200 rifles and Southern Rhodesia somewhat belatedly contributing two obsolete machine-guns and 200 drill rifles. In the end African divisions, not imperial co-operation, determined the fate of the rebellion. Between 10,000 and 15,000 Ngoni were called in as auxiliaries, and were promised all the booty they could carry away, including women and children. Thus, by condoning terrorism and slavery, the Portuguese broke the back of the rebellion by the end of 1917.[287]

Neither the Makonde nor the Makombe responded in any obvious way to the possibility of German support. The north-east of the Portuguese colony remained settled throughout the German invasion, an indirect tribute to the Portuguese army's work, and Lettow never penetrated Zambezia. But almost wherever they went the Germans were well received. The Yao in the north-west had accommodated those fugitives from the 1915 Chilembwe rebellion who

---

[286] Pélissier, *Naissance du Mozambique*, ii. 704; see also 699–703.
[287] Ibid., ii. 650–79; Ranger, *St Antony's Papers*, XV (1963), 54–80.

had escaped into Portuguese East Africa, and had also welcomed the 1917 German expedition. The Lomue, south of the Lurio, and the Angoche, along the coast beneath Mozambique, proved equally hospitable. The Germans, for all that their paper money was worthless, did at least pay for their goods rather than seize them. German doctors attended to the sick. But Lettow did not take the opportunity to turn opposition to Portuguese rule into revolution. The Germans neutralized the African population rather than armed it. Thus, even in 1917–18, and even in Lettow's own hands, the anxiety to buttress collective European colonial rule outweighed immediate military advantage. Lettow still rejected a true strategy of revolutionary warfare.

Nonetheless, with his entry into Portuguese territory Lettow's actual style of operations for the first time conformed to that of a guerrilla leader. His supply position had forced him to reduce his fighting strength. Thus he had to quell his predilection for the offensive. He fought to feed, and to feed he had to keep moving to fresh sources of supply. Mobility, not striking power, was henceforth his major asset. When he crossed the Ruvuma his column was 30 kilometres long, the main body separated by one day's march from its advanced guard and two days' from its rear. Confined to jungle paths, frequently crossing precipitous terrain, the Germans trudged in single file. In such circumstances rapid concentration for battle was impossible. Lettow reorganized his forces into three columns, his own, Wahle's, and Kohl's, each with its own supply train and field hospital. By following parallel routes the columns overcame the worst dangers of dispersion. The Germans marched for six hours a day, with a half-hour halt every two hours, and aimed to cover 24 to 32 kilometres a day. It was a considerable achievement. The porters frequently carried additional loads weighing up to 30 kilos; the askaris bore iron rations for fifteen days as well as their rifles and ammunition; their wives on occasion gave birth on the line of march and within hours had rejoined the column.[288]

The greatest potential impediment to mobility, the bush apart, was ill-health. In this respect Lettow's force began its trek with several advantages: only the fittest were selected, thirteen doctors were among them, and the small European complement was adjusted to the available supply of quinine. Plunder made good many deficits in medical supplies. But the Portuguese had done little to eradicate disease within their colony. Locally recruited porters and prolonged residence in native settlements introduced new sicknesses. Smallpox appeared in February and July 1918. In August 1918 pneumonia (not, the German doctors were sure, influenza) struck 250 of the force and killed at least twenty-two. By then only eighty sick could be carried. Periodically they would be collected into a hospital and left, together with a

---

[288] Schnee, *Deutsch-Ostafrika*, 353–5; Lettow-Vorbeck, *Reminiscences*, 233–4, 271, 280; Miller, *Battle for the Bundu*, 299–305.

doctor, for the British. By the end of the war Lettow had only six doctors remaining.[289]

The area between the Ruvuma and the Lujenda did not prove as rich as Lettow had hoped. Game formed much of the diet, but the thick, tall vegetation made stalking and shooting difficult. However, now the Germans, effectively for the first time since Tanga, could plunder. The Portuguese frontier forts along the Ruvuma provided arms, ammunition, and European food. At Ngomano, on 25 November 1917, the Germans surprised 1,200 Portuguese troops and captured 600 rifles and 250,000 rounds. Three more forts were taken in December, and the *Schütztruppen* thus re-equipped themselves with Portuguese rifles and almost a million rounds.

Lettow commenced his march south before the rains ceased, so as to maintain his lead over Deventer. Two British battalions from Fort Johnston began to advance on Mwembe in January 1918, and Lettow concentrated around Nanungu at the end of February. As the rains eased the Germans were able to rig up a wireless. In late March they heard the news of the German victories in France, and of the imminent capture of Amiens. Their purpose in maintaining a German presence in Africa reaffirmed, Lettow briefly flirted once again with offensive options. His central position seemed to give him the chance to strike enemy forces in isolation, particularly those with longer lines of communication coming from the west. In late April and early May Lettow placed Kohl at Medo to guard him from the east, while he concentrated five companies for a blow to the west. The action at Kireka mountain on 5 May cost him 27 per cent of those engaged.

Deventer's concern was still to stop the Germans going north. He therefore planned to create a line of posts from Port Amelia to Fort Johnston, via Medo and Mahua. The conception was ridiculous: he never possessed the resources to create an impermeable barrier 560 kilometres long. His main base was still at Dar es Salaam. Therefore goods from Britain proceeded via the Cape and Dar, before being transshipped and routed south again to Port Amelia. The conviction that Lettow was about to be defeated had not, despite all the evidence to the contrary, dissipated. Thus, when Port Amelia and later Mozambique were established as intermediate bases, provision was made for 12,000 men to be fed up to 320 kilometres from the coast. Ultimately 33,000 men were dependent on the two ports.[290]

Deventer's other major obstacle was the Portuguese. The presence of Portuguese troops did little more than create supply dumps from which Lettow could replenish his food and ammunition needs. They also antagonized the local population, making it increasingly hard for the British to recruit

---

[289] Taute, *Tanganyika Notes and Records*, VIII (1939), 3, 6, 10, 18–20.
[290] The English-language sources on this phase of the campaign are few; see Fendall, *East African Force*, 114–42, and Moyse-Bartlett, *King's African Rifles*, 390–414.

porters. The British paid the hut tax of those Africans who enlisted as carriers. The effect, however, was to antagonize the local administrators, who were in the habit of appropriating a percentage of the tax for themselves. Ultimately the King's African Rifles lived largely off the land, an expedient which slowed their pursuit as they foraged over areas through which the Germans had already passed. The campaign was fought on Portuguese territory but increasingly without Portuguese participation. In July 1918 Sousa Rosa was recalled to Lisbon and arrested.

On 22 May Lettow got his major battle. Kohl's column, now effectively his rearguard, was nearly trapped by the British forces from Port Amelia at Korewa, near Maketi. He managed to extricate himself, but at the price of losing all his supplies, including 70,000 rounds, 30,000 rupees, and all Schnee's official documents; Schnee himself was lucky to escape. The British completed their junction from east and west, and the Germans marched south.

On 16 June Lettow captured a Portuguese map showing the area as far as Lugella and Quelimane. Anxious to capitalize on what little intelligence he could garner, he pressed on, aware that the Lugella Company's base might provide rich pickings. He found them at Namakura on 1–3 July. The defences, 3,000 yards in extent, proved too great for the combined Portuguese-British garrison of 1,030 men to hold. Neither ally fought well; in their efforts to escape along the Namakura river many were drowned or eaten by crocodiles; the Germans lost nine men, the British and Portuguese 200 dead and 543 captured. Far more importantly, the booty included ten machine-guns, 350 rifles, 350 tonnes of food, and large quantities of ammunition. The Germans were almost entirely re-equipped with modern British and Portuguese rifles, and had a stock of 813,800 rounds. While the pursuing forces pressed on to Quelimane, anticipating that the next German move would be to strike the harbour there and then go up the Zambezi, the Germans rested at Namakura, drinking the abundant quantities of schnapps which they had looted, and then doubled back to the north-east.

Across the River Namirrue Lettow attacked an isolated British force on the night of 22/3 July, and then captured Namirrue itself. On 28 July he paused at Chalaua, recruiting and training 310 porters as askaris. A captured letter alerted Lettow to the next British move and on 8 August he quitted Chalaua. His direction at first was north-east, but then, having deceived his opponent, he switched to due west, reaching Numarroe on 24 August. The British hoped that Lettow would attack Regone, but their intention of enveloping him while he did so was known to Lettow. He marched north to Lioma. Here he was hard hit by three battalions of the King's African Rifles, losing 48,000 rounds and large quantities of stores. His total casualties between 27 August and 6 September included thirty-nine Europeans, 184 askaris, and 317 porters (242 were reported as missing). His intention now was to aim through the Livingstone

Mountains, around the northern end of Lake Nyasa, and then turn west. He calculated that Deventer would rein in his pursuit and reconcentrate on the central railway to cover Tabora. He was only partly right. Intelligence acquired on 22 September suggested that there were no troops on the Ruvuma, but that there were major concentrations in Nyasaland. Morale was slipping. Lettow's refrain, that their efforts were tying down 30,000 enemy troops, was less persuasive as the *Schütztruppen*'s strength dwindled, their supply and health problems multiplying. On 28 September the Germans recrossed the Ruvuma; they again speculated about a push to the north, aiming to get beyond the Ruaha before mid-December and the advent of the rains.

The projects discussed on 29 September bordered on the fantastical. Some favoured the northern thrust, even as far as Abyssinia, in the hope that it might be pro-German. Others suggested taking ship for Afghanistan (presumably via Persia). But opinion veered once again towards the west, and a march to Angola.[291] The morale of the askaris recovered as they regained their own territory. At Songea, the local population welcomed and resupplied them. At Ubena on 18 October Lettow found papers alerting him to the situation in Europe; thereafter, a number of reports confirmed that Germany was seeking an armistice. The British prepared their defences at Mahenge, Iringa, and Tabora, and, forewarned by the example of Wintgens's raid to the north, anticipated a dash across the central railway. But round Dodoma the requisitioning of grain and livestock in 1915–16 had driven those of the population not taken as porters into the forests and mountains. Cultivation had declined, and the lateness of the rains in 1918–19 meant that shortages turned into famine.[292] Lettow struck west towards Fife, not north. His intention was to raid the depots on the Kasama–Fife road, working along Northey's line of communications, and then push west between lakes Bangweulu and Mweru.

It was a brilliant move. Relations between the administrations of Rhodesia, the British South Africa Company, and the War Office, deteriorating from autumn 1916, had finally collapsed in September. The Company was alarmed by its increasing deficit, forced up by the costs of the war, and above all by the requisitioning of carriers for Northey's columns. The Makombe rising, just across the border from Northern Rhodesia, had been a salutary reminder of the need to reward and compensate, not to terrorize and compel, the local population into war service. The strain of sustaining Northey's operations had rebounded. Colonial authority was itself being undermined by their side-effects: crime, illegal repression, and famine. The Colonial Office backed the company; the War Office and the Treasury did not. In September 1918 the Colonial Office acted unilaterally and banned compulsory war recruitment in

[291] Deppe, *Mit Lettow-Vorbeck*, 30, 368–9, 396–402.
[292] Maddox, *Journal of African History*, XXXI (1990), 183–5.

Northern Rhodesia. When Lettow entered Northern Rhodesia, Northey's forces could not move for lack of porters. In two weeks the Germans advanced 160 kilometres.[293]

On 9 November 1918 Lettow's advance guard entered Kasama. The position of Major E. B. B. Hawkins and his 750 King's African Rifles was unenviable. Lettow was in unknown country but so, effectively, was Hawkins; his only map was a world atlas on a scale of 200 miles to the inch. Lettow's invasion had smashed British prestige, fomenting panic and looting. British askaris were deserting; the Northern Rhodesia Police was mutinous.[294] On 12 November the two sides clashed in the last engagement of the Great War.

The following day Lettow received the news of the armistice. The formal surrender at Abercorn on 25 November revealed a fighting force that, given the chaos in Northern Rhodesia, could easily have sustained itself well into 1919. Lettow's strength was 155 Europeans and 1,156 blacks, armed with thirty-seven machine-guns, 1,071 British and Portuguese rifles, and 208,000 rounds. They had captured sufficient quinine to last until June.

The real restraint on what Lettow might have achieved in November 1918 lay not in the possible efforts of his enemies—he had, after all, successfully struck at their weakest point—but in his own reluctance to embrace a revolutionary strategy. Lettow was an officer of resource and determination, ruthless in war and honourable in peace. He was not a guerrilla. He had proved reluctant to exploit the collapse of Portuguese authority for the purposes of the war. There is no reason to assume he would have behaved any differently in the case of Britain.

Lettow justified his entire campaign in terms of the number of Entente soldiers committed to the East African theatre. About 160,000 British and Belgian troops, including naval forces, were engaged during the course of the war against the *Schütztruppen*; Smuts had 55,000 men in the field in 1916.[295] However, very few of these, if any, would have been available for the western front. The only point where the British consciously weighed Europe against Africa was over the deployment of the South Africans in 1916; but at that stage, given the political divisions within the Union, the existence of the East African theatre was a convenience rather than an embarrassment. Thereafter the Africans themselves took the burden. Total British losses in East Africa were 3,443 killed in action and 6,558 died of disease.[296] It is only with the inclusion of porters, a local resource not readily employable elsewhere, that casualty figures reach levels commensurate with the length and breadth of the campaign:

---

[293] Yorke, 'Crisis of colonial control', 272–370.

[294] Ibid. 362–70; Moyse-Bartlett, *King's African Rifles*.

[295] The first figure is from Crowder, 'The First World War', 291; the second from Moyse-Bartlett, *King's African Rifles*, 413. Boell, *Operationen*, 32, gives 240,000.

[296] Iliffe, *Tanganyika*, 246.

British losses then rise to over 100,000 dead.[297] Africans, and to a lesser extent Indians, were Lettow's major foe, at least in numerical terms. Their only likely alternative area of operations was the Middle East, not Europe. In practice, Lettow's real diversionary achievement was to be measured in its maritime, not military, effects. In 1917–18, with U-boat warfare at its height, the length of the voyage around the Cape to Dar es Salaam engaged merchant vessels on long-haul voyages when they were badly needed elsewhere. The need for ships, not the need to defeat Lettow per se, underpinned the British war cabinet's impatience with Hoskins's lack of movement in February to May 1917.

During and after the war the Entente powers tried to appropriate the war in Africa as a war for liberalism, a crusade for civilization and enlightenment against repression and brutality. There is little evidence that those who did the fighting, and on behalf of whom these grand claims were advanced, thought in such terms. Many askaris had, by the end of the war, fought for the Germans and the British, and had done their duty to both. Their loyalty was that of the professional or the mercenary—the soldier who takes pride in doing his job well and who fights because that is his vocation. Similarly, the attractions of portering, if there were any, were pecuniary: the pay was better than in other comparable occupations. The causes so vehemently espoused in Europe relied on a well-developed sense of nationalism; in Africa no such nationalism yet existed, and if it had it would have undermined, not supported, the war efforts of both sides.

The Great War was the prelude to the final stage of the scramble for Africa, played out at Versailles. Despite all their misgivings at the outset, the European powers advanced rather than retarded the cause of colonialism between 1914 and 1918. The opposition which they encountered was tribal and traditional; glimmerings of modern resistance—the involvement of educated elites in the Chilembwe rebellion, inter-ethnic unity in the Makombe rising—remained short-lived. Instead, the marches of the armies, the wiles of the recruiting parties, the supply needs of their men, spread the colonial nexus through the agencies of the market, of cash, of cartography, and of communications. Because, by 1914, colonialism had begun to move from conquest to civilization, the armies' contribution to its advancement was not apparent: what the European powers saw was the withdrawal of white administrators and the Africanization of missions. But the war reinvigorated territorial ambitions dormant since the turn of the century. Annexation or retention remained the dominant European motivation in the war in Africa, even if not so clearly elsewhere. Ebermaier's and Schnee's primary concern was to sustain Germany in Africa, not Germany in Europe. Similarly, Smuts's emphasis on manoeuvre rather than on battle derived from his principal objective, the conquest of

[297] Hodges, *Journal of African History*, XIX (1978), 115.

territory. Lettow-Vorbeck's principal achievement was, perhaps, the thwarting of the full extent of South Africa's annexationist ambitions.[298] He himself appeared a guerrilla because his interpretation of colonialism was contrasting, not congruent; for Lettow, as for Zimmerman, in the last analysis Germany's African claims resided not in the preservation of land but in the unity of the *Schütztruppen* themselves. In a war redolent with eighteenth-century parallels, it was perhaps appropriate that the heirs of Frederickian Prussia should still interpret the army as the embodiment of the state.

[298] Wolfgang Petter, 'Der Kampf um die deutschen Kolonien', in Michalka (ed.), *Der Erste Weltkrieg*, 406

8

TURKEY'S ENTRY

THE ESCAPE OF THE *GOEBEN* AND THE *BRESLAU*

Shortly after 10.30 on the morning of 4 August 1914 Captain Francis Kennedy, commanding the British battle cruisers *Indomitable* and *Indefatigable*, sighted the two German cruisers, the *Goeben* and the *Breslau*. Kennedy was sailing westwards, north of Bône and south of Sardinia, under orders to close the exit of the Mediterranean at Gibraltar, and so prevent the *Goeben* and the *Breslau* escaping into the Atlantic. However, the course being steered by the German ships was to the east. Earlier that day the *Goeben* had bombarded Philippeville and the *Breslau* Bône. Both were embarkation ports for the XIX French corps, en route from North Africa to metropolitan France. Although his ships had done little damage, Rear-Admiral Wilhelm Souchon had broken off the action and was now proceeding to the Straits of Messina. As the four cruisers converged, they kept their guns trained fore and aft. They passed each other at a distance of 8,000 yards without an exchange of either shots or courtesies. The British ultimatum to Germany was not due to expire until midnight.[1]

Kennedy swung his ships round and set off to shadow the Germans. In her trials the *Goeben* had achieved a speed of 27 knots. But she had been sent out to the Mediterranean precipitately in 1912, during the first Balkan war, and her engines had created problems ever since. She had spent July in dry dock at Pola, Austria's naval base at the head of the Adriatic, in order to change her boiler

---

[1] The broadest accounts of the *Goeben* and the *Breslau* incident are Halpern, *Naval war*, 12–26; Trumpener, *Canadian Journal of History*, VI (1971), 171–87. Exhaustive from the British perspective is Miller, *Superior force*; operational descriptions are Corbett, *Naval operations*, i. 54–71; Marder, *From the Dreadnought*, ii. 21–41; Hough, *Great War at sea*, 69–86.

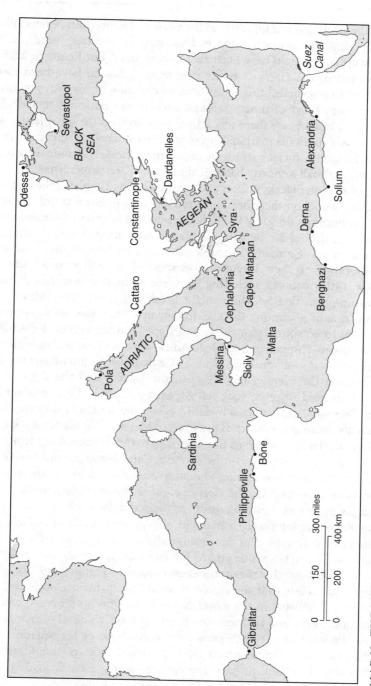

MAP 23. THE MEDITERRANEAN

tubes. In the ensuing chase three out of the *Goeben*'s twenty-four boilers failed, and, although she occasionally managed 24 knots, her average speed was 22. The battle cruisers should have been able to keep pace. But Kennedy, admittedly ignorant of the *Goeben*'s boiler problems, seems to have been more conscious of the Germans' theoretical superiority than of his own potential. *Indomitable* was short of ninety stokers, and he was reluctant to redeploy gunners to the task in case there was action. Souchon, on the other hand, was determined to exploit his marginal advantage. His stokers fell unconscious in the effort to raise sufficient steam in the summer heat, and four died from scalding. By nightfall Kennedy had lost sight of the German cruisers.

The combination of leaky boilers and great speeds had depleted the *Goeben*'s coal supplies. Souchon therefore bunkered at Messina but was only allowed twenty-four hours to do so by the Italians, who had affirmed their neutrality on 2 August. Admiral Sir Berkeley Milne, commanding the Mediterranean Fleet, knew of the Germans' probable whereabouts by the afternoon of 5 August, but not of their intentions. Respectful of Italian neutrality, he deployed his major forces, including his three battle cruisers, west of Sicily on the assumption that Souchon might break out north from Messina to resume his task of disrupting the French convoys. The other option open to Souchon was to go south, past the Italian Cape, and then enter the Adriatic to join the Austro-Hungarian fleet. Rear-Admiral Ernest Troubridge, with four armoured cruisers, was cruising west of Cephalonia to guard against this eventuality. On the evening of 6 August, the *Goeben* and the *Breslau*, the former still in need of more coal, left Messina and steered a course for the Adriatic. They were duly spotted by HMS *Gloucester*, a light cruiser stationed to observe the southern exits from the strait of Messina. *Gloucester* stuck close to the German cruisers, observed that the entry to the Adriatic was a feint, and reported that their course was now towards Cape Matapan and the Greek Peloponnese. Souchon was hoping to rendezvous with a collier in the Aegean. *Gloucester*'s task was to delay the *Goeben* and the *Breslau* sufficiently to allow Troubridge's squadron, steaming south, to intercept them.

Although grossly inferior in armament, *Gloucester* engaged the *Goeben* on the evening of 6 August. But Troubridge did not follow suit. On 30 July Churchill had instructed Milne and Milne had told Troubridge not to attack a 'superior force'. Churchill meant the fleets of Austria-Hungary and Italy, and his orders made clear that the *Goeben* was Milne's principal objective. But Troubridge was unusual in the Royal Navy: he had been an observer in the Russo-Japanese War, and had seen the effects of modern naval ordnance. He knew that the *Goeben*'s 11–inch guns outranged those of his squadron. An exercise in 1913 had demonstrated that armoured cruisers should remain concentrated if they were to have any chance against a battle cruiser. One option was to attack the *Goeben* at night, but the light cruiser *Dublin*, detailed for this duty, failed to make contact. Another was to catch the *Goeben* in narrow waters so as to lessen the range. However, such calculations were further complicated by Troubridge's continuing uncertainty as to Souchon's true course, whether he would continue to the south-east or double back to the north-west, and, if the latter, by the possibility that the Austro-Hungarian fleet might come out. Counselled by his flag captain, Troubridge allowed prudence to overcome his own offensive instincts. At 3.47 a.m. on the morning of 7 August he turned away. He was in tears as he did so. But he went further: shortly after 4 a.m. he signalled to Milne that he had abandoned the chase.[2]

Troubridge's grief, which would have been even greater had he anticipated the vituperation subsequently to be heaped upon him, could not at the time have seemed wholly warranted. The real threat to the *Goeben* lay with the French Mediterranean fleet under Admiral Boué de Lapeyrère and with Milne's battle cruisers. However, the French fleet (in direct contradiction to its pre-war orders) had forsaken offensive operations for convoy duties. Milne was dilatory. His respect for Italian neutrality had prevented him from following Souchon south through the Straits of Messina on the evening of 6 August. He had therefore failed to support HMS *Gloucester*. By passing Sicily to the west, he had guarded against the the danger of Souchon doubling back towards the Algerian coast. During the night he learned that the French escorts were now sufficiently organized to counter such a threat. But instead of dispatching the almost fully coaled *Indomitable* east in hot pursuit, he bunkered in Malta. While there, at 1.45 a.m. on the 8th, he received a message which originated from the head of the British naval mission in Greece, Rear-Admiral Mark Kerr, to say that the *Goeben* was at Syra (now Siros) in the Aegean. But at noon the Admiralty signalled that hostilities had begun against the Austrians. They had not, and would not until 12 August. At 2.30 p.m., therefore, Milne abandoned the Aegean for a watch on the Adriatic. Although the Admiralty acknowledged its mistake eighty minutes later, it still said the situation was 'critical', and Milne concluded that keeping the Austrian navy under observation took priority over the pursuit of the *Goeben*. His signal to that effect was received in the Admiralty at 6.15 p.m., but not digested until 2 a.m. on the 9th, and was then reckoned to have pre-dated his receipt of the cancellation of hostilities with Austria-Hungary. Not until 2.35 p.m. did Milne receive definite instructions to 'continue to chase the *Goeben* which passed Cape Matapan early on the 7th steering north-east'.[3]

Milne still expected Souchon to double back westwards, either to the Adriatic or to Gibraltar, or to extend his North African depredations to a raid on Alexandria and the Suez Canal; speed was not, therefore, of the essence.

[2] For a fuller consideration of Troubridge's position, see Miller, *Superior force*, esp. 26–32, 84–111, 270, 293–4.
[3] Lumby, *Policy and operations in the Mediterranean*, 197; Lumby gives the signals, as well as the proceedings of the court of inquiry and the court martial. See also Miller, *Superior force*, 90–3, 120–33, 279.

Thus Souchon enjoyed an uninterrupted sixty hours in the Greek archipelago, completing a leisurely coaling in the early hours of 10 August. With the intensity of British signals traffic revealing the proximity of his pursuers, Souchon moved northwards. At 5 p.m. on 10 August his two ships anchored at the entrance to the Dardanelles. Milne had received no information on the political situation in Turkey, and he believed that the Dardanelles were mined and barred to all warships. The subsequent news that the Turks were guiding the *Goeben* and *Breslau* into Constantinople came as a complete surprise to him. The Germans' escape rendered the actions of every British naval commander, with the distinguished exception of Kelly of the *Gloucester*, not prudent but incompetent.

Much indeed of the conduct of the operation did not reflect well on the Entente fleets, and specifically on the Royal Navy. Milne and Troubridge received the ire of the Admiralty, but the Admiralty itself had done no better. Its orders, transmitted by wireless, displayed an imprecision which suggested that London should have abandoned the attempt to direct operations at long range. Troubridge had interpreted the 'superior enemy' as the *Goeben*, when the reference was to Austria-Hungary; Milne was told that the dual monarchy was in the war when it was not. Most crucial of all, the Admiralty did nothing to correct the fundamental assumption that the Germans would be aiming for the western Mediterranean and not the eastern. Joint French and British planning for operations in the Mediterranean in the event of war was scanty. The rough division giving responsibility for the western end to France and the eastern to Britain reflected French concerns for the security of North African communications. The raids on Bône and Philippeville, along with subsequent but false reports of the *Goeben* and the *Breslau* moving west, combined to fix Boué de Lapeyrère's attention in that quarter. Milne's instructions from the Admiralty of 30 July had told him to aid the French in the transport of troops and only to attack superior forces in combination with the French. Despite his difficulties in establishing direct contact with Lapeyrère, Milne had therefore conformed with the French. In Britain the Foreign Office knew something of Germany's contacts with Turkey by 6 August. In Athens, Kerr had been told by King Constantine that the *Goeben* and the *Breslau* were bound for Constantinople as early as 4 August. But Constantine knew because his cousin, the Kaiser, was trying to bludgeon him into a pro-German Balkan alliance. Kerr was sufficiently acquainted with the Kaiser to have appreciated the distinction between his impetuous correspondence and German policy. Furthermore, he could not compromise his source. He therefore routed the information via the British naval attaché at St Petersburg, and it was not received at the Admiralty until 1.15 a.m. on 9 August.[4] It need not have been a surprise: the Admiralty was

---

[4] Miller, *Superior force*, 179–88, 278–9, 281–2.

apparently decrypting most of the key signals between Berlin and Souchon.[5] And yet London did not respond to the course adopted by the *Goeben* and the *Breslau* on 7 August to correct Milne's assumption that Souchon's move eastwards was a feint.

Conspiracy theories as to Britain's behaviour are easy to hatch. The Russians had repeatedly warned Britain of their fears for the naval balance in the Black Sea, either through an addition to the Turkish fleet or (more recently) through the presence of German or Austrian vessels. But Turkish naval strength could block a Russian presence in the straits and the eastern Mediterranean; thus the *Goeben* and *Breslau* served Britain's longer-term, imperial needs.[6] More immediate was the argument that the delivery of the two ships into Ottoman hands took them out of the Mediterranean. This not only served the interests of Britain and France but also those of Greece. By making sure that the *Goeben* and the *Breslau* went to Constantinople rather than to the Piraeus, the Greek prime minister, Venizelos, undermined the Germans' pressure on the king to abandon his neutrality while making it more probable that Greece would eventually join the Entente in the furtherance of its ambitions in the Aegean.[7]

At one level the episode's outcome was entirely satisfactory to the Entente. If the Triple Alliance had any potential for joint operations, it was as a naval force in the Mediterranean. The *Goeben* and the *Breslau* in combination with the Austro-Hungarian and Italian fleets presented a formidable threat. But the Italians had declared their neutrality on 2 August, and in isolation the Austro-Hungarian fleet had immediately become conscious of its inferiority to the French. Its principal mission was to secure the Adriatic coast, to blockade Serbia, to watch Montenegro, and so to support the army's land operations in the Balkans. The postponement of hostilities with both France and Britain was therefore entirely in its immediate interests. By breaking through to the Black Sea, the *Goeben* and the *Breslau* ensured that there was no German reinforcement of the Austro-Hungarian fleet. Furthermore, the two vessels did not re-enter the Mediterranean until 1918, and their neutralization in relation to that sea was indeed rapidly adopted by the Entente as a rationalization of what had happened.

In reality, the mood of the opening days of August was not so considered; the uncertainty as to who was at war with whom, the emphasis on concentration on the western front, the expectation of a decisive battle in the major naval theatre, the North Sea—none of these was conducive to sustained attention to Souchon's two cruisers. Indeed, although Souchon himself was decisive and energetic, his instructions from Berlin revealed a comparable German uncer-

[5] Santorini, *Revue internationale d'histoire militaire*, 63 (1985), 101.
[6] Gottlieb, *Studies*, 43–6; Weber, *Eagles on the Crescent*, 75–6.
[7] Miller, *Superior force*, 190–5, 277.

tainty which—even when known to London—did not necessarily clarify the situation.

Souchon's orders up until 2 August were exactly those reflected in Entente dispositions—he was to operate in the western Mediterranean or break through to the Atlantic. But on that day Turkey and Germany formed a secret alliance. Tirpitz and Pohl, the chief of the naval staff, therefore agreed that Souchon should go to Constantinople; Souchon had received these orders even before the attacks on Philippeville and Bône. On 5 August the Germans asked the Austro-Hungarian fleet to leave its bases and move into the southern Adriatic to help the *Goeben* and *Breslau* break out of the Messina strait. The Austro-Hungarian naval commander, Anton Haus, was hesitant. The mobilization of his fleet had only been ordered the previous day and was not yet complete. He was therefore even more anxious to avoid meeting the French fleet. Furthermore, he was simultaneously under contradictory pressures from Berchtold. The foreign office wanted him to break through to the Black Sea in order to bolster Turkey and to persuade Bulgaria and Romania to join the Central Powers. But to do so (even if technically practicable—and Haus was clear that it was not) would court the naval action with the British and/or French which he had been told by the foreign ministry to avoid. He therefore stayed put.

The Germans renewed their request with greater urgency on 6 August. Souchon was told that the Turks did not want him to appear in the straits just yet, and he was running out of options. Haus still refused to come south, but he agreed to escort the *Goeben* and *Breslau* into Austro-Hungarian territorial waters: in Pola expectations of major fleet action—certainly with the British and possibly with the French—soared.[8] That evening Haus learnt that Souchon's course had been a decoy, and that he was now on the way to the Dardanelles. Given these tergiversations on the German side, Milne's expectation that Souchon would break back to the west and even the Admiralty's failure to alert Milne to the Turkish possibility become more comprehensible. It was Souchon himself who forced the pace of events. By presenting his ships at the entrance to the straits he obliged the Turks to come off the fence.

The significance of the *Goeben* and *Breslau* to Turkey's decision to enter the war on the side of the Central Powers is perhaps more debatable than tradition allows. But what the episode does reveal is the difference in attitude to Turkey, and Turkey's role in their respective strategies, enjoyed by Britain and Germany. Britain's immediate response was to play down the political importance of what had occurred. The fiction of Germany's sale of the two cruisers to Turkey was readily accepted. Churchill fumed, but Asquith was complaisant: 'As we shall insist that the Goeben shall be manned by a Turkish instead of a

---

[8] Halpern, *Haus*, 143–54.

German crew, it doesn't much matter: as the Turkish sailors cannot navigate her—except on to rocks or mines.'[9] Bethmann Hollweg, reluctant to credit the Admiralty with incompetence, construed the British response as a desire to limit the war.[10] He was partially right, but for the wrong reasons. Britain did not propose to moderate its efforts against Germany, but it was anxious to restrict the war to Europe by preserving Turkish neutrality. The belief that Souchon would try to turn back to the Atlantic represented wishful thinking. Souchon's push to the east showed how different was Germany's understanding. Britain and Russia were Asiatic powers, France an African one. Their vulnerabilities lay as much outside Europe as within it. The voyage of the *Goeben* and the *Breslau* was an opportunity to widen the war, not restrict it.

TURKEY'S DECISION TO JOIN THE CENTRAL POWERS

In the second half of the nineteenth century the Ottoman empire bore at least a superficial comparison with Austria-Hungary. In an era of increasingly strident nationalism, it rested its claims to great power recognition on the principle of supra-nationalism. Of a population of 39 million in 1897, only half were Turks. Macedonia embraced Slavs and Greeks; eastern Anatolia had a sizeable Armenian minority; Kurds bridged the frontier with Persia; and to the south were Jews, Circassians, and above all Arabs. Much of Ottoman greatness had rested on religious and racial toleration: Greeks and Armenians in particular had played a major part in the empire's administration and in the development of its commerce. But towards the end of the nineteenth century the importation of European nationalism had fostered terrorism, particularly among the Macedonian and Armenian populations. Racial divisions were not marked out with geographical neatness. The cities of Macedonia were predominantly Muslim and Greek, while the countryside was Muslim and Slav; in none of the six provinces of eastern Anatolia did Armenians enjoy an absolute majority. In both areas the Muslim population was as much sinned against as sinning. But reprisals followed terrorism. The Ottoman empire's multinational legacy became the victim of violence and European propaganda: the Turk was portrayed as—and increasingly became—a bloodthirsty bigot.

Like the Habsburg empire too, the Ottoman empire owed its continued integrity to the conduct of international relations. The orderly management of

[9] Brock (ed.), *Asquith: Letters to Venetia Stanley*, 168.
[10] Egmont Zechlin, 'Cabinet versus economic warfare in Germany', in Koch (ed.), *Origins*, 228; Hörich, *Deutsche Seekriegführung*, 26.

Macedonia lay in Russian and Austrian interests as well as Turkey's; Britain maintained Turkey as the buffer to Russian expansion into the eastern Mediterranean, the Middle East, and the route to India. But in 1878, at the Congress of Berlin, the great powers changed tack. They were happy to affirm the independence of Romania, Serbia, and Montenegro, to grant autonomy to Bulgaria, to let Austria administer Bosnia-Herzogovina, to allow Britain control of Cyprus, and to give France a free hand in Tunisia. In 1897 they forced the Sultan to grant autonomy to Crete. Britain in particular, for so long Turkey's guarantor, now centred its strategy on Egypt (another Turkish loss) and the Suez Canal. As importantly, irridentism within the empire could henceforth look to external sponsors; the emergent Balkan states encouraged their fellow nationals in the rump of European Turkey; Armenian nationalism enjoyed French and Russian encouragement.

To counter this process of disintegration the Ottoman empire had no cultural identity save that of Islam. The progressive loss of European Turkey, the consequent decline in the number of Christians, and the emigration of its Muslim population to Constantinople and points east increased Muslim predominance. Furthermore, Islam provided the unifying link whereby the Arabs could be restrained from political separatism. The fact that the European powers used religion as a mantle for their own penetration of Turkey— the Orthodox churches were vehicles for Russian, Greek, and Bulgarian agitation, and France claimed the protection of the empire's 750,000 Roman Catholics—heightened Islamic awareness. Sultan Abdul Hamid emphasized his claim to the caliphate, fostered the use of Arabic, revived Muslim schools, and repaired the mosques. Ottomanism was redefined in increasingly Islamic terms in order to counter irridentist nationalism.

However, any tendency towards direct ideological competition and even overt religious hostility was moderated by the principle of economic self-interest. When Abdul Hamid had come to the throne in 1876, 80 per cent of Turkey's state revenues were devoted to meeting its foreign debts. The cost of the war of 1877–8, the subsequent indemnity to Russia, and the loss of so much productive territory exacerbated the position to the point where Turkey's finances were about to fall under overseas control. The Sultan's solution was to consolidate the debts, to create a public debt commission with representatives from Germany, Britain, Holland, France, Italy, Austria-Hungary, and Turkey, and to allocate direct to the commission certain state revenues, and in particular customs duties, for the purpose of reducing the debt. Having compartmentalized the debt, Abdul Hamid was then free to develop the remaining sources of revenue in order to compensate. This he accomplished with a fair degree of success. But by 1908 foreign economic control of Turkey had nonetheless extended far beyond the bounds set by the public debt commission. In part this was the Sultan's own fault: he encouraged

European economic competition as a substitute for territorial ambitions; his drive to create the conditions for industrialization (and thus increased revenues), particularly the construction of railways, required foreign investment; the burdens of an expanded army and an inflated bureaucracy needed fresh loans. However, in addition, the industrial powers had no desire to foster Ottoman economic independence. The 'capitulations'—privileges granted to foreigners in the days of Ottoman might, and allowing them exemption from Turkish law and taxation—became the symbol and instrument of the Sultan's weakness. Businessmen in Turkey were foreign residents or Ottoman citizens of non-Turkish race. Turkey itself was predominantly an agricultural country. In Abdul Hamid's reign the value of Anatolian grain exports went from 465 million kurus to 754 million, and the peasantry's contribution to state revenues grew from 77 per cent of the total to 87 per cent between 1872 and 1910.[11] But the capitulations prevented any increase in tariffs to protect Turkish industry from imports or to generate state wealth from exports. The exploitation of coal and mineral resources was limited; investment in industrial infrastructure could only proceed by way of foreign concessions and foreign loans. Thus, the Imperial Ottoman Bank was under British and (increasingly) French control, and 22 per cent of the public debt was owed to the former and 63 per cent to the latter. Thus too, despite a flourishing overseas commerce, Turkey had a trade deficit of 1.5 billion kurus in 1907–8.

The central aim, therefore, of the Young Turks' coup in 1908 was modernization, and modernization for a specific end, that of reversing Ottoman decline. Abdul Hamid, although aspects of his administration had been marked by success, had ruled as an absolute despot and had created an administration centred around the court rather than parliament. The revolutionaries aspired to restore the constitution of 1876. Their inspiration was thus in part western, liberal, and democratic: 'la Jeune Turquie' had been founded in Parisian exile in 1889. But the émigrés had split, some rejecting foreign influences and embracing centralization and others not. Within the empire the growth of professional education, particularly in the army and the civil service, sponsored an indigenous political awareness. Secret societies of young Ottoman officers drew inspiration not just from the west, but also from Japan, for Japan had managed to modernize without destroying its traditional society, and had given evidence of its emergence with victory on the battlefield. The Turkish army was convinced that fears of a coup had caused its neglect at Abdul Hamid's hands, and that if allowed a free rein it could crush terrorism and assure Ottoman integrity.

[11] On the general background, see Shaw and Shaw, *Ottoman empire*, ii. 201–41; Feroz Ahmad, 'The last Ottoman Empire', in Kent (ed.), *The great powers*; Macfie, *End of the Ottoman empire*.

In 1906 a post office official, Mehmed Talaat, formed the Ottoman Freedom Society in Salonika. The young officers of the 3rd army proved particularly enthusiastic adherents, and its ideas were carried to the 2nd army at Monastir. In September 1907 the Ottoman Freedom Society merged with the centralist arm of the exile movement, the Committee of Union and Progress, and adopted its name. It also absorbed a smaller but older organization, *Vatan* ('Fatherland'), which had been formed by Mustafa Kemal, who returned to Macedonia from a posting in Syria, also in September 1907. The initiative for action in 1908 came from within the empire rather than without—from Salonika and from the 2nd and 3rd armies.

In a sense the 1908 revolution was not a revolution. Parliament was restored (not introduced for the first time); the sultanate was not overthrown; grand viziers of the pre-revolutionary period held the same office afterwards; and the Young Turks themselves did not seize power. The class origins of the Young Turks were relatively humble; they lacked both the age and experience seen as necessary for government. The Committee of Union and Progress, therefore, preferred to exercise influence on government through indirect means and to continue to make a virtue of its quasi-secret arrangements. The result was a power struggle between and within the old political elites and the newly established political parties.

If there was a revolution it occurred in 1909, and it did so as the result of a largely fabricated counter-revolution. The grievances of the army were central to the 1908 coup. Demonstrations over arrears of pay and the failure to release conscripts at the conclusion of their terms of service had turned to mutiny on several occasions between 1906 and 1908. Of 505 members of the Salonika group of the Committee of Union and Progress in 1908, 309 were officers. Themselves products of military academies, they were anxious to reduce the army's reliance on officers promoted from the ranks. In April 1909 the mutiny of a Constantinople-based battalion, feeding on Islamic fundamentalism and probably stoked by discharged ex-ranker officers, was dressed up as a counter-revolution. The Sultan, almost certainly wrongly, was implicated. Mustafa Kemal created an Action Army from elements of the 2nd and 3rd armies, and became its chief of staff. Under the guise of restoring order it declared martial law, cracked down on those parties opposed to the Committee of Union and Progress, purged the older Ottoman elites, and deposed Abdul Hamid.

Thus the army, not the Committee of Union and Progress, provided such semblances of political order as existed between 1908 and 1913. Mustafa Kemal himself proposed that officers should disengage from politics. Mahmud Sevket Pasha, the commander of the 3rd army, led the Action Army and subsequently became inspector-general of all the troops in the region and then minister of war. Sevket put the weight on patriotism and national security ahead of liberalism and social reform. He was tolerant of the Committee of Union and Progress rather than supportive of it. The latter divided against itself, the soldiers being more extremist than the civilians, and their political influence thriving on crisis but languishing without it.[12]

The initial reaction of the great powers to the Young Turks' revolt was supportive, if condescending. The Committee of Union and Progress saw the objectives of the new Turkey as a revived Ottomanism, resting on a programme of capitalism and westernization. Its members, therefore, expected the backing of Britain in particular. Throughout the nineteenth century Britain had urged such reforms as means to Turkish reinvigoration. More specifically, the conviction that the meeting between Edward VII and the Tsar at Reval in 1908 presaged Russo-British intervention in the problems of Macedonia had been a key cause of the coup: domestic reform was seen as a preventive to foreign support for irridentism and eventual partition.

But the hopes of the Young Turks were soon dashed. Grey was ready to 'give sympathy and encouragement to the reform movement', but otherwise proposed 'to wait upon events'; he would not, in other words, use Britain's external clout to aid the establishment of internal order.[13] The cycle of coup and counter-coup, the violence of Turkish politics over the next five years, did nothing to persuade him to adopt a more positive line. Nor did the revolution staunch the loss of territory. The Austrian annexation of Bosnia-Herzgovina, still nominally Ottoman, was the first blow, and elicited—it seemed—only weak protests from the Entente powers. Italy's attack on Tripoli appeared also to enjoy great-power collusion. As the Italians' allies, the Germans were reluctant to intervene, and the British did not respond to Turkey's appeals. The culmination of this process, the Balkan wars and the effective extinction of European Turkey, confirmed for the Young Turks the notion that the international system would provide them with no succour.

The visible erosion on the frontiers was coupled with the latent threat of partition from within. Germany's debates with Russia, Britain, and France over the apportionment of Turkish railway construction carried with them the implication that the powers were dividing even Asiatic Turkey into spheres of influence—a process confirmed by Russia's proposals for the protection of the Armenians. Thus France sketched out its claim to Syria, Britain to southern Mesopotamia and the Gulf, Russia to the Caucasus, and Germany to central Anatolia. In reality, each of these powers pursued a policy designed to sustain the Ottoman empire, albeit in a weakened state. But by preparing its claim should the actions of another power trigger Turkey's final partition, it fuelled great-power rivalry and Ottoman mistrust.

---

[12] Ahmad, *Young Turks*, esp. 1–56; Zürcher, *Unionist factor*, 19–51; Macfie, *End of the Ottoman empire*, 18–19, 22, 24–5, 42–56.
[13] Miller, *Straits*, 31–2.

Thus, the revolution produced no change in Turkey's economic subservience. Many of the Young Turks were themselves government employees whose salaries or pensions determined the size of the public debt. The army's hold on politics made increased military expenditure, not budgetary cuts, the order of the day. In 1910–11 the government collected 2.88 billion kurus but disbursed 3.37 billion. The frustration with foreign economic dominance—by 1911 the public debt organization employed a staff of 8,931, and was larger than the ministry of finance itself—fuelled antipathy to western capitalism and further undermined politicial liberalism. Djavid, the Young Turk minister of finance, struggled to establish Ottoman independence of French financial control, both in the public debt and in the Ottoman Bank. However, in so doing he weakened one of the few external bulwarks against the empire's partition. The French government's support of the political status quo was conditional on the interests of its own bondholders. Djavid resigned in May 1911.[14]

In none of the key areas, therefore, had the revolution of 1908 reversed the decline. And by 1912 the Committee of Union and Progress itself seemed a spent force, reliant on an increasingly authoritarian army and responsible for the alienation of Britain and France. Political parties, themselves offshoots of the Committee, entered the lists as its opponents. In November 1911 the Liberal Union was formed, pledged to the ideals of 1908 and 1909, ideals to which the Young Turks themselves seemed increasingly hostile. In January 1912 the Committee of Union and Progress exploited its hold on the provincial administration to ensure a triumphant, albeit corrupt, success at the polls before the Liberal Union could organize itself. With its parliamentary position shored up for the time being, it pushed through an amendment to article 35 of the constitution, allowing the Sultan to dissolve parliament, and so swinging the balance of power from the chamber to the executive. Such cynical manipulation of the constitution infuriated a group of junior officers with liberal links, who in July 1912 threatened a coup. The Sultan appointed a fresh government, without Young Turk members, and with a fixed determination to root the Committee of Union and Progress out of politics altogether. Using the weapon provided by the Committee itself, the government dissolved parliament under the amended article 35. The Young Turks had a foothold neither in cabinet nor in chamber.

The Committee saved itself from political extinction by playing the patriotic card. The outbreak of the first Balkan war at the beginning of October 1912 diverted the government's attention from domestic affairs, but also at first persuaded the Young Turks not to react until peace had been restored.

[14] Ahmad, *The young Turks*, 75–80; Shaw and Shaw, *Ottoman empire*, ii. 285–7; Macfie, *End of the Ottoman empire*, 92, 110–12; Hayne, *French foreign office*, 26, 180, 185.

However, by December the Turkish army in the Balkans had fallen back almost to Constantinople. It seemed possible that the government would confirm Turkey's loss of Adrianople in an effort to get peace. On 23 January 1913 a hot-headed army officer of Macedonian origins, and (since he was only 31) a Young Turk in more than name, Enver, stormed into a cabinet meeting at the head of a group of soldiers. The minister of war was shot dead and the grand vizier forced to resign. Another Unionist, Djemal Pasha, took over the 1st army based at Constantinople. Enver then asked the Sultan to form a coalition government with Mahmut Sevket at its head. The external crisis presented by Adrianople had provided the Committee of Union and Progress with the means to resuscitate its domestic fortunes.

Even now, however, its hold on power was far from assured. Enver had acted out of frustration with the military situation rather than in pursuit of political self-advancement.[15] Only three Unionists were in the cabinet, all of them moderates, and the new grand vizier was tolerant rather than supportive of the Committee. Adrianople fell on 26 March. Conspiracies against the government abounded; in Cairo the ousted grand vizier, Mehmed Kamil Pasha, was believed to be in cahoots with the British. The Young Turks' policy was, in the circumstances, prudent. They harped on the theme of national unity; they formed a committee of national defence to mobilize the country's war effort. Opposition to the government, therefore, smacked of betrayal. Kamil's return to Constantinople on 28 May to head a coup and Sevket's assassination on 11 June played into the Unionists' hands. The coup was crushed, Djemal imposed martial law, the Liberal Union was suppressed, and four more members of the Committee of Union and Progress were brought into the government. The new grand vizier, Mehmed Said Halim Pasha, was himself a member of the Committee; Djemal became minister of public works, and Mehmed Talaat minister of the interior. The appointment of Enver as minister of war in January 1914 brought together the triumvirate—Enver, Djemal, and Talaat—most associated with Turkey's entry into, and prosecution of, the war. Enver purged the officer corps in a reasonably successful attempt to remove the army from politics. The Committee itself—reputed to consist of about forty members—drew the strings of patronage into its own hands. The recovery of Adrianople in July 1913 gave the new government at least some consolation in foreign affairs, greater authority with the army, and success where its predecessors had failed.

The fact that it had taken five years for the Young Turks to assume power made it easy for foreign observers to underestimate the hold which they now exercised on Turkish politics. Those five years, although characterized by coups, assassinations, and defeats, proved vital in shaping the

---

[15] Haley, *Middle Eastern Studies*, XXX (1994), 16.

Committee of Union and Progress's attitude to power. First and foremost, the young and inexperienced officers and bureaucrats of 1908 had served an apprenticeship in the exercise of government. Secondly, the Unionists' interpretation of modernization had been defined. In shedding its liberal support, the Committee had become a leaner but more compact body. But equally, its desire to westernize and to secularize, through the emancipation of women, through the reform of education, through the introduction of civil law, distanced it from the more conservative interpretations of Islam. Turkey remained Muslim—in some respects it became more so—but a division between faith and state was inaugurated. Pan-Islam was associated with the Hamidian regime. The Committee's aim was to centralize the state's administration. In their political philosophy, therefore, both Islam and Ottomanism— the universality of one and the multinationalism of the other—took on subordinate roles.

What replaced them in importance was Turkish nationalism. The loss of European Turkey and the inability to ensure the loyalty of Greeks or Armenians helped restate the Islamic identity of the empire by reducing the influence, as well as absolute numbers, of Christians. But Muslims too, most notably at the empire's peripheries in Albania and the Yemen, resisted the revival of Ottomanism through centralization. Therefore the setbacks of 1908– 12 put the weight on the Anatolian heartland. All three—Djemal, Talaat, and Enver—hailed from the lost territories; yet their response to defeat was positive rather than negative. What was left them was racially and culturally more homogeneous. What it lacked was a sense of identity. This they endeavoured to provide, through language and literature, through youth movements, through 'Turk Ocagi' (the Turkish Hearth Society).

The origins of this movement were intellectual and academic. The study of a decaying culture of a backward society had flourished among exiles in France; it had assumed an increasingly political texture in response to European nationalism. Ziya Gokalp, its principal spokesman and a member of the Central Council of the Committee of Union and Progress, was a student of Le Bon and Durkheim, and professor of sociology at the new University of Istanbul. But if its bottom was western, its bulk was eastern. Its most vociferous advocates included a disproportionate number of Tatar, Azeri, and Uzbek exiles from Russia. After the 1905 revolution the Turkic peoples of the Russian empire hoped for greater autonomy. At first censorship was slack—250 journals were published by Turkic groups in Russia between 1905 and 1917—but as controls were reimposed so the focus of agitation moved across the Caucasus to Constantinople. This flight from the repression of a Christian power highlighted the fact that the Tatars and others were Muslims as well as Turks. Therefore Turkish nationalism provided a third way, at once both an alternative to and a synthesis of westernization and Islam.

Gokalp defined nationalism in terms of culture and sentiment. His aim was to get the average Osman to identify less with the cosmopolitan stock of the empire's administrative and business world and more with the illiterate Anatolian peasant. Thus, ethnic and political limits were not clearly drawn. Thus too, the distinction between Turkism and pan-Turkism became confused. Turkism's basic proposition suggested that, by being racially more united, the state would gain in vigour what it had lost in size. Pan-Turkism, on the other hand, was openly irridentist and expansionist. In its most extreme forms Magyars and Finns, Tamils and Chinese, were numbered as Turkic peoples. The Young Turks never went this far. But the thrust of their message was nonetheless visionary, its penumbra romantic. Gokalp directed the Turk's gaze not to the west but to the east, identifying Turks with Tatars, with the populations of the Russian Caucasus, of Azerbaijan, Turkestan, Persia, and Afghanistan. 'For the Turks,' Gokalp wrote in 1911, 'the fatherland is neither Turkey nor Turkestan; their fatherland is a great and eternal land: Turan.'[16]

The implications of pan-Turanianism, or even of Turkish nationalism, for Turkish policy in 1914 should not be exaggerated. Turkey did not enter the Great War with the intention of turning Gokalp's cultural reveries into political reality. Nor could the Committee of Union and Progress publicly define Turkification so narrowly that it excluded non-Turkish Muslims (such as the Arabs) or non-Muslims of other races (such as Armenians or Greeks). At a secret meeting of the Committee of Union and Progress in August 1910, the Young Turks declared their resolve to uphold Muslim supremacy and to ensure the dominance of the Turkish language, but in endorsing those objectives Talaat (who, one observer concluded, had no commitment to any religion, including Islam)[17] stated that their objective remained that of 'Ottomanizing the Empire'.[18] Both Ottomanism and Islam continued to coexist with Turkism. For those reluctant to embrace the new thinking, Turkification carried a measure of intolerance and xenophobia. But its purpose was consolidatory, not revisionist. A common religion and a common language would serve the Young Turks' objective, a stronger and more united Turkey that could stand on its own feet, and so preserve itself from economic subordination, territorial partition, and nationalist irridentism.

Such objectives could not, however, be achieved independently of the great powers. Turkey's survival, in which the powers were mildly interested, was not the same as Turkey's recrudescence, in which they were not. Not only would the latter threaten their own established interests, it also seemed inherently improbable of fulfilment. To the external observer there was little reason to

---

[16] Jaschke, *Die Welt des Islams*, XXIII (1941), 5; see also Landau, *Pan-Turkism*, 28–42; Larcher, *La Guerre turque*, ch. 2; Bihl, *Kaukasus-Politik*, 143–50.

[17] Morgenthau, *Ambassador Morgenthau's story*, 20.

[18] Macfie, *End of the Ottoman empire*, 63; also 84–90.

expect the new government of 1913 to be any more stable than its predecessors. Furthermore, its espousal of Turkification, and its employment of the metaphors of French Jacobinism, suggested excesses which did not appeal to liberal sensibilities. Turkey, rightly, had no faith in the concert of Europe to protect its interests. It needed an ally—an ally for whom Turkey's strength would be an asset, not a threat. The trouble was that, while Turkey itself was still weak, such an alliance held little appeal to any potential partner.[19]

In 1908 it had been Britain that had inspired the Committee of Union and Progress in its political reforms, and which had provided a possible break with the pro-German policies of the Sultan and of the army. But, in so far as British responses were positive, they were swayed not by Turkey as a European power but as an Asiatic one. 'I think', wrote Sir Arthur Nicolson in January 1911, 'that this Pan-Islamic movement is one of our greatest dangers in the future, and is indeed far more of a menace than the "Yellow Peril".'[20] With a large Muslim population in India, and indeed elsewhere in the empire, it behoved Britain to cultivate good relations with the Caliphate. Moreover, in Mesopotamia and in the Persian Gulf British interests in Ottoman stability took on a more practical form. The British India Steam Navigation Company had the shipping rights on the Euphrates and the Tigris; they, and other British and Indian companies, had—in 1906—79 per cent of the total Gulf trade; and—a growing concern now that oil-burning warships were under construction—the Anglo-Persian Oil Company and Shell (which although Dutch had a minority British interest) owned 75 per cent of the shares of the Turkish oil company. Germany's construction of the Baghdad railway and an increase in German shipping in the Gulf represented a converging challenge to the complacency of British business in the area. But Germany was less of a challenge to Britain in Asia than was Russia: in 1903 it preferred to see the former, not the latter, on the Mesopotamian littoral. In seeking protection for its interests, Britain maintained that it was buttressing the status quo; remarkably, in meeting most British desiderata in 1913 and 1914, both Germany and Turkey agreed.

[19] The literature on Turkey's entry to the war is sadly deficient. Reflecting the available sources, most academic work approaches the problem from the viewpoint of a particular great power rather than from the Turkish end. Kent (ed.), *The great powers*, provides a country-by-country survey; on Britain and Turkey, see Heller, *British policy*, and Miller, *Straits*; on the Central Powers and Turkey, Trumpener, *Germany and the Ottoman empire*; Silberstein, *Troubled alliance*; Weber, *Eagles on the crescent*, and—older but still valuable—Mühlmann, *Deutschland und der Türkei 1913–1914*. An excellent recent survey, but focused on 1913–14, is F. A. K. Yasamee, 'Ottoman empire', in Keith Wilson (ed.), *Decisions for war*. A brief synthesis from a Turkish perspective is Y. T. Kurat, 'How Turkey drifted into World War I', in Bourne and Watt (ed.), *Studies in international history*. Also helpful: Shaw and Shaw, *Ottoman empire*; Ahmad, *Young Turks*; Larcher, *La Guerre turque*; Howard, *Partition of Turkey*; Emin, *Turkey in the World War*; Trumpener, *Journal of Modern History*, XXXIV (1962), 369–80.

[20] Heller, *British policy*, 39; in addition to Heller on Turko-British relations, see also Cohen, *British policy in Mesopotamia*, and Marian Kent, 'Great Britain and the end of the Ottoman empire 1900–23', in Kent (ed.), *The great powers*.

But what set the overall tenor of Turkish–British relations was not the success of British concerns in Mesopotamia but the death of Turkey in Europe. Sir Edward Grey regarded the Concert of Europe as the best device for managing Turkish decline without triggering Turkish partition; he also felt that the demise of European Turkey might consolidate Turkey in Asia. Thus, British support for Ottoman grievances over the Austrian annexation of Bosnia-Herzogovina involved financial compensation, not the return of territory. Apart from the Concert of Europe, the other—and progressively more important—plank to British foreign policy was the solidity of the Triple Entente. Russia was Britain's ally; Russia was also Turkey's putative foe—at least on its northern frontiers. Russia had fought Turkey in 1828, 1854, and 1877; it was a sponsor of the Balkan states, a coadjutor of the Armenians in eastern Anatolia, and an interested party in the fate of the straits and Constantinople; it was also frightened by pan-Islamism and pan-Turkism. Such a combination of interests was potentially lethal to Turko-British rapprochement. Britain's policy was determined by the needs of the Entente, not of empire. In 1910 the India Office's commercial and strategic priorities in Mesopotamia were subordinated to the Foreign Office's fear that a forward policy in the region would increase Turkey's reliance on Germany. In 1911 Britain did not restrain Italy in Tripoli for fear of driving that country back into the arms of the Triple Alliance.

Britain's military and naval weakness in the region was a driving factor in its diplomacy. Even in the 1890s Britain realized that it could not prevent Russia seizing the straits without exposing itself to France in the western basin of the Mediterranean or in the channel. The Defence Committee therefore concluded in 1903 that the strategic position would be no worse if Russia had free access to the eastern Mediterranean, and in 1906 the Committee of Imperial Defence made it clear that Britain was bereft of coercive powers in relation to the straits. In reflection of these views, Grey expressed sympathy with regard to Russia's ambitions in the area, thus fomenting Izvolsky's bargaining with Aehrenthal over Bosnia-Herzogovina. Therefore, the Anglo-Russian entente had a European as well as an Asiatic naval dimension, even if the first was never part of the formal agreement. Much of the ire of the Foreign Office over the Admiralty's plans to withdraw from the Mediterranean was concerned specifically with the role of sea-power in giving stability in an area where Britain's ambivalent diplomacy left it unable to play a more positive role.[21]

One indirect substitute for the erosion of British naval power in the eastern Mediterranean was the British naval mission established in Turkey in 1908. Fisher favoured the incorporation of Turkey as a fully-fledged member of a formalized entente, and Churchill took a similar line when he entered the Admiralty. But the navy for which Britain assumed responsibility had been

---

[21] Macfie, *End of the Ottoman empire*, 114–18; Miller, *Straits*, 17–22, 25–7, 111–12, 147.

deemed 'practically non-existent' in 1904: in 1908 vegetable gardens grew on the decks of its obsolete vessels. British naval advisers, perhaps also reflecting Fisher's advocacy of flotilla defence for enclosed home waters, urged the Turks to acquire torpedo boats rather than more sophisticated and demanding ships. But maritime inadequacy in the face of Italy in 1911 and Greece in 1912 made the Turks determined to have Dreadnoughts. The tensions which therefore emerged were exacerbated by Constantinople's conviction that the completion of the two ships it had eventually ordered from British yards was deliberately delayed. Nonetheless, in 1913 Vickers secured a thirty-year contract to upgrade and maintain Turkey's dockyards, and in May 1914 a third ship was ordered from Armstrongs.[22]

This most obvious, if fraught, symbol of Turko-British co-operation was also vulnerable to Entente concerns. The Russians were less relaxed about Turkish naval power: for them its focus was the Black Sea, where their own fleet was still weak and unmodernized. The fact that Turkey's naval ambitions in 1913–14 were directed not against them but against Greece complicated the situation rather than resolved it. The British also maintained a naval mission in Athens. The Greeks were as resistant as the Turks to the idea that torpedo boats would suffice, and ordered a battle cruiser from Germany in 1912. Britain favoured the Greeks rather than the Turks, but they were determined not to allow either party to play off the great powers against each other in its search for domination of the Aegean. In Greece the case for a pre-emptive attack before Turkey received its Dreadnoughts was vitiated by exhaustion after the first Balkan war. In Turkey the determination to recover the forfeited islands of Chios and Mytilene was held in check by the fact that the Dreadnoughts had not arrived and by the vulnerability of its position in Thrace.[23]

At its best, therefore, British policy towards Turkey was cautious, not warm. Its worst was represented by Sir Gerard Lowther, ambassador in Constantinople from 1908 to 1913. Lowther was slow to gather information on the Committee of Union and Progress, and when he finally did so he saw it as an aggressive and chauvinistic organization, committed to Turkish nationalism. Lowther emphasized the splits in Islam, Shi'ite versus Sunni, Arab versus Turk, and did not therefore share the fears for Muslim loyalty in the British empire; when the Young Turks spoke in a western voice, he bracketed them with the Terror of the French Revolution. In July 1913 Lowther was replaced by Sir Louis Mallet, an orientalist and an advocate of improved Turkish relations. But by 1913 British foreign policy was even more set in the mould of European policies, and of its Entente commitments. Mallet's desire to rebuild Ottoman

---

[22] Miller, *Straits*, 59, 78–83, 96–7, 140–3, 184; Marian Kent, 'Constantinople and Asiatic Turkey 1905–1914', in Hinsley (ed.), *British foreign policy under Grey*, 158–9; Marder (ed.), *Fear God and dread nought*, ii. 197–9, 384–6, 389–90.
[23] Miller, *Straits*, 190–1, 204–6; Miller, *Superior force*, 152–7, 163–72.

strength was bridled by his belief that it must be done in conjunction with the other powers; he feared that unilateral action would trigger the very scramble for territory that it would be designed to avoid. Mesopotamia could still be resolved as a local issue; but it could not be the vehicle for a broader Turko-British alliance. Thus, on three occasions—in 1908, 1911, and 1913—the Turks sought an agreement with Britain, and on all three were met with coolness. On the last, in June 1913, Turkey offered Britain a defensive alliance. But Turkey was seen as too weak and the proposal too challenging to the European powers for its risks to be acceptable to Britain.

Historically, Germany was not a major player in Ottoman affairs. By 1913 the value of its exports to Turkey was still inferior to those of Britain and Austria-Hungary, and the value of its imports to those of Britain, Austria-Hungary, and France. Germany was restricted in Turkey, as elsewhere, by its lack of mobile capital: in 1910 Germany had provided Turkey with the loan which France and Britain had refused, but in 1913 Germany could not lend and the Turks had reverted to the French. On the other hand, the cause of Germany's lack of liquidity was the pace of its own industrialization, and what was striking—and alarming to those powers alert to German expansionism—was the growth of German imports to Turkey. France dominated the Ottoman public debt, but saw its share of Turkish imports fall from 18 per cent of the total in 1887 to 11 per cent in 1910. Over the same period Germany's share rose from 6 per cent to 21 per cent, and Austria-Hungary's from 13 per cent to the same figure; Britain's fell from 60 per cent to 35 per cent.[24] Thus, selective examination suggested a higher German profile in the Turkish economy than did crude aggregates. Two specific areas were of special significance, since their impact was as much strategic as it was economic.

In 1903 the Deutsche Bank secured a ninety-nine-year concession for the construction of the Baghdad railway, together with branch lines in Mesopotamia and Syria. A subsidiary company, the Baghdad-Eisenbahn-Gesellschaft, was formed, and was guaranteed a minimum income on the operating costs: the first 4,500 francs earned on each kilometre of track per annum were to go to the company, sums above 4,500 francs and below 10,000 to the Turkish government, and profits over 10,000 francs were to be split 60 : 40 between the government and the company. German heavy industry thrived on the export of rolling-stock and steel rails. The grandiloquent title the 'Berlin-to-Baghdad railway', and the connotations of German expansionism which it contained, tended to obscure the fact that commercial rather than strategic considerations underpinned German involvement. Indeed, the very fact that the railway did not meet the needs of the Turkish army caused friction between

[24] Gottlieb, Studies, 21.

the company and German officers.[25] In so far as the railway was used as an adjunct of policy, it became the means for détente, not confrontation. The Germans respected the Russians' wish that the course of the line should pass through southern Anatolia rather than open up the north-eastern part of Turkey; thus, they deliberately forfeited the opportunity to threaten the Caucasus and so draw Russian troops away from the European front. Britain and Germany agreed to divide the Mesopotamian parts of the line into southern and northern sections. Compromise with France over Syria proved more difficult. But again the German objectives were economic: the financial viability of the line rested in large part on its links with Aleppo and Alexandretta. Germany's priorities with the Baghdad railway stand comparison with France's control of the public debt and Britain's interests in Mesopotamia; over the long term Germany wanted to establish its stake in the event of Turkey's partition, and the foreign ministry worked closely with the Deutsche Bank, but in the meantime it intended to compete in this, as in other, overseas markets.

The second obvious symbol of the German presence in Turkey was its military mission. It was the reaction of the other powers, and specifically Russia, to the Liman von Sanders affair in early 1914 that set the military mission in an international political context. Liman himself stressed that his task was entirely technical, to help in the training and rebuilding of the Turkish army after the defeats of the Balkan wars.[26] Furthermore, the invitation originated with the Turks; it balanced the comparable roles of the French with the Turkish gendarmerie and the British with the Turkish navy. The decision to approach the Germans in 1913, which ran counter to the Young Turks' own proclivities in foreign policy, was thus a product of the need for equipoise, and also the fruit of history. German advice to the Turkish army began in the 1830s under the elder Moltke; many senior Turkish officers, including Sevket and Ahmed Izzet Pasha (grand vizier and minister of war respectively at the time the invitation was issued), had been attached to the German army in their early careers; and Colmar von der Goltz, who had served in Turkey from 1883 to 1895 and again in 1909–10, enjoyed an intellectual, if not practical, influence in Constantinople that enhanced Germany's military reputation. Liman van Sanders's mission therefore represented continuity for an army already influenced by German military practices, and which in its anxiety to restore its fighting capacity as soon as possible could not afford the time lost in a change of style. Germany's acceptance of the Turkish invitation was defensive more than it was aggressive. At stake was the German army's *amour propre*; a refusal would be tantamount to the acceptance of

[25] Trumpener, *Journal of Contemporary History*, I (1966), 180–1; see also id., *Germany and the Ottoman empire*, ch. 9.

[26] Liman von Sanders, *Five years in Turkey*, 1–4; see also Trumpener, *Germany and the Ottoman empire*, 13–14.

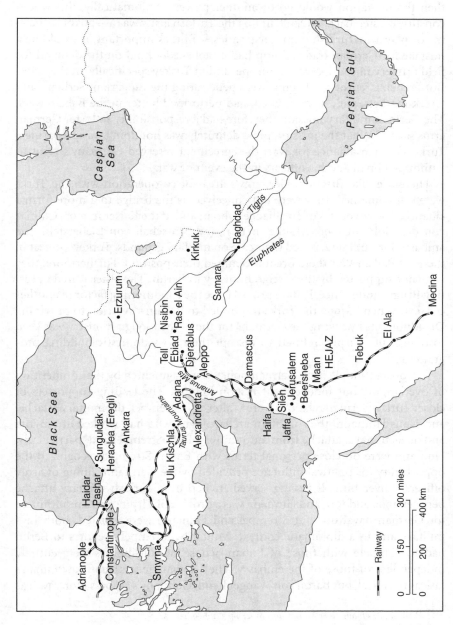

MAP 24. THE OTTOMAN EMPIRE'S RAILWAY COMMUNICATIONS

Caspian Sea

Black Sea

Persian Gulf

Adrianople
Constantinople
Haidar Pashar
Sunguldak
Heraclea (Eregli)
Ankara
Smyrna
Ulu Kischla
Adana
Taurus Mountains
Alexandretta
Amanus Mts
Erzurum
Nisibin
Tell
Ebiad
Ras el Ain
Djerablus
Aleppo
Kirkuk
Samara
Baghdad
Tigris
Euphrates
Damascus
Haifa
Jaffa
Sileh
Jerusalem
Beersheba
Maan
HEJAZ
Tebuk
El Ala
Medina

——— Railway

0   150
0   200   400 km

0   300 miles

responsibility for the defeats of the Balkan wars. If Germany did not accept, then the invitation would go to another power. Diplomatically, this would constitute a step back; after all, in 1913 the Turkish army was a—possibly the— major player in Turkish domestic politics.[27] But, as important, it would be a mistake for German trade. Krupp had established a hold on the demand for field artillery in south-eastern Europe, and in Turkey specifically, in the 1880s. But French Creusot-made guns were penetrating the Bulgarian, Serbian, and Greek markets, and, it was argued, had performed better in the Balkan wars. The German military mission therefore had a responsibility to foster German arms sales.[28] What the mission most definitely was not doing was preparing a Turko-German alliance for war; the agreement reserved Germany's right to withdraw Liman and his officers in the event of war.

Therefore, like Britain's, Germany's areas of co-operation with the Turks were self-contained; they were not conceived as the bridge to a more formal alliance. The advocates of an alliance, who included the Kaiser in 1905, Colmar von der Goltz in 1909, Moltke in 1911, and Marschall von Bieberstein, the ambassador until 1912, rested their case on military grounds. Turkey's defeat in the First Balkan War therefore undermined their position. Furthermore, they were not supported by the foreign ministry in Berlin. The latter feared upset-ting Britain and France. Britain proved to be the conditioning factor in another context. When in 1909 the Turks responded to Britain's aversion to providing Dreadnoughts by asking the Germans for them, the foreign ministry was keen to oblige, but Tirpitz refused to disrupt the navy's domestic building pro-gramme.[29]

In Constantinople itself German policy was fragmented by the competition of overlapping but independent responsibilities. The leading supporters of closer Turko-German relations were Walter von Strempel, the military attaché, and Hans Humann, the son of an archaeologist who had worked at Smyrna and de facto naval attaché from autumn 1913. Both Strempel and, particularly, Humann were on close personal terms with Enver; Strempel recognized the opportunity for political influence provided by the German training of army officers, Enver himself having served in Berlin as Turkish military attaché between 1909 and 1911, and Humann was a protégé of Tirpitz and a mouthpiece for German navalism. But Strempel and Humann were isolated, both in a military and in a diplomatic context. Militarily, Strempel's reports to Berlin had to compete with those of Liman, whose responsibilities were entirely independent of those of the embassy. The German general staff saw Liman's task as technical, but Baron von Wangenheim, Germany's ambassador, saw it as

[27] Wallach, *Anatomie einer Militärhilfe*, 91–2, 94–5, 108–9, 111–13.

[28] Schulte, *Vor dem Kriegsausbruch*, 19–35.

[29] Hagen, *Türkei im ersten Weltkrieg*, 31–2; Epkenhans, *Wilhelminische Flottenrüstung*, 305; Mombauer, 'Moltke', 115–16.

political. Moltke would have been content to dispatch a team of junior but professionally proficient advisers; Wangenheim wanted a figurehead capable of exploiting the Turkish army's clout in domestic politics for the benefit of Germany's eastern policy. This did not mean preparation for war. When Liman stressed the strategic needs of the Baghdad railway, Wangenheim countered by emphasizing its economic rationale and its function in great-power détente. Liman huffed and puffed over the salaries and ranks of his officers—both inflated in Turkish eyes—and threatened to resign: Enver did not object. Most importantly, Liman dismissed the Turkish army as being of no military value in the immediate future. Accordingly, in March and again in May 1914 Moltke wrote off Turkey as a potential ally.[30] Diplomatically, Strempel and Humann found themselves countered by Wangenheim. The key to Wangenheim's policy was Germany's need to find an accommodation with Russia. Thus, Wangenheim had been a prime mover in seeking a settlement of the Liman affair, suggesting compromises in his status unacceptable to the general himself, and so aggravating their poor relations. If a synthesis of German policy towards Turkey before the First World War is possible, its complexion would differ little from that of other powers. Co-operation with Turkey was seen as desirable, but its pursuit should come second to the management of the Triple Alliance and its needs. On this broader stage Turkey, particularly after the defeats of the Balkan wars, threatened to be a liability rather than an asset.[31]

Not that Turkey in 1914, at least to begin with, was actively seeking a German alliance. The great powers inevitably interpreted the position of Turkey against the background of their alliance networks. This impression was confirmed by Said Halim and Talaat, both of whom reckoned that Turkey needed the protection of one or other of the two blocs. But actual policy was determined by local considerations, by the balance of power in the Aegean and the Balkans, and by Russian ambitions in the area. Turkey had two main aims. First there came the recovery of Chios and Mytilene from the Greeks. Both the French and the British were pro-Greek, but the British were building the Dreadnoughts Turkey needed to counter the Greek navy, and the Kaiser, bound to King Constantine by Hohenzollern blood, was unlikely to support an anti-Greek policy for Germany. Secondly, Turkey wanted to come to terms with Bulgaria. Both powers had an interest in the revision of the Treaty of Bucharest, and Turkey was anxious to stabilize its position on the European side of the straits. Here the policy of the Central Powers was divided: Austria-Hungary was anxious to establish a fresh Balkan League around Bulgaria, but Germany was not. As late as mid-July 1914 Pallavicini, the Habsburg representative in Constantinople, found his advocacy of a new Balkan grouping built around

---

[30] Mühlmann, *Das deutsch-türkische Waffenbündnis*, 14; Wallach, *Anatomie einer Militärhilfe*, 150–2.
[31] Weber, *Eagles on the crescent*, 17, 19–20.

Austria-Hungary, Bulgaria, and Turkey blocked by both Jagow and Wangen-heim. Like the Austrians, the Turks had an interest in overthrowing the verdict of the Balkan wars, and some of them, Enver in particular, were prepared to fight to achieve that. What made such a policy thinkable was the fact that Russia, the power with the weakest economic stake in the Ottoman empire and no seat on the Ottoman public debt commission, appeared less of a threat than theretofore. Russia had not a single Dreadnought (although four were under construction) available in the Black Sea. For the time being at least, a weakened Turkey in control of the straits was a better proposition for Russia than their possession by a strong power other than Russia.

Thus, in May 1914 pro-Germanism aroused as divided reactions in Turkey as did pro-Turkism in Germany. German efforts to renegotiate the financial clauses of the 1903 railway agreement, and a conviction that Germany was just as bent on Turkish partition as the other powers, fuelled the pro-Entente lobby. Rejected by Britain, Turkey first turned not to Germany but to Russia and then to France. In May itself Talaat floated the idea of an alliance with the Russians. Sazonov was sufficiently taken by surprise not to seize his opportunity. In July Djemal visited France to attend the naval manoeuvres off Toulon. Distrustful of Germany's ulterior motives, Djemal argued that France, if allied to Turkey, would restrain Russia. But his timing was unfortunate. Poincaré and Viviani were about to depart for St Petersburg; thus the French could excuse their own support for the Greeks and their sensitivity as to Russian reactions with postponement.[32]

By late July 1914, therefore, Turkey still had no alliance and had been rejected by each of the Entente powers. The case for a German alliance became proportionately more convincing. Germany's attraction was its combination of military strength on the continent with its weakness in Asia Minor. Germany had taken no Ottoman territory, as Britain had done in Egypt or Cyprus; Germany was not a Mediterranean or Gulf naval power and therefore could not threaten Turkey's long coastline, as Britain or France could; Germany had no Muslim colonies to create a clash of interests with Islam. Instead, Germany's interests were purely commercial; therefore, self-interest would determine German willingness to fight in Turkey's defence. Put in the context of the great-power alliances, the Turks were invoking the principles of deterrence—of the threat that the partitioning of Turkey by the Entente powers would trigger war with the Triple Alliance—in order to buttress their own integrity. More immediately, a treaty with Germany would become the means to persuade Romania and Bulgaria to ally with Turkey, and so create a fresh Balkan bloc which would isolate Greece.

---

[32] For Djemal's own account, see his Memoirs, 101–8; also Corrigan, Past and Present, 36 (1967), 144–52.

It was therefore Turkey, not Germany, which initiated the alliance between the two powers, and it did so for reasons largely independent of the July crisis and its impact on European politics. The advocates of the alliance—Turkey's ambassador in Berlin, Said Halim (the grand vizier), Talaat and Djemal (after their rejections by the Russians and the French respectively), and, above all, Enver—were still in a minority both in the cabinet and in the Committee of Union and Progress. The offer made by Enver on 22 July 1914 was consequently kept secret from the cabinet as a whole.

However, while Turkey's offer reflected a long-term policy, Germany's acceptance was determined by short-term considerations. After all, nothing had happened in Asia Minor to make Turkey a more seductive mate. Only four days before the Turkish offer Wangenheim had reported that,

without doubt, Turkey today is still an unsuitable alliance partner. They only want their allies to take on their burdens, without offering the slightest gains in return... The policy of the Triple Alliance must be to shape relations so that, if the Turks should after years finally become a major power, the threads will not have been cut.[33]

The author of the change in German perceptions was the Kaiser himself. Wilhelm's dynasticism had caused him to favour Greece and to dislike Enver's radical politics. But by 24 July immediate military imperatives had become more compelling. A Balkan grouping of Turkey, Bulgaria, and Romania linked to the Triple Alliance would transform the prospects for Austria-Hungary and the balance of forces on the eastern front. The alternative, particularly given the Turkish approach to the Russians in May (which was known to the Germans), might be a Turkish-led Balkan grouping on the side of the Entente. Furthermore, Wilhelm's views were fully in accord with those of his Austro-Hungarian ally. Pallavicini argued that the swift defeat of Serbia would create the opportunity to form—with Turkey's adherence—a Balkan constellation favourable to the dual monarchy.[34]

What came back from Berlin was therefore not the same proposal which the Turks had originally offered. Foreign ministry opposition to a long-term alliance persisted. Instead, the German objective, reflecting the dominance enjoyed by the military in decision-making in the last four days of July, was the fulfilment of immediate military needs. It has been argued that Bethmann Hollweg hoped, through the agreement, to frighten Britain towards neutrality.[35] But in reality Bethmann's role was reactive rather than creative. Moltke now saw some relief from his worries with regard to the eastern front, and,

---

[33] Mühlmann, *Deutschland und der Türkei*, 39.

[34] Weber, *Eagles on the crescent*, 52–5; Corrigan, *Past and Present*, 36 (1967), 150–1; A. May, *Passing of the Hapsburg monarchy*, 140; Silberstein, *Troubled alliance*, 10–16. But F. R. Bridge, 'The Habsburg monarchy and the Ottoman Empire, 1900–18' in Kent (ed.), *Great powers*, 43–6, suggests Austria-Hungary was more cautious.

[35] Mühlmann, *Das deutsche-türkische Waffenbündnis*, 18.

putting aside his earlier reservations concerning Turkey's military capabilities, posited a Turkish attack on Russia. Liman seemed optimistic with regard to Turkey's military potential, and reckoned that four to five army corps would soon be ready to take the field. Bethmann Hollweg accepted the argument, contenting himself with the thought that the agreement should be limited to the immediate military crisis.

Enver and his colleagues, therefore, found themselves no longer engaged in their primary task of resolving their Balkan problems but of committing themselves to war against Russia. The fact that they were prepared to do so must in retrospect be seen as evidence of their brash foolhardiness. But at the time the arguments for following Germany were not without conviction. The immediate confrontation was that between Austria-Hungary and Serbia; in the calculations of Said Halim there would be a short war which would impel Bulgaria into the Triple Alliance and effect a new balance of power in the Balkans. Serbia and Greece would be squeezed, disgorging the Aegean islands and western Thrace, and Germany's principal function would be to guarantee the consequent settlement.[36] Thus, a defensive alliance with Germany against Russia did not necessarily betoken involvement in a wider European war, and did provide a guarantee against Turkey's most long-standing military threat. Secondly, given all the indications that the European powers were bent on the partition of the Ottoman empire, if a wider European war did break out it might trigger a scramble for Turkey. In particular, the straits, the waterway which linked Russia to its allies, could never remain truly neutral. Both sides would see their control as crucial to the war's outcome. In these circumstances neutrality did not seem a viable option; certainly it had not profited Turkey in the recent past. On 2 August 1914 Germany and Turkey formed an alliance. Austria-Hungary adhered three days later.

The hasty improvisation which had characterized Germany's acceptance of the Turkish offer continued to determine its dealings with the Ottoman empire in the autumn of 1914. Having secured an ally, Germany's main need was to make sure that the ally became a belligerent. In particular, the knowledge that only a minority of the Turkish cabinet had negotiated the treaty, and that parliament had been adjourned rather than risk its rejection of the alliance, coupled with the well-established volatility of Turkish politics to suggest that the opportunity to get Turkey into the war on the side of the Central Powers might be fleeting. But Turkey's military weakness, which had argued against an alliance in May, had not been eradicated by August. Turkey was not ready for war; mobilization would take months; its European frontier was unsecured, and the Dardanelles were inadequately defended. None of these considerations stopped Moltke and, in particular, Conrad from hatching hare-brained

---

[36] Yasamee, 'Ottoman empire', in Wilson (ed), *Decisions for war*, 237–8.

schemes for execution by Turkish forces.[37] Wangenheim tried to console the intemperate soldiers by arguing for the advantages of Turkey's benevolent neutrality. The alliance had forestalled the formation of a hostile Balkan league, and by remaining out of the war Turkey minimized its material demands on the Central Powers.[38] But the effect of Wangenheim's approach was to keep alive the division in German policy which had existed before the conclusion of the alliance.

For the moment, therefore, the Turks were in a strong bargaining position. German splits and German needs gave them the upper hand in negotiations. On 6 August Said Halim took the opportunity presented by Germany's request that Turkey admit the *Goeben* and the *Breslau* to the straits to spell out to Wangenheim what he believed the implications of the treaty to be. Germany was to support the abolition of the capitulations, to aid Turkey in the recovery of its 1878 frontiers in the Caucasus, to reconsider Turkey's Balkan frontier, to promote understandings with Bulgaria and Romania, and, if Greece joined the Entente, to help Turkey regain its Aegean islands. In addition, Germany was not to make peace while any Turkish territory remained in enemy occupation, and was to ensure that Turkey received a war indemnity. Prudently, Wangenheim made his acceptance of these terms conditional on Turkey's belligerence and Germany's ability to dictate the peace. But neither then, nor with the *Goeben* and the *Breslau* flying Turkish colours, did Turkey abandon its neutrality.

Bulgaria was the key to Turkey's position. The Ottoman empire could not fight Russia with its back exposed to a potentially hostile Balkan neighbour. But on 9 August the Turkish cabinet's Unionist members went even further: they proposed to await the outcome of negotiations with Greece and Romania as well. Thus they could benefit from the protection of the Central Powers while postponing the costs of fighting. Said Halim in particular effectively saw the Turko-German alliance as the means to create a four-power Balkan bloc. The negotiations surrounding such a configuration—the Bulgarians would not act without a guarantee from the Romanians, and by September the Greeks were embracing neutrality—became so protracted as to be a means by which those favouring neutrality could postpone entry into the war indefinitely.[39]

The ambivalence of the Turkish cabinet, while it represented a source of strength in negotiation with Germany, was an indication of the limitations on Enver's power. Opinion in Constantinople was divided four ways. Around Enver were those convinced of German military prowess and of the need to hitch Turkey's star to a Triple Alliance victory as quickly as possible. Opposed to him was the economic realism of those who argued that Turkey should be

[37] Pomiankowski, *Zusammenbruch*, 80–2.   [38] Silberstein, *Troubled alliance*, 91–2.
[39] Yasamee, in Wilson (ed.), *Decisions for war*, 242, 245, 247–8; Miller, *Straits*, 224–6, 234, 283–5.

allied to the Entente, the potential victors because of their greater resources. The neutralists fell into two groups: those in favour of strict neutrality, and those who favoured armed neutrality and an alignment with Germany as a defence against Russia.[40] The fact that policy lay in the hands of the Committee of Union and Progress as well as the cabinet, that the divisions were replicated there, and that its membership was unclear, doubled the uncertainties created by these splits. Britain's abandonment of neutrality, the failure of Italy and Romania to honour their obligations to the Triple Alliance, and—in due course—the defeat on the Marne all progressively weakened the hands of the pro-German lobby. Each of the steps taken by Turkey in August prolonged the ambiguity. The simultaneous declaration of neutrality and of mobilization, approved by the cabinet on 3 August, appeased all parties: the warriors had put war preparations in train, the neutralists had approved those preparations so that Turkey could protect its neutrality. Even the acceptance of the *Goeben* and the *Breslau*, which seemed bound to force Turkey's hand, was accomplished without a change of stance.

Vital to Turkey's ability to resist German pressures was the support it received from the Entente powers in the maintenance of its neutrality. Turkey got away with the most flagrantly un-neutral behaviour in August because at that stage neither Russia nor Britain could afford to interpret Turkish behaviour in an adverse light. Moreover, Turkey's own approaches to the Entente at first suggested that its commitment to the Central Powers was not as rigid as its actions increasingly implied.

On 5 August Enver, of all people, reassured Giers, the Russian ambassador, as to the purposes of Turkish mobilization. He said it was not directed against the Russians, and that indeed the Turkish army could be employed in the Balkans against Austria-Hungary. The conditions that Turkey would set for such an alliance would be frontier ratifications in western Thrace and the return of the Aegean islands. From the great-power perspective Turkey's offer was rank duplicity; from the Turkish perspective Turkey's Balkan and Aegean objectives remained totally consistent. The attractions to Russia were obvious. The straits question would be settled on sufficiently favourable terms, at least for the time being, and the Russian army in the Caucasus could be switched to the European theatre. But the consequence would be a Turkish-led Balkan grouping, reactivating European Turkey. This caused Sazonov to pause, since he preferred the idea of Russia as the orchestrator of Balkan affairs. More importantly, it led both Britain and France, with their pro-Greek sympathies, to favour Turkish neutrality rather than Turkish belligerence. Thus the Entente reply, delivered on 18 August, offered Turkey territorial integrity in exchange for Turkish neutrality. If Turkey accepted the Entente's terms, the German

---

[40] Kurat, in Bourne and Watt (eds.), *Studies*, 293.

military mission and the German cruisers would have to depart. The capitulations and the territorial grievances would continue. Russia would grow militarily stronger through Dardanelles-directed imports. On one interpretation the Entente offer betokened not even the maintenance of the status quo, but a further reduction in Ottoman power.[41]

The failure of these negotiations, together with the arrival of the *Goeben* and *Breslau*, increasingly convinced Sir Edward Grey of the eventual outcome. Turko-British relations had received a major blow on 29 July 1914, when Britain had impounded the two Turkish Dreadnoughts under construction in British yards. According to the terms of the contract Britain acted within its rights. Moreover, although this was not known to the British, on 1 August Enver and Talaat did offer the first vessel to the Germans. The decision was therefore fully justified in terms of the naval balance in the North Sea. It also protected a potential ally, Greece, from attack in the Aegean, and calmed Russian worries about the balance in the Black Sea. But it was a gift to Young Turk propaganda. The ships had been funded by popular subscription, deliberately engineered to heighten Turkish national awareness, and were the symbol of Turkish resolve over the question of the Aegean islands. The howls of the Turks were not without effect. They popularized the German alliance, justifying the arrival and purchase of the *Goeben* and the *Breslau* as substitutes for the forfeited battleships, and contributing to the Entente's acceptance that the sale of the cruisers did not infringe Turkish neutrality. On 20 August Kitchener persuaded the cabinet to reject Venizelos's offer of a Greek alliance for fear that further inflammation of Turkish sentiment would threaten Egypt. Just over a month later, a date by which the Foreign Office in London—if not Mallet, the ambassador—was convinced that Turkey would soon side with the Central Powers, Britain even offered to return the two battleships: the offer was not taken up.[42]

The explanation for the confusion in British policy is largely personal. Churchill, the First Lord of the Admiralty and therefore primarily responsible for the appropriation of the battleships, had been much impressed in 1911 both with the Young Turk leadership and with Turkey's ability to cause mayhem as Germany's proxy in southern and central Asia.[43] His attitude, compounded by frustration at the escape of the *Goeben* and the *Breslau*, and then by his reading of intercepted signals traffic between Germany and Turkey, was correspondingly firmer. By the beginning of September he was initiating plans for storming the straits; on 27 August and again on 8 September he told Troubridge 'to sink the Goeben and Breslau, under whatever flag, if they come out of the

[41] Howard, *Partition*, 96–104; C. J. Smith, *Russian struggle*, 70–5.

[42] Weber, *Eagles on the crescent*, 79.

[43] Heller, *British policy*, 63–4; see also Churchill to Enver, 15 Aug. 1914, in Gilbert, *Churchill*, vol. III, *Companion*, 38–9.

Dardanelles';[44] and on 25 September he authorized Vice-Admiral S. H. Carden,
who had succeeded Troubridge, to attack any Turkish vessel. On 2 October, the
Turks having closed the straits to foreign shipping on 26 September, the British
blockade of Turkey began.

Limpus, the head of Britain's naval mission in Constantinople, sent reports
to the Admiralty emphasizing Germany's increasing hold on Turkey; Mallet,
writing from the same city to the Foreign Office, stressed the strength of
Turkish neutralism. The ambassador was absent from the capital at the beginning of August, and his appreciation of what followed was correspondingly
weakened. It was he who argued that the presence of the *Goeben* and *Breslau*
was in British interests, since they protected the straits against Russia;[45] and it
was he who, at the end of September, advised British ships to back off from the
Dardanelles rather than risk a clash with the Turks. But in October even Mallet
began to accept that war looked probable. His aim now was to prolong Turkish
neutrality for as long as possible.

Such conduct was unsustainable. By the beginning of October British policy
towards Turkey was no more genuinely neutral than was Turkey's own. Grey's
diplomacy from August onwards concentrated on the formation of a Balkan
confederation, under Venizelos's leadership, with Turkey as its implicit foe.[46]
But the immediate pressure was imperial, not European. The proximity of
Arabia and Mesopotamia to India, their position on the route to the subcontinent, and the fear that the collapse of Turkish power in the southern half of
the Ottoman empire could destabilize British imperial authority prompted
forward action, albeit for conservative reasons. The preservation of the status
quo in the Gulf would be undermined if Arab rebellions were successful and
Britain had become too closely associated with Ottoman rule. Hardinge, the
viceroy of India, feared that if, as a result, Persia extended into southern
Mespotamia, Russia would not be far behind. On 25 September Sir Edward
Barrow, the military secretary at the India Office, suggested that the 6th Poona
division should be dispatched to Shatt-el-Arab, at the head of the Persian Gulf.
Ostensibly its task would be to defend the Admiralty's oil supplies; in reality it
was to signal support to the Arabs, to block the spread of a holy war to the east,
and to 'steady' Turkey.[47] On 24 September Kitchener, reflecting parallel concerns to those of India but from an Egyptian perspective, instructed that secret
negotiations should be opened with the Hejaz Arabs. Hardinge reported
himself confident that the Muslim population of the subcontinent would

[44] Gilbert, *Churchill*, vol. III, *Companion*, 101.
[45] Weber, *Eagles on the crescent*, 75.
[46] C. J. Smith, *American Historical Review*, LXX (1965), 1015–34.
[47] Heller, *British policy*, 146; also J. Nevakivi, 'Lord Kitchener and the partition of the Ottoman
empire 1915–1916', in Bourne and Watt (eds.), *Studies*, 317–19; Olson, *Anglo-Iranian relations*, 34;
Popplewell, *Intelligence and National Security*, V (1990), 143.

remain loyal in the event of a holy war. But he remained anxious not to provoke Turkey without call. In deference to these concerns, the 6th Poona division, or Indian Expeditionary Force D as it became on 16 October, was diverted from the oilfields at Abadan and halted at Bahrain on 23 October.[48]

Such self-imposed restraint, major at a local level, was nonsensical against the broader background. Turkey's declaration on 6 October that the Shatt-el-Arab constituted Turkish territorial waters forced Britain to a decision—either to abandon its Gulf interests or to reassert them. On the Egyptian frontier minor clashes occurred between the Turks and the British. Russian agitation amongst the Armenian population in Persian Azerbaijan threatened the stability of the Caucasus front. The Turks responded by appealing to the Kurds, and both sides involved troops in support of their propaganda by October.[49] In fomenting Arab nationalism, in exploiting the aspirations of the Balkan powers, and in their primary alliance with Russia, the British were abetting Turkey's partition as surely as they had already commenced hostilities, albeit of a low intensity.

Thus Britain, for all its apparent desire to restrict the war and to ensure Turkey's continued neutrality, made, in the furtherance of that policy, not a single concession of any real significance to Turkey. The contradiction implicit in British policy since 1908, and even before, was forced into the open. Support for a liberalized, reformed Ottoman empire was incompatible with continued stability in the Middle East.[50] In Constantinople Germany's credit gained from the comparison.

The most significant convert to the German cause was Talaat. He had hoped that the Entente powers would offer terms sufficiently attractive to enable him to isolate Enver and his policies. But their collective failure to end the capitulations, and Britain's and France's inability to provide Turkey with any long-term guarantees against Russia, swung him round in favour of intervention. Talaat remained more cautious than Enver, in particular wanting Bulgaria as an active participant in any war with Russia. But the opponents of intervention, Said Halim and Djavid, were now losing influence. As minister of war, Enver had enhanced his domestic authority by mobilization and the imposition of martial law. As minister of finance, Djavid countered by offering the war minister only a quarter of what he deemed necessary to fund the army.[51]

Mobilization had deepened Turkey's economic plight; so too had the outbreak of war in Europe. Business in Constantinople collapsed as shipping and insurance were unobtainable. Panic on the markets generated a run on the

[48] Cohen, *British policy in Mesopotamia*, 298–308; Busch, *Britain, India and the Arabs*, 12–15.
[49] Gehrke, *Persien in der deutschen Orientpolitik*, i. 15–20.
[50] Kedourie, *England and the Middle East*, 11–17.
[51] Yasamee, in Wilson (ed.), *Decisions for war*, 249–50.

banks. On 3 August the Ottoman treasury had only £Turkish 92,000 in cash.[52]
On the following day a moratorium was declared. Foreign loans dried up. But
the effects, although adverse, included an enforced economic independence.
On 5 September Enver proposed that Turkey default on its repayments to the
Ottoman public debt and to the Banque Perrier. Djavid was outraged. Instead,
on 8 September Turkey abrogated the capitulations and on 1 October, as
evidence of its freedom from great-power control, raised customs duties by 4
per cent and closed foreign post offices. This was one decision in which the
whole cabinet, not just a Young Turk clique, was involved. The assertion of
national sovereignty unleashed a wave of popular enthusiasm, both spontaneous and orchestrated. Flags appeared on shops and houses, a national festival
was announced, and the rhetoric of Turkism declaimed.[53]

Germany was as uncomfortable about Turkey's economic policy as were the
other powers. But, since the capitulations were only enforceable through great-
power collaboration, Germany and Austria-Hungary made no economic
sacrifice when they prudently supported the Ottoman decision. Moreover,
with trade at a virtual standstill the abrogation of the capitulations was of
political rather than financial significance. Turkey's need for cash was not
thereby averted. Britain's blockade made further temporizing hard to sustain.
Turkey had to choose between demobilization or bankruptcy, but the former
was as incompatible with robust neutrality as it was with active belligerence.
On 30 September Enver asked the Germans for a loan of £T 5 million in gold.
Bethmann Hollweg and Zimmerman wanted to make the loan conditional on
Turkey's entry into the war. Both sides had strong hands to play. The Turks
needed the money whatever their foreign policy; the Germans knew that the
Turks could not fight without their financial aid, given the Entente's effective
control of the Imperial Ottoman Bank. Wangenheim was still uncertain of the
wisdom of securing as an ally a power ostensibly prostrated by wars in Libya
and the Balkans. The foreign ministry, therefore, extracted Richard von Kühlmann from its Stockholm embassy and sent him to Constantinople, his birth-
place, specifically to get Turkey into the war.[54] At a meeting at the German
embassy on 11 October Enver, Talaat, Djemal, and Halil agreed that they would
authorize Admiral Souchon to attack the Russians in the Black Sea when the
Germans had deposited a first instalment of £T 2 million in Constantinople.
The balance would follow when Turkey was in the war.[55] Germany's stake in
Ottoman public finance thus began to grow at the Entente's expense. At the
same time the hesitations of those Turks convinced of Entente economic and
maritime superiority, especially Djemal, began to be undermined.

[52] Ahmad, in Kent, *Great powers*, 16.
[53] Ahmad, *Studies in Ottoman Diplomatic History*, IV (1990), 46–54.
[54] Kühlmann, *Erinnerungen*, 440–1,448.
[55] Trumpener, *Germany and the Ottoman empire*, 48–9, 51.

The idea that a foray by the *Goeben* and the *Breslau* into the Black Sea would mark the initiation of Turkish belligerence is the clearest indication of the significance of the two cruisers' escape for the development of the war. By the end of October the defence of Constantinople and the straits, the pivot of Turkey's communications, its naval base, and its economic and administrative centre, had been secured. Germany had sent both sailors and mines to upgrade the Dardanelles' defences. A defensive agreement with Bulgaria, settled on 18 August, although it had not included any alliance for offensive purposes in the Balkans and had done nothing, therefore, to alleviate the military position of Austria-Hungary, had reassured the Turks with regard to the landward approaches to the straits on the European side. But, three months after mobilization had begun the Turkish army was still not fit for offensive operations. Hafiz Hakki Bey, the deputy chief of staff, said that another six months were required, and argued that with winter approaching war was now impossible; on 4 October Enver even ordered token steps towards demobilization.[56] The fleet was no readier. Souchon was convinced that the British naval mission had deliberately undermined the fitness of the Turkish navy[57]—although the experience of the Germans with the army would suggest that the fault lay with the Turks themselves. The German cruisers therefore provided the most battleworthy means by which hostilities could be precipitated.

The frustrations of the German officers, stranded in Turkey while their colleagues fought in Europe, had mounted with their inactivity. Liman, isolated from Turko-German negotiations, had requested his return to Germany, albeit without success. Souchon similarly chafed at the incarceration of his cruisers. An early plan that he should be reinforced by the Austro-Hungarian fleet from Pola had come to nought on technical grounds. Berchtold's and Conrad's enthusiasm for a naval presence to help persuade Romania and Bulgaria into support for the Central Powers was countered by the lack of appropriate bases and fuel problems.[58] On 14 September Enver secretly authorized Souchon to enter the Black Sea, but on the 19th the government realized what was afoot. Souchon protested at this denial of his duties as a German officer, in other words, to engage the enemy. So on 24 September he became a Turkish officer with instructions not to undertake warlike acts without Turkish orders. Thus, when Souchon finally was allowed into the Black Sea the responsibility for what he did lay with Turkey and not Germany. Cruises of limited range by isolated vessels of the Turkish fleet were conducted without incident, largely because the Russians stayed in harbour in their anxiety to avoid provocation. But on 25 October Enver gave Souchon specific instructions to 'gain command of the Black Sea', and to seek out and attack the

---

[56] Yasamee, in Wilson (ed.), *Decisons for war*, 253–4.   [57] Halpern, *Naval war*, 49–50.
[58] Ibid. 19–20.

Russian fleet. The support of the Turkish cabinet for war was still far from certain, and what Enver had in mind may have been a manufactured incident on the high seas.[59] Souchon's own orders went further. On 29 October the Turkish fleet raided Sevastopol and Odessa, and bombarded Theodosia and Novorossisk. The damage inflicted on either side was minimal; certainly the opportunity to inflict a pre-emptive and disabling blow on the Russian Black Sea fleet had gone begging. But the political purport of the act was unequivocal.

With hindsight, Turkey's entry to the war was ordained from the moment it admitted the *Goeben* and the *Breslau* to the Dardanelles. The subsequent delay had been a product of Turkey's lack of war-readiness and of Bulgarian neutrality, not of uncertainty in regard to its eventual policy.[60] But an observer in Constantinople on the days subsequent to Souchon's attack still felt that the overall disposition of the government was against belligerence, and that the Russian response to the attack—a request for the removal of the German naval and military missions—gave Turkey an option for peace which a majority wished to exercise.[61] Enver's orders to Souchon had been known beforehand to Talaat and Djemal; indeed, it was the winning of the latter from his pro-Entente stance that proved crucial to Enver's resolve. But the triumvirate was sufficiently conscious of its numerical weakness in the cabinet to sidestep the request that the latter convene on 29 October. Instead, Talaat contrived that the government should meet with the central committee of the more bellicose Committee of Union and Progress on 30 October. Enver had anticipated a government crisis, and in particular the opposition of Said Halim, the grand vizier, and Djavid. They and three other ministers resigned, but then gave in to the pressure of the central committee, which supported the war by seventeen votes to ten. Some of the support for neutrality did not represent a predilection for peace per se; it was grounded on the army's continuing low estimate of its combat-readiness.[62] Thus, even the lines in the debate for peace or war were not clear cut. Governmental unity was sustained by the dispatch of a conciliatory, albeit—in its account of Souchon's attack—fictitious note to Russia on 1 November. Said Halim's inclination was still to resign: Enver's and Talaat's pressure, probably not gentle, ensured that he did not. Their hold on government was not so secure, their power not so untrammelled, that they could afford to do without him. Their achievement was considerable. Djavid and three other opponents of intervention did go, and Enver was able to exaggerate the size of the anti-war lobby in order to increase his leverage on Germany. But

---

[59] Wallach, *Anatomie einer Militärhilfe*, 165–6; Trumpener, *Germany and the Ottoman empire*, 53–5.
[60] Mühlmann, *Deutschland und der Türkei*, 64–5.
[61] Pomiankowski, *Zusammenbruch*, 87.
[62] Kurat, in Bourne and Watt (eds.), *Studies*, 311–14; more generally, Trumpener, *Germany and the Ottoman empire*, 56–61, and id., *Journal of Modern History*, XXXIV (1962), 369–80.

in effect Turkey embraced a war united in its government and in its purpose; neutralism before the war did not spill over into lack of patriotic resolve during it.

The Ottoman empire therefore entered the First World War through its own devices, and in pursuit of its own interests. It was neither the innocent pawn in Germany's more ambitious concepts, nor the victim of Russian and British imperialism. A combination of rationality—represented by Djemal, and arguing that the costs of neutrality had ceased to make the latter a sensible option—and emotion—represented by Enver, and fusing pan-Turanianism with nationalistic fervour—made a strong domestic argument in favour of intervention. But Turkey's commitment notwithstanding, it is also true that neither Germany nor Britain in the end acted to stop Turkey. This failure was born of the circumstances generated by the onset of the war itself rather than of the long-term agents for Ottoman decline.

More problematic is the question of Russian responsibility. Russia's policy in the first half of 1914 had become unwontedly conciliatory towards Constantinople, and its strategic interests in the second half demanded a concentration on the European front, not on the Caucasus. The arrival of the *Goeben* and the *Breslau* had renewed the threat of naval inferiority which the Turks' pursuit of Dreadnoughts had already promised for the years 1914 to 1916. On paper the *Goeben* could outrun and outfight the Black Sea fleet: her broadside was as heavy as that of all three Russian pre-Dreadnoughts combined. Sazonov's diplomatic instructions confirmed Stavka's prudence (if not the fleet commander's inclination), and contrasted with the response of the British navy on the other side of the straits: the Black Sea fleet was not to provoke Souchon nor to challenge the fiction of his ships' neutrality. But Russia's ambitions to control the straits had been fostered by its own brand of navalism and by the long-term plans for the build-up of the Black Sea fleet.[63] The determination that if Turkey did not control the Dardanelles Russia should was reawoken by the boost to partition provided after the Turko-German alliance. Turkey's closure of the straits at the end of September re-emphasized Russia's economic vulnerability. Thus, while Russian policy still favoured Turkish neutrality, Russian sentiment greeted war against Turkey with acclaim. From the Entente's viewpoint, the dangers that Russia's efforts on the eastern front might be distracted by Turkey were offset by the consequent hardening of Russia's commitment to the war itself.

Russia's handling of the developments of September and October had been significantly aided by decrypts of the signals between Pallavicini and the foreign ministry in Vienna. It had passed the contents of these to London, but the impression of imminent Turkish belligerence which they conveyed was at odds with the more reassuring reports from Mallet and from Britain's military attaché in Constantinople, Francis Cunliffe-Owen. Britain did not appreciate that it was receiving top-grade political intelligence until 20 October.[64] Thereafter its expectation of war with Turkey meant that Souchon's attack caused little surprise. Together with France, Britain broke off diplomatic relations with Turkey on 30 October. On the next day Churchill, cock-a-hoop, signalled the commencement of hostilities, and ordered the bombardment of the Dardanelles. Technically Britain and Turkey were not yet at war, and indeed Sazonov's reply to the Turkish note did leave open the possibility of negotiation. On 2 November Russia declared war, and on 3 November Carden opened fire on the outer fortifications of the Dardanelles. On 4 November Grey was still hoping to postpone Britain's war with Turkey, but the Royal Navy's actions had forced the hand of the Foreign Office, and indeed of the cabinet. On 5 November both Britain and France followed Russia's lead.[65]

TURKEY'S CAPACITY FOR WAR

'Turkey is militarily a nonentity! . . . If Turkey was described before as a sick man, it must now be described as a dying man . . . Our military mission is like a medical board, that stands by the deathbed of a hopeless invalid.'[66] These were the words with which Moltke had assessed the military capacities of his new allies when writing to Conrad on 13 March 1914. But within days of 2 August both chiefs of the general staff were sketching out offensives for this 'dying man' that simultaneously embraced the Caucasus, Bessarabia, Odessa, and the Suez Canal. Rational assessment was prey to wishful thinking: once again the push to extremes—world power or decline, annihilating victory or defeat— failed to include the possibility of a middle way. The Turkish army was a far more potent force than Moltke's March 1914 assessment allowed for: by the beginning of 1916 it had achieved major defensive victories; throughout the war it would tie down large numbers of British and Russian troops; the Dardanelles would remain closed to Entente traffic; and Turkey's defeat would come no sooner than that of Germany itself. But equally, the Turkish army was not a finely honed instrument well adapted for modern war, and nor was the Turkish economy sufficiently advanced to support it even if it had been.

[64] Sheffy, *British military intelligence*, 90.
[65] David, *Inside Asquith's cabinet*, 205; Gilbert, *Churchill*, iii. 215–19; Miller, *Straits*, 326–30.
[66] Wallach, *Anatomie einer Militärhilfe*, 150; see also Mühlmann, *Oberste Heeresleitung und Balkan*, 22–3.

   The army to which Liman von Sanders was appointed in January 1914 was a
bewildering blend of the new and the unreformed. One historian of modern
Turkey has written of officers 'with up-to-date training for an out-of-date
army'.[67] But even this oversimplifies the issues. Abdul Hamid had opposed
modernization for fear of the army's potential role in domestic politics. In von
der Goltz's day the activities of the German military mission were circumscribed, its pressure for reform contained. The effect was to channel the
Germans' efforts into military education, and specifically into the service
academies. In the 1890s up to twenty young officers a year had gone to
Germany for further tuition. Finally, in 1907, six model battalions under
German-trained Turkish officers were established for the instruction of officers
and NCOs. Two main consequences accrued. First, at least until 1907, training
was theoretical rather than practical, confined to the classroom and the
barrack-yard. Secondly, its beneficiaries were regimental officers, not generals.
Only once, in 1894, was von der Goltz allowed to conduct a staff ride. The
formation of the model battalions confirmed the generational division within
the officer corps.[68]
   The frustrations of internal policing, which had fostered the army's politicization despite Abdul Hamid's best endeavours, and the aftermath of the 1908
revolution served to deepen this split. The older generation, pre-eminently
Sevket himself, argued that the army's political role was disinterested, finite,
and above party. Some of the younger generation, notably Mustafa Kemal
(later Ataturk), agreed in principle but acted very differently in practice; many
identified with the Unionists. Thus, to professional fissures were now added
political differences.
   Most officers, whatever their age, liked to see their loyalties as Ottoman
rather than Turkish. After all, many were Macedonian in origin or had found
in Macedonia the forcing ground for their political and professional motivations. In reality, the supra-national ideal found only weak expression within
the army. Although the latent conflict between Ottomanization and Turkification was no more explicit than it was elsewhere, it was not possible for either
idea to provide the means to reunify the officer corps. The conscription law of
1886 made all male Muslims aged over 20 liable for three years' active service
and for a total of seventeen in the various categories of reserve.[69] But Kurds,
Arabs, nomads, and the inhabitants of Constantinople were all exempt. Thus,
less than half the population was eligible for service, and its burden fell
disproportionately on the Anatolian peasant. A revised recruitment law introduced in 1912 and promulgated in May 1914 embraced non-Muslims who did
not pay taxes (but not those who did). It posited an army of 1.2 million men,

[67] B. Lewis, *Modern Turkey*, 201.   [68] Wallach, *Anatomie einer Militärhilfe*, 64–89.
[69] Shaw and Shaw, *Ottoman empire*, ii. 245–6.

but as only two of its twenty-five annual classes served in the active army the regulars' peacetime establishment was set at 200,000. The lack of population registers for many parts of the country made evasion easy. Non-appearance meant that the actual strength was probably nearer 150,000, rising on mobilization to 800,000, or only about 4 per cent of the population. Sevket simplified the arrangements for mobilizing the massive number of reservists required to flesh out this diminutive force by introducing a regional corps organization. He established four army 'inspections' (Constantinople, Erzincan, Damascus, and Baghdad) and a total of thirteen corps, each of whose divisions (thirty-six in all) recruited locally.[70] But thus was Ottomanization forfeit. Furthermore, the army did not even have a common language. Only 40 per cent of the total population spoke Turkish; Said Halim, the grand vizier, could not write it. The script was a problem, particularly for the transmission of orders by telegraph. It took four different forms, and—because the Turks wrote Arabic and Persian words phonetically—the spelling lacked standardization. The Young Turks, partly to ease commercial transactions and partly through their support for Turkification, were committed to the standardization and Latinization of the language. Enver, when he became minister of war, struggled to introduce into the army a common form of Arabic, but by the second year of the war had to abandon the attempt.[71]

Sevket was the dominant figure in the army's reform between 1909 and 1913. The suppression of the so-called 'counter-revolution' of 1909 was the first step in the elimination of the older generation of officers, and it was his authority that papered over the political and professional fissures of the officer corps.[72] His initial aim was simply to make good the perceived deprivations of the Hamidian era. As minister of war in 1910 he refused to allow his department's budget to be subject to the ministry of finance's controls, and successfully demanded an extraordinary credit of £T5 million as well as an ordinary budget of £T9.5 million.[73] Modern equipment was ordered from Germany. But in 1912 either this had yet to be delivered or Turkish soldiers had still to be trained in its use; thus, not only was the Turkish army defeated, the empire's foreign indebtedness was increased. Sevket, now grand vizier, rethought his approach. He aimed for financial retrenchment. His assumption in 1913 was that Turkey would not face war for some time. Its immediate target should therefore be a small, professional army, capable of expansion in case of crisis—hence the 1914

---

[70] Larcher, *La Guerre turque*, 65–6; Erik Zürcher, 'Little Mehmet in the desert: the Ottoman soldier's experience', in Cecil and Liddle (eds.), *Facing Armageddon*, 232–3; Sheffy, *British military intelligence*, 34; Ahmad, *Kurdistan*, 52–3.

[71] Emin, *Turkey in the World War*, 225–6; Bihl, *Kaukasuspolitik*, 140, 153, 158, 161, 200; Guse, *Kaukasusfront*, 18.

[72] Haley, *Middle Eastern Studies*, XXX (1994), 17–18, 23.

[73] Ahmad, *Young Turks*, 68–74.

recruitment law and the corps organization.[74] Enver continued on the same lines. The War Ministry's budget for 1914/15 showed a 30 per-cent cut, partly achieved by lowering the soldier's pay. His attention was on increasing the pace of mobilization through the improvement of roads and through the training of reservists. In February 1914 he reckoned that the army would be fit for war in five years.[75]

It is customary, when explaining Turkey's military performance in the First World War, to set it in the context of the two Balkan wars, to argue that Turkey was at war continuously from 1912, or even—if the rebellions in the Yemen, Lebanon, Albania, and Macedonia are included—from 1910. Thus, by 1918 the empire was militarily exhausted. But this interpretation misses the point. The experience of the Balkan wars proved crucial to the reform and reinvigoration of the Turkish army. The major problems that Turkey encountered in embarking on a fresh war in 1914 were less the consequence of economic strain than of the fact that the transformation of the army initiated by Sevket was incomplete, that the army was caught between having partially abandoned one system and having not yet fully embraced another. Furthermore, the war for which this army was being prepared in 1913 was presumed not only to be more distant in time than 1914, but also to be a Balkan, not a world war.

When Turkey opted for intervention its army was indeed ill-equipped. It was short of 280 guns and 200,000 rifles; it had only 150 small-arms rounds per man, and 1,088 shells per gun. Lack of animals deprived it of mobility. The Anatolian horse was too small for the cavalry, which was 20 per cent below its establishment, and too weak for the draught of artillery; the low number of pack horses had been reduced yet further by the depredations of the Balkan wars. Efforts in the 1890s to form an irregular Hamidieh cavalry from the Turkoman and Kurdish tribes had floundered after 1909: the lack of horses meant that half of them were in fact infantry. Even more problematic than their locomotion were their loyalties. Raising men eroded the authority of the tribal chiefs, and those they procured were largely motivated by hatred of the Armenians; nearer the Persian frontier their sympathies frequently lay with Russia.[76] For the army as a whole, as significant as lack of stocks and lack of horses was lack of standardization. Some of the Turkish army's equipment was excellent: they had Mauser magazine-rifles and French 75 mm quick-firing field guns. But within the same units were found weapons of different bores, and different vintages, and different nationalities. The Mausers were of two calibres, and alongside them were single-shot Martinis. The heavy artillery was antiquated; Turkey's field guns came from Schneider in France, its field howitzers from Krupp in Germany, and its mountain artillery from Skoda in

[74] Djemal, *Memoirs*, 67.
[75] Ahmad, *Young Turks*, 68–74; Pokrowski, *Die internationalen Beziehungen*, series 1, ii. 61–3, 193–4.
[76] Ahmad, *Kurdistan*, 53–8.

Austria-Hungary. The supply services, already primitive, were presented with a logistical problem far more complex than that of any of the major European powers. Turkey's equipment problems were characterized as much by the transitional stage of its modernization as by the exhaustion of the Balkan wars.[77]

Furthermore, not until January 1914, and the appointment of Enver as minister of war, were the professional and political splits of the officer corps properly addressed. The need to neutralize the army politically, to force officers to choose between membership of the army and membership of the Committee of Union and Progress, had been recognized by Sevket and advocated by a group of younger officers, including Mustafa Kemal.[78] In addition, the Balkan defeats had highlighted the incompetence of many senior officers. But Sevket was assassinated and Izzet Pasha, minister of war in 1913, proved reluctant to execute the purge of the officer corps widely recognized as essential. This, therefore, was Enver's major task on appointment. At a stroke he removed both military inefficiency and political opposition from the army. The total number of officers dismissed is variously given, with figures ranging from 200 to 2,000, and a safe average would be over 1,000. Most generals aged over 55 were out; so too were those promoted from the ranks without professional education; young majors found themselves in command of regiments, lieutenant-colonels in charge of divisions. Many German observers argued that Enver had done no more than buoy up his own political position, and that the current of promotion was still determined—and continued to be throughout the war—by political favouritism. But they missed the point. Enver did use the army as his political base; his 'Special Organization', or *Teskilat-i Mahsusa*, formed in 1914, was a secret service responsible to him alone and funded by the war ministry. Built on the experience of terrorist and guerrilla operations in Macedonia and Libya, it became the vehicle for his political objectives, foreign and domestic, pan-Islamic and pan-Turkic.[79] But in the army as a whole ability was not placed second to political reliability; Kemal himself, whose calls for the army's political neutrality were in reality cloaks for his own enormous ambition, and who was opposed to Turkish intervention in the war, was not a victim of Enver's purge. What German officers were often reacting to was less politicization per se than democracy; officers from humble backgrounds, without the breeding or the aristocratic pretensions of German officers, and schooled by the events of 1908 to 1913, seemed lacking in the sense of duty and personal honour which German observers expected.[80]

[77] Larcher, *La Guerre turque*, 70; Muzaffar Erendil, 'The Ottoman empire in World War I', in Kiraly *et al.* (eds.), *East Central European society*, 371–2; Shaw and Shaw, *Ottoman empire*, 246.
[78] G. Dyer, *Journal of Contemporary History*, VIII (1973), 125–33.
[79] D. Rustow, *World Politics*, XI (1959), 518–19; Zürcher, *Unionist factor*, 50, 59, 83.
[80] Schulte, *Vor dem Kriegsausbruch*, 131–5; Guse, *Kaukasusfront*, 21, gives a different view from his compatriots.

Enver's refashioning of the army's officer corps masked the commencement of an assumption of overall strategic control that was completed by the autumn. His friends dubbed him 'Napoleonlik'; Pomiankowski, the Austrian military attaché, called him a dilettante. Both descriptions were merited, but neither was true. Enver's ambitions, both for himself and for Turkey, were Napoleonic; his abilities—at least as a commander—were not. A 'matinee idol', in the words of the American ambassador Henry Morgenthau, Enver also impressed another advocate of action rather than reflection, Winston Churchill, who described him as 'A charming fellow—vy good looking & thoroughly capable'.[81] Enver's self-belief derived from his successful organization of the defence of Libya; significantly, he had not even won that campaign, but he had established the infrastructure for a protracted defence. His strengths were administrative rather than operational. The war ministry was the basis of his political power both domestically and internationally; his mastery of it was what forced the Germans, hitherto wedded to the older, Hamidian generation of officers, to take him seriously. As Francis Cunliffe-Owen, Britain's military attaché, observed, Enver made his department 'as up to date in its methods as the *Kriegsministerium*'.[82] During the course of the year the range of Enver's responsibilities rapidly expanded. The committee of national defence, created by the Committee of Union and Progress in 1911 in response to the invasion of Libya, and taken formally within the purview of government after the coup of January 1913, was placed under the ministry of war. Reflecting the rhetoric of the French Revolution and charged with social and economic mobilization for war, it gave Enver a role in agriculture, industry, commerce, and education.[83] The arrival of the *Goeben* and the *Breslau*, and the consequent de facto subordination of the navy to German control, weakened the hold on the fleet of Djemal, the minister of marine. Not until September was Limpus's naval mission asked to leave; thus, Souchon's dealings were with Enver, and Djemal's role became secondary. With the outbreak of war Djemal went to Syria as military governor and commander of the 4th army, delegating the daily running of his ministry to Enver. Meanwhile, on 21 October 1914 the Sultan became titular commander-in-chief, and appointed Enver as his deputy. Enver thus gathered into his hands responsibility for both services, and for command as well as administration.

The transformation of the Turkish army between 1913 and 1914, therefore, owed much more to Sevket and to Enver than it did to Liman von Sanders. This was not, in fact, what Sevket had intended. He had planned 'a German military mission on the grand scale', thus giving the Germans the real influence

---

[81] Morgenthau, *Ambassador Morgenthau's story*, 31–2; Soames (ed.), *Speaking for themselves*, 31; generally, Haley, *Middle Eastern Studies*, XXX (1994), 1–51, 224–51, esp. 1–15.

[82] Miller, *Straits*, 178.

[83] Ahmad, 'War and society under the Young Turks', 128–32.

which the Hamidian regime had denied them. But his plan 'to appoint a German general to command a Turkish army corps, and to have German staff and regimental officers in command of every unit comprising it, and in this way form a model army corps',[84] fell foul of the diplomatic crisis generated by the German mission. Liman was appointed inspector-general of the Turkish army. Therefore his orbit was restricted almost immediately on arrival. His main efforts were channelled into improving conditions of service. This suited Enver very well. The new minister of war was as impressed as Sevket by German military methods; the Turkish general staff was reorganized on the German model, with three sections for each of operations, intelligence, and railways; and a German, Bronsart von Schellendorf, was appointed its chief. But Enver was equally determined that the Turkish army should be employed in the Turkish national interest, not in that of Germany. The German military mission had risen to a strength of seventy by the summer of 1914. Its task, however, remained advisory and technical. Germans became chiefs of staff; they did not command.

Furthermore, temperamentally Liman and Enver found themselves at odds. By the end of the war Liman had proved himself an able commander and a sympathetic judge of Turkish troops. But he antagonized many of his colleagues. One of his German subordinates in Turkey, Kress von Kressenstein, described him as 'self-confident and conceited, temperamental and hot-tempered, mistrustful and sensitive'.[85] He had been judged unsuitable for a corps command in Germany. Thus, status was to Liman an important aspect of his Turkish service. But he was then undercut by Enver's appointment as minister of war. Deprived of the coveted corps by diplomatic pressure, he had to be promoted a general of cavalry in the German army and a marshal in the Turkish army as consolation. This preoccupation with rank and rewards, combined with his prior commitment to Germany's, rather than Turkey's needs, provided the basis for a series of clashes with the equally explosive character of Enver.

In sum, the influence of the German military mission was marginalized. Liman played only a minor part in the negotiations leading to the Turkish alliance and then to Turkish intervention. He had no co-ordinating role in German strategy in Turkey. Indeed, the divisions between German departments played a major part in strengthening Enver's hand; Wangenheim and Liman bypassed each other; Souchon, Admiral Usedom (the officer sent out to improve the Dardanelles' defences in September), and the military and naval attachés all reported independently to Berlin. Paragraph 3 of the Turko-German treaty of 2 August stated that in the event of war the military

[84] Djemal, *Memoirs*, 67.
[85] Wallach, *Anatomie einer Militärhilfe*, 137; see also Haley, *Middle Eastern Studies*, XXX (1994), 30–4, 40–2.

mission would be left at Turkey's disposal, and that relations between the head of the mission and the Turkish war minister would be direct and so established as to have 'an effective influence on the general conduct of the army'. Bethmann Hollweg interpreted this clause as giving the military mission the supreme Turkish command in all but name. What actually happened was that Liman was appointed to the command of the 1st army in Thrace. The German presence at Turkish GHQ was headed by Bronsart von Schellendorff, as Enver's chief of staff.

Bronsart was responsible for such war planning as Turkey had achieved by October 1914, and for its mobilization plan. The fact that both were chaotic may be an indictment of Bronsart, or of his ability to stand up to Enver: the winter campaign in the Caucasus in 1914–15 would support such judgements. The Austrian military attaché called him 'petty, excessively nervous, glory-seeking and an intriguer'.[86] But even the most able staff officer would have had difficulty resolving the problems with which Bronsart was confronted. The war plan, which he drew up on 4 July 1914, reflected priorities in Turkish foreign policy: it concentrated on a war with Russia in the area of the Dardanelles and the Bosphorus, and on a possible conflict in the Balkans. Turkey would adopt a defensive posture in the Caucasus and would redeploy the troops in Palestine and Mesopotamia to Anatolia.[87] What happened between August and November was that a world war was grafted onto a Balkan war. Turkish plans grew accordingly, but the basic assumption—that the major concentration should be around Constantinople—was not altered.

Moltke's enthusiasm for the Turkish alliance rested not so much on the aid it could provide in the Balkans as on its ability to distract Russia and Britain. At a meeting on 16 August the representatives of the German military mission discussed with Enver and Hafiz Hakki, the deputy chief of staff, the possibilities for amphibious operations in the Black Sea and for a thrust against the Suez Canal. The orders for the 2nd army in Syria and VIII army corps in Palestine to move to Anatolia were revoked; instead, both were earmarked for the Egyptian offensive, and two divisions from Mesopotamia, also originally destined for Anatolia, were given the task of parrying any British landing in northern Syria. By mid-September the German sailors, Souchon and von Usedom, were dismissive of landings on the Black Sea coast: the Turks would need to defeat the Russian fleet first, but without the ability to blockade the Russian ports they would not be able to force the Russian navy to battle. They, together with Wangenheim, therefore favoured a concentration against the British in Egypt. Liman von Sanders was opposed: if the army protected the straits it would at least guard the navy's back and so give Souchon the freedom

[86] Bihl, *Kaukasuspolitik*, 223.
[87] Erendil, in Kiraly *et al* (eds.), *East Central European society*, 372; Sheffy, *British military intelligence*, 35.

to fight for control of the Black Sea. Enver agreed; on 22 October he accepted that Bulgaria's failure to ally itself with Turkey meant that considerable forces should remain in Thrace. But at the same time he did not renounce the offensive in Egypt, and moreover he declared his support for operations in the Caucasus.[88] His response to German pressure, and his anxiety to assert Turkish worth, led him to produce an inclusive list rather than to establish priorities.

Therefore, the mobilization ordered on 2 August lacked a clear operational focus and was carried out by an army in the throes of reorganization. When the orders went out the full instructions for mobilization under the terms of the 1914 recruitment law were not yet issued. In their peacetime state divisions were formed of six or nine battalions, totalling 5,000 or 6,200 men; many units were in fact under establishment, some companies mustering only twenty soldiers. Those aged 23 to 30, the reservists who were to complete the active corps, and those aged 30 to 38, who were to form corps depots, were ordered to report within three days. Even the disabled were to attend, in order to have their disability registered. Units were then doubled in size. The economic crisis of August, with overseas trade suspended, boosted unemployment and provided a ready reservoir of manpower. But the army could not cope with the influx. The reservists were told to bring food for three days. Thereafter there were insufficient rations for the swollen battalions. The local population, its economic life already shattered by the loss of the adult male population, was plundered for food. The only financial compensation was to the state, which at least received the payments of those able to buy themselves out. The purge in the officer corps had, as result of the consequent acceleration in promotion, created gaps in the junior ranks; the NCOs of the Turkish army were mostly re-enlisted men, peasants, frequently illiterate and lacking in initiative. Thus, old methods of training were mixed up with new. In September the territorials, those aged 38 to 45, were called up; in October they were sent home again. By the end of October full Turkish mobilization was still not implemented, but there was a danger that the strains it imposed would cause its collapse before its completion.[89]

Enver's attention, reflecting the original war plan, had been on the assembly of the 1st and 2nd armies (a total of 200,000 men) around Constantinople, and of the 3rd army (120,000 men) around Erzerum, facing the Caucasus. The transport system was sufficient to move 10,000 reservists a day, and therefore the concentration of the whole army would take between four and five months.

[88] Mühlmann, *Deutschland und der Türkei*, 101–2; Macfie, *End of the Ottoman empire*, 124; Sheffy, *British military intelligence*, 35–6; Miller, *Straits*, 307–8, 321.

[89] Larcher, *La Guerre turque*, 66–7; Emin, *Turkey in the World War*, 107–8; Aaronsohn, *With the Turks*, 16–23; Miller, *Straits*, 237. On its impact in Mesopotamia, see Moukbil, *La Campagne de l'Irak*, 11–15; and in Kurdistan, see Ahmad, *Kurdistan*, 133–6.

When Turkey went to war its southern borders, the responsibility of the 4th army in Syria and of four divisions in Iraq, were still not covered. The security of the south was rendered secondary to the needs of the north. Iraq in particular was used as a reserve for the other fronts, three of its four divisions going to reinforce the 4th army in Syria and the 3rd in the Caucasus. And yet, thanks to Indian Expeditionary Force D, the first Turkish soldiers engaged in action were the diminutive garrison at Fao on the Persian Gulf. Furthermore the southern areas, because of their distance from Constantinople, had been those least affected by the German military mission and other reforming agencies; pay was frequently in arrears, and Arab disaffection (albeit at this stage exaggerated) created doubts about the troops' loyalty.

The fact that Britain and France, as well as Russia, were at war with Turkey transformed the Ottoman empire's strategic position. Its extended coastline, with its accessibility to naval power, its joint frontier with British-controlled Egypt, and the Government of India's interests in Mesopotamia meant that the entire perimeter lay under potential threat. The concentration planned in July, in Turkey's north-western corner, had by November to be balanced with the defensive needs—and the offensive possibilities—at each of its other apexes, in the north-east and the Caucasus, in the south-west and the Suez Canal, and in the south-east and Iraq. The ability to concentrate rapidly, to exploit interior lines in order to be able to transfer troops from one sector to another, would be pivotal to Turkey's ability to wage war. Turkey had an elaborate telegraph system but no efficient means of internal transportation.

Before the war much of Turkey's traffic was carried around its perimeter, by sea. But the British had instituted a blockade in the Mediterranean even before the declaration of hostilities, and Russia began to assert its dominance over the Black Sea during the course of 1915. Therefore the difficulties of the land communications, masked before the war, were exposed. Turkish railway construction between 1888 and 1914 showed an impressive rate of growth, from 1,780 kilometres of track to about 5,800, but its density—for 1.76 million square kilometres of territory—remained sadly deficient.[90]

Furthermore, from the military perspective the situation was even worse than the crude statistics suggested. In May 1914 Major Theodor von Kubel reported that the railways in Iraq and Anatolia required an investment of 100 million marks in order to bring them up to military needs.[91] Von Kubel's recall, as a consequence of the ensuing fracas with the Deutsche Bank's railway subsidiaries, highlighted the commercial priorities that underpinned even German railway construction. Each nation built according to its own local

---

[90] On Turkey's railways, see esp. Trumpener, *Germany and the Ottoman Empire*, ch. 9; Larcher, *La Guerre Turque*, 57–9; W. Stanley, *Journal of Transport History*, VIII (1966), 189–204; Mühlmann, *Das deutsch-türkische Waffenbündnis*, 31–4.

[91] Wallach, *Anatomie einer Militärhilfe*, 148–9.

needs, establishing not an Ottoman network but a juxtaposition of single-track links, of different gauges, without interconnections. The fact that Constantinople, the potential hub of a railway system had there been one, was on the periphery of Turkey confirmed the inappropriateness of the routes for the purposes of national defence. Such military needs as were served by the railways were for the movement of troops from Asia Minor to European Turkey, not for a two-way flow across the Asiatic heartland of the empire.

Thus, of the four major fronts envisaged by Enver in his 22 October memorandum only the Balkan and the Constantinople areas were adequately provided for. Deliberately neglected, in deference to Russian objections on strategic grounds, was eastern Anatolia. The nearest railheads were Ulu Kischla, north of the Taurus Mountains, and Tell Ebiad, east of the Euphrates, 700 and 400 kilometres respectively from Erzurum, itself some distance from the frontier and the putative battle-front.

Syria was better endowed, and superficially seemed to be well adapted for a push towards Egypt. But British and French efforts in the regions had been designed to link the Mediterranean ports to commercial centres inland, and not to provide a north–south connection. Thus Jerusalem was linked to Jaffa, but there was no line south to Beersheba, and that to the north and to the Haifa–Damascus line was begun but not complete. Further east, the line from Damascus through Maan to Medina, the Hejaz railway intended to transport pilgrims to the holy cities, was narrow gauge, and between Tebuk and El Ala had to carry its own water (in addition to the water for the troops in the blockhouses guarding the line), so reducing its capacity.

During the course of the war the lines within Palestine were reorganized, redirected, and extended with comparative speed. But the whole theatre of operations remained isolated from Constantinople by the breaks in the southern Anatolian section of the line in the Taurus and Amanus mountains, northwest of Aleppo. When war was declared 37 kilometres were still to be cut through the Taurus range and twelve tunnels were required: not until January 1917 was a narrow-gauge link effected, and not until September 1918 was this upgraded to a standard gauge. The Amanus link was 97 kilometres long, and was completed early in 1917. Until then all equipment for not only the Syrian but also the Mesopotamian fronts had to be unloaded and reloaded twice, and had to be carried by pack animal or by human labour across the two ranges. Those disqualified on religious or national grounds from military service formed labour and porter battalions, numbering 110,000 men as early as October 1914.[92] Each 100-kilometre stretch across the mountain ranges was—by late 1915—allocated 3,500 to 4,000 baggage animals—camels, buffaloes, and horses. But the standard of veterinary care was appalling: sixty

---

[92] Bihl, *Kaukasuspolitik*, 193.

to seventy died each day. Furthermore, the retired officers of the Hamidian army, pressed back into service for duties in the rear, proved limited and slothful, leaving their NCOs to manage matters and to sell the camels to the neighbouring Kurds.[93]

The Taurus and Amanus links were not the only incomplete sections in the celebrated Berlin–Baghdad railway line. A total of 825 kilometres of track was still to be laid in August 1914. The Euphrates bridge near Djerablus was not finished; from Tell Ebiad to Samara, north of Baghdad, only the first 103 kilometres to Ras el Ain had been begun, and by the war's end the line had been extended 200 kilometres from Tell Ebiad to Nisibin. The 1903 agreement with the Turkish government was increasingly squeezing the Baghdad railway company's profits as operating costs rose, thus reducing the capital available for further investment. Labour was lost not only through the mobilization of the army but also because the workers were not paid. The war worsened the company's financial position, as military needs ousted commercial traffic but military goods were only charged one-third the standard rate. In 1914 the company registered a 1.2 million franc loss, and in 1915 1.7 million francs, while the Turkish government netted 8 million francs. In November 1914 the company reckoned that a forced construction programme could complete the Taurus and Amanus sections in April 1916, and the Iraq section in May 1917. But the German government was slow to interpret the line in strategic terms rather than economic. It had to accept that the war was going to be sufficiently long for the imperatives for completion to be military. Not until March 1915 was OHL convinced by the German foreign ministry of the military import-ance of the line. Then the Turks themselves proved reluctant to support what they saw as the furtherance of German interests. Negotiations with Turkey over the terms of a German government loan to aid construction continued throughout the war without reaching a conclusion. By 1917 the Baghdad railway company was effectively bankrupt, setting its accumulated losses since 1914 at 6 million marks. It was saved in July by the German government, which provided a prepayment of 100 million marks secured in Baghdad rail-way bonds and most of the company's shares. The solution, intended as an interim one pending fresh negotiations with the Turks over the revenue arangements, fell foul of the intransigence of the Ottoman government. By the end of the war the German government had diverted a total of 360 million marks towards the line.[94]

Initially, however, it was not the Turkish section of the Berlin–Baghdad railway line that gave cause for major concern but the European. On 6 August 1914 Enver asked the Germans for half-a-million artillery shells and 200,000

[93] de Nogales, *Four years beneath the crescent*, 164–7.
[94] Trumpener, *German and the Ottoman Empire*, ch. 9; Feldman, *Deutsche Bank*, 141–4.

rifles. The Turkish shopping list lengthened as mobilization proceeded: mines, howitzers, trucks, electrical equipment, and even boots, blankets, and uniforms were requested. Progressively more pressing were the demands for German coal. In 1911–12 Turkey produced 700,000 tonnes of coal from its mines at Eregli; the balance of its needs, 421,000 tonnes, were imported, 88 per cent from Britain.[95] In September 1914 British imports ceased. Turkey's own production in that year reached 651,240 tonnes; in 1915 it fell to 420,317 tonnes, and in 1917 to 146,000. Such coal as there was did not necessarily reach its major consumers—the city of Constantinople and the railways themselves.[96] Before the war the coal had been shipped from Sunguldak in the Black Sea to the Bosphorus; from late 1914 the Russians mounted a blockade on the port and bombarded its facilities. The Turks were not able to use the *Goeben* and the *Breslau* to break the blockade, principally because if the *Goeben* was employed as an escort she consumed almost as much coal as the colliers could carry.[97] Nonetheless, the blockade was not sustained continuously; the bombardments, for all that there were twenty-five, including an air raid, were not definitive.[98] Thus, coastal traffic continued to trickle through at a rate sufficient to deprive of urgency pressure for a railway to link Sunguldak to Turkey's interior. Opponents of the line argued that coastal traffic would make any line redundant with the advent of peace. Thus, both Turkey's major sources of fuel, Britain and Eregli, were affected by the outbreak of war.

Broadly speaking, Germany was willing to provide its ally with coal and munitions. But with Serbia undefeated, the Berlin–Constantinople line passed through Romania and Bulgaria, both still neutral. The route was mostly single track, and at Giurgevo goods had to be unloaded, taken across the Danube by barge, and reloaded at Rustchuk. However, the technical difficulties were second to the political. Initially Romania co-operated with Germany, albeit with restrictions, allowing no more than eight freight cars a day. In September the Romanian attitude became stickier, and by 17 September only thirty-three of 116 cars sent by Krupp had passed through Romania. On 2 October the Romanian government finally stopped all shipments to Turkey.[99] The Germans tried every possible way of reopening the route; they considered shipments down the Danube in the teeth of Serb artillery; plans to airlift goods by Zeppelin foundered on the weight of the load and on the lack of facilities for airships in Turkey; one scheme suggested the release of forty balloons in south Hungary when the wind was favourable.[100] Ultimately there was no real

[95] Larcher, *La Guerre turque*, 603.
[96] Bihl, *Kaukasuspolitik*, 204.
[97] Neulen, *Feldgrau in Jerusalem*, 43.
[98] Allen and Muratoff, *Caucasian battlefields*, 550–2; Nekrasov, *North of Gallipoli*, 26, 36.
[99] Trumpener, *Journal of Modern History*, XXXII (1960), 145–9.
[100] Mühlmann, *Das deutsche-türkische Waffenbündnis*, 48–9.

solution other than the defeat of Serbia. Not until 17 January 1916 would the first train from Berlin pull into Constantinople. By and large Turkey conducted its first year of operations with its own resources.

The victories which the Ottoman army secured at Gallipoli and at Kut, therefore, provide further confirmation that material exhaustion after the Balkan wars was not such a major factor affecting Turkey's fighting capacity. Even the railway problems of the southern parts of the empire should not be exaggerated—at least for 1915: the inhospitability of the terrain, the problems of water and of supply, kept armies in those regions relatively small irrespective of the limitations imposed by railway capacities. Much more important was the fact that the Turkish army, thanks principally to Sevket and Enver, had been reforged in 1913 and 1914 sufficiently to sustain major operations with success in 1915.

Virtually lost amidst a welter of damning evidence gathered by British military intelligence was the report filed by Cunliffe-Owen, the British military attaché, on 10 October 1914:

There is no doubt that very considerable progress is being made in [the Ottoman army's] efficiency, and that it will be far superior to that in existence before the Balkan war. The continuous training . . . and the time which has elapsed for the deliberate organisation of mobilisation and administrative arrangements must cause the Turkish forces to be now regarded as a factor . . . to be taken seriously into account.[101]

Moltke's sudden enthusiasm for the Turkish army had some basis in military reality, rather than solely in political opportunism. Moreover, the early defeats in the Balkan wars, when Turkey had fought offensively, had obscured the later successes in defensive battles. These were the qualities—the hardiness, the doggedness of the Anatolian peasant—on which the Turkish leadership was able to build, and which made Turkey a worthy ally of the Central Powers.

[101] Sheffy, *British military intelligence*, 61.

9

GERMANY'S
GLOBAL STRATEGY

HOLY WAR

Both the British and the French official histories described the First World War as the Great War. In English that remained the common practice until 1939; in France even today 'la grande guerre' is used more frequently than 'la première guerre mondiale'. But from its outset the German official history was dubbed, simply and massively, *Der Weltkrieg*, 'the world war'. The distinction is of more than verbal significance.

France and, even more, Britain possessed colonial empires. During the course of the war they used their overseas resources to conquer the Central Powers. But their principal objective, to defeat Germany within Europe, shaped their conception of the war's military dimensions. Although global in their dominions, they did not embark on world war. Britain's efforts outside Europe in 1914 were designed to restrict the war, to eliminate Germany as a global force, to drive its cruisers from the seas, to close down its African and Pacific colonies.

It was not the Entente but the Central Powers that broadened the war in 1914; it was not Britain but Germany that pursued a peripheral strategy and aimed to strike its opponents at their weakest points in Africa and Asia. *Der Weltkrieg* was therefore not simply a title adopted in the 1920s; it was current in Germany throughout the war; it was even coined before it. In some cases the pre-war use of *Welt* lacked geographical precision; it was a synonym for 'great'.[1] Friedrich von Bernhardi's *Deutschland und der nächste Krieg* (1912) used *Weltkrieg* in this way, and so too did the luminaries of the centre and left, Matthias

---

[1] Raithel, *Das 'Wunder' der inneren Einheit*, 119–25, 133.

Erzberger and August Bebel.[2] Others employed it to warn of the danger that a local Balkan conflict could escalate, because of Russia's intervention, into a general European war. Thus, Franz Joseph spoke to Conrad of *Weltkrieg* in January 1913.[3] Four months later Bethmann Hollweg said: 'If there is a war, it will be a world war, and we will have to fight on two fronts ... It will be a battle for existence.'[4] But in Germany (as opposed to Austria-Hungary) *Weltkrieg* also implied a war that went beyond the confines of Europe. Bethmann Hollweg's predecessor as chancellor, Bülow, reckoned that Germany's great-power status within the continent was conditional on its activity in the wider world.[5] The Anglo-German antagonism, which Bülow's *Weltpolitik* fomented, prompted naval planners to speak of world war by 1905.[6] And it was the prospect of Britain's intervention which, on the night of 30/1 July 1914, led Moltke to say to his adjutant, Hans von Haeften, 'This war will grow into a world war'.[7] Moreover, in this context a world war could carry precise strategic meaning. In 1913 Friedrich Grautoff published a fictional account of a war in Europe, in which only a Muslim rising and then revolution in Africa brought Britain and France to the peace table.[8]

The obvious land bridge to the implementation of a German global strategy was the Ottoman empire. Its potential was evident to German Turcophiles from the 1890s. A strong Turkish army could, in Colmar von der Goltz's view, do two things. The first, primarily European in orientation, was to create a threat in the Caucasus sufficiently great to force the Russians to divert troops from East Prussia. The second was much more ambitious. The Turks, launching themselves from southern Syria, could seize the Suez Canal, become once again masters of Egypt, and so cut Britain's communications with India. Indeed, given Germany's naval inferiority, an alliance with Turkey seemed to be the only means by which to administer a direct blow to Britain's vital interests.[9]

The ramifications of such a coup were tantalizingly broad. Paul Rohrbach, writing in 1902, anticipated the collapse of Britain's position in Central and East Africa.[10] More influential, at least with the Kaiser before the war and with the foreign office during it, were the opinions of Max von Oppenheim, an archaeologist, a Christian convert from Judaism, an expert on Arabic and Islamic affairs, and a former adviser to the German consul-general in Cairo. In 1908 he told Bülow that, in the event of

[2] Herrmann, *Arming of Europe*, 183.   [3] Jerabek, *Potiorek*, 100.
[4] Schulte, *Vor dem Kriegsausbruch*, 116.   [5] Schöllgen, *Escape into war?*, 123.
[6] Herwig, *International History Review*, XIII (1991), 281.   [7] Mombauer, 'Moltke', 185.
[8] Jost Dülffer, 'Kriegserwartung und Kriegsbild in Deutschland vor 1914', in Michalka (ed.), *Der Erste Weltkrieg*, 784–7.
[9] Schulte, *Vor dem Kriegsausbruch*, 19, 40–6, 123; von der Goltz, *Denkwürdigkeiten*, 318.
[10] Gottlieb, *Studies*, 23.

a great European war, especially if Turkey participates in it against England, one may certainly expect an overall revolt of the Muslims in the British colonies ... In such a war, those colonies would be, along with Turkey, the most dangerous enemy of an England strong on the seas. British soldiers would be unable to invade Inner Turkey, and, in addition, England would need a large part of its navy and almost its entire army in order to keep its colonies.[11]

Thus, German rejection of revolutionary warfare in sub-Saharan Africa was the exception, not the rule. Elsewhere the horror of revolution at home was turned inside out, to become the agent of warfare abroad. Relatively unfettered by colonial responsibilities of its own, and comparatively secure in its ethnic homogeneity, Germany agitated among the subject peoples of Britain, France, and Russia; not only Muslims (although they constituted the largest single group), but also Irish, Jews, Poles, Finns, Estonians, Letts, Balts, Ukrainians, and Georgians. It was a process that, in its final form, aligned Hohenzollern with Bolshevik. Furthermore, this use of revolution was not, at least in the first instance—and in some areas of the world not ever—directed at creating German global domination.[12] The pillars of the world order were to be shaken with no idea beyond the collapse of the existing edifice. Political objectives were subordinated to military necessity; revolution was an unguided missile, its purpose to turn Germany's encirclement and its naval and colonial inferiority to good account. On 30 July the Kaiser wrote of Britain:

Now this entire structure must be ruthlessly exposed and the mask of Christian peacefulness be publicly torn away ... Our consuls in Turkey and India, our agents, etc., must rouse the whole Moslem world into wild rebellion against this hateful, mendacious, unprincipled nation of shopkeepers; if we are going to shed our blood, then England must at least lose India.[13]

This was not the Schlieffenesque stuff of pre-war military planning. Von der Goltz's brushstrokes of 1899 had not been transmogrified into alliances, mobilization procedures, and deployment areas. On 2 August 1914 Moltke wrote to the foreign office demanding revolution in India and Egypt, and pressure on Persia to expel the Russians and make common cause with Turkey. Like the Kaiser, he was mouthing the pan-Islamic rhetoric of press and propaganda; like the Kaiser, he was short on specifics. On 5 August he added the Caucasus to his Islamic revolutions, and on the 20th Morocco, Tunisia, Algeria, and Afghanistan.[14] By now, too, he was ranging Zionism alongside Islam. On 7

[11] Landau, *Politics of pan-Islam*, 97.
[12] Even Fischer concedes this point; see *Germany's aims*, 120. Ibid. 120–53, and Zechlin, *Aus Politik und Zeitgeschichte* (1961), 269–88, 325–37, 341–67, are the best accounts of revolutionary strategy in 1914–15. Kimche, *Second Arab awakening*, is in English but overstated. McKale, *War by revolution*, makes good use of German materials, but focuses on the Arabs.
[13] Gehrke, *Persien in der deutschen Orientpolitik*, i. 1.
[14] Ibid. 22; Bihl, *Kaukasus-politik*, 40–1.

August Dr Otto Sprenger told the political department of OHL that 4 million of the 7 million Jews in Russia were Zionist in sympathy, and that the Zionists were permeated with German influences; he imagined a Jewish network operating in the rear of the Russian army, collecting intelligence, preparing supplies for the advancing Germans, and ultimately carrying revolution, sabotage, and terror into Russian ranks. A precondition of such a movement was Turkey's acceptance of Germany's protection of the Jews in Palestine, a subject on which Talaat had given assurances to the German ambassador.[15]

In just over two weeks Moltke had drawn up a shopping list that embraced, as the Kaiser told Enver on 15 August, Asia, India, Egypt, and Africa. But, to continue the metaphor, he had no money with which to purchase his wants. Most obviously, the army's prior commitment to Europe left it without men and munitions for other theatres. Overland communications between Germany and the Near East were rudimentary, if not non-existent. The insulation of the German army from the rest of the world had left it deficient in expertise in the areas in which it was now to seek influence. Broadly speaking, Moltke was looking to diplomacy to create a myriad revolutionary armies. And yet, while he required the foreign office to conjure up the troops, he was determined to retain control of the objectives which these troops were to pursue.[16]

Thus, a course was set which was bound to generate friction between OHL and the foreign office. Jagow's deputy, Arthur Zimmermann, embraced with enthusiasm the idea of a revolutionary strategy, pivoting on Constantinople and pan-Islam. Zimmermann's keenness was buttressed by Oppenheim, who joined the foreign office on 2 August. Other apparent experts, notably Ernst Jäckh, Professor of Turkish History at Berlin University but recruited by the foreign office in 1912, aided and abetted. From Constantinople, Wangenheim, while realistic in his assessment of Turkey's military capacities, reported on Enver's plans for revolutions throughout Central Asia and North Africa, so confirming Berlin in its grandiose schemes. By November 1914 Zimmermann was the outstanding spokesman in government of von der Goltz's strategy. Turkey, he argued, was the key to the rest of the world. The Near East and the Balkans should therefore be the crux of Germany's effort in the war. But, while Zimmermann wanted troops diverted to Serbia to open the direct route between Berlin and Constantinople, Falkenhayn was still locked in a desperate battle on the western and eastern fronts.[17] OHL, having given birth to the global strategy, now insisted that its execution was the task of the foreign

---

[15] Friedman, *Germany, Turkey, and Zionism*, 200–1; Zechlin, *Aus Politik und Zeitgeschichte* (1961), 341–67.

[16] Gehrke, *Persien in der deutschen Orientpolitik*, i. 6, 23, 326.

[17] Janssen, *Der Kanzler und der General*, 41–8; Fischer, *War aims*, 122–4; Mühlmann, *Oberste Heeresleitung und Balkan*, 52–64.

office. Foreign office exasperation was increased by the anomalous position of the political section of the general staff. Stationed in Berlin, remote from OHL, headed by a career diplomat, Rudolf Narodny, rather than a professional soldier, it manufactured an independence that in the field cut across the work of the foreign office, preferring military action to negotiation, directness to diplomacy.

German policy was therefore riven with internal divisions. It was also built on a fundamental contradiction. Moltke's initiatives in August 1914 depended on the Turkish alliance for their legitimacy; and yet all too frequently they were launched as German projects without regard for Turkish national sensibilities. Turkey entered the war to secure its freedom from great-power involvement. It had no intention of becoming Germany's proxy. In North Africa, Central Asia, and the Near East Turkey had its own foreign-policy objectives. For much of the war they coincided with those of Germany, but there was no necessary congruence. And, as the war went on, Turko-German relations deteriorated, the former gaining in self-assurance, and the latter all too frequently insensitive to emergent national feeling.

Moltke's memorandum of 2 August suggested that the prime objective of German strategy through Turkey was to be Britain. In fact, however, Britain was not yet in the war. Some—possibly including Moltke, for all his realism about Britain's position—perhaps hoped that a German–Turkish alliance would compel the latter's neutrality at the eleventh hour. Germany accepted the alliance to meet immediate military needs, not distant and grandiose objectives. Its purpose was to engage the Turkish army not with the British empire, but with Russia.

On 1 August Enver and Liman von Sanders assured Wangenheim that within thirty days of mobilization 120,000 Turkish troops could be in Thrace for a joint advance with Bulgaria and Romania against Russia; a further 90,000 could follow a month later.[18] The Turks' initial task, therefore, was not global revolution but direct support for the Austrians in Galicia. Romania's subsequent neutrality lessened the Turks' enthusiasm while increasing the Austrians' needs. At the end of August Conrad proposed that 50,000 men be landed at Odessa. Turkey was still not even in the war. Pomiankowski, the Austrian military attaché, to whom Conrad looked for support, poured large doses of realism onto the scheme. Turkey had not got 50,000 men assembled; even if it had, lack of transport vessels would mean that it would take eight to ten convoys and up to three months to ship the troops across the Black Sea. Pomiankowski convinced Liman, but Conrad continued the hunt for naval support. His frustration might have been better founded if the Austro-Hungarian fleet had responded to the German appeal and quitted the security

---

[18] Trumpener, *Journal of Contemporary History*, I (1966), 182–3.

of the Adriatic for the Black Sea. But Haus set impossible conditions. The supply needs of a full fleet, particularly of coal and oil, could not be met, and he demanded an intermediate base between Pola and Constantinople.[19] So Conrad's hopes were pinned on Souchon. But Souchon was as cautious as Pomiankowski. He was sufficiently Tirpitzian to believe that *Goeben* and *Breslau* achieved their objectives as a fleet in being; their use in war should be confined to attacks on isolated Russian vessels. By insisting that Russia's Black Sea ports be blockaded before the expedition got under way (a task beyond the capacity of the Turkish navy), he scuppered the proposal.[20]

Conrad remained fixed on Turkey's role in the war with Russia. In September and October he hatched a plan to send 50,000 Turkish troops and 500 Ukrainians under an Austrian officer who was the brother of the Metropolitan of Halyc to rouse the Kuban Cossacks in revolution against the Tsar. Desperation had forced him into the realms of cloud-cuckoo land. The Turks still had not got 50,000 men available, nor had they control of the Black Sea; Austrian command, even if its purpose was to undermine German influence in the Ottoman empire, was not congenial to Constantinople; Ukrainian volunteers came forward in insufficient numbers and on terms incompatible with Conrad's aims; the confusion of Orthodox and Islamic objectives created tension; and the Kuban Cossacks remained loyal to Russia.

The effective focus of the Central Powers' designs for Turkish attacks on Russia was now the Caucasus. At the beginning of August Moltke, reflecting Liman's advice, had eliminated the Caucasus as a possible theatre for offensive operations. He was apprehensive about the Turks operating in isolation against the Russians. Neither the terrain nor the communications favoured anything more than an active defence to tie down such Russian forces as held the Caucasian frontier.[21] But in the course of August and September the other options fell away. At the same time both the Austrian and German ambassadors in Turkey reported risings against the Russians by the Muslim populations of the area, and the preparation by Enver of the 3rd Turkish army for an offensive. By November mobilization on this front at least was complete.[22] For those in Berlin looking for signs of pan-Islamic fervour, and for its conjunction with Turkey's belligerence, the Caucasus seemed to be about to deliver. Furthermore, while not exactly a southern front against the Russians in Galicia, operations in the Caucasus would certainly go some way to meet Conrad's desiderata.

[19] Halpern, *Haus*, 149–51, 155–64.
[20] Ibid. 186–7; Kurat 'How Turkey drifted into World War I', in Bourne and Watt (eds.), *Studies*, 305–6; Mühlmann, *Waffenbündnis*, 109–10; Pomiankowski, *Zusammenbruch*, 81–2; Bihl, *Jahrbucher für Geschichte Osteuropas*, NS, XIV (1966), 362–6.
[21] Mühlmann, *Oberste Heeresleitung und Balkan*, 42–3.
[22] Bihl, *Kaukasus-politik*, 59, 219, 230–1; Conrad, *Aus meiner Dienstzeit*, iv. 389.

But between the outbreak of war and late autumn German priorities and perceptions had been fundamentally altered, first by Britain's belligerence and secondly by the defeat on the Marne. Both suggested that the war would be long. The Kaiser and Tirpitz found an increasing number of adherents to their view that the real enemy was Britain, the economic hub of the Entente but extraordinarily difficult for Germany to attack. On both these counts the importance of a strike on the Suez Canal loomed ever larger in German calculations. In August the navy hatched a plot to sink a merchantman, the *Barenfels*, in the channel. It misfired, but Bethmann Hollweg was supportive of the intention.[23] His priorities began to change. A telegram, dispatched by the chancellor to Wangenheim on 7 September, showed at once the transitional state of his thought and the confusion which it spelled for the strategy of the Central Powers: 'We are forced to exploit every suitable opportunity to break England's resistance. For the time being [*zunächst*] your excellency will do everything to demand the attack of Turkey on Russia.'[24]

In August and September Wangenheim entered into direct negotiations with the Khedive of Egypt, Abbas Hilmi, who was holidaying in Constantinople when war began. The Germans advanced Hilmi 4 million gold francs. The Austrians were appalled—and not simply because of Germany's progressive reorientation away from what, for Vienna, was the major threat. Success in Egypt could rouse Turkish and Islamic feeling to such a pitch as to threaten the precarious Italian foothold in Cyrenaica. The likelihood of Italy honouring its obligations to the Triple Alliance would be diminished. Zimmermann turned this argument on its head: if the Central Powers controlled Egypt, Italy would be less likely to respond to Entente overtures.[25] In a major memorandum composed in October, Max von Oppenheim, perhaps reflecting the bias of his own expertise, summarized the shift in German thought. The first priority in a pan-Islamic holy war was to be an attack on the Suez Canal and a revolution in Egypt and India; a campaign in the Caucasus came second, and rebellion in French North Africa third.[26]

Within Turkey, Germany's new direction accorded with the hopes of the Young Turks. Enver, whose reputation rested in large part on his determined resistance to the Italian invasion of Cyrenaica, aspired to recover Egypt and Turkey's other former North African provinces for the Ottoman empire. Provided the campaign was secured as a joint, and predominantly Turkish, venture, German and Ottoman objectives could coincide. On 2 August the mobilization orders of the 4th army embraced the possibility of an attack on

---

[23] McKale, *War by revolution*, 52–3.
[24] Mühlmann, *Oberste Heeresleitung und Balkan*, 48; see also L. L. Farrar, *Short-war illusion*, 27. The precise sequence intended is unclear because of the ambiguity in *zunächst*.
[25] Weber, *Eagles on the crescent*, 88–94; Trumpener, *Germany and the Ottoman empire*, 36–8.
[26] Bihl, *Kaukasus-politik*, 41–2.

Egypt. Liman von Sanders alone rejected the notion, recognizing its logistical difficulties and still favouring an expedition to Odessa. On 17 September he was told by Bethmann Hollweg and OHL to fall into line, and three days later Kress von Kressenstein was appointed chief of staff to VIII corps of the 4th army. Kress joined Curt Prüfer, a former dragoman in Cairo, who had arrived in Constantinople on 3 September. Prüfer's task was to further Zimmermann's plan for an Egyptian revolt against British rule. Secret agents were to infiltrate into Egypt in order to recruit terrorists and unleash a campaign of murder and sabotage. Thus, Britain's forces would be committed to the maintenance of internal order and so scattered in advance of a Turkish attack from the east. Kress's job during October was to reconnoitre the south Syrian approaches to the Sinai desert and to calculate the requirements for an attack on Suez.[27] In the same month an impetuous young German officer was checked by Turkish gendarmes from breaching Turkish neutrality and making a dash to the canal, with a view to sinking a vessel and so blocking navigation.[28]

On 22 October Enver sent to OHL the Turkish war plan. It contained six options. The fleet was to attack the Russian fleet in the Black Sea. A holy war was to follow against the enemies of the Central Powers. In the Caucasus the Turks would hold the Russians. In Syria, VIII army corps, possibly supported by XII army corps, would launch an attack on Egypt, although this would not be possible for a further six weeks. If Bulgaria joined the Central Powers, Turkey would join it in a thrust on Serbia; such a combination might bring in Romania and thus enable Turkey to be part of a Balkan league against Russia. Sixthly, Enver included a possible expedition with three or four corps to Odessa.[29]

Enver's plan was, in truth, not a plan. It was a list of possibilities; there was no evidence of any staff-work to support the propositions; any rank order of priorities was implicit, not explicit. Odessa figured in it, although that had already been eliminated; the putative Balkan allies were notable for their absence; the Caucasus was mentioned as a limited operation but was already bulking larger in some quarters. On the other hand, the commitment to the offensive in general and to the Suez attack in particular could only please the Germans. If Turkey did not attack, it would not draw in sufficient British or Russian troops to render its belligerence of value to the Central Powers. By making the advance on Egypt the most specific aim in terms of timing and troops, Enver ensured that Turkish and German objectives remained in step. On 24 October OHL signalled its approval.

---

[27] Liman, *Five years in Turkey*, 26–7; Wallach, *Anatomie einer Militärhilfe*, 191–2; Mühlmann, *Waffenbündnis*, 89; McKale, *War by revolution*, 55–6.

[28] Trumpener, 'Suez, Baku, Gallipoli: the military dimensions of the German–Ottoman coalition 1914–18', in Kiraly *et al.* (eds.) *East Central European society*, 390.

[29] Mühlmann, *Deutschland und der Türkei 1913–1914*, 101–2, gives the text.

What Enver's war plan revealed was that Turkish strategy was shaped disproportionately by political factors rather than by operational considerations. Between August and October projects had been added without earlier ideas being taken away; to the original target of Russia was now grafted Germany's concentration on Britain; the specific and limited focus of the alliance on 2 August had been turned into a grandiose array of schemes with shallow foundations, spanning three continents, and requiring a decaying empire to take on Russia and Britain simultaneously and virtually unaided. Enver gave no attention to either of the major areas of vulnerability, the Dardanelles and Mesopotamia; the two theatres of attack were at different apexes of the empire from the major areas of defence and from each other. Both embodied the political philosophy of the Young Turks more than they represented military sense. Enver's strategy was at once pan-Turk, in that the Caucasus stretched its fingers towards Turan, and pan-Islamic, in its appeal to the Arab world and the recapture of Cairo.

The confirmation of this policy came on 14 November, with the declaration of an Islamic holy war by the Sheikh-ul-Islam in the presence of the Sultan. All believers throughout the world were called upon to fight Britain, France, Russia, Serbia, and Montenegro. The first three were accused of enslaving Moslems. The Crimea, Kazan, Turkestan, Bokhara, Khiva, India, China, Afghanistan, Iran, and Africa were urged to make common cause with the Ottoman empire. The appeal was translated into Arabic, Persian, Urdu, and Tatar; it was extended to Shi'ites as well as to Sunni Muslims.[30]

In this call the religious and secular enjoyed a complex relationship. The Sultan claimed the Caliphate, a function inherited through the Abbasids of Egypt, and confirmed by the Ottoman empire's custodianship of the holy cities Mecca and Medina. Implicit in the Caliphate was temporal authority over all the Muslims of the world; such a combination of spiritual and political authority had become unfamiliar to Christians.[31] Enver had realized the value of the Caliphate for Ottomanism in Libya; he rallied the Arabs not by dint of his own authority but as the future son-in-law of the Sultan and Caliph.[32] And it was in these terms that the Kaiser appealed to Enver to launch a holy war, or jihad, in August 1914.[33]

Technically jihad concerned the spiritual striving of man to overcome his baser instincts. But the *fatwas* of November took 'the form of general mobilization'. They set their demands in the context of universal conscription for all Ottoman subjects aged 20 to 45, but then added a summons to 'the ulema,

[30] Landau, *Politics of pan-Islam*, 99–101; Bihl, *Kaukasus-politik*, 37.
[31] Larcher, *La Guerre turque*, 7–10; Bihl, *Kaukasus-politik*, 36–7.
[32] Haley, *Middle Eastern Studies*, XXX (1994), 4–5.
[33] Martin Kröger, 'Revolution als Programm. Ziele und Realität deutscher Orientpolitik im Ersten Weltkrieg', in Michalka (ed.), *Der Erste Weltkrieg*, 371.

professors and teachers, and all students of the religious and profane sciences ... together with most officials, and the young men of the motherland who are the protectors of helpless families, [and] of frail old parents'.[34] The language was reminiscent of one of the founding documents of the nation state, the French declaration of *la patrie en danger* of 1793. The secular and modernizing agenda of the Young Turks was thus grafted onto the appeal of Islam.

There were up to 270 million Muslims in the world in 1914, about 170 million of them in Asia and 50 million in Africa. A jihad on this scale potentially doubled the impact of the original outbreak of war in August. But only about 30 million Muslims were ruled by other Muslims. Almost 100 million were governed by Britain; Russia and France each had about 20 million; less than 2 million, most in East Africa, were ruled by Germany.

Muslims in the empires of Britain, France, and Russia who opposed the Caliphate were promised 'the fire of hell', while those who committed the lesser offence of fighting Germany and Austria-Hungary would 'merit painful torment'.[35] Holy war was not, therefore, simply religious in its implications; it was also proto-nationalist, a counter to European imperialism.

However, the declaration of holy war was not the key to unlocking pan-Islamic fervour that it seemed. The politics of its conception robbed it of doctrinal purity. This was not a war of believers against unbelievers. The Muslims under German and Austro-Hungarian rule were not enjoined to turn against their masters; the Italians, for all that they had given the greatest recent offence to Ottoman sensibilities, were exempted as enemies in reflection of the continuing Austrian hope that they would honour their alliance obligations. None of the 10 million Shi'ites and few Sunni Arabs recognized the Sultan's claim to the Caliphate. The Young Turks, after all, had overthrown the Caliph, Abdul Hamid, and had downplayed Hamidian pan-Islamism in preference for pan-Turkism. The convenient revival of Islam in Ottoman interests smacked of expedience.

The summons to holy war, although not unanswered, did not set Asia and Africa alight. For Turkish commentators in the 1930s and for most western historians until the 1980s the cause of its comparative failure was self-evident: nationalism, not religion, was the popular rallying cry of the twentieth century. The Committee of Union and Progress was a part of this process, the self-acknowledged agent of modernization, committed to Turkism and to Turkification. Its circular on the war to its local bodies, dated 11 November 1914, thus emphasized secular objectives rather than religious. 'The national ideal of our people and our land', it ran, 'drives us toward destroying the Muscovite foe and toward achieving in this manner the natural frontiers of the state in which our brothers in race will be included and united.' Only then did it add: 'Religious

---

[34] Lewis, 'The Ottoman proclamation of Jihad in 1914', 160, 163. [35] Ibid. 160.

considerations drive us toward liberating the Islamic world from the domination of the Infidel.'[36]

And yet an explanation that discounts the strength of Islamic fundamentalism looked less satisfactory as the twentieth century closed than it did at its midway point. In 1914 the national identities of the Muslim world were confused and embryonic. The war itself and the peace settlements helped sharpen them. But nationalism did not thereby supplant religion. Instead, the two coexisted and even merged, allowing Islam to restate its political, social, and legal functions.

The ambivalence of the Turkish appeal operated in another dimension. The pan-Islamic afterthought of the Committee of Union and Progress statement spoke of freedom. It suggested that interdependence of Muslim ethnic groups, probably through an alliance with Turkey, was the aim. The Turks themselves envisaged a Central Asian bloc of three sovereign states, Turkey, Persia, and Afghanistan. But the pan-Turkish summons implied the reinvigoration of Ottoman imperialism, thrusting into the Trans-Caucasus, and inviting the Muslim peoples of the world to trade one domination for another. The blending of Turkism and Islam thus robbed the holy war of its political purity.

The Turks, therefore, forfeited the advantages in propaganda with which in November 1914 they seemed so amply endowed. Despite the illiteracy of many to whom their appeal was directed, and despite the poverty and slowness of communications, Islam was a powerful means for spreading the message. The Sultan's summons reached Yola in Nigeria; it was relayed through Zanzibar to Uganda, the Sudan, and the Congo; it was passed through German East Africa to Nyasaland.[37] Furthermore, the Committee of Union and Progress had itself developed the arts and machinery of propaganda in the years immediately preceding the war. Much of the original effort was pan-Turkish in focus. The Committee had organized branches in the Caucasus and Turkestan by 1911; it had established contacts with Azerbaijan; it sent its first agents to Afghanistan in 1910. Pan-Islamic structures came later and were primarily a result of the Libyan war with Italy. Enver rallied the tribes, using the appeal of a jihad, and learning that pan-Islam could be exploited for political purposes. Italy's short-sighted recognition of the Caliph's continuing religious supremacy in their new North African colony confirmed the wisdom of this approach. The Benevolent Islamic Society (or Pan-Islamic League), founded in January 1913, ostensibly for educational and philanthropic purposes, was in reality dedicated to operations in countries where the Turkish army was not capable of direct intervention. It published a fortnightly magazine, *Jihan-i Islam* ('The

[36] Jaschke, *Welt des Islams*, XXIII (1941), 12; the translation is from Swietochowski, *Russian Azerbaijan*, 76. See also Hagen, *Die Türkei im Ersten Weltkrieg*, 28.
[37] Osuntokun, *Nigeria in the First World War*, 149; Landau, *Politics of pan-Islam*, 141–2; Shepperson and Price, *Independent African*, 405–8.

World of Islam') in Turkish, Arabic, Persian, and Urdu. *Jihan-i Islam* was taken over by the Ministry of War in 1914. A parallel institution, the Society for the Progress of Islam, was set up on what would become neutral ground, in Geneva.[38]

These threads were drawn together on 5 August 1914 when a secret order issued by Enver established the *Teskilat-i Mahsusa* or 'Special Organization'. Although it was built on pre-existing secret groups, the *Teskilat-i Mahsusa* became specifically Enver's creation, staffed by his nominees, free from the jurisdiction of the government or of parliament, and secretly financed by the Ministry of War. Propaganda was only one of its tasks; the others included subversion, terrorism, and sabotage. It served both pan-Turkism and pan-Islam, but its antecedents in the Libyan war and its success in that theatre put the weight on the latter rather than the former. The senior figures were mostly Turks, but the heads of regional cells were often locally recruited. About 700 of them were ranked as 'brethren', empowered to receive operational instructions and to distribute propaganda; they in turn controlled about 30,000 supporters.[39]

Of primary concern to the *Teskilat-i Mahsusa*, and a principal motivation in sustained resistance to Italian rule in Libya, was the loyalty of the Arabs within the Ottoman empire. The Ottoman claim to the Caliphate rested crucially on their support; Arabic was the language of the Koran, Arabia was the land in which the Holy Places were situated. And yet the apparatus which Enver had developed by 1914 became preoccupied with the projection of Turkish and Islamic influences abroad, beyond Ottoman frontiers. Not until April 1916 were journals established specifically to put the Ottoman case to the Arabs. They were too late.[40]

In fact, both Ottoman domestic opinion and Islamic world views received far more attention from Berlin than they did from Constantinople. Of seventeen enemy tracts circulating in French Algeria between October 1914 and December 1916, only three were printed in the Turkish capital; most of the rest emanated from Berlin or Berne.[41] The Germans recognized the shaky foundations of the Sultan's claim to the Caliphate, and appreciated that pan-Turkism could prove a two-edged sword to a multinational empire. However, the effect of their intervention proved equally ambivalent.

The underlying problem was organizational confusion. The Germans knew that the Turkish War Ministry had a centralized propaganda agency: Enver told them so in September 1914, and claimed he had a network which

---

[38] Landau, *Politics of pan-Turkism*, 49–51; Landau, *Politics of pan-Islam*, 92–4, 104, 108, 134–8.

[39] Simon, *Libya between Ottomanism and Nationalism*, 125–8.

[40] William L. Cleveland, 'The role of Islam as political ideology in the First World War', in Edward Ingram (ed.), *National and international politics in the Middle East*, 85–98.

[41] Meynier, *L'Algérie révelée*, 509.

stretched from India to Morocco, and from the Caucasus to the Yemen. But the Germans did not believe his claims. Moreover, they were not aware of the existence of *Teskilat-i Mahsusa*. Thus, their own efforts functioned independently of those of the Turks, and were always in danger of being wrong-footed by them.[42]

Germany itself did not lack the tools in 1914 to influence opinion in the Ottoman empire. Its central dilemma was the choice of language in which to communicate its message. French was the language of the educated elite. This, as well as German, was the means of communication favoured by *Osmanischer Lloyd*, a newspaper founded by German commercial interests in the region and launched following the 1908 coup. After the outbreak of the war *Osmanischer Lloyd* tried to expand its appeal by publishing an exclusively French edition in print-runs of up to 10,000. But plans to produce separate Turkish and Arabic editions came to nought, not least because of shortages of paper. Supplied with material by the foreign office, *Osmanischer Lloyd*'s reporting had to satisfy the censors of both powers. Thus, it generated a blandness unlikely to appeal to the intellects of its restricted readership. During the period of Ottoman neutrality the foreign office sought alternative outlets by pumping money directly into Turkish newspapers. The dissatisfaction of German businessmen was manifested in the private news services operated by the Anatolian railway and the German-run Ottoman Bank, both of which disseminated the dispatches provided by the Wolff Agency (the only government-approved press agency in Germany during the war).

To compound Germany's problems, the language issue became fused with that of religion. In 1911 the Prussian Ministry of Culture recognized the possibility of linking missionary activity to the promotion of German influence overseas. The foreign office was supportive, not least because it saw French missionaries in Syria and Palestine as agents of France rather than as promoters of Catholicism. Ostensibly the outbreak of war created the opportunity to oust the French. The driving force of the *Zentralstelle für Auslandsdienst*, founded to co-ordinate the overseas propaganda of the different departments of state, was the leader of the Catholic Centre party, Matthias Erzberger. But there was clearly a contradiction in using the opportunity of an Islamic holy war to promote Catholicism.

The French language was too entrenched and the proclivities of the Young Turks too nationalistic for this religious dilemma to become really significant. In 1913 France had over 500 schools in Turkey, with 54,000 pupils, to Germany's thirty schools with 3,000 pupils. On 11 February 1914 Jagow took the chair at a meeting to establish an organization to promote German culture, the Deutsche-Türkisch Vereinigung. Under the guidance of Ernst Jäckh, the

[42] Müller, *Islam, Gihad*, 197, 239–43.

DTV promoted German schools and German-language teaching in the schools of other nationalities. It backed a scheme, which also enjoyed foreign office patronage, for a Deutsch-Türkischen Hochschule. But in September 1915 the Turks banned foreign organizations from opening schools, and made further progress contingent on the principle of reciprocity and on the recognition of the abrogation of capitulations. Professor Schmidt, who had been attached by the Foreign Ministry to the Turkish Ministry of Education at the beginning of the year, recognized that Germany's best hope for influence was through the medium of Turkish. The Hochschule scheme languished, but the German professors who were appointed to the University of Constantinople gained kudos precisely because they learnt the local language.[43]

Despite its enjoyment of foreign ministry backing, the DTV was not a fully fledged German propaganda agency for Turkey. No such body was up and running until 1915 or even 1916. Thus, German propaganda was reactive rather than innovative, a response to the lukewarm reception to the declaration of holy war rather than a clarion call when it was originally published. Like Turkey's efforts in the Arab world, Germany's publications peaked in 1916—after the major successes of Ottoman arms in 1915 and even longer after the initiation of a German revolutionary strategy in 1914.

Max von Oppenheim suggested a bureau to translate war news for Muslims and to educate Muslim opinion in the ideas of pan-Islam and the Turko-German alliance on 18 August 1914. It was also a theme of his lengthy October 1914 memorandum advocating revolutionary activity in the Islamic territories of Germany's enemies. With Jagow's and Zimmermann's support, he got 100 million marks to establish the Nachrichtenstelle für den Orient. He recruited orientalists from universities, and the office was organized according to their academic specialisms. In 1916, by which time the department in Germany was headed by an Egyptologist from Berlin University, Eugen Mittwoch, the Nachrichtenstelle für den Orient was spending 300 million marks a year. The diplomats now saw it as marching to the individual enthusiasms of the scholars it employed rather than submitting to the discipline of the foreign ministry. The doubters, already vocal in December 1914, reckoned that Oppenheim had exaggerated the strength of the indigenous revolutionary movements and of Germany's influence on the ground.[44]

It was in recognition of this point that Oppenheim himself went to Constantinople to establish an office there early in 1915. The embassy resented the 'doubtful-looking' characters who now arrived at its door with 'promises to stir up some Mohammedan people for the "Djihad"'.[45] By the autumn of 1916

[43] Dahlhaus, *Möglichkeiten und Grenzen*, 117–37, 151–69, 186–200, 221–30.

[44] Müller, *Islam, Gihad*, 193–8, 204–7; Martin Kröger, 'Revolution als Programm', in Michalka (ed.), *Der Erste Weltkrieg*, 368–75.

[45] Stuermer, *Two war years*, 147.

the Constantinople station administered twenty-five head offices and sub-offices throughout the east, most of them functioning under the umbrella of the local German consulate. Oppenheim also created a network of seventy information rooms and correspondence offices for the perusal of war reports, newpapers, and other publications throughout Asia Minor and eastern Arabia. In 1917 he established the Balkan-Orient Film GmbH, and rented the largest theatre in Constantinople for cultural shows.[46] Relations with the foreign office, or at least with the German embassy in Constantinople, became progressively more fraught, and in April 1917 Oppenheim's department was hived off as an independent company, Deutschen Überseedienst GmbH, and told to concentrate on establishing Germany's commercial position in the east. Military and political material remained in the hands of the embassy's own press office and of the Nachrichtenstelle in Berlin.

Oppenheim appreciated the importance of providing information in as many languages as possible. A war chronicle covering the main events was published in Arabic, Thai, Russian, Urdu, Hindi, Chinese, Turkish, and in the dialects of the Tatars and of the Maghreb. Leaflets, pamphlets, books, and brochures in a similar range of tongues poured off the presses. The Nachrichtenstelle claimed that between October 1914 and July 1918 it produced 1,012 publications in nine European and fifteen eastern languages, a total of 3 million copies.[47]

The initial image of Germany in the Muslim world was an extraordinarily favourable one. Its embodiment was the Kaiser. His picture, his posturing in flamboyant full-dress uniforms, which worked against German interests in westernized societies, worked for them in the Middle East. Wilhelm's reputation derived from his visit to Jerusalem and Damascus in 1898 and his declaration of solidarity with Islam. He was dubbed 'Haj Wilhelm', implying that he was a 'saint' who had made the pilgrimage to Mecca. Arabs 'considered the Kaiser King of all Kings of this world'.[48] In 1914 Germans were esteemed honorary Muslims, and their military might was a given in popular assumptions.

But Germany's handling of its religious credentials was bound to be delicate. Late in 1914 Max Roloff caused outrage in the Islamic world by an account of his mission to Mecca to recruit Muslims; the knowledge that he was a fraud who had drawn a fat salary to go no further than Holland did not negate the fact that the German government had proposed to insert an infidel into the holy city. The following year Oppenheim toured Syria, Simi, and north-western Arabia, attired in Arab dress and praising Islam while condemning

[46] Hagen, Die Türkei im Ersten Weltkrieg, 41.

[47] For this and most of what follows, see Bihl, Kaukasus-Politik, 51, 102–12; Jacobsen, Revue d'histoire Maghrebine, 59–60 (octobre 1990), 95–100.

[48] Aaronsohn, With the Turks, 27; also 36. See Meynier, L'Algérie révelée, 250–1.

Christianity. Although the British took him seriously, Djemal did not.[49] Thereafter, Oppenheim's propaganda distanced itself from religious themes. The European idea of holy war as a mass movement sweeping across national boundaries and directed against western culture in general and Christianity in particular was not one with which Germany could, for obvious reasons, identify too closely.

The fact that the reality was different from the image helped. Over four years of war the portrayal of German invincibility wore thin. Publications such as the Arabic *Al 'Adl* harped on a succession of German victories, illustrating their claims with photographs of battleships and Zeppelins. But for those on the periphery of the Ottoman empire, awaiting the results of these German triumphs, the actual evidence in their localities receded rather than multiplied. Therefore, too, holy war where it occurred was a local response. Oppenheim emphasized this element. His department's propaganda constituted a series of individual initiatives whose commonest themes were opposition to Britain and France. Holy war, in so far as it was invoked, lost its aggressive thrust and became defensive, protecting Islam from the encroachments of godless French *civilisation* and rapacious British imperialism.[50]

The Germans were therefore portrayed not as Muslims, but as Turkey's allies. This carried a double danger. First, it suggested that Turkey was being exploited by Germany, that the holy war had been subverted for the purposes of European imperialism. Increasingly, actual contact with Germans, and the high-handed behaviour of some of them, endorsed that view. Alternatively, Germany's aim could be seen as the triumph of the Caliphate. Indeed, by 1916, in its advocacy of holy war, Germany made no secret of this objective. But that could imply not liberation but the extension of the Ottoman empire. Germany's propaganda became more strident, not more subtle, as its situation became desperate.

The question of the Caliphate, and its claim to secular as well as religious suzerainty, was a fundamental one for both Turkey and Germany. The summons to holy war in November 1914 had minimized the Caliphate, presenting the Sultan as the organizer of a joint Muslim war effort. Islam was to be the midwife of nationalism and anti-colonialism. A pamphlet, 50,000 copies of which were published in Turkey to coincide with the declaration of holy war, concluded that 'Hindustan belongs to the Muslims of India, Java to the Muslims of Java, Algeria to the Muslims of Algeria, Tunisia to the Muslims of Tunisia'.[51] But in 1916 this acknowledgement of nationalist pretensions rebounded on the Ottoman empire. The Arab revolt argued that the war would be the vehicle, not for an Islamic confederation with Constantinople

[49] McKale, *War by revolution*, 62, 111–12, 159–60, 165.
[50] Müller, *Islam, Gihad*, 177–85, 198–201, 333–9, 353–7.
[51] Meynier, *L'Algérie révelée*, 514; for what follows, see 510–17.

at its heart but for the disintegration of Turkish power. Thereafter Constantinople's emphasis on the war as a holy war was redoubled, and the temporal authority of the Caliphate reaffirmed.

However, Germany's response to the Arab revolt was diametrically opposed, and thus further confusion entered the propaganda message. The Nachrichtenstelle set itself up as the sponsor of exiled nationalists. Arabs and orientals in Switzerland were observed by a network of Armenian and Tatar agents, answerable to the embassy in Berne, and some of these émigrés became the authors of German propaganda. In June 1915 the director of a German Persian carpet company, Heinrich Jakoby, set up an agency in Switzerland to co-ordinate these efforts. But his work was hampered by the counter-activities of spies from Switzerland as well as from the Entente. Moreover, his own sources of information were poor, and his contact with the German embassy limited. He failed to establish relations with Muhammed Bas Hamba, a Tunisian exile, who in May 1916 began to publish the *Revue du Maghreb* with Turkish money. Although the *Revue* owed no special loyalties to Germany, it pursued freedom for the countries of North Africa, and the Nachrichtenstelle took 200 to 300 copies of each issue. Contact between Jakoby and the Nachrichtenstelle was also minimal, and so in April 1916 the latter opened a Swiss office, which established contacts with the *Gazette de Lausanne* and acquired its own publishing house, the *Librarie nouvelle*. In 1917 the Nachrichtenstelle published *Islam dans l'armée française* in Lausanne, the work of a Tunisian lieutenant in the French army, Raban Boukabouya, who had deserted in 1915. The coping-stone, and legitimization, of these efforts were the national independence committees set up for India, Persia, Georgia, and Tunisia.[52]

These committees were not simply vehicles for the policies of the Central Powers. They included some of the leading intellectuals of their parent societies, and the latter's publications—notably the *Revue du Maghreb* and the Persian *Kaveh*—put scholarly understanding of their indigenous cultures on a new footing. The role of German academics in German propaganda helped serve the wider purposes of Islam's culture and history, and the Nachrichtenstelle financed Muslims to study in Berlin. But from this work developed not an acceptance of the Sultan as the Caliph but a demand for autonomy. In the case of the Algerians at least their ambitions were so out of line with Turkish objectives as to include the possibility of reform within the existing political structure rather than its total overthrow. In the second half of the war, therefore, German propaganda in some cases was serving not the needs of Turkey but of Islamic nationalisms.

A prime, and utilitarian, reason for the absorption of German propaganda in the culture of the Middle East was the need to educate opinion in Germany

---

[52] Müller, *Islam, Gihad*, 209–10, 284–95, 347–9.

itself. The foreign office was concerned that the popular image of their Turkish allies was as bloodthirsty bigots. Holy war was seen as a weapon that could rebound in the hands of its instigators. The Nachrichtenstelle was therefore charged with the education of European opinion, both within the Central Powers and in neutral countries, in oriental and Turkish affairs. It commissioned Salih ash-Sharif al-Tunisi, a Tunisian nationalist and friend of Enver, to write *Die Wahrheit uber den Glaubenskrieg* (The truth about the war of the creeds) (1915), and sponsored him to tour Germany so that he could explain Islam's aims.[53] Its major effort to influence the European press was its publication *Korrespondenzblatt für den Orient*, recast in April 1917 as a fortnightly periodical, *Der neue Orient*, with a print-run of 5,000.

The Nachrichtenstelle was therefore pointed in two directions at once. It had to educate the east in the affairs of the west, and the west in the affairs of the east. Its functions were simply too diverse and too broad. It had to monitor the oriental press for government departments, to translate oriental documents, to censor oriental post, and to advise on the handling of Muslim prisoners of war. The assimilation of incoming material took up most of the working day, and the distribution and dissemination of outgoing propaganda became a secondary exercise. Even the mechanics of adequately addressing its material were neglected. Its geographical orbit embraced all Asia, North Africa, and the Pacific, including the western Americas. The department could not concentrate on a simple purpose with a simple message.

Ultimately, however, Oppenheim's work, whatever its range of responsibilities, was fatally debilitated by two further factors, one external and one internal, that were probably beyond rectification in the time available. The bottom line in the Nachrichtenstelle's tasks was to create an awareness of German culture. The Germans were understandably amused by the Austrian propaganda effort, which aimed to supplant Parisian influences with Viennese. It brought opera to Constantinople, sponsored a fashion show in the Pera Palace Hotel, and arranged for a tour by the band of the Hoch-und-Deutschmeister Regiment Nr. 4.[54] But although all this suggested the frivolity of a dying empire, it also recognized that without a general cultural empathy Turkish receptivity to European propaganda would be limited. Curt Prüfer suggested that German propaganda reorientate itself along comparable lines in 1917, but the response was limited. Support for an archaeological institute meant that Theodor Wiegand, the director of antiquities at the Berlin museum, was attached to the 4th Turkish army in Palestine in 1917–18—just as the sites he was sent to visit were being overrun. Germany's idea was that his finds might be used to liquidate Turkey's debt. An exhibition of German art,

[53] Heine, *Revue de l'Occident Musulman et de la Mediterranée*, 33 (1982), 89–95; also Müller, *Islam, gihad*, 271–80.
[54] Bihl, *Kaukasus-politik*, 124; Pomiankowski, *Zusammenbruch*, 325–6.

held in Constantinople in April and May 1918, was more successful.[55] Second, and interlocking with the first, was the fact that the Nachrichtenstelle could never rid itself of the scholarly backgrounds of its members or of the scholasticism of its message. Karl Schabinger, who ran the office between Oppenheimer's departure for Constantinople and Mittwoch's succession the following year, said of his colleagues (and, significantly, he was a dragoman and not an academic): 'they operated—and this was truly German—much too much with logical and legal concepts, they appealed little or barely at all to the feelings, they had no pathos nor sense of theatre.'[56] Most of their publications appeared in print-runs of between 500 and 3,000, reflecting the selective nature of their appeal. But if literacy was low, influencing opinion-makers would not have the same impact as if literacy were high and newspaper-reading were customary. The German consul in Damascus in 1915 arranged for traditional storytellers in the coffee-houses to recount the tales of Germany at war. He at least appreciated that, where the press was weak and governmental authority in question, Germany's attention should be to the local common denominator.

Finally, the pay-off for all propaganda lay on the battlefield. With the declaration of holy war, both Germany and Turkey hoped to destabilize Entente governments and win allies throughout the east. Very quickly it became evident that the power of the sword was mightier than the pen: the Central Powers had to provide men and munitions, and victories, to redeem their pledges.

THE CAUCASUS, 1914–1915

Russia's military concern for the Caucasus in 1914 was not its defence against Turkey but its internal security. Until 1864 Georgia had been Russia's principal frontier problem, guerrilla warfare in the region shaping the soldiering experience of many, including Tolstoy. The extension of the Russian border in 1878 to a line south of the River Aras had increased the polyglot composition of the province's peoples. It also re-emphasized the colonial nature of Russian rule. In 1897 only 34 per cent of the population was Ukrainian or White Russian; the balance included three major groupings: Georgians (11.6 per cent), Armenians (12 per cent), and Tatars (16.3 per cent). The Georgians were concentrated in the west and centre, around Tiflis, and the Tatars to the east around Baku. The Armenians, as in Ottoman Turkey, had no obvious geographical focus, although they did constitute a narrow majority in Erivan. Thus, the region

---

[55] McKale, *War by revolution*, 201; Dahlhaus, *Möglichkeiten und Grenzen*, 204–13.
[56] Hagen, *Die Türkei im Ersten Weltkrieg*, 48.

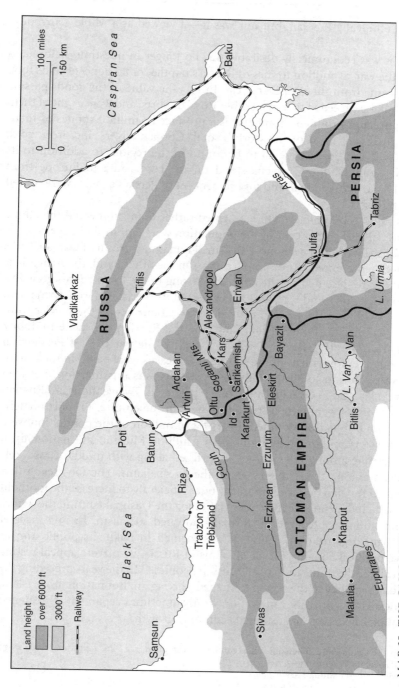

MAP 25. THE CAUCASUS

was not ethnically Russian, but nor was it—if viewed as a whole—anybody-else's.[57]

That it was economically desirable was no longer in question. Before and during the war 7.5 million tonnes of Russia's naptha, or 80 per cent of its total supply, came from the area every year. In 1913 the value of the goods passing through Baku exceeded that of all other Russian ports, and 85 per cent of them were petroleum products. Transcaucasia produced 1 million tonnes of manganese in 1913, a third of the world's total. Copper, silver, zinc, iron, gold, cobalt, salt, and borax were all to be found in the region. In addition to its natural resources, the Caucasus stood on the land route to Europe from Central Asia. Between 1908 and 1914 70 per cent of Persia's exports were routed through Russia.

This rapid economic growth confirmed rather than submerged the ethnic tensions. In 1897 79 per cent of the population were employed in agriculture; Georgians, Tatars, and even more the small remaining group of Osman Turks were over-represented in peasant farming. On the other hand, the Armenians were under-represented on the land, and strong in the towns. Tiflis grew five times between 1876 and 1912, and 71 per cent of its merchants were Armenian. Urban growth and the pattern of trade drew labour across the border from Persian Azerbaijan. Between 1891 and 1904 the Russian consulate in Tabriz issued 312,000 entry visas to Persians.[58] Eighty-one per cent of Persians in independent employment in the southern Caucasus were based in the towns.

Russia's solution to all this inherent volatility was Russification. Between 1878 and 1880 75,000 Osman Turks were repatriated. Twelve thousand Russian peasant families were settled from elsewhere in the empire. Proportionately, the Muslim population declined. In 1897 4.59 million of the population were Orthodox, 1.13 million Gregorian, and 3.2 million Muslim. But nationalism, already strong among the Georgians, surfaced along with middle-class intellectualism among the Armenians and the Azerbaijanis. The 1905 revolution moderated Russian policy temporarily but sufficiently to increase the foothold of the local independence movements. In 1907 the Dashnaktsutiun, the Armenian revolutionary federation, formally adopted socialism. In 1912 a secret Azerbaijani organization, Musavat, was formed in Baku, its public aim to achieve political equality for all Muslims in Russia, its private appeal resting on its call for the unification of all Muslim peoples.[59] In the years preceding the war Russia's policy in the region tightened once again. But nationalism, Islam, and socialism, sometimes in conjunction, sometimes separately, threatened the stability necessary to sustained economic growth.

[57] On the Caucasian demographic and economic background, see Bihl, *Kaukasus-politik*, 17–27; Geyer, *Russian imperialism*, 330–6.

[58] Swietochowski, *Russian Azerbaijan*, 65.

[59] Ibid. 73–4; Hovanissian, *Armenia*, 13–23.

Russian diplomacy in the pre-war years aimed to neutralize and isolate eastern Anatolia, not overrun it. Its expansionism was directed towards Persia. By creating a *cordon sanitaire* between its own interests and Turkish irredentism, it freed itself for a forward policy in Azerbaijan. The southerly route adopted for the Baghdad railway was the most obvious manifestation of Russian success. In 1911 Germany recognized Russia's sphere of interest in northern Persia, and the two powers agreed that Russia would build the line from Teheran to Khanikin, south of Kirkuk, to link with the Berlin–Baghdad route. Eastern Anatolia seemed condemned to backwardness.[60] Its principal cities, Erzurum and Trabzon, were already in decline before 1914.[61] The railway from Tabriz to Tiflis sucked the Tatars and Turkic populations of Persian Azerbaijan northwards into the economic nexus of Russia, not westwards into holy alliance with Turkey.

Almost every scenario concerning the Caucasus suggested to Russia's military planners that the front would retain this secondary status.[62] In the case of war with Germany and Austria-Hungary, but not Turkey, the three Caucasian corps were to be used to feed Russia's western front. If Turkey joined the Central Powers, Russia still planned to concentrate in the west, leaving two of the three Caucasian corps to conduct an active defence. In August 1914 the first of these contingencies was fulfilled, and II and III Caucasian army corps left for the west. One corps remained. However, the alliance with Britain removed the possibility of a clash between the two Entente powers in Persia. Therefore the two corps in Turkestan could be released for the Caucasus front, bringing Russian strength there to about 100,000 infantry, 15,000 cavalry, and 256 guns.[63] A mishmash of reservists and volunteers, Cossack brigades (or 'plastouns'), and so-called Caucasus Chasseurs added about 60,000 more: the numbers are imprecise because there was insufficient equipment for the 150,000 men available. Stavka did not, therefore, discount Turkey's joining the enemy. But the advice from the Russian ambassador in Constantinople was that the Turkish efforts would be directed towards the Balkans.[64]

The Russians took the Turkish military threat with sufficient seriousness to raise the number of divisions which they reckoned they might confront in the Caucasus from eleven to eighteen. But they seem to have done little else to explore Turkish intentions. Perhaps this was no more than a reflection of the fact that the Ottomans' plans were themselves in flux. More probably the

[60] Howard, *Partition of Turkey*, 46, 51; Alan Bodger, 'Russia and the end of the Ottoman Empire', in Kent (ed.), *Great powers*, 79, 89–92.

[61] Guse, *Kaukasusfront*, 8.

[62] The fullest operational account of the Caucasian front is in Allen and Muratoff, *Caucasian battlefields*.

[63] Ibid. 240–1; Danilov, *La Russie dans la guerre mondiale*, 339–40, and Larcher, *La Guerre turque*, 375–7, have slightly different totals.

[64] Wm. C. Fuller, Jr., 'The Russian Empire', in E. R. May, *Knowing one's enemies*, 120–3.

Russians were bewitched by the excellence of their own maps. Any perusal of the terrain argued that an offensive in the Caucasus was a doubtful proposition. The theatre of operations was effectively an enormous valley bounded by two mountain ranges, the Caucasus to the north and the Taurus to the south. The Russian railway to the front followed a circuitous route that showed both its commercial priorities and its respect for the Caucasus barrier. From Vladikavkaz, it proceeded south-east to Baku before doubling back north-west to Tiflis, and then to Poti and Batum on the Black Sea. A line south from Tiflis forked at Alexandropol, one route thrusting towards Kars, Sarikamish, and the Turkish frontier, the other going to Erivan and then along the Aras valley to Julfa and Tabriz. The configuration of this line made Batum and Kars the pivots of defence; neither it nor they were adapted as bases for attack. Given their own assumptions, it was not surprising that the Russians anticipated similar conclusions to be drawn by the Turks. The latter's railheads at Ulu Kischla, at the northern end of the Taurus mountains and at Tell Ebiad, at the head of the Euphrates and actually behind the Taurus range, were 1,120 and 640 kilometres respectively from Erzurum. The only good road ran from Erzurum to Trabzon and the Black Sea. The poverty of the area meant that even in peacetime its subsistence economy could barely support the indigenous population. Thus, there were neither the lines of communication nor the local means to supply a large army entirely dependent on baggage animals.

Russian insouciance had no cause to be shattered when finally Turkey did reveal its hand at the beginning of November. Winter had already begun. In the Asiatic interior it could be expected to last until at least March and even May. The snow in December might fall for up to a week, and then lie at depths of 2 metres in the valleys and 4 metres in the mountains.[65] Temperatures would drop to minus 20 degrees centigrade and below.

Russian assumptions were right. The reports sent back from Constantinople by Wangenheim and Pallavicini, talking of Enver's plans for a Caucasian offensive, were pap, designed presumably to keep the Germans in play. Between August and November 1914 little was done to prepare the Turkish 3rd army for major operations. Its commander, Hassan Izzet, was not forewarned of Souchon's sally into the Black Sea and was taken by surprise when war was declared.[66] Of his two corps, IX corps, based in the area Trabzon–Erzurum–Erzincan, was by virtue of its proximity to the main towns and the sea-lanes of the Black Sea fully mobilized. XI corps, inland at Malatia, Kharput, and Van, had had more problems, resting on poorer communications and reliant on recalcitrant Kurdish reservists. To these six infantry divisions Izzet could add about 20,000 Kurdish irregular cavalry, which proved useless, and a few frontier and gendarmerie battalions, which did not. His maps of the area,

[65] Guse, *Kaukasusfront*, 7–8.   [66] Allen and Muratoff, *Caucasian battlefields*, 243.

on a scale of 1:200,000, were good on land forms, less good on roads and paths. His staff lacked the knowledge of the country to tell him which routes were accessible and which not, and local lore proved unreliable. His chief of staff, Felix Guse, one of the few Germans in the 3rd army, had only arrived at Erzurum on 1 June. Erzurum's fortifications were outmoded and incomplete. Izzet's principal task was therefore defensive, to protect the town by anticipating the likely lines of Russian advance from the direction of Kars and Oltu. The basic stance of Turkish deployments was confirmed by the role of X corps, placed in reserve to the rear of 3rd army around Samsun and Sivas. X corps had suffered heavy losses in men and material in the Balkan wars, and was not yet up to strength. Its task was to go to Thrace or to the Caucasus according to the situation; it was not finally allotted to the 3rd army until early November. The outbreak of war thus brought the nominal strength of the 3rd army to 190,000 men, but of these 66,000 only could be classed as combatants. It was deficient in artillery (it had 168 guns) and cavalry. The summer had not been used to collect transport or to preposition supplies.[67]

Efforts to make up the deficit in the autumn were not helped by the failure of the Turkish navy to assert its command of the Black Sea after Souchon's strike at the end of October. Stavka, to which the Russian navy was subordinated, was sufficiently concerned by the prospect of Turkish amphibious landings to demand that the Black Sea fleet disperse to protect the Russian coastline. But the fleet's commander, Eberhardt, believed that pure defence would expose his ships to defeat in detail. His answer to the firepower of the *Goeben* was to seek battle on his own terms, with his three pre-Dreadnoughts concentrated. A brief action off Cape Sarych in the the Crimea, as his ships were returning to Sevastopol on 18 November 1914, vindicated his tactics. Despite the failure of the Russians' centralized gunnery control, the *Goeben* suffered some damage and over 100 casualties. Eberhardt's sweeps along the Anatolian coast in November and December sank troop transports and coastal shipping. Russian mines closed the harbour at Trabzon, leaving only Rize open, and on 25 December the *Goeben* struck a mine in the Bosporus and was out of commission until 3 April 1915. Although Eberhardt's strategy left both Poti and Batum vulnerable to offshore bombardment, it also ensured that the Turks could not derive compensation for the deficiencies of their landward communications in northern Anatolia by the exploitation of the maritime route.[68]

The Russians were, therefore, correct. The external danger was manageable and secondary. The primary threat was internal. The propaganda of the Committee of Union and Progress and the covert activities of Turkish agents in the Russian Caucasus before the war were an indirect recognition of the

[67] Guse, *Kaukasusfront*, 11–28; Larcher, *La Guerre turque*, 378–9.
[68] Nekrasov, *North of Gallipoli*, 27–39.

same fact. What pushed Enver into action on the Caucasian front was less a belief in his own pan-Turanian rhetoric than a need not to lose the initiative to others.

In September 1914 a Georgian nationalist committee, under the direction of Prince Georg Matschabelli and Michael Tserethelis, was established in Berlin. Germany recognized a potentially independent Georgia. Matschabelli asked the Germans for 50,000 rifles and 5 million rounds. Falkenhayn offered 14,000 outmoded rifles and 1.4 million rounds, but then, owing to the blockage of the Budapest–Bucharest route, could not deliver them. German support for Georgia was therefore nominal rather than actual. But its motivation—to create an army out of nothing but diplomacy—was one which Matschabelli kept in play. In April 1915 he would talk grandly of raising a force of 500,000 Caucasians in two or three months.[69]

Given the fact that Germany could not prime the pump with munitions, the Georgians had in addition to speak to Talaat and Enver. This Leo Keresselidse did in September. The Georgian aim was independence for Georgia and neutrality in the Caucasus; their kingdom, once independent, would embrace not only its Christian population but also the Muslims. Keresselidse's object-ive, therefore, was an alliance with Turkey, not Turkish suzerainty. Enver could not afford to renounce Georgian manpower, but nor could he bring himself to abandon the pan-Turkish dream. If Turkey wished to have a say in the settle-ment of the region it would have to use its own forces and upstage its German ally.

Other German initiatives in the autumn also threatened to steal a march on Turkey. In September and October 1914 schemes were floated variously to exploit Armenian nationalism, Azerbaijani nationalism, and revolutionary socialism in order to bring Baku's oil production to a standstill. Paul Schwarz calculated that the destruction of the stocks of crude oil and the disruption of production in the region would halt Russia's railways in two to three months, thus causing the collapse of the entire eastern front. Schwarz was appointed Germany's consul-general in Erzurum, specifically to advance this scheme.[70]

The political effects of German involvement confirmed that Enver's putative allies in the Caucasus were more often Christian than they were Muslim. In 1912 the Armenians in Turkey had appealed to Russia, and by 1914 aspired to autonomy within the Ottoman empire under great-power protection. One answer to Russia's own Armenian problem had thus become Russian guard-ianship of Armenians elsewhere. In the summer of 1914 the Young Turks tried to turn the tables by asking the Dashnakists at Erzurum to incite rebellion within Russia in order to support a Turkish invasion of Transcaucasia. As a

---

[69] Bihl, *Kaukasus-politik*, 60–1, 63–4, 74, 234–5; Jaschke, *Welt des Islams*, XXIII (1941), 13–14; Zechlin, *Aus Politik und Zeitgeschichte* (1961), 354.
[70] Bihl, *Kaukasus-politik*, 65–6; also 57–8.

quid pro quo, the Turks offered to create an autonomous Armenia formed of the Russian Armenian territories, plus the *vilayets* of Erzurum, Van, and Bitlis. The Armenians refused, but they confirmed their allegiance to Turkey.[71]

Pan-Islamic feeling seemed, therefore, to play little part in the destabilization of the Russian Caucasus in 1914. Indeed, the Muslim population of Russia remained, broadly speaking, loyal throughout the war. Muslims were exempt from military service, and therefore any immediate crisis of conscience was avoided. The Caucasus committee, founded by an Ottoman senator, Fuad Pasha, in August 1914, embraced the recognition that independence and nationalism were the goals of all the Caucasian peoples, while trying to harness these forces to Turkish ends by achieving those objectives under Turkish protection. By the winter of 1914, therefore, Enver was having to recognize that the strength of opposition to Russian rule lay in directions which might take the peoples of Turan away from Turkey, not towards it. Equally, that opposition was not in itself so broad as to cause the collapse of the Russian position in the Caucasus without an external nudge. The 3rd army would have to attack if Turkey was to retain control of its own foreign policy.

Once again, however, the actions of others more than his own pan-Turkism shaped Enver's strategy. The structure of the Russian command was confused. The Russian viceroy in the Caucasus, Count Vorontsov-Dashkov, an ailing man without military experience, delegated effective command to his deputy, Myshlayevskii. The latter had been shunted out to the Caucasus by Sukhomlinov because his narrow-mindedness and conservatism had created obstacles to reform on the general staff.[72] His headquarters constituted a small and able team headed by Nicolai Yudenich. Both it and Myshlayevskii's general reserve were based on Tiflis. The main Russian concentration, I Caucasian corps under General Bergmann, was formed up in the area Alexandropol–Kars–Sarikamish–Karakurt to guard the approaches from Erzurum to Oltu and Kars. Lesser formations blocked the other main routes across the frontier, at Batum, from Bayazit to Erivan, and from the Persian Azerbaijan. The whole front was 600 kilometres long. Therefore, in order to shorten the Russian front, Bergmann was ordered forward to the line Bayazit–Eleskirt–Id. By 5 November this manoeuvre had been completed.

Bergmann now decided to exceed his instructions and push on to Hasankale on the main road to Erzurum. The Turks used IX corps to hold what they took to be the main Russian concentration (in fact only a brigade) advancing south from Oltu and Id, while assembling XI corps at Hasankale and Köprüköy against Bergmann's right. Their counter-attack on 6 November, carried out in snow and rain and with insufficient reconnaissance, was driven back. But on the 9th Izzet himself arrived on the battlefield, and with the weather clear could

---

[71] Hovanissian, *Armenia*, 30–4, 37–8, 41–2.   [72] Suchomlinow, *Erinnerungen*, 284.

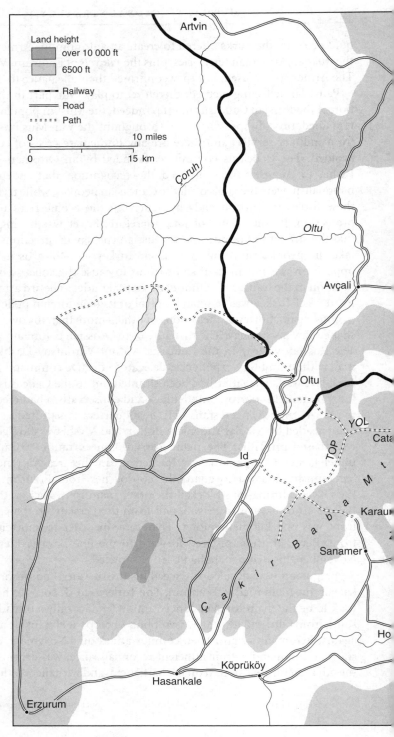

Land height

- ▨ over 10 000 ft
- ▨ 6500 ft
- ┅ Railway
- ── Road
- ┈ Path

| 0 | | 10 miles |
| 0 | | 15 km |

Artvin

Çoruh

Oltu

Avçali

Oltu

YOL

TOP

Cata

Karau

Çakir Baba Mt

Id

Sanamer

Ho

Köprüköy

Hasankale

Erzurum

MAP 26. THE SARIKAMISH REGION

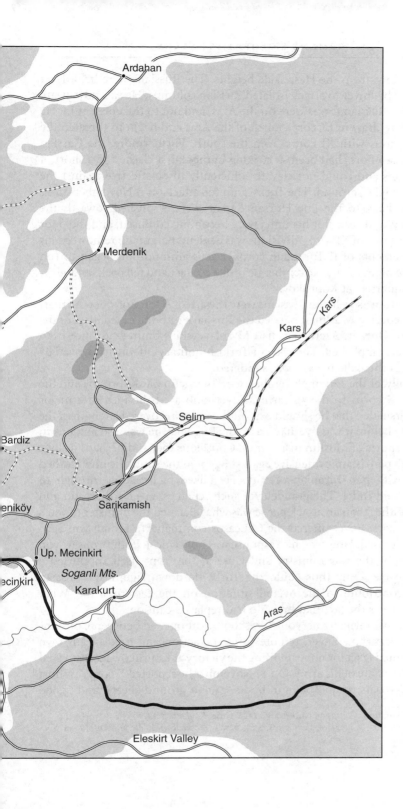

direct operations from the Hasankale heights. The Russians were held. Izzet had been told by Enver to attack isolated Russian columns. He was now aware that the major Russian forces were on the Aras, and not to the north at Id. He could therefore draw in IX corps north of the Aras and begin to threaten the Russian positions with XI corps from the south. Furthermore, the Russian artillery, whose efforts had been so striking in these first clashes, was short of mountain guns and could not elevate sufficiently to be effective against the Turks on the higher ground. The Turks' counter-attack on 11 November drove the Russians back to the line Horsan–Sanamer. Izzet pushed towards the Russian flanks and rear. But his units were becoming confused, and the poor state of at least one of XI corps' divisions was evident. Bergmann reinforced his right with elements of II Turkestan corps. Izzet's ammunition began to run short. On the night of 21/2 November he broke contact and fell back, establishing his headquarters at Köprüköy.[73]

Around Batum as well, the Russians were thwarted. A force of 5,000 Adzhari guerrillas (Georgian Muslims) harried the Russians into the evacuation of the lower Çoruh. Only in Azerbaijan had Myshlayevskii's limited advance been successfully accomplished. The spell of Turkish military inferiority, woven by the defaults of the Balkan wars, was sundered.

Thus, finally, at the end of November, with the victory at Köprüköy and the accession of X corps to the 3rd army, Enver embraced the idea of a major offensive. Persuaded that he should exploit the newly recovered strength of the Turkish army before it was overhauled by the Russians, he was also anxious to exploit the reports of Muslim insurgency. Conscious too, and perhaps jealous of[74] Djemal's pan-Islamic offensive against Egypt in the south, he now clothed his project with pan-Turanian oratory. He talked of breaking through to Afghanistan and India. The grandeur of such schemes, given the season and the terrain, rather than an attack per se was what alarmed the minister of war's German advisors. Enver offered the Caucasus command to Liman von Sanders. Liman refused. However, his response was not typical. Both Bronsart von Schellendorff at the war ministry and Guse at the front itself supported a limited offensive. Only thus could the Turks tie down significant Russian forces and contribute to the overall situation on the eastern front. What worried them was the fact that bravado had replaced caution.

It worried the normally nervous Izzet too. A rift opened between Constantinople and Erzurum. Enver, remote from the action and fired by his own schemes, blamed Izzet for not exploiting the victory at Köprüköy. Izzet stressed the incomplete state of his army. On 29 November he reported X corps as short of 17,000 overcoats, 17,400 pairs of boots, 23,000 ground-sheets, and 13,000

---

[73] Allen and Muratoff, *Caucasian battlefields*, 244–8; Guse, *Kaukasusfront*, 29–33.

[74] This is the theory of Nogales, *Four years*, 25; generally see Haley, *Middle Eastern Studies*, XXX (1994), 227–8.

knapsacks.[75] Enver's response was to send Hafiz Hakki,[76] the 30-year old, thrusting deputy chief of the general staff, to form a personal view. Hakki stoked Enver's ambitions. He glossed over the difficulties and announced that the envelopment of Oltu would take the Russians completely by surprise and open the way to Kars. On 10 December Enver appeared at Izzet's headquarters. Guse briefed Enver in Izzet's presence. Nine days later Izzet was relieved, and Enver himself took over the 3rd army, with Bronsart as his chief of staff and Guse as Bronsart's deputy. Hakki was given the task of putting fire into the belly of X corps.

After Köprüköy the Russians had consolidated their positions for the winter, describing an arc round the Soganli Mountains, their right resting on the Çakir-baba ridge and their left along the Aras, so guarding the railhead at Sarikamish to their rear. Enver's plan reflected the lessons of Tannenberg, that the Russians were vulnerable to attacks against their flanks.[77] He reinforced XI corps's right with two divisions originally bound for Iraq and Syria, and gave it the immense task of fixing by frontal attack the main weight of two Russian corps (both bigger in establishment than a Turkish corps and totalling about 54,000 men). Meanwhile IX corps was to follow a path along the Çakir-baba ridge. This path, the *top yol*, was known to the Russians but was considered impracticable for large bodies of troops. Enver reckoned that its exposed position would keep it swept of snow, and would take it above the ravines which would otherwise impede IX corps's progress. IX corps was to begin its march on 22 December so as to reach Çatak on 24 December. Çatak lay on a transverse track connecting Oltu to Bardiz and Sarikamish. The Turks would therefore be able to fall on the Russians' main base and railhead from the north-west on Christmas day.

But it was to X corps that the task of deep envelopment fell. A single Russian brigade (8,000 men) held Oltu. Therefore X corps was to set out from Id on 22 December and take Oltu on the 23rd. Parts of X corps were then to use the Oltu–Bardiz path to reinforce IX corps, although it was left open to Hakki to press on 73 kilometres to Merdenik and thence to Ardahan (a further 42 kilometres and held by 2,000 men). X corps's northward drive would be facilitated and supported by the eastward attack of elements of the 32nd division, which were to be landed at Rize on the coast and were to advance on Ardahan by way of Artvin.

After the battle Liman blamed Bronsart von Schellendorff for the plan and its execution. He called on Bronsart to resign. Enver protected him, not least because to have done otherwise would have acknowledged that a German, not

[75] Schwarte, *Weltkampf*, iv. 422.

[76] Guse refers to Ismael Hakki; Allen and Muratoff to Hafiz.

[77] Inostransev, *Revue militaire française*, 165 (mars 1935), 334. Inostransev's articles; Guse, *Kaukasus-front*; and Allen and Muratoff, *Caucasian battlefields* are the principal sources for Sarikamish.

he, was the de facto commander. Bronsart himself both downplayed the scale of the disaster and claimed that his advice had not been heeded by Enver. Thus German military thought evaded its share of responsibility.[78] But the whole of Enver's conception bore Schlieffen's stamp. It concentrated strength against weakness. It left weakness to fix strength. It put the weight on planning and timetabling, not on flexibility and improvisation. It set a march programme that took little account of human frailty or of supply problems. And it sketched out the entire campaign right through to its victorious denouement.

The public confrontation on the planning for Sarikamish focused on Liman von Sanders and Enver. The subtler and implicit, but far more important differences must have occurred between Bronsart and Guse. By December 1914 Guse had been with the 3rd army for six months. He did not oppose the attack, as Liman did. Indeed, the idea of an envelopment of the Russian right through Id and Oltu had been germinating at 3rd army headquarters before the arrival of Enver and Bronsart. But Guse did favour a plan that was grounded in reality. The advance from Köprüköy had shown him the problems of forced marches. The 3rd army was capable of short leaps after careful preparation, not of deep penetration. It would need one day's rest for every three or four days' advance. Guse knew, therefore, that the terrain and the weather would present far greater constraints than the Russian deployments. The snows had just begun. And yet IX corps was told to leave its coats and packs behind to ease the burden of its march through the drifts. X corps was given the greatest distance to go. Nonetheless, its forward formations were recalled by Hakki to Erzurum so that he could concentrate his corps before beginning. Thus, X corps's climb was extended. Its equipment was still incomplete. The only comprehensible element in the preparations was the rigidity of the timetable: the absence of transverse links between the three corps and of wireless communications between them and Enver's headquarters left no other option if a plan of this ambition was to be executed.[79]

Up until Christmas Eve the Turkish plan unfolded with reasonable success. Hakki talked of a 'race to Sarikamish' and announced that he would need only 'a few hours' to destroy the Russians.[80] In fact the advance of X corps was slow, but it took Oltu on 23 December. The leading division of IX corps entered Bardiz on the 24th. Bronsart now urged a day's rest. X corps had not pursued the Russian garrison in its retreat from Oltu to Avçali; Hakki's men were exhausted by the march and the battle, and disordered by looting. IX corps was strung out, the 17th division in its rear reporting 40 per cent of its strength

[78] Bihl, *Kaukasus-politik*, 223–4; Wallach, *Anatomie einer Militärhilfe*, 175–7; Haley, *Middle Eastern Studies*, XXX (1994), 229.

[79] Guse, *Kaukasusfront*, 34–5, 38–9; Pomiankowski, *Zusammenbruch*, 103–4. Guse himself is always complimentary about Bronsart: *Kaukasusfront*, 36, 54.

[80] Haley, *Middle Eastern Studies*, XXX (1994), 227.

as stragglers. But a Russian prisoner of war told Enver, who was himself well forward at Bardiz, that Sarikamish was only weakly held. Furthermore, the Turks' supplies were scheduled to run out on 25 December; by then they must have secured the Russians'. The 29th division of IX corps was therefore pushed on to Sarikamish. At the same time Enver issued fresh orders to X corps. He was alarmed by the reports of a Russian concentration at Yeniköy, south of Bardiz; presumably this was the right flank of II Turkestan corps, centred on Karaurgan. Enver requested X corps to move on Bardiz. By now, however, two of its divisions had already set off down the road to Ardahan.

Turkish intentions began to become evident to Myshlayevskii's headquarters from 20 December. The Oltu garrison reported movements from Id. Yudenich had tried to make preparations for Bergmann to reinforce Oltu. But the threat to Oltu, at least from Bergmann's perspective, seemed exaggerated. He knew that XI corps faced him; he did not know of X corps' presence. Not until 22 December had the Russians identified X corps, and on the 24th Bergmann still insisted that its attack was a local affair. Bergmann's solution was to advance I Caucasian corps towards Köprüköy, thus threatening the rear of IX and X corps. For Yudenich, on the other hand, the threat to Sarikamish and to the right and rear of II Turkestan corps was the immediate priority. Indeed, he had already begun moving reinforcements towards Sarikamish. Thus, Myshlayevskii was caught between two opposing interpretations of what was afoot. He compromised, and then compounded the split by appointing Yudenich to the command of II Turkestan corps.[81]

At 11.30 a.m. on 24 December Myshlayevskii finally cancelled Bergmann's attack and ordered the withdrawal of I Caucasian corps. On the following day the commander-in-chief was shot at on the road to Mecinkirt. In his subsequent panic he ordered a general retreat to Kars, emphasizing the need to withdraw through Sarikamish before the Turks seized the railhead. Bergmann's advance, although criticized by Yudenich's supporters, had retained for the Russians freedom of manoeuvre. I Caucasian corps put pressure on Turkish XI corps, not vice versa; nor had the Turks mastered the Karakurt–Sarikamish road. Thus the Russians still had the advantage of interior lines. The longer Sarikamish could hold, the more feasible became the prospects of a Russian escape.

The Turkish attack on Sarikamish did not begin in earnest until 27 December, two days later. The 29th division, leading IX corps, was misled in its march from Bardiz by the inaccuracies of its maps. The night of 25/6 December was particularly cold. By the morning, the 29th division, without having yet

---

[81] Inostransev, *Revue militaire française*, 164 (février 1935), 203–5, emphasizes the logic of Bergmann's thinking and actions, and throughout plays little regard to Yudenich. Allen and Muratoff, *Caucasian battlefields*, see Yudenich as the hero of Sarikamish, and indeed of the Caucasus war as a whole.

fought a major action, was reduced by frostbite and exposure to half its strength. Furthermore, the Turks, confident of being unopposed, placed three out of their eight mountain guns too far forward, where they were silenced by the two Russian pieces in Sarikamish. Enver therefore decided to await the arrival of the corps' other division, the 17th, and of X corps. Given his belief that XI corps would stop the main Russian forces from redeploying, the delay seemed acceptable.

Between 25 and 27 December the Russian garrison at Sarikamish was swelled from two reserve battalions, one squadron of cavalry, and two guns, to ten battalions, seven squadrons, and six guns. By the 27th, with the advent of the 17th division, IX corps mustered about 10,000 of its original complement of 25,000. Its attacks, although determined, were held. Not until 29 December did Hakki's X corps enter the battle from the north. Following its original orders, it had reached Merdenik before doubling back to Bardiz. Its march across mountain peaks, reaching heights of 3,000 metres, where the snow was above waist level, took nearly four times longer than anticipated by its German chief of staff, and reduced its strength by a third. On 28 December it had to rest. On the 29th both IX and X corps attacked Sarikamish, bringing a total of 18,000 men against 14,000 Russians, and cutting the latter's communications with Kars. In the night the 17th division got into the town, but it was repelled. The crisis at Sarikamish had passed. Enver's orders of 31 December did no more than express the hope that his troops could hold their positions on the morrow.

The Russian opportunity to turn desperate defence into devastating counter-attack was recognized by Yudenich. During the evening of 26 December the chief of staff of the Turkish 28th division was captured. From him Myshlayevskii learnt the full scope of Enver's intended envelopment. Sarikamish he counted as lost: his only hope lay in blocking the Turks between Sarikamish and Kars. On the 27th Myshlayevskii was far from the front, in Tiflis, spreading panic and telling his forces in Persian Azerbaijan to fall back. Using the same information, Yudenich came to different conclusions. Both the Turkish enveloping corps were grouped on one line of communications passing through Bardiz; they could not, in the middle of a Caucasian winter, hold their ground long. Moreover, to pull back the two Russian corps while they were engaged with Turkish XI corps risked turning retreat into rout. Therefore, for Yudenich, Sarikamish, far from being abandoned, should become the pivot of a manoeuvre of the Russians' own. His II Turkestan corps was to hold the line Mecinkirt–Karaurgan–Yeniköy, so guarding Bergmann's left flank. From his own right he spurred on the two regiments at Yeniköy to march north across mountain passes, and so strike the communications of IX and X corps at Bardiz. The guns of this column opened fire on Bardiz on 30 December.

Yudenich's powers of persuasion had now to be applied to Bergmann rather than Myshlayevskii. Bergmann was a brave, if foolhardy man, committed to the offensive; there is no reason to believe Yudenich's supporters who bracket Bergmann's conduct with that of Myshlayevskii's in the crucial days of 27–30 December. Certainly his intention was to pull back from his forward position, still 13 kilometres south-west of Mecinkirt on the 28th; certainly too he continued until at least 31 December to envisage the possibility of a full-scale retreat back through Sarikamish. On the other hand, he left two divisions to shore up Yudenich's front. Thus a general retreat was not the only option in his mind. He sent the equivalent of two Cossack cavalry divisions under Baratov east of Sarikamish to link with reinforcing elements moving south from Kars. By the night of 2/3 January 1915 Baratov's group was near Selim, on the railway north of Sarikamish, ready to threaten the retreat of Hakki's X corps. Bergmann was slow to take the opportunity thus presented: he had envisaged Baratov's primary task as that of clearing the Sarikamish–Kars railway. But it seems far-fetched to give the credit for this manoeuvre to Yudenich, given the fact he had no direct responsibility for Baratov and was preoccupied with a desperate battle on the Russians' other flank. Indeed, by this stage the thrust which Yudenich was advocating was a Russian advance from Sarikamish, a much more limited envelopment and one probably beyond the physical powers of the exhausted garrison despite its growing numerical superiority. Ironically, neither Yudenich nor Bergmann saw the opportunity for Baratov to strike X corps; the idea was Myshlayevskii's. Thus all three had a role in the great Russian counter-envelopment, and the manoeuvre itself was the product of improvisation and of flexibility, not of long-term planning. But on 6 January Yudenich replaced Bergmann as the commander; Yudenich's was therefore the version of events that came to dominate.[82]

Yudenich's contribution to victory between 31 December and 6 January was nonetheless vital, albeit more prosaic. With IX corps reduced to 1,000 men fit, Enver recognized that his only hope lay in XI corps' frontal attack between Yeniköy and Karaurgan. He himself escaped through the Russian net to join XI corps. The withdrawal and redistribution of I Caucasian corps left II Turkestan corps holding the line with nineteen battalions to the Turks' thirty. It did so. On 10 January II Turkestan corps counter-attacked, a column of 1,500 men passing through the mountains on the Turks' left, covering 3 to 5 kilometres a day across thick snow, to strike at Zivin in their rear. On 16 January XI corps commenced its retreat.

[82] Inostransev, *Revue militaire française*, 164 (février 1935), 207–8, seems to imagine that the whole Russian manoeuvre was conceived on 27 December. If that were the case, and following Allen and Muratoff, *Caucasian battlefields*, 268–9, 272–4, Yudenich would have to have been its author. But Inostransev, *Revue militaire française*, 165 (mars 1935), 329–32, then gives Bergmann the credit for Baratov's manoeuvre and for seeing the opportunity for envelopment on 2/3 January 1915. Allen and Muratoff, *Caucasian battlefields*, 276–80, see Bergmann as still devoid of insight and delaying Baratov's manoeuvre till 6 January.

X corps began to pull back from its position north of Sarikamish on the night of 1/2 January. Baratov's manoeuvre was both delayed, partly thanks to fog on the 3rd, and frontal, principally due to Bergmann telling him to conform to the movements of those on his left. X corps described an arc around Sarikamish and then trudged back along the Çakir–baba ridge. The Russians retook Ardahan on 3 January and Oltu on the 12th, but halted at Id on the 18th. Hakki led 3,000 men back into Hasankale. The remnants of IX corps, taken in the rear from Bardiz and in the front from Sarikamish, surrendered on 4 January.

Only at the very end of the battle had the Russians outmanoeuvred the Turks. Guse concluded that, up until the night attack on Sarikamish on 29/30 December, Enver might have succeeded. But Guse's conclusion, that the outcome was therefore dictated by the Turks' inexperience in night operations, seems far-fetched. It was the terrain and the weather, and the failure to plan for these, not fighting the Russians that broke the Turkish 3rd army. The Turks had already lost 25,000 men, and with them their numerical advantage, before they had even made contact with the Russians. The temperature at Ardahan never rose above minus 31 degrees centigrade, and dropped as low as minus 36 degrees. The Russians found 30,000 frozen bodies around Sarikamish alone, and reckoned that 20,000 lightly wounded Turks died through lack of medical care. The precise figures for Turkish losses are nonetheless elusive. Russian calculations included 27,000 prisoners of war and 30,000 dead; 12,000 deserters were rounded up in Erzurum: 75,000 as a total is the lowest estimate; some rise to 90,000. The 3rd army's effective strength on 23 January was put at 12,400 men.[83]

The significance of Sarikamish lies not only in the operational defeat, but above all in its strategic repercussions. Enver had broadcast his offensive as the beginning of a great pan-Turanian movement. The panic in Tiflis had aroused Georgian expectations; in the area around Batum the Adzharis had risen in support of the Turks. But most Muslims had preferred to wait and see. The Russian Armenians had declared their hands, calling for popular resistance to the Turkish invasion and raising units of volunteers. Enver's defeat was followed by ruthless Russian repression of the Adzharis, the Muslim population of the Çoruh valley falling from 52,000 to 7,000 between February and April 1915. Elsewhere conciliation was more prevalent than persecution.[84]

The defeat of pan-Turkism and the consequent loyalty of the Caucasian populations to Russia freed Stavka from worries about its southern front in

[83] Bihl, *Kaukasus-politik*, 222–3; Guse, *Kaukasusfront*, 49–50; Pomiankowski, *Zusammenbruch*, 103–4; Allen and Muratoff, *Caucasian battlefields*, 283–4; Larcher, *La Guerre turque*, 389; Falls, *First World War*, 96.

[84] Hovanissian, *Armenia*, 47–8; Jones, *Military–naval encyclopedia*, iv. 218–20.

1915. However, the strategic ramifications of Sarikamish were more extensive and decisive than that.

Pan-Turkism regained vitality as Russia weakened in 1917. Pan-Islam never recovered. Although pan-Islam was not a primary objective in the campaign, its melding with Ottoman and pan-Turk objectives made it also a loser. The defeat came within six weeks of the summons to holy war. Victory in the Caucasus might well have provided the impetus to turn aspirations into reality. But the conjunction of the declaration and of the catastrophe were too close to be subsequently erased. However considerable the Turkish military achievements of 1915, and however strenuous the efforts of German and Ottoman propaganda, first impressions proved vital. Throughout Asia, Sarikamish confirmed the image of Ottoman decline. It was a major coup in limiting a war that otherwise had only expanded during its first six months. It was a decisive battle.

SUEZ, EGYPT, AND LIBYA

In Germany the planned attack on Egypt was a means to an end; for Turkey it was an end in itself. The Suez Canal constituted the most direct route between Britain and its eastern empire. To threaten it would draw off British and Indian troops that might otherwise be destined for Europe; to seize it would cut British trade and maritime power in half. The project was, therefore, clearly related to the wider objectives of the war.

Turkey, however, had little interest in blocking the Suez Canal per se. Much more important was the integrity of the Ottoman empire and the loyalty of its Arab population. Formally speaking, Egypt was still part of that empire, but since the nationalists' revolt of 1881–2 the Sultan's sovereignty had been no more than nominal. Real power was exercised by Britain through its consul-general, Lord Kitchener. To the south the Sudan was governed as an Anglo-Egyptian condominium, although its governor-general and the sirdar of the Egyptian army was an Englishman, Sir Reginald Wingate. To the west of Egypt lay the lands of Libya, Cyrenaica and Tripolitania. Here Turkey had been obliged to cede its sovereignty, but as recently as September 1912, and not without first reminding Italy 'that to demand that the Imperial Government amputate from itself so vital a member of its Empire was equivalent to proposing that it commit suicide'.[85] Turkey wanted back its lost territories.

The fulfilment of Turkey's aims would still serve Germany's. But the reverse did not also apply. Conquest of such a large land mass would require

---

[85] Quoted by Herrmann, *English Historical Review*, CIV (1989), 345.

considerable planning and a numerous army. The logistical considerations in a theatre made up predominantly of desert argued that preparations on a sufficient scale would be so lengthy as to stretch almost to infinity. What the Germans wanted was action now. Thrusts on Egypt, however ill co-ordinated or weakly mounted, would be sufficient to draw British troops from other theatres.

The grander Ottoman conception created a second tension with its ally. On 2 August 1914 Moltke called for revolution in Egypt. Thus, during the period of Turkish neutrality Berlin looked to Egyptian nationalism to effect its strategy. Wangenheim's negotiations in Constantinople with Abbas Hilmi, the Khedive of Egypt, alarmed the Turks. Abbas was recovering from an assassination attempt which he attributed to a conspiracy on the part of the Turkish government. He hoped to exclude the Turks from his dealings with the Germans. But the Turks had no intention of presiding over the birth of full Egyptian independence. Said Halim, the grand vizier and also an Egyptian, was rumoured to aspire to be Khedive himself. Enver was angered by Abbas's claim to be Caliph of all the Arabs. The Turks therefore emphasized the spiritual authority of the Ottoman Caliphate, while playing down its corollary—the temporal rule of the Sultan. Both powers pinned their hopes of military success on local Egyptian support, and yet the message they conveyed to the nationalists was contradictory. Germany held out the prospect of full independence, but to achieve that it ended up using Turkish troops, who—if successful—would replace one suzerainty with another.

In any case, Egyptian nationalism, although the fundamental premiss on which the campaign rested, was at a low ebb. Strong enough in 1882 to throw off the Turks, and able in 1921 to command full independence, in 1914 it was fractured and incoherent. The larger of the nationalist parties, the Watanists, simultaneously advocated Egyptian territorial patriotism and solidarity with the Ottoman empire. The contradictions in this position were more evident at the religious level than at the political: the Watanists embraced pan-Islam while preaching the unity of Muslim and Copt within Egypt. Politically, the two threads fused as means and ends: Ottoman rule was a stick with which to beat the British so as to achieve independence. The smaller of the nationalist groupings, the Umma party, was more logical in resolving these conundrums. Its leader, Ahmad Lutfi al-Sayyid, rejected any political links with Turkey, and embraced British economic and social reforms as a preliminary to formal Egyptian independence from Constantinople. Although isolated from majority Egyptian feeling when pan-Islamic nationalism revived during the Turks' war with Italy, Lutfi enjoyed British backing. The Watanists, on the other hand, fell into disarray after the death in 1908 of their main spokesman Mustafa Kamil. His followers welcomed the Young Turks' revolution, but at that stage the Committee of Union and Progress was more concerned to secure British than Egyptian backing, and thus the Watanists received no encouragement in return. By the time the Committee took a more positive line, in 1911–12, the Watanists were in no position to respond. Sheikh Abd al-'Aziz Jawish went into exile in December 1911, and became a spokesman of pan-Islam rather than of Egyptian nationalism, eventually editing *Die islamische Welt* from Berlin. Kamil's successor, Muhammed Farid, refused the financial support of the Khedive, broke with his more prosperous Egyptian supporters, and followed Jawish to Constantinople in March 1912. The Watanist press folded. The Umma party's paper, *al-Jarida*, survived, its more moderate line earning it British toleration and the British being rewarded with wartime loyalty, even as the Turks advanced on the Suez Canal. Thus, in 1914, when probably most Egyptians were sympathetic to the Ottoman cause, the party best qualified to articulate their feelings was in confusion. At the same time the more resilient of the nationalist parties was the smaller in terms of popular support.[86]

Neither party, however, was a fully fledged organization with a broad base of followers. Instead, each was a grouping of political thinkers and activists, rooted in the urban middle class and themselves the products of a Europeanization which sat uncomfortably with Islamic rhetoric. They constituted an educated and professional élite, frustrated by an increasingly direct British rule which blocked them from major office. Their ideologies paid no attention to the economic plight of the fellahin, the Egyptian peasantry. In 1904 929,000 fellahin farmed individual plots of less than 5.5 acres. Kitchener, as consul-general from 1911, set out to improve the material conditions of the fellahin, prohibiting mortgages on these smallholdings in order to curb indebtedness, and protecting the rights of primary producers in their negotiations with the cotton dealers. Conflicting commercial interests, therefore, cut across nationalist or Muslim fusion.[87]

In August 1914 Kitchener was in London, the Khedive was recuperating in Constantinople, and the newly formed legislative assembly was adjourned. Lutfi urged the prime minister, Hussein Rushdi Pasha, to declare war against the Central Powers, demanding that Britain in exchange acknowledge Egypt's independence of Turkey. Rushdi recognized that the British occupation made neutrality unsustainable, but proved too weak to exploit the opportunity for any reciprocal concession. On 5 August Egypt declared war on the Central Powers.

The position of the Khedive was thus increasingly awkward. His anti-British sympathies were overt; but his dealings with the Germans made him progressively more dependent on the almost equally uncongenial Turks. It is not clear

---

[86] On Egyptian nationalism, see Gershoni and Jankowski, *Egypt, Islam, and the Arabs*, 4–24; Goldschmidt 'The Egyptian Nationalist Party'; M. W. Daly, 'Egypt' in A. D. Roberts (ed.), *Cambridge History of Africa*, vii. 745; Landau, *Politics of pan-Islam*, 122–33.

[87] Elgood, *Egypt and the army*, 19.

precisely how either Abbas Hilmi or Wangenheim imagined they would execute a German-sponsored coup in Cairo. Most probably they looked to the army and the police. But in that case they were naive: fourteen of the seventeen infantry battalions of the Egyptian army were stationed not in Egypt but in the Sudan. However, on 4 September Enver revealed that forty senior Egyptian officers had pledged loyalty to the Committee of Union and Progress. If Abbas Hilmi was to return to Cairo in triumph it had to be with Turkish sponsorship. He was therefore forced to accept Enver's challenge that he place himself at the head of a Turkish army to invade Egypt.

The British, angered by the Khedive's past conspiracies against them and still anxious to preserve Turkish neutrality if possible, saw Abbas Hilmi rather than Enver as the villain of the piece. London's ambassador in Constantinople, Sir Louis Mallet, therefore completed the transformation of the Khedival holiday into permanent exile. Within Egypt the convening of the legislative assembly, scheduled for November 1914, was postponed, and on 20 October Rushdi outlawed assemblies of more than five people. On 2 November martial law was established. Thus, when on 7 November war with Turkey was announced in Egypt, possible pro-Ottoman demonstrations had already been pre-empted. Under the provisions of martial law, the legislative assembly was prorogued *sine die*. As importantly, several hundred Egyptian officials with nationalist leanings were interned or exiled. If there was an underground conspiracy in favour of the Khedive or of Turkey (and the direct evidence that there was is confined to Wangenheim's reports from Constantinople),[88] it was now definitively quashed. On 18 December Britain declared Egypt a protectorate, thus terminating Ottoman sovereignty. On the following day Abbas Hilmi was deposed, and his uncle, Hussein Kamil, declared Sultan.

Therefore, as 1914 closed the British hold on Egypt tightened. But German and Turkish hopes of a popular rising did not diminish. Deprived of up-to-date intelligence, they listened to exiled nationalists who assured them that the first Turkish soldier to arrive on the Suez Canal would cause all Egypt to rise.[89] This chimed in well with Oppenheim's exaggerated predictions from Berlin. More tangible were the offers of support from the Bedouin of the Sinai desert. About 50,000 Arab volunteers, including Syrians and Druses, joined the Turkish 4th army. Their role was to agitate among the Muslims of the Indian and Egyptian armies along the canal.[90] But the educated Egyptians of 1914 were contemptuous of the nomads to the east, and were reluctant to subscribe to

[88] Weber, *Eagles on the crescent*, 88–91. Macmunn and Falls, *Military operations: Egypt and Palestine*, i. 35, mention a possible German coup; Gershoni and Jankowski, *Egypt, Islam and the Arabs*, 25, say a conspiracy was rumoured but not confirmed.
[89] Kress von Kressenstein, *Mit den Türken*, 75–6.
[90] Bihl, *Kaukasus-politik*, 43; Newell, 'British military policy in Egypt', 43–5.

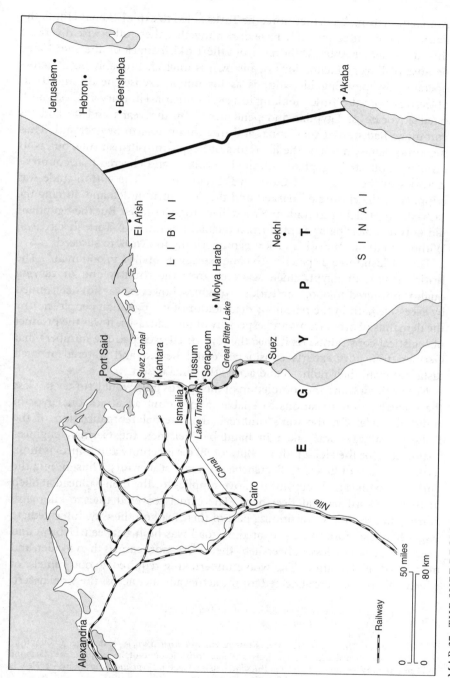

MAP 27. THE SUEZ REGION

Arab nationalism.[91] Furthermore, the Turks failed to exploit Abbas Hilmi, the figure who might conceivably have drawn together these otherwise divergent threads. Whether Abbas withdrew from the Turkish attack on the Suez Canal because of Enver's inclinations or his own is unclear. Probably both factors operated. By pleading his wounds as his public excuse, he distanced his objectives from the Turks', looking instead to Austria-Hungary as a less interested advocate of Egyptian independence.[92] By the year's end he and his entourage had moved to Vienna, and in autumn 1915 to Switzerland. Thus the Turks came on not as the liberators of Egypt from British rule, but as its invaders. Educated Egyptians admired Germany, and cheered that country's victories in the cinemas of Cairo in February 1915.[93] The cotton trade was crippled by the closure of markets and the downturn in demand, forcing the cash-hungry fellahin to trade their jewellery to meet taxes. But the Egyptians did not turn their passive anti-British inclinations into pro-Turkish activism. Without that, the Turkish attack was numerically too weak to succeed.

The Turkish force dispatched to conquer Egypt totalled 19,000 men.[94] The British troops in Egypt, albeit scattered over the country and of varying quality, mustered 70,000. The Turkish weakness, however, was not determined by excessive faith in the rebellious demeanour of the Egyptian people, nor by the demands of other fronts and especially of the Caucasus. It was the product of logistical constraints. As it was, the force used exceeded the numbers that German transport experts considered could be fed and watered at such distances from their railhead and across the Sinai desert.

Not until 1918, and the completion of the Taurus link, would Turkey possess the railway communications to enable it to mount an attack on Egypt in sufficient style. On the war's outbreak the internal reorganization of the Palestine railways was taken in hand by Meissner, the German engineer responsible for the Hejaz railway. But, for all his ingenuity and improvisation, Jerusalem was not linked to Beersheba until 17 October 1915. Thus, in 1914 the Turks relied on camel columns to move supplies for the then-railhead at Sileh to their forward base at Beersheba. The camels covered the 170-kilometre journey in eight days, consuming part of their load on the way. Intermediate stages had therefore to be prepared. A road was built between Hebron and Beersheba. Nonetheless, at Beersheba there were more camels than fodder, and many died of starvation. The whole undertaking required 30,000 camels, of which only 11,000 were allocated for the actual advance across the Sinai desert.

[91] Gershoni and Jankowski, *Egypt, Islam, and the Arabs*, 15–17.
[92] Bihl, *Kaukasus-politik*, 118–19, 214–15.
[93] Fewster, *Bean*, 41.
[94] This figure is derived from Kress van Kressenstein, *Mit den Türken*, 85–6; the other account from the Turkish side, Djemal, *Memoirs*, 150–1, gives 25,000. British accounts of the campaign are Macmunn and Falls, *Military operations: Egypt and Palestine*, i. 19–52; Elgood, *Egypt and the army*, 108–37; Newell, 'British military policy in Egypt and Palestine', 64–78.

Such demands drove up prices, and the camel-dealers insisted on payment in gold, which came from Germany. Drivers and overseers proved as hard to procure as the camels themselves. Enver, in his plan of 22 October, promised an attack within six weeks. That proved impossible.

The 4th Turkish army had been warned on mobilization in August that its probable role would be the invasion of Egypt. But both the army's commander, Zekki Pasha, and his chief of staff opposed the scheme. Zekki was concerned for internal order in Syria and for the vulnerability of the coastline to British naval attack. Enver therefore passed the task direct to VIII corps, circumventing Zekki, and appointing Kress von Kressenstein as the corps's chief of staff. VIII corps's commander embraced the task with zeal, but not until mid-November was Zekki relieved of his command. His replacement was Djemal, the minister of marine. Thus, at a stroke, Enver resolved two problems. His most obvious rival in Constantinople was moved to Syria, enabling Enver to assume de facto command of the navy as well as the army. Secondly, the 4th army became the vehicle for pan-Islamic aggression. Djemal ordered a holy flag to be brought from Mecca. On 20 December it was paraded through Jerusalem, and it, together with a number of Arab priests, accompanied the expedition. The symmetry and virtual simultaneity of the two offensives— Enver's pan-Turanian attack in the Caucasus and Djemal's pan-Islamic thrust on Egypt—revealed the personal rivalry that underpinned (and undermined) the direction of Turkish strategy. Djemal was no soldier. His relationship with his chief professional adviser, Kress von Kressenstein, was therefore of fundamental importance. British intelligence thought it fraught from the outset; certainly by 1917 the clash between the two on operational matters had become fundamental. But in his memoirs Kress was restrained, and even at times complimentary, in his account of Djemal. Djemal spoke French but was not himself, Kress concluded, anti-German. The problem was one of access. Not until later in 1915 would Kress actually become chief of staff in the 4th army; in 1914–15 that post was held by Werner von Frankenberg. But Kress felt that if he could get to see his army commander, then on the whole they could resolve their differences.

Kress had completed his reconnaissance of southern Syria on 23 October. He had conducted it without adequate maps and with insufficient intelligence. The only German map was on a scale of 1 : 1,400,000. Captured British maps on scales of 1 : 250,000 and 1 : 125,000 would compensate, but not until 1916. Nonetheless, Kress plumped for the most difficult of the three possible routes across the Sinai desert.

The obvious line of march lay along the Mediterranean coast from El Arish. But the water here was brackish, the going soft and sandy, and progress observable by the British vessels off the coast. The southern route, by way of Akaba and Nekhl, used by pilgrims from Egypt to Mecca, was lengthy and also vulnerable to British sea-power in the headwaters of the Red Sea. The central approach, tracing a virtually direct line from Beersheba to Ismailia, had countervailing advantages. It promised the greatest chance of surprise. Being across limestone, the going was good. The expedition would have to carry its own water for three or four days, but there were cisterns at Moiya Harab. The rains of November 1914 were unusually heavy; they frustrated the Turks' road and railway construction in Syria, but they filled the wells in Sinai. From Moiya Harab the Turks could strike the canal at two points where it could be bridged and where it was close to the adjacent sweet-water canal.

The central route, nonetheless, confirmed the small size of the Turkish force. The three divisions of VIII corps were under strength and, more significantly in the demonology of the Ottoman army, made up of Arabs; two Anatolian divisions reinforced the corps, but were kept back in the attack.[95] There were those who wanted to postpone operations until the expedition could be better equipped and prepared. Kress may have been among them. Certainly Djemal saw himself as the deliverer of Egypt from British bondage. He wanted a supply dump in the desert sufficient to keep his forces active on the Suez Canal for a month, not a week. Falkenhayn at OHL disagreed. For him a rapid thrust on the canal now, with its impact on other theatres, was more important than a major victory later. After his defeat at Sarikamish Enver followed the line of the German high command. The effect of this division of objective was to please neither side. The Turkish advance did not get under way until 14/15 January 1915, three weeks after Kress's original starting date. But when it did leave it was short of artillery and ammunition, of all that it needed to sustain operations for more than a brief period.[96]

Djemal's command was divided into two echelons. The first included two small columns, advancing from El Arish to Kantara and from Nekhl to Suez, along the northern and southern routes. Their task was diversionary. The first echelon's main column, about 10,000 men, with pontoon equipment and a 15 cm heavy howitzer battery, was to attack south of Ismailia. The second echelon, totalling 8,000 men, was to follow sufficiently slowly to allow the transport of the first echelon to return and the wells to refill. Meanwhile the first echelon was to pause until the second came up. Djemal planned to get across the canal at the first rush, securing a bridgehead on the western bank, and then holding Ismailia for four to five days until he could concentrate his forces there. By then, he hoped, all Egypt would have risen in his support.

In 1907 the idea that rebellion was the greatest danger to the British in Egypt was one shared by the Committee of Imperial Defence. In a study prompted by a dispute over the frontier with Palestine, it accepted the general staff's verdict that only a small raiding force of 1,000 to 3,000 men, mounted on camels,

[95] Sheffy, British military intelligence, 47–8.   [96] Mühlmann, Waffenbündnis, 88–91.

could cross the Sinai desert. The effectiveness of such an attack would therefore be contingent on its domestic impact.

But not all participated in the general staff's equanimity about the scale of the external danger. Sir John French said that the Turks could get a force of 100,000 men to the Suez Canal. By 1911–12 the War Office was more receptive to such calculations, partly because it was anxious to prevent the Admiralty abandoning the eastern Mediterranean. The intelligence network created to provide early warning of any attack found several routes across the desert and more abundant water supplies than previously imagined. Transport replaced water as the most likely constraint on an Ottoman army. In 1913–14, with the archaeologists Leonard Woolley and T. E. Lawrence as cover, the Palestine Exploration Fund extended the surveying work of British intelligence towards Palestine, and in particular monitored the progress of the railway. Estimates of the size of the Turkish army in Syria climbed as 1914 unfolded, not least because the Bedouins the British used as spies tended to exaggerate what they saw. Tighter border controls after August, although they blocked the flow of human intelligence, did not revise the totals downwards. On 10 January 1915 Gilbert Clayton, the head of military intelligence in Egypt, echoed French's fears of almost a decade earlier; he reckoned that there were 100,000 men available for the invasion of Egypt, and that they could be on the canal in two weeks' time.

The potential for panic was obvious. The fear of revolution could now be allied to the threat of a full-dress invasion, and Milne Cheetham, acting chief at the British residency in Cairo, took exactly that line.[97] But neither Kitchener in London nor the commander-in-chief in Egypt, Sir John Maxwell, would support him. Maxwell, appointed on 18 August 1914, was an old Egyptian hand. He had, in T. E. Lawrence's words, 'a mysterious gift of prophesying what will happen, and a marvellous carelessness about what might happen. There couldn't be a better person to command in Egypt. He takes the whole job as a splendid joke.'[98] He saw the Sinai not as a military highway but as an obstacle. He also shared the widespread belief, based on the Balkan wars and confirmed by most of the British army's reports since, that the only strength of the Turkish army was the hardiness of the Anatolian peasant, and that even he was ill trained and ill motivated.

For much of 1914 the War Office persuaded itself that the main offensive orientation of the Turkish army was towards the Caucasus and Russia. By the end of November both the director of military intelligence in London and the intelligence department in Cairo had reversed this assumption. They now saw the principal danger in Egypt and regarded the deployment in the Caucasus as

[97] McKale, *European History Quarterly*, XXVII (1997), 206.
[98] J. Wilson, *Lawrence of Arabia*, 173.

defensive. Nonetheless, the Ottoman concentration in Syria could also be seen as defensive: the build-up might be designed to parry a British amphibious landing from the Mediterranean.

The Committee of Imperial Defence had canvassed this very option in 1906–7. Its secretary, Sir George Clarke, said that the best defence of Egypt would be a pre-emptive thrust against Turkish communications, aimed either at Haifa or at Alexandretta. Maxwell's underestimation of the threat from Palestine was therefore driven by contradictory but ulterior motives. At one level he recognized the diversionary thrust of German strategy, determining that he should not be caught by it but should ship troops to France as fast as possible. Yet at another, the shield of the Sinai was the means to enable a sword to be thrust into Syria. In November 1914 an amphibious operation at Haifa was proposed; in December Maxwell, Kitchener, and Sir Charles Callwell (the director of military operations) focused on Alexandretta, the hinge of Turkish communications from southern Anatolia to its Arab possessions. Thus the defence of Egypt would be given an offensive form. British counsels were therefore sorely tempted by exactly the considerations which had fired the fears of Zekki and the hopes of Germany. In January, however, the War Office calculated that such an undertaking would require 21,000 men; its scale and its likely duration led to its postponement.[99]

Meanwhile, Maxwell had received abundant intelligence of Turkish intentions. Robert Mors, a German by descent but a lieutenant in the Egyptian police, who had been recruited by Prüfer to co-ordinate terrorism in Egypt, was captured in late October. On the strength of the information he provided the British rounded up possible supporters of the Central Powers.[100] Kress's reconnaissance was reported by the Greek consul in Damascus. From November onwards accounts of a Turkish build-up in Syria reached Cairo by way of refugees and of the British military attaché in Sofia. On 15 January British intelligence reckoned that the Turks had six infantry divisions between Adana and Beersheba. Although the Turks advanced by night, aerial reconnaissance—conducted by long-range French seaplanes—enabled their movements to be followed. Bad weather disrupted observation for almost two weeks after 5 January, but on 18 January between 30,000 and 40,000 troops were spotted in the sector Beersheba–Libni–El Arish. What had been seen was VIII corps, bound for the central route, in the act of passing the diversionary forces destined for the northerly route. However, the first impressions were of a larger body designed to follow the coast road alone. Cloud prevented further reconnaissance until the 24th, by which time there was no evidence of major forces to the north, and by 27 January the intelligence department was clear

---

[99] Newell, 'British military policy in Egypt and Palestine', 46–59; J. Wilson, *Lawrence of Arabia*, 134–8, 167–72.
[100] McKale, *War by revolution*, 53, 576, 71.

that the principal thrust was in the centre. But Maxwell could not divest himself of two preconceptions—that the Turkish forces in Sinai were possibly twice as strong as they were, and that they would use the northern route for the larger body.[101]

By the end of January Maxwell had remarkably precise and accurate details as to the Turks' dispositions at either end of Lake Timsah. Although he reinforced the central sector around Ismailia accordingly, he could not bring himself to abandon entirely the defences to north and south. The former, facing the coastal route used in reverse by Napoleon, would enable him to employ the support of the Royal Navy; the latter, the Red Sea approaches, figured (albeit probably unknown to Maxwell) in the hare-brained schemes of German naval officers.[102] Nine British warships patrolled the channel. He therefore treated the canal as a line of defence, placing his forces on the western rather than the eastern bank. The two Indian divisions deployed were in reality a hastily formed collection of brigades with indifferent artillery, and incorporating many Muslims of perhaps doubtful loyalty. The commitment to a static defence was therefore total—so much so that the intelligence on the Turks was not relayed in full from Cairo to the forward units. Britain had been the first to breach the neutrality of the canal zone: the need thereafter was to underline that the justification for British action was Turkish aggression and the protection of neutrals' rights of navigation.

The Turkish march was a triumph of good management. Baggage was cut to a minimum, officers being allowed only 15 kilos each. The soldiers' daily ration was restricted to tea, biscuits, and dates. And yet there were no losses and the sick rate was kept to one man per thousand. It was on the day of the attack that things went wrong.

Kress's plan was for half the central force to advance on Ismailia on 2 February, drawing the British into the defence of the area to the north of Lake Timsah. The Turks would then move to their left and to the south, to support the main attack which would strike the canal between Tussum and Serapeum at 10.30 p.m. Divided into eight columns, some hundreds of metres apart, and each including three pontoons and a half-company of pioneers, the Turks would cross to the west bank under cover of dark. Surprise was all. Therefore the howitzers, there being only four of them, were not employed in advance of the attack on the slow-moving traffic in the canal. Nor did the infantry fire as the pontoons were being dragged into position.

A sandstorm on the night of 2/3 February caused the bridging train to lose its way and the attack to be delayed until 2 a.m. Not until 3.25 a.m. was the British observation post at Tussum aware of the attack. Three pontoons reached the far bank, but then daylight exposed the bridging equipment to the fire of the

---

[101] Sheffy, *British military intelligence*, 53–4.   [102] Neulen, *Feldgrau in Jerusalem*, 64–5.

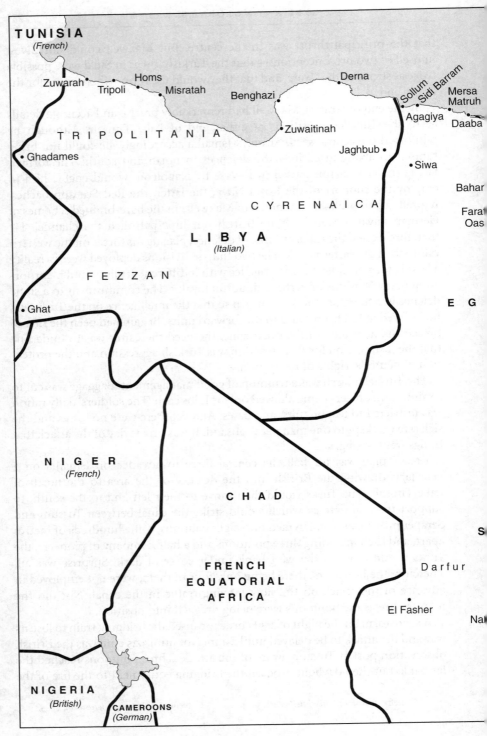

MAP 28. LIBYA, EGYPT, AND THE SUDAN

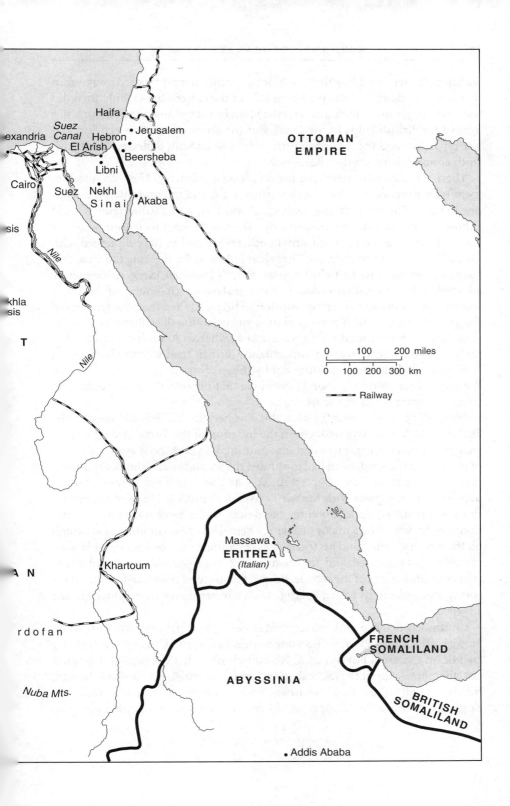

Haifa

Suez
Canal
exandria

Jerusalem

OTTOMAN
EMPIRE

Hebron
El Arîsh
Cairo   Beersheba
            Libni
Suez   Nekhl
S i n a i   Akaba

sis

Nile

khla
sis

T

Nile

0   100   200 miles
0   100   200   300 km

━━ Railway

A N   Khartoum

Massawa
ERITREA
(Italian)

rdofan

FRENCH
SOMALILAND

Nuba Mts.

ABYSSINIA

BRITISH
SOMALILAND

Addis Ababa

Indian defenders, enabling them to hole the pontoons and floats. At 7.45 a.m. a torpedo boat destroyed the pontoons left on the eastern bank. Only then did the Turks begin using their artillery, the 15 cm howitzers making good practice against the British ships in the canal. But the attack of the first echelon had already failed, and the feints to north and south had not deflected the British from concentrating on the vital sector.

There was a case for renewing the attack on 4 February. The 10th division, forming the second echelon, had remained fresh and uncommitted throughout the day. But the bridging equipment was lost, and further failure could expose the entire force to annihilation. Djemal decided to withdraw under cover of dark that night. The German officers seemed to have disagreed with Djemal's decision: certainly, the Turks blamed them for pressing the attack on the 3rd when surprise had already been lost.[103] However, Kress subsequently concluded that Djemal's decision was correct. For him the source of the defeat was less the sandstorm and its disruption to his plans than the poor training of the Turkish troops which prevented their surmounting the subsequent confusion. Although the 10th division was Turkish, whereas Arabs had been used in the attacks on 3 February, the Turkish and German tendency to blame all on their Arab soldiers was not borne out by the gallantry of those who did cross the canal. There was no reason to conclude that the 10th division would have fared any better on the morrow.

Maxwell did not pursue. In part, this was because the British expected the Turkish attack to be renewed. Given the inflation of the Turks' strength, there were presumed to be troops as yet uncommitted. In part too it was a reflection of ignorance: the sandstorm had grounded the seaplanes and the Turks' movements were not so clear after 3 February as they had been before. But the decision was of a piece with Maxwell's overall approach. None of his formations was really equipped to enter the desert. There were no mobile formations. Water would be a major problem. Djemal lost 7,000 out of 11,000 camels on the return journey, and his total losses (excluding the Bedouin irregulars)—192 killed, 375 wounded, and 727 missing—were considerably increased by the transport difficulties of the retreat. Both echelons were now moving simultaneously, not separately, with a baggage train smaller than that employed in the advance.

Continued defence also reflected Maxwell's principal priority. Just as the Turkish attack hinged on an uprising within Egypt, so his main vulnerability lay not on the canal but in Cairo. He himself never left the capital. He could not, therefore, exploit the tactical opportunities available on 3 and 4 February. But he could ensure that the newly arrived forces of Australia and New Zealand, en route for Europe, would impress the civilian population. The

---

[103] Larcher, *La Guerre turque*, 253–4.

pivot of the successful defence lay not where the action occurred, but where it was prevented from occurring.

Moreover, as a military headquarters Cairo enjoyed a central position. The Turkish threat to Egypt came not only from the east but also from the west. Ottoman resistance to the Turkish invasion of Cyrenaica had forged the reputation of Enver and grafted pan-Islamic awareness onto pan-Turanianism. Although Italy had consolidated its hold on Tripolitania, the western half of Libya, between 1912 and 1914, its progress in the eastern part, Cyrenaica, had been slower and remained incomplete.

Therefore, despite Constantinople's formal concession to Rome, local resistance to the Italians had never died. In recognizing the Caliphate, Italy allowed Islam a role in Libya that, because it was religious, became also secular. The war pitted Muslim against Christian. Funds to support the fighting flowed from believers throughout the Islamic world, from Afghanistan, Morocco, and India, and were channelled into Libya via Egypt and Tunisia. The struggle, therefore, changed character. In 1911 and 1912 one colonial power fought another; after 1912 nationalism, of a sort and charged with religion, took up the cudgels.

Freed of the incubus of empire, Turkey could pose as the Islamic ally. By putting itself at the head of a holy war with Italy, Constantinople justified its claim to the Caliphate and its continuing dominion over other Arab peoples, those of Syria, Hejaz, and Iraq. In late 1913 the Turks set about the resumption of their involvement in Libya. In August of the following year Enver recommended that Sulayman al-Baruni be sent to lead the struggle against Italy. Baruni and his colleagues represented the new Ottoman approach: as Libyans, rather than Turks, they were intended to build on the strength of local resistance.[104]

But, formally speaking, Turkey and Italy were not at war. Furthermore, Italy was the ally of Germany and Austria-Hungary, and might still be prevailed upon to acknowledge its obligations to the Triple Alliance. Baruni's rhetoric was therefore directed less at Italian rule in Libya than at British rule in Egypt. Enver tried to argue that Italy could remain neutral while eastern Cyrenaica became a conduit for an attack on Britain. He hoped thereby to be able to divide British troops in Egypt over two fronts, thus enhancing the prospects of success for Djemal's 4th army.[105] But Constantinople did not control events in Libya. The reciprocal effect for which Enver was striving eluded him. Baruni, seen in Cyrenaica not as a Libyan but as an Ottoman, was arrested by those he

[104] R. Simon, *Libya between Ottomanism and nationalism*, 87–105, 155–6, 305. Simon is fundamental on Libya in the war, and largely replaces the older work of E. E. Evans-Pritchard, *The Sanusi of Cyrenaica*. O. Meynier, 'La Guerre sainte des Senoussya en Afrique (1914–1918)', *Revue militaire française*, 131, 138, 139, 140, 148, 149, 152, 153, (1932–4), has a wider geographical remit than Simon.
[105] Trumpener, *Germany and the Ottoman empire*, 115–17, 119–21.

was meant to lead and his movements restricted thereafter. As Djemal prepared his thrust across Sinai, Turkish strategy in the western desert stood in tatters.

What gave coherence to anti-Italian resistance in Libya was not Ottoman leadership but the Senussi. The Senussi were a puritan sect of Islam, fundamentalist in their beliefs but latitudinarian in their appeal. From their bases among the Bedouin of the Libyan desert, by 1882 they claimed between 1.5 and 3 million adherents across the Sahara and into equatorial Africa. Their role in the fighting of 1911 and 1912 was not major, but after 1913 their Islamic credentials and their ability to unite the tribes made them natural allies for the Turks. When Enver left Cyrenaica in September 1912 he entrusted the struggle to Ahmad al-Sharif, who was elected leader of the Senussi on the death of his uncle Mohammed el-Mahdi, owing to the youth of Mohammed's own sons. Ahmad's status as the leader of an emergent independent state in Cyrenaica was confirmed with a victory over the Italians near Derna in May 1913. Although the Senussi were cleared from western and central Cyrenaica by the outbreak of the First World War, about 10,000 continued to hold out in the east, close to the Egyptian frontier. Economically, therefore, the Senussi depended on British toleration. For them the enemy was Italy: hence Baruni's downfall.

Senussi activity increased between August and November 1914. Nadolny had sent a five-man expedition to Tripoli on the second day of mobilization. Its leader, Otto Mannesmann, travelled under an alias and was a reserve officer, but the German foreign ministry insisted he was a consul. The Italians were fearful of British and French reactions, and their protests meant that by the end of August only Mannesmann remained. Without his colleagues he reduced his brief, which had originally embraced almost the entire North African coastline, to the establishment of links with the Senussi. German efforts to appease the Italians by trying to persuade the Senussi to stop fighting them were undermined by events.[106] In Tripolitania, where Italian conquest seemed to be complete with the acquisition of Ghat in its south-western corner in August, the tribes rose in the Italian rear. The Italians evacuated first Ghat and then Ghadames, the garrisons of both withdrawing across the frontier into French territory. But it was the summons to holy war in November that really gave focus and impetus to the Senussi efforts. The Senussi responded more wholeheartedly to the call than perhaps any other single Muslim group: in Libya, if nowhere else, the idea of holy war found its fulfilment. The consequence of the Senussi's purity of doctrine meant that the Italians could not, as the *fatwa* from Constantinople had specifically requested, be exempt. Ahmad raised the standard of holy war in Fezzan, in southern Libya, remote indeed from British interests.

---

[106] Müller, *Islam, Gihad*, 187–9, 268, 377–80.

Thus, from their nadir before 14 November Senussi–Ottoman relations began to improve. Money and equipment, initially smuggled in on Greek boats and from late 1915 in German U-boats, increased Senussi reliance on the Turks. Sollum, on the Libyan–Egyptian border, was the main point of entry. And it was here that Nuri, Enver's younger brother and another veteran of the Libyan war of 1912, landed on 23 March 1915. Nuri was accompanied by fifty Turkish officers. The Turks were initially accorded little more trust than had been given Baruni and his colleagues. But Nuri proved politically more astute. He exploited latent splits among the Senussi leaders. He flattered Ahmad, appealing to his vanity and conferring on him the title of vizier (or the Caliph's representative) for North Africa. On 20 August 1915 Italy's declaration of war on Turkey united the narrower objectives of the Senussi with the broader aims of the Ottomans. For the Senussi the First World War became the means by which the Italians could be ejected from Libya.

The resurgence of Senussi activity in Fezzan and in southern Tripolitania culminated in the summer of 1915. The Italians who had withdrawn into Algeria re-entered Libya to take Ghadames in February. To the north-west, a policy of vicious repression had aimed to clear the hinterland around Tripoli so as to prevent supplies reaching the Senussi through Tunisia or from the sea. But by April plundered Italian equipment left the insurgents well stocked with rifles, artillery, machine-guns, and ammunition. In May Italy declared war on Austria-Hungary; its troops in Libya, which had reached 100,000 in 1912 and still totalled 60,000 in 1914, were refused reinforcements. They evacuated Ghadames again on 19 July, and by the end of the same month were confined to a coastal foothold at Tripoli.

The crisis in Fezzan and Tripolitania eased the military position of the Senussi in eastern Cyrenaica. Italian troops were pulled westwards; yet others were sent to Eritrea. But at the same time British policy towards the Senussi hardened. In 1914 Cairo had appreciated that the Senussi's enemy was Italy, not Britain, and had concluded that a policy of appeasement would be sufficient: the 320,000 square kilometres of desert between the Libyan frontier and the Nile constituted a buffer more considerable than the Sinai desert. But in May 1915 Italy's commitment to the Entente required Britain to prevent the Senussi using Egypt as their base. British pressure on the Senussi to recognize Italian rule was sustainable; the block to trade across the Egyptian frontier was not. Economic necessity increased the Senussi's reliance on German and Turkish imports; it also forced them to move in order to feed. On 15 August Mannesmann tried to manufacture an exchange of fire between the Senussi and the British. He failed, and the Senussi, still reluctant opponents of Britain, apologized.[107] But they were becoming increasingly open to the blandishments of Nuri.

[107] McKale, *War by revolution*, 146–51.

Senussi penetration of Egypt had begun with an element of British conniv-
ance. But by November 1915 main force had replaced trade as its vehicle.
Sollum and its environs were in Senussi hands. The British withdrew along
the coast to Mersa Matruh, a more effective base for operations, suppliable
from Alexandria by rail (as far as Daaba) and by sea. Immediately, however, the
evacuation expanded Senussi success, sucking them further into Egypt. The
British reckoned that the Senussi force of 3,000 to 5,000 could be swelled by
local support to 50,000. In fact—although some Egyptian troops deserted to
join the Senussi—those calculations proved exaggerated. The Senussi taxed the
local population for payments in kind and in cash, and thus alienated rather
than wooed it.

In Enver's plan, Egypt would have been attacked simultaneously from east,
south, and west. In October 1915 Ahmad, the Senussi leader, spoke of acting in
conjunction with Ali Dinar in western Sudan, and sent letters to the eastern
Arabs urging them to join the jihad. But the idea that insurgents operating over
such a vast area, lacking any means of direct communication with each other
and, in the final analysis, without a sizeable body of regular troops is testimony
to the grandiloquent absurdity of Enver's strategic thought. The strength in
such situations rested not with exterior but with interior lines; the British on
the Nile enjoyed an immediate operational advantage.

Efforts to construct a southern front, inherently fantastic in any case, were
further vitiated by being pulled in two directions. German agents saw in
Somalia, Ethiopia, and the Sudan the possibility of a campaign which might
jeopardize British East Africa and so relieve the pressure on Lettow-Vorbeck.
Plans developed on these lines early in 1915 by Adolf Friedrich zu Mecklenburg,
a former governor of Togoland, and Fritz Bronsart von Schellendorff were
seized on by the German colonial secretary, Wilhelm Solf. For Solf the attack
on Egypt was the route to the conquest of Central Africa. But efforts to
establish contacts across the Red Sea from Arabia showed such schemes to
be fantasies. In the winter of 1914–15 the combination of religious sensitivities
close to Mecca and British patrols in the Red Sea thwarted the expeditions of a
Hungarian officer, Franz Gondos, Major Schwabe, and Bernhard Moritz. Leo
Frobenius, 'the ethnographer and German agent, well known . . . from French
West Africa for his liking for absinthe and negro women and his Teutonic
brusqueness',[108] was marginally more successful. In Constantinople he haggled
over titles and orders rather than the men and equipment which the Turks
refused him, but he managed to sail down the Red Sea to Massawa. There the
Italians turned him back, and on Wangenheim's advice he was not re-employed.
He did, however, manage to establish contact, via the German minister in

---

[108] Stuermer, *Two war years*, 146; also Martin Kröger, 'Revolution als Programm', in Michalka (ed.),
Der Erste Weltkrieg, 378; Hagen, *Türkei im Ersten Weltkrieg*, 37; McKale, *War by revolution*, 63–5, 104–5,
156–8.

Addis Ababa, with Lij Yasu, the youthful emperor of Abyssinia, who was promised that a Turco-German victory in Egypt would give him Eritrea, parts of the Sudan and Kenya, as well as Italian and British Somaliland.

Hitherto Abyssinia had adopted an attitude favourable to Britain, reflecting its hopes that it too might benefit from the partition of Somalia. However, by 1915 Lij Yasu was more concerned to cement unity within his domains by merging Muslim and Copt in a common cause, although hopes of a joint Somali-Abyssinian attack on Berbera underestimated the strength of their mutual distrust. Ironically, Lij Yasu's flirtation with Islam prompted Sayyid Mohammed, or the 'Mad Mullah', to negotiate with Britain. Although Sayyid Mohammed overplayed his hand, Somali tribal leaders were impressed by tours of the Egyptian front and news of the Arab revolt in June 1916. Adolf Friedrich zu Mecklenburg and Wilhelm Solf hoped the Somalis would attack British East Africa, and so provide succour from the north for Lettow-Vorbeck. But the Somalis' distrust of Abyssinia, supplemented by the British and Italian ministers' courtship of the latter's Christian leadership, left Lij Yasu's schemes for an Islamic empire in East Africa exposed. In September 1916 a Christian-led coup against Lij Yasu in Addis Ababa resulted in civil war in Abyssinia. In the same month Italy, Britain, and—more reluctantly—France agreed to ban arms sales in the region.[109]

In the Sudan, reports that Turkish agents were active in Darfur arrived in Khartoum from December 1914 onwards. Enver wrote to Ali Dinar, the Sultan, asking him to join the war on Britain on 3 February 1915. However, the letter took over a year to reach its destination. Nuri wrote in August, but the first Senussi to visit Darfur did not arrive until March 1916. Ali Dinar had already threatened the adjacent town of Nahud, in Kordofan, with attack in November. The problems of Darfur had emerged before the outbreak of the war, and were therefore of longer standing than the Senussi threat to Egypt. The British had wanted to leave it as a self-governing buffer between Sudan and Chad; the French, advancing from the west, had demanded a clearer demarcation. Ali Dinar was frustrated by the Sudan government's failure to protect his position. Sir Reginald Wingate, the governor-general, initially would have preferred the resolution of the Darfur issue to have been postponed until after the war. But Ali Dinar's behaviour increasingly threatened the stability of the tribes of Kordofan. The issue was therefore essentially a local one. Turco-Senussi contact may have influenced Ali Dinar, but the notion that his campaign would sweep on to Khartoum, and then advance up the Nile in co-ordination with the Senussi advance on Egypt was laughable. Cairo opposed Wingate's taking pre-emptive action in Darfur; London approved it (Wingate circumvented the

---

[109] Kakwenzaire, *Transafrican Journal of History*, XIV (1985), 36–45; Marcus, *International Journal of African Historical Studies*, XVI (1983), 263–79; McKale, *War by revolution*, 168–9, 193–6.

proper channels to write direct to Kitchener), but would not pay for it. By maximizing any wider relationship between Ali Dinar and the world war, Wingate stood to justify his actions and transfer the expense.[110]

To the east, Djemal's 4th army—bled to meet the demands of Gallipoli, Mesopotamia, and the Caucasus—was in no position to renew its advance across Sinai. Thus the Senussi offensive from the west lacked any direct support. Nuri divided his thrust in two. The coastal advance, which he accompanied, was commanded by Jafar al-Askari, an Arab officer in the Ottoman army. Jafar had organized his forces into four brigades, each of four battalions of 400 men, and from them had fashioned the principal striking force. Inland, Ahmad al-Sharif led a second column from Jaghbub to the Siwa oasis. From Siwa further oases opened two routes to the Nile. But tactically, as well as strategically, the British had the upper hand. Aeroplanes enabled them to watch the Senussi movements; armoured cars gave them the mobility to turn local defence into counter-attack. Jafar could do no better than adopt defensive positions and then make good his escape. Thus were the months of December 1915 and January 1916 occupied.

In February 1916 Maxwell's forces had accumulated sufficient camels, 2,000 of them, to enable sustained offensive operations west of Mersa Matruh. Their aim was the reoccupation of Sollum. On 26 February, at Agagiya, 24 kilometres south-east of Sidi Barrani, Jafar again adopted a good defensive position, manned by 1,600 troops. As the British attack took effect the Senussi–Ottoman forces moved off to the south. However, the pursuit of three squadrons of British cavalry turned retreat into rout, crushing the Senussi rearguard and capturing Jafar himself. The Senussi did not again stand their ground. Sollum was reoccupied on 14 March.

To the south Ahmad al-Sharif pushed forces forward to the Bahariya, Farafra (only briefly), and Dakhla oases, equidistant between Siwa and the Nile, in February. Maxwell restricted his initial response to aerial observation and the occasional air raid. At first his ground forces lacked the mobility to take the offensive westwards from the Nile into the desert itself. Gradually, however, the Imperial Camel Corps (in reality a brigade, built up company by company from Australians, New Zealanders, and British territorials) created a network of patrols. To the camels were added armoured cars. As the Senussi oases became isolated, so the British consolidated their hold with railways pushing on Bahariya and Dakhla. Both oases were occupied in October 1916. Siwa was cleared of Senussi in February 1917 in a raid launched with armoured cars from Mersa Matruh, 320 kilometres distant.[111]

---

[110] Evans-Pritchard, *Sanusi*, 128, says Ali Darfur was not sympathetic to the Senussi. Macmunn and Falls, *Egypt and Palestine*, i. 135, 147–51, assume wider co-ordination. Daly, *Empire on the Nile*, 171–87, is exhaustive.

[111] Macmunn and Falls, *Egypt and Palestine*, i. 101–47.

The threat from Ali Dinar was over before it had begun. The Sultan of Darfur could not begin operations until the wet season in July. Wingate had to decide whether to wait until the rains, when there would be water but the ground would be glutinous, or to act in the dry season, when the going was firm but there would be little water. He opted for the latter, advancing on the capital of Darfur, El Fasher, in April and May 1916. What enabled Wingate to spurn the climatic and geographic constraints that had hitherto restricted the penetration of European armies in colonial wars was—as in the north—the internal combustion engine. By using light lorries forward from the railhead at Rahad, speed of movement and rapidity of resupply minimized the water problem. Four aircraft, on loan from Egypt, replaced mass with force. On 23 May Ali Dinar and 2,000 followers quitted El Fasher, his march south harassed by aerial attack. The completion of the Cameroons campaign to the west enabled the French in Chad to turn east and to co-operate with the British in boxing in the Darfur rebellion. Ali Dinar's support ebbed. By the time he met his end, on 6 November, his power had long since been crushed.[112]

The Sudan as a whole was unaffected by Ali Dinar's efforts. Indeed, the stability of the area was surprisingly consistent throughout the war. Outwardly, the Anglo-Egyptian condominium had good cause for concern in 1914. The inspector-general of the Sudan, Rudolf von Slatin, was an Austrian citizen unable to return from leave in Vienna in August. The Central Powers were therefore better placed with regard to political intelligence (for which Slatin had been responsible) than for any other area of the Middle East or Africa. And yet Slatin, although he offered his services, was never used; he spent the war working for the Austrian Red Cross. Worries about Turkish and German propaganda proved so ill-founded that censorship was abandoned in December 1916. The Islamic appeal of the Caliph found no answering chord in the Sudan. The Mahdists saw the Turks as effete and corrupt, and preferred the temporary inconvenience of British rule to the return of Turkey or the reimposition of Egypt. The Mahdi had been Britain's scourge in the 1880s and 1890s; his son, Sayyid Abd al-Rahmin, became Britain's prop, acting as a counterweight to Ali Dinar's summons to holy war. Prosperity served to consolidate Britain's position. In 1914, when the rains and the Nile flood both failed, famine was averted by food imports from India. In the four subsequent years harvests were abundant, Sudan becoming an exporter of grain and cattle. In each of the years 1915–18 the real value of Sudan's exports was 20 to 25 per cent higher than in 1911–14. Furthermore, because taxation was light, the proceeds went (by and large) into Sudanese pockets. British penetration in the south was suspended

---

[112] Ibid. 147–53; O. Meynier, *Revue militaire française*, 153 (mars 1934), 418–26; Osuntokun, *Nigeria in the First World War*, 153–4; Wingate, *Wingate of the Sudan*, 183–5.

for the duration of the war. A single rising in the Nuba in 1915 was the only blemish on a peaceful scene.[113]

The Senussi were fractured internally as well as worsted militarily. Friction between Turk and Arab had increased rather than declined with the advance into Egypt. Nuri's expectations of military discipline had been frustrated by the Bedouin's independent ways. More seriously, the position of Ahmad al-Sharif was under challenge. The sons of Mohammed el-Mahdi were now of age, and the elder, Mohammed Idris, laid claim to the leadership. Idris had visited Egypt on his return journey from Mecca in 1914, and had received Kitchener's support in his pretensions. When Ahmad led the Senussi into Egypt Idris remained behind in Cyrenaica, free to consolidate his following. Ahmad's defeat at the hands of the British discredited his pro-Ottoman policy while validating Idris's conciliation of Cairo. Mannesmann was shot in 1916, possibly by Idris, although conceivably by the Turks, who were jealous of German influence. The Germans themselves concluded that the Senussi would follow their own agenda.[114] By April 1917 Ahmad's supporters were reduced to about 200; he abandoned Cyrenaica to Idris and moved to Tripolitania. But his status here was as a religious, not a temporal, leader.

Idris opened negotiations with the British in March 1916, saying that he was ready to expel the Turks and the Germans from Cyrenaica, and to make peace with Italy and Britain. However, despite the wish of both sides to resolve their differences, the continuing obligation of each to its ally confounded the possibility of speedy resolution. Idris was no friend to Turkey; the Turks in his army at Zuwaitinah, south of Benghazi, were virtual prisoners. But he could not afford to dispense entirely with them or with Ahmad, if he was to support his diplomacy with the threat of a return to military solutions. The British, for their part, had agreed with Italy not to make a separate pact with the Senussi. And yet that was exactly what Idris wished to achieve: he trusted the British, but not the Italians.

In May 1916 Idris proposed that the Senussi be accorded recognition in all their existing areas of control, from Cyrenaica through Tripolitania to Tunisia, and that Italy be confined to the coast. Left to their own devices, the British might have accepted this package. As sponsors of Arab nationalism in Arabia, it behoved them to adopt the same mantle in North Africa; moreover, Idris's proposal would secure Egypt and free the British to get on with defeating Turkey. It seemed to many that Italy was more concerned to use Britain's military prowess to make good the lack of its own, its aim thereby being to

---

[113] Daly, *Empire on the Nile*, 152–91, is the main source on these points. See also G. N. Sanderson, 'The Anglo-Egyptian Sudan', in Roberts (ed.), *Cambridge History of Africa*, vol. VII; 'Abd al-Rahim, *Imperialism and nationalism in the Sudan*, 96–9; Warburg, *The Sudan under Wingate*, 106–7, 152–4.

[114] Müller, *Islam, Gihad*, 327–9, 373, 385; Neulen, *Feldgrau in Jerusalem*, 102.

secure its Libyan empire rather than to fight the First World War. However, Britain's obligations to Italy proved stronger than its cynicism. By September negotiations with the Senussi had collapsed.

The fear that Idris and Ahmad would be pushed together again, and that the Senussi threat in Cyrenaica would reappear, was ill-conceived. British control of Sollum and of the coastal frontier enabled Cairo to sustain economic pressure on Idris. In January 1917 talks were resumed, and in April agreement was reached. The Italians and the Senussi were each accorded zones in Cyrenaica, with free passage between each. Sollum was opened to the Senussi. Italy's gains were limited: its sovereignty in the area was still unconfirmed and its position would continue to rest, ultimately, on force of arms. Idris, on the other hand, had, by dint of hard negotiation, gained diplomatic recognition for the Senussi. The Senussi, although moved to war by Islam, had laid the foundations of Libyan nationalism.

Italy accepted this uncongenial treaty for fear of something worse. The Turks, thwarted in Cyrenaica and Egypt, switched their attentions to Tripolitania. In May 1916 Italy had retaken Zuwarah, on the coast between Tripoli and Tunisia, and seemed well placed to exploit the tribal rivalries of the region. The French agreed to co-operate with a blockade of Tripolitania, thus cutting the caravan routes of the Sahara. But by the end of the year Zuwarah was back in the hands of the insurgents. Both the blockade and the division of power among the Senussi served to increase Turco-German credit. Although Ahmad el-Sharif joined Nuri, the Senussi's status was religious rather than political, and Ahmad depended on Nuri rather than the other way round. Temporal authority resided with the chiefs, some of whom were supporters of the Senussi but others not. Nuri was therefore able to use his skills in playing off one against the other in order to maximize his own position.

The main base for Turco-German operations in Tripolitania was Misratah, along the coast from Homs. Although the German navy regarded it as a waste of resources, in 1917 U-boats called at Misratah every two or three weeks. They brought Mauser rifles, armoured cars, and even light aircraft; on one return journey *UC20* brought a young riding camel as a present from the Arabs for the Kaiser. In May 1917 a fresh German mission, originally sent to establish Mannesmann's fate, undertook the erection of a wireless station and the manufacture of small-arms ammunition. Nuri continued to be jealous of the Germans' influence, and the mission's leader, Wolffron Todenwarth, told Berlin that all equipment should be delivered in the name of the Turks. Although the Germans criticized Nuri, by the year's end they had effectively lost contact with the Senussi. The Turks had established twenty posts on the Mediterranean coast. In 1918 their total strength included 20,000 regular troops, a comparable number of reservists with only limited training, and a further 40,000 reservists without training.[115] The combination of Italian defeats and German imports meant that arms were abundant.

However, unlike Cyrenaica, Tripolitania was not in the grip of a new nationalism. Traditional rivalries simmered, and after 1918 would provide the splits which enabled a reassertion of Italian power. Around Misratah the most powerful personality was Ramadan al-Shitawi; although a supporter of the Central Powers, his methods of taxation and sequestration had the effect of driving others towards Italy. Inland, the Awlad Sulayman tribe resisted Turkish control. The Turks responded by using another tribe, the Urfella, to curb the Awlad Sulayman, who then threw in their lot with Idris. To the west, Mohammed Suf al-Mahmudi, although himself a Senussi, clashed with Khalifa ben Asker who was eager to broaden the insurrection and push into the adjacent French territories.

The Turks' ability to control and exploit these conflicts was weakened through the erosion of Nuri's power. In October 1916 Sulayman al-Baruni returned to Libya as the governor of Tripolitania. Militarily Nuri, as supreme commander for all Libya, remained superior, but Baruni's immediate political master was Ahmad, whose power was now broken. In December 1916 Nuri switched his own headquarters to Misratah. Throughout 1917 the clashes of the two Ottoman leaders forced each tribe to decide with whom its loyalties lay. The Italians, reinforced in the spring of 1917, and equipped with gas and aircraft, cleared the coast between Homs and Zuwarah in a series of limited offensives. Civilian mortality in this area and along the Tunisian frontier was appallingly high. The 1917 harvest was poor and combined with the blockade to produce famine. To this the Italians added atrocity and massacre.

However, Italy had no intention—and no capability, given its commitments in the Trentino and on the Isonzo—of doing more than consolidating its foothold around Tripoli. The defeat of Caporetto in October and the danger of collapse in Italy itself served to underline the point. They also rallied the tribes, forced into co-operation by hunger and Italian success. Once again the Italian bridgehead was reduced, this time to Tripoli and Zuwarah.

At the end of 1917 Nuri was replaced by Ishak Pasha. At first Ishak succeeded in subordinating Baruni and in reuniting civil and military authority. But his own power, like Nuri's, was purely military, and his tough policies lost him local support. In May 1918 Constantinople made a final effort to retrieve the situation, sending Prince Osman Fuad, the grandson of Murad V, as the Sultan's personal representative. Fuad endeavoured to break the power of the chiefs by ceasing to distribute recruits on a tribal basis and by centralizing the allocation of fodder, arms, and other supplies. The effect, however, was to

[115] Simon, *Libya between Ottomanism*, 233; see more generally 131–2, 169–83, 219–39, for what follows, and also G. Meynier, *L'Algérie révelée*, 489–96; Müller, *Islam, Gihad*, 387–9, 415–16; Neulen, *Feldgrau in Jerusalem*, 103–5.

foster tribal resistance to Ottomanism. Desertion increased. In a final bid to unify the movement in Tripolitania, and to fuse the tribes of Libya with the Ottoman empire, Fuad named Ahmad as leader of an insurrection to embrace all North Africa from Egypt to Morocco. It was an abject failure. In August Ahmad left Libya for Constantinople.

Italy ended the war on an upbeat note, anxious, no doubt, to consolidate its claim to Libya at the coming peace conference. Giovanni Ameglio, an ever-present figure since 1912, was replaced as governor by Vincenzo Garioni. Idris now co-operated with the Italians as they pushed on Misratah. The Turks, although anxious to continue the fight with Italy even after the armistice, were once again the prisoners of the Senussi, not the manipulators of an emergent nationalism. Paul Kutzner, a German commanding an Arab machine-gun section, remained unaware that the wider war was over until he was captured by the Italians in autumn 1919.[116]

The Senussi front thus remained active throughout the war. In this it was perhaps the most successful of the Turco-German initiatives in revolutionary warfare. Nonetheless, its effect on the broad strategic picture was minimal. The threat to Egypt was remote and short-lived. The total British and Dominion forces committed to the western desert may have been 40,000 men. But in January and February 1916, Egypt as a whole was host to 370,000 men. Of these only 2,400 were engaged at Agagiya. Italy was the power more directly threatened, and yet Italy was not the object of (at least) German strategy. Nor did Rome really rise to the bait. It was prepared to let the bulk of Libya go, retaining only a foothold sufficient for a renewed post-war effort.

The war in Libya stood independently of the First World War. It had begun in 1911 and it was to continue until 1931. It is best characterized as a colonial war—which originated as colonial warfare's first stage, that of resistance to European imperialism by a traditional society, and then developed into its second, that of national liberation. Its tactical features also simultaneously embraced backwardness and modernity. The use of air-power, not simply for reconnaissance but also for direct attack, initiated by the Italians in Libya, was carried on by the British. In the context of relative technological superiority and small force-to-space ratios, industrialized warfare made for decision and mobility, not—as on the western front—for indecision and immobility. The absence of fixed lines and the difficulties of transport meant that the contribution of artillery was negligible. Armoured cars, on the other hand, could—in the right circumstances—prove more effective, operationally and tactically, than the camels and cavalry which otherwise constituted the bulk of the contending forces. In this respect, the war against the Senussi was of immediate relevance. The tactical ingredients which brought success in the eastern

---

[116] Neulen, *Feldgrau in Jerusalem*, 105; McKale, *War by revolution*, 190–1 .

desert and Syria in 1917–18 found their origins in the western desert and Libya in 1915–16.

FRENCH NORTH AFRICA

Before the war Germany's most conspicuous bid for colonies had been in North-West Africa. The two crises over Morocco, in 1905 and 1911, were significant stepping-stones in the development of pre-war tensions. German agents were reported as active throughout the Maghreb. Many of the imputations were no doubt false: the legitimate activities of German priests, businessmen, scientists, and academics could be imaginatively re-created as a part of a wider conspiracy as easily here as in Britain or in metropolitan France. Some, whose conduct may well have been perfectly proper before August 1914, were recruited for state service thereafter: Leo Frobenius, who had already roused French suspicions before the war because of his frequent visits to Algeria, resurfaced as a German agent.[117] The French had good cause to be nervous. Their hold on northern Tunisia and on the Algerian coastline might seem secure, but their penetration of the southern Sahara was incomplete, and the pacification of Morocco still in train. And yet, when the war broke out, for all its apparent vulnerabilities French North Africa received comparatively little attention from the Central Powers.

A process of inversion took place. Because in 1914 the main German armies were grappling with those of France on French soil, the need to undermine France's power through its colonies was less pressing. Because Germany could not come to grips directly with Britain, the use of revolutionary warfare against its possessions assumed a much higher priority. Russia, through Germany's need to back up Austria-Hungary, occupied an intermediate position in the rank order of subversive schemes.

There were, in addition, practical constraints. When the *Goeben* and the *Breslau* bombarded Philippeville and Bône the French feared rebellion, but that had never been Souchon's mission. Thereafter, the German naval presence in the western Mediterranean (and, for that matter, off the Atlantic coast of Morocco) was negligible. The first U-boats were sent to the Mediterranean in April and May 1915, but their activities (and their bases, at Pola and Cattaro) were concentrated at its eastern end. Their numbers were not significantly augmented until spring 1917. Turkey was neither contiguous nor particularly influential in the region. Both Algeria and Morocco had claims to be

---

[117] On German agents, see Meynier, *Revue militaire française*, 14, (mars 1933), 396–8, and as a corrective, G. Meynier, *L'Algérie révelée*, 249–52.

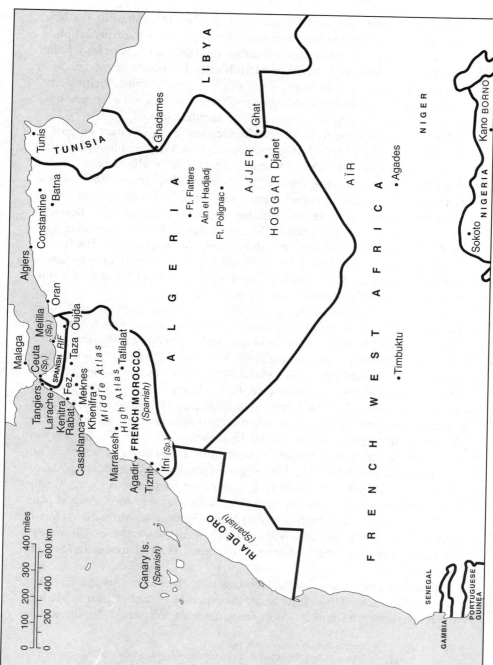

MAP 29. FRENCH NORTH AFRICA

independent states before the French arrived, and the Sultan of the latter averred that he—not the Sultan in Constantinople—was the true Caliph.[118] Strong Islamic sentiments meant respect for the Turks as religious leaders, but this did not extend to their temporal authority. 'Le panislamisme que nous connaissons en Afrique du Nord', wrote an Algerian nationalist, Victor Barru-cand, in 1912, is 'un sentiment de legitime défense, [qu'] il a son siège, non pas à Constantinople mais dans la coeur de tous les mussulmans.'[119]

Enver's response was to bypass existing leaders and give direct support to any rebels. But in Morocco the Germans at first took a different line, preferring to develop their pre-war links with Moulay Abd al-Hafiz, who had been ousted from the Sultanate by the French. The Turks had to co-operate with the Germans because the latter had money and arms, and the Germans had to work through the Turks because they had the personnel. Asif Tahir Bey, who had headed a short-lived Turkish military mission to Morocco also dislodged by the French, made contact with Abd al-Hafiz in October 1914. The former Sultan had just moved from Tangiers to Spain, and he showed no eagerness to return to Morocco. The hazards of an aeroplane flight or passage in a sub-marine were much less attractive than quiet retirement.[120]

The lure of Morocco was its accessibility from Spain. Spain's frustration at the poor deal it had got from France in the area made it sympathetic to Germany. Ernst Kühnel, an archaeologist and art historian, was dispatched to Larache, on the Atlantic coast of Spanish Morocco. His task was not only to work with the consulates of the Central Powers in Larache and Melilla in the distribution of propaganda (a job complicated by the fact that the German and Austrian consuls in Larache suspected him of being a French spy rather than a German one), but also to foment rebellion and to blow up railways in French Morocco and Algeria. Kühnel stayed in Larache until 1917, but he was too remote from the interior to have a major impact. Moreover, although Spain was prepared to overlook the distribution of propaganda and the dispatch of financial subsidies to tribal leaders, it took exception to gun-running. Weap-ons could be turned against the Spanish as easily as against the French. A plan to ship 5,000 rifles and 500,000 rounds from Argentina to Morocco via Spain was blocked, and the police at Malaga impounded 3,000 carbines. Ultimately, Germany's principal intermediary in these deals, its naval attaché in Madrid, was expelled.[121]

Almost as problematic for the Germans were their allies. Austria-Hungary restricted its support to a rather feeble summons by its ambassador in Madrid to French—but not Spanish—Morocco to launch a holy war.[122] Turkey, which

---

[118] Landau, Politics of pan-Islam, 139.
[119] Akhbar, 14 Apr. 1912, quoted in G. Meynier, L'Algérie révelée, 248.
[120] Müller, Islam, Gihad, 93–4, 241–2, 299–308.
[121] ibid. 394–9.   [122] Bihl, Kaukasus-politik, 117.

Germany badly needed to legitimize its standing as an insurgent rather than colonial power, proved lackadaisical. *Teskilat-i Mahsusa* was reported to maintain large numbers of agents in North Africa, but in reality they seem to have numbered no more than eight: at best, two were operating in Morocco.[123] In November 1915, after much German prodding, the Turks established a mission in Spain. Its second-in-command was Asif Tahir Bey, but its leader, Prince Aziz Hasan, was a liberal opponent of the Committee of Union and Progress. During the course of 1916 the Turkish mission broke up, clashing with its allies over its funding, and its Arab members sympathizing with Hussein's revolt in the Hejaz.[124] From 1916 onwards German propaganda had little alternative to working through the committees for national independence in Berlin rather than mouthing the pan-Islamic objectives of the Caliph.

The threat of holy war was something which France, like Britain, took seriously from the outset of the war, and even before. Both powers had, after all, devoted much recent campaigning effort to countering tribesmen fired with religious fervour. In February 1912 Clemenceau anticipated that war within Europe would give rise to a jihad outside it. In Algeria the governor-general, Charles Lutaud, anticipated rebellion as early as August 1914. On 5 November he pre-empted Constantinople's summons with a declaration of his own, in which he made a distinction between the Young Turks (presented as Jews and Greeks, not Anatolians—lackeys of the Germans rather than true Moslems) and the Turkish people.[125] Because France recognized the possible force of German and Ottoman propaganda it made strenuous efforts to intercept and to counter it. Suggesting that French fears were exaggerated may, in reality, be a reflection of French success.

The two pillars of their effectiveness were, first, speed off the mark (and here the battle of the Marne was a vital asset in denting from the very outset the image of German military superiority), and secondly, superior intelligence. By 1915 the French were reading German diplomatic signals from Madrid. Co-operation with the British, given the ability of the Royal Navy to decipher German codes, enabled them to track U-boat movements off the North African coast.[126] Thus, much that the Central Powers initiated could be anticipated and pre-empted. Within Morocco, the fact that penetration and pacification were in progress meant that an extensive intelligence network was already up and running when war began. The Bureau des Affaires Indigènes

---

[123] G. Meynier, *L'Algérie révelée*, 510; Burke, *Francia*, III (1975), 459.
[124] Burke, *Francia*, III (1975), 458–60, 463.
[125] Ageron, *Les Algériens musulmans*, 1175. Algeria in the First World War is the subject of two fine and thorough studies: Ageron, and G. Meynier, *L'Algérie révelée*. Meynier revises (and amplifies) Ageron's picture in many ways, particularly in seeing the First World War as giving rise to a sense of Algerian nationalism and the beginnings of the move for independence. Ageron, by contrast, emphasizes the stability of Algeria during the war itself.
[126] Burke, *Francia*, III (1975), 449–50.

maintained posts on the frontiers of the occupied zone which, as well as pushing French influence forward, channelled information back.

The recent experience of French military prowess, particularly in Morocco, where French diplomatic success had been at German expense, was the bottom line in ensuring North African loyalty. To reinforce it, German prisoners of war were put to work on the roads of Algeria and (especially) Morocco. Indications of support for France for more positive reasons were sedulously exploited by the French. Most of the loyal statements in Algeria came from those already compromised by the French government—the tribal chiefs, the magistrates, the functionaries—and from the more prosperous areas. Nonetheless, the Maghreb was not immune from some of the more spontaneous manifestations of the *union sacrée* common to metropolitan France. One butcher perched a red fez adorned with a crescent on the ox's head displayed outside his shop: beneath it was inscribed the legend 'viande de bocherie'. For each of the main groups in Algerian society the *union sacrée* had particular force. French settlers were given the chance to reassert their European status by a sense of solidarity with metropolitan France. The Algerians themselves experienced a suppression of racism in the outburst of fraternity generated by military service.[127]

The Algerian government began the publication of an official news bulletin, *Akhbar al Harb*, in August 1914. However, this was soon recognized for what it was, and the *Service d'Afrique* in Paris, in addition to producing its own material, decided to allow in other, unofficial, publications. A propaganda office was established in Cairo in order to work with the British in preparing items for the Arab press. But, inevitably, Britain's and Egypt's preoccupations were not France's, and so relevant articles were selected from the Cairo journals for reproduction in *Akhbar al Harb*. An Arabic newspaper, *Al Mustaqbal* ('The Future'), began publication in Paris on 1 March 1916. At the same time all these strands were pulled together with the appointment of Edmond Doutte, a teacher in Algeria, who at last co-ordinated the Moslem-orientated propaganda of the Maghreb, eliminating its more obvious contradictions. Doutte's contribution, above all, was to recognize the importance of the picture and of the cinema in the portrayal of France's war effort. He established a network of press offices in the major centres designed not only to disseminate information, but also to monitor local opinion the better to be able to reflect it in future publications.[128]

French rule in North Africa rested as much on collaboration as on confrontation. Formally speaking, both Tunisia and Morocco were protectorates, their indigenous and traditional rulers enjoying France's recognition, and the Islamic faith receiving full support. Algeria was a proper colony, but its

---

[127] G. Meynier, *L'Algérie révelée*, 269–70, 605, 616.
[128] Ibid. 533–40; Landau, *Politics of pan-Islam*, 120–1; Bihl, *Kaukasus-politik*, 38–9.

conquest had begun as far back as 1830, and particularly around Oran and Algiers its economic life and its political stability were now interlocked. Italy had forced the tribes of Libya into union by insisting on annexation and on sovereignty, and by giving its campaign the status of a crusade. France made no such mistake. Both before the war and again in February 1915 the German ambassador in Lisbon gave it as his view that the Arabs were unlikely to rise against the French.[129]

French colonialism was nonetheless divided in its philosophy. Some, including Lutaud and his military commander in the Algerian Sahara, Octave Meynier, reflected a belief in France's civilizing and republican mission. The ultimate objective was assimilation. The peoples of North Africa would be incorporated into the French empire by French education and French political ideas: traditional forms of Arab life would be suppressed. Others, most notably Hubert Lyautey, *résident général* of Morocco, and Charles Jonnart, both Lutaud's predecessor and in 1918 his successor as governor-general of Algeria, wanted to proceed by association. Temperamentally, Lyautey was entirely out of tune with the radical jacobinism of Lutaud and Meynier, as well as of political circles in Paris. His sympathies were with the aristocracy; he was a snob; he regarded metropolitan France and the Third Republic as decadent. France's power should, for him, rest on the traditional elites of the Maghreb. Neither school was interested in an emergent nationalism. Both were united in wanting an extension of the French empire. Their difference was over the most appropriate means—social revolution or aristocratic government.

Elements of both can be found in French policy in North Africa in the First World War. Clashes were not infrequent, but the war also introduced an element of pragmatism. Proposals for political reform in Algeria were adumbrated throughout the war, ultimately to little effect; but in this way the assimilationists had their run and the ambitious young Algerian bourgeois, the *jeunes algériens*, were kept in play. The corollary of citizenship would have been full conscription. But, at least until 1918, the call-up was kept small and the right of exemption if a substitute could be bought was maintained. The sons of chiefs and notables who did join the army received privileged treatment. Incorporated into a particularly useless form of irregular cavalry, the *spahis auxiliaires*, or (from 1916) drafted into a special military school, either way they were spared the horrors of warfare experienced by humble *tirailleurs* on the western front.[130]

If, politically, French colonial rule drew from both points of view, militarily it had less choice. The challenge confronting the ambitious soldier was no longer in the Sahara but on France's own frontiers. It had been axiomatic for

[129] I am grateful to Dr Gregory Martin for this information.
[130] G. Meynier, *L'Algérie révelée*, 540–7.

many colonial conquerors that aggression and boldness, finding their culmination on the battlefield, were the methods with which to overawe a native
opponent. In North Africa Charles Mangin embodied such a view. He went to
Europe to apply similar precepts on the battlefields of Verdun and the Marne,
but he left some of his disciples behind. In the circumstances of 1914–18,
however, France wanted not fighting but pacification. This, at least ostensibly,
was the method of Lyautey. His strategy was to combine the occupation of
permanent posts with the formation of mobile columns. Without the latter,
the former could do little more than protect the ground on which they were
erected: the columns enabled France to dominate the area beyond the posts.
But, without the posts, France's military presence would not be transformed
into something more enduring. Lyautey said that his posts would become
centres of commercial activity, drawing in the tribesmen, and so converting
them from war to trade. The soldier was to become the agent of civilization.
When Lyautey lost most of his regular troops in August 1914, and received aged
territorials instead, he was not displeased. Both the Arab respect for seniority
and the territorials' civilian skills made them assets, not liabilities. Much of
Lyautey's strategy—his celebration in May 1917 of 'the grandeur and beauty
of colonial war... [which] ... on the very day following the cessation of
fighting... begins to create life'[131]—was rhetoric. In reality, his opponents
were happy to trade one minute and plunder the next; in reality, raids and rape
were as much part of his repertoire as of any other colonial conqueror. But the
words had a role to play. They convinced Paris of the virtues of the empire, and
made it prepared to compromise when the corruption of the Caids or sherifs
seemed at odds with France's civilizing mission. Furthermore, Lyautey's per-
suasiveness won sufficient allies within Morocco for 'native politics' to be a
partial substitute for manpower.[132]

However, the new military threat which confronted French North Africa in
1914 was not on Lyautey's patch but to the east, on its frontier with Libya.
French expansion into the Sahara, both south and east, had forced the Senussi
to concentrate their activities in Tripolitania and Cyrenaica. The possibility in
August of 1914 of setting the Senussi on the French rather than on the British
occurred to the Germans. But the Germans, unlike the Turks, were respectful
of Italian neutrality, and the Turks themselves were more anxious to gain Libya
and Egypt than Tunisia and Algeria. Moreover, the Senussi were for the most
part happy to leave the French alone, recognizing that the defeat of Italy was a
military target quite sufficient for their slender powers.

[131] Quoted in Scham, *Lyautey in Morocco*, 34.

[132] Porch, *Conquest of Morocco*, and 'Bugeaud, Gallieni, Lyautey: the development of French colonial
warfare', in Paret (ed.), *Makers of modern strategy*, 388–95, puts Lyautey in his place. See also Bidwell,
Morocco under colonial rule, 12–25; Le Révérend, *Lyautey*; P. Lyautey (ed.), *Lyautey l'africain*, for his
correspondence; Rivet, *Lyautey et l'institution du protectorat français au Maroc*, which is exhaustive but
organized thematically, and therefore hard to use specifically for the First World War.

But the combination of Senussi success and Italian neutrality made it impossible for France to remain uninvolved. The defeated Italian garrisons from Ghadames and Ghat crossed into the safety of southern Algeria in December 1914. The French policy, that of benevolent neutrality, demanded that the belligerents of either side, whether Italian or Senussi, be disarmed and interned on entering French territory. The French did disarm the Ghadames garrison, but they did not disarm that of Ghat. Instead, in January 1915 the latter re-entered Libya with a view to retaking Ghadames. Furthermore, it was supplied with French military equipment to enable it to do so.

As a European power engaged in a major war, France was understandably anxious to avoid offending Italy in the hope that Italy might be won over to the Entente.[133] But the confusion in France's responses arose less from the split between its priorities as a European and an imperial power, and more from the division in attitudes to colonial government. The 'associationists', especially the French resident in Tunis and General Moinier, commanding XIX corps, were anxious not to inflame the Senussi for fear of repercussions in southern Tunisia and the Sahara. They feared that Italy's savagery close to the Tunisian frontier could have destabilizing consequences for France if France were too closely linked with it. Even after Italy had joined the Entente in May 1915, the governor of Algeria, Lutaud, told Moinier to treat developments in Libya as the result, 'not of a foreign war but of an internal revolt'.[134] Meynier, on the other hand, as the local commander, was anxious to extend French rule, an objective in which Lutaud was prepared to connive. Ghat commanded Ajjer, the south-eastern corner of French Algeria, into which French influence had scarcely penetrated. For Meynier, the war was an opportunity to occupy Ghat and Ghadames preventively, and to subordinate the Touareg of the southern Sahara.[135]

Meynier's policy was the reverse of Lyautey's—to harass and humiliate the Touareg of the Ajjer into action, so that they could then be crushed. On 6 March 1915 500 Senussi, using captured Italian artillery, attacked the French post at Djanet, just inside the Algerian frontier from Ghat. Moinier's corps plan in such circumstances was to abandon all south-eastern Algeria. He agreed, however, to allow Meynier to form two columns in order to reinforce forts Flatters and Polignac, the latter still 250 kilometres in a direct line from Djanet. Meynier's force of 600 men required over a thousand camels; the heat necessitated halts between 11 a.m. and 6 p.m., and it marched in three- or four-day stages. Movement, at about 50 or 60 kilometres per day, was therefore slow

---

[133] Ferry, *Carnets secrets*, 43; Farrar, *Principled pragmatist*, 183.

[134] J. L. Miège, 'La Libye, l'Italie et la France entre 1914 et 1917', in Guillen (ed.), *La France et l'Italie*, 468.

[135] G. Meynier, *L'Algérie révélée*, 489–505; and also O. Meynier, *Revue militaire française*, 148 (octobre 1933), 120–42; 149 (novembre 1933), 336–53; 152, (février 1934), 214–37 (By Commdt. Filio).

in relation to the distances to be covered. But as wireless was not available in the Saharan theatre until 1916, intelligence was at a premium and direct control from on high hard to enforce. Lutaud asked for Meynier to be allowed to retake Djanet, to suppress the Ajjer region, and march on Ghat. In May Meynier set about doing exactly that. On 3 June, however, Moinier instructed Meynier to abandon his attack on Ghat, and on 30 June the French refused a request from the Italian government for joint action. The whole of the Ajjer was now in revolt, or close to it. With a line of communications 900 kilometres long and with only four useable companies for the entire eastern Sahara, Meynier was in danger of exposing his force to defeat in detail. On 3 July he abandoned Djanet once more, falling back north of the Ajjer to Fort Polignac. Even here supply problems triggered the onset of scurvy, and the post to its west, Ain el Hadjadj, was hemmed in by the Touareg.[136]

What Moinier had feared had come to pass. Khalifa ben Asker, flouting the wishes of the Senussi leadership, had broken off relations with the French. In September 1915 he crossed into southern Tunisia, raising the standard of rebellion against the French. French rule in northern Tunisia remained stable. Les jeunes tunisiens, a small group of educated, liberal reformers, had shot their bolt in 1912. Protests and strikes had resulted in the arrest and exile of their leaders, and the banning of their publications. Furthermore, their westernizing and modernizing inclinations had driven the traditional Muslims into closer alliance with the 'associationists' of France, so preventing the formation of an anti-colonial, nationalist bloc.[137] But, if ultimately France's political position seemed secure, its military situation—with Meynier gallivanting far away in the southern Sahara—did not. France all but charged Italy with complicity with the Senussi, claiming that its new Entente partner was deliberately giving ground in Libya so that the rebels would be encouraged to divert their attentions to French territory.[138] Meynier redeployed northwards with deliberate slowness, creating a scratch force near Ghadames, and asserting that the real threat lay to the south, with up to 12,000 Senussi massing to invade Algeria. The southern Tunisian frontier was held by a force of territorials and over-age reservists. What really checked Khalifa ben Asker was the fury of Mohammed Suf al-Mahmudi, who arrested him.

No sooner had Moinier and Alapetite, the French resident in Tunisia, surmounted one crisis than they faced another. Italy requested that France co-operate in the blockade of Tripolitania by stopping the caravans which entered from Tunisia and southern Algeria. Both recognized that to do so would weaken Suf's hand with Khalifa ben Asker, inflame the Senussi, and inflict economic hardship on their own domains. However, a combination of

[136] Raynaud-Lacroze, Méharistes au combat, provides a memoir, although it confuses 1915 with 1916.
[137] Perkins, Tunisia, 92–5.
[138] J. L. Miège, 'La Libye, l'Italie et la France', in Guillen (ed.), La France et l'Italie, 470.

Entente loyalty and pressure from Lutaud and Meynier overrode wiser counsels. Khalifa ben Asker was then released and the Senussi attack on southern Tunisia resumed in 1916. The exiled *jeunes tunisiens* had come to rest in Berlin, and through their national independence committee stepped up anti-French propaganda. The French garrison—although mostly local troops deemed unusable on the western front—peaked at 15,000 men. By October 1916 they had regained the upper hand, and the Turkish leadership in Tripolitania persuaded ben Asker to concentrate his efforts on Italy. In 1917 the French strength in Tunisia fell back to 8,000 men. Khalifa ben Asker had a final flurry in August and October 1918, renewing his attacks in response to Prince Osman Fuad's call.

The effect of the fighting and, principally, of the blockade was destitution on both sides of the frontier. To the south, Senussi and Touareg joined hands to defend their way of life. The Touareg of Air, across the border of southern Algeria in Niger, had never submitted to French rule, and one of their leaders, Mohammed ben Khaossan, had taken refuge in Fezzan. In December 1916, with Senussi support, Khaossan struck south-west from Ghat, raising the banner of holy war from Ajjer through Hoggar to Air. Tagama, Sultan of Air, joined the insurgents. The whole French position in the central and southern Sahara, from Lake Chad to Timbuktu, and as far north as Fort Polignac, was threatened. On 17 December 1916 Khaossan and 1,200 men, accompanied by Turkish and German advisers and equipped with captured Italian artillery and machine-guns, laid siege to Agades. The French garrison of ninety men was devoid of artillery and encumbered with 165 women and children. In an independent development, resistance to recruiting and to its concomitant—the extension of French rule—had thrown the mountainous areas of Dahomey, Togo, Haut Senegal, and Niger into open rebellion, and French West Africa was ill-prepared to meet the new threat. France appealed to Britain. Movements of the Nigeria Regiment to East Africa were halted, and in January 1917 the British columns marched northwards from Kano and Sokoto into French Niger. They in turn relieved the French garrisons of the Niger, 2,000 of whom were freed to relieve Agades. On 3 March the siege was raised.

The Touareg broke up, some returning whence they came and others fleeing into northern Nigeria. Kano had been affected by the suppression of Saharan trade, and Senussi lodges had been established there and in Borno. During the war years 20,601 Nigerian Muslims made the pilgrimage to Mecca, but 24,633 returned. The Germans, raiding across the Cameroons border at the beginning of 1915, had distributed pan-Islamic propaganda. The possibility of influences subversive to British rule entering from the north and west, therefore, created grounds for concern in Nigeria. The French claimed that the Sultan of Sokoto was in league with Khaossan. But the emirs of northern Nigeria did not move. Lugard's policy of indirect rule, like Lyautey's of native politics, provided a dyke against which the tide of Senussi influence broke and then retreated.[139]

In Algeria the rebounding of Meynier's forward policy resulted in his removal. 'The main danger in the Sahara', Moinier reported at the end of 1916, 'is Meynier.'[140] The French minister of war, albeit briefly, was Lyautey. He created a temporary joint command for the whole Sahara, thus bypassing the governors of Algeria, Mauretania, the French Sudan, and the Niger, and gave it to his own protégé and a veteran of the region, Henri Laperrine.

The key to Laperrine's policy was the loyalty of Moussa ag Amestane, chief of the Hoggar Touareg. Moussa had managed to stay on the fence as Khaossan passed through, and in the spring of 1917 co-operated with the French in driving the Senussi back into Tripolitania. Laperrine aimed to solicit local support rather than to antagonize it, but he sustained his efforts with an active military presence. In a previous incarnation as commander in the Algerian Sahara he had formed mobile, camel-mounted columns. Meynier preferred to employ *goums*, unreliable local levies, in heavy columns. Laperrine now supplemented his original concepts by using cars, aeroplanes, and wireless as the means to ubiquity. With longer lines of communication, mechanization confronted greater difficulties than in the British sphere of operations: camels were still needed to convey the petrol for the cars. But broadly speaking, and despite obstruction from Lutaud and from Moinier's successor Nivelle, Laperrine's strategy worked. By the time Laperrine met his death in an air crash in 1920, France controlled the Ajjer.[141]

The crisis faced by France on the southern frontiers of Algeria in 1916–17 coincided with the only major threat to its hold in the north of the country. Early German efforts to promote rebellion in Algeria revolved around the reinsertion of former members of the Foreign Legion to persuade those Germans still serving to mutiny. Ernst Kühnel made contact with one former legionnaire, Adolf Staringer, in his bid to sabotage the Algerian railways. But these plots had come to nothing.[142] Thus, if the twin crises of 1916–17 were linked by Turco-German agitation (and this cannot be proven), it seems likely to have come via Libya rather than via Morocco. The mountainous region around Batna, in eastern Algeria and inland from Constantine, was close to Tunisia and only 600 kilometres from Tripoli. A proclamation from Sulayman al-Baruni calling for holy war had arrived in the area only weeks before

---

[139] G. Meynier, *L'Algérie révelée*, 500–2; Osuntokun, *Nigeria in the First World War*, 139–61; Michel, *L'appel à l'Afrique*, 118; Haywood and Clarke, *West African Frontier Force*, 252; Crowder, 'The 1914–1918 European war and West Africa', 500, 508–9.

[140] G. Meynier, *L'Algérie révelée*, 501.

[141] Ibid. 502–5; Porch, *Conquest of the Sahara*, 299–302; Clayton, *France, soldiers and Africa*, 101–2.

[142] Müller, *Islam, gihad*, 371–2, 395.

violence erupted in November 1916. But the causes of the Batna rising can be explained in local terms, without reference to external pressures.

Throughout the war the area around and south of Constantine showed itself the least supportive of France in all Algeria. Oran provided 43.6 per cent of those who joined the army, when it contained 21.9 per cent of the population; central Algeria (including Algiers itself) had 32 per cent of the population and produced 33.2 per cent of recruits; eastern Algeria, however, could only muster 24.2 per cent of the army, although possessing 44.9 per cent of the population. Furthermore, the rate of desertion among the Constantinois was double. When it came to war loans, Oran raised 287 francs per inhabitant, Algiers 270 francs, and Constantine 60 francs. In part, this was no more than a reflection of the backwardness of the region. The real incomes of those peasants who farmed cereals fell to 95 per cent of their 1914 level in 1916, but in Constantine to 80 per cent. Elsewhere the boom in agricultural export crops, particularly tobacco and wine, enriched many Algerians, so that over the war as a whole the real incomes of agricultural workers in Oran rose 50 per cent and in Algiers 30 per cent. But in Constantine they fell 14 per cent.[143]

The triggers to rebellion were two decrees issued in September 1916, conscripting the class of 1917 and requisitioning workers for industries in France. Resistance to conscription had briefly flared among the Beni Chougram in October 1914. Otherwise, as elsewhere in the French empire, men took to the mountains and to brigandage to avoid enlistment. What gave the Batna rising its character, and its seriousness, was the element of leadership provided by major families and by the petty bourgeois. Both were concerned by reports that the privilege of buying replacements would be removed. The violence was concentrated in three areas, divided from each other but linked in that French penetration was recent without being complete or militarily strong. Where the French were present in numbers, or where the French had yet to reach, all remained quiet.

The rebellion found Lutaud in a weak position. There were only 3,000 troops in the area, and about 8,000 in Algeria as a whole. He gave the dissidents until the end of November to come to order, and asked Paris for 16,000 men, artillery, aircraft, and armoured cars. The repression began in December and lasted five months. The effort was out of all proportion to the original end, employing 14,000 men to bring in 1,366 reluctant conscripts (many of whom may have come in by 30 November in any case). What, in reality, was at stake was the extension of French rule. Formally, Lutaud's policy was one of conciliation. Sheikh Beloudini, in whose house the first steps towards rebellion had been hatched, was fined and imprisoned for a year; of 805 men convicted, only eight were executed. But the Senegalese soldiers raped and pillaged.

[143] G. Meynier, *L'Algérie révelée*, 279–80, 602, 638, 658–61.

Livestock and grain were requisitioned by the soldiers, fines were levied in kind, and the loss of manpower ravaged cultivation. The 1917 harvest was bad, and famine followed.[144]

The rest of Algeria watched. However sympathetic others were to the response of the Constantinois, they were not prepared to revolt against French rule. The First World War may have marked a step in the emergence of an Algerian national consciousness, but the behaviour of the population as a whole was characterized by *attentisme*, not by action.

Most significant was the passivity of the mountains around Oran and of the western Sahara, for it served to isolate Morocco. Oran itself was the most Europeanized of Algerian conurbations; southern Oran and the desert beyond had felt the hand of the French army shortly before the outbreak of war. Senussi influence penetrated no further westwards; equally, the adjacent centres of Moroccan resistance, in the middle Atlas Mountains and around Tafilalat, did not spread eastwards. Morocco, like Lyautey, remained a law unto itself.

In May 1914 Lyautey declared France master of 'le Maroc utile'. By taking Taza, he had opened the route from Fez to Oran. The coastal areas, the ports, and the towns were in French hands, and their inhabitants were benefiting from the order and commerce brought by French rule. Resistance was confined to rural areas and was divided—not least by the small Spanish holdings to the north at Ceuta and Melilla, and to the south at Ifni.

But to achieve this France's military commitment to Morocco jumped from 38,000 men to 80,000 between 1911 and 1914. On 27 July 1914 the foreign minister told Lyautey that the fate of Morocco would be resolved in Lorraine. He was to withdraw to the line Kenitra–Meknes–Fez–Oujda, abandoning the hinterland and the whole of central and southern Morocco, thus releasing all European, Algerian, and Tunisian units for the western front, a total of thirty-five battalions. Lyautey argued that such a precipitate withdrawal would trigger a general insurrection. Instead, he released twenty of the sixty battalions available to him with immediate effect, promising a further twenty as the situation developed. By June 1915 forty-two battalions had returned to France. Rather than concentrate his forces on an inner perimeter which would still be too extensive for effective defence, Lyautey proposed instead to maintain forward positions and to continue with an offensive posture. This would enable him to strip his interior, the cities, and the coast to meet the needs of metropolitan France. His object, he insisted, was not territorial extension: 'si nous avons attaqué c'était pour nous défendre mais non pour conquérir.'[145] He

---

[144] Ibid. 575–98; Ageron, *Les Algériens musulmans*, 1150–7.

[145] Memorandum by Lyautey, Dec. 1914, in P. Lyautey (ed.), *Lyautey l'africain*, ii. 316. In addition to the works already cited in footnote 132, see also Michael Brett, 'The Maghrib', in Roberts (ed.), *Cambridge History of Africa*, vol. VII.

aimed to hold for France that which France already occupied. In this he succeeded.

Nonetheless, the main French concentrations were in the north, and their obvious weakness to the south. Lyautey's defences around Marrakesh rested on the co-operation of the great Caids of the High Atlas. His principal threat was Ahmad Haybat Allah, also known as el Hiba, who used Spanish territory around Ifni as an enclave and had a base at Tiznit. Although he had been roundly defeated by Mangin in 1912, el Hiba was reactivated by the war and its promise of German assistance. Now, however, his former ally Haida ou Mouis threw in his lot with France, and by 1915 Haida had driven el Hiba south of Tiznit. In July 1916 el Hiba made contact with the Germans operating out of the Canary Islands. They provided him with a subsidy. In November 1916 a submarine landed a Turco-German mission headed by the former German consul at Fez, Edgar Pröbster. Pröbster bore the promise of weapons, also to be delivered by submarine, but French cruisers foiled any further landing. Nonetheless, el Hiba triggered a rising along the High Atlas to the Tafilalat, and in January 1917 Haida was killed. Threatened with the collapse of their position south of the Atlas, the French committed 4,000 troops. Formally speaking the policy of collaboration remained unchanged: Arabs still outnumbered soldiers in the mobile column, and whenever it appeared the local tribesmen denounced el Hiba. But Henri Gouraud, who had replaced Lyautey while the latter was minister of war in Paris, refused to create any permanent garrisons, with the result that the situation was no more than contained and el Hiba remained at large.[146]

To the north the main apparent threat in August 1914 came from the Berbers of the Middle Atlas. Furthermore, Lyautey had to contend with the thrusting instincts of those raised in the Mangin school and anxious to finish with Morocco in order to return to the real war in France. On 13 November 1914, in direct defiance of Lyautey's instructions, Colonel Laverdure mounted a raid on Moha ou Hammou and his Zaian followers, the winter having brought them down from the mountains to el Herri, near Khenifra. Initial success turned to disaster. Laverdure and 622 men were killed, and the French garrison driven back to Khenifra for the rest of the war. Only in 1917, when Gouraud penetrated the Middle Atlas from north-west to south-east, dividing the Beni Oudren from the Zaians, did the French again resume the offensive. Lyautey began to plan a second road through to Algeria.

Although the Middle Atlas proved the most protracted and insoluble of French military problems in Morocco, it was too isolated from the coast—and the Berbers too internally divided—for it to be easy for the Germans to aid the

---

[146] Burke, *Francia*, III (1975), 448–9; Usborne, *Conquest of Morocco*, 230–1; Hoisington, *Lyautey*, 93–107.

insurgents there. Much more accessible were the Mediterranean coastline and the mountains of the Rif, buttressed at one end by neutral Spanish territory. Ahmad al-Raysuni received a total of a million pesetas, in instalments, from the Germans. But it was almost entirely wasted money. Raysuni's enemy was Spain, not France, and he was quite happy to pass the war playing off the three European powers against each other and drawing in the proceeds. The likelihood of his co-operating with the Central Powers was yet further diminished with the emergence of a rival leader in the Rif.

Abd el Malek was an Algerian living in Tangiers. More importantly, he had been an officer in the Ottoman army and was the grandson of Abd el Kader, the hero of Algerian resistance against France between 1830 and 1847. In March 1915, accompanied by German and Turkish advisers and aided by German deserters from the Foreign Legion, Abd el Malek left Tangiers for the country around Taza. By the end of the year he had raised a force of 1,200 men, and in the summer of 1916 was reckoned to have 1,500 operating north-east of Taza. The Turks declared him to be emir of Morocco. More helpfully, the Germans gave him 100,000 pesetas a month, rising to 300,000, and by March 1918 to 600,000. Nonetheless, Abd el Malek's relations with his German advisers were fraught. The first, an engineer called Franz Far, came without weapons and was reported by Asif Tahir Bey to be no more than a mouthpiece for German propaganda; he died in isolation in November 1915. The second, Friedrich Albert Bartels, also did not bring weapons, and his military effectiveness was achieved principally through his rallying of ex-legionnaires. The French persuaded the Spanish to tighten their customs arrangements, thus interrupting the flow into the Rif of smuggled rifles. Nonetheless, arms were abundant. The problem for both Far and Bartels was that weapons were successfully smuggled into the Rif, but that they tended to fall into the hands of those tribesmen closest to the coast. In July 1916, for example, a consignment of 3,000 rifles and 2 million rounds got through to the tribes.[147] In early 1918 the German military attaché in Madrid, who co-ordinated the agents in Morocco, decided to push Kühnel out of his lair in Larache in the hope that he could get on better than Bartels. France put a price of 250,000 francs on Kühnel's head, but he remained at large until the armistice. In June the French concentrated 6,000 men to defeat Abd el Malek, driving him north to Kifan. Germany's money enabled Abd el Malek to compensate those tribesmen who accompanied him for the crops which they forfeited, but in September 1918 they were beaten again in a five-day battle at Kifan. With the approach of winter Abd el Malek's tribesmen began to surrender. On 1 November he fled to Spanish Morocco.

[147] Burke, *Francia*, III (1975), 446–7, 451–4; P. Lyautey, *Lyautey l'africain*, iii. 107, 298; Müller, *Islam, Gihad*, 308–18, 400–4, 407–10.

Lyautey's dispatches to Paris anticipated co-ordinated action by the tribes, prompted by German agents and sustained by German subsidies, in each of 1915, 1917, and 1918.[148] This may have been a device to prevent further reductions in the strength of the French army of occupation. In practice, Germany's activists in Morocco consistently failed in their efforts to produce synchronized action among the tribal leaders. France's commitment was to guerrilla operations little different from those which they might have anticipated without war in Europe. Lyautey's penetration of Morocco did not advance, but nor did it retreat. And within the periphery the inner core remained secure. Indeed, the French hold became stronger, not weaker. Lyautey took the threat which Germany posed to the coast and towns with seriousness. In many other colonies, both French and British, German citizens found their activities only gradually curtailed in 1914–15. In Morocco, Carl Ficke, a German businessman, and three colleagues were summarily executed on 2 August 1914. Lyautey became increasingly preoccupied with the U-boat threat to Rabat and Casablanca. But if these were reflections of exaggerated fears, outwardly his demeanour was calm, confident, and authoritative. Morocco played host to three trade fairs during the course of the war. Agricultural improvement and road construction continued. The message to those resident in Morocco's cities was clear enough: France's power was immediate, Germany's remote and apparently ineffective.

The forty-two battalions which Lyautey returned to France did not represent a net saving in manpower. Their places were taken by the territorials and reservists who policed and developed the interior, while the Foreign Legion and Senegalese *tirailleurs* held the outer edge. The total number of French troops in North Africa during the war varied little from pre-war totals— approaching 200,000, with 100,000 in Morocco. But plan XVII had envisaged that XIX corps, at 55,000 men in 1911 the largest of France's corps, would release twenty-nine battalions for service in France. In practice 104 battalions were sent. Of forty battalions of Algerian and Tunisian *tirailleurs*, thirty-two went to France, six to Morocco, and only two remained in Algeria. Of the European population of Algeria, 73,000—or 10 per cent of the total—were called up to serve in their land of origin.[149]

French North Africa, therefore, probably gave more than it took. And certainly this is the case if local recruitment is added to the equation. Tunisia raised 63,000 soldiers and 29,000 labourers, Algeria 173,000 soldiers and 78,000 labourers, and Morocco 37,000 soldiers and 35,000 labourers. Lyautey justified his policies by what Morocco could do for France. On balance he was probably right. Certainly the French public thought so. The loyalty of the North Africans

---

[148] P. Lyautey, *Lyautey l'africain*, iii. 17–19, 29–42, 249, 262, 293–303; see also Lyautey's two major reports on his wartime work, of November 1916 and June 1919: ibid., iii. 129–72, 333–49.
[149] Larcher, *La Guerre turque*, 526–8; G. Meynier, *L'Algérie révelée*, 88, 260, 523–4, 529.

to France, the image of cheerful courage associated with the *tirailleurs*, helped transform French colonialism from a minority interest to one of national self-esteem.

PERSIA AND AFGHANISTAN

Throughout the nineteenth century Britain had made it abundantly clear that it took very seriously any threat to India's north-west frontier. In 1904, a year in which the German general staff concluded that an invasion of India from Russia was out of the question, the Committee of Imperial Defence gave consideration to Kitchener's calculation that Britain would have to send 135,614 men to ensure the security of the subcontinent.[150] The method whereby the British Expeditionary Force could be divided and its concentration in Europe prevented was therefore clear enough. From 1912 on, Moltke's staff developed an increasing interest in India. But the paradox that confronted them did not admit of an easy resolution. The defence of India was a military responsibility and could not rest on Britain's major bulwark, the Royal Navy; hence its attraction. But without themselves possessing mastery of the seas, the Germans were unable to threaten India in the first place. The chances of revolution from within the subcontinent diminished as British rule solidified—or so at least von der Goltz and others reported. There remained the overland route. After all, Napoleon had tried it.[151]

However ambitious Moltke's proposals for extending the war on 2 August, they did not reach this level of unreality. He spoke of rebellion in India; he suggested, too, an alliance with Persia. But he did not connect the two: the former he saw as self-contained, the latter as a buttress to Turkey and a challenge to Russia.

Responsibility for suggesting that the threat to India might be directed through the Khyber Pass belongs not with anybody in Germany but with Enver. On 11 and 14 August 1914 the Ottoman minister of war spoke in extravagant terms to Wangenheim of the Islamic fervour of Habibullah, the Emir of Afghanistan. He implied—falsely, the Germans subsequently concluded—that officers of the Turkish army were already in contact with the Emir and with Muslims in the subcontinent. A word to Habibullah would be sufficient to unleash an Afghan invasion of India. The German foreign ministry was almost totally devoid of expertise in, and information on, Central Asia. But those whom they consulted endorsed Enver's encouraging scenario. Oppenheim, whose expertise lay in Egypt, and Professor Ernst Jäckh,

---

[150] Gooch, *Plans of war*, 215.   [151] Barooah, *India and the official Germany*, 74–5, 80–1, 168–9.

retained by the foreign ministry since 1912 as an adviser on Turkey and the Near East, served only to reinforce each other's optimism. The former told Bethmann Hollweg that Afghanistan had 50,000 troops ready to invade India, and a Swedish explorer, Sven Hedin, said that Habibullah was 'burning with desire to attack the British rule in India'.[152] Significantly, Hans von Seeckt, a staff officer of considerable accomplishments who had visited the Khyber Pass in 1907/8, was not consulted. By 26 August the foreign office had collected a group of fifteen people to form a German mission to Afghanistan.

They arrived in Constantinople disguised as a travelling circus. Enver was not impressed: the decline in Turkish enthusiasm for the scheme can be charted from this moment. The only member of the party who was a Persian speaker was Wilhelm Wassmuss, who had been a dragoman and a fomentor of anti-British tribes in Bushire.[153] The foreign office had been unable to provide maps specifically of Afghanistan; those that had been issued were copied from W. and A. K. Johnston's general atlas of the world. Some of the group imagined that they might drive to Kabul, using oil and petrol from Baku. The fact that its task was in the first instance diplomatic, and even commercial (its organizing committee contained representatives of shipping and of industry), was reflected in its equipment and structure. The Turks relieved the Germans of the two machine-guns with which they had been provided, leaving them only with small arms of varying calibres. Administration was in the hands of a committee of five. When the military attaché at Constantinople negotiated for Wassmuss to take over the command, the others objected. They bickered all the way down to Aleppo.

By this time the party had been reinforced to twenty-five, the new participants including Oskar von Niedermayer. Niedermayer had travelled extensively in Arabia, Persia, and India before the war; he was also an officer in the army, convinced that military organization was essential if the expedition was to succeed. Wassmuss was instructed in October that Wangenheim, as ambassador in Constantinople, was responsible for the expedition. In December Wangenheim appointed Niedermayer to the command, in Wassmuss's stead. But Niedermayer regarded himself as the leader of an independent military force, answerable to the general staff and not the foreign office, to Berlin and not to Constantinople.

The conflict as to the ultimate responsibility, whether it was the army's or the foreign office's, and the friction between the leading personalities at the local level were exacerbated in April 1915 when Berlin decided on a second mission. In January 1915 Mohamed Barkatullah, an Indian revolutionary who

[152] McKale, *War by revolution*, 52; Vogel, *Die Persien- und Afghanistanexpedition Oskar Ritter v. Niedermayers*, 139; also 49, 138–9, 188–9.
[153] Wassmuss has a somewhat overblown biography in English: Sykes, *Wassmuss*.

had been resident in Japan and then the United States, presented himself at the German consulate in Geneva. Barkatullah claimed a friendship with Habibullah's brother, Nasrullah. The foreign ministry agreed to send a group of Indians, including Barkatullah, Kumar Mahendra Pratap, and six erstwhile prisoners of war, under the management of Werner Otto von Hentig to Kabul in order to foment rebellion across the frontier. Hentig was a diplomat who had served in Teheran. As the creature of the Indian committee in Berlin, Hentig's party was clearly the foreign office's pigeon, not the general staff's. But in June 1915 Hentig and Niedermayer met in Teheran and agreed to proceed together. Nobody could decide who was the senior. The foreign office preferred to treat the two as independent. All those in the joint expedition took sides in the ensuing squabbles. Pratap—considered by his German companion to be 'fanatical, moody and egocentric',[154] and convinced that he himself was the real leader—took delight in stoking these disputes. Ultimately, the issue became that of the subordination of the military to political control. But, even on ostensibly neutral territory, practicality gave the weight to the former, not the latter. Whatever were the achievements of the mission to Afghanistan, the credit is Niedermayer's.

In the autumn of 1914, therefore, German policy focused on Afghanistan, not Persia. The German ambassador in Teheran had not encouraged Moltke's proposed alliance with the Shah: Persia was a country 'without patriotic energy and for the moment powerless'.[155] It therefore became the high road to Afghanistan, not an end in itself.

Germany's assessment of Persia's weakness was well founded and widely shared. Revolution in 1906 had destroyed the traditional bases of authority without creating a substitute. The Shah had accepted the election of an assembly (the *Majlis*) and the creation of a constitutional monarchy. But the liberalizing inclinations of the *Majlis* upset Islamic interests, and the two groups which had united to effect the revolution—the commercial classes and the *ulema*—burst asunder. Muhammed Ali, who succeeded as Shah in 1907, exploited the clash to close the *Majlis* in 1908. Those democratic nationalists who escaped his purge rallied in Tabriz, the capital of Azerbaijan and the centre—by virtue of its trade with Russia and Turkey—of liberal as well as commercial activity. The siege of Tabriz was ended by Russian intervention. But the popular guard of Tabriz sallied forth along the Caspian shore, in an advance on Teheran. Simultaneously, the Bakhtiari tribe seized Isfahan and then marched on the capital from the south. In July 1909 the two forces converged, and the Shah fled to Russia.

[154] Vogel, *Persien-und Afghanistanexpedition*, 173; see also 7, 23–4, 57, 66, 137–76, 197–202.
[155] Gehrke, *Persien in der deutschen Orientpolitik*, i. 22. Gehrke's work has proved invaluable, and is the source for much of what follows. Hopkirk, *On secret service*, provides a recent general account in English of the main German efforts in Persia, Afghanistan, and India.

His successor and son, Ahmad, was a minor: he was crowned in July 1914, aged 17. Power, therefore, remained divided. Ahmad's regent drove many educated liberals into exile; the authority of the mullahs waxed as that of the nationalists waned; and beyond the purlieus of Teheran, especially to the south, tribal independence multiplied.[156]

Superimposed on this confused domestic picture, and interacting with it, was an international position that only confirmed the fissures. Throughout the nineteenth century Persia had served as, and profited from being, a buffer between Russian expansion into Central Asia and Britain's defence of India. But in 1907 the two powers, while formally recognizing Persia's integrity, had allocated each other spheres of interest, Russia's to the north and Britain's to the south. A central band remained unapportioned. In the decade between the revolution and the world war Russia became the most consistent authority in northern Persia. In addition to 5,000 troops who remained in Azerbaijan, Russians officered the Persian Cossack brigade in Teheran. Aided by their railway to Tabriz, Russian economic interests came to dominate Persia. In 1913–14 Russia's imports from Persia were five times those of its principal rival in the region, Britain, and its own exports to Persia double. In 1911, when Persia struck out for independence by calling in a neutral American, Morgan Shuster, to reform its finances, Russia once again intervened in force, ensuring his dismissal and precipitating the dissolution of the *Majlis*. In June 1914 Sir Edward Grey described northern Persia, and specifically Azerbaijan, as 'a Russian province ruled by Russian officials'.[157]

Formally speaking, Britain had no interest in the domestic politics of Persia; London's concern was India's concern, to create a buffer in order to secure the subcontinent. But the Shah's powerlessness in the south prompted the British to make independent bargains with local leaders. Thus, they too contributed to the undermining of central authority. Furthermore, the fact that real power came increasingly to be exercised by Russia meant that, despite the 1907 agreement, tensions between the two allies mounted. Russian intervention in 1911 had been prompted because Morgan Shuster wanted an efficient gendarmerie in order to ensure the collection of taxes. He proposed that it should have British officers, some of whom would have been deployed in the northern zone. The British agreed not to press the point, and Swedes were appointed instead.

India's security made Britain's interest in Persia, however long-standing, indirect. But in the years immediately preceding the war commercial considerations began to mesh with strategic, so making British involvement more

---

[156] For background, see Peter Avery, *Modern Iran*; Nikki Keddie and Mehrdad Amanat, 'Iran under the later Qajars, 1848–1922', in Peter Avery et al. (eds.), *Cambridge History of Iran*, vol. VII.

[157] Rose Greaves, 'Iranian relations with Great Britain and British India 1798–1921', in Avery *et al.* (eds.), *Cambridge History of Iran*, vii. 421; see Geyer, *Russian imperialism*, 334–7.

immediate. Britain owned the Imperial Bank of Persia and printed Persia's money. In 1901 Britain was granted the oil concessions for all of Persia except the five northernmost provinces. In 1908 oil was found in the neutral zone. The Anglo-Persian Oil Company established a refinery at Abadan, and constructed a pipeline along the Karun river. HMS *Queen Elizabeth*, the super-Dreadnought laid down in 1912, was the first battleship to burn oil, not coal; in 1913 the company secured the contract to supply the Admiralty with fuel oil. The following May the British government became the company's majority shareholder. Oil output that year reached 273,000 tons. Outwardly, Britain did not wish to partition Persia; privately, the Foreign Office had ceased to regard it as an independent nation.[158]

The Shah's cabinets were, therefore, seen as the tools of foreign powers. And indeed Russia and Britain constantly intervened in order to fashion a cabinet favourable to Entente interests. The result was chronic governmental instability. Sixteen cabinets were formed during the war. Nonetheless, the clique through whose hands power rotated was small. Three prime ministers held office more than twice, and Mustaufi ul-Mamalik did so four times. His attraction was his weakness, as he was able to compromise with more than one group at the same time. Thus, beneath the flux and the intrigue there was an underlying continuity. Its effect was to keep out the democrats and the nationalists, although they had a small majority in the *Majlis*, which reconvened in the autumn of 1914. The latter, therefore, turned to Berlin. Germany was the opponent of both of Persia's major interventionist powers; it had no great stake in Central Asia; its victories in Europe might serve to oust Russia from Azerbaijan; at the least, it could be the means to resurrect Persia's buffer status, so preserving independence.

As early as October 1914 the German chargé d'affaires in Teheran (the ambassador was on leave) began to argue for the resuscitation of Moltke's proposed alliance. He was persuaded that so positive were feelings in Persia towards Germany that only money and munitions were required to trigger a rising. Zimmermann promised 50,000 marks to fund the rebellion and an exiled Persian prince, Salar ad-Daula, to lead it. In Constantinople Wangenheim and the Turks knew Salar ad-Daula for what he was, an opportunist who had forfeited all credibility in his homeland. On 1 November the Shah responded to Turkey's entry to the war by declaring Persia neutral. Perversely, the enthusiasm of the German embassy in Teheran for rebellion now waned and its hopes of persuading the Shah to reconsider increased. More logically, the Turks turned away from the Shah and became keener on an uprising. But they nonetheless interned Salar ad-Daula when he arrived in Constantinople.

---

[158] Charles Issawi, 'European economic penetration 1872–1921', in Avery *et al.* (eds.), *Cambridge History of Iran*, vii. 606–7; Olson, *Anglo-Iranian relations*, 6–22.

Germany's precipitateness had weakened its credibility not only in Persia but also in the Ottoman empire.[159]

Technically, Persia's neutrality was a status which remained unchanged over the next four years. In reality, the statement was meaningless before it was issued. The Shah lacked an army able to ensure his country's integrity. Belligerent forces were already deployed inside his frontiers. Russia refused to withdraw from Azerbaijan. Britain, for all its attempts to get its ally to comply with Persian requests, was guilty of a double standard. It had undertaken punitive action against the Gulf tribes in 1909, 1911, and 1913, and had stationed small bodies of Indian troops at Bushire and Bandar Abbas. Their presence became justified by the Turkish thrusts across the Mesopotamian frontier against the Karun pipeline.

However, it was Azerbaijan's geographical position and cosmopolitan status which marked most clearly the impossibility of Persia's remaining untouched by war. Between 1906 and 1909 Tabriz became the home not only of Persian liberals but also of exiled Russian revolutionaries. Persian workers found seasonal employment in Baku and Elizavetpol. Furthermore, of the 2 million Turks reckoned to live in Persia (out of a total population of 9 million), the greatest concentration was in Azerbaijan. From this mixture emerged a pan-Azerbaijani sentiment, which looked to link Persian and Russian Azerbaijan, and which found echoes across the frontier in Baku with the formation of Musavat. Azerbaijani aspirations were nourished in Constantinople. Divisions between Sunni and Shi'ite were minimized, links with Turkism maximized.[160]

The campaign in the Caucasus gave these trends a pressing relevance. On 6 November Sazonov justified Russia's refusal to withdraw from Persia by arguing that the most accessible Turkish route into Transcaucasia lay though Azerbaijan rather than across the Caucasus mountains. The Turks, naturally enough, responded by pointing out that the Russians in Tabriz constituted a threat to their flank. Even before hostilities were formally announced, both sides began fomenting discord between the Armenians and the Kurds around lakes Urmia and Van.

On 23 November the Russians appointed the former governor of Tabriz, Shuja ud-Daula, exiled as a result of his corrupt administration and disregard for the Shah's government, governor-general of Azerbaijan. His task was to form a force under Russian auspices. The Shah's protests at Russia's high-handedness were interpreted by Sazonov as evidence of Persia's pro-Turkish inclinations. Therefore the Persian government, in a bid to regain control of the situation, declared that the task of Shuja's troops was to defend Persian neutrality. In late December Shuja was defeated south of Lake Urmia by the

---

[159] Olson, *Anglo-Iranian relations*, 21–2, 65–7; Gehrke, *Persien*, 38–41.
[160] Swietochowski, *Russian Azerbaijan*, 64–77.

Kurds, who then advanced on Tabriz and entered it on 8 January 1915. Enver saw the opportunity to offset the defeat of his pan-Turanian offensive at Sarikamish. He followed up the Kurds' success with the Turkish divisions, commanded by his uncle, Halil, which had arrived from Mesopotamia too late to take part in the battle in the Caucasus. He also, in his customary grandiose fashion, named Omar Nadji, a hero of the revolution of 1906, inspector-general of Azerbaijan and the eastern Caucasus, thereby implying that the area was one and so capitalizing on pan-Azerbaijani sentiment. The Armenians fled north to Tiflis. Enver imagined that a popular rising was imminent and that it would sweep Turkish forces into Baku.

In reality, the Turkish victory was more apparent than actual. On 30 December 1914, faced with the prospect of defeat at Sarikamish, Vorontsov-Dashkov had ordered the evacuation of all northern Persia, presenting the move as a concession to Persia's protests. The Turks and Kurds had driven against an open door. Furthermore, when the situation in the Caucasus was restored the Russians had regular battalions available and intact with which to crush Halil's weak and disorganized forces. Tabriz was retaken on 31 January, and the Turks driven back across the frontier.[161]

The British ambassador in Teheran, Sir Walter Townley, was infuriated by Russia's forward policy. Britain's high moral stance, that it had entered the war to defend the neutrality of small states, was being undermined by the behaviour of its ally. Even more importantly, by encouraging Armenians to set on Kurds, Russia was stoking hatreds between Christians and Muslims. Britain, as a ruler of both (as, for that matter, was Russia), was determined to deny, not to affirm, that the war was a holy war. The effect of Russian policy might be to drive Persia into the hands of the Central Powers, and so help construct an Islamic bloc from Constantinople to Kabul. Such an alliance would increase the pressure on India's Muslims to challenge British rule. Certainly the Persian democrats, encouraged by the German chargé d'affaires, attributed to Entente intervention the problems of Persia and began in January 1915 to use their majority in the *Majlis* to topple the cabinet. Finally, Townley saw in Russia's behaviour a direct bid to extend Russian control into southern Persia.

In London Grey, with his determination that diplomacy should now serve the needs of the war, was able to take a somewhat broader view. The survival of the Entente was not to be prejudiced by the particularisms of Persia. In April Townley was replaced by Charles Marling. Simultaneously, Sazonov relieved Russia's minister in Teheran. The personal animosity between the two allied representatives was thus quashed. At the same time the Persian policy of the two powers was put on a new footing. In March 1915 Britain and France agreed that Russia should have control of Constantinople and the straits after the war.

---

[161] Ibid. 78–9; Allen and Muratoff, *Caucasian battlefields*, 288–9, 295–6; Gehrke, *Persien*, 44–51.

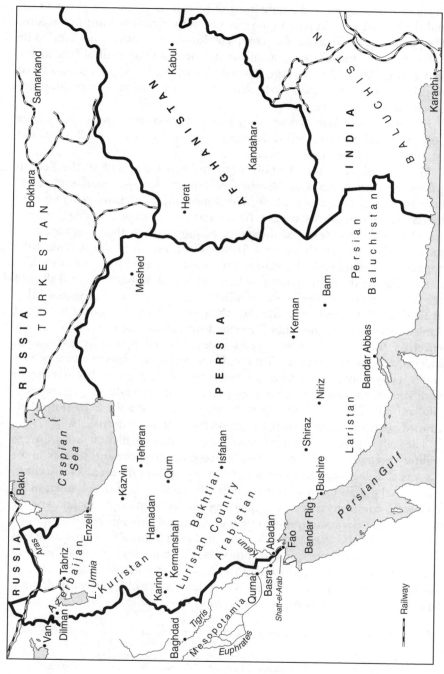

MAP 30. PERSIA AND AFGHANISTAN

In exchange, Grey secured a tightening of British control in the Persian Gulf and the Middle East, hoping in the short term to minimize Muslim tensions. The partition of Persia was thus complete: Russia was given a free hand in its northern zone, but all the rest, including the erstwhile neutral belt in the centre, was allocated to Britain. It would be wrong to say that Russian and British policy in Persia then proceeded in tandem, but direct competition and covert hostility were ended.[162]

However, Azerbaijan had not only revealed tensions between the Entente powers, it had also exposed differences between Germany and Turkey. The latter were to prove more intractable.

The Caliph's summons to holy war, although welcomed by the Persian colony in Constantinople and by the Kurds on the Turko-Persian border, had little impact in Persia as a whole. The Sunni–Shi'ite division remained too fundamental to be glossed over by Turkey's pan-Islamic appeals. The Committee of Union and Progress, therefore, employed the other weapon in its propaganda armoury, that of pan-Turanianism. But in so doing it shed the appeal of religious brotherhood in pursuit of a more naked annexationism. The nationalists, as the opponents of Britain and Russia, were the natural allies of the Central Powers in Persia. But Halil's thrust into Azerbaijan suggested that Turkey's aims were no more altruistic than Russia's. Furthermore, the rout at Sarikamish hardly argued that Enver and his colleagues would be militarily effective. In looking to Germany as a disinterested party, the nationalists therefore specifically rejected Turkey. Thus, by January 1915 the two powers were on divergent courses. Germany was increasingly prepared to curry favour with Persian nationalism, but only in pursuit of its more distant objectives in Afghanistan. Turkey, on the other hand, was bent on the extension of its immediate frontiers and was therefore no friend to the nationalists.[163]

The split in policy was not immediately evident at the highest levels. Enver's military pretensions in Central Asia had received an enormous setback in the Caucasus; Falkenhayn had no resources to pump into the area. As elsewhere, each could pursue his own strategy under the pretence that in conjunction the two were complementary. At a meeting in Constantinople in January the Austrian and German representatives en route for Teheran hammered out a proposal with the Persian ambassador in Constantinople to activate Persia with propaganda, money, and weapons: 'Persia for the Persians' was the cry. At the same time Enver proposed Turkish invasions across Persia's western frontier in the north and south, and Falkenhayn agreed.[164] The contradictions in all this manifested themselves at the local level.

[162] Olson, *Anglo-Iranian relations*, 35–53, 61–71; C. J. Smith, *American Historical Review*, LXX (1965), 1015–34; id., *Russian struggle for power*, 83–8, 216–30; Neilson, *Britain and the last Tsar*, 362.
[163] Gehrke, *Persien*, 32–3, 114–15; Vogel, *Persien- und Afghanistanexpedition*, 191–2.
[164] Pomiankowski, *Zusammenbruch*, 150; Mühlmann, *Waffenbündnis*, 69; Gehrke, *Persien*, 67, 84–5.

Enver's proposal in February was to renew the attack in Azerbaijan first. Colmar von der Goltz, who had just arrived in Constantinople, supported him: Azerbaijan was the key to Persia and commanded the route to Teheran. Halil's force of 12,000 men concentrated on Bitlis, south of Lake Van, in April, and took Dilman, at the northern end of Lake Urmia, on the 29th. But a rising of Armenians at Van to their rear, and the overawing of the Kurds by the Russians to their front, compelled the Turks to fall back.[165] Subsequent activity in the region in 1915 was sustained not by Turkish force of arms but by Omar Nadji and his contacts with Emir Aslan Khan Choiski. However, Aslan's concerns were with the eastern Caucasus and a raid on Baku; the direction of these negotiations was therefore to the north, into Russia, not to the south-west, into Persia.[166]

Setback in the north meant that the weight of Turkish efforts for 1915 lay less in Azerbaijan and more in Luristan and Arabistan. In Baghdad, however, the 6th army was facing in two directions at once. The British force that had been landed in Mesopotamia on the war's outbreak occupied Basra and Qurna by the year's end. The primary threat was therefore to the south. But the principal opportunities lay to the east. In January 1915 two groups of Germans reached Baghdad. The first was Niedermayer's, compelled by Russian presence to take a route through central or southern Persia to Afghanistan. The second was under the command of Fritz Klein, a former military attaché in Teheran, who had been given the task of seizing the oil refinery at Abadan and of rousing the Shi'ite tribes to holy war.

This German activity in what they saw to be their theatre of operations unnerved the Turks. They imputed to Niedermayer and Klein those same imperialist ambitions which they nurtured themselves. Enver saw Klein's plan, which would allow the Central Powers to operate the oilwells for their own needs, as evidence not of wartime priorities but of a long-term German ambition to replace Britain and Russia as the arbiter of the Middle East. The fact that the Germans opposed his idea of destroying the pipeline and using a block-ship to close the Shatt-el-Arab confirmed his suspicions. He therefore worked to have both Klein's and Niedermayer's expeditions subordinated to Turkish command, justifying the arrangement by allocating a division to their support.[167]

Defeat in the Caucasus deprived Niedermayer and Klein of their division. Thus, the Turks once again confronted the possibility that the Germans alone would carry the cause of the Central Powers into Persia and Afghanistan. When Suleyman Askeri Bey, commanding the 6th army, announced that he needed the services of the Germans in his preparations for an offensive against

---

[165] Allen and Muratoff, *Caucasian battlefields*, 298–301.
[166] Bihl, *Kaukasus-politik*, 65–6, 71, 240–1.   [167] Weber, *Eagles on the crescent*, 170–1.

the British in Mesopotamia, Niedermayer was irate. The Turkish abandonment of the Afghanistan expedition despite the slender resources it required;
orders that his personnel should be redistributed among the Turkish supply
services and that they should help with training; the fact that in January he and
his colleagues were effectively confined to Baghdad—these led him to suspect
that not military necessity but competition for political primacy in Persia was
the issue. His views were confirmed when it transpired that Hassan Rauf Bey,
the Turk originally named to command the joint undertaking to Afghanistan,
was secretly pressing ahead with independent Turkish operations into Persia.
Rauf believed that the appeal of pan-Islam would draw in the border tribes of
Luristan and open the way to Kermanshah.[168]

Wangenheim told the Germans in Baghdad to co-operate with the Turks,
and Klein was disposed to comply. But Niedermayer's inclination to press on
regardless of Turkish obstructionism was confirmed from two directions.
Reconnaissances into Persian territory showed that the Turks were not trusted,
but that the Germans would be welcomed. From Berlin came word that
Nadolny was increasingly supportive of a line independent both of Turkey
and of the German foreign ministry. Nadolny used his position in the political
section of the general staff to bypass the ambassadors in Constantinople and
Teheran, and to communicate directly with the military attachés in both
places. By the end of March he hoped 'to light a torch from the Caucasus to
Calcutta'.[169]

These arguments were not in themselves responsible for Klein's failure to
secure the Abadan oilfields before the British did. But the fact that the latter
had accomplished that objective by early November meant that Klein's task
became one of destruction and demolition. On 5 February 1915 his group,
operating in conjunction with two Turkish regiments, succeeding in damaging
the Karun pipeline. On 22 March and several times in April Hans Lühr blew up
the pipeline, claiming that 290,000 tonnes of oil had been destroyed. The effect
of these attacks was to justify the British in more direct efforts to protect their
interests in south Persia. In 1912 the daily output from Persia's oilfields was
1,600 barrels; by 1918 it would be 18,000 barrels.[170] Klein astutely accepted his
subordination to Turkey's military command in Iraq, and joined with the
Turks in agitating for holy war in Arabistan. Simultaneously, Wassmuss,
profiting from the temporary break-up of the Afghanistan expedition, and
glad to escape its bickering, set off on an independent mission as German
consul in Shiraz. Finally, Niedermayer, breaking his command into separate
components to escape Turkish attention, sent advance parties forward to
secure his communications through Kermanshah and Hamadan to Isfahan.

---

[168] Vogel, *Persien- und Afghanistanexpedition*, 55–9; Gehrke, *Persien*, 54–6, 68–72.
[169] Gehrke, *Persien*, 84–7, 99–100; Moberly, *Operations in Persia*, 74–84.
[170] Kröger, 'Revolution als Programm', in Michalka (ed.), *Der Erste Weltkrieg*, 379–80.

Further delay, he was convinced, would only allow Russia and Britain to tighten their hold on Persia.

At the beginning of 1915, therefore, Germany's desire to reach Afghanistan, and Turkish obstacles to that aim, forced the Germans to develop their own policies for Persia rather than simply follow those of Constantinople. But in the process they had engendered not one design, but several.

Niedermayer's plan was to create a line of communications across central Persia to Afghanistan, so exploiting the corridor between the Russian and British zones. On 13 April he entered Kermanshah; on 6 May Seiler arrived in Isfahan; Erich Zugmayer (a professor of natural history) and Walter Griesinger left Isfahan in June and reached Kerman on 4 July. To the south Wassmuss, who nurtured hopes of eventually reaching India, suffered an initial setback. Wrongly told that the British would respect Persian neutrality, he and his caravan were ambushed by Indian troops and local tribesmen at Bandar Rig on 7 March. Wassmuss lost his maps and codebooks; the British gained valuable intelligence on the composition of Niedermayer's group and its intentions. But Wassmuss himself escaped. The result was to reorientate and harden his resolve. By May he had rallied the Tangistani tribe, establishing a dominance in the interior of southern Persia which boxed the British in at Bushire. Germany's consuls in the towns of central and southern Persia cast off their diplomatic credentials and openly agitated on behalf of the Central Powers. A wireless station, able to communicate with Nauen, was erected at Isfahan. Only in east Persia, in Baluchistan close to the Indian border, did the Germans encounter difficulties. The British consuls were driven out of Kermanshah, Shiraz, and Isfahan in August and September, and from Kerman in December.[171]

The German consuls' military clout rested on two bodies of support. First, von Kardoff, the German chargé d'affaires in Teheran, had won over the gendarmerie. The thirty-four Swedish officers both admired the Prussian army and believed that Sweden would side with Germany; the 120 Persian officers belonged to the educated and liberal classes predisposed to nationalism; nobody had been paid since the summer. In December Sweden recalled its regular officers from Persia, but the result was to leave the command in the hands of an actively pro-German reserve major. In February 1915 a scheme was devised to enable twenty Swedish reserve officers secretly to join the German army; their tasks were to increase the size of the gendarmerie from 6,000 men to 12,000, and to win over and lead the Persian tribes whose independence they had so recently been endeavouring to curb.[172]

The tribes were, therefore, the second and potentially more numerous component of Germany's secret army. But their local effectiveness as guerrillas

---

[171] Vogel, *Persien- und Afghanistanexpedition*, 63–5, 102–7; Gehrke, *Persien*, 77–82, 124–31, 149–64, 193–4.   [172] Gehrke, *Persien*, 57–60.

could be deceptive. In defence of their own grazing areas, commanded by a leader such as Wassmuss whose personal influence could be felt in small bodies of men, their contribution was vital to the German consuls of the central and southern towns. But they demanded money for their services. One cynic reckoned it cost 10 gold marks a day to keep a tribesman in the field, despite the fact that he was totally untrained for modern war; Germany disbursed about 50 million marks in Persia and Afghanistan.[173] The tribesmen were not nationalists, and they had little enthusiasm or capacity for operations outside their own territory. Nonetheless, Graf Kanitz, who arrived as military attaché in Teheran in February, argued that cash would unlock weapons already to be found in Persia, and that the revolutionary eddies would be felt as far north as the trans-Siberian railway. He believed that with £ Turkish 100,000 and 1,000 kilos of explosives he could raise 50,000 tribesmen, drive the Russians out of Azerbaijan, and then turn on India and Afghanistan. The foreign office disliked the scheme; after all, the route through the Balkans to Constantinople was still closed, and Germany could not get arms to Turkey, let alone Persia. But Falkenhayn nonetheless endorsed it on 25 July. And Nadolny undermined foreign office opposition by going direct to Austria-Hungary for its approval and half the costs.[174]

All that Niedermayer, Nadolny, and Kanitz proposed rested on bluff, and therefore speed. The Russians and the British were both potentially stronger in the region than Germany could ever be, and yet in the first half of 1915 there seemed to be an opportunity to make something out of nothing and pass the point where the Entente powers could recall the situation. The need to act quickly was also generated by the fear that hostility towards the Turks in west Persia could undermine the German advantage almost as fast as it was built up. Wangenheim put pressure on Enver to stop Rauf. He failed. In the summer of 1915 Rauf's advance into western Persia triggered Shi'ite risings; forced to retreat, and no doubt ill-supplied, the Turks resorted to plunder, looting, and devastation. Rauf's men even ruptured German communications by destroying the Teheran–Baghdad telegraph line at Karind.[175]

Niedermayer's and Nadolny's strategy was also revolutionary. In subverting the gendarmerie and in fomenting the tribes, it struck at the roots of the Shah's authority. Niedermayer's concern, after all, lay not with the stability of Persia but with the security of his route to Afghanistan; Nadolny and Kanitz focused more on Persia itself, but their methods for bringing it into the war were direct, not diplomatic.

---

[173] Neulen, *Feldgrau in Jerusalem*, 205–6, 212.
[174] Gehrke, *Persien*, 137–8, 167–71; Vogel, *Persien- und Afghanistanexpedition*, 204–6.
[175] Gehrke, *Persien*, 73–5, 121–2, 135–6; Vogel, *Persien- und Afghanistanexpedition*, 61–2; Nogales, *Four years*, 226.

The army's methods were not the foreign office way. Germany's representation in Teheran from August 1914 to April 1915 was weak and inexperienced. Prince Heinrich XXXI Reuss, the ambassador, was on leave; when war broke out, so unimportant did Persia seem that he was diverted to Belgium. Kardorff, only 33 and with little experience of the region, while responding to approaches from Persian nationalists, thought also that negotiations should be continued with the Shah. He did not despair of being able to construct a nationalist, pro-German government that would then encourage the Shah to seek an alliance with Germany. Such a policy was abetted by contacts between Wangenheim and the Persian ambassador in Constantinople. When Reuss returned to Teheran in April 1915 the possibility of a Perso-German alliance received fresh impetus. But while he patiently and soberly worked to create a pro-German Persian government, Germany's consuls in the south were systematically destroying the authority of that government. The fact that the wireless station at Isfahan was in Niedermayer's territory, not his, increased Reuss's frustration. In July Niedermayer suggested that the Shah shift his capital to Isfahan. Reuss protested (rightly) that Niedermayer was becoming too involved in Persia and neglecting Afghanistan.[176]

Reuss's policy began to bear fruit in August. Germany's stunning victories against the Russian armies in Poland offset the impact of the British advance on Baghdad. In a cabinet crisis spanning all July and August, the contenders for power in Persia, although tacking between the two opposing alliances, recognized that a treaty with Germany could bolster their standing with the democrats in the *Majlis*. But in Berlin the foreign office warned that Persia, while weak and divided, would be a liability, not an asset. The continued closure of the Berlin–Constantinople railway meant that arms could not be delivered; the Germans tried to ship money through Bombay, but the negotiations and the passage were slow, and while the pay of the gendarmerie could not be guaranteed nor could its loyalty. On 18 August Mustaufi ul-Mamalik formed a government. His reliance on democrat support obliged him to ask Germany for an alliance, and specifically for a guarantee of Persia's integrity and independence, as well as for gold and munitions. Germany could not provide such a guarantee unless Persia was in a state to defend itself. And yet, as Reuss appreciated, if Germany rebuffed the Persian approach the chances of an alliance would be gone for ever. Jagow therefore reversed the Persians' priorities. Germany promised the money and the weapons as soon as the route through Turkey could be opened. If Germany won the war, it would guarantee Persian sovereignty.[177]

[176] Gehrke, *Persien*, 40–3, 62–3, 102–3, 108–9, 142–6, 153–4; Vogel, *Persien- und Afghanistanexpedition*, 68–70, 161–2.
[177] Gehrke, *Persien*, 165–81.

Germany's negotiations with Teheran were unilateral. But Berlin could not give effect to any alliance without the co-operation of Turkey. By October 1915 the rivalry between the two powers seemed to make that impossible. The Persians did not trust the Turks, the Turks did not trust the Germans. The Persians wanted a senior German officer appointed to Persia, the Turks insisted on retaining the primary role in the Islamic world. Enver cut through the impasse. He proposed that Colmar von der Goltz be sent to Persia. On 5 October Falkenhayn agreed, and added the suggestion that von der Goltz also take over the Mesopotamian command so that Iraq and Persia could be treated as one theatre.

It was an inspired move. Von der Goltz, now aged 72, enjoyed a respect in the Ottoman army accorded to no other German officer. He had been summoned to Constantinople in December 1914, in a bid by Wangenheim to oust Liman von Sanders and to heal the divisions generated by the latter's egotistical behaviour. But Wangenheim had failed; his hopes had rested on Liman accepting the command of the 3rd army in the Caucasus, thus leaving a vacancy as head of the German military mission in Constantinople. Although Enver, on his return from the Caucasus in February 1915, had employed von der Goltz as an adviser at his headquarters, and had later given him the command of the 1st army, the latter was frustrated to find himself 'the fifth wheel to the coach'.[178]

Von der Goltz was to secure fame, and death, as commander of the 6th army in Mesopotamia. But the origins of his appointment, and its rationale, lay in Persia, not Iraq. His status was being used to woo the Persians, to soothe Turkish sensibilities, and to fuse the divergent policies of the German army and foreign office. It was from the latter that he encountered most resistance: Enver's original brief, giving him supreme powers from Lake Van to the Persian Gulf, was moderated by his subordination to Germany's conventional diplomatic service (although he remained in charge of the military attachés and the consuls in southern Persia). His task, Enver instructed him, was 'to prepare an independent war against India'.[179] To this end he was to win Persia to the Central Powers, to drive out Britain and Russia in the process, to secure Persia's freedom and independence, and to establish the foundations of a Persian army.

For von der Goltz, such a mission was a fulfilment of his life's work. He did not underestimate the hazards, the supply and equipment problems, the difficulties of terrain and communications; and if he had been minded to forget, a morose letter from Moltke urging him not to sacrifice himself in Mesopotamia made him appreciate that failure was more probable than

[178] Wallach, *Anatomie*, 183; see also 170–4, 182–4; Trumpener, *Germany and the Ottoman empire*, 72–9.
[179] Mühlmann, *Waffenbündnis*, 71–4; see also Gehrke, *Persien*, 185–91; von der Goltz, *Denkwürdigkeiten*, 419.

success. But he was convinced that Britain could be brought down only by a direct threat either to its own shores or to India. Since German naval inferiority ruled out the former, the latter alone could be decisive.[180]

Von der Goltz appreciated that his first task would be to secure Turkey's position in Baghdad from the British advance up the Tigris. Although operations in Persia would therefore be delayed, he was convinced by talks in Constantinople with the Persian ambassador and with a Swedish gendarmerie officer that conditions there were very favourable. As he boarded the train on 15 November he was confident that the gendarmerie was efficient, the *Majlis* would be welcoming, and that all southern Persia could be won with relative ease.[181] When he arrived in Baghdad on 6 December the Turko-German position in Persia had almost entirely collapsed.

British policy in Persia, after settling its differences with Russia in March, fell prey to its own internal divisions. The plan initiated by Mushir ud-Daula's cabinet in April 1915, and eventually endorsed by the Foreign Office in London, was for Britain to provide a loan so as to prop up the government and thus enable it to sustain its neutrality. The loss of customs revenue through the collapse of the Gulf trade on the outbreak of war had deprived the Shah of much of his income—hence the problems in paying the gendarmerie. Moreover, Persia's existing debts were secured on the same customs receipts. A direct loan from the Entente powers would have provoked the ire of the nationalists, and have therefore failed to achieve its objectives. What was proposed instead was a moratorium on Persia's existing debts. The allies would suspend interest on current loans and would give the government a monthly subsidy equivalent to the lost customs duties.

But governmental instability made the negotiations protracted. A run on the silver reserves of the Imperial Bank of Persia, initiated by the German agents in April, confirmed the interaction of financial chaos and cabinet weakness. Marling in Teheran, therefore, wavered. He oscillated towards bringing Russian troops into Teheran. London, still clinging to the figment of Persia's neutrality, disliked the idea.[182]

Moreover, British foreign policy in Persia was not the exclusive domain of the Foreign Office. The consuls of southern Persia wore two hats: they were responsible to the Foreign Office, but they were also political agents of the Government of India.[183] German penetration in 1915 generated increasing concern for India's security. On 2 July the viceroy told the consuls to meet fire with fire, and to raise their own local forces to stop the Germans reaching

---

[180] von der Goltz, *Denkwürdigkeiten*, 413, 421, 426.
[181] Ibid. 423–4.
[182] Olson, *Anglo-Iranian relations*, 57–9, 73–92.
[183] John S. Galbraith and Robert A. Huttenback, 'Bureaucracies at war: the British in the Middle East in the First World War', in Ingram (ed.), *National and international politics*, 105–6, 114–16.

Kabul. An eastern cordon, formed of British troops in the south and Russian in the north, was created as a barrier between Persia and Afghanistan.

On 12 July Wassmuss and 300 to 400 tribesmen assembled outside Bushire. The British advanced to reconnoitre, and in the subsequent engagement two officers were killed. Marling now felt that Russian military intervention was fully justified. But India suddenly became cautious. A forward policy could drive Persia into the arms of the Central Powers and take Afghanistan with it. The viceroy preferred a more limited approach, including the payment of compensation for the British casualties. Thus, rather than give the Persians money, the Foreign Office was being urged to take it from them. Finally, in September, it was agreed to ask Persia to provide guarantees against further incidents in the south, and to offer in return a moratorium and subsidy. In October the first instalment of the subsidy, set at 200,000 tumans per month, was paid. But by now this was no more than a holding operation. On 21 October the India Office authorized an advance on Baghdad. Military action in Mesopotamia might resolve, at least in part, Britain's predicament in Persia.[184]

To those bewitched by maps rather than by the realities of movement in an impoverished and increasingly lawless land, the British march up the Tigris was part of a massive converging operation. Ultimately it would link with the fronts in the Caucasus and Azerbaijan, outflanking the Turkish armies to the north of the Taurus Mountains and threatening to isolate those in Kurdistan and Iraq. There is no evidence that General Sir J. E. Nixon, for all the over-extension of his forces now put in train, thought in these terms; there is some that the Russians did.[185]

In March the Russians landed a detachment at Enzeli, on the Caspian Sea, and then pushed it forward to Kazvin. The Russians said they were relieving the troops already at Kazvin; the Persians detected a threat to Teheran. On 18 May the manager of a Russian bank was murdered in Isfahan. Two days later more Russian troops arrived at Enzeli. Throughout the summer the Russian and British ministries advocated further Russian intervention; by September both deprecated the policy of drift favoured in London and Delhi, arguing that only an ultimatum to Persia could check the increase in German influence. Sazonov supported this line; neither Yanushkevitch at Stavka nor Yudenich at headquarters in Tiflis felt able to do so. For them, Persia was no more than a continuation of the Caucasian front; at the beginning of September Yudenich released only 1,200 more troops. Then, on 24 September, Vorontsov-Dashkov was replaced as governor-general of the Caucasus by Grand Duke Nicholas. Nicholas overruled Yudenich and approved a Russian expeditionary force of

[184] Olson, Anglo-Iranian relations, 57–9, 93–113.
[185] Allen and Muratoff, Caucasian battlefields, 257–8.

8,000 cavalry and 6,000 infantry, under the command of Baratov. It landed at Enzeli on 12 November, and occupied Kazvin on 1 December. Its instructions were to isolate Teheran, but not occupy it. On 7 November the Russians already at Kazvin demonstrated in the direction of the capital.[186]

The Russian military build-up, therefore, constituted a gradual and sustained threat rather than a sudden and decisive attack. Its effect on the Perso-German exchanges was to increase the German sense of urgency while strengthening the Persian ability to negotiate. On 28 October Mustaufi ul-Mamalik pointed out to the Germans that if Persia declared war, its richest provinces were those that could be most quickly seized by the Entente powers. Teheran would therefore need a monthly subsidy of at least 2 million marks, and after the war it would require a loan of 100 million marks as well as the repayment of its war costs. Reuss, breathing the frenzied atmosphere in Teheran, felt that Germany had no choice but comply. Jagow in Berlin preferred to leave matters to military solutions and von der Goltz.

Recognizing that the Russians could get to Teheran before von der Goltz could even reach Baghdad, Reuss decided that the Persian government should be persuaded to move to Isfahan. On 10 November he took it upon himself to agree a twenty-year defensive treaty with Persia without reference to Berlin. But on the 12th the Shah insisted that Berlin should be asked for its approval and so postponed its ratification for a fortnight. By now the Russians were encamped four hours' march from Teheran. *Muharram*, the month of mourning for the Shi'ite holy men massacred by the Umayyad Caliphs at Kerbela, added to the tension in the city. Kanitz decided that military action should replace negotiation, and urged the Persian Cossack brigade to turn against its Russian officers and escort the Shah and his government from the capital. The Russians got wind of the plan. The brigade was paraded, declared its loyalty to the Tsar (not the Shah), and the Russians threatened to restore Muhammed Ali, Ahmad's deposed father.

The German mission, its supporters, and most of the democrats had already fled to the holy city of Qum. The Shah was due to follow on the morning of 15 November. But without the pressure of Reuss or the nationalists, his resolve weakened. At 9 a.m. he decided to stay. The German attempt to seize control of the Persian government had failed. Its major ally, the nationalist lobby of the *Majlis*, had dissipated, and the *Majlis* itself did not reconvene until after the war. The nationalists established a rump parliament, the committee of national defence, in Qum. Reuss first stayed at Qum, then returned to Teheran, and finally concluded that he had failed and retired to Berlin. Kanitz still pressed for military action. But without arms the Persians could not and

---

[186] Ibid. 322–4; see also Moberly, *Operations in Persia*, 87–9, 102–8, 117–19; Gehrke, *Persien*, 105–7, 140–1, 175.

would not turn against the Russians. The gendarmerie in Teheran, uncertain whether its loyalty lay with the Shah or with the Germans and the nationalists, opted for neutrality.[187]

Thus, the effect of the attempted coup was to leave the capital clear for the Entente powers. The Persians agreed to a policy of benevolent neutrality on condition that the Russians halted 32 kilometres from Teheran. Farman Farma, an Anglophile, came in as minister of the interior, and on 24 December he formed his own cabinet. His policy was to seek an alliance with Britain and Russia. The Shah was anxious to make amends, even suggesting his own abdication but accepting instead an allowance as an indication of his dependence. The Cossack brigade was increased to 10,000 men under Russian officers. Teheran remained an Entente enclave for the rest of the war.[188]

Kanitz's hopes of forming a front on Qum proved short lived. Within the city the nationalists and the clericalists fell out. Outside, Nizam as-Saltana, the governor of Burujird, accepted a subsidy in exchange for 4,000 armed men. But his troops proved of little military worth. Baratov occupied Hamadan on 14 December, and on the 20th entered Qum. Kanitz and his tribesmen fell back to Kermanshah, which had been secured by Klein's group in September. Here they linked up with the German military mission sent by von der Goltz to form the Persian army. Commanded by Colonel Bopp, and bearing six machineguns and 20,000 rifles, it was also accompanied by three Turkish battalions, a mountain battery, and a machine-gun company. The Kurds in the surrounding area, rallied by a German agent, helped provide a block to direct Anglo-Russian collaboration.[189]

The retreat of Kanitz, and of as-Saltana and the nationalists, to the fringes of western Persia initiated the collapse also of much of the German strength in central and eastern Persia. In November the Germans staged a coup in Shiraz, only to lose control again in December. Seiler advanced from Isfahan to Kerman in November, but found his line of retreat exposed. Zugmayer, who was even further to the east at Bam, and aiming for Baluchistan, fell back on Kerman in March 1916. The two then returned westwards, but Seiler was captured in Shiraz and Zugmayer in Niriz. The British occupied Bandar Abbas on 16 March 1916, and the Russians entered Isfahan three days later. Only Wassmuss with the Tangistani and Kardorff with the Bakhtiari remained at large. Therefore, while Niedermayer and Hentig negotiated in Kabul, their lines of communications across Persia collapsed behind them.

The German expedition to Afghanistan successfully evaded the Russians of the eastern cordon and crossed the frontier on 19/20 August 1915. Hentig wore a cuirassier's white tunic and helmet to enter Herat;[190] the governor of the town

---

[187] Gehrke, *Persien*, 192–215; Moberley, *Operations in Persia*, 119–28.
[188] Olson, *Anglo-Iranian relations*, 118–33.
[189] Ahmad, *Kurdistan*, 98.   [190] Sykes, *Wassmuss*, 155.

was polite but unenthusiastic. He had received the Caliph's summons to holy war some time previously but had elected not to forward it to Kabul. Now the Germans found themselves virtual prisoners while the governor awaited instructions as to whether they could proceed. On 1 October the expedition reached the Afghan capital—their journey had taken a year. But here too their status was that of captive guests; they were not allowed into the city and their activities were circumscribed. Furthermore, the Emir was away at Paghman, his summer residence.

Habibullah was astute, realistic, and hard-headed. He was guided by practical politics and not by religious fervour. His aim was to use the German mission to regain Afghan sovereignty. In 1880, after the Second Afghan War, Britain had taken control of Afghanistan's foreign policy. This treaty had been renewed in 1905, and in 1907 Russia had accepted that Afghanistan was outside its sphere of interest. The advent of Germany enabled Afghanistan, like Persia, to exploit its position as a buffer state in pursuit of its own independence. Habibullah wanted weapons, money, and a seat at the peace conference. The German expedition became a pawn in his efforts to exact these concessions from Britain.[191]

Under the terms of the treaty Britain had no direct representation at Kabul; its diplomacy on the empire's most volatile frontier was likened by one observer to 'navigating a ship in a fog'.[192] Hardinge, as viceroy of India, was not unduly worried. The Afghans were frightened that the Russians would use the war as an excuse to invade; the British could argue that their alliance represented security against that. German intentions were known in Delhi by December 1914. Thereafter intelligence on Niedermayer's progress was full and reasonably up-to-date. British intercepts, particularly after the windfall of Wassmuss's papers in April 1915, enabled Britain's policy in Kabul to anticipate that of Germany. In July Hardinge forewarned the Emir of the German arrival, and emphasized British friendship for and protection of Islam. On 29 October Britain increased its subsidy to Afghanistan to 2 lakhs of rupees.

Nonetheless, Habibullah could not appear too openly to favour the British. The British received no acknowledgement of the increased subsidy until December, and the Emir then complained that it was too small. His aim was not simply to extract further concessions from Delhi. He had also to counter a pro-German lobby within his own court, headed by his brother Nasrullah and supported by the Young Afghans, a small nationalist and constitutionalist movement founded in 1908 in emulation of the Persians. In itself this radical fringe was weak, but it had the potential to rally the more traditional sectors of society, the religious establishment and the frontier tribes. The one Afghan

[191] In addition to Vogel, *Persien- und Afghanistanexpedition*, esp. 45–6, 72–101, 217–30, 254–71, 277–8, see also Adamec, *Afghanistan*, 86–107.
[192] Rumbold, *Watershed in India*, 23.

newspaper, *Siraj al-Akhbar,* embodied this fusion, appealing to pan-Islam, pro-Ottomanism, and Afghan nationalism. Some Afghans had joined the Mohmands in fighting on the frontier in 1915.[193] Habibullah's neutrality was therefore double-sided—outwardly between the Entente and Central Powers, inwardly between the competing camps in Kabul.

On 26 October the Germans were granted their first audience with Habibullah. The Emir stalled. As the Germans waited for the next summons the friction within the party, particularly between Hentig and Pratap, flared. By mid-December both Hentig and Niedermayer had concluded that their mission had failed and that they should return home.

The danger of losing his lever on Britain prompted Habibullah to summon the Germans once again. He told them on 23 December that Afghanistan had decided to seek a treaty with Germany before it declared war; the terms of the treaty were to include a guarantee of territorial integrity, a seat at the peace conference, £10 million, 100,000 rifles, and 300 guns. Nasrullah encouraged Niedermayer to think that if Germany would give sufficient aid to Afghanistan, rather than just expect Afghanistan to sacrifice itself for Germany, the chances of an agreement were good.

Niedermayer now felt justified in exercising his military skills. He asked Germany to send immediately £1 million and large quantities of arms. He drew up plans for an Afghan army 70,000 strong, with officer schools and a demonstration company; he initiated training in musketry and tactics. But as January gave way to February and then March, his pessimism returned. At a durbar on 23 January Habibullah announced Afghanistan's neutrality. The Germans thought this might be another tactical ploy, but the Afghans knew of the collapse of Germany in Persia. Niedermayer's frustration led him in directions that show he had lost contact with the broad thrust of the war. He developed a plan for contacting the Russians in Meshed in order to propose a joint German-Russian advance on India; his respect for the status of Afghanistan had become secondary to the local balance of power. He also spoke of organizing a coup in Kabul. The British intercepted Niedermayer's communications and informed Habibullah. On 12 March Habibullah said Afghanistan would not enter the war unless two prior conditions were met—that there should be revolution in India, and that at least 20,000 German or Turkish troops should attack Baluchistan. Both sides knew that both conditions were impossible of fulfilment. The negotiations were at an end.

Hentig argued that, as he had been offered terms by Kabul his diplomatic mission was fulfilled. Niedermayer wanted to stay in order to foment action in India. The Emir would have no truck with this. A weakened German mission would incur danger without diplomatic advantage. Both made their own way

---

[193] Rumbold, *Watershed in India,* 23.

home. Hentig travelled north through China, and reached Berlin on 9 June 1917 via the United States, Halifax, and Bergen. Niedermayer slipped the Entente patrols by passing through Russian Turkestan, where he was robbed and left for dead. He eventually arrived back in Teheran on 20 July 1916. In September he rejoined the Turko-German forces at Kermanshah. Nadolny tried to prevail upon him to lead a second expedition, but Niedermayer refused. He reported that in theory a force of up to 300,000 men could be raised in Afghanistan, but the tribes were too divided and the frontiers too exposed for an Afghan invasion of India—even with 20,000–50,000 German troops in support—to get any further than the Indus.

Desultory communications between Kabul and Berlin were relayed through Kermanshah. An emissary from the Emir arrived in December, but with no powers to negotiate. A forward German base was maintained in Herat until October 1917, but by then its members had heard nothing from Germany for eight months and they decided to leave. The Central Powers' representation in Kabul devolved onto the Austro-Hungarian prisoners of war who had escaped Russian captivity. They had formed the potential nucleus of Niedermayer's fantasy army, but their real desire was to avoid the war and marry the local women. Their amorous inclinations posed sufficient threat to the domestic order of an Islamic society to result in their internment.

Both Pratap and Barkatullah remained in Afghanistan. Despite the impeccability of their pan-Islamic credentials, Habibullah remained the servant of *Realpolitik* and not of religious idealism. He nonetheless tolerated the declaration, on 1 December 1915, of a provisional government of India, Pratap being named as life president and Barkatullah as prime minister. The letters which Pratap bore from Bethmann Hollweg to the princes of India were entrusted to Harish Chandra. On arrival in the subcontinent Chandra promptly became a British agent, revealing much about the intentions both of German propaganda and of Indian nationalism. The provisional government claimed as adherents fifteen Muslim students who had quitted Lahore and Christian rule for Kabul and Islamic government, and half-a-dozen Afridi deserters from the Indian army. With this unpromising nucleus the provisional government hoped to exploit the frontier tribes and fuse invasion from Afghanistan with uprising in India.

INDIA

For much of the nineteenth century the economic strength of Britain's overseas position rested not on 'formal' but 'informal' empire. Its status as the world's first industrialized nation enabled its goods to penetrate world markets by virtue of their quality and uniqueness. Without effective competition, free trade constituted its own imperialism. But in the last quarter of the century the industrialization of the continental powers, and the advantages which they derived from coming later into the field, challenged the ability of British exports to dominate the world's commerce. The debate on free trade, and particularly the split over the repeal of the Corn Laws in 1846, had shaped the thought and composition of both the Liberal and Conservative parties. The political past, therefore, determined the response to economic change: protection was rejected. Instead, Britain adopted two alternative strategies. First, London became the centre of the world's banking, shipping, and insurance markets: invisible exports compensated for the relative decline in sales of manufactured goods. Secondly, formal empire supplemented informal. The colonies became significant markets for British goods, and in turn themselves became exporters of commodities and raw materials. In 1850 much of the empire was a network of ports and trading stations, giving access to a hinterland over which direct control was unnecessary. By 1900 that hinterland had itself been brought within the pale of empire. And at the heart of the formal empire was India.

In 1914 India took 16.1 per cent of all British exports. Most importantly, India bought 42 per cent of Britain's textiles at a time when cotton goods constituted a quarter of all British exports and the cotton industry employed a tenth of all workers in manufacturing. India paid for this not by its exports to Britain but by its earnings in other industrialized countries, so gaining foreign exchange for London and financing two-fifths of Britain's deficits.[194] Nor was the relationship simply economic. The fabric of imperial defence, at least in military if not naval terms, was constructed around the sub-continent. The security of the route to India had determined many of the campaigns of the late nineteenth century; the stability of South Africa, Egypt and the Sudan had all been related to the question of imperial communications.[195] Secondly, India was the principal garrison of the Empire. In 1914 76,953 British troops served in India, and the Indian army itself totalled a further 239,561 (of which 159,134 were active). The beauty of the arrangement was that the cost was borne by the taxpayers of India and not of Britain. In 1902 it was agreed that the Indian government should be responsible for financing military operations in Afghanistan, Persia, the Gulf, and as far as the Suez Canal. By 1914 the Indian army provided garrisons for Egypt, Singapore, and China.[196]

But to say that the task of the Indian army had become the mounting of imperial expeditionary forces is to exaggerate. India did provide battalions for service in China, Abyssinia, and the Sudan after 1861. It continued and

---

[194] Dignan, *Indian revolutionary problem*, 4–6, 13.
[195] R. Robinson and J. Gallagher, with A. Denny, *Africa and the Victorians*.
[196] Jeffery, *British army and crisis of empire*, 3.

confirmed the trend in 1914. Five Indian Expeditionary Forces were sent abroad, A to Europe, B and C to East Africa, D to Mesopotamia, and E to Egypt. However, none of these can be considered a contribution commensurate with the Indian army's size. The major operations from 1815—the Crimean War, the Boer War, and (in effect) the Western front in the First World War—were left to British units; most colonial wars fought beyond India's own immediate frontiers between these dates did not involve Indian troops. The primary job of Indian soldiers was the defence of India, both on its north-west frontier and, within its borders, against internal sedition. Furthermore, the dispatch of Indian Expeditionary Force A apart, its overseas operations both before and during the First World War were extensions of, rather than divergences from, this primary task. Indian troops in the Persian Gulf and even on the Suez Canal were engaged in forward defence. They took over the task of garrisoning the route to India from British units, so releasing the latter from imperial duties for continental ones.

Nonetheless, the effect of the outbreak of war was to leave India itself remarkably exposed in military terms. By late 1914 the British garrison had tumbled to 15,000 men. In March 1915 all eight regular battalions still in India were stationed on the north-west frontier. In the course of the year territorial battalions came out to replace the regulars. But the British numbers remained, in relative terms, exiguous. In June 1918 the British troops in India mustered 93,670 compared to 388,599 Indian soldiers. In 1922, when the Indian population totalled 315 million, the British official presence (troops apart) embraced 1,200 in the Indian civil service, 700 policemen, and 600 medical officers.[197] For a group for whom the memory of the mutiny of 1857 remained traumatic, the inability to balance Indian troops with British was indeed worrying. Hardinge, who remained remarkably phlegmatic throughout, still observed in August 1914: 'after all it is the Native troops that present the greatest danger so, say I, the more that go to the war the less danger there is at home.'[198]

Hardinge himself was the target of an abortive bomb attack in 1912. Terrorism flourished, particularly in Bengal. Curzon, as viceroy from 1899 to 1905, had both ridiculed and radicalized Indian nationalism. His final gesture, the partition of Bengal, had fuelled Hindu ire and had been interpreted as an effort to divide Bengali sentiment. British policing, anxious not to alienate moderate opinion, lagged behind the growth of political crime. Its efforts were concentrated in the cities, not the countryside, and its officers too often could not speak Bengali. Its opponents were organized in self-contained cells, their only obvious centre being the French enclave of Chandernagore. The reunification

---

[197] Judith M. Brown, 'War and the colonial relationship: Britain, India and the war of 1914–18', in Ellinwood and Pradhan (eds.), *India and World War I*, 24–7; War Office, *Statistics of the military effort*, 30, 777.

[198] Quotation provided by Dr G. Martin.

of Bengal in 1911 did not curb the problem. On 26 August 1914 the Bengali revolutionaries seized fifty pistols and 46,000 rounds from a Calcutta arms dealer. Thus armed, the terrorists committed twice as many atrocities in 1915 as in the previous year (thirty-six to seventeen). Perhaps because they themselves were from educated and comparatively prosperous backgrounds, they failed to raise active popular support. But witnesses were reluctant to testify against them. Twenty-five incidents in the first half of 1916 culminated in the murder of a Bengali policeman in broad daylight in a Calcutta street. Nobody would come forward to give evidence. Now at last the Government of India was prepared to use the powers accorded it by London under the Defence of India act in March 1915. The act gave the criminal intelligence department powers of surveillance. Between August 1916 and June 1917 705 people were placed under house arrest and a further ninety-nine imprisoned without trial. Furthermore, the outbreak of war brought French co-operation in Chandernagore. Only nine outrages were committed in 1917.[199]

The conspiracy to attack Hardinge had only one root in Calcutta, the department of criminal intelligence established in February 1914. Many of the major activists in the Indian revolutionary movement were no longer in India but in Europe and North America.

In 1905 Shyamaji Krishnavarma had opened a house in London which became a focus for westernized middle-class intellectuals studying in the capital. Inspired by Mazzini, and encouraged by British socialists and by Irish and Egyptian nationalists, the exiled Indians moved from boycotts and the hope of autonomy within the empire to terrorism and complete independence. In 1908 V. D. Savarkar, the author of what was seen as a subversive history of the Indian mutiny, tried to organize the collection of arms outside India and the creation of revolutionary cells within the country, and specifically the army. On 1 July 1909 the political aide-de-camp to the secretary of state for India, Sir Curzon Wyllie, was assassinated in London. Suppression both in the metropolis and in the subcontinent forced Shyamaji's group to disperse. Although the effect was to divide the movement, it also augmented the difficulties confronted by British counter-intelligence. The Indians were no longer concentrated in one place, and they ceased to be resident within British jurisdiction. Many went initially to Paris, France being seen as a natural home for advocates of liberty and nationalism. But European responses were not all that the Indians might have hoped for. The international socialists took the chicken-and-egg view that, as India possessed no indigenous socialist party, it could not be represented at their conferences. With the outbreak of war France showed itself prepared to intern Indian revolutionaries. Most

---

[199] Popplewell, 'British intelligence and Indian subversion', 56–113; Rumbold, *Watershed in India*, 14–16, 32–3, 43–4.

decamped across the Atlantic to the New World's haven of democratic ideals.[200]

The result of the move was to give a small group of intellectuals, anarchists, and nationalists a popular base. The Pacific coast of North America was short of labour in relation to the land available. Indians, particularly Punjabis, emigrated in search of work, establishing themselves around the rim of the Pacific, in China as well as in British Columbia and California. However, their arrival provoked racial animosity. Labour movements in Canada, Australia and the United States emphasised the rights of whites. Australia excluded Indians. Between 1904 and 1908 about 5,000 Indians arrived in Canada. In the latter year, Canada ruled that only those who had travelled direct from India (there were no regular direct sailings) and possessed $200 would be admitted. What infuriated the Indians was that they too were citizens of the empire, but London did not intervene, preferring to leave such a thorny issue to the Dominions themselves. The Government of India did not check emigration; Canada became increasingly opposed to immigration. Those Sikhs who left but failed to secure entry gravitated to other points on the Pacific littoral. Some looked to Japan, a hero of Asian resistance after the defeat of Russia and the victim also of white exclusion. They found that Tokyo protested more strongly on their behalf than did Delhi. Others moved across the American border, although here too they encountered racial discrimination.[201]

America, like Europe, had its share of small Indian intellectual groups. But the Punjab emigrants provided the basis for mass support. In 1911 the revolutionaries in Paris asked Lal Har Dayal, recently appointed to a post at Stanford University, to co-ordinate the activities of the Sikh groups on the Pacific coast. Har Dayal aimed to unite both students and labourers, and to turn the movement from assassination and anarchy to full-scale revolution. To him was attributed a key role in the Hardinge bomb attack. In 1913 his work led to the establishment of a joint organization for the pre-existing societies, best known by the name of its newspaper *Ghadr* ('mutiny'). From its headquarters in San Francisco copies of *Ghadr* made their way all round the Pacific. It banned religious discussion, arguing that divisions of faith should not prejudice the achievement of national unity and independence. Its aim was to overthrow British rule in India through armed revolution and in its stead to establish a democratic republic. The alliance between the intellectuals, predominantly Bengali and high-caste Hindus, and the labourers, mostly Punjabi and Sikh, was cemented with the voyage of the *Komagata Maru*. Chartered to carry Indian immigrants direct to Canada, she was turned away at Vancouver, refused entry in Hong Kong but admitted to Kobe, and eventually returned

[200] Sareen, *Indian revolutionary movement*, 1–48.
[201] Ibid. 53–79; Offer, *First World War*, 164–209.

to Calcutta on 26 September 1914. Her disappointed passengers had been educated in the ideas of *Ghadr* on their voyage. Those who arrived back in India marched into Calcutta, and in the ensuing struggle twenty-six died.

The Punjabis on *Komagata Maru* may well have been the dupes of a conspiracy designed by *Ghadr* to create a revolutionary core in India. Certainly that was the effect. On 15 August 1914 *Ghadr* concluded that the time had come for open war with Britain and that, in its bid to establish a sovereign republic, the organization would accept help from whatever quarter it was offered. The Punjabi peasantry not only constituted the majority among Indian emigrants, it also provided the core of the Indian army. Having remained loyal in 1857, the Sikhs were seen as pre-eminent among the 'martial races' of India. About half the soldiers sent overseas in 1914–15 were Punjabis: many who served on the Western front were appalled by the conditions of modern war and urged their kinsmen not to enlist. *Ghadr*'s aim, therefore, was to build on the *Komagata Maru* incident, to win over units of the army, and so compensate for its own lack of arms. Between 500 and 1,000 agitators returned to India in the autumn of 1914. Turkey's entry into the war enhanced the possibility that Muslims would join Sikhs and Hindus in the conspiracy. Among the revolutionaries a false optimism grew. The extent of nationalist feeling was exaggerated, wishful thinking substituted for money, arms, and leadership.

British counter-intelligence had recovered from its earlier setbacks. In London the police had lacked the expertise to penetrate Shyamaji Krishnavarma's organization. The Indian criminal investigation department had therefore taken on the task. By 1910 a network of agents was being established in Europe. On the Pacific coast, a former Indian policeman employed by the Vancouver immigration department established sufficiently good links with the San Francisco authorities to penetrate the *Ghadr* organization. In March 1914 Har Dayal was charged with anarchism and deported from the United States. The return of the *Komagata Maru* was carefully monitored, and many of the revolutionaries were interned on arrival in India.[202] The British knew from a Sikh soldier, Kirpal Singh, that Rash Behari Bose planned to trigger the revolution with a mutiny of the 23rd Cavalry in Lahore on 21 February 1915. Bose suspected a leak and brought the rising forward to the 19th. But the 23rd Cavalry was paraded for the entire day, so thwarting the conspiracy. The police raided the *Ghadr* headquarters; what violence followed was sporadic and isolated; most of the country, including Bengal, remained quiet. Bose escaped to Japan. Empowered by the Defence of India act of 17 March 1915 to try by tribunal rather than by the normal judicial procedures, the government arraigned 291 individuals on charges of conspiracy. Forty-two were condemned to death, 114 were transported for life, and ninety-three were

---

[202] Popplewell, 'British intelligence and Indian subversion', 114–36, 145–65.

imprisoned. The army took its own measures against the 12th Cavalry, which had been provoked into mutiny on 23 February: twelve out of the eighteen men sentenced to death were executed. In the Punjab the lieutenant-governor, Michael O'Dwyer, imprisoned 400 people and confined a further 2,500 to their villages. He balanced his harshness by his success in enlisting rural notables to prop up the British administration at the local level and so sustain recruiting: landowners and gentry continued to look to the Raj for preferment, and they were abetted by Sikh religious leaders who condemned *Ghadr* as apostasy.[203]

The coincident ripples in the Indian army outside India seem in reality to have had little association with the revolutionary movement. Mutiny in the 130th Baluchis in Rangoon was headed off in January 1915. More serious was the rising of the 5th Light Infantry in Singapore. The battalion (unusually) was entirely Muslim. No evidence exists to support the argument that two members of *Ghadr* played a leading role, and, although elements of another Indian-recruited regiment, the Malay States Guides, were affected, the 36th Sikhs, also in Singapore, were not. Thus, if the mutiny is to be set in any general context it should be that of pan-Islam, not of Indian nationalism. But the real problems were specific to the regiment. The commanding officer was incompetent and distrusted by the other officers. Poor leadership allowed lesser issues to fester—the promotion prospects of the NCOs, inadequate rations, the uncertainty as to the regiment's eventual destination. The battalion planned to mutiny on 17 February, the day before its embarkation for what it feared would be a fight with the Turks. In the event, the sailing was brought forward and action was improvised on the 15th. Outwardly, the situation was serious. There were only 231 European regular troops on the island to face as many as 800 mutineers. Thirty-two British soldiers and civilians were killed. In practice, the danger was past almost as soon as it had begun. A landing party from HMS *Cadmus* checked the mutineers from advancing into Singapore, and by the morning of 16 February an improvised force had relieved the 5th Light Infantry's commanding officer, besieged in his bungalow. The rising collapsed from within. The right wing of the battalion, who were Rajputs, initiated the mutiny, but were at odds with the left wing, who were Pathans, and with each other. The German prisoners of war on the island, whom it had been planned to release and arm, were in the main less inspired by the Indians than frightened by them. Those few Germans who did act preferred to take the opportunity to escape rather than to prosecute the war. From 16 February onwards flight was the main preoccupation of the mutineers also. In the subsequent days the arrival of French, Russian, and (most significantly) Japanese sailors made little contri-

---

[203] Dignan, *Indian revolutionary problem*, 40–7; Sareen, *Indian revolutionary movement*, 95–110; Tan, *Journal of Military History*, LXIV (2000), 398–9; also 374, 381–3, 387–8. Hopkirk, *On secret service*, 83, gives different totals for those tried and convicted.

bution to the restoration of order, but did underline Britain's military and naval weakness in the Far East. In the subsequent courts martial 213 men were tried, of whom all except one were convicted; forty-seven were executed.[204]

By the spring of 1915 the revolutionary movement within India and within the Indian army had shot its bolt. Only in Bengal did the Indian nationalists retain a foothold in the subcontinent. Germany had played no part in the events. And yet what had happened was enough to convince Germany that the basis for revolution existed.

Germany's pre-war attitude to the revolutionary movement was justifiably sceptical. Although the Kaiser and the general staff hoped that the north-west frontier would tie down significant British forces, until 1907 they assumed that the source of the threat would be Russia. After 1907 the possibility of a native uprising became more important in their calculations. But their focus was on the Muslims, not on the Sikhs or Hindus. Graf von Luxburg, the German consul-general in India, went furthest in anticipating a Muslim rising, noting the support of Indian Muslims for the Turks in 1912 and 1913, praising their manly and military qualities, and even adumbrating the possibility of co-operation with the Hindus. But the general tenor of Germany's attitude was to buttress British rule, not undermine it. As a colonial power in East Africa, Germany stood to lose if the principle of white supremacy was undermined. Between the late 1880s and 1913 Germany's share of India's exports tripled; commercial considerations therefore determined that Germany would avoid giving offence to the British in India.[205]

The initiative in involving the Germans in the cause of Indian nationalism was taken not by the Germans but by the Indians themselves. Two Indian students in Germany in August 1914, Virendranath Chattopadhyaya and Abinash Bhattacharya, made contact with Clemens von Delbrück, the minister of the interior. In September an office for Indian activities was opened in Berlin. Religious tensions cut across much of the office's work, not least in its efforts to subvert Indian troops in Egypt and Mesopotamia. Although Chattopadhyaya and Bhattacharya were Bengali and Hindu, the Germans—largely thanks to Oppenheim—tended to place their contribution in an Islamic and Turkish context. Har Dayal had been sufficiently impressed by *Deutschland und der nächste Krieg*, in which Bernhardi had highlighted Britain's vulnerability in India, to have made contact with the German consul in San Francisco in 1913.[206] Either of his own volition, or because he was recruited by the German

[204] Precise figures vary, see Dignan, *Indian revolutionary problem*, 48–9, and Sareen, *Indian revolutionary movement*, 106–10. Both Dignan and Sareen place the mutiny firmly in the context of the *Ghadr* revolution. Beckett, *Journal of the Society for Army Historical Research*, LXII (1984), 132–53, sees the issue as primarily professional, as does Omissi, *Sepoy and the Raj*, 149. Harper and Miller, *Singapore mutiny*, is the fullest account. See also Murfett, et al., *Between two oceans*, 125–44.

[205] Barooah, *India and the official Germany, passim.*　　　　[206] Hopkirk, *On secret service*, 51.

consul-general in Geneva (accounts vary), he went to Constantinople in September. Dayal had extraordinarily grandiose notions. He hoped to launch an invasion from Afghanistan, and to establish an enclave in Kashmir from which terrorism could flourish throughout India. The other notable recruit to the Berlin group, Barkatullah, was wedded to a similar approach. But many were less sure; Indian nationalism stood poised to be usurped by German imperialism or Turkish pan-Islamism. Neither the grand old man of the revolutionaries, Shyamaji Krishnavarma, now resident in Geneva, nor Lajpat Rai, a leading Punjabi in the United States, would join the Berlin Committee. India, the latter argued, must gain its independence through its own efforts.

In December 1914 these views found at least some reflection within the Berlin Indian Committee. It threw off Oppenheim's suzerainty and affiliated itself directly to the foreign office. Its members did not dispense entirely with the Islamic link and the overland route. But their preference was to generate revolution from within India itself, and to use the revolutionary communities already established in the United States, Shanghai, Siam, and the Dutch East Indies in order to prepare the ground. Oppenheim's departure for Constantinople in 1915 and Barkatullah's participation in Hentig's expedition both confirmed the diminution of the Islamic thread in Berlin. The dominant influence now was Chattopadhyaya. Under his guidance the Berlin Committee was directed by Indians in the interests of Indian nationalism. But it had made two interlocking decisions, both of which weakened its chances of success. It had emphasized political purity rather than military effectiveness. And it had also based itself in Germany, and so dented its claim to neutrality.

The willingness of the German Foreign Ministry to accommodate *Ghadr*'s approach was a reflection both of weakness and of ignorance. Lacking naval power and recognizing that Niedermayer's expedition was a long shot, the Germans could do little but accept what opportunities there were. Moreover, the advice which they took confirmed the reasonableness of what was now proposed. None of Germany's former consuls in India, whose judgements might have had a distinctly sobering effect, was consulted. Instead, the report of the Austro-Hungarian consul-general in Calcutta, Count Thurn, was circulated. Thurn had left India on 3 October; he reckoned that there were 250 secret societies in existence, and that 10,000 revolutionaries could possess themselves of weapons and would act at the first indication of outside support.[207] Thurn had, of course, served in Bengal, and it was the situation there, rather than in India as a whole, which spurred his excessive optimism.

---

[207] Barooah, *India and the official Germany*, 167–210; Fraser, *Journal of Contemporary History*, XII (1977), 258–60; Sareen, *Indian revolutionary movement*, 117–25.

Therefore, not until the New Year of 1915 was any link forged between *Ghadr* and Germany. The co-ordination of the two was in the hands of H. L. Gupta, the Berlin Committee's emissary in America and then the Far East, and Johann Heinrich Graf von Bernstorff, Germany's ambassador in Washington. Until 1917 the United States took a lenient view of *Ghadr*. The state secretary, William Jennings Bryan, had written supportively of Indian nationalism. The Germans were careful to cover up their more flagrant breaches of American neutrality. And the British ambassador, Sir Cecil Spring-Rice, took the view that a protest against *Ghadr*'s activities in the United States would provoke anti-British feeling.

Bernstorff reckoned in December 1914 that $2.5 million would be required to purchase arms in the United States and ship them to India. Germany spent a great deal, but probably not as much as that. Franz von Papen, the military attaché, bought over 10,000 rifles and 4 million rounds through Krupp's American representative, announcing that they were destined for Mexico. They were loaded on a small schooner in San Diego, the plan being that they would be transshipped to a tanker, the *Maverick*, for the onward journey to Batavia. Twice the two ships failed to rendezvous. In June the schooner returned to the United States and the arms were seized. A second consignment of 7,300 rifles, 1,920 revolvers, ten Gatling guns, and 3 million rounds was collected in New York for shipment in a vessel belonging to the Holland–America Line. British intelligence traced the cargo, tipped off the line, and the company refused to carry the goods.

The empty *Maverick* arrived in Batavia on 19 July 1915. Emil Helfferich, Germany's agent in the Dutch East Indies, felt understandably frustrated. During the course of the previous six months he had established contact with Jotindra Nath Mukherjee, the leader of a revolutionary group in Bengal. Mukherjee reckoned that, if he could win over the 14th Rajput Rifles at Calcutta and cut the line to Madras at Balasore, he could be master of Bengal. He intended to strike on Christmas day, when the Europeans' revelries would slow their responses. His emissaries had persuaded Helfferich that *Maverick*'s cargo should be landed not in Karachi, as Helfferich intended, but in Bengal. But then, early in July, assuming that 50,000 rifles would arrive, the Bengalis said they needed only 15,000 of them and that the rest could go to Karachi and Pondicherry.

Smaller shipments to different destinations would indeed have presented British intelligence with a more difficult task. As it was, an increasingly effective organization was established with its base in Singapore. With no existing network in the Far East in 1914, and with little time to develop one, Dudley Ridout, the military commander on the island, put his main effort into counter-espionage on his own patch rather than into far-flung activities elsewhere. Thus, the confusion in the plans emanating from the Dutch East Indies

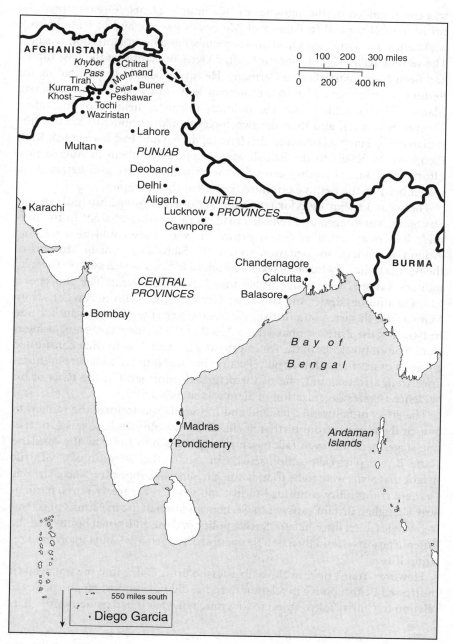

AFGHANISTAN

Khyber
Pass • Chitral
Tirah • Mohmand
Kurram • Swat • Buner
Khost • Peshawar
Tochi
Waziristan

• Lahore

Multan • PUNJAB

Deoband •

Delhi •

Aligarh • UNITED
Lucknow • PROVINCES
Cawnpore

• Karachi

CENTRAL
PROVINCES

• Bombay

Chandernagore •
Calcutta •
Balasore •

BURMA

Bay of
Bengal

• Madras
Pondicherry

Andaman
Islands

0   100   200   300 miles

0   200   400 km

550 miles south

• Diego Garcia

MAP 31. INDIA

was compounded by the activities of two double-agents. 'Oren' warned the British consul-general in Batavia of *Maverick*'s passage and of its links with Mukherjee. The latter was killed on 9 September and his organization crushed. The second agent, Georg Vincent Kraft, a German planter in the East Indies, had been court-martialled in Germany. He saved his skin by persuading the Berlin Committee of a plan to use German settlers in a raid on the Andaman Islands. They would release the political prisoners held there (including Vinayak Savarkar), and then the two forces would combine to land on the Indian coast. Having conceived this fanciful design and had it accepted, Kraft then sold its details to the British when captured by them in August 1915. Efforts in Shanghai to ship arms for the expedition were also betrayed. In December 1915 the Berlin Committee cancelled the operation.

The second major base for revolutionary operations against India in 1915 was Siam. The rugged and remote northern mountains adjacent to the Burmese border appealed to *Ghadr* before the war. They could be a training ground and a base for agitation among the Sikhs and Punjabi Muslims of the Burma police. By July 1915 several hundred Indians as well as three German military advisors were active. What they lacked were arms. The efforts of a Chicago antiques dealer and two other German-Americans to run guns from Manila were thwarted by a British representation to the American authorities. In Bangkok the British ambassador asked that the Siamese government intervene. The ambivalence of the Americans and the Dutch as to what constituted a breach of neutrality found no reflection in Thailand. Six Indian revolutionaries were arrested, and one of them turned informer. On the basis of his evidence *Ghadr*'s organization in Siam was smashed.[208]

The effect of failure in Thailand and Indonesia was to force the Indians to launch their efforts from further afield. The most obvious base was China; at one stage there was even talk of smuggling arms into India by the overland route. But its physical position apart, China had other attractions. Civil strife meant that arms were to be found; Sun Yat-sen was supportive; and a sizeable German community continued to live and work in the treaty ports, particularly Shanghai. Britain's answer to German and Indian use of China's ports was to inveigle China into the war. Such a policy had the additional bonus that the Entente powers would then be able openly to buy arms in China in order to re-equip Russia.

However, Yuan's offer in November 1915 to bring China into the war, while it buttressed British policy in relation to India, did not support Japan's policy in relation to China. Tokyo stood to lose much of what it had gained through its

---

[208] On operations in the Dutch East Indies and Thailand, see Fraser, *Journal of Contemporary History*, XII (1977), 261–8; Sareen, *Indian revolutionary movement*, 130–44; Dignan, *Indian revolutionary problem*, 55–69; Doerries, *Washington–Berlin 1908/1917*, 174–9; Popplewell, 'British intelligence and Indian subversion', 103–4, 232–8; Emily Brown, *Har Dayal*, 202–3.

participation in the war and through the twenty-one demands. Japan success-fully blocked Yuan's proposal. But India, therefore, served to underscore the ambivalence in Anglo-Japanese relations. Japan's naval contribution was a vital element in Britain's ability to control the illicit arms trade across the Pacific. Japanese warships pushed south, operating out of Singapore into the Indian Ocean. But this assistance, vital in the short term, carried with it a long-term challenge to Britain's grip on the economy of the subcontinent. In 1916 Grey remained loyal to his broader perspective and to the needs of the war: he therefore advocated that Japan's growth should be recognized and accommod-ated. But for others, not only in India but also in the embassies of the Far East, Japan took on the mantle of bogeyman once enjoyed by Russia.

What served to underpin these fears was Japan's ambivalent handling of the Indian revolutionaries. Japanese sponsorship of Sun Yat-sen and the rebels of southern China confirmed for Indian intelligence that the real danger by 1916 lay not in China but in Japan. Pan-Asian groups in Japan had played host to Indian nationalists since 1910. Barkatullah had used the country as a base for propaganda that fused three disparate strands—pan-Islam, Asia for the Asians, and Indian revolution. In 1913 he had been appointed to a lectureship in Urdu at the University of Tokyo. British protests led to his removal in March 1914. But in May 1915 Delhi's fears were re-excited when Rash Behari Bose entered Japan after his flight from India, posing as the agent of the Indian author Rabindranath Tagore. H. L. Gupta joined Bose in August. When the British appealed to Ishii's government to deport the two revolutionaries, the Japanese gave the fugitives sufficient notice to enable a pan-Asiatic protest to be mounted by the Japanese nationalists. Gupta made his escape to the United States. Bose went into hiding in Japan. Britain had refused to set up an intelligence network in Japan before the war; it now did so. Furthermore, its focus became not its Indian enemy but its Japanese ally. By 1917 the British felt clear that the Japanese police were protecting Bose, and began to suspect that the minister of the interior, Baron Goto Shinpei, was not entirely averse to the Indians' hope that Japan might be prised from the Entente.[209]

India increased the tension in Anglo-Japanese relations in the war. But in the final analysis it did not undermine them. By the beginning of 1916 the threat to Indian domestic order posed by *Ghadr* could be regarded with justifiable complacency. On 20 January the navy guaranteed that no major landing was possible, and expressed the view that even if a landing was affected it was unlikely to get support.[210] Although false illusions continued to appear in the German Foreign Ministry, Germans closer to the action were increasingly contemptuous. The Indian nationalists, one agent reported in a dispatch

[209] Dignan, *Indian revolutionary problem*, 76–121, 137–201; Fraser, *History*, LXIII (1978), 366–82; Popplewell, 'British intelligence and Indian subversion', 260–78.
[210] Dignan, *Indian revolutionary problem*, 71–2.

destined to fall into British hands in May 1916, 'are heroes only in words...
Until the day for action arrives they are prodigal of grandiloquent phrases—
when it comes they at once seek, and always find, reasons to avoid their
obligations.'[211]

In January 1916 the Indian Committee in Berlin began to share these
reservations about *Ghadr*. It sent Dr C. K. Chakravarty to co-ordinate its
American operations. Chakravarty was bullish; the organization in India, he
claimed, was complete; all that was required were arms. Although Lansing had
become secretary of state in place of Bryan in August 1915, and although the
evidence of the Lahore trials could be used to substantiate the accusations
against *Ghadr*, Spring-Rice remained reluctant to push the Americans on the
Indian issue. And when he did push, the Americans did nothing. India's
counter-intelligence therefore adopted a more indirect approach. The division
between the Bengalis and the Sikhs reappeared. The latter claimed that they
made the greater financial contribution; the former argued that the Sikhs were
prompted by British agents. Both were right. The Berlin Committee advised
the German Foreign Ministry to suspend payments to *Ghadr*. In January 1917
Ghadr conducted an internal review of its accounts. A British agent, Pratap's
erstwhile emissary Harish Chandra, said that Ram Chandra, who had succeeded H. L. Gupta in the United States late in 1915, had misappropriated
funds. The Sikhs used Harish Chandra's report to turn on Ram Chandra; the
Ghadr movement split into its two component parts in February 1917.

Meanwhile the head of British intelligence in America, William Wiseman,
passed directly into the hands of the New York police the details of a bomb plot
implicating Chakravarty and linking Indian revolutionary activity to Germany. Wiseman therefore undercut the procrastination of the United States
federal authorities and of Spring-Rice. On 17 March 1917 the American government agreed to act against the Indian revolutionaries in the United States. One
hundred and twenty-four Indians were indicted on charges of conspiracy to
breach American neutrality. The trial, held in San Francisco between November 1917 and April 1918, was a showpiece; only thirty-five of the accused were
apprehended and the sentences were mild. But it confirmed that *Ghadr* had
destroyed itself as much as it had been destroyed from outside. A Sikh,
convinced that Ram Chandra was a British agent, shot and killed him in
court.[212]

Ghadr re-emerged in the United States after the war, although its German
associations and the racism of labour organizations limited its influence. But
American entry into the war completed its extinction as an effective belligerent. Siam followed the United States's lead and declared war on the Central

[211] Ibid. 72; cf. Doerries, *Washington–Berlin 1908/1917*, 178.
[212] Sareen, *Indian revolutionary movement*, 193–205; Dignan, *Indian revolutionary problem*, 122–35;
Sareen, 204, says 97 were indicted.

Powers on 22 July 1917. China did so a month later. Thus, all but the Dutch East Indies were removed as possible neutral bases within the Pacific.

The failure of the Hindus and the Sikhs, the hopelessness of operations involving sea-power—both of these had been anticipated in Berlin before the war. Germany's preferred area of operations had always hinged on the activation of the north-west frontier and on the potentiality of its appeal in pan-Islamic circles. The Muslim population of India was a minority, but it nonetheless mustered 57 million. Furthermore, it was concentrated in the north, adjacent to Afghanistan. And yet the Islamic challenge to British rule in India proved even more feeble than that of *Ghadr*.

Ostensibly, pan-Islamic feeling had made considerable inroads among younger, better-educated Muslims before the war. As elsewhere, the defeat and the reduction of Turkey in Europe and in Libya triggered a popular response. Indians collected funds, sent medical aid, and bought Ottoman bonds. In 1913 the society for the servants of Kaaba, *Anjuman-i-Khuddam-i-Kaaba*, was founded in order to form a military force to protect the holy places. The viceroy insisted that the purposes of the society were political; its members were less sure. It was not unaffected by the example of the Young Turks or by the propaganda of the Committee of Union and Progress. During the war it actively encouraged Indian soldiers to desert to the Turks.

Moreover, it seemed that the corollary of this growth in pan-Islamic sentiment was an estrangement from British rule. As a minority group, Muslims had profited from British protection against the Hindu majority. But after Curzon's departure it seemed that Britain's response to the growth in political activism in India would be to give way to the larger, more vocal, and more violent groups. The partition of Bengal which had so roused the Hindus had suited the Muslims. But it was annulled in 1911. The proposal to create a centralized Muslim university at Aligarh was overthrown in favour of local, residential universities. And a minor issue—the realignment of a road in Cawnpore so that it required the demolition of a mosque's washing-place—triggered violent riots in 1913.

When the war broke out both of these themes found expression in the Muslim press. The hope in August was that war between the Christian powers of Europe would create the opportunity for a neutral Turkey to recover its losses. *Al-Hilal*, an Urdu weekly edited by A. K. Azad, blamed Britain for France's acquisition of Morocco, Russia's of Persia, and Italy's of Tripoli. Despite a police warning, it went on in October to describe the British withdrawal from Antwerp as evidence of cowardice. *Al-Hilal* was closed. It was also more outspoken than most. Other journals confined their doubts about the Entente to criticism of Russia. When Britain and Turkey found themselves at war with each other in November, most bemoaned a situation that demanded they divide their loyalties. But for all their formal allegiance to Britain, sympathy for Turkey and anxiety for the security of the holy places could never free them for a wholehearted commitment to the war effort. Most of the more obviously anti-British publications were silenced by the end of 1914. Mohamed Ali, the owner and editor of two newspapers, and his brother Shaukat were interned in 1915. Nonetheless, the news of the Arab revolt in 1916 still revealed a range of responses potentially more worrying to the British. Rather than welcoming the revolt as an Islamic response to Turkish misrule, and as an indication that Britain had in the Arabs active Muslim allies, most Indian Muslims condemned the rising. Furthermore, such sentiments were not confined to pan-Islamic radicals. Loyalty to Britain could be justified by the need to accept the established temporal authority; by the same token, the Arabs should have acknowledged Ottoman rule, especially when the Turks were their co-religionists. All Muslims were alarmed that the Sherif of Mecca had made the holy places a battleground; many were not reassured by British assurances that the sites would be respected. The Government of India liked to see its own military initiative in Mesopotamia as the principal bulwark against pan-Islamism; it concluded that the Arab revolt was an impediment to the effectiveness of the campaign and stopped all reporting from the Hejaz.[213]

The activities of the *Khuddam-i-Kaaba*, and of *Al-Hilal* and similar publications, contained sufficient inflammatory material to give British alarmism good grounds. But in reality the Indian Muslims were too deeply divided amongst themselves to provide a coherent threat to the Raj. The Muslim League was founded in 1906 as a counter to Hindu dominance in the Indian National Congress. Its aim was not political activism but quietism. It feared constitutional reform as the path to Hindu domination. It reckoned that the best future for Islamic interests would be secured by education; this would qualify professional Muslims for office in collaboration with the British. Increasingly, too, it saw its task as directing the enthusiasms of the younger, more radical group into legitimate channels. But the divisions were not simply generational. They were also bounded by language, literacy, and wealth. Those Muslims who constituted a majority in their area saw the future of India differently from those who did not. The issues of pan-Islam and of religious fundamentalism were embraced less as ends in themselves than as rallying cries. They enabled the western-educated professional elite to broaden its appeal to traditionalists and to the peasantry. The substance was not the war and its outcome, but the quest for political influence within India.[214]

Thus, the move from rhetoric to revolution was embraced by very few. The key figures were Mahmudul Hasan and his pupil Obeidullah Sindhi, a convert from Sikhism. Hasan used his seminary at Deoband as a base for arguing that

[213] Prasad, *Indian Muslims and World War I*, 1–121; Rumbold, *Watershed in India*, 26–7, 41–2.
[214] Judith Brown, *Gandhi's rise to power*, 29–32, 138–40.

British government cut across religious freedom. He taught that it was the duty of Muslims to go to a country under Muslim rule, and he was the inspiration to the fifteen students who left Lahore in 1915 to join the Turkish army via Kabul. Hasan and his pupils agitated among the tribes of the north-west frontier, particularly the Wahabi communities in Buner.

The Wahabi numbered at most 800 fighting men. In the estimation of the British the key to the behaviour of the frontier tribes was the Afridi. They divided the restless Mohmands, north of Peshawar and adjacent to Buner, from the Mahsuds in Kurram and Waziristan. The allowances paid by India to the Afridi were doubled in February 1915. But of the 2,500 Afridi serving with the Indian army, over 600 had deserted by June. Moreover, across the border Habibullah's authority in Khost was weak. Raids from Khost into the Tochi valley in 1915 and five attacks in the Peshawar region were described by Hardinge as the most serious frontier operations since 1897. Operations against the Mohmands, numbered by the British in tens of thousands, extended throughout the summer. But in 1916 they were quieter until later in the year, and were then contained by a network of blockhouses. In these operations the British used both aircraft and armoured cars in the North-West Frontier Province for the first time. The nominal strength of the forces in the area—three infantry divisions, one cavalry brigade, and three frontier force brigades—remained unchanged throughout the war, but the quality declined. Thus the application of new technology, combined with the opening of a mountain warfare school in May 1916, offset the worst deficiencies in training and experience. Crucially, Waziristan remained quiet until 1917, with the result that each clash on the north-west frontier remained isolated rather than part of a general rising. The bulk of the Afridi remained loyal; the Khans in Chitral, the Swat valley, and the Khyber aided the government.[215]

In August 1915 Obeidullah and three other *mujahedin* left the tribes for Kabul. He was rewarded with the home portfolio in Pratap's provisional government. However, his major creative effort went into the organization of the 'army of God'. He dubbed the Wahabis the 'Hindustani fanatics' and saw them as the advance guard in a general Muslim rising in India. To support them there would be an Islamic army with its headquarters in Medina, and branches in Constantinople, Teheran, and Kabul. He seems to have been more concerned with the distribution of senior rank than with the operational effectiveness of the 'army of God'. Both he and Hasan were to be generals; he named the Sherif of Mecca, who by the time he penned this ridiculous farrago in July 1916 was already on the other side, a field marshal.

Hasan himself had gone to the Hejaz in September 1915, ostensibly as a pilgrim, in reality to organize the Turkish end of Obeidullah's scheme.

[215] Baha, *Asian Affairs*, NS, LVII (1970), 29–34; Macmunn, *Turmoil and tragedy in India*, 133–45; Moreman, *Army in India*, 99–102.

The Turks were wary; they recognized that ultimately Indian nationalism and pan-Islam were incompatible. Moreover, the capricious and unsympathetic behaviour of Har Dayal had resulted in a fragmentation of the Berlin Committee's efforts in the Ottoman empire. Har Dayal had initially imagined that Enver was supportive of the Hindus, and that Muslim religious feeling could therefore be subordinated to Indian nationalism. But he also concluded that the Indian middle class was effete, and therefore preferred to answer directly to the German foreign office than to the Berlin Committee. Thus, although Har Dayal was co-ordinating Indian propaganda in Damascus, he inflamed both Turks and Indians.[216] Similarly, a proposal to raise an Indian legion from the prisoners of war captured in Mesopotamia foundered, caught between the Turks' wish to incorporate only Muslims in the Ottoman army and the Berlin Committee's fantasies of an Indian national army.

The governor of the Hejaz, therefore, received Hasan with politeness, but suggested he might be better advised to work on the revolutionary organization within India. Hasan declined to return himself, but sent two of his acolytes. In Persia two of the Lahore students entrusted with the task of opening overland contact between Obeidullah and Constantinople were interned in May 1916 and handed over to India. Obeidullah himself wrote a long account of what had so far been achieved, the so-called 'silk letters', which he entrusted to an emissary to take to Hasan in Arabia. The messenger promptly handed them over to the commissioner of police in Multan, and on the basis of his evidence and of the 'childish rot' (the police's description) in the letters, Obeidullah's Indian associates were exposed. Hasan was arrested in Jedda in December 1916.[217]

The intrigues of the *mujahidin* and of the Turkish agents among the frontier tribes, abetted by Nasrullah, had results only marginally less feeble. In June 1916 a Turkish colonel and a former Indian army NCO rallied about 400 Afridi in Tirah. But in September they were ousted by the pro-British faction and in June 1917 the Turks returned to Afghanistan. The Mohmands were stirred into activity between October 1916 and July 1917, but then settled with the British. And to the south the Mahsuds became gradually bolder in the area beyond the Indus. In 1917 a punitive expedition was organized in Waziristan and the Mahsuds were subdued. The ambivalence of Afghanistan, the tendency of the Turkish agents to agitate in the winter when the Afridi looked to move into the lower ground, and the British use of aeroplanes rather than troops all contributed to curtail the seriousness of the frontier threat.[218]

---

[216] Emily Brown, *Har Dayal*, 190–3, 210–13.
[217] Prasad, *Indian Muslims*, 127–44; Sareen, *Indian revolutionary movement*, 172–84.
[218] Baha, *Asian Affairs*, NS, LVII (1970), 36–7; Baha, *Journal of the Asiatic Society of Pakistan*, XIV (1969), 185–92; Macmunn, *Turmoil and tragedy*, 191–2.

The schemes of Pratap, Barkatullah, Obeidullah, and Hasan were as riddled with fissures as those of *Ghadr*. Obeidullah pledged his allegiance to a provisional government of India, and even established a branch of the Indian National Congress in Kabul. But his own commitment was to Islam, not to India, and he was using the latter to advance the cause of the former. These contradictions would only have been more evident had the hare-brained schemes which underpinned them been more successful. An Afghan invasion, as the Germans recognized, stood in direct opposition to the achievement of Indian independence. To the westernized and professional elites of the Indian cities the tribes of the frontier represented backwardness, not advance.

The hopes for revolutionizing India, whether Hindu, Sikh, or Muslim, depended on long-range thrusts delivered from outside. Never was there an internal movement of sufficient robustness to overcome the splits within Indian society and to rally mass support.

Although the divisions—of race, religion, caste, language—were the most obvious feature of Indian political life in 1914, the latter's small base was equally important. The Indian National Congress was founded in 1885, and was accepted as an effective spokesman for Indian demands. But its activities did not reflect the preoccupations of the bulk of the Indian population. Whole swathes of territory, including the Punjab, the Central Provinces, and the United Provinces, were barely represented. The kernel of Congress was the high-caste Hindu of Bombay, Madras, and Bengal. British rule relied on collaboration, and western education became the means by which the professional classes could ensure their places in the civil service and in municipal self-government. Congress, therefore, directed its attention not to the politicization of the masses but to securing the power-base of its own members. The Morley–Minto reforms of 1909 introduced communal electorates. The indications were that co-operation with the British—moderation, not extremism—would expand the influence of the western-educated Indian elite. In 1914 the Indian politician, however radical he might sound, was committed to change through constitutional methods and to co-operation with the Raj.[219]

The impact of the war did affect the tempo of political life, principally because of the economic and social change engendered by the war effort. But the consequences of rising prices, of major recruiting efforts, and of shortages of imported foods were manifest in 1917–18, not earlier. In 1914 the Government of India was agreeably surprised by the level of popular support for Britain's entry to the war. In September the legislative council agreed to India bearing the normal costs of Indian Expeditionary Force A while it was in France. Enlistment, which had averaged 1,250 men a month in peacetime, reached 10,000 a month by the end of 1915. Two divisions in Egypt had

[219] Judith Brown, *Gandhi's rise to power*, 17–24.

been earmarked for dispatch to India in the event of a major rising on the north-west frontier or of invasion from Afghanistan. But in late 1916 the commander-in-chief in India was confident he could meet such a threat from his own resources. In March 1917, as war-weariness manifested itself, India set a target of 17,500 recruits a month, and in fact enlisted 276,000 in the course of the year 1917–18, more than twice its total for 1916–17. All these were voluntary engagements, even if disproportionately from the Punjab. Moreover, in another indication of popular support for the imperial war effort, war loans were successfully floated in India in 1917 and 1918.[220] The Government of India never felt sufficiently challenged to extend its control of the press to censorship before publication or to central direction; active propaganda in favour of Britain remained local and self-generated until 1918.[221]

Nonetheless, in 1916 Congress recognized that the war was a good moment to press the British for constitutional concessions. Moreover, they could use the threat of their own extremists and of the young Muslims to argue that without reform the viability of moderation would be under severe challenge. Congress accepted that there should be separate Muslim electorates, and proposed that no bill would be passed if it was opposed by 75 per cent of any one community. In December 1916 the Muslim League responded to this package by joining Congress in calling for change. In a striking, though still limited, departure from previous political behaviour, two Home Rule Leagues were formed to carry the demand for self-government into areas and castes that previously had remained unpoliticized.

Two factors prevented this movement becoming the internal focus for a radical Indian nationalism which the revolutionaries abroad hoped to establish. The first was that British policy was rooted in moderation and concession, and therefore kept the professional and educated classes within its thrall. And the second was that the unity of 1916 was only apparent. The Muslim League did not represent the Muslim community of India.

The idea that India's contribution to the war should be repaid by voluntary concessions had already been embraced by Hardinge in 1915. In November 1916 his successor, Lord Chelmsford, reflected the views of the provincial governors when he advised that a measure of political reform be granted as soon as possible. By setting self-government as the ultimate, if long-term, objective he hoped to pre-empt India's home-rule movement, and by broadening the franchise he planned to undermine the dominance of the legal profession on the local and imperial legislative councils. The Government of India's proposals were sent to London on 24 November 1916, and were thus temporarily

[220] Rumbold, *Watershed in India*, 20–1, 28–30, 130; Lucas, *Empire at war*, v. 190–3, 198–201; Bogart, *War costs*, 184–5.
[221] N. Gerald Barrier, 'Ruling India: coercion and propaganda in British India during the First World War', in Ellinwood and Pradhan (eds.), *India and World War I*; Brown, *Modern India*, 195.

submerged by the death throes of Asquith's coalition government. However, the secretary of state for India, Austen Chamberlain, survived the reshuffle. As the son of Joseph, whose career had been defined by Ireland, he was persuaded that extremism was best avoided by the early concession of home rule, freely and ungrudgingly given. The Lucknow Declaration threatened Chamberlain and Chelmsford with the loss of initiative, and on 20 March 1917 the Council of India too favoured swift action, cautioning against 'a formula of political progress, hedged with restrictions that nullify its meaning'.[222] India was accorded membership of the Imperial War Conference, despite the opposition or indifference of the white Dominions, and thus acquired de facto Dominion status. But Conservative resistance delayed any further announcement. In June the publication of the report of the Mesopotamian commission lambasted the Government of India, and Chamberlain by implication. Chamberlain resigned.

At this stage there was still little sense, particularly in London, of a long-term progression towards British withdrawal or even Indian self-government. Curzon, who was now lord president and a member of the war cabinet, saw self-government to mean 'responsible government', not parliamentary democracy. Any suggestion that India should be rewarded for its contribution to the war effort was therefore laughable, for, as he roundly declared on 27 June 1917: 'The classes to whom it is now proposed to offer additional concessions [i.e. the educated, professional middle class] have no right to claim them on the ground of war service, for they have rendered no such war service.'[223]

But he was outflanked by the appointment of E. S. Montagu as Chamberlain's successor. The Conservatives were not the only ones to be appalled; Asquith, who admittedly felt that Montagu had robbed him of Venetia Stanley, tersely observed that 'a Jew was not a fit person to attempt to govern India'.[224] Only weeks before Montagu had used the debate on the Mesopotamian commission to argue that the inflexibility of the Government of India and the circumlocution of the India Office might be corrected by the establishment of more representative institutions. In August 1917 he publicly promised that India could aspire eventually to become a self-governing Dominion. By himself visiting India and by producing with Chelmsford a joint report on the self-government of the country, published in July 1918, he identified himself with the ideas of decentralization and popular participation. But his aim was as much expedience as any commitment to liberalism. He was anxious to ward off political extremism. Like Chamberlain, he used Ireland as a cautionary tale, but for that very reason had regarded his predecessor as a man 'intent on mending the lavatory tap when the house is on fire'. The real reason for political reform was 'to fit Indian organisation to a part of the world war'.[225] Montagu and

[222] Rumbold, *Watershed in India*, 69; see generally 48–50, 54–64, 69–126.
[223] Rumbold, *Watershed in India*, 69; see generally 91.
[224] Turner, *British politics and the Great War*, 223.   [225] Ibid. 222.

Chelmsford wanted to provide the underpinnings for India's war effort, for the expansion of the Indian army, and continued withdrawal of British troops.

Montagu's declaration was a pragmatic recognition that during the war years British rule had come to rest even more on the co-operation of the moderates. Its effect was to justify their reliance on Britain. It confirmed the Indian view of Britain as an enlightened and impartial ruler. But the proposals themselves were not as extensive as such Indians might have expected. The moderates did not want to criticize for fear of wrecking what had been gained; equally, they could not appear to praise them for fear of alienating potential supporters. In the 1918 Congress, which attacked the proposals, the moderates abstained. Furthermore, the new constitution continued specifically to recognize the interests of minority groups. What, therefore, Montagu had also done was to reopen the divisions which had apparently begun to close in 1916.

But the 1917 declaration was also the agent of political and social change, as well as its reflection. The combination of the economic strains now evident in 1917–18, and the expansion of political awareness generated as Indian politicians fought for their power-base and for their interests in the new conditions, all helped nudge India towards a political system that rested on mass support. The politician who would most obviously profit from this in the immediate post-war era was Mahatma Gandhi. But in the conditions of 1918 his influence served to divide yet further India's body politic. Although himself the product of India's westernization, and although building his plans for India on British co-operation, he broke with the political styles of the professional classes. He used the Hindu heritage of India, the ashram, to build his following; he urged his followers to use objects made in India and so indirectly reverted to a peasant economy; and his advocacy of passive resistance created a political technique that allowed mass political mobilization. But while traditional in some ways, he sought alliance with the Muslims and worked with low-caste Hindus. From this Gandhi was to fashion Indian nationalism. But its effect in 1918 was to divide Indian politics in yet another direction. And even when Indian nationalism gained momentum it remained more dependent on British co-operation than directed at revolution.[226]

In reviewing the German exploitation of its alliance with Turkey and the threat of holy war from Morocco to India, it is too easy to criticize. The Germans over-extended themselves; they never had the manpower to back up their demands on others, and their aspirations conflicted with the war aims of the Turks. The British and the French are, therefore, mocked for taking too

---

[226] Brown, *Gandhi's rise to power*, 40–51, 123–40; id., 'War and the colonial relationship: Britain, India and the war of 1914–18', in Ellinwood and Pradhan (eds.), *India and World War I*; id., *Modern India*, 193–4, 198–9.

seriously a threat that never became substantial. They were the powers in possession; they had the resources to hand.

But in the years 1919–21 ample proof was provided of just how unsteady the European hold on the Muslim world could be. The reduction and partition of Turkey in the peace settlement provided the general context for more specific frustrations. Egypt threw off British rule in 1922; Libya continued its resistance to Italy for a further decade; Algeria was ravaged by strikes in 1919 and 1920. In Central Asia, a coup ended Britain's indirect control of Persia in 1921 and eventually installed Reza Pahlavi as Shah in 1925. Habibullah, the prudent Emir of Afghanistan, was assassinated in February 1919, and his brother Nasrullah led Afghanistan into its third war with British India. And in India itself the emergency measures of 1919, the Rowlatt acts, carried the provisions of the Defence of India act into the peace. The Punjab, which had failed to rise in 1915, seethed in 1919, and British anxieties were reflected in overreaction and massacre at Amritsar. The pan-Islamists seized control of the Muslim League in December 1918, and the priesthood mobilized the fanaticism of the masses in the Khilafat movement. Much of this had its roots in post-war problems. But it is hard to conclude that Germany had been barking up the wrong tree.

The corollary, therefore, of German failure was Entente success. In the end, French and, particularly, British rule rested on their reputations as liberalizing and progressive powers. The educational and legal systems which they established gave them a following within the indigenous populations which the Germans could never fully match. But these were passive, not active reasons for their defensive triumph. The positive contribution was the quality of their intelligence. In North Africa it enabled French propaganda to stay one step ahead of the Germans. In India counter-intelligence penetrated all the major revolutionary groups, and to such an extent that Indian revolutionaries were set working against each other. Britain did not in the end mobilize large forces to hold India or its forward defences. It did not do so because it was always in a position to deal with certainties rather than contingencies.

By 1916 Germany had begun to recognize that the appeal of holy war was, for too many Muslim states, an indirect form of Ottoman imperialism. Thereafter, Berlin's propaganda relied on nationalism. But this carried two attendant difficulties. First, Germany thus placed itself athwart the intentions of its Turkish ally. Secondly, the strongholds of nationalism tended to be the middle-class professionals, very often small in numbers, the recipients of western education who were impressed by French and British liberalism. Nor were they likely to be traditional Muslims.

The shift to the use of nationalism emphasized the revisionist nature of Germany's revolutionary strategy. German support of the Young Tunisians and of the Persian nationalists was not primarily a covert form of German imperialism. In May 1917 the Germans were happy for the Berlin Indian Committee to establish a propaganda bureau in Stockholm and so formalize its links with international socialism. The Indians now looked increasingly to Russia rather than to Germany. In November 1917 the Berlin Committee briefed the Bolsheviks; in December 1918 it would move its activities to Petrograd. The German foreign office did not obstruct such obvious manifestations of Indian independence.[227] The Germans' espousal of the nationalism of others could be real enough. In October 1915 Colmar von der Goltz wrote, as he was about to take command of the 6th Turkish army for its push into Persia and India:

If we are defeated this time, perhaps we will have better luck next time. For me, the present war is most emphatically only the beginning of a long historical development, at whose end will stand the defeat of England's world position. The hallmark of the twentieth century must be the revolution of the coloured races against the colonial imperialism of Europe.[228]

[227] Sareen, *Indian revolutionary movement*, 207–10, 218–21.
[228] von der Goltz, *Denkwürdigkeiten*, 421–2.

10

FINANCING
THE WAR

Of the two main arms of economic capability in the First World War, industry and finance, current scholarship is far more preoccupied with the former than the latter. It was not always so. Before 1914 the competition in arms had created such abundance that there seemed little need to consider wartime procurement. How the war would be paid for promised to prove much more intractable. And, in the 1920s, the assessment of reparations and the urgent need to understand the sources of inflation—whether it had been generated in the war or in its aftermath—provided the study of wartime finance with a continuing relevance.[1]

The comparative neglect of finance by modern scholars can no doubt be explained by the fact that its administration was not apparently decisive to the outcome of the war. By 1918 goods were running out faster than cash; the maximization of resources was much more important than the management of money. Few had anticipated this. On finance, the banker I. S. Bloch, so often cited as the perceptive but unheard prophet of the true nature of the war, was wrong. Bloch, on the basis of tactical and technological development, correctly anticipated that a future war would be protracted and indecisive. Extrapolating from the evidence on expenditure in earlier European wars and from defence budgets at the end of the nineteenth century, he anticipated that even the advanced nations would have considerable difficulties in funding

---

[1] The only recent general treatment of the subject is Hardach, *First World War*, ch. 6. Balderston, *Economic History Review*, 2nd series, XLII (1989), 222–44, is important but focuses on Britain and Germany only. Soutou, *L'Or et le sang*, a work of considerable intelligence, is concerned primarily with war aims. However, his essay, 'Comment a été financé la guerre', in La Gorce (ed.), *La Première Guerre Mondiale*, makes salient observations in a brief compass. Of the older literature, Bogart, *War costs and their financing*, and Knauss, *Die deutsche, englische, und französische Kriegsfinanzierung*, are comparative and helpful.

this long war; smaller nations would find it unattainable. Bloch's implicit, if optimistic, conclusion was that war between the powers of Europe might now be impossible.[2]

Most of his contemporaries in the world of finance disagreed; they reckoned that a war would occur but that it would be short. Bloch had begun with the tactics and saw that the finance did not fit; they—in so far as they thought through the problem—went the other way, shaping the operational model to the financial imperative. They were more realistic than Bloch, in that they did not think that the probable nature of the war would deter the powers from fighting. They were, of course, wrong about its length. Nonetheless, their pre-war orthodoxy, that the war would be short, continued to shape financial thought well into 1915. At a dinner party on the occasion of Kitchener's visit to France on 1 November 1914, the assembled statesmen and soldiers of the Anglo-French Entente deliberated over the length of the war. Ribot, France's finance minister, cut across Kitchener's pronouncement that Britain would not be fully mobilized for another year by saying that finance would determine the war's duration, and that it would end by July 1915 because the means to pay for it would have been exhausted. Accordingly, at the beginning of that year, on 30 January, *L'Économiste français* announced that the war would not last longer than another seven months. In May Edgar Crammond opined in the *Journal of the Royal Statistical Society* that economic exhaustion would force some belligerents to stop fighting from July.[3]

Crammond was no doubt entitled to feel surprised that poverty did not force states to fall out of the war. Pre-industrial societies like Turkey and Serbia were at war virtually without ceasing from 1912, and yet continued the struggle as long as the major powers. Their prostration by 1918 followed from the depletion of their resources in kind, not from the expenditure of cash. Of the principal belligerents, Russia's early exit in 1917 was not in any direct sense a consequence of its small taxable base or its limited capacity for further borrowing. Financial primitivism did not betoken a lack of military staying-power.

For the perceptive few this point had already been demonstrated by the Balkan wars. Lack of money, Raphael-Georges Levy pointed out in the *Revue des deux mondes* in 1912, had never stopped a nation from fighting. Paul Leroy-Beaulieu extended the argument in *L'Économiste français* on 23 August 1913. A major European war could be sustained over a long period despite a shortage of funds. Money was needed before the war for its preparation, and afterwards to settle the consequent debts. But during the war states survived by requisitioning, by price control, and by credit: thus, paying for a war could in large part be postponed until after its conclusion.[4]

[2] I. S. Bloch, *Modern weapons*, pp. xliv–xlv, 140–6; Jean de Bloch, *Guerre future*, iv. esp. 321–9.
[3] Brécard, *En Belgique*, 95; Bogart, *War costs*, 52.
[4] Charbonnet, *Politique financière*, 9–10.

Such faith in the flexibility and extendability of credit in wartime ought to have been a logical consequence of the policies of the European states in peacetime. Between 1887 and 1913 France's national debt rose 39 per cent (from an already high base-point), Germany's 153 per cent, and Russia's 137 per cent. However, the burden of borrowing declined in real terms owing to the economic growth of the three powers. Germany's fell from 50 per cent of net national product to 44.4 per cent, and Russia's from 65 per cent to 47.3 per cent. Most of Leroy-Beaulieu's contemporaries were more alarmed by the absolute figures than they were reassured by the net cost. This tendency was encouraged by the example of Britain, which over the same period cut its debt by 5 per cent. In 1913 Britain's public debt was only 27.6 per cent of net national product, and a bare 10 per cent of total expenditure was allocated to its service.[5]

Britain's intolerance of debt, intensified by the burdens of the Napoleonic wars, had been reinforced by the costs of the war in South Africa. In reality, the message of that conflict was reassuring; a cavalry captain, R. S. Hamilton-Grace, writing on finance and war in 1910, observed that two-thirds of its costs had been funded by borrowing and one-third by taxation, exactly the same proportions as those of Britain's wars between 1688 and 1785. Hamilton-Grace's conclusion was unequivocal: borrowing in wartime was easy, and Britain in particular was well placed to do it. Moreover, he argued, in contra-distinction to Bloch, 'it is improbable that any nation with reasonable chances of victory will be deterred from declaring war owing to lack of funds'.[6]

Nonetheless, the Gladstonian orthodoxy persisted: war should be paid for out of current income. Thus, British economists tended to underestimate the resilience of credit. In the autumn of 1914 J. M. Keynes predicted that Germany's use of credit would give rise to inflation, and that Britain would be better able to stand the strain of a long war. Not until September 1915 did Keynes clearly articulate the argument that note inflation itself would not bring the war to an early end. 'As long as there are goods and labour in the country the government can buy them with banknotes; and if the people try to spend the notes, an increase in their real consumption is immediately checked by a corresponding rise of prices.' What would determine Germany's eventual economic exhaustion, therefore, was not financial catastrophe but the deple-tion of commodity stocks. However, the bogey of credit inflation was not laid to rest; it was simply reassigned. In Keynes's analysis the power which it now endangered was Britain, which through the importing of resources and the subsidy of allies was spending far more lavishly than Germany.[7]

---

[5] Ferguson, *Pity of war*, 126–30; Ferguson's focus is Anglo-German, but he is unique among recent writers in integrating war finance with a general account of the war.

[6] Hamilton-Grace, *Finance and war*, 43, 53, 57, 62, 71–2.

[7] Johnson (ed.), *Collected writings of Keynes*, xvi. 23, 39, 123–5.

Keynes was not necessarily wrong in his analysis of the economic effects. But he exaggerated their impact on strategy. The problem with his warnings about inflation was that their focus was on the long term. Financial theory looked to the post-war world more than to the winning of the war itself. In the short term the war put into reverse most nostrums about economic behaviour. The tempo of the war economy was set by consumption, not by production. Thus, worries about overproduction were no longer a concern. Capital investment was nonetheless limited to the satisfaction of immediate needs. The primary purchaser of the goods that resulted was the state rather than the private sector. Therefore the state replaced the individual in requiring credit. Most perverse of all, a nation's standing could depend, not on its solvency or its financial prudence or even its international trading position, but on its military performance. Victory, after all, was the pay-off for a war economy. 'Success', Lloyd George instructed the cabinet in 1916, 'means credit: financiers never hesitate to lend to a prosperous concern.'[8] The position of the German mark on the New York exchange proved his point. In October 1917 100 marks bought $13.73; by April 1918, after Russia's humiliation at Brest-Litovsk and Ludendorff's offensives in the west, 100 marks stood at $19.58.[9] Short-term military outcomes, not long-term economic management, could determine foreign financial confidence.

THE GOLD STANDARD

What shaped the distant perspectives of economists was faith in the gold standard—belief that it had regulated international finance before the war, that it continued to operate after a fashion during the war, and that it would be fully restored when the war was over.

By July 1914 fifty-nine countries were on the gold standard.[10] In other words, they used gold coin or backed their paper money with a set percentage of gold, and they determined a gold value for their currency and guaranteed its convertibility. Domestically, this discipline was believed to check inflation since it regulated the money supply. Internationally, the gold standard maintained the balance of payments. If one country had an adverse trade balance, it would pay out in gold. The process might be corrected spontaneously, as the weakened exchange rate would encourage owners of foreign funds to speculate on the gains to be made when the losses were stopped. Ultimately, the central bank could raise interest rates, so sucking back into the country the gold that

---

[8] Skidelsky, *Keynes*, i. 334.   [9] Roesler, *Finanzpolitik des Deutschen Reiches*, 229.
[10] Ally, *Journal of Southern African Studies*, XVII (1991), 222.

had emigrated. If this happened, prices rose and the demand for imported goods fell. Thus, the balance of payments was restored by adjusting the balance of trade. The system was therefore deeply inimical to the requirements of a war economy: it limited note issue, it pivoted around international commerce, and it normally stabilized the economy without active government intervention.

But for all its overt commitment to international finance, the gold standard in practice was shot through with national considerations. Only active co-operation between the central banks enabled the system to cope with major crises, and the experience of those crises could encourage the hoarding of gold, even in normal times. In 1903 a third of the world's gold was either in domestic circulation or held by the Banque de France. In 1914 two-thirds of France's holdings of gold, a total of 4,104 million francs against a note circulation of 5,911 million, were in the bank: 475 million francs were added in the first six months of the year.[11] Gold, therefore, acted as its own protection without frequent changes in French interest rates. In 1907 both the Banque de France and the German Reichsbank had to draw on their reserves in order to support the Bank of England, caught by heavy American borrowing. In November 1907 the Reichsbank's interest rate, which had stood at 4.5 per cent in 1906, reached 7.5 per cent: the flow of gold to the United States was still not checked. By 1910 31 per cent of the world's official gold reserves were held in the United States, but much of it was immobilized in the Treasury, and America still financed its trade through London. Almost 60 per cent of the world's gold money supply had now been appropriated for official reserves, as opposed to 31 per cent in 1889.[12] The Germans, therefore, concluded that they too should increase their holdings of gold, so as to use it in the same manner as the French. Their resolve was hardened by the 1911 Moroccan crisis. In 1909 the Reichsbank's purchases of gold totalled 155,241,225 marks; in 1913 they reached 317,450,056 marks.[13] This 'monetary nationalism'[14] carried clear implications for the financial management of all types of crisis, that of war as well as those of peace.

Britain alone did not build up its reserves. The Bank of England's holdings of gold rarely exceeded £40 million, as opposed to £120 million in France.[15] It helped that three of the world's principal sources of gold, South Africa, Australia, and the Klondike in Canada, lay within the empire; furthermore, India's favourable balance of trade buttressed the market against the seasonal highs and lows of American demands. The Bank of England, therefore, argued that gold was a commodity to be used, and that, because London's money market was the world's largest, its manipulation of interest rates was more

---

[11] Eichengreen, *Golden fetters*, 52; Knauss, *Kriegsfinanzierung*, 21.
[12] de Cecco, *International gold standard*, 115–21.
[13] Zilch, *Reichsbank*, 40–59, 124; Knauss, *Kriegsfinanzierung*, 21.
[14] de Cecco, *International gold standard*, unpaginated preface.
[15] Eichengreen, *Golden fetters*, 49.

effective than would have been French or German use of the same policy. The
fact that foreign bankers kept their sterling balances in London meant that a
balance of payments' deficit did not necessarily draw on the Bank's own
reserves. London's strength was its liquidity. In appearance, therefore, the
gold standard worked because it was 'essentially a sterling exchange system';[16]
in reality, it did so only because of the collusion of the other central banks. As
the Bank of England ensured stability and harmony in normal times, so the
central banks of other nations supported it in times of crisis.[17]

The Committee of Imperial Defence did consider the imbalance between
Britain's gold reserves and its national wealth, but was content to accept the
Treasury's assurances that in the short term interest rates could be used to
check a run on gold, and that in the long term a free market for gold would
ensure the continuance of trade through London. The clearing banks were less
confident. They, and not the Bank of England, held an increasing proportion
of the country's gold reserves, and yet the Bank was their lender of last resort.
In a crisis the Bank of England would be pulled in two directions: as a central
bank it had to increase interest rates to draw in gold, but such action would run
counter to its obligations as a commercial bank providing services to its clients.
Two dangers confronted the Bank. One was that the joint-stock banks had
power without responsibility, since they were under no formal obligation to
make their reserves available for patriotic purposes in the event of a crisis. The
second was the ability of a foreign power to create a run on British gold; many
British merchant banks (or acceptance houses) were heavily implicated in
German overseas trade, which was paid for by bills drawn on account in
London. At the beginning of 1914 the clearing banks lobbied for a royal
commission on the country's gold reserves. They noted that the existing
reserves of forty-six banks in England and Wales represented only 4.04 per
cent of their deposits: 5 per cent was their recommended target. They anticipated two pressures on gold. The first, an external one, would come from
foreign powers anxious to exchange their bills. The second would be domestic—a desire from the British public to hoard cash. They therefore proposed
that in an emergency the Bank of Engand should produce additional currency
for the clearing banks, secured as deposits by the banks of one-third gold and
two-thirds bills. Thus, the Bank of England would increase its holdings of gold
and the public would get its money. Neither the Bank of England, still a private
not a government institution, nor the Treasury was supportive of this suggestion. Rather than a royal commission, the banks were fobbed off with a
Treasury memorandum affirming the status quo. External calls for gold
would be met by increased interest rates, and excessive domestic demand
would result in a suspension of the 1844 Bank act (which fixed the ratio

---

[16] Brown, *Gold standard*, xiii.   [17] Eichengreen, *Golden fetters*, 3–9, 29–66.

between gold and the Bank's note issue). Therefore the most likely initial outcome of a war would be an increase, not a reduction, in Britain's gold reserves. The memorandum made the obvious point that, if such optimism proved unfounded, no gold reserves, however large, would be sufficient to prevent the suspension of cash payments: 'regarded as a preparation for war, our Gold Reserves are either adequate in amount or else are incapable of being raised to a figure which would make them more adequate.'[18]

The Treasury reported on 15 May 1914. Already the beginnings of the run on gold could be detected. Demand for short-term securities in London grew throughout May and June, as an economic downturn created pressure to have assets liquid and available. From 24 July, after the Austrian ultimatum to Serbia, the continental powers called in their assets via London. Foreign capital applications in London totalled over £150 million in 1914, almost all of them before August: France alone withdrew £1,358,000 in the last week of July. Selling became so general as to threaten a collapse in the price of securities. Between 18 July and 1 August Russian 4 per-cent government bonds fell 8.7 per cent, French 3 per-cent bonds 7.8 per-cent, and German 3 per-cent bonds 4 per cent.[19] The pressure on London increased as stock exchanges elsewhere closed, beginning with Vienna on 25 July. On 30 July only London, Paris, and New York were functioning, and on 31 July Paris announced it was postponing settlement for a month. At 10 a.m. on the same day, for the first time in its history, the London stock exchange closed its doors.

The problem for sterling was London's inability to meet new demands for capital. Most foreign balances were already committed to current trade. The loss of business from the continent meant that new funds were not forthcoming. Government-imposed moratoriums left foreign debts unpaid; of £350 million outstanding in bills of exchange, £120 million was owed either by the Central Powers or by Russia, and was therefore unlikely to be recovered even when the moratoriums were lifted. All foreign exchange rates, except France's, moved in favour of London, increasing the reluctance to settle debts. Shipping had all but halted. Payments in gold were suspended by the Russian state bank on 27 July; the other central banks followed suit early in August.[20] Catastrophe confronted the London commercial banks. Representatives of twenty-one merchant banks met on 5 August and reckoned that over £60 million in acceptances was owed them by enemy firms, but that their own capital was only £20 million.[21] The

[18] R. S. Sayers, *Bank of England*, ii. 19; see generally i. 60–3; ii. 3–30. Seabourne, 'Summer of 1914', 79–82, puts the banks' case, and de Cecco, *International gold standard*, 132–41, 191–3, is critical. See also Paul Kennedy, 'Great Britain before 1914', in E. R. May (ed.), *Knowing one's enemies*, 200–1; Johnson (ed.), *Collected writings of Keynes*, xvi. 4–6; D. French, *British economic and strategic planning*, 16–18, 67–70.
[19] Ferguson, *Pity of war*, 192.
[20] The main accounts of the crisis used here are Brown, *Gold standard*, 1–23; Morgan, *British financial policy*, 1–32; Seabourne, 'Summer of 1914'.
[21] Roberts, *Schröders*, 153.

practice of acceptance houses was to rediscount bills when they neared maturity with the clearing banks. The clearing banks' room for manoeuvre was restricted by the closure of the stock exchanges, and by their own refusal to extend credit.

On 30 July the Bank of England advanced £14 million to the discount market and a comparable sum to the banks.[22] But having gone some way to fulfilling its function as the lender of last resort, it then had to protect its own reserves in its capacity as a central bank. It raised the interest rate from 3 per cent to 4 per cent on 30 July, to 8 per cent on 31 July, and to 10 per cent on 1 August. The rate was excessive. The problems on the external market were generated less by the policy of the Bank than by the hoarding instincts of the central banks of other nations. Foreign firms trying to remit to London were being prevented by their governments from doing so. Nonetheless, the last week of July showed a net influx of gold from abroad of £1.4 million. At the same time the Bank's holdings of securities and stocks recovered, but its gold reserves fell from £29.3 million to under £10 million. The pressure was now more internal than external.

The fall in the stock exchanges had wiped out the margins on securities used by stockbrokers as collateral for bank advances. The banks had called in their loans, so forcing further selling of shares and further reductions in the margins on collateral. The closure of the stock exchange had then rendered any remaining shares non-negotiable. The bill brokers, under pressure from the clearing banks, rediscounted bills with the Bank of England, so increasing the Bank's deposits but reducing its gold. The banks, anticipating the storm from the acceptance houses, also drew on the Bank's gold. Simultaneously, however, they refused to give the public payments in gold, and insisted they accept the smallest-denomination note, £5, which was too large for normal use. The banks were convinced that their customers wanted to hoard. Their customers were more pragmatic: they wanted cash to cover the impending August bank holiday weekend. They therefore took their notes to the Bank of England to exchange them for coin. Keynes, a severe critic of the clearing banks' instincts for individual self-preservation, observed the collective consequence of their actions: 'our system was endangered, not by the public running on the banks, but by the banks running on the Bank of England.'[23]

Not only the clearing banks but also the Treasury—with its refusal to engage in pre-war planning and its lifting of the Bank rate to 10 per cent—had deepened the crisis. All sides now gave themselves breathing-space by adding three extra bank holidays, so that business would not resume until Friday 7 August. The clearing banks had asked the Bank of England to implement its earlier recommendations for creating emergency currency; indeed, their hope that their request would be met was an additional factor in their holding gold.

[22] Ferguson, *Pity of war*, 197.   [23] Morgan, *British financial policy*, 30.

Told on 2 August that their suggestion was still not acceptable, they made four demands—that emergency currency be issued nonetheless, that the 1844 Bank act be suspended, that specie payments be halted, and that there should be a general moratorium. All of these proposals were debated at a conference convened by the Treasury on 4 August.

The 1844 Bank act was suspended, but it was not (as the banks had assumed it would be) a necessary corollary of the issue of additional notes. The emergency currency (£1 and 10 shilling notes) was issued by the Treasury and not by the Bank of England. This was to ensure its acceptability in Scotland and Ireland. A maximum issue of £225 million (20 per cent of the banks' liabilities) was authorized at the Bank rate of interest. The banks rightly argued that the rate should be reduced. Externally it was not helping as the problems were not of Britain's making, and domestically it was creating panic and depressing business. The Bank of England's commercial concerns helped it accept the clearing banks' case; if the differential between the Bank's rate and that of the clearing banks were too great, then the former's creditors would shift their business to the latter, so enabling the clearing banks to profit from the crisis.[24] The interest rate was reduced to 5 per cent by 8 August. The final issue was convertibility. The banks had assumed that suspension of the Bank act and the issue of emergency currency would oblige the Bank of England to abandon the gold standard.

On 3 August J. M. Keynes, not yet employed by the Treasury but consulted by it, hammered home two vital points. The first was the difference between the internal demand for gold and the external demand. The purpose of the Treasury currency notes was to meet the former—and, although strictly speaking they were convertible, this was not an option likely to be exercised. By easing the domestic calls on gold, the Bank had more gold available for exchange purposes. His second major message, therefore, was the vital importance of continued convertibility. As he reiterated throughout the war, it was 'useless to accumulate gold reserves in times of peace unless it is intended to utilise them in time of danger'. By maintaining convertibility, Britain would sustain its purchasing power in international markets and would retain foreign confidence and therefore foreign balances in London.[25]

At the outset of the conference Lloyd George, the chancellor of the exchequer, had been sufficiently in the thrall of the clearing banks to have been considering the cessation of convertibility. But, as Keynes and the Treasury stressed, the gold which the crisis had siphoned off from the Bank of England had not gone abroad; it had flowed to the clearing banks because of the latter's squeezing of credit and their determination to seize the opportunity which the war offered of fulfilling their pre-war agenda. The only foreign power which could demand gold from Britain was France, a British creditor in July 1914; in general terms the world was Britain's debtor, and London was therefore well able to sustain its overseas purchases. Lloyd George was convinced. Britain stayed on the gold standard. On 6 August a royal proclamation postponing payments on bills of exchange for a month was confirmed by act of parliament. When the banks reopened on 7 August the domestic crisis had passed.

But if the maintenance of convertibility was to have any meaning, it was the exchange market—not domestic confidence—which required reassurance. On 13 August the Bank of England agreed to discount all approved bills accepted before 4 August 1914. The government was to guarantee the Bank against any eventual loss. However, no protection was accorded the acceptance houses, which remained reluctant to undertake new business. Therefore, on 5 September the Bank announced that it would advance funds at 2 per cent above Bank rate to enable the repayment of pre-moratorium bills on maturity; these advances would not be reclaimed until one year after the war's end. By the end of November most of the £120 million's worth of bills discounted by the Bank under its arrangements of 13 August had been redeemed.

The government's handling of the crisis reflected the view that the key to economic management lay in finance, not in industry. Having initially treated the crisis like any other, with the raising of interest rates and the suspension of the Bank act, it had then stepped up a gear to more direct interventionism. Furthermore, it had accomplished this at the urgent behest of that stronghold of free-trade principles, the City of London. Neither the Bank of England nor the clearing banks had cause for complaint. The arrangements for pre-moratorium bills gave the former good business without major risk; the moratorium protected the latter, sandwiched between the absence of overseas remittances and the persistence of domestic demands for payments. One effect, therefore, was to redistribute the pressure generated by the international crisis away from the City to the manufacturers and small traders of Britain. They found themselves subject to a moratorium which starved them of cash but which still required them to pay wages. The government exhorted them to maintain full employment while extending the moratorium for two further months. The fact that the latter was not lifted until 4 November reflected the sway of finance in governmental calculations. The fact that the economic life of Britain continued nonetheless demonstrated the banks' increasingly relaxed attitude to the formal protection which it provided.[26]

Critics of the government said that it had put itself too much in the hands of the banks. A moratorium on past acceptances and a guarantee of new ones,

---

[26] Peters, *Twentieth century British history*, IV (1993), 126–48; see also Skidelsky, *Keynes*, i. 291, for a critical view of the banks.

leaving the banks to hold the debts themselves, would have been sufficient. The measures that were adopted were inflationary. The bills rediscounted by the Bank appeared as 'other deposits' and securities in the Bank's accounts, and thus by a bookkeeping transaction could be the basis for advancing fresh credit. But even if the banks were rewarded with an injection of cash, the resumption of business proved sluggish. Overseas trade had fallen. The stock exchange did not reopen until 4 January 1915, and when it did the Treasury—with a view to giving the government first call on available capital—had to approve all new issues. Between 1915 and 1918 new overseas issues totalled £142 million, as against £159 million in 1914 alone. A merchant bank like Schröders, which had been heavily reliant on German business, limped along for the rest of the war. The Bank of England's arrangements for pre-moratorium bills did not cover all their advances to enemy clients, and their acceptances in 1918 were valued at £1.3 million, as against £11.7 million in 1913. Schröders returned losses in every year until 1919.[27]

The key outcome of the 1914 financial crisis was that Britain remained on the gold standard. From their low of £9,966,000, the Bank of England's gold reserves reached £26,352,000 by the end of August, and £51,804,000 by the end of the year. Freed of the obligation to issue its own notes by the Treasury, and drawing in gold from the clearing banks, its reserves reached 34 per cent of its deposits by 18 November 1914. On the same date the Bank's issue of gold coin and bullion, which had fallen to £26,041,000 on 5 August, peaked at £72,018,000. These were highs not to be repeated for most of the war; for much of the time, and continuously after June 1916, the proportion of reserves to deposits hovered at under 20 per cent, and not until October 1918 did the issue of gold coin again reach its November 1914 figure. But over the war as a whole the gold reserves of Britain increased by 109 per cent, and by 210 per cent when the currency note reserve was included.[28]

This achievement was set against a decline in the world's production of gold. Russian output fell from 146,470 pounds (weight) in 1914 to 66,960 pounds in 1916—the victim of a loss of labour, increased production costs, and transport problems. Payments to the producers, which had been fixed at a profit of 30 per cent in November 1915, were increased to a 45 per-cent profit in November 1916, but with negligible results on output.[29]

Output in the British empire, which reached almost £60 million in 1916, fell thereafter.[30] Australia imposed an embargo on the export of gold in 1915; designed to ensure sufficient cover for the commonwealth's expanding note

[27] Roberts, Schröders, 160–4.
[28] Seabourne, 'Summer of 1914', 94–5; Morgan, British financial policy, 160–1; Brown, Gold standard, 100, 108–11.
[29] Michelson et al., Russian public finance, 393–4, 439–41.
[30] Morgan, British financial policy, 335–6.

issue (by 1918 the note issue had risen from £9.5 million to £52.5 million, but the gold reserve had only fallen from 42.9 per cent to 33.6 per cent), the embargo depressed the price of Australian gold in international terms. Australia's output, which had totalled £8.7 million in value in 1914, fell to just over £5 million in the last year of the war.[31] But more important than any decision in Australia was the Bank of England's fixing of the gold price. Two-thirds of Britain's imperial gold came from South Africa. On 14 August 1914 the Bank of England secured an exclusive agreement with the mining companies of the Union, which fixed the official rate of gold at £3. 17s. 9d. per standard ounce. Given the wartime problems of freight and insurance, the Bank's terms were attractive as 97 per cent of the purchase price would be advanced before shipment. Similar arrangements were concluded with Australia. The gold could therefore remain in the Dominions without incurring the risk of loss at sea, and the advances made by London could go towards the issue of Dominion notes to fund the imperial war effort. But as mining costs rose, so the companies' profits fell. Britain was able to buy gold at a fixed rate and sell it on to neutrals at the market price. The quantity of gold mined fell in 1917 and again in 1918. By then relations between the mines and London were fraught.[32]

Initially, a further source of gold was the United States. The outbreak of the war coincided with the period before the autumn sales of corn and cotton, when America was normally in debt to London. Domestic depositors, unable to export their produce, withdrew cash from branch banks, which in turn—fearing a run—drew from the reserve city and central banks. As other stock exchanges across the world closed, dealing concentrated on New York. In the week before its closure on 31 July New York's sales of securities increased sixfold. By 8 August 1914 European withdrawals had reduced the gold reserves of the New York banks by $43 million. By the end of the year short-term debts to the tune of $500 million had been called in by the belligerent powers, and gold exports had totalled almost $105 million. Although share prices recovered sufficiently to enable the New York stock exchange to reopen on 15 December, trading remained restricted until April 1915.

The domestic crisis was surmounted by the use of emergency currency, and by the issue of 'clearing house loan certificates' to permit banks with unfavourable clearing balances to pay other banks. Externally, New York was determined to remain on the gold standard. But the exchange rate with sterling began to approach $7 to the £, when par was $4.87. With short-term bills falling due, further gold would have to be shipped abroad to hold the exchange rate. American companies placed the value of their stock held abroad at $2,400 million. The closure of the stock exchange forestalled the immediate danger of

[31] Scott, *Australia during the war*, 503–7.
[32] Ally, *Journal of Southern African Studies*, XVII (1991), 221–38; Grady, *British war finance*, 41–4.

these holdings being redeemed, but it did not obviate the possibility of other debts being called in. The US Treasury reckoned that $450 million would mature in London by 1 January 1915, and a further $80 million was owed by the city of New York to London and Paris. Given that the crisis would be circumvented once American exports began to move, and given New York's desire that the United States hold its gold, the preferred solution of the banks was for their overseas stockholders to accept credits in New York. This Britain refused to do, insisting on the shipment of gold. Britain's stance confronted the United States with a choice. Either it declared a moratorium or it maintained payments in gold. By opting for the latter, New York sustained its financial prestige in international markets. Furthermore, it signalled to the world that other countries' floating capital would be safe in the United States. In the event, it achieved this at minimal cost to itself. The clearing houses established a gold fund of $100 million, to which $108 million was actually subscribed, and of which $104 million was earmarked for deposit at par in Ottawa on the Bank of England's account. The resumption of American exports meant that the dollar was back to par by November 1914, and in December the United States achieved a net import balance of almost $4 million in gold. Only $10 million, therefore, was actually deposited in Ottawa.[33]

Britain's final source of overseas gold was its Entente allies. By the end of the year Entente orders to the United States were stimulating a revival in American exports: in December sterling was already 1 cent below par on the New York exchange. In 1915 British imports from the United States would be 68 per cent higher than they had been in 1913. The fall in the pound was therefore a reflection of Britain's need for foreign exchange to pay for American goods, and the weaker the pound the more expensive they would be. By June 1915 the pound stood at $4.77.[34]

London channelled orders to the United States not only on its own account but also on those of its allies. Its status as the world's financial capital persisted despite the war. It did so, the Treasury argued, because it remained on the gold standard, and therefore its allies France and Russia, which had not, had an obligation to help keep it there. Crudely put, Britain required its co-belligerents to ship gold to London, overtly to pay for munitions in America, indirectly to keep the sterling–dollar exchange in equilibrium.

Initially the Russians proved more co-operative than the French. In October 1914 the Treasury agreed a loan of £20 million secured by the issue in London of Russian treasury bonds valued at £12 million and the shipment of £8 million in gold bullion. But when the Russians came back for a second loan in December,

<hr/>

[33] Gilbert, *American financing*, 14–18; Burk, *Britain, America and the sinews of war*, 55–62; Brown, *Gold standard*, 16–21; Morgan, *British financial policy*, 21–2; Noyes, *American finance*, 60–1, 82–8; Chandler, *Strong*, 55–60.
[34] Burk, *Britain, America*, 61–2.

provisionally pitched at £100 million, they baulked at the Treasury's insistence that they should support it with a further shipment of gold.[35] Simultaneously the French began negotiations for a loan of £10 million. They had opened an account with the Bank of England at the beginning of the war to fund purchases which passed through London; by the end of the year £9.3 million had been paid out of this account, and expenditure was beginning to run away from income. The Bank of England demanded that the loan be secured with gold. The French refused.[36]

France had abandoned international convertibility precisely in order to buttress the franc domestically; the spectre of the *assignat*, which had promoted galloping inflation in the wars of the French Revolution, promoted conservatism in relation to gold in the war of 1914–18. By December 1915 the Banque de France had added a further 1,000 million francs to its gold reserves, thus prompting the British to see its governor, Georges Pallain, as obstinate and stupid. But Pallain also represented an alternative approach to war finance: by abandoning peacetime norms, France was confident of its ability to restore them once the war was over. In the interim finance would be the servant of war, not an objective in itself. France's only concession was to agree to spend the loan exclusively in Britain.[37]

Keynes had little truck with the French or Russian attitudes. In a memorandum prepared for a meeting of the three powers' financial ministers in February 1915, he came back to his arguments of August 1914. Gold was to be used, not hoarded. '*They* think that we want their gold for the same sort of reason that influences them in retaining it namely to strengthen the Bank of England's position on paper. And our *real* reason, namely the possibility of our having actually to export their gold and so *use* it, they look on as little better than a pretext.'[38] Increasingly the British aim was less the gold standard per se, and more a gold-exchange standard.[39] The French were nonetheless right to observe the long-term intention, the maintenance of British international credit in the post-war world. Octave Homberg, advising the French government before the same conference, reported that the British aim was to increase their gold stock, and that they intended to remain the clearing house for the world, not just during the war but after it as well.[40]

The French saw a potential symmetry, rather than clash, of interests. The French had the gold, the British had the international credit. Therefore when

  [35] Neilson, *Strategy and supply*, 54–7, 65–6.
  [36] Petit, *Finances extérieures de la France*, 59, 181–6.
  [37] Horn, *Guerres mondiales et conflits contemporains*, 180, (1995), 11–13; Horn, *International History Review*, XVII (1995), 52–4, 56–8.
  [38] Johnson (ed.), *Collected works of Keynes*, xvi. 72.
  [39] Soutou, *L'Or et le sang*, 224; for a development of this theme, see Soutou, in La Gorce (ed.), *La Première Guerre Mondiale*, 286–8.
  [40] Soutou, *L'Or et le sang*, 222–3.

the representatives of the three powers met in Paris on 2 February 1915, Alexandre Ribot, the French finance minister, proposed the issue of a joint allied loan of perhaps £800 million. The British opposed, arguing in part that the total sum would be so large that the issue would fail. Privately they felt that such an arrangement would suit the French and Russians, who would get the loan more cheaply than they would on their own, but that British credit would be undermined by its association with its allies. The outcome was that Britain and France supported Russia, the former to the tune of £25 million and the latter with 625 million francs. In exchange, Britain's allies agreed that if the Bank of England's reserves fell by more than £10 million in the next six months—in other words, below £80 million—the Banque de France and the Russian State Bank would each advance in equal proportions £6 million in gold, to be reimbursed within a year. The French reserved the right to use American dollars for this purpose.[41]

Mutual mistrust persisted. The Anglo-French exchange rate, although now approaching par, had been in France's favour thus far in the war. Ribot was sure the Bank of England was withholding credit with the aim of getting the pound to rise against the franc, and so oblige France to consign gold to Britain.[42] This would have happened anyway. In the first quarter of 1915 the French deficit in Anglo-French trade rose to 400 million francs per month, and Ribot reckoned he needed a credit of up to £12 million per month to cover French purchases in the United States and Britain. The French could not obtain credits in America. So, at the end of April Ribot asked Lloyd George for £62 million to cover French orders over the next six months. The French agreed that two-fifths of their American expenses payable in sterling would be backed by gold sent to the Bank of England.[43]

France remained a reluctant and obstructive disgorger of its gold. It stuck to the principle established in February, that it would not grant the gold but lend to the Bank of England in exchange for British credits to the French government. By the end of the war France's gold reserves had nominally increased 56 per cent, but the reserves actually held in France had fallen by 2 per cent.[44] The gold was effectively being used twice over, by the French to support their currency, and by the British to support their interpretation of the gold standard.

The Treasury did two things with the gold. First, it prepared the US stock market for eventual allied borrowing by flushing American business with cash and keeping American interest rates low. Secondly, and relatedly, it exported gold to hold the sterling–dollar exchange steady. The French pooh-poohed the first objective, recognizing that the scale of allied credit operations was likely to

---

[41] Michelson *et al.* (eds.), *Russian public finance*, 294.   [42] Ribot, *Letters to a friend*, 90.
[43] Petit, *Finances extérieures*, 62, 71, 196–7.   [44] Brown, *Gold standard*, 100.

outstrip the ameliorative effects of comparatively small consignments of gold. By 1916 their expectations were proved well founded. But the export of gold did fulfil the Treasury's second aim, albeit in desperate circumstances.

In November 1915, after the pound had fallen to $4.56, the chancellor of the exchequer appointed an exchange committee formed of representatives of the Treasury and the Bank of England. Using an account in New York in the name of the Bank of England, underwritten by the Treasury, the committee purchased sterling for dollars in order to peg the exchange rate. Between 1915/16 and 1918/19 this account disbursed $2,021 million on exchange, compared with $5,932 million on supplies.[45] Furthermore, although the French never fought as hard to control their exchange rate, they derived benefit from the stability imparted to the sterling–dollar rate. If France had bought abroad without credit from Britain, French exchange on London would have been weakened, without any effects on the sterling–dollar or franc–dollar exchanges. The opportunity for profit through the sale of francs for dollars, dollars for pounds, and pounds for francs would have further depreciated the franc.[46] By the end of March 1916 the franc, for which par was 25.22, stood at 28.50 to the pound. Negotiations initiated by the central banks of the two powers, designed to get credit for French companies to buoy French exchange, and to secure gold for Britain, concluded that Britain should provide a credit of £120 million, a third of which was to be secured in gold. Ribot wanted more; Reginald McKenna, Lloyd George's successor in London, much less. He feared that fresh advances to France would hit the British exchange in the United States. The outcome of their meeting was that France received only £60 million, with a third still secured in gold. But, most importantly, the agreement was to be suspended if the pound fell below 27 francs. The effect, therefore, was not only to stabilize the sterling–franc exchange, but also to hitch France to the Anglo-American financial nexus.[47]

Overtly, the surprising aspect of this reconstruction of foreign exchanges was the co-operation of the United States. The European currencies did not depreciate against the dollar as fast as European wartime inflation exceeded American inflation. In other words, it was cheaper to buy goods in the United States than to produce them in Europe, because the European exchange rates were pegged at levels that overvalued the pound by 10 per cent (by 1918) and the franc by 35 per cent.[48] The effect was to pass on the price inflation of the belligerents to the neutrals, and so distribute the war's costs.

Voices in the United States objecting to the rise in domestic prices as a consequence of the belligerents' demands made little headway, because by the

[45] Morgan, *British financial policy*, 356–7; Sayers, *Bank of England*, i. 89–91.
[46] Brown, *Gold standard*, 75–6.
[47] Petit, *Finances extérieures*, 211–16; Ribot, *Letters to a friend*, 104–5.
[48] Eichengreen, *Golden fetters*, 73; Pigou, *Political economy of war*, 184–5.

time the effects were felt the United States was already too deeply implicated. Entente orders had pulled American industry out of recession, and what worried W. B. McAdoo, the US secretary of the Treasury, in August 1915 was that further depreciation of sterling would undermine Britain's ability to pay for its purchases.[49]

McAdoo was not a financier but (in the words of a British Treasury report of June 1917) 'a Wall Street failure with designs on the Presidency'.[50] His political ambitions aside, his long-term objective was to use Europe's indebtedness to the United States to enable the expansion of American business. Outwardly similar were the priorities of Benjamin Strong, governor of the Federal Reserve Bank in New York. Strong was anxious to use the opportunity which the war provided for the United States to prise from London's grasp control of foreign (and especially American) debt, and to establish an acceptance market in dollars, not in sterling. But his policy for doing this was to keep 'our rates as . . . the lowest in the world, [and] as . . . the steadiest in the world, and make the New York market so attractive that the business will come willingly'.[51] America had only established a centralized banking structure, the Federal Reserve System, in December 1913, as a consequence of the 1907 crisis. Its purpose, and one which Britain strongly endorsed, was the creation of an agency which would avert or minimize future domestic panics by greater international financial integration. Its sympathies were Republican, and its determination was to establish an identity independent of the US Treasury. In the early part of 1916 Strong toured Europe in order to give the Federal Reserve System a clear profile overseas. His discussions in March with the governor of the Bank of England, Lord Cunliffe, resulted in a memorandum of agreement and Britain's acceptance of the principle of Anglo-American financial equality. The declared aim was joint action to ensure stability in the post-war period; its necessary corollary during the war was America's collusion in the maintenance of British (and French) exchange.

The crunch for America, whether it was to follow McAdoo or Strong, and indeed the crunch for Britain came after the United States's entry to the war, in the summer of 1917. Britain was anxious that the United States should take over its role as Entente financier, but it did not want at the same time to forfeit its international position. McAdoo had to seek the approval of Congress for the legislation which would enable the American government to purchase Entente bonds. Some Congressmen disliked New York bankers as much as the British; furthermore, McAdoo needed Congress's support if he was to advance his political career. He objected to Britain using funds derived from the United States to pay off debts incurred in New York and to sustain sterling on the

---

[49] Nouailhat, *France et États Unis*, 283.
[50] Burk, *Economic History Review*, 2nd series, XXXII (1979), 408.
[51] Chandler, *Strong*, 91.

foreign exchanges. He was prepared to see Britain sell its remaining gold and suspend convertibility. Forced to choose, Keynes was prepared to overturn his previous policy: £305 million in gold had been sent to the United States since the war began in order to peg the rate of exchange, and Keynes now advised that convertibility be suspended before the Bank of England's gold was exhausted. Throughout June 1917 the crisis for Britain's wartime finances deepened, and a suspension of convertibility seemed imminent. Then, on 3 July the US president, Woodrow Wilson, agreed to new American advances, not without conditions but accepting the principle of American support for sterling. Because the American loans were short term, the Treasury continued on a knife-edge for the rest of the war. But the cardinal point was that the United States did not take the opportunity to force Britain off the gold standard.[52]

Strong's commitment to international financial stability did not, however, extend to a British approach to the hoarding of gold. By 1916 many American pundits, observing the neutrals' accumulation of gold as a result of the belligerents' adverse trade balances, favoured not the acquisition of gold but its repulsion. America could have allowed the free export of gold without undermining either the gold cover for its currency or the redeemability of credits based upon gold. However, Strong feared that after the war the gold acquired from Europe during it would be withdrawn, so causing the deflation of domestic credit. On 16 November 1914 the Federal Reserve act, by reducing the reserve requirements of the member banks, had created excess reserves of $465 million. Strong's policy was to promote this trend through the issue of Federal Reserve notes and the withdrawal of gold from public use and from the member banks. He also opposed the Treasury's accumulation of gold, as he felt the government could never redeem paper currency without deepening what would already be a crisis.[53] In 1916 the system held 28 per cent of the nation's gold. By the end of 1918 it controlled 74 per cent. Strong's policy was therefore adopted—albeit not for his reasons. It followed from American belligerency. The export of gold was banned in September 1917, partly so that there was no danger of its falling into German hands, but principally so that it could be a basis for the government's own domestic borrowings to fund its war effort.

This ambivalence about the desirability of gold was evident in the policies of other neutrals. Gold accumulation proved no longer to be a hedge against inflation. The use of gold as a basis for the money supply meant that the latter increased at a greater rate than the stock of purchasable commodities. Even in the United States, whose exports boomed, the growth of business between 1913 and 1918 was only 13 per cent as against a growth of actual money in circulation of 60 per cent and in bank deposits of 94 per cent.[54]

[52] Soutou, L'Or et le sang, 120–7, 344–53, 462–3; Burk, Economic History Review, 2nd series, XXXII (1979), 405–16.   [53] Chandler, Strong, 63, 83–6.   [54] Bogart, War costs, 356–7.

By 1916 the response of the Swiss and the Swedes was that they wanted no more of the belligerents' gold. Switzerland, whose gold cover grew from 46.8 per cent in July 1914 to 61.4 in December 1916, reduced it to 41.5 in October 1918. The note issue and the gold supply roughly doubled during the war. Sweden, which enjoyed a gold cover of 45.4 per cent in July 1914, managed to reduce it to 38.2 in April 1918, but still saw its holdings of gold more than double and its note issue triple. The experience of neutrals that were not so firm showed their gold cover increasing to 74 per cent (from 28.1) in the case of Spain and 74.9 (from 38.9) in that of the Netherlands. Both powers, while seeing their gold reserves increase by over 350 per cent, managed to restrict the increase of their note issue—Spain's grew by a third, Holland's by a half.[55]

The neutrals' implicit rejection of the gold standard did place the whole intellectual edifice in jeopardy at the end of 1916. Exchange rates, having been remarkably stable for most of that year, began to wobble as the Entente's trade imbalances with the United States multiplied. American entry to the war was therefore vital for the resilience of the idea of the gold standard. As the erstwhile leading neutral, it set a trend in favour of gold rather than of its rejection. Its own purchases in neutral countries and its embargo on gold exports drove up neutral exchanges; to stop lesser powers from hiving off, the United States (and the other Entente allies using American banking) demanded that the neutrals accord them credits.[56] And it was prepared to support the pivot of British policy, the maintenance of the sterling–dollar exchange. Therefore, while Britain acted as the mainstay of convertibility, America vindicated its judgement.

In the sense of an overarching international financial system, the gold standard did collapse in 1914 into a series of lesser financial units. But the importance of the Anglo-American nexus, and its commitment to a gold exchange system, meant that the basis for the revival of the pre-war gold standard seemed to survive. Pars on the foreign exchanges remained those set before the war, and at the armistice many responded to the expectation that that was the level to which they would return, whatever the financial predicaments of individual countries. The wartime practice changed in order to preserve the peacetime theory; countries went 'off' gold in 1914 precisely in order to be able to go 'on' it again when normality returned.

FINANCIAL MOBILIZATION

In Berlin on 2 August 1914 Hans Peter Hanssen, a Reichstag deputy, offered a waiter a 100-mark note. It was refused: the waiter complained that all his

---

[55] Helfferich, *Money*, 216–17; Brown, *Gold standard*, 46–7, 100, 104–5.
[56] Brown, *Gold standard*, 66–7.

customers were proffering large bills and he was running out of change. The following day Hanssen tried to pay for a meal with a 20-mark note. On this occasion the waiter grumbled, saying he would prefer silver, and went away to get change. Fifteen minutes later he returned empty-handed. Hanssen's solution was to ask for an extension of credit.[57]

In August 1914 such trials were not confined to Reichstag deputies in Berlin; they were commonplace throughout Europe. Only in Britain had cheques begun to replace cash in private transactions (it required the war to popularize them in France and Germany). Two pressures produced a shortage of cash. The first of these was hoarding by private citizens. As in Britain, it was more often the banks or their governments which—by a sudden rise in interest rates or by the threat of a moratorium—created the panic. Thus, a run on the banks was as likely to be a pre-emptive response to pressure not to withdraw money as a considered initiative in the face of international crisis. The second constraint, however, was real enough. As the armies of Europe mobilized, their need for ready money to buy horses and to secure fodder and provisions sapped the liquidity of the states they were defending.

Germany, with its commitment to rapid deployment and swift victory, was not unmindful of this aspect of its military preparations. But in some respects its response remained extraordinarily rudimentary, rooted in the experiences of 1870–1 and a desire to avoid their repetition.[58]

Frederick the Great's conservative economics had included the accumulation of bullion in a war chest to finance future conflict. In 1871, after the defeat of France, Germany used the indemnity it received to establish a Reich war chest of 120 million marks in the Julius Tower at Spandau. This sum remained unchanged until the 1913 army law, which doubled it to 240 million gold marks, and threw in 120 million in silver for good measure. By 1914 205 million marks had been raised towards the new total. The arrangement was doubly absurd. In peacetime it tied up money unproductively, so that it neither earned interest nor was a basis for note issue. In war, the provision was too limited for even the most optimistic of short-war advocates. The Reichsbank in 1913 concluded that mobilization alone would cost 1,800 million marks; actual expenditure in the month of August 1914 totalled 2,047 million marks.[59]

German estimates of total war costs varied so wildly as to be meaningless. In 1905 the optimistic General Blume suggested between 4,680 million marks and 5,760 million; four years earlier J. Renauld had reckoned on an annual

[57] Hanssen, *Diary of a dying empire*, 14, 17–18.

[58] Reichsarchiv, *Der Weltkrieg: Kriegsrüstung und Kriegwirtschaft*, i. 417; see, in general, i. 417–79, and documents in app., 293–354.

[59] Burchardt, *Friedenswirtschaft und Kriegsvorsorge*, 8; Helfferich, *Weltkrieg*, 211. On German financial preparations and mobilization in general, see Roesler, *Finanzpolitik*, 18–54; Lotz, *Deutsche Staatsfinanzwirtschaft*, 16–26; Zilch, *Reichsbank*, 83–141. There are also important observations in Holtfrerich, *German inflation*, 102–16.

requirement of 22,000 million a year. In 1913 the general staff put its campaigning costs at 10,000 to 11,000 million marks a year. In the event, Germany's annual expenditure during the war averaged 45,700 million marks.[60] However, most official calculations were confined to the period of mobilization only. In 1891 Johannes von Miquel, the Prussian finance minister, managed to establish an annual review by the minister of war of the financial resources available for the first thirty days of hostilities. This, it was felt, would take the war up to the first German victory, after which—as in 1870—German credit would be secure on the foreign exchanges.[61]

To bridge the gap between the holdings of the state (the war chest plus other cash balances) and the anticipated mobilization costs, the government planned to turn to the Reichsbank for credit. Founded in 1875, not least with the needs of war in mind, the bank was independent of the state but obliged by law to provide it with services free of charge. The bank was required to cover at least a third of its note issue with gold, coin, or treasury bills. This—the gold standard—was the rock on which the Reichsbank's proposals for war foundered. In 1891 the bank wanted to issue smaller-denomination notes in peacetime so as to wean the public gradually from its reliance on coin, and to make preparations to suspend convertibility. Miquel opposed: notes, he argued, should not have the character of money. The smallest note in circulation remained 100 marks. All that could be agreed on was the maximum compatible with the maintenance of the gold standard: on the outbreak of hostilities the issue of short-term treasury bills should be increased, and these, together with the war chest and other government balances, should be transferred to the Reichsbank to form the basis for an expanded note issue.

However, in the decade immediately before 1914 the policy of the Reichsbank changed sufficiently to make it far better prepared for war. This shift of direction could be taken as evidence of Germany's role in the war's origins. Certainly, the need to cope with the crisis of mobilization was part of the argument for change. But in 1904, when a law to suspend convertibility in time of war was drafted, the potential needs of an economy at war did not override the immediate desiderata of an economy at peace. Proposals to increase the war chest and to introduce smaller-denomination notes were both rejected. Twenty-mark and 50-mark notes were at last authorized at a crown council in February 1906. Two hundred million marks' worth were for immediate circulation, and 800 million were to be held in reserve. The basis for this decision was the revelation that 2,500 million marks would be needed for the first three months of hostilities (1,300 million in the first thirty days), and that the Reichsbank had neither enough gold nor enough notes to cover this. But the problems thereby addressed show the interaction between the possible but distant requirements of war and the immediate difficulties of German finance, and that it was the urgency of the latter which gave direction to the solution of the former.

The expansion of German business was constrained by a lack of liquidity. And in 1907 the Reichsbank's support of the Bank of England reduced its gold cover to 41.3 per cent of note issue, perilously close to the 33 per cent legal requirement. The response of the bank's governor, Rudolf Havenstein, was to create a buffer against future crises by withdrawing gold from circulation, and by expanding alternative types of currency. In 1909 the 20- and 50-mark notes were made legal tender, and the use of cheques as exchange and the introduction of postal orders were both designed to reduce the demand for coin. Between 1908 and 1913 the Reichsbank's note issue increased from 1,951 million marks to 2,574 million. In addition, the circulation of treasury notes (*Reichskassenscheine*) more than doubled, from 62 million marks to 148 million. Clearing accounts handled cashless transactions worth 163,632 million marks in 1908 and 379,157 million in 1913. One inflationary trend was in place before the war.[62]

More striking evidence of the relative balance between the priorities of peacetime finance and those of wartime is provided by the attitude of the German Treasury. Given the widespread contemporary recognition of the problems of financial mobilization, the Treasury's neglect of the issue was remarkable—and was commented on even at the time. The second Morocco crisis caused major falls on the Berlin stock exchange in September 1911, and the banks said they could not finance a war without borrowing; the French exploited the situation by withdrawing short-term funds and so causing a liquidity crisis.[63] But the Treasury spurned a call in 1911 for a financial general staff; its profile in the standing committee on the economic problems of mobilization, established in December 1912 by the minister of the interior, was low.[64] Indeed, its behaviour provides further evidence of the limited impact of the resolutions of the so-called 'war council' of that month. Adolf Wermuth, secretary of state for the Treasury from July 1909 to March 1912, was more preoccupied with restraining the pressure of defence spending on the current budget than in making future provision. Wermuth lost his battle, but the financial significance of the 1913 army law resided in its projected impact on Reich expenditure over five years of peace. The law did rather less to address the finances of a Reich at war. It doubled the war chest, and it increased the circulation of short-term treasury bills by 120 million marks. But Havenstein reckoned that, in view of the public's hoarding of gold in the 1911 Moroccan

[62] Feldman, *Great disorder*, 28.   [63] Stevenson, *Armaments and the coming of war*, 193.
[64] Zilch, *Reichsbank*, 83–8; Burchardt, *Friedenswirtschaft*, 74; C. von Delbrück, *Wirtschaftliche Mobilmachung*, 64, 77.

crisis, 3,500 million marks would now be needed to cover the period of mobilization.[65]

His worries were increased by the growth of the German credit banks. Deposits tripled and acceptances almost doubled in the decade before the war. This expansion was predicated almost entirely on the banks' close relationship with German business; they were not in the practice of holding either treasury bills or other reserves to cover their own obligations. Havenstein was therefore concerned that in a crisis the banks would deplete the Reichsbank's gold reserves precisely when it itself needed them to fulfil the purposes of the government. Although on 10 June 1914 the Berlin bankers rejected Havenstein's suggestion that they should accept a 10 per-cent liquidity requirement, they saw the wisdom of permitting the Reichsbank to act as a controlling authority. Therefore, it was the Reichsbank and not the credit banks which dictated policy in late July.[66]

Financial circles were made aware of the possibility of mobilization on, or soon after, 18 July 1914.[67] As in Britain, therefore, any sense of crisis began with the banks more than with their customers. The banks' resolve to persuade their clients to deal in paper fostered the clients' determination to do the opposite. The emergency (and unauthorized) issue of 5- and 10-mark notes deepened fears more than it eased circulation. Paper currency was exchanged at a 10 per cent discount, and was refused even by large institutions like the railways. Small savers stormed the banks on 27 July. About 7,000 depositors in Berlin withdrew 935,000 marks, and the totals were only slightly lower on the following day: between 27 July and 8 November 1914 11 million marks were withdrawn but only 2.5 million paid in.[68]

The pressure was, however, almost entirely domestic. Being comparatively isolated, the German money market was spared the flurry of foreign withdrawals. Between 23 July and 31 July 1914 the Reichsbank's holdings of gold only fell from 1,356.9 million marks to 1,253.2 million.[69] To check withdrawals, commercial interest rates rose from 1.5 per cent to 4.5 per cent by 1 August, and the Reichsbank's discount rate was fixed at 6 per cent on 31 July. By 7 August, partly through the addition of the war chest, the gold losses of the last week of July had been nominally recovered. Gold reserves rose 225 million marks in August as a whole.

On 4 August the Reichstag approved a package of proposals, including a short-term credit of 5,000 million marks secured on treasury bills lodged in the

---

[65] Zilch, *Reichsbank*, 126–7.

[66] Gall *et al.*, *Deutsche Bank*, 130–3; de Cecco, *International gold standard*, 110; Ferguson, *Pity of war*, 33.

[67] Ferguson, *Paper and iron*, 99.

[68] Verhey, 'The "spirit of 1914"', 132, 135, 187–8; also Raithel, *Das 'Wunder' der inneren Einheit*, 225; Mai, *Das Ende des Kaiserreichs*, 10.

[69] Zilch, *Reichsbank*, 139–41.

Reichsbank. The convertibility of both notes and treasury bills was suspended: it was argued that the international element in the gold standard was temporarily redundant, and that domestic confidence could be sustained by an enhancement of the status of the Reichsbank and by the knowledge that the one-third cover for notes still pertained. One of the symbols of this changed relationship between the Reichsbank and the government was the bank's release from the tax on any uncovered notes. Treasury bills and treasury bonds were both declared secondary reserves against note issue. In addition, the task of providing credit to the private sector was delegated to loan banks, *Darlehenskassen*, created specially for the purpose.

The *Darlehenskassen* were another symbol of the continuity in German thinking on war finance. Prussia had used them in 1848, 1866, and 1870. Their purpose was to ensure liquidity so that business and local government could continue without adding to the demands on the collateral of the Reichsbank. They were authorized to give loans of up to 50 per cent of the value of goods, and up to 75 per cent on stocks and shares. Their interest rate was fixed to fall above that of the discount banks and below that of the Reichsbank. They were authorized to issue their own bills, *Darlehenskassenscheinen*, 550 million marks-worth of which had been printed in preparation for the possibility of war in 1912.[70] While not legal tender, they were exchangeable for notes (but not, of course, for gold) at the Reichsbank. Their initial circulation was fixed at 1,500 million marks, but the Bundesrat was empowered to raise this—which it did. The *Darlehenskassen* proved as attractive to the communes and states of Germany as to the business world. Cut out from the normal loan market by the Reich's needs, they could now get credit and at a rate lower than that of the Reichsbank. The effect was indirectly to draw their reserves, from whose exploitation the Reichsbank would otherwise have been excluded, into the base for an increase in note issue. The Reichsbank could substitute *Darlehenskassenscheinen* (as well as treasury bills) for bullion in the one-third reserve for its notes. Moreover, in practice if not in theory, the *Darlehenskassenscheinen* themselves became currency. Their low denominations (initially down to 5-mark notes, and from 31 August 1914 1- and 2-mark notes) filled the need for small change which had so preoccupied Hanssen and his waiters at the beginning of the month.[71]

The *Darlehenskassen* were a device to help bridge the shift from peacetime finance to wartime finance. Germany played down the significance of this shift. Alone of the major belligerents, it eschewed the declaration of a general moratorium. But this was more of a gesture to boost confidence and ensure credit than it was a reality. Individual states were allowed to take their own

---

[70] Ferguson, *Paper and iron*, 117.
[71] Holtfrerich, *German inflation*, 115; Roesler, *Finanzpolitik*, 41–3; Knauss, *Kriegsfinanzierung*, 54–5, 57.

decisions. The law of 4 August permitted the postponement of payments, and on 6 August the settlement of bills and cheques was extended to thirty days. Pre-war debts could be put off for between three and six months. The stock exchange, which closed on 30 July, was subject to a moratorium on 14 August which was not lifted until November 1915. Officially, the stock exchange never reopened—although in practice trading, particularly in the shares of arms firms, persisted.[72]

The process of German mobilization had worked a more fundamental revolution in the mechanism of German credit than was realized at the time. The Reichsbank's reserves were increased through treasury bills and *Darlehenskassenscheinen*. On 7 July, against a note circulation of 2,192 million marks were entered 1,626 million marks in gold and 1,025 million marks in treasury bills and other forms of security. On 31 August a note circulation of 4,235 million marks was covered by 1,606 million marks in gold and 4,897 million marks in treasury bills, *Darlehenskassenscheinen*, and exchange bills. The bills served as the basis for the growth in currency, but were themselves not subject to restriction. The supply of money had become effectively autonomous. Total German circulation of all types rose from 5,893 million marks in May 1914 to 8,436 million in September.

Currency inflation was indeed the simplest and most effective means of shifting to a war economy. Britain had incorporated elements of the same approach, particularly in the issue of treasury notes. But in Germany the possibility of the quantity of money itself creating inflation was not seriously entertained. Inflation, in German theory, could only be the consequence of a shortage of commodities, which would generate rising prices. The control of inflation could therefore be managed by the control of prices. And the law of 4 August included the power to fix prices.[73]

Inflation also played an important role in the financial mobilization of Germany's principal ally, Austria-Hungary. And yet the overt manifestations were different, as the shortage of small change was much more persistent. The army's need for cash was a clear lesson of the partial mobilization during the Bosnian crisis, but no preparations were made to meet the sudden demand for currency in August 1914. Although temporary use of 20- and 10-crown notes had been permitted on occasion, the smallest note in normal circulation was 50 crowns. A decision on 14 August to issue notes in denominations of 5 crowns, 2 crowns, and 1 crown was never fully implemented. The 2-crown note was available on 18 August 1914, but so hurried had been its printing that the Hungarian version had mistakes. The 5-crown note was not produced. In May 1915, to meet the demand for coin, a 'new silver' coin (in reality 50 per cent

---

[72] Knauss, *Kriegsfinanzierung*, 33–4, 56–7; Dix, *Wirtschaftskrieg*, 213–15; C. von Delbrück, *Wirtschaftliche Mobilmachung*, 109–10, 118–19.

[73] Krohn, 'Geldtheorien in Deutschland', 44–5; Roesler, *Finanzpolitik*, 46–8, 52, 216.

copper, 40 per cent zinc, and 10 per cent nickel) was minted, but the supply of copper began to run out in 1916. From March of that year small coins were fashioned from iron. Finally, in December 1916 the 1-crown note made its belated appearance. Only now was the need for small-denomination currency fully satisfied.[74]

Ironically, rather than help Austro-Hungarian financial preparedness for war, the Bosnian crisis undermined it. In 1908 Austria-Hungary was feeling the benefits of five years of industrial growth. Interest rates were set at 4 per cent in March, and in 1909 gold cover averaged 70 per cent of note issue. But, despite their best intentions, the finance ministers of Austria and Hungary found themselves unable to pay for the partial mobilization of 1909 out of tax income, and had to resort to treasury bills and an increase in the national debt. The spurt in arms spending which followed meant that by 1912 the state owed 541 million crowns in government stocks, against an average of 149 million in the decade up to 1909. Capital became increasingly hard to find, especially as the government's needs competed with those of industry. Interest rates rose to 6 per cent in November 1912, and liquidity problems either dampened business expansion or encouraged a search for funds overseas, so contributing to Austria's balance of payments' deficit. Then the 1911 Moroccan crisis and the 1912 Balkan war took their toll. Foreign (particularly French) capital departed, and the confidence of domestic investors was shaken, leading them to place their capital overseas. The Austro-Hungarian Bank had to sell gold abroad to defend the exchange rate. In 1912 its gold cover averaged 45 per cent, and by the year's end had fallen to 1,210 million crowns against a note issue of 2,816 million. Military mobilization was clearly a costly exercise—and, some argued, war itself could not be more damaging.[75] One of the strongest exponents of this view was the common finance minister, Bilinski; for him, finance had become the servant of war even while peace still prevailed.[76]

The task of funding mobilization had been given to the Austro-Hungarian Bank in 1887. The bank was a private company, although its governor was appointed by the emperor on ministerial advice, and the board included representatives of the two monarchies. It was obliged to maintain a cover of two-fifths of its note issue, although this could include up to 60 million crowns in British, French, and German deposits. The effect of the run on gold was that by 1912 the bank could not fund mobilization and adhere to the terms of the Bank act. The requirement for two-fifths cover reduced the possible additional note issue to 950 million crowns. The cost of the first three months of

[74] Popovics, *Geldwesen*, 34, 56, 94–8; Müller, *Finanzielle Mobilmachung*, 28–30. These are the principal sources on Austro-Hungarian war finance, together with März, *Austrian banking*.

[75] Williamson, *Austria-Hungary*, 157–9; März, *Austrian banking*, 27–32, 99–100; Popovics, *Geldwesen*, 27–9, 39.

[76] Leslie, *Wiener Beiträge*, XX (1993), 360, 363, 367.

mobilization was estimated at 1,850 million crowns, without any allowance for an intervening increase in prices.[77]

The fact that war would require the suspension of the Bank act was emphasized by the governor, Alexander Popovics, at a conference of the banks and of representatives of the finance ministries in Budapest in November 1912. The conference thought that the normal credit machinery—existing cash, the placing of loans at home and abroad—could produce 800 million crowns for the first eight days, and that thereafter 1,700 million crowns could be borrowed from the clearing banks (*Notenbanken*). But the talk remained general. No draft laws or regulations were prepared. And consideration was given only to the first three months of war.[78] Privately, the finance ministries thought that the empire could not fund hostilities for more than one or two months.[79]

Austro-Hungarian accounts showed some signs of stabilization in 1913–14. Gold reserves picked up, and the interest rate was reduced to 4 per cent in March 1914. But Popovics had had insufficient time to reduce Austria's overseas holdings or to win back domestic capital. Furthermore, the response of the Austro-Hungarian Bank in the course of the July crisis was always late and inadequate. Popovics's problem was that of Austria-Hungary writ small: he did not know whether he should be anticipating partial mobilization, general mobilization, or war, and he was subject to a timetable that was constantly foreshortened rather than lengthened.

On 19 July he was warned that an ultimatum would be delivered to Serbia, but was told that this would happen on 25 July. On 20 July he learnt that the deadline for the ultimatum was now 23 July, and that he should anticipate the mobilization of eight corps. As a result of his experience in the earlier crises he knew that this could not be achieved by normal credit operations. Nonetheless, the easier conditions in the money market encouraged the banks to accept that the message should be one of calm and continuity. Foreign withdrawals of gold had begun after Franz Ferdinand's assassination. The bank raised the interest rate to 5 per cent on 26 July, but still the withdrawals continued. Its holdings of gold and foreign exchange fell by 148 million crowns in the last week of July. Nonetheless, Popovics had room for manoeuvre. He had actually reduced liquidity in the first three weeks of the month—total circulation had fallen by about 200 million crowns[80]—and therefore a decision to print 400 million crowns on 23 July to meet the army's cash needs still left a cover—despite the outflow of gold—of 58 per cent on 26 July.[81]

Then, on 30 July, the ground shifted again. General mobilization was ordered for 31 July. So far provision had been made to cover the costs of partial mobilization for fifteen days from existing sources. The finance ministers of the

[77] Popovics, *Geldwesen*, 23–5, 32, 39–40.   [78] Ibid. 34–7.
[79] Regele, *Conrad*, 155; N. Stone, 'Austria-Hungary', in E. R. May (ed.), *Knowing one's enemies*, 50.
[80] Müller, *Finanzielle Mobilmachung*, 25–6.   [81] März, *Austrian banking*, 130.

two monarchies had begun discussions with a view to borrowing 600 million crowns from an Austrian banking consortium and 340 million from a Hungarian consortium in the event of partial mobilization running beyond fifteen days. The governments planned to borrow at a rate of 5 per cent and repay their debt on 1 February 1917. Now 2,000 million crowns, 1,272 million from Austria and 728 million from Hungary, were required; the state would pay interest at 1 per cent and the Austro-Hungarian Bank, through whom the loan would be channelled, was relieved of the burden of tax payments on note circulation.

On 31 July the interest rate was raised to 6 per cent, and on 2 August, following the Bank of England's rise to 10 per cent, to 8 per cent. But Austria-Hungary's only real protection from the run on gold was to come off the gold standard. On 5 August the policy settled between the finance ministers and the bank reserved gold for military and state use; foreign payments were banned. On the previous day the Bank act was suspended, relieving the Austro-Hungarian Bank of the need for its 40 per cent gold cover. The security on the bank's note circulation now became the loans which the bank provided the government to enable it to wage the war. By the year's end the money in circulation had increased 91 per cent on its 31 July figure.[82] When current account deposits are included and the comparison shifted back to 23 July, the total circulation had grown from under 2,500 million crowns to over 6,500 million.[83]

The confusion of Austria-Hungary's financial mobilization was compounded by its use of the moratorium, first imposed on private transactions for a two-week period on 31 July. It created panic and contributed to the shortage of small change. But it was then extended to 30 September, to allow people to accustom themselves to the new economic conditions. By the time of the third extension, on 27 September to 30 November, creditors were becoming restive. The moratorium was therefore partial, providing for the settlement of 25 per cent of a debt after 15 October. At the same time the legal machinery was set up to protect small businesses which had valid reasons for not satisfying their creditors; the effect was to allow enterprises that would not have been viable in peace to limp on in war. Up to 31 August 1917 2,552 concerns became subject to this legislation, but of 1,885 cases actually referred to the courts only 110 resulted in bankruptcy. The moratorium itself was extended three more times, on 25 November 1914, 25 January 1915, and 22 December 1915, each extension permitting settlement of further tranches of debt (normally 25 per cent of a demand at a time). The moratorium was not fully lifted until 31 December 1916. Inflation over this period meant that many debts were effectively wiped out by the time they fell due.[84]

[82] Gratz and Schüller, *Wirtschaftliche Zusammenbruch*, 181.
[83] März, *Austrian banking*, 141; the key account of the crisis as a whole is Popovics, *Geldwesen*, 41–58.
[84] Müller, *Finanzielle Mobilmachung*, 12–24; Popovics, *Geldwesen*, 161–2, gives different dates for the later stages.

The impact of the moratorium on private credit had national repercussions. Savings banks, deposits having been withdrawn in the period up to 31 July 1914, could not win them back again until 1915. The government, having moved to credit operations at the outset, found that the banks could not unlock their deposits, and—after securing its first advance—had to turn directly to the Austro-Hungarian Bank for funds. By the same token, loans could not be floated for public subscription.

Partly in order to meet this last need, but principally to finance business, Austria-Hungary aped its German ally and set up *Kriegsdarlehenskassen* on 20 September 1914. The aim was to meet the demand for cash and at the same time to furnish credit against exports whose markets had been cut off by the war. However, the shortage of goods in relation to purchasing power meant that commodities tended to find a domestic market: sugar was the only major product to be mortgaged in quantity. More significant in the books of the *Kriegsdarlehenskassen* were shares (by the end of 1915 they had accounted in Austria for advances of 140.77 million crowns, as against 18.7 million in goods and 0.96 million in book credits). With the empire's stock exchanges having closed after 24 July,[85] assets had become frozen at an early stage in the crisis. Initially the *Kriegsdarlehenskassen* would only take over the rather conservative range of stocks admitted as security by the banks before the war, but the list of negotiable shares was gradually extended. The *Kriegsdarlehenskassen* issued in exchange non-interest-bearing treasury notes, which were effectively treated as money and were exchangeable for cash at the Austro-Hungarian Bank. However, the *Kriegsdarlehenskassen* did not have the inflationary effects of their German prototypes. The maximum issue was set at 500 million crowns for Austria and 290 million for Hungary. By the end of 1915 231.27 million crowns had been disbursed in Austria, but only 105.36 million was still in circulation. In Hungary the peak demand of 22 million crowns had already fallen to 16 million by the end of 1915. As liquidity returned and the moratorium eased, and as savings banks' deposits recovered, so the *Kriegsdarlehenskassen* became redundant and their loans repaid. In 1916 only 62 million crowns were issued in Austria. The quantity of notes in circulation never even approached the legal maximum until the final collapse of the empire in October 1918.[86]

In Germany and Austria-Hungary the establishment of the *Darlehenskassen* relieved the central banks of the day-to-day deposit business, thus enabling them to concentrate on a much closer relationship with the state. In neither

---

[85] Most histories, e.g. Popovics, *Geldwesen*, 46–7, and Reichsarchiv, *Weltkrieg: Kriegsrüstung*, i. 478, give 27 July. However, März, *Austrian banking*, 141–2, says the stock exchanges were closed on 24 July for three days: 25 and 26 July fell on Saturday and Sunday.

[86] Müller, *Finanzielle Mobilmachung*, 72–5; Popovics, *Geldwesen*, 86–90; März, *Austrian banking*, 154–5.

Russia nor France was this the case. In the two Entente powers the central banks simultaneously funded their states' mobilization needs and supported the continuation of commerce.

Nonetheless, when considering Austria-Hungary's mobilization, Popovics—even in 1925—could look ruefully across to the comparatively greater financial preparedness of his country's major foe in 1914, Russia.[87] In the run-up to the outbreak of the war Austria was struggling to recoup its gold reserves, while Russia's monetary base looked impressively strong. On 29 July 1914 2,357 million roubles were in issue: 1,633.4 million of them were in notes, and 48.2 per cent of those were in small denominations. Only 463.7 million roubles in gold were circulating, and 260 million in other metal. Most of Russia's gold was in the bank: 1,603.8 million roubles were held in the State Bank at home and 140.7 million abroad or in foreign drafts.[88] The note cover was thus approximately 100 per cent.

Like Germany in 1870–1 and Austria-Hungary in 1908–9, Russia had an experience of financial mobilization on which to draw. On 14 January 1906, as a consequence of the Russo-Japanese War and the 1905 revolution, Russia's gold reserve was reduced to 700 million roubles against a note issue of 1,207.5 million. But Russia was not forced off the gold standard. Foreign loan stock boosted the gold reserves back up to 1,190.6 million roubles within a year, as against a note issue of 1,194.5 million. Russia paid over the odds for its foreign money (as it kept interest rates high), and it needed a lot of it; therefore, despite its grain exports, it had a balance of payments deficit. In addition, the costs of military re-equipment and re-expansion after 1905 pushed the budget into deficit, even if the size of the deficit was obscured.

Russia was financially more ready for war in 1914 than this recent history might suggest. The pace of its economic growth was reducing its burden of debt in real terms. In 1913 increased state revenues and a good harvest meant that the surplus on the ordinary account wiped out the debt on the extraordinary account. Moreover, its response to the confrontations and mobilizations in the Balkans was not the hawkishness of Bilinski but renewed caution. On 27 March 1914 Peter Bark, the finance minister, declared that 'at the present time we are far less prepared for war than ten years ago'.[89] He was wrong, but it was this conservative approach to monetary matters which determined Russia's pecuniary preparedness in 1914.

Russia's international credit was of short duration and its fiduciary reputation slender. Witte had established a gold standard in 1897 far more rigorous than that applied elsewhere: foreign confidence was essential if Russia was to attract foreign investment. Thus, the State Bank was required to maintain a

[87] Popovics, *Geldwesen*, 40–1.   [88] Michelson *et al.*, *Russian public finance*, 364.
[89] Spring, *Slavonic and East European Review*, LXVI (1988), 570.

minimum gold cover of half its note circulation; if the latter exceeded 600 million roubles, then the cover for the excess was to be of equal value. The greatest demand for notes fell in the autumn, when the crops were harvested but before overseas remittances were received. Therefore the gradual increase in the State Bank's gold reserves in the first half of 1914 reflected its desired annual cycle.[90]

The determination with which Russia cleaved to the gold standard displayed a greater awareness than was necessarily shown elsewhere of its two distinct functions—its external as opposed to its internal role. On 5 August Russia suspended specie payments, thus making its notes unconvertible. But the State Bank's own holdings of gold only dipped slightly, to 1,558 million roubles in January 1915, and by 14 January 1916 had reached a high of 1,613 million. During 1916 gold reserves fell, to 90 million roubles in May, but domestic production brought them back up to 1,474 million in January 1917. What forced Russia finally to abandon the international gold standard in March 1917 was the domestic depreciation of the rouble, not an inability to export gold abroad.

On 5 August 1914 the State Bank was authorized to issue 1,200 million roubles above the legal maximum. The Treasury, with cash balances of only 580 million roubles in hand, was, therefore, turning to the State Bank to fund mobilization. In return, the bank discounted short-term treasury bills, but never to the same value as the notes required by the Treasury. Thus, on 1 January 1915 the State Bank held 656 million roubles in treasury bills, but the note circulation had increased by 1,171 million roubles.[91]

In addition to its role as a central bank tied to a close relationship with the government, the State Bank was also the linchpin in commercial credit. Therefore, the peacetime official rate of interest was—unusually for a central bank—below the market rate: in 1912 the State Bank's rate was already 5 per cent, and the market rate was 6 or 6.5 per cent. With rates set deliberately high to attract foreign funds, an increase in the official rate to 6 per cent on 29 July was not unsettling. The message of the State Bank was calm and continuity. The moratorium was limited and brief. Its only major sign was the closure of the stock exchange on 29 July. As the government feared a flood of redeemed Russian securities from abroad it remained closed, except for a limited period in February 1917.

However, in the five years before 1914 Russian commercial banking had expanded significantly. In 1908 2,969 million roubles were held in deposits and current accounts; by 1913 the total was 5,228 million. In 1909 the share capital of the thirty-one commercial banks was 236.6 million roubles. In 1910 eleven of these banks increased their capital by 70 million roubles, and in 1911

[90] Michelson *et al.*, *Russian public finance*, 342–66.
[91] Claus, *Kriegswirtschaft Russlands*, 16; also more generally 14–19.

thirteen banks increased theirs by 80 million and in 1912 by 100 million. In 1912 there were 776 credit houses, of which 172 had been founded in 1911: their capital totalled 120 million roubles as against deposits of 500 million roubles. This rapid growth relieved the State Bank of much of its commercial business, but it underlined its role as banker to the banks. The expansion relied on the State Bank for credit, and in 1912 the government slowed its pace by insisting that new banks pay between 25 and 50 per cent of their original capital to the State Bank.

The outbreak of the war prompted a massive withdrawal of deposits.[92] Thus the State Bank, while simultaneously addressing the needs of the Treasury, was also required to support the commercial banks. Some of the deposits withdrawn from the credit houses were reinvested in the State Bank. But in the month between 14 July and 14 August the State Bank's accounts showed an increase in bills and other securities from 521.8 million to 963.8 million roubles, 425 million of which were deposited after the outbreak of the war.[93] Thereafter the position stabilized. Funds were reinvested, and by January 1915 deposits were approaching their pre-war levels. But the commercial sector was slow to extend credit to industry. Lending remained below its pre-war level throughout the second half of 1914 and all of 1915. Not until 1916 did this aspect of banking activity revive. Thus, the war industries too turned to the State Bank.

In France, as in Russia, the central bank performed both commercial and state functions. But the burdens on the Banque de France were that much greater than they were on the Russian State Bank, undertaken as they were in the context of overt confusion in public finance, compounded by a particularly fierce moratorium.

However, France was like Germany in one respect. The experience of 1870 determined the obligations imposed on the Banque de France in the event of another war. Then the bank had been relieved of its obligation to redeem notes for currency, and had made advances to the state in the shape of an increased note issue. On 11 November 1911, in the aftermath of the second Moroccan crisis, Lucien Klotz, the finance minister of the day, put these principles into more concrete form. Convertibility would be suspended. The Banque de France was to advance the government 2,900 million francs. As security, the bank would receive treasury bills, paying 1 per cent interest, with an initial life of three months but renewable. Five hundred million francs of the advance would be immediately distributed throughout the country as credits to fund mobilization. To meet the anticipated demand for small change, the bank prepared a supply of 5-franc and 20-franc notes. On 30 November 1911 a

---

[92] The figures given by Claus, *Kriegswirtschaft Russlands*, 41–2, and Michelson *et al.*, *Russian public finance*, 375–6, show the position after it had stabilized. But see, in general, Claus, 39–48, and Bernatzky in Michelson *et al.*, 354–8, 374–6.

[93] Claus, *Kriegswirtschaft Russlands*, 17.

comparable arrangement, this time for an advance of 100 million francs, was reached with the Bank of Algeria.[94]

The end of July 1914 found the Banque de France, unlike the government, in a financially healthy position. Its concentration of gold gave it a 69 per-cent cover on a note issue of 6,800 million francs. France did not require its central bank to have a fixed gold reserve. But public confidence in the bank and its notes was amply justified by a perusal of its accounts. In addition to its 4,141 million francs in gold it held 625 million francs in silver, 1,373 million francs in Paris securities, 1,071 million francs in its branches, and 744 million francs in advances on shares. Its active balances, therefore, totalled 7,954 million francs, against notes actually in circulation of 6,683 million.[95] In addition, France had healthy overseas balances, and further gold—to the tune of 4,500 million francs—in private hands.[96]

The public's faith in the bank, however, was not matched by its faith in the nation's capacity to organize itself for war. Between 27 and 31 July 1,500 million francs were withdrawn from the banks.[97] In Pau savings banks withdrawals rose fourfold on 27 July, sixfold on the 28th, and twentyfold on the 29th.[98] On 30 July the savings banks limited withdrawals to a maximum of 50 francs every fortnight. On 31 July a one-month moratorium was imposed on all trade settlements. The interest rate was raised from 4 per cent to 6 per cent on the same day. But the banks were complaining that they were rich in paper and poor in specie. So, on 1 August they too became subject to a moratorium. On 5 August convertibility was suspended. On 6 August withdrawals on deposits were limited to a maximum of 250 francs and 5 per cent of the balance. On 9 August the trade and banking moratoriums were combined. On 14 August a moratorium was imposed on rents. Six days later the bank rate was lowered to 5 per cent. But further moratoriums followed. On 30 August all local-government bodies were relieved of the obligation to redeem debt, and on 23 September they no longer had to pay interest or dividends. On 27 September insurance companies became subject to a moratorium, although most had already been postponing premiums for the previous six weeks.[99]

Many of these moratoriums could be justified, at least temporarily, because of the confusion created in financial transactions by the operations of war. Those living in occupied areas could not remit rent to those residing elsewhere in France; war-related damage to property would require assessment and arbitration. And there was the threat to Paris itself. Many banks had decamped,

[94] Jèze and Truchy, War finance of France, 190, 228–30, 236–7; Klotz, De la guerre à la paix, 16–17.
[95] Charbonnet, Politique financière de la France, 36; Duroselle, La France, 206.
[96] Petit, Finances extérieures, 74.
[97] Becker, 1914, 513–15; Duroselle, La France, 217.
[98] Pourcher, Les Jours de guerre, 58.
[99] Knauss, Kriegsfinanzierung, 66; Fisk, French public finance, 80.

along with the government, and could not be traced by their account-holders. Between 18 August and 3 September 36 million francs in silver, 4,000 million francs in gold, and 14 million francs in share certificates were removed from the capital to the south-west.[100]

But on 24 November 1914, when the situation had stabilized, the government, instead of removing the moratoriums, announced that they would continue until the end of the war. Although that in Algeria was lifted in March 1916,[101] in metropolitan France they persisted until December 1920. Of course there were modifications. On 16 August 1914 war ministry contractors were allowed funds to buy raw materials or to pay wages. However, there was no provision for investment in new plant, and on 29 August their right of withdrawal was modified to the extent that they received advances direct from the state.[102] The same decree on 29 August charged debtors with accrued interest and therefore encouraged them to settle if they could. The maximum withdrawal from a deposit was raised to 1,000 francs and 50 per cent of the balance by 27 October. But the net effect remained deadening for industry and for commerce. Employers could not buy raw materials and workers were not paid. Deposits flowed out but not in: the discount portfolio of the Crédit Lyonnais on 31 March 1915 was half its end-of-year total in 1913 (746 million francs as against 1,518 million), and its deposits had fallen from 913 million francs to 620 million. Nationally, all credit houses showed a decline in deposits from 7,500 million francs to 4,270 million in 1914.[103] The total annual house rent that remained unpaid was reckoned to be 1,500 million francs.[104] In the short term landlords confronted bankruptcy, but in the long run the calling in of the accumulated debt threatened tenants with penury.[105] The bad debtor was protected, the creditor was not. The French economy carried an immense burden for the rest of the war.

Gradually the banks and other institutions began to disregard the moratorium. But, particularly in 1914–15, it was the Banque de France that enabled any semblance of economic activity to continue. The bank's commercial portfolio doubled between 27 July and 1 August 1914, from 1,583 million francs to 3,041 million. By 1 October it was carrying 4,476 million francs in deferred bills. This total declined as banks elsewhere defied the moratorium. On 31 December 1915 the figure was 1,838 million francs, and by December 1918 1,028 million.[106] In the rented property market, although the government provided an indemnity for up to 50 per cent of a loss scaled according to the population size of the town, it was again the Banque de France that carried most of the obligations.[107] And it was the bank that provided the kick-start to activity in the share market.

[100] Klotz, De la guerre, 18–19.   [101] G. Meynier, L'Algérie révelée, 366–7.
[102] Jèze and Truchy, War finance, 122–3, 128.   [103] Olphe-Galliard, Histoire économique, 34.
[104] Knauss, Kriegsfinanzierung, 67.   [105] Flood, France 1914–18, 47–8.
[106] Olphe-Galliard, Histoire économique, 20, 24.   [107] Bogart, War costs, 35.

The Paris bourse reopened for cash business on 3 August, but then migrated to Bordeaux on 2 September, and did not return until 7 December. It remained closed for business that had been settled in late July 1914, but in September 1915 the Banque de France made 250 million francs available to the Chambre Syndicale des Agents de Change to settle floating commitments. Debtors were required to pay a tenth of their outstanding debt and interest on the remainder: the principal was then paid off in tenths, so that the debt was fully redeemed in July 1916.[108]

In none of this activity did the bank enjoy any form of government guarantee. Thus, while the Bank of England moved from a position of commercial independence to one where it was underwritten by the Treasury, the Banque de France was effectively self-reliant. Alexandre Ribot, who became finance minister on 26 August 1914, made a virtue of the relationship. By keeping the bank's credit separate from that of the government, the bank would act as a restraint on the state's increasing its issue. On 21 September Ribot committed the state to pay 3 per cent interest on the bank's advances after the end of hostilities, rather than the nominal 1 per cent set at the start of the war. This, he believed, would be a symbol of the state's financial self-discipline: the bank could put the extra 2 per cent into a sinking fund to wipe out the debt.[109]

In reality, however, any discipline in the relationship between government and bank would be undermined if there was no necessary internal self-control in the fiscal affairs of either party. On 5 August, when the 1911 agreement came into force and the bank duly advanced the government 2,900 million francs, the authorized note issue was increased to 12,000 million. The bank, with no requirement to maintain a set gold reserve, and now also released from convertibility, effectively had a free hand. Its note issue could be enlarged by decree of the council of state without reference to the assembly. At the same time the latter gave to the council of state the right to open extraordinary credits for the duration of hostilities. Ribot's financial purism on 21 September was set against a request for a further advance from the bank of 3,100 million francs, making 6,000 million in all. When the assembly next reconvened, on 22 December, it found that the government had voted itself 6,441 million francs in extraordinary credits. Thus, the primary pressure to increase the bank's note issue was not to ensure liquidity for the sake of business (this, after all, was effectively curtailed by the moratorium), but to meet the fiscal needs of the government. The enlargement of note circulation was the main method of state borrowing, and would in turn lead to currency inflation, the depreciation of the franc, and rising prices.[110]

[108] Knauss, *Kriegsfinanzierung*, 65.
[109] Ribot, *Letters to a friend*, 29–32; see also Charbonnet, *Politique financière*, 107–8.
[110] Bogart, *War costs*, 112; Fisk, *French public finance*, 40–4.

France, of course, was not alone in using currency inflation as a means to cover its mobilization costs. Without a rapid increase in available cash the liquidity necessary for paying suppliers, financing industry, or staving off public panic would have been forfeit. Without it, too, the switch from the requirements of a peacetime economy to those of war would have been much more protracted. The success of these methods is perhaps best rendered in negative terms: none of the major powers, not even Austria-Hungary, was constrained militarily in those first few weeks of 1914 because of financial problems. But the powers were prepared to act as they did, to suspend convertibility and to borrow from their central banks, in response to what they saw as an immediate crisis, not as a long-term situation. The crucial question, therefore, would be how they managed war finance and its inflationary effects over the long term. This would require them to pace themselves, but in a race of whose ultimate length they had no better knowledge than (mostly) over-optimistic guesses.

THE LOSS OF BUDGETARY CONTROL

In January 1917 an Australian division had one officer and fifty men continuously employed in salvage operations.[111] There is no reason to think that they were atypical. But their attentions were concentrated on the items that could be reused, not on those which could not. When visitors toured the battlefields of France and Flanders after the war they saw piles of rubbish—the refuse of industrialized war. Rusting rifles, rent helmets, and spent shell-cases were the obvious signs of fighting. But also there were old tin cans, discarded corrugated iron, and broken bottles, the remnants of the daily needs of millions of men over four years. The First World War was fought with equipment that was both more sophisticated and yet more vulnerable than its predecessors, that proliferated spare parts and spawned its own obsolescence. The destructiveness of its weapons was in part responsible for its wastefulness. But in addition, standards and expectations—of medical care, of rationing, and of creature comforts—were all higher. The litter sprang above all from abundance; lavishness proceeded from lack of financial limitation.

War reversed the relationships between exchequers and their spending departments. The treasuries of Europe saw their task no longer as one of restraint but as one of enablement. Karl Helfferich, an economist, a former director of the Deutsche Bank, and Reich secretary of state for finance from

[111] Cutlack, *War letters of Monash*, 160; see also Chapman, *Passionate prodigality*, 266–7; Binding, *Fatalist at war*, 165–6.

February 1915 to May 1916, declared after the war that he had little enthusiasm for thrift. His task, as he saw it, was not to deny departments what they wanted but to work with them. He boasted that he had acceded to every request that the army had made. The watchword in Germany—for all Helfferich's empty efforts to rebut it—was 'money plays no role'.[112] And attitudes were little different among the Entente powers. Lloyd George, as Britain's chancellor of the exchequer on the war's outbreak and prime minister at its conclusion, set the tone. Although chancellor since 1908, he never, in Keynes's view, 'had the faintest idea of the meaning of money'.[113] After resolving the crisis of July 1914, Lloyd George neglected his departmental business for the wider world of the war as a whole. Octave Homberg, meeting him in December, reported to Ribot that he 'seems to know nothing of financial affairs and is above all a politician'. By May 1915 discontent within the Treasury made his continuation there insupportable.[114] His transfer to the government's prime spending department, the Ministry of Munitions, completed the erasure of any instincts for economy he had once possessed. For the rest of the war the only limits on Lloyd George's mobilization of resources for the purposes of victory were those imposed by physical availability, not those suggested by cost.

That governmental restraints on spending were easing was evident—albeit to different degrees—before 1914. The demands of the pre-war arms race had already pushed back the frontiers of financial control. In Britain the quest for 'national efficiency', not least in relation to defence, had forced the Treasury to defer to specialist advice, regardless of financial orthodoxy.[115] Between 1900 and 1913 Britain had the highest defence spending per capita in the world.[116] But Britain could afford it: it also had the highest per capita income. And so it was able to observe two cardinal principles before 1914: expenditure should be paid for out of revenue, and parliament had the ultimate authority to approve the budget. In the other belligerent countries the combination of weak parliamentary systems, ill-developed systems of taxation, and of rising defence budgets at a time of increasing expenditure on social benefits fostered devices and deceits in peace which would flourish and grow in war. Accounting ploys and deficit financing were lessons already well learnt by 1914. Helfferich and Lloyd George might therefore protest that they did no more than preside over trends already in place.

[112] Helfferich, Weltkrieg, 200–1, 210–14.
[113] Skidelsky, Keynes, i. 300; see also Stamp, Taxation during the war, 32–4; Hirst and Allen, British war budgets, 44–5, 53.
[114] Ribot, Journal, 23; Gilbert, Lloyd George 1912–16, 200–2; David, Inside Asquith's cabinet, 182, 230.
[115] Pugh, Making of modern British politics, 103–4.
[116] Davis and Huttenback, Mammon and the pursuit of empire, 160. For an important corrective to Davis's and Huttenback's calculations, see Hobson, Journal of European Economic History, XXII (1993), 461–506.

Helfferich's predecessor but one, Adolf Wermuth, finance minister from 1909 to 1912, had argued as a British chancellor of the exchequer would have done. Without a thriving economy and a secure financial base, an enhanced defence capacity would have nothing to protect. Wermuth resigned rather than preside over the 1912 and 1913 army laws. The 1912 budget approved defence expenditure up until 1917 without making clear how it was to be funded; the army, like the navy, was manoeuvring into a position where its growth would be autonomous, independent of Reichstag control. The 1913 budget appropriated 61.8 per cent of its total for military purposes: military spending rose 62.9 per cent from 1910, when it had been 49.1 per cent of the total budget. Thus the Reich's financial arrangements were already being 'militarized' before the war broke out. The Bavarian finance minister said of the tax which resulted, 'in truth it is . . . a war contribution in advance . . . not a tax, but a sacrifice, a patriotic gift'.[117]

The new tax, a direct levy on property to run for three years, meant that Germany's 1914 budget—although drawn up in peace—contained an element which suggested that it was appropriate for war. Hermann Kühn, Wermuth's successor, did not see the need to revise the budget when war broke out, and Helfferich followed its outline in 1915 and to some extent in 1916. However, the new principles of the defence tax were overshadowed by a legacy of financial laxity, manifested in two interlocking elements in the budget.

The first of these was the burden of debt. On 31 March 1914 the Reich's total debt was 5,441,897,600 marks, all but 524 million of which was long-term and interest-paying.[118] The second significant continuity was the extraordinary budget. Technically this was for capital improvements and was therefore self-amortizing: it was funded by loans, the interest and redemption of which were met by the ordinary budget. But the strain of rising defence costs before the war had eroded the rigour implicit in these arrangements. Loans were being used to meet recurrent expenditure, including not only defence costs but also interest and redemption payments. Furthermore, the expenditure for the redemption of debt appeared as a charge on the ordinary account, but as an income on the extraordinary. Provided ordinary receipts, including new loans, met ordinary outgoings, and provided transfers to the extraordinary account covered that element of the budget's outgoings, the Reich avoided declaring a deficit. Formal deficits or surpluses could appear because it was possible to carry forward extraordinary allocations from the previous year as income for the new year. This rolling over of accounts obscured whether the deficit was real or not—and in any case, even if it were, it could be simply resolved by the contraction of fresh debt.[119]

---

[117] Witt, *Finanzpolitik des Deutschen Reiches*, 364; see generally, Kroboth, *Finanzpolitik des Deutschen Reiches*, 127–30, 161–4, 192–4, 301.
[118] Lotz, *Deutsche Staatsfinanzwirtschaft*, 6.   [119] Ibid. 7–8; Williamson, *Helfferich*, 123.

It was intended in the 1914 budget to break this cycle by balancing the ordinary budget through the defence tax. But with the outbreak of war all the additional military costs created by hostilities were pushed into the extra-ordinary account, which was funded through credits. In 1915 and subsequently even peacetime defence expenditure was shifted out of the ordinary account, and thus that aspect of the budget was reduced in line with the reduction in the receipts for ordinary income.[120]

The effect was to remove from Reichstag supervision the auditing of the war's financing. The Reichstag's concerns were effectively narrowed to those costs which could not be transferred to the extraordinary budget. Not once throughout the war did it review Germany's financial policy as a whole.[121]

Arguably this would have happened anyway. On 4 August the Reichstag itself voluntarily gave up what oversight it had by empowering the Bundesrat to adopt the financial measures it deemed appropriate. Thereafter, so compelling and immediate were the needs of the war that no nation, including Germany, could manage its funds according to an annual budget: what mattered was the monthly cash flow. In addition, as elsewhere, proper controls were the casualty of conscription: insufficient men remained to keep tallies and to collect taxes.

Germany's domestic political agenda—the services' battle to be independent of parliamentary control, the Bundesrat's clash with the more liberal and more democratic Reichstag—created the context into which the issues of war finance irrupted. Thus, its experiences were more characteristic of its forms of government than of its military situation. In this it had at least something in common with its main ally Austria-Hungary. Admittedly, the latter's difficulties in central control and accountability, with its finances divided between the two monarchies in war as in peace, were entirely *sui generis*. But, like Germany, the best of the finance ministries' staffs, at the top as well as the bottom, were called to other duties. When Alexander Spitzmüller, who had left the Austrian government's employ to become president of the Creditanstalt bank in 1909, was appointed to head the Austrian finance ministry in December 1916 he found that it had been split into too many departments, that it lacked strong leadership to give it unity, and that it was 'no longer the elite instrument of national and political economy'.[122]

In many ways, however, the more obvious comparison between Germany and its allies was with Bulgaria, which joined the Central Powers in July 1915. Bulgaria, like Germany, used the device of an extraordinary budget to fund its war effort. As a result, its ordinary account showed a surplus in 1917 and 1918. Only in the latter year did the outgoings on the ordinary account increase, by

[120] Roesler, *Finanzpolitik*, 67–70.
[121] Ibid. 102, 105, 119, 174; Dix, *Wirtschaftskrieg*, 215.
[122] Spitzmüller, *Memoirs*, 158–9.

about 41 per cent, and in real terms inflation meant that the expenditure charged to the account was constant. Indeed, the depreciation of the Bulgarian currency, the lev, ensured that by 1918 actual spending on the ordinary account had fallen to 27 per cent of its 1914 value. Even in 1911, the last full year of peace for Bulgaria, 21.7 per cent of the budget was devoted to direct defence spending, and debt charges, many of which arose from the acquisition of military equipment abroad, was responsible for a further 20 per cent. After 1915 all military expenditure, including the peacetime costs of the army, was shifted into the extraordinary account. Beginning in 1916, any attempt at an annual statement was abandoned in favour of monthly credits in twelfths. The extraordinary account duly multiplied by a factor of 14.4 between 1914 and 1918. Again, depreciation limited the real cost, which peaked at a threefold increase on the 1914 figure in 1917, and by 1918 the combined values of both ordinary and extraordinary accounts had declined 45 per cent on their 1914 totals. But the accounts understate the price of Bulgaria's war. About half of wartime expenditure was simply unbudgeted. Using the protocols of the civil and military authorities, the state borrowed from the national bank of Bulgaria, Bulgarska Narodna Banka, without cover or with, at best, the security of provisional receipts or anticipated post-war extraordinary credits. At any one time the Treasury had no idea of its current commitments, let alone its anticipated outgoings.[123]

Of the Entente powers, Russia was most akin to Bulgaria in its practices. Between 1900 and 1913 Russia's state spending rose 93 per cent, but its national income increased only 80 per cent. The finance minister and future chairman of the council of ministers, V. N. Kokovtsov, alarmed by military spending which accounted for 43 per cent of the budget in 1909–10, tried to bring the armed services under control. He did reduce the national debt, from 9,054 million roubles in 1908 to 8,825 million in 1913, so that its cost was 13.7 per cent of the budget as against 16 per cent. Nonetheless, military spending rose over the same period. The navy's expenditure grew 178.4 per cent and the army's 43.1 per cent. Russia's ostensible financial health was confined to its ordinary budget, whose revenue was derived from the state railways, state monopolies, and taxation, and a quarter of whose expenditure was allocated to the services. Its extraordinary budget, funded through loans, was what shouldered spending on railways and on the major arms programme of 1914.[124]

As in Germany, the principle of the extraordinary budget was extended on the outbreak of hostilities. Russia's fundamental laws gave the Tsar the power to authorize additional wartime spending for all government departments,

---

[123] Danaïllow, *Les Effets de la guerre en Bulgarie*, 69–70, 496–512.

[124] Geyer, *Russian imperialism*, 255–7; David Jones, 'Imperial Russia's forces at war', in Millett and Murray (eds.), *Military effectiveness*, i. 258–9; Michelson, 'Revenue and expenditure of the Russian government during the war', in Michelson *et al.*, *Russian public finance during the war*, 15–72.

and also to raise state loans to fund it. The war could effectively be financed out of the war fund, and be totally independent of the Duma. The ordinary budget continued as it had before the war—and remained subject to the Duma and to the state council. The absurdity of this position was clear from even the most superficial glance at the accounts as presented to the Duma. Those for 1914 showed a deficit of 242.7 million roubles on the ordinary and extraordinary budgets; those for 1915 moved into surplus, and for 1914–17 as a whole recorded a favourable balance of 2,190.7 million roubles. Ordinary spending in 1915 was actually recorded as 452 million roubles below that of 1913.

Two things were happening to obscure the true state of Russia's finances. First, into the war's expenditure were transferred not only the additional military costs generated by the fighting but also the normal expenses of the services' peacetime establishment. Secondly, many items of non-military expenditure, particularly spending on state railways, but also other capital projects, were billed to the war. By 1916 10 per cent of all civil outgoings were channelled through the war fund. Between the outbreak of war and August 1917 41,392.7 million roubles had been appropriated for the war fund, 20 per cent of it for government departments other than the army and the navy. Thus, even the apparent health of the ordinary budget was in reality misleading: ordinary revenue was not covering ordinary expenditure. The gravity of the position was further underlined by the fact that much of the revenue in the ordinary budget was generated by the profits of war industry or by customs duties on the services' imports. If the war had ended in 1916 the ordinary budget was likely to have been up to 2,000 million roubles in deficit.

The principal cause of Russia's loss of budgetary control was artifice. The opportunity afforded the Tsar to undermine the Duma made the war fund an instrument in the battle for autocratic control. The Duma protested about the bookkeeping fictions over which it retained oversight, but to little avail. However, incompetence also played its part. Ribot expressed the view of many of his Entente colleagues when he described Peter Bark, a banker and Russia's minister of finance throughout the war, as 'a child who knows nothing, neither of his resources, expenses, nor budget'.[125] Even if Bark had wished to assert control, he probably lacked the machinery to do so. The execution of the 1914 Finance act was the last on which the state audit department was able to report: the growth of the budget and the diminution of the department's staff through the demands of military service spelt the end of any rigour in accounting controls.[126]

France before 1914, like Germany and Russia, paid for the growing costs of central government, particularly the military ones, by borrowing. Unlike

[125] Schmidt, *Ribot*, 125; Keynes was perversely complimentary, see Johnson (ed.), *Collected writings of Keynes*, xvi. 130–3.

[126] Michelson *et al.*, *Russian public finance*, esp. 75–8, 119–21, 125, 129, 138, 145, 157, 214, 215.

Germany and Russia, it made rather less effort to disguise the fact. In 1907 it budgeted for a deficit of 295 million francs, in 1908 for 54 million, in 1909 for 45 million, and in 1910 for 48 million. In 1912 Klotz showed a surplus, but only by an accounting sleight of hand, which was repeated in 1913. The 1914 budget anticipated a deficit of 794 million francs, all of it and more generated by the 1913 three-year service law. Between 1904 and 1914 fresh expenditure totalled 1,777 million francs, but normal income only netted an additional 800 million francs. France's consolidated debt in July 1914 was 27,000 million francs, its annual arrears on that 967 million francs, and all its obligations of whatever description 34,188 million francs.[127]

Perhaps more surprising than the pre-existing burden of debt which France carried into the war was the ease with which such a fiercely republican country could slough off the principles of parliamentary control. Caught up in the symbolism of 1793, the assembly's authorization of extraordinary credits by decree was a willing delegation of power to the centre in a time of crisis. Even when parliamentary activity resumed in December, Ribot was surprised to find that the financial committee of the senate was only interested in matters of secondary importance: 'we did not speak of the general financial position and of the possible means to provide the treasury with the sums it needs.'[128]

The chamber agreed that the government should have provisional credits, given in twelfths, and in December accorded the government six twelfths (in other words, cash for six months) to the tune of 9,000 million francs. When, in June 1915, fresh credits were needed the period was reduced to three months, and there it remained for the rest of the war. Although in December 1914 the government had drawn up a list of headings under which the money would be disbursed, the allocations were not binding and the credits were effectively voted as undivided blocks. The assembly was authorizing expenditure without any calculation as to income; lacking a firm hold on how the money was meant to be spent, it possessed no means of monitoring how it had been spent. Its limited knowledge led it to encourage expenditure without regard to revenue. The credits voted in 1915 totalled 22,804.5 million francs. They then rose by approximately 10,000 million francs in each year of the war, to reach 54,537.1 million in 1918.[129]

In practice, actual spending in France exceeded the credits voted. Moreover, their global figures did not encompass the special accounts created at the beginning of the war to ensure food supplies. Technically, the accounts could show favourable balances, since they sold commodities as well as bought them.

[127] Charbonnet, *Politique financière de la France*, 21–35; Duroselle, *La France*, 205; Jèze and Truchy, *War finance*, 187.
[128] Ribot, *Journal*, 24.
[129] Jèze and Truchy, *War finance*, 22, 160–75; Renouvin, *War government in France*, 109–11; Charbonnet, *Politique financière de la France*, 43–53.

The most important embraced wheat, sugar, petrol, coal, and the merchant marine. Their foreign purchases, as well as their multiplicity, made proper control problematic—even after the war had ended. In 1920 30,000 million francs passed through the special accounts. During the war their adverse balances amounted in all to 10,305 million francs, including 3,904 million in 1916 alone.[130]

What the special accounts highlighted was the difficulty for a country that was itself a major battlefield in distinguishing between civil and military expenditure. The voting of lump-sum credits meant that even without the device of the extraordinary budget France lost control of its peacetime disbursements as surely as did Germany and Russia. Parliament lacked the information to be able to balance non-military spending against normal income.

In December 1914 the assembly left itself with two instruments with which it could scrutinize the government's financial affairs—the budget committee of the chamber and the finance committee of the senate. Although passive at first, these two bodies—especially the latter—became more assertive as the war lengthened. In particular, they tried to get the ministry of war to justify the credits it requested and to monitor the disbursements it then made. The ministry's hand was not strong: a law of 1869 permitted the commander-in-chief at the front to authorize expenditure. Much of France was a front, and Joffre reasonably protested that his headquarters had more pressing concerns than the keeping of accounts. Army commissaries and paymasters-general were requested to produce monthly statements—a request honoured as much in the breach as in the observance. The ministry of finance, under pressure from the two committees of the assembly, tried, somewhat feebly, to get the ministry of war to channel orders through it, and to control prices through the centralization of the competing demands of the service departments.[131]

Ribot's determination to establish control was not strong. His financial advisers, including the same Paul Leroy-Beaulieu who had recognized before the onset of hostilities that a long war could be funded on credit, were unconcerned about the loss of budgetary control. Debt mounted in proportion to the government's existing borrowings, not according to its receipts, which did not even match its normal peacetime outgoings. Ribot defended his position by reference to the military situation: with so much territory under occupation normal fiscal self-discipline was irrelevant. At the end of 1915 he drew up a draft law which aimed to compare total credits with total expenditure, and thus show whether France was in balance or deficit. Nothing came of it. In May 1916 he engaged in a similar exercise when, in order to argue for

[130] Jèze and Truchy, War finance, 40–7.   [131] Ibid. 173–83; Schmidt, Ribot, 123.

increased taxation, he tried to match outgoings to income. But the first promise of a proper budget had to wait until June 1917, when Thierry, finance minister in the Painlevé government, projected his expenditure and his receipts for the third quarter of 1917, and announced his intention to produce a proper annual budget in 1918. His aim, minimal as it might seem, was to stabilize France's non-war costs, and to end the system of provisional credits.

It was not fulfilled. When Clemenceau became prime minister in November 1917 France adopted the principles of Lloyd George to the securing of victory. To mix national metaphors, Klotz, who succeeded Thierry as minister of finance, belonged to the Helfferich school. 'He signed cheques', Clemenceau said of him, 'as though he was signing autographs.'[132] After the war Klotz boasted that, while on the chamber's budget committee, he had never obstructed an order placed by the ministry of war—indeed, quite the reverse—and he rationalized his position—as Helfferich did—by saying that the payment by a defeated enemy of an indemnity would solve the problem of accumulated debt. Ribot's horror at Klotz's ambition to be minister of finance proved well founded.[133]

Klotz kept the provisional twelfths for war credits. He followed Thierry in announcing his intention to meet the costs of civil administration and of servicing the debt from ordinary income, but he did not achieve it. France in 1918 was still budgeting for a deficit in its ordinary accounts. But at least parliamentary control was reasserted to the point where on 29 June 1918 the first budget of the war was approved.[134]

Perhaps Thierry need not have worried. Britain had a budget for every year of the war, but parliament still lost control of expenditure. The chancellor of the exchequer dutifully informed the House of Commons what he anticipated the country's disbursements would be in the coming year, and how he proposed to fund them. But when the cost of war exceeded its budgeted figure, the government supplemented its receipts with emergency votes of credit. On 12 February 1917, for example, the House of Commons voted £350 million to see the government through until the end of May. But on 9 May Bonar Law, the chancellor since December 1916, was back asking for £500 million. Furthermore, he told the House that the average daily cost of the war was £7.45 million, when only a week before he had declared it to be £5.5 million. These were extremes, but in such circumstances it was impossible for Members of Parliament to grasp the full financial picture.[135]

The British annual budget, nonetheless, served three principal functions. First, the debate which it engendered showed that, except during the

[132] Duroselle, *La Grande Guerre des français*, 157. See also Martin, *Les Finances publiques de la France*, 132–5, 140; Martin, *La Situation financière de la France*, 216–22.
[133] Klotz, *De la guerre*, 43–6; Ribot, *Journal*, 28–9, 46–7.
[134] Knauss, *Kriegsfinanzierung*, 129–34.   [135] Hirst and Allen, *British war budgets*, 186.

chancellorship of Reginald McKenna (May 1915 to December 1916), the House was inclined to greater financial radicalism than the government. Thus, the cabinet was not held back from potentially unpopular taxation for fear of its political effects. Secondly, the appearance of parliamentary accountability and of financial rigour was enormously important in sustaining domestic confidence and foreign credit. And thirdly, the effective result was that Britain, alone of all the European belligerents, continued to cover its peacetime expenditure through income. A calculation that aggregated revenue through taxation and then deducted interest charges and the pre-war civil budget showed that over the war years Britain generated a surplus of $5,396 million. By contrast, Germany showed a deficit of $4,180 million, Russia (to 1917) of $1,142 million, France of $3,346 million, Austria-Hungary of $401 million, and Italy of $787 million.[136]

The controls that Britain lost were specifically over war costs. Furthermore, they were willingly forfeited. Neither the War Office nor the Admiralty was used to ordering without restraint. It required Lloyd George to tell the War Office in October 1914 not to come to the Treasury for approval for orders.[137] Even then the culture of penny-pinching was sufficiently ingrained for the chancellor to have to continue hectoring, and eventually—as minister of munitions—to take over the job of spending himself. In other words, in Britain civilian government deliberately loosened the reins rather than having them prised from their grasp.

Responsibility for their daily handling lay, of course, not with parliament but with the Treasury. But in 1914 the Treasury was ill-prepared to supervise the expenditure of an empire in a world war. It mustered thirty-three officials in its administrative class.[138] It then found itself neglected and humiliated by its political head. Keynes reflected the Treasury's disillusionment. Lloyd George 'soon got bored with' Sir George Paish, one of his principal financial advisers, 'and stopped reading his lengthy memoranda. [Paish] was, however, given a good salary and an exalted title...and...a room set at a considerable distance.'[139]

McKenna, when he succeeded Lloyd George in May 1915, found 'hopeless financial disorder at the Exchequer, so great indeed that we could not have carried on for another three months'.[140] He himself had served as financial secretary a decade before, so he ought to have known what he was talking about. But, somewhat surprisingly, that was not the prevailing view. His own financial secretary, Edwin Montagu, agreed with him that the department was in confusion, but on little else. His political colleagues felt that he was simply

---

[136] Bogart, War costs, 316–18.
[137] Kathleen Burk, 'The Treasury: from impotence to power', in Burk (ed.), War and the state, 91.
[138] Ibid. 85.   [139] Skidelsky, Keynes, i. 299.
[140] David, Inside Asquith's cabinet, 247; see also Farr, 'McKenna', 57, 70–1, 154, 238.

keeping the seat warm for Lloyd George, and that therefore calls for fiscal rectitude ill behoved him. On finance itself, E. C. Grenfell of Morgan Grenfell characterized him 'as a very ignorant man . . . [who is] inclined to try to appear wise'.[141]

Some, at least, of McKenna's problems derived from the fact that by the time he assumed office the new culture had taken hold in the departments of disbursement. In a memorandum of February 1916 Keynes showed how munitions orders were being increased. The War Office added a margin over what it reckoned it needed, and the Ministry of Munitions then made a similar supplement to the War Office's already inflated request: thus, a scheme for 3,404 guns had been elevated to one for 4,362.[142] McKenna complained that Lloyd George was not only ordering more munitions than he could use but that, in the process, he was actually impeding output rather than promoting it. A retrenchment committee was created in July 1915, and in November McKenna secured an undertaking that all contracts worth more than £500,000 would be referred to the Treasury.[143]

For the Treasury, the key issue was whether finance should be the regulator of British policy or its servant. One traditional interpretation of British strategy contended, in the words of Austen Chamberlain in 1903, that 'Our defensive strength rests upon our financial not less than upon our military and naval resources'.[144] Britain's determination to cling to its international convertibility in 1914 reflected its commitment to this approach. But the actual experience of major war injected pragmatism into its formulation, not least for McKenna. Outwardly, his policies seemed to accommodate the needs of the City of London. He was, for example, loath to use compulsion when securing control of American securities, not because of any political commitment to Liberal principles, but because he feared that foreign investors would withdraw their deposits. His ultimate objective, therefore, was not to prop up the City but to preserve Britain's liquidity.[145] And it was this pragmatism which made him a shifty and even uncongenial ally for any one camp. McKenna saw funds not as an end in themselves but as the means to purchase goods for the prosecution of the war. Therefore, at bottom he reckoned production, not purchasing power, to be the regulator of British strategy. The key issue was the division of manpower between output and military service. If Britain's productive effort was directed to the latter to the detriment of the former, it would have to buy the munitions its armed forces and its allies would need from overseas, and so jeopardize its financial supremacy.[146] Herein was the nub of British strategy. It was a battle which McKenna fought in the cabinet from late 1915 until the early summer of 1916, and lost.

[141] Burk, 'A merchant bank at war', 162.   [142] Johnson (ed.), *Collected writings of Keynes*, xvi. 173.
[143] French, *British strategy and war aims*, 128.   [144] Neilson, *Britain and the last Tsar*, 129.
[145] Farr, 'McKenna', 186, 211.   [146] Ibid. 169–71.

Ultimately, controls on British spending were reimposed not by parliament or by the Treasury, but by the United States. Britain's need for American credit provoked the United States into demanding co-ordination among its new allies in their overseas purchasing. The scale of British and French orders made the management of the exchange rate a key aspect in regulating their cost. The bankers regarded this as their business, and Lord Cunliffe, the governor of the Bank of England, was convinced that the accumulation of gold and its export when required were the keys to its regulation. By appointing Cunliffe as chairman of the London Exchange Committee McKenna hoped to defuse a fraught situation. Cunliffe was not an easy man: E. C. Grenfell thought the problem was his teeth, and that if he had only seen a dentist all would have been all right.[147] But the underlying difficulty was that neither the Bank nor the London Exchange Committee had real bite. His deputy, Montagu Norman, was as frustrated with the Treasury as Cunliffe: 'one might as well talk to an airball as them.'[148] By 1917 Cunliffe was openly undermining the Treasury's policy in the United States, insisting that Britain should ship gold. In July he challenged the Treasury's increasing intervention in the management of the exchange rate. Bonar Law, as chancellor, told Cunliffe that in war the Bank must be subordinate to the national interest and follow the Treasury. Cunliffe huffed and puffed, was overruled, and resigned in April 1918.[149] The confrontation did more than mark the completion of the process by which the Bank of England became a central state bank. It gave the Treasury the whip hand in the key component of British financial policy: control of foreign dealings became the substitute for the lack of control of domestic disbursements.

Some of the same effects could be observed in France. The efforts to reimpose peacetime budgetary procedures in 1917–18 coincided with American pressure on France to reduce its call for American credits. Furthermore, the squeeze which the United States placed on Britain was relayed to Paris in British restrictions on French borrowing through London. The inter-allied purchasing committee forced on the Entente by McAdoo in August 1917 therefore provided the external constraint on France's spending departments which its government had failed to impose internally. The value of its imports fell from over 3,000 million francs to under 2,000 million in the autumn of 1917. In 1918 France found it was underspending on the credits afforded it in the United States, and in the summer the franc rose against the pound and the dollar.[150]

The United States thus imposed some discipline on its allies. But it too found that domestically the control of the war's costs was not necessarily easier

[147] Burk, 'A merchant bank at war', 167.
[148] Norman, 27 June 1916; I am grateful to Dr Martin Farr for this quotation.
[149] Burk, *Historical Journal*, XXII (1979), 361; Sayers, *Bank of England*, i. 99–109.
[150] Petit, *Finances extérieures*, 101–7, 133–47, 248–52, 282–303, 433–6, 446–69, 477–93, 497–8.

for a democratic power than an autocratic one. Like Britain, it sustained the outward form of public accountability. However, its spending on the war far exceeded that of any other nation, averaging $42.8 million per day between 1 July 1917 and 30 June 1919. That of each of the other major belligerents hovered around $32 million over the same period. Federal expenditure rose 2,454 per cent between 1916 and 1919.[151]

The contrast in financial management between the United States and, say, Austria-Hungary was therefore much less striking than the difference in their political structures might have suggested. Austria did not even consult its parliament between 1914 and 1916. But its principal fiscal problem, that of controlling the army's expenditure, was a difference of degree rather than of substance. The complaints of the Austrian finance minister[152]—that the army paid for its needs without regard to the market rate, that efforts to control costs in the higher administration of the army were undermined by independent commanders in the field, that civilian procedures had been usurped by military necessity—found echoes throughout the nations. Whatever their nominal controls, all powers were operating some form of arrears to fund their war efforts. Britain's wartime budget deficit, if calculated in current prices, was 60.6 per cent of its pre-war national income; Germany's, at 64 per cent, was little higher.[153] All powers, therefore, ended up borrowing. The crucial questions were how they managed that borrowing, and how they juxtaposed it with taxation.

TAXATION

The choice between taxation and borrowing as means to finance the war was at bottom a choice between taxation now or taxation in the future. Loans contracted during the war would have to be repaid on maturity through tax receipts. They could, of course, be postponed by contracting fresh debt, but even if the state thereby retained the principal over a longer period taxation would still be required to pay the interest.

Servicing the debt made loans more expensive than taxation. But it did not follow that the state should therefore tax heavily in order to pay for as much of the war as possible out of current income. Part of the case against such a policy rested on the principle of equity. Those fighting the war were making sufficient sacrifices for the future well-being of their societies for it to be reasonable to expect not them but their successors to meet the financial costs. In addition

---

[151] Gilbert, *American financing*, 65, 221–3.   [152] Popovics, *Geldwesen*, 167.
[153] Balderston, *Economic History Review*, 2nd series, XLII (1989), 229.

there was an economic argument. The taxable capacity of a country was a reflection not simply of the money in circulation but also of the goods and services for which the money was the means of exchange. Waging the war depressed both commerce and those industries which were not war-related. Peace would revive normal business. Thus, a higher tax burden would be easier to sustain after the war than during it.

The problem of post-war reconstruction was therefore a material consideration in the development of intra-war taxation. But it was one which split both ways. The easing of taxation after the war would boost consumer spending and so help reactivate peacetime markets. This, then, was a case for a short, sharp shock—heavy taxation in the war. The opponents of such an approach contended that excessive taxation during hostilities would erode individual savings. Consequently, potential consumers would be too impoverished to be able to buy goods when they were once again available.

The real difficulty with not taxing heavily during the war was that those whose incomes were left relatively untouched could not be relied upon to save the money they earned. Inflation eroded the real value of capital. Goods seemed a securer investment. But because the state was increasingly taking over the means of production for the needs of the war, goods were in short supply. The consequent monetary overhang—the problem of too much money chasing too few commodities—prompted price inflation. An effective system of wartime taxation which reduced the purchasing power of the consumer was therefore an essential element in the armoury of price control in particular, and of inflation control in general. Because there were few goods to buy, heavy taxation was unlikely to curb actual consumption any more than it was already depressed by the war. And since the war made the state the most important arbiter in the investment of capital (as well as the most significant consumer of its products), there seemed little short-term case for saying that taking such decisions out of private hands restricted industrial growth.

Government policy, therefore, had to strike a balance between on the one hand actively dampening consumer activity over the short term and on the other securing immediate and, above all, future capital investment. The result was a taxation pattern that in its final form inverted peacetime priorities. Broadly speaking, taxation ceased to be socially progressive. It needed to shore up the wealth of the rich, since this might be invested in goods and services over the long term, and it needed to reduce the disposable income of the less affluent, which would otherwise contribute to price inflation.

The most striking illustration of this process was the declining significance of inheritance tax. Death duties had generated major constitutional struggles in Britain in 1909–10 and in Germany in 1906–13. In both cases expenditure on armaments had been the prime motor for change. But during the war the egalitarian argument for the direct taxation of large estates was offset by a desire not to penalize patriotism. The deaths of heirs in action threatened families with payments in unexpectedly rapid succession. Britain in 1914 granted relief to those estates where war casualties resulted in the ownership changing more than once. A single transfer caused by a war-related death could be offset by deferring payment until three years after the war's conclusion.[154] Thus, yields rose only marginally and then stabilized. No alternative emerged, despite pressure from the Trades Union Congress in September 1916. Sidney Webb called for a levy on accumulated wealth to reduce government debt and as an alternative to higher rates of income tax. He argued that interest payments would fall, with the result that the profits of rentiers would slump and investment in production rise. But the Treasury rejected the idea for fear that property sales to release cash would cause a slump in values, and that individuals would therefore borrow to pay the levy rather than invest in government bonds.[155] In France the return on inheritance tax averaged 100 million francs less than the 1913 total in each of 1914, 1915, and 1916. Only in Germany did the annual income on death duties rise progressively—from 47.1 million marks in 1913 to 77.8 million in 1918.[156] And even here the increase was not proportional to the growth in direct taxation in general.

The declining significance of inheritance tax was, above all, relative. In Britain it accounted for 13.8 per cent of all direct taxation at the war's outset, and 3.4 per cent at its conclusion.[157] Other forms of direct taxation, therefore, grew at a much faster rate. In Britain the most important was income tax, which netted £47.2 million in 1913, £205 million in 1916, and £291.1 million in 1918. None of the other major belligerents possessed an effective form of income tax in 1914. Nor did they develop one during the war. Their major revenue producer, a tax also introduced in Britain, was a duty on excess profits arising from or during the war. Delays in its introduction and problems in its assessment meant that the duty varied in its application from country to country, and that it only made an effective contribution in 1917 and 1918. But by the last year of the war it provided France with just under a quarter of its direct taxation, Britain with nearly a half, and Germany with almost all.

A major question in relation to excess profits duty was the identity of the ultimate payer. Ideally the burden would be shifted onto the consumer. Levies on excess profits would therefore constitute a form of indirect tax, and could depress consumer demand.[158] But such theorizing harboured a logical inconsistency. The industries making large profits in wartime were doing so out of the war; their principal client was not the public but the state. But the state's spending was not easily curbed. Thus, if the war profits tax was borne by the prime consumer it would not inhibit inflation but promote it. The tax would

[154] Stamp, *Taxation*, 143.   [155] Daunton, *English Historical Review*, CXI (1996), 890–1.
[156] Knauss, *Kriegsfinanzierung*, 135–6.   [157] Ibid. 136.   [158] Gilbert, *American financing*, 62–3.

drive up prices which the state could only then pay by further taxation (and a further increase in prices) or by borrowing. The corollary of an excess profits duty, if it was not to stoke credit inflation, was an effective policy of price control.

The crux of the debate between state and business over war profits was, therefore, the question of what constituted a reasonable return on capital. Firms argued that a radical reduction in their profits would inhibit reinvestment and reduce the plant devoted to war production. Taking the average of pre-war profits as a basis for comparison, which is what most states did, had the disadvantage that firms producing war goods reckoned on a high level of profits during the course of hostilities to sustain them in peacetime when orders were slack. On the other hand, the three years before 1914 were marked by unwonted activity in the armaments industries of Europe. The distinction between war and peace might be less immediate in terms of war profits than it was in many other areas.

What was clear was that a levy on excess profits could only reduce the demand for goods where peace industries flourished alongside war industries. In these circumstances the duty would act in the same way as indirect taxation. This argument was advanced in the United States. But there, as elsewhere, the nominal returns on indirect taxation fell. In 1916 excise duty accounted for 47.6 per cent of federal revenue; in 1918, 17.9 per cent. Customs receipts declined from 27.2 per cent to 4.4 per cent over the same period.[159] In Germany indirect taxation fell from 81.3 per cent of ordinary receipts in 1913 to 47.9 per cent in 1918; in Britain from 46 per cent to 21.2 per cent; and in France from 53.5 per cent to 43.1 per cent.[160] The goods were simply not available in sufficient quantity to produce the cash required. Industry's production for public consumption was pared to essentials. Imports of luxuries and non-essentials were limited in order to maximize shipping space and foreign purchasing power for war goods.

Much of the increase in direct taxation was therefore no more than relative—a response to a decline in absolute yields elsewhere. Germany between 1913 and 1918 increased its direct tax from 3.5 per cent of its ordinary receipts to 47.9 per cent without establishing a proper Reich income tax. The growth looked so dramatic because, for example, customs, responsible for raising 679.3 million marks in 1913, fell, under the impact of the blockade, to 133 million marks in 1918.[161]

Falling real levels of indirect taxation meant that direct taxation was the only effective tool with which to control consumer-led inflation. The major

[159] Gilbert, *American financing*, 76.
[160] Knauss, *Kriegsfinanzierung*, 148; Daunton, *English Historical Review*, CXI (1996), 896, gives the British figures as 42.5% in 1913–14 and 20.4% in 1918–19.
[161] Knauss, *Kriegsfinanzierung*, 142, 148.

potential change in taxation policy was that which made income tax a burden on all wage-earners and not just on the wealthy. But the belief that the principal aim in war finance should be the securing of cash, not the curbing of consumption, died hard. Even in 1921 a distinguished British economist, A. C. Pigou, observed that a man who paid his income tax by reducing his consumption might manage—because he would avoid indirect taxes on goods—to pay less tax, not more. Pigou's attention was on the need to raise money to cover the real costs of the war.[162] But in practice the function of wartime taxation was less important to this than to the reduction of the monetary overhang created by credit inflation.

In these terms, no power, not even Britain, taxed as heavily as it needed to or could have done. But, arguably, the possibility of harsher regimes became more evident after the war and with hindsight than it was at the time. Taxation itself was a cumbersome instrument of economic control, in that its burdens were slow to take effect. New areas of liquidity became evident in retrospect; new taxation was applied in future. The time-lag between cause and result was therefore at least a year. The war, however long, presented rapidly changing economic conditions, but conditions whose longevity was of uncertain duration. Pacing the financial effort and retaining a system which would enable a swift change to peace were both factors inhibiting innovation. The taxation systems of most belligerents, therefore, changed little and late. Those states that taxed most efficiently were those that had the appropriate taxes already in place when the war began.

In Britain income tax was first adopted, in 1799, specifically as a war tax. It was the engine by which the nation harnessed its commercial strength to military applications. But in 1842 Sir Robert Peel employed the tax in peacetime, albeit still on a temporary basis, to enable a reduction in indirect taxes in his bid to stimulate the expansion of commerce and consumption through free trade. So apparently successful was this policy that Gladstone felt consistently able to promise its abolition. But in reality the burdens of colonial defence made the financial distinction between peace and war increasingly irrelevant. Gladstone's logic, that Britain would be unlikely to go to war if income tax resumed its primary status as a war tax, and if—broadly speaking—liability for the tax correlated with the parliamentary franchise, proved unfounded. The rebuilding of the Royal Navy under the pressure of competition with France raised the basic rate from 5d. to 8d. in the £ in 1885. The Boer War pushed it up to 1s. 3d. in 1902–3, and in the five years before 1914 it stabilized at 1s. 2d. In 1900–14 the average tax burden per person per year in the United Kingdom was £3.44, about £1 more than in the other developed countries of the world.[163]

[162] Pigou, *Political economy of war*, 48.
[163] Davis and Huttenback, *Mammon and the pursuit of empire*, 225–6.

Britons avoided the necessity of conscription by virtue of their dependence on the navy for primary defence. But they paid for the privilege in cash.

The result was that in 1914 Britain possessed, as no other nation did, the basis for a system of war finance. It had developed the machinery which enabled it to draw on the nation's liquid assets. The Dreadnought revolution was funded not through loans, as was half of Germany's spending, but through income. Britain's lead over Germany was not only naval but also fiscal. Therefore, unlike Germany or France, its stock market was not already encumbered with a superfluity of government stocks. Indeed, in 1914 Britain budgeted for a surplus which was to be applied to the reduction of the national debt.[164]

Pre-war opponents of the naval programme argued that the revenue implications were eroding Britain's fiscal base—that the wealth required in the event of war was being spent before the war broke out.[165] In reality income tax, despite its high rate compared with other countries, had plenty of spare capacity. Real earnings per worker rose 36 per cent between 1875/6 and 1889–1900, and yet most did not become liable for direct taxation. In 1913–14 only 1.13 million of the country's electorate of 8 million were paying direct taxes. The political acceptability of the 'people's budget' of 1909 resided in the fact that its principal burden fell on 11,000 payers of supertax and on the heirs of estates valued at £20,000 or more. With allowances for children and reduced rates on small earned incomes, it exempted most working-class and many married middle-class men. Those taxes which did affect the working class, indirect duties, fell from 70 per cent to 55 per cent of the total tax yield; the cost of customs and excise per head of the population rose a mere 2 per cent. The bulk of the British population, therefore, was encumbered with taxation that was no more than nominal. The country, the supporters of Liberal defence policies contended, was getting financially stronger, not weaker; the total wealth not taken by taxation was put at £1,747 million in 1904–5 and £2,020 million in 1914.[166]

The advice of the Treasury to the chancellor of the exchequer on the war's outbreak, therefore, was that he should increase income tax. By November 1914 Britain's liquidity was rising as the government spent the money it had borrowed to pay for the war. But Lloyd George's budget of that month, the first of the war, was, by common consent, not as fierce as the circumstances demanded or as parliament was prepared to accept. On the advice of Austen Chamberlain (speaking for the Conservatives) he did not expand the levying of direct taxation to embrace all income-earners. Liability remained confined to those earning £160 or more per annum, and Lloyd George restricted himself to

[164] Sumida, *In defence of naval supremacy*, 196, 336.
[165] French, *British economic and strategic planning*, 14–15.
[166] Balderston, *Economic History Review*, 2nd series, XLII (1989), 231–3; Stamp, *Taxation*, 11–12; Daunton, *English Historical Review*, CXI (1996), 885–6.

doubling the basic rate from 9d. in the £ to 1s. 6d. and to proportional increases in the higher rates. To compensate for his feebleness over direct taxation, the chancellor increased the duty on tea from 5d. to 8d. in the £, and on beer from 7s. 9d. to 25s. per barrel. But as he aimed to reduce consumption of the latter by 35 per cent through restricting the hours of opening of licensees, the total increase from both sources in the first full year of operation, 1915–16, was reckoned to be about £20 million. Lloyd George's arrangements increased the revenue for the year 1914–15 from its peacetime target of £207 million to an actual figure of £226.7 million. And yet he was anticipating expenditure of £555.4 million, of which £348.5 would be attributable to the war. One of his parliamentary critics, Thomas Lough, pointed out that six-elevenths of the costs of the Crimean War were covered by tax, and two-fifths of those of the Boer War, but on present reckoning only one-seventy-fifth of the current war.[167]

The shortfall between Lloyd George's rhetoric and the financial substance continued into his second war budget, in May 1915. In the first he had warned of a long war. In February 1915 he continued in a similar vein, calling for Britain to be fully mobilized for total war by 1916.[168] But in his budget speech he projected two alternatives—a war lasting until the end of September 1915 and one continuing until March 1916. He put the cost of the latter at £1,136.4 million, but then said that most of that sum would be spent on the army and the navy and would be covered by votes of credit. He acknowledged a probable deficit of £800 million without explaining how he would cover it. He observed the growing liquidity of Britain, prompted by government spending; he noted the rise in earnings; he adumbrated the possibility of an excess profits duty. But the budget contained no increases in direct taxation. When tackled on these points, the chancellor replied 'with a speech full of taxing precepts, but no taxes'.[169]

What really concerned Lloyd George was his political position—his status as the representative of radical nonconformity and of its preoccupation with temperance. Growing individual incomes were manifesting themselves in the consumption of spirits, which in turn contributed to gains in the yield on customs and excise. In December 1914 beer-drinking fell 38 per cent, in response to the augmentation in duty, but spirit sales increased 3 per cent. In January spirit sales rose 6 per cent, in February 15 per cent, and in March 26 per cent. Lloyd George attributed falling productivity in war industries to drink. At the beginning of April thirty-three Special Branch men in plain clothes investigated the shipyards, and reported that the problem was local and specific: Clydebank

[167] Hirst and Allen, *British war budgets*, 22–35; Morgan, *British financial policy*, 89–90; Stamp, *Taxation*, 24–8; Gilbert, *David Lloyd George*, 139.
[168] French, *British strategy and war aims*, 92.
[169] 'F. W. H.' in *The Economist*, 8 Apr. 1916, cited in Hirst and Allen, *British war budgets*, 135.

was more affected than Plymouth, and riveters were the principal offenders, especially on Mondays. The king, under Lloyd George's influence, was persuaded to take the pledge for the rest of the war, but the cabinet decided it would be inexpedient to extend prohibition to his subjects. It also rejected, after somewhat greater deliberation, the notion of a national monopoly. Finally, five days before the budget itself, Lloyd George proposed a doubling of the duty on spirits to 29s. 6d. per gallon, and an addition of 12s. per barrel on strong beers and of 15s. per gallon on sparkling wines. Increases in indirect taxation were to substitute for the failure to grasp the nettle of direct taxation.

The effect was to threaten simultaneously two props of Asquith's tottering Liberal government. The Conservatives, on whose tacit support the cabinet relied in order to be able to offset its own radicals, were the traditional spokesmen of the drink interest. Even more seriously, the Irish MPs saw the new duties as an attack on the only major manufacture of southern Ireland. Arthur Henderson, for the Labour party, added his voice to the protest: Lloyd George's assumptions about its drinking habits were a gross calumny on the working class. On 29 April 1915 the government withdrew its proposed increases in duty, and confined itself to a restriction on immature spirits and to local regulation under the Defence of the Realm act. By failing to take the whole matter of excise within the budget proper, it prevented a full discussion of the financial provision for the coming year.[170]

Thus, when Reginald McKenna became chancellor later in the same month he inherited a catalogue of missed opportunities, a Treasury anxious to tax more fiercely, and a parliament predisposed to accept its advice. Moreover, in a memorandum of 9 September 1915 Keynes alerted his political superior to the fact that the issue was not simply that of financing the war but of controlling inflation. The war had diverted 'a greater part of the income of the nation than ever before into the hands of those classes of the population which are not much affected by direct taxation and are not accustomed, or likely at any time, to subscribe largely to Government loans'. In a crude calculation, Keynes reckoned that half the industrial population was employed directly or indirectly by the state, but much less than half its money income was being appropriated by the government.[171]

McKenna raised income tax by 40 per cent in his first budget (the third of the war), in September 1915. He lowered the threshold from £160 per annum to £130. Given the rise in nominal wages, McKenna's measure was the vital step in expanding the number of taxpayers. At a stroke, their number was all but doubled. Furthermore, inflation made the effect progressive. Two million

---

[170] Hirst and Allen, *British war budgets*, 36–50; Gilbert, *David Lloyd George*, 159–71; Grigg, *Lloyd George 1912–1916*, 230–7.

[171] Johnson (ed.), *Collected writings of Keynes*, xvi. 117–19.

wage-earners became taxpayers between 1916/17 and 1918/19. Arguably, those on lower incomes were still spared at the expense of those with higher earnings. Farmers were to be assessed on their whole rental, not on one-third as in the past. Rates on incomes over £8,000 were increased to 2s. 8d. in the £, and the scale thereafter rose in three further steps, so that an income of £100,000 or more was taxed at 6s. 10d.

But McKenna's approach was two-pronged. He doubled duties on tea, tobacco, coffee, cocoa, chicory, and dried fruits, and increased the levy on sugar from 1s. 10d. per hundredweight to 9s. 4d. Imported luxuries were subject to a tax of one-third of their value. McKenna's motivations were pragmatic. He wanted to depress consumption, to free shipping space for goods vital to the war effort, and to husband Britain's foreign exchange. He was not a Liberal betraying the party's cardinal principle of free trade. But inevitably his critics, and particularly the radical opponents of the war policies of Asquithian Liberalism, saw the new tariffs as a sell-out to the Conservatives and to protectionism. Their fears were justified, not by the principle but by the practice: the universal applicability of free trade had been breached.[172]

Import duties may have generated the major controversy, but the real innovation of McKenna's budget lay elsewhere. A duty of 50 per cent was to be levied on all profits earned during the war which were in excess of peacetime norms. In most cases assessments were based on the best two of the three trading years before 1914. For business as a whole, 1912 and particularly 1913 had been highly successful. Therefore this method, not least because it eliminated from the calculation the effects of low profits in any one pre-war year, mitigated the effects of profits made during the war. Big firms making big profits before the war could continue to make comparable gains during it without showing any growth in profit. McKenna himself made the point that no firm would pay anything unless during the whole of the three years 1914 to 1917 it had made an average profit equal to that of the best two out of the three years preceding the war.[173] Those companies which still felt themselves harshly treated because they had suffered a more sustained depression could ask to be assessed on the best four years of the six preceding the war. Firms for whom capital formation was relatively more significant (particularly, therefore, those businesses commencing activity or undergoing expansion just before the war) were permitted to base the calculation on a percentage of capital invested. The norm was 6 per cent on 5 August 1914, but private firms were allowed 7 per cent, and a prima facie case for a greater proportion could be made to the Inland Revenue for arbitration by a board of referees. Allowances under this head were particularly frequent in small businesses where capital was necessarily at stake or in larger concerns where the case for capitalizing the profits was linked

[172] Soutou, L'Or et le sang, 205–8.   [173] Hirst and Allen, British war budgets, 114.

to such factors as the rapid depreciation of equipment or the expansion of war production. Under the first head, West End theatres were permitted 15 per cent, and under the second aircraft construction was also granted 15 per cent, mining 14.5 per cent, and the iron and steel industries 8.9 per cent.[174]

Ironically, therefore, the initial impact of the excess profits duty was not on firms directly engaged in weapons production, not on the profits arising from warfare itself, but on profits made during the war through unwarlike activities. McKenna himself said that the issue was not that of profits from war production per se, 'but that during the war persons are enjoying profits more than the average'.[175] Indeed, the arms manufacturers were specifically exempted under the terms of the Munitions of War act of June 1915. This act gave the government the power to take over control of the arms firms, fixing their wages and salary scales, and setting their profits at 20 per cent of the average of the last two pre-war years. The wartime profits which had drawn the attention of the public and of the Treasury were those generated in grain and food production, in the manufacture of boots and clothes, and in the chemical and soap industries. Profits were generated through the creation of new markets for war services; through the curtailment of supplies from overseas, and particularly from belligerents; through population movements within Britain itself; and through the rapid working up to a proper return on new fixed capital unrelated to the war. The Treasury's survey showed that those industries which were doing well were doing very well, with profits in excess of 10 per cent of capital.[176]

One principal attraction of excess profits duty to the Treasury was its simplicity. In 1916/17 56,430 firms were assessed, and the collection of the tax could have proved extraordinarily complex. But its calculation was based on data which the Inland Revenue already possessed. And it operated through self-assessment, relieving the Revenue of the principal onus at a time when it was short of manpower. But the corollary was the possibility of evasion. In a sense this was recognized in legislation that condoned laxity. The state appropriated no statutory powers to examine the books of companies. Many concerns escaped entirely. Agriculture was exempted—partly because it had already been hit by the new assessment of rentals, partly because of its importance to the war effort, but principally because many farmers failed to keep proper accounts. More controversially, shipping also escaped: the formal explanation was that the Admiralty had already commandeered much British-registered tonnage, and that it was now hard to distinguish between the contributions of British vessels and of neutral ships in the transport of British trade.[177] The tax was levied on firms, not individuals: thus, for example, a lawyer whose income increased through war-related business would escape the

---

[174] Grady, *British war finance*, 111–12; Stamp, *Taxation*, 170–8.
[175] Public Record Office T 170/212; I am grateful to Dr Martin Farr for this reference.
[176] Stamp, *Taxation*, 146–9.   [177] Farr, 'McKenna', 262.

duty, but a small business which had been struggling to make its way before the war would be hit with disproportionate severity.

Business critics elevated their opposition to a high moral plane by talk of principles. They objected to the principle of retrospectivity; they pointed out that the first year of assessment included months in 1914 when Britain was not at war. Neither criticism recognized the two fundamental objections to the tax. First, it failed to distinguish between profits derived from speculation and profits generated through hard work and increased productivity (both desirable elements in a war, as in any other, economy). The duty effectively penalized good management; cash was capitalized for the development of production but diverted into direct taxation; wastefulness, in so far as it was reflected in low profit margins, was rewarded. As a corollary, new businesses with low profits before the war but which became established during it were hit harder than pre-existing large and over-capitalized firms.[178] Secondly, firms were not prevented, particularly in the early stages of the duty's operation, from setting prices to include the tax element. The government was therefore creating profits through its own contracts which it then clawed back again in taxes. Even one of its principal architects, Josiah Stamp, was tempted to conclude that the whole exercise might have been an illusion.[179] In so far as the cash gained represented goods and services, he may have been right. But in the struggle to soak up the liquid money supply the excess profits duty became an important, if imperfect, weapon in the government's armoury.

McKenna tackled the most obvious anomaly, the simultaneous continuation of both the munitions levy and the excess profits duty, in his second wartime budget of April 1916. The arms firms maintained that their agreement with the Ministry of Munitions exempted them from liability to the new tax. McKenna accepted rates of depreciation which would write off the extra capital invested in new plant within the period of the war. But he insisted that the administration of the munitions levy should be in the hands of the Inland Revenue. The first 20 per cent of the new profit was made liable for excess profits duty; any profit beyond that was forfeited to the munitions levy. The merger of the two taxes was completed in January 1918.

In other respects the budget of April 1916 contained no major innovations. It was, however, widely seen as an assault on the rich. The rate of excess profits duty was raised to 60 per cent; income tax was increased to 5s. in the £ on earned incomes above £2,500 and on unearned incomes over £2,000. Those liable to excess profits duty, surtax, and income tax could find themselves liable to pay joint rates of 77 per cent. The growth in income tax yield was anticipated to be £43.5 million, roughly double that budgeted for in additional customs and excise.[180]

[178] Daunton, *English Historical Review*, CXI (1996), 898. [179] Stamp, *Taxation*, 216; also 118.
[180] Hirst and Allen, *British war budgets*, 129–33.

McKenna's tenure of the chancellorship earned the praise of the *Economist*: 'The public credit stands unshaken,' F. W. Hirst averred on 8 April 1916, 'thanks to the principle of providing new taxes in advance sufficient to cover both interest and a liberal Sinking Fund on the new debt.'[181] Presumably the Gladstonian ring of sound financial management in these precepts compensated for the sin of McKenna's challenge to free trade. In addition, the chancellor had spurned the apparent attractions of many small taxes, costly to assess and complex to collect. Instead, in embracing the excess profits duty, he had established before any other power one of the principal revenue producers of the war. He anticipated a yield, admittedly highly speculative, of £30 million in its first full year of operation. In practice only £140,000 was netted in the half financial year to March 1916.[182] But in 1916/17 the tax totalled £140 million against an expected £86 million.[183] By 1918/19 it was budgeted to produce £300 million, putting it on a par with income tax, and thus contributing almost half of Britain's direct tax and over a third of its total revenue.

McKenna's credentials were those of Liberal economic orthodoxy, even if his operation of them was stamped with pragmatism. He stood for a strategy built on sound finance. He was therefore a necessary casualty of Lloyd George's accession to the premiership in December 1916. Bonar Law, the Conservative leader, succeeded him at the Treasury.

Law was less bound by the legacy of free trade than McKenna. He was therefore able to introduce an increase in duty from 3.5 per cent to 5 per cent on Lancashire cotton goods imported to India. The package was reciprocal; it included a contribution to the costs of the war of £100 million from the Government of India, to be funded not only by the new import duty but also by a war loan. The Lancashire Liberals saw the tax as a protectionist assault on free trade and expected McKenna and Walter Runciman, the former president of the Board of Trade, to lead the attack from the opposition front bench. They did not do so. For them the issues were not those of Liberalism or of free trade, but of effective government, both in Britain and in India.[184]

McKenna's respect for Law's position was well founded. His successor added nothing to the principles which he had established, and indeed consulted him regularly on financial issues and retained Keynes as his advisor. Law's priorities were to manage his party, to deputize for Lloyd George, and to lead the House of Commons. The Treasury spared him the accusation of neglect. But it was surprised that his reputation as a practical businessman did not transform itself into consistency of purpose and firmness of execution.[185]

---

[181] Hirst and Allen, *British war budgets*, 136.   [182] Ibid. 84; Morgan, *British financial policy*, 92.
[183] Hirst and Allen, *British war budgets*, 128.
[184] Rumbold, *Watershed in India*, 65–6; Turner, *British politics*, 188–90, 346.
[185] Stamp, *Taxation*, 107–8; also Hirst and Allen, *British war budgets*, 199; Farr, 'McKenna', 236.

His first budget, the fifth of the war, in May 1917 was widely criticized for its failure to increase income tax. He raised the duties on tobacco and entertainments. But in doing so he netted only £26.1 million, or sufficient to fund five days of the war.[186] Even his fierceness over the excess profits duty, boosted to 80 per cent, was moderated by concessions. Assessments on the basis of capital were raised from a profit of 6 per cent to 9 per cent (or from 7 to 11 per cent in the case of private companies).

Law went some way to meeting his critics in the final budget of the war, that of April 1918. The standard rate of income tax was increased to 6s. in the £. The maximum rate of supertax was raised to 4s. 6d., and the income threshold for the tax was lowered from £3,000 to £2,500. Farmers, whose exemption from the excess profits duty aroused controversy, were assessed on double their annual rental. Indirect taxes targeted luxuries, and the duties on beer and spirits were doubled. In increasing the tax on tobacco to 8s. 2d. in the £, Law justified its use of shipping space by saying that 'in importing tobacco we are almost importing money'.[187]

Law failed to note the implication of his claim. If the consumption of alcohol and cigarettes continued despite high levels of duty, taxation generally was making insufficient inroads into the fiscal base of the country. In each of the previous two financial years, 1916/17 and 1917/18, excess profits duty and income tax had brought in yields over budget. The chancellor's tax provision was not keeping pace with the growth of the money supply. In 1913/14 the gross income of the nation for tax purposes was estimated at £1,167 million; tax was received on £791 million. In 1917/18 the gross income was put at £1,967 million but tax was received on only £1,083 million.[188] Income tax peaked as a percentage of the total tax yield in 1915/16; by 1918/19 it had fallen from 38.10 per cent to 32.75 per cent.[189] The government response, that the excess profits duty over the same period climbed from 0.04 per cent of the tax yield to 32.06 per cent, assumed that that tax was a direct tax on income. That was the view of business, and as its consent was central to the tax's collection the exchequer tended to share its view. But most of the government's critics argued that it was an indirect tax passed on to the consumer, and that in consequence the increase in direct taxation claimed by the government, as well as the corresponding fall in indirect tax, were exaggerated. On their calculations the excess profits duty increased wages and inflated credit, thus multiplying, rather than reducing, the need for harsher income tax.[190]

During the war the income tax yield rose six times. This was the multiple by which a typical supertax payer saw his tax burden grow. Somebody earning £50,000 a year paid tax at 8.4 per cent at the beginning of the war but 50.6 per

---

[186] Knauss, *Kriegsfinanzierung*, 115.   [187] Hirst and Allen, *British war budgets*, 211.
[188] Ibid. 176.   [189] Grady, *British war finance*, 78.   [190] Kirkaldy, *British finance*, 204–6.

cent at its conclusion. But the numbers earning such large incomes were small, and did not grow as much as war-inflated incomes might have led one to expect. Those in Britain with annual incomes of £75,000 to £100,000 increased from sixty-five to ninety-eight over the whole war. In 1913/14 13,664 individuals were assessed for supertax. This total had already jumped to 30,211 in 1914/15, and it actually fell in 1915/16 and 1916/17. It rose to 35,564 in 1917/18 and 46,107 in 1918/19.

The attention to the affairs of the wealthy led to an underestimation of the tax's impact on the waged. The government seems to have imagined that it was more lenient than in practice it was with those on lower incomes. A person already paying tax at the bottom end of the scale in 1914 saw his tax burden increase twofold during the war to 9 per cent. However, the more realistic picture was not of somebody on a small fixed salary but somebody on a low but increasing wage. The 2.4 million taxpayers who entered the system during the war constituted two-thirds of all taxpayers by 1918/19. The contributions of a waged member of the working class multiplied 3.7 times. The pre-war system of income tax had been a means by which to bind the working classes to the state; wartime levels threatened to undermine this consent.[191] But protests were surprisingly muted. Many Labour leaders felt that direct taxation would inculcate political awareness in the working class, and were, accordingly, not opposed to the trend. A perverse proof of their argument was provided in March 1918 when the desperate situation on the western front prompted the Scottish miners to shelve their opposition to income tax on patriotic grounds. But the amenability of the miners also suggests that the collective phenomenon was more significant than the individual burden. In 1919 only 4 per cent of the total revenue from income tax was derived from the direct taxation of wage-earners. The system of allowances removed the liability of many men who were eligible in terms of gross earnings. In 1914 allowances for children were doubled for those on incomes of less than £500, and in 1918 extended to incomes below £800 (and for larger families below £1,000). In the latter year allowances for wives or other adult dependants were introduced. Thus, only 25 per cent of wage-earners earning between £130 and £160 per annum actually paid income tax in 1916/17. Although the reliefs did not keep pace with the money supply, the proportion had only risen to 32 per cent in 1918/19. Of 5.75 million people with incomes in excess of £130 per annum, 2.2 million were exempted by virtue of the system of allowances.[192] Not for nothing did the working class dub income tax the bachelor's or spinster's tax.

This did not mean that the breadwinners in working-class families escaped tax; they just paid it indirectly. The 2.6-fold increase in customs and excise and the possible operation of the excess profits duty as an indirect tax hit the low

---

[191] Daunton, *English Historical Review*, CXI (1996), 887, 903, 915.   [192] Ibid. 889.

wage-earner with several mouths to feed proportionally harder. In 1919 a married man with three children earning £200 a year was not liable for income tax but still paid 10 per cent or more of his income to the Inland Revenue. Indirect taxes, however, were less visible and caused less grumbling. The fact that different taxes hit the working classes in variable ways fragmented possible opposition. And the net effect was to leave taxation operating rather more as Keynes wished it to: it was reducing the consumptive capacity of the bulk of the population.[193]

What mattered as much as anything else was the perception that Britain was taxing effectively. It was important for the control of domestic inflation; it reassured international credit. The belief that Britain had got it right, primarily through its income tax but also through the excess profits duty, acted as a benchmark for the other belligerents.

In practice, only the United States followed the lead. The incidence, distribution, and yield of federal taxes were all transformed by the war, and because the period of active American belligerency was so short it is not unreasonable to call the effects revolutionary. Nonetheless, as in the British case, the practice fell short of the declared intentions. In April 1917 McAdoo announced his belief that taxation was the main method to finance war, and that he hoped in this way to cover half the war's costs. So vociferous was the response from those who argued that such rates would reduce the incentives to investment that McAdoo reduced his target to one-third. Moreover, he was too optimistic with regard to outgoings. He budgeted for total expenditure of $8,400 million in 1917/18; in reality federal spending was $13,000 million, and in 1918/19 it reached $18,515 million, twenty-four times its 1916/17 level.[194] The ratio of budgeted war revenue to war expenditure fell continuously between 1917 and 1919, averaging below 29 per cent. The actual ratio of war revenue to war expenditure was only 23.3 per cent.[195]

In 1916 74.8 per cent of total revenue was raised through customs and excise. The latter, increased by the Emergency Revenue act of October 1914 to compensate for the loss of the former, accounted for 47.6 per cent of the whole. By contrast, only 16 per cent was derived from taxes on incomes and profits. Income tax, levied on net receipts over $3,000 per annum or $4,000 for a married person, supertax, which began on incomes over $20,000, and corporation income tax, charged on net profits over $5,000, were all introduced in 1913 at a rate of 1 per cent. Supertax rose to 6 per cent on incomes over

[193] Whiting, *Historical Journal*, XXXIII (1990), 895–916; Balderston, *Economic History Review*, 2nd series, LXII (1989), 235–6; Grady, *British war finance*, 75–83, 95–9, 102; Stamp, *Taxation*, 219; Hirst and Allen, *British war budgets*, 176.
[194] Chandler, *Strong*, 99–101.
[195] Gilbert, *American financing*, 74, 82–91, 221–3.

$500,000, producing a maximum combined rate of 7 per cent. There was therefore plenty of slack in the system.[196]

Although in 1915 the new excise duties only produced $52 million against an anticipated $100 million, Wilson's initial preference was to increase them rather than to move to direct taxation. Congress disagreed. Therefore, the Revenue act of 8 September 1916, designed to cover the defence programmes of that year, marked a significant shift in principle. Income tax and corporation tax were raised to 2 per cent. The top rate of supertax was set at 13 per cent (i.e. 15 per cent when combined with income tax) on incomes over $2 million per annum. Inheritance tax, hitherto levied by forty-two states, was appropriated for federal purposes. Beginning on estates of over $50,000, it was charged on a scale rising from 1 per cent to 10 per cent on $5 million or more. The final major innovation was a form of excess profits duty, a tax on munitions' manufacturers of 12.5 per cent of the entire profit for 1916. In aggregate, federal receipts were increased 70 per cent and exceeded the budget forecast of $975.5 million by $142.4 million. But their incidence was borne chiefly by the wealthy, and (in the case of the munitions levy) the Entente. In 1913 49.7 per cent of the tax yield was paid for by those whose incomes exceeded $20,000. Under the terms of the 1916 act this same group paid 95.4 per cent of the yield. The government was therefore appropriating savings, not purchasing-power, and so failing to deter consumption.

On the other hand, the United States had made effective the two major taxes of war finance, income tax and excess profits duty, in advance of its actual entry to the war. The Revenue act of 3 March 1917 never became operational, but it serves to underline the point. It proposed a duty on the excess profits of all companies, at a rate of 8 per cent on profits of over 8 per cent.

Not until 3 October 1917 was the United State's first War Revenue act passed, six months after its entry and at a stage when the monthly deficit was already over $400 million. The delay was less attributable to the fact that the system of war finance had been anticipated before April 1917, and more due to the pleading of special interests. The casualty was the rate of excess profits duty, which, although a great fiscal success ($2,227.6 million was raised in the year ending 30 June 1918), was insufficiently severe. Net profits equal to between 7 and 9 per cent of the capital invested in 1911, 1912, and 1913 were exempt. Thereafter 20 per cent was payable on the first 15 per cent of profits, 25 per cent on the next 5 per cent, 35 per cent on the next 5 per cent, 45 per cent on the next 7 per cent, and 60 per cent on the remainder. The tax on munitions' manufacturers was reduced to 10 per cent, and this, together with a generous depreciation policy, halved its yield in 1918.

---

[196] Gilbert, *American financing*, 26–7, 54–5, 76; Bogart, *War costs*, 264–7. These constitute the principal sources for what follows; see Gilbert, *American financing*, 70–114; Bogart, *War costs*, 264–95.

That McAdoo's taxes were failing to anticipate new areas of liquidity was reflected, as in Britain, by yields over budget. The year ended 30 June 1918 showed a surplus of nearly $300 million on a budget of $3,400 million. Furthermore the taxes lacked simplicity. Their temporary nature was emphasized by dubbing each of the new direct levies a war tax, and they operated alongside the existing bands. Thus, the war income tax was superimposed on the prevailing income tax. The new threshold was fixed at $1,000 for a single person and $2,000 for a married person, and was charged at 2 per cent. The surtax liability was also lowered, beginning at $5,000, not $20,000. The initial rate remained 1 per cent, but those earning $20,000 or more were liable to pay a rate of 8 per cent. Somebody earning $2 million paid 13 per cent under the old surtax arrangements plus 50 per cent under the new. A war estate tax was added to the existing inheritance tax to give a maximum rate of 25 per cent on estates over $10 million, but estates worth under $50,000 were exempt from the old duty and paid only the new one at a rate of 2 per cent.

The combined effect was to continue to load the burden onto the rich and so to tax savings rather than purchasing power. Seventy-seven per cent of taxpayers earned less than $3,000 per year, but they contributed only 3.6 per cent of income tax. Indirect taxes targeted luxuries, including cars, jewellery, cameras, cosmetics, and boats, not major consumer items. By 1918 customs and excise contributed 22.3 per cent of federal revenue, as against 67.8 per cent generated by incomes and profits.

McAdoo's proposals for 1918 included increased taxes on lower incomes and a maximum rate of 80 per cent on war profits. If the latter had been passed on to consumers it could have operated to curb demand and so check inflation. But Congress was more worried about the elections impending in November 1918, and preferred to meet a deficit—accumulating at over a $1,000 million a month by July—through reducing expenditure. The debate dragged on in the Senate until February 1919, and the War Revenue act of 1918 was therefore not effective until 1920.

Thus, even though the United States swung the balance of its revenue from indirect to direct taxation during the war, it found itself unable to effect major changes during the period of its active belligerence. An addition to the principles on which taxation rested proved extraordinarily difficult in wartime. No country demonstrated this more graphically than the third major financial power of the Entente—France.

In June 1914 France was poised to introduce individual income tax. For the radicals it was the denouement to a struggle begun by Caillaux in 1909 but prolonged by the recourse of successive governments to loans and deficit financing. In 1913 Barthou had promised income tax as the corollary of the three-year service law. He then did nothing. The success of the left in the 1914 elections put the three-year law under sufficient threat to make tax reform the quid pro quo of its retention. However, what followed was a feeble response to the length and depth of the debate. Eligibility for the tax, introduced on 15 July 1914, began with incomes of over 5,000 francs, but allowances for spouses of 2,000 francs and for each child of 1,000 francs raised the practical threshold to that comparable with supertax across the Channel. The full rate of 2 per cent was only applicable to incomes over 25,000 francs. Moreover, the opportunity to overhaul the existing tax structure was spurned. Four taxes—the ground tax, the door and window tax, the personal furniture tax, and the business tax—dated from the Revolution and were to a large extent dependent on regional variations in property values. They rested on the principle of equality of incidence rather than on social progressivism. Although a fifth, taxing the income on capital, had been added in 1872, whole areas of wealth and actual incomes were untouched.[197]

Almost immediately, the entire economic life of France was thrown into disarray. The implementation of a new tax seemed impossible when so many tax collectors were ordered to report for military service. Those that remained were instructed not to prosecute the families of servicemen. Tax collection never recovered from the initial disruption of invasion and mobilization. In 1913 10 million Frenchmen paid personal taxes, however low and however antiquated. During the war only 557,000 paid income tax. About 2.5 million were taxed on industrial and commercial profits in 1913, but only 1 million between 1914 and 1919. Certain classes were almost entirely exempt: only 120,000 farmers paid tax and only 32,000 members of the liberal professions (of four times that number practising) paid duty on their profits.[198]

Administrative confusion was not the only cause of falling revenue. Military service and the loss of north-eastern France also reduced France's fiscal base. The moratorium cut off rental income, rendering landlords unable to pay taxes. Import duties on foodstuffs were suspended. The return on customs, which had increased sixfold between 1870 and 1913 to produce a total of 777.9 million francs, fell to 548.3 million francs in 1914. Between August and November 1914 yields on indirect taxes and monopolies were 43 per cent below their total for the first six months of the year; they were still 35 per cent down in December and only recovered to 22.21 per cent below in the first half of 1915. Indirect taxes did not rise significantly above their 1914 total until 1916, and monopolies not until the following year. In fact 1917 was the first year in which the revenue raised through France's existing taxes exceeded its pre-war level.[199]

[197] Krumeich, *Armaments and politics*, 138–40, 213; Knauss, *Kriegsfinanzierung*, 36–40; Ferguson, *Pity of war*, 120–1.

[198] Charbonnet, *Politique financière*, 347; Eichengreen, *Golden fetters*, 75–6.

[199] Olphe-Galliard, *Histoire économique*, 161; Knauss, *Kriegsfinanzierung*, 41–2, 142; Jèze and Truchy, *War finance*, 192; Fisk, *French public finance*, 72, 186.

The appointment of Alexandre Ribot as finance minister on 26 August 1914 was not calculated to reassure the radicals. An opponent of income tax, he proposed to delay its introduction from 1 January 1915 to 1 January 1916. The practical impediments to change gave legitimacy to his argument that France had more than enough problems to cope with. His preference was to wait until economic activity had recovered sufficiently to enable the new tax to be the basis for a balanced budget. As an interim measure he offered to double existing taxes. But the budget commission of the chamber was concerned that by doing so he would entrench the old system and provide an excuse for further procrastination on the new. France went into 1915 without any significant increase in its rates of tax.[200]

The problem for both Ribot and the budget commission was that the situation was no more settled by the end of the next year. In December 1915 Ribot proposed once again to postpone the introduction of income tax. This time he argued that the yield would be too low to warrant the trouble of change, as the richest part of France remained in enemy hands. He was voted down in the chamber. In response, Ribot not only introduced income tax, albeit at the low rate of 2 per cent and at the unnecessarily high starting point of 7,000 francs for a married man, but he also promised a war profits tax.[201]

Ribot modelled his war profits tax on Britain's. As on the other side of the Channel, agriculture was excluded. But France's tax, unlike its ally's, made some effort to target the profits of individuals as well as those of companies. The average of the last three years of peace was to form the basis for judging the profits gained between 1 August 1914 and 31 December 1915. Those who refused to supply information to enable assessment were to have their normal profits assessed as thirty times the yield of the business tax. The first 5,000 francs of profit were to be exempt.[202] In practice, the spectacular yields on the war profits tax were retrospective. A law of 1920 providing for the revision of all contracts formed during the war, and establishing 10 per cent as a reasonable profit, netted 2,937 million francs in 1920 and 3,313 million in 1921.[203] But in the war itself 10 per cent was the effective rate of the tax. Fear of the moratorium's effect on banking activity and the latter's support for business were partly to blame. The government was too fearful of reducing output by removing the profit incentive. Thus Citröen, who showed a profit of 6.1 million francs between 1914 and 1917, paid only 60,000 francs in tax.[204] Fiscal lag did the

---

[200] Charbonnet, *Politique financière*, 63; Duroselle, *La France*, 208–10; Schmidt, *Ribot*, 117.
[201] Schmidt, *Ribot*, 133; Knauss, *Kriegsfinanzierung*, 120–1.
[202] Ribot, *Letters to a friend*, 62; Knauss, *Kriegsfinanzierung*, 122.
[203] Jèze and Truchy, *War finance*, 152–8.
[204] Gerd Hardach, 'Industrial mobilization in 1914–1918', in Fridenson (ed.), *French home front 1914–1918*, 77–8; also Alain Hennebicque, 'Albert Thomas and the war industries', in ibid. 110–12.

rest. The tax was enacted on 1 July 1916, and produced a mere 192.5 million francs in 1917 and 521.5 million in 1918.[205]

In May 1916 Ribot sounded a more robust note. He proposed to double all the existing direct taxes, except the door and window tax, and to increase income tax to 5 per cent. Although an attempt at last to recognize the mismatch between France's outgoings and her declining revenues, the positive effects on revenue would have been minimal and the fiscal implications regressive. The inadequate levels of new taxation were being compensated for by the perpetuation of the old. As a result, the system was becoming more complex at a time when the tax authorities were understaffed, and individually each tax was producing a return too small for the effort required to collect it.

The law of 30 December 1916, therefore, seemed a better answer to the problem. Income tax was raised to 10 per cent, and liability was to begin on incomes of 3,000 francs. Furthermore, the rates were progressive, rising in steps of 10 per cent so that all income over 150,000 francs was forfeit. A war tax, modelled on that adopted by Napoleon, carried a further 25 per cent surcharge on income tax (or a flat rate of 12 francs per annum for those not liable for income tax) payable by men of military age not in the services. The war profits tax was raised to 60 per cent of profits over 500,000 francs. But total receipts in 1916 did little more than match those of 1913, and even in 1917 the yield on direct taxes only exceeded its 1914 total by a third. The effect of the new rates of income tax was moderated by exemptions. Duties on consumption—on beverages, sugar, alcoholic drinks, and tobacco—were raised and an entertainments tax introduced. Therefore, of the extra revenue for 1917 206.5 million francs derived from direct taxation and 379.6 million from indirect.

The fundamental reform of direct taxation, repeatedly postponed since 1914, was finally effected by Thierry on 31 July 1917. Thierry established seven schedules which combined to levy taxes on capital (on property and mobile capital), on capital and income combined (on business and agriculture), and on income (pensions, wages, and profits on trade). By including farming, Thierry closed the obvious loophole for evasion. But the rates, although progressive, were not high. Agriculture was assessed on half the annual rental; rates in other areas began at 3.75 per cent over 3,000 francs or 4.5 per cent over 5,000 francs, with reductions for income below these levels and exemptions according to the size of family. The new taxes, which came into force on 1 January 1918, brought in 411 million francs of additional revenue. But, as the old system was finally abandoned, income of 325 million francs was simultaneously forfeited.

[205] Jèze and Truchy, War finance, 152; Fisk, French public finance, 186, has radically different figures—634 million francs for 1917 and 1,780 million for 1918. Knauss, Kriegsfinanzierung, 136, gives 363.7 million for 1917 and 350.2 million for 1918.

France, therefore, entered the final year of the war at last possessed of a machinery for taxation appropriate to the undertaking. But the levels of tax were still low. Thierry anticipated increasing the rates of income tax, making the war profits tax truly progressive, and introducing a turnover tax. Klotz, his successor, was reluctant to increase income tax. However, in February he raised the rate from 12.5 per cent to 14 per cent. In December 1917 he adopted an estate tax and increased rates of inheritance tax. But France's preoccupation with its declining birth rate once again moderated a tax into virtual ineffectiveness. Only an owner of an estate of over 50 million francs with no children faced a significant burden, fixed at 24 per cent. The owner of a similar estate but with three children paid only 3 per cent. A comparable fate overtook Thierry's plan for war profits, which Klotz also accepted. He established a rate of 50 per cent on profits under 100,000 francs, rising to 80 per cent on those over 500,000 francs. But he then introduced lower rates for newly established war industries, for businesses in war areas, and for companies in which workers held up to a quarter of the total capital. Postponements of the tax were so freely given that of 720 million francs owed up to November 1918 only 24 per cent had been collected.[206]

Thus Klotz, like his predecessors, could not escape an excessive reliance on indirect taxation. A turnover tax of 2 per cent was charged on all payments of more than 10 francs if a receipt was issued, and of more than 150 francs if not. Luxuries, including first-class hotels and restaurants, were subject to a 10 per-cent levy. The tax was pointless. In wartime the yield was small: by definition, luxuries found few markets in the conditions of 1918. In peacetime, industrial interests argued, the duty would hamper France's post-war recovery, since French exports were led by luxury products.[207]

Therefore, the profile of French taxation during the war changed remarkably little. It was still heavily weighted towards indirect duties. In 1913 27.8 per cent of taxation was direct, in 1918 39.1 per cent; indirect taxation stood at 53.5 per cent in 1913 and 43.1 per cent in 1918. Income tax raised less than 1,000 million francs by the war's end.[208] A distinctive feature of France was the relatively high burden of trade taxes (including the post and railways), which, at 18.7 per cent of the whole in 1913 and 17.8 per cent in 1918, remained virtually unchanged.[209]

After the war France's defenders would argue that the taxes on consumption and the registration and stamp duties constituted not-ineffective substitutes for income tax.[210] The former depressed the demand generated by rising nominal incomes; the latter represented a levy on cash as it circulated. If the

[206] Knauss, *Kriegsfinanzierung*, 123–35; Charbonnet, *Politique financière*, 77–81.
[207] Olphe-Galliard, *Histoire économique*, 430–1.
[208] Duroselle, *La Grande Guerre des français*, 155.
[209] Knauss, *Kriegsfinanzierung*, 148–9.   [210] Jèze and Truchy, *War finance*, 218–19, 223–5.

population of France was characterized by a mass of small-income earners, rather than by great concentrations of wealth, and if the retrospective purpose of war taxation was the control of inflation, not the covering of war costs, then French policy was not as ill-conceived as its critics sometimes maintain. But the problem for France after the war remained that of paying for the war. France spent 223,000 million francs in the years 1914–19. It raised 32,000 million through taxation: this was not enough to cover its normal peacetime budget, let alone the servicing of the war debt. By November 1918 France had yet to pay for a single centime of its direct war costs.[211]

France's problems were more those of forwardness than of backwardness. Its old tax structure, hallowed by the triumphs of the Revolution and of Napoleon, was the product of a transformation in the power of the state over a hundred years earlier. Administrative innovation had therefore preceded rapid economic growth. Its principal continental ally, Russia, confronted a range of issues that superficially were similar. Like France, Russia was considering the introduction of income tax in 1914; like France, Russia saw its tax yield decline in 1914/15; and, like France, it planned major reforms, embracing income tax and a war profits tax, in 1916/17. But there was a cardinal difference. Russia was backward, in an administrative as well as in a fiscal sense. It lacked the developed economic base possessed by its major Entente partners. It then compounded its weakness by decisions calculated to worsen its position. By the time of the Bolshevik revolution, it had—again like France—failed to cover any of its war costs, including the servicing of its debt, through taxation.

In 1911 76.8 per cent of Russia's revenue was derived from indirect taxation, and only 13.7 per cent from direct. By 1913 the latter figure had fallen to 8 per cent.[212] The principal sums were raised through excise rather than customs, the latter being designed principally to protect Russia's nascent industries rather than to contribute to the exchequer. Of 1,606.9 million roubles generated by customs and excise in 1913, only 352.9 million came from customs. The impact of the war on overseas trade was therefore less burdensome than for other powers. The main sources of excise duty were sugar, beer, tobacco, petrol, matches, and—above all—spirits. In 1912 the combination of the duty on spirits and the state's monopoly of their sale produced net profits of 626.3 million roubles, or about a quarter of all state revenue.

Direct tax was levied on land, on urban property, and on commerce and industry. The yield of all three doubled between 1903 and 1913. But the total, 272.4 million roubles, remained low. Russia was too predominantly

[211] Georges-Henri Soutou, 'Comment a été financée la guerre', in La Gorce (ed.), *La Première Guerre Mondiale*, 284; Knauss, *Kriegsfinanzierung*, 175.

[212] Michelson *et al.*, *Russian public finance*, 24, 47. Michelson remains the only English-language source on the subject; some additional comments can be found in Claus, *Kriegswirtschaft Russlands*, 31–6.

agricultural for the increases in commercial and industrial taxation arising from urbanization to have significant effect. Land values were falling. Estate duties, levied on the transfer of land, including death, were minimal: the top rate was 12 per cent and the bottom (for a widower or for children) only 1.5 per cent.

A bill for the introduction of income tax was drafted in 1905 and introduced in 1907. In 1914 it still languished in committee. The case against its implementation in peace was real enough. Russia was not a rich country; its geographical size and its population density would make assessment and collection complex. A low threshold would therefore be difficult to administer and possibly not very productive. A high threshold (the 1907 bill planned to exempt incomes below 1,000 roubles per annum) would discourage the accumulation of capital and its subsequent investment. Thus, the possible net returns on income tax were murky. Moreover, Russia before the war did not need direct taxation to soak up surplus cash. During the war it did.

On 28 July 1914 the state liquor shops were closed as a temporary measure to expedite mobilization. On 3 September the Duma extended the closure for the duration of the war, and a month later authorized local governments to intensify the ban. Temperance, it was hoped, would help the war effort by raising standards of public health and boosting industrial productivity. But it had two fiscal disadvantages. First, it contributed to monetary overhang, increasing the quantity of unspent cash in private pockets. Secondly, it diverted the trade in alcohol into illicit channels, so passing profits from the state to speculators. The gross loss to governmental revenues was 432 million roubles in 1914 and 791.8 million in 1915.

Even without such self-administered wounds, the war eroded Russia's fiscal base. Loss of territory accounted for a decline in revenue of 69 million roubles in 1914 and 226.7 million in 1915. Customs receipts were hit by the closure of the western land frontier and of the Dardanelles. Railway traffic in the combat zone fell by two-thirds (and by a quarter elsewhere), so reducing returns on the railway tax. The budget of June 1914 had assumed an income for that year of 3,585.5 million roubles. In practice it sank to 2,898.1 million, and receipts for the second half of 1914 totalled 1,130.5 million roubles as against 1,804.8 million for the comparable period in the previous year. Revenue for 1915 continued at a similar level, 2,827.6 million roubles, when a rise to 3,132 million had been forecast.

The growth in income budgeted for 1915 rested on increases in almost all Russia's existing taxes in 1914. The most contentious of these was the railway tax, whose abolition had been anticipated as part of an effort to encourage trade. As a result of its intensification, it became cheaper to move cargo on passenger trains and humans on freight trains. The only significant innovation of 1914 was a tax on the carriage of goods. Calculated by weight, it was particularly designed to restrict the movement of raw materials, so curbing demand which was exceeding supply. In practice, both the railway tax and the duty on the carriage of goods formed the beginnings of a vicious circle in which the government levied taxes on itself. The increase in military transport more than compensated for the loss in volume of civilian railway traffic; the ministry of war therefore paid the railway tax, albeit at half rates. The carriage of goods tax fell on materials destined for the production of munitions, and its burden was therefore passed on by industry in the price paid by the government for the finished article. A related point could be made about customs duties, which were revised in February 1915: 25 per cent of customs were paid by the Ministry of Finance for imports for military purposes.

The full force of this bogus income was revealed in the 1916 budget. Only minor changes were made to taxation in 1915, and the revenue anticipated for 1916 was 2,914 million roubles, a level comparable with the previous year. In the event, receipts totalled 3,974.5 million. The depreciation of the rouble played its part in creating a nominal increase. But that, in its turn, was partly fostered by the government's taxation policy which was stoking cash inflation. About 70 per cent of the total revenue for 1916 was contributed by the state itself.

The 1916 budget, unlike that of 1915, did, however, recognize the need to plan for a long war followed by a sustained period of post-war recovery. The burden of indirect taxation had been significantly reduced by the ending of the monopoly on spirits, and it was proposed to continue the trend to direct taxation by the establishment of progressive income tax and of an increased tax on industrial profits. The target was not only to cover Russia's ordinary expenditure during the war, but also to establish its taxation system on a new permanent basis appropriate to peace.

In the event, less was achieved than Bark's ambitious programme promised. He wanted to exempt incomes below 700 roubles, recognizing that Russia's population was becoming increasingly wealthy in nominal terms, and was being spared a significant burden of indirect tax. The Duma, arguing that Russian workers were poor and their cost of living high, was more concerned with the social than the inflationary implications. Its members pushed for a threshold of 1,000 or even 1,500 roubles. A compromise was struck at 850 roubles. Depreciation did mean that this level embraced about half the households of Russia, and its progressive effects put the top level of taxation higher than that of any other European country except Britain. But the tax was not to come into force until 1917. And the yield budgeted for that year, 178 million roubles, was still small alongside the forfeited spirit revenue.

The same point could be made in even stronger terms in relation to the new levels of tax on industrial profits, scheduled to produce only 55 million roubles in 1917. Companies whose profits exceeded 8 per cent of their invested capital and of their average profits for 1913/14 were liable for tax on sums over 2,000 roubles. Individuals were taxed on emoluments over 500 roubles. The bottom rate of tax was 20 per cent; the top rate, including the existing direct tax and income tax, was not to exceed 50 per cent.

In many ways the fiscal policy of the Provisional Government of March 1917 built on the programme developed by the Tsar's ministers in the previous year. Nor was what it proposed dissimilar to the thinking displayed by the other Liberal governments of the Entente at this stage of the war. It planned to increase rates of income tax, setting a combined top level of 90 per cent. As the assessment was based on 1916 incomes, which in some cases had fallen in 1917, the new taxes could in theory have exhausted a taxpayer's total salary. The war profits tax was to be subject to progressive rates, so that individuals were liable to a maximum of 60 per cent and publicly audited companies to one of 80 per cent. The maximum combined level of tax on businesses was again 90 per cent. Speculators and middlemen, who had effectively escaped the 1916 legislation, were liable to be taxed on income rather than on profits from capital. Plans were also afoot to increase indirect taxes and establish new state monopolies.

But the Provisional Government was the victim of its predecessors' weaknesses, of fiscal lag, and of its own flabby-mindedness. It increased salaries and allowances, promising to pay them out of its tax reforms. But taxation was too slow in its effects. In the short term it could only do so through monetary inflation. Between January 1917 and the Bolshevik revolution in November Russia's note issue doubled. Little of this additional cash could be soaked up by the fiscal structure inherited from the Tsarist government. Thus the Provisional Government contributed to the very process which its harsh fiscal policy was designed to check. Inflation was not the least of the factors making Russia ungovernable in the autumn of 1917.

Russia had only a limited fiscal base. The increased money supply generated by the war, therefore, bore less and less relationship to the availability of goods and services. But a limited fiscal base did not mean that a state had to wave farewell to an efficient system of war finance. Good administration could in theory—by tight control of the money supply and by severe taxation—compensate for limited wealth. During the war and after the commentators of the major economic powers of the Entente, including Keynes, remarked approvingly on the performance of Italy. In 1914 Italian taxation drew off a higher proportion (about 10 per cent) of the gross national product than that of any other major European power.[213] Throughout the war, Italy made, it was maintained, a real effort to service its war-related borrowings from current revenue. Some thought it had succeeded.[214] It had not, but E. L. Bogart's 1921 calculation of Italy's deficit on normal expenditure plus interest charges for the

[213] Forsyth, *Crisis of Liberal Italy*, 3, 326; what follows relies almost exclusively on Forsyth, whose work revises Luigi Einaudi, *La guerra e il sistema tributario italiano* (Bari, 1927).
[214] Teillard, *Les Emprunts de guerre*, 73, 127; Forsyth, *Crisis of Liberal Italy*, 69.

war, $786.5 million, compared favourably with his reckonings for France ($3,346 million) and Germany ($4,180 million).[215]

Economic growth had enabled Italy to generate budget surpluses between the financial years 1897–8 and 1910–11. But the campaign in Libya then combined with Giolitti's social reforms to push the national account into deficit. Although Italy did not join the Entente until April 1915, the burden created by military expenditure was exacerbated by preparations for war from 1914. Thus, Italy had been living with some of the features of a war economy for three years before it commenced active belligerence. Like France and Germany, it entered hostilities with an exchequer already encumbered by pre-war debt.

The period of budget surplus was, with hindsight, an ideal opportunity to restructure Italy's taxation system. Taxes were levied under three heads—direct taxes on land, buildings, and mobile capital; transaction taxes (including inheritance duty); and consumption taxes. In 1913 only 27 per cent of Italy's revenue was generated through direct taxation, as opposed to over 40 per cent in the 1870s. Fifty-eight per cent derived from the taxes on consumption, and 15 per cent from transaction taxes. Personal income tax was advocated, but as a measure of social justice, not as a means to increase revenue.

Italy's tax structure remained unreformed in 1914. Its post-war critics would accuse it of inflexibility. But as serious as its increasingly antiquated structure was the fact that its stringency was more apparent than real. A powerful argument against personal income tax and in favour of the high rate of indirect tax was the relative poverty of Italy compared with its western European neighbours. The difficulties generated by relatively low incomes and high rates of taxation were resolved by the Ministry of Finance in a series of personal negotiations between individuals and the state as to their commitments. Published rates, therefore, did not reflect actual payments. Nor was the system of assessment only unfair, it was also inefficient. The direct tax on land was levied on the basis of an incomplete land register. Italy had voted to draw up a national register in 1886. Those provinces which expected their assessments to fall as a result co-operated in its establishment; the majority did not. Thus the yields on land tax fell. Thus too the tax on mobile capital became a proportionally greater element of direct taxation. However, this latter tax assessed each source of income separately, rather than considering each person's total holdings. A taxpayer who divided his wealth over several heads therefore paid less on the same income than a taxpayer who concentrated his investments.[216]

Italy entered the war with much trumpeting about fiscal rectitude. Unable to claim that its purpose was defensive, it could harbour no latent hopes for an indemnity, and had therefore to confront its own capacity to pay for what it was about. But by the end of the war the structure of its taxation was little

---

[215] Bogart, *War costs*, 317–18.   [216] Forsyth, *Crisis of Liberal Italy*, 5, 28–33.

changed. In 1917/18 direct taxes still only contributed 36 per cent of total revenue, transaction taxes remained virtually constant at 14 per cent, and consumption taxes had yet to fall below 50 per cent. By the same year the burden of taxation, expressed as a proportion of gross national product, showed no more than a marginal increase to 10.9 per cent (expenditure rose from 11.2 per cent in 1913/14 to 36.7 in 1917/18).[217] The accusation of inflexibility was justified.

The rates of direct tax were, of course, increased. Indeed, the three permanent direct taxes carried a 5 per-cent surcharge from October 1914, and a 10 per-cent increase followed in December of the same year. But these rises were low compared with the increased liquidity created by the war. Efforts to introduce progressive taxation, in November 1916 and September 1917, foundered on the illogicalities of the basic structure. Property in different regions continued to be assessed separately; distinctions as to earned, unearned, and mixed income persisted; investments in different businesses were not aggregated. Evasion was simple. Like France, Italy fell into the trap of an excessively diverse structure, complex and confusing in its administration, and with each tax generating only small returns. Like France, these pinpricks included a levy on those of military age not in the services (introduced in November 1916), and taxes on luxuries that were in limited demand.

Italy's reputation for fiscal prudence was, nonetheless, sustained by its early introduction of a war profits tax. Indeed, the Italian duty actually became law in November 1915, ahead of the British scheme. Its basic structure aped the British proposal. Profits over 8 per cent of invested capital were defined as excessive, unless firms could prove that they had made higher profits in the three years preceding the war. The basic rate of tax was 20 per cent, rising to 60 per cent on profits over 20 per cent. As at first in Britain, the duty was not accompanied by a policy of price controls. Potentially, therefore, the tax operated not as direct tax on industry but as an indirect tax on the consumer. But, unlike Britain, the profits subject to assessment were not all the profits generated during the war but only those profits derived from the war. The excess profits duty adopted by Westminster did not have the munitions firms as its primary target; that embraced by Rome did. Therefore, the consumer which would bear the indirect burden would be the state. In Britain the excess profits duty had at least some impact in the battle to absorb private purchasing power. In Italy it did not.

A tax regime favourable to heavy industry was justified on strategic grounds and on Italy's need to compensate for its economic backwardness by an accelerated programme of investment. War profits were therefore seen as an opportunity to write off debts and to develop fresh plant. State controls on

---

[217] Ibid. 326, 327; also 93–4.

industry were reduced, not tightened. Fiscal privileges were extended to equipment which did not necessarily need to be written off during the war but which could be used for peacetime purposes. To achieve all this, the state took, in the form of increased prices for war goods, the burden of its own excess profits duty. Similarly, a tax on all payments of the state to private parties (the *centesimi della guerra* introduced at 1 cent in November 1915, and then raised to 2 cents in July 1916, and 3 in June 1918) could be reflected back in the form of prices. The Italian exchequer's creation of fictitious revenue bore at least a passing resemblance to that of Russia.[218]

Italy's failure to control costs meant that, although during the war 23 per cent of its expenditure was nominally covered by revenue, the wholesale price index stood at 364 in 1919, if 1913 is taken as 100.[219] But what, of course, is surprising in the Italian story is the reputation for fiscal rigour, not the fact of post-war inflation. The Liberal government of Italy was weak, its foreign policy misguided and unpopular, and its economy ill-developed. Italy was the least of the great powers of Europe in 1914.

Much more complex, and much more alluring to scholars in the 1920s and ever since, was the failure of Germany to manage its war finances. In 1919 its wholesale price index was 415, and it would quintuple by the end of 1922. Germany was not only the mainstay of the Triple Alliance, it was also, in economic as well as in military terms, the greatest of the continental powers. And yet, if the existing deficit in 1914 is included, German revenue between 1914 and 1918 met only 13.57 per cent of expenditure.[220] Its total tax yield from all sources throughout the war was less than Britain's revenue from its excess profits duty alone.[221] It thus failed to cover not only the servicing of its war-related debt but also its ordinary peacetime outgoings.

Self-evidently, Germany's difficulty with taxation was not primarily the consequence of insufficient wealth (however illiquid much of it might be, compared, say, with France). It did not begin the war, as Russia and Italy did, with an already limited fiscal base. The problem was political: it was in origin the consequence of the circumstances of the Reich's foundation.

Broadly speaking, Bismarck had left the power of direct taxation to the individual states. To the Reich he had appropriated indirect taxation, and particularly stamp duty and customs and excise. In the circumstances of 1871 the Reich and not the states possessed the major producer of revenue. Furthermore, the states were obliged to contribute to the running of the Reich at a level set by the Reichstag. These two elements, Reich customs duty and the states' *Matrikularbeiträge*, were set in an interlocking relationship in 1879. The Centre party agreed to support Bismarck's programme of tariffs, on condition that

[218] Forsyth, *Crisis of Liberal Italy*, 7–9, 64–5, 70–99.   [219] Ibid. 76.   [220] Lotz, *Deutsche Staatsfinanzwirtschaft*, 105.   [221] Balderston, *Economic History Review*, 2nd series, XLII (1989), 230.

when the yield on customs exceeded 130 million marks the excess would go to the states. The ceiling set on the Reich's share was sufficiently low to necessitate the survival of the *Matrikularbeiträge*. The arrangement worked to the Reich's advantage until the end of the century. Thereafter it did not. Central government activity expanded faster than the consumption of the population. Between 1875 and 1913 the Reich's net expenses grew five times, but its population only increased by 57 per cent.[222] The fact that the per capita income of that population was also rising meant little when the Reich had no constitutional right to tax it. Nor did the *Matrikularbeiträge* provide the flexibility Germany required. They were a head tax, not an income tax: thus their burden on the poorer classes in the more impoverished states of Germany was already heavy. Indeed, the population of Germany, when it aggregated the taxation levied by Reich, state (*Land*), and commune (*Gemeinde*), considered itself hard pressed. The exemption level in Prussia was set at the equivalent of £45 (as opposed to £160 in Britain), and by 1903 there were already 3.9 million taxpayers in Germany. In 1913 local authorities (including the states) were responsible for 66.9 per cent of government spending, the Reich for only 33.1 per cent, and 22.6 per cent of the total was funded by income tax.[223]

Between 1906 and 1913 the Reich was locked in battle with the states in an effort to appropriate some element of direct taxation, and so cover its increasing expenditure on the armed forces. However, this struggle was not simply an issue of governmental centralization; it was also a matter of party politics. The Socialists were in favour of progressive direct taxation; they were prepared even to support a larger army and navy to achieve that aim. The Conservatives were opposed to duties on property, particularly on land, but were compromised by their wish to strengthen the services. The objective of Bethmann Hollweg, in particular, was as much to secure an ongoing majority in the Reichstag as it was to reform Germany's finances.

The Conservatives' alarm at the implications of *Weltpolitik* seemed justified in 1906 itself, when a Reich inheritance tax was imposed. Their opposition rendered it a tax without teeth. In 1911 Wermuth proposed to make death duties effective in order to end the Reich's deficits. Bethmann Hollweg sought a solution that would be less offensive to the Conservatives. By taxing all property, he hoped to draw more on the wealth of industry. But the opposition of the states to an inheritance tax prompted Wermuth to resign in March 1912. The subsequent budget did no more than adjust indirect taxation, although the Reichstag budget commission required the government to formulate a new universal property tax by 1913. The Conservatives and the Centre party hoped

---

[222] Knauss, *Kriegsfinanzierung*, 30; see also 24–30; Roesler, *Finanzpolitik*, 13–17; Carl-Ludwig Holtfrerich, 'The modernisation of the tax system in the First World War and the Great Inflation, 1914–23', in Witt (ed.), *Wealth and taxation*, 126–8.

[223] Roesler, *Finanzpolitik*, 134; Daunton, *English Historical Review*, CXI (1996), 886.

this would be a duty on mobile capital, and wanted it raised by the states; the Progressives and the SPD advocated a central tax on all property.

Wermuth's successor at the Treasury, Hermann Kühn, planned a tax on capital gains. By not appropriating any of the states' taxes, by leaving existing wealth untouched and yet imposing a levy on all types of property, he produced a workable and sensible compromise. As originally proposed, this *Wehrbeitrag* would have taxed any increase in value of over 2,000 marks on all property worth more than 6,000 marks. As enacted, the thresholds were 10,000 marks and 20,000 marks. Most small tradesmen, skilled craftsmen, and peasant farmers were thereby exempted. The rate was progressive, between 0.75 per cent and 2.5 per cent according to the size of the unearned increment.[224] The right was appeased by two concessions: agricultural land was assessed on its fictional yield value, which was below the real value on sale; and the total package for 1913 still included increases in indirect taxation. But in overall terms the shift in policy between 1906 and 1913 favoured the less privileged. Consumption taxes over that period rose 19.3 per cent, transport taxes 71.8 per cent, and direct taxes 71.7 per cent. The total Reich yield borne by each of these elements in 1913 was 34 per cent, 9.1 per cent, and 56.8 per cent.[225]

Nonetheless, it is exaggerated to claim that the Reich had made the breakthrough to a system of progressive taxation, which favoured the poor and milked the rich.[226] Such an argument is essentially counter-factual. In 1912/13, at least temporarily, the financial implications of the arms policy created a form of social fusion; that fusion possibly prefigured the liberal Reichstag majority of 1917/18. But the tax that had made this possible was not envisaged as part of the normal peacetime financial arrangements of the Reich. The *Wehrbeitrag* was a one-off contribution to defence, to last three years only. The direct tax levied on each individual was still only half that of Britain, and the total tax burden little more than that.[227] The *Wehrbeitrag* was a reflection of international tension more than a reform of fiscal principles.[228]

Above all, there had been no intellectual shift in the Reich. The acquisition of limited powers of direct taxation did not produce the determination that taxes rather than loans should be the main means of financing a war. Even in peacetime, borrowing was the means by which to finance increased defence spending. This was a principle established by the build-up of the navy, and by 1913/14 65.3 per cent of all Reich debt had been incurred through expenditure on the colonies, the army, and the navy. As a corollary, servicing the debt which

[224] Witt, *Finanzpolitik*, 370.
[225] Kroboth, *Finanzpolitik*, 302.
[226] Ibid. 284–9, 321; also Holtfrerich, 'The modernisation of the tax system', in Witt (ed.), *Wealth and taxation*, 128; Knauss, *Kriegsfinanzierung*, 28; Witt, *Finanzpolitik*, 372–6; Ferguson, *Historical Journal*, XXXV (1992), 725–52, provides a historiographical survey in English.
[227] Kroboth, *Finanzpolitik*, 304.
[228] Holtfrerich, *German inflation*, 110.

the armed forces largely generated itself became a significant element of Reich expenditure—about 11 per cent of the whole in 1913.[229] In an influential text of 1912, *Kriegssteuer oder Kriegsanleihe?*, Heinrich Dietzel argued that war should be paid for out of loans, or in other words, that taxation should be deferred. He anticipated that wartime taxation would reduce consumption and encourage the withdrawal of investments: given a limited understanding of inflation, both consequences seemed to him undesirable. Dietzel was anticipating a short war. Taxation, because of the lag in its collection, would be much slower in raising money than the issue of government loans. Finally, Dietzel warned against fostering a divisive political debate just at the point when the nation needed to be united.

Dietzel did not go unanswered. Jakob Riesser, a National Liberal and a banker, called for a sound budget resting on direct and indirect taxation in *Finanzielle Kriegsbereitschaft und Kriegführung* (2nd edition, 1913). Riesser advocated what became the orthodox rule of thumb for liberals, that one-third of a war's costs should be met through tax.[230] But it was the writings of Dietzel, not of Riesser, that found reflection in what Helfferich did. The fact that Dietzel's title posited taxation and loans as competing alternatives encouraged the view that one was the replacement for the other; the possibility that both might be required was neglected. Indeed, Helfferich even harboured the hope that the loans would not be redeemed by deferred taxation but by payments from the defeated enemy. When he took over from Kühn at the Treasury on 26 January 1915 he already had behind him the experience of advising the chancellor on appropriate levels of enemy indemnity.[231]

However, Helfferich's major concern as finance minister was not pecuniary but political. The *Burgfrieden* was too recent, too fragile, and too precious for it to be sacrificed on the altar of fiscal rectitude. Any increase in direct taxation would please the left and would augment the power of the Reichstag; therefore it could be calculated to antagonize the right and the *Bundesrat*. Helfferich received clear warning of the limits this imposed on his effective powers in July 1915. The *Bundesstaaten* told the Reich that it would not be allowed to renew the *Wehrbeitrag*.[232]

The German government was therefore caught in a cleft stick. Its traditional source of revenue, indirect taxation, was a wasting asset. The Socialists would only agree to increased duties on consumption if they were accompanied by the taxes on income opposed by the right. But more significant than the political arguments were the falling returns on existing rates of duty because

---

[229] Ferguson, *Historical Journal*, XXXV (1992), 748; also Ferguson, *Pity of war*, 129.
[230] Manfred Ziedler, 'Die deutsche Kriegsfinanzierung 1914 bis 1918 und ihre Folgen', in Michalka (ed.), *Der Erste Weltkrieg*, 418–19.
[231] Hecker, *Rathenau*, 178.
[232] Williamson, *Helfferich*, 129–30; Helfferich, *Weltkrieg*, 224–5; Roesler, *Finanzpolitik*, 71, 104–5.

of the war. Customs were eased in an effort to attract goods to Germany despite the blockade. In 1913 they had raised 679.3 million marks (or 30.8 per cent of Reich revenue); in 1915 they contributed 359.9 million, and in 1918 133 million. Domestic duties were caught by the decline in national income. Taking 1913 as 100, the most optimistic index shows a fall in national income to 88 by 1918, and the most severe to 57.[233]

Neither the 1914 budget, introduced by Kühn, nor that of March 1915, the first actual war budget and the first proposed by Helfferich, showed any change in the structure or rates of tax. Without the *Wehrbeitrag*—which produced 637.4 million marks in 1914 and 307.8 million in 1915—the position would have been bleak. Receipts under most of the major traditional heads fell. The exception, significantly, was the Reich printing works, busy producing notes for the government, the Reichsbank, and the *Darlehenskassen*. The *Matrikularbeiträge* remained constant (as they did throughout the war) at 51.9 million marks. Total Reich income in 1914 was 2,471.1 million marks (excluding the net profits on postal services and railways); in 1915 it fell to 1,825.2 million marks.

In 1916 the *Wehrbeitrag* would decline to 19.5 million marks. Rebuffed over its renewal, Helfferich had to find a substitute. He suggested a tax on all wartime profits, to be levied on a scale of up to 15 per cent of the increase in value of property or 30 per cent of the income. But inherited property and corporate profits would be excluded, and he did not envisage introducing the tax until after the war. Helfferich found he had struck a chord both with the Bundesrat and with the public. On 30 November 1915 he formally introduced a proposal for a war profits tax.

This time company profits were included. Businesses were to deposit 50 per cent of gains in excess of their pre-war average over five years in a special reserve fund. The tax would be drawn from the fund. The complicated arrangement was designed to forestall the distribution of the profits on the second year of the war before a definitive law had been passed. The proposal and the debate were uncontentious. By building on the principles of the *Wehrbeitrag*, the tax could be construed as a once-and-for-all levy on capital gains accrued in the calendar years 1914, 1915, and 1916. The income which had been consumed or capitalized during this period would be liquidated without the imposition of a direct income tax at a time when the cost of living was increasing. The Bundesrat was therefore convinced that the states' rights to income tax were unimpinged. Conversely but conveniently, the Socialists—although wanting the tax to be at a higher rate than was the case—were persuaded that the tax was a Reich levy on income. Even the industrialists had little to complain about. At first only public companies were affected, and they—by virtue of Helfferich's notice in July—had had time to take evasive

---

[233] Holtfrerich, *German inflation*, 224–7, on these indexes and their variations.

action. Furthermore, they could still draw on the special fund in order to subscribe to war loans. Private companies and individuals remained exempt until June 1916. The Reichsbank alone was severely handled. Its release from the tax on its note issue and the increased circulation of notes had boosted its profits, three-quarters of the excess on which were now diverted from its private shareholders to the government.

Helfferich's budget of March 1916 therefore marked a first attempt to put Germany's war finances on a firmer foundation. The war profits tax was set at a rate of 10 per cent on a 2 per cent excess, rising in steps to 30 per cent on sums above 15 per cent. If average profits were more than 25 per cent of paid-up capital and reserves, then a surcharge of up to 50 per cent was payable.[234] Similarly for individuals, 50 per cent was the maximum rate of tax on the nominal increase in their assets (on an increase of more than 400,000 marks).[235] Property, provided it retained 90 per cent of its value as at 31 December 1913, was taxed at 1 per cent; increased wealth derived from inheritance or from insurance payments was exempt. None of this became law until June, and it had little impact on revenue until 1917.

The remainder of Helfferich's budget rested on more traditional devices. Excise duties began to climb back to their pre-war yield, principally thanks to an increased duty on tobacco; the rates on alcoholic drinks were untouched, and continued to fall. His proposal to impose a stamp duty on almost all transactions was thrown out by the budget committee of the Reichstag, on the grounds that it would inhibit business. Goods tended to change hands many times on the market, and commercial circles therefore preferred a sales tax on finished goods. The budget committee replaced Helfferich's proposed duty with a charge of one-thousandth on the value of sales in kind, a tax that hit small shopkeepers more than the powerful figures represented in the chambers of commerce.[236] Although a potentially powerful generator of revenue, a value-added tax in prototype, the tax's rate was too low to be of much short-term significance. The combined outcome was disappointing. Helfferich had projected revenue of 2,749.2 million marks for 1916, hoping thus to balance the ordinary budget (including debt charges of 2,308.7 million marks). Actual income was only 2,122.2 million marks, and ordinary expenditure rose to 3,066.8 million marks.[237]

Helfferich's move to the Ministry of the Interior resulted in the appointment of Graf Siegfried von Roedern as his successor at the Ministry of Finance on

---

[234] Roesler, *Finanzpolitik*, 71–4; Williamson, *Helfferich*, 130–4; Lotz, *Deutsche Staatsfinanzwirtschaft*, 54–5, 60–1; Knauss, *Kriegsfinanzierung*, 97–100; Helfferich, *Weltkrieg*, 229–31.
[235] This follows the table in Roesler, *Finanzpolitik*, 189; Lotz, *Deutsche Staatsfinanzwirtschaft*, 60, gives 50% on an increase of 1 million marks in personal wealth.
[236] Ferguson, *Pity of war*, 130–1.
[237] Roesler, *Finanzpolitik*, 68; see also Williamson, *Helfferich*, 133–43.

1 June 1916. Roedern's budget of February 1917, although apparently harsh, was rightly criticized in the Reichstag for not going far enough. Roedern announced that he needed an additional 1,250 million marks to be raised through taxation in order to cover interest payments. He got 1,473 million. But in 1917 the net debt increased by 36,092.9 million marks, with the result that the interest payments alone were running at 3,250 million marks on 1 April 1917.

Furthermore, much of the increased revenue was the legacy of Helfferich's 1916 budget, now fully operational. Total receipts for 1917 were projected at 4,026.7 million marks; in the event 8,010.1 million were raised. Half of this came from Helfferich's war tax, to which Roedern added a 20 per cent surcharge. Roedern was also the beneficiary of Helfferich's budget in the duty on tobacco, whose yield—at 419.5 million marks for 1917—was double that of 1916 and eight times its pre-war level. His own principal innovations fell into the trap of creating revenue that was largely fictitious. Coal was taxed at 20 per cent of its sale price at the mine. The attractions of the coal tax were its ease of collection (only about 500 firms were involved) and the possible stimulus to neutral imports through an increased domestic price. But the principal consumer of coal was ultimately—via the arms industries and its products—the government. To spare it a double burden, coal was exempted from the other major new tax, on the transport of goods and individuals.

Reich revenues for 1918 fell to 7,395.2 million marks. Principally, this was because the war profits tax was a one-off arrangement, which required renewal or reconstruction to be effective for 1918. Roedern felt that direct taxation was incompatible with the government's preferred method of war finance, that of loans. Both could be seen as chasing the same wealth, and appropriation through the former might inhibit voluntary subscription to the latter. Furthermore, Roedern still preserved the notion that direct taxation had not become a permanent feature of the Reich's finances: he was prepared to use it only to reduce accumulated debt and not to cover current deficits. Therefore, although his budget of July 1918 contained a dozen new laws, and effectively ten new taxes, it was heavily weighted towards indirect taxation. The war profits tax produced only 791.8 million marks under the 1916 law and 1,617.2 million under Roedern's 1918 provisions. The tax on company profits was set at 60 per cent, but was reduced for profits of under a million marks, and could also be set against any losses registered in previous years. Increases in income were taxed on a scale beginning at 5 per cent for the first 10,000 marks and which rose in five steps to 50 per cent over 100,000 marks. The tax on property, although levied not on the increase in value but on the sum itself, was presented as a tax on accumulated income which had been capitalized. It was applied at a rate of one-thousandth on the first 200,000 marks, and also rose in five gradations, to five-thousandths on more than 1 million marks. Most of the indirect taxes fell on drinks, both alcoholic and non-alcoholic. Luxuries carried a purchase tax of 10 per cent. The biggest change was to the turnover tax, which at 5 per cent on all dealings not only produced 823.4 million marks in 1919 but also forced a foreshortening in the number of transactions and so discouraged specula-tion.[238]

Roedern's 1918 budget showed how little the fundamental lineaments of German thinking had shifted throughout the war. His indirect taxes were meant to yield an additional 1,564 million marks in 1918; they actually pro-duced 486 million.[239] Germany's failure to milk fresh areas of liquidity was therefore more than a simple matter of fiscal lag. Peacetime yields were still being expected of taxes on consumption despite the facts that national income was diminishing and that the state had appropriated the powers of production.

By the same token, Germany fudged the issue of direct taxation in new areas. War profits, after all, might be deemed sufficiently exceptional to be outside the ambit of the peacetime restrictions on direct taxation by the Reich. But Germany failed to establish a coherent model for the management of its war industry. The question of excess profits prompted the Reichstag to establish a committee on war supplies in June 1916, but it did not meet for the first time until December and it ended its proceedings, after fourteen meetings, in February 1918.[240] In July 1917 Wilhelm Groener, as head of the newly created war office, proposed controls on profits and wages and urged a sharpening of the war profits tax. Shortly thereafter he fell victim to the machinations not only of heavy industry but also of OHL itself.[241]

Industry successfully resisted government management. Only one company in Germany became subject to direct state control: on 6 March 1918 the Daimler motor works were placed under the oversight of the army. Daimler's shares, which had stood at 317 at the end of 1913, rose to 630 by 1916 and 1,350 in 1917: in 1916 and 1917 dividends of 35 per cent and 30 per cent were distributed. In the financial year 1916/17 the firm wrote off 100 per cent of the book value of its plant. Such accounting practices and their consequent profits did not prevent Daimler's management from asking the War Ministry for a 50 per cent increase in the prices of automobiles and spare parts for aero-engines at the beginning of 1917, and threatening to suspend night shifts and overtime if its demands were not met in February 1918.[242]

The difficulty in assessing the impact of the war profits tax is knowing how far a firm like Daimler was typical. Industries that were not benefiting from

[238] Roesler, *Finanzpolitik*, 109–18, 189–94, 196; Lotz, *Deutsche Staatsfinanzwirtschaft*, 62–79; Knauss, *Kriegsfinanzierung*, 100–7.

[239] Roesler, *Finanzpolitik*, 120–1.

[240] Wette, *Militärgeschichtliches Mitteilungen*, 36 (1984), 34–5.

[241] Feldman, *Army, industry and labor*, 385–404; Feldman, *Great disorder*, 68–70.

[242] Wette, *Militärgeschichtliches Mitteilungen*, 36 (1984), 44; Bellon, *Mercedes*, 89–90, 102–12; Burch-ardt, *Zeitschrift für Unternehmensgeschichte*, XXXII (1987), 98, 103.

army orders were likely to experience decline; dividends as a whole, if related to the movement of prices, fell.[243] But many firms kept both their dividends and their balances low in order to avoid tax demands from the government and increases in pay for their workers. Their profits were hidden in increased capital and reserves. The sixteen most important steel and mining firms in Germany—admittedly businesses likely to benefit from the war—entered net profits of 285 million marks over its first three years. The dividends of iron-processing firms rose on average 175 per cent when allowance is made for inflation, and those of the chemical industry 200 per cent. The most successful heavy industries showed an eightfold increase in profits even against 1912/13, itself a peak year, and Rheinmetall a tenfold increase.[244]

But Rheinmetall's major rival, and Germany's principal armaments firm, Krupp, displays the danger of snap judgements. Shortly after the war's outbreak Gustav Krupp von Bohlen und Halbach declared to the firm's directors that he did not intend the company's profits to be any greater than was normal in peace. The firm's accounts suggest that this was not the empty rhetoric it was long assumed to be. In the immediately pre-war years average net profits had been 20 per cent of turnover; during the war they ran at 8.4 per cent, much lower than those of other major companies. Furthermore, Krupp's dividends, which had averaged 12 per cent in the three years up to and including 1915/16, fell to 10 per cent in 1916/17, and no dividend was paid in 1917/18. The key to the question as to whether Krupp made vast profits from the war but hid them lies in its depreciation policy. During the course of the war it wrote off 85 per cent of its plant. But factory space increased 170 per cent, and housing was provided for the workforce, which tripled. So, writing off assets was not simply an accounting device. Munitions production constituted about 80 per cent of its business, and drastic depreciation was its only protection against the end of the war. Even so, its reserves were not sufficient to prevent the firm confronting crisis in 1919/20.[245]

Krupp's ability to carry through such accounting policies was enhanced by the fact that, after the efforts of 1915/16, the fiscal grip of the state on war industry relaxed. Helfferich, enamoured of the workings of the free market, used his shift to the Ministry of the Interior to make sure that the apparent rigour of his 1916 budget was not sustained. He was to be counted among Groener's opponents in 1917.[246] When Hindenburg took over at OHL in August 1916 he set a programme of increased munitions production which effectively elevated output over price control. The conservative instincts of Bethmann Hollweg's government, reflected in economic liberalism, had been a

[243] Mommsen, *Journal of Modern History*, XLV (1975), 535.
[244] Wette, *Militärgeschichtliches Mitteilungen*, 36 (1984), 42–3; see also Feldman, *Great disorder*, 79.
[245] Burchardt, *Zeitschrift für Unternehmensgeschichte*, XXXII (1987), 71–123.
[246] Chickering, *Imperial Germany's Great War*, 182; Groener, *Lebenserinnerungen*, 368.

partial restraint on costs; they were elbowed to one side by radical militarism. Because firms were left to bear their own investment costs in order to create sufficient plant for war needs, the state was required to be generous in the matters of depreciation and capitalization. Munitions manufacturers, like Krupp, aimed to write off their equipment costs in one or two years. But indulgence became laxity, and even collusion. Businesses could evade taxes, a once-and-for-all loss, by subscribing to war loans, a temporary sacrifice compensated for by the government. The obstructiveness of war industry in revealing the details of its accounts was borne with unreasonable patience by the War Ministry. Firms got into the habit of not operating to fixed prices, but of setting the final cost after delivery. The raw materials section of the War Ministry made allowances to employers for wage increases.[247] Thus the state, as the principal consumer, became the main bearer of the burden of the war profits tax. Germany had embraced the principle of price control, albeit unevenly in 1914; as its effectiveness waned after 1916, so the real returns on the war profits tax fell. Without price control, taxation—and certainly taxation levied at a lower rate in 1917 and 1918 than in 1916—was stoking inflation, not retarding it.[248]

The failure of the Reich to tax real incomes directly was made more severe by a shift in the financial policies of local governments. During the war they multiplied their spending four times (as opposed to five times for the Reich). They covered 35 per cent of it through borrowing, despite possessing the power to impose direct taxation, and, moreover, they moved from long-term debt to short-term. The federal states between 1914 and 1923 raised 6.1 billion marks through taxation, but required 3.5 billion of it to service their debts.[249] Thus, it was not only the company but also the individual for whom the impact of taxation was loosened in the war, rather than tightened. The legacy of Germany's failure to tax directly was not, therefore, the amount by which it failed to cover its war costs but the degree to which it bequeathed the post-war government with the problems of monetary overhang.

The post-war focus on Germany has, however, served to obscure the even more dire position of Austria-Hungary's revenues. In Austria itself, the reluctance to introduce new taxes was not the consequence of a lack of pre-war powers or of a pre-war infrastructure. In 1913 total net revenue was 3,122.9 million crowns. Direct taxes on property and income produced 431.5 million crowns, customs 199.9 million, excise duties 418.1 million, charges on stamps and railways 265.5 million, state monopolies 433.1 million, state-run businesses (including the roads) 1,208.1 million, and income from administration 166.7

---

[247] Feldman, *Army, industry and labor*, 387–9.
[248] Roesler, *Finanzpolitik*, 99–102, 129–30, 163–6.
[249] Ferguson, *Paper and iron*, 116; Witt, 'Tax policies, tax assessment and inflation: towards a sociology of public finances in the German inflation, 1914–23', in Witt (ed.), *Wealth and taxation*, 141–3.

million. By the end of the war current prices had risen fifteenfold, but ordinary revenue in 1917/18 had only increased by a quarter in current prices, to 4,194 million crowns. Furthermore, Austria stubbornly maintained the fiction that the war was working no change in the value of money. If the crown was held at its pre-war value, the net revenue for 1917/18 fell to 417.7 million crowns. By the same token, government spending also fell. If war costs for 1914/15 stood at 100, the ratio in peace prices was 77 for 1915/16, 46 for 1916/17, and 36 for 1917/18. The proportions for the armed services were even more alarming: 100; 74; 41; and 27. Austria was spending less in real terms on the war at the end than it was at the beginning.[250]

The suspension of parliamentary activity in Austria until 1917 proved both a blessing and burden. On the positive side, government by decree removed the problems of parliamentary obstructionism and delay. On the negative, any new taxation lacked the imprimatur of popular approval and thus threatened to exacerbate internal tensions. The effect was to encourage the government to build on existing patterns of tax, but to fail to tap new sources. The first additional taxes of the war, not introduced until September 1915, were increases to existing levies—an addition to the duty on beer, and to the charges for inheritances, gifts, and social welfare. But these were not prompted by the war: they had been long debated in parliament and could now be imposed because of the latter's absence. They were therefore irrelevant to Austria's new circumstances. The yields on beer and spirits fell in line with the fall in consumption: indeed, because 77 million crowns of beer duty had to be passed over to the provinces, this particular account moved into deficit by the end of the war. The September 1915 increases netted a paltry 23 million crowns of additional income.

The decline in consumption, therefore, rendered indirect taxation an inadequate tool with which to tackle the government's target of covering the interest charges on war debt. But the principle of building on the existing system persisted. In September 1916, citing the precedent of the Italian war of 1859, the government introduced special war surcharges on existing direct taxes. Overtly, these struck at the wealthy and relieved the less affluent: the threshold for liability to personal income tax was raised from 1,600 crowns to 3,000 crowns. With indirect duties failing to tax lower incomes because of falling consumption, this was not a route to social harmony but to monetary inflation. Moreover, the new rates appeared fiercer than they were. The surcharges were expressed as percentages on the existing levels of taxation, not on the principal to be taxed. The surcharge on incomes between 3,000 crowns and 20,000 crowns was only 15 per cent. But the scale after that rose with apparent steepness to 100 per cent on incomes over 140,000 crowns, 120 per cent on

---

[250] Winkler, *Einkommensverschiebungen in Österreich*, 68–75.

incomes over 200,000 crowns, and 200 per cent over 1 million crowns. However, all these percentages were the supplements applied to existing (low) rates of tax, not to the income itself. Thus, the net additional yield remained relatively small. The tax on interest payments was expressed as a 300 per-cent surcharge; in practice this meant an increase in the basic rate from 2 per cent to 8 per cent, which was— furthermore—to be levied only when the money was withdrawn. The surcharge on the duty on share dividends was 20 per cent, raising the rate from 10 per cent to 12 per cent—with a complicated additional scale graduated according to the level of profit on the invested capital. The tax on business profits suffered a 100 per-cent surcharge when the tax yield exceeded 60 crowns, and 60 per-cent when it was below that. The only group for whom the real burdens increased were landowners, whose effective rate of tax had fallen by half between 1898 and 1914. The 80 per-cent surcharge imposed on ground tax bit more deeply because the basic rate was 19.3 per cent, and the new effective rate became 34.7 per cent.[251] But the empire's agricultural heartland, Hungary, was left unaffected for fear of antagonizing Magyar farmers: throughout the war there was virtually no change in Hungary's fiscal policies.[252] In 1917/18 Austria's yield on direct taxation had risen to 676.8 million crowns, but that was expressed in current values: in peace crowns it had fallen to 67.4 million.

The difficulties of genuine innovation, directed at new areas of liquidity, were amply illustrated by the travails of Austria's efforts to milk war profits. A royal decree of April 1916 aimed to tax the increased profits of all companies (not just companies benefiting from war industries) generated in the war years 1914, 1915, and 1916. When parliament reconvened in 1917, its deputies argued that the provisions of April 1916 were insufficiently rigorous. They wanted severer rates to be incorporated in a new scale which subsumed individuals as well as companies. However, the Upper House construed the proposals of the Lower as a socialist-inspired attack on productivity and capital formation. Conscious that a simple rejection of the deputies' proposals would give time for profits to be dissipated before legislation was in place to tax them, the Upper House proposed a short-term solution—which was promptly rejected by the Lower House in case it transmogrified into a long-term arrangement. The final result was compromise. For public companies, the basis of comparison was the average of the highest and lowest profits in the years 1909 to 1914; the first 10,000 crowns of war-related profit was not liable for tax, and thereafter a levy on a scale of 10 to 35 per cent was applied. For private firms and individual businessmen 1913 was the point of comparison, the first 3,000

[251] Müller, *Finanzielle Mobilmachung*, 157–8, 161–2, 164–9; Josef Wysocki, 'Die Österreichische Finanzpolitik', in Wandruszka and Urbanitsch (eds.), *Habsburgermonarchie*, i. 101–3; Wegs, 'Austrian economic mobilization', 27–8.
[252] Popovics, *Geldwesen*, 171–2.

crowns were not liable, and the rate was 5 per cent on the next 10,000 crowns, 10 per cent on the next 10,000, 15 per cent on the next 20,000, and 20 per cent on the next 20,000. But the law only applied to 1916 and 1917, and the whole debate was therefore rerun in 1918. On this occasion the scale for private firms was widened, so that profits over 300,000 crowns were taxed at 60 per cent—a ceiling set by the Upper House. The Lower House wanted the same principles applied to public companies, but the Upper House insisted that account should be taken of the profitability on capital investment, and the scale was set at two-thirds that of private firms in order to allow the creation of reserves. The effect of all this parliamentary rancour was inefficiency. Many profits earned in 1914 and 1915 escaped entirely; the yield for 1916/17, budgeted at 169 million crowns, proved to be 90 million; an anticipated return of 300 million crowns for 1917/18 came in close to target, but this was only 29.9 million peace crowns. Austria's hope was that it would make up the leeway—to the tune of 2,000 million crowns—after the war was over.[253]

Parliament's inability to embrace innovation was clearly recognized in Austria's first proper war budget, introduced in September 1917 and designed to cover the year July 1917 to June 1918. It revealed that normal receipts had risen (in current crowns) from 3,080 million in 1913 to 4,062.6 million in 1917, and that the surcharges and war profits tax added a further 720 million crowns. But normal expenditure had outstripped the additional yield, jumping by 2,220 million crowns to 5,681 million. Furthermore, the interest charges on the war debt—which Austria had previously hoped to cover through the surcharges of 1916—were running at 1,795 million crowns. Despite this clear evidence that Austria was no longer even covering its peacetime costs, the budget did no more than reiterate the policy of surcharges on existing sources of revenue. A suggestion that a property tax be introduced was crushed with the observation that the idea was 'not yet topical'.[254] So palpable was the budget's failure that new taxes had to be introduced long before the planned date of June 1918. These measures—adopted in January 1918— continued the notion of wartime supplements to existing direct taxes. The main novelties—a coal tax modelled on that of Germany, and a railway tax—had the effect of driving up production costs, and therefore committed the error of indirectly taxing the state itself. By these means the January 1918 interim budget added 820 million crowns to the existing total for war-related taxation of 720 million. But such figures were doubly insignificant—meaningless in the context of a total state expenditure for 1917/18 of 22,169 million crowns, and expressed in a currency that to all intents and purposes was fast becoming valueless.[255]

[253] Müller, *Finanzielle Mobilmachung*, 158–9, 169–74.
[254] März, *Austrian banking*, 192–3.
[255] Müller, *Finanzielle Mobilmachung*, 159–60, 163–4; Winkler, *Einkommensverschiebungen*, 71–3.

When Bulgaria entered the war in 1915 its Finance Ministry had succumbed to pressure from both left and right and accepted the principle of progressive direct taxation. But the government's enthusiasm for the idea was distinctly limited, not least because the bulk of foreign loans it had contracted in 1904, 1907, and 1909 were secured on the receipts from indirect taxation and from customs and excise. Between 1889 and 1911 Bulgaria's yield from direct taxation remained roughly constant, totalling 38.2 million gold leva in 1889, peaking at 49.1 million in 1905, and falling back to 41.6 million in 1911. By contrast, indirect taxation grew from 9.3 million leva to 83.6 million over the same period. The government used its entry into the war to argue that any change in the balance should be postponed until the return of normal conditions. Although a war profits tax was proposed in December 1916, it was not adopted until May 1919. Direct taxation produced 24 per cent of Bulgaria's revenue in 1914, and 21 per cent in 1918.

A significant pressure against radical change was Bulgaria's reliance on agriculture, and the effect on it of war. The mobilization of the army drained the land not only of men but also of draught animals and vehicles. In 1912 17 per cent of the land was fallow; in 1917 29 per cent. Grain production fell from 2,876,000 tons in 1911 to 1,065,000 in 1918. About half of Bulgaria's direct taxation was derived from land tax. It netted 17.33 million leva in 1911, but under the impact of the First Balkan War slumped to 4.54 million in 1913.

By 1917 its yield had recovered to 13.96 million leva, and in 1918 to 19.26 million. The growth was principally due to depreciation. But it also highlighted a shift to so-called industrial crops, and particularly tobacco. Bulgaria's production of tobacco multiplied 3.5 times between 1912 and 1918. In meeting the cravings of the soldiers of the Central Powers, Bulgaria ensured that its balance of trade moved from deficit in 1914 to surplus in 1915, 1916, and 1917. By the latter year tobacco accounted for 70 per cent of Bulgaria's exports, as opposed to 9.9 per cent in 1909. Thus, the government could offset its reluctance to move on the issue of direct taxation by focusing on customs and excise, as well as its own monopolies, including patents for the production and sale of tobacco.

Total tax income, which stood at 120 million leva in 1914, fell to 97 million in 1916, but recovered to 151 million in 1917 and 278.7 million in 1918. In real terms, however, the tax yield was a third that of 1914, and thus made no contribution to the costs of the war. Nor did it soak up the increased money supply, which saw the note circulation rise from 226.5 million leva to 2,298.6 million. Peasant debt was reduced, and bank deposits rose.[256]

---

[256] Danaïllow, *Les Effets de la guerre en Bulgarie*, 61–4, 512–30; Crampton, *Bulgaria*, 479–87; Lampe, *Bulgarian economy*, 33–4.

If any of the belligerents had a weak administrative structure accompanied by a limited fiscal base, it was Turkey. When the tax on cattle was quadrupled, Kurdish breeders simply moved beyond the reach of the Turkish army.[257] On the other hand, the abrogation of the capitulations did create the opportunity, previously denied the Sublime Porte, to levy customs and excise. However, the tariff structure, designed on a provisional basis before 1914, charged imports according to weight, not value. During the war the latter rose while the former fell, but the Turks were reluctant to change for fear of trade suffering even more than was already the case. More successful were domestic taxes on non-essential items of consumption imposed in 1916/17. These included sugar, petrol, matches, coffee, tea, and playing-cards. The duty on alcoholic drinks was revised in 1918.

Arguably, the empire's most effective direct tax was the power to requisition goods in kind. A war tax for those of military age but exempted from service was a failure. The idea of war profits tax was canvassed by Djavid, the finance minister, in a budget speech on 3 March 1917. But he then affirmed his defence of the rights of private property and reassured his listeners by emphasizing his belief that in war as in peace personal profits added to the nation's wealth. His budget for 1917/18 assumed that outgoings of £T52 million would be offset by receipts of up to £T23 million, but it also reckoned on peace within six months. At that point the tax system would be revised to raise the state's income to £T35 or £T36 million. In November 1917, when it was clear that the war would not end as he anticipated, income tax was introduced, but it was not effective during the war itself.

Revenue therefore declined during the war, but the scale is hard to estimate. In 1913/14 Turkey's receipts were £T29,201,865. In October 1914 monthly spending if Turkey entered the war was projected to be £T500,000, but by February 1915 it had risen to £T1 million. In 1915/16 receipts fell to £T22,325,793, and although they rose by almost £T3 million in the following year the currency was rapidly depreciating and the cost of the war up to March 1917 averaged out at £T5 million a month. At that stage Djavid reckoned actual monthly war spending to be £T7 million.[258]

After the war Karl Helfferich averred that Britain had covered only about 12.5 per cent of its war expenditure from taxation. While conceding that Germany had not done so well, he nonetheless argued that at least a small part of its war spending had been met through tax. Recent calculations suggest that Helfferich claimed too little for both powers: Britain covered 18.2 per cent of its war expenditure from taxation, and Germany 13.9 per cent.[259] But his

[257] Ahmad, *Kurdistan*, 136.
[258] Emin, *Turkey in the world war*, 157–9; Dschawid, *Türkische Kriegsfinanzwirtschaft*, 9–11, 30–1, 34–5.
[259] Helfferich, *Money*, 227; Ferguson, *Pity of war*, 323.

central point remains valid. None of the belligerents was capable of meeting the major part of its war costs from taxation. Helfferich's case contains less special pleading than might at first appear. More united the belligerents in their fiscal policies than divided them. All could have taxed with far greater severity than they did. All could have made those rates of tax that they did in fact adopt more realistic if they had accompanied them with truly effective prices-and-incomes policies.

But it is this latter point that constitutes the basis for the criticism of Helfferich. The former minister of finance was still seeking an explanation of war finance that related outgoings to income. What he had still not comprehended was the relationship between taxation and the money supply. During the war inflation had positive effects: it meant that some of the war's costs were met by those whose incomes could not stay abreast of rises in prices. It therefore functioned as a form of indirect, discreet, and immediately productive taxation. If those on falling real incomes ultimately ceased to buy goods, they released productive capacity for other forms of (ideally) war-related production. Simultaneously, those who profited from inflation simply became liable for higher rates of tax. Josiah Stamp, reflecting Britain's relaxed view on inflation, concluded that 'the illusion of prosperity, and the incentive to production created by inflation have their real value in war-time, provided that they are not carried out of hand'.[260]

It was this final caveat which Helfferich failed to grasp. All the belligerents proceeded cautiously in relation to taxation for fear of undermining the principle of consent on which its collection (especially when tax authorities were understaffed) rested. But taxation managed inflation by drawing in the surplus cash of consumers, and so moderating prices. Helfferich's anxiety concerning the fragility of the *Burgfrieden* seems to have blinded him to this relationship.

Inflation also eroded the real value of the national debt. Given Helfferich's preference for loans, herein is a further reason for his blindness to the wider functions of taxation. By reducing the value of investments, inflation had taxing effects. But again, the value of inflation as a mechanism for wartime finance depended on its relationship to taxation. Investors had to be persuaded to invest in government bonds. Fiscal rectitude, even if more an appearance than a substitute, helped sustain confidence at home and credit abroad. The former was an important prerequisite for domestic borrowing; the latter was part of the armoury for seeking foreign loans.

---

[260] Farr, 'McKenna', 241–2.

DOMESTIC BORROWING

The principal functions of taxation in the First World War were the suppression of inflation and the maintenance of creditworthiness. Taxation did not cover the daily expenses of fighting—or at least not to any significant degree. At best (in the United States and Britain), taxation paid for less than a quarter of the war's ongoing costs; at worst (in France, Austria-Hungary, and Russia) for none of them. The war was therefore predominantly funded by borrowing—and this is a generalization applicable to all belligerents.

In August 1914 borrowing reinforced two aspects of the popular response to the outbreak of the war. The first was the sense that the war had healed social divisions, and so united the nation; the second was the belief that the war would be short. Unlike taxation, which was compulsory, loans were voluntary. They therefore enabled the warring peoples to cement their enthusiasm into positive action without at the same time courting the odium and awakening the divisions generated by proposals for new taxes. Furthermore, those most likely to contribute were the wealthy; levels of popular consumption remained unaffected. Thus, liquid capital could be mobilized with far more rapidity and far less pain than through taxation.

However, as it became clear that the war was not going to be short, the initial attractions of borrowing turned to disadvantages. On the one hand, loans put the burden of war finance on a minority of the population, who might feel aggrieved that others were not making a comparable contribution. On the other, the more loan stock an individual acquired, the more he was enabled to increase his wealth at the expense of the masses. The interest and principal would be paid off through taxation levied on the entire population. Moreover, the attractions of the investment were diverting capital from productive uses to unproductive. The long-term cost would be a reduction in national wealth which would afflict the population as a whole rather than the owner of the original capital. Thus, a continuation of borrowing on the principles applied at the beginning of the war made less and less sense as the war continued. Social division would replace social unity.

But it was no solution to this conundrum to switch from borrowing to taxation. Fiscally, it would be insufficiently productive; socially, the same problems would resurface, albeit in different form. Once they had begun borrowing, the nations had little choice but to continue. The buoyancy of war loan stock became an indication of confidence in ultimate victory; to change horses might set prices tumbling and so erode a state's creditworthiness. To maintain the latter governments had to show that they could raise fresh loans, with the result that borrowing promoted more borrowing. The task of the government was to find a sensible balance in the management of debt. War loans had to be issued in denominations sufficiently low to draw in the small investor as well as the big; they had to offer a rate of interest sufficiently high to ensure success, but not so high as to suggest financial desperation or to saddle the taxation system with an insupportable burden of interest payment; finally, they had to be the means by which short-term borrowing and floating debt were converted into long-term obligations.

Most governmental debt was taken up not by private investors but by financial institutions. Short-term treasury bills were the dominant and immediate means by which governments procured the cash to pay for the war. The treasury bills were discounted by the banks. Having acquired the status of securities, the bills could then become the basis for new note issue. Thus, at the cost of expanding the money supply governments could extend their credit indefinitely. By spending the money so generated on war production, the state put the cash back into circulation. War loans were therefore a means of soaking up surplus money, and of shifting the government's short-term borrowing at the bank into long-term debt with the people. But the circle was not thereby broken, because war loan stock could itself be bought by the banks or be treated as security by them. So it too became the basis for an increase in the money supply. Therefore, domestic currency was freed from the restraint of a set percentage of gold cover. But the goods and services procurable with the purchasing power that the money represented were diverted from private individuals to the state. A. C. Pigou argued that bank credits therefore constituted a concealed form of taxation, albeit an inefficient one.[261] The most immediate and evident form of state credit was the quantity of unearned currency in circulation—'a form of interest-free forced loan'.[262]

The banks, therefore, became the essential intermediaries in the onward transmission and multiplication of government debt. Throughout the belligerent countries the banks saw an increase in deposits and in credits. In France the deposits of the Banque de France and the six leading commercial banks rose from 7,058 million francs on 30 June 1914 to 10,882 million by the end of 1918; their credit expanded 242.58 per cent, from 17,289 million francs to 41,937 million.[263] In Austria the deposits of the major Viennese banks rose from 163,628,000 crowns at the end of 1913, to 324,700,000 at the end of 1918, and of credits from 3,252,061,000 to 11,498,642,000.[264] In Italy, the deposits of the four Italian banks increased 344 per cent between 1914 and 1918.[265] In Germany the holdings of the seven major Berlin banks rose from 7,661 million marks to 21,979 million over the same period, and their credit from 4,508 million marks to 17,126 million.[266] The deposits of the Russian state bank grew from 184.7 million roubles in July 1914 to 2,454.7 million in

---

[261] Pigou, *Political economy of war*, 107–8.   [262] Knauss, *Kriegsfinanzierung*, 69.
[263] Fisk, *French public finance*, 40.   [264] März, *Austrian banking*, 223, 224.
[265] Teillard, *Emprunts de guerre*, 222.   [266] Roesler, *Finanzpolitik*, 220.

September 1917, of savings banks from 2,073 million roubles to 6,739.8 million between the same dates, and of private banks from 3,393.3 million roubles in August 1914 to 9,153.3 million in July 1917.[267] In Britain the deposits and current accounts of the joint stock banks of England and Wales (excluding the Bank of England) grew from £809.4 million on 31 December 1914 to £1,583.4 million on 31 December 1918, and of all banks from £1,032.9 million to £1,988.3 million.[268] Although this expansion was expressed in depreciating currencies, the point was often lost on bankers gratified by the ease with which they had shuffled off the blows to private business and international commerce. The president of the Deutsche Bank, Arthur von Gwinner, was entirely positive in his annual report for 1917: 'the placement of deposits in the Treasury bills of the Reich, the federal states, and the large cities now offers the easiest opportunity to invest every available sum in a short-term and secure manner at acceptable interest rates which run at an average of $4\frac{1}{4}$ per cent to $4\frac{1}{2}$ per cent.' Not until the end of the following year would he recognize 'monetary depreciation' rather than real wealth as the source of the bank's increase in business.[269] Moreover, the key point remained: the banking systems of the belligerents proved capable of sufficient growth to keep pace with the demands of war finance.

Broadly speaking, the structural changes which underpinned this enlargement were in place before the war; the war accelerated their development rather than originated them. Most significant and most fortuitous was the establishment in the United States of the Federal Reserve System. Until 1914 the banks of America lacked any central organization, with the result that their reserves were scattered and immobile and their capacity for development severely restricted. Three months before the outbreak of war the Federal Reserve act divided the country into twelve districts, with a Federal Reserve bank for each district. All national banks were obliged to join the system, and others were encouraged to do so. The member banks subscribed capital to the regional Federal Reserve bank, and in return the reserves required to be held against deposits were reduced in varying percentages according to the size and status of the member bank. The interest rates of the Federal Reserve banks fell by up to 2 per cent between 1914 and 1916. In practice, the decline in the reserve ratios was offset by the gold imports generated through the war: on 5 April 1917 the reserve ratio was still 89 per cent, and on 17 November 1916 the reserves of the member banks were $2,536 million, of which only $1,510 million was actually required. The United States therefore possessed a flexible system for credit expansion of considerable capacity.[270]

[267] Michelson et al., Russian public finance, 402–5; Claus, Kriegswirtschaft Russlands, 17. Claus (p. 38) says savings banks' deposits grew from 1,704 million roubles to 4,915 million between July 1914 and October 1917; the figures in the text are from Michelson .
[268] Brown, International gold standard, 116; Morgan, British financial policy, 228.
[269] Gall et al., Deutsche Bank, 134–5, 161–2.
[270] Gilbert, American financing, 47–51; Bogart, War costs, 135–7.

Although no other belligerent underwent reforms so crucial to its capability to finance war industry, all saw an alteration in banking profiles. In Italy the issue banks' proportion of the total assets of all banks rose from 23.9 per cent in 1913 to 46.1 per cent in 1918, largely at the expense of the savings banks and popular banks. The four or five largest credit banks expanded their assets from 16.7 per cent of the whole in 1914 to 33.9 per cent in 1919. And the government and the Bank of Italy combined forces in 1914–15 to create a new commercial bank, the Banca Italiano di Sconto, to contest the field with two Milanese banks, the Banca Commerciale Italiana and the Credito Italiano.[271] In Germany the existing banking structure was reinforced by the *Darlehenskassen*, which moved from being upmarket pawnshops to full-blown credit institutions. In Britain the process of bank amalgamations, already evident before the war (the number of British banks halved between 1895 and 1914), continued during it. Twelve of the largest London banks formed the 'big five'. The gap between them and their medium-sized competitors widened: the former commanded 70 per cent of deposits by 1918, and were able to write down their capital to only 5 per cent of deposits (when 13 per cent had been normal in 1910).[272]

Two general and interlocking trends predominated. First, the central banks were increasingly required to fall into step with government policy. In Britain this was symbolized by the Treasury's defeat of the nominally independent Bank of England over the policy to be followed on gold reserves and interest rates in July 1917. Secondly, the central banks became bankers to the commercial banks. In Russia the balances of fifty banks (representing a total of 782 branches) with the Russian State Bank increased from 64 million roubles at the beginning of 1914 to 160 million two years later.[273] Thus, the commercial banks as well as the central banks were enlisted for government service.

The banks therefore grew, but by means of state credit and at the expense of private business. In Germany trade bills constituted 17 per cent of the Reichsbank's assets in 1914 but only 0.7 per cent in 1918: the bank's role in refinancing commerce had been all but extinguished. Meanwhile, the credit banks themselves acquired 'the character of deposit banks lending chiefly to public authorities'; by 1918 government treasury bills constituted the bulk of the Deutsche Bank's liquid engagements.[274] At the other end of the banking spectrum the deposits of the savings banks grew 50 per cent during the war, but almost entirely through their handling of war loan stock: in Bavaria the savings banks dealt with 66 per cent of all war loan transactions.[275] In Italy the

---

[271] Forsyth, *Crisis of Liberal Italy*, 143–7, 310, 317.
[272] Grady, *British war finance*, 213–26, 247–50.
[273] Claus, *Kriegswirtschaft Russlands*, 43.
[274] P. Barret Whale, quoted in Gall *et al.*, *Deutsche Bank*, 130–1.
[275] Caesar, *Zeitschrift für bayerische Sparkassengeschichte*, V (1991), 72, 85–91.

commercial portfolio of the banks declined 25 per cent between 1914 and 1916, its gross increase in these years being attributable to the discount of treasury bonds.[276] In the joint stock banks of Britain the ratio of other securities to British government securities declined from 86.8 per cent in 1913 to 24.6 per cent in 1918. The entire increase in bank deposits between June 1917 and December 1918, a total of £467 million, representing 40 per cent of total deposits, was generated by the needs of war finance.[277] In France in December 1914 31.07 per cent of all advances from the banks were made to the government; four years later this figure stood at 63.7 per cent. The gross profits of the Banque de France itself, which had averaged 52 million francs a year up to 1913, had reached 344 million in 1919—almost entirely through state business.[278]

Long-dated government stock and its absorption in a pattern of long-term bank deposits—for all its discounting and the consequent expansion of the money supply—had one major anti-inflationary effect: it reduced liquidity. The latent inflation generated by wartime borrowing could therefore be kept in check; the fact that governments adopted deficit financing during the war did not in itself guarantee hyperinflation after the war.

Germany's declared policy at the war's outset—that of borrowing—was certainly in marked contrast to Britain's formal position. But, to reiterate a point, its gross effect in cash terms was less different. By the end of the war 90 per cent of the ordinary budget was devoted to interest payments on war debt; in other words, Germany—unlike some other belligerents—serviced its war debt out of ordinary revenue and still had a surplus. Taxation made at least some contribution to Germany's war costs: the customary calculation is 6 per cent.[279] But total tax revenue, if the states are included, was at least 16.7 per cent, and possibly 17.7 per cent, of all wartime spending.[280] The significant difference is the fate of the 94 per cent of Reich war costs not funded through taxation. In 1918 only 60 per cent of the debt was fixed in long-term loan stock, and fully 34 per cent consisted of floating debt. This was high, although certainly in France and possibly in Italy it was higher. But by 1920 the floating debt of the last two had fallen, while Germany's had grown to over 50 per cent.[281] Germany's primary problem at the war's end was excessive liquidity.

What was a vice in 1918 had been a virtue in 1914. At the war's beginning Germany's financial policy was directed to the achievement of liquidity.

[276] Teillard, *Emprunts de guerre*, 225.

[277] Grady, *British war finance*, 261; Morgan, *British financial policy*, 246–7.

[278] Fisk, *French public finance*, 42; Charbonnet, *Politique financière*, 143.

[279] Knauss, *Kriegsfinanzierung*, 175.

[280] Balderston, *Economic History Review*, 2nd series, XLII (1989), 228. By contrast Witt, 'Tax policies, tax assessment and inflation: towards a sociology of public finances in the German inflation, 1914–23', in Witt (ed.), *Wealth and taxation*, 141, reckons 97.7% of all expenses authorized during the war were covered by loans.

[281] Forsyth, *Crisis of Liberal Italy*, 101; Forsyth's figures give Germany's floating debt as 31% in 1918.

Borrowing was one manifestation of this overarching principle; the rejection of a formal moratorium was another. The limited and short-lived hike in interest rates served the same end: the Reichsbank's rate rose from 5 per cent to 6 per cent, but fell back to 5 per cent on 23 December 1914, and stayed there for the rest of the war. Anticipating that mobilization would not only generate a shortage of cash but would also leave industry short of hands, so causing unemployment and rendering plant idle, Germany flushed its economy with cash in order to stimulate activity. It recognized the danger of inflation, but believed that the evidence would be found not in the growth of the money supply but in the movement of prices. Price controls appeared reasonably effective in 1914 because prices were restrained by short-term unemployment But, as employment levels rose and war orders generated competition for increasingly scarce goods, Germany needed to throttle back on liquidity. It could have applied harsher taxation or increased interest rates in order to draw in deposits. It did neither.

Symptomatic of the failure to rethink financial policy in terms of a long war and full employment rather than a short war and unemployment was the development of the *Darlehenskassen*. The *Darlehenskassen* offered an interest rate of up to 6.5 per cent (as against the Reichsbank rate of 5 per cent), and only required deposits to be fixed for between three and six months. Thus, cash remained effectively on call. Although designed to help commerce and private business surmount the liquidity crisis of mobilization, their attractions soon drew in a different range of creditors. By 1916 25 per cent of their loans were to states and communes; a further 28.2 per cent were to banks; only 12 per cent were to trading and transport interests, 3 per cent to industry, and 0.7 per cent to agriculture. In 1917 74.9 per cent of loans were to states and communes. By then, of 7,700 million marks held in securities, only 89 million represented goods in kind; the vast majority were paper. At the end of the war the total issue of *Darlehenskassenscheine*, 15,626 million marks, was ten times the original authorization of 1,500 million. But, because the *Darlehenskassen* relieved it of a major burden, particularly in the funding of local government, the Reichsbank had little interest in calling a halt to what was going on. Moreover, the *Darlehenskassenscheine*, although currency in practice, were still not legal issue, and thus helped disguise the real—as opposed to the theoretical—increase in total circulation.[282]

The *Reichskassenscheine* (treasury notes) were declared legal tender on mobilization, and the Reichsbank intensified its efforts to trade these notes for gold. On 22 March 1915 10-mark notes—both the Treasury's and the Reichsbank's own—were introduced, and the total note issue was raised by

---

[282] Knauss, *Kriegsfinanzierung*, 56; Bogart, *War costs*, 116–17; Dix, *Wirtschaftskrieg*, 216–17; Roesler, *Finanzpolitik*, 212–14.

120 million marks. Thus, three types of irredeemable notes were in circulation—*Reichsbanknoten*, *Reichskassenscheine*, and *Darlehenskassenscheine*. Currency creation had become effectively autonomous, because it no longer rested on a combination of credit, goods, and gold but on credit itself. By the end of the war a third of the *Reichskassenscheine* in circulation were covered by deposited *Darlehenskassenscheine*, and a third of the *Darlehenskassenscheine* were held by the Reichsbank as security against their own note issue. In July 1914 total German circulation was 6,970 million marks: 2,909 million in Reichsbank notes, 172 million in treasury notes, 157 million in private bank notes, and 3,732 million in coin. In December 1918 circulation totalled 33,106 million marks: 22,188 million in Reichsbank notes, 10,109 million in *Darlehenskassenscheine* (i.e. minus the *Darlehenskassenscheine* held by the Reichsbank), 356 million in treasury notes, 283 million in private bank notes, and only 170 million in coin (as against a wartime low of 69 million in April 1918).[283] The quantity of notes and coin in circulation in Germany increased from 110 marks per head in 1914 to 430 million in 1918.[284] Most of this was in notes. Note circulation in Germany rose 1,141 per cent between late 1913 and late 1918, whereas the lack of small coin prevented shopkeepers giving change by 1916–17, and the coins that were in circulation were made of nickel and iron rather than silver and gold.[285]

Germany issued nine war loans between September 1914 and September 1918, with the purpose of redeeming its treasury bills and so wiping out its floating debt. Up until the issue of the fifth loan, in September 1916, this policy appeared to work.

The absence of a moratorium and the high level of liquidity at the war's outset enabled Germany to issue its first loan with alacrity. Given the underdeveloped nature of Germany's money market and the existing glut of government debt with which it was encumbered, it was essential that Germany exploit the initial mood of war enthusiasm in order to put its borrowing policy on secure foundations. In these terms, the first loan was a success. A total of 4,460 million marks was subscribed, producing a surplus of 1,832 million over the existing debt. The second, in March 1915, raised 9,060 million, a surplus of 1,851 million; the third, in September 1915, 12,101 million, a surplus of 2,410 million; and the fourth 10,712 million, a surplus of 324 million. But although the sums subscribed continued to rise in the subsequent loans, up until the eighth (issued in March 1918 and netting 15,001 million marks), they failed to keep pace with the growth in floating debt. The fifth loan was 2,114 million marks short of its target, the sixth (in March 1917) 6,732 million, the seventh (in September 1917) 14,578 million, and the eighth 23,970 million. The total of the

[283] Roesler, *Finanzpolitik*, 217–18.
[284] Bartholdy, *War and German society*, 58; Cooper, *Behind the lines*, 119, 177.
[285] Hardach, *First World War*, 171.

last loan, issued in September 1918, fell back to 10,443 million marks, and left a shortfall of 38,971 million.[286] Thus, the Reich's floating debt doubled in the second half of 1916 from 7,000 million marks to 13,000 million, doubled again to 28,000 million by the end of 1917, and almost doubled again to 50,000 million by November 1918. Furthermore, these figures understated the problem, because war loans were directed at mopping up the short-term debt of the Reich and ignored its increasing use by local government.[287]

Even before the fifth issue in September 1916 disquieting cracks were emerging. From 1915 the increase in subscriptions was falling behind the growth in the money supply and in the rise in prices. Thus their real value was declining. Indeed, the war loans were themselves contributing to this process. They were accepted as security by the *Darlehenskassen*, which issued their notes in exchange; these notes could be used by subscribers to buy more war loan stock, and by the Reichsbank as collateral for its own note issue. It was the war loan that gave the *Darlehenskassen* a higher profile: 70 per cent of their lendings were for subscriptions to the first issue, although their role declined thereafter.[288] Other credit institutions played key roles in the success of the scheme, but in doing so monetized goods or rendered liquid cash that was fixed. The savings banks were responsible for 19.8 per cent of the first subscription. For the third loan, in September 1915, the banks proposed special terms to those who had subscribed to the first and second issues. They would advance 75 per cent of their nominal value, and four times that amount could be subscribed to the new issue provided this stock too was deposited as collateral: thus, an initial investment of 10,000 marks in the first loan could grow to 36,997 marks over the nine loans of the war with no further cash payment.[289] The war loans were therefore mopping up money which they were helping to create.

The ability of the scheme to make real inroads into Germany's monetary overhang depended not on the financial institutions but on the loans' attractiveness to individual investors of modest means. Success here could compensate for a lack of rigour in direct taxation.

Overtly, this side of the story was more successful. The first loan offered individuals an interest rate of 5 per cent (as against an existing rate of 4 per cent on government stocks), convertible in tranches after ten years. Institutional investors were channelled towards treasury bonds which matured in five years. Subscribers totalled 1,177,235 and the stock, issued at 97.5, reached par very quickly. Helfferich capitalized on this success, which he felt justified the generous terms of the issue, by stressing the notion of 'financial conscription':

[286] Helfferich, *Money*, 228.
[287] Manfred Ziedler, 'Die deutsche Kriegsfinanzierung 1914 bis 1918 und ihre Folgen', in Michalka (ed.), *Der Erste Weltkrieg*, 427; Chickering, *Imperial Germany's Great War*, 177.
[288] Helfferich, *Weltkrieg*, 211; Roesler, *Finanzpolitik*, 56–7.
[289] Bogart, *War costs*, 190; Feldman, *Great disorder*, 35.

loans were the contribution which those safe at home could make to the war effort. Available in small denominations, advertised in posters and the press, and sold through post offices and banks, they were bought by increasing numbers of private citizens. The second attracted 2,691,060 subscribers, the third 3,966,418, and the fourth 5,279,645.[290] But these aggregates, as Helfferich's socialist critics were quick to point out, disguised some disquieting features. Of the total subscribed, 57 per cent had been taken up by 227,000 individuals, as opposed to 4 per cent by 3.3 million.[291] What concerned the socialists was that a few people in Germany still had the larger share of wealth; what concerned the organizers of the war loans was that the majority were not subscribing more.

The fifth war loan, that of September 1916, provided clear confirmation that the war loans policy was no longer meeting the objectives Helfferich had assigned it. Not only did it produce a shortfall on the floating debt to be consolidated, it also saw a decline in the number of subscribers to 3,809,976. Those contributing less than 200 marks fell from 2,406,118 for the fourth issue to 1,794,084: only for sums above 50,100 marks were the numbers of individual subscribers increased. The few were giving more; the majority less. In part this was a reflection of the cost of living, but it also bore testimony to the relatively depressing military situation. This interpretation is borne out by the sixth loan, issued in March 1917. Individual subscribers reached their highest total of the war (7,063,347) and those investing less than 200 marks more than doubled. Its success reflected the greater liquidity created by Hindenburg's programme for increased munitions output.[292] But it also coincided with two promises of ultimate victory—revolution in Russia and the move to unrestricted U-boat war. The seventh loan (September 1917) witnessed another fall in the number of subscribers, to 5,530,285, and it required the March 1918 offensives on the western front to pull the eighth back up to 6,869,901. The ninth, issued in September 1918, could draw in only 2,742,446 investors, with the wealthy minority making a disproportionate contribution. By 3 October exchanges were refusing to buy war loans, and the market price in Bavaria had fallen to 70 per cent of par.[293]

The volatility of popular support for the war loans after 1916 prompted the government to pursue the big investor with more ardour. The consequences were doubly damaging. First, those workers who were in employment, and especially in war-related industries, were left with money in their pockets. Secondly, industry and finance insisted that they needed their resources in

---

[290] Helfferich, *Weltkrieg*, 217–19; Roesler, *Finanzpolitik*, 54–7, 206–7; also Lotz, *Staatsfinanzwirtschaft*, 32–41.
[291] Williamson, *Helfferich*, 138.
[292] Knauss, *Kriegsfinanzierung*, 152.
[293] Hanssen, *Diary of a dying empire*, 310–11.

sufficiently liquid form to be available at the war's end for demobilization, reconstruction, and the recapture of export markets. Short-term loans at 4.5 per cent were not sufficiently disadvantageous, given a rate of 5 per cent on longer-term stock, to encourage a shift from the former to the latter. In March 1917, anticipating the redemption of the treasury bonds of the initial war loan issues in 1918, the Reich tried to lure institutional investors to convert their short-term stock into longer-term capital growth. Treasury bills, still paying 4.5 per cent, were offered at 98 but would be redeemable at 110. Redemption was phased according to the date of the war loan which was to be converted, and would be completed in fifty years, in 1967. But the possibilities for exchange were too limited, and only 2,100 million marks were consolidated in this way.[294]

Therefore, in 1917–18 large credit balances were accumulating in bank accounts, earning rates of interest comparable with, or little below, war loan stock. In the first half of the war, three-quarters of the floating debt was held by the Reichsbank; this changed after 1916, and by 1918 well over 50 per cent was taken up by the money market. The balances of the seven major Berlin banks rose from 11,140 million marks in 1916 to 21,979 million in 1918, the bulk of the increase being attributable to treasury bills. From here it entered the secondary reserve against note issue. But over the same period, 1917–18, the velocity of circulation more than halved. Money was not being spent, it was being hoarded. In the short-term, therefore, Germany's liquidity did not create hyperinflation. But the preconditions were in place.[295]

The broad intentions of Austria-Hungary's policy were the same as those of its ally, to finance the war primarily through borrowing. However, Austria-Hungary was less wealthy. The creation of liquidity was not, as in Germany, simply a matter of realizing goods and assets; it also necessitated raiding the empire's pre-war capital. There was a limit to what could be monetized. By 1918 Austria-Hungary's war expenditure, alone of that of all the belligerents, was below its pre-war annual national income.[296] Furthermore, a corollary of relative poverty was an underdeveloped money market. The postal savings bank was designed in 1910 to lead consortiums of banks in the raising of national credits; it failed to raise a loan of 100 million crowns in 1912, and during the war it remained more subject to the banks' views than vice versa.[297] As elsewhere, the activities of commercial banks expanded under the stimulus of war, but they did so from a lower base point than in Germany, and accordingly the government's debt was less widely distributed. In

[294] Roesler, *Finanzpolitik*, 132–3; Lotz, *Staatsfinanzwirtshaft*, 35–9.
[295] Roesler, *Finanzpolitik*, 220, 91–5; Balderston, *Economic History Review*, 2nd series, XLII (1989), 238–40 .
[296] Bogart, *War costs*, 106.
[297] Spitzmüller, *Memoirs*, 62–3, 161.

Austria-Hungary, therefore, a greater burden fell on the central bank. In Germany the advances made to the government by the Reichsbank were comparable in frequency with loans raised from the public; in Austria-Hungary the Austro-Hungarian Bank contributed twice as often as the public.[298]

The suspension of the Bank act on 4 August proved to be the first step towards a laxity in accounting from which the government benefited and of which parliament (because it did not meet) could not disapprove. Weekly accounts ceased to be published. Not until December 1917 did the bank hold its first general meeting of the war—when the close relationship between bank and state was at last fully revealed. In February 1918 a further meeting adopted in one fell swoop all the accounts for the years 1914, 1915, 1916, and 1917. By then the bank had advanced 13,000 million crowns to Austria and 6,000 million to Hungary.[299] At the end of the war these figures stood at 25,060 million crowns and 9,909 million.

The relationship between the bank and the empire, called into being by the mobilization and prolonged by the moratorium (which denied other possible approaches to the money market), was put onto a regular footing on 15 July 1915. The bank advanced the two governments 1,500 million crowns, secured on treasury bills paying 1 per cent interest per annum. No pattern of repayment was fixed; this was to be discussed six months after the war's end. No limit to the number of loans was agreed; by October 1918 the two governments had taken out twenty-one such loans. Each advance was for the same amount, but the periods between loans became progressively shorter: whereas Austria did not exhaust its first tranche for three months, its final instalment ran out in two weeks. In exchange, the two governments agreed not to issue any state paper currency. Therefore the bank had total charge of the note issue. It vowed to do its best to limit this. But the security on which the circulation rested was the loans which the bank advanced to the government, and these were unlimited.

After the war Popovics maintained he had done no more than his patriotic duty. He also suggested that the alternative to the July 1915 agreement was a takeover by the army. But, on his own account, his underlying fear was the threatened assumption of note-issuing powers by the two governments. Conversely, he regarded his primary achievement as the involvement of the issuing banks in the system of war finance: it was now up to them to offer interest rates high enough to absorb the currency which would enter circulation.[300] What he forebore to mention were the increased profits accruing to the Austro-Hungarian Bank as a result of government business. In 1914 the bank's profits had been 57.9 million crowns; in 1916 they reached 136.9 million. Although

[298] März, *Austrian banking*, 208.   [299] Müller, *Finanzielle Mobilmachung*, 33–41.
[300] Popovics, *Geldwesen*, 70–9.

these were gained at the state's expense, they were—through the war profits tax and the tax on banknotes—in part recouped. Furthermore, the interest rate was reduced to 0.5 per cent because the income of the two governments could not keep pace with the increase in their debt. But Popovics still hoped to use the profits to build a reserve in gold and foreign exchange in 1917 and 1918. Ultimately, however, the bank's solvency had become dependent on the solvency of the empire itself.[301]

The yield of each loan was divided so that Austria received 954 million crowns and Hungary 546 million. The split, therefore, followed the budgetary allocation of financial responsibility. But it did not mirror the rate of wartime spending. Hungary's demand for cash was much less pressing than that of Austria. In part this reflected a slightly more vigorous pursuit of the alternative forms of credit, but more significant was the difference in burden assumed by the two monarchies. Austria was more industrialized and involved in more areas of warlike activity; it was also much more generous in welfare payments. At the war's end Austria owed the bank 25,560 million crowns, Hungary 5,740 million. Furthermore, Austria had exhausted its credit on 30 October 1918; Hungary still had 5,500 million crowns in hand. The loans were therefore raised in accordance with the constitutional needs of the empire, not according to its spending requirements. However, it would be unreasonable to leave this as further evidence of a rapacious and parasitical Hungary. The currency which the borrowing policy depreciated was an imperial one, but the main cause of the depreciation was Austria. Thus, 'the forced loan' which the note issue represented was levied disproportionately on Hungary.[302]

Banknote circulation in the dual monarchy increased 1,396 per cent during the war. The average monthly circulation was 2,405,350,660 crowns in July 1914, and 34,888,999,890 in December 1918.[303] Metallic cover slumped from 40 per cent to 2.7 per cent by the end of 1917. Almost half of the note increase occurred in 1918 itself. Popovics blamed the recall of the Austrian parliament on 30 May 1917. Until then the balance in the relationship between Austria and Hungary had been preserved; after it Austria's bank debt all but doubled (from 13,000 million to 25,000 million crowns), whereas Hungary's grew by a third (from 6,200 million to 9,900 million).[304] Parliament spent money on reconstruction and on family allowances which pushed cash back into private pockets. However, unlike in Germany, money was not hoarded. The commercial banks saw a large increase in their business, but no proportionate growth in private deposits. Clients moved away from savings banks as they preferred to keep

[301] Müller, *Finanzielle Mobilmachung*, 38–41.
[302] Gratz and Schüller, *Wirtschaftliche Zusammenbruch*, 171–6; Winkler, *Einkommensverschiebungen*, 272.
[303] Walvé de Bordes, *Austrian Crown*, 46–7.
[304] Popovics, *Geldwesen*, 154.

their cash on call.[305] Popovics's strategy depended on the issuing banks fixing the inflated currency through attractive interest rates. So comprehensively did the policy fail that in March 1918 the governments effectively reneged on their agreement not to issue their own currency by introducing *Kassenscheine*, treasury bills designed to mop up the excessive banknotes.

Austria-Hungary found itself locked in a paradoxical spiral of excessive liquidity and insufficient cash. Banking had too weak a foothold to cope with the liquidity created by the mobilization and government spending. Small firms found their debts rapidly written off, not least by depreciation; the banks were then bypassed in the bid to acquire raw materials before prices rose. Consequently money was moved into goods as soon as possible, and the competition to do so—given the shortage of goods—forced up prices, therefore creating the need for yet more cash. Rising prices meant that assets in kind could always be sold at a profit, and the difference between the cost of borrowing and the growth in prices assured the middlemen of a dividend. Thus, in Austria-Hungary the velocity of circulation grew even during the war, and—unlike in Germany—hyperinflation was already entrenched in 1918.

The publicly issued war loans could not in these circumstances be used to redeem the advances made by the Austro-Hungarian Bank. Rather, they were spent directly on the procurement of war-related goods. Short-term debt was not consolidated; instead, it was renewed and extended.[306]

Although the watchword of the dual monarchy became 'the war finances the war',[307] Vienna was slower off the mark in issuing its first loan than Berlin. The moratorium made it difficult for those with assets to get access to them; domestic liquidity remained low until government spending entered circulation; and the military victory required for a successful flotation proved stubbornly slow in coming. Despite the continuing lack of the latter, the exhaustion of credit and the return of liquidity led to the first war loan in November 1914. In Austria the stock was offered at 97.5, paying interest of 5.5 per cent, and redeemable in 1920. In Hungary the price was 96.5 and the interest rate 6 per cent. No upper limit was set. Austria raised 2,153.5 million crowns and Hungary 1,184.98 million.

The banks agreed to lend against the collateral of the war loans at the current discount rate to 75 per cent of their face value. On this basis the loans were an attractive proposition. The continued closure of the stock exchanges shut off other avenues for speculation, and borrowing from the bank to lend to the state would show a profit. However, the effect was to draw in capital rather than income. Industrial investment was therefore undermined. Efforts were made to encourage the small subscriber: the lowest denomination was 100

[305] Müller, *Finanzielle Mobilmachung*, 67–72.   [306] Bogart, *War costs*, 195.
[307] Müller, *Finanzielle Mobilmachung*, 10.

crowns, and units of 25, 50, and 75 crowns were offered through post offices. But the principal element in the subscriptions were advances of between 10,000 and 50,000 crowns. The lenders were drawn disproportionately from Vienna, the Alps, Bohemia, and Moravia—and in Hungary from the Magyars. Thus, despite the apparent success of the first loan, it already lagged behind the increase in circulation; and its claim on patriotism showed that feeling to be as unevenly distributed as the empire's private wealth.

The first three Austrian loans were issued as treasury bills, the maturity extending to ten years on the second and fifteen on the third. However, the fourth loan, framed in April 1916, offered a choice between a forty-year bond at 93 or a seven-year bill at 95.5, both paying interest at 5.5 per cent. The aim was, of course, to reduce the short-term debt and dampen domestic liquidity. Small savers—those investing in 100-crown units—constituted 258,000 of the loan's subscribers, as against 55,000 for the first issue. But the institutions were reluctant to commit funds for so long a period. As Austrian finance minister, Spitzmüller despaired of the commercial banks: 'I had to consider myself lucky if I succeeded in the conversion of at least one of the earlier war loans.'[308] And in subsequent loans the banks became the dominant element. Having taken 40.6 per cent of the first loan, they subscribed to 58.5 per cent of the eighth and last. They did not retain the stock which they acquired but quickly redis-counted it. Thus, the war loans were achieving neither of their principal fiscal roles—they were not absorbing privately held cash, and they were not shifting floating debt into long-term borrowing.

Austria's eight loans netted a nominal 35,129.3 million crowns. Hungary floated thirteen government loans, seven at 6 per cent and the others at 5.5 or 5 per cent, and a further four through the banks: they raised 18,851.8 million crowns. The greater frequency and better rates of Hungary's issues helped explain its lesser dependence on the Austro-Hungarian Bank. The ratio of sums raised between the two monarchies was in line with their budgetary relationship—64.7 : 35.3. But Hungary floated its stock on the Austrian market, and therefore added 3,200 million crowns to the burden borne by Austria.[309] Of the Austrian loans, the seventh, which totalled 6,045.9 million crowns, was nominally the most successful. In terms of real purchasing power, however, only the third raised more than the first; the seventh was worth 41 per cent of the first, and the eighth 24 per cent.[310]

The fragility of Austria-Hungary's economic and industrial development confronted it with irreconcilable demands in its credit operations. It might have soaked up more note issues if it had raised interest rates. But it was

[308] Spitzmüller, *Memoirs*, 161.
[309] Gratz and Schüller, *Wirtschaftliche Zusammenbruch*, 176–7.
[310] März, *Austrian banking*, 134–42, 189–91, 208, 236–7, 243; Popovics, *Geldwesen*, 59, 65–6, 81–2; Winkler, *Einkommensverschiebungen*, 78, 272.

pathetically anxious not to divorce itself from the patterns adopted by the other banks of Europe. Only too aware of its own underdeveloped money market, it mortgaged its short-term position in the hope of retaining its post-war status. But, even if the Austro-Hungarian Bank had increased its discount rate, the effect might well have been either neutral or nugatory. The war needs of the state were so insistent as to overwhelm the deflationary effects of any interest rate, however high. And ultimately, higher rates would only have added to the burdens of war finance already borne by the dual monarchy.[311]

Of the Entente powers, Russia's position was that most akin to Austria-Hungary's. Its banking system and money market were underdeveloped. The profits to be gained by the quick turnover of goods in a depreciating currency encouraged the growth of middlemen and caused the banks to be bypassed. These factors accelerated circulation. But, unlike Austria-Hungary, hoarding then had a dampening effect. Peasants reverted to type and simply opted out of the cash economy; one estimate has calculated that perhaps half the total note circulation was hoarded.[312]

The corollary of hoarding in Russia was the failure of the publicly issued war loans to draw in privately held funds. Russia issued seven war loans between November 1914 and March 1917. Most had a fifty-year life (the seventh was to run for fifty-five years) but could be redeemed after ten years. The first was offered at 95 and paid 5 per cent. It totalled 466.6 million roubles. The third, issued in May 1915, brought the price up to 99, but in return paid 5.5 per cent interest over the first six years and 5 per cent thereafter. The fourth (November 1915), fifth (March 1916), and sixth (October 1916) combined both the induce-ment of a low price, 95, and the higher interest rate of 5.5 per cent. The seventh, the so-called Liberty Loan issued by the Provisional Government, brought the interest rate down to 5 per cent, but went on sale at 85. This provided a total annual yield to the investor of 5.88 per cent (as opposed to 5.318 for the first loan), and brought in the highest nominal subscription, 3,841.4 million roubles. The combined proceeds from the seven loans were 11,378,289,000 roubles against a theoretical target of 12,010,000,000.[313]

The lowest unit offered in the first loan was 50 roubles. As elsewhere, press and propaganda campaigns tried to lure the small investor. The subscription period was extended from seven days for the first loan to forty-six for the fifth. But private individuals were reluctant to respond. The seventh loan was offered in units of 20, 40, and 50 roubles. The Provisional Government harped on its claims to popular support, and the soldiers' and workers' soviet hinted at more direct methods. But by July 1917, after three months, only 2 per cent of the Petrograd population and 4 per cent of Moscow's had subscribed.[314]

[311] Popovics, Geldwesen, 163–5.   [312] Hardach, First World War, 168.
[313] Michelson et al., Russian public finance, 249–56; Bogart, War costs, 176–80.
[314] Michelson et al., Russian public finance, 274–5; Claus, Kriegswirtschaft Russlands, 4–6.

The success of the loan issues, therefore, rested with the banks. They took about three-fifths of the first two issues, and about half overall. Their commission—3 per cent at first, and 2 per cent on later issues—was high, and substantially reduced the total yield. Many of their subscriptions were in the form of paper securities. By December 1915 the State Bank's advances on paper reached 877 million roubles, and by May 1917—after a lull in 1916—topped 1,000 million roubles. The State Bank itself thus kept its own holdings of paper relatively constant, while the government found itself rediscounting existing government debt rather than clawing back circulating cash.[315] Indeed, the effect of the banks' involvement was to increase circulation, not reduce it. The savings banks drew in money that its owners intended to hoard, and which would therefore have been withdrawn from circulation. But by subscribing to war loans they put this money back into the hands of the government, who then spent it and so restored it to circulation.[316]

The actual note issue effectively doubled in each year of the war. From 1,633.3 million roubles at the end of July 1914, it rose to 2,946.5 million at the beginning of 1915, 5,617 million at the beginning of 1916, and 9,097.3 million at the beginning of 1917. By November 1917 and the Bolshevik revolution 18,917 million roubles were in circulation. The impact of mobilization and then of the Provisional Government's policies can best be illustrated by the average monthly issue, which hit 310.4 million roubles after the outbreak of war in 1914, but fell in 1915 and 1916, only to rise after March 1917 first to 1,083 million and then—by October—to 1,516 million. The state printing works could not keep pace, and the involvement of private firms eased the path to counterfeit production.[317]

The State Bank's note issue was secured on the collateral of 5 per cent treasury bills. The initial authorization for 400 million roubles in treasury bills had risen to 6,000 million by the end of 1915, 12,000 million by October 1916, and 25,000 million by October 1917. The actual amounts outstanding never reached these ceilings. The vast majority were taken by the State Bank: it held 82.4 per cent of the total in July 1915. Efforts were made to distribute the short-term debt more widely. The bills became increasingly negotiable, and advances on them of 95 per cent of par at 5.5 per cent were authorized. The Provisional Government made payments in treasury bills for contracts, rising to 50 per cent of the total over 200,000 roubles. But although the State Bank's holdings reduced to 65.3 per cent of all treasury bills in June 1916, they climbed back to 73.7 per cent in September 1917. Efforts to convert this floating debt into long-term loans were no more successful. The interest rate on the treasury bills was sufficiently high to drive out treasury bonds by 1915—the 4 per cent 'series',

---

[315] Claus, *Kriegswirtschaft Russlands*, 6–7, 43.
[316] Michelson *et al.*, *Russian public finance*, 265–9.
[317] Ibid. 379–80; Claus, *Kriegswirtschaft Russlands*, 14–16, 18–19.

interest-bearing notes with a life of four years which circulated like currency, raised only 850 million roubles.[318] By October 1917 48 per cent of Russia's debt was in short-term treasury bills.[319]

Russia's borrowing, therefore, rested just as much as Austria-Hungary's on an interlocking relationship between the government and the central bank. Of 38,649 million roubles of war expenditure, 16,426.5 million were funded through treasury bills, the majority of them lodged with the State Bank; of a further 11,408.2 million raised through domestic loans, over half was generated through the banks.[320] But the short-term treasury bills held by the State Bank as collateral did not keep pace with the note issue held by the Treasury in exchange.[321] Thus, the government's debt was not even notionally covered by the credit-creating devices of the day. The issue of paper notes, over and above government borrowing, covered 31.1 per cent of war expenditure.[322]

Italy's story ought to have been similar—and in some respects was. The poverty of the population and the low level of national wealth both ensured that propaganda drives to urge small investors to subscribe to war loans would not prove particularly lucrative. Industry was urged to use its wartime profits to write off its own debts, not to buy government stocks. Thus, as in Russia, the state looked to the banks. But the inflationary implications were kept in check by relatively low levels of liquidity and by the consolidation of a higher proportion of the total borrowing in long-term debt.

Italy's first war loan was floated before it entered the war, in January 1915. Its arms spending prompted an issue of 1,000 million lire in twenty-five-year obligations, offered at 97 and paying 4.5 per cent in interest. Only 881 million was subscribed—a reflection, it was argued, of public support for Italy's neutrality. But in any case, the terms of the loan were not particularly attractive and the financial community proposed to wait until the government came back to the market with a better offer. A banking consortium, headed by the Bank of Italy, which had underwritten half the issue had therefore to produce the shortfall, 119 million lire. By late May 1915 the price of the stock had fallen to 95.32.

The concessions to experience in the second war loan, issued in July 1915, were minimal. The only change in the terms was the reduction in price from 97 to 95, and for subscribers to the original loan to 93. Once again the banks had to come to the rescue—underwriting 200 million lire and making loans of up to 95 per cent of the amount subscribed. A total of 1,145.8 million lire was eventually raised, but by the end of September 1915 the price was 93.92 and falling.

[318] Michelson *et al.*, *Russian public finance*, 280–6, 373–4, 381; Claus, *Kriegswirtschaft Russlands*, 7–9.
[319] Ferguson, *Pity of war*, 326.
[320] Michelson *et al.*, *Russian public finance*, 324.
[321] Claus, *Kriegswirtschaft Russlands*, 16.
[322] Michelson *et al.*, *Russian public finance*, 220.

The terms of the third loan, in January 1916, were more attractive: a price of 97.5 at an interest rate of 5 per cent produced a real return of 5.13 per cent per annum. The target figure of 1,500 million lire was exceeded. Pre-war treasury bonds were accepted for up to half the total; most of the first and second war loans were converted. A total of 3,018.1 million lire was raised, 891.4 million of it in securities. But again the price fell: in October 1916 it stood at 93.7.

The fourth war loan, that of January 1917, was a perpetual rent, and the government stated it would not be converted for fifteen years. Issued at 90 and paying 5 per cent interest, it raised 3,798.5 million lire, a third of which represented conversions of earlier stocks. Initially the price rose, but by June it had settled below 90. The final wartime issue, in January 1918, was offered in the aftermath of Italy's defeat at Caporetto. The banks thought 2,000 million lire a realistic ceiling, but Francesco Nitti, the finance minister, was determined to engineer a propaganda and political triumph out of the loan drive, and set a target of 6,000 million. By dint of extending the subscription period to March, and of offering life insurance policies against subscriptions, he succeeded. Two-thirds of the total was raised in cash, and one-third in securities.[323]

As elsewhere, the banks' support of the war loan issues provided the basis for the expansion of credit rather than for the absorption of cash. Industry was encouraged to take on loan stock; from October 1915 contractors could be paid in treasury securities; and from January 1918 firms could treat their loan subscriptions as capital exempted from war profits tax.[324] But having acquired the stock, companies rapidly disposed of it. Hence the fall in prices, which hit—and in due course deterred—the small investor. The government's securities were therefore taken on by the banks as collateral, so expanding their commercial portfolios. In December 1918 approximately 2,800 million of 10,845 million lire in treasury paper securities were held by the four largest commercial banks.[325]

But what was significant in the Italian case was that this process took root relatively late in the war. The first three war loans caused an expansion of credit as investors borrowed to subscribe to the issues, but contraction followed as banks called in their debts and as the stock price fell. Not until 1917, as the institutional share in the high targets increased, did the expansion of credit fail to fall after the issue of the loan.

Furthermore, the proportion of short-term debt to long-term also remained relatively low until late in the war. In 1914 5.59 per cent of the national debt was floating; in 1915 14.85 per cent; in 1916 15.6 per cent; in 1917 22.07 per cent; and in 1918 27.06 per cent.[326] The major increase in floating debt did not occur until

[323] Forsyth, *Crisis of Liberal Italy*, 105–11, 117–21, 306.
[324] Teillard, *Emprunts de guerre*, 277–8.   [325] Forsyth, *Crisis of Liberal Italy*, 115–16.
[326] Fisk, *French public finance*, 139; Forsyth, *Crisis of Liberal Italy*, 101, gives 5.9% in 1914 and 34% in 1918.

the summer of 1916. Between July 1916 and November 1917 almost 1,000 million lire were advanced—in secret—by the Bank of Italy to the government on the security of low-interest treasury bills. In the twelve months after July 1916 short- and medium-term securities accounted for 58 per cent of all government securities (as against 20 per cent in the preceding year). But much of this was fixed in three or five year bonds, and much also was consolidated in the fifth war loan in 1918.[327]

Both Antonio Salandra, Italy's prime minister between March 1914 and June 1916, and the Bank of Italy pursued a policy of tight monetary control. The August 1914 crisis in the Italian case arose from the panic on the stock exchanges; falling prices for industrial shares hit the mixed banks that had financed industry, and undermined the value of the collateral held by the credit institutions. Salandra allowed only a small increase in note circulation, preferring to back the Bank of Italy's wish for a moratorium. The Bank remained liable for tax on additional note issue. Furthermore, it feared that any government guarantees on the lines followed by London would enable the commercial banks to pass on their bad debts to the state. Thus Italy risked recession in 1914—which it evaded through the war-led boom—rather than inflation.[328]

Italy's total note circulation rose 504 per cent in the First World War.[329] Between 1914 and 1919 the issue of the banks rose 618.75 per cent, and the issue of state notes 355.08 per cent.[330] The restraint of the government is evident in its handling of state notes, whose maximum, fixed at 500 million lire in December 1910, rose in steady but small steps to 2,200 million in November 1918. The main injection of cash came in the wake of Caporetto: the note issue expanded 23 per cent in 1914, 31 per cent in 1915, and 27 per cent in 1916, but 59 per cent in 1917 and 38 per cent in 1918. The total, which stood at 3,530 million lire on 31 December 1913, had by the end of 1916 doubled in three years, but by the end of 1918—after a further two years—had doubled again, amounting to 15,900 million lire.[331]

France funded 83.5 per cent of its wartime expenditure through loans.[332] In 1919 its debt charges were 7,900 million francs a year, the equivalent of 120 per cent of its income from taxation.[333] By 1920 its internal debt expressed as a ratio of its national product was 1.64, as opposed to 1.26 for Britain and 0.27 for the United States. And yet its public debt grew more slowly in the war than did that of either of its western allies. This was a reflection of how high were the

[327] Forsyth, *Crisis of Liberal Italy*, 111–16; Teillard, *Emprunts de guerre*, 168–73.
[328] Forsyth, *Crisis of Liberal Italy*, 125–30.
[329] Hardach, *First World War*, 171.
[330] Teillard, *Emprunts de guerre*, 338.
[331] Forsyth, *Crisis of Liberal Italy*, 134, 309.
[332] Jèze and Truchy, *War finance*, 193.
[333] Duroselle, *La Grande Guerre des français*, 154.

existing borrowings of the French government in 1914.[334] France's public
capital was doubly immobilized at the outbreak of war—first by this debt
and secondly by the moratorium.

The vital role played by the Banque de France in ensuring liquidity during
the mobilization persisted for the rest of the war. On 4 May 1915 Ribot signed a
new convention, setting a ceiling of 9,000 million francs (in place of 6,000
million) on the bank's advances to the government. In February 1917 the
maximum was fixed at 12,000 million, in October at 15,000 million, in August
1918 at 21,000 million, and in June at 24,000 million. The Banque d'Algérie had
advanced 75 million francs by December 1915, and contributed a further 45
million between then and May 1917, 80 million between May 1917 and January
1918, and 580 million over the last ten months of the war.[335] The principle of
state financial probity, enunciated by Ribot, was affirmed by regular repayments of the debt from the yields of publicly issued war loans: by the end of
1918 7,400 million francs of Banque de France advances had been redeemed in
this way, and 8,850 million in all. But 4,650 million francs were still outstanding. The practice was absurd, as the repayments in turn required the
government to come back for regular increases in credit. A mechanisim
devised to surmount a short-term crisis became a funding method for conducting long-term war.[336] These advances constituted 10 to 15 per cent of total
receipts from all sources between 1914 and 1919.[337]

The bank's loans took the form of an increase in note circulation. The
maximum note issue, fixed at 12,000 million francs on 5 August 1914, settled
at 40,000 million on 17 July 1919. Circulation rose progressively and evenly
from 10,042 million francs at the end of 1914, to 13,216 million at the end of 1915,
16,580 million at the end of 1916, 22,336 million at the end of 1917, and 30,250 at
the end of 1918.[338] The total increase over the war as a whole, 533 per cent, was
comparatively modest.[339] Indeed, Keynes, in January 1915, felt that the Banque
de France was being too conservative.[340] The emphasis on holding gold,
almost for its own sake, meant the cover for notes was still 42.4 per cent in
1917. Thus, note circulation seemed to be set more by the needs of commerce
and industry than by state policy. But the fact that it increased in line with the
government's debt meant that for its critics the state was not as innocent as it
claimed. In the first five months of 1918 circulation rose by 5,676 million francs,
a rate of 247 million per week; one commentator averred that this was 'the
only financial practice of a government whose chief blessed heaven that

[334] Eichengreen, *Golden fetters*, 78–9.
[335] Charbonnet, *Politique financière*, 110–11, 145.
[336] Jèze and Truchy, *War finance*, 233–7; Martin, *Les Finances publiques de la France*, 132–5, 140.
[337] Fisk, *French public finance*, 14.
[338] Jèze and Truchy, *War finance*, 237–9.
[339] Hardach, *First World War*, 171.
[340] Johnson (ed.), *Collected writings of Keynes*, xvi. 48.

he had not been born an economist'.[341] By then too a major pressure for the increase in fiduciary circulation was the spending of the British and American armies, who purchased francs for pounds and dollars.

Treasury bills were—alongside the bank's advances—the other main method of French government borrowing in the early stages of the war. France used three main forms of floating debt. One, the advances of the *trésoriers-payeurs généraux*, was a revival of an earlier but dwindling practice. Two, national defence bonds and national defence obligations, were similar to the treasury bills used by other nations but were given more catchy titles to reflect the immediate needs of the state.

The advances of the *trésoriers-payeurs généraux* were effectively mortgages taken out by the government on taxation revenue that had yet to come in. By 1914 these loans, paying interest of 1.75 per cent, had fallen to 30 million francs. Ribot tried to revive them in December 1914, setting the interest rate at 2.25 per cent. But, although the return eventually rose to 3.5 per cent, only 285 million francs were raised in deposits.[342]

The most powerful competition to the advances of the *trésoriers-payeurs généraux* was national defence bonds. Before the war the ceiling on treasury bonds was fixed at 600 million francs, and the subscribers were banks and large companies. On 1 September 1914 the maximum was raised to 940 million francs, but only 350 million were in circulation. Ribot decided to rechristen them national defence bonds, and to invite public subscriptions. Paying 5 per cent free of tax, and sold in units of 100, 500, and 1,000 francs, for periods of three, nine, or twelve months, they proved immediately attractive. They functioned both as savings accounts for those looking for a hedge against wartime inflation and current accounts for those anxious to expand their businesses in wartime. They circumvented the constraints of the moratorium, they facilitated tax avoidance, and they did so against a background rhetoric of patriotic duty. They were fully subscribed by the end of November. A new maximum, of 1,400 million francs, was soon exceeded. National defence bonds raised 1,618.8 million francs in 1914, 7,985.8 million in 1915, 12,372 million in 1916, 12,630.7 million in 1917 and 16,429 million in 1918. The monthly increase in circulation—576 million francs in 1915, 785 million in 1916, 912 million in 1917, and 1,400 million in 1918—is probably a better indication of their enduring popularity. On 31 December 1918 22,000 million francs were in circulation.

National defence bonds were so easily convertible as almost to constitute currency; hence the importance of regular repayment if required so as to limit their inflationary effect. The Banque de France secured advances on the bonds of up to 80 per cent of their value. But, for all their importance in raising

[341] Martin, *Les Finances publiques de la France*, 142; Duroselle, *La France et les français*, 211.
[342] Charbonnet, *Politique financière*, 150–4; Jèze and Truchy, *War finance*, 244–6.

revenue the bonds were less successful in drawing in the deposits of small investors. Three-quarters of those subscribing in 1915 did so in blocks of 10,000 francs or more, and 34,692 subscribed for 100,000 francs each. For the rural smallholder, distant from a bank, the bonds' short-term convertibility was less useful: most in this category subscribed for one year, and many did not subscribe at all. Thus, the multiplication of types of unit available, not only upwards to 10,000-franc and 100,000-franc denominations but particularly downwards to 5- and 20-franc investments, was not as significant as might at first appear. In June 1918 the bonds were offered for periods as short as one month. By then the full 5 per cent was payable only on one-year investments; one-month bonds paid 3.5 per cent, three-month bonds 4 per cent, and six-month bonds 4.5 per cent. The disparity in interest rates was to some extent evened out by the price of issue, which for a three-month bond at 98.75 was closer to par than a one-year bond at 95.[343]

The success of the national defence bonds was both a blessing and a curse. The blessing consisted in France's success—at least compared with the other belligerents—in mobilizing the wealth of the public. Elsewhere almost all treasury bills and much of the war loan were taken up by financial institutions; in France most of the war loan and many of the treasury bills were held by private investors. The danger was the product of the very attractiveness of the national defence bonds: they were too nearly liquid. Little of the floating debt was fixed: between 1914 and 1919 76,000 million francs were raised in short-term debt and only 24,000 million in long-term. Furthermore, as the war ended Klotz loosened, rather than tightened, an already relaxed fiscal hold: 54,000 million francs of the short-term debt were issued between 1916 and 1919.[344] France's position seemed far more perilous than Germany's.[345]

What worried the government was less the spectre of inflation and more the fear that all its creditors would call in their debts at the same time. Ribot's intention was to consolidate far more of the debt represented in national defence bonds than actually proved to be the case.[346]

His first attempt, in January 1915, was to offer a series of ten-year national defence obligations at 96.5, paying 5 per cent interest free of tax. But the obligations failed to strike a chord with either the business community (who were reluctant to forfeit liquidity) or the public (whose enthusiasm was not encouraged by the obscure and complex methods of purchase). A second series was issued in February 1917. The five-year obligations were offered at par but

[343] Jèze and Truchy, War finance, 246–54; Charbonnet, Politique financière, 156–79; Ribot, Letters to a friend, 34–8; Martin, Les Finances publiques de la France, 149–55.
[344] Duroselle, La Grande Guerre des français, 160.
[345] Soutou, 'Comment a été financée la guerre', in La Gorce (ed.), Première Guerre Mondiale, 284; Eichengreen, Golden fetters, 79.
[346] Schmidt, Ribot, 121–2.

paid a 2.5 per cent premium on maturity, and were thus designed to be held as investments until then.[347] They enjoyed no more success.

Initially Ribot was very reluctant to launch funded war loans. The evacuation of the government to Bordeaux, the desperate military situation, the closure of the bourse, and the effects of the moratorium—all militated against a successful issue in 1914–15. Most immediate was the effect of all these circumstances on the absorption of the 805 million franc perpetual loan (*rente*) issued at 3.5 per cent on 7 July 1914. The loan, intended to cover the equipment implications of the three-year service law, was nominally forty times oversubscribed. But it had been offered at a reduced price to institutions which then planned to pass it on to private clients at a profit: the outbreak of the war had checked this flow, requiring the institutions to pay the government but preventing the onward transmission to private investors. Thus, the credit houses were immobilized. By the end of August 1914 the price of the *rente* had already fallen from 91 to 82, and over half of the total had yet to be paid. The government was obliged to rescue those who had speculated on its stock if it was to free the market and guarantee its own credit. On 11 September 1914 it admitted the principle of conversion at the issue price provided the seller subscribed to future loans; it also used Banque de France advances to buy up the stock. By February 1915 all but 30 million francs of the target had been realized. The way was now open for the launch of the first public war loan.[348]

Ribot's rescue package had effectively committed France to a policy on war loans that followed the dictates of prestige and propaganda ahead of those of fiscal prudence. To ensure success all four of France's war loans were offered at rates well below par, with high levels of interest and free of tax. The first and second loans (those of 1915 and 1916) were issued at 88; the third (1917) was offered at 68.6 and the fourth (1918) at 70.8. Low initial prices guarded against a fall in values and encouraged investment for capital growth. However, the effect for the state was a decline in short-term revenue and an increase in future debt. The necessary corollary of such a policy ought to have been a low rate of interest. But France paid 5 per cent on the first two loans and 4 per cent on the last two.

This triumvirate of government forfeits was justified by the need to consolidate the floating debt. The right to convert short-term stocks to long-term issues was fundamental to the purpose of the scheme. But in fact much pre-war debt, as well as all four war loans, were in the form of perpetual *rentes*. And yet conversion from these as well as from national defence bonds was permitted in at least some of the war loan offers. Effectively, a fourth inducement was

[347] Charbonnet, *Politique financière*, 191–203; Jèze and Truchy, *War finance*, 254–8; Knauss, *Kriegsfinanzierung*, 163.
[348] Charbonnet, *Politique financière*, 29–31, 35, 221–8; Ribot, *Letters to a friend*, 47–8; Johnson (ed.), *Writings of Keynes*, xvi. 51; Jèze and Truchy, *War finance*, 259–62.

granted—the opportunity to transfer an existing long-term investment to yet more advantageous terms. For the state, the advantage in popularizing the *rentes* lay in the right of the government to choose when to repay its debt. Thus, it could stage its payments and so spread the burden; it could time redemption for when the price was low; and it could postpone it for so long that depreciation had eliminated the differential between the issue price and par.

The first war loan was launched in November 1915 and marked a definitive step to longer-term financial planning for the war. Individual subscribers totalled 3,133,389. Of 13,308 million francs raised, 6,285 million came in cash and 2,244 million in national defence bonds; the rest—national defence obligations, 3.5 per-cent 1914 *rentes*, and the pre-war 3 per cent *rentes*—represented existing long-term debt that was traded for more favourable terms. For the second loan, floated in October 1916, payments in instalments could be extended over six months, and pre-war 3 per-cent *rentes* were not convertible: it thus constituted a drive to draw in cash and national defence bonds. Of 10,082 million francs contributed, 5,425 million were subscribed in cash and 3,693 million in national defence bonds; 956 million came from national defence obligations; and just under 8 million from 3.5 per-cent *rentes*.

The profile of the third loan, opened on 26 November 1917, was remarkably similar—partly because Klotz set a target of 10 million francs, arguing that the length of the war now required regular, staged subscriptions rather than unlimited but less frequent drives for as much money as possible. Klotz put aside a small fund to enable the government to intervene in the market so as to keep up the price of the stock. The fourth loan, first offered on 20 October 1918, did not close until 24 November, and was dubbed the 'liberation loan'. Unlike the third, it was unlimited, and 7 million individuals subscribed 22,163 million francs—including conversions of 239 million francs of Russian government stocks.[349]

The relative success or failure of France's war loans policy can be measured in different ways. It never fully caught up with its late start: pundits in 1919 reckoned that France was two years behind on its loan issues. Their nominal yield—55,600 million francs—was reduced to 24,000 million net when allowance is made for the conversion of existing stocks.[350] Thus, they paid for a tenth of France's war expenditure, and their effective contribution was only a third that of national defence bonds. On the other hand, the issues never developed the institutional reliance on the banks characteristic of Austria-Hungary, Italy, and Russia. This is not to say that public subscription embraced large numbers of small investors. French sources are coy as to how many individuals subscribed to the second and third loans: the implication is that there were fewer than to the first. In the industrial area of Le Creusot

[349] Charbonnet, *Politique financière*, 254–320; Jèze and Truchy, *War finance*, 259–84; Ribot, *Letters to a friend*, 72–7.
[350] Duroselle, *La France et les français*, 214–16.

subscriptions fell successively over the first three loans.[351] The average gross contribution per Frenchman in metropolitan France to all four loans was 1,405 francs; by contrast his compatriot in Algeria subscribed 1,633 francs.[352] The crux was the big private investor. Tax exemptions encouraged the very wealthy to advance more, and from 1917 the government accepted loan stock in payment for the war profits tax.[353]

France's management of its borrowing was, by the standards of pre-1914 financial orthodoxy, relatively cautious. It restricted its note issue as best it could; it fought to conserve its gold; its devices for domestic debt drew in privately owned deposits. By these criteria it should have been in a far stronger financial position after the war than Britain. Britain's total circulation in the war increased 1,154 per cent[354]—double France's and even slightly more than Germany's; it argued that gold was to be used, not hoarded; and it issued only three war loans, of which the first was directed at the banks and the last was offered as early as January 1917. Its annual average rate of borrowing as a proportion of its 1913 national income was, at 57.3 per cent, not significantly less than Germany's 62 per cent.[355] By the end of the financial year 1918/19 its total internal debt was £6,142 million, almost a tenfold increase on the national debt as it stood at the beginning of the financial year 1914/15.[356] Interest payments on the debt rose from 9.6 per cent of budgeted receipts in 1913/14 to 22.4 per cent in 1920/1.[357] And yet Britain escaped the levels of inflation suffered by either France or Germany after the war.

It started the war with its debt at a historic low, and thereafter the sophistication of Britain's financial structure enabled it to withstand better the effects of wartime liquidity. Its patterns of borrowing—and indeed its sources of revenue as a whole—were much more diverse than those of other belligerents. It found it easier to change tack in its policies, and it was readier to do so. As the world's financial centre, London possessed a money market of greater sophistication and greater confidence. These qualities were important in enabling Britain to export its debt, to sell its stock overseas. Hence, much government debt did not enter the domestic banks' secondary reserves and so did not fuel the note issue; hence too, much of the interest paid by the government went to fill the pockets of overseas investors, so stoking inflation elsewhere rather than feeding monetary overhang at home.[358] But in addition, the confidence in Britain's credit which reinforced the marketability of its stock elsewhere, and especially of course in New York, was also an important element

[351] Becker, *The Great War and the French people*, 147.   [352] Meynier, *L'Algérie révelée*, 602.
[353] Jèze and Truchy, *War finance*, 278.   [354] Hardach, *First World War*, 171.
[355] Balderston, *Economic History Review*, 2nd series, XLII (1989), 229.
[356] Morgan, *British financial policy*, 114–15; Hirst and Allen, *British war budgets*, 14.
[357] Daunton, *English Historical Review*, CXI (1996), 883.
[358] This is the central argument of Balderston, *Economic History Review*, 2nd series, XLII (1989) 222–44.

in enabling the absorption of government debt at home. The maintenance of the gold standard, however fictional in practice, may have had its most potent effects on the sterling–dollar exchange, but it was also a symbol of financial strength to investors in Britain.

The most obvious illustration of these points was the management of the increase in Britain's circulation. In June 1914, of a total circulation of £199 million, £161 million was in coin. By June 1918 £148 million was still in coin: an underpinning of hard currency was thus preserved. The significant change was, of course, the rise in note issue, from £38 million to £311 million over the same period. However, the impact of this expansion was diffused by the fact that it was accomplished in large part by the use of treasury notes. They were payable in gold, but because they had the imprimatur of the government their convertibility mattered less to the public than did that of banknotes. Initially the commercial banks made only limited use of them: authorized to accept the equivalent of 20 per cent of their deposit liabilities, a total of £225 million, they actually took only £13 million. Treasury notes entered the circulation, there-fore, not in a flood but in a steady trickle. Government payments for contracts were their most obvious route. As the quantity increased so their issue was secured less by the gold reserve, which settled at £28.5 million in June 1915, and more by government securities. In August 1915 the ratio of gold to currency notes was 61 per cent; in August 1918 it was 16.9 per cent and, of £168.5 million in outstanding notes, £141.6 million were backed by government securities. Currency notes, therefore, freed both the government and the note circulation from the disciplines of the Bank of England. The government's credits were secured by loans, and it then transferred its credits back to its creditors so as to enable them to exchange the credits for the legal tender which the government also created. As long as no treasury notes were withdrawn, cash reserves increased in step with the government's borrowing.

The inflationary implications were immense. But two factors dampened their effects. The first was that, after the initial surge of liquidity on mobiliza-tion, the total circulation remained comparatively steady until 1917. The increase in the note circulation between 1915 and 1917 was offset by the with-drawal of £35 million in gold, and the total circulation rose by £56 million between June 1915 and June 1916, and by £42 million between June 1916 and June 1917. Not until after the summer of 1917 did the growth in the money supply again rise steeply. The pressures for cash included the desire to evade the excess profits duty, the need (as a result of inflation) for notes larger than £1 or 10 shillings, and the reluctance to use cheques after they became subject to stamp duty. Between June 1917 and June 1918 £98 million were added to the total circulation. The major increase, though large, was late.[359]

[359] Grady, *British war finance*, 14–36, 187, 194; Morgan, *British financial policy*, 216–26; Brown, *Gold standard*, 111–17.

The second prop to domestic confidence in the note issue was its quarantin-ing of the Bank of England. The beauty of treasury notes was that they ensured the liquidity required to fuel the war economy without impugning the status of the Bank of England's own currency or its gold reserves. Although the Bank act was suspended in 1914, the first major pressures on the Bank to increase its issue were not felt until 1917. By then the ultimate source of legal tender was no longer the Bank but the Treasury.

This reversal in the balance of the relationship between the two would have been hard to predict in 1914. The principal agent in the creation of government credit on the outbreak of war was the Bank of England. Between August and November 1914 the government borrowed £35 million from the Bank. Known as 'ways and means advances', these funds represented the Bank's own borrow-ings from the commercial banks. When spent by the government, the money returned to the banks, so increasing their deposits and enabling them once again to lend to the Bank. The flow thus ran in parallel with that of treasury notes. The Bank's commanding position in this relationship was determined by its manipulation of its interest rate, which normally hovered two percentage points above the market rate. In 1915 the Bank rate was at times up to 3 per cent higher than that of the market. Internationally, the effect of the Bank's control was to give the London market a consistency and stability which it would not have enjoyed if the price for money had been determined by stockbrokers: this was the case in New York, and the rate there varied daily according to the dictates of the stock exchange. Domestically, the rate at which the Bank borrowed was ordinarily 0.5 per cent below that at which new treasury bills were issued. Thus, the Bank helped establish treasury bills, and hence govern-ment securities became much more attractive vehicles for investment than general deposits.[360]

The closure of so many stock exchanges in 1914 left many would-be investors searching for outlets for their funds. On 19 January 1915 the Treasury imposed an embargo on fresh capital issues that were not in the public interest. The effect was to reserve the London money market for government use. In 1916 the total value of capital issues in the United Kingdom was £585.6 million, as against £512.6 million in 1914, but of this total only £31.5 million (as opposed to £180.1 million in 1914) were not earmarked for government loans. The issues in 1917 were valued at £1,338.7 million, and all except for £40.9 million were government securities. The stock exchange was effectively regulated by the issue of treasury bills.[361]

By 4 November 1914 £82.5 million in six-month treasury bills had been sold at rates of between 3.5 and 3.75 per cent. Their issue was then suspended to

[360] Grady, British war finance, 66–8, 272–4; Sayers, Bank of England, i. 82–3.
[361] Grady, British war finance, 65; see also 59–66, 143–5, 276–9.

allow the first war loan to be offered. The intention was to repay the 'ways and means advances' and redeem the outstanding treasury bills. Priced at 95 and paying 3.5 per cent, the war loan's effective yield on maturity (between 1925 and 1928) would be 3.7 per cent. The Bank of England supported the issue by lending up to the full issue price at 1 per cent below the Bank rate. Not only did it lose on this deal (as the price fell to 90), but it also underwrote £113 million to enable the target figure of £350 million to be reached. The banks collectively subscribed £100 million as opposed to £91 million from the public. There were only 25,000 individual contributors. By pitching the minimum subscription at £100 (albeit payable in instalments over six months), and by keeping the interest rate low, the Treasury had deterred the public, and so failed to use the loan as an anti-inflationary device.[362]

With the launch of the first war loan completed the issue of treasury bills was resumed—initially with five-year exchequer bonds, and then with three-, six-, and nine-month bills, paying 2.75 per cent, 3.6 per cent, and 3.75 per cent respectively. Their aim was less to raise money than to stabilize the market rate of discount.[363]

In June 1915 McKenna launched the second war loan. Its aims were Keynes's—less the raising of new money and more the countering of domestic inflation by attracting small investors and the steadying of international exchange by pulling in American funds. Bonds of £5 and £25 and vouchers for 5 shillings were offered through post offices. McKenna employed Hedley Le Bas of the Caxton Advertising Agency, who had promoted army recruiting, to popularize its terms. 'We must give the investor something for nothing to make him lend his money to the country,' Le Bas observed. 'In other words, why not make patriotism profitable?'[364] Although the stock was issued at par, the interest rate was set at the much more attractive level of 4.5 per cent. The banks grumbled at the competition, but were softened by the Bank of England's readiness to lend to them so that they could in turn enable their customers to borrow in order to subscribe. The units were repayable in 1945, although they were redeemable at the government's option after ten years and could be converted for any later long-term loans at par. The principle of convertibility was also recognized for past issues, and accounted for £313 million (about a third of the government's outstanding stock) of the £900 million raised. McKenna had hoped for £1,000 million. Although the loan attracted over a million subscribers, over half of them bought units of £100 or more, and one-third of the new money was contributed by the banks.[365]

[362] Knauss, *Kriegsfinanzierung*, 155–6; Johnson (ed.), *Collected writings of Keynes*, xvi. 95; Sayers, *Bank of England*, i. 79–81.
[363] Morgan, *British financial policy*, 108.
[364] Farr, 'McKenna', 119–20; see also 154–6 .
[365] Ibid. 108–9, 189–90; Knauss, *Kriegsfinanzierung*, 156–7; Johnson (ed.), *Collected writings of Keynes*, xvi. 103–5; Hirst and Allen, *British war budgets*, 57–64.

In 1916 government issues were dominated by medium-term stocks. Five-year exchequer bonds, paying 5 per cent, were issued in December 1915. In February 1916 war savings certificates, offered at 15s. 6d. but realizing £1 on maturity after five years, were aimed at the small investor. They were followed in June by war expenditure certificates, repayable in two years but convertible to war loans. In October a significant barrier was breached when exchequer bonds, convertible and paying interest free of tax, were offered at 6 per cent.

The 6 per-cent exchequer bond, designed to attract foreign funds, told a desperate story. Determined to reject exchange restrictions, the Bank had to counter the lure to investors of the New York market. In July it raised its rate to 6 per cent, far higher than that of any other belligerent. Three-month treasury bills, which paid 4.5 per cent in March 1916, were offered at 5.5 per cent in July; one-year bills earned 6 per cent between July and September. Outstanding treasury bills, to the tune of £800 million, clogged the money market in the late summer. The City was unhappy, as government rates were effectively depreciating existing stock. But the issue of a new war loan seemed inopportune as the battle of the Somme dragged on.[366]

Treasury bill rates fell in the autumn to accommodate the issue of exchequer bonds, and their sale was suspended altogether in January to allow the flotation of the third war loan. By now the American money market had eased, and the loan could be offered at a rate lower than 6 per cent. It was available in two forms—5 per cent stock issued at 95 and repayable in 1947, and 4 per cent stock issued at par, repayable in 1942, and free of income tax but not supertax. The former raised £2,075 million and the latter £52 million. The success of the 5 per-cent stock was interpreted as a reflection of confidence that taxation would fall after the war. But it was also a product of conversion rights: almost all the second war loan was exchanged for the third, and its price soared to 99. The first war loan, which did not enjoy convertibility, fell to 84.75. The arrangements for the third loan, therefore, included provision for a sinking fund to buy war loan bonds when they fell below the issue price. Just under half the total raised constituted new money.[367]

The third loan was the last of the war. Between 1914 and 1917 government policy was to consolidate floating and short-term debt through the periodic issue of long-term stock. Thus, devices like treasury bills covered the gaps between the major flotations. But after January 1917 short-term and medium-term debt dominated. The effect was to bring interest rates down and so make domestic borrowing cheaper. From April 1917, when treasury bills were available on tap once more, their rate fell until in February 1918 they paid only 3.5 per cent. The commercial deposit rate declined even further to 3 per cent.

[366] Knauss, *Kriegsfinanzierung*, 157–8; Grady, *British war finance*, 143–4; Sayers, *Bank of England* i. 95–7.
[367] Morgan, *British financial policy*, 110–12, 192–4; Grady, *British war finance*, 131–3; Hirst and Allen, *British war budgets*, 169; Knauss, *Kriegsfinanzierung*, 158–9.

The first consequence of this policy was an inability to attract foreign investment. In normal times the Bank would have responded to the market and raised its rate. Its subordination to the requirements of the state meant that it did not. But in November 1917 a differential rate was established for foreign balances, which paid 4.5 per cent.[368]

The domestic consequence was a disincentive to the private investor. By the end of 1917 the number of individuals holding government securities had swollen from 345,000 in 1914 to 16 million. Of these, 10.5 million owned war savings certificates.[369] Lowering interest rates could jeopardize this success, fostering liquidity and pushing up prices. That the situation did not get out of hand was the result of extending the policy of medium-term stocks begun in 1916. Five-year exchequer bonds paying 5 per cent were made available again in April 1917, but they only netted £82 million. In September they were withdrawn, and replaced by national war bonds. Marketed in several different guises, but embodying the principle of convertibility and interest rates of between 4 and 5 per cent, they raised £649 million in 1917–18 and £987 million in 1918–19.[370] Thus, unlike the shorter-term debt of the other belligerents at the end of the war, much of Britain's was both more fixed and better adapted to absorb private purchasing power.

Nonetheless, the increase in medium-term bonds could not prevent a major surge in the floating debt. 'Ways and means advances', which had not been used in 1915 or for most of 1916, were resumed at the end of the latter year. By 31 March 1918 treasury bills totalling £973 million were outstanding. The debt was absorbed by the commercial banks. They contributed £400 million to the government's financing of the war between June 1914 and June 1917, but provided £470 million between June 1917 and December 1918. This represented the entire increase in the banks' deposits over the last eighteen months of the war; commercial advances fell from 49.6 per cent of their deposits at the beginning of the war to 32.5 per cent at its conclusion. The banks had become the creditors not of trade and industry but of the government.[371]

Britain, like the other belligerents, had a floating debt problem at the end of the war. But it was manageable and its reduction could be staged. Of its total domestic debt at the conclusion of the financial year 1918/19, £6,142 million, only £1,412 million was floating; £1,040 million was in medium-term debt due to mature in 1925. Furthermore, Britain had managed to distribute its debt over many sectors: by 1924 £765 million was held in extra-budgetary funds, £740 million in the banking system, £790 million by small savers, £1,775 million

[368] Morgan, *British financial policy*, 112–13, 179–80, 196.
[369] Knauss, *Kriegsfinanzierung*, 157–8; Bunselmeyer, *Cost of the war*, 137–8.
[370] Knauss, *Kriegsfinanzierung*, 160; Morgan, *British financial policy*, 113–14.
[371] Morgan, *British financial policy*, 246–8, 296.

by larger individual investors, and £2,315 million in foreign and corporate holdings.[372]

Thus, through medium-term stock and through the spread of its creditors Britain contrived to mitigate the more inflationary aspects of its change in borrowing policy after 1917. Furthermore, its corollary, the low rate of interest, itself created a continuing confidence in British financial strength. Hindsight, conditioned by the knowledge that ultimately the international money market would shift from London to New York, from sterling to the dollar, might suggest that this was a false optimism. Remarkably, however, London's status as the world's creditor emerged from the war comparatively intact. In the month of the armistice the London banks accepted $500 million worth of business compared to New York's $210 million.[373]

The crisis in British government borrowing had come in the autumn of 1916, when the interest rate peaked at 6 per cent. Domestically, short-term debt expanded to the detriment of long-term, while the Treasury faced a mounting burden of debt repayment. Internationally, Britain had a double dilemma. To maintain its hold on the money market, its rates had to remain competitive with New York. To draw in overseas funds it could, of course, let its rate rise, but to export its domestic debt it had to offer terms no more advantageous than those prevailing across the Atlantic. Its ability to surmount this crisis lay only partly in its own hands. The reduction in the cost of its own borrowing relied in turn on the maintenance of low interest rates in America. The sequence of exchange-rate crises and the complaints of harassed Treasury officials obscure the two fundamental financial advantages the United States conferred on Great Britain. It followed a policy of low interest rates, and it fostered the developing machinery of credit. Without the creation in New York of favourable conditions for the flotation of debt, the battle to preserve the sterling–dollar exchange would have been meaningless.

In April 1917 the banks of the United States were in an extraordinarily strong position, flush with gold, their structure reformed, and free of debt. But the American Treasury was still concerned that the Federal Reserve System was insufficiently flexible for the demands which it anticipated the United States's entry to the war would generate. On 21 June 1917 the legal reserve requirements of the member banks were reduced by 5 per cent. The effect was to create excess reserves which could then be used to expand deposits. Between June and December 1917 all deposits increased by 39.3 per cent and government deposits by 65.1 per cent. The member banks were required to pass their excess reserves over to the Federal Reserve district bank, so increasing the reserve ratio from 70.9 per cent to 78 per cent by August 1917. Between March 1917 and November the reserves of the district banks grew by 77 per cent, and by December 1919 by

[372] Morgan, *British financial policy*, 114–15, 136.   [373] Bogart, *War costs*, 80–1.

125 per cent. On this basis the discounts of the Federal Reserve banks increased by a massive 2,548 per cent.[374]

Expanded reserves also enabled an extension of the note issue. The crisis of August 1914 was bridged by the terms of the 1908 Emergency Currency act, fortuitously extended in 1914 for the purposes of covering the establishment of the Federal Reserve System. The act allowed up to $500 million to be added temporarily to the circulation on the security of shares and bonds. By mid-October 1914 $363.6 million were outstanding, but in November the Federal Reserve System became fully operational and the emergency currency was retired.[375]

The Federal Reserve act did not establish an absolute ceiling on American circulation; it confined itself to stipulating that a gold reserve of 40 per cent should be held against outstanding notes. The memory of the Civil War served to persuade Americans that the danger of inflation lay primarily in uncovered notes. Thus, their worry in the summer of 1917 was that for the first time since the war began their exports of gold exceeded their imports. Their response, to ban the export of gold and to concentrate holdings in the Federal Reserve System, meant that America ended the war with a gold reserve of $2,090 million against a Federal Reserve note issue of $2,802 million.[376] By then the Federal Reserve Bank held 74 per cent of the United States's monetary gold stock as opposed to 28 per cent at the end of 1916.[377] Even in relation to total circulation the gold cover looked more than adequate. In December 1916 $3,679 million were in circulation, in December 1917 $4,086 million, and in December 1918 $4,951 million. The ratio of Federal Reserve notes to the total circulation grew from .044 in June 1916 to .530 by December 1918.

But America's experience proved an object lesson in the dangers of simple or single explanations for inflation. Federal Reserve note issues rose 754 per cent between March 1917 and December 1919.[378] The money supply swelled by 60 per cent between 1913 and 1918, bank deposits increased by 94 per cent, but business only grew by 13 per cent. Thus, the mismatch between the availability of cash and the goods for purchase fed price increases.[379] America's industrial boom, fuelled by the Entente's orders for war goods, only exacerbated the problem. The pegging of exchange rates fixed American products at—by European wartime standards—artificially low prices. Thus, goods were taken out of domestic consumption while simultaneously overseas payments augmented domestic purchasing power.[380]

---

[374] Gilbert, *American financing*, 177–88; also Petit, *Finances extérieures*, 439–43.
[375] Noyes, *American finance*, 77–81.
[376] Helfferich, *Money*, 232; see also Petit, *Finances extérieures*, 440–3, 460–1.
[377] Chandler, *Strong*, 104.
[378] Gilbert, *American financing*, 188.
[379] Bogart, *War costs*, 356–7.
[380] Brown, *Gold standard*, 97; Gilbert, *American financing*, 43.

If inflation was the downside of American policy, the expansion of the stock market was the upside. Low interest rates contributed to liquidity but encouraged lending and investment. The Dow Jones index, which fell to 54.63 in January 1915 had recovered to 99.15 by December of the same year. From April 1915 New York was the only stock exchange which did not restrict the trade in foreign securities. As a consequence the growth in loans and non-governmental investments in 1916 was valued at $3,188 million.[381] Thus, the private financial sector was gearing up for wartime expansion before the American government itself generated any demands of it.

In April 1917 the United States's national debt was small and the burden of interest payments trivial. The scope for extension was considerable. But the success of McAdoo's borrowing policy was vitiated by the maintenance of low rates of interest. Already, between January and April 1917, government bonds suffered a slight fall, thus providing a clear indication that the popular success of war loans would depend on the attractiveness of their terms. McAdoo, however, was persuaded that patriotic sentiment, not financial self-interest, would woo the small subscriber. He insisted on selling government bonds at rates of interest less than those of the market. In doing so he helped keep down the price of money, to the benefit both of America's allies and of the industries of the United States. Expansion was never slowed because money was either unavailable or too costly. But the effect on government loans themselves was less positive. The price of the stock was depressed to below that at which it was issued and ultimately deterred the public. Consequently, America's war loans did not divert the growing purchasing power of its lower-income groups, and so failed to staunch inflation. Instead, the banks became increasingly important to government borrowing. The government's policy was that, by limiting credit to essential purposes and by encouraging the acquisition of long-term government securities, the war should be funded by 'the thrift of the people'. But in the three years up to June 1919 the commercial banks' credit increased by $11,350 million, while their holdings of Treasury obligations and the loans on them rose by only half that. Thereafter the favourable conditions for credit were being exploited for non-essential purposes, and—as elsewhere— the expansion of the secondary reserve meant that war loans fuelled rather than quenched the money supply.[382]

McAdoo's general principle was that the war would be paid for by a mix of taxation and long-term war bonds. He met the government's current expenditure through short-term certificates of indebtedness. The Revenue act of 3 March 1917 authorized the issue of certificates of indebtedness to a ceiling of $300 million dollars; they paid 3 per cent interest. The legislation was linked to

[381] Gilbert, *American financing*, 37, 42; Noyes, *American finance*, 101–8.
[382] Gilbert, *American financing*, 52–4, 117–19; Chandler, *Strong*, 109–18.

the receipt of taxation and therefore permitted a maximum maturity period of one year. But with the entry to the war the Treasury issued certificates of indebtedness which anticipated the four major war loans (or Liberty Loans, so called as they were to be used to wage war against autocracy). The first tax anticipation certificates were not offered until August 1918, and proved relatively unpopular—partly because their interest rate of 4 per cent was less than that then available through the loan anticipation certificates, and partly because the latter were more attractive to the banks. The Treasury prompted the banks to take up loan anticipation certificates so that subscriptions to the Liberty Loans proper would effectively be paid for before they were issued. It thus avoided large transfers of cash at any one time, and so prevented temporary restrictions on credit. From February 1918, anticipation certificates were marketed at fortnightly intervals; the banks were urged to subscribe 1 per cent of their gross earnings a week, and from April 5 per cent per month. The interest rate was fixed at 4 per cent in November 1917, and 4.5 per cent in February 1918. The banks responded by taking 83 per cent of the third and fourth Liberty Loan anticipation certificates. Non-bank subscribers, despite various taxation exemptions comparable with those available to holders of Liberty Loans, accounted for only 17 per cent. By 1 July 1919 48 series had been issued, totalling $21.9 million; 79.4 per cent of the Liberty Loan proceeds were used to refund Liberty Loan anticipation certificates.[383]

The first Liberty Loan was issued at par on 24 April 1917. The banks advised that a maximum of $1,000 million dollars could be placed at an interest rate of 4 per cent. McAdoo, persuaded by his own faith in popular patriotism, opted for $2,000 million at 3.5 per cent. The bonds matured in 1947, but the Treasury could redeem them after fifteen years. The smallest unit was $50, but special bonds of $10, which could be grouped into units of $100, were made available. Employers allowed employees advances on their salaries; firms fostered liquidity by declaring extra dividends; payment could be spread over five instalments. McAdoo's faith was rewarded with $3,035 million, subscribed by 4.5 million individuals. The bond-holding public in the United States expanded over ten times. Applications were therefore scaled down. Of the total subscribed, 42 per cent was in blocks of between $50 and $10,000; but of the $2,000 million of allocated units, 65 per cent was in this lower range. The effect was to restrain the benefits of the generous tax exemptions which the bonds offered. They were liable only for estate and inheritance duties, and thus a person paying income tax at the top rate of 67 per cent was being given the equivalent of 10.6 per cent in interest.[384]

[383] Chandler, *Strong*, 145–61.
[384] Ibid. 120–3; Bogart, *War costs*, 208–10; Petit, *Finances extérieures*, 444; Noyes, *American finance*, 183–7.

McAdoo had been authorized to take out a loan of $5,000 million. He had therefore $3,000 million in hand. In August 1917 he requested authority to float the second Liberty Loan, which would incorporate the unused $3,000 million and add a further $4,500 million. His aim was to withdraw the privileges which the first loan had accorded the wealthy and to woo those on lower incomes. The new loan was therefore liable to supertax and to excess profits duty. In return the interest rate was raised to 4 per cent. The loan attracted 9.4 million subscribers, and raised $4,617.5 million. Only $568 million of the first loan was converted: for most of its holders tax exemptions were more valuable than an increase in interest rate.

By the time McAdoo applied to issue the third Liberty Loan, in April 1918, his policy was showing signs of strain. It had failed to win over the excess purchasing power of lower-income groups; its low rate of interest meant that the existing Liberty Loans traded below par; and only after the first loan had the government—albeit briefly—been free of debt. Local quotas were set as targets to popularize the new loan. McAdoo wanted to issue the stock at 4.25 per cent, in ten-year non-convertible bonds. The banks advised that non-convertibility should be compensated for by a rate of 4.5 per cent, not least because the government would not have to bear the higher rate on its earlier issues. The Treasury was authorized to buy up to 5 per cent of any of the issues in any one year in order to sustain the market price. To encourage investors to hold the bonds, they were made redeemable at par plus interest in payment of estate and inheritance taxes. No provision was made for purchase in instalments. The effect was, once again, to make the issue relatively more attractive to the wealthy. Of 18,376,815 subscribers who put up $4,176.5 million, 18,354,315 contributed $2,770.9 million in units ranging from $50 to $10,000. Thus, 99.8 per cent of subscribers received 66.5 per cent of the issue.

For the fourth Liberty Loan, in October 1918, the Treasury gave in to the market. All the Liberty Loans were trading below par, but the first had remained better priced than the others because of its tax exemptions. Therefore the fourth loan was exempt from surtax, excess profits duty, and war profits duties. For those who bought the fourth loan the exemption was extended to their holdings of the second and third issues. On this basis the interest rate could be held at 4.25 per cent, and the fifteen-to-twenty-year bonds made inconvertible. Over 22 million people subscribed $6,993 million for an issue of $6,000 million: most of these (85 per cent) wanted $50 and $100 bonds, but that accounted for only 9.8 per cent of the total sum.[385]

Including the Victory Loan (issued after the war had ended), only 20 per cent of the debt outstanding in June 1920 was held in units of $50 or $100, and

---

[385] Gilbert, *American financing*, 124–42; Bogart, *War costs*, 210–24. Bogart's figures occasionally differ from Gilbert's, and in these cases Gilbert's have been followed.

some of these smaller denominations had been bought by companies as dividend payments for their shareholders. Thus, the bulk of American war loans were subscribed by the wealthy. Companies themselves had significant holdings: the United States Steel Corporation took almost $128 million of Liberty Loan stock.[386] But the failure of McAdoo's grandiose vision was only relative to its own ambition. Over a fifth of the population of the United States applied for the fourth loan. Moreover, McAdoo himself recognized that alternative devices were needed to reduce the purchasing power of lower-income groups, and in January 1918 imported from Britain the idea of war savings certificates. Denominations of $5 were sold at $4.12, and gained 1 cent towards their final redemption value in each succeeding month. Thrift stamps, valued at 25 cents, could be collected towards the price of one war savings certificate. Monthly sales averaged $50 million, and in July 1918 they peaked at $211.4 million. In 1918 as a whole $962.6 million was raised through war savings certificates. But the scheme was too late in adoption and maturity too short-term for it to have a major deflationary effect.[387] McAdoo had been determined to restrict short-term debt, but in June 1919 it stood at 14 per cent, less than elsewhere but not significantly below that of Britain.[388] If McAdoo had really wanted to draw in the subscriptions of those on lower incomes, to attract spenders not savers, he would have had to forgo tax exemptions and to raise interest rates.

However, it was only the post-war preoccupation with inflation that cast the policy of low interest rates into doubt. During the war their effect was not entirely nugatory. Obviously the state, as the principal borrower in the market, benefited from the cheapness of money. This was a direct advantage. Indirectly, the success of the whole Liberty Loans scheme came to rest on low interest rates. The Liberty Bond act banned banks from using the bonds as security for note issues. Formally speaking, their task was to take up the certificates of indebtedness—the short-term stock, not the long-term. However, the act permitted all banks, including those which were not members of the Federal Reserve System, to accept deposits; it also released member banks from their reserve requirements in relation to deposits of government funds. The Federal Reserve banks increased their loans to commercial banks from less than $20 million in early 1917 to around $2,000 million in mid-1919. The commercial banks then offered preferential rates to clients seeking advances to buy Liberty Loans. The discounts of the members became increasingly secured by government stocks, and their own rediscounts were then secured on their holdings of these stocks. In January 1918 31.9 per cent of the banks' rediscounts were secured by government obligations; by the end of the year the figure was 70

---

[386] Noyes, *American finance*, 189.
[387] Gilbert, *American financing*, 163–70; Bogart, *War costs*, 228–30.
[388] Chandler, *Strong*, 112.

per cent. The banks' holdings of government obligations rose 233 per cent, from $1,546 million in June 1917 to $5,147 million in June 1919. Thus, subscriptions to the loans rested on bank borrowings which themselves relied on low rates of interest.[389]

The consequent increase to the money supply was not more damaging because the United States's entry to the war was late, and its experience of war finance more restricted in time than that of the other belligerents. But of course low interest rates did not only serve America's own liquidity requirements in 1917–18. They were essential to the finances of its Entente partners. By April 1917 British, French, and Italian spending in the United States, funded principally through debt contracted in America in the first place, was so great that only America's active belligerence seemed capable of shoring up their international credit.

FOREIGN BORROWING

Foreign borrowing fulfilled two main and interlocking objectives. First, it provided the funds with which to buy in imports. In peace, imports were—in ideal circumstances—paid for through exports, but in the war military demands on domestic industry eliminated any surpluses for overseas trade. Secondly, it could be used to manipulate exchange rates. The pressures of the war on a belligerent—a fall in exports, an increase in inflation, the possibility of defeat—tended to depreciate its currency against those of neutral powers. But by acquiring foreign funds for its own purposes, the belligerent could staunch depreciation. Thus the costs of foreign purchases could be controlled and, in the longer term, the path to post-war reintegration in international commerce eased.

However, Germany's need to achieve these two objectives was rendered ambiguous by the blockade. With the loss of 44 per cent of its merchant fleet and the curtailment of its exports, not only through the blockade but also by dint of domestic demand, invisible earnings slumped. The tendency of its wartime rhetoric was to make a virtue of necessity. 'Das Gelde im Lande',[390] the retention of wealth at home through the inability to import, became a clarion-call of propaganda; Helferrich lauded autarky as Germany moved towards a form of neo-mercantilism, stressing the economic reinvigoration that would be achieved through reliance on domestic resources and industrial ingenuity.[391]

[389] Gilbert, *American financing*, 189–97; Brown, *Gold standard*, 122–3.
[390] Dix, *Wirtschaftskrieg*, 243.
[391] Williamson, *Helfferich*, 132; Lotz, *Staatsfinanzwirtschaft*, 92; Knauss, *Kriegsfinanzierung*, 174.

At first policy followed the public posturing. Foreign creditors were denied access to German courts, and neutral funds thereby rebuffed.[392] But in practice Germany could not continue to be so xenophobic. Imports, albeit in smaller quantities, continued to arrive through the neutral states on its borders, and they had to be paid for. Its conquests, especially in France and Russia, forced it to acquire francs and roubles in order to administer the occupied territories. Warburgs called in short-term foreign assets to the tune of 241 million marks, particularly from the United States, via Amsterdam.[393] In 1915 the Russians suspected that roubles reached the Germans from Sweden.[394] In 1916 both francs and dollars were channelled through Switzerland. Thus remittances continued, not only between the Central Powers and their non-aligned neighbours, but even between the two opposing camps by way of neutral intermediaries.[395] Ethel Cooper, an Australian living in Leipzig, continued to receive payments in sterling into 1917, and did so at increasingly favourable rates of exchange.[396]

The exchange rate which mattered most was that between the mark and the currencies of those neutrals with whom Germany traded. By January 1916 the mark had lost a third of its pre-war value in the Hague, New York, and Stockholm. The Bundesrat therefore made efforts to eliminate speculation on the foreign exchanges and to curb the demand for foreign exchange from importers. It gave the Reichsbank the task of preparing a list of permitted imports, and it and the other main banks were formed into a consortium licensed to deal in foreign exchange. A year later all transactions in foreign exchange, not just trading agreements, were made subject to Reichsbank control. Steps were also taken to improve the inflow of exchange.[397] Both allies and neutrals importing from Germany were required to pay in their own currencies. German coal exports to Holland and Switzerland brought in a steady flow of Dutch florins and Swiss francs. In December 1917 Germany refined the system by issuing invoices in German marks but demanding payment in the appropriate foreign currency at the rate prevailing on the day of payment, thus contriving to generate a profit from its own depreciating currency. Its bid in 1918 to be paid for goods that had yet to be delivered was less successful.[398]

Efforts to gain control of Germany's foreign investments charted a similar path from voluntarism to compulsion. Germany held between 20,000 million

[392] Bartholdy, War and German society, 47–9.
[393] Bogart, War costs, 75; Frey, Militärgeschichtliche Mitteilungen, 53 (1994), 330–1; Ferguson, Paper and iron, 102.
[394] Michelson et al., Russian public finance, 409–10.
[395] Petit, Finances extérieures, 603; Brown, Gold standard, 13–14.
[396] Cooper, Behind the lines, 32, 119, 184, 218.
[397] Knauss, Kriegsfinanzierung, 73–4; Lotz, Staatsfinanzwirtschaft, 86–7; Helfferich, Money, 259–62; Brown, Gold standard, 61–3.
[398] Petit, Finances extérieures, 311.

and 28,000 million marks of foreign investments at the outbreak of the war. In 1915 the Reichsbank encouraged shareholders in possession of foreign bonds to sell them to the bank in exchange for marks. In this way it acquired $470 million on the New York stock exchange in 1915 and 1916.[399] But at the same time legislation in the enemy countries was confiscating German holdings; after America's entry and by the war's end 16,100 million marks were forfeited.[400] In August 1916 the Reichsbank calculated that, of 15,000 million marks of foreign holdings, only 2,148 million were 'seizable', and that of that 1,334 million marks were held by neutral powers (excluding the United States) or Germany's allies. As 700 million marks of this final figure represented investments in Austria-Hungary which were to all intents and purposes worthless, a bare 634 million marks remained that could be easily sold.[401] Efforts to encourage the transfer of privately held foreign securities and foreign currency to the Reichsbank were stepped up in August 1916, and in the new year it became mandatory to lend them to the state for the duration of the war.

In the circumstances the mark enjoyed an extraordinary stability on the international exchanges. Germany's efforts in January 1916 were rewarded with only a 4 per-cent variation in the position of the mark in Zurich between then and November. But the United States's entry into the war had the effect of aligning neutral markets with those of the Entente, and so isolating the Central Powers. By October 1917 the mark had fallen 50 per cent. It recovered after Soviet Russia's acceptance of humiliating peace terms at Brest-Litovsk, and it did not go into steep decline until the second half of 1918.[402] Germany believed that the international position of the mark, in so far as it reflected inflation, did so because inflation was a product, not of domestic fiscal policy but of an adverse balance of payments. On this interpretation the recovery of Germany's ability to trade after the war would soon restore the mark to parity. The fact that this view was shared elsewhere had its effects in wartime too, since it prevented the mark from falling as far as other economic factors might have suggested was likely.[403]

At one level the comparative strength of the mark was a reflection of German weakness—an inability, thanks to the blockade, to import more. Because Germany imported less, it needed less foreign currency. Thus, the impediments to commerce also rendered less debilitating the consequences of Germany's comparative inability to place a greater proportion of its debt abroad.

The most important neutral money market until 1917, New York, remained all but closed. One problem was that of Germany's representation. A secret

---

[399] Frey, *Militärgeschichtliches Mitteilungen*, 53 (1994), 342–3; Frey, *International History Review*, XIX (1997), 547–8.
[400] Ferguson, *Paper and iron*, 102–3; also Ferguson, *Pity of war*, 253–4.
[401] Frey, *Militärgeschichtliche Mitteilungen*, 53 (1994), 346.
[402] Brown, *Gold standard*, 62–6; Knauss, *Kriegsfinanzierung*, 72; Roesler, *Finanzpolitik*, 139.
[403] Holtfrerich, *German inflation*, 163; G. H. Soutou, 'Comment a été financée la guerre', in La Gorce (ed.), *La Première Guerre Mondiale*, 291 .

mission headed by Heinrich Albert of the Interior Ministry in August 1914 was both over-sanguine concerning Britain's observance of the declaration of London, and too dependent on the use of German treasury bills as payment for American goods. In spring 1915 the American moratorium on the purchase of belligerents' loan stock was breached by the Entente's representative, J. P. Morgan. Although in theory the path to the floating of a loan in the United States was now as open to Germany as it was to Britain, in practice Berlin had to deal with Morgan's dominance of the market. Only the comparatively unknown firm of Chandler and Co. would act for Germany: it took $10 million in treasury bills. By the end of 1915 the Reichsbank regarded the US bill market as effectively closed. The blockade, in addition to strangling German–American trade, also checked the movement of promissory bills and other commercial paper across the Atlantic. Three American institutions were prepared to handle German business: the National City Bank of New York, the Equitable Trust Company, and the Guaranty Trust Company; but in autumn 1916 the first of these capitulated to British threats to blacklist neutral banks which dealt with Germany. Germany's best hope seemed to be Kuhn Loeb, an associate of Warburgs. However, a plan to float a loan on behalf of the cities of Berlin, Hamburg, and Frankfurt in late 1916 was forestalled by Woodrow Wilson himself. Germany raised $27 million in the United States, just over 1 per cent of the total borrowed by the Entente over the same period.[404] The blockade meant that most of the proceeds were used to fund purchases from the border neutrals rather than the United States. The money that was spent in America was allocated to funding German propaganda, and so made no direct contribution to Germany's exchange problem or to its balance of trade.[405]

The problems of access to the New York money market and of the shipment of American goods made Holland, rather than the United States, the main focus of Germany's international borrowing by the end of 1915.[406] Germany centralized its purchases and so controlled prices through the establishment of the Zentral-Einkauf Gesellschaft. By November 1915 the ZEG had imported agricultural goods valued at 684.5 million marks since January, and reckoned it needed 25.3 million marks a month. A consortium of the Deutsche Bank, Diskonto-Gesellschaft, and Warburgs, formed in the summer of 1915 to fund the ZEG's buying, was no longer equal to the task. With the mark having depreciated 32 per cent against the guilder and with Germany importing goods

---

[404] Soutou, 'Comment a été financée la guerre', 282; Manfred Zeidler gives $35 million in 'Die deutsche Kriegsfinanzierung 1914 bis 1918 und ihre Folgen', in Michalka (ed.), *Der Erste Weltkrieg*, 424.

[405] Helfferich, *Weltkrieg*, 221; Knauss, *Kriegsfinanzierung*, 74; Nouailhat, *France et États-Unis*, 108; Petit, *Finances extérieures*, 409–10; B. Gilbert, *Lloyd George 1912–1916*, 371; Bernstorff, *Deutschland und Amerika*, 78–9, 97–9; Frey, *Militärgeschichtliche Mitteilungen*, 53 (1994), 330–8.

[406] The entire discussion of German-Dutch finances relies on Frey, *Militärgeschichtliches Mitteilungen*, 53 (1994), 340–53. The principal points are also made by Baer, 'Anglo-German antagonism and trade with Holland', 214, 220, 300–1.

to the tune of 100 million marks a month (as opposed to exports of 30–40 million), the German ambassador, Richard von Kühlmann, anticipated the collapse of German credit. By August Germany's Dutch imports had reached 100 million marks per month, and a credit of 100 million guilders negotiated by the Dresden Bank was not even sufficient to cover the ZEG's monthly purchases. The Dutch banks were of course flush with funds, but pressure from London hampered the negotiation of credits. On 16 December 1916 the German banks which had been authorized in January to deal in foreign currency came to an agreement with a consortium of Dutch banks based on the exchange of Dutch food for German coal and steel. The Dutch banks committed themselves to monthly credits of 6 million guilders for six months, at a 5 per-cent rate of interest. But it was still not enough: ZEG's total imports for 1916 were valued at 2,100 million gold marks, and after America's entry the exchange rate slumped to 2.68 marks to the guilder (pre-war parity having been 1.69). The Reichsbank shipped 50 million marks in gold at the end of June, but the principal effort was to try to get the Dutch banks to lend to German cities and communes: the local governments which co-operated with the Reich in this way were to get special treatment in the allocation of food supplies. But the terms on which settlement was reached obliged the cities to repay the marks which they borrowed from Dutch (and Swiss) firms in ten years' time in a currency of the lender's choice at pre-war parity.[407] The Dutch were becoming fearful of their dependence on Germany and were only too aware of the mark's vulnerability. Although gold and Belgian notes were used to help cover the trade gap over the summer of 1917, both devices were exhausted by September. Using its neighbours' reliance on German coal once again, Germany negotiated a new credit agreement in October 1917, handled for the sake of neutrality by the Diskonto-Gesellschaft; it provided 13.75 million guilders for six months. Despite further crises in German–Dutch relations in the following spring and summer, a fresh credit of 14 million guilders was negotiated on 24 August 1918. By the end of the war Germany owed Holland 1,600 million gold marks.

This constituted about half Germany's total debt to all neutrals. The leverage of Germany's coal enabled the contracting of debt in Switzerland (the Reichsbank had secured credits of 335 million gold marks by October 1917), and also in the two other border neutrals with which Germany sustained major trade— Sweden and Denmark (Reichsbank credits of 285 and 180 million gold marks respectively by October 1917). About 3,000 million marks had been raised through the sale of foreign securities and a further 1,000 million through the disposal of German shares; exports of gold totalled about 1,000 million marks.

---

[407] Roesler, *Finanzpolitik*, 172; Feldman, *Great disorder*, 45; also Petit, *Finances extérieures*, 608.

Germany, therefore, paid for its imports primarily with notes; to that extent its foreign purchasing was deflationary. The consequences were inflationary in that virtually all Germany's debt was held domestically, and most of it in the Reichsbank. Thus, far more of Germany's debt was monetized than was the case in Britain. Germany's monetary base increased 56 per cent between 1913 and the end of 1917 and 76 per cent by the end of 1918; by contrast, Britain's grew 12 per cent by the end of 1917 and 32 per cent by the end of 1918.[408] Moreover, if war represents an unproductive use of capital, then Germany loaded the responsibility onto its own money market rather than onto those of others. Nonetheless, German bankers and shipowners were not over-anxious about the consequences of inflation for international reintegration as the war came to an end. Indeed, they saw the depreciation of the mark on the international exchanges as the fastest route to the recovery of Germany's export trade and the readjustment of its balance of payments. As Albert Ballin of Hapag put it in September 1917: 'The American who no longer gets for his dollar 4.21 marks worth of goods from us, but 6.20 marks worth, will rediscover his fondness for Germany.' Max Warburg was inclined to agree.[409] Therefore, the assumption in commercial circles was that the best policy after the war would be a quick return to pre-war parity.

A further source of consolation was the fact that, unlike the import-dependent Entente powers, Germany had avoided the need to export gold to support the exchange rate. Indeed, the Reichsbank's holdings of gold, pursuing the policy established by Havenstein before the war, swelled by 93 per cent during it.[410] Some of this gold was the fruit of conquest. The persistence into 1918 of the notion of the gold standard and of the faith in indemnities was confirmed by the Treaty of Brest-Litovsk, whose clauses included the requirement that the Russians surrender to the Germans 245,564 kilograms of fine gold valued at 200 million marks.[411] Much of it came from Germany's own population, the result of successive propaganda drives linking gold in the Reichsbank to an increased money supply. A great deal of it came from Austria-Hungary. Germany may not have borrowed abroad to any great extent, but its allies borrowed from Germany. Berlin did not lose the opportunity to confirm its economic suzerainty.

The pattern of Austro-German financial relations was set by the end of 1914. Austria-Hungary had a balance of payments problem before the war. Even in 1913 the empire had not managed to cover its own cereal needs, and in 1914 the harvest fell yet further; the pattern was to be repeated in every subsequent year, although the decline was less precipite in 1917 and 1918. To feed it had to

---

[408] Balderston, *Economic History Review*, 2nd series, XLII (1989), 237; Feldman, *Great disorder*, 38.
[409] Ferguson, *Paper and iron*, 150.
[410] Brown, *Gold standard*, 94–5, 100; Roesler, *Finanzpolitik*, 171–2.
[411] Michelson *et al.*, *Russian public finance*, 452–5.

import, and to do that it needed foreign exchange. In November 1914 German banks, with the backing of the government, advanced 300 million marks on the security of Austrian and Hungarian treasury bills. Not all of this sum was released, because of constraints on the German capital market.[412] The notes paid 6 per cent up until 23 December 1914 and 5 per cent thereafter, and had a life of one year, although this was renewable. By July 1918 Austria had received credits of 2,124 million marks and Hungary 1,336 million; in the first six months of 1918 Germany was advancing the dual monarchy 75 million marks a month on condition that Austria-Hungary met the costs of German soldiers serving on its soil.

However, in addition to the needs of the two governments the Austro-Hungarian Bank required marks to service foreign trade. From the Bank Berlin demanded not paper securities but gold. Between December 1914 and December 1915 the Bank's holdings of gold fell from 1,055 million crowns to 684 million. By 31 October 1918 its stocks had dwindled to 268 million crowns.[413] In December 1918 Vienna's gold reserves were 79 per cent below those of December 1913, a collapse unparalleled in the finances of any other belligerent.[414] Only a decisive victory and a massive indemnity, it seemed, could restore the empire to the international gold standard. What rankled in Vienna was that the cause of this fall seemed to be not the war but the empire's ally.

Austria-Hungary's obvious route to salvation was to lessen its dependence on its gold-hungry partner and to increase its reliance on the gold-satiated neutrals. In January 1916 the leading banks undertook to negotiate loans with their peers in Switzerland, Holland, Denmark, and Sweden. But their success was limited. The banks themselves charged commission and they did not halt the haemorrhage of gold, being prepared to advance up to a third of their collateral in this form. Only the Dutch advanced significant sums, and even here talk of an Austro-Dutch trading company came to nought.

Intergovernmental arrangements secured in treasury bills promised to be much less costly. In November 1916 Austria and Hungary each concluded a loan with Holland, whereby the Dutch accepted two-year treasury bills paying 5 per cent to the value of 45,560,000 guilders and in exchange advanced 70 per cent of that sum in nine monthly instalments. In November 1917 a second agreement gave the dual monarchy a further 24 million guilders, and in three separate deals over 1917 Austria used its tobacco monopoly to get more Dutch advances. Denmark, between late 1917 and early 1918, advanced 20,569,150 Danish crowns to Austria and 8,815,350 to Hungary on the security of renewable, non-interest-bearing treasury bills. In late 1917 Sweden lent 4.2 million Swedish crowns to Austria and 3,755,707 to Hungary in exchange for

[412] Rauchensteiner, *Tod des Doppeladlers*, 149.
[413] Popovics, *Geldwesen*, 120–5; März, *Austrian banking*, 137, 194.
[414] Brown, *Gold standard*, 100, 106; see also Spitzmüller, *Memoirs*, 115.

a combination of exports and treasury bills. Switzerland proved the most reluctant, but Swiss francs were promised by a group of companies in late 1917 in exchange for deliveries of kerosene, benzine, and sugar.[415] As in Germany's case, the American market remained closed: contacts through Warburgs with Kuhn Loeb in New York came to nothing. Even where these deals were successful, they bore witness to Austria-Hungary's impoverishment: the nominal credits were vastly in excess of the cash advanced. Furthermore, although Austria-Hungary's dependence on Germany was eased, it was far from eliminated: of 717,234,000 crowns in foreign credits outstanding in February 1918, 510,790,000 were German.[416]

But the frustration was not all on one side of the relationship. What irked Germany was that the Austro-Hungarian Bank used the better-priced mark, rather than the rapidly depreciating crown, to finance its foreign purchases. Thus, Berlin's own efforts to sustain the mark were undermined by Vienna's tendency to spend the German currency it borrowed not in Germany but in the adjacent territories. Furthermore, Berlin felt, with good reason, that Vienna could make more strenuous efforts to curb its flow of imports, and thus reduce its foreign-exchange dealings.

Germany's establishment of its own foreign exchange control mechanisms in January 1916 served to alleviate, at least temporarily, some of these tensions. Austria-Hungary collaborated with the German scheme. Central offices for foreign-exchange dealings were set up in Vienna and Budapest under the auspices of the Austro-Hungarian Bank. But the scheme was voluntary, demand exceeded supply, and the price of foreign exchange on the open market rose. In December 1916, under German pressure, the arrangements became mandatory: foreign dealings were confined to a list of approved firms, and foreign exchange gained through exports was to be handed over to the foreign-exchange office. In March 1917 all imports became subject to the approval of the two finance ministries. Finally, in June 1918 these various acts were consolidated, and ministerial and bank approval for imports had to be granted before negotiations began, not once they were in train.[417]

The depreciation of the crown on the international market suggested that all these measures were little and late. Like the mark, the crown stabilized in 1916, fell in 1917, recovered in early 1918, and plunged in September 1918. In July 1914 the crown traded against the dollar at 4.9535; by January 1916 it had reached 8.1440; in October 1917 it exchanged at 11.498, a rate which was not exceeded until eleven months later, when the crown stood at 12.010. In Zurich 100 crowns bought 105 Swiss francs at par, but 66.75 in June 1916, 44.02 in June

[415] Popovics, Geldwesen, 126–8, 140–2; März, Austrian banking, 196, 232–3.
[416] Popovics, Geldwesen, 133–4.
[417] Ibid. 118–19, 136–47; Walvé de Bordes, Austrian Crown, 108–9; Lutz, Fall of the German empire, ii. 208–9.

1917, and 43.01 in June 1918. During the war itself what mattered most of course was the crown–mark exchange. Depreciation here accelerated the exodus of gold and increased the cost of German imports. In January 1916 the crown stood 27 per cent over par; it reached 32.5 per cent by the end of 1917, recovered briefly with the hopes of victory at the beginning of 1918, and fell back to 47 per cent in December 1918.[418]

Nonetheless, what is surprising about this picture is not that it was bleak, but that it was not bleaker. The efforts to control imports in 1917–18 and the securing of credits in neutral nations over the same period helped slow the fall of the crown until it was overtaken by military collapse in the autumn of 1918. Moreover, the depreciation on the international exchanges bore no relationship to the increase in circulation in 1914–16 or to the rise in prices in 1916–18. Both the latter soared, undermining the value of the crown in a way that was not reflected on the international money markets during the war. The blockade, by controlling Austria-Hungary's balance of payments' deficit as it did that of Germany, hid the true decline in the crown until trade resumed at fuller levels on the conclusion of the war.

Germany's role as banker to its allies was even more pronounced in the case of Turkey. But, unlike Austria-Hungary, the Ottoman empire managed to resist exploitation by its powerful coadjutor. Arguably the ultimate destination of the gold provided by Vienna was not Berlin but Constantinople. Of 900 million marks in gold surrendered by Germany by June 1918, 844 million represented payments to the other Central Powers,[419] predominantly Turkey. Efforts by Berlin to get long-term concessions from Constantinople in return foundered repeatedly on the rock of immediate military necessity. The provision of ready cash seemed the only way to cut through Ottoman procrastination. Furthermore, Turkey's use of the aid it received was very different from that of the other belligerents: its economic backwardness curbed the implications of the balance of payments problem and Turkey's standing on the international exchanges was proportionately irrelevant. The Sublime Porte's foreign borrowing was applied predominantly to domestic purposes. Germany's task, therefore, was nothing less than to be the main financier of Turkey's war effort.

Turkey made this plain even before it entered the war. Enver's demand for a loan of £Turkish 5 million was set as a precondition of Turkey's fulfilment of its alliance obligations. The Germans wisely made full payment conditional on active belligerence, and thus £T2 million was advanced in mid-October before Souchon's sally into the Black Sea, and the balance followed in six monthly instalments beginning on 1 December. The loan was secured in Turkish

<hr>

[418] Walvé de Bordes, *Austrian Crown*, 114–15, 145, 146; Gratz and Schüller, *Wirtschaftliche Zusammenbruch*, 182; Popovics, *Geldwesen*, 115–16, 147, 151–3, table IX.
[419] Feldman, *Great disorder*, 44.

treasury bills, paying 6 per cent per annum, and redeemable a year after the end of the war.[420]

What alarmed Germany was that the export of its gold promised to continue for the duration of the war. The issue of paper money was in the hands of the Imperial Ottoman Bank, but the bank was effectively administered from Paris. The British and French managers of the bank in Constantinople were not removed from their posts until January 1915. Djavid, as finance minister, was reluctant to break the French link, a reflection of his pro-Entente sympathies as well as a recognition of the likely importance of France's investments to Turkey's post-war position. Ninety per cent of the £T40 million in circulation in 1914 was metallic, and the faith in notes was proportionately slender. Paper currency issued by any authority, and certainly paper money issued by any authority other than the Imperial Ottoman Bank, was unlikely to command confidence. Thus, it seemed that liquidity could only be maintained by further shipments of gold.

Djavid's solution was to propose that the Ottoman public debt be used as a bank of issue on a temporary basis. Helfferich favoured the idea but not its corollary—that, to gain public confidence, the notes be fully covered by German gold. The compromise was to make the notes redeemable in gold six months after the conclusion of hostilities, but in wartime to keep the gold in Berlin, in the Deutsche Bank, for the account of the Ottoman public debt. On this basis 80 million marks were advanced in the spring of 1915.

For subsequent note issues the Turks agreed to accept the security of German treasury bills rather than gold. Furthermore, although the bills too were redeemable in gold, the period for repayment was progressively extended. For the second and third issues, in November 1915 and February 1916, payment was due a year after the end of the war. The fourth (August 1916) was not due to be fully redeemed until five years after the peace, and the fifth (February 1917) would not begin to be repaid until the redemption of the fourth issue was complete. On this basis Turkey added £T160 million to its note circulation. But the increased currency did not, as in the case of other belligerents, constitute a forced loan from its own public; it was instead a loan, worth almost 4,000 million marks, from Germany.[421]

Germany's financial obligations to its ally were not thereby resolved. The lack of public confidence in paper currency was not overcome. Before the war notes were issued in high-value denominations, £T100, £T50, and £T5, and were therefore rarely seen in market-place transactions. On 10 August 1914 the

---

[420] Trumpener, *Germany and the Ottoman empire*, 48–9, 51, 271–2; Silberstein, *Troubled alliance*, 81–2, 93–4.

[421] Trumpener, *Germany and the Ottoman empire*, 272–83; Emin, *Turkey in the World War*, 161–2; Bihl, *Kaukasus-Politik*, 54–5; Helfferich, *Weltkrieg*, 232; Williamson, *Helfferich*, 119; Gall et al., *Deutsche Bank*, 141.

banks were relieved of the obligation to redeem notes for metal, and notes valued at £T1 and £T$\frac{1}{2}$ were issued. The result was that coin disappeared, not because it had been withdrawn from circulation but because it was hoarded. Notes were progressively less acceptable the further one moved from Constantinople. Their rejection contributed to paper's depreciation, as its availability exceeded its marketability. By 1916 paper money was exchanged even in Constantinople at 40 per cent below its face value, and in the provinces at 80 to 90 per cent. By 1917–18 £T1 in gold traded for £T6 in notes, and in Syria and Arabia for £T8 or £T10.[422] Lack of faith in paper currency was therefore a major cause of rising prices. Efforts to reform the currency had no appreciable impact. In April 1916 the currency was unified, but its primary aim was to prevent further deterioration in the value of Turkish paper money and common valuations of the same denominations did not follow.[423] On 1 January 1917 the National Credit Bank was founded, but as it had no powers of issue the dilemma created by the French management of the Imperial Ottoman Bank was not resolved.[424]

Lack of liquidity jeopardized military effectiveness. Between 1916 and 1918 the major Turkish war zones were in the southern parts of the empire, remote from the note-using metropolis. In Syria and Mesopotamia only gold was negotiable. Even in April 1916, when the Turkish 6th army was in the ascendant in Iraq, it found itself unable to buy food or horses for lack of gold.[425] In 1918 each Turkish army was given a float of £T1 million in paper. But the Arabs would only sell their goods for gold, and therefore preferred to trade with the British.[426] Thus, German support of the note circulation was not in itself sufficient to shore up Turkey's currency. Shipments of gold were required to enable the Ottoman armies to stay in the field. To all intents and purposes, Turkey reversed the normal pattern of foreign borrowing: it contracted debt in Germany to enable it to buy war goods within its own frontiers, and it imported, rather than exported, gold in order to try to stabilize the regional variations in the domestic exchange rate between metal and notes.

The most direct manifestation of the indissolubility of the link between German gold and Turkish military effectiveness was provided in May 1917. Berlin was scaling down its credit operations in the Ottoman empire, but its commitment to an offensive planned to recapture Baghdad required it to provide £T200,000 a month in gold, with a willingness eventually to allocate £T5 million.[427] If Germany wanted to ensure that Turkey conformed to its

[422] Pomiankowski, *Zusammenbruch*, 263, 319; Emin, *Turkey in the World War*, 144–7; Bihl, *Kaukasus-Politik*, 204; Dschawid, *Türkische Kriegsfinanzwirtschaft*, 9, 24, 29.
[423] Emin, *Turkey in the World War*, 166; Bihl, *Kaukasus-Politik*, 202; Stuermer, *Two war years*, 131–2.
[424] Bihl, *Kaukasus-Politik*, 202; Trumpener, *Germany and the Ottoman empire*, 282.
[425] Moukbil, *Campagne de l'Irak*, 184–6.
[426] Wallach, *Anatomie*, 262–3; Liman, *Five years in Turkey*, 236; Nogales, *Four years*, 284.
[427] Wallach, *Anatomie*, 213.

strategic priorities, it had little choice but to fund them directly. Thus, German gold and silver, valued at £T17.5 million, was pumped into pan-Islamic propaganda.[428] Since the notion of holy war furthered the principles of the Caliphate as well as the anti-British objectives of the Germans, Turko-German tensions were not thereby revealed. But when in 1915 the German foreign ministry offered an advance of 40 million marks to hasten the completion of the Baghdad railway, Djavid objected that the purposes were German and that a hasty and improvised construction would fulful the short-term needs of Berlin, not the long-term objectives of Constantinople. Terms were finally settled in January 1916, but only because Germany, not Turkey, provided the financial guarantees needed by the Bagdad-Eisenbahn-Gesellschaft.[429]

The Baghdad railway also highlighted how much Germany's financial aid was supplemented by the provision of equipment. Locomotives, machinery, and raw materials allocated to the railway by Germany were valued at 435 million marks. Total military supplies from Germany were estimated at 616 million marks.[430] The Foreign Ministry's final calculation of Germany's contribution, aggregating aid in kind as well as in cash, was £T235,056,344 or 4,700 million marks.[431]

Germany tried to get Austria-Hungary to take a share of the burden. The Turks preferred Skoda's artillery to Krupp's, and by April 1916, according to the calculations of the latter, its Austrian competitor had secured orders worth £T4.2 million. These were paid for by loans from Austria-Hungary: an advance of 47 million crowns, agreed in May 1915, had risen to 240 million by January 1917. Gwinner of the Deutsche Bank was furious: 'German money is being used for Turkey via Austria and competes or directly damages German interests.'[432] The transaction was handled by the Orient Group, a consortium of Austro-Hungarian banks which hoped to develop Austro-Turkish trade after the war. But Skoda's primary obligation was to the Austrian army itself, and it never delivered the full consignment of guns. Thus, the Orient Group did not fulfil its aspirations, the Turks were left short of artillery, and the Germans concluded that the proceeds of Berlin's loans to Turkey were being spent in the dual monarchy and not in the Reich.[433]

Austro-German competition was also fuelled by the efforts of the two allies to get Turkey to deliver raw materials to them and to agree post-war economic concessions. Germany established a central purchasing agency in Turkey in 1916, and Austria accepted that its ally should act on behalf of both powers,

[428] Larcher, La Guerre turque, 96.
[429] Trumpener, Germany and the Ottoman empire, 292–7.
[430] Wallach, Anatomie, 238.
[431] Trumpener, Germany and the Ottoman empire, 283; Bihl, Kaukasus-Politik, 5.
[432] Gall et al., Deutsche Bank, 146.
[433] Pomiankowski, Zusammenbruch, 321; Bihl, Kaukasus-Politik, 120–1; März, Austrian banking, 229–31.

with the produce being split in a ratio of 11 : 10 between Germany and Austria-Hungary. Efforts focused on foodstuffs and metals. However, once again Turkey got the better of the deal. By 1 October 1916, the Germans reckoned that they had sent 600 million marks' worth of goods to Turkey but had received only 50 million marks' worth in return. Moreover, Turkey contrived a profit of 200 per cent on their exports and insisted on payment in advance in cash. Even in 1918, when Ludendorff and OHL used the leverage of German loans in a bid to get industrial and raw material concessions, the Turks avoided any significant reciprocal obligations to their allies.[434]

Turkey's strength in these negotiations derived ultimately from Germany's strategic dependence. However, in 1918 it also resulted, ironically enough, from Germany's refusal to extend credit. Turkey was forced into launching its first and only war loan. Thus, Constantinople diminished its reliance on Berlin's funding. The terms of the loan were generous— interest was payable in gold at 5 per cent—and it raised £T17,851,120. But the target was £T37 million. In July Djavid was back, asking Germany for more money. By August so desperate was the position of the Central Powers that Ludendorff was robbed of the will to push for concessions in return, and £T45 million was advanced without conditions.[435]

The costs of the war to Turkey were, in fiscal terms, minimal. The public rejection of the note issue dampened its liquidity and curbed monetary overhang. In March 1917, when Djavid computed that his country's war debt would reach £T180 million by August, only £T15 million was domestic, and even that had been generated indirectly—through requisitions. At that stage of the war he still did not anticipate launching a war loan, and when one was eventually issued it was limited and late. Almost all of Turkey's war debt was external, and most of it was held by Germany. During the war Turkey was able to brush off domestic anxieties about its borrowing, claiming that it was guaranteed by the German government, whose ordinary budget (at least formally) had no deficit and whose international standing ensured that it would not default. Djavid reckoned Turkey would pay off its combined pre-war and wartime borrowings (calculated in March 1917 to be £T330 million) within twelve years of the war's end. In the event, the German debt was repudiated on Turkey's behalf by the Entente after the war. But Djavid's wartime declarations were not simply wishful thinking. If Turkey had had to pay Germany, the burden would not have been great. Turkey's foreign debt in 1914 was already large, £T161 million; it did not quite triple by 1918, when it totalled £T454.2 million.[436] Depreciation

[434] Wallach, *Anatomie*, 204–5; Bihl, *Kaukasus-Politik*, 122, 204; Trumpener, *Germany and the Ottoman empire*, 317–48; Emin, *Turkey in the World War*, 134–5 .

[435] Trumpener, *Germany and the Ottoman empire*, 344–8; Emin, *Turkey and the World War*, 164–5; Larcher, *La Guerre turque*, 137–8.

[436] Larcher, *La Guerre turque*, 541. Macfie, *End of the Ottoman empire*, 150, and Ahmad, *Kurdistan*, 131, give slightly different but comparable figures. See also Dschawid, *Türkische Kriegsfinanzwirtschaft*, 12–14, 30.

within Turkey—the domestic exchange rate—kept the real value of this debt remarkably low.

Very similar points emerge from an examination of Bulgaria's management of its financial relationship with Germany. It had funded the Balkan wars by three forms of credit. It borrowed from the national bank against increased note issue; it levied a compulsory domestic loan; and it raised funds from banks in France, Russia, and Austria-Hungary. Anxious in July 1914 to consolidate these floating and short-term debts, it secured 500 million gold leva at 5 per cent over a fifty-year period from a consortium headed by the Diskonto-Gesellschaft. The deal was not without its domestic critics, both those averse to aligning Bulgaria with the Triple Alliance, and those angry at the rights over Bulgarian coal, railway construction, and post development which were conceded in exchange. The first tranche of 250 million leva was due on 30 September 1914, but when the war broke out Germany, as allowed under the terms of the agreement, made the funds conditional on Bulgaria's political alignment. An indication of Sofia's ability to manipulate Berlin was the fact that it secured 150 million leva in February 1915 not for belligerence but for its continuing neutrality. Moreover, Bulgarian obstructionism ensured that the benefits Germany derived from the mining concessions were minimal.

Therefore, Bulgaria did not enter the war in September 1915 to secure funds, but having done so ensured that its own disbursement on the war's conduct was matched—virtually in a 50:50 relationship—by Germany.[437] Germany agreed to provide its ally with a subsidy of 50 million leva a month at 5.5 per cent. The money was lodged in the Bulgarian national bank's account with Diskonto-Gesellschaft in exchange for Bulgarian treasury bills. Bulgaria's claim that its domestic economy thus derived no direct benefit was spurious. A law passed in 1912 allowed the national bank to treat foreign loans as metallic cover for its note issue. The bank's reserves of gold and silver rose only from 83.6 million leva in 1914 to 103.78 million in 1918 (as opposed to a tenfold increase in note circulation). By contrast, Germany's advances totalled 350 million gold leva. Thus, the German loans underpinned the growth in Bulgaria's money supply, which was in turn reflected in bank deposits. Those of the national bank rose from 42 million leva in 1914 to 85 million in 1917, those of the Bulgarian Agricultural Bank from 8.9 million leva to 14.1 million, and those of the Central Cooperative Bank from 8.4 million to 79.9 million. Flush with funds, the banks were able to support the creation of 155 new companies with a total initial capital of 156.7 million leva between 1913 and 1918; by contrast, in the first of these years only five new companies had been set up and their combined capital was a mere 4.5 million leva. Germany's frustration was

---

[437] This is the calculation of Lampe, *Bulgarian economy*, 44; in general, see Danaïllow, *Les Effets de la guerre en Bulgarie*, 496, 530–45; Crampton, *Bulgaria*, 429–34.

compounded by the fact that Bulgaria's tobacco exports kept the leva strong against the mark, thus enabling the Bulgarian banks to buy their allies' notes at low rates and sell them in Germany and Switzerland at a profit.[438]

Germany's toleration of this relationship did not—unlike that with Turkey—extend beyond December 1917. For the last year of the war Bulgaria had to fall back on domestic borrowing, primarily by discounting treasury bills with the national bank. Its debt in paper leva doubled from 319.99 million in 1917 to 688.88 in 1918, and at the year's end it had 822 million leva outstanding with the Bulgarska Narodna Banka. Inflation was no longer held in check, and prices doubled.

Nonetheless, although Bulgaria bore more of the real monetary costs of its war effort than did Turkey, it was far from facing them in their entirety. It never launched a domestic war loan, and its domestic debt, even in 1917, was a third that of its foreign borrowing. Moreover, the latter was written off by the peace settlement. Put crudely, the experience of both powers showed that the financial burden of fighting a world war for an underdeveloped power was less than that for a state possessed of industrial abundance. In this respect Turkey, and to a lesser extent Bulgaria, fulfilled at least some of the expectations of pre-war economists concerning the greater financial resilience of the more backward nations.

But the explanations for strength in the management of wartime finance are not monocausal. Forwardness was also an advantage; sophistication in the machinery of credit created flexibility. The Entente powers proved adept at externalizing their debt, and displayed in doing so a degree of mutual support which, however tinged with exploitative overtones, provided a clear instance of co-operation within the alliance. Admittedly this co-ordination was the consequence of one power's financial supremacy at any one time—Britain's in the early stages of the war, and the United States's in the latter. Moreover, pre-war national rivalries were not simply forgotten. France resented Britain's presumption of financial leadership, and was restrained largely by Ribot's Anglophilia and his determination not to compromise relations between the two powers.[439] Britain financed Belgium in the Congo because France was funding the Belgian army: 'we believe', wrote a member of Asquith's cabinet in December 1914, 'that France would like to get the Belgians in her pocket—but we have not resisted a German protectorate over Belgium in order to have a French one.'[440] However, neither this jockeying for position nor the relative lack of collaboration between the military high commands of the allies until

[438] Crampton, *Bulgaria*, 487.

[439] Horn, *Guerres mondiales et conflits contemporains*, 180, (octobre 1995), 7–8, 27; Horn takes a harsher line than that adopted here.

[440] David (ed.), *Inside Asquith's cabinet*, 209.

1918 should obscure a much more broadly based and fundamental sharing of monetary and other resources from 1915 onwards.

The prime mover in effecting such a rapid progression towards financial fusion was not the wealth of Britain but the impoverishment of Russia. Russia's leverage over its allies in 1914–15 bore comparison with that of Turkey over Germany. Both Britain and France regarded their eastern ally as a source—by dint of its manpower—of latent military supremacy. Money was the oil to ease the machinery of the Russian 'steamroller'.

Neither Britain nor even France confronted major problems in their foreign borrowing until 1915 or possibly 1916. But much of Russia's pre-war industrialization was already predicated on investment by both London and, especially, Paris.[441] It filed its first request for British funds almost as soon as the war began, and in October 1914 the Treasury agreed to advance £20 million. Russia went on to borrow £568 million from Britain, almost £200 million a year for each year of its belligerence. Of £974.7 million in British loans to the Dominions and allies outstanding at the end of the financial year 1916–17, almost half, £400.6 million, was Russian debt.[442] France, which found itself shoring up the finances of Serbia, Belgium, and Montenegro as well, allocated at least a third, and by some calculations almost a half, of its foreign credits to Russia. At the war's end Russia owed Paris 3,530 million francs.[443]

Only a small proportion of this debt was contracted in order to purchase war materials directly from Russia's Entente partners. Its immediate purpose was to pay dividends on the shares and interest on the government loans already held abroad before the war. The few Russian stocks belonging to German and Austrian investors in 1914 migrated to neutral markets. Thus, there was no relief from the need to continue payment even on these.[444] Since 80 per cent of Russia's foreign cash balances were in France and consequently were caught by the French moratorium, they could be only gradually released. French government loans to Russia were therefore being used to reward the pre-war speculation of French private investors.[445] In August 1915 Bark told the Duma that of Russia's new, wartime debt 500 million francs and £10 million had been used to cover the cost of borrowing contracted before the war.[446]

Even without this prior call on Russian borrowing, little could have been spent within Britain and France. The war industries of both were fully taken up by their own nations' needs. The major source of Russian munitions was the United States. But Russia had no entrée to the American money market. A

[441] Trebilcock, *Industrialization of Continental Powers*, 244–7, 278–81.
[442] Morgan, *British financial policy*, 317.
[443] Petit, *Finances extérieures*, 164–6; Knauss, *Kriegsfinanzierung*, 93.
[444] Claus, *Kriegswirtschaft Russlands*, 9.
[445] Michelson *et al.*, *Russian public finance*, 288–90; Schmidt, *Ribot*, 124.
[446] Claus, *Kriegswirtshaft Russlands*, 11.

Jewish lobby in America, headed by one of the managers of Kuhn Loeb, and outraged by the anti-Semitism of the Tsarist government, blocked Russia's attempts to raise loans in New York before the war. Thus, although American policy sought improved relations with St Petersburg from July 1914, the infra-structure for the extension of American credit was not in place. Not until 1916 did a determination that America should dominate Russo-American trade lead the National City Bank to become active in the Russian loan market. In the first year of the war the Russians tried to borrow in the region of $1,000 million but came away with only $60 million. However, the barriers to American money did not constitute barriers to American goods.[447]

On 17 August 1914 Britain and France, as a result of a French initiative, established the Commission Internationale de Revitaillement. Its task was to co-ordinate and control allied purchasing, so as to keep down prices and to prevent inter-allied competition. Neither Britain nor France intended the Commission to become an agent of Anglo-French financial co-operation: they did not use it to obtain funds, and France placed orders outside it. But both did use it to manage the spending of their allies. In September Russia and Belgium joined the Commission, and in due course the other allies followed suit.[448] The effect was to give the weaker financial powers the credit status of Britain in international markets. Russia could therefore buy American produce under Anglo-French auspices, and pay for it with the debt that it contracted in London and Paris rather than in New York. American exports to Russia grew from a value of $32.2 million in 1913 to $640 million in 1916. The United States's funding of Russia was prodigious: by November 1917 $2,615 million had been advanced, $1,229 million between January 1916 and April 1917, and $902 million between the two revolutions. But of this, only $435 million constituted direct advances and only $840 million was secured in Russia's own name: $460 million was debt contracted in the name of France and $880 million in that of Britain. Thus, when Britain and France borrowed in the United States between 1914 and 1917, more often than not they did so on Russia's behalf. Over 70 per cent of American funds lent to the two west European powers in the period of American neutrality were destined for Russian use.[449]

By April 1917 58 per cent of all Entente borrowing, both that contracted between the belligerent powers themselves and that from the United States, had been generated by the needs of Russia.[450] Much of it was misapplied. Britain and France felt that their funds were being used not for the purposes of

[447] Owen, *Historical Journal*, XIII (1970), 253–60; Parrini, *Heir to empire*, 59–60.
[448] Burk, *Britain, America and the sinews of war*, 44–5; Petit, *Finances extérieures*, 129, 181–3; Horn, *Guerres mondiales et conflits contemporains*, (octobre 1995), 9 .
[449] Owen, *Historical Journal*, XIII (1970), 261–7; see also Michelson *et al.*, *Russian public finance*, 312–17.
[450] Harvey, *Collision of empires*, 289–90.

the war but to improve Russia's peacetime industrial infrastructure. Part of the problem was the difficulty of distinguishing what was civil from what was military in the conduct of war in the industrial age. Railway investment would benefit Russia after the war but was also vital during it: in 1916 and 1917 many of the goods shipped from the United States remained mired at Archangel for lack of transport.

Like that of other belligerents, the deficit in the balance of Russia's trade grew. But to blame the depreciation of the rouble on the balance of trade, as Bark did, was misleading.[451] The rouble fell 28.2 per cent against the dollar by August 1915, 41.8 per cent by January 1916, and 43.9 per cent by April 1917.[452] At their conference in February 1915 the finance ministers of Britain and France pledged to hold the rouble at par with the pound and the franc. As Russia paid for most of its imports with money borrowed from Britain and France, they— not Russia—bore the brunt of the rouble's depreciation. London, rather than Petrograd, was the main international market for roubles. The Russian government, therefore, used Barings to buy roubles in London so as to shore up their value. In 1916, with the support of British Treasury funds, it set up an intervention account operated by Barings. However, these operations had little effect in halting the rouble's downward slide.[453]

London felt that the heart of the problem lay in Petrograd. Part of its solution was political: military victory and governmental reform would generate greater international confidence. But there was also a monetary aspect. The purchase of roubles on foreign markets had to be accompanied by effective blocks to the exodus of funds from Russia. Without them, there would always be more roubles on the international market than the market could absorb. No effective controls were ever put in place.

In November 1914, as part of an effort to prevent trade with the Central Powers, a ban was imposed on the export of money or precious metals worth more than 500 roubles. The order was doubly inadequate. First, no limit was put on the number of transactions for sums of less than 500 roubles; thus, large amounts could be moved in successive small tranches. Secondly, the prohibition only applied to the physical transfer of metals and money, not to their consignment to overseas concerns.

However, the biggest weakness in the policy was that Bark did not believe in it. He argued that some export of cash would facilitate Russia's foreign purchasing, and that the notes would eventually return to domestic circulation. Thus, by the summer of 1915 the Ministry of Finance was itself authorizing exemptions to permit the migration of Russian capital. The trade was monitored by controls set up in July 1915, and centralized in a single department

---

[451] Claus, *Kriegswirtschaft Russlands*, 26.   [452] Brown, *Gold standard*, 49.
[453] Michelson *et al.*, *Russian public finance*, 431–3.

in January 1916. But no further efforts were made to restrict the movement of money until June 1916, and even the measures then adopted did little more than regularize existing practice. Large banks were allowed to consign sums to allied and neutral countries, and private individuals could do so to Britain and France. The exemptions granted in 1915 were not ended until December 1916. The legislation of the Provisional Government under this head also lacked substance. Payments abroad were prohibited unless they enjoyed the approval of the Ministry of Finance. But as the original allowance permitting exports of up to 500 roubles remained in place, those anxious to move large sums continued to transfer the permitted maximum every day.[454]

London's frustration at Russia's failure to control its foreign exchange was cumulative. Russia's resentment at the terms attached to Britain's first loan was immediate. The demand for gold worried a power whose perch on the gold standard was so precarious. It also bridled at the Treasury's efforts to determine how the proceeds of the loan should be spent. When the Russians asked for a second loan, of £100 million, in December 1914 the Treasury said that Russia's war needs suggested it only required £40 million, and that 40 per cent of any part of the loan spent outside Britain should be backed by gold. Britain justified its demand for gold by saying that it was acting on behalf of all the Entente powers in the neutral markets of the world.[455]

This, then, was the background to the tripartite allied conference on finance held in February 1915. At that meeting the French and Russians, albeit reluctantly, supported the British lead on the gold exchange standard.[456] The Russians, for their part, got about half of what they wanted but more than the British Treasury thought they needed—£25 million and 625 million francs.

The Russians were proved right. On Kitchener's suggestion the War Office set up a Russian purchasing committee in May 1915. Running in parallel with the Commission Internationale de Revitaillement, its job was to channel orders for munitions to the United States on Russia's behalf. But Russia persisted in buying outside both organizations. So great were Russian demands that a fresh loan was needed by June, and pressure on Britain to export gold to America followed in July. During the late summer orders were processed without the credit to fund them. On 30 September the British agreed to advance the Russians £25 million per month for the next twelve months. The money was secured by Russian treasury bills, but Petrograd was to be prepared to ship £40 million in gold within twelve months. The threat to the rouble caused by the export of gold was to be offset by a British credit of £200 million, on the basis of which new paper money could be issued. The agreement thus marked a further meshing of Entente finances. The Russians accepted that

---

[454] Michelson *et al.*, *Russian public finance*, 407–24.
[455] Neilson, *Strategy and supply*, 54–7; Grigg, *Lloyd George*, 190–1.
[456] See above, 828–30.

their gold could be advanced for the purposes of securing the credit of the whole Entente—not just of Russia—in the United States; they also acknowledged—in principle, if still not in practice—that they had no powers to purchase munitions abroad on a unilateral basis. Britain, for its part, had sacrificed long-term financial prudence for immediate victory.[457]

Bark, his negotiations in London complete, then crossed over to Paris at the beginning of October. His demands of the French were exorbitant, but he had most, if not all of them, met. He put Russia's needs at 1,500 million francs over the next twelve months. This total included provision for municipal loans, for the acquisition of foreign exchange for trade and industry, and for the maintenance of credits in Italy. In exchange he offered a hypothetical condition— the shipment of wheat and alcohol on the assumption that the Dardanelles would be reopened. Ribot refused to support Russia's Italian borrowing but he did accept the rest, for all its lack of direct application to the war effort. On 4 October 1915 Bark was given 125 million francs a month by France—a rate of payment endorsed in July 1916 and sustained until November 1917.[458]

The irony of Russia asking France to support its borrowing in Italy cannot have been lost on Ribot. Italy entered the war on the Entente's side on 24 May 1915. By the time of Bark's request the Entente had already had to come to terms with the indigence of its new ally. Indeed, both Britain and France had used the offer of loans from the outset in their wooing of Italy. Thus they accepted, at least implicitly, that if Italy waged war it would be at their expense. What was surprising was the low price Salandra, the Italian prime minister, put on Italy's entry on the Entente side. He demanded £50 million, a figure arrived at without discussion with the Ministry of Finance. Its small size reflected Salandra's conviction that the war would be short, and that Italy's primary objectives—not to be forfeited to requirements generated by financial necessity—were political and territorial. Nobody pretended that it was likely to be adequate.[459] By the end of the financial year 1918/19 Italy owed Britain £412.5 million.[460]

Italy had had a healthy balance of payments in August 1914, but by April 1915, even before its entry to the war, its holdings of foreign exchange were running low. The war demands of the belligerent nations had meant that for the first time exports had exceeded imports. Nonetheless, the total volume of trade had declined, and the visible surplus was not sufficient to offset the loss of invisible earnings. Tourism, a major earner of foreign exchange for Italy, collapsed with

---

[457] Neilson, *Strategy and supply*, 100–7; Michelson *et al.*, *Russian public finance*, 305–9, 311; Neilson, *Britain and the last Tsar*, 353–4; Neilson, 'Managing the war: Britain, Russia and ad hoc government', in Dockrill and French (eds.), *Strategy and intelligence*, 108–9.

[458] Michelson *et al.*, *Russian public finance*, 296–9; Petit, *Finances extérieures*, 61.

[459] Forsyth, *Crisis of Liberal Italy*, 152–4.

[460] Morgan, *British financial policy*, 317.

the outbreak of war. More serious still was the decline in remittances from Italian emigrants. In 1913 these totalled 828 million lire; by 1915 they had fallen to 497 million lire, or 390 million in 1913 prices. Much of the fall was in US dollars, and was not balanced by any compensating increase in exports to America.[461] Italy tried to float treasury bonds on the American market in the autumn of 1915, but found themselves cutting across the negotiations of their more senior Entente partners, and had to be content with $25 million raised in October 1915.[462]

Italy's principal pre-war creditor was France. In 1911–12 the latter recovered about three-quarters of Italy's foreign debt repayment, and in 1914–15 France used this status in its bid to break down Italian neutrality. But the leverage vouchsafed France by its money market diminished as Italy increased its ability to contract debt at home: in 1909–10 only 11.8 per cent of Italy's debt was placed abroad, as opposed to nearly half in 1892–3. Furthermore, the balance of French loans was skewed to public funding rather than to private investment; here Germany was an increasingly important player. France therefore saw Italy's decision to join the Entente as an opportunity to re-establish its suzerainty over Italian finance. Its efforts focused on the Banca Commerciale Italiana, which in 1914 had eleven German directors to four French, although Frenchmen were responsible for six times more business than were Germans. By the end of 1915 France had two plans—one drawn up by a banker, Guiot, and driven by financial considerations, and the other developed by an industrialist, Devies, of Creusot. The Foreign Ministry went for Devies's scheme, principally because it could not agree on Guiot's. Its objective was to gain control of the Banca Commerciale Italiano, and then to establish a Franco-Italian industrial consortium as a basis for cornering the Italian import market for France. But Germany's pre-war influence in Italian finance was a paper tiger; Italy, with seventeen directors, already dominated the board of the Banca Commerciale Italiano, and it had no intention of using its escape from Germany's thrall (if such it was) to resubordinate itself to France's. Italian industry boomed on the back of the war, and it did so in conjunction with a banking sector that was increasingly independent of foreign influences. France failed in its bid to re-establish pre-eminence in post-war Italian industry, and the focus of its efforts diverted it from a primary role in funding Italy's war effort. That responsibility passed to Britain.[463]

The terms agreed between Britain and Italy in Nice on 5 June 1915, a month after Italy's formal entry to the Entente, reflected the principles thrashed out by

[461] Forsyth, Crisis of Liberal Italy, 12–13, 56–9, 150–1, 154, 321.
[462] Ibid. 163; Nouailhat, France et État-Unis, 278; Petit, Finances extérieures, 349, 357.
[463] Raymond Poidevin, 'Les Relations économiques et financières', and Pierre Milza, 'Les Relations financières franco-italiennes pendant le premier conflit mondial', in Guillen (ed.), La France et l'Italie; also the comments by Leo Valiani on both essays, ibid. 348–9.

the three original partners in Paris in February. Italy, to its surprise, was required to transfer £10 million in gold to the Bank of England. In addition it deposited sterling treasury bills to the value of £50 million; the British then sold treasury bills for the same amount on the London market. The total credit of £60 million was made available at the rate of £2 million per week. The funding was therefore deemed sufficient for about seven months.

In fact it was in November 1915 that Italy's monthly credit was increased from £8 million to £10 million with effect from April 1916. As in their earlier negotiations, Britain insisted on a deposit of gold—a tenth of the total. Revealing of new pressures, however, were the restrictions on Italy's use of the money in the United States. Not more than £65 million could be spent in America, and Britain reserved the right to reduce Italy's dollar credits after March 1916 in the event of London being unable to procure sufficient loans in New York.[464]

The machinery of Entente finance that evolved in 1915 therefore rested on a fundamental premiss—that of British credit in international markets, and specifically in the largest neutral market, New York. Thus, while Britain and France extended loans to Russia and Italy, they in their turn had to seek advances from the United States. France's experience over the first year of the war suggested that this would not be straightforward.

On 3 August 1914 the French government approached Rothschild's in Paris and J. P. Morgan in New York about the possibility of placing a loan for $100 million in the United States. Morgan's advised against. Both the fall of European trade and the sale of European stocks on the outbreak of war suggested that the American market was not primed to react positively. These commercial causes for hesitation were reinforced by political factors. William Jennings Bryan, the secretary of state, argued that loans to the belligerents were incompatible with American neutrality. He saw money as the most powerful contraband of all, since it directed all other commodities, and he feared that once Americans invested their wealth in the outcome of the war their loyalties would be divided, domestic disharmony would follow, and the United States itself might be propelled into hostilities.

In October the French government renewed its efforts in a much more modest form. It approached the head of the National City Bank, a Frenchman called Maurice Léon, with a view to placing £10 million in French treasury bonds. Léon consulted Bryan's subordinate, Robert Lansing. Lansing's response was predicated not on political principle but on financial self-interest. He argued that, if the United States blocked the belligerents' efforts to get credits, they would take their trade elsewhere and the American economy would remain depressed. He saw no incompatibility between neutrality and

[464] Forsyth, *Crisis of Liberal Italy*, 162–3.

the private issue of bank loans to belligerents; America's objection was to the public flotation of government stocks. Thus, the National City Bank loan went ahead, and an important precedent was set.[465]

By the beginning of 1915 the contribution to American economic recovery of allied orders for munitions and other supplies was manifest. Between August and December 1914 French payments in America averaged 53.8 million francs a month; in February 1915 they rose to 76.9 million, in March to 135 million, and in April to 186 million.[466] British imports from America in 1915 were 68 per cent greater by volume and 75 per cent by value than they had been in 1913; they cost £237.8 million.[467]

To administer these orders, and to prevent confusion and competition between government departments, Britain appointed J. P. Morgan and Company as its sole agent in January 1915. Morgan's took a 2 per cent commission on the net price of all goods up to £10 million, and 1 per cent thereafter. To some the appointment seemed perverse: finance, not purchasing, was Morgan's forte. These doubts were allayed by the fact that it was indeed as financial agents that Morgan's fulfilled their most important services. Their attraction to Britain was their combination of Wall Street expertise and Anglophilia. As they emphasized discount business rather than the integration of industry and investment banking, their style and expertise accorded with British practices. Their profits derived from the flotation of loans, not from securing a niche for American exports. Thus, they were not exploiting Britain's short-term need in order to undermine Britain's long-term economic position. Others in America, particular Frank Vanderlip of the National City Bank, took a diametrically opposed line. But until 1918 it was the Morgan's approach which dominated American finance.[468]

With associated firms in London (Morgan Grenfell) and Paris (Morgan Harjes), Morgan's were well poised to represent the interests not just of Britain but of the Entente. Lloyd George pressed this point on Ribot in the aftermath of the February 1915 conference. As a result France agreed on 1 May to appoint Morgan's as its representative, but the relationship never became as close or as comprehensive. France appreciated full well how handsomely Morgan's was doing out of the Entente's needs. Between May 1915 and November 1918 Morgan's handled 2,445 French contracts, worth a total of $1,073.2 million, and paid out £18,000 million on behalf of the British. Octave Homberg was convinced that the cushion provided by their Entente contracts prevented Morgan's taking sufficient initiative on their clients' behalf. He accused them

[465] Nouailhat, *France et États-Unis*, 96–100; Renouvin, *Annales*, VI (1951), 289–94.
[466] Nouailhat, *France et Etats-Unis*, 109.
[467] Burk, *Britain, America and the sinews of war*, 62, 267.
[468] Ibid. 20–2; Burk, 'A merchant bank at war', 158–9; id., 'The Treasury: from impotence to power', in Burk (ed.), *War and the state*, 89–90; Sayers, *Bank of England*, i. 86–8; Parrini, *Heir to empire*, 59–65.

of favouring firms to which they were financially linked and of failing to
increase their staff in line with the increase in business for fear of reducing
their profits. In 1917 both governments reflected these criticisms by increasingly representing their own interests—France through Homberg himself.[469]

The basis of the French dislike of Morgan's was established in March 1915.
Ribot sought to place $50 million in treasury bonds in America. Morgan's and
the National City Bank were both keen to act, but proposed to buy the bonds in
francs and sell them in dollars so as to elevate their own commissions. Ribot
rejected their terms. The two banks, now joined by the First National Bank,
came back, agreeing to take $25 million in French treasury bonds and to offer a
further $25 million at option. Only $1.2 million of the second instalment was
subscribed, despite the fact that France was paying a higher rate of interest (5.5
per cent) than that prevailing in the United State (4.5 per cent). French
government credit was thereby impugned. Ribot's solution in June 1915 was
to use French holdings of US railway stocks as security. Not only did Ribot
raise $42 million in this way, but he also did so on very advantageous terms: he
borrowed from the Banque de France at 1 per cent to buy shares selling at up to
4.56 per cent. In September he repeated the formula through Kuhn Loeb, and
raised a further $2.5 million.[470]

Despite the eventual success of this operation, France never took a tight grip
of foreign securities and thus failed to maximize their use in generating foreign
credits. This caused particular annoyance in Britain. France's foreign investments in 1914 were as high as half those of Britain, but during the war it sold
only 8 per cent of its entire foreign security portfolio. Part of the problem was
that France's foreign investment was concentrated in the wrong places—
countries like Russia where payments were slowed or blocked by moratoriums,
and where military self-interest worked against their withdrawal. Not enough
had been invested in the United States. But a further significant factor was
France's reluctance to coerce the market. Thus, 30 per cent of privately held
dollar securities still remained in individual ownership at the war's end.[471] Fear
that restrictions on the market would forfeit France's international status
circumscribed policy. Between 1915 and 1917 efforts focused on preventing
the settlement in Paris—through the mediation of neutral banks—of shares
held by the Central Powers. Even in 1917 French citizens holding neutral shares
came under no more than moral pressure to pass them over to the government. The contrast with Britain was instructive. The Bank of England began
buying dollar securities on the Treasury's instructions in July 1915. By the end of
1915 $233 million had been acquired in this way. The government then went

---

[469] Nouailhat, *France et États-Unis*, 241–9; Nouailhat, *Revue d'histoire moderne et contemporaine*,
XIV (1967), 366; Schmidt, *Ribot*, 125–6.
[470] Nouailhat, *France et États-Unis*, 110–13; Petit, *Finances extérieures*, 71, 339–42.
[471] Knauss, *Kriegsfinanzierung*, 82; Eichengreen, *Golden fetters*, 83.

public, offering either to buy securities at the current price or to borrow them at 0.5 per cent over their actual return. It thus approached the American money market as an owner, and could threaten to sell if New York did not lend. More significantly, stick followed carrot. In the April 1916 budget foreign securities became liable to punitive rates of income tax, and in January 1917 the Treasury was empowered to requisition all such securities.[472]

Nor was France any firmer in its management of foreign exchange. When Ribot suggested on 1 July 1915 that controls on foreign exchange might be appropriate, the Banque de France argued that the market was too sophist-icated for controls to be possible: all that followed was a voluntary code. A whole succession of regulations, based on postal and commercial intelligence garnered by the general staff and by the organizations responsible for the blockade, took the form of advice and lacked legal penalties. After the entry of the United States the pressures on France were political as well as fiscal: France's western allies, fierce with themselves, expected France to fall into line. By not doing so, Paris was increasing the burden borne by New York and London. But the commission on exchanges, established by the Ministry of Finance in July 1917, built on the established regulations rather than began afresh. The banks were invited to restrict their sale of foreign exchange to legitimate operations, but their freedom of operation was circumscribed only by an appeal to their patriotism, not by the law.[473]

The combination of laxity in relation to foreign exchange and a severe imbalance in payments was soon evident in France's faltering exchange rate. In August 1914 the franc had gained 3.5 per cent on the dollar. However, by February 1915 the exchange was back to par, by April 1915 the dollar was trading at 8.5 per cent above the franc and by August at 15 per cent. The Swiss franc stood at 6.5 per cent above par in July 1915 and the Dutch florin at 9.69 per cent.[474]

The weakness of the franc generated friction within the alliance. French imports from Britain more than doubled in value in the second quarter of 1915, and, with the pound at a premium of 7.3 per cent over the franc at the end of June, a significant element of this expense was going on exchange. France protested that it was denied the access to the London money market promised it in February in Calais, but for the time being London itself remained unresponsive. Partly this was due to surprise; as recently as the new year France had seemed second only to Britain in its strength on international markets. But it was also due to McKenna's own priorities.[475]

[472] Morgan, *British financial policy*, 327–31; Stamp, *Taxation*, 101; Brown, *Gold standard*, 60–1; Farr, 'McKenna', 185.

[473] Petit, *Finances extérieures*, 66–7, 103–19.

[474] Jèze and Truchy, *War finance*, 289–90; Petit, *Finances extérieures*, 63.

[475] Horn, *International History Review*, XVII (1995), 62–3.

966   FINANCING THE WAR

The London–New York axis was more important to the pound than that between London and Paris. At the start of the war sterling too rose against the dollar, but by December 1914 it had fallen back to par, $4.86. In June 1915 it stood at $4.77. Morgan's reminded the Treasury of the surcharge thus being put on Britain's American purchases, but McKenna seemed relatively indifferent to exchange-rate problems. His fear was British indebtedness to the United States. His policies came under attack from two directions. Cunliffe resented the fact that the Bank of England was battling with the exchange rate single-handed, and in the cabinet both McKenna's predecessor at the Treasury, Lloyd George, and his successor, Bonar Law, were less fearful of American credits. The wavering market reflected the conflicting policies which emanated from London.

On 25 July Asquith told McKenna that contracts were not to be lost through lack of exchange.[476] In that month Morgan's arranged a loan of $50 million, four-fifths of which was guaranteed by American securities and one-tenth in gold from the Bank of England. But by August almost all this loan had gone and the exchange rate was still tumbling. On 14 August alone it fell from $4.73 to $4.64. Four days later the cabinet agreed to ship $100 million in gold to America, as well as to buy up British-held American shares.[477]

The decline of the British and French exchanges caused almost as much concern in New York as it did in London and Paris. McAdoo was well aware how contingent American prosperity was on Entente purchasing: he could not afford to let the value of the dollar price American goods out of the market. The behaviour of the Federal Reserve Board reflected these commercial inter-ests. Benjamin Strong was keen to use the war to promote the use of dollar acceptances for two reasons. First he saw no reason why trade between the United States and the rest of the world, particularly South America, should be funded by credits from London. Secondly, the alternative, for American exports to be paid for in gold, would render the United States vulnerable to the return of normal trading conditions, when the gold would emigrate once more. The Board adopted the principle of rediscounting commercial accept-ances in April 1915, but made an exception for arms and munitions. In August, under pressure from McAdoo, the Board revised its policy, and banks were permitted to rediscount all commercial acceptances. Politically too—although the president remained reluctant publicly to commit himself—the mood changed. America's protest to Germany over the torpedoing of the *Lusitania* with the loss of American lives on 6 May prompted the strongly neutralist Bryan to resign. He was succeeded as secretary of state by Lansing, who had of course already shown himself sympathetic to the financial needs of the

[476] Farr, 'McKenna', 158.
[477] Burk, *Britain, America and the sinews of war*, 62–4; Sayers, *Bank of England*, i. 89; Soutou, *L'Or et le sang*, 225–7.

Entente. On 19 August 1915 a German U-boat sank the *Arabic*, and two more Americans were drowned. Not for the last time the German use of submarines came to the rescue of Britain's imperilled finances. When Britain enquired at the end of the month about the possibility of publicly launching a government loan in the United States, it was accorded muted approval. Wilson would not give any flotation his public benediction, but nor would he oppose it.[478]

McKenna's anxiety to enforce the primacy of British finances in the Entente remained. Thus, he proposed that a government loan launched in America should be in Britain's name only, although France and Russia should share the proceeds. Similarly, the cabinet decision of 22 August to ship gold rested on the presumption that both Britain's Entente partners would contribute to the pot. Ribot was not happy with either idea. At Boulogne on 21 August, the two finance ministers agreed that the loan would be joint, and that gold would not be sent immediately but that each power would hold $200 million in reserve in case it was needed. The speed with which the meeting was convened prevented Russia from being represented, but the two western allies shed few tears: they recognized that Russia's poor reputation in America could cause the failure of the loan.

However, the converse did not apply. Russia's exclusion did not guarantee the loan's success. Lord Reading, who was sent by the British government to negotiate the loan's terms, was told by McKenna that he would be happy with $100 million; his aim was to get America used to the idea of foreign loans.[479] In the event, the nominal capital of the issue was $500 million. It was sold at 98 and paid 5 per cent. But American investors were used to a rate of 5.5 or 6 per cent. Furthermore, they were not accustomed to a loan on this scale nor one which lacked collateral. Only $33 million was subscribed by individuals; on this evidence American sentiment remained strongly neutral—whatever the popular responses to the sinking of merchant ships or the financial self-interest generated by Entente purchasing. Indeed, without the latter the loan would have flopped completely. Six companies with major allied orders brought £100 million of the stock. Little interest was shown in the Midwest, where German agitation was strong. By the close, on 14 December 1915, $187 million was still unsold and had to be taken by the banks which had underwritten the issue. The banks' price was 96, the stock rapidly fell to 94 and, despite Morgan's intervention, it was trading even lower by the end of February 1916.[480]

Nonetheless, the loan achieved a number of important objectives. At the price of growing indebtedness in New York, it secured British exchange rates.

---

[478] Nouailhat, *France et États-Unis*, 272–85; Renouvin, *Annales*, VI (1951), 294–6; Chandler, *Strong*, 86–92.

[479] Farr, 'McKenna', 164.

[480] Petit, *Finances extérieures*, 73–5, 200–1, 347–8; Nouailhat, *France et États-Unis*, 287–91; Burk, *Britain, America and the sinews of war*, 67–76; Burk, *Historical Journal*, XXII (1979), 353–4.

By the beginning of 1916 the pound exceeded \$4.77, and it never fell below \$4.76 for the rest of the war. The loan thus provided a secure platform from which the British exchange committee could begin its operations in November 1915.[481] Furthermore, it linked the franc to the pound, thus stabilizing the former as well as the latter. The pegging of the exchange rate kept the dollar artificially weak, but in so doing sustained Entente orders and thus deepened America's own need to support sterling and its associated currencies.

The focus in the literature is on the sense of continuing crisis generated by the battle to secure American funds and to maintain the convertibility of sterling in New York. But the irritability and frustration which bubbled up in London should not be allowed to obscure the specific advantages which accrued to Britain from the Anglo-American financial relationship. Nor should the attention to the deficit in Britain's Atlantic trade overshadow the broader picture of Britain's balance of payments. Shipping profits helped offset the loss of other earnings. In 1913 Britain's trading surplus (aggregating visible and invisible trade) was £181 million; during the war it still averaged £50 million; and only in 1918 did the account show a major deficit, £204 million.[482] Furthermore, Britain's economic leadership of the Entente helped compensate for the imbalance in its American trade. France spent almost as much in Britain during the war, 23,000 million francs, as it did in the United States (between 26,000 and 27,000 million francs). In 1913 French visible exports to Britain were worth 1,453.8 million francs, and its imports 1,115 million; by 1915 this modest French surplus had been turned into a deficit of 2,938.7 million francs, and in 1917 the deficit was 5,791.2 million francs.[483]

Britain therefore became the banker not only to Russia and Italy but also to France. Ribot opened an initial credit of £400,000 at the Bank of England at the outset of the war, and French treasury bills to the tune of £2 million were placed in London in October 1914. Negotiations for a loan of £10 million continued during the winter of 1914–15: Ribot felt the total was too low, but Cunliffe feared the short-lived strength of the franc and the possible depreciation of the pound. The fall of the franc and the February 1915 conference cleared the way for an Anglo-French deal in April. Ribot asked for, and got, £12 million to cover France's purchases in Britain for the next six months, and a further £50 million for acquisitions in North America: two-fifths of France's American costs in sterling were to be backed by gold sent to the Bank of England. In November 1915 Britain moderated its closure of the stock exchange to foreigners, allowing France to sell its first war loan stock, an operation which raised over £19 million. A continuation of the April 1915 agreement was negotiated in February

---

[481] See above, p. 830.
[482] Peter Dewey, 'The new warfare and economic mobilization', in Turner (ed.), *Britain and the First World War*, 82–3.
[483] Petit, *Finances extérieures*, 44–6, 49–50, 696.

1916. Britain agreed to discount French treasury bills at the rate of £4 million per month from the end of June; it also advanced £6 million a month for three months from mid-April to cover French payments in New York. In exchange France shipped £1 million in gold to Britain for each of February, March, and April, so allowing Ribot to conclude the total credits were £11 million per month rather than £10 million, as the British reckoned.[484]

The two powers concluded their February 1916 discussions by saying they would meet again at the end of the year to concert their financial plans for 1917. But McKenna had promised that London would take measures to support the franc when the pound passed 25.50 francs. By the end of January it had risen to 28 francs. Paris's position in the United States had been secured until mid-April by the Anglo-French loan, but its deficit in Britain was increasing at the rate of 100 million francs per month. Cunliffe was prepared to make a sufficiently large advance to buoy the French exchange rate and to continue the migration of French gold to Britain: he suggested a credit of £120 million, to be divided between the Banque de France and the state, and to be secured one-third in gold and the balance in treasury bonds. Ribot regarded £120 million as insufficient: he wanted £160 million. McKenna, however, feared that a large British loan to France would hit the dollar–sterling exchange, and stipulated a maximum of £30 million over three months. On 14 April Ribot got £60 million, one-third covered by gold. The exchange rate, which had reached 29 francs to the pound, stabilized at 27 francs.

By May 1916 France had become dependent on British guarantees for its overseas purchases. Well over a third of Britain's advances to France in the war, £177.2 million of £445.75 million, were made in 1916. France's subordination was evident in the terms to which Ribot was bound in April. The agreement was to be suspended if the exchange rate became any more favourable to the franc, and the level of interest on the loan—when the 6 per cent payable on the treasury bonds was added to the loss of interest on the gold—aggregated at 9 per cent.[485]

While France was negotiating with Britain, its credit with the United States was ebbing away. By 8 July 1916 France owed Morgan's $726,686, and the payments on the Ministry of War's orders due in August totalled 264 million francs. The ministry's American purchases in 1916 were running at double the level of 1915. But Morgan's counselled delay in the issue of a fresh loan. The 1915 Anglo-French loan stock remained depressed until April; the danger of a war between the United States and Mexico created the possibility that the American government itself would enter the loans market; and confidence in French military prowess as well as French financial strength was low.

[484] Horn, *International History Review*, XVII (1995), 68.
[485] Petit, *Finances extérieures*, 59, 77–9, 183–6, 196–7, 206–16; Jèze and Truchy, *War expenditure of France*, 299–301, 305–7.

France needed Britain's name to get credit in New York. In mid-July Ribot canvassed the notion of a second Anglo-French loan at a conference in London attended by all four Entente powers. But the remit of the conference was economic in its widest sense: it followed on a discussion of economic war aims in Paris in June, and its focus was as much material as financial. The need for munitions generated by the battles of Verdun and the Somme was as pressing a consideration as the method of paying for them. Lloyd George, driven as usual by the former rather than the latter, argued that America was more dependent on Entente orders than the Entente was on American money: he felt that presidential support for an Anglo-French loan would be forthcoming and therefore supported Ribot. However, McKenna reckoned America would not lend. His priorities were unchanged: to extract gold from Britain's allies, to curb Britain's indebtedness to the United States, and to float loans in Britain's name only.

Ribot left the conference under a misapprehension. He had shifted his own ground since December. He was now less determined in his subordination of war finance to the imperatives of strategy, and more appreciative of McKenna's general point, that the military effort might have to be scaled back so that it was more in step with financial capacity. France's overseas payments had totalled 282 million francs in January, and had risen to 500 million by June. But the fears he expressed domestically had been moderated by at least some of his allies. Asquith had intervened in April to overcome McKenna's doubts about the increased British loan to France. Now Lloyd George seemed similarly bullish. Ribot and McKenna agreed that the launch of any joint loan should be postponed until after the American presidential election in November. But their policies, although driven by similar interpretations of their own nations' individual needs, took divergent courses.[486]

Ribot pressed ahead with a scheme on which Homberg had been working since January. The evidence of 1915 showed that France would not be able to raise a loan on its own account without collateral. This upset Ribot: the name of the French government should be sufficient credit in itself. Homberg's solution was to form a banking syndicate, the American Foreign Securities Company, backed with $120 million in neutral shares. On this basis a loan for $100 million was issued on 19 July 1916, and was oversubscribed three days before it was due to close. The credit of the French government—or perhaps more properly Ribot's *amour propre*—remained inviolate.[487]

[486] Horn, *International History Review*, XVII (1995), 69, and for what follows 73–4; see also Horn, *Guerres mondiales et conflits contemporains*, 180 (octobre 1995), 21–6.
[487] Nouailhat, *France et États-Unis*, 363–7; Nouailhat, *Revue d'histoire moderne et contemporaine*, XIV (1967), 356–74; Petit, *Finances extérieures*, 217–19, 378–83.

But Britain too needed credit in America. McKenna and Keynes felt that all that had saved the situation so far was the failure of American firms to deliver contracts to time and the lack of cargo space to ship those orders that had been completed.[488] But as American industry accustomed itself to allied war needs the first of these constraints on Britain's spending was eased. At the beginning of May 1916 the Treasury thought that the country could be bankrupt by the end of June, and McKenna warned Ribot that he might not be able to stick to the February 1916 agreement.[489] On 19 May the Treasury calculated that $434 million was required by the end of September, just to cover its existing commitments. At the end of August the British government, acting on the advice of Morgan's but against that of the Bank of England, floated a loan of $250 million. Britain, unlike France, acted in its own name, and furthermore provided as collateral North American and neutral securities worth $300 million.[490] The effect was to trigger a fall not only in the 1915 Anglo-French stock but also in the new French loan of July 1916. Ribot was furious. He had not been consulted. The principle which he had contested with Homberg had been subverted by the unilateral action of France's ally. A precedent had been set which France, partly through its reluctance to commandeer the neutral shares of its own citizens, could not follow. Henceforth an unguaranteed loan would be impossible, and in the short term the American Foreign Securities Company could not return to a market glutted with British stocks. British credit, which Ribot had understood from the July conference was being held in reserve for joint use, had been expended. Moreover, the issue was not particularly successful: only $200 million was subscribed and its price fell.

McKenna and Ribot met at Calais on 24 August to rebuild the bridges of cross-Channel financial co-operation. McKenna denied that he had breached any earlier agreements but was probably more apologetic than he need have been. He said that the loan was a response to an immediate crisis on the exchanges. More to the point was the fact that Britain's action on the exchanges and in the export of gold was not entirely self-interested; it was designed to support the American purchases of all the Entente. He offered to increase French credits to £25 million per month for six months; £10 million of this was to be used by the Banque de France to support the franc. In return, Britain's allies were to disgorge a further £100 million in gold—half of which was to come from France, £40 million from Russia, and £10 million from Italy.[491] The real opposition to these proposals came not from Ribot but from Bark. Russia had not yet shipped £20 million of the £40 million in gold agreed on in September 1915. At the London conference in July Britain had accorded Russia

[488] Farr, 'McKenna', 245.
[489] Horn, *Guerres mondiales et conflits contemporains*, 180 (octobre 1995), 22.
[490] Burk, *Britain, America and the sinews of war*, 78–80.
[491] Schmidt, *Ribot*, 134–5; Petit, *Finances extérieures*, 225–32, 384–6.

credits of £25 million per month for the next six months, in addition to £63 million for immediate use in military orders and to a further £63 million in the autumn provided Russia held £40 million in gold ready for shipment. The Foreign Office feared that the Treasury was blackening Britain's image in Russia in its pursuit of gold, and McKenna moderated his demands. If the £20 million outstanding under the September 1915 agreement was remitted, Britain would only require a further £20 million; the first instalment was received in November 1916 and the second in February 1917.[492]

Neither Britain nor France could afford to be soft with their ally. McKenna had accepted at Calais that an Anglo-French committee on finance should be set up, and it held its only meeting between 3 and 10 October 1916. The two powers calculated that their spending in America over the six-month period October 1916 to April 1917 would total $1,500 million. France expected its monthly deficit to run at between £8 million and £10 million despite the £25 million British credit. Two-fifths of Britain's daily spending on the war was disbursed in the United States, giving a monthly expenditure of $250 million.[493] In the five months ending on 30 September 1916, three-fifths of British spending in America had been covered by gold or by existing British investments in the United States and two-fifths by loans. The allied agreement to raise £100 million in gold could contribute $500 million towards the $1,500 million required, but prudence suggested that half this gold should be kept back. Thus, perhaps five-sixths of allied spending in the United States over the next half-year would have to be funded by loans—a total of $1,250 million. Borrowing on this scale would itself clog the market, as each issue would compete with the last. The principal problem was its pace: 'the question', Keynes wrote, 'is whether the money can be turned over in America and brought back to us in the form of loans as fast as we are spending it.'[494] Furthermore, nobody had any idea how the war could be financed beyond April 1917. McKenna, reflecting advice from Keynes, reckoned that by June 1917 the United States would be in a position to dictate terms.[495]

The only break in a dark and troubled sky was Morgan's view of the short-term state of the New York market. They reckoned it to be in a much more receptive mood. Britain therefore issued loans worth $300 million in October, half offered at 99.25 and maturing in 1919, and the other half at 98.5 and maturing in 1921: both paid 5.5 per cent. A credit for $50 million for French industry was organized by a group of American bankers in November 1916. At

[492] Neilson, *Strategy and Supply*, 202–3, 237–8; Michelson *et al.*, *Russian public finance*, 307–9; Neilson, *Britain and the last Tsar*, 355–6; Neilson, 'Managing the war: Britain, Russia and ad hoc government', in Dockrill and French (eds.), *Strategy and intelligence*, 112 .

[493] Burk, *Britain, America and the sinews of war*, 81–2; Petit, *Finances extérieures*, 236–9, 401.

[494] Johnson (ed.), *Collected writings of Keynes*, xvi. 207; see also 197–209.

[495] Soutou, *L'Or et le sang*, 367–8.

the end of September the city of Paris successfully floated a loan for $50 million, which it then transferred to the government; on 24 November Lyons, Marseilles, and Bordeaux followed suit.[496]

The French cities loan quickly raised $34.5 million, and then shuddered to a halt on 28 November 1916. On that day the press published a warning from the Federal Reserve Board to its member banks, advising against the purchase of foreign treasury bills. The announcement also carried an injunction to private investors to consider carefully the nature of their overseas investments, particularly in the case of unsecured loans. Allied shares fell, and $1,000 million was wiped off the stock market in a week. The ensuing run on the pound could only be staunched with the shipment of more gold. To save its exchange, Britain stopped its American orders and tried to curb those of its allies.

London's ire over the Board's declaration was directed more towards Morgan's than it was towards Washington. Morgan's had advised the British and French that an unsecured joint loan could be issued by both governments in January 1917. H. P. Davison, a partner in Morgan's, met the Federal Reserve Board on 19 November and told them that up to $1,000 million in treasury bills would be issued in the near future. Davison's manner, despite the fact that the Board had already halved the projected value of the French industry loan in the same month, was not conciliatory. He miscalculated the mood of the Board. Its membership was already divided as to future financial strategy. Benjamin Strong was most favourable to the Entente's position: he saw the creation of foreign credit as a hedge against the end of the war, when the gold that had poured into the United States during hostilities would move again. But Strong was ill. Possessed of the opposite view was Paul Warburg, a German by birth, who played on the fears generated by American dependence on allied orders. Inflation and a rising cost of living were only the obvious manifestations. In 1915–16, when allied purchases were predicated on shipments of gold, the war had boosted the reserve status of the banks and so brought forward the full effectiveness of the Federal Reserve act. But once unsecured medium-term loans began to oust gold the reverse process occurred. Moreover, these foreign obligations were denying short-term funds to domestic business and so distorting America's industrial growth. Thus there were long-term adverse implications in America's short-term prosperity. By extending credit, America was investing not only in the continuation of the war but also in the prospects of Entente victory: a sudden end to hostilities or—or even, and—the defeat of the Entente would cause an economic crash. On this interpretation America's best policy was to let allied orders wind down as the Entente's power to pay also declined. Thus, the adjustment could be gradual. These views convinced the Board's president, W. P. G. Harding.

[496] Petit, *Finances extérieures*, 94–5, 400–10; Morgan, *British financial policy*, 325.

The prime motor in the Board's declaration, therefore, was financial. But the force of its views was also political. In the recent presidential elections Morgan's had supported the Republicans, while the Democrat, Woodrow Wilson, campaigned on a neutralist ticket. Wilson was re-elected. By curbing Entente credits, he could pressurize the allies into peace negotiations. If this policy failed, then the probability was that America would be forced into the war on the Entente side. From an economic perspective its investment would give it little choice; from the political, German policy seemed to be eliminating any room for manoeuvre. If America joined the war it would need its domestic loan market for its own military effort, flush with liquid funds and not already committed to medium-term foreign stocks.[497]

The Federal Reserve Board did not formally revise its statement of November 1916 until 8 March 1917. It then declared itself to have been misunderstood in November, said that it had no intention of impugning foreign credit or of limiting exports, and announced its permission for all forms of allied loans without any requirement for gold as cover. Thus, the immediate advice to the cabinet of Asquith and McKenna against precipitate action was wise. The London exchange committee wanted a moratorium on payments to the United States, but this would have effectively ended the convertibility of sterling. A few days later both Asquith and McKenna were out of office, replaced by Lloyd George as prime minister and Bonar Law as chancellor. The new cabinet reflected the British frustration with Morgan's, and decided it needed direct Treasury representation with the Federal Reserve Board. Accordingly Sir Hardman Lever arrived in New York in February: Harding, already modifying the Board's position, responded to Lever's pressure.[498]

Until March, however, Britain had no choice but to muddle through the winter of 1916–17 as best it could. It shipped $300 million in gold; it let £358 million in uncovered debt accumulate with Morgan's; and it issued $250 million in stock in January 1917.[499]

It also reviewed its position with its allies. Unable to launch a major American loan for $100 million until late March, France could only raise $15 million from Morgan's and $17 million through a credit with the National City Bank.[500] On 19 January 1917 the Bank of England revised the April 1916 agreement with the Banque de France, increasing its credit from £60 million to £72 million, but requiring the French bank to boost its deposit of gold from

[497] Burk, *Britain, America and the sinews of war,* 83–90; Soutou, *L'Or et le sang,* 373–8; Renouvin, *Annales,* VI (1951), 297–303; Nouailhat, *France et États-Unis,* 373–8; J. M. Cooper, *Pacific Historical Review,* XLV (1976), 222–5; Petit, *Finances extérieures,* 411–22.

[498] Fiebig-von Hase and Sturm, *Militärgeschichtliche Mitteilungen,* 52 (1993), 32; Burk, *Britain, America and the sinews of war,* 89–93; Nouailhat, *France et États-Unis,* 416–18; Soutou, *L'Or et le sang,* 406–9.

[499] Morgan, *British financial policy,* 324–5; Soutou, *L'Or et le sang,* 388–90.

[500] Petit, *Finances extérieures,* 424–30; Nouailhat, *France et États-Unis,* 381–2.

£20 million to £24 million. Further negotiations in March, designed to update the terms of the Calais accord of August 1916, were blocked by a French refusal to ship more gold. A compromise extended the existing arrangements for a further month.[501] Italy and Russia were easier to deal with, as all their American orders were effectively channelled via London, and by blocking them exchange could be saved.[502]

Nonetheless on 1 April 1917 Britain's cash in the United States was all but exhausted. In New York, against an overdraft of $358 million and a weekly spend of $75 million Britain had $490 million in securities and $87 million in gold. At home the Bank of England and the joint stock banks could command a reserve of £114 million in gold.[503] But just at the point when the exhaustion of Britain's finances was about to cut the Entente's Atlantic trade Germany declared unrestricted U-boat warfare, with the intention of achieving the same result. The effect was finally to precipitate the United States's entry into the war. Although Germany's U-boat campaign represented strategic miscalculation at a number of levels, this was the most significant in the long term. The submarine constituted the most serious threat of the war to Britain's maritime supremacy, but on one interpretation it saved Britain.[504]

The failure of German intelligence which produced this blunder cannot be attributed to lack of raw data. Britain's financial plight was evident to every American investor. Rather, what it displays is the narrow framework within which German strategy was shaped. Winning the war was seen to be a matter of operational solutions, whether by sea or by land, and the expanding power of OHL militated against a broader conception. Finance, seen by many before 1914 as the component which would end war soonest, had dropped out of German strategic calculations by 1917. Max Warburg, an opponent of U-boat warfare, declared in February 1916 that, 'If America is cut off from Germany, that means a 50 per cent reduction in Germany's financial strength for the war and an increase of 100 per cent for England's and France's.'[505] But Warburg was a representative of the very commercial interests which the industrial associations had already begun to marginalize before the war and which were now increasingly isolated thanks to it. The liquidity in industry generated by war-related profits made the big firms independent of the banks, and this found reflection in German economic thought more generally. Helfferich, minister of the interior and deputy chancellor since May 1916, opposed unrestricted U-boat warfare during the course of 1916, but declared his support in the Reichs-

[501] Petit, *Finances extérieures*, 241–3.
[502] Forsyth, *Crisis of Liberal Italy*, 169–70; Neilson, *Strategy and supply*, 213–14.
[503] Burk, *Britain, America and the sinews of war*, 95.
[504] Cooper, *Pacific Historical Review*, XLV (1976), 228.
[505] Ferguson, *Paper and iron*, 134; also 108–9; see Gall *et al.*, *Deutsche Bank*, 155–8; Feldman, *Stinnes*,
501.

tag in January 1917. Even in his post-war reflections he could do no more than acknowledge in passing the financial boost American belligerence gave the Entente:[506] because he himself saw financial policy as the servant of Germany's war effort, not its master, or even its partner, he could not envisage its potentially decisive implications for the Entente's war effort.

Many Germans did, of course, feel that the United States, by dint of its supply of munitions and of the availability of its credits for war orders, was already a covert belligerent before April 1917. On this reading America's formal entry to the war did no more than make public and legal what was already practice. By contrast, there were moments in the ensuing eighteen months when some in Britain felt that the shift in American policy after April 1917 was not sufficiently dramatic or altruistic to represent a full acceptance of alliance obligations. Certainly, those in the Treasury who hoped that Britain, having financed the Entente and its overseas orders for three years, would now be able simply to pass that particular function over to the United States proved to be both optimistic and naive.

The American Treasury did not, as the British had done, take finance as a self-contained component of the war economy. McAdoo wanted to create an inter-allied economic committee, but his objective was to restrict and co-ordinate Entente purchasing in America, not to pursue a joint policy in relation to borrowing. By eliminating wastefulness in the orders of the European allies, he would of course reduce their need for credits. But he did not see the support of their rates of exchange as a component of this strategy. Nor did he see the undertaking of long-term financial support to the allies as desirable or sensible. Indeed, he argued the reverse: by restricting American support to short-term funds he would force the allies to confine their demands to immediate necessities.

Thus, America's entry helped develop the machinery for the acquisition and distribution of commodities. The joint committee on war purchases and finance was established in August 1917. But Britain's pre-existing leadership in the area of co-ordinated purchasing (particularly for wheat) and Woodrow Wilson's insistence that America was an 'associate' rather than an 'ally' of the Entente both militated against true American economic leadership. Even on the basis of co-ordinated and restricted orders, the Entente's demand for goods exceeded the United States's ability to deliver. The committee's remit therefore came to embrace purchases in neutral countries as well as in the United States. However, since America banned the export of gold in September, it could not aspire to the dominant position in Entente overseas finance enjoyed by Britain. America resisted British pressure to take over the Entente's debts in the United States and yet at the same time insisted that the allies should spend their

---

[506] Helfferich, *Weltkrieg*, 355; on his Reichstag speech, see Hanssen, *Diary*, 164–5.

American credits in America. Consequently America's entry helped soften adverse balances of payments. But it did not ease the pressure to husband gold reserves or to acquire foreign exchange. Nor did it enable the weaker Entente currencies to use dollars to bolster their own credit. Finance itself became subject to largely bilateral negotiations, and Britain, for all its huffing and puffing, found that its primacy in the field was never as comprehensively usurped as its parlous position suggested.[507]

Lever told the US Treasury on 9 April 1917 that Britain needed $1,500 million as soon as possible, with a third of that necessary just to cover the spending of the next thirty days. On 25 April McAdoo began to eke out a succession of short-term loans to America's new allies. Britain got $200 million, France and Italy $100 million each, and a further $100 million was pledged to Russia and $45 million to Belgium. The effect was to displease everybody. The advances were not only insufficient to meet the Europeans' demands, but they also gave them no idea as to what they could expect on a regular monthly basis. On the other hand, they were sufficient to threaten America with a mounting short-term debt which could reach $7,000 million in six months.[508]

McAdoo's response in June was to try to cut the Entente's demands for credits. Britain, as the biggest American borrower and also the biggest Entente creditor, was the principal victim. It was running an overdraft of $400 million with Morgan's, was confronting earlier loans which were now falling due, and was continuing to provide more than twice as much financial support for its allies as the United States. On 20 June Lever demanded $50 million with immediate effect and a promise of funding for the next two months. When McAdoo only agreed to $15 million, Britain threatened to default in the United States. If this had happened the dollar–sterling exchange would have collapsed, and with it the whole structure of Entente finance. Confronted by a choice that was no choice, McAdoo conceded the full $50 million. But he still refused Britain satisfaction on its basic demands—that America should pay the debt with Morgan's, that American loans could be used to support the exchange, and that America should take over from Britain responsibility for Entente purchasing in the United States. McAdoo complained of a lack of information. The Americans were being asked to take on trust the British claim that it was carrying the burden for the Entente. This was the premiss on which Britain demanded that the pound be held at $4.76 and that it receive seven-tenths of the American funds available for foreign loans. If it were not true, British policy smacked of self-interest rather than of alliance altruism.[509]

Britain was in part paying the penalty for its reliance on Morgan's to speak for its interests in America—a dependence ingrained in 1915 and 1916. Its

---

[507] Soutou, *L'Or et le sang*, 479–80, 510–17.   [508] Petit, *Finances extérieures*, 436–7, 440–1.
[509] Burk, *Britain, America and the sinews of war*, 195–203.

experience in those years had been with Wall Street, which was Republican in sympathy, rather than with the American government and its Democrat president. The declaration of the Federal Reserve Board in November 1916 had warned of the need to change tack. However, Lever's mission, for all its short-term success, did not establish the ideal basis for Anglo-American financial relations at the governmental level. McAdoo did not get on with Lever; he did like Lord Northcliffe, who was appointed to co-ordinate all the British missions in America on 31 May 1917, but Northcliffe lacked financial expertise. Moreover, Northcliffe's presence crystallized a bifurcation in British representation in America: on the one hand were the wartime missions speaking for economic interests and concentrated in New York, and on the other was the embassy, focused on traditional diplomacy and based in Washington. On 5 September 1917 Lord Reading was appointed to succeed Northcliffe. Reading, though Lord Chief Justice, had worked in the City of London and in the wartime Treasury. In February 1918 he replaced Sir Cecil Spring Rice as ambassador, and thus the two arms of British policy were united under one head.[510]

Reading's frankness with McAdoo helped transmute the latter's reluctant and short-term concessions to British demands into a more pragmatic relationship. On 23 July 1917 the United States agreed to a pattern of monthly advances—$185 million for August and $400 million for September. On 16 August McAdoo accepted in practice, if not in principle, that the United States would sustain the sterling exchange rate at $4.76. The resolution of the Morgan's overdraft proved more protracted and tested the patience in particular of the British government's principal financial adviser, J. M. Keynes. Between February and September 1918 the American Treasury helped Britain meet its maturities and outstanding debts, but did so while subrogating Britain's collateral. Keynes's sense of humiliation found reflection in a draft memorandum of May 1918 which, although never sent in its entirety to Reading, reflected the fact that, for all the latter's success, McAdoo's policy was still guided by the same principles as it had been twelve months earlier. The conditions of the Americans' financial support were unpredictable; their understandings were committed not to paper but to 'vague oral assurances'.[511]

But Keynes's frustration conveniently neglected the fact that his own advice of 28 July 1917, that Britain abandon the gold standard, had not had to be followed through. In the final analysis, the United States did not use the war to force out sterling as the principal medium of international exchange; it was instead prepared to see the dollar shore up the pound, and thus sustain both as

---

[510] Ibid. 10, 65, 138–43, 163–6, 167–8, 175–7, 181, 185; Petit, *Finances extérieures*, pp. 439–40 .

[511] Johnson (ed.), *Collected writings of Keynes*, xvi. 287; for all above see Burk, *Britain, America and the sinews of war*, 202–20.

convertible currencies.[512] In March 1918 Bonar Law went so far as to suggest that America should finance the purchases of France and Italy in the United States, while Britain continued to carry this responsibility elsewhere in the world. France and Italy were to pay Britain in dollars obtained from the American government. Thus, Britain's own need for dollars would be limited, its pivotal position in the world's trade would be protected, and yet America would relieve it of final responsibility for the borrowings of its Entente partners.[513] Although this suggestion reeked of British self-interest and was understandably not accepted as it stood, much of its spirit was reflected in Entente practice in 1918. That this was so was largely due to the changed, and improved, tenor in Anglo-French financial relationships prompted by America's entry.

Bonar Law effectively outflanked the United States by reorganizing Anglo-French relations in advance of Anglo-American. On 29 May 1917 France accepted that its purchases in Britain would be limited to goods originating in Britain; thus, Britain's credit to France for June was fixed at £14 million. France was to forward francs to cover the expenses of the British Expeditionary Force and Britain would reimburse France in sterling. France accepted that it would pay Britain in dollars for all the expenses that it incurred on France's behalf outside the British empire, and that it would be responsible for its own dollar exchange and its own American payments.

However, America's reluctance to move to firm arrangements for lending to its allies drove back up France's need for sterling. At the end of June Britain suggested it advance £16 million a month for two months from July and France countered with a request for £18 million a month for three months. But America's attitude also increased Anglo-French solidarity. Because the franc rested on the pound, the French had a direct interest in measures designed to reinforce the pound against the dollar. On 7 August the French agreed to pass over to Britain $40 million for that month, and to pay in dollars for goods bought through the Entente purchasing machinery, including food acquired from within the British empire. McAdoo's frustration at Entente measures calculated to weaken the dollar was countered by allied sophistry, to the effect that if the Allied Wheat Executive had not provided wheat from India bought with sterling it would have had to do so with wheat from America secured through American credits.

At the same time, however, Britain used America's pressure for the allies to co-ordinate and control their overseas purchasing to reinforce its own efforts in the same direction. France's regulation of its imports was still lax: about £4 million of its monthly imports in mid-1917 were generated by private

[512] Soutou, *L'Or et le sang*, 467–76; see also Parrini, *Heir to empire*, 10, 259.
[513] Johnson (ed.), *Collected writings of Keynes*, xvi. 281–3; Skidelsky, *Keynes*, i. 344, 348.

commerce, and the French government knew the exact use of, at most, two-thirds of its British credits. On 1 March 1918 Law reckoned that Britain's loans to France had climbed back to £22 million a month. He tried to get all French orders, not just those of the government, channelled through the Commission Internationale de Ravitaillement. Klotz resisted this, but in July 1918 the French government began at last to put its own house in order, grouping and monitoring the main categories of import, and their cost. Britain's credits to France tailed off as 1918 progressed: Law had been anxious to keep them below £20 million a month, and the final average for the year was only £10.5 million. On 13 August 1918 the exchange rate fell below 27 francs to the pound, the basis of the agreement of August 1916. France reckoned that the recovery of the franc should mark the return to a self-regulating market. But the Treasury went further and called on France to reimburse its bonds. France countered with a request for interest on the gold France had transferred to Britain. This formed the basis for a trade-off in October 1918.[514]

Like Britain, France created its own governmental missions to represent its interests in the United States, with André Tardieu as its high commissioner. Ribot put his country's needs at $218 million a month, of which $133 million would be spent in the United States and $85 million elsewhere in the world. McAdoo advanced $100 million for each of May and June 1917, plus $10 million for the population of the battle zones of northern France. Firmer arrangements would, he said, have to await the outcome of the first American loan issue in July. He suggested that the French could then expect $150 million a month until the end of 1917. The French were disgruntled on three counts. First, the British were doing better out of the United States than they were. Secondly, they resented America's demand that the money be spent on the purchase of American goods, and that it be channelled through the banks of the Federal Reserve System. Thirdly, the Americans wanted to know how the money was spent. The French in Paris responded by demanding $160 million a month. The French in Washington told their compatriots not to antagonize the Americans, and that $130 million would be enough. In the event, so successful were American efforts to control France's imports—or so profligate had been France's policy hitherto—that the full monthly credit was not actually spent. France disbursed $150 million in July and only $130 million in August. By the end of 1917 the United States had advanced France $1,130 million since May, but the latter had spent only $1,082 million.

Nonetheless, Franco-American tensions multiplied. Only a third of France's expenditure, $355 million, represented government purchases in the United States. The proportion of private buying funded through government loans, $250 million, was comparable with the pattern of French purchasing in Britain.

[514] Petit, *Finances extérieures*, 100–1, 248–326.

But most vexing for McAdoo was the fact that $331 million of the total had been transferred to Britain. France, for its part, was having to refinance loans contracted with American banks early in the war, but was doing so without the public backing of the American government, and in one case at an interest rate of 7.5 per cent. In October 1917 France's interest and redemption payments totalled $38.5 million. Thus both powers approached the negotiations at the beginning of 1918 on a collision course. Although French spending in January totalled $134 million, Klotz wanted $170 million for the month. McAdoo, mindful that American troops were now spending dollars in France, and anxious to confine France's credits to French payments in America, envisaged $60 million as an appropriate credit for February.

McAdoo came off worst. On 12 March he suggested that the French should hold a maximum reserve of $30 million, and that they should only seek fresh credits when their cash in hand fell below this sum. On this basis each advance remained higher than McAdoo wanted, between $100 million and $150 million, but the period for which it lasted was not fixed and was related to the size of the unexpended balance. Nine days after France accepted these terms, on 21 March, the Germans mounted the first of a series of successful offensives. The loss both of territory and of population reduced France's yield from loans and taxation. At the same time the growth of the allied armies in France increased the note circulation. On this basis France secured a modification of the agreement of 12 March. Rather than reduce American credits to France as France's receipt of American army dollars rose, the Americans continued to give credits in dollars to France and used dollars to buy francs for their troops. The French intention was to continue to fund current purchases in America through American credits while creating a reserve of dollars in France for post-war use. In June 1918 Clemenceau, France's prime minister since the previous November, intervened, adding to France's demands a delivery of gold to cover the note increase generated by the expenditure of the American army. The Americans refused the gold but agreed to an extraordinary credit of $200 million in August. When this was added to ordinary credits of $895 million for the year, America's support for 1918 was only marginally less than that for May to December 1917. The dispute over the trade-off between French credits in America and the spending of American troops in France continued until 1919. But procrastination was now in France's interests. The franc recovered against the dollar from late August, and thus the relative cost of the redemption of maturing French loan stock diminished with each succeeding day.[515]

At times between 1917 and 1918 France felt itself squeezed between Britain and the United States. But given the reluctance with which it curbed its

[515] Petit, *Finances extérieures*, 446–56, 464, 472–98, 501–9, 515–29; Jèze and Truchy, *War finance*, 315–16; Kaspi, *Le Temps des Américains*, 51–7, 330–3.

overseas purchasing, such sentiments reflected more the needs of self-justification than of legitimate grievance. McAdoo would no doubt have argued the reverse—that the United States was being squeezed between France and Britain.

In the case of Italy the United States was more successful in warding off British efforts to secure dollars in compensation for its credits. By 31 March 1919 Italy owed 10,676 million lire to Britain as opposed to 8,332 million to the United States.[516] But Anglo-Italian financial links were not as embedded by April 1917 as those between Britain and France, and the United States therefore found it easier to insert its own concerns into the relationship. Moreover, the picture was complicated by the fact that the growth of French and Italian trade during the war (it roughly quadrupled in value) made the flow of funds four-sided rather than tripartite.[517]

Britain's call on the dollars lent by the United States to Italy was couched in terms similar to those developed in the French case. In 1917, to save on Mediterranean shipping, Britain ceased to provide coal for Italy, and the responsibility was taken up by France. But Britain continued to demand compensation as France replenished its own coal stocks by increasing its imports from Britain.[518] In the same fashion, Britain contended that if it exported steel to Italy it, in its turn, had to increase its steel imports from the United States. Ultimately Britain could, by using these arguments, make things sufficiently unpleasant to get its own way at least some of the time. Thus Italy, like France, paid Britain in dollars for wheat imported from India on the grounds that Britain had to import a similar quantity from the United States. On 27 July 1918 British credits to Italy were fixed at £8 million a month, of which £1.5 million was useable outside the British empire; the United States, by contrast, agreed to provide $10 million per month to be used by Italy in neutral markets, and to allow a proportion to be transferred to Britain so that it could purchase on Italy's behalf.[519]

The crucial check on the extent of British control was the fact that the lira never came to depend on the pound in the way that the franc did. In 1916 the lira was left to float freely; in 1917 it depreciated rapidly, and after Caporetto it crashed. Nitti immediately set about its stabilization. His objective in doing so was to facilitate a massive increase in Italy's foreign debt. He aspired not only to get the British and Americans to pay Italy's war costs, but also to enmesh them in a commitment to Italy's post-war recovery. The Americans responded to the crisis of Caporetto with an advance of $230 million.[520]

But Nitti's initial efforts to control Italy's foreign exchange were frustrated. The Finance Ministry lacked the manpower for the job and the Bank of Italy

[516] Teillard, *Emprunts de guerre*, 175–6.   [517] Petit, *Finances extérieures*, 623.
[518] Ibid. 629.   [519] Forsyth, *Crisis of Liberal Italy*, 173–4, 186–7.   [520] Ibid. 175–8.

opposed the thinking behind the scheme. In January Nitti formed a national institution for exchange with the co-operation of the seven principal commercial banks. Only they were authorized to deal in foreign currency; all imports required a licence and all foreign-exchange earnings had to be passed over to the national institution for exchange. The institution began operations in March, but it lacked sufficient reserves, and contracts were therefore concluded in lire at rates below those fixed by the institution. Thus the depreciation of the lira was not halted.

Italy's proposal to deal with the problem was an inter-allied exchange office. This might have commended itself to the American Treasury if the latter's approach to allied financing had been similar to that of Britain. But it was not. The United States wanted Italy to redeem its debts first, and thus France—which, like Italy, stood to benefit from such an arrangement—withdrew its backing. Therefore, the pattern of bilateral agreements continued.[521] The significant outcome was that the United States supported the lira on the foreign exchanges through the establishment of a joint committee of the Italian national institution for exchange and the Federal Reserve Board. In June 1918 the Americans undertook to finance Italy's commercial deficit in the United States, and the Federal Reserve Board advanced $100 million for the support of the lira. The Americans correctly reckoned that with the end of the war emigrant remittances to Italy would recover and that as demand for America's holdings of lire increased the exchange rate would go up.

The effect of the agreement was to exclude Britain from the routing of dollars to Italy. Britain's first response was to refuse to co-operate in support of the lira. But as the gap between the value of the lira in New York and the value in London widened, Britain found itself being confronted with exclusion from Italian trade. This threat to the City of London's international position compelled the modification reflected in the agreement of 27 July 1918.[522] On 4 August France too came to the support of the lira. Compensation for existing debts was settled and Italian advances for French troops in Italy regulated. France opened a monthly credit of 25 million francs for Italian payments in France, secured on Italian treasury bonds.[523] The lira recovered rapidly against the dollar in July and August, and more steadily against the pound and the franc.

The United States's entry to the war may ultimately have ensured the Entente's victory, particularly if in twentieth-century warfare such outcomes rest on economic resources. But to the allies in 1917 and 1918 there were times when dollars seemed as hard to come by as they had been before 1917. America's decision to create a mass army, effectively from scratch, meant

---

[521] Petit, *Finances extérieures*, 147–9.   [522] Forsyth, *Crisis of Liberal Italy*, 178–87.
[523] Petit, *Finances extérieures*, 638–41.

that its government wished to reserve a larger proportion of New York's money market for its own use. British, French and Italian loans had to compete with American.

Thus, the last eighteen months of the war accelerated and deepened the need to expand the network of borrowing to other nations. Neutrals acquired gold and dollars as they exported commodities to the belligerent states; their holdings exceeded their domestic needs and threatened inflation. The logical step for the belligerents was to borrow from this neutral wealth in order to pay off their debt in the United States. McAdoo, however, insisted that Britain use the dollar proceeds to fund its current purchasing in America, and so ease the burden on the US Treasury. Bonar Law agreed to this in April 1918, provided the United States would replace the funds so raised if Britain was required to repay its American debt.[524]

Two factors dictated the geographical spread of this borrowing. The first was the need to focus purchasing in states that were geographically contiguous in order to economize on shipping; this pressure was, of course, particularly acute after Germany's declaration of unrestricted U-boat warfare in 1917. The second was the necessity to acquire food, particularly meat and grain. The combined result was to concentrate the acquisition of credits in neutral Europe and in South America.

By 1915 France was already aware of its changing trading relationship with the neutral European powers. Its lack of shipping increased the need to import from Spain, Switzerland, and Scandinavia. But the effect was to upset the balance of trade and to depress the franc against other European currencies. By August 1915 the peseta had gained 11 per cent on the franc. In May 1916 France negotiated its first Spanish credit, for 200 million pesetas. The deal, which was secured on French holdings of Spanish shares, fell foul of Spanish nationalist efforts to repatriate foreign holdings and to prevent the export of capital. But its pattern was repeated elsewhere that summer. Between June and August banks in Switzerland, Sweden, Norway, Holland, and Denmark all opened credits for the French government. In the Dutch case, the advance, for 12 million florins to buy food, was secured against French shares with a margin of 30 per cent. But in the other instances the securities were principally French holdings of shares of the country in which the loan was contracted.[525]

The continuation of this policy, therefore, depended on France's ability to command the foreign shares held by its citizens. The rejection of compulsory sequestration curtailed its development. After April 1917 Britain and the United States increasingly restricted their credit to sums sufficient to meet France's expenses only in those two countries, but France's efforts to extend its

[524] Burk, *Historical Journal*, XXII (1979), 370–1.
[525] Petit, *Finances extérieures*, 89–92, 539–47, 601–4.

borrowing among the neutrals were hamstrung for lack of sufficient appropriate guarantees. Norway accepted French treasury bonds deposited in the Banque de France, and Swiss credits were secured on French railway stock. But in Spain France had to sell French holdings of Spanish shares and of Spain's own overseas debt.[526] France's strength in international finance no longer rested on its pre-war position as an exporter of capital.

Instead, what gave France leverage in the money markets was its membership of the Entente. By 1917–18 the alliance constituted the most powerful economic bloc in the world's commodity markets. Central allied ordering, beginning with the Allied Wheat Executive in 1916, and continued with McAdoo's policies in 1917, created near-monopolies in the purchasing of major foodstuffs. The implementation of the blockade and the control of shipping (in itself another near-monopoly) conferred on the allies the power of coercion. Neutral producers of raw materials still needed markets, and access to those markets, for their goods. Thus neutral credits could be turned on through the tap of trade.

Franco-Spanish bilateral negotiations over finance foundered in 1917. The Spanish were sympathetic to the Germans and were opposed to exports; the French refused to requisition the Spanish shareholdings of their citizens. Since Spain did not need to import from France, France lacked the foothold to clinch a lasting agreement. But Spain did need coal from Britain and cotton and oil from the United States. Furthermore, its agricultural produce was more dependent on overseas markets than some chauvinists cared to admit. Therefore, it was on Spain's initiative that a central bureau for allied purchases in the peninsula was created in December 1917. Spain was still not keen to advance credits to France. But the United States suspended exports to Spain and put an embargo on Spanish ships until it did so. In March 1918, a Spanish banking consortium advanced 350 million pesetas, at a rate of 4.5 per cent per annum, and secured in French treasury bonds. France was required to spend a proportion of the money on Spanish wine and fruit, but it also got metals and pyrites.[527]

The United States gave France comparable support in its negotiations with Switzerland. The Swiss too had an export problem: demand for Swiss luxuries, and particularly chocolate, had fallen. But France could not afford to make its acquisition of Swiss credits conditional on increased French consumption of Swiss chocolate. The Swiss needed American wheat, and this was channelled through France. In December 1917, in exchange for easing the blockade and for a limited French purchase of Swiss luxury goods, the Swiss government permitted the Swiss banks to open credits for the French government of up to 150 million francs.[528]

[526] Petit, *Finances extérieures*, 102, 123–5.   [527] Ibid. 548–97.   [528] Ibid. 607–17.

The fact that America itself was buying goods in Spain and Switzerland also in due course helped to stabilize the franc. The United States had turned its face against the export of gold and also found its dollar advances committed to Entente needs. Imports from neutral powers were therefore most easily paid for in the currencies of its associates, and especially in francs. But the effect was to depreciate the franc yet further, and so increase the dollar credits required by Paris. At first America's solution was to buy pesetas and Swiss francs with dollars, but as the demand for pesetas increased it negotiated credits to buy pesetas from France and thus simultaneously supported the franc.[529]

The strength which America's entry gave the Entente in its negotiations for European credits was made most manifest in its handling of Sweden in May 1918. The Swedes agreed to channel their purchases of food, and particularly of wheat, via the Entente. In exchange, the Entente bought timber and minerals from Sweden, and the Swedes provided a credit of 50 million crowns to facilitate this. Thus, Germany was elbowed out of the Baltic trade, and finance was fused with economic warfare.[530]

Wheat was the centrepiece of this strategy. By monopolizing its purchase, the belligerents could control its price for themselves and secure neutral exchange through the surpluses they sold within Europe. Most of Europe's major suppliers—the United States, Canada, Australia, and India—lay automatically within the Entente's nexus. The principal exception—and, of course, an outstanding meat producer as well—was Argentina. In the first three months of 1917 France spent 860 million francs on Argentinian produce.

In July 1917 the Allied Wheat Executive proposed to buy the entire Argentinian harvest. On the face of it much conspired against Argentinian co-operation. The 1917 harvest was low and initially exports were banned. Argentina could best exploit its position as a food producer in an open market. But, like other South American countries before the war, Argentina had been heavily reliant on foreign capital. Hostilities had switched off the flow of overseas funds while boosting trade; the cost of servicing the foreign debt expressed as a percentage of the value of exports halved between 1913/14 and 1918/19. By the end of 1917 the consequent strength of the peso, although reducing the burden of foreign debt, threatened to be an embarrassment to Argentinian exports. What was therefore attractive about the allied desire was its potential to stabilize the exchange. But the United States blocked Britain and France from using either gold or dollars in the proposed purchase. The two European partners therefore wished to fund their acquisition through a credit of 200 million gold pesos raised in Argentina: the effect would be to settle the peso and facilitate exports. No doubt American inducements to facilitate Argentina's imports of coal, or allied threats to block them, also

[529] Ibid. 510–14.   [530] Ibid. 124–5.

prompted Argentina's decision. In January 1918 Britain and France were accorded credits to buy 2.5 million tons of cereals at fixed prices.[531]

The need to shorten shipping routes focused these credit negotiations on the western hemisphere. The extension of foreign borrowing to the Pacific basin was confined to powers that were themselves belligerent. Japan opened credits for Russia, France, and Britain in 1917, primarily to pay for munitions for the first-named. After Russia's exit from the war, both France and Britain carried on with the combination of selling bonds and retiring existing loans. Japan raised a total of 860 million yen.[532]

For those historians who see London's money market and its pre-1914 domination of world finance as evidence of 'informal' empire, neither Argentina nor Japan was as independent of Britain's thrall as their political status nominally suggested. But the biggest burden on the pre-war exchequer was the defence of the 'formal' empire. After 1914 that relationship changed in military terms: imperial forces made significant contributions in all theatres of war. But Britain proved less successful in changing the arrangements for funding the empire's war effort. The Dominions did not become, in net terms, creditors of Britain itself. Outstanding loans to the empire as a whole rose from £39.5 million in 1914/15 to £194.5 million in 1917/18.[533] The debate in India was instructive. Formally speaking, India was precluded from paying for military operations carried on by Indian army troops beyond India's frontiers. Its patriotic contribution was to accept the same financial responsibility for its forces as it would have incurred if the troops had remained on the subcontinent, a total of £26.4 million.[534] Britain met the balance.

Given the demands of the war, the Treasury was anxious to restrict the use of British credits for the capital development of the empire during the course of the war itself. At a conference in March 1915 it stipulated that the Dominions should use the London money market to settle maturing obligations, to meet commitments under contracts placed before the war's outbreak, and to pay for expenditure necessarily incurred in respect of works already in progress. But it was unsuccessful. In Australia the individual states increased their total debt from £387.6 million to £417.3 million during the course of the war, without making any direct contribution to the war's costs. In 1917 London suggested Australia should shift its borrowing to New York, but the latter resisted on the grounds of imperial loyalty.[535]

[531] Petit, *Finances extérieures*, 306–7, 645–54; Albert, *South America*, 65–6, 143–8; Forsyth, *Crisis of Liberal Italy*, 170–1.
[532] Petit, *Finances extérieures*, 92–3, 122–3; Morgan, *British financial policy*, 321; Michelson *et al.*, *Russian public finance*, 317–18; Claus, *Kriegswirtschaft Russlands*, 13; Dua, *Anglo-Japanese relations*, 181–2.
[533] Morgan, *British financial policy*, 317; also Bogart, *War costs*, 129–30, 184–5; Brown, *Modern India*, 188; A. J. Stockwell, 'The war and the British empire', in Turner (ed.), *Britain and the First World War*, 37.
[534] Lucas, *Empire at war*, v. 197–8.
[535] Scott, *Australia during the war*, 481–93.

Britain effectively funded a war-related boom in each of Canada, Australia; and New Zealand. Demands for commodities—wheat from Canada, meat and wool from the Antipodes—ensured that the current accounts of all three moved into surplus on the back of customs and excise receipts. Britain's subsidy extended to the provision of a guaranteed market at prices in excess of those prevailing within the United Kingdom or within the Dominions' domestic markets. Beginning in 1916/17, London bought the entire wool clip of Australia and New Zealand at a price 55 per cent higher than that pertaining before the war.[536] The shipping shortage ensured that Australia and New Zealand revenues fell after 1917, but not to the point where their public accounts went into deficit. New Zealand had accumulated £11.5 million by the war's end, but none of it was used to pay off the public debt, which had doubled from £92 million in 1914 to £201 million by March 1920. Instead, it was retained as a reserve fund and invested in British government securities.[537] Canada, whose greater proximity to Britain meant that its boom coincided with the shipping shortage, and therefore began later and lasted longer than those of Australia and New Zealand, retired $113 million of its eventual public debt of $1,200 million by March 1918.[538]

The change that the war did accelerate was the domestication of this debt. Australia borrowed £43.4 million from Britain but £188 million through seven domestic war loans; New Zealand raised £26 million from Britain but £54 million internally; and $700 million of Canada's debt of $1,200 million represented Canadian investment in Canadian war loans.[539] To that extent, therefore, the Dominions were funding their own military costs. The success of war loans, however, also shows the growing wealth of the Dominions' farmers and rentiers. Tax regimes were light, justified in the cases of Canada and Australia by the argument that the power of direct taxation lay with the individual provinces or states. Canada introduced a business profits tax in 1916, but reduced the liability of individuals for income tax, which was adopted in September 1917, in proportion. Australia was braver, embracing estate duty in 1914, income tax in 1915, and a war profits tax in 1917, with the result that by 1920 revenue had covered £71 million of the total £333.6 million which the war had cost. New Zealand increased taxes on land and income in 1915, and added an excess profits tax in 1916. It was abandoned in 1917, although higher incomes now became subject to tax rates of up to a third. By putting the weight less on tax than on war loans offered at very attractive rates of interest, the Dominions enabled those who had already profited from the war to do even better.[540]

---

[536] Andrews, *Anzac illusion*, 71–2; Lucas, *Empire at war*, iii. 241.
[537] Lucas, *Empire at war*, iii. 249–52.
[538] Ibid. ii. 59.   [539] Ibid. ii, 59; iii. 251–2; Scott, *Australia during the war*, 496, 500.
[540] Lucas, *Empire at war*, ii. 11–13, 14–16, 27–9, 39–41, 59–60; iii. 235–49; Scott, *Australia during the war*, 481, 495–6.

Each of the Dominions made a significantly greater financial contribution to military expenditure than it had before 1914. But their own healthy balances of payments did not affect the imperial relationship as radically as they might have done: Britain still felt beholden to subsidize their efforts despite the self-sufficiency of their economies. India offered £100 million towards the cost of the war, £78 million of which was raised by the issue of a war loan within India and the balance by taking on the interest payments on an equivalent sum in British war loans. Such devices simply enabled Indian princes to widen their investment portfolios.[541] Canada alone used its position on the Atlantic trade route and its adjacency to the United States to change the imperial relationship from that of debtor to creditor. In 1918/19 its debt to Britain stood at £72.4 million, but Britain's to Canada at £135.4 million (£91.8 million of which was lent by the government, and the balance by bankers for the purchase of wheat and munitions).[542] This was a process commenced in November 1915: 'Canada the borrower', McKenna then declared, 'has become Canada the lender.'[543]

Entente yields from credit operations in neutral or non-North American markets were small. Of 43,585 million francs borrowed overseas by France between 1914 and 1919, 40,839 million were derived from Britain and America.[544] Britain's external debt at the end of the financial year 1918/19 stood at £1,364.8 million: of this £1,162.7 million was owed in the United States and Canada.[545] But neutral credits were symbols—first, of the diversification of the international money market which the war set in train, and secondly—but paradoxically—of the increasing leverage which the Entente came to exercise within that market.

The fact that the United States did not opt to maximize its opportunities for full financial leadership in 1917–18 left the initiative with the allied purchasing agencies, themselves based in Europe and more the product of British shipping dominance and of the British-led blockade than of McAdoo's policies in 1917. Thus, the picture remained more variegated than a crude shift in the balance of power from London to New York. Moreover, through the alliance machinery London was able to continue to exercise more influence than the real strength of sterling suggested was probable.

Part of this resilience was itself a product of Britain's and France's success in exporting their debt. Britain funded about 25 per cent of the gross increase in its national debt through foreign borrowing, and France 19 per cent of its total war costs.[546] They thereby reduced domestic inflation in two ways. First, such

[541] Lucas, *Empire at war*, v. 198; Sanjay Bhattacharya, 'Anxious albatross: British India and the armistice', in Cecil and Liddle (eds.), *At the eleventh hour*, 189, 196.
[542] Morgan, *British financial policy*, 317, 320.
[543] Lucas, *Empire at war*, ii. 29.   [544] Jèze and Truchy, *War finance of France*, 286.
[545] Morgan, *British financial policy*, 320–1.
[546] Balderston, *Economic History Review*, 2nd series, XLII (1989), 238; Soutou, 'Comment a été financée la guerre', in La Gorce (ed.), *Première Guerre Mondiale*, 284.

debt did not enter their secondary reserves and so was not monetized. Secondly, they reduced the interest and maturity payments due on loans extracted from their own citizens. At the same time they pegged their exchange rates, and so made overseas purchases artificially cheap; this boosted the demand for imports, but once again exported and diffused excessive liquidity. These operations sustained their presence in the international market during the war, and so limited the consequences of its revitalization after the war. Germany was, therefore, doubly disadvantaged. During the war its debt was concentrated at home, with the attendant implications that followed from that. After the war the reopening of trade and the accessibility of foreign credit became key factors—in the view of some historians—in creating the excessive liquidity which spawned hyperinflation in the early 1920s.[547]

Foreign borrowing in wartime was by its nature short-term. In this it contrasted starkly with peacetime debt, which was intended to pay for capital investment and thus generate income for the borrower (as well as for the lender) over the long term. However, the choice in the war lay not between those two sorts of overseas credit, but between short-term and relatively unproductive foreign debt and the spending of domestic capital. All the Entente powers had in varying degrees to employ the latter as well as the former. The Central Powers had no choice. The Entente's readier access to foreign credits is crucial to explaining the proposition that the war cost twice as much to win as to lose, $147,000 million as against $61,500 million.[548] Those figures focus on direct fiscal input—taxation and borrowing; they leave disinvestment and potential investment foregone out of the account. Effectively denied access to overseas money markets, Germany and Austria-Hungary—having taxed their populations and having borrowed from them—could do no more than spend their accumulated assets. National wealth in Germany in 1913 totalled 350,000 million marks; 220,000 million was invested in buildings and land, which could not be realized; 50,000 million represented machinery and plant; 75,000 million was liquid. The latter having been spent, the residue of war expenditure was funded through disinvestment. This traded not only on the future, through a failure to reinvest, but also on the past, through the consumption of existing wealth. It was manifested in two ways, falling real incomes and declining output.[549]

The relative availability of foreign borrowing was not in itself decisive for the war's outcome. Overseas credits, although possessed of signal fiscal benefits, remained means to an end—the procurement of materials with which to wage the war. Ultimately, the war was paid for not through money or credit but through the goods and services which they could command. The long-term

[547] Holtfrerich, *German inflation*, 75–7.   [548] Ferguson, *Pity of war*, 322.
[549] Roesler, *Finanzpolitik*, 151–8; see also Winkler, *Einkommensverschiebungen*, 14–15, 60, 69–70, 81–2, for similar points in relation to Austria-Hungary.

significance of disinvestment lay in the houses that were not built and the plant for peacetime production that was not renewed. The short-term significance lay in defeat on the battlefield, the result of the Central Powers' inability to match the Entente in a strategy determined by the application of superior resources.

The argument that finance played a role in the immediate outcome of the war commensurate with pre-war expectations has to proceed counterfactually. If the United States had not been propelled into the war by Germany's decision to adopt unrestricted U-boat warfare, would it have left Britain, and with Britain the whole of the Entente, to confront its effective bankruptcy? The American ambassador in London, Walter H. Page, cabled the president on 5 March 1917 to point out the implications for the United States of not sustaining Franco-American and Anglo-American exchange.

The inevitable consequence will be that orders by all the Allied Governments will be reduced to the lowest possible amount and that trans-Atlantic trade will practically come to an end. The result of such a stoppage will be a panic in the United States. The world will therefore be divided into two hemispheres, one of them, our own, will have the gold and the commodities: the other, Great Britain and Europe, will need those commodities, but it will have no money with which to pay for them. Moreover, it will have practially no commodities of its own to exchange for them. The financial and commercial result will be almost as bad for the United States as for Europe.[550]

The financial collapse of the Entente would have triggered economic crisis in the United States. The corollary of continued American neutrality, therefore, might not have been a cessation of American credits and an end to American warlike supplies. American self-interest alone suggested that the reverse was more likely. Indeed, for all the long-term implications for sterling in such an outcome, it could be argued that in the short-term American neutrality might have proved as beneficial to the Entente as American belligerence. Its own military preparations would not have competed with the needs of the Entente in the American domestic money market and in the productive capacity of American industry, while at the same time the financial commitment to the Entente would have bound the United States to its survival and even victory, whatever America's formal position in relation to hostilities.

The fact that the Balfour mission emphasized Britain's financial peril in April 1917 as greater than the submarine threat[551] reflected Britain's sense of how America could best contribute to the war effort in the short term. The creation of a sizeable American army seemed two years distant; credits to procure munitions for the existing allied armies would have more immediate effect. But in venting such views Balfour revealed how powerful in British strategy pre-war fiscal orthodoxies remained. Indeed, they became stronger in

---

[550] Hendrick, *Page*, ii. 270.   [551] Ibid. ii. 268.

1917–18 as the Treasury, through its negotiations in the United States, re-asserted its suzerainty not only over the spending departments of Britain but also over the extravagance of Britain's allies. McKenna's values may have been routed in a political sense with Lloyd George's triumph in December 1916, but they remained enmeshed in the counsels of Keynes and others. Britain's gloom about its financial position in 1918 was less a realistic response to the current position than a continuing coda on the prevalence of pre-war views on the limits of war finance.

11

INDUSTRIAL MOBILIZATION

SHELL SHORTAGE

On 24 September 1914 Joffre's headquarters signalled to all army commanders: 'rear now exhausted. If consumption continues at the same rate, impossible to continue fighting for lack of munitions within fifteen days.'[1] Three days later each 75 mm field gun was limited to a supply of 300 rounds. For the batteries in static positions this allocation was to last until 26 October. By the end of the month the combined stocks of front and rear averaged 400 rounds per 75 mm, and the allowance issued to the armies was clipped to 200 rounds per gun. The balance was constituted as a reserve under the control of the commander-in-chief. Joffre used it to supplement the batteries on the French left, manoeuvring northwards towards Flanders. Attacks without clear objectives were proscribed; if the French army had ever been gripped by 'the spirit of the offensive', it was now formally renounced. Material considerations had triumphed over moral.[2]

France's shell shortage was deeper, more dramatic and, above all, earlier than those of the armies of other powers. But the phenomenon was universal. The Germans became aware of the problem in September, and it deepened in October. Some batteries were limited to five rounds a day (or less than one round per gun). At the beginning of November the field guns of the German 4th army, fighting at Ypres, were cut to a daily allowance of half a train of shells (13,440) and the field howitzers to a third of a train (4,000). On 14 November Falkenhayn reckoned that there were enough shells for four more days' fighting

---

[1] Hatry, *Renault*, 25.
[2] Ministère de la guerre, *Armées françaises*, vol. I. 4e vol., 393–5, and vol. XI, 65; also Gamelin, *Marne*, 310, 315–16.

in Flanders.[3] On the same day Alfred Knox, serving with the Russian 9th army in Poland, reported that, on the assumption that each gun would fire an average of fifty rounds per day, his corps had sufficient shells for seven more days.[4] In fact the Russian allocation per gun was set at 300 rounds for the month.[5] In the spring of 1915 Russian allowances were down to four rounds per gun per day,[6] and in one case five rounds per battery.[7] On some fronts and sectors the British were in as parlous a position. In February 1915 allowances of one round per gun per day were reported;[8] at Gallipoli in May 1915 each howitzer was limited to two rounds and each field gun to four.[9] The origins of Britain's difficulties, like those of Germany, lay in the first battle of Ypres. On 29 October 1914 the field guns were restricted to firing nine shells for the day, and two days later Sir John French reckoned his stocks to be 837 rounds of all calibres.[10]

Even as the shell crisis bit, a palliative was at hand. The shorter days and limited visibility of Europe's winter months curtailed the opportunities to fire. Throughout the war high shell consumption was seasonal. In 1915 Germany's monthly expenditure of field gun ammunition was five times greater at its highest point (2.5 million shells) than its lowest (584,640).[11] If the war had broken out later in the year the shell crisis might have taken longer to develop and the available stocks come nearer to meeting the six-month expectations of the general staffs and the pace of conversion of civilian industry.

Longer days and better weather apart, the common precipitant of crisis was the first big battle of positional warfare. The French suffered soonest because of the battle of the Marne. Indeed their shell shortage is further indirect evidence that for most of the French armies, from Foch and the 9th army eastwards, the battle was not one of manoeuvre but of dogged resistance. For the French heavy artillery, because of the fighting around the fortified positions on the eastern frontier, the situation was already acute by 4 September, before the drama on the left around Paris had begun to unfold. For the 75 mm field guns the next five days were pivotal. Between mobilization and 5 September the reserves of 75 mm shells fell from 530,000 rounds to 465,000; by 10 September they had slumped to 33,000. In August the average consumption of 75 mm shells was 200 rounds per gun; in September it was more than double that.[12]

[3] Schoen, *Geschichte de deutschen Feuerwerkswesens*, 614, 622, 642, 646, 989; Reichsarchiv, *Weltkrieg*, vi. 12, 93; for the quantities in a train (*Zug*), see Schwarte, *Weltkampf*, vi. 92.
[4] Knox, *With the Russian army*, i. 174–5.
[5] Danilov, *Russie*, 327.
[6] Gourko, *Memories*, 100.
[7] Lobanov-Rostovsky, *Grinding mill*, 96.
[8] Dunn, *The war the infantry knew*, 116.
[9] Fewster, *Bean*, 113.
[10] Farrar-Hockley, *Death of an army*, 136, 148; see also Holmes, *Little field marshal*, 248–53; *Ministry of Munitions*, vol. I, pt. 1, 22, gives French's limit on 29 October as 20 rounds per gun per day.
[11] Benary, *Ehrenbuch der deutschen Feldartillerie*, 56.
[12] Ministère de la guerre, *Armées françaises*, vol. I, 3ᵉ vol., 1314–15, and annex no. 2657; also vol. XI, 65.

Shell shortage was not the result of pre-war neglect. In 1906 Messimy, then chairman of the commission on the French army's budget, secured an agreement that the reserve of shells should be increased from 700 rounds per 75 mm gun to 1,200 by the end of 1912. When Joffre became chief of the general staff in 1911 Messimy's target was close to realization: 940 shells per gun were assembled, and the components of 200 more were ready in case of mobilization. In the wake of Agadir, and with Messimy now minister, the target was again revised upwards, to 1,500 rounds per gun. When war broke out France had in hand 1,397 rounds for each 75 mm gun, 1,212 of them assembled and ready to fire.[13]

What Joffre did not know was how much would be enough. Partly this was a reflection of the French army's reliance on the 75 mm. In theory it could dispatch fifteen shells a minute. Sustained combat at that rate would quickly outstrip both existing stocks and current productive capacity. The French lacked sufficient battlefield experience with quick-firing artillery to know what would happen in practice. However, they did realize that, with decisions on divisional heavy artillery still pending, they would be forced to use their field guns more frequently and across a wider spectrum of tactical roles than would the Germans. Therefore, the only obvious objective criterion was comparability with the Germans. But herein lay two difficulties. First, the Germans too lacked recent battlefield experience, and were therefore also groping in the dark as to the effects of quick-firing artillery. Secondly, French intelligence projected onto the Germans its own preoccupations, those of rapid mobilization and of the first clash of arms. The focus was on a standing start: what was at issue was the size of current German shell stocks. In this respect the information available to the French, while patchy, was reassuring.[14]

In January 1912 the Prussian War Ministry agreed to maintain a peacetime stock of 1,200 rounds per field gun, but this target had not been reached by 1914. In November 1912 each corps had 400 rounds per field gun, and there were a further 200 in reserve; the position with regard to light field howitzers was marginally worse, and that for heavy field howitzers somewhat better. Moltke reckoned such stocks would be exhausted in forty days. He and Ludendorff lobbied for more at regular intervals from 1909 onwards. However, after 1912 they undermined the effects by also calling for more men. Overall stocks rose between November 1912 and August 1914, but the simultaneous expansion of the army prevented the ratio of firepower to manpower improving in proportion. In August 1914 Germany had 5,096 field guns and 1,230 light field howitzers. If the available shells had been equally distributed between all the available pieces, each field gun would have been allotted 750 rounds and each light field

---

[13] Ministère de la guerre, *Armées françaises*, vol. XI, 940–1. No figures on French stocks in August 1914 tally precisely. For different totals see ibid., vol. XI, 61; Joffre, *Mémoires*, i. 75–8; Contamine, *Révanche*, 107, 130.

[14] Joffre, *Mémoires*, i. 75–6.

howitzer 712. In reality, the allocation for each gun on field service was higher and that for guns kept in reserve or fortifications lower. The official history states that the total horsed for the field was 4,200 guns and 1,230 light field howitzers, and that the allocation for these was raised to 864 and 882. Other sources suggest that in fact as few as 3,042 field guns and 720 light howitzers were put into the field, at least initially; they therefore conclude that each field gun had 987 shells and each light howitzer 973.[15] But the corollary of this procedure was that, as the reserve guns were mobilized (and in October five new corps were created), the existing shell stocks had to be divided over more pieces and the allocation per gun reduced accordingly. The sense of crisis in shell supply was therefore exacerbated, not because aggregate shell stocks had fallen but because more guns had to be supplied. In general, Germany's artillery was, depending on its calibre and on whether it was in the field or in garrison, between 20 and 50 per cent below its target shell stocks on mobilization.

However, what France's preoccupation with German stocks failed to high-light was Moltke's constant emphasis on the need for the rapid expansion of shell production on mobilization. The German chief of the general staff recognized the trade-off between peacetime holdings and wartime deliveries. If production was slow to get into its stride on mobilization, then the German army would have to have large reserves ready for use. But, as Einem recognized when minister of war, stockpiling devoted resources to shells which might be obsolete before they could be fired. Furthermore, Moltke reckoned that the opening engagement, spread over several days, and likely to be fought in the longer daylight hours of summer, would consume the seemingly enormous total of 500 rounds per gun. Rather than crack the intractabilities of shell consumption in such circumstances, he urged the need to maintain sufficient plant to replace existing stocks within six weeks. Resupply should begin on the twenty-first day of mobilization and be sustained at monthly intervals there-after. The Germans prepared to vary their standards of production and to incorporate fresh plant in the manufacture of munitions at short notice. This, and not the relative size of their stockpiles, was the cardinal difference between them and the French.[16]

Both the French and the Germans cited the Balkan wars as evidence of increased rates of consumption. But more immediately influential in shaping

---

[15] Max Schwarte, 'Waffen und Munition—Erzeugung und Verbrauch', in Jost and Folger (eds.), *Was wir vom Weltkrieg nicht wissen*, 337. Benary, *Ehrenbuch der deutschen Feldartillerie*, 35, 55, gives similar stocks per gun, but like other sources omits the distinction between guns in the field and guns in reserve (see e.g. Reichsarchiv, *Der Weltkrieg*, ix. 383; Wrisberg, *Wehr und Waffen*, 53–4). Schoen, *Geschichte des deutschen Feuerwerkswesens*, 581, gives 3,762 guns in the field on mobilization. The planned targets are given in Reichsarchiv, *Der Weltkrieg*, ix. Anlage 3.

[16] Ludendorff, *Urkunden der Obersten Heeresleitung*, 2–16; Reichsarchiv, *Der Weltkrieg: Kriegsrüstung und Kriegswirtschaft*, i. 379–403. Germany's calculations concerning shell production were promised serious attention in vol. ii of the latter, but this work never appeared.

Russian thinking was the war in Manchuria. During the most intensive fighting at Mukden shell consumption had risen to 375 rounds per gun. Total expenditure over the war as a whole averaged 730 rounds per gun, and the highest in any one army was just over 1,000 rounds per gun.[17] These demands had far outstripped the capacity of Russia's state-owned arms industry, and Russia had to turn to foreign producers. To obviate such measures in future it increased the flow of peacetime orders to private manufacturers.[18] But, as in France, the basic emphasis lay on initial stocks more than on long-term capacity. 'Previous wars', the director of the main artillery administration (or GAU) explained in May 1915, 'provided clear evidence that an army got along on that reserve of munitions which existed in peacetime. Everything ordered with the declaration of war was caught up with only after the war's conclusion and served to make good on expended reserves.'[19] The plan was to create a stock of 1,000 rounds, thought to be enough for four to six months fighting. But manoeuvres in 1911 and in April 1914 suggested that more than 400 shells per gun might be fired in a single battle. In 1914, as Russia closed on its target of 1,000 rounds, the general staff persuaded the GAU that it should be revised to 1,500.[20]

This figure was also that chosen by the other belligerent with recent experience of quick-firing artillery in combat, even if the quick-firers had been in the hands of the enemy. In the Boer War the British found, as the Russians were to discover in Manchuria, that domestic orders for shell did not keep pace with consumption. The problem was that no peacetime organization could prepare production adequate to meet the theoretical capabilities of modern quick-firing field artillery. In 1905 Britain's Army Council reckoned that a six-gun battery could fire between 3,600 and 5,400 shells in an hour. A horse-drawn supply system could only sustain such guns for two hours. The Army Council therefore adopted what was effectively an arbitrary ruling: each field gun would have 500 rounds, with a further 500 in reserve.[21] By 1913 the scale was 1,500 rounds per 18-pounder field gun, and 1,200 per 4.5-inch howitzer. Provision was made for an additional 500 for the first and 400 for the second after six months of fighting.[22] Britain's reserves of shell in 1914 were two-and-a-half times greater than they had been in 1899. They were reckoned to be sufficient for four major battles, each of three days, during the first two months of war.[23]

[17] Stone, *Eastern front*, 49; Danilov, *Russie*, 79–81.
[18] Siegelbaum, *Politics of industrial mobilization*, 27–8.
[19] Menning, *Bayonets before bullets*, 255.
[20] Danilov, *Russie*, 79–81; Suchomlinow, *Erinnerungen*, 270, 400.
[21] French, *Journal of Strategic Studies*, II (1979), 193–4; see also Clive Trebilcock, 'War and the failure of industrial mobilisation: 1899 and 1914', in Winter (ed.), *War and economic development*, 144–51.
[22] *Ministry of Munitions*, vol. I, pt. 1, 21; Bidwell and Graham, *Fire-power*, 96.
[23] Llewellyn Woodward, *Great Britain and the war*, 38.

The armies of Europe had not not thought about the problems of shell consumption. Broadly speaking, they had doubled the figure they had first thought of. Moreover, shell shortage was not, in the first instance, precipitated by an underestimation of the length of the war. France reckoned its shell stocks would be sufficient for three months,[24] but confronted crisis within six weeks (or within a month of the commencement of active operations). Britain's plans assumed that its allocation per gun would see it through the first six months of hostilities; in fact it lasted less than half that time. The German munitions services (*Feuerwerkswesen*) had made a similar calculation, and were comparably confounded.[25] The Russian general staff was proved more accurate in its predictions, arguing that 1,000 rounds per gun would last four months, but it encountered opposition from the main artillery administration which claimed that such provision would last four times as long.[26] Thus, the supplies available in August 1914 were almost universally reckoned to be sufficient for a longer period than proved to be the case. The shells crisis of the autumn of 1914 was emphatically not a manifestation of a belief that the war would be short.

The immediate causes of shell shortage lay in the fact that the manner of fighting was so different from pre-war expectation. This point can best be demonstrated negatively. The attention to shell shortage in 1914 causes scholars to neglect the problem of shell abundance. The all-big-gun ship, the Dreadnought, and the complexities in the production of its projectiles generated major pre-war worries concerning supply. The ability to fire rapidly at a long range implied increased consumption, but nobody had any direct experience on which to base rational calculations. The British government erred on the side of over-provision. Although it manufactured its own cordite at the Royal Gunpowder Factory at Waltham Abbey, its demand exceeded the capacity of its own plant, and even in peacetime absorbed 60 to 80 per cent of that of the private sector. Conscious of the dangers of monopoly relations between government and business, it endeavoured to promote competition among the eight leading firms engaged in the manufacture of high explosives. Unbeknownst to the Admiralty, however, Nobels controlled directly or indirectly five of the eight, and by 1913 provided 75 per cent of the British government's needs. After a loss in 1908, Nobel returned significant profits in each of the last four years before the war despite the fact that not a shot had been fired in anger. On the outbreak of war the Admiralty stepped up production once more, telling its principal cordite contractors to increase output to the maximum possible. By the end of 1914 the private firms had orders for 16,000 tons of cordite, approaching double their annual pre-war capacity of 10,000 tons. Some of this was destined for the army, but one constraint on the army's

---

[24] Ministère de la guerre, *Armées françaises*, xi. 61.
[25] Schoen, *Geschichte des deutschen Feuerwerkswesens*, 581. [26] Danilov, *Russie*, 79–81.

shell supply was that the navy continued to have first call on cordite production. As early as 14 October Churchill reluctantly acknowledged the navy's
over-provision when he sanctioned the transfer of 1,000 tons of the increased
supply to the army.[27] By the end of 1915 the Royal Navy had fired only 5,000
large-calibre shells, and in the war as a whole it expended only 29,200.[28] In its
case the accumulation of stocks, not their lack, was the primary cause of
embarrassment. Britain had plenty of certain sorts of shells, and could have
fought a long war without any crisis if the nature of the war had been different.

The British example is obviously an extreme. The continental powers did at
least anticipate major land operations. But what they had reckoned on was
manoeuvre warfare. This is not to say that mobility could not generate shell
shortage, but it tended to be local and limited, the product of transport
problems rather than of low aggregate stocks. The pace of the opening
advances frequently outstripped the logistical capabilities of the armies. This
was the German and the British problem on the Marne and even at the first
battle of Ypres.[29] It also explains the apparent discrepancy between the
shortages experienced on both Russian Fronts, North-West and South-West,
in late August 1914, and the simultaneous reassurances concerning shell supply
emanating from Sukhomlinov in the rear.[30] The lack of railways and the poor
state of the roads continued to be major determinants in shell supply on the
eastern front in 1915. But because the front was more fluid than in the west, the
requirement for shells was not itself so great: the Germans (unlike the Russians) insisted that shell shortage was not a factor in their operations in the
east.[31]

Thus, manoeuvre warfare created a virtuous circle. As long as armies
remained mobile, their pauses to fire were less frequent and so their shell
consumption was restrained. When armies were stopped and trenches were
dug, both attack and defence became more dependent on artillery. The guns
themselves could identify more fixed targets, and could rely on securer lines of
supply: both became factors fostering prodigality in munitions expenditure.

The shift to positional warfare also had the effect of generating a need for a
different balance in types of shell. Pre-war thinking had assumed that the
principal targets for field artillery would be infantry scattered in skirmishing
formation. Shrapnel, which exploded in the air sending fragments over a wide

---

[27] *Ministry of Munitions*, vol. I, pt. 1, 96; Reader, *Imperial Chemical Industries*, i. 191–3, 300–1; see also
Lambert, *Journal of Military History*, LXII (1998), 33–7.
[28] Sumida, *Journal of Military History*, LVII (1993), 453–4.
[29] Groener, *Lebenserinnerungen*, 174, 190; Gudmundsson, *Stormtroop tactics*, 6; Brown, *British
logistics*, 62–3.
[30] David Jones, 'Imperial Russia's forces at war', in Millett and Murray (eds.), *Military effectiveness*, i.
266; Knox, *With the Russian army*, i. 186; Pearson, *Russian moderates*, 26.
[31] Ludendorff, *War memories*, i. 121; Wrisberg, *Heer und Heimat*, 20; Wrisberg, *Wehr und Waffen*, 95;
Benary, *Ehrenbuch des deutschen Feldartillerie*, 56.

area, was the most appropriate shell for this sort of tactical application. However, in position warfare high explosive was preferred, as it was better adapted to the destruction of field fortifications; the most useful function that shrapnel could perform in these circumstances was to cut barbed wire. The Serbs had used high-explosive shells in field guns to good effect in 1912, but in 1914 the field artillery of all the major belligerents was—to varying degrees— shrapnel dominated.

Most extreme were the British. The equipment of their field howitzers and heavy guns was 70 per cent shrapnel, and in August 1914 all their 13- and 18-pounder guns were entirely supplied with shrapnel. The reasons were largely technical. The tactical value of an effective high-explosive shell was recognized, but that used in South Africa, lyddite (made from picric acid), was liable to detonate either prematurely or not at all. The latter was particularly the case in guns of smaller calibre. Therefore, high-explosive shell was reserved in the field artillery for the 4.5-inch howitzer. The decision was justified by Britain's adoption of the 18-pounder as its quick-firing field gun in 1903. With a calibre equivalent to 83.8 mm, its power was much greater than the field guns of other armies. Trials suggested that an 18-pounder shrapnel shell could do much of the work of high explosive, including hitting infantry in entrenchments, putting a shielded gun out of action, and penetrating the walls of an ordinary building before exploding. The dominance of shrapnel was endorsed as late as 1913.[32]

In Britain tactics were used to justify technological retardation; although in Germany the reverse occurred, the result was no better. Shrapnel had not worked against field fortifications in Manchuria or in the Balkan wars. The Germans had, therefore, adopted common shell for their field howitzers in 1906. By sacrificing some high explosive the common shell made room for shrapnel, but in doing so it risked fulfilling the roles of neither. Although the common shell was also formally adopted for field guns in 1911, its technical sophistication and the cost of its manufacture militated against mass production and rapid replacement. Once the war broke out it was soon abandoned. In 1914 half of the German army's shell supply for field guns was still made up of shrapnel.[33] The French occupied an intermediate position: rather more than half their 75 mm shells were shrapnel.[34]

Thus the early shell crises were not often manifestations of a general shortage but of a specific one. Confronted with field fortifications, armies fired high explosive in preference to shrapnel, and, given their limited stocks of the former, ran out of it sooner than they did of the latter. Joffre's exhortations

[32] *Ministry of Munitions*, vol. I, pt. 1, 26–7; Gudmundsson, *On artillery*, 7, 12; Headlam, *History of the Royal Artillery*, ii. 72–6, 112–14, 233; McCallum, *War Studies Journal*, IV (1999), 69–72.

[33] Reichsarchiv, *Weltkrieg: Kriegsrüstung und Kriegswirtschaft*, i. 240–2; Müller, *Militärgeschichtliches Mitteilungen*, LVII (1998), 398, 401–2, 408; Gascouin, *Le Triomphe de l'idée*, 199.

[34] Ministère de la guerre, *Armées françaises*, xi. 61.

to his generals in mid-September dwelt on the merits of shrapnel, so urging them to make the best of what they had rather than to request what was not available.[35]

There were other remedies as well. Heavy artillery was designed to fire high explosive, and at a slower rate than quick-firing field guns. The French and Russians had allocated their heavy artillery to fortresses rather than to the field armies. Joffre was forced, through his lack of divisional heavy artillery, to strip coastal defences and fixed positions of fortress artillery in order to press it into field service. In doing so he was able to liberate shells that would otherwise have been unuseable: half the stocks of Verdun, Toul, Épinal, and Belfort were plundered in this way.[36] Russia was not so resourceful. The upgrading of the Polish fortresses before the war attracted funds that could have been allocated to the field artillery, but the resources so committed were not redistributed in 1914. When the Germans captured Kowno and Novo Georgievsk in 1915 they seized 3,000 guns and nearly 2 million rounds of ammunition.[37]

High-explosive shell became the technological panacea for the new tactical conditions in which armies found themselves. It could blast a way through deep defences supported by barbed wire and machine-guns. The prime mover in Russia's attention to its Polish fortresses, Grand Duke Nicholas, wrote to the main artillery administration at the end of September that, in default of 'the liberal employment of artillery fire', 'no tangible result can be achieved'.[38] Such pronouncements formed an oft-repeated litany that frequently smacked of rhetoric rather than of reflection. Thus, Douglas Haig voiced a common orthodoxy when he told the military correspondent Charles Repington in January 1915 that, 'as soon as we were supplied with ample artillery ammunition of high explosive, I thought we could walk through the German line at several places'.

Significantly, however, Haig believed that the major effect of higher rates of shelling would be not material but moral.[39] This approach made the case for more shells open-ended. Even if there were sufficient shells to meet the material objectives, failure could still be accounted for in moral terms. Moreover, the generals' analysis of why more munitions were required was itself productive of shell shortage. It implied that the only solution to the stalemate was an even more prodigal use of artillery. Few paused to ask, as did the deputy Prussian war minister General Franz Wandel, whether shortages were not the product of excessively lavish expenditure.[40] In the French and the Russian

[35] Ministère de la guerre, *Armées françaises*, vol. I, 3ᵉ vol., 394, and annexes 3236 and 4741.
[36] Ibid. xi. 66; Gascouin, *L'Évolution de l'artillerie*, 100, 104.
[37] David Jones, 'Imperial Russia's forces at war', in Millet and Murray (eds.), *Military effectiveness*, i. 263.
[38] Wildman, *End of the Russian imperial army*, 83.
[39] De Groot, *Haig*, 176.
[40] Wild, *Briefe*, 40.

armies in particular, the infantry were criticized for becoming over-dependent on artillery support. A German serving in the Ypres sector at the end of October 1914 noted that the French artillery opened fire on a single horse-man.[41] Thus, while commanders-in-chief wrote to ministries of war, threatening an imminent cessation of hostilities for lack of shells, their subordinates in the field began to appreciate that the consequences of restraint were not necessarily so deleterious. A British infantry officer recorded in his diary in January 1915 that a more limited and systematic use of artillery had made the crises of October and November a thing of the past.[42]

The rhetoric of shell shortage not only boosted shell expenditure. It could also generate false shortages. Russian batteries responded to the infantry's continuous demands by hoarding shells. This became known to the main artillery administration, which in its turn treated calls for munitions from the front with increasing scepticism. Therefore, by 1915 the artillery administration was secreting shell stocks in order to resist what they saw as rapacious battery commanders, and battery commanders were underestimating what they held in order to increase their leverage over the artillery administration. The result was to obscure the true position on munitions, and to make appearances worse than reality.[43]

Accurate accounting would have cleared the air. It would have revealed the real position and facilitated the planning of production. But Joffre's insistence that each army report its munitions stocks every night was not typical.[44] Although by the autumn of 1914 the German armies in the west were required to report their stocks each day, the Prussian Ministry of War was not getting regular returns of consumption until 1915, and even then only on a monthly basis. The scope for each party to deceive the other was acknowledged by the head of the munitions section at general headquarters, who prided himself on his inner sense of what was reasonable but recognized that that itself rested on each report's comparability with the last return. In the winter of 1914–15 his tendency was to bypass the Ministry of War entirely. The need to split his stocks between west and east became a source of flexibility, as he met crises in one army or on one front by calling on the resources of another, rather than by adding to the already excessive demands on home production.[45] In Russia orders for shell passed from the Fronts to the rear, bypassing Stavka: at the end of 1914 Stavka could only account for a third of the shells with which it had

[41] Binding, *Fatalist at war*, 22; also Gascouin, *L'Évolution de l'artillerie*, 89. See, for Russia, Taslauanu, *With the Austrian army*, 141.

[42] Terraine (ed.), *General Jack's diary*, 96, 99.

[43] Wildman, *End of the Russian imperial army*, 84; Stone, *Eastern front*, 132; David Jones, 'Imperial Russia's forces at war', in Millett and Murray (ed.), *Military effectiveness*, i. 267.

[44] Ratinaud, *La Course à la mer*, 40.

[45] Wrisberg, *Wehr und Waffen*, 94–5; Schoen, *Geschichte des deutschen Feuerwerkswesens*, 615–16, 622, 996–7.

been supplied. When Grand Duke Nicholas complained about shell shortage he did not really know, in any detail, what he was talking about.[46]

The demand for munitions generalized and made acute a problem that was more specific, in its operational implications as much as in its geographical incidence. Greater knowledge of what was really going on would have aided proper tactical analysis. Too often shell shortage acted as its substitute. It elevated material considerations over all others in the achievement of victory, denigrating training and instruction. It destabilized morale: soldiers without artillery regarded themselves as already defeated.[47] And its circumvention demanded solutions that were much more multifaceted than simply that of increased production. In June 1915 one French general, Fayolle, questioned—in the privacy of his diary—whether, when shells did become available in abundance, breakthrough would then become possible.

To do that it will be necessary to knock out the enemy artillery. Is that really possible? If there are several successive lines of defence, the second sufficiently far in the rear to make it impossible to prepare simultaneously against them both, it is clear that there will have to be a pause and that everything will be begun afresh.[48]

Some generals appreciated, in line with Fayolle's logic, that the most appropriate palliatives to shell shortage could be tactical rather than industrial. If methods of fighting were adopted that were less reliant on high explosive rather than more, then the edge would be taken off the crisis. In December 1914 the French 10th army ordered two twenty-minute gaps between three twenty-minute bursts of artillery fire; Fayolle himself, as a corps commander, preferred continuous fire, but with the heavy artillery preceding the 75 mms.[49] Both aimed to limit consumption. For the British attack at Festubert on 16 May 1915, Birch, the 7th division's artillery commander, devised a scheme using bluff and pauses so as to draw the Germans out of their shelters. He followed a three-minute bombardment with a two-minute pause, and then resumed with a two-minute bombardment.[50] Thus, working within the context of restricted supplies generated tactical innovation.

Shell shortage may have been exaggerated in the winter of 1914–15, but belief in it as a conditioning phenomenon was real enough. It became the means by which failure could be rationalized and strategy justified. In the recriminations prompted by the setbacks of 1914–15 shell shortage generalized problems that were more specific, and gave objectivity to grievances that were frequently

---

[46] Knox, *With the Russian army*, i. 219; David Jones, 'Imperial Russia's forces at war', in Millett and Murray (eds.), *Military effectiveness*, i, 267.

[47] For these sorts of arguments, admittedly from a self-interested paticipant, see Baquet, *Souvenirs*, 164–9.

[48] Fayolle, *Cahiers secrets*, 118.

[49] Ibid. 64.

[50] Farrar-Hockley, *Goughie*, 156–7.

fuelled by no more than personal animus. The case of Austria-Hungary illustrated both of these tendencies.

On 18 September 1914 the Austrian commander on the Serb front, Potiorek, complained to Bolfras, the head of the emperor's military chancellery, of a shortage of munitions. Austrian shell shortage was characterized by many of the features current elsewhere. Although Vienna seems to have learnt less from the use of artillery in the Balkan wars than did Paris or Berlin, its shell stocks—800 rounds for each field gun—were not so very different from those of other armies. What made the Balkans significant as a precursor to the conditions of the First World War were their mountains, their passes, and their defiles. The geography of south-eastern Europe favoured positional warfare and defensive battles. Thus, the timing of Potiorek's complaint, Austria-Hungary's first major encounter with field fortifications, mirrors that of Joffre's on the Marne. But although the Austrian War Ministry responded that it had no reserves of shell, Potiorek's problems were not simply created by lack of stocks. The inadequacies of an outdated mountain gun had encouraged his artillery to put its faith in howitzers; thus, the shortage was greater in shells for the latter than the former. Secondly, pre-war calculations had pitched the consumption of small-arms ammunition at much higher levels than proved to be the case; so even Austria-Hungary had its own modified form of munitions abundance. And third was the issue of transport: when, in November, Potiorek renewed his offensive into Serbia his line of communications became extended over glutinous tracks, awash with melted snow. By the end of November munition wagons took four days to cover 20 kilometres. Even if the empire had been producing sufficient shells, Potiorek's men would still have suffered shell shortage.

Potiorek could, therefore, have taken steps to ameliorate his position—tactically, by urging his troops to use what they had rather than call for what they did not have; operationally, by setting more limited objectives. But to do this would have required him to sacrifice quick strategic success. This he could not do, not just because of the political pressures for victory, but also because he wished to establish his personal primacy over Conrad von Hötzendorff, and to assert the priority of his own front over that of Galicia. Potiorek's complaints infuriated Conrad on both counts: his appeal to Bolfras bypassed the army high command, and Conrad regarded Potiorek's claim that the guns on the Russian front were being favoured over those on the Serb as false. Shell shortage became a fulcrum for their personal and professional rivalry. Ultimately it became the means by which Potiorek—thrice thwarted by the Serbs in five months—endeavoured to explain away his own failings as a commander.[51]

---

[51] Jerabek, *Potiorek*, 150–6, 170, 178–9, 186; Conrad, *Aus meiner Dienstzeit*, iv. 933–40; Österreichrischen Bundeseministerium, *Osterreich Ungarns letzter Krieg*, ii. 16–17. Rothenberg, *Army of Francis Joseph*, 174, says 550 rounds were in stock per field gun and 330 per howitzer.

What was unusual about Potiorek's expedients was their employment in the furtherance of rifts within the high command. Much more typical was their application by soldiers against outside bodies. Politically, shell shortage became the stick with which generals beat civil administrations: in Britain it was to be an agent in the fall of Asquith's Liberal government in May 1915.

In these circumstances, shell shortage coloured discussions between soldiers and civilians in the winter of 1914–15. It was an important factor in the shaping of their decisions over strategy. Britain and France looked to Russia to take the principal burden in the fighting of the following year. Their eastern ally pleaded lack of munitions as a reason for being unable to mount an offensive before July.[52] By then Germany's concentration on the eastern front would turn such thoughts into pious hopes. But for Germany too a conditioning factor in their switch to the east was shell shortage. Lack of munitions had curbed operations in Flanders in November 1914; relative mobility on the Russian front in 1915 would make shell supply less critical.[53]

THE SHORT-WAR ILLUSION

On 1 November 1912 Moltke wrote to the Prussian War Ministry scotching the notion of a quick campaign culminating in decisive victory. 'We must prepare ourselves,' he went on, 'for a long campaign, with numerous tough, protracted battles, until we defeat one of our enemies; the application of effort and the consumption of resources must increase, if we have to achieve victory in different theatres in west and east successively and have to fight with inferior forces against superior.'[54]

As Moltke was pleading for increased munitions production, he had a vested interest in making the case against the expectation of a short war. But his remarks were not at odds with sentiments he expressed elsewhere. Famously, he told the Kaiser in 1906, when he took up his appointment as chief of the general staff, that the next war 'will not be settled by a decisive battle but by a long wearisome struggle with a country that will not be overcome until its whole national force is broken'; it would be 'a war which will utterly exhaust our own people, even if we are victorious'.[55] He wrote in similar terms to his wife. And much that he did over the next nine years bore testimony to these convictions. The decision to bypass Holland, the caution in his undertakings

[52] Neilson, *Strategy and supply,* 58–9.
[53] Farrar, *Short-war illusion,* 137–8; Reichsarchiv, *Weltkrieg,* vi. 93; Kraft, *Staatsräson und Kriegs-führung,* 30.
[54] Ludendorff, *Urkunden der Obersten Heeresleitung,* 14.
[55] Tuchman, *August 1914,* 34.

to Austria-Hungary concerning the eastern front, the call for the creation of an economic general staff—all are evidence of his willingness to follow up his predictions with practical remedies.

It has become a truism of 1914 that men went off to fight in the expectation of a short war. But overstatement has led to misrepresentation. Many soldiers before 1914 anticipated that the next European war would be long. The fact that this was so is remarkable, not simply because it is at odds with the conventional wisdom concerning 1914. Optimism in the face of adversity is almost a requirement of successful command. Generals, after all, need to temper the rendering of sober advice in peacetime with sufficient faith in their own abilities and in the strengths of their armies to ensure victory if hostilities begin. The belief in the possibility of a quick war crowned by a triumphant denouement can be a basis for professional success. Rare indeed is the commander who allows his realism about the nature of war to become pessimism concerning its outcome or its duration. Moltke did, but Moltke was not alone in 1914. Professional wisdom on the likely nature of the First World War was remarkably uniform.

Kitchener was already predicting a war of three years in 1909. On 7 August 1914, at his first cabinet meeting as secretary of state for war, he repeated this view and then set about the creation of a mass army to give it effect. Typically, he did not vouchsafe to his colleagues in government the inner workings of his calculations. He later claimed to have been influenced by the American Civil War. But more immediate was his own experience in South Africa: in 1899 the Boers had no more been defeated by Christmas than the Germans would be in 1914.[56] Kitchener was not an isolated voice in the army. Two of the 1914 corps commanders, whose careers would prosper thanks to the war's length, were of a similar persuasion. One was Henry Rawlinson.[57] The other, Douglas Haig, told the council of war held on 5 August that the war could last for years, and that the BEF should be the basis for the creation of an army of a million men.[58]

Across the Channel Joffre predicted a long war, albeit without Haig's effort to be precise. In saying this, he was doing no more than reflect the teaching of Commandant Benneau at the École de Guerre in the 1880s,[59] and the views of one of France's most perceptive military theorists, General Langlois, expressed in 1911.[60] In Morocco, Lyautey was in no hurry to leave when the war broke out. He reckoned that he could finish his work there and still have time to move to a major post (he already had the Ministry of War in mind) in the metropolis.[61]

---

[56] French, *British economic and stragegic planning*, 125; id., *British strategy and war aims*, 24; id., *English Historical Review*, CIII (1988), 387–8; Simkins, *Kitchener's army*, 38; Stone and Schmidl, *Boer war*, 169; Huguet, *Britain and the war*, 37.
[57] Prior and Wilson, *Command on the western front*, 11.
[58] Terraine, *Haig*, 70–4.
[59] Contamine, *Révanche*, 60, 165; Farrar, *Short-war illusion*, 6.
[60] Reboul, *Mobilisation industrielle*, 3–4.   [61] Le Révérend, *Lyautey*, 375.

Further east, Schemua, Conrad's stand-in as chief of the general staff during the latter's fall from grace, told Franz Joseph on 13 February 1912 that the next war would be a *Volkskrieg*: all industry would be mobilized in its prosecution and armies would fight until utterly broken. Certain quarters in the Austrian military press were of the same view.[62] In Russia, the fragmentation and diversity of doctrine spawned by the war in Manchuria included powerful writers who warned against the ideal of short, sharp campaigns. General N. P. Mikhnevich, the chief of the main staff, saw advantages for Russia in a protracted war: 'Time is the best ally of our armed forces', he wrote in *Strategiia* in 1911. 'Therefore, it is not dangerous for us to adopt "a strategy of attrition and exhaustion", at first avoiding decisive combat with the enemy on the very borders.' In taking this line he was opposed by General A. A. Neznamov, who—while affirming his faith in a short war—warned that firepower would dominate and that the decision would be reached, not in a single climactic engagement but in sequential battles of exhaustion. A theorist who became much better known after the war than he was before it, A. A. Svechin, pragmatically concluded in 1913 that armies should plan for an early victory but prepare for a protracted conflict.[63]

The military view that the war would be long and indecisive was rooted in three factors. First, the creation of armed alliances had made the swift victories of 1866 and 1870, achieved against single powers, unrepeatable. This was the basis of Moltke the elder's gloomy forecast to the Reichstag in 1890. Echoing historical precedent, he warned of a war lasting seven or even thirty years. Caprivi, Bismarck's successor as chancellor, was accordingly persuaded of the need to plan for a long war. In this respect, as in others, Moltke the younger was the heir to his uncle's realism.[64]

Secondly, the adoption of universal military service enabled a state to draw on its full resources in the event of war while making it unlikely that it would go to war unless the cause was right. The vocabulary of social Darwinism, of cultural decline and regeneration, provided a framework within which such concepts could be subsumed and which made the prospect of early (or any) surrender remote.[65] The combination of national mobilization and deeply felt motivation would prompt states to fight on until their reserves were exhausted. Both Wilhelm von Blume and Colmar von der Goltz, two of the most important German writers on strategy before 1914, recognized that in such circumstances victory would not be ceded easily or quickly.

[62] Regele, *Conrad*, 67, 172.
[63] Menning, *Bayonets before bullets*, 208–13, 216; Jones, *Military–naval encyclopedia of Russia*, iv. 119, 136.
[64] Ritter, *Sword and the sceptre*, ii. 197; Elze, *Tannenberg*, 28; Burchardt, *Friedenswirtschaft und Kriegsvorsorge*, 162–3, 170–80.
[65] See Mackensen's views on 3 August 1914 as an example: Schwarzmüller, *Zwischen Kaiser und 'Führer'*, 93.

Thirdly, most soldiers were sensitive to the implications of the revolution in firepower effected between 1871 and 1914. The advent of breech-loading rifles and quick-firing artillery, allied to field fortifications and barbed wire, pointed to the strength of the defence. Attackers committed to a frontal assault were unlikely to make rapid progress. Battle would be robbed of its decisiveness. Major-General Ernst Köpke, quartermaster-general on the German general staff, warned in 1895 that an attack on France's eastern frontier by way of Nancy would soon resemble siege warfare: gains would be limited and there could be no expectation of quick, decisive victories.[66] The Germans' emphasis on operational envelopment sprang precisely from the awareness of possible tactical stalemate.

The problem for the German general staff was that it could not live with the implications of this logic. Protracted warfare implied not victory for Germany, but defeat. In terms of combined resources and of total manpower the Triple Alliance was inferior to the Triple Entente: if Italy did not fight and Austria-Hungary proved as militarily weak as the Germans feared, then the staying-power of a coalition would be an advantage enjoyed only by the enemy. Furthermore, the internal picture was as depressing as the external. The army's self-appointed role as the bulwark of domestic order against socialism made it acutely sensitive to the strains which a long war would generate.[67] Schlieffen thus found himself confronted with a contradiction between his strategic sense and the needs of national policy. The tension this created was reflected in his response to the tactical conditions prevailing in the Russo-Japanese War. 'Out there in Manchuria', he wrote,

they may face each other for months on end in impregnable positions. In Western Europe we cannot allow ourselves the luxury of waging a war in this manner. The machine with its thousand wheels, upon which millions depend for their livelihood, cannot stand still for long ... We must try to overthrow the enemy quickly and then destroy him.[68]

Therefore Schlieffen's advocacy of a short war sprang precisely from his recognition of the possibility of a long one. The best, indeed the only prospect of a German victory, given Germany's confrontation by superior numbers, lay in a rapid campaign of annihilation. Such an outcome would, of course, endorse the *amour propre* of the army and the status of the general staff within it. Having embraced this conclusion, Schlieffen had to find evidence to support it. Unable to do so on the basis of recent military experience, he began to argue that the next war would be short because the structure of international

[66] Förster, *Militärgeschichtliche Mitteilungen*, 54 (1995), 74–5.
[67] Borgert, 'Grundzüge der Landkriegführung', 460.
[68] Hardach, *First World War*, 55; see also Reichsarchiv, *Weltkrieg: Kriegsrüstung und Kriegswirtschaft*, i. 326–34.

trade and the mechanism for domestic credit could not enable it to be long. And so, in a circular process, he could fulfil his own professional need, as a strategist in the Napoleonic tradition, to plan for a short, decisive, and victorious war.[69]

But here he was in uncharted waters. The German general staff was no more geared for the formulation of grand strategy, embracing economics and politics, than was any other general staff of the day. Indeed, it was the narrowness of its thinking about war that enabled it to interpret Frederick the Great's strategy in the Seven Years War in such radically different terms from its great academic critic, Hans Delbrück. Delbrück saw the wars of Frederick as a whole, spread over years, punctuated by battles that did not in the long run necessarily prove decisive: what he dubbed an *Ermattungsstrategie*, a strategy of attrition. When he shifted his gaze to the present, the strength of the tactical defensive served to confirm his grasp of this continuity. Schlieffen's thinking, like the general staff's history, saw each campaign as an independent operational undertaking. Thus, he could effectively shrink the coming war in Europe, and the apocalyptic imagery associated with it, to a single campaign against France, rationally conceived in the tradition of cabinet warfare.[70]

Schlieffen's success as a propagandist for the idea of a short war created confusion. Moltke the younger could not abandon his predecessor's plan for quick victory for exactly the same reasons that had led Schlieffen to adopt it in the first place. But at the same time Moltke could not delude himself as thoroughly as did Schlieffen. Thus, he ended up developing operational plans for a short war while urging civilian administrators to prepare for a long one. In doing so he achieved little more than to confirm his reputation for indecisiveness.[71]

The effects on Falkenhayn were even more ambivalent. It was Falkenhayn's task, as minister of war, to respond to many of Moltke's pre-war demands for greater preparation for a long war and for the industrial mobilization to sustain it. Ludendorff, as head of operations, seconded his chief in very similar terms,[72] and these general staff views were echoed within Falkenhayn's own ministry by Franz Wandel.[73] Any lingering hesitation on the point entertained by either departmental head was quashed by Britain's entry. On the night of 30/1 July 1914 Moltke told Hans von Haeften that if Britain joined the Entente nobody could foresee either the length or the outcome of the conflict.[74] A few

[69] Snyder, *Ideology of the offensive*, 108, 123, 139, embraces elements, but not all, of this interpretation.
[70] Bucholz, *Delbrück and the German military establishment*; Förster, *Militärgeschichtliche Mitteilungen*, 54 (1995), 80; Scheibe, ibid. 53 (1994), 358–60; Lange, *Delbrück*; Raschke, *Der politisierende Generalstab*.
[71] Burchardt, *Friedenswirtschaft und Kriegsvorsorge*, 24–7.
[72] Schoen, *Geschichte des deutschen Feuerwerkswesens*, 990.
[73] Storz, *Kriegsbild und Rüstung*, 327.
[74] Mombauer, 'Moltke', 185.

days later, and in the knowledge that Britain was indeed a belligerent, Falkenhayn tried to be more precise: speaking to an American diplomat, Henry White, he anticipated a war of three to four years.[75] The Kaiser spoke in comparable terms to White's superior, the American ambassador James Gerard, and neither Bethmann Hollweg nor Kurt Riezler dissented.[76] While minister of war, Falkenhayn's actions conformed to these prognostications. But when Falkenhayn himself became chief of the general staff he seemed determined to prove himself the worthy heir of the Schlieffen tradition in this respect as in others. The minister of the interior, Clemens von Delbrück, who before the war had been the subject of Moltke's call for an economic general staff, once the war began found Falkenhayn particularly dismissive of the need for long-term planning. Similarly, in November and December 1914 Groener and Helfferich could not get the chief of the general staff to consider new railway construction on the grounds that the war would be over before it was complete.[77]

Schlieffen had built his short-war illusion on the financial impossibility of sustaining a long war. This was the explanation for the probability of a war of limited duration most commonly embraced by soldiers in all the belligerent nations. It coloured the views of the Prussian War Ministry.[78] It persuaded Sir Archibald Murray, the British chief of the imperial general staff in August 1914, that the war could only last for eight months. And those who disagreed, like Murray's superior Lord Kitchener, did so by taking issue with the financial argument: Kitchener pointed out, somewhat naively and certainly irrelevantly, given the preparations for a great continental war over which he was presiding, that colonial wars had been fought on a 'financial shoestring'.[79] Neither side tested their assumptions with the same rigour as they put into staff rides or war games. Few had the courage to confess, as did the French intendant général Ducuing, in 1912: 'Nobody can foresee the length of a future war nor the protraction of which it will be capable. Many think that it will be short because of the enormity of the expenditure before there can be a result. But in reality we do not know anything about it.'[80]

The second main foundation of the short-war argument built on by the military was socio-economic. Here too general staffs were happy to draw major conclusions from largely untested hypotheses. The German manual, *Grundzüge der höheren Truppenführung*, published in 1910, refrained from the explicit statement that the next war would be short, but still stated: 'The levy of

[75] Afflerbach, *Falkenhayn*, 171.
[76] Gilbert, *First World War*, 39; Raithel, *Das 'Wunder' der inneren Einheit*, 406.
[77] Delbrück, *Wirtschaftliche Mobilmachung*, 116; Groener, *Lebenserinnerungen*, 211; Helfferich, *Weltkrieg*, 158.
[78] Wrisberg, *Heer und Heimat*, 5.
[79] French, *English Historical Review*, CIII (1988), 387; id., *British strategy and war aims*, 24.
[80] Pedroncini, *Histoire militaire de la France*, iii. 304.

all able-bodied men, the strength of the army, the difficulty of supplying it, the cost of being under arms, the interruption to trade and traffic, commerce and agriculture—for the purpose of having an army ready to fight and easily assembled—all that presses for a quick end to the war.'[81] The French equivalent, published in 1913, pointed to similar conclusions.[82] Both armies feared that general mobilization would give rise to strikes and demonstrations. They expected domestic disaffection to deepen rather than to dissipate. After all, in the 1880s Engels had anticipated with relish the possibility of a war lasting three to four years precisely because it could create the conditions for the victory of the working class. In 1914 the German Social Democrats appreciated that a long war enhanced the likelihood of fundamental domestic change.[83] Thus, in this respect the armies' search for a short war was driven by resistance to social change, and was at least based on matters closer to their own interests than was any expectation derived from the workings of international credit.

None of the economic arguments anticipating an early end to the war rested on the possibility that the belligerents would run out of the munitions with which to fight it. After all, Europe underwent an arms race between 1911 and 1914 of sufficient intensity to suggest that both stocks and plant would be available in abundance. Indeed, the state of the arms industry was evidence to support those who expected a long war, not a short one. It was precisely because they could foresee industry's capacity to continue supplying armies in the field until those armies destroyed each other that so many generals summoned up images of future war that proved to be all-too accurate. The possibility of large-scale industrial mobilization was a key element in the 'long-war assumption'.

The mix of these military and economic arguments produced an understandable ambivalence in Germany. Somewhat more surprisingly, it also caused confusion in Britain. As a trading and maritime empire, with a strong money market and a small army, the United Kingdom stood to gain from a long war. Sir Charles Dilke made this very point in 1887.[84] Anticipating a long war on 8 September 1914, Lloyd George said, 'that is where our resources will come in, not merely of men, but of cash. We have won with the silver bullets before.'[85]

Britain's principal weapons, sea-power, and specifically blockade, were also agents appropriate to a war of extended duration. Common to both sides of the debate on British strategy at the Committee of Imperial Defence on 23

[81] Borgert, 'Grundzüge fur Landkriegführung', 475.
[82] Krumeich, *Armaments and politics*, 118.
[83] Gunther Mai, '"Verteidigungskrieg" und "Volksgemeinschaft"', in Michalka (ed.), *Der Erste Weltkrieg*, 586–7; also Pick, *War machine*, 56.
[84] Gooch, *Prospect of war*, 38.
[85] Hazlehurst, *Politicians at war*, 176.

August 1911 was the presumption that the war should be made to be long. Henry Wilson wanted to commit the British Expeditionary Force to the continent so as to forestall any danger of a quick German victory: Britain's staying-power was to be pitted against the German army's initial impact. On this occasion Churchill said that British influence on the war would be greatest after twelve months.[86] But on the war's outbreak he told the Admiralty departments to proceed on the assumption that the war would only last twelve months, and that the greatest effort would be required in the first six.[87] The Admiralty, while expediting the completion of ships under construction, cancelled all other contracts.[88] Logistically, it was completely unprepared for a long war. The building of the fleet had been achieved at the expense of the dockyards and shore bases needed to sustain protracted operations in the North Sea. Fuel stocks were sufficient for four-and-a-half months.[89] Not until October 1914 did Fisher begin to plan for a long war: on 3 November he drew up a scheme for a fleet of 600 vessels.[90]

Part of Britain's problem was the trade-off between the sort of long-term planning represented in cabinet by Kitchener, Lloyd George, and Maurice Hankey, and the short-term crises generated by the military situation on the continent. Arguably, the pursuit of fleet action early in the war by Jellicoe would have militated against a long war, and would have rendered the short-war idea not illusion but reality. In other words, the conservatism of Britain's naval leadership helped make the war protracted.[91] Converse pressures applied on land. Those at GHQ in France, and especially Henry Wilson, railed against Kitchener's emphasis on preparing for the long haul at the expense of current needs.[92] If these were not met in the short term, there would be no long term.

Ultimately, British strategic thought lacked consistency for reasons very similar to those found on the continent. Military and naval professionals made assumptions about areas outside their ken, and in their hands commercial and trading vigour became a source not of strategic strength but of vulnerability. In 1901 the head of the strategic section of the Directorate of Mobilization and Intelligence, E. A. Altham, rested his plans for the defence of the empire on the assumption that a trading empire would have to fight a short war.[93] On 5 August 1914 Beatty wrote to his wife that the war would be over by winter: his opinion did not rest on the capabilities of his battle cruisers or on the role of sea-power, but on his belief that 'There is not

[86] Herrmann, *Arming of Europe*, 156–7.
[87] Gordon, *Rules of the game*, 624, n. 20.
[88] Goldrick, *King's ships were at sea*, 33.
[89] Sumida, *Journal of Military History*, LVII (1993), 450, 456–7; Patterson, *Jellicoe*, 52–3.
[90] Goldrick, *King's ships were at sea*, 170–1; Marder, *From the Dreadnought*, ii. 93–4.
[91] Farrar, *Short-war illusion*, 115.
[92] Grieves, *Politics of manpower*, 9; Cassar, *Tragedy of Sir John French*, 183.
[93] Gooch, *Plans of war*, 178–9.

sufficient money in the world to provide such a gigantic struggle to be continued for any great length of time'.[94]

The failure of soldiers and sailors to test their assumption about the workings of economies in wartime was mirrored by the failure of politicians to revise their expectations in the light of military advice. Bethmann Hollweg frequently referred to a war of three or four months. Such hopes, derived from the wars of 1866 and 1870, were not challenged in the light of military developments since then. Instead, they were nurtured by staff officers who rested their hopes on financial guesswork rather than on military probability. The short-war illusion was therefore sustained by the failure to co-ordinate differing perspectives on the next war.

What does seem unambiguous is the nature of popular belief. The public imagined a short war would be even more brief than that of the most optimistic of policy-makers. Men responded to the call to arms, and their families bade them farewell, precisely because they believed they would be back home before the leaves fell. The only counterbalance to this naivety was the apocalyptic notion of the next war as Armageddon—a vision peculiarly appropriate to 1914 but not exclusive to it. In this context the long-war idea belonged in the imaginings of pessimists, while the short-war illusion reflected most of mankind's continuing optimism concerning the human condition. Thus, wishful thinking—rather than either military or economic analysis—gave the short-war notion universality.

When the war was not over within a month, men adjusted by thinking of it as a series of short episodes. The short-war illusion therefore persisted throughout the war. Conceptually, the idea of a long war remained hard to grasp.[95] The French victory on the Marne clearly signalled that the fighting would continue for some while yet. But few could conceptualize a war lasting years. A soldier of the Royal Welch Fusiliers on 5 November 1914 wrote, 'I am getting awfully bored by the trenches and am feeling fearfully tired. I hope we won't be in them much longer.' The combination of his current predicament and his future aspiration produced the calculation that the war would last two to three months more.[96] Sandor Ferenczi, serving as an assistant medical officer with a Hungarian reserve cavalry regiment, told his friend Sigmund Freud in January 1915 that the war would be long, which meant an end 'perhaps in October'—of the same year.[97] The tendency, among policy-makers as much as at the front line or on the shop-floor, was to site the conclusion of the war at some point in the middle distance. Few of these predictions were accompanied by realistic explanations as to how the war would be ended, and therefore the time-lapse had to be sufficient for a new element to enter the equation. But it

[94] Roskill, *Beatty*, 79.   [95] Becker, *1914*, 491–7.   [96] Dunn, *The war the infantry knew*, 90.
[97] Falzeder and Brabant (eds.), *Correspondence of Freud and Ferenczi*, ii. 42.

was reckoned that when this new element was felt the end would be rapid. Typically, such events were reckoned to be six months hence. Not until 1917 would it become common to predict the war's continuation in terms of years. Significantly, when the popular expectation of a short war was finally ousted, crises in morale soon followed.[98]

These popular misapprehensions confirm how relative was the notion of what was long or short. For pre-war planners a two-year war was deemed long; for post-war analysts such a conflict would have been deemed short. Even those who before the war reckoned on a short war had no common scale to define what they meant. In Germany most predictions oscillated between four and nine months, but some ran up to a year.[99] In Britain in 1912 the general staff said that a war would last longer than six months, but wisely refused to give an upper limit.[100] Furthermore, views changed as the war progressed. Kitchener's belief in a long war, shaped at least in part by the experience of colonial operations, wobbled in the face of the intensity of European warfare and its attendant shell shortage.[101]

Predictions of a short war or long war were therefore themselves a cloak for imprecision. Variations of two to three months, given the scale of national mobilization envisaged, were fraught with significance for the consumption of resources and the pace of industrial mobilization. From this point of view the debate was of value only in the most general sense. Neither set of predictions was translated into policy before the war, or even into plans for implementation on mobilization, in any of the belligerent powers. In this most reductionist sense too, the problems of industrial mobilization were not contingent on any pre-war expectations concerning the war's length.

RAW MATERIALS, MUNITIONS PRODUCTION, AND THE CENTRAL POWERS, 1914–1916

On 8 August 1914 Walther Rathenau, of the German electrics giant AEG, called on Colonel Heinrich Scheüch, head of the *Allgemeine Kriegsdepartement* of the Prussian War Ministry. Scheüch was responsible for all orders for munitions. The immediate object of Rathenau's visit was to discuss the exploitation of Belgian industry. Rathenau seems to have envisaged a quick campaign, but a long war. He appreciated that Britain's entry would prevent a rapid victory in the west having decisive effects. But the territorial gains could provide the

---

[98] Becker, *Revue historique*, CCLXIV (1980), 71–2.
[99] Burchardt, *Friedenswirtschaft und Kriegsvorsorge*, 14–20.
[100] French, *British strategy and war aims*, 14–15.   [101] Koss, *Asquith*, 170.

wherewithal to enable Germany to sustain protracted operations. Scheüch was of a like mind. He reported the exchange of views to his minister, Falkenhayn. Falkenhayn then invited Rathenau to meet him on the following day.

By the time Rathenau saw Falkenhayn on 9 August he had digested a memorandum written on the 8th by his AEG colleague Wichard von Moellendorff. Moellendorff was worried by the implications of a British blockade for German imports of raw materials. His immediate concerns were those of the AEG, and in particular its reliance on imported copper. But he nurtured a longer-term objective. He envisaged the creation, through the central allocation of raw materials, of a 'deutscher Gemeinwirtschaft'—a state-led centralized economy. Thus, onto his original preoccupation with Belgian booty Rathenau now grafted a scheme for the central appropriation, allocation, and distribution of raw materials in order to benefit war industries. Rathenau prepared a memorandum for Falkenhayn along these lines. The Prussian war minister was convinced. He asked Rathenau to head a new office, the Kriegsrohstoffsamt (KRA or war raw materials office). To give the KRA some military clout, a passed-over colonel, Boehme, was hauled out of the clothing office of II corps to be Rathenau's nominal collaborator. On 13 August 1914 the KRA began business.

The story of the establishment of the KRA is bewitching in its suddenness and in its completeness. Particularly compelling is the ease with which a Jewish businessman stormed the ramparts of the apparently conservative and anti-Semitic Prussian army. Far from being doubly disqualified, Rathenau—at least on his own account—found himself being pressed into service. And it is that version of the story, framed in December 1915, which has generated the principal controversy surrounding the episode.[102]

Rathenau's account failed to give credit to his subordinate, Moellendorff. The hinge of their argument—whether or not Rathenau was already convinced of the need for the central control of raw materials before he read Moellendorff's memorandum—puts the emphasis on the precise sequence of events on 8 and 9 August. Thus, the effect of the debate was to heighten the stress on the short-term and the immediate. The decisiveness and urgency of both entrepreneurs was contrasted with the previous procrastination and inaction of the German government. The consensus that Germany had made no pre-war preparations for economic mobilization became the essential foil to the events of early August. Scheüch and Falkenhayn were only accorded walk-on parts.[103]

---

[102] Rathenau's version, albeit abridged, is to be found in English in Lutz, *Fall of the German empire*, ii. 77–91.

[103] Burchardt, *Friedenswirtschaft und Kriegsvorsorge*, comes to conclusions about Germany's lack of economic preparation which at times are at odds with his own evidence. On the Rathenau–Moellendorff debate, Burchardt, *Tradition*, XV (1970), 169–96, points up Moellendorff's role; Pogge von Strandmann, *Rathenau*, 157–9, takes a balanced view; Hecker, *Rathenau*, 201–12, differs in some details.

But a reconsideration is required. First there is Scheüch. His response is evidence that the need to prepare for a long war had penetrated the bowels of the War Ministry. Secondly, there is the picture of Falkenhayn created by Rathenau's version of events. Clear-headed, masterful, and decisive, his focus was on the long term, uncluttered by the immediate trivia of mobilization. Whether Moellendorff or Rathenau should get the credit is largely beside the point: both were preaching to the converted.

Schlieffen's replacement by Moltke had given the prophets of a long war an audience. Hitherto Schlieffen's need for a quick victory had brooked no argument; thereafter, there was at least debate. From 1906 the Prussian War Ministry, previously sidelined by the dominance of the chief of the general staff, took a larger share in the formulation of policy. The military authorities conferred with the civilian concerning the economic preparations for war. An intellectual conversion began.

That ideas did not become policy was largely attributable to institutional impediments. The Reich minister responsible for the economy was the secretary of state for the interior, but so broad was his portfolio that many issues were more pressing than those of contingency planning for war. Furthermore, as Clemens von Delbrück, the minister from 1909, quite reasonably pointed out in his otherwise self-serving memoirs, economic preparation for war frequently conflicts with the needs of an economy in peace: concentration on the former can ultimately undermine the latter.[104] With the Interior Ministry inactive, the Ministry of War felt itself powerless. Although a standing committee was established by the two departments in 1906, it contented itself with the calculation that Germany had sufficient stocks of food and raw materials to survive nine months of fighting.

However, in 1911 the second Moroccan crisis caused the War Ministry's fears to overcome its sense of restraint. Heeringen proposed a ban on exports to Delbrück. Perturbed by the slowness of the latter's response, Heeringen then appealed to Bethmann Hollweg. The Balkan war reinforced Heeringen's concerns. It may also have played its part in converting Delbrück, for in 1912 he expressed his agreement with Emil Ludwig Possehl, who used the forum of the Army League to advocate a department of wartime economic planning.[105] In November Delbrück—probably under instructions from Bethmann Hollweg (although Delbrück denied this)—convened a conference of interested parties to discuss economic mobilization. Constituting itself as a standing commission, much of its work in 1913 was undertaken by subcommittees devoted to the collection of information. A plenary meeting in May 1914 was the first

---

Falkenhayn's most recent biographer does not probe the minister of war's position: see Afflerbach, *Falkenhayn*, 172–4.

[104] Delbrück, *Wirtschaftliche Mobilmachung*, 64. [105] Coetzee, *German Army League*, 106–7.

opportunity to formulate policy. By now, however, Delbrück was the activist and Bethmann Hollweg his opponent. The chancellor was fearful that overt economic preparation for hostilities would further destabilize an already fraught international situation. When war broke out it seemed that in absolute terms Delbrück had failed: Germany had recognized the possibility of a long war, conceivably on a global scale, but it had taken no significant steps to prepare for it.[106]

This stress on outcomes and its accompanying denigration of deliberation serve to heighten the importance of Rathenau's intervention in August 1914. Nor does this interpretation seem to be undermined by a closer examination of the contents of the pre-war discussions. Their focus was less on the raw-material needs of the war industries than on the maintenance of food supplies. The initial involvement of the general staff in the issue of economic mobilization was motivated by the need to feed the army. Of related concern were the problem of liquidity (as cash was needed to buy food, fodder, and horses), and the interruption to civilian transport (particularly that carrying foodstuffs to major cities) through the army's commandeering of the railways. Therefore mobilization, and its implications for Germany as a whole, was the point at which the general staff's concern with war touched the army's more general preoccupation with internal order. The possibility of domestic opposition to, and disruption of, its plans for war fed on the fear of socialism. Nor was this bogey confined to the army. The threat of revolution was a more continuous pressure on the Ministry of the Interior than the contingency of war. Both departments linked economic questions to social ones, and for both this convergence resulted in a preoccupation with food stocks.

The propaganda emanating from Tirpitz's Imperial Naval Office both reinforced and eased their fears. In 1907 Tirpitz described with extraordinary accuracy the pattern and long-term effects on Germany of a British blockade. But in stressing the threat, he was developing the case for the navy's expansion, not for amassing sufficient food for a long war. At one level his success in achieving the former was evidence of the seriousness attached to the latter. But at another, and particularly as the fleet grew both in size and as a burden on the exchequer, the navy had to acquire a more positive rationale. Tirpitz was just as capable of stressing Britain's dependence on overseas trade, and therefore Britain's, not Germany's, vulnerability to blockade. It was this dimension to Tirpitzian thought that underpinned the complacency of the president of the Imperial Statistical Office at the first meeting of the standing committee on wartime supplies on 11 June 1906.[107]

[106] Burchardt, *Friedenswirtschaft und Kriegsvorsorge*, 249; also generally 165–241.
[107] Baer, 'Anglo-German antagonism and trade with Holland', 13–20, 25–6, 30.

Food would, of course, not be the only commodity whose importation would be checked by a British blockade. Delbrück flagged the issue of raw materials at the May 1914 conference. But the stockpiling of metals and chemicals in peacetime carried a direct challenge to the economic liberalism espoused both by Delbrück himself and by his predecessor as minister of the interior, Bethmann Hollweg. In 1908 the latter rejected a proposal to amass stocks in peacetime on the grounds of cost. In 1912 the former recoiled from a suggestion that an economic general staff be formed precisely because of its connotations for state intervention. Procuring raw materials in excess of industry's peacetime needs and planning for their allocation in the event of war implied the subordination of individual enterprise to state direction. Similar calculations determined Bethmann Hollweg's reluctance to ban the export of arms in 1913.[108]

However, if economic liberalism was sufficient explanation for the refusal of the German civil authorities to consider the establishment of the KRA in advance of war itself, it was not in the case of the army. In 1905–6 the Imperial Naval Office reported that 922 firms in the Ruhr, employing a total of 400,000 workers, said that their business was dependent on imported raw materials. Germany produced only a fraction of its requirement for nickel, manganese, aluminium, copper, wool, and flax; all of its rubber, cotton, jute, saltpetre, and oil was imported. The firms considered by the navy in 1905 held, on average, sufficient stocks of imported raw materials for three months production; 20 per cent had enough for six to eight months, and only 2 per cent for more than twelve months. A second survey, conducted by the Interior Ministry in 1913, found little change. Furthermore, these figures almost certainly put a favourable gloss on the true position. They did not take account of the fact that firms included orders which had been placed with the trade although the goods themselves had yet to arrive in Germany. Imports peaked in the autumn, and thus a war which broke out in late summer would coincide with the period when real stocks were at their lowest.[109] All the pre-war indications seemed to suggest that German industrial productivity would fall for lack of raw materials long before the German population would starve through the shortage of imported food.

Therefore, the central conundrum must be the insouciance of the chief of the general staff concerning raw materials. Moltke, in his pre-war injunctions about shell supplies, stressed sustained production during the war rather than the amassing of stocks before it. His neglect of raw materials—as opposed to food supplies—seems bizarrely at odds with his own expectations concerning the length and nature of the next war.[110]

[108] Burchardt, *Friedenswirtschaft und Kriegsvorsorge*, 86–92, 140, 169–73, 188, 206–8.
[109] Ibid. 79–81, 92–3, 169–70, 246; Burchardt, *Tradition*, XV (1970), 172–3; Goebel, *Deutsche Rohstoffwirtschaft*, 13–18.   [110] Burchardt, *Friedenswirtschaft und Kriegsvorsorge*, 169–73.

Part of the explanation is, once again, institutional: Moltke did not see it as his job to sort out industry's problems for it. But much the most important reason was that the raw materials position was, in reality, not as dire as either the pre-war propaganda of the navy or the post-war explanations of German historians (anxious in many cases to play down any suggestion that Germany was preparing for war) suggested. The naval survey was one devoted to all types of industry in the Ruhr; it failed to distinguish between those producing for the home market and those for export. The blockade would eliminate the need for raw materials dedicated to the latter. Secondly, it did not distinguish between the munitions industries and the rest. Moltke's preoccupation was only with the former; provided they continued to secure the raw materials they needed, then the German armies could carry on fighting. Finally, the navy failed to take account of the fact that many raw materials—including nickel and chrome—were imported from overseas because they were cheaper than those produced in Germany. If Germany's foreign trade was blocked, then the economic viability of mining those metals available within Germany itself would increase.

The navy's presumption was that the blockade would be total and immediate in its effects; this was not the army's view. Moltke, as his decision not to invade Holland testifies, hoped to continue importing through the border neutrals. The German market seemed too important to the United States for the latter to allow itself to be excluded from it.[111] In particular, Germany's most significant import for military purposes, iron ore, seemed relatively impervious to maritime intervention. Its main suppliers were Sweden and France. But the trade with the former was conducted through the Baltic, and was therefore not so vulnerable to the Royal Navy's attentions. French supplies might be temporarily cut off by hostilities, but they could then fall to Germany by right of conquest.

Most important of all to Moltke's calculations was the scale of Germany's own stocks of raw materials. Germany may have increased its imports of iron ore by 350 per cent between 1900 and 1913,[112] but well over half of its consumption was domestically produced, and that proportion could increase significantly if rising demand increased the profitability of domestic extraction. In terms of coal Germany was completely self-sufficient. Its production had increased from 34,485.5 million tonnes in 1871 to 190,109.4 million tonnes in 1913. Furthermore, coal was the single most important raw material in the chemical industry, a sector in which Germany was the world's leader.[113]

[111] Egmont Zechlin, 'Cabinet versus economic warfare in Germany', in Koch (ed.), *Origins of the First World War*, 234–5.

[112] Fischer, *War of illusions*, 320–1.

[113] Reichsarchiv, *Weltkrieg: Kriegsrustung und Kriegswirtschaft*, i. 380–2.

None of this, however, should be taken as confirmation that the army was complacent about the problems of wartime production. Stockpiling on a narrow base—that is to say, of the imported raw materials vital for munitions production—was fostered by the Ministry of War in 1913. The immediate consequences of this effort were absorbed by the race to equip the new formations sanctioned in the army laws of 1912 and 1913. The fact that these were ready for war in 1914 is evidence that Delbrück's belated efforts were not without some immediate consequences.[114]

Most revealing of how appearances belied reality was the position of Germany's major private armaments manufacturer, Krupp. In 1913 Krupp was reported as holding sufficient raw materials for two months' production; on the outbreak of war its stocks of iron ore totalled 420,000 tonnes against an annual consumption in 1912–13 of 2.5 million tonnes. But between 1888 and 1913 Krupp had been buying up its own iron-ore fields: thus, although high extraction costs had depressed actual production, Krupp had reserves in hand. The combination of these and the continuation of supplies of iron ore from Sweden and France meant that the firm's output of armaments was never threatened during the war. In 1914, of the specialist metals which it imported, Krupp had sufficient nickel for two years and sufficient chrome ore for one. Domestic production of both increased during the war, and Krupp imported further nickel from Norway and more chrome ore from Serbia. It covered two-thirds of its copper requirement during the war from existing stocks. By the expectations of the day Krupp was ready for a long war.[115]

The effect of the pre-war thinking on supplies of food and of raw materials was that Germany responded to the British blockade before it was even effective. On 3 August an agreement was drawn up between the Ministry of the Interior and the Hamburg–Amerika Line, putting the organization of the latter at the disposal of the former for the import of foodstuffs and raw materials.[116] In the British view Germany was more worried about its raw-material stocks than the situation warranted. By October there was clear evidence of Germany's bid to increase its indirect trade via its border neutrals. Norway's export of pig iron to Germany quadrupled between 1913 and 1914. Between August and December 1913 Germany had imported 729 tons of iron ore a month from Sweden; over the same period in the following year monthly imports totalled 2,310 tons. German imports of Swedish aluminium, which had been non-existent in 1913, totalled 5,511 tons in the last four months of 1914.[117] In addition, Germany overran France's main iron-ore fields in Longwy-Briey, thus doubling its reserves at a stroke.[118] Symbolic of the

[114] Schulte, Vor dem Kriegsausbruch, 100–1, 105–7.
[115] Jindra, Jahrbuch für Wirtschaftsgeschichte (1976), Teil I, 140–50.
[116] Delbrück, Wirtschaftliche Mobilmachung, 110–11.
[117] Bell, Blockade of Germany, 40, 52–3, 150–1, 192, 243.   [118] Fischer, Germany's aims, 257–8.

abundance at its disposal was Germany's inefficiency in the exploitation of the occupied zone: total production of iron ore in the Aubon area during the war was 46 per cent of that achieved in the comparable period before the war.[119]

Therefore, Rathenau's visit to Scheüch was not an isolated act by a determined individual; it was effective precisely because it fitted into an existing context. Furthermore, part of that context were the views developed and espoused by Rathenau himself in the years immediately preceding the war: his own long-term perspective was Rathenau's best answer to the accusation that in the hectic days of August 1914 the ideas he expressed were not his own but those of Moellendorff.

As an industrialist, Rathenau was keenly aware of the economic rivalry between Germany and Britain. He therefore shared the expectations of those who feared a long war, who saw the blockade as a key element in its outcome, and who believed that national mobilization and the control and distribution of resources would be pivotal to its conduct.[120] In July 1912 he had advocated the idea of a German-led European customs union, *Mitteleuropa*, as a counterweight to the other main economic blocs in the world—the United States and the British empire. For Rathenau the war was an opportunity for the reordering of Germany's position on the international economic stage.[121] It was also the moment for a radical domestic restructuring which would produce a more rational division of resources and labour within German industry. Together with Moellendorff and others (including Kurt Riezler), Rathenau favoured a modified form of collectivism. He rejected the economic liberalism of the older generation in favour of greater state regulation. The KRA was thus not simply a wartime expedient but a stepping-stone to a new economic order. It built on pre-war demands for an economic general staff, and it projected its continuation into the post-war world.[122]

The rhetoric of the KRA was therefore socialist. But the criticism most frequently levelled at it was its imprisonment by capitalism. Its ethos, according to Otto Goebel, was more that of a private company than was suggested by Moellendorff's corporatist vision.[123] Rathenau's opponents saw the KRA as the creature of AEG's own interests, and observed with cynicism the transfer of staff (including Moellendorff) from one to the other. But the truth was that practicality had to be the parent of compromise. The state lacked both the credit to finance the acquisition of raw materials and the power to direct the work of

[119] Louis Kroll, 'The civilian population of Aubon, during the German occupation', in Patrick Fridenson (ed.), *1914–1918*, 47 (this essay is not reprinted in the English edition); see also Gatzke, *Germany's drive to the west*, 36.

[120] Hecker, *Rathenau*, 63, 68–9, 70, 82–5, 94.

[121] Ibid. 172–5; Fischer, *Germany's aims*, 28–9, 101–3.

[122] Hecker, *Rathenau*, 168; Burchardt, *Friedenswirtschaft und Kriegsvorsorge*, 147–9; Lutz, *Fall of the German empire*, ii. 90–1; Riezler, *Kurt Riezler*, 213, 261.

[123] Goebel, *Deutsche Rohstoffwirtschaft*, 23; Burchardt, *Tradition*, XV (1970), 180–6.

industry. Put negatively, the KRA was therefore a paradox, built on competing principles—those of collectivism on the one hand and of industrial self-government on the other.[124] Put positively, it was both a product and a promoter of the *Burgfrieden*, an attempt to pioneer a third way, which would end the polarity between capitalism and socialism by combining the best of both.[125]

The KRA itself was a state-run government department staffed largely by personnel seconded from industry. Its tasks were administrative, and embraced the collection of statistics, the maintenance of accounts, and (reflecting Rathenau's original concern) the management of Belgian resources. It initiated the policy of developing substitutes for those vital commodities that were increasingly unobtainable. It pioneered the imposition of price controls from the autumn of 1914. What it could not do, given the scale of the problem, was undertake the detailed work of managing the distribution and allocation of raw materials to specific industrial sectors.[126]

To do this it created *Kriegsrohstoff-Gesellschaften* (war raw-materials companies—normally abbreviated to *Kriegsgesellschaften*) for each category of raw material. The first of these was that for the metal industry, established on 2 September. Wool and chemicals soon followed. These, especially the first, were giants. The Kriegsmetall Aktiengesellschaft reckoned it had about 30,000 firms under its aegis. The tasks of reporting on metal stocks every two months and of fixing allowances of raw materials on a half-yearly basis were delegated to local intermediaries, *Metall-Vermittlungsstellen* or *Metall-Beratungsstellen*; although they encouraged convergence and centralization, these subordinate organizations had still swollen in number to about seventy by 1918.[127] At the opposite end of the scale, in cases where the handling and distribution of an individual raw material was not too great, *Abrechnungstellen* (clearing offices) were established rather than separate companies. Most *Kriegsgesellschaften* were established as joint stock companies, some as limited liability companies. The businessmen who ran the companies provided the initial capital at a fixed rate of interest (in most cases 4 per cent, but in some 5 per cent). No dividends were payable, and any profits accrued by the companies at the war's end reverted to the Reich. The job of the companies was to acquire the use of raw materials, either by requisition within Germany and its occupied territories or by importation from neutrals and allies. However, the ownership

[124] Ehlert, *Wirtschaftliche Zentralbehörde*, 45.
[125] Wolfgang Michalka, 'Kriegsrohstoffsbewirtschaftung, Walther Rathenau und die "kommende Wirtschaft"', and Dieter Krüger, 'Kriegssozialismus. Die Auseinandersetzung der Nationalökonomen mit der Kriegswirtschaft 1914–1918', in Michalka (ed.), *Der Erste Weltkrieg*; Rürup, 'Der "Geist" von 1914', 18–19; Kruse, *Krieg und nationale Integration*, 116–23.
[126] Hecker, *Rathenau*, 216–18, 235; Williamson, *Zeitschrift für Unternehmensgeschichte*, XXIII (1978), 124–8.
[127] Richard Tröger, 'Technik in der Metallwirtschaft', in Schwarte (ed.), *Technik im Weltkriege*, 516–18.

of the raw materials remained vested in individuals and not in the Reich: what was controlled by the *Kriegsgesellschaften* were the uses to which the materials were put. It was the responsibility of the companies to allocate resources according to the needs of their consumers. But those consumers were in many cases also the directors of the *Kriegsgesellschaften*, and were thus in a strong position to favour the interests of their own enterprises. They derived personal advantages from price control and efficient distribution. What Rathenau had done was to take the principle of cartelization and the German penchant for large company size, and put them at the centre of the war economy.

The workings of free enterprise, or—as the small firms who were not directly represented on the boards of the *Kriegsgesellschaften* saw it—of big business, were subject to three controls. First, the Reich could withdraw its guarantees which underwrote the companies' debts. These were often massive in relation to their share issue. In 1915 the Kriegsmetall Aktiengesellschaft had a share issue of 6 million marks, but a debt of 300 million; in the case of the Kriegswollbedarf Aktiengesellschaft the ratio of shares to debt never fell below 6:100 between 1916 and 1918, and on occasion rose as high as 6:150.[128] Secondly, central or local government commissioners served on the boards of the individual companies. Thirdly, the KRA itself, acting in the name of the government, had the final say in all decisions.

By the end of the war the KRA was a massive organization, employing over 20,000 people and divided into twenty-five departments with over 100 sections. There were 200 *Kriegsgesellschaften*.[129] The formation of such an important new governmental department could not be accomplished without generating bureaucratic friction, particularly at the outset. The amount of booty captured in Belgium and north-eastern France was exaggerated, and disappointment fostered suspicions that rival organizations had been favoured. An official report of 28 December 1914, commenting on these tensions, observed that the source of the problem was that nobody knew who owned the expropriated materials. Business organizations, like the chambers of commerce and the industrial associations, ranged themselves against the government's agencies, the KRA and the general staff. Clarity was not served by the friction between the latter two departments.[130]

The KRA was a creature of the army. Its legal basis was the Prussian law of siege of 1851, which appropriated emergency powers to the government in the

---

[128] Wiedenfeld, *Organisation der Kriegsrohstoff-Bewirtschaftung*, 47; generally on the workings of the KRA see Hecker, *Rathenau*, 220–67; Williamson, *Zeitschrift für Unternehmensgeschichte*, XXIII (1978), 118–36; Ehlert, *Wirtschaftliche Zentralbehörde*, 44–7.

[129] Pogge von Strandmann, *Rathenau*, 195–7; Wiedenfeld, *Organisation der Kriegsrohstoff-Bewirtschaftung*, 43; Feldman, *Great disorder*, 56.

[130] Hecker, *Rathenau*, 228.

event of war. It was subordinated to the Prussian War Ministry. This carried advantages: its philosophy was shaped by the collectivist needs of the war economy, not the more liberal patterns of peacetime thinking. Its relations with the War Ministry remained cordial and supportive throughout its existence. But its status also made the KRA vulnerable to the interventions both of OHL (which under Hindenburg and Ludendorff after 1916 took an increasing role in the war economy) and of the deputy commanding generals of corps areas (who were the local military commanders under the law of siege). Furthermore, it made the KRA specifically Prussian rather than German. Although the war ministries of Bavaria, Saxony, and Württemberg were quick to recognize the KRA, it had always to be wary of the accusation that it was acting in the interests of Prussian industry. Finally, the KRA was not recognized by the navy, which insisted that firms supply it with raw materials without having to be part of the KRA structure.

Nor did creation of the KRA in itself end the responsibility of the Ministry of the Interior for economic matters. On the very day that Rathenau saw Scheüch, Delbrück attended the first meeting of the war committee of German industry, formed three days previously by the central association of German manufacturers (Centralverband Deutscher Industrieller) and the manufacturers' league (Bund der Industrieller). He established a formal liaison between his department and the committee, as did the Prussian Ministry for Trade and Industry and the Imperial Naval Office. Although there were overlaps in personnel between the KRA and the war committee of German industry, the latter's agenda was different. Formed on the initiative of Heinrich Class of the Pan-German League and Alfred Hugenberg of Krupp, it was dominated by the banks and heavy industry: these were the people who were already manufacturing munitions, or who might do so. Their interests were those of capitalism; they wanted to regulate labour and to contest government bans on exports. Thus, the committee became the focus of liberal economic thought. It sought, in a resolution passed in December 1915, to hive off responsibility for trade, manufacturing, and industry from the secretary of state for the interior. By creating a separate ministry, business would be given a more powerful voice and German war production could be wrested from the growing grip of collectivism represented by the KRA.[131]

The battles which these disputes generated may have been a factor in spurring Rathenau's resignation on 1 April 1915. The accusations of profiteering, the feeling that large firms were benefiting at the expense of small, the backbiting over the links with AEG—all soured his enthusiasm for the task. Equally, however, Rathenau might reasonably have concluded that he had

---

[131] Ehlert, *Wirtschaftliche Zentralbehörde*, 40–1, 53–7; Gutsche, *Zeitschrift für Geschichtswissenschaft*, XVII (1970), 881–6; see Feldman, *Stinnes*, 382–3.

completed his mission, that the KRA was fully operational, and that he wished to be available in case he were offered the secretaryship of state at the Treasury (he was not).[132] His departure did not set back the advance of the KRA. His successor, groomed by Rathenau himself, was Major Joseph Koeth, who had headed a section in the Prussian War Ministry before 1914. Koeth confirmed the military, rather than entrepreneurial, ethos of the KRA. He appreciated the distinctive qualities and characteristics of a war economy. He enthused his colleagues, shaping the KRA according to his principles, and enthroning system and method in its workings.[133]

Four imported raw materials were particularly vital to Germany's war industry in 1914. These were cotton from the United States, camphor from Japan, pyrites from Spain, and saltpetre from Chile. All were ingredients in the manufacture of gunpowder. Powder production was the bottleneck in the German munitions industry.[134] It determined the pace in the expansion of German armaments as a whole: there was little point in having more guns if there was nothing for them to fire.

Furthermore, gunpowder's requirements for raw materials interacted with the needs of Germany's food supply. Saltpetre was not only employed in the production of nitric acid for explosives but also of nitrates for fertilizers: before the war Germany used a maximum of 40,000 tonnes of fixed nitrogen a year for industrial purposes (including many non-military ones), while 200,000 tonnes were consumed by the needs of agriculture.[135] The trade-off between powder production and food production was further highlighted when domestically produced raw materials were taken into account. Glycerine was derived from fats and oils; alcohol was distilled from potatoes. During the war sugar was fermented to produce both. Thus, agricultural yields would fall for lack of fertilizers, and an increasing proportion of those yields would themselves not be used as foodstuffs. Germany, it seemed, could not have guns *and* butter (or at least their equivalents), and would probably have neither.

In the long-war scenario the production of fixed nitrogen appeared to be Germany's most obvious and most significant vulnerability. But it was rarely alluded to in the discussions before 1914. Perhaps this was lack of foresight. However, in August 1914 Gustav Krupp von Bohlen und Halbach, of the armaments firm, was confident that Germany would be producing synthetic nitrates within a year.[136] The Kaiser Wilhelm Society for the Advancement of the Sciences, established in 1911, had spawned a series of research institutes

[132] Pogge von Strandmann, *Rathenau*, 195–7; Hecker, *Rathenau*, 244–67.
[133] Wiedenfeld, *Organisation der Kriegsrohstoff-Bewirtschaftung*, 38–9; Goebel, *Deutsche Rohstoffwirtschaft*, 23–4.
[134] Schwarte, *Weltkampf*, vi. 79; see also Geyer, *Deutsche Rüstungspolitik*, 104–5.
[135] Helfferich, *Weltkrieg*, 201, reckons the industrial requirement for pure nitrogen was 40,000 tonnes; Schwarte, *Technik im Weltkriege*, 538, gives 20,000 tonnes.
[136] Manchester, *Arms of Krupp*, 319.

designed not least to develop applied research for the purposes of international competition. As a result Germany's chemical industry was the most advanced in the world. It had already experimented with two processes for the production of fixed nitrogen. Germany generated nitrogen gas as an automatic by-product of its gasworks and coking plants. Adolph Frank and Nikodem Caro distilled the gas into liquid, and introduced it into electrically heated cylinders containing a mixture of calcium carbide and lime. The result—calcium cyanamide or lime nitrogen (*Kalkstickstoff* in German)—was therefore dependent on a combination of readily available raw materials and massive quantities of electricity. From it could be derived ammonal and ammonium nitrate. In 1914 two German factories produced 25,000 tonnes of calcium cyanamide. The second process, developed by Fritz Haber while professor of physical chemistry at Karlsruhe College of Technology, established that a mixture of nitrogen and hydrogen gases, when cleared of carbon dioxide and heated to between 500° and 550° centigrade, synthesized ammonia. Haber was well aware of the uses of chemistry in war, the army less so. In 1912, after his appointment to the Kaiser Wilhelm Institute for Physical Chemistry, Haber, a Jew, was rebuffed in his efforts to establish contact with the Prussian War Ministry. However, Carl Bosch at the Badische Anilin- und Sodafabrik (BASF) transferred Haber's laboratory findings to industrial production. In July 1914 BASF reckoned its annual output was 30,000 tonnes of sulphate of ammonia, equivalent to 6,000 tonnes of nitrogen.

On 1 October Emil Fischer, the presiding genius of the Kaiser Wilhelm Society and Germany's leading organic chemist, called at the War Ministry. His explanation of the infant processes for the production of nitrates laid the basis for links between science, industry, and army. The War Ministry established the 'Bureau Haber' as the basis for its own chemical section, and Moellendorff took the ammonia programme as a model for the new corporatist economy.[137] The impediments to the maximization of the synthetic fixation of nitrogen proved to be financial rather than scientific. Investment in new plant was held back for lack of agreement on its funding and on the fixing of prices. The deadlock was broken by Helfferich who, with his customary unconcern about fiscal rectitude, was prepared to put enhanced productivity ahead of any controls on profits. Most of the army's needs for ammonia were covered by the Badische Anilin- und Sodafabrik, which increased its annual output of nitrogen to 200,000 tonnes a year. The manufacture of calcium cyanamide was largely assumed by a state factory, the Bayerische Stickstoffwerke, taken over on the initiative of Helfferich after prodding by Gwinner of the Deutsche Bank, and able to produce 175,000 tonnes a year. Between February and December 1915 Germany's total output of calcium cyanamide was 380,000

---

[137] Johnson, *Kaiser's chemists*, esp.187; also Harris, *German History*, X (1992), 28–9.

tonnes, which corresponded to 76,000 tonnes of nitrogen. By the year's end industry was meeting 90 per cent of its needs, and agriculture 70 per cent. Over the war as a whole, Germany's production of nitrogen was two-and-a-half times greater than its total pre-war consumption over a comparable period.[138]

The fixing of nitrogen was only the most important of the chemical industry's contributions to the production of explosives. Spirits of turpentine were found to do just as well as Japanese camphor in the powder for all arms except infantry rifles. A substitute for nitrocellulose or gun cotton was developed through soaking paper in cellulose derived from wood. Wood was also the primary material in the production of acetone, which was used in the manufacture of the nitroglycerine powder needed for heavy artillery. Picric acid and trinitrotoluene were substituted for up to two-thirds of the nitroglycerine used in powder production, so freeing glycerine for explosives.[139]

Before the war German shells were filled with trinitrotoluene (TNT), prepared by acting upon toluene with a combination of sulphuric and nitric acid. Toluene itself was produced from coal, but efforts to improve the process in order to increase output and to economize on sulphuric acid were not particularly successful. Experiments with other coal-tar derivatives—benzol and phenol—produced explosives with only limited applications: trinitroanisol was suitable for mines and large-calibre guns, picric acid was manufactured in small quantities and used in fuses, and dinitrobenzol was poisonous and required great care when being loaded into shells. But the mixture of nitrocompounds (either TNT or dinitrobenzol) with the increasingly abundant ammonium nitrate in a ratio of 60 : 40 gave an explosive viable in most shells, known as ammonal. The loss of explosive power was compensated for by the economy in the use of TNT. The Germans found that a greater proportion of ammonium nitrate in the mixture made the ammonal harder to pour.[140]

This emphasis on powder and explosives was the reverse of what the War Ministry had anticipated before the war. It thought that the major block to increased munitions output would be the production of fuses and of the shells themselves.

Part of its concern was generated by Germany's dependence on imported copper. Germany continued to get some copper during the war from Norway, and later from Sweden and Bulgaria; it also produced its own, not least by telling the civilian population to disgorge its pots and pans in the winter of

---

[138] N. Caro, 'Die Stickstoffgewinnung im Kriege', in Schwarte (ed.), *Technik im Weltkriege*, 537–51; also ibid. 92–6; Schwarte, *Weltkampf*, ii. 80–2; Helfferich, *Weltkrieg*, 201–7; Gall *et al.*, *Deutsche Bank*, 145; Reichsarchiv, *Der Weltkrieg*, ix, 393.

[139] Schoen, *Geschichte des deutschen Feuerwerkswesens*, 1075–6.

[140] Schwarte (ed.), *Technik im Weltkriege*, 98–113; Wrisberg, *Wehr und Waffen*, 26, 64–6.

1915–16.[141] Brass was used in fuses and bullet cases, and the copper content of the second was 72 per cent. For the former, pressed zinc or zinc alloy was substituted; for the latter, iron stood duty. The driving rings for shells were also made of copper: therefore the shape of the ring was changed and the ring itself was made of soft iron. The number of driving rings on the 120 mm shrapnel shell was cut from five to two, and on the 150 mm shell from four to one. By the last year of the war only the 210 mm still used copper.[142] Copper consumption in munitions production was cut by seven-eighths.

The most pressing worry was the production of high-quality compressed steel, itself dependent on manganese. During the war Germany's only sources of manganese were Hungary and, after the end of 1915, Serbia.[143] In anticipation of this problem the War Ministry planned before the war to use shells made of cast iron, bored out of whole ingots. Thus, factories with simple turning-lathes and milling machines could be brought into service with immediate effect. Ultimately about 230 firms were involved in their manufacture. But the Germans lacked sufficient inspectors to ensure the maintenance of standards across so many establishments. Prussia struck a middle course between late delivery and high prices, whereas Bavaria opted for high prices and delivery within three months. The casting was not easy: inspectors reported holes right through the wall of the shell, slag and fragments in the casting, poor finishes at the mouth of the shell, and improperly fitted driving rings, all of which carried the risk of premature explosions. The shell itself was heavy, because weight of iron had to compensate for the robustness of compressed steel, and so it increased barrel wear. The thickness of the casing also reduced the space available for high explosive. Much of the pre-war effort had been devoted to finding acceptable explosives, and those types that were used, produced from derivatives of coal, attracted and retained excessive moisture. The shells could only take a simple contact fuse. The lower quantity of high explosive generated less smoke and so made observation hard and the correction of fire difficult, and the cast iron broke into fewer splinters. The gunners regarded the shells as fit only for training. Quality was therefore deliberately sacrificed to the interests of speed and scale of production. The first deliveries of the auxiliary ammunition were received in the third week of September, and they were issued to the front in mid-October. The original intention was to produce cast-iron shells for the field artillery only, but on 14 September the scheme was extended to shells for heavy guns. The production of cast-iron shells ceased after July 1915 when cast steel, rolled in the Thomas process, began to become available. The production of cast-steel shells continued—albeit

[141] Reichsarchiv, *Der Weltkrieg*, ix. 351; Cooper, *Behind the lines*, 114–15.
[142] Schoen, *Geschichte der deutschen Feuerwerkswesens*, 1055–7, 1060.
[143] Reichsarchiv, *Der Weltkrieg*, ix. 351.

with intermissions—alongside that of compressed steel for the rest of the war.[144]

The steel production problem also had its impact on the manufacture of the guns themselves. Before the war the steel for gun barrels was cast in crucibles to make it impermeable. But the expansion of production meant that steel produced in open hearths and furnaces, principally by the Siemens-Martin and Thomas processes, had to be used. The Siemens-Martin process was heavily dependent on aluminium, and most of Germany's bauxite came from France. The best steel before the war used 30 per cent tungsten, much of it imported from Spain. And nickel, which was employed to strengthen the barrels and gun shields, came from French New Caledonia. No shortages in any of these areas delayed munitions production during the war. Partly, this was achieved through a reduction in their use: the quantity of tungsten in high-quality steel was halved, and the proportion of nickel employed was cut from between 4 and 8 per cent to between 1 and 3 per cent. Partly, overseas supplies were maintained in spite of the blockade: nickel was received via France until 1915, was shipped from the United States in the cargo submarine *Deutschland* in 1916, and—together with aluminium—was exported from Scandinavia throughout the war. But the chief source was the expansion of domestic production—tungsten from Saxony, nickel from Silesia, and aluminium from bauxite deposits in Austria-Hungary.[145]

The primary responsibility for the administration of all orders for warlike material was vested in the ordnance depot (*Feldzeugmeisterei*) created in 1898 as a section subordinate to the *Allgemeine Kriegsdepartement* of the Prussian War Ministry. Comparable arrangements applied in Bavaria, and Saxony—although not in Württemberg, which had no state-run ordnance factories. Six workshops—four in Prussia, one in Bavaria, and one in Saxony—were responsible for the production of artillery of calibres up to 210 mm. Others manufactured rifles and ammunition. But, as elsewhere in Europe, the state did not sustain an arms industry large enough to equip its forces in the event of war. The primary functions of the government workshops were to regulate prices and to set standards to which private industry could conform. They kept in play some elasticity in productive capacity: in producing a single item of equipment they might give contracts to over 100 small firms which would otherwise have been driven out of the arms industries by the big cartels. They also provided technical training for the army's own supply and repair services. But in general their key characteristic was that they were adapted to the limited

---

[144] Schoen, *Geschichte des deutschen Feuerwerkswesens*, 586, 647, 1045–6, 1050–1, 1060–1, 1066–7; Schwarte (ed.), *Technik im Weltkriege*, 82–91, 523; Wrisberg, *Wehr und Waffen*, 22–3, 63, 66, 89; Schwarte, *Weltkampf*, vi. 72.

[145] Schwarte (ed.), *Technik im Weltkriege*, 83, 91, 519–24; Jindra, *Jahrbuch für Wirtschaftsgeschichte* (1976), Teil I, 147–50.

peace of peacetime replacement: the ordnance depots in combination employed only 16,000 workers. They were not even big enough to cope with the rate of expansion between 1911 and 1914: in the last full year of peace 60 per cent of the funds spent on war materials went to private industry, and only 40 per cent to cover procurement from the state's own factories.[146]

The War Ministry was therefore well aware that in the event of hostilities it would be dependent on the productive capacities of independent firms. The sector comprised about twenty-four businesses before 1914, with between 156,000 and 212,000 workers, or a maximum of 1.9 per cent of the industrial labour force.[147] Only three of these manufactured artillery, and the most important was Friedrich Krupp. The link between the rise of Krupp and the forging of the German nation, symbolized by the performance of the firm's steel breech-loaders in 1870, was sustained by the close links between the Kaiser and the Krupp family.[148] But both sides saw the dangers in an excessively monopolistic relationship. Orders for artillery were not sufficient to sustain Krupp in peace, and the company could not afford to hold idle plant against the contingency of a possible spurt in demand in wartime. Between 1910 and 1914 only 12.8 per cent of the firm's artillery and munition orders were for delivery to the German army.[149] In the financial year 1913/14 war material accounted for only 54 per cent of the turnover of Krupp's Essen works (and therefore an even smaller percentage of the whole), and armour plate a further 11 per cent.[150] Krupp diversified into railways, shipbuilding, and iron and steel production. It also built up its export markets. The Ministry of War actively supported the latter policy, recognizing that foreign purchases could enable Krupp to carry an additional capacity for armaments production in peace which would become available for the German army's use in war.[151] Thus, foreign powers—including Belgium, which bought Krupp quick-firers as well as heavy artillery for the defences of Antwerp—were indirectly covering many of Germany's research and development costs. Nor was it only through the encouragement of exports that the Ministry of War applied the discipline of the market to Krupp. It also promoted competition within the German arms business. The Rheinischen Metallwaren- und Maschinenfabrik was founded in 1889. Although far behind Krupp in scale of output (its workforce in 1914, at 8,000, was only just over a tenth of that of the Essen giant), its technical

---

[146] Reichsarchiv, *Weltkrieg: Kriegsrüstung und Kriegswirtschaft*, i. 391–4; Erzberger, *Die Rüstungsausgaben des Deutschen Reichs*, 40–3.

[147] Epkenhans, *War in History* (forthcoming).

[148] Pogge von Strandmann, 'Der Kaiser und die Industriellen. Vom Primat der Rüstung', in J. Röhl (ed.), *Der Ort Kaiser Wilhelms II*, 120–4.

[149] Stevenson, *Armaments and the coming of war*, 25.

[150] Burchardt, *Zeitschrift für Unternehmensgeschichte*, XXXII (1987), 74, 78.

[151] Manchester, *Arms of Krupp*, 315; Stevenson, *Armaments and the coming of war*, 37; Epkenhans, *War in History* (forthcoming).

competence was highly rated. Under its director Heinrich Erhardt, Rhein-metall developed a quick-firing field gun which won it orders from Britain, Russia, Norway, and Austria-Hungary. Persuaded by its success in overseas markets, the German army bought artillery from the firm after 1905. The Prussian War Ministry, like the Imperial Naval Office, used the competition for its orders to force down prices. By 1905 the price which had been quoted by Krupp in 1897 for steel for 15 cm artillery shells was cut through competitive tendering by 50 per cent, and that for ready-use ammunition for the same gun by up to 40 per cent. Contracts won from the army by Krupp stagnated, and constituted only about 40 per cent of the firm's turnover after 1900.[152] In 1912 it was revealed that Krupp had been bribing members of the artillery testing commission, and that secret documents had been passed from the ministry to the firm. But, although outwardly this suggested a dependence that would prefigure the notion of a 'military-industrial complex', in reality it confirmed the highly competitive nature of the business. The main thrust of the Reichstag committee of inquiry into the scandal was not to impugn the need for the close relationship between Krupp and the services, but to ensure that the state was getting value for money.[153]

The astuteness of the War Ministry's management of Krupp was testified to by the company's state of readiness for industrial mobilization in 1914. Between 1903 and 1908 it added 2.1 hectares per annum to its workshop area; between 1906 and 1914 it expanded at a rate of 2.6 hectares. In the summer of 1914 it increased its share capital from 180 million marks to 250 million, so providing it with the finance to enable a further addition to its plant. In the first year of the war it added thirty-five new workshops in Essen alone, and in the first half of 1915 it built a new shell factory from scratch. Krupp's plant grew at the rate of 18.7 hectares a year between 1915 and 1918, resulting in a doubling of its overall size.

The army's problem in 1914 was not its relationship with the existing producers, but its failure to anticipate the need to draw in new ones. Krupp itself, aware that a long war and increased munitions consumption could break its monopoly, had no interest in promoting a rethink.[154] By the summer of 1914 the firm's monthly peacetime output was 280 light and medium guns and four heavy guns. The targets set by the mobilization plan generated by the War Ministry were little different: 200 field guns and 144 torpedo-boat guns. The ministry aimed to reach a monthly production figure of 200,000 field artillery shells within twelve to sixteen weeks of mobilization. Krupp alone already

[152] Reichsarchiv, *Weltkrieg: Kriegsrüstung und Kriegswirtschaft*, i. 386–7; Mollin, *Auf dem Wege*, 336–7; Epkenhans, *Wilhelminische Flottenrüstung*, 197; Erzberger, *Die Rüstungsausgaben des Deutschen Reichs*, 36, 51–6, 64–5.

[153] Epkenhans, *Wilhelminische Flottenrüstung*, 366–90; Manchester, *Arms of Krupp*, 312–15.

[154] Feldman, *Stinnes*, 395.

manufactured 150,000 shells of all calibres every month, and Germany's output for August, in other words within four weeks of mobilization, was 170,000.[155]

The ministry's thinking on wartime production was determined by the need to make good existing stocks, to replenish ammunition as it was fired, and to repair or replace damaged or captured artillery pieces. What it had not considered was the possible pressure to augment its overall equipment levels. In 1914 the War Ministry requisitioned from Krupp 108 7.5 cm field guns ordered by Brazil. It appropriated other smaller orders placed by foreign powers, allocating many of them to Turkey.[156] But it did not place massive orders over and above its existing contracts. In December daily production of rifles was 2,300, only just above the figure of 1,900 planned for the war's outbreak, and the result was that the army had received only a sixth of the rifles it needed. The manufacture of small-arms ammunition had not risen beyond its initial target. When five new reserve corps were created in October 1914 their field artillery was organized in four-gun, rather than six-gun, batteries not for tactical reasons but because of shortages of pieces. By the end of 1915 the army had only 5,300 field guns, when it had originally hoped to have 5,588 on mobilization. The stocks of heavy artillery had risen, but through the capture of fortresses such as Antwerp (armed with a total of 2,500 guns, including Krupp 15 cm howitzers), Maubeuge (600 guns), and Longwy (which yielded a further 100 guns and 250,000 rounds), rather than through domestic production. Actual output of heavy artillery did not rise until after 1916. Only in the case of machine-guns (from 2,400 to 8,000—and 1,900 more were captured) and of field howitzers (from 950 to 1,700) was there a significant growth in initial holdings by the end of 1915.[157]

Heavy industry, the armaments sector apart, was slow to respond to the opportunities presented by the war between 1914 and 1916. To many the arms business seemed a risky undertaking: entrepreneurs reckoned that investment in the appropriate plant might soon prove redundant, especially given the evidence of the early German victories. And the Treasury's espousal of liberal economic principles left the issue of industrial conversion to the workings of profit incentives rather than to state direction. Even those firms ready to convert to war production found the task far from straightforward. In peacetime the War Ministry had set stringent specifications. The new contractors found it hard to meet these standards, and the ministry was slow to relax its expectations. In September 1914 AEG contracted to produce 150,000 shells a

[155] Burchardt, *Zeitschrift für Unternehmensgeschichte*, XXXII (1987), 74–5; Reichsarchiv, *Der Weltkrieg*, ix. Anlage 5.

[156] Jindra, *Jahrbuch für Wirtschaftsgeschichte* (1976), Teil I, 152–5, 159–60; Manchester, *Arms of Krupp*, 330.

[157] Mollin, *Auf dem Wege*, 329; Wrisberg, *Wehr und Waffen*, 53–4; Reichsarchiv, *Der Weltkrieg*, ix. 380–7, and Anlage 3; Schoen, *Geschichte des deutschen Feuerwerkswesens*, 615, 782, 901–3, 968–72; Benary, *Ehrenbuch der deutschen Feldartillerie*, 36.

month, but its first delivery was only 80,000, and many of those did not satisfy the inspectors.[158]

The onset of position warfare lowered the levels of technological sophistication required, at least in some respects. The Germans embraced one weapon of eighteenth-century warfare, the hand grenade, because it used muscle power rather than scarce powder as a propellant.[159] Siege conditions also enabled the *Minenwerfer*, a small artillery piece which fired mines at high angles over short ranges (effectively, in other words, a trench mortar), to come into its own. In August 1914 the German army possessed seventy heavy and 110 medium *Minenwerfer*; by January 1918 total deliveries amounted to 1,322 heavy *Minenwerfer*, 2,476 medium, and 13,329 light.[160] The *Minenwerfer* was simpler to construct than a field gun—indeed, the slowness in the increase of their output in 1915 encouraged the infantry to improvise their own—and thus foundries without a pre-war background in the arms business could be drawn into their production. Furthermore, the fact that they fired projectiles over short ranges also economized in powder.

The *Minenwerfer* was symptomatic of a broader trend—a proliferation in types of artillery and of the shells fired from them. Fifty-three different guns were in use at the front in 1916, and seventy-seven by April 1917.[161] Shells diversified according to their precise applications so as to make the best use of explosives: firing at flatter trajectories but with less powder reduced the wear on the gun. Germany produced 200 different sorts of shell in the war, and of these ninety were still in production at the war's end.[162] As a result, twenty-five factories were able to produce complete guns, 463 produced components for gun carriages, and forty-five produced components for gun barrels.[163] In late 1916 Hamburg still had fifty-eight firms appropriate to the production of munitions that were not being used. But the accusation that the structure of the war economy, and the workings of the KRA in particular, favoured large firms was not wholly true: of ninety-two firms which had munitions contracts, only fifteen employed more than 100 people.[164] Artillery specifications were adapted as much to the capabilities of German industry as they were shaped to the requirements of trench warfare.

Standardization was therefore sacrificed. A massive expansion in orders was accompanied by a multiplication of types. Thus, a double strain was put on Germany's procurement organization. On the outbreak of war over forty different agencies had responsibilities for procurement. The individual states

[158] Hecker, *Rathenau*, 306–7.
[159] Schoen, *Geschichte des deutschen Feuerwerkswesens*, 618.
[160] Schwarte, *Technik im Weltkriege*, 47–59; Wrisberg, *Wehr und Waffen*, 76.
[161] Wrisberg, *Wehr und Waffen*, 59, 99.
[162] Schwarte, *Weltkampf*, vi. 91; Gascouin, *L'Évolution de l'artillerie*, 119–20, 124–8.
[163] Wrisberg, *Wehr und Waffen*, 17.   [164] Ferguson, *Paper and iron*, 105.

and the individual services were only a part of the structure: within the army each branch—artillery, pioneers, communications, infantry—had its inspectorates responsible for the acquisition of its own equipment.[165] Before 1914 the War Ministry had developed an innovative approach to new technology; it recognized that sophisticated machinery could substitute for manpower as a force multiplier. But this approach was most deeply embedded in the lower echelons, and many of the ministry's technical specialists left their posts for service at the front.[166]

At the interface between the War Ministry and the general staff stood the *Feuerwerkern*, literally 'fireworkers', who were responsible for the testing, development, production, and inspection of munitions. In 1901 they had been detached from the siege artillery and placed under the command of the Ordnance Department, the *Feldzeugmeisterei*, itself subordinate to the War Ministry. The *Feuerwerkern* served at artillery depots, in munitions factories, and on testing commissions; they were responsible for the research, development, production, and inspection of all forms of shell. But, as technical specialists, they lacked authority in an army which put weight on field command and officer status. The *Feuerwerker* was frustrated by holding an intermediate appointment, not unlike that of the *Deckoffizier* in the navy. Promoted through the ranks, he would be in his mid-forties by the time he reached the equivalent of captain, and even then was subordinate for disciplinary purposes to artillery officers who were his juniors. The nature of his expertise alerted him to the relationship between technology and tactical innovation, but it was not an awareness vouchsafed to the general staff. Franke, the *Feldzeugmeister* in 1914, said that he had not once been called to a meeting to address the issue of the army's ammunition supply in the event of war.[167]

The consequences of treating its technical advisers as part of a peacetime establishment for home service went beyond personal disgruntlement (although this continued throughout the war), and even beyond the failure to relate operations to new technology. The army tripled in size on mobilization but the establishment of *Feuerwerkern* did not. Their technical school, closed on the outbreak of war, only reopened in March 1918. Efforts to recall retired *Feuerwerkern* were not likely to prove successful: they were too old on retirement to constitute an effective reserve, and innovation rapidly rendered their expertise obsolete. As the German armies advanced into Belgium, they did so without an establishment of *Feuerwerkern* at their headquarters. Captured munitions stocks were destroyed for lack of technical advice. As the war

[165] Feldman, *Army, industry and labor*, 57–9; Geyer, *Deutsche Rüstungspolitik*, 103.

[166] Geyer, *Deutsche Rüstungspolitik*, 91–2; Hecker, *Rathenau*, 105–11, for examples; Wrisberg, *Wehr und Waffen*, 115–17.

[167] Mombauer, 'Moltke', 39; on *Feuerwerkern*, see Schoen, *Geschichte des deutschen Feuerwerkswesens*, in particular 332–42, 584–9, 589, 598, 607–9, 623, 982, 988–9, 994–8, 1059.

stabilized, dumps in the field were left in the hands of reservists who did not know what they were looking after, who sometimes issued shells of the wrong calibre, and who lost ammunition (and lives) through negligence or ignorance. The guns themselves were not properly cleaned or maintained. These problems were exacerbated as the types of ordnance and the shells they fired proliferated, thus increasing the requirement for specialist knowledge. They were never fully overcome: in April 1917 one German battery on the Aisne fired 27,000 rounds of blank ammunition, as it had been issued with the wrong charges. From 1915 *Feuerwerkern* were allocated to jobs in the field and, even if too few to micro-manage such situations, they could at least combat shell shortage through the introduction of better systems for reporting and distribution. But the corollary of efficiency gains at the front was a loss of inspectors at the rear just as new firms were entering production. Their frustrations were not eased as they dealt with gunners firing shells whose manufacturing defects they themselves could have prevented if they had been given the power of ubiquity.

One—if hardly the only—cause of the *Feuerwerker*'s travails was the confusion between the respective provinces of the War Ministry and the general staff. Tensions between the two had been worsened by the increases of 1912 and 1913. The Prussian War Ministry, assailed in the Reichstag by south Germans and socialists, felt undervalued by the general staff, and was increasingly convinced that its chief was dominated by, in the words of Franz Wandel, 'unruly and ambitious heads'.[168] After 14 September 1914 Falkenhayn, as Prussia's war minister, was also de facto chief of the general staff. The daily demands of the latter office tended to take priority over the longer-term considerations of the former. It was often not clear in which capacity Falkenhayn acted. In the autumn of 1914 he used Max Bauer to liaise directly with the armaments industry on munitions production. Before the war Bauer had worked with Krupp on the development of the 42 cm gun required to deal with the Liège fortifications. That was a task generated by the general staff's adaptation of the war plan, and Bauer saw himself as a representative of the interests of OHL. He railed against the War Ministry for its bureaucratic ways and its slowness to widen the network of firms with which it placed orders. By July 1915 he had created an independent section within the general staff, thus heightening departmental sensitivities.[169] Falkenhayn was relieved of the Ministry of War in January 1915, but the step did little to clarify the division of its responsibilities from those of the general staff. His successor, Adolf Wild von Hohenborn, had been his deputy; the experience did not stimulate his appetite for the task. As early as 1912 Wild had resolved that he would not become war

[168] Granier, *Militärgeschichtliche Mitteilungen*, 38 (1985), 142; see also 124, 145–6, 147.
[169] Vogt, *Bauer*, 30, 40–4; Bauer, *Grosse Krieg im Feld und Heimat*, 25, 61.

minister 'at any price', and when patriotic duty left him no option his response was not to rise to the challenge but to tell his wife 'it's too much'.[170] He remained in thrall to Falkenhayn, and infuriated the commanders at the eastern front by preferring to spend his time at OHL rather than in Berlin.[171]

Thus, in the post-war historiography, dominated by Hindenburg, Ludendorff, and the preoccupations of the third OHL after 1916, the War Ministry was easy meat. Failures in productivity were attributed to its methods of management. Wandel, who had been deemed physically unfit to command a division in 1913, was nonetheless recalled to be Wild's deputy. Like Wild, he preferred the ambience of general headquarters to Berlin, and he saw it as no part of the ministry's job to be on close terms with industrialists or to acquire specialist knowledge.[172] The ministry was, therefore, not its own best advocate. Its response to the central question of powder production was to split the difference between what was needed and what could be manufactured. Powder production, therefore, lagged behind both the demands of the front and the ministry's own projections. The effect was to turn comparative success into apparent failure. Germany's monthly powder production in August 1914 was only 1,240 tonnes, when the ministry's own calculations suggested that 7,000 were required—a total only just exceeded for the four months to the year's end. An interim target of 3,500 tonnes per month was raised to 4,500 tonnes in December 1914, a month in which actual production reached 2,170 tonnes. By the time output had reached 4,750 tonnes (in October 1915), the goal had been raised again (in February 1915) to 6,000 tonnes. A revised figure of 8,000 tonnes, established in December 1915, was attained in April 1917, and one of 10,000 tonnes, adopted in July 1916, in October 1917. The effect of the targets was to create an impression of ministerial inefficiency when, in reality, the expansion of production was continuous. The figure of 8,000 tonnes was achieved only a month behind schedule, and from March 1918 production was exceeding expectations. The growth in powder production set the pace of gun production, but here too there was relative success. Germany's monthly output of field guns was 100 in December 1914, 270 in the summer of 1915, and 480 at the year's end. By then 3,500 new field guns had been manufactured since the war's commencement. Krupp's figures make it clear that 1915, not 1916, saw the most significant increases in output. The proportion of the firm's Essen works devoted to war material rose to 79 per cent of turnover in 1914–15 (as opposed to 54 per cent before the war), and reached what became a plateau of 82 per cent in 1915–16. Actual output of new guns of all calibres doubled in the second year of the war, 1 August 1915 to 31 July 1916, to 2,481; it fell back to

[170] Wild, *Briefe*, 4, 53.   [171] Janssen, *Der Kanzler und der General*, 80.
[172] Granier, *Militärgeschichtliche Mitteilungen*, 38 (1985), 134–5.

2,276 in the following year. Germany's overall stocks remained low, not so much because of inadequate output but because of damage and destruction at the front. Every month, over the war as a whole, an average of 3,000 guns of all calibres required some form of repair. In the first year of the war Krupp mended more guns than it made new ones, 1,535 compared to 1,264. In 1915 improvised shell production was responsible for as much damage as enemy fire: 2,300 field guns and 900 light howitzers were destroyed through premature explosions. The 6th army reckoned to lose 20 per cent of its guns every day in a major battle, and attributed only 2 to 4 per cent of those losses to enemy action. Germany's artillery was lost three and a half times over during the course of the war.[173]

The most obvious manifestation of the War Ministry's success was that shell shortage figured only rarely as a constraint on operations in 1915. Between August and December 1914 total consumption of field gun, light and heavy field howitzer, 10 cm gun, and mortar ammunition was 260 per cent of output. But in December 1914 monthly shell production for field artillery reached 1.2 million rounds and for light howitzers 414,000, almost a sevenfold increase on August. By the end of 1915, when output of field-gun shells had reached 2.1 million per month and of light howitzer ammunition 800,000, only 73 per cent of the year's production had been fired—and this despite the fact that in the autumn battles field guns had been firing 349 rounds a day and light howitzers 325. Falkenhayn himself declared that there were no problems after the spring of 1915, and this situation persisted until June 1916.[174]

However, the achievement of this short-term objective should not be allowed to gainsay the existence of longer-term structural problems within the war industries and their management. The War Ministry persisted in seeing the production of munitions in isolation from the German economy as a whole. By 1915 Germany's net national product had fallen to 79 per cent of its 1913 total. It continued to fall, and so did aggregate industrial production, which declined from 81 per cent of its 1914 total in 1915 to 77 per cent in 1916. Within heavy industry, coal production in 1915 was 78 per cent of its 1913 total, iron and steel 68 per cent, and non-ferrous metals 72 per cent. Germany was, of course, an exporter both of coal and of iron and steel before the war, and in 1914 it had lost many of its export markets. Thus, the implications of the fall should not be exaggerated. Outputs in all three categories would rise again in

[173] Wrisberg, *Wehr und Waffen*, 16–17, 60, 88–9, 91–4; Max Schwarte, 'Waffen und Munition-Erzeugung und Verbrauch', in Jost and Felger (eds.), *Was wir vom Weltkrieg nicht wissen*, 343; Reichsarchiv, *Der Weltkrieg*, ix. 383, and Anlage 5; Burchardt, *Zeitschrift für Unternehmensgeschichte*, XXXII (1987), 76–8; Schoen, *Geschichte des deutschen Feuerwerkswesens*, 625.
[174] Reichsarchiv, *Der Weltkrieg*, ix. 394, and Anlage 5; Schoen, *Geschichte des deutschen Feuerwerkswesens*, 619; Falkenhayn, *General headquarters*, 45–6; Wild, *Briefe*, 163. For local shortages, see Rommel, *Attacks*, 83.

1916 and 1917—although only that of non-ferrous metals would exceed its 1913 figure.[175]

The ultimate constraint on increased productivity was the labour supply. But explanations for the initial problems of 1914–15 are more specific. In 1914 the war industries lost more workers in reserved occupations than did the civil industries. In the chemical sector, mobilization deprived Bosch of 52 per cent of its workforce and Bayer of almost 50 per cent. In 1915 the situation began to be rectified, and the total number in reserved occupations in civil industries was halved, but not until 1917 would those in war production exceed the pre-1914 total.[176] The pressures within, and from, war industry caused the commanding generals in certain districts to plan for the militarization of the labour supply. In October 1914 a scheme was bruited in Allenstein to make war-related work compulsory for the entire population, and regulations to limit the mobility of workers, as competition between firms drove up wages, were introduced in Würzburg in March 1915.[177] Falkenhayn proposed to incorporate such steps in a co-ordinated plan for all Germany in June 1915, but he was dissuaded by Wandel, who preferred to rely on voluntarism and patriotism. Wandel argued, moreover, that skilled workers in sufficient numbers had already been released from the army back to industry.[178]

One calculation suggests that between 30 and 40 per cent of skilled workers were called up in 1914.[179] Even if Wandel was right, and the army had returned many of these workers by 1915, military service continued to reduce the skills base of Germany's workforce. Industrial training was forfeit to short-term necessity, and by 1916 the numbers of apprentices in Berlin had fallen from 25,000 to 7,800.[180] This loss of skills has been adduced as one explanation for the fact that while output fell, the number of workers in key industries rose.[181] But the implication in such an argument is an acceptance of conservatism in relation to the management of labour. The point has, after all, been developed in precisely opposite terms for Britain; there the status of the skilled worker, largely protected in the war, is seen as a restraint on the introduction of new methods of production and so a block on increased output.

The essential point in Germany is that labour shortages in 1914 were not sufficiently acute to demand new practices. Germany, after all, conscripted far fewer of its urban workers than did France. Moreover, the short-term effect of

[175] Roesler, *Finanzpolitik*, 64–7, 221; Feldman, *Great disorder*, 78; Kocka, *Facing total war*, 27; Ferguson, *Pity of war*, 249–50; Ferguson, *Paper and iron*, 110; Mai, *Das Ende des Kaiserreichs*, 108.

[176] Mai, *Das Ende des Kaiserreichs*, 94–5, 110; Ferguson, *Pity of war*, 264, 267.

[177] Kruse, *Krieg und nationale Integration*, 173.

[178] Afflerbach, *Falkenhayn*, 317–20.

[179] Gunther Mai, '"Verteidigungskrieg" und "Volksgemeinschaft"', in Michalka (ed.), *Der Erste Weltkrieg*, 587.

[180] Eve Rosenhaft, 'Restoring moral order on the home front: compulsory savings plans for young workers in Germany 1916–19', in Coetzee and Shevin-Coetzee (eds.), *Authority, identity*, 90.

[181] Ferguson, *Pity of war*, 264; Ferguson, *Paper and iron*, 107.

mobilization was to create unemployment, as firms which lost a sizeable proportion of their labour to the services or which manufactured goods for which demand tumbled felt it was uneconomic to continue. In December 1914 unemployment in Germany was three times higher than usual for the time of year.[182] War industries proved more prodigal in their use of labour, not less. At Daimler, the leading manufacturer of aero engines for the War Ministry, the number of workers per machine rose from 1.8 to 2.4 over the war as a whole. What is striking, therefore, is the failure of Daimler to change their production processes in order to maximize output per machine. The guaranteeing of profits and of manpower by the state made for conservatism in the production methods employed.[183]

In this respect the KRA proved a false dawn. Germany circumvented both of its immediate crises—that of raw materials and that of munitions output. The compromise which the KRA embodied worked for the time being. But it did so without forcing a conclusion between two rival economic philosophies—that of collectivism and that of free enterprise. It therefore postponed any final resolution of the dilemma as to which government agency was to direct Germany's economic mobilization—Prussia's War Ministry or the Reich's Interior Ministry. And implicit in this tension was the continuing lack of an industry ministry for Germany as a whole.

The absence of overall co-ordination was played out in sharpening relations between the War Ministry and the manufacturers. The ministry's policy of proliferating orders did not include concentrating contracts for specific types of munitions with particular firms, and thus industry complained of a lack of continuity. The War Ministry, for its part, found that a rapid increase in the number of contractors in 1914 resulted in a loss of price control. When, early in 1915, it began to exercise greater direction, the representatives of heavy industry squealed.[184] In April 1915 a long-term plan for the development of the war economy centralized army orders, and tightened controls over exports and imports. The *Kriegsgesellschaften* were treated increasingly as representatives of the central authorities rather than of independent companies.[185] Industry responded that it could only maximize its productivity if it were free to do so; the army saw control as the only means to eliminate waste. Some soldiers, like Bauer, may have had close relationships with some firms, like Krupp. But ultimately the objectives of the army were the waging of war while those of industry were the maximization of profit. Conflict was more likely than collusion.

Domestically, therefore, the establishment of the KRA proved a less dazzling triumph than its initial success promised. Internationally also, the con-

[182] Armeson, *Total warfare and compulsory labor*, 7.   [183] Bellon, *Mercedes*, 91.
[184] Feldman, *Army, industry, and labor*, 55–64.   [185] Goebel, *Deutsche Rohstoffwirtschaft*, 28.

sequences of Rathenau's efforts turned out to be rather mixed. His pre-war notion of a Central European economic bloc, based on Germany and Austria-Hungary, was pressed into a quasi-existence by the enforced dependence generated by the war. The pooling of raw materials, and their distribution according to the needs of war-related industries, seemed likely to achieve their greatest efficiencies through economies of scale. Thus, the most readily available device for giving *Mitteleuropa* practical effect was the extension of the principles of the KRA from Germany into the Habsburg empire. But in both objectives—the establishment of a common trading area and the direction of their industries towards a common goal—the Central Powers were disappointed.

Again, initial success raised expectations of more. Austria-Hungary was critically dependent on Germany for trade even before the outbreak of war. Of its annual imports of 22.6 million tons, 16.5 million were derived from Germany or transshipped through Germany from the harbours of northern Europe. The Habsburg empire, for all its size, was effectively landlocked: only 11 per cent of its imports and 13 per cent of its exports were seaborne.[186] Its principal port, Trieste, was at the end of a maritime cul-de-sac, and easily blockaded. Once war was declared, Italy remained a southern conduit for Mediterranean trade, but after May 1915 even this route was closed. Therefore, Germany's economic controls—and particularly its curb on exports in anticipation of Britain's blockade—had an immediate effect on Austria-Hungary. Transshipments routed to Austria via Holland and Germany ceased. Austria-Hungary was similarly unmindful of its ally in the application of comparable laws, which, although less significant, checked the movement of goods via Italy or Trieste to Germany. At a conference in Berlin on 24 September 1914 the two powers moved swiftly to re-establish unrestricted trade across their mutual frontier, and in particular to restore the movement of transshipments. Germany insisted, however, that the goods it exported to its ally must not be for the purposes of speculation but must be consigned to the war administration. Germany's co-operation in securing raw materials for the Austro-Hungarian war effort was conditional on its ally establishing an organization comparable to the KRA.[187]

The trading agreement of 24 September, therefore, pointed forward to the creation of a joint Austro-German economic organization. However, in practice the exploitation of occupied areas produced friction, not collaboration. Talk of a customs union, developed in 1915, foundered, not least over the issue of Poland. Germany was prepared to let Vienna control Poland—the so-called 'Austro-Polish solution'—but on condition that Austria-Hungary was in its turn subordinated to Berlin. Caught increasingly in the thicket of war aims,

---

[186] Bell, *Blockade of Germany*, 362, 366.　　[187] Riedl, *Industrie Österreichs*, 24–8.

immediate economic co-operation was confined to the procurement of only a few raw materials. In August 1915 Germany assumed responsibility for the entire rubber supply of the Central Powers. In January 1916 Austria-Hungary did the same for textiles and leather. The two powers also avoided competing against each other for food imports. But there was no reduction in tariffs in order to stimulate trade.[188] By late 1915 evidence that Austria was pursuing its own economic objectives in eastern Europe, including covert trade with Russia, soured the relationship yet further.[189]

Austria-Hungary's industrial mobilization was, therefore, accomplished much more independently of Germany than either the empire's comparative economic backwardness or its relative military unpreparedness suggested was probable. The process was facilitated by the experience of the economic consequences of mobilization in the Balkan crisis. The emergency war law of 1912 gave almost unlimited powers to the joint War Ministry in the event of hostilities. Although drafted to enable the requisitioning of transport, supplies, billets, and manpower in the area of operations, its remit extended to the whole empire. Entire businesses engaged in the production of war-related material were eligible to be taken over by the army; their employees became liable to military law and were subject to the army's direction. What concerned most commentators were the implications for civil liberties. Workers as well as soldiers were conscripted. The war could become the means to enable 'unlimited internal reaction' against irridentist nationalists.[190] In economic terms, however, the significance of the act was that it enshrined the principles of collectivism and state control from the war's outset.

The war, therefore, transformed the joint War Ministry from an agency responsible for the army's budget and for the procurement of weapons into a surrogate economic ministry for the empire as a whole. Eleven new departments were grafted onto its existing fifteen. More importantly, a war supervision office (Kriegsüberwachungsamt—significantly translated by the liberal Josef Redlich as war surveillance office) was created by the supreme army command (AOK) and the ministry. Although administered and chaired by a general, its meetings were attended by representatives of the ministries of finance, the interior, trade, justice, transport, and foreign affairs. But the war supervision office did not evolve into a supreme direction for the dual monarchy's war economy. From the outset Hungary refused to recognize its authority. Its remit was thus confined to Austria and Bosnia-Herzogovina. Furthermore, a decree of 10 October, following the spirit of the Austro-German agreement of the previous month, empowered the Austrian Ministry

---

[188] Wegs, 'Austrian economic mobilization', 70–80; on war aims, see also Soutou, L'Or et le sang, 92–102; Fischer, Germany's aims, 200–12.
[189] Weber, Eagles on the crescent, 119–25.
[190] Redlich, Austrian war government, 62.

of Trade to take charge of the supply of raw materials and the organization of production. Thus economic authority, even within Austria alone, was divided. Many decisions taken by the war supervision office were no more than the basis for further negotiation both within Austria and with Hungary.[191]

Business response to the establishment—at least in theory—of state control was less hostile than any dogma about the virtues of capitalism might have suggested. Army contractors before the war had already bound themselves to holding raw material stocks sufficient to be able to increase their deliveries two- or threefold on mobilization. In other words, security of orders and of resources could offset loss of economic freedom. A similar response was evident when the 1912 law was applied. Those firms put under military administration knew they were assured of raw materials and of labour, that strikes would be curbed, and that their businesses would remain in operation.[192]

The danger that confronted the Austro-Hungarian war economy seemed to be less that of opposition to collectivism and more the loss of entrepreneurial flair. Of the three forms of military administration, one involved ownership by the army and another management by it (the third left the owner *in situ*). The soldiers who ran these firms tended to be reservists, unfit for active service, and more interested in the discipline of the labour force than in the processes of production.[193] Under the decree of 10 October 1914 the business activity of Austria was divided into two heads. Those businesses dependent on imports or exports, that used ships or were in shipping, that needed their paths eased by foreign negotiations, were put under the commercial policy section of the Trade Ministry. The ethos here was that of self-administration. Those that were reliant on domestically produced raw materials, including the iron and metal industries, chemicals, and coal-mining, were incorporated in the industrial section of the ministry. Here the influence of the army was more evident. Central direction prevailed: industry was a milch-cow whose output could be regulated by order, and whose principal sectors were treated as support services, not as independent businesses.

The principal device for the management of industry, modelled on Germany's *Kriegsgesellschaften*, were the Centrals (*Zentralen*). The name was indicative of their function—to centralize raw materials within a particular industrial sector. The first three, created in October and November 1914, covered cotton, wool, and metal. But further progress was slow. Many did not come into existence until 1916 and 1917, including those for petroleum and for rubber. Chemicals proved to be too diverse to be centralized at all. Oxen

[191] Wegs, 'Austrian economic mobilization', 12–14, 34–5, 40–2; Redlich, *Austrian war government*, 85–6, 124–7; Riedl, *Industrie Österreichs*, 20–3.
[192] Riedl, *Industrie Österreichs*, 3–7, 47–53.
[193] Egger, 'Heeresverwaltung und Rüstungsindustrie', 83, 85–6.

were governed by five Centrals—those for leather, meat, bones, fats, and fodder.[194] Nor was the Central a consistently applied model. War associations were formed of all enterprises producing the same commodity; some Centrals provided services rather than goods. Ultimately ninety-one Centrals were created.

The key distinction between the Centrals and the *Kriegsgesellschaften* was that the Austrian system did not rest on government guarantees. The Austrian minister of finance argued that it was in an industry's own interest to organize its supply of raw materials, and that consequently it could be left to invest in its own Central. The share capital of the Centrals was generated by the particular industry and by the investment banks. Thus, the pre-war role of the major Viennese banks in Austrian industrialization was perpetuated during the war itself. The interest rate was limited to 5 or 6 per cent; any profits above this were transferred either to the Central's reserves or to the state. The ostensible collectivism of the army's control provided a forceful contrast with this degree of potential self-government on the part of individual industries: the ministers of war and trade had no more than a power of veto within the Centrals.

However, the fact that the Centrals were more truly private companies than were their equivalents in Germany made it harder for them to extend their authority, particularly in the matter of monopolizing imports. It also made them vulnerable, albeit with little justification, to accusations of profiteering. But the real limitation on their powers of control was the refusal of Hungary to co-operate. Initially the Centrals functioned in both segments of the empire, but from the beginning of 1915 Hungary broke away to create its own parallel structure. In Austrian eyes Hungary was using the Centrals to further the cause of its own industrial development, not that of the war economy. When, in 1917, the War Ministry finally endeavoured to rationalize its demands on the iron industry by creating dumps in Vienna, Graz, Cracow, and Budapest, the obstructionism of the Hungarian trade minister delayed the establishment of the last until too late in 1918 to be of any value.[195]

Administrative complications, even if evidence of major issues—of Magyar particularism against imperial unity, or state centralization against the spirit of free enterprise—played no more than a small part in the fall in productivity evident in 1914. On mobilization the army's pre-war contracts overloaded existing firms while failing to draw in new; the delay in creating Centrals and imposing their monopoly status made raw materials scarcer and more expensive. But the decline in output was too deep, too quick in its impact and too brief in its duration, to have been the result simply of managerial confusion. Iron-ore output in 1914 fell 25 per cent from that of 1913, and the wholesale iron

[194] Egger, 'Heeresverwaltung und Rüstungsindustrie', 87.
[195] Riedl, *Industrie Österreichs*, 28–43; Redlich, *Austrian war government*, 117–18, 51–2; März, *Austrian banking*, 117–19; Wegs, 'Austrian economic mobilization', 14–23.

trade in August 1914 ran at 72 per cent below its August 1913 level.[196] High interest charges after the 1912 mobilization were already causing stagnation in the economy; mobilization pushed it into recession. Loss of labour was the immediate precipitant. The northern Bohemia metal manufacturing industries, which had employed 24,887 workers in 1912, retained only 9,706 in August 1914. Between August and December 1914 25 per cent of miners were drafted into the army. Those businesses not secured by army contracts were left short of hands, transport, and raw materials. In Austria in 1914 15,154 businesses closed, and 211,677 workers were laid off.[197]

Crucial to the resumption of output was a recovery in coal production. Coal yields in 1914 declined—by 6 per cent in the case of bituminous coal, 13 per cent in the case of lignite, and 25 per cent in the case of pit coal. Behind these figures lay further fuel problems. First, Austria-Hungary was strong in lignite but short of coking coal: in 1913 it had imported 12 million tons of coal.[198] Most of this came from Germany. To limit its dependence on its ally, the army maintained production in the conquered regions of southern Poland, but the Germans claimed that the area was theirs.[199] Moreover, gains in one direction were effectively eliminated by losses in another. Austria-Hungary produced nearly 2 million tons of oil before the war. However, its fields were in Galicia and fell victim to the Russian advance: production in the second half of 1914 was 68 per cent below that of the first half. When the Russians retreated in May 1915 they destroyed the wells, and the total output for 1915 was 54 per cent of 1914's.[200]

Interacting with fuel shortages were the problems of transport. Landlocked, with its heavy industry concentrated in Bohemia and Moravia, and with the Danube of little use as an alternative, the Austro-Hungarian economy was critically dependent on its railways. On mobilization the army took over the entire network, and then bent its efforts towards concentrating its rolling stock in Galicia. Much was lost in the subsequent retreat, including 15,000 freight cars, or more than the total production for 1915. By June 1915 only eighty-six locomotives had been added to the 12,000 available in August 1914. By now the system was having to sustain armies at three extremities of the empire. Furthermore, the performance of the railways was not as efficient as it had been. The copper fire-boxes were taken for munitions production and replaced with iron boxes, which could not generate so much pressure. Thus, loads fell. The loss of skilled labour, through military service and natural wastage, was not made up: at any one time 5,000 locomotives were under repair. Shortage of

[196] Wegs, 'Austrian economic mobilization', 85–91.
[197] Ibid. 182, 212; Wandruszka and Urbanitsch, *Habsburgermonarchie*, i. 59–60.
[198] Winkler, *Einkommensverschiebungen*, 49; Wegs, 'Austrian economic mobilization', 180–8.
[199] Leslie, 'Austria-Hungary's eastern policy', 151–2.
[200] Wegs, 'Austrian economic mobilization', 190.

rolling stock meant that even where coal was mined it could not be moved. In December 1914 only 20 to 30 per cent of the cars required to move lignite from Bohemia were available; in the first quarter of 1915 the coal-mining areas got only two-thirds of the rolling stock they needed. The cycle of fuel shortage and railway bottlenecks was thus a circular one.

The fact that production recovered in 1915–16 was a reflection of an improvement in the transport position. The output of cars, which had totalled 3,500 in 1914, reached 12,000 in 1915 and 18,000 in 1916; in 1915 Germany lent its ally 4,786 captured trucks. In the first three months of 1916, of 685,887 wagons due to collect coal 641,165 actually arrived.[201] Coal production, already recovering in 1915, in 1916 exceeded its 1913 output by 8 per cent in the case of bituminous coal and 5 per cent in that of pit coal; lignite still lagged by 16 per cent. With its supply of coal sufficiently restored, and with the consolidation of labour accomplished by the closure of non-essential industries, ferrous metal production also began to recover in 1915. By 1916 Austria was producing 3.9 million tons of iron ore (as against 3.43 million in 1913), 1.9 million tons of pig iron (1.63 million in 1913), and 2.75 million tons of steel (1.84 million in 1913).[202]

As in Germany, the war made viable previously uneconomic sources of tungsten (mined in Bohemia) and nickel (from Salzburg). Manganese production fell in 1914 but by November 1915 had risen to 77 tons per day. Austria-Hungary's domestic output of copper increased from 4,052 tons in 1913 to 6,528 in 1915. A combination of tight controls, requisitioning, and overseas purchases made 36,227 tons available for military purposes that year. Output rose again in 1916, to 7,774 tons, and the total from all sources to 44,698, but increased munitions production meant that, whereas in 1915 the army's needs were frequently met in full, in 1916 they were satisfied only 65 per cent of the time. Austria's ability to use iron, aluminium, and zinc as substitutes for copper was dependent on German co-operation. In 1915 Austria-Hungary hoped to get 1,639 tons of refined zinc each month from Germany, not least because the latter had access to Belgium's supply, but in fact it received only 670 tons. Co-operation was better in the case of aluminium, partly because Austria produced bauxite which Germany processed, and partly because both allies had an interest in controlling the prices set by the Swiss.[203]

Broadly speaking, the picture was one of industrial recovery in 1915 and 1916. In Hungary the industrial workforce as a whole rose by 12 per cent, and in the war-related industries by 30 or 40 per cent.[204] Particular sectors of the chemical

[201] Wegs, 'Austrian economic mobilization', 178–9, 185, 203–7; J. Robert Wegs, 'Transportation: the Achilles heel of the Habsburg war effort', in Kann et al. (eds.), Habsburg empire in World War I; Herwig, First World War, 239.

[202] Winkler, Einkommensverschiebungen, 49; Wegs, 'Austrian economic mobilization', 85–100, 183–4.

[203] Wegs, 'Austrian economic mobilization', 92–100, 118–28, 136–44.

[204] Wandruska and Urbanitsch, Habsburgermonarchie, i. 521.

industry grew with remarkable rapidity: Austria-Hungary produced 20,000 tonnes of nitrogen per annum in 1914, but with German co-operation added the equivalent of a further 40,000 tonnes through the production of 200,000 tonnes of calcium cyanamide.[205] In 1914 four firms produced shells; in 1916 forty-seven did so.

Austria-Hungary had lagged behind in the arms race of 1911–14. Naval expansion had not helped: of 757.7 million crowns voted in January 1911 for a five-year programme, 312.4 million had been earmarked to cover the entire shipbuilding budget. For the army, material had to be sacrificed for man-power.[206] The early campaigns, therefore, created a munitions crisis that was different in nature from that of Germany. More than replacing lost or damaged equipment, more than arming an enlarged army, Austria-Hungary had to create in war the stocks it had failed to form in peace. Despite increased production, it never fully caught up.

Although this was a war dominated by artillery, Austria-Hungary also had a small-arms crisis. Rifles were manufactured by the state-owned Austrian weapons company at Steyr, and also by the Hungarian works at Győr, established in 1912 and just coming on stream in 1914. But so infrequent were orders from its own army that Steyr was not geared to the domestic market; it received none in 1910, and contracts for 6,500 small arms in 1911 and 2,700 in 1912. By contrast, in 1913 Greece placed orders for 200,000 rifles and Romania for 230,000; in early 1914 Steyr joined with Mauser, the German firm, to clinch a deal for 200,000 rifles for Serbia.[207] Steyr produced 34,000 rifles in January 1915, a tenfold increase on its output for September 1914. But some divisions that winter had only 3,000 to 5,000 rifles for between 12,000 and 15,000 men: only one-third were of the new 1895 model, and the remainder were of six different calibres. In September 1915 Steyr produced 74,000 rifles and the Győr works a further 18,000, but still the army's demand was double their output. Monthly production finally exceeded 100,000 rifles a month in the second half of 1916. One reason why the Austro-Hungarians had an abundance of small-arms ammunition was that it had too few rifles from which to fire it.[208]

The production of artillery, and especially of heavy artillery, was concen-trated at the Skoda works in Pilsen. Skoda was a private firm, but worked closely with the technical committee of the War Ministry. Testimony to this relationship was the massive 30.5 cm mortar adopted in 1911. In November of the following year the Inspectorate of Technical Artillery was created, an indication that some quarters of the Austro-Hungarian War Ministry were

[205] Schwarte, *Technik in Weltkriege*, 544, 548.
[206] Stevenson, *Armaments and the coming of war*, 137–40.
[207] Rauchensteiner, *Tod des Doppeladlers*, 38.
[208] Wegs, 'Austrian economic mobilization', 160; Österreichischen Bundesministerium, *Österreich-Ungarns letzter Krieg*, ii. 14–16, and vi. 60–1.

as persuaded as their German counterparts that machines could substitute for men. The inspectorate established itself as the co-ordinating body between government and private industry—a function which by 1915 would embrace the metal Centrals and would give the inspector a status comparable to the war minister himself.[209] Skoda flourished partly for these reasons, but principally thanks to naval orders and exports. Its workforce increased 60 per cent between 1910 and 1913, to reach 9,600. It jumped again in 1914 to reach 14,000; in 1916 it was almost 30,000.[210]

The Skoda heavy mortar was exceptional, the result of a secret and unauthorized deal. Before 1914 Austria-Hungary held back from the costs of modernization and innovation in many categories of artillery. Conrad, an advocate of new models and involved in the development of the heavy mortar, found himself baulked until the war showed the inadequacies of the existing armament. In October 1914 he demanded that the new models of field howitzer, 10 cm gun, and mountain artillery, all designed before the war, be put into production and adopted forthwith. In February 1915 a programme was drawn up which specified that each division should have twenty-four field guns, thirty-six light field howitzers, four 10 cm guns, and four 15 cm howitzers. Thus, while more than half the army's artillery holdings were to be exchanged for new types, the divisional artillery establishment was to be increased by at least a third.[211] The effect of these overlapping programmes was to swell the different types of guns in use to a total of forty-five, making the logistic and maintenance problems more complex, and increasing the difficulty of maintaining a satisfactory supply of the appropriate shells.[212]

The position was exacerbated by the pre-war neglect of the heavy artillery, the 30.5 cm mortar apart. Here the key weapon was the 15 cm howitzer, but with a bronze barrel it deepened the copper shortage and could only range 5,000 metres. The decision to upgrade to steel barrels, taken in 1915, coincided with demands to repair and replace worn-out field guns. The production of gun barrels in the second half of 1916 stood at 3,554, as opposed to 240 for the comparable period in 1914. But all new construction had been halted in June to meet the needs of existing ordnance, and by the end of 1916 total output for the year was 3,650 of all calibres. Although a significant increase on the 1,463 manufactured in 1915, the Austro-Hungarian army still had only 5,000 of the 13,300 guns it reckoned it needed.[213]

[209] Wegs, 'Austrian economic mobilization', 42–3; Wandruszka and Urbanitsch, *Habsburgermonarchie*, v. 447; Regele, *Conrad*, 521–3.
[210] März, *Austrian banking*, 69–71, 123–4, 169–70.
[211] Österreichischen Bundesministerium, *Österreich-Ungarns letzter Krieg*, ii. 17–18.
[212] Stone, *Eastern front*, 123; Österreichischen Bundesministerium, *Österreich-Ungarns letzter Krieg*, vi. 62, says there were 29 different types of gun in 1915.
[213] Österreichischen Bundesministerium, *Österreich-Ungarns letzter Krieg*, vi. 57–61; vii., Beilage 2, Tabelle 10; Krauss, *Ursachen unserer Niederlage*, 94–6.

The struggle to increase the production of guns was less severe in its impact than it might have been, because of the persistence of shell shortage. Indeed, the position was the opposite of that for small arms: more artillery would only have exacerbated the problems of shell supply. Stocks per gun have been variously calculated at 250 and 500 rounds:[214] even the higher figure is significantly lower than that of the other major powers. Shell production at the outbreak of war was 7,400 rounds per day, or three rounds per gun. In December 1914 it was running at 17,000 rounds per day, or seven rounds per gun, and by August 1915 at 43,000 rounds per day or fourteen rounds per gun. In 1915 as a whole monthly output averaged 950,000 rounds, as against 375,000 in 1915, but in 1916 it only increased to 1.4 million—as opposed to Germany's 7 million.[215] Although daily output was 60,000 rounds by the end of 1916, it could still be exceeded by daily consumption and the army's target was 800,000 per week, or twice what was being achieved.[216] Furthermore, the global figures obscure even greater shortages for specific calibres. The proliferation of ordnance meant that by 1915 twenty-nine types required 100 different sorts of ammunition. Austria-Hungary, like Britain, had favoured shrapnel over high explosive and struggled to fill its shells. The decision to replace the 7 cm mountain gun and the 10 cm field gun meant that stocks of shell for these pieces were already being run down when the war broke out, although both guns still figured in Austria-Hungary's order of battle.[217]

The confusion of the empire's bureaucracy are only a partial explanation for the failures of procurement from 1916. The dual monarchy could not do more; it had reached the limit of its capacity for industrial expansion. Raw materials were running short. Supplies of vital commodities like manganese and copper could not keep pace with the growth in the army's needs for munitions. Transport bottlenecks were already re-emerging in the second half of that year. As the shell-production figures for 1916 themselves made plain, the dependence of Austria-Hungary on its more industrialized ally would grow in the second half of the war.

Between 1914 and 1916 Germany was protected from the consequences of its position as the economic leader of the Central Powers. Austria-Hungary's industrial response in 1915 kept its dependence to manageable levels. Bulgaria did not join the Central Powers until September 1915, and therefore generated no demands on Germany's productive capacity before that. The effect of

---

[214] Herwig, *First World War*, 13; Krauss, *Ursachen unserer Niederlage*, 95.
[215] Österreichischen Bundesministerium, *Östereich-Ungarns letzter Krieg*, vii. Beilage 2, Tabelle 10; Wegs, 'Austrian economic mobilization', 156, 159–60; Stone, *Eastern front*, 123–4. Wegs's figures, which disagree with Stone's for late 1914, convey a more positive picture than Stone's.
[216] Österreichischen Bundesministerium, *Österreich-Ungarns letzter Krieg*, vi. 62–3; Herwig, *First World War*, 242.
[217] Rauchensteiner, *Tod des Doppeladlers*, 148; Österreichischen Bundesministerium, *Österreich-Ungarns letzter Krieg*, vi. 62; Krauss, *Ursachen unserer Niederlage*, 94–5.

Bulgaria's entry was to outflank Serbia and so open the route to Turkey. Until then, however insistent the demands for munitions from Constantinople, Berlin could plead quite genuinely that it was in no position to respond. But from 1916 all three of its allies would increase their requests for raw materials and finished goods. Up until 1916 German industry, and the compromise structure adopted for the management of the German war economy, proved equal to the task because the demands made of them were comparatively limited. Thereafter, the structure would have to have the resilience both to cope with a more sustained and more intensive version of industrialized warfare, and to be able to do so on several fronts simultaneously.

THE MUNITIONS CRISIS AND THE ENTENTE, 1914–1916

By 10 September 1914, after little more than three weeks of active operations, the French army had lost a tenth of its field artillery, 410 75 mm guns, and 750 limbers.[218] By January 1915 its holdings of the 1886 Lebel rifle had fallen from 2,880,000 to 2,370,000, a loss of over half-a-million.[219] Some of these guns and rifles were no doubt smashed beyond repair. But many lay on the battlefield, salvageable or even intact. The soldiers of France, anxious to expedite their retreat and exhausted by its pace, did not encumber themselves with excessive burdens.

The allies' abandonment of equipment in the first few weeks of the war was the most immediate economic consequence of the opening German advance. Particularly in the supply of rifles, it created considerable short-term strains for the French army. But in the long term it was not the most deleterious aspect of Germany's territorial gains. After the stabilization of the front, France's industrial heartland lay either under German control or within the battle zone. In 1913 the north-east of France was responsible for 74 per cent of the nation's coal production, 76.5 per cent of its coke, 81 per cent of its pig iron, 63 per cent of its steel, 94 per cent of its copper, 76.5 per cent of its lead, 60 per cent of its manufactured iron and steel, 25 per cent of its engineering products, 81 per cent of its wool, and 44.5 per cent of its chemicals.[220] Heavy industry was hit with particular ferocity. Eighty-five out of 170 blast furnaces were lost, forty-eight out of 164 Siemens-Martin furnaces, and fifty-three out of 100 convertors. By 1915 French coal production had tumbled from 40 million tonnes to under 20 million, its iron ore output from 22 million tonnes to 620,000, and its steel

[218] Ministère de la guerre, *Armées françaises*, xi. 71.   [219] Hatry, *Renault*, 48–9.
[220] Fontaine, *French industry*, 16–17.

production from 4.6 million tonnes to 1.1 million.[221] Furthermore, France was already a laggard in the more obvious indices of European industrial strength. In 1913 Britain produced 270 million tonnes of coal and Germany 220 million to France's 37 million; and Britain produced 11 million tonnes of iron and Germany 17 million to France's 5 million.[222] Given such a proportionately high loss of such a comparatively low productive capacity, how could France sustain and equip its armies over four-and-a-half years of industrialized warfare? For not only did it do so, but it also rearmed the Serbs in 1915, provided artillery for the Americans and Greeks, and supplied aircraft to the British.[223]

Not all the answers can be found within France. In 1915 France's imports of steel matched its domestic production, in 1916 and 1917 its steel imports tripled, and in 1918 they fell back to parity with domestic production only because of the shortage of shipping.[224] For France was part of an alliance that included the world's third industrial power, Britain, and was able to continue trading with the world's first, the United States. From the latter came Remington rifles, and Colt and Hotchkiss machine-guns. In February 1916 Fiat in Italy contracted to deliver munitions and trucks, and later aero-engines and tanks.[225]

But there were within France strengths obscured by the overall aggregates. The concentration of French industry in the north-east had left underexploited the resources of other regions: Normandy and the Ardèche had iron ore, the water-power of the Pyrenees and Alps could generate electricity. Thus, the abandonment of the north and east was offset by a rise in production in the centre, the south, and the west. In December 1915 42.5 per cent of France's labour force was employed south of a line from Mont-Saint Michel to Geneva; by January 1917 that figure had risen to 55 per cent. In every *département* of the same area the number of businesses which had been forced to close in the first seventeen months of the war was below the national average of 10.3 per cent. Most striking was the Rhône. Its workforce engaged in the defence industries swelled 35.5 per cent by December 1915 (when over France as a whole it declined by 4.2 per cent). Between then and January 1917 the number of newly opened firms in the region was less than the national average (41.4 per cent as against 92.1 per cent), but the workforce nonetheless grew by a further 215.7 per cent, against a national average of 58.7 per cent. In other words, the Rhône attracted big business.[226] Therefore, one effect of the war was to promote the industrialization of the rest of France. Furthermore, one consequence of defeat was

[221] Jèze and Truchy, *War finance*, 189; Duroselle, *La France*, 217–19.
[222] Knauss, *Kriegsfinanzierung*, 14.
[223] Falls, *First World War*, 355.
[224] Duroselle, *La Grande Guerre des français*, 173.
[225] R. Poidevin, 'Les Relations économiques et financières', in Guillen (ed.), *La France et l'Italie*, 287–8.
[226] Dereymez, *Cahiers d'histoire*, 2 (1981), 159–61, 174–6.

that fewer of France's own resources were being siphoned off to support the manufactures of the north. France's imports of coal, coke, and related fuels remained relatively constant (at about 20 million tonnes per annum) both before the war and during it: the loss of domestic output in the war was balanced by a decline in domestic consumption.

The results were particularly apparent in the steel industry. The production of the high-grade steels needed for military purposes depended on crucibles and electric furnaces. These were already concentrated in the centre before the war. Whereas 64 per cent of France's pig iron production for 1913 came from areas that had been overrun, the same applied to only 58 per cent of its crude steel and 54 per cent of its finished steel. Therefore, in 1913 unoccupied France had already produced about 500,000 tonnes of munitions-quality steel, when the annual requirement of the land armaments of industry was only 5,000 tonnes.[227] Its needs did, of course, grow from September 1914, to 200 tonnes a day, with targets of 500 tonnes a day by early November and 800 tonnes thereafter. But the problems of 1914 were less those of capacity and more those of labour. Furnaces were extinguished for lack of manpower. Output for August 1914 in the war-free zones slumped from 3,000 tonnes a day to 250. As existing furnaces were relit, new ones were added. France more than doubled its numbers of Thomas convertors and of crucibles, and increased its holdings of Martin furnaces by 94 per cent and of electric furnaces by 75 per cent. Steel output in the Loire rose by between 60 and 80 per cent, and in the south and west by between 15 and 30 per cent. By 1918 new furnaces increased France's capacity to produce cast iron by 590,000 tonnes a year, and steel by 1,760,000 tonnes. By December 1914 steel production was already able to keep pace with the needs of the munitions industry, then set at 1,140 tonnes a day, and rising to 1,800 tonnes a day by May 1915. By 1916 France's aggregate production still lagged significantly behind its pre-war output—just under 1.5 million tonnes of pig iron as opposed to 5.2 million in 1913, and just under 2 million tonnes of steel as opposed to 4.7 million. Furthermore, after 1916 France was actually unable to maximize its productive capacity in iron and steel owing to labour shortages, lack of fuel, especially coke, and transport difficulties. In 1918 output of steel was 59 per cent of capacity and of pig iron 56 per cent. But in central France output had swelled from 527,952 tonnes to 763,159, in the south-west from 159,994 tonnes to 207,347, in the south-east from 120,258 tonnes to 176,463, and in the west from 184,144 tonnes to 207,649.[228]

The adaptive strengths of the French iron and steel industry were becoming evident in the two decades before the war. Its rate of growth in that period had

[227] Crouzet, *Revue historique*, CCLI (1974), 78.

[228] Fontaine, *French industry*, 271–9; Birkett, *Journal of the Royal Statistical Society*, LXXXIII (1920), 377–83; Baquet, *Souvenirs*, 52–3.

exceeded those of Germany, the United States, and Britain, and by 1913 it ranked fourth in the world to those three. By 1914 France was reaping the advantages of backwardness. A selective look at its industries showed that its late spurt had given it a lead in precisely those technologies to become relevant to modern war, including the manufacture of automobiles and aircraft, and certainly not neglecting artillery.[229]

The switch from bronze and iron guns to steel had given Schneider-Creusot its opening to the arms trade. By 1900 Schneider had secured orders for quick-firing artillery in twenty-three countries, and between 1904 and 1907 it delivered 300 complete field and mountain batteries, two-thirds of them to Balkan states. The performance of Schneider-Creusot's guns in the Balkan wars presented a serious challenge to Krupp's domination of overseas markets. Domestically, the navy was a bigger buyer from private industry than the army. The latter ordered components from the arms trade but preferred to assemble whole systems itself. The position changed with the tentative development of orders for heavy guns from 1912. Schneider-Creusot received contracts for half the 220 long 105 mms ordered in April 1913, for eighteen 280 mm mortars in November 1913, and for 120 long 155 mms in June 1914. The combination of the army's uncertainty over heavy artillery doctrine and the competition with the attractions of aircraft and the infrastructure costs of the three-year law kept these orders small. Moreover, ensuring that the state ordnance factories also received contracts subdivided the investment (Bourges was asked to produce the other half of the long 105 mms) and so retarded serial production.[230] Thus, the biggest initial industrial impediment to the expansion of munitions production was neither resources nor location (Schneider-Creusot, like many other arms factories, was in Saône-et-Loire); it was the lack of machine tools. At the war's outset part of France's productive capacity was devoted to the preparation of plant as a preliminary to the manufacture of guns.[231]

This was hardly a situation unique to France. There, as elsewhere, the real difficulties in expanding munitions production were organizational. Mobilization disrupted the manufacture of shells until the sixty-fifth day of hostilities.[232] Exemptions from the call-up were extended only to 11,000 of the 45,000 to 50,000 employed in the French arms business: 7,600 of these worked in the state-owned factories. Renault, for example, which during the war would expand its production of aero-engines as well as diversifying into shell production and tank design, at first received no exemptions. Even Schneider-

[229] Godfrey, *Capitalism at war*, 13–14; McNeill, *Pursuit of power*, 299–300; Stone, *Europe transformed*, 280–2.
[230] Crouzet, *Revue historique*, CCLI (1974), 58, 64–7, 412–14, 417; Stevenson, *Armaments and the coming of war*, 29–30, 37, 223–4; Baquet, *Souvenirs*, 37–40.
[231] Baquet, *Souvenirs*, 51, 58, 127; Gamelin, *Manoeuvre et victoire*, 317.
[232] Duroselle, *La France*, 98.

Creusot found its labour clipped from 12,000 to 6,600. Twenty-five per cent of the whole French workforce was mobilized, but the rate in the metal industry was 33 per cent, and in the chemical industry 42 per cent. In August only about half the businesses and a third of the workers in the Paris-Seine area remained active. The production of 75 mm shells, due to double to 13,600 a day at the war's outset, fell to 7,000 by the beginning of September.[233]

Although France had failed to think through the economic implications of mobilization, the Ministry of War was not slow to anticipate crisis. At about the same time that Falkenhayn was planning the establishment of the KRA with Rathenau, Messimy was expressing his concerns for shell production to Renault. He was warned by Joffre immediately after the opening encounters in Alsace that shell consumption had exceeded all expectations and that he should aim to multiply output more than tenfold, from an anticipated 6,000–8,000 shells per day to 100,000.[234] On 14 August Messimy met the representatives of France's leading private arms manufacturers, Schneider-Creusot and St-Chamond, and on the following day he initiated co-operation with the Comité des Forges, the trade association of the major iron firms. The ministry still had little idea as to what the actual level of shell expenditure would be: not until the closing stages of the Marne, on 14 September, was it fully informed as to the disparity between consumption and output.

The effects of Messimy's initiative at the local level were virtually instantaneous. On 15 August itself an iron foundry at Renage in the south-east was visited by an officer from the Intendance Militaire based at Lyons: within two days the firm had received an order for 200,000 pickaxes, and within a week its workforce had increased from fifty to sixty-five, including four soldiers released from the army. Prompted by his anxiety concerning employment for those not mobilized, the president of the Paris chamber of commerce had already issued a national call, urging firms to compete for army contracts. Departmental committees to maintain employment, ranging over the entire field of economic activity and embracing the heads of local business, deputies, and trade unionists, sprang into life. That for the Isère was formed on 19 August. The principal members were the town *maires*, and their significance lay not least in their marriage of business and government at the local level.[235]

This combination—the fusion of national with local responses, and the incorporation of private enterprise in the affairs of the state—was confirmed on 20 September. Millerand, who had replaced Messimy at the end of August, summoned a meeting of the representatives of heavy industry at the government's new headquarters, Bordeaux. He set a production target of 100,000

[233] Reboul, *Mobilisation industrielle*, i. 7; Hatry, *Renault*, 20–3; Gerd Hardach, 'Industrial mobilization in 1914–1918: production, planning and ideology', in Fridenson (ed.), *French home front*, 59–61.
[234] Messimy, *Mes souvenirs*, 326.
[235] Flood, *France 1914–18*, 57–63.

shells a day. To achieve this, he recalled General Louis Baquet from the front to be director of artillery. Baquet was a designer of guns, and in particular was responsible for the 75 mm high-explosive shell which had so proved its worth at the Marne. France was divided into twelve regions, each regional head being responsible for the allocation of resources and contracts. The Comité des Forges profited from its tight organization and its early involvement: under its secretary-general, Robert Pinot, it dominated the regional structure, manip-ulating resources, prices, and orders for the advantage of its own members. Millerand effectively bound himself over to the abilities of heavy industry to manage its own affairs. He met the heads of sectors every eight days (at least at first), but accepted their assurances rather than testing them. He promised the release of skilled labour from the army: this was ordered on 11 October. In November a central labour exchange was established to recruit for the muni-tions industry. By June 1916 287,000 workers had been returned from the army, and by the end of 1915 the workforce engaged in the metal industries was fully up to its pre-war level; that of the chemical industry had recovered to 93 per cent of its pre-war level. Renault's payroll, which had peaked at 6,300 in 1914, reached 12,800 in 1915.[236]

At the Bordeaux meeting the representatives of industry told Millerand that they could deliver 40,000 shells per day by the beginning of December. On the following day, buoyed by their bullishness, Millerand informed Joffre that he could expect 30,000 rounds per day in three to four weeks time. But output in August had averaged 6,000 shells a day, and it had first exceeded 10,000 a day only six days previously, on 15 September. Eight days later Millerand revised his estimate downwards, informing the commander-in-chief that 20,000 rounds per day would be the norm until the beginning of November, but that the rate would then rise to 33,300 rounds. Even on 3 November Joffre was being assured that the daily rate of production would jump from 13,000 rounds to 23,000 by the middle of the month. But on the 14th he was told to expect only 18,000 shells per day. In the event, output for November remained stubbornly fixed at 13,000. The state-owned workshops were meeting their mobilization targets, but private industry could not yet fulfil its. The latter's total deliveries on 10 November were 2,000 rounds, against the 7,000 that had been promised. Its orders for the coming six months were ten times a full year's peacetime production. On 28 September Bouchayer and Viallet in the Isère were told to install a forge to produce 1,000 shells a day: that was their total output by the year's end. In October the Societé des Constructions Mécaniques undertook to produce 1.2 million shells in plants at Paris and Lyons. But by the end of March

[236] Hatry, *Renault*, 26–8; Godfrey, *Capitalism at war*, 48–50; Fridenson, *Renault*, 90–1, 93; Hardach, 'Industrial mobilisation', in Fridenson, *French home front*, 59–61; Miquel, *Grande Guerre*, 235–8; Baquet, *Souvenirs*, 7, 18, 20, 70–1; Farrar, *Principled pragmatist*, 162–4; Dereymez, *Cahiers d'histoire*, 2 (1981), 165.

1915 it was over 800,000 rounds in arrears, and the Lyons factory had yet to deliver any.

Baquet reckoned that the corner was turned in December, others somewhat later. He calculated that the new factories produced 32,500 shells a day in the last month of 1914, as against their target of 50,000. In addition, the existing major munitions firms delivered 7,500 shells a day and the state workshops 16,000. Other accounts claim that daily production did not reach 50,000 rounds until March (when in fact it averaged 62,173), and that the production target set for January 1915, 80,000 shells per day, was not attained until July. By then the army was abundantly supplied with 75 mm shells. On 10 August 1915 the stocks under Joffre's own control (excluding those already in the hands of army commanders) totalled 2,681,486 shells. The number had almost doubled during December and January, from 301,361 to 573,696; more than doubled in February, March, and April, to 1,202,670; and more than doubled again during the next three months.[237] As in Germany, the Ministry of War, by setting objectives which were not met on schedule, undersold its own achievement.

By the summer of 1915 the problem was no longer quantity but quality. The state factories apart, in 1914 only Schneider-Creusot and St-Chamond possessed the hydraulic presses required to forge shells. Production methods, therefore, had to change in order to convert other plants to the needs of war industry. On 23 August 1914 Renault told Messimy that automobile factories could manufacture shells by boring out the interior of steel ingots, a process which would require a turning-lathe rather than a hydraulic press. But forged steel was stronger: a shell made before the war could take a water pressure of 1,400 kilos per square centimetre, whereas one made in the straitened circumstances of 1914–15 could only cope with 400 kilos per square centimetre. Moreover, the turning process could not fashion the nose-cone of the shell, and the shell therefore had to be made in two parts. Renault's shells were nicknamed 'bi-blocs', as opposed to the 'monoblocs' produced in the state arsenals. Techniques were developed to reinforce the more delicate parts of the shell, but they mitigated the problems rather than removed them. Inspection standards were inevitably lowered in the rush to boost output. Problems with fuses had caused many French shells to misfire even at the outset of the war, when production had been the monopoly of properly constituted arms factories. At Muhlhouse the Germans found pits which the French gunners had dug to bury their defective shells. In January 1915 one German observer calculated that 50 per cent of French rounds fired in a single day were duds. Some had problems with the charges, others had fuses but no charges, and a

[237] Baquet, *Souvenirs*, 44–5, 67–76; Flood, *France 1914–18*, 58; Menu, *Revue militaire française*, 149 (1933), 185–90; Ministère de la guerre, *Armées françaises*, xi. 203, 205, 210–12, 1004–5; see also Fayolle, *Carnets secrets*, 120, 127, 129.

few were even training rounds filled with sawdust.[238] Moreover, the French lost over 600 guns in 1915 through premature explosions. Before the war one gun burst for every 500,000 rounds; in the spring of 1915 one gun burst for every 3,000 rounds. On 1 March 1915, with shell production now in full swing, the decision was taken to abandon the 'bi-bloc', and on 15 April the pre-war standard for forged steel was reapplied. However, not until late 1916 would the quality of shell production equal that of peacetime.[239]

Nor were guns and their crews the only casualties of the drive to increase shell production. The complexities of shrapnel were beyond the capabilities of the firms suddenly drafted into the ordnance business. The pre-war ratio of production, 15/26 shrapnel to 11/26 high explosive, had altered by December 1914 to 1/7 shrapnel and 6/7 high explosive. The construction of trenches had, of course, increased the need for high explosive beyond pre-war expectations, but in the French case the constraints of munitions production pushed the pendulum too far in the other direction: the gunners were left with insufficient shrapnel for interdiction and harassing fire.[240]

Most of these problems were ironed out in the course of 1915. Citroën expressed an interest in the production of shrapnel in January, and by the end of September private industry was delivering 10,000 rounds per day. Renault devised a system for manufacturing the cone of the shell under heat. Car and bicycle factories proved well suited to the production of *gaines* (the metal casings for shell fuses), and textile firms made fuses. Copper shortages, which threatened to curtail the output of the driving rings for shells, were mastered in part by the recovery and reworking of those sent back from the front. The rate of premature explosions was halved in the summer of 1915, and the problem was more fully mastered in 1916, as hydraulic presses become widespread in private firms. By the end of the war France, the biggest single producer of shells in the Entente, had 375 businesses engaged in their production.[241]

In France, as opposed to Germany, the pace of shell manufacture was never determined by the output of powder. As a detonator, France used a solution of gun cotton in a mixture of alcohol and ether, called powder B. The plan on mobilization was to increase the daily peacetime production of 15 tonnes to 25 tonnes by the end of the second month of the war. But the problems of shell fabrication meant that at first powder output exceeded the army's requirements. Demand was also suppressed by a reduction in the individual charge from 0.665 kilograms to 0.620 as part of the bid to avoid premature

---

[238] Schoen, *Geschichte des deutschen Feuerwerkswesens*, 772, 801.

[239] Baquet, *Souvenirs*, 77–9, 92.

[240] Reboul, *Mobilisation industrielle*, 21–7; Hatry, *Renault*, 26, 28–9, 42–3; Gascouin, *L'Évolution de l'artillerie*, 139–40; Gilbert Hatry, 'Les Rapports governement, armée, industrie privée pendant la Première Guerre Mondiale: le cas des usines Renault', in Canini (ed.), *Les Fronts invisibles*, 175–6.

[241] Hardach, 'Industrial mobilization', in Fridenson (ed.), *French home front*, 63, 67.

explosions.[242] Not until early 1915 did the need for powder run ahead of domestic capacity. In January France produced 50 tonnes a day, and by October 100 tonnes. The rate of shell production meant that 80 tonnes a day was needed in January and 150 in October. The deficit was made good by purchases from the United States, and by favouring shell production over that of small-arms ammunition.

More immediate was the pressure to expand explosives output, as a result of the switch from shrapnel. The French chemical industry grew at a rate of almost 5 per cent per annum between 1895 and 1913; one of its strengths was the sulphuric acid works of St Gobain. But in 1914 domestic production of explosives still remained small. Stocks, primarily melinite or picric acid, totalled 2,400 tonnes at the war's outbreak. On 18 August Messimy was told that these stocks had been prepared for an output of 8,000 shells a day, and that there were only enough for three more weeks. Schneiderite, used by Schneider-Creusot for its exports, was employed from October 1914, but it was derived from ammonium nitrate, whose output was itself limited, and it was disliked by gunners as the colourless gas emitted on impact made fire hard to observe. By January total explosive stocks had dwindled to 700 tonnes, and the daily output of melinite was 16 tonnes, enough to load 20,000 75 mm shells. These worries were stoked by Joffre, who—as an insurance measure—pitched his expectations ahead of his likely consumption. But they were also fuelled by the nature of the business: its close links with Germany before the war generated suspicions, and they were not allayed by the high prices secured as a result of government demand. However, the government saw in the war an opportunity to foster the growth of an indigenous chemical industry, free of German influence and control. Thus, the concentration of the business in fewer hands was encouraged by the state. So too was the emphasis on sulphuric acid, whose output rose from 1.16 million tonnes in 1913–14 to 1.611 million in 1916–17.[243] All in all, the production of explosives proved relatively easy to set in train. In 1914 France imported its benzol from Britain and Germany; after 1915 it was manufacturing between 35 and 40 tonnes a day. In 1914 its output of phenol was 1 tonne a day; at first this too came from Britain, but by December 1915 it was producing 60 tonnes a day. The production of chlorates, which was still minimal in December 1914, reached 40 tonnes in May 1915 and 100 in March 1916. In July 1917 France was producing 985 tonnes of explosives a month, thereby exceeding its target of 900 tonnes.[244]

[242] Ministère de la guerre, *Armées françaises*, xi. 211; see generally Reboul, *Mobilisation industrielle*, 115–34.

[243] Godfrey, *Capitalism at war*, 120–6, 157–76; Fontaine, *French industry*, 136–68; Saatmann, *Parlament, Rüstung und Armee*, 223–5; Baquet, *Souvenirs*, 89–90; Messimy, *Mes souvenirs*, 326–7; see also Robert O. Paxton, 'The calcium carbide case and the decriminalization of industrial ententes in France, 1915–26', in Fridenson (ed.), *French home front*, 153–80.

[244] Reboul, *Mobilisation industrielle*, 123–8, 131–2.

By the summer of 1915 efforts to boost the production of 75 mm shells had proved almost too successful. Sufficient shells highlighted the lack of sufficient guns from which to fire them. Burst barrels as a result of premature explosions compounded the losses incurred in the initial retreat. Between 30 November 1914 and 1 May 1915 the number of 75 mm guns available fell by a further 468, to leave a total of 3,071. In mid-April Joffre reckoned he needed 805 new field guns; even if he had had them he would still have been short of over 700 guns compared with the number at his disposal on mobilization. Not least because the scale of loss through premature explosions was not evident until the new year, Baquet had been reluctant to place fresh orders in the first six months of the war. Schneider-Creusot and St-Chamond each received contracts for eighty guns after the Marne, but both firms accepted that the work would compete with their efforts to increase shell deliveries, and in November Schneider-Creusot was persuaded to withdraw from a contract for a further 160 guns because of its commitment to the production of heavy artillery. The 75 mm manufactured by the private firms was regarded as inferior to that produced in the state ordnance factories. But by the time the problem became urgent, in February 1915, the state workshops were largely taken up with repair work, replacing barrels on guns damaged by premature explosions. Thus, private industry received the lion's share of the contracts for new guns, 500 to 100, but the state factories also repaired a further 458 guns. The situation at the front did not improve until the autumn. By 1 October 1915 the armies had 3,524 guns, and production in the last quarter of the year for the first time exceeded its pre-war level of 500 guns to reach 700. In the first quarter of 1916 1,000 guns were completed, almost as many as in the whole of 1915.[245]

In the first year of the war the position in regard to heavy artillery was even more desperate.[246] In 1911 the Conseil Supérieur de Guerre favoured long 105 mms in the field howitzer role, as they were mobile and ranged 10 kilometres. But the gunners, Baquet among them, protested that at that range, with a light shell, the fall of shot would be at such a low angle as to be hard to observe and correct. They favoured the 155 mm, whose shell could contain 10 kilos of high explosive. The tendency in the debate was therefore for heavy artillery designed for the field either to be pulled in a direction where its performance was sufficiently akin to the 75 mm as to make the latter a satisfactory substitute, or to align it with siege artillery and so jeopardize its mobility. When the fighting began the tactical arguments at least spawned routes out of the impasse, particularly in the employment of the 75 mm—an

[245] Ibid. 24, 32–40; Menu, *Revue militaire française*, 149 (1933), 196; Ministère de la guerre, *Armées françaises*, xi. 216–17; Baquet, *Souvenirs*, 105–11.

[246] Porch, *March to the Marne*, 233–45; Ripperger, *Journal of Military History*, LIX (1995), 599–618; Baquet, *Souvenirs*, 27–37; Messimy, *Mes souvenirs*, 84–7; Dieter Storz, 'Die Schlacht der Zukunft', in Michalka (ed.), *Der Erste Weltkrieg*, 269; Rouquerol, *Le Canon*, 31–3.

example of ideas as alternatives to material inferiority. But the immediate result of deep thought for actual armament was stasis. In 1914 France's heavy guns were almost all antiquated and of limited range; few were quick-firers. Only about 300 were ready to take the field. Joffre was able to circumvent the immediate crisis by plundering fortresses, coastal defences, and the navy. This was a slow process: their carriages had to be adapted, harness had to be procured, and teams of horses—most heavy guns required eight and the heaviest ten—assembled. Even by 15 November 1914 only 724 heavy guns had been put into the field. Few were howitzers. Numerically the most significant was the long 120 mm Bange gun, made between 1877 and 1882, of which there were ultimately 2,400 available. Also present in large numbers was another siege gun, the long 155 mm: there were 1,400 of these. Having been designed for static warfare, they remained ponderous in their deployment and could take the best part of a day to bring into action. Lacking manoeuvrability, punch, or high rates of fire, many in the French army remained sceptical of heavy artillery while the war remained mobile. Of the short guns, there were only 200 of the 120 mm and 400 of the 155 mm. The latter included 100 quick-firing guns (the Rimailho model of 1904). Orders had been placed for 220 105 mms, due for delivery in 1914–15, and 120 long 155 mms, due in 1916–17.

The shells crisis, followed by the pressure to rebuild the stocks of field guns, had knock-on effects in the procurement of heavy artillery. When GQG felt able to move its attention from the former to the latter, in April 1915, it opted to concentrate on the types of gun already in use so as to maximize existing machine tools. The effect was to postpone any move to serial production until 1917. In the first year of the war the only new heavy guns received by the army were 110 long 105 mms from Schneider-Creusot. In the second half of 1915 Schneider-Creusot delivered a further seventy 105 mms, and St-Chamond added forty short 155 mms: the total output in all calibres was 140. Even in 1916 deliveries only reached 245 in the first half of the year and 345 in the second.

The lack of heavy artillery under Joffre's command in 1914 delayed the onset of shell shortage for these larger calibres. Although consumption was high during the battle of the Marne, the stocks in the eastern fortifications averted crisis. But most of these were cast iron, as this had been deemed sufficient for defensive purposes in the 1880s. They carried, at most, a third of the high explosive of a steel shell and, with a weaker charge, they generated less smoke, making the fall of shot hard to observe. Total daily production of steel shells for all calibres of heavy artillery was about 1,000 rounds for the first three months of the war, rising to 2,000 in December. By then Joffre wanted 3,000 shells a day for the 155 mms alone, when the planned production on mobilization was 465 and actual output in December 400. In January the problems with the 75 mm increased the army's reliance on the 90 mm and 95 mm guns as substitutes, and as a result Joffre wanted 6,000 rounds a day for the former. The expedients used in the production of 75 mm ammunition were not appropriate for shells of larger calibres, and Baquet's short-term response was to revert to cast iron. Although massive orders for steel shells were placed, 660,000 rounds for calibres between 90 and 105 mm, 340,000 for 120 mm and 155 mm, and 50,500 for 220 mm and above, they were way beyond the immediate capacity of the contractors. The retention of steel for heavy artillery shells restricted their manufacture to the major armaments works already equipped with hydraulic presses; it also prevented the same plant from being used for 75 mm shells, and so indirectly increased the number of premature explosions in field guns. A process to harden cast iron with steel was developed late in 1914, and production of shells made in this way began in March 1915. On 5 July 1915 Joffre suggested production targets of 3,000 shells per day for the 220 mm, 12,000 for the 155 mm, 10,000 for the 120 mm, 4,600 for the 105 mm, 10,000 for the 95 mm and 12,000 for the 90 mm. But the previous month's output for each of these calibres had been respectively 100, 2,500, 3,000, 1,500, 1,500, and 1,000. Joffre's figures would not be reached until March 1916, and then only in part.[247]

Joffre knew of the German adoption of the *Minenwerfer* in 1913, and recognized that this was a weapon whose simpler technologies could be more easily mastered by civilian industries. They could also be adapted from existing but otherwise redundant equipment. Black-powder 152 mm mortars made in 1839 were deployed in September 1914. The obsolete 80 mm Bange mountain gun was adapted as a spigot mortar, with the bomb placed over the barrel. Dubbed the *lance-mine* Goutard, it entered service towards the end of the year. The 58 mm mortar devised by Major Duchêne had a barrel developed from the 105 mm recoil mechanism, shell cases from the obsolete 150 mm mortar, and explosive that was too unstable for artillery proper. Trials at the front in February 1915 proved Duchêne's improvisation entirely satisfactory in practice, so enhancing French firepower by widening its sources of supply.[248]

Although the army's worries focused on artillery, the attention of its critics concentrated on the provision of rifles. The mathematics of the problem were much simpler: the army needed virtually as many rifles as it had men under arms. It had begun the war with 2.8 million Lebel rifles; it had expanded its manpower to 2.5 million; but it had lost 850,000 rifles in the first six months of the war.[249] The difficulty in making good the deficit was that the three state factories at St Étienne, Chatellerault, and Tulle had long since ceased production of the Lebel, and only Tulle still possessed the machine tools to resume

[247] Reboul, *Mobilisation industrielle*, 40–56; Gascouin, *L'Évolution de l'artillerie*, 19–21, 27–36; Ministère de la guerre, *Armées françaises*, xi. 66–9, 72–3, 212–13, 217–19; Menu, *Revue militaire françaises*, 149 (1933), 197–8, 205–7; Baquet, *Souvenirs*, 96–102, 118–28.
[248] Linnenkohl, *Vom Einzelschuss zur Feuerwalze*, 198–9; Gudmundsson, *On artillery*, 75–6.
[249] Klotz, *De la guerre à la paix*, 43–4; see also Ferry, *Carnets secrets*, 48, and Saatmann, *Parlament, Rüstung und Armee*, 178–9.

output. All they could do was increase their output of artillery carbines and of rifles designed for Indo-China. Private industry was not interested in contracting for the Lebel, and in any case protested that it was too busy responding to the needs of the artillery. The Ministry of War fell back on its stocks of the obsolete 1874 Gras rifle. It had 600,000 of these, and up to 200,000 were converted from their original calibre of 11 mm to 8 mm, the calibre of the Lebel. Small parcels of rifles were secured from Japan (50,000) and the United States (30,000), but significant imports, principally American, could not be expected until 1916. In February 1915 the army was still short of 700,000 rifles.

The rifle issue was taken up with vehemence by the senate commission on the army, which resumed its activities with the reconvening of the assembly in Paris in December 1914. On 28 January 1915 the director of artillery met representatives of private industry, who were now cautiously optimistic about developing the manufacture of rifles. The principal obstacles were the high specifications required of machine tools—tolerances were often no greater than a hundredth of a millimetre—and the division of labour to compensate for the loss of skilled workers and to enable serial production. Those firms already producing small arms had greedily accepted contracts, but had not rejected those for shells or fuses; moreover, they soon found that military requirements differed from sporting. And so the backlog of orders cascaded. One small-arms firm, which had promised 1,000 rifles a day in September 1914, delivered 100 in March 1915. A Paris consortium due to begin deliveries in May 1915 did so in June 1916. When Millerand met Renault at the beginning of March 1915 he received the same response as Baquet in January. But the Paris manufacturers agreed that they could contribute more effectively if they concentrated on parts rather than entire rifles. Conversion of the Gras rifle was suspended. Output of the Lebel reached 46,000 by August, and over double that a year later. By then stocks were sufficient to enable production to be throttled back.[250]

Nothing could have been achieved, in the view of Charles Humbert and other senators, if they had not intervened. They magnified their role by using calculations which exaggerated the possible shortfall in rifles in 1915. Their solution to artillery orders was to increase the flow of orders to firms which had still not delivered on the contracts they had already received. But in this they were being manipulated by the arms dealers themselves, principally Schneider. The effect was to compound the very backlog the parliamentarians were committed to removing. The Senate saw the failure to produce more Lebels sooner, like the shells crisis and then the artillery shortage, as a symptom of the dilatoriness and defensiveness of the Ministry of War. What actually produced delay was the conversion of peacetime industry to wartime needs.

[250] Reboul, *Mobilisation industrielle*, 59–65; Hatry, *Renault*, 48–50; Baquet, *Souvenirs*, 136–53.

But the senate commission preferred to find its explanations in scapegoats rather than structures.

The output of munitions, therefore, became the peg on which the Third Republic hung its fears of military domination. The effect of the German invasion and of the government's evacuation of Paris had been to elevate the political power of the army to the point where one of its critics could describe it as a ministry within itself. The military coup which had haunted the government since 1871 seemed to have been effected by indirect means. But neither Viviani's cabinet nor the senate commission could easily reassert itself, given the continuance of the immediate danger and the obfuscation and secrecy of Joffre's GQG. They therefore focused their attacks on the hinge of the civil–military relationship, the Ministry of War. Millerand became the butt of his own government as much as of its opposition. But Millerand's defences included the danger that his fall would also entail the collapse of the ministry as a whole. Thus, Viviani had to cast about for another answer to the commission's attacks than simply resorting to the obvious remedy of removing Millerand.[251]

His answer, on 18 May 1915, was to appoint Albert Thomas as undersecretary of state at the Ministry of War, with particular responsibility for artillery and munitions. A month later General Baquet was removed from his post. Thomas was a socialist. Many of Millerand's critics saw him as their ally within the War Ministry.[252] Both descriptions were only partly true. Thomas was a reformer rather than a revolutionary, a pragmatist rather than a theorist. He was also a great admirer of Millerand, and his involvement in munitions production dated back to October 1914 and the initiative of the latter, rather than to May 1915 and his appointment by Viviani.[253]

Thomas's appointment did not, therefore, mark a radical change in course. It did, however, coincide with major increases in output, and he therefore benefited by association. Thomas's role was to give shape and method to war industry. The conversion in 1914–15 was improvised and confused: expedience had of necessity triumphed over system. Senator Charles Humbert reckoned that there were over 900 contracts awaiting signature, and that skilled labour was still being taken from industry for military service.[254] Thomas's answer to this was not collectivism or the requisitioning of factories. He numbered industrialists and members of the Comité des Forges among his friends. His aim was to secure their co-operation. Profits were controlled, but they were

---

[251] Saatmann, *Parlament, Rüstung und Armee*, 178–203; M. Farrar, *French Historical Studies*, XI (1980), 577–609, esp. 595–8. For a contemporary record, see Ferry, *Carnets secrets*, ch. 2.

[252] See e.g. the favourable remarks in Ferry, *Carnets secrets*, 79, 91, 97. Saatmann, *Parlament, Rüstung und Armee*, 182–3, 194, suggests the Senate was less easily gulled.

[253] Godfrey, *Capitalism at war*, 181–5.

[254] Saatmann, *Parlament, Rüstung und Armee*, 194.

preserved. The role of the state, in Thomas's eyes, was to intervene in order to co-ordinate and to arbitrate, to maximize output through a sensible division of resources and of labour.[255] Raw materials were distributed, not through the state but through the development of monopolies organized within specific industries. The regular meetings between the service chiefs and the heads of industry, initiated by Millerand in Bordeaux, were continued and developed under Thomas.[256]

Thus, workers' rights took second place to war needs. Thomas supported employers in their call for more hands, but his goal was an organized economy. He embraced the principles of Taylorism, of scientific management through the division and dilution of labour. Typical of this philosophy was the 'loi Dalbiez', first introduced on 17 August 1915 and amended in October. Designed to winkle out the shirker, its initial purpose was to put into uniform those who had no particular skills. It therefore set limits to the number of exemptions in each industry, thus threatening to constrain rather than promote production. However, thanks largely to Millerand, its revised form did as much to ensure its corollary, a secure supply of skilled workers for industry. The total numbers working in arms production and its related industries swelled from 313,000 in May 1915 to 425,000 in December, and 880,000 in June 1916. The law created a powerful instrument against the obstructionism of a general staff desperate for soldiers, and retained the rights of the state over the individual in time of war. It established the notion of a 'military worker', a man released from military service because of his skills, whose right to shift his place of employment was dependent on the Ministry of War and the imperatives of war production.[257] In theory, such workers enjoyed the wages and privileges appropriate to their jobs; in fact, they lost the right to strike and found their wages depressed by their employers. Thus, for his socialist critics, Thomas gave with one hand—creating workers' committees within the ministry—but took with the other.

The withdrawal of labour for the army was only one of the obstacles which the state had erected in the path of war industry. The other was the moratorium. Manufacturers fulfilling state contracts were permitted to use any working capital they had deposited in the bank, but they could not negotiate fresh loans. A decree of 16 August 1914 permitted the state to pay advances to its contractors, but only to cover raw materials and wages. There was no allowance for plant. Furthermore, the amount of cash that could be withdrawn from

---

[255] Alain Hennebicque, 'Albert Thomas and the war industries', in Fridenson (ed.), *French home front*, 93–108; see also Becker, *La France en guerre*, 54–6.

[256] See Hardach, 'Industrial mobilisation', in Fridenson (ed.), *French home front*, 78–80.

[257] Hatry, 'Les Rapports gouvernement, armée, industrie privée', in Canini (ed.), *Les Fronts invisibles*, 173–4; Flood, *France 1914–18*, 65–6; Duroselle, *La Grande Guerre des français*, 180; Farrar, *Principled pragmatist*, 177–9; Dereymez, *Cahiers d'histoire*, 2 (1981), 157.

the bank was modified by the value of the advance. The conversion of civilian industries to war production was thus vitiated by lack of funding.

A decree of 15 July 1915 enabled the state to advance money for plant. However, the implications were not fully considered. Thomas's policy was to control profits through fixing prices. But it was patently absurd for the state to pay the same prices for goods manufactured in existing factories and for goods from plant financed through a state advance. By asking for interest on its advances, and later for securities as well, the state cut out the more flagrant routes to profiteering. During the late summer and early autumn of 1915 it also refined other methods for funding conversion. At one extreme the Ministry of War could provide all—the plant, the labour, and the orders: in these circumstances the role of business was to do no more than contribute the management. At the other, the state could increase the price paid for the product so that it included an element for capital depreciation: on 22 September 1915 the ministry's artillery and munitions committee took the view that the ministry would in this way become the ultimate owner of any premises. The middle path was for the ministry to provide a direct subsidy for an undertaking. This lessened the risk to be borne by a reluctant businessman, while at the same time reducing the cost to the state of the final product.[258]

This last device widened the circle of firms involved in the arms business. Small firms, which had been slow to convert to war production, now did so. But the general thrust of the development under Thomas was seen to be towards the growth of monopolies, not their reduction. Small workshops were consolidated under one head. Large factories replaced small. In 1921, as in 1911, 99 per cent of French businesses employed fewer than 100 workers; but in arms production this was true of only just over 25 per cent of firms.[259] For his critics, Thomas's actions were at odds with his philosophy: his management of the war economy was strengthening capitalism rather than replacing it. The provision for direct state ownership was not acted on—or at least not immediately. Like Rathenau, Thomas—albeit approaching from a different political direction—pursued compromise in the interests of immediate effectiveness. It was a solution, as in Germany, that proved equal to the demands of 1915. But in 1916 the need for munitions would be cranked up once more. The improvisation of shell production lay within the competence of all large, well-equipped engineering firms. But heavy artillery required massive equipment capable of operating to exact specifications. France had still not attended to these needs, and it was to these that Joffre drew attention in a lengthy list on 30 May 1916.

In 1916 France would no longer enjoy one advantage which had accrued to it in 1914. Because at the outset of the war it was the senior military partner in the

[258] Jèze and Truchy, *War finance*, 119–48.
[259] Reboul, *Mobilisation industrielle*, 158–9; Dereymez, *Cahiers d'histoire*, 2 (1981), 158.

Entente, it could reasonably expect Britain to act as its economic prop. Its drive to boost its munitions output could be built in part on raw materials imported from its ally. In 1913 France had bought 11 million tonnes of coal from Britain. In 1915 it acquired 18.9 million tonnes. In January 1916 France's orders for British iron were running at 115,000 tons per month. Through these imports France was both compensating for its lost territories and budgeting for further industrial expansion. The fact that Britain could supply them is, in its turn, witness to the comparative slowness of British industrial conversion. But in 1916, as its war industries gathered pace and as it fielded a major army, Britain had to hold back on the export of raw materials to its ally. France was told it could only have 40,000 tonnes of iron a month, and its imports of British coal stabilized at 18.17 million tonnes for the year.[260]

Britain's industrial mobilization was not constrained by a lack of raw materials. Its exports of iron and steel had already fallen from 5 million tons in 1913 to 3.9 million in 1914. Under the impact of the prohibitions of 1916 they dwindled to 2.3 million tons in 1917. At the same time imports of ferrous material rose, approaching a million tons in 1915. Thus, total steel production grew year on year, from 7.6 million tons in 1913 to almost 9 million in 1916.[261]

The slowness of Britain's industrial mobilization appears paradoxical for another reason. In 1914 it spent more on defence per head of its population than any country in the world. Furthermore, because Britain's per capita income was higher than that of its rivals, the burden of military spending was low in relation to net national product. It therefore had both the highest level of defence spending in absolute terms and the greatest capacity for further expansion.[262] Most of this money was disbursed domestically, and 70 per cent of it was channelled towards private manufacturers. Furthermore, its leading arms producers, pre-eminently Vickers but also Armstrong Whitworth, had firmly established themselves in export markets. On the face of it, Vickers enabled Britain to respond to industrial mobilization more effectively than did Krupp enable Germany or Schneider-Creusot France.

In reality the outlook was less positive, for three reasons. First, the British armaments sector was less internally competitive than appearances suggested. Armstrong was in decline; many of the other firms in the business, like Maxim-Nordenfeld or William Beardmore, were wholly or partly owned by Vickers. Secondly, much of Vickers's overseas business was conducted through subsidiary companies established abroad: thus, its success in Sweden, Spain, Austria-Hungary, France, Italy, Russia, Japan, and Turkey was represented—at least in part—in plant available to those nations and not, as was the case with

[260] Knauss, *Kriegsfinanzierung*, 51; Godfrey, *Capitalism at war*, 222–3.
[261] Birkett, *Journal of the Royal Statistical Society*, LXXXIII (1920), 355, 360.
[262] Davis and Huttenback, *Mammon and the pursuit of empire*, 161; Hobson, *Journal of European Economic History*, XXII (1993), 461–506.

Krupp in Germany, to Britain. Thirdly, Britain was a sea-power. Vickers was able to secure orders for warships because of the Royal Navy, just as Krupp could sell its guns on the back of the reputation of the German army. 'The old-fashioned little British Army', Kitchener told the president of the Board of Trade in August 1914, 'was such an infinitely small proportion of the world's demand that looking after its equipment was not much more difficult than buying a straw hat at Harrods.'[263] British industry was not adapted to the maintenance of a large army for protracted land operations.

Indeed, it could almost be argued that the greater the focus on naval building the greater were the obstacles to Britain in the race to convert its industry to wartime production. Fleets were more expensive in terms of capital equipment than armies. Therefore the export of warships and of naval ordnance was a much bigger money-spinner than that of field artillery or rifles. To concentrate on naval armaments was sound business sense. Between 1900 and 1914 British exporters secured 63.2 per cent of seven overseas markets; France got 9.4 per cent and Germany 7.6 per cent. But Britain's reinforcement of its commercial gain worked against the achievement of a balance in capabilities. Furthermore, the principal strategic function of large fleets was not war but deterrence. They were adapted to the maintenance of stability and order in international relations. Navalism was costly but—crudely put—it concentrated on equipment, not projectiles, on gun turrets and armour plate rather than on shells and mines. It was therefore not about the creation of large numbers of expendable units for the fighting of a major war.[264]

The British government's policy in the event of war was simply to increase the flow of orders to private firms. In the 1890s the private arms companies had received 45 per cent of the amount spent annually on munitions; during the Boer War they got 75 per cent. But British arms firms, no more than other businesses in Britain or other arms firms elsewhere, could not afford to keep plant idle. The flood of orders in 1899 had resulted in a backlog of between one and two years in the deliveries of field guns by May 1901. Then, in 1902 orders evaporated and productive capacity languished. In 1905 the War Office divided a major order for new field guns between Vickers, Armstrong, and—in a deliberate bid to promote competition—the Coventry Ordnance Works. But the army turned to outside competition precisely because of the transitory nature of the demand. Its long-term policy, affirmed in a report on government factories in 1907, was to keep the Royal Arsenal fully employed in peacetime. Eighty per cent of the army's orders for guns and shells between 1909 and 1914 were placed with the Royal Ordnance Factories. The government

---

[263] Crow, *Man of push and go*, 71.
[264] Trebilcock, *Vickers*, esp. 9, 21–4, 123; also Clive Trebilcock, 'The British armaments industry 1890–1914: false legend and true utility', in Best and Wheatcroft (eds.), *War, economy and the military mind*, 89–107.

workshops were therefore restricted to regular work, but were left without spare capacity for wartime expansion. The effect was to increase the government's reliance on private industry in an emergency, but without any effort to provide a flow of business sufficient to maintain the latter's plant in the interim. In 1908–9 the trade received only 44 per cent of government munitions orders. Although work increased after 1909, it was stimulated by the naval competition with Germany, and army orders constituted only a tiny fraction of the 70 per cent of government munitions orders passed to private industry by 1914. Vickers received no army contracts in 1911, and were asked for a mere twenty-two field guns in 1913–14.[265]

Nobody had planned for an expansion of the army on the scale undertaken by Kitchener. In 1914 the army had 795,000 rifles in stock. All but 70,000 of these were already in use or had to be issued on mobilization. Its holdings of field guns, including heavy artillery designed for field service (the 60 pounder), amounted to 906 pieces, sufficient to equip the BEF and a further five divisions. But between 4 August and 12 September 1914 478,893 men joined the army: guns were needed not for five but for fifty divisions. Kitchener's New Armies trained with antiquated weapons if they were lucky and broomsticks if they were not. By November 1914 the first New Army had only 30 per cent of the modern rifles and 11 per cent of the field guns it required. For later formations such equipment levels would seem lavish. Britain's problem in creating a mass army was not so much manpower as munitions.[266]

The War Office duly increased its orders to the arms trade. By 21 October 781,000 rifles were under contract for delivery by 1 July 1915. Orders for 878 18-pounders were placed with the Royal Gun Factory, Vickers, and Armstrong, and for 150 4.5-inch howitzers with the Coventry Ordnance Works and the government factories. The arms trade performed as best it could in the circumstances. Firms increased their plant and their working hours to boost output. The government works at Enfield doubled its weekly production of rifles to 3,000 by 14 November; the London Small Arms Company reckoned it could produce 700 rifles a week at the outset, but had raised this to 1,500 by January 1915. Output of 18-pounder shell, planned to reach 162,000 in the first six months of the war, actually totalled 409,000. The total stocks of 18-pounder ammunition available at the outbreak, 654,000 rounds, were made to last until February 1915, and by March 2 million rounds of all calibres had been received at the front.[267] Munitions output in August 1914 had been increased 90 per cent

[265] Clive Trebilcock, 'War and the failure of industrial mobilisation: 1899 to 1914', in Winter (ed.), *War and economic development*, 139–64; Trebilcock, *Vickers*, esp. 74–80; French, *British economic and strategic planning*, 44–8; Stevenson, *Armaments and the coming of war*, 26, 29.

[266] Simkins, *Kitchener's army*, 279, 282, 290, 292; French, *British economic and strategic planning*, 139–40; also Hankey, *Supreme Command*, 257.

[267] *Ministry of Munitions*, vol. I, pt. 1, 34–5.

by October, 186 per cent by January 1915 and 388 per cent by March.[268] The response was sufficiently impressive to argue that the effects of munitions shortage were more severe at home than in France.

Where the crisis was really evident was on paper. Deliveries did not keep pace with contracts, and the arrears accumulated as the army grew and further orders were placed. More men meant that 'the maxima of one month became the minima of the next'.[269] The BEF grew 320 per cent in 1915. The rise in demand, therefore, constantly challenged the increase in production. Moreover, ammunition scales were increased, so deepening the appearance of crisis. In February 1915 the establishment of shells per field gun in France was raised from 1,500 shells to 2,000. After the battles of Aubers Ridge and Festubert stocks of 18-pounder shells dropped from over 800 to 600. Although they rose to 1,000 by the year's end, and although the number of guns they were designed to serve also rose, shell supply per gun was still only half the established scale. And so the figures highlighted a failure to meet an ever expanding target and obscured a major increase in production in absolute terms.[270]

Deliveries of rifles were closest to target: by June 1915 rifle production was only 12 per cent in arrears, and 1,153,000 rifles had been issued (excluding a further 410,000 foreign and drill rifles). In other categories of weaponry the problems of rapid conversion were writ large. The output of shell was the most alarming: by 29 May 1915 38,806,046 rounds of all calibres had been ordered but only 1,972,558 delivered. This at least made the implications of the shortfall in the production of field guns less acute: only 800 of 2,338 18-pounders had been received. The criticisms of the army for its failure to use more machine-guns were singularly ill-directed when Vickers had managed to manufacture only 1,022 of the 1,792 due for delivery by July 1915. More contracts for more machine-guns would not have added to the firepower of the army when industry could not cope with its existing orders. Piling contract on top of contract did not in itself create the plant or provide the labour necessary for production.[271]

The fact that Kitchener, as secretary of state for war, recognized this essential truth has formed the basis for a reversal of his status in the history of British munitions production. In the hands of Lloyd George and his acolytes, the War Office's management of munitions supply in 1914–15 was the embodiment of conservatism. It failed to prepare big enough orders, and it restricted its dealings to an established circle of arms producers. When the government

---

[268] Dewar, *Great munitions feat*, 127.
[269] *Ministry of Munitions*, vol. I, pt. 1, 14.
[270] Brown, *British logistics*, 92–5, 103.
[271] Ibid. 146–50; Simkins, *Kitchener's army*, 283–5; Trebilcock, 'War and the failure of industrial mobilisation', in Winter (ed.), *War and economic development*, 154–6. Trebilcock's calculation of arrears seems to embrace all items not delivered even if they were not behind schedule.

issued contracts in excess of the capacity of the arms firms, it left those firms to subcontract without itself checking on the ability of the subcontractors to meet their delivery dates or to satisfy the army's inspection standards. But, Kitchener's advocates point out, delegation made administrative sense. The War Office was stripped of personnel by the need to staff the BEF. Restricting the management problems to a small group of known private firms made the task of the officer responsible, the master general of the ordnance, a realistic one. Moreover, it worked. By 31 December 1915 shell deliveries totalled 16,460,501, 88 per cent of which had arrived in the last six months. But 13,746,433 rounds were on the War Office's account and only 2,714,468 on that of the Ministry of Munitions. Although the Ministry of Munitions was created under Lloyd George's aegis at the end of May 1915, none of its products was received until late October, and War Office orders were still being received well into 1916. The growth in output achieved in the course of 1915 was a consequence, not of the establishment of a dedicated ministry halfway through that year but of the steady conversion and expansion of war industry since August 1914.[272]

However, as with the war ministries in Germany and France, the British War Office was frequently its own worst enemy. Kitchener's resistance to outside advice could manifest itself as insouciance. Most notoriously, he informed Asquith that growing public anxiety concerning the army's shell supply was misplaced. The basis for this advice, which formed the thrust of a speech by Asquith on 20 April 1915, was an assurance given to Kitchener by Sir John French.[273] But it also reflected Kitchener's own intention, that his New Armies should not be committed to the continent until 1917, by which time war industry would be well into its stride.[274]

A telling and much cited instance of War Office conservatism was its reaction to the Stokes mortar. The tactical value in trench warfare of the *Minenwerfer* and its French equivalents did not escape the British. The Royal Gun Factory produced its first mortars in December. Simultaneously, Wilfred Stokes, chairman of Ransomes and Rapier, an East Anglian engineering company producing locks and cranes and totally unconnected with the arms trade, devised a 3-inch mortar of the simplest construction. It was little more than 'an educated drain-pipe', without wheels and divisible into man-portable loads. Its bomb was detonated by a firing pin as it fell to the bottom of the tube, and it could fire quickly enough to have three rounds in the air simultaneously. Made in six compartments, the bomb exploded at unequal intervals, bouncing around the enemy trench. The Board of Ordnance rejected the Stokes mortar

[272] Simkins, *Kitchener's army*, 324; for similar points, Cassar, *Kitchener*, 330–60; Harvey, *Collision of empires*, 282; Chris Wrigley, 'The ministry of munitions: an innovatory department', in Burk (ed.), *War and the state*, 34–5; *Ministry of Munitions*, vol. I, pt. 1, 150; Crow, *Man of push and go*, 71–2.
[273] Koss, *Asquith*, 181–2; also 171.
[274] French, *English Historical Review*, CIII (1988), 390.

twice, in January and March 1915. Not only had the War Office failed to recognize its tactical effectiveness, it had also failed to appreciate its significance for industrial conversion. Stokes rightly stressed that his tube and its bomb could be produced by firms that were not capable of producing high-explosive shell. The establishment of an engineer munitions branch to deal with weaponry for trench warfare might have advanced Stokes's case, if the master general of the ordnance had not concluded that weapons using explosive propellants should be handled by the directorate of artillery. Not until June 1915, when it was transferred to the Ministry of Munitions as its trench warfare department, was the engineer munitions branch given responsibility for mortars. In August 1915 the directorate of artillery approved the Stokes mortar, and in September the War Office ordered 200. But Lloyd George took the credit: in the same month the Ministry of Munitions ordered 1,000. A total of 11,421 were manufactured in the war, and it became the prototype for all modern mortars.[275]

Kitchener's biggest vulnerability, therefore, was his protection of Major-General Sir Stanley von Donop, the master general of the ordnance. Christopher Addison, who became Lloyd George's parliamentary private secretary at the Ministry of Munitions, said of von Donop, he was either 'incompetent or a traitor. I am inclined to the latter view.'[276] The master general's Teutonic name did nothing to remove such aspersions. But the problem was also organizational. The office, historically significant but castrated in 1855, had been enhanced after the Boer War in recognition of the importance of munitions supply in modern war. But its powers were still insufficient. On the one hand Kitchener recruited men oblivious of equipment considerations; on the other, the army contracts department negotiated with firms while remaining independent of the master general. Not until January 1915 was the contracts department subordinated to the master general, and until then von Donop's task was little more than the assessment of demands.[277]

The first clash between von Donop and Lloyd George flared in October 1914, when the chancellor of the exchequer discovered that the master general of the ordnance had not told the arms firms that the Treasury had made £20 million available to increase plant. Von Donop was still observing the cost controls and auditing procedures appropriate to peacetime orders; Lloyd George was not. As a result, a cabinet committee on munitions was formed. Its first three meetings, between 12 and 21 October, were concerned with the supply of guns, powder, and rifles. Its solution to these problems was to add to the

[275] Scott, *Army Quarterly*, CXI (1981), 205–28; Adams, *Arms and the wizard*, 151–2; Linnenkohl, *Vom Einzelschuss zur Feuerwalze*, 200–4.

[276] Wrigley, 'The ministry of munitions', in Burk (ed.), *War and the state*, 38.

[277] Adams, *Arms and the wizard*, 10; French, *British economic and strategic planning*, 133–4; *Ministry of Munitions*, vol. I, pt. 1, 46–71.

number of orders: contracts for guns were raised from 878 to 1,608. But, beyond urging the armaments firms to increase their plant and the War Office to widen their range of contractors, the committee had no formula to expedite the process of industrial conversion. Its work, therefore, heightened the difference between demand and supply, fuelling a sense of crisis rather than resolving it. After October it did not meet again until December, and by January it was moribund.[278]

However, the demise of the committee was not entirely self-generated. It also owed something to the reluctance of Kitchener to co-operate. The more Lloyd George chivvied, the more the secretary of state for war was anxious to show that his own ministry could cope without external intervention. Part of the confusion in attributing credit for industrial mobilization in Britain arises precisely from the duplication of initiatives which followed. Furthermore, it is clear that, although Lloyd George was the cabinet's spokesman, he was not necessarily the originator of its policies.[279] The role of the chancellor was above all rhetorical: he created a public awareness of the need for full mobilization. Kitchener's devices were more discreet. The central theme around which these issues were played out was not resources (as in Germany) or plant, but labour.

The trade-off between the creation of a voluntarily enlisted mass army and the manpower needs of industry did not become acute until 1915. By the middle of that year mining had lost 21.8 per cent of its workforce, iron and steel 18.8 per cent, engineering 19.5 per cent, electrical engineering 23.7 per cent, shipbuilding 16.5 per cent, small-arms manufacturers 16 per cent, and chemicals and explosives 23.8 per cent.[280] But within the arms industry specifically, the loss of skilled labour—although in aggregate terms small in number—had an effect much earlier. In December it was the principal explanation by the arms firms for their failure to meet existing contracts. Armstrong needed 4,150 skilled workers, and Vickers 1,676. By June 1915 the two government factories and sixteen private firms engaged on munitions work were short of 14,000 skilled workers.[281] Plant lay idle as a result: in July four-fifths of munition-making equipment was employed for a single shift only, and even in December 750 presses and other machines were not being used. The numbers employed in the iron and steel industry only reached their pre-war totals after July 1916.[282]

Vickers had already led the way in pioneering two responses to the problem. In September 1914 they suggested that skilled workers engaged in arms

[278] *Ministry of Munitions*, vol. I, pt. 1, 93–9; Hankey, *Supreme command*, 309.
[279] Gilbert, *Lloyd George*, 157.
[280] Adams, *Arms and the wizard*, 72.
[281] *Ministry of Munitions*, vol. I, pt. 2, 1–3. For what follows, see ibid. pt. 2, *passim*; Adams, *Arms and the wizard*, 71–82; Grigg, *Lloyd George*, 216–21; Gilbert, *Lloyd George*, 155–8, 171–8.
[282] Dewar, *Great munitions feat*, 48; Hughes, 'Monstrous anger of the guns', 66; Birkett, *Journal of the Royal Statistical Society*, LXXXIII (1920), 373.

production should be given badges, to show the importance of their jobs and to quarantine them from the social and moral pressures to enlist. The cabinet approved the idea of 'badging' in December, and it was adopted by the Admiralty in the same month. The dilemma confronting the army was greater: it needed more men in the army and it needed more munitions. The War Office did not endorse 'badging' until March 1915. However, in January it began, albeit tentatively, to release skilled men who had already enlisted, and in May it produced its first list of exempted occupations.

The second solution was the 'dilution' of labour, the substitution of skilled jobs by unskilled. In November 1914 the trades unions and the management of the Vickers works at Crayford agreed that unskilled workers could be used on fully automatic machines. But Vickers was unable to get an extension of the agreement to its other works, and the negotiation of any relaxation in restrictive practices fell prey to union leaders' fears that they would forfeit their members' support. Kitchener refused to intervene, and in January the Board of Trade appointed Sir George Askwith as chairman of a committee on production. Askwith's remit embraced a wide range of manufacturing industries, of which the most important was shipbuilding. However, the only substantive outcome was the so-called shells and fuses agreement of 5 March, thrashed out between the Engineering Employers' Federation and the Amalgamated Society of Engineers. The two bodies accepted the principle of dilution, but only for the duration of the war and only in the production of munitions.

Dilution could work within the armaments business because precision engineering and machine tools working to tolerances of a hundredth of an inch enabled their manufacture to be broken up into a large number of distinct operations. The Lee-Enfield rifle had 131 distinct parts, and the barrel alone involved eighty-five separate machining operations. Standardization was ensured by the use of 1,250 gauges. Thus, the ratio of skilled to unskilled labour could fall. Kynochs, who at their peak produced 25 million small-arms rounds a day, expanded their labour force from 2,051 in 1913 to 15,435 by 1916, but their skilled workers fell to 250. As a post-war propagandist trumpeted: 'Working within fine limits on a great manufacturing scale by hundreds of thousands of unskilled hands supervised by a sprinkling of skilled is one of the chief discoveries of the war.'[283]

By March 1915 a second aspect of the labour problem was looming in the government's calculations. This was the right to strike. The threat to the completion of contracts through strike action grew as unemployment receded and workers felt themselves caught in a spiral of rising prices and falling real wages. The effect was to give a twist to the government's amendment to the Defence of the Realm act. Under the original act, passed in August 1914, the

---

[283] Dewar, *Great munitions feat*, 111; also 82, 84, 86.

government had appropriated to itself the right to requisition the means of munitions production. The amendment to the act, adopted in March 1915, was a reflection of the slowness with which other engineering firms had switched to war production. It was designed to enable the government compulsorily to direct firms from private manufacturing to government work. But its formulation and introduction coincided with strikes on Clydeside. Grafted onto the bill, therefore, were clauses prohibiting strikes, insisting on compulsory arbitration, and restricting the freedom of movement 'of any workmen or class of workmen whose services may be required'. Such an affront to trade-unionism required a sop. The corollary to the loss of rights inflicted on employees was a limitation of the profits enjoyed by employers.

The amendment to the Defence of the Realm act acquired these wider ramifications for labour and for war profits because it coincided with Lloyd George's efforts to give bite to Askwith's work of the previous month. On 17 March he convened a conference at the Treasury to which he invited trade-union leaders. The proposals of Askwith's committee embracing dilution, compulsory arbitration, and suspension of the right to strike were accepted on the 19th—or at least so Lloyd George averred. In reality, proof would await practice. Those trades-union leaders present said no more than that they would recommend the committee's suggestions to their memberships; the Amalgamated Society of Engineers came to a separate deal; and the Miners' Federation was never party to the agreement.

Through leaving the issue of labour relations to the Board of Trade's committee of production Kitchener found that, within two months, the initiative in munitions production was passing from the War Office to the cabinet, and specifically to the Treasury. The marginalization of the War Office became clear on 22 March, when Asquith appointed a committee to plan the formation of a new committee on munitions. It was to be subordinate to the cabinet and not to the War Office, and it was to have the power to place contracts. Lloyd George attended; Kitchener was not invited. The secretary of state for war protested and then threatened to resign if the new committee was given executive powers. On 31 March he endeavoured to regain the ground he had lost by establishing a specifically War Office body, the armaments output committee.[284]

The remit of the committee, according to the official announcement of its formation, was to take steps to provide additional labour for war production. Kitchener's first priority was to ensure the full utilization of existing plant through the replacement of the workers lost by Vickers and their ilk. But behind this apparently narrow definition of the committee's responsibilities lay a broader agenda. On the one hand it was to exploit the amendment to the

---

[284] Cassar, *Asquith*, 85–6; see, in general, Fraser, *Canadian Journal of History*, XVIII (1983), 74–9.

Defence of the Realm act by diverting labour from other industries, and on the other it was to spread munitions contracts to a wider range of firms through the establishment of co-operative groups. The latter built on steps already taken in conjunction with the Board of Trade to establish local organizations for production. Many businesses could not produce complete items but could manufacture parts. For example, thirty-seven firms were asked to tender for the production of shell on 19 October 1914; only six were able to do so, but 129 offered to supply individual components or undertake particular processes.[285] In January the Board of Trade and the Engineering Employers' Federation began to argue that rather than develop arms production through the existing major firms, both by encouraging them to subcontract and by diverting labour from other work to munitions production, it would be more advantageous to offer direct contracts to minor firms. These businesses would act as co-operatives, pooling their resources on a regional basis. The first such group was formed in Leicester in January. The armaments output committee developed both of the principles embodied in these initiatives—the regional structure (borrowed in its turn from France) and direct contracts. By May 2,500 firms would be operating under War Office contract.

Its work, therefore, anticipated and shaped that of the Ministry of Munitions. Nor were these the only significant innovations that came to be associated with the latter, but in reality had their origins in the War Office. Lloyd George, as minister of munitions, made great play of his recruitment of 'men of push and go', of businessmen rather than civil servants. But Lloyd George was less original than he claimed. Initially the War Office was fearful of employing outsiders, and particularly businessmen whose firms stood to profit from any consequent contracts. But it was Kitchener who called in the barrister and scientist Lord Moulton to chair a committee on explosives in November 1914. When the committee found it needed executive powers, Kitchener appointed Moulton head of the explosives supply department. The composition of the armaments output committee confirms the point. Of its six members, only two (Kitchener and von Donop) came from the army. A prime mover in shaping its agenda was Allan M. Smith, secretary of the Engineering Employers' Federation. The committee's chairman was George Macaulay Booth, a Liverpool shipowner. Booth had been consulted by Kitchener in December 1914, and at a meeting on 16 March 1915, convened by Kitchener to discuss the labour problem, Booth used the Leicester model to press on the secretary of state the wisdom of spreading munitions contracts to every suitable engineering workshop in the land. It was largely by dint of Smith's and Booth's efforts that the regional structure took shape. Co-opted to

---

[285] *Ministry of Munitions*, vol. I, pt. 1, 104.

aid the committee was Sir Percy Girouard who, although a former soldier, was by then the managing director of the Armstrong works at Elswick.[286]

In Booth's hands the armaments output committee would form the embryo of the Ministry of Munitions. But the parentage became confused by Asquith's announcement on 8 April of another body, the Treasury munitions of war committee, under the chairmanship of Lloyd George. This was the product of the preliminary meeting on 22 March; it continued to exclude Kitchener, but it did embrace von Donop as well as Booth and, in due course, Girouard. The remit of the committee was couched in the widest possible terms, and Lloyd George described its function as that of policy. For the chancellor, the armaments output committee was the executive arm of his committee. In the personal battle between Kitchener and Lloyd George the latter had regained the initiative. In itself, the munitions of war committee achieved little, but in institutional terms it gave the armaments output committee a status which made its subordination to the War Office progressively less sustainable.

Rumbling away on the margins of the management of munitions were the bigger issues of state control, so central to the comparable debates in Germany, but overshadowed in Britain by the clash of personalities. Kitchener's resolve to manage the labour question implied the central organization of manpower. On 5 March 1915 a committee set up to deal with labour problems on Clydeside proposed, among other things, that the government should take over the munitions industry. The proposal divided the cabinet, but not along predictable lines. Runciman, the president of the Board of Trade, favoured such ideas, despite his free-trade credentials. Churchill, on the other hand, who had endorsed a proposal for the co-ordination of industry throughout the empire in September 1914, criticized Runciman's scheme as 'socialite and anarchic'.[287] The cabinet member closest to New Liberalism before the war, Lloyd George, endorsed the sort of corporatism advocated by the unionist business committee, a Conservative backbench group formed in January 1915. Its leader, W. A. S. Hewins, was a tariff reformer, who described 'putting our economic resources on a war footing' as a long-held objective of the imperial preference movement.[288] Less divisive politically was the model of France, whose national organization of its resources was more immediately related to the onset of war. The potential beneficiaries from a rationalization of existing plant were the big firms. G. H. West, seconded from Armstrong Whitworth to the War Office to advise on shell production, favoured a census of all machinery, and the subsequent allocation of plant from small firms to those that could make

---

[286] *Ministry of Munitions*, vol. I, pt. 1, pt. 3, *passim*; Moulton, *Life of Lord Moulton*, 179–82, 271; Crow, *Man of push and go*, 87–106.

[287] David (ed.), *Inside Asquith's cabinet*, 225, also 228; see also Fraser, *Canadian Journal of History*, XVIII (1983), 77–9; Dewar, *Great munitions feat*, 31, 117–18.

[288] Hewins, *Apologia of an imperialist*, ii. 5 (diary entry of 16 October 1914).

better use of it; furthermore, local groups of those involved in arms manufacture should be subordinated to the management of one of the principal existing manufacturers. Thus, capitalism and rationalization would go hand in hand, to the advantage not only of national output but also of Armstrong and its pre-war rivals.

By April a sort of stalemate had been reached in which no one individual and no one ministry had overall responsibility for munitions production, but in which the principal players—including Lloyd George—seemed content to collude. Kitchener acknowledged the reality on 26 April when he authorized Girouard and Booth to act without further reference to him.[289] At the macro-level control of munitions was divided between Kitchener and Lloyd George; at the micro, between Girouard and Booth. The depth of ill-feeling between the former was not reflected in the relationship of the latter, but they did diverge in their solutions to the problem. Girouard preferred the establishment of state factories to Booth's spreading of contracts. The result was compromise. Britain was divided into two zones, 'A' and 'B'. 'A' areas were those within 20 miles of existing arms factories: the policy here was to direct labour to the established plant. 'B' areas were those distant from arms works: in these cases contracts would be shared among new firms on the co-operative basis.

Compromise was also in evidence in von Donop's report to the munitions of war committee on 13 April. The master general outlined the programme for the next four months. It was shaped neither by anticipated demand nor by likely supply, but by balancing the two. At the end of 1914 Sir John French had pitched the required output of 18-pounder ammunition at fifty rounds per gun per day. This was excessive: the French advised Kitchener that twenty-five would be enough, but the War Office adopted twenty as their target and seventeen as their minimum. On the supply side, von Donop almost halved the quantity of shell promised by the contractors, from 420,000 to 215,000. In this fashion his estimates of production and consumption all but matched. But his calculations in achieving this satisfactory outcome proved ill-conceived on both sides of the equation. On demand, it is not clear that his requirement for 18-pounders incorporated the growth in that period from two armies to six (although that for 4.5-inch howitzers certainly did). On supply, contractors delivered half of what von Donop hoped for, and therefore a quarter of what they had promised.

Von Donop did all that Lloyd George's munitions of war committee asked him to do. A balance sheet after his fall concluded that he had 'started [the war] with 27 large contracts; those developed into 279, and those again with sub-contractors into 3,000'.[290] But his supply-side calculations and measured approach were driven from the field on 14 May 1915. Sir John French and *The Times*, for long an advocate of a Ministry of Munitions, attributed the setback

[289] Cassar, *Kitchener*, 346–7.   [290] David (ed.), *Inside Asquith's cabinet*, 250.

at Aubers Ridge on 9 May specifically to a lack of 18-pounder high-explosive shell. So armed, the British would have been able to level the German parapets, as the French (once again the models) had done. The subsequent furore obscured the fact that the real focus of the report of Repington, *The Times* correspondent, was on the need for heavy artillery, not more shells for field guns; the latter would never break down deep defences.[291] But it was the shells issue which rekindled Lloyd George's attack on Kitchener. Moreover, it was the shell shortage which revealed Asquith's public assurances at Newcastle the previous month as a sham. The fall of the Liberal government which followed was not precipitated solely by the issue of munitions, nor was the division between French and Kitchener solely over the technical issues. But the effects of both were to complete the restructuring of the management of Britain's war industries. At first Asquith was not persuaded of the need for a new government department, but he was convinced that his government's credibility needed Kitchener. The king pointed out that Kitchener's continuation at the War Office could only be sustained politically if he was relieved of responsibility for production. On 9 June 1915 the Ministry of Munitions was created, and Lloyd George was appointed to head it.

Lloyd George's move from the Treasury made sense, given his instincts in war, which were those of expenditure rather than economy. 'The munitions conception', one Treasury official reported to McKenna in October 1915, 'is "all of everything".'[292] Lloyd George's own credo was: 'Take Kitchener's maximum; square it, multiply that by two; and when you are in sight of that double it again for good luck.'[293] Much of this was said for effect, but there were practical consequences: his critics argued that the multiplication of orders drove up prices rather than output. Sir G. Gibbs gave Kitchener sage advice: the munitions issue was 'not a question of the allocation of contracts, but of the organization of production'.[294]

Lloyd George's principal contribution to the management of the war economy, therefore, was to shift from supply to demand as its key determinant. In June he accepted Sir John French's suggestion of a ration of twenty-five rounds per field gun per day, and in 1916 he moved to the original target of fifty— although this did indeed prove excessive. On 19 June 1915 he asked Major-General J. P. Du Cane: 'Given an army of 1,000,000 men what would your requirements be in guns and ammunition in order to deliver a decisive and sustained attack to enable you to break through the German lines?' Du Cane's reply formed the basis of Lloyd George's programme. The contractors' current capabilities were not consulted.[295]

[291] Fraser, *Canadian Journal of History*, XVIII (1983), 70–3.
[292] Public Record Office T 170/73/6.10.15; I am grateful to Dr Martin Farr for this reference.
[293] Farr, 'McKenna', 253.   [294] Hewins, *Apologia of an imperialist*, ii. 37–8.
[295] *Ministry of Munitions*, vol. I, pt. 1, 23–6, 38–42.

The detail of what Lloyd George did was almost entirely derived from others. Much came from the War Office via the armaments output committee. Much, too, was culled from the example of France. Albert Thomas established a close relationship with Lloyd George. Thus, while in Paris the French Ministry of War was earning the brickbats of the senate commission on the army, in London it was winning the plaudits of its British allies.

Lloyd George borrowed ideas but then took them much further. Most striking in this respect was the recruitment of businessmen to the new ministry; within three months he had enlisted over ninety. Negatively, this was a product of necessity: there were not enough civil servants to do the job.[296] Positively, it reflected Lloyd George's distrust of experts: Sir Percy Girouard, the first director-general of munitions supply in the new department, was an early casualty on these grounds.[297] What he wanted was managers—and not cautious men, but improvisers who would respond to crises. His recruits, who included Samuel Hardman Lever, Eric Geddes, and William Beveridge, came from the City and from the distillers Johnny Walker, as well as from the obviously relevant industries of coal, shipbuilding, machine tools, and armaments. Among the most important was Kitchener's protégé, George Macaulay Booth.

Booth, initially in conjunction with Girouard, developed the organization of the new ministry. He confronted two obstacles, both of which meant that the structure was shifting and uncertain. The first, predictably, was Kitchener, and the second, less predictably, was Lloyd George.

Kitchener himself was entirely supportive in his personal dealings with the new ministry, but his demeanour—at least at the outset—may have been the product of a misapprehension. He seems to have believed that the Ministry of Munitions remained under the War Office's purview. The various agencies involved in munitions production were only gradually transferred from one to the other. Shells made under the auspices of the ministry were sent to Woolwich to be filled in the ordnance factories, which were still under the aegis of the War Office. In mid-August the latter were said to turn out 100,000 shells per week fewer than did the former. The ordnance factories were transferred to the Ministry of Munitions in the same month, but the process of inspection remained centralized at Woolwich.[298] The research-and-development functions of the Board of Ordnance were not transferred until November. Until then, too, the War Office remained the conduit for discussions on munitions with the India Office.

The problem with Lloyd George was that he shared at least one attribute with Kitchener—both were unsystematic. The Welshman appointed Girouard

[296] French, *British strategy and war aims*, 117.
[297] Grigg, *Lloyd George*, 259–60; Gilbert, *Lloyd George*, 211; Adams, *Arms and the wizard*, 47–8; Addison, *Four and a half years*, i. 83, 86–7.
[298] Addison, *Four and a half years*, i. 83, 105, 115–17, 134.

as director-general of munitions but then sacked him without fully replacing him. Neither Girouard nor Lloyd George himself favoured the creation of a board of munitions. Thus, each department within the ministry went its own way, a trend encouraged by the appointment of captains of industry accustomed to running their own affairs. Lloyd George's tendency to say one thing to one person but something else to another did not help. Booth's answer was to meet his fellow departmental heads over lunch; he would also write down what Lloyd George told him to do, read it back to him, and then get him to sign it.[299]

The ministry was divided into four principal departments—a secretariat (under Beveridge), explosives (Lord Moulton), engineer munitions (Brigadier-General L. C. Jackson), and munitions supply (Girouard, at least at first). The latter, developed from the armaments output committee, had three sections—artillery production (Geddes), artillery ammunition (G. H. West), and organization and labour (Booth). In July Geddes's section was divided, so that Geddes retained responsibility for rifles and machine-guns, and artillery formed a new section under Charles Ellis. The subdivision and musical chairs of the munitions supply department continued throughout the next twelve months: by 1 July 1916 it contained ten sections. Trench warfare supply was not, however, one of them. Acquired by the ministry on 23 June 1915, it was responsible for the new weapons generated by the conditions of the western front—grenades, gas, flamethrowers, and mortars. Like explosives supply, it constituted a separate supply department of its own; unlike munitions supply, it contained its own research-and-development capability.

The real organizational strength of the ministry lay not at the centre but in the localities. The ministry was not primarily a producer of weapons; it was a co-ordinator and facilitator. Its first task, carried through in the second half of June, was to conduct a national survey of engineering resources. This having been completed, the country, as France had been, was divided into regions—at first ten and later twelve. Each region had an area office which provided specifications for weapons and helped with labour supply and the allocation of raw materials. The ministry rejected the War Office's preference for subcontracting in favour of direct contracts. The arms firms, as principal contractors, had proved unable to enforce delivery dates or to prevent small firms from bidding up prices through the competition for their services. The issue of the contracts was put in the hands of local boards of management, subordinate to the areas, and formed of businessmen who were deemed to know local capabilities and who served without pay. The boards of management could opt for one of three different structures. The first was to establish national shell factories directly under the board: this was a scheme pioneered

[299] Grieves, *Geddes*, 14, 17; Crow, *Man of push and go*, 117, 125.

by Kitchener at the end of April 1915, and by December there were seventy-three such factories. They mostly produced shell for field guns: fifteen out of forty-seven boards went down this route. The second structure was the co-operative scheme developed by Booth, and appropriate to areas where the concentration of processes in a single factory was impossible: eighteen opted for this solution. The third was a mixture of both methods.

Through the national shell factories the ministry expanded the scope of state production. The manufacture of heavy-artillery shells was entrusted to national projectile factories, fifteen of which were built in 1915 and 1916, and these were placed under the management of the major arms firms. The shells produced in this way were filled in national filling factories, run on lines similar to those for the national shell factories. The effect was to reassert the power of the state in controlling prices, a function effectively forfeited by the contraction of the ordnance workshops before 1914. It also made the state the principal purchaser of a whole range of commodities—metals, coke, dyes, and gas among them—which enabled it to regulate costs through central buying.[300]

The state's relationship with the employers was not an antagonistic one. The national factories were attached to and integrated with existing plant. The ministry enlisted the co-operation of businessmen both directly and indirectly. Certainly, the construction of new government-owned workshops symbolized the much more assertive line taken by the state in Britain than was the case in either Germany or France in 1915. But a principal motivation was not the curbing of capitalism but the taming of the trades unions. National factories appealed to the minister of munitions because, as new institutions, they could become models of best practice, both technically and managerially, for emulation elsewhere in British industry. Above all, they were not so bound by restrictive practices as the older workshops. Significantly, the Munitions of War act of 2 July 1915 was, despite its grandiose title, concerned almost exclusively with the regulation of labour. It built on the shells and fuses agreement and the Treasury agreement to establish compulsory arbitration, the prohibition of strikes, and the curtailment of the freedom to change jobs. Admittedly, the loss of workers' rights was confined to the munitions industry, and those workers were rewarded with 'badges' effectively exempting them from military service. Moreover, these measures, by being clearly related to the duration of the war only, implicitly gave long-term protection to past practices. But trades unionists could legitimately argue that the state's intervention in the munitions industry bore harder on them than on employers. Lloyd George paid lip service to controls on profits, but they were only applied to

[300] Adams, *Arms and the wizard*, 56–69; Grigg, *Lloyd George*, 211–21; *Ministry of Munitions*, vol. III, pt. 1, 1–46, 243–5; Chris Wrigley, 'Ministry of Munitions', in Burk (ed.), *War and the state*, 47–51.

certain enterprises and were set at low levels: indeed, it could be said that Lloyd George, like Thomas in France, used the power of the government to institutionalize the notion of excessive profit-taking by arms firms in wartime.

The Munitions of War act did not, however, resolve the main bone of contention between Lloyd George and the trades unions, that of dilution. Lloyd George harangued the TUC on the issue in September 1915. On 23 December a speech he made in Glasgow was so heckled that he used the powers of the Defence of the Realm act to suppress an accurate report of its contents. The ministry argued that the aim of dilution was not the reduction of skilled jobs but their redistribution and reallocation so that they helped to create opportunities for unskilled workers. Although the ministry established a central labour supply committee in September, progress was limited. By the summer of 1916 about 10,000 unskilled women had replaced 7,436 unskilled men in 150 controlled establishments. Furthermore, for all his talk Lloyd George was much more in the thrall of the unions than he could afford to admit. Confrontation could suspend production; conciliation tended to mean concession.[301]

Lloyd George staked all, therefore, on raising output to meet demand. His policy was to budget for a surplus, to set orders sufficiently high and to enter into contracts sufficiently far into the future to sustain the stimulus to industrial conversion and enhanced production. Arguably, Kitchener's orders in themselves would not have resulted in deliveries in the medium term without the security to industry which Lloyd George's commitment provided.[302]

Furthermore, Lloyd George made a second major contribution. His programmes were dominated by heavy artillery. In the year that Lloyd George was at the Ministry of Munitions the production capacity of lighter guns was reduced 28 per cent, that of medium guns was increased 380 per cent, and that of heavy guns 1,200 per cent.[303] In 1915 both Germany and France were concentrating on field artillery in order to meet immediate crises; they thus postponed consideration of their heavy-gun output until 1916, and saw no significant increases until 1917. In Britain 134 60-pounders were delivered in 1915, and 640 in 1916. Total output of all calibres apart from the 13-pounder, 18-pounder, and 4.5-inch howitzer (i.e. the principal field guns) was eight in 1914, 200 in 1915, and 1,714 in 1916.[304] Britain led the way in changing the balance in artillery armament and thus equipping itself for the *Materialschlachten* of 1916.

The fact that this shift was achieved was a reflection of the capacities of the private arms firms—of Armstrong (primarily responsible for the 60-pounder) and of Vickers (primarily responsible for the other workhorse of the heavy artillery, the 6-inch howitzer). The pressures on them to maximize production

[301] Adams, *Arms and the wizard*, 91–110; Gilbert, *Lloyd George*, 242–50.
[302] Grigg, *Lloyd George*, 271–3.   [303] Adams, *Arms and the wizard*, 172.
[304] *Ministry of Munitions*, vol. X, pt. 1, 96.

in too many directions simultaneously, multiplied in 1914, were relaxed in 1915. Of 10 million shells ordered by the end of 1914, 6.25 million were due from arms firms although their manufacture lay within the competence of many less specialized engineering businesses.[305] In 1915, not least thanks to the network of national shell factories, this responsibility was spread more sensibly. Similarly, orders for field guns could level off as those in place early in the war were met. By the end of 1914 contracts for 3,628 18-pounders had been signed, principally with Vickers and Armstrong, and for 812 4.5-inch howitzers, principally with Coventry Ordnance Works. The army had received 2,672 and 601 of these respectively by the close of the following year; deliveries of 18-pounders could therefore fall to 1,492 in 1916.[306] The pressure on field-gun manufacture also relaxed as production of the Stokes mortar developed in the summer of 1915.

But the heavy-guns programme was a matter of doctrine as well as of capacity. In this respect it was the fruit of Lloyd George's relationship with General Du Cane. In 1914 Du Cane was appointed by French to head an experiments committee with the BEF. Thus, as was to happen in other areas of policy, GHQ set up an alternative source of wisdom to that of the War Office. Lloyd George was not slow to exploit the division, using Du Cane to advise him at the Anglo-French munitions conference in Boulogne on 19 June 1915, and bringing Du Cane in to head design within the ministry when that function was transferred from the Board of Ordnance in November. At Boulogne Du Cane told Lloyd George that the army needed as many heavy guns as light, and that before an attack was launched each heavy gun should have 1,000 rounds, all high explosive with delayed-action fuses. Each field gun would need 2,000 rounds, three-quarters of which should be high explosive.

The programme developed at GHQ on the back of the Boulogne conference called for an additional 400 60-pounders, 400 6-inch howitzers, and 290 8-inch and larger howitzers. This, 'gun programme A', set a total for the army of 8,881 guns of all calibres, both existing and new, of which 7,240 were to be in the field by March 1916. The programme assumed an army of fifty divisions. But by July the War Office was reckoning on an army of seventy divisions. 'Gun programme B' therefore increased French's targets for additional heavy guns to 641, 458, and 316 respectively. In August Lloyd George argued that production should be geared to 100 divisions. 'Gun programme C' now aimed for 920 60-pounders, 980 6-inch howitzers, and 925 larger howitzers by December 1916. The implication was the production of 1,035 more guns than were required for an army of seventy divisions. Kitchener said he could not possibly find the 4,980 officers and 119,198 other ranks that would be required to fire these guns.

[305] Scott, *Vickers*, 98, 101.
[306] *Ministry of Munitions*, vol. I, pt. 1, 45, and vol. X, pt. 1, 9; Dewar, *Great munitions feat*, 123.

Training artillerymen was a more complex and lengthy process than training infantrymen. Thus, at the end of 1915 the British army was actively trying to slough off guns rather than clamouring for more.[307]

As complex a consequence of Lloyd George's programmes as gun crews was ammunition. The shift to high-explosive shell favoured by Du Cane conformed to the pressures to widen the circle of shell manufacturers, as the production of high explosive was simpler than that of shrapnel. But four problems were generated by the change. First was the propellant. Shrapnel used gunpowder, but high explosive—principally thanks to the navy's needs for a more stable propellant—used cordite. Cordite was made of nitroglycerine and gun cotton, the two being gelatinized by the incorporation of acetone, a distillate of wood. In 1914 most acetone came from the United States. Secondly, the switch from lyddite to the more stable TNT as the bursting charge for high-explosive, foreshadowed in trials in 1908, had been confirmed by TNT's effectiveness against the Belgian forts in 1914. But TNT production was still in its infancy, and one-and-a-half tons of TNT required 1 ton of toluene, which itself needed 600 tons of coal. Third was the lack of a reliable fuse for high explosive shells: the fuse in use in 1914 had been designed for the high-angle fire of howitzers and was not adapted to ricochet and grazing fire. And, finally, the shift in favour of high explosive did not automatically rule out all uses of shrapnel for field guns: in determining a long-term munitions programme it was essential that the proportions of the two be fixed, but this was difficult when each day brought fresh and not necessarily convergent experiences of trench warfare.

The domination of the Nobel Dynamite Trust, an Anglo-German cartel, in the private production of propellants meant that research and development had been concentrated in Germany. Germany too produced the phenol which went into lyddite. Nonetheless, the narrowly chemical problems were resolved more speedily than the technical gunnery ones. Chaim Weizmann, the Zionist and professor of chemistry at Manchester University, developed a process for producing acetone from maize mash, as a by-product of his research on synthetic rubber. The alternative method of synthetic production depended on large quantities of potatoes to manufacture inadequate amounts of acetone.[308] The shortage of TNT was circumvented, as in Germany, by its incorporation with ammonium nitrate to produce amatol. Although Britain knew of the Haber process in outline, its access to Chilean saltpetre relieved it of the

[307] Adams, *Arms and the wizard*, 164–72; *Ministry of Munitions*, vol. X, pt. 1, 6–27; Gilbert, *Lloyd George*, 224–30. Hughes, 'Monstrous anger of the guns', 63–4, describes 'gun programme A' as that designed by the War Office for an army of 20 divisions, 'gun programme B' as that developed after Aubers Ridge, and 'gun programme C' as issued on 8 September 1915; his running totals differ, and he says that Kitchener concluded that the final programme would require 6,876 officers and 162,328 gunners.
[308] Reinharz, *English Historical Review*, C (1985), 575–95.

pressure to develop the process's industrial application. In May 1915 approval
was given for the same 60 : 40 mix of TNT and ammonium nitrate as used by
the Germans. But experiments with loading shells by pressing rather than
melting got over the problems in filling encountered by the Germans, and
allowed the British to use TNT and ammonium nitrate in a ratio of up to
20 : 80. To maximize the production of toluene the government requisitioned
all toluol manufactured by coal-tar producers in November 1914. The raw
material constraints on TNT production, as well as the navy's appropriation
of the purest TNT for its guns, meant that the army continued to use lyddite
for the time being. The production of picric acid only ceased in 1918, ironically
just after large-scale phenol factories came on stream. In this fashion Britain
resolved the problem of filling shells before that of making empty shells. The
total output of high explosives and propellants, 434 and 5,298 tons respectively
in the last four months of 1914, reached 20,206 and 25,973 tons in 1915. In the
spring of 1915 Britain had accumulated stocks of TNT and picric acid, and was
already able to pass over its surpluses to its allies. The build-up to Lloyd
George's three successive gun programmes of 1915 created worries in May
and June, but by August and September Moulton could again face the future
with equanimity.[309]

Fuses proved much more difficult. As with chemicals, Britain had become
accustomed to rely on others' expertise, as it lacked the skills' base for fuse-
production, an indigenous clockmaking industry. The no. 44 fuse, that
designed for howitzers, could not be relied on to detonate when fired at low
angles. It was adapted for air explosions, but this was not much use against
entrenchments and field fortifications. In February 1915 a graze action fuse, the
no. 100, was adopted, but it caused premature explosions both in the gun and
in flight. By December 1915, although only one 18-pounder was being destroyed
for every 27,650 rounds fired, the rate of premature explosions for the 4.5-inch
howitzer was one round in 5,000. Even when the no. 100 performed as expected
there was still a delay between impact and detonation, with the result that the
shell had begun to bury itself before taking effect. The no. 106 fuse, which gave
much better results, was introduced in July 1916, but was not widely used in the
field until 1917.[310]

The fact that the fuse was at the base of the high-explosive shell was what
gave rise to the danger of premature explosions. But delayed detonation, after
the shell had penetrated its target, also depended on the fuse. The best use of
TNT, therefore, depended on the development of a satisfactory fuse. The
difficulties of doing so prejudiced gunners against the use of high explosive.
Indeed, at one stage the high incidence of premature explosions was attributed

[309] *Ministry of Munitions*, vol. I, pt. 1, 32, 110–12; vol. III, pt. 1, 30–1; vol. X, pt. 4, 4–76, 127–40;
Moulton, *Life of Lord Moulton*, 187–207, 272; McCallum, *War Studies Journal*, IV (1999), 70–5.
[310] *Ministry of Munitions*, vol. X, pt. 2, 46–9, 55.

not to the fuse at all but to amatol: its 80 : 20 mix required the fuse to have a greater force on explosion than did the 60 : 40 mix. Amatol was also unpopular because its detonation produced little smoke and it was therefore difficult to observe the fall of shot. Eighteen-pounder high-explosive shell was only of value in field guns for its destructive effect when it burst on graze, and for its man-killing effect when it burst after ricochet. Thus, the army's demand, so insistent for more high explosive at the beginning of the war, changed in the second year of fighting. On 6 November 1914 GHQ had requested that 25 per cent of its field-gun ammunition should be high explosive, and in June 1915 Sir John French raised this to 50 per cent. But as early as January 1915 some gunners were arguing that shrapnel was better at cutting wire, and after the experience of the battle of Loos in September 1915 the view gained ground that a 50 : 50 split was mistaken. With the initial assault completed, fighting had been sufficiently open to make shrapnel the more valuable ammunition, and its use also left the ground less broken up and therefore more passable for advancing infantry. In April 1916 GHQ requested that future production be set at 70 per cent shrapnel to 30 per cent high explosive. The effect of this reversal of opinion was, of course, to make the fuse issue less pressing.[311]

Both problems—the quality of the fuse and the most appropriate ratio of shrapnel to high explosive—provided fuel for the continuing acrimony between the War Office and the Ministry of Munitions. The latter blamed the former for not adopting the high-explosive shell and fuse used by the French in the 75 mm gun:[312] the Ministry of Munitions, in its enthusiasm for all things French, overlooked the high rate of premature explosions in their allies' field guns. The former blamed the latter whenever it ran short of high explosive, conveniently neglecting the variations in scales preferred by the army itself.

The battle of the Somme, which began on 1 July 1916, made it clear that Britain had not yet surmounted its munitions problems. Twenty-five per cent of guns were put out of action owing to design faults and inferior materials, as well as to poorly trained gun crews.[313] Thirty per cent of shells were reported as duds. In particular, the process of pressing amatol into shells did not give the density required for detonation.[314] Undoubtedly some of the defects were the consequences of the rapid expansion of production—the lowering of inspection standards, the incorporation of ill-qualifed firms, the dilution of skilled labour. Equally, however, these were the penalties of any massive industrial conversion, and the tendency to heap responsibility on the Ministry of Munitions should not obscure the point that whoever presided over shell production confronted a short-term choice between quality and quantity.

[311] *Ministry of Munitions*, vol. X, pt. 2, 2–7; see also vol. I, pt. 1, 29–30.
[312] Cassar, *Kitchener*, 336.
[313] Bidwell and Graham, *Fire-power*, 98–9.
[314] Terraine, *Smoke and the fire*, 113; Hughes, 'The monstrous anger of the guns', 72.

More telling is the criticism that quality had been forfeited without a sufficient increase in quantity. Some divisions, for at least some of the time, still experienced shell shortage. Those guns not engaged at the Somme were restricted to one or two rounds a day in order to feed the main battle.[315] Such shortages, however, were no more susceptible to global explanations than those of 1914. Total orders for field gun and 60-pounder shell exceeded 10 million rounds by June 1915, and these contracts were fulfilled by July 1916. But the constraints in perfecting the field-gun high-explosive shell meant that 8.6 million of the total were shrapnel. Furthermore, 8.4 million were for field guns, because the heavy-gun programme had not been completed.[316] The dominance of shrapnel and of field artillery were key explanations for the failure to inflict greater damage on German defences. While the BEF lacked sufficient heavy guns it relied disproportionately on the 18-pounder, and while it did that it elevated shrapnel over high explosive. But it could not get the specialist arms firms to produce more heavy artillery when they were still being chased for shrapnel, and the new firms could not maximize output for 18-pounder high-explosive shell until its design problems were overcome. Not until mid-1917 would British shell production overhaul that of France, and not until 1918 would shells be available in abundance. By then too, improving tactics would make more effective use of the shells that were provided. Thus, the remedies lay on both sides of the equation.

In the short term one solution was to place contracts overseas. Three million of those shells ordered by June 1915 were due from North America. On 24 August 1914 Kitchener wrote to the minister of militia in Ottawa asking him to get 18-pounder empty shrapnel shell, with or without fuses, from the American trade. The War Office's action both pre-dated any direct British experience of shell shortage and gave the lie to the accusation that it was reluctant to explore alternative sources of production.

Kitchener's presumption was that the United States would provide shell. It did: in 1915 imports of finished munitions from the United States totalled 54,500 tons, and in 1916 547,500.[317] But Canada responded to Kitchener's query by saying that its own manufacturers reckoned they could produce 4,000 rounds a week. It had the raw materials—apart from zinc and copper, which it could get from the United States—and by the end of October it had identified the capacity to manufacure 80,000 shells a month, assuming round-the-clock working. Gauges arrived on 31 October, and in December the master general of the ordnance accepted that Canadian basic steel could substitute for British 'acid' steel. By the close of 1914 Canada had orders for 400,000 18-pounder empty shrapnel shells and 1,100,000 complete shells. The

[315] Falls, 36th (Ulster) Division, 68.
[316] Figures from Hughes, 'Monstrous anger of the guns', 67–70.
[317] Birkett, Journal of the Royal Statistical Society, LXXXIII (1920), 355.

production of TNT began in April 1915, as soon as Canada had taken receipt of the plant to recover the waste gases from coke. By June 10 million rounds were on order, including 4.5-inch and 60-pounder high-explosive shells.

The expansion of Canadian production was in the hands of a shell committee set up at the instigation of the minister of militia, Sir Sam Hughes, and formed of those with industrial, technological, and military backgrounds. Its policy from the outset was not to place orders for whole shells but for components. Thus, manufacturers were able to tender for those elements for whose production their plant was best suited. By 31 March 1915 155 factories and 25,000 employees were engaged in shell production, and five new industries had been established in Canada. The shell committee's policy made sense of the fact that Canada lacked an indigenous arms industry while enabling the rapid conversion of the plant which it possessed. But in June 1915 it ran foul of the Ministry of Munitions, and from London it received not orders (no fresh contracts were placed between 21 June and 2 September) but a visitation.

D. A. Thomas, the ministry's emissary, criticized the shell committee for failing to concentrate its orders on the larger firms, so as to encourage them to invest in plant. Underpinning his comments was a wider agenda. The shell committee saw 'themselves as contractors selling to the British Government [rather] than as government agents'.[318] It had rejected competitive tendering on the grounds that Canadian manufacturers did not know enough about shell production to quote sensibly, and instead had fixed prices. But it was therefore accused of allowing subcontractors excessive profits, and of awarding contracts on the basis of political favouritism. Fundamental to the whole inquiry was the fact that in Canada, as elsewhere, orders had stacked up while deliveries had not yet come on stream. By the end of November 1915 the shell committee had only shipped 1 million complete 18-pounder rounds out of 8.6 million under contract. In all, it had placed orders for 22 million shells, but had only 3 million dispatched or ready to go.[319]

The committee of investigation established as a result of Thomas's visit gave the Canadian government two options: either it should itself take over the supply of munitions and emulate Britain by establishing its own ministry for the purpose, or it should allow the British Ministry of Munitions to create its own agency in Canada. The Canadian government opted for the second alternative, and the Imperial Munitions Board was formed at the end of November. Publicly the new structure was justified on the grounds that the work was now administrative rather than technical; in reality the philosophy was commercial. The manufacturers of the shell committee were replaced by bankers. The board was divided into five departments—contracts and

---

[318] Carnegie, *Munitions supply in Canada*, 93; see more generally 1–93, 292–3, 307–13; also *Ministry of Munitions*, vol. II, pt. 4, 14–18.

[319] Carnegie, *Munitions supply in Canada*, 58, 107–8.

purchasing; technical; inspection; secretarial; finance and accounting—and it emulated its London parent in establishing national factories for fuses, explosives, and shells. Also like the Ministry of Munitions, it drew credit for the groundwork done by others. When the shells committee was wound up the monthly output of empty shells had reached 700,000 and of complete rounds 400,000. In 1916 Canada shipped almost 20 million shells, and for a time it was responsible for the production of between a quarter and a third of the British army's entire munition supply.[320]

A quarter of Canada's 1916 ouput constituted shell for heavy artillery, and this proportion increased in 1917; in 1918 it was over 40 per cent of the whole. Canada was therefore able to follow the shifting emphases of gun programmes A, B, and C. Moreover, in its case the penalty of distance, a slowness in responding to changing specifications, was minimized by the comparative shortness of the Atlantic route. Both Australia and India, being much further away, found themselves unable to keep pace and, having geared themselves up to increase field-gun shell production, were stood down again as the emphasis swung to heavy artillery in the early summer of 1916.

Determined to be self-sufficient in its entire military effort, Australia had established state factories for the production of small arms and cordite before 1914. India too was geared up to the armament of its own army, and in 1914 had the capacity to manufacture 6,000 shells and 13,000 fuses a week. By taking up the slack on mobilization, India more than quadrupled its output of most munitions between October 1914 and March 1915, and sent both shell and cordite to Britain. The May 1915 shells crisis had its repercussions in the empire. Australia, which had expressed its determination to produce its own 18-pounder guns and shells in September 1914, renewed its efforts, and created a federal munitions committee in June. India increased its shell production by incorporating the workshops of the Railway Board. By September it had twenty-five factories producing shells, and reckoned it could be manufacturing 40,000 4.5-inch, 40,000 13-pounder, and 10,000 18-pounder shells each month by the year's end. In July 1916 it actually exceeded those targets, with a monthly output of 130,000. But the Ministry of Munitions now turned off the tap. Bent on enhancing Britain's own output, it had been reluctant to divert scarce expertise to either India or Australia to aid them in the development of plant or to inspect their output. Britain's own conversion was now largely complete. Furthermore, high-explosive shell, which was technically easier to produce, could not be shipped filled because of the attendant dangers. Australia produced only 15,000 18-pounder shells and ceased production at the end of June 1916. In April India was asked to shift to manufacture of 18-pounder shrapnel, reflecting the recovery of the BEF's demand for this type of shell. But

[320] Ibid. 107, 127, 133, 294, 314–15.

India needed all its shrapnel for the Indian Expeditionary Force in Meso-potamia. In July 1916 the Ministry of Munitions told India that no more high-explosive shells were wanted. When it changed its mind in December, the organization had been broken up and the shell steel used for other purposes.[321]

Britain was therefore cutting back on some sorts of munitions production just as the battle of the Somme opened: shell abundance had resurfaced. The problems of industrial mobilization could not be solved as simply as Lloyd George's inclination for improvisation and grandiose targets suggested: muni-tions production had to be sensitive enough to respond to tactical evolution and technological innovation, without simultaneously losing system and certainty. The Ministry of Munitions would only shake down under Lloyd George's successors. When he moved to the War Office, after the death of Kitchener in June 1916, he took many of his 'men of push and go' with him. E. S. Montagu assumed responsibility for a ministry shattered by his prede-cessor's self-interest. And when Churchill arrived in the office in July 1917 he found that the proliferation of departments had gone so far that fifty were directly responsible to himself.[322] Britain was the first of the belligerents to establish a ministry specifically to tackle the problems of industrial mobiliza-tion, but it did not thereby resolve all the attendant problems at a stroke. Innovation did not always equate with efficiency.

Britain was an industrialized society; its major eastern ally, Russia, was not. In 1913 Russia's gross domestic product per head of the population was a third of Britain's and a half of France's. But there is no neat correlation between economic backwardness and Russia's more protracted experience of shell shortage. In the first place, Russia's size meant that its gross domestic product when aggregated was greater than that of any other European power, including both Britain and Germany. Secondly, the travails of the latter two powers illustrate the point that economic strength did not automatically transmute into military effectiveness. Political decisions and managerial efficiency were vital elements in the mobilization of war economies. France committed to munitions production resources almost as great as did Britain, although its gross domestic product was a third less. By such steps an economically weaker power could compensate sufficiently to ensure that backwardness did not necessarily betoken military inferiority. But Russia did not do this. Its total financial outlay was about a third that of the other powers, and its actual output about a quarter of France's. The Russian effort, therefore, fell below

[321] *Ministry of Munitions*, vol. II, pts. 5 (India) and 6 (Australia); Scott, *Australia during the war*, 236–48.
[322] Grieves, *War & Society*, VII (1989), 45; Wrigley, 'Ministry of Munitions', in Burk (ed.), *War and the state*, 43–6; Harvey, *Collision of empires*, 293; Farr, 'McKenna', 254.

that of the other countries not only absolutely but also in relation to its own resources.[323]

Russia's average annual growth rate before the war was 3.25 per cent; one calculation suggests that for 1914 itself it was 14 per cent.[324] Between 1908 and 1913 the value of consumer goods produced in Russia rose 32.8 per cent and of textiles 46 per cent. But most spectacular was the performance of heavy industry. The output of capital goods manufactured over the same period increased 84 per cent as a whole, and in the metal industries 88.9 per cent.[325]

Both defence spending and arms production formed key elements in this growth. The successive rearmament programmes of 1908, 1910, and 1912 produced an average annual increase in expenditure on the two services of just under 6 per cent. In 1900 14.6 per cent of the manufactures of the Putilov works were defence-related, in 1912 45.8 per cent.[326] The output of iron and steel climbed from 2.42 million tons in 1908 to 4.04 million in 1913: of the latter, 1.6 million tons, or two-fifths of the total, were allocated to government orders.[327]

In general terms, therefore, Russia's arms industries supported its claim to great-power status in 1914. More specifically, its stocks of shell and its output of guns were both comparable with those elsewhere. But three features were evident in the management of Russia's war industries which would hinder the maximization of its potential.

First, production costs were comparatively high. The cost per ton of build-ing a warship in Russia in 1908–9 was £85 as opposed to £80 in Germany and £71 in Britain.[328] If this had been a reflection of high levels of investment in new plant it would have represented reasonable capital investment. But Russia achieved its growth more through increasing its labour force than through the replacement of men by machines. Between 1908 and 1913 the total number of those employed in Russia's defence industries rose by 40 per cent, from 86,000 to over 120,000. Output per worker was constant. Furthermore, the majority were young males, the very category most liable for military service in the event of hostilities. Wages were low but labour costs were high because on-the-job training was poor and employee turnover frequent. Pre-industrial work practices persisted. Skills, in an industrial sector which made particular demands on them, were at a premium.[329]

Russia's second major difficulty was the fact that the relationship between the state and the private arms sector was adversarial rather than symbiotic. The

[323] Gatrell and Harrison, *Economic History Review*, XLVI (1993), 430–2.
[324] Keith Neilson, 'Russia', in Wilson, *Decisions for war*, 98; Pearson, *Russian moderates*, 10.
[325] Geyer, *Russian imperialism*, 265.
[326] Keith Neilson, 'Russia', in Wilson, *Decisions for war*, 103.
[327] Gatrell, *Government, industry and rearmament*, 139, 176–8.
[328] Ibid. 288.
[329] Ibid. 223, 243–52, 257; see also Neilson, *Britain and the last Tsar*, 101.

government preferred to order arms from its own enterprises rather than from those in other forms of ownership. It was fearful of a private sector monopoly sufficiently powerful to drive up prices. Not until 1913 was the official position in relation to the formation of syndicates moderated—a belated recognition that Russia was losing in international competitiveness as a result of a lack of internal organization. Iron and steel firms, in their turn, protested at what they saw as unfair government subsidies for state-run businesses, and pointed out that through their ability to import cheaper raw materials from overseas they could frequently undercut state enterprises committed to the use of domestically produced materials. Most telling of all was the private sector's argument that its associations with foreign companies—pre-eminently Schneider and Vickers—made it technologically far more innovative.[330]

After 1910 the pace of rearmament gave the government no choice but to concede. Orders were placed with private firms. But—and this was the third structural defect—the consequent growth in the private arms trade took place disproportionately in shipbuilding. Russia was effectively creating two Dreadnought fleets from scratch, one for the Baltic and one for the Black Sea. The workforce in private shipyards tripled between 1908 and 1913, and in the latter year private yards accounted for three-fifths of all workers in naval construction.[331] Thus, Russia's capacities were better developed in relation to its fleet than to its army. The navy's budget grew by 18.6 per cent between 1911 and 1914, but the army's only by 6 per cent. Plant for the production of rifles languished, underused: in 1912 the three state armourers could have manufactured 525,000 rifles, but actual output was 47,000. In Russia it was not the private sector but the state that was seeking other markets for land weapons.[332]

When the war broke out the navy proved all but redundant. While the distortions generated by navalism in pre-war arms procurement bore comparison with Britain, the actual consequences had more in common with Germany. Russia was effectively blockaded. The German fleet, although overshadowed in the North Sea, enjoyed a superiority in the Baltic which cut Petrograd's main outlet to the world. To the south, Turkey's entry to the war sealed off the Black Sea. The overland connections to European markets lay through the territories of the Central Powers. The consequences for war-related industries looked dire. In 1913 almost half of Russia's imports came from Germany.[333] Principal among them was industrial machinery, 70 per cent of which was received from overseas.[334]

Four alternative trading routes were available. The first lay through Sweden and Finland. But Sweden was pro-German, and the British were fearful that goods transshipped via Stockholm might be destined for their enemies rather

[330] Gatrell, *Government, industry and rearmament*, 167–70, 197–8, 277–80.
[331] Ibid. 199, 215–16, 226.   [332] Ibid. 139, 209.   [333] Florinsky, *End of the Russian empire*, 34.
[334] Siegelbaum, *Politics of industrial mobilization*, 31.

than their allies. Thus, the Russians complained, the British blockade was operating against them as much as against the Germans.

The other three options were maritime, but nonetheless possessed of drawbacks. Vladivostok was ice-free but was on the Pacific coast and 5,600 kilometres from the front: every two trains running to the port and back required 120 engines.[335] Archangel was much closer, but being on the White Sea was only open for half the year. Here too railway connections were unsatisfactory: the link to the main network was narrow gauge. Murmansk was closest to Britain and remained free of ice throughout the year, but had no rail connection to the interior.

By forcing commerce to deviate from its customary pathways, the blockade of Russia therefore highlighted the inadequacies of the empire's internal communications. The pre-war take-off in Russia's armaments industries had been accomplished at the expense of the further development of its railways. The annual average addition to the nation's track between 1909 and 1913 was a third that of the years 1899 to 1903. Orders for locomotives and rolling stock declined after 1908. On the outbreak of war not only was Russia's railway density low, but also three-quarters of what there was remained single track. The network was short of 2,000 locomotives and 80,000 wagons.[336] The war served to exacerbate these trends. Munitions production continued to take precedence over railway production. Freight levels rose while the availability of rolling stock fell.

From the outset the railways were unable to meet the demands imposed on them by the mobilization of industry. Petrograd had imported coal from Britain via the Baltic. The closure of that route forced the city to turn to the Donetz Basin in the south. Although the output of Donetz coal fell by a third between June and August 1914, this proved immaterial. Production in the latter month still totalled 80 million puds, when in June the railways could shift 75.5 million puds and in July only 44.3 million. In 1915 the Donetz Basin produced 181.2 million puds more coal than in 1913, and in April 8,132 wagonloads were dispatched, as opposed to 4,500 in January. But in the last quarter of the year one-third of the coal produced could not be transported. In October Petrograd received 49 per cent of the coal assigned to it and Moscow 40 per cent.[337] In December the factories of Petrograd were close to exhausting their fuel stocks, only twenty-nine wagonloads of coal having arrived from the Donetz Basin since September. The Putilov works closed some workshops. The situation did not improve in 1916. In June Alekseev told the Tsar that 'Petrograd's private defence industries... are receiving at best some 50 to 60 per cent of the

---

[335] Golovine, *Russian army*, 37.
[336] Gatrell, *Government, industry and rearmament*, 148, 187–8, 305.
[337] Siegelbaum, *Politics of industrial mobilization*, 21–2, 136.

necessary materials'. By the year's end many war industries were forced to halt production for a week or longer; seventy-nine plants were idle.[338]

The fact that Russia's supplies of raw materials and Russia's industrial centres were so far apart was not the only source of strain on either coal supply or railway communication. Loss of territory also played its part. The overrunning of Poland in 1915 resulted in the forfeiture of one-fifth of Russia's coal production, one-tenth of its iron ore, and two-thirds of its chemicals, as well as of the industrial centres of Lodz, Warsaw, Radom, and Lublin.[339] In July the German advance in the north-west, towards Vilna and Riga, prompted the evacuation of 166 enterprises eastwards. Priority was given to machine tools, but dismantling plant proved easier than shifting and re-erecting it. One train arrived in the Caucasus, 2,000 kilometres away from its destination. More frequently, goods remained loaded on wagons, their terminus uncertain and their use as temporary storage deemed preferable to leaving machinery out in the open to rust.[340]

Thus, like France, Russia lost resources through defeat, but unlike France found it hard to compensate through imports. Both comparisons are matters of degree. Russia lost a smaller proportion of its total, and the loss came later. It remained well endowed with many raw materials vital to munitions production, including copper and manganese, as well as coal and iron.

What made Russia's experience of industrial mobilization different from that of France, and from those of the more advanced economies, was the pace and pattern of its industrialization before the war. The latter's quickening tempo and its bias towards heavy industry meant that it outstripped any increase in the capacity of Russia's indigenous extractive processes. In the quinquennium 1909–13 Russia imported annually 316 million puds of coal, 12 million puds of chemical products, and nearly 3 million puds each of iron and lead. Imports as a whole rose 45 per cent over 1904–8.[341] In these circumstances the underlying economic trends of the war were less different from what had gone before than was the case elsewhere. First, armaments production already enjoyed a disproportionately high profile in the economy as a whole. Secondly, the pressure to maximize domestic resources for the purposes of heavy industry (and so save on foreign exchange) was not new. And thirdly, the constraints on the development of the war economy were, as the case of the railways so graphically illustrated, as much symptoms of belated industrialization in general as of the difficulties of conversion to wartime production. Russia's allies frequently complained that their aid, whether financial or material, was

---

[338] McKean, *St Petersburg*, 323–4.
[339] Lincoln, *Passage through Armageddon*, 165.
[340] Siegelbaum, *Politics of industrial mobilization*, 148; Claus, *Kriegswirtschaft Russlands*, 68–70; Frantz, *Russland auf dem Wege*, 264.
[341] Zagorsky, *State control of industry*, 14–15.

being adapted to the industrial advance of the empire as a whole rather than to the needs of the war in particular. They were not wrong: by 1916 Russia's national income had grown by 21.5 per cent on that of 1913, and its industrial output by 17 per cent.[342]

In other countries industrial mobilization was a matter of conversion, of adapting peacetime industries to wartime needs. In Russia the war forced the pace of industrialization in general, drawing labour not from businesses that the war made redundant but from the land. By the autumn of 1915 one male factory worker in seven in Petrograd had lived in the city for less than a year: the city's workforce grew by a fifth in each year of the war, and Moscow's grew by a tenth.[343] Between 1913 and 1917 employment in the metal industry rose by 61 per cent, and in coal mining by 66 per cent.[344] The role of the war in promoting industrialization in general is graphically illustrated by the phenomenal growth in the proportion of the industrial working class engaged in war production, from 24 per cent in 1914 to 76 per cent in 1917: in the more industrialized nations war workers remained a minority in the industrial working class as a whole.[345] The fact that what Russia was undergoing was something with wider implications is demonstrated by the building trade. Elsewhere construction was a casualty of the war: Britain built, on average, 72,000 new houses a year before the war but only 17,000 in 1916. But in Russia during the war the workforce in the building industry increased by a third.[346]

The migration of labour from country to town confirmed the continuity of two pre-war patterns. First, Russia used manpower rather than plant to expand production. Secondly, output per worker, already low relative to other states before the war, declined during it.

The expansion of the industrial workforce was accomplished by the incorporation of women, children, and prisoners of war. At the same time skilled men departed for the front. Men constituted 50 per cent of the workforce in Moscow in 1914, and 82.7 per cent of that of the metal industry; in 1917 these figures were 37 per cent and 69.7 per cent. The working day was lengthened and more days were worked, but yields still fell. In the Donetz Basin the annual output of coal per head of the workforce declined from 9,054 puds in 1914 to 7,451 puds in 1916, and of iron from 21,590 puds to 12,543.[347]

In aggregate, Russia's production of key commodities fell despite both the continuing growth of the economy and the addition to the industrial workforce. Fundamental, because of its impact on other industries, was the fall in

---

[342] David Jones, 'Imperial Russia's forces at war', in Millett and Murray (eds.), *Military effectiveness*, i. 270; Ferguson, *Pity of war*, 249–50.
[343] Lincoln, *Passage through Armageddon*, 94, 220–6; Stone, *Eastern front*, 284–5.
[344] Zagorsky, *State control of industry*, 53.
[345] Ferro, *Great War*, 120.
[346] Dewey, *Historical Journal*, XXVII (1984), 208; Stone, *Eastern front*, 285.
[347] Zagorsky, *State control of industry*, 54–6; see also Claus, *Kriegswirtschaft Russlands*, 83–4, 87.

coal output from 2,213.8 million puds in 1913 to 1,946.6 million in 1915. Thus, even had the railways been able to move the coal that was produced, shortages would have persisted. As it was, lack of coal meant that some locomotives were fired by wood or peat, thus reducing their carrying capacity. In December 1915 forty blast furnaces in the Urals were idle for lack of fuel. Russia mined 562.4 million puds of iron ore in 1913 but only 331.4 million in 1915. The output of pig iron, which ran at 282.9 million puds in 1913, tumbled to 225.2 million in 1915. This was a result not only of the lack of coal (charcoal was used instead) but also of the loss of Poland. The story in non-ferrous metals was no different. The Urals produced 300 puds of platinum in 1913 but 215 in 1915. Copper output fell from over 2 million puds to 1,587 million in 1915.

Copper was exceptional in showing no improvement in 1916 (output fell again to 1.3 million puds). Most other commodities displayed a marked improvement. Coal recovered to 2,092.4 million puds for the year, and pig iron to 232 million. Regionally, some areas exceeded their pre-war levels, particularly in the coal industry. But the combined effect was mitigated by the persistence of the transport problem as much as by the consequences of actual hostilities. Thus, copper production in the Caucasus was halved between 1914 and 1916, and this was blamed on the operations in the area. But the same explanation could not explain the decline of copper output by four-fifths in Siberia (where there was no fighting), nor the consistent and improving levels of naphtha production in Baku (where the war impinged somewhat more).[348]

Nonetheless, the dismal picture in relation to raw materials did not result in a comparable fall in munitions production. If Russia's entry into the war had resulted in no more then a continuation of the same trajectory of industrial-ization as that marked out immediately before the war, then falling armaments output might have been the consequence. The fact that this was not the case highlights the point that Russia underwent two experiences between 1914 and 1916—one being a continuity, that is, the acceleration of industrialization broadly defined; and the other a change, the conversion of industry to wartime purposes. Ultimately, coal shortages meant the withdrawal of supplies for civil consumption: heat and light suffered more than munitions. Lack of iron resulted in a cutback in agricultural machinery, not in guns. To this extent, as elsewhere, political and managerial decisions played their part.

One reason for the underestimation of the achievements of Russia's war production is the bureaucratic confusion which attended its implementation. The main artillery administration (Glavnoe Artilleriiskoie Upravlieniie or GAU) of the War Ministry was responsible for the supervision of production as well as for the state arsenals. It had coped with the rearmament programmes

---

[348] Zagorsky, *State control of industry*, 39–45, 347–8; Claus, *Kriegswirtschaft Russlands*, 86–91.

of the pre-war years, and had ensured that in most cases the army's stocks of
munitions in 1914 were close to the norms established by the general staff in
1912: in the case of rifles and 3-inch (or 76 mm) shell they exceeded them.[349] In
September 1914 its structure was reformed and revitalized.

But the GAU was sandwiched between Stavka and the military council of the
War Ministry. It reckoned that the former inflated its orders for shell and was
profligate in its use of artillery. Its relationship with the latter was bedevilled by
a rivalry between GAU's head, the Grand Duke Sergei Mikhailovich, and the
war minister, Sukhomlinov. Stavka's requests, already reduced by GAU, were
cut yet further by the ministry. In September 1914 GAU approved orders for 2
million shells; the military council pared them down to 800,000.[350]

Parallel with the friction between Stavka and the War Ministry was the
tension between the state and the private arms sector. Their mutual distrust
had been modified between 1910 and 1914, but not removed. In September the
existing contractors could produce only 500,000 shells per month, when the
army wanted 1.5 million. Sukhomlinov's solution was to advance sufficient
capital to the existing munitions firms to enable them to expand their plant
and hence their output to 1 million shells per month by the autumn of 1915.
Rather than draw in other firms to war production, Sukhomlinov preferred to
limit the orders he placed with Russian industry, and instead to direct the
additional demand abroad. No further orders were placed after October.

The scepticism towards the government entertained by most industrialists,
briefly stilled by the nationalist enthusiasms of the opening weeks of the war,
therefore resurfaced as 1914 drew to a close. Hopes that industry might become
the partner of government in the prosecution of the war effort had been
dashed. The Association of Trade and Industry tried to build bridges in
January. It suggested that orders should be channelled direct from Stavka to
the arms firms, thus removing the War Ministry from the chain. The big firms
should be allowed to contract to smaller concerns, so facilitating the conversion of industry to war production. Skilled labour should be returned from the
front.[351]

Both the demands of Stavka and the proposals of the Association were meat
and drink to the progressives within the Duma. In April Rodzianko, the
president of the Duma, visited the front and reported on the shortage of shells
and on the tensions between Stavka and the War Ministry; not Grand Duke
Nicholas but Sukhomlinov was responsible for Russia's lack of success. Thus,
the attack on the War Ministry's management of industrial mobilization

---

[349] Gatrell, *Government, industry and rearmament*, 299.
[350] D. Jones, 'Imperial Russia's forces at war', in Millett and Murray (eds.), *Military effectiveness*, i.
267–8; Jones, *Military–naval encyclopedia of Russia*, ii. 154.
[351] The main sources for what follows are Siegelbaum, *Politics of industrial mobilization*; Roosa,
'Russian industrialists during World War I'.

became fused with an attack on the Tsar's prerogatives. The net effect was to deepen the divide between Russia's government and Russia's industrialists. The former blamed the falling coal yields of the Donetz Basin on the latter's harsh exploitation of its labour force; the latter attributed the crisis to the railways, the responsibility of the government's minister of transport.

The politicization of the Association of Trade and Industry became evident at its 9th Congress, in June 1915. The agenda for the meeting did not reflect the frustration now felt by many industrialists, particularly in Moscow. The latter argued that the flow of government orders had favoured the traditional arms suppliers in Petrograd, and that in consequence Petrograd had also received the lion's share of raw materials. On the second day of the congress the vice-chairman of the Moscow exchange committee, Riabushinski, who had just returned from the front, called for full industrial mobilization. The congress scrapped its agenda, set up a special commission, and then adopted a series of resolutions. It declared that its intention was to harness all the unutilized power of Russia's industry for the purposes of state defence. To achieve this it planned a series of regional committees to co-ordinate production in accordance with local capacities. A central War Industries Committee would be established in Petrograd, not only to oversee the regional bodies but also to liaise with other interested parties, including the Union of Zemstvos, the Union of Towns, the Duma, the railways, and the scientific community.

The most important task of the War Industries Committee was to win the co-operation, rather than the hostility, of the government. Its progressive credentials, its call for the convening of the Duma, and in due course its appointment of a politician, Alexander Guchkov, as its chairman—these were manifestations likely to deepen the rift between state and industry rather than to rally the two to serve the common cause. Mindful of this, Riabushinski himself used conciliatory language, emphasizing co-operation rather than confrontation.

On 2 May the Central Powers had delivered a stunning blow at Gorlice Tarnow. The subsequent 'great retreat' helped achieve—albeit briefly—the fusion the War Industries Committee sought.

Rodzianko returned from the front and reported his findings to a private meeting of members of the Duma. On 1 June 1915 the government tried to pre-empt the mounting opposition to its running of the war by appointing a special commission to supervise the supply of the army. On 20 June, co-incident with the formation of the War Industries Committee, this was replaced by a 'special council for the co-ordination of measures directed to the regular supply to the army of munitions'. Answerable to the Tsar, its powers were comparable with those vested in the minister of war at the outbreak of hostilities: it could requisition businesses and it could direct private industry to accept government orders. However, it did not attempt to regulate the market nor did it intervene in the internal workings of industry. Its real novelty, therefore, was not economic but political. Its membership embraced the appropriate government ministers, the president of the Duma, four members of the Duma chosen by the Tsar, and four representatives of commerce and industry.[352]

Needless to say, Sukhomlinov was not happy with this dilution of his ministerial authority. He persuaded himself that shell shortage was more the fantasy of the Petrograd press than the reality of the front.[353] He continued to resist any wider distribution of arms orders. But evidence of his unwisdom was mounting.

In January 1915 a French technical mission visited Russia to relay the benefits of its experience. It argued that 3-inch shell production could be simplified and expedited if high explosive was given preference over shrapnel. Fuses could then be made in one piece and inspection standards lowered, so that orders could be spread to firms new to war production. GAU was sceptical: the French concluded that Russia's artillery administration had learned nothing from the war. But General Vankov, head of the Bryansk arsenal, was impressed by the advice of the French. He offered contracts for 3-inch shell to firms not already employed by GAU: by the end of the war his organization had distributed orders for 12 million rounds, and was responsible for 44 per cent of total Russian output. Vankov demonstrated not only that production in quantity was possible but also that a balance could be found between industry's need for sufficient profit to cover its conversion costs and the government's need to control expenditure. Vankov guaranteed a gross profit of 47 per cent. But Sukhomlinov persevered in his preference for traditional contractors: on 19 June 1915 he placed an order with the Putilov works for 3 million 3-inch shells at a price 20 per cent above that paid by Vankov.[354]

Sukhomlinov's refusal to change his practices and his obstruction of the new special council smacked of the bloody-mindedness of a doomed man. His credibility had already been shattered by the exposure—possibly through a Stavka conspiracy[355]—of one of his protégés as a spy. On 26 June 1915 he was dismissed. A year later he was arrested and imprisoned.

His replacement was A. A. Polivanov. Polivanov possessed impeccable anti-Sukhomlinov credentials. He set about making the ministry a conduit rather than an obstruction. He reversed previous policy, settling demand before supply. He diligently attended Stavka briefings, however unhelpful he found

---

[352] The chronology of these events is very confused in the published sources. That followed here is from Zagorsky, *State control of industry*, 82–6.

[353] Suchomlinow, *Erinnerungen*, 419–21.

[354] Knox, *With the Russian army*, i. 272–3; Stone, *Eastern front*, 162–3; Siegelbaum, *Politics of industrial mobilization*, 35–9.

[355] Stone, *Eastern front*, 197–8; see also Suchomlinow, *Erinnerungen*, 430–7, 472–7.

them, arguing that plans at home had to be shaped by events on the front.[356] Having been an assistant minister of war for six years, between 1906 and 1912, he had got to know members of the arms industry, and showed himself much more adroit in his relations with them than had his predecessor. The weighting of the special council in favour of Petrograd firms was modified: the representation of the War Industries Committee was increased. Polivanov's policy was justified by a report to the special council on the state of the Putilov works: racked by debts, which had been contracted in the bid to expand their shipyards as orders flooded in before the war, it was postponing old orders and allowing real wages to fall. Under Polivanov's guidance the special council advanced 43.3 million roubles—principally for plant—to co-operatives outside the traditional arms firms: the War Industries Committee received almost half, but the Union of Towns and the Union of Zemstvos were also major beneficiaries. By the end of August the central committee of the War Industries Committee was handling orders for 5 million hand grenades and 1.7 million shells.[357]

Nonetheless, Polivanov was unable to surmount the underlying political tensions. The council of ministers took fright at the prospect of a state organization, the special council, becoming subservient to a private one, the War Industries Committee. The progressives wanted to go further: a fusion of all the interested parties in a Ministry of Munitions. Not even the majority of the Duma was happy with such a close identification of industry and government. Instead, the industrialists found themselves marginalized. On 30 August three further special councils were added to the existing council on defence. The new ones embraced fuel, food, and transport. But, whereas the War Industries Committee retained its representation on the special council for defence, it was not included in the other three.

The effect was to break the alliance between the Duma and the War Industries Committee. Rodzianko, as the former's president, was more anxious to preserve the unity of the assembly than to pursue wartime coalitions of interest: concessions to Duma conservatives therefore took precedence over the pressure of the progressives. The industrialists, for their part, began to fear that excessive progressive pressure on the regime could backfire and work against the interests of business.[358]

Ostensibly, the War Industries Committee enjoyed a rapid success. Building on existing local organizations, it had attracted seventy-eight regional committees and seven affiliated bodies to its first all-Russia Congress in August 1915. But in reality fragmentation soon followed. The Association of Trade and Industry tried and failed to retain control. The Moscow War Industries

---

[356] Frantz, *Russland auf dem Wege*, 235–7, 246–9.
[357] Siegelbaum, *Politics of industrial mobilization*, 69–72.
[358] Pearson, *Russian moderates*, 44–5, 73.

Committee, dominated by textile and commercial firms rather than heavy industry, and originally closer to the progressives in the Duma, overshadowed the central committee in Petrograd. Petrograd firms first sought the creation of their own committee and then began to move away from the organization as a whole. The War Industries Committee was accused of showing little interest in regional development outside Russia's two main cities, and of failing to protect and encourage small firms. The accusation was not really justified: of orders distributed up to March 1916, 33 per cent went to Petrograd but only 11.5 per cent to Moscow. What was much more significant was the fact that the fragmentation of the War Industries Committee made its services redundant to the large firms naturally favoured by the state. By 1916 the War Industries Committee had secured only 7.6 per cent of the orders placed within Russia since its inception. Its ambition—to become a *Kriegsrohstoffsamt* or a key component in a Ministry of Munitions—was shattered as much through its own fissiparous tendencies as through the backlash of a conservative government.[359]

Therefore the successes of the War Industries Committee lay on the margins. As elsewhere, plant was adapted to new purposes more rapidly when the technology of the weapon was simple and some at least of the production processes familiar. The Fabergé workforce was doubled through its conversion from jewellery to grenades. The War Industries Committee was responsible for about half the grenades and half the gasmasks made during the war. It also sponsored the growth of the Russian chemical industry. In Baku toluene was manufactured for high explosive. The Kiev branch established a close relationship with the Kiev Polytechnical Institution, and manufactured optical instruments, pharmaceuticals, and iodine. In advertising its harnessing of science and technology, the War Industries Committee had one eye on the post-war position of Russian industry.[360]

In spite of the obstacles to its trade and in spite of its loss of territory, Russia's output of munitions had been transformed by 1916. The average monthly output of 3-inch shell had grown fifteenfold since 1914, from 103,000 rounds to 1,618,000; that of the guns to fire the shell tenfold, from fifty-seven pieces to 603.[361] The increase in shell production was continuous over the two years 1915 and 1916, but was particularly dramatic between May and July 1915, when it doubled from 440,000 rounds to 852,000. It continued to rise, reaching 1,512,000 in November, and then levelled off, before leaping again from May 1916.[362]

The role of the War Industries Committee in this transformation should not be exaggerated. The central committee was much better at accepting orders

[359] Siegelbaum, *Politics of industrial mobilization*, 49–50, 58–68, 85–102.
[360] Ibid. 54, 95–6, 100–5.   [361] Andolenko, *Histoire de l'armée russe*, 379.
[362] Stone, *Eastern front*, 210.

than at fulfilling them: indeed, its record in this respect was worse than that of the traditional contractors it sought to challenge. Some of the delays were not the fault of the War Industries Committee but the result of a slowness in delivering blueprints, of transport difficulties, or—most frequently—of a lack of working capital. However, the small firms operating within the War Industries Committee were also to blame. By accepting government orders they could secure a share of the labour and fuel that would otherwise be channelled to the big producers. Having got the resources necessary to maintain production, they then continued to fulfil contracts for the private sector as well as for the state.[363]

The new weapons of trench warfare apart, like the mortar and the grenade, the bulk of Russia's armaments during the war were produced by those same firms that had been in the business before the war. The state ordnance factories concentrated on heavy artillery and small arms, the large private concerns on machine tools and shells. Putilov moved away from shipbuilding to the manufacture of detonators and grenades. In June 1915 it received an order for 3 million 3-inch high-explosive shells and 700 field guns, and to meet this it established a consortium of nine firms, with the assistance of Schneider-Creusot. The combination of GAU advances, bank credits, new capital flotations, and war profits enabled the expansion of plant. In a process of vertical integration the arms businesses acquired raw-material companies. Thus, the large firms got larger. They were able to work round the clock and to achieve economies of scale. In Petrograd the net profits of six major metalworking and electrical companies grew from 10.4 per cent of working capital in 1913 to 79.5 per cent in 1916.[364] The metallurgical committee—established at the beginning of 1916 as a joint state–industry enterprise to manage unfulfilled orders, to allocate metals, and to set prices—was dominated not by the War Industries Committee but by Prodamet, a pre-war syndicate of iron and steel firms. The dismissal of Polivanov on 16 March 1916 completed the sidelining of the War Industries Committee. Its share of orders declined, and its activities seemed increasingly self-interested and political rather than nationalist and economic.[365]

Thus, the vilification of the Ministry of War in the winter of 1914–15 had—as elsewhere—less economic substance than its popular impact suggested. For all its caution, the GAU remained the body most obviously responsible for the abundance of Russian shell by 1916. It expanded its network of firms from the spring of 1915, and output even began to rise from January 1915, well before the significant administrative changes in May. Grand Duke Sergei

---

[363] Siegelbaum, *Politics of industrial mobilization*, 105–19; Knox, *With the Russian army*, 524.
[364] McKean, *St Petersburg*, 324–6.
[365] Siegelbaum, *Politics of industrial mobilization*, 117–19, 183–91, 210; also Gatrell, *Government, industry and rearmament*, 216–23.

Mikhailovich stressed that his policy was to increase plant so as to boost domestic production, and both he and Sukhomlinov regularly forecast that the situation would not come right until the autumn.[366] Nor were they as consistently conservative in regard to production methods as their numerous detractors suggested: GAU established a chemical committee, chaired by an academic, to work on explosives and designed to compensate for Russia's pre-war dependence on Germany.[367]

Chronology, therefore, suggests many parallels between Russia and other countries. One obvious theme is that all the ministries of war deserved more credit for expanding output than their contemporaries were wont to give them. Nonetheless, Russia remains an exception. For, although munitions production reached levels comparable with those of other belligerents, shell shortage went deeper and persisted longer. The complaints from the front continued throughout 1915 and even into the winter of 1915–16: not until the spring of 1916 would abundance in the rear be reflected in abundance at the front.[368]

Part of the explanation lies with Stavka. It had grown used to deflecting blame from its own shortcomings on to lack of shell; moreover, it was less adept than the Germans at changing artillery techniques to compensate for inferior stocks. Another major factor was transport. The strain on the railways which hamstrung the mobilization of industry also delayed deliveries to the front. The fact that Stavka was not responsible for supply meant that shells could be sent forward by the ministry while the Front commanders remained oblivious of their arrival: Sukhomlinov claimed that Ruszkii at South-West Front complained of shell shortage when there were never less than 400 wagonloads sitting on his rail network.[369] Thirdly, the 'great retreat' of 1915, although it shortened the army's lines of communication, exacerbated the problem of wastage. Abandoned equipment, most notably the guns and shells locked up in the fortresses on the Russo-Polish border, was not regained in any subsequent advance.

In two areas, however, the continuing shortage of armaments was quite genuinely a production problem. One was small arms, and the other heavy artillery.

Russia's most obvious resource was its manpower: the size of its population gave it the potential to create the largest army of any European power. But to maximize that resource it needed rifles. Small-arms production was far more complex and far less easily improvised than that of shells, grenades, or mortars. In July 1914 Russia's stocks of rifles exceeded those required under its 1912

[366] Neilson, *Strategy and supply*, 75–6.
[367] D. Jones, *Military–naval encyclopedia of Russia*, ii. 161.
[368] See Knox, *With the Russian army*, 270, 317, 319; Lobanov-Rostovsky, *Grinding mill*, 144, 160.
[369] Suchomlinow, *Erinnerungen*, 400–1.

mobilization plan by 3 per cent—even if its holdings of the ammunition required for them was below the target.[370] Although maximum annual production was high at 700,000 rifles, the combination of losses in the field and of the expansion of the army created a requirement for 200,000 rifles a month. Output rose to 865,000 in 1915, and to 1,321,000 in 1916, less than double the pre-war level.[371] Units trained with one rifle for five men;[372] in the winter of 1915–16 companies shattered in the retreat were reformed with two platoons armed and two not;[373] and the rifles themselves included captured models as well as imports from Japan, France, Britain, and Italy.[374]

At the opposite end of the armaments scale was the heavy-artillery problem. In 1914 Russia had in the 3-inch gun (or 76 mm), an excellent light field gun. But, like France, it had been unable to decide about heavy artillery. Partly this was due to the animosity between Sukhomlinov and Grand Duke Sergei Mikhailovich, the procurement of heavy guns being GAU's responsibility. But it was played out against the state's distrust of the private arms firms, and in particular of their subservience to foreign direction. Sukhomlinov was anxious to promote the Russian-owned factories at Tsaritsyn and Perm, but was accused of lining his own pockets in doing so. The Grand Duke favoured Schneider-Creusot, whose guns were completed at the Putilov works. Field artillery was a high priority in each of the 1910, 1912, and 1913 programmes, but the last, in setting a target of 8,558 guns by 1917, included 2,110 heavy pieces. On completion each corps would have 108 field guns and thirty-six heavy guns. But in 1914 much of what had been acquired was allocated to Russia's fortresses, and its principal howitzer, the 4.8-inch (or 122 mm) made by Krupp, was a corps, not a divisional, weapon. In any case there were only 534 of them. The heaviest gun, of which the army had 173, was the Schneider-Creusot 6-inch (152 mm).[375] In the first two years of the war GAU concentrated on multiplying stocks of existing patterns rather than introducing new equipment. Thus, massive increases in the output of guns and shell obscured an inferiority in the heavier calibres of increasing—and from 1916 acute—significance. In January 1917 the number of heavy guns deployed on the eastern front by Russia was half that allocated to the same theatre by the Central Powers. The sparseness of large-calibre artillery was a defining characteristic of the eastern front, and one not explained by the fact that it was twice the length of the western

[370] Gatrell, *Government, industry and rearmament*, 299; Menning, *Bayonets before bullets*, 255; Fuller, *Strategy and power*, 449.

[371] Golovine, *Russian army in the World War*, 126–7; for different figures, see Andolenko, *Histoire de l'armée russe*, 379

[372] Miquel, *Grande guerre*, 253.

[373] Lobanov-Rostovsky, *Grinding mill*, 160.

[374] Gourko, *Memories*, 103.

[375] Gatrell, *Government, industry and rearmament*, 132–4, 299; Suchomlinow, *Erinnerungen*, 327–9; Menning, *Bayonets before bullets*, 231–2, 234.

front: the British had thirteen heavy guns per kilometre, the French ten, and the Russians one.[376]

The obstacles to importing weapons to compensate for these shortages were not confined to the problems of ports. Russia had its foreign exchange to consider; its allies had to attend to their own shipping needs; and in 1914–15 all arms firms, not just those of the belligerents, found themselves inundated with orders way beyond their current capacities.

The power most obviously poised to exploit this opportunity was the United States. Competition between allies would not only enable American companies to raise prices but also to juggle and vary delivery dates. The need for the Entente to co-operate in its purchasing was immediately recognized, and found reflection in the French and British decision to establish the Commission Internationale de Ravitaillement (CIR) in August 1914. Russia joined the Commission the following month. However, the CIR did not thereby become the exclusive overseas purchasing authority which logic suggested. Many Russians believed it was corrupt, and saw no reason to channel their orders for American arms through an allied organization. Others were under the impression—thanks largely to the grandiose image of Vickers, established in the pre-war years—that Britain was awash with weaponry which only its miserliness was failing to release. Indirectly, here was another distortion generated by the naval arms race. The fact that neither the engineering nor the artillery department of the War Ministry was represented on the CIR was taken to justify independent ordering. The situation was improved with the creation in January 1915 of a Russian government committee in London, charged with arranging all Russian purchasing in Britain. Its head, General Timchenko-Ruban, could speak for the engineering department of the War Ministry, and the membership of his committee overlapped with that of the CIR.[377] The dispatch of the GAU representatives to Britain also helped. Nonetheless, the domestic friction between the Ministry of War and Stavka continued to create an ambiguity about policy in regard to overseas purchasing which perplexed Russia's allies and opened the door to middlemen anxious to exploit the opportunity for profits. Thus, in March 1915 Grand Duke Sergei Mikhailovich declared that GAU's policy was to import the plant in order to enable Russia to boost domestic production: this quelled Sukhomlinov's fear, justified particularly in relation to small arms, that a multiplicity of foreign imports would diversify the number of calibres in use.[378] But in May Stavka espoused the opposite approach. Grand Duke Nicholas appointed Kitchener

[376] Knox, With the Russian army, 547; also Gourko, Memories, 219–20.
[377] Keith Neilson, 'Managing the war: Britain, Russia and ad hoc government', in Dockrill and French, Strategy and intelligence, 106–7.
[378] Golovine, Russian army, 127–9.

the agent of the Russian government in the ordering of shells, small-arms ammunition, machine-guns, and rifles.[379]

British frustration with the consequences of bureaucratic competition in Russia should not be allowed to obscure the duplication that was also at work in Britain itself. Kitchener received his mandate from Grand Duke Nicholas just as the Ministry of Munitions was being called into life. But he construed his responsibility to be a consequence of his personal intervention with Stavka, and—rather than hand the business over to the new ministry—created a Russian purchasing committee within the War Office. Because British productive capacity was fully absorbed with the needs of its own army, the principal task of the Russian purchasing committee was to channel orders to the United States. This was exactly the job now being done for the British army by the Ministry of Munitions.

The War Office had entered into its first contract for American-made munitions in October 1914, and by the time J. P. Morgan was appointed the government's agent in January it reckoned that it had already placed the bulk of its orders. It anticipated that at most a further £10 million in contracts would be required. But by mid-May deals to six times that value had been struck. Rumblings concerning Morgan's role related not just to the fat commissions landing in the firm's lap. They were also provoked by the continuing competition of other nations, by the tendency of brokers to play off the War Office against Morgan's, and by the delays in actual deliveries.

In June 1915 Lloyd George sent D. A. Thomas to investigate whether Morgan's were adequately representing British interests. Thomas quashed some misconceptions: he reported that Morgan's were so zealous on Britain's behalf that they were making themselves unpopular with American firms, and were so embarrassed by the size of their profits that they were prepared to revise the basis on which their commission was calculated. The real issues lay elsewhere. One was that of standards. Morgan's were reluctant to place contracts with unproven businesses. Therefore established companies were overloaded with orders while other plant languished underused. Another was exchange. An independent Russian purchasing committee was established in New York in May 1915, but its London analogue was Timchenko-Ruban's Russian government committee, not the War Office's Russian purchasing committee. All three bodies were operating outside Morgan's framework, effectively causing Russian to bid against Russian, and ally against ally. The Ministry of Munitions was not only adjudicating between the Russians and the British, but was also in competition with the War Office. The Russians continued to block centralized purchasing into 1916, but the exchange-rate crisis in July and August 1915 at

[379] Neilson, *Strategy and supply*, 52–3, 74–9, 87. Neilson is fundamental for what follows; see also Neilson, *Slavonic and East European Review*, LX (1982), 572–90; Neilson, *Russia and the last Tsar*, 351–6; *Ministry of Munitions*, vol. II, pt. 8.

least rationalized Britain's own buying. On 5 September 1915 the British experts in North America were combined into a British Munitions Board. This was entrusted with the investigation of new firms and with following up their progress on contracts. In December 1915 E. W. Moir was appointed to head the board, which henceforth became known as the 'Moir organization'.[380] Relations between Moir and Morgan were not easy, but in conjunction they at least provided a reasonable structure. Certainly, Britain's approach was more coherent than France's.

On 12 September 1914 France ordered 29,000 rifles, valued at $1,537,000, from the United States. Its first contract for shells followed a month later. By April 1915 the artillery mission in the United States had entered into 318 contracts. But the artillery mission was only the most important of a range of independent bodies, each operating under the Ministry of War but each purchasing particular commodities without liaison with the other. By April 1915 113 Frenchmen, many of them unable to speak English or without commercial experience, were representing the French army's need for remounts, powder, engineering equipment, clothing, food, medical supplies, and aeroplanes. In theory, France's appointment of Morgan's in May limited the role of the missions, to technical advice and inspection. The trouble was that some American firms persisted, as a consequence of their dislike of Morgan's, in pursuing independent contacts with the French missions, and Ribot remained willing to condone this. Not until June 1916 did France emulate the British example and create a single purchasing mission under Colonel Vignal, previously the military attaché to the French ambassador. By then the size of the missions had swollen yet further (their personnel numbered 209 in November 1916), and the two principal agencies—artillery and remounts—had become so powerful that Vignal struggled to assert his authority.[381]

Arguably, this network of competing authorities ought to have produced a surfeit of deliveries, albeit at inflated prices. In fact, what happened was the reverse. The arms industry of the United States was not in a position to meet the demands made of it in 1914. A French Senate report reckoned that there were about 15,000 businesses in the United States producing arms and munitions, but most of these were engaged in the manufacture of small-arms. The United States had only one major producer of shells (Bethlehem Steel) and only one of powder.[382] These firms accepted more orders than their plant was capable of delivering. By the end of 1915 the United States had supplied Britain with 189 field guns and 3.5 million shells. Its most important contribution— 17.5 million rounds of small-arms ammunition in 1914 and 178 million rounds in 1915[383]—reflected its real strength. But the small-arms business in particular

---

[380] Burk, *Britain, America*, 30–42; Gilbert, *Lloyd George*, 211–13; *Ministry of Munitions*, vol. II, pt. 3.
[381] Nouailhat, *France et États-Unis*, 91–5, 241–6, 380–1.
[382] Ibid. 91–2, 94.   [383] *Ministry of Munitions*, vol. II, pt. 3, 127.

had been sustained by private trade. The belligerent governments—particularly, but not only, Russia—were reluctant to modify their expectations in the light of firms' capacities. They even compounded the problem by altering specifications in mid-contract. In June 1916, of 1 million rifles ordered by Britain, only 480 had been both delivered and accepted.[384] Of 1.8 million rifles ordered by Russia from Westinghouse, 216,000 had been delivered by February 1917, together with 27,000 of 300,000 due from Winchester and 180,000 of 1.5 million from Remington.[385]

Russia's response to late delivery was to postpone the placing of further foreign orders until existing contracts were fulfilled.[386] France, reflecting its loss of raw materials as well as the belief that the maintenance of standards was easier with domestic manufacturers, adopted a different approach.

The demand which the United States could satisfy much more readily than that for instant armaments was the need for materials from which munitions could be fabricated. Over the period 2 August 1914 to 30 June 1915 American exports of munitions to France were valued at over $15 million, but they represented only 13 per cent of France's US purchases for the purposes of the war. French policy in 1914–15 was to boost domestic arms production, so using the war to buttress French wages and French profits, but to do so with imported steel, copper, cotton, benzol, toluene, and picric acid.[387]

Another approach, and one adopted by France in placing orders for weapons in Spain and Italy, was to seek alternative markets. For Russia, Vladivostok made the Far East an obvious source of armaments, and one, moreover, which would minimize demands on Entente shipping. China was believed to have imported over 150,000 German Mauser rifles during the revolution, many of them still unpaid for. Britain graciously decided that Russia should have first call on these. But by October 1915 the total available had dwindled to 26,000, and in the event it was the British who got 10,919 of them; not a single rifle reached Russia.[388] The Japanese were opposed to the withdrawal of China's rifles, the arming of the warlords being a means to encourage the country's disintegration. The British, therefore, promoted direct trading between Russia and Japan. In August 1915 Grey pointed out to the Japanese that, by arming Russia so that it could defeat Germany, they would prompt the Russians to remain a European power rather than an Asiatic one—an outcome which would, of course, serve Britain's interests as well as Japan's. Japan replied that it had already supplied Russia with 430,000 rifles

[384] Burk, *Britain, America*, 41–2.
[385] D. Jones, 'Imperial Russia's forces at war', in Millett and Murray (eds.), *Military effectiveness*, i. 268–9.
[386] Knox, *With the Russian army*, 276, 411, 416.
[387] Nouailhat, *France et États-Unis*, 91–5; Jèze and Truchy, *War finance*, 119–21.
[388] Jones, *Britain's search for Chinese co-operation*, 50–1, 54–61, 105–6.

and 500 heavy guns and ammunition in the first year of the war. Certainly, Russia had turned to Japan from the outset, but whether it got as much satisfaction from its orders as the Japanese claimed is doubtful: the British military attaché in Russia reckoned only 200,000 rifles were delivered (of 1 million ordered), and made no reference to heavy guns.[389]

American deliveries of finished armaments did not really come on stream until the second half of 1916. Having delivered 480 rifles to Britain by early June, the Americans handed over 200,000 by September.[390] Total supplies for the year included 398 field guns, 20.9 million shells (a sixfold increase on the previous year), and 554 million rounds of small-arms ammunition. Although deliveries of guns and rifles rose again in 1917, shell and small-arms ammunition supplies fell back to their 1915 levels.[391]

The explanations for this decline are fourfold. First, British domestic production was still rising, and in so doing was gradually lessening Britain's dependence on American finished goods. Secondly, by opting, as the French had done, for raw materials Britain could save on foreign exchange. Thirdly, America was arming itself in 1917. Fourthly, and most importantly, the combination of U-boat warfare and declining Entente tonnage was forcing a careful weighing of shipping priorities.

The effect of these pressures on France worked somewhat differently. Being to a large extent reliant on British shipping, its preference for the importation of materials—which were more bulky than finished goods—was more costly in shipping charges and therefore in foreign exchange. The manufacture of 1 tonne of gunpowder required 12 tonnes of raw materials.[392] It therefore became relatively cheaper, as well as more economical in shipping, to buy finished goods abroad. Imports fell by weight but rose by price. In 1916 French imports weighed 44 million tonnes, but in 1917 they fell back to 34.5 million, close to their levels in 1914 and 1915. However, the total cost of these imports leapt from 20,640 million francs in 1916 to 27,554 million in 1917. Much of this jump was attributable to imports of manufactured goods, which rose in value by 2,863 million francs, whereas those of industrial raw materials rose by 2,123 million francs. Having imported 267,000 quintals of explosives in 1916, the French brought in 763,000 in 1917.[393] Thus France's imports of munitions from the United States in 1917 climbed from 37,853 tonnes in 1916 to 98,505 tonnes.[394]

Resolving their allies' needs in relation to munitions production—and particularly the Russians' demand for rifles and heavy artillery—made strategic sense for Britain. Opponents of conscription in 1915 argued that British munitions output would be better applied arming the manpower of Russia

[389] Knox, *With the Russian army*, 216; Rothwell, *History*, LVI (1971), 39; Nish, *Alliance in decline*, 162.
[390] Burk, *Britain, America*, 41.   [391] *Ministry of Munitions*, vol. II, pt. 3, 127.
[392] Reboul, *Mobilisation industrielle*, 133–4.   [393] Petit, *Finances extérieures*, 28, 35–44.
[394] Nouailhat, *France et États-Unis*, 253.

than the workforce of Britain.[395] Even when this argument had been lost, an active eastern front remained an essential element of a successful western front: the more the Russians could be enabled to engage the Germans, the easier would be the lot of the French and the British. Therefore both Kitchener, as secretary of state for war, and Lloyd George, as minister for munitions, were united on broad principles.

But their application caused division. By October 1915 the Ministry of Munitions was already looking forward to the day when it had a munitions surplus available for redistribution to its ally. The manner of its allocation could, in a resource-driven war, have an effect on the direction of operations. The War Office, however, could not so readily embrace the notion of abundance, particularly when the material needs of the British army were far from satiated.

Even while he was chancellor of the exchequer Lloyd George had seen in the principle of inter-allied munitions co-operation a lever by which he could take a share in the direction of strategy. This was the subtext of the February 1915 allied conference on finance. However, the Anglo-French meeting at Boulogne in June was the first devoted specifically to munitions. It was followed by further deliberations in July and October. Both powers quickly agreed that any surplus to the requirements of one country would 'be freely accessible to the other country without any question of a *quid pro quo*'. Albert Thomas went on to declare: 'I do not consider the Ministry of Munitions in London or my own office in Paris to be two separate institutions. I consider there is one Munitions Ministry for both countries.'[396]

Two obstacles lay athwart the fulfilment of such high-minded objectives. First, Italy and—particularly—Russia were badgering their more industrialized allies for weaponry: consequently the two ministries had not only to regulate their own relationship but also to harmonize it with that of their poorer partners. Secondly, the question of who should get what from any big allied pot did not necessarily depend on equal shares for all but rather on the strategic priority accorded to each front. Such calculations could cut many ways. Not even the two ministers for munitions were in accord. In October Thomas considered that France was readier to act and so should have priority over Russia; Lloyd George thought that by arming Russia he would enable the latter to aid Serbia and so keep the Balkan front active. Thus, for all his overt solidarity, Thomas's actual priorities were closer to those of the War Office than of the Ministry of Munitions.[397]

When all four allies met in London at the end of November 1915 to discuss munitions the show of co-ordination proved much greater than the

[395] Roskill, *Hankey*, 220, 225.   [396] *Ministry of Munitions*, vol. II, pt. 8, 20.
[397] Ibid. 20; Neilson, *Strategy and supply*, 116.

subsequent practice. A resolution, proposed by Thomas, that a central munitions office for the allies be established, was quickly approved. But it remained a dead letter. Part of the problem was over what the office would have done if it had been given life. G. M. Booth's suggestion, for pooling all allied resources on an equal basis, was the only viable option in the circumstances of 1915–16, and it was therefore the only principle on which such an office could have functioned. The alternative, an agreement as to the differentials to be applied in the allocation of arms to different fronts, would have had to be predicated—as Lloyd George recognized—on a concerted allied plan of campaign. Lloyd George's hope, that the centralization of munitions orders could force the centralization of strategic direction, foundered on its inversion of the natural order in which to proceed.[398]

The western allies wanted centralization not for strategic but for economic reasons, to curb Russia's independent purchasing and to protect their own exchange. The Russians did not want that, but they did like the idea of pooling resources, a process from which they were the power most likely to benefit. The trouble was that the British and the French had no intention of equipping the Russians on the same scale as themselves. Furthermore, even the most ardent of Russia's supporters found themselves wrong-footed by the exorbitant nature of Russia's demands. It came to the November conference with a request for 1,400 4.8-inch howitzers, 250 8-inch siege howitzers, ninety 6-inch howitzers, and fifty-four 12-inch howitzers. Furthermore, it soon became clear that the Russians hoped that the conference would also resolve its small-arms needs. Britain did not have heavy artillery to offer. It had put the larger calibres at the centre of gun programmes A, B, and C precisely because they were its own priority: what it anticipated releasing to the Russians by the spring of 1916 was the resulting surplus in field guns, specifically 18-pounders.[399] Even if Britain had been able to release bigger pieces, they might well not have met the high standards set by Russia's inspectors. The Russian army relied even more than the British on horse-drawn transport. Therefore the barrels of its guns were made of higher quality and thinner steel, in order to make them lighter than the comparable British piece.[400]

Lloyd George offered Russia 300 4.5-inch field howitzers to be delivered in three consignments in February, March, and April 1916. Thomas said that France would contribute one out of every three 105 mm howitzers it produced, plus two 280 mm guns a month.[401] Ultimately France delivered to Russia a total of 100 105 mms, 160 long 120 mms, fifty short 155 mms, and sixteen 220 mms.[402]

Lloyd George's promise, small though it was in relation to the original Russian request, still seemed massive to the new chief of the imperial general

[398] *Ministry of Munitions*, vol. II, pt. 8, 20–3.   [399] Addison, *Four and a half years*, i. 130.
[400] Crow, *Man of push and go*, 131–2.   [401] Neilson, *Strategy and supply*, 129–34.
[402] Reboul, *Mobilisation industrielle*, 50.

staff, Sir William Robertson. The British army had been promised 100 heavy howitzers for January 1916 but had got only fifty-one. His case against fulfilling Lloyd George's undertaking was augmented by the problems of shipping the guns to Russia, and of railway communication at the ports once they were there.

Thus, easing Russia's shortage of heavy artillery became embroiled in two further issues. First, there was the question of allied shipping control: the Russians were reluctant to cede management of their tonnage to Britain, but without it Britain was not confident that the shipping made available to Russia would be used for the purposes of the war rather than for those of commerce more generally. Secondly, the difficulty of shifting the guns from the port area suggested that railways should take priority over guns—and indeed that the latter could not be properly exploited without more of the former. Therefore, Russia's particular need for heavy artillery touched more general sensitivities. It was becoming clear to the Entente that the prosecution of the war might make it impossible to service Russia's war effort in isolation: Britain and France were being called on to support Russia's industrialization on a broader front.[403]

Albert Thomas visited Russia in May 1916. He returned convinced, as he told Lloyd George, that the Russians had plenty of plant and should be left to sort themselves out. The implication was that Britain should devote any munitions surplus to France rather than to Russia.[404]

Neither Lloyd George nor Kitchener was disposed to take this view. But both needed to have a clearer picture as to the true nature of Russia's needs in order, on the one hand, to fend off the more outrageous Russian demands, and on the other to enable them to handle the French. On the outcome of this mission would also depend allied financial policy in the United States, so much of which was predicated on Russia's arms orders.

Both men were obvious candidates for such an embassy, but the Easter Rising in Dublin detained Lloyd George on other business, and Kitchener went alone. The cruiser on which he sailed, HMS *Hampshire*, struck a mine off the Orkney Islands at 7.45 p.m. on 5 June. Kitchener was drowned.

The abrupt conclusion to Kitchener's mission meant that the dilemmas of allied co-ordination in the face of Russia's demand for arms remained unresolved. But it did at least end the bureaucratic confusion over the administration of orders in London. The War Office's Russian purchasing committee was wound up, its personnel moving to a Russian supply committee within the Ministry of Munitions, and its purchasing functions being absorbed by the Commission Internationale de Ravitaillement. Furthermore, Lloyd George was appointed Kitchener's successor at the War Office. Thus, strategic debate

[403] Neilson, *Strategy and supply*, 172–98.   [404] Gilbert, *Lloyd George*, 349.

was focused where it belonged, and the Ministry of Munitions could concentrate its attention on the business of procurement.

The political debates over industrial mobilization in the first phases of the war gave each nation's experience a complexion peculiar to it alone. But the frustration which found a voice in the course of these discussions was very often a manifestation of problems that were common to most of them. All powers, including the United States, experienced delays in production caused by the conversion of industry; all the belligerents had to regulate their labour supply and had to harness their scientists in the development of new processes. What is striking is how nearly simultaneous the main troughs and peaks of enhanced munitions production were, regardless of the relative states of industrial development. Thus, beneath the rhetoric the actual achievement of increased output owed less to changing administrative structures and more to continued plugging away by ministries of war, very often operating in established grooves.

Nevertheless, the political flashpoints mattered. At one level they were part of a debate about whether state collectivism or liberal capitalism was the most appropriate ideology with which to tackle the issue of industrial mobilization. Uniformly, at least at this stage of the war, the answer was compromise. This particular choice was stated most starkly in the autocracies. In Germany Rathenau and Moellendorff put the case for state control, even if the result of their efforts was somewhat different. In Russia the rallying of the Duma to the War Industries Committee testified to the continuing antagonism between liberalism and commerce on the one hand and Tsarism and state enterprise on the other.

The other dimension was less socio-economic, and was more in evidence in the western democracies of the Entente. The parliamentary assault on Millerand, Lloyd George's clash with Kitchener—these were symptoms of an effort to curb the powers of the army. The munitions issue was therefore the first phase of a struggle to control and direct strategy. In the second half of the war the tensions of civil–military relations would be played out in different forums—for the Entente in a strategic direction itself, and for the Central Powers in the army's direction of the inner workings of the state. But no greater evidence could be afforded of the demands which the war was making on its participating societies than the fact that the practical issues of enhanced munitions productivity touched such fundamental political themes.

Furthermore, by the summer of 1916, although this effort had ensured that the war percolated through to the bowels of the belligerents, it had still not resolved many of the armaments issues which the war had thrown up. Armies had, broadly speaking, either procured more of the same—more field guns and more rifles—or had opted for low-technology solutions, such as grenades and mortars, which were not dependent on the sophisticated plant of the major arms firms. Only Britain had begun to assimilate the massive increase in heavy artillery demanded by position war. This could not be improvised, but was a high-technology option, dependent on sophisticated machine tools of exact specifications and massive weight and size. Russia's strident call for heavy guns was echoed in cries emanating from all armies in 1916.

The battle of the Somme would, therefore, create a fresh munitions crisis and demand a further progression in industrial mobilization. Not until then would the Germans coin the word *Materialschlacht*, a battle of material. Not until then would machines really begin to substitute for men, and so permit a reduction in manpower as a trade-off for the enhancement of firepower. Perhaps it was the last argument of navalism that it was Britain, and not France or Germany, that led the way in this ultimate intensification of continental warfare.[405]

[405] Strachan, *Journal of Strategic Studies*, XXI (1998), 79–95.

12

CONCLUSION: THE
IDEAS OF 1914

Within three months the third Balkan war had embroiled the bulk of the world's three most populous continents, Europe, Africa, and Asia. It had, moreover, embraced two more, Australia and—via Canada—North America. 'The war', Alfred Baudrillart, wrote in his diary on 31 October 1914, 'is extending to the whole universe.'[1]

Baudrillart's hyperbole reflected the global status of the European powers. Africans found themselves fighting because they were the subjects of Britain, France, Germany, or Belgium, not because they were Africans. Furthermore, London's primacy as the world's financial capital and Paris's status as an international lender meant that even those nations that were formally independent could not remain untouched by the war's outbreak in 1914. Neutrality in the political sense did not result in immunity from the war's effects in every other sense. Neither the United States nor China became formal belligerents until 1917, but their domestic politics, their diplomacy, and their wealth were all contingent on the war from its very outset.

To contend that the war was truly global throughout its duration is, of course, not the same as also saying that its purposes were commensurate with its scale. Indeed, it has been the presumption of hindsight that they were not. The Great War has often been portrayed not as a world war but as a European civil war, a squabble between brothers, united—if only they had realized it—by more than divided them, a struggle where the means were massively disproportionate given the ends.

The now-considerable literature on war aims reinforces this approach, because it states the objectives of each power in geographical or economic

---

[1] Baudrillart, *Carnets*, 92.

terms. Being drawn up as agendas for peace settlements, war aims—however extensive—rested on the presumption that negotiation would become possible. Their implication is some form of limitation, even if those limits tended to be set far beyond the bounds of acceptability for the enemy and, often, for allies. War aims were a retrospective effort to give shape to something bigger. They did not cause the war. Even those of Germany were developed during the conflict, not before it. The powers of Europe entered the war without clearly defined geographical objectives; if they had, the First World War might indeed have been nearer to the 'cabinet wars' of Bismarck or even of the eighteenth century than it was. When the war broke out, it was not a fight for the control of Alsace-Lorraine or Poland or Galicia. It was, as Bethmann Hollweg melodramatically anticipated in 1913, 'a battle for existence'.[2]

Big ideas, however rhetorical, shaped the war's purpose more immediately and completely than did more definable objectives. 'The War of 1914', an Oxford classics don, Alfred Zimmern, told an audience from the Workers' Educational Association at its summer school that year, 'is not simply a war between the Dual Alliance and the Triple Entente: it is... a war of ideas—a conflict between two different and irreconcilable conceptions of government, society and progress.'[3] Later that year H. G. Wells published *The war that will end war*. 'We fight', he declared, 'not to destroy a nation, but to kill a nest of ideas... Our business is to kill ideas. The ultimate purpose of this war is propaganda, the destruction of certain beliefs and the creation of others.'[4]

Wells was no more a militarist than Zimmern was a Germanophobe. For all Wells's use of the word 'propaganda', his book was not propaganda in the narrowly defined sense: neither he nor Zimmern held the views they did because they were mouthpieces for the British government. In due course the ideas with which they were concerned did indeed become the meat of official propaganda; but their emotional charge derived precisely from the personal conviction that underpinned them. The issues were moral and, ultimately, religious.

In a sectarian sense, the Thirty Years War was the last great European war of religion. Thereafter notions of just war atrophied, and vindications for the recourse to arms were couched in political and national terms. In the First World War neither alliance was shaped by a clearly defined creed. Muslim and Christian, Catholic and Protestant, were to be found on both sides of the line. Germany stressed its Lutheran credentials within Europe, but became—by virtue of its pact with Turkey—the spokesman for Catholicism in the Holy Land. The same alliance also made it the protector of the Jews. In this case, however, the function was replicated rather than reversed within Europe itself:

[2] Schulte, *Vor dem Kriegsausbruch*, 116.
[3] Seton-Watson *et al.*, *War and democracy*, 318.
[4] Marrin, *Last crusade*, 98.

France, the persecutor of Dreyfus, and Russia, the architect of anti-Semitic pogroms, were Germany's enemies. Zionism, however, found its advocate in Britain. In confessional terms Britain and Germany should have been aligned. The fact that they were not shattered German theologians like Adolf von Harnack. Their disillusionment was deepened by Britain's readiness to ally with Shinto Japan and to deploy Hindu troops in Europe. Ernst Troeltsch described the consequences for international Christianity, ' the religion of the white race', as 'a downright catastrophe'.[5]

Troeltsch's despair went further. The destruction and hatred which the war unleashed seemed to make Christianity itself 'an alien message from an alien world'. This was not a new lament: its origins were both pre-war and domestic. Church–state relations in many of the belligerent countries were increasingly fraught. Societies had become sufficiently secularized in their pursuit of material progress for church leaders to be tempted to see the war's advent as divine retribution. For them, the war could be welcomed as a necessary and God-given process of cleansing and rejuvenation.

Paradoxically, therefore, optimism trod hard on the heels of pessimism. The response of many on mobilization was to turn to religion for guidance and comfort. In Hamburg church attendance rose 125 per cent in August. In Orcival, in France, 4,115 people received communion in 1913 but 14,480 did so in 1914.[6] Much of what moved congregations was spiritual and mystical. In a sermon delivered in October 1914 Pastor L. Jacobsköller saw the war as a new Whitsun, the coming of the Holy Ghost 'like a mighty, rushing wind'.[7] God acquired a fresh immediacy, awesome and judging as well as loving and compassionate. Ernst Barlach's lithograph for *Kriegszeit*, a weekly magazine, entitled *Holy War*, showed a robed figure, his identity obscured, with sword poised.[8] Its message was ambiguous. Was this a vengeful God, purging the world of decadence and unbelief, or could it be a more partial God, punishing only His chosen people's foes?

Much of the rhetoric of holy war delivered from the pulpits of Europe in 1914 opted for the second interpretation. The *Solingen Tageblatt* on 5 August declared that this is 'a holy war': 'Germany can and is not allowed to lose . . . if she loses so, too, does the world lose its light, its home of justice'.[9] In Britain, the bishop of London, Arthur Winnington-Ingram, was of the view that 'the Church can best help the nation first of all by making it realise that it is engaged in a Holy War, and not be afraid of saying so'.[10] The cellist Maurice Maréchal, then a 22-year-

[5] Rubanowice, *Crisis in consciousness*, 101; also Pressel, *Kriegspredigt*, 128–30; Huber, *Kirche und Öffentlichkeit*, 171–3, 181–2.
[6] Hope, *German and Scandinavian protestantism*, 591; Becker, *Great War and the French people*, 188.
[7] Pressel, *Kriegspredigt*, 17–18; also 188–91.
[8] Cork, *Bitter truth*, 47.
[9] Verhey, 'The "spirit" of 1914', 273.
[10] Marrin, *Last crusade*, 139.

old music student, wrote to his mother on 2 August 1914 in terms that were more emotive and romantic. He had that day passed Rouen cathedral on his way back home: the building was saying, 'I am the Glory, I am the Faith, I am France. I love my children, who have given me life, and I protect them.'[11]

The crux of such pronouncements was their identification of church with state. Nowhere was this more evident than in the only formal declaration of holy war, that made in Constantinople and issued in the name of a spiritual leader, the Caliph, who, as Sultan, was also a temporal ruler. In Russia the Orthodox church fused its own proselytization with the Russification of the empire's ethnic communities. Under the leadership of the minister of religion, the church used the opportunity of the war not only to intensify its persecution of Jews and Muslims but also to root out Lutherans in the Baltic states, Catholics in Poland, and above all, Uniates (or Greek Catholics) in the Ukraine.[12] In a series of fourteen lithographs entitled *Mystical Images of War* Natalia Goncharova subscribed to this fusion of Russia's history with its religion, her final print showing the spirit of St Alexander Nevsky, who routed the Teutonic knights in 1242.[13] Significantly, the *lubok*, a traditional form of popular broadside, was revived in Russia in 1914–15. Although the *lubki* rarely referred to the church, they used iconic elements to emphasize the holiness of the struggle, with the Entente as the Trinity and Russia and the Russian soldier as mother and child.[14]

In western Europe the fact that Catholics were committed to both sides reduced the Vatican to virtual silence. But the German invasion of Belgium and northern France acquired the trappings of a holy war with almost immediate effect. The German army was heir to two traditions. The first, forged by the French army in the Vendée and in the Peninsular War, saw Catholic priests as the orchestrators of local guerrillas and resistance movements. The second was Bismarck's anti-Catholic *Kulturkampf*. The stories of German atrocities often had priests and nuns as their victims. If they accepted the accusations, German soldiers excused their actions as responses to 'conspiratorial Catholicism';[15] if they denied them, their prosecutors cited as evidence the physical destruction suffered by churches, notably at Louvain and Reims.

For the Catholics themselves, their sufferings were an opportunity to re-establish the links between church and state. In Belgium Cardinal Mercier, archbishop of Malines, became a symbol of resistance. In his 1914 Christmas message he told his flock that, 'The religion of Christ makes patriotism a law:

[11] Guéno and Laplume, *Paroles de poilus*, 11.
[12] Pares, *Fall of the Russian monarchy*, 64–5; Rauchensteiner, *Tod des Doppeladlers*, 29; Zeman, *Break-up of Habsburg empire*, 5–6.
[13] Cork, *Bitter truth*, 48.
[14] Jahn, *Patriotic culture in Russia*, 24, 28.
[15] Horne and Kramer, *Journal of Modern History*, LXVI (1994), 24.

there is no perfect Christian who is not a perfect patriot.'[16] In occupied France the mobilization of teachers and then the severance from Paris could leave the curé as the most important local figure. Indeed, the Germans' victimization and even execution of the clergy may have reflected the latter's exercise of secular rather than spiritual leadership. The archbishop of Verdun told Baudrillart of one curé who had been stripped and flogged in front of his parishioners, and of another who had been clothed in his vestments and then forced to watch the rape of his maid.[17] However much exaggerated by French and British propaganda, such stories were almost certainly not without some foundation.[18] More importantly, they were believed at the time. Baudrillart established a Catholic committee to produce anti-German propaganda, and in April 1915 it published *La Guerre allemande et le catholicisme.* Thus the war provided the opportunity for France's Catholics both to challenge republican aspersions on their loyalty, and to win back Frenchmen for Rome.

In 1429 Joan of Arc had passed through Auxerre on her way to raise the siege of Orléans. In 1914 the city's cathedral church of St Étienne commissioned a stained glass depiction of the maid directing operations: it carried the words attributed to Joan—'I have been sent by God the King of Heaven to drive you out of all France.' The ambiguity as to whom her words were addressed proved helpful. A declaration directed at the English in 1429 could in 1914 be targeted at the Germans. Before the First World War's outbreak the cult of Joan of Arc promoted political division more than patriotic unity. The campaign for her canonization and for her appropriation as a national symbol was orchestrated by the Catholic right. But there existed another image of Joan, not of the church militant or of martial success, of Joan clad not in armour but in a dress; this was a peasant girl betrayed by the king whose coronation she had achieved and burned at the stake by the church which she had served. Both images carried patriotic overtones, even if the second was of a revolutionary France rather than a royalist one. The outbreak of the war, and particularly the bombardment of Reims cathedral, where Charles VII had been crowned under a standard held aloft by Joan, permitted these divergent interpretations to be integrated. At one level, therefore, the iconography of Joan in late 1914 was simply further evidence of the *union sacrée* and its capacity for reconciliation. But it carried a further message. The posters and postcards bore a legend that was both a reminder and a promise: 'Dieu protège la France.'[19]

[16] Stengers, *Guerres mondiales et conflits contemporains,* 179 (July 1995), 31.
[17] Baudrillart, *Carnets,* 100.
[18] The subject of atrocities and also of their relationship to propaganda will be dealt with in a subsequent volume. Trevor Wilson challenged the evidence of atrocities in Belgium used by the British, *Journal of Contemporary History,* XIV (1979), 369–83; John Horne and Alan Kramer are exploring the truth—see *Journal of Modern History,* LXVI (1994), 1–33.
[19] The Auxerre window is by Edmond Socard, from a painting by Paul Louzier. See also Krumeich, *Jeanne d'Arc,* esp. 10–12, 187–99, 216–18.

Catholicism was hardly the monopoly of the Entente. Austrian fealty to the Vatican contrasted strongly with the anticlericalism of the Third Republic. And the latter made France an even greater threat in the adjacent territories of Catholic south Germany. Efforts were made to render Freiburg's cathedral as symbolic as those of Reims or Louvain. *Illustrierte Zeitung*, a Leipzig journal, highlighted its vulnerability with a picture of a French air raid over the city on 13 December 1914. Alsatian priests were not martyrs but traitors; the number reported by the German press as having been executed for treason proved to be double the number actually in orders. Thus, the themes of allied propaganda and the accusations of Entente Catholics were turned. The fact that Germany's propaganda in neutral states was entrusted to the leader of the Catholic Centre party, Matthias Erzberger, reinforced the specifically Catholic dimension to the German riposte. The charges levelled by Baudrillart's committee received a point-by-point rebuttal in a volume written by A. J. Rosenberg at Erzberger's request, and Georg Pfeilschifter presided over a collaborative volume, *Deutsche Kultur, Katholizismus und Weltkrieg* (German culture, Catholicism, and world war). Significantly Pfeilschifter's contributors, like Rosenberg himself, were predominantly academic theologians rather than clerics. The Vatican had asked Erzberger to keep the episcopate out of the controversy.[20]

The Germans were portrayed not merely as anti-Catholic but frequently also as anti-Christian. The root of this second charge was liberal theology. In Germany biblical scholarship had neglected faith in favour of research, religion in favour of rationality, and so removed the moral force from Christian teaching. The invasion of Belgium was cited as evidence, the act of a society which denied the natural law of the civilized world. Adolf von Harnack and Ernst von Dryander, the primate of the German Evangelical church, rejected these allegations. In late August the first of a succession of manifestos was drawn up under their aegis, and addressed to Evangelical churches abroad— particularly in the United States. Its distribution was entrusted to the Deutsche Evangelische Missions-Hilfe, created in December 1913 to promote missionary work in the German colonies. The fusion of Evangelism and propaganda, the broadening in focus from Germany's own overseas possessions to the world as a whole, helped redefine the church's mission in political and cultural as well as religious terms.[21]

The result was a new theology. The war enabled orthodox Lutherans and liberal theologians to converge. Both saw victory as the means to the applica- tion of the kingdom of God within an ethical community; Protestantism could be confirmed as the religious bedrock of the German cultural state.[22] The

[20] Geinitz, *Kriegsfurcht und Kampfbereitschaft*, 280, 398; Epstein, *Erzberger*, 101–2; Erzberger, *Erleb- nisse*, 11–18; Pfeilschifter (ed.), *Deutsche Kultur, Katholizismus und der Weltkrieg*.
[21] Andresen, *Dryander*, 313–16, 331–3, 346–8; Pressel, *Kriegspredigt*, 108–18.
[22] Huber, *Kirche und Öffentlichkeit*, 145, 168–9.

Lutheran church's evangelism, therefore, embraced the spirit of 1914 as an opportunity to relaunch itself not only in the wider world but also at home. Preachers did not move from their texts to contemporary life, but vice versa, addressing their parishioners' immediate experiences and using the Bible to reinforce the message. The Old Testament acquired a fresh relevance—evidence of God's use of war as judgement, and of his endorsement of a chosen people seeking a political and cultural independence.[23]

Luther himself became a hero—the fusion, like Joan of Arc in France, of religion, nationality, and historical identity. The Reformation joined the wars of unification in the historical foundations of the German state. The early Protestant church had relied on the secular powers for its survival, and was thus prey to state intervention from the outset of its existence.[24] Luther had recognized the dangers by propounding his doctrine of the two kingdoms. But, in seeking to separate the spiritual from the temporal, he had curtailed the church's role in national life while not preventing its appropriation for the purposes of nationalism. The Pan-German League and, particularly, the Army League were overwhelmingly Protestant in composition.[25]

God, therefore, became an active participant in the historical process. His nature in these circumstances was not determined by the needs of private morality but of public. The crowds on 1 August 1914 sang Luther's great hymn, 'Ein feste Burg ist unser Gott', a song that was at once both national and religious. Ernst Troeltsch moved under the impact of the war from theology to history, because the German form of Christianity was Lutheranism and the German state embodied the best form of Lutheranism in political practice. Patriotism, therefore, became both a source of faith and a Christian duty.[26]

On the occasion of the opening of the Reichstag on 4 August 1914 Ernst von Dryander preached in Berlin cathedral. The Kaiser was in the congregation. Dryander was entirely persuaded of the significance of this marriage of church and state. As he was later to say, 'I owe the best that I have to my fatherland not *in spite* of, but *because* of, my being a Christian—the best not only in time, strength and wealth, but also in the marrow of my strength, my relationship to God and to my faith'.[27] His text on 4 August was St Paul's Epistle to the Romans, chapter 8, verse 3: 'If God be for us, who can be against us?' His assumptions were cultural, in his rejection of materialism and his hopes of national regeneration, and they were historical. He cited Treitschke, and he summoned up Luther and 'the old heroes of 1813'. 'We march to the fight for our culture against unculture, for German morality against barbarity, for the free, German, God-fearing person

---

[23] Pressel, *Kriegspredigt*, 35–44; Doehring, *Ein feste Burg*, ii. 363–5.
[24] Marrin, *Last crusade*, 109–18.
[25] Ferguson, *Pity of war*, 18.
[26] Pressel, *Kriegspredigt*, 75–6, 176, 202–4; Rubanowice, *Crisis in consciousness*, 102–3, 107–9.
[27] Pressel, *Kriegspredigt*, 203.

against the instincts of the uncontrolled mass . . . We know that we fight not only for our existence but also for the existence of the most holy of possessions that we have to perpetuate.' The key issue, he concluded, was not 'whether God is with us, but whether we are with God'.[28]

Dryander explored themes which became central to Germany's sense of purpose, whether expressed by believers or agnostics. Bernhardi, the military publicist, wrote in *Internationale Monatsschrift* in November 1914: 'God reveals himself in victory by which He makes truth defeat appearance. It is God's law that condemns the vanquished, and it is, therefore, His will that the conqueror should dictate such peace terms as shall display his inner strength by his external power and greatness.'[29] The philosopher and, in due course, founding father of sociology Max Scheler, who was the son of a Protestant and a Jew, but who later converted to Catholicism, contended that the war was a holy war precisely because it was about fundamental issues associated with the existence of the nation. War was the moment when God passed judgement, and the mobilization of the state's resources as it put its fate in God's hands in itself made the war a just one.[30]

For thinkers in France and Britain the Nietzschean spin in this sort of thought—'the religion of valour, the religion of might is right', in the words of *The Times* on 10 September 1914[31]—suggested not a reworked Christianity but a departure from it. Baudrillart's Institut Catholique saw the root of the problem as Kant, Nietzsche's logical predecessor. In asserting that God was beyond human comprehension and that man could know only himself, Kant had, in the eyes of French Catholics, elevated man and with him the law and the moral authority of the state. For republicans, socialists, and anti-Catholics in France, Kant's emphasis on rationality was of course right and Catholicism superstitious and wrong. Conveniently too, Kant had written about perpetual peace.[32]

The divisions in French approaches to Kant highlighted not only the split between church and state in the republic but also the pre-war French conviction that there were two Germanies. Kant personified the cerebral, spiritual, and reasoned Germany; Hegel the materialist, militarist, and nationalist. During the war itself this division would find another, more practical interpretation, that of a German people (presumably Kantian) being guided, gulled, and misled by a German leadership (presumably Hegelian). In due course much Entente propaganda came to rest on the conviction that the

[28] Doehring, *Ein feste Burg*, i. 14–18; see also Andresen, *Dryander*, 319–20.
[29] Verhey, 'The "spirit" of 1914', 289; see also Lange, *Marneschlacht und deutsche Öffentlichkeit*, 113–16.
[30] Scheler, *Der Genius des Krieges* (first published in article form in October 1914, and as a book in 1915), 55, 86–8.
[31] Martin, *Times Literary Supplement*, 5 Aug. 1994, 11–12.
[32] Hanna, *Mobilization of intellect*, 108–18, and for what follows 9–10.

German masses were fundamentally liberal and rational. But the corollary of such a belief was that the allied purpose was itself revolutionary. Its task was not only to clear the Germans out of France and Belgium but also to overthrow the Kaiser and establish a German republic. Guided by their hopes of internationalism and perpetual peace, French socialists were as intellectually committed to the dismemberment of Germany—and therefore to a big war for big ideas—as were French Catholics and German Protestants.[33]

For many French intellectuals the notion of the two Germanies was scuppered by the manifesto of ninety-three German university teachers published by the *Berliner Tageblatt* and other major newspapers on 4 October 1914. Provocatively addressed 'An die Kulturwelt' (to the world of culture), it made clear that the unity of orthodox Lutherans and academic theologians which underpinned the August manifesto had now been extended. The ideas embraced by the church were endorsed by professors from throughout the Reich, of all religions and of all disciplines. Most claimed to be apolitical in the sense of being above party, but all parties bar the SPD were represented.

The signatories had international reputations as well as international contacts. Their pre-war assumptions were neither insular nor chauvinist. One of the most distinguished was the classicist Ulrich von Wilamowitz-Moellendorff. Wilamowitz orchestrated the preparation of a further manifesto published on 16 October 1914 in English, French, Italian, and Spanish as well as German. Thanks to the efforts of Dietrich Schäfer, professor of history, pupil of Treitschke, and pre-war stalwart of the Army League, virtually the entire German academic profession—over 4,000 names, including almost every professor at every German university—endorsed the declaration. Numbered among them were closet socialists, future pacifists, and sceptics, including Max Weber and Albert Einstein. The professors rejected the accusations that Germany had caused the war, had broken international law in its invasion of Belgium, and had committed atrocities against the civilian populations of that country and of France. Their list of denials concluded with two assertions: first, that the future of European culture rested on the victory of German so-called 'militarism'; and secondly, that in defining this militarism there was no distinction to be made between Prussia and the rest of Germany, or between the German army and the German nation: 'both are one.'[34]

A third manifesto, emanating from the University of Tübingen and entitled 'Appel au monde civilisé', was published on 17 October. In the long run their combined effects were counter-productive: they disseminated the charges

---

[33] Robert, *Les Ouvriers*, 28–30; also Milner, *Dilemmas of Internationalism*, 214.
[34] Brocke, 'Wissenschaft und Militarismus', 649–64; Schwabe, *Wissenschaft und Kriegsmoral*, 22–4; I have not been able to consult Jürgen Ungern-Sternberg von Pürkel and Wolfgang von Ungern-Sternberg, *Der Aufruf an die Kulturwelt. Das Manifest der 93 und die Anfänge der Kriegspropaganda im Ersten Weltkrieg* (Stuttgart, 1996).

against Germany by repeating them. But the immediate consequences arose from their association of German *Kultur* with German militarism.

The world of scholarship and the arts fragmented into national components. Sigmund Freud, writing in the spring of 1915, mourned science's loss of 'her passionless impartiality'.[35] The Institut de France dismissed from its honorary membership all those German professors who had signed the manifesto, and on 3 November 100 members of the French literary and artistic world countered with their own declaration. The signatories, who included representatives of the left like Georges Clemenceau, and of the right like Maurice Barrès, as well as Debussy, Gide, Matisse, and Monet, declared that 'the intellectual and moral richness of humanity is created by the natural variety and independence of all nations' gifts'. The Académie des Sciences replied on the same day in terms which were both more chauvinistic and more questionable: 'Latin and Anglo-Saxon civilisations are those which have produced the majority of the great discoveries in the mathematical, physical and natural sciences in the last three centuries.' It was left to historians like Ernest Lavisse, director of the École Normale Supérieure, to explain the roots of pan-Germanism and to work out the implications of German culture for the German 'theory and practice of war'.[36]

On 12 December 1914 Henri Bergson, the doyen of French philosphy, delivered his presidential address to the Académie des Sciences Morales et Politiques. For Bergson the union of the two Germanies had been effected not in 1914 but in 1871. Germany had opted not for an organic, natural unification, but for a mechanical and artificial form derived from Prussia. The basis of Germany's victories was material prosperity, and the ideas that followed did so as an effect of unification, not as its cause. Germany's philosophy was 'a translation into intellectual terms of her brutality, her appetites, and her vices'. German atrocities, and the belief of German academics that the ends justitifed such means, were evidence of 'barbarism reinforced by civilisation'.[37]

For Bergson individually, and for French academics collectively, herein was the key to the war's purpose. The defence of France was transformed into the defence of civilization. Once again the Huns were at the gates, and this time the threat was far greater because they had harnessed to the cause of barbarity the machinery of the state and the material advantages of industrialization. For those on the left the civilization which they were protecting was the legacy of 1789, equality and fraternity, principles of universal application. For those on the right the sources lay further back, with Charles Martel and Charlemagne. Common ground was a recovery of classicism. Athenian republicanism appealed to the left, the reinvigoration of Latin teaching favoured the

---

[35] Freud, 'Thoughts for the times', 275.
[36] Hanna, *Mobilization of intellect*, 78–90; Brocke, 'Wissenschaft und Militarismus', 667–8.
[37] Bergson, *Meaning of war*, 18–20, 29–33.

church. Both saw in the classics an enduring and international definition of civilization which endorsed France's mission.[38]

Bergson's lecture on the meaning of the war was published in English in 1915, and reprinted several times. But British philosophers were hesitant about following his example, for two reasons. The first was the uncertainty of some about making the leap from academic to public life. The war promoted emotion and instinct to the detriment of reason and law, and herein lay the second difficulty. The former qualities were more characteristic of the European philosophical tradition, which included not only Nietzsche but also, as the liberal and would-be neutral L. T. Hobhouse, pointed out, Bergson himself.[39]

More representative of the British academic profession as a whole than Hobhouse's doubts about public involvement was an initial reluctance to nationalize the world of learning. A group of nine scholars, mostly from Cambridge, wrote to *The Times* on 1 August 1914 to protest against a war with Germany, which was 'leading the way in Arts and Sciences', on behalf of Serbia and Russia, which most certainly were not. Six weeks later fifty-three writers, including G. K. Chesterton, Arthur Conan Doyle, Rudyard Kipling, and H. G. Wells, were prompted by the government to address the editor of the same newspaper in order to condemn Germany's appropriation of 'brute force to impose its culture upon other nations', but they still confessed their high regard for that same culture. Even on 21 October 1914 117 British academics prefaced their reply to the German professors' manifesto with an expression of their deep admiration for German scholarship and science, and an affirmation of their 'ties with Germany, ties of comradeship, of respect, and of affection'.[40]

The sequence of letters shows a conversion that marches in step with, but not ahead of, the pattern of popular recruiting. Its significance lies less in the fact that British intellectuals, like those of Germany, came to endorse the government line, and more in their determination, again as in Germany, to forsake reflection and research for action. The Oxford History School produced a succession of pamphlets concerning the causes of the war from mid-September 1914. Like the manifestos of the German professors, these publications became the foundation for more officially directed propaganda. But the dons insisted that their reaction was spontaneous: the initiative was their own.

Like those of France, the scholars of Britain were clear that the cause on which their country had embarked was a universal one. The assumption of this burden was a consequence of empire because, in the words of Alfred Zimmern, 'Of the Great Powers which between them control the destinies of civilisation

[38] Hanna, *Mobilization of intellect*, 142–5, 155–6, 166, 174; also Raithel, *Das 'Wunder' der inneren Einheit*, 379–80.
[39] Wallace, *War and the image of Germany*, 48.
[40] Brocke, 'Wissenschaft und Militarismus', 670; Wallace, *War and the image of Germany*, 24–5.

Great Britain is at once the freest, the largest, and most various'.[41] Britain, therefore, supported France not because it now finally felt able to endorse the claim of the ideas of the French Revolution to universality, but out of respect for France's own evolution to democracy: France, as another Oxford man, the historian Ernest Barker, said, is 'one of the great seed-beds of liberal thought and ideas'.[42]

Civilization, a key word in France, was also a central concept in Britain. However, Alfred Zimmern was clear that its meaning was different in Britain: 'it stands for something moral and social and political. It means, in the first place, the establishment and enforcement of the Rule of Law... and, secondly... the task of making men fit for free institutions.' Britain was fighting for 'Law, Justice, Responsibility, Liberty, Citizenship', concepts which 'belong to civilised humanity as a whole'.[43] The Oxford historians agreed. In their first pamphlet, *Why we are at war: Great Britain's case*, they said that Britain was fighting for 'the public law of Europe'.[44]

Law in this case meant the natural law to which the church too subscribed, and which Christianity had appropriated from the Greeks. It meant less international law in a legal sense and more a common morality; it implied that treaties had a sanctity which derived not merely from the honour of those who signed them but also from a Christian world order. 'If', G. W. Prothero wrote, 'international morality is regarded as of no account, a heavy blow is dealt at commercial and private morality as well. The Reign of Law, the greatest mark of civilization is maintained in all its parts.' Law was, therefore, indivisible: the law which regulated international relations was in principle the same as that which upheld the rights of property, the sanctity of marriage, and the workings of credit.[45]

The problem was that of giving such academic concepts immediacy. The Oxford historians tried: 'We are a people in whose blood the cause of law is the vital element.' Alfred Zimmern went further. As the author of *The Greek commonwealth*, he was appalled that Wilamowitz-Moellendorff, whose scholarship he admired, could regard Prussia as superior to Athens because Prussia was a monarchy. Zimmern therefore spurned any constitutional definitions of democracy for something much more organic: 'Democracy is a spirit and an atmosphere, and its essence is trust in the moral instincts of the people.' He sidestepped the troubling issues of empire, crown, and franchise to emphasize the responsibility which British democracy cast on the individual citizen.[46]

[41] Seton-Watson *et al.*, *War and democracy*, 371.
[42] Wallace, *War and the image of Germany*, 62.
[43] Seton-Watson *et al.*, *War and democracy*, 363–4.
[44] Oxford Faculty of Modern History, *Why we are at war*, 115–16.
[45] Gullace, *American Historical Review*, CII (1997), 722–3.
[46] Seton-Watson *et al.*, *War and democracy*, 1–2.

Bethmann-Hollweg helped. His contemptuous reference to the Belgian guarantee as 'a scrap of paper' gave a force to what was otherwise in danger of being either theory or rhetoric. The Belgians became the personification of ideas. Hensley Henson, the dean of Durham, likened them to the Israelites in their sufferings under the tyrannies of Egypt and Babylon.[47] 'A democracy armed with faith is not merely strong,' Zimmern explained: 'it is invincible; for its cause will live on, in defeat and disaster, in the breast of every one of its citizens. Belgium is a living testimony to that great truth.'[48] Walter Sickert gave these words visual expression. His own opposition to violence was first undermined by the emotional jingoism of the music halls which he painted so well. But it was Belgium that rationalized the shift: in October 1914 he painted *The soldiers of King Albert the Ready*, based on the defence of Liège, and in January 1915 he exhibited *The integrity of Belgium*.[49]

Thanks to Belgium, the Asquith cabinet had been able to rally round the rights of small nations and the sovereignty of international law. Thereafter Asquith was able to invert the sequence. Britain fought not for Belgium, but for what Belgium represented. In a speech on 19 September the prime minister defined Britain's reasons for entering the war as threefold: first, to uphold 'the public law of Europe'; secondly, 'to enforce the independence of free states'; and thirdly, 'to withstand ... the arrogant claim of a single Power to dominate the development of the destinies of Europe'.[50] By elevating the principles over the principality, Asquith evaded the knotty issues of Belgium's pre-war record as a colonial power. The good ousted the bad. For Germany the opposite was the case. Monolithic and militarist, its crime was the assumption that its culture, a product of the state, was appropriate to peoples whose languages and traditions were different. In the circumstances, the notion of there being two Germanies was a difficult one to sustain.

Surprisingly, Lloyd George tried to do so. In a speech in Bangor on 28 February 1915 he expressed his admiration for German music, German science, and 'the Germany of a virile philosophy that helped to break the shackles of superstition in Europe'. Even now he saw the issue of which Germany would dominate as unresolved, comparing it to a Wagnerian struggle 'between the good and the evil spirit for the possession of the man's soul'. The outcome would depend on who won the war. If Germany was victorious, then 'we shall be vassals, not to the best Germans', but 'to a Germany that talks through the vacuous voice of Krupp's artillery'.[51]

[47] Marrin, *Last crusade*, 129.
[48] Seton-Watson *et al.*, *War and democracy*, 2.
[49] Cork, *Bitter truth*, 54–7; also *The Times Review*, 14 Nov. 1992, pp. 38–9.
[50] Seton-Watson *et al.*, *War and democracy*, 239.
[51] Grigg, *Lloyd George*, 216; also 161–6.

A few others could still see the distinction. Dean Inge took Nietzsche on his own terms, highlighting his praise of individualism and stressing that his writings justified neither militarism nor racism.[52] Alfred Zimmern resisted the temptation to cull extracts from 'Treitschke's brilliant and careful work', or to forget that 'Nietzsche, like many other prophets, wrote in allegory'.[53] But they were increasingly isolated, Zimmern even within his own university. Sir Walter Raleigh, Oxford's professor of English literature, was delighted to have the excuse 'to be rid of the German incubus ... It has done no good, for many years, to scholarship;—indeed, it has produced a kind of slave-scholarship'.[54] Even Zimmern's fellow classicist Gilbert Murray, a Liberal, a would-be neutral before the war and an ardent internationalist after it, saw the opportunity to reassert a specifically British approach to learning, based on 'feeling and understanding' rather than research for its own sake: 'we are always aiming at culture in Arnold's sense not Bernhardi's'.[55]

Whether Murray read Bernhardi may be doubted; unlike some other British academics, he had never studied at a German university. Ignorance, not least of the German language, underpinned many of the portrayals of German ideology. In France, Bergson's idea that German philosophy had become the pawn of an alliance between militarism and industrialism was vital to his optimism concerning the war's outcome: material resources could be exhausted, those of the spirit could not. But Bergson's interpretation was flawed. It rested on his memories of 1870, and of France's awareness ever since of its growing inferiority, both demographically and economically. In 1914 Britain's entry into the war ensured that collectively the Entente had a combined national income 60 per cent greater than that of the Central Powers.[56] Not Germany but France now stood to gain from a war of materialism.

Germany's awareness of its economic inferiority directed its thinking on war along routes very different from those which Bergson—or for that matter Murray—imagined. Despite his place in Entente demonology, Bernhardi perhaps matters least as an indicator of military thought, since he was at odds with much of the prevailing ethos in the general staff. But it is nonetheless worth pointing out that, according to *Germany and the next war*, war was not to be undertaken lightly, it should be fought according to moral conventions, and it should be limited in its objectives.[57] Effectively, Bernhardi gave himself little choice, since he was highly critical of 'material prosperity, commerce and money-making',[58] the very means which would enable the war to be fought at

---

[52] Marrin, *Last crusade*, 103.
[53] Seton-Watson *et al.*, *War and democracy*, 350.
[54] Wallace, *War and the image of Germany*, 36.
[55] Ibid. 38; see also 105.
[56] Ferguson, *Pity of war*, 248.
[57] Marrin, *Last crusade*, 108 (citing Bernhardi, *Germany and the next war*, 18–19, 45, 48, 79, 85–7).
[58] Offer, *Politics and society*, XXIII (1995), 216.

greater intensity and for more grandiose aims. In this respect at least, Bernhardi aligned himself with the German army collectively. It feared economic
progress as a threat to its warlike and warrior qualities.[59] Material and demographic inferiority in 1914 confirmed its predisposition to trust in alternative
strengths. As the year ebbed away, Moltke pinned his hopes of ultimate German victory not on superior armament or even on greater military efficiency
but on 'the high idealism of the German people'.[60]

Things of the spirit were the key: *Geist* was the catchword. Moltke himself
was an anthroposophist; in private he admitted, 'I live entirely in the arts'.[61] On
the eastern front one of his army commanders, August von Mackensen, put his
faith in 'our inner strength'.[62] This was not the vocabulary of professionalism
or modernism, let alone materialism. Moreover, these soldiers were expressing
themselves in terms similar to those used by academics. In *Die Nationen und
ihre Philosophie* (1915), Wilhelm Wundt rejected the British idea that individual
progress was linked to industrial development. He condemned British ethics,
which harnessed economic growth to utilitarianism and materialism to positivism, as the path to shallowness and mediocrity.[63] The sociologist Werner
Sombart produced the most extreme version of this thesis. In *Händler und
Helden* (Traders and heroes) (1915) he described man as living two lives on
earth, one superficial and the other spiritual: life itself was a continuing effort
to pass from one to the other. The struggle was essentially a personal one, but
war gave it transcendant qualities. In these circumstances the free response to
duty's call and the willingness to sacrifice self characterized Sombart's 'hero'.
Therefore, the significance of war for the state lay not in social Darwinism, not
in terms of the state's standing in relation to its neighbours, but in the nation's
ability to elevate the spirit and will of its people. War found the state at its
acme. 'The sword and the spirit', Max Scheler wrote, 'can create a beautiful,
worthy marriage.' Its fertility was proved for him by the link between the
Persian wars and Greek philosophy and between the Napoleonic wars and
Hegel. 'The war of 1914', Sombart concluded, 'is the war of Nietzsche.'[64]

Both Sombart and Scheler, born in 1863 and 1874 respectively, belonged
to that younger generation which had come to maturity in Wilhelmine
Germany after Bismarck's fall. By contrast, Rudolf Eucken was already 20
when 1866 had inaugurated a promise that he felt had not yet been fulfilled.
Before unification Germany had found its identity not in politics but in
philosophy, literature, and music. Since then Germans had worked hard to
improve their material lot, but in so doing had lost their vocation. Eucken,
a Nobel prizewinner and the dominant figure in German philosophy,

---

[59] Echevarria, *War & Society*, XIII (1995), 23–40.   [60] Verhey, 'The "spirit" of 1914', 311.
[61] Eksteins, *Rites of spring*, 89.   [62] Schwarzmüller, *Zwischen Kaiser und 'Führer'*, 98.
[63] Ringer, *Decline of German mandarins*, 185.
[64] Sombart, *Händler und Helden*, 53, 61–5; Scheler, *Genius des Krieges*, 34–5, 94–5.

particularly in spiritual existentialism, hankered for his subject's return to the centre of national life. The outbreak of the First World War provided him with the opportunity to fulfil his aspirations. Like Sombart, Scheler, and the leaders of the church, he celebrated war's power to reinvigorate the moral health of the individual. And he went as far or even further in pursuing its collective implications. His 1914 publication, on 'the world historical significance of the German spirit', asserted that Germany could not be defeated while it remained truly united and stood fast in its inner strength.[65]

If *Geist* was a word that concerned the feelings of the individual but could be extended to the community, *Kultur* embraced concepts that began with the community but were defined nationally. Sombart quoted Novalis to the effect that 'all culture derives from the relationship of a man with the state'.[66] *Kultur* was shaped by language and history, but its vitality rested also on the civic virtues to which *Geist* gave rise—idealism, heroism, subordination to the community.[67] Thus, the German professors declared in their October manifesto that 'Our belief is that the salvation of all European culture depends on the victory for which German "militarism" is fighting, the discipline, the loyalty, the spirit of sacrifice of the united free German people'.[68]

Kultur's opponent was 'civilization'. There was, of course, a paradox here. Germany was civilized, in the sense that it had benefited as much as any state from the advances in science and technology so fundamental to Europe's primacy in the world at the beginning of the twentieth century. Even Eucken acknowledged this: the distinction of Germans as technicians, traders, and industrialists meant that 'today people are in the habit of calling us the Americans of Europe'.[69] But the civilization which Thomas Mann saw as the opposite of *Kultur* was itself more cultural than technological.[70] In part it was materialistic, and hence damaging to the heroic spirit; in part it was egalitarian, a fruit of 1789. Civilization, according to another philosopher, Paul Natorp, was the culture of society, and that meant a levelling down of the best to conform with the average. It could make a man a slave. *Kultur*, on the other hand, was liberating. The contrast was Kant's, but the context in 1914 was no longer moral but political.[71]

The clash between civilization and culture took German thought back to its late-eighteenth-century roots. In condemning civilization, the philosophers of 1914 were reflecting the rationality of the Enlightenment and the consequences of the French Revolution. They argued that, following what was essentially an alien, French track, philosophy had elevated the rule of law and the rights of

---

[65] Lübbe, *Politische Philosophie*, 176–84; see, in English, Mommsen, *Imperial Germany*, 206–14.
[66] Sombart, *Händler und Helden*, 74–7.   [67] Chickering, *Imperial Germany*, 135.
[68] Kruse, 'Kriegsbegeisterung', 85.   [69] Sieferle, 'Der deutsch–englische Gegensatz', 159.
[70] Mann, 'Gedanken im Kriege', 7.
[71] Lübbe, *Politische Philosophie*, 190–1; Scheler, *Genius des Krieges*, 50.

the individual, and so had promoted selfishness and materialism. At one level, therefore, the summons of 1914 was a call to rediscover the ideas of the *Aufklärung* and to refurbish the memory of 1813. More important even than Kant or Hegel in the nationalist context was Fichte. Fichte's *Reden an die deutsche Nation* (Speeches to the German nation) (1808) symbolized the engagement of the philospher with the life of the state, and his endowment of the nation with its own identity and his subordination of the individual to the nation connected the themes of the war of liberation with those of 1914. Between 1890 and 1900 Fichte's philosophy was the subject of only ten noteworthy studies; between 1900 and 1920 over 200 appeared. The context of Fichte's writing, the defeat at Jena in 1806, and the long path from there to liberation, ensured that his relevance did not dwindle as the adversities of the war multiplied.[72]

Although France was home to the Enlightenment and to the alleged triumph of its ideas in politics, France was not, in 1914, Germany's principal ideological foe. As Paul Natorp was prepared to concede, Germany had derived from revolutionary France both its sense of nationalism and the idea of the nation in arms.[73] For writers like Sombart and Scheler, the clashes between Germany and France, or even between Germany and Russia, were second-order issues tacked onto the war of real significance for world history, that between Germany and Britain. The enemy was capitalism, because this was the true threat to the spirit.

Sombart, like Wundt, characterized British philosophy as preoccupied with economics. It had neglected matters of the spirit for practical problems, and the consequences had permeated British life. The elevation of trade resulted in the pursuit of economic self-interest and the subordination of the state. The latter was seen as no more than a necessary evil. War, which for Scheler found the state in its highest form, was for the British superfluous. In their ideal world it would not exist, and when they did fight they did so for economic objectives and, very often, by economic means. The aristocracy was motivated by commerce rather than by honour, and the army and navy were no more than instruments for armed trade and colonial plunder. But the British practised cultural as well as economic imperialism. Their empire swamped alternative languages and traditions. Its aim, J. A. Cramb was quoted as saying, was 'to give all men within its bounds an English mind'. The ideal of gentlemanly self-restraint curbed the dynamic effects of personality and character. Even in international relations Britain, by the use of balance-of-power theory, elevated weak powers at the expense of the strong. Its own credentials as a democracy were doubtful: it was a colonial power abroad and a centralized state (rather than a federal one, like Germany) at home. Britain nonetheless

---

[72] Lübbe, *Politische Philosophie*, 194–201.   [73] Ibid. 188.

was bent on persuading the rest of the world that freedom should be defined solely in political terms. The fear, above all, was that the 'cant' of capitalism and its political expression, liberalism, was sapping even German culture of its own identity.[74] The greatest danger to Germany, in the view of Max Weber's brother Alfred, was 'Anglicization'.[75]

Implicit in Weber's formulation was his recognition that the threat was insidious. Even in late July 1914 Germany had preferred to see itself as the guardian of the civilization of western Europe against Russia. Animosity towards Britain was moderated by the common inheritance of Protestantism. But by the same token, Britain's decision to side with the enemy required more explanation. Its entry into the war was construed as a massive betrayal. Within days, Britain had replaced Russia as the focus for German hatred. Friedrich-Wilhelm Foerster rationalized Britain's behaviour in terms of a dualism not unlike that used by British commentators in regard to Germany. In 1914 the evil, imperialist side of Britain had triumphed over its better, peace-loving aspect. Others were less forgiving: Britain's decision was selfish and exploitative. The war did not confront Britain itself with any direct threat, and its effects could not be morally uplifting when Britain had no intention of committing itself wholeheartedly to its conduct. War, by definition, could not be a source of spiritual elevation when its motivation was economic gain. The clash of philosophies was rendered in popular terms. Britain's decision to side with France and Russia was evidence of its perfidy, and its determination to do so was driven by its pursuit of mammon. Neither honour nor spirit was part of its conceptual vocabulary.[76]

Thus, the outbreak of the war itself marked a change in patterns of thought. Ernst Troeltsch saw it as evidence that ideas stemmed from events, not events from ideas.[77] The reworking of the legacies of the Enlightenment and the French Revolution was not simply a means by which Germany rediscovered its cultural roots; it also helped put a shape on time. The long nineteenth century, which began in 1789, had ended in 1914. If the first date marked the French Revolution, the second marked the German one. The 'ideas of 1914', however much they tapped into the thought of Kant, Hegel, or Fichte, were essentially a new departure. In *Die Ideen von 1914* (The ideas of 1914) (1915), Rudolf Kjellen, a Swedish economist, associated the French Revolution with freedom and the ongoing German revolution with its replacement by order and responsibility. Johann Plenge picked up these points in 1916 with *1789 und 1914. Die*

[74] Sombart, *Händler und Helden*, esp. 4–43; Scheler, *Genius des Krieges*, 25–31, 53–4; Kjellen, *Politischen Probleme*, 130–4.

[75] Sieferle, 'Der deutsch–englische Gegensatz', 142.

[76] Schwabe, *Wissenschaft und Kriegsmoral*, 27–8; Pressel, *Kriegspredigt*, 128–30; Raithel, *Das 'Wunder' der inneren Einheit*, 102–4, 215; Horn (ed.), *Stumpf*, 26–7; Kennedy, *Anglo-German antagonism*, does of course trace deeper roots.

[77] Pressel, *Kriegspredigt*, 20.

symbolischen Jahre in der Geschichte des politischen Geistes (1789 and 1914. The symbolic years in the history of the political spirit).

Germany's mission, according to Kjellen, was 'leadership without domination'. World powers had followed one of two models—the Roman, with its tendency to centralize and dominate in a political sense, and the Greek, with its patriarchal presumption of superior values. Britain had veered to the latter, but had not abandoned the former. Germany's task was to promote a third way.[78] 'German freedom', Ernst Troeltsch explained, 'has no craving for world domination, either materially or spiritually. Germany wants freedom of co-existence for various peoples and not the extermination of different possibilities of development nor stereotyping in the name of some alleged law.'[79] Herein were the intellectual foundations for the national liberation movements which Germany sponsored for India, Persia, Tunisia, Egypt, Ireland, and elsewhere. The challenge was to relate means to ends. To beat the British, it had first to join them. Germany's ability to implement the new order was predicated on its achieving world-power status through victory on the battlefield.[80]

Britain was a declining power, as Gerhart von Schulz-Gaevernitz had argued in 1906.[81] It therefore had a vested interest in the status quo, because only thus could it buttress a position which it could no longer sustain by other means. Germany, on the other hand, was in the ascendant, a young nation with a young Kaiser, prepared to embrace innovation in the sciences and the arts. The world's need to advance forced it to fight: progress was impossible without Germany's acceptance of its role as a revisionist power. The idea that Germany went to war as an escape from its domestic dilemma, as a way of resolving the challenge to its conservative elites and of evading pressure for constitutional change, assumes a mood of cultural despair. But many of the Kaiser's own generation saw doors opening, not closing. Adolf von Harnack, the first president of the Kaiser Wilhelm Society, expected the marriage of traditionalism and modernism to lead 'to an unprecedented increase in the vitality of the German organism'.[82] Karl Helfferich, banker not Junker, born in 1872, likened Wilhelm's reign to the Renaissance. In *Deutschlands Volkswohlstand 1888–1913* (Germany's national wealth, 1888–1913), published in 1913, he believed that Germany's economic development was proving Marxism wrong.[83] For many Germans the example of France suggested that full-blown parliamentary government implied atrophy, decay, and disorder. The war intensified Germany's responsibility for renewal. 'The German eagle', Paul Natorp wrote in *Krieg und Friede* (War and peace) in 1915, 'is not like the bird of Minerva,

---

[78] Kjellen, *Politischen Probleme*, 134.   [79] Rubanowice, *Crisis in consciousness*, 112.
[80] Ringer, *Decline of the German mandarins*, 186; Huber, *Kirche und Öffentlichkeit*, 151; Schwabe, *Wissenschaft und Kriegsmoral*, 112.
[81] Sieferle, 'Der deutsch–englische Gegensatz', 144.   [82] Johnson, *Kaiser's chemists*, 16.
[83] Williamson, *Helfferich*, pp. v–vi, 111–14.

which, according to Hegel, first begins its flight at dusk. We signify the morning chorus of a new day not only for Germany, but also for mankind.'[84]

The so-called failure of German liberals and social democrats to remain true to their beliefs in 1914 becomes more comprehensible when set against the rhetoric of reform rather than reaction. During August 1914 the SPD press was ready to redirect its ire from Russian tsarism to the British bourgeoisie.[85] In *Die Sozialdemokratie* (1915) Paul Lensch used Hegel to argue that Britain had fulfilled its world-historical role, that individualism and liberalism, the British way, had been absorbed, and that now it was Germany's turn to pioneer the nationalization of social democracy.[86] For the liberals, national survival and national identity were sufficiently central to make the appeals of 1914 not uncongenial. Friedrich Naumann argued that British liberalism was inappropriate to Germany, with its different traditions and its greater deference to order and authority. Neither he nor Max Weber could embrace full-blooded parliamentary government with the enthusiasm of a Gladstonian. While their suspicions of the popular will would not have been unfamiliar to mid-nineteenth-century British liberals, their articulation of the alternatives carried collectivist overtones that sprang from very different roots. The people and the state should be united in terms which clearly tapped into the ideas of *Kultur*. The state itself would implement social reform on the worker's behalf but without itself being fully democratic. Instead, a dualism of democracy and monarchy, *das soziale Volkskaisertum*, would represent a new synthesis.[87]

The immediate effect of the war was to solidify the intellectual underpinnings of the monarchy rather than undermine them. The balance of the Bismarckian constitution provided a security against the irrational excesses of the masses, while the unity provide by the crown eliminated the divisions and instability characteristic of republican France. 'We Germans', Kalweit, the chairman of the Danzig church consistory explained, 'are born monarchists.' That did not mean blind allegiance to princes, but that they saw the value in the embodiment of the idea of the state's unity and will in a living person. The words 'monarchy' and 'democracy' too easily suggested an antithesis, Kalweit argued. He preferred to use *Kaiserherrlichkeit* and *Volksmacht*, which not only linked abstractions to people but also—more debatably—implied convergence.[88]

Therefore, for many liberals and even some socialists German freedom was distinct from the freedoms of revolutionary France or liberal Britain. In December 1915 Kurt Riezler tried to define these opposing conceptions of

[84] Lübbe, *Politische Philosophie*, 186.
[85] Kruse, *Krieg und nationale Integration*, 70–6, 92–3, 124–30.
[86] Sieferle, 'Der deutsch–englische Gegensatz', 149–55.
[87] Sheehan, *German liberalism*, 267–78; also Naumann, 'Deutscher Liberalismus', in *Werke*, iv. 316–20; Mai, *Ende des Kaiserreichs*, 33; Struve, *Elites against democracy*.
[88] Doehring, *Ein feste Burg*, ii. 370.

freedom. The west European powers practised 'freedom without regulation, with the fewest possible concessions by the individual to the state, freedom through equality, the formula of the French Revolution'. German freedom, on the other hand, had evolved out of its reaction to the ideas of 1789, and had been defined by Fichte as freedom through the state, an organization set above the individual. The latter was 'ready to concede to the state in all respects, as the state's strengths should be the function of a freedom in which every man is ranked according to his own strengths, but not valued equally'.[89] One gain for the individual was the sense of meaning which arose from sharing in a common endeavour. But more important was the freedom for the spirit which order bestowed. Ernst Troeltsch, who before the war had written on the significance of Protestantism for the modern world, was the key figure in linking this balance between public duty and inner life to Lutheranism. In *Die deutsche Freiheit* (The German freedom) (1915) he emphasized that the 'progress in the idea of freedom' which 1914 signified 'in the first place must be a thing of feeling and life style, but then also the clearly recognisable spirit of our public arrangements'.[90]

The war, therefore, conferred on Germany the opportunity to propagate 'a third way' in political thought as well as in international relations, a path between capitalism and Marxism, individualism and collectivism. Johann Plenge's celebration of the 'ideas of 1914' argued that 'under the necessity of war socialist ideas have been driven into German economic life, its organization has grown together into a new spirit, and so the assertion of our nation for mankind has given birth to the idea of 1914, the idea of German organization, the national unity of state socialism'.[91] Rathenau, who through the KRA had tried to apply the principles of corporatism to public life, was therefore both putting the *Burgfrieden* into practice and testing the principles of 'the new economy' for possible post-war application. Reflecting later in the war on what had been achieved, he was more hesitant than Plenge in referring to socialism. 'The new economy' was not so much a creation of the state as an organic growth, established through the resolve of citizens, enabled by the intermediary of the state freely to unite to overcome rivalry between themselves and to co-ordinate their different achievements and qualities. The key words were rationalization and responsibility rather than self-interest and profit: the result would be—and here Rathenau used the title of Wichard von Moellendorff's 1916 publication—a *Gemeinwirtschaft*.[92]

[89] Diary entry, 4 Dec. 1915, Riezler, *Tagebücher*, 317–18; see also 325.
[90] Lübbe, *Politische Philosophie*, 227–30.
[91] Michalka, 'Kriegsrohstoffbewirtschaftung, Walther Rathenau, und die "kommende Wirtschaft"', in id. *Der Erste Weltkrieg*, 497.
[92] Ibid. 494–5; also Michalka, 'Kriegswirtschaft und Wirtschaftskrieg', in Böhme and Kallenberg (eds.), *Deutschland und der Erste Weltkrieg*, 189–90.

For Paul Lensch, one of the advocates of state socialism, it was the primacy of the community which defined Germany as a modern state, just as it was the principle of individualism which now characterized Britain as backward. Lensch saw Germany's lead over Britain as manifested in three fundamental attributes—universal compulsory education, universal suffrage, and universal military service.[93] Militarism and socialism were therefore not in tension, but were supporting attributes of the new state. The pre-war argument of the right, that the army was the school of the nation by virtue of its ability to inculcate subordination and service to the community, was now assimilated further to the left. Scheler saw militarism in the sense of conscription as evidence not of barbarism but of a form of higher state development. This admiration for the close links between army and society in Germany was increasingly couched not in the Rousseauesque vocabulary of the nation in arms or of the citizen soldier, but in metaphysical exuberance. For Troeltsch, the *Volksheer*, 'an army of the people', was 'flesh from our flesh and spirit from our spirit'.[94] For Scheler, war was a manly activity which elevated honour and nobility, while subordinating the individual to the state. The experience of war made the collective person-alities of nations self-aware: it realized the nation as a 'spiritual total person'.[95] Militarism in this sense not only gave meaning to the community, it also elevated *Kultur* over civilization. Nachum Goldmann, in *Der Geist des Militarismus* (The spirit of militarism) (1915), described the military spirit as the means to human progress because it combined equality of opportunity with the virtues of a meritocracy.[96] A state which honoured the achievements of soldiers over all others also rewarded obedience, courage, self-confidence, and discipline: 'order inside and order outside', as Sombart put it. But in linking militarism back to spirit and to culture Sombart was moved to some of his more excessive statements. Militarism was 'the manifestation of German heroism', the union of Potsdam and Weimar: 'It is *Faust* and *Zarathustra* and Beethoven scores in the trenches. Then the Eroica and the Egmont overture are also the most real militarism.'[97]

Sombart's hyperbole, its reference to Goethe as well as Nietzsche, encapsulated the core of Entente objections to the German ideologies of 1914. Both Goethe and Nietzsche described themselves as Europeans who happened to be Germans. The presumption in Sombart's writing was the opposite, that the rest of Europe needed to be Germanized. He saw the German people as the chosen people of the twentieth century; they were as much an elect as the Greeks and the Jews had been. Such a status imposed on Germany hard obligations.[98] Ultimately it might have to fight the world to save the world. The messianic implications—and Gotthilf Herzog likened Germany's burden

[93] Sieferle, 'Der deutsch–englische Gegensatz', 153.   [94] Rubanowice, *Crisis in consciousness*, 103.
[95] Scheler, *Genius des Krieges*, 34, 81, 91.   [96] Sieferle, 'Der deutsch–englische Gegensatz', 146.
[97] Sombart, *Händler und Helden*, 84–6.   [98] Ibid. 136–43.

to that of Christ[99]—incorporated the sense of mission developed by the war theology of the Lutheran church. Religion and nation became indistinguishable. In a sermon delivered in 1915 in celebration of the Reformation, Friedrich Rittelmeyer asserted that, 'The German ability for understanding makes us particularly suited to be the nation to bring other, non-Christian nations to Christendom, the German capacity for honesty makes us especially suited to fight the fight between religion and natural science, and the German spiritual sense makes us particularly fitted to fight today's battle against superficiality and shallowness, against the entire culture of materialist ostentation, which will invade mankind'.[100]

One German soldier wrote in August 1914: 'Our victory enables Europe's survival with an infusion into German culture of fresh blood. The victory will not come easily for us. But if there is any sense of right and of God's direction in history... then the victory must be ours, sooner or later.'[101] Eucken argued that it was this sense of mission which made Germany invincible.[102] Germany *could* not lose, because 'the defeat of Germanness would signify the collapse of mankind',[103] and it *would* not lose because defeat was impossible for a nation of believers. The longer the war lasted, the more Dryander and others harped on these aims. The very duration of the conflict became a test of faith and of spiritual resolve.[104]

Sombart was at pains to stress that the aim was not German expansion in a territorial sense: 'we have more important things to do. We have our own spiritual existence to unfold, the German soul to keep pure.'[105] For some commentators, including Paul Lensch on the left and Oswald Spengler on the right, it was this very characteristic of the First World War—that it was about ideas and principles, and their claims to universality—which likened it to a civil war. And that carried for them not the pejorative connotations of later generations, of brother fighting brother, but the devastation, intensity, and length of the Thirty Years War. Such conflicts were about the issues that really mattered, not about territory or treasury. The difference between civil war as traditionally defined and the world war as they defined it was that now nations rather than classes or social groups appropriated the monopolies in ideas, social structures, and economic organization. In this sense the *Weltkrieg* was a *Weltbürgerkrieg*.[106]

For Scheler, what determined whether a war was just was the commitment of those fighting it to the ideas that were at stake. The quality of those beliefs mattered less than the depth of conviction itself.[107] Many of the 'ideas of 1914' were as subjective as Scheler's definition implied; they represented sloppy

[99] Pressel, *Kriegspredigt*, 165.   [100] Ibid. 117.   [101] Rürup, 'Der "Geist" von 1914', 4.
[102] Lübbe, *Politische Philosophie*, 183.   [103] Pressel, *Kriegspredigt*, 120.
[104] Ibid. 217–19; Andresen, *Dryander*, 328–9, 341.   [105] Sombart, *Händler und Helden*, 143.
[106] Sieferle, 'Der deutsch–englische Gegensatz', 153–4, 160.   [107] Scheler, *Genius des Krieges*, 101.

thinking by academics anxious to integrate their disciplines with the currents of the day. Lumping was more important than splitting, connections more significant than divisions. The results were unscientific. Historians were happy to collude in history as spirit rather than as objective reality; philosophers sought to make politics moral, but instead politicized morality. By late 1915 some, not least in Germany, began to have second thoughts. A minority of German academics, including Troeltsch, recognized the need for an eventual accommodation, particularly with liberalism and the west. Max Weber and Hans Delbrück were both patriots, but were contemptuous of patriotic emotion. Delbrück was one of the few professors who had refused to sign the manifestos of October 1914, and he continued to emphasize more traditional definitions of militarism, with the consequent need for the army and the conduct of war to be subordinated to political direction.[108] In 1917 the historian Friedrich Meinecke, who charted a course from enthusiasm to moderation, called for the demobilization of the intellect as a precondition for peace.[109] But for most the war's very nature confirmed and deepened the ideas first hatched in 1914. Its duration and intensity, its geographical extension, its effects on the state and its relationship with its citizens, endorsed rather than undermined the idea that 'the war', as the Kaiser wrote to Houston Stewart Chamberlain on 15 January 1917, 'is the battle between two world views'.[110]

The Kaiser's conclusion was that such polarities could never be resolved by reconciliation or negotiation: 'One must *win*, the other must *go down!*' On his enemy's side, J. W. Carliol saw the war in very similar terms, albeit much closer to its outbreak: 'Underneath, and at the root of this Titanic conflict, antagonistic principles and powers, irreconcilable ideas and ideals, the ideals of faith and the ideals of force are contending. These are the sap of the contention: the very breath of its nostrils and the source of its vigour. But for them this war, with its world-encompassing issues, would never have come into being; and until one of them has been utterly vanquished it cannot reach its end.'[111]

Of course, an assessment of the impact of the 'ideas of 1914' requires some quantification of the transfer from published page to public thought. How successful were the intellectuals in shaping their contemporaries' views of the war? By September 1915 the eighty-seven pamphlets so far published as a result of the initiative of the Oxford History School had a total print-run of 500,000 copies.[112] Most of the German pamphlets appeared in a comparable series, *Der deutsche Krieg*. The absorption of this output in officially directed propaganda

[108] Brocke, 'Wissenschaft und Militarismus', 682–3; Ringer, *Decline of the German mandarins*, 193–7; Schwabe, *Wissenschaft und Kriegsmoral*, 24–5, 32–3, 49, 55; Huber, *Kirche und Öffentlichkeit*, 179.
[109] Verhey, 'The "spirit" of 1914', 301.
[110] Hartmut Zelinsky, 'Kaiser Wilhelm II, die Werk-Idee Richard Wagners und der Weltkampf', in Röhl (ed.), *Der Ort Kaiser Wilhelms II*, 303.
[111] Pick, *War machine*, 141–2.   [112] Ferguson, *Pity of war*, 235–6.

confirms at one level that what these economists, historians, and sociologists were doing was no more than saying what their governments wanted them to say. On the other hand, the effectiveness of propaganda is measured not by the nature of its message but by the degree of receptivity it encounters. On this reckoning, the determination of the belligerent states to appropriate the 'ideas of 1914' suggests that they were also what the people wanted to hear. Soldiers' letters, not only of 1914 but later in the war, frequently mouthed the phrases and ambitions of the academics' outpourings.[113]

This should not be surprising, for many of the ideas flowed in the opposite direction from that which normally preoccupies historians. Anxious to illustrate the influence, or lack of it, of intellectuals, they labour over inadequate evidence in order to show transfers from high culture to popular thought. But in 1914 the experiences of August prompted the intellectuals to assimilate the pre-war nostrums of the populists. Many of the ideas embraced and developed by Troeltsch, Scheler, Sombart, and others in Germany were already common currency in the publications directed at, and produced on behalf of, the veterans' organizations before the war.[114] The responses of the intellectuals were frequently uninhibited and altruistic. But their openness to ideas from below was also a recognition of the opportunity which the war conferred for internal reintegration. Britain became the vehicle for Germany's worries about its own culture; internal threats were externalized, and so could be attacked; the process of unification from below could be completed by defence against the danger from without. The maintenance of the *Burgfrieden*, or of the *union sacrée*, itself became a condition for victory. In this sense war aims were domestic: Troeltsch told his readers 'to become more German than we were'.[115]

The assimilation of the 'ideas of 1914' had two consequences. First, it removed any effective limits on the objectives of the war very soon after its onset. The ideas applied a vocabulary of absolutes which justified all that followed. Indeed, they could rationalize even defeat, both because it was only material and because its consequences need only be temporary. Secondly, it meant that final victory could not be achieved until one side had reversed the process, most probably by absorbing the ideas of the other. The advocates of 'state socialism' in Germany, like Lensch and Plenge, saw constitutional reform and the abolition of the Prussian three-class franchise as the most important step required of Germany in its role as modernizer. But that was also an objective of the Entente, not because liberals wished to install state socialism

[113] See, for Germany, Witkop, *Kriegsbriefe gefallener Studenten*; for Britain, Hynes, *War imagined*, 119; for France, Hanna, *Mobilization of intellect*, 24, 211–16, and Audoin-Rouzeau, *À travers leurs journaux*, 203.
[114] Rohrkrämer, *Militarismus der 'kleinen Leute'*, 178–258.
[115] Rubanowice, *Crisis in consciousness*, 107; see also Schwabe, *Wissenschaft und Kriegsmoral*, 13; Ringer, *Decline of the German mandarins*, 187; Pressel, *Kriegspredigt*, 23.

in Germany but because they saw democratization as a check to militarism. Thus, for a general like August von Mackensen the enemy was parliamentary government, whether without or within.[116]

The effect of enshrining the war as a conflict between liberalism and militarism, between individualism and community, between anarchy and order, between capitalism and state socialism, was to make its immediate focus the Anglo-German antagonism. But the values which Britain claimed to defend in 1914 were as deeply, or more deeply, etched in the United States of America. Furthermore, as the exigencies of the war forced Britain to modify its liberalism in the pursuit of greater military effectiveness—to conscript, to curb free trade, to control profits—so its ideological differences seemed much less striking to Germans than did those of the United States. The Entente's ease of access to American markets, and America's condoning of the blockade which denied Germany comparable status, confirmed that the sin of perfidy and the pursuit of mammon were even more firmly entrenched across the Atlantic than across the Channel. The consequence of the 'ideas of 1914' was the extension of the war, not only ideologically but ultimately geographically.

---

[116] Schwarzmüller, *Zwischen Kaiser und 'Führer'*, 150.

BIBLIOGRAPHY

The Bibliography includes works relevant to the war as a whole and to this volume specifically. It does not incorporate material relevant to aspects of the war to be covered in subsequent volumes.

The most recent guide to the English-language published sources is A. G. S. Enser, *A subject bibliography of the First World War books in English 1914–1978* (London, 1979). Older, but particularly helpful for works published during the war and its immediate aftermath, are the *Subject index of the books relating to the European war, 1914–1918, acquired by the British Museum, 1914–1920* (London, 1922) and Sir George Prothero, *A select analytical list of books concerning the Great War* (London, 1923). Both of these embrace foreign langagues, but, like Enser, they eschew critical comment. Cyril Falls, *War books: a critical guide* (London, 1930) fills the gap, at least for military history, and its 1989 edition makes some attempt to come up to date. However, Jürgen Rohwer (ed.), *Neue Forschungen zum Ersten Weltkrieg* (Koblenz, 1985), is far more wide-ranging, and is particularly good for Austria-Hungary and for many of the minor belligerents. Of the major ones, Germany can be followed through two excellent critical guides, both strong on the First World War: Dennis Showalter, *German military history 1648–1982: a critical bibliography* (New York, 1984), and Keith W. Bird, *German naval history: a guide to the literature* (New York, 1985). Listings of older German works are to be found in the *Bibliographen der Weltkreigsbucherei*, published by the Bibliothek für Zeitgeschichte, Stuttgart. Now dated, and focused tightly on military events, but still useful for France is the publication of the Ministère des Armées, État-Major de l'Armée, Service Historique, *Guide bibliographique sommaire d'histoire militaire et coloniale française* (Paris, 1969). French war literature received a thorough going over from Jean-Norton Cru, *Témoins: essai d'analyse et de critique des souvenirs de combattants édités en France* (Paris, 1929). Possibly the most exhaustive national bibliography is that for Belgium: Patrick Lefèvre and Jean Lorette, *La Belgique et la première guerre mondiale: bibliographie* (Brussels, 1987): it interprets its brief in the widest possible terms.

The most recent chronology of the war, and the best, is Randal Gray, with Christopher Argyle, *Chronicle of the First World War,* 2 vols. (Oxford, 1990–1). The older ones have all been recently reprinted, and are: Lord Edward Gleichen, *Chronology of the Great War,* 3 vols. (London, 1918–20; reprinted in one volume with a new introduction by Gwyn Bayliss, London, 1988); Historical Section of the Committee of Imperial Defence, *History of the Great War based on official documents: principal events 1914–1918* (London, 1922; reprinted London, 1987); and *The Times diary and index of the war* (London, n.d.). David F. Burg and L. Edward Purcell, *Almanac of World War I* (Lexington, 1998) tries to roll a war diary in with a select bibliography and a number of potted biographies.

Atlases are much more problematic, and not just because of changing place-names or fashions in spelling. The contemporary fashion is to use historical atlases to tell a story in ideographic form: the atlas most widely available, Martin Gilbert, *First World War Atlas* (London, 1970; reprinted many times), is an example of this. It is almost totally devoid of physical information, and therefore useless for understanding operations. Anthony Livesey, *The Viking atlas of World War I* (London, 1994), is much better on this score, but is still no substitute for those published at the time or soon after. *The Times war atlas and gazetteer* (London, n.d.) is invaluable, although less good for theatres outside Europe. E. O. Volkmann, *Strategischer Atlas zum Weltkrieg* (Leipzig, 1937), illustrates individual campaigns.

Among other works of reference, mention should be made of Holger H. Herwig and Neil M. Heyman, *Biographical dictionary of World War I* (Westport, Conn., 1982).

Aaronsohn, Alexander, *With the Turks in Palestine* (London, 1917).

Adamec, Ludwig A., *Afghanistan, 1900–1923: a diplomatic history* (Berkeley, 1967).

Adams, R. J. Q., *Arms and the wizard: Lloyd George and the Ministry of Munitions* (London, 1978).

—— and Philip P. Poirier, *The conscription controversy in Great Britain, 1900–18* (London, 1987).

Addington, Larry H., *The Blitzkrieg era and the German general staff* (New Brunswick, 1971).

Addison, Christopher, *Four and a half years: a personal diary from June 1914 to January 1919*, 2 vols. (London, 1934).

Afflerbach, Holger, *Falkenhayn. Politisches Denken und Handeln im Kaiserreich* (Munich, 1994).

—— 'Wilhelm II as supreme warlord in the First World War', *War in History*, V (1998), 427–49.

Afigbo, A. E., *The warrant chief: indirect rule in southeastern Nigeria 1891–1929* (London, 1972).

Ageron, Charles-Robert, *Les Algériens musulmans et la France (1871–1919)*, 2 vols. (Paris, 1968).

Ahmad, Feroz, *The Young Turks: the Committee of Union and Progress in Turkish politics 1908–1914* (Oxford, 1969).

—— 'Ottoman armed neutrality and intervention August-November 1914', *Studies in Ottoman Diplomatic History*, IV (1990), 41–69.

—— 'War and society under the Young Turks, 1908–1918', in Albert Hourani, Philip S. Khoury, and Mary C. Wilson (eds.), *The modern Middle East: a reader* (London, 1993).

Ahmad, Kamal Madhar, *Kurdistan during the First World War* (London, 1994).

Ajayi, J. F. A., and Michael Crowder (eds.), *History of West Africa*, vol. II, (London, 1974).

Akavia, Gideon Y., *Decisive victory and correct doctrine: cults in French military thought before 1914. A rereading of Ardant du Picq, Ferdinand Foch, and Loyzeau de Grand-maison* (Stanford, 1993).

Albert, Bill, with Paul Henderson, *South America and the First World War* (Cambridge, 1988).

Albertini, Luigi, *The origins of the war of 1914*, 3 vols. (London, 1957).

Allen, W. E. D., and Paul Muratoff, *A history of the wars on the Trans-Caucasian border 1828–1921* (Cambridge, 1953).

Ally, Russell, 'War and gold—the Bank of England, the London gold market and South Africa's gold, 1914–1919', *Journal of Southern African Studies*, XVII (1991), 221–38.

al-Rahim, Muddathir 'Abd, *Imperialism and nationalism in the Sudan: a study in constitutional and political development* (Oxford, 1969).

Anderson, Ross, 'The Battle for Tanga', *War in History*, VIII (2001), (forthcoming).

Andolenko, C. R., *Histoire de l'armée russe* (Paris, 1967).

Andresen, Bernd, *Ernst von Dryander: eine biographische Studie* (Berlin, 1995).

Andrew, Christopher, *Secret service: the making of the British intelligence community* (London, 1985).

Andrew, Christopher M., and A. S. Kanya-Forstner, *France overseas: the Great War and the climax of French imperial expansion* (London, 1981).

—— and ——, 'France, Africa, and the First World War', *Journal of African History*, XIX (1978), 11–23.

—— and ——, 'The French colonial party and French colonial war aims 1914–1918', *Historical Journal*, XVII (1974), 79–106.

Andrews, E. M., *The Anzac illusion: Anglo-Australian relations during World War I* (Cambridge, 1993).

Anglesey, Marquess of, *A history of the British cavalry*, 8 vols. (London, 1973–96).

Army Quarterly, 'The Lemberg campaign: August-September, 1914', XXII (1931), 23–40.

Armeson, Robert B., *Total warfare and compulsory labor: a study of the military-industrial complex in Germany during World War I* (The Hague, 1964).

Arnold, Joseph C., 'French tactical doctrine, 1870–1914', *Military Affairs*, XLII (1978), 61–7.

Ascher, Abraham, 'Radical imperialists within German social democracy 1912–1918', *Political Science Quarterly*, LXXVI (1961), 555–75.

Aschheim, Steven E., *The Nietzsche legacy in Germany 1890–1990* (Berkeley, 1992).

Asprey, Robert B., *The German high command at war: Hindenburg and Ludendorff and the First World War* (London, 1993; first published 1991).

Assmann, Kurt, *Deutsche Seestrategie in zwei Weltkriegen*, (Heidelberg, 1957).

Avery, Peter, *Modern Iran* (London, 1965).

—— Gavin Hambly, and Charles Melville, *From Nadir Shah to the Islamic Republic: The Cambridge History of Iran*, vol. VII (Cambridge, 1991).

Audoin-Rouzeau, Stéphane, *À travers leurs journaux: 14–18. Les combattants des tranchées* (Paris, 1986); English edition, *Men at war 1914–1918: national sentiment and trench journalism in France during the First World War* (Providence, 1992).

Austen, Ralph A., *Northwest Tanzania under German and British rule: colonial policy and tribal politics, 1889–1939* (New Haven, 1968).

Aymérich, J., *La conquête du Cameroun 1er août 1914–20 février 1916* (Paris, 1933).

Baer, Alexander, 'The Anglo-German antagonism and trade with Holland, with special reference to foodstuffs, during the First World War', Cambridge University Ph.D. thesis, 1997.

Baha, Lal, 'Activities of Turkish agents in Khyber during World War I', *Journal of the Asiatic Society of Pakistan*, XIV (1969), 185–92.

—— 'The North-West Frontier in the First World War', *Asian Affairs*, NS LVII (1970), 29–37.

Baker, Paul, *King and country call: New Zealanders, conscription and the Great War* (Auckland, 1998).

Balck, Wilhelm, *Entwicklung der Taktik im Weltkriege*, 2nd edn. (Berlin, 1922); *Development of tactics—World War* (Fort Leavenworth, 1922), is translated from the 1st edition.

Balderston, T., 'War finance and inflation in Britain and Germany, 1914–1918', *Economic History Review*, 2nd series, XLII (1989), 222–44.

Balfour, Michael, *The Kaiser and his times* (London, 1964).

Baquet, Louis H. A., *Souvenirs d'un directeur de l'artillerie: les canons—les munitions: novembre 1914–mai 1915* (Paris, 1921).

Barbellion, W. N. P., [B. F. Cummings], *The journal of a disappointed man and a last diary* (London, 1984; first published 1919 and 1920).

Barnett, Correlli, *The swordbearers* (London, 1963).

Barooah, Nirode Kumar, *India and the official Germany 1886–1914* (Frankfurt, 1971).

Barrett, John, 'The rank and file of the colonial army in Nigeria', *Journal of Modern African Studies*, XV (1977), 105–15.

Barthas, Louis, *Les Carnets de guerre de Louis Barthas, tonnelier, 1914–1918*, ed. Rémy Cazals (Paris, 1997; first published 1978).

Bartholdy, Albrecht Mendelssohn, *The war and German society: the testament of a liberal* (New Haven, 1937).

Baudrillart, Alfred, *Les Carnets du Cardinal Baudrillart (1914–1918)*, ed. Paul Christophe (Paris, 1994).

Bauer, Max, *Der grosse Krieg in Feld und Heimat* (Tübingen, 1921).

Beadon, R. H., *The Royal Army Service Corps*, vol. II (Cambridge, 1931).

Becker, Jean-Jacques, *1914: comment les français sont entrés dans la guerre* (Paris, 1977).

—— 'Union sacrée et idéologie bourgeoise', *Revue historique*, CCLXIV, (1980), 65–74.

—— *The Great War and the French people* (Leamington Spa, 1985; first published 1983).

—— 'L'Union sacrée: l'exception qui confirme la régle', *Vingtième siècle revue d'histoire*, 5 (1985), 111–20.

—— *La France en guerre 1914–1918: la grande mutation* (Brussels, 1988).

—— and Stéphane Audoin-Rouzeau, *Les Societés européennes et la guerre de 1914–1918* (Paris, 1990).

Beckett, Ian F. W., 'The Singapore mutiny of February, 1915', *Journal of the Society for Army Historical Research*, LXII (1984), 132–53.

—— and Keith Simpson, *A nation in arms: a social study of the British army in the First World War* (Manchester, 1985).

Beckmann, Max, *Briefe im Kriege* (Munich, 1984; first published 1916).

Beesly, Patrick, *Room 40: British naval intelligence 1914–18* (London, 1982).

Belgique, Royaume de: Ministère de la Défense Nationale—Etat-Major Général de l'Armée Section de l'Historique, *Les Campagnes coloniales belges 1914–1918*, 3 vols. (Brussels, 1927–32).

Bell, A. C., *A history of the blockade of Germany and of the countries associated with her in the Great War, Austria-Hungary, Bulgaria, and Turkey* (London, 1937; actually published 1961).

Bellon, Bernard P., *Mercedes in peace and war: German automobile workers, 1903–1945* (New York, 1990).

Benary, Albert (ed.), *Das Ehrenbuch der deutschen Feldartillerie* (Berlin, [*c.* 1930]).

Bennett, Geoffrey, *Coronel and the Falklands* (London, 1962).

—— *Naval battles of the First World War* (London, 1968).

Berend, I. T., and Gy. Ránki, *The development of the manufacturing industry in Hungary (1900–1944)* (Budapest, 1960).

Berghahn, V. R., *Germany and the approach of war 1914* (London, 1973).

—— *Modern Germany: society, economy and politics in the twentieth century*, 2nd edn. (Cambridge, 1987).

—— and Martin Kitchen (eds.), *Germany in the age of total war* (London, 1981).

Bergson, Henri, *The meaning of the war: life and matter in conflict* (London, 1915).

Berliner Geschichtswerkstatt (ed.), *August 1914: ein Volk zieht in den Krieg* (Berlin, 1989).

Bernard, Philippe, and Henri Dubief, *The decline of the Third Republic 1914–1938* (Cambridge, 1985; first published 1975–6).

Bernhardi, Friedrich von, *Germany and the next war* (London, 1914).

Bernstorff, Johann-Heinrich, *Deutschland und Amerika. Erinnerungen aus dem fünf-jährigen Kriege* (Berlin, 1920).

Beztuzhev, I. V., 'Russian foreign policy February–June 1914', *Journal of Contemporary History*, I (1966), 93–112.

Bidwell, Robin, *Morocco under colonial rule: French administration of tribal areas 1912–1956* (London, 1973).

Bidwell, Shelford, and Dominick Graham, *Fire-power: British army weapons and theories of war 1904–1945* (London, 1982).

Bihl, Wolfdieter, 'Das im Herbst 1914 geplante-Schwarzmeer-Unternehmen der Mittelmächte', *Jahrbücher für Geschichte Osteuropas*, NS XIV (1966), 326–66.

—— *Die Kaukasus-Politik der Mittelmächte. Teil 1. Ihre Basis in der Orient-Politik und ihre Aktionen 1914–1917* (Vienna, 1975).

Binding, Rudolf, *A fatalist at war* (London, 1929).

Birkett, M. S., 'The iron and steel trades during the war', *Journal of the Royal Statistical Society*, LXXXIII (1920), 351–400.

Bitsch, Marie-Thérèse, *La Belgique entre La France et l'Allemagne 1905–1914* (Paris, 1994).

Blake, Robert *The unknown prime minister: the life and times of Andrew Bonar Law 1858–1923* (London, 1955).

—— (ed.), *The private papers of Douglas Haig 1914–1919* (London, 1952).

Blenkinsop, L. J., and J. W. Rainey, *History of the Great War based on official documents: veterinary services* (London, 1925).

Bloch, I. S., *Modern weapons and modern war* (London, 1900).

Bloch, Jean de [i.e. I. S.], *La guerre*, 6 vols. (Paris, 1898).

Bloem, Walter, *The advance from Mons 1914* (London, 1930; first published 1916).

Boell, Ludwig, *Die Operationen in Ostafrika* (Hamburg, 1951).

Boemeke, Manfred F., Roger Chickering, and Stig Förster (eds.), *Anticipating total war: the German and American experiences 1871–1914* (Cambridge, 1999).

Bogacz, Ted, ' "A tyranny of words": language, poetry, and anti-modernism in England in the First World War', *Journal of Modern History*, LVIII (1986), 643–68.

Bogart, Ernest Ludlow, *War costs and their financing: a study of the financing of the war and the after-war problems of debt and taxation*, (New York, 1921).

Bogros, Denis, 'L'Anglo-Normand, cheval de la cavalerie métropolitaine de la IIIe République (1874–1914), *Guerres mondiales et conflits contemporains* 185, (janvier 1997), 7–12.

Böhme, Helmut, and Fritz Kallenberg (eds.), *Deutschland und der erste Weltkrieg* (Darmstadt, 1987).

Bond, Brian (ed.), *The First World War and British military history* (Oxford, 1991).

Borgert, Heinz-Ludger, 'Grundzüge der Landkriegführung von Schlieffen bis Guderian', in Militärgeschichtliche Forschungsamt, *Handbuch zur deutschen Militärgeschichte 1648–1939*, vol. IX (Munich, 1979).

Bosworth, Richard, *Italy and the approach of the First World War* (London, 1983).

Bourne, J. M., *Britain and the Great War 1914–1918* (London, 1989).

Bourne, K., and D. C. Watt (eds.), *Studies in international history* (London, 1967).

Brécard, Général, *En Belgique auprès du Roi Albert: souvenirs de 1914* (Paris, 1934).

Breguet, Émmanuel, and Claude Breguet, 'La Reconnaissance aérienne et la bataille de la Marne (30 août–3 septembre 1914), *Revue historique des armées*, 166, mars 1987, 92–100.

Bridge, F. R., *From Sadowa to Sarajevo: the foreign policy of Austria-Hungary 1866–1914* (London, 1972).

——— and Roger Bullen, *The great powers and the European states system 1815–1914* (London, 1980).

Brock, Michael, and Eleanor Brock (eds.), *H. H. Asquith: letters to Venetia Stanley*, (Oxford, 1985; first published 1982).

Brocke, Bernhard vom, ' "Wissenschaft und Militarismus". Der Aufruf der 93 "an der Kulturwelt!" und der Zusammenbruch der internationalen Gelehrtenrepublik im Ersten Weltkrieg', in Wm. M. Calder III, Hellmut Flashar, and Theodor Linken (eds.), *Wilamowitz nach 50 Jahren* (Darmstadt, 1985).

Brodie, Bernard, *Sea power in the machine age*, 2nd edn. (Princeton, 1943).

Brooks, John, 'All-big-guns: fire control and capital ship design 1903–1909', *War Studies Journal*, I (1996), 36–50.

Brown, David, 'The Russo-Japanese War: technical lessons as perceived by the Royal Navy', *Warship* (1996), 66–77.

Brown, Emily C., *Har Dayal: Hindu revolutionary and rationalist* (Tucson, 1975).

Brown, Ian Malcolm, *British logistics on the western front 1914–1919* (Westport, Conn, 1998).

Brown, Judith, *Gandhi's rise to power: Indian politics 1915–1922* (Cambridge, 1972).

——— *Modern India: the origins of an Asian democracy* (Delhi, 1985).

Brown, William Adams, jr., *The international gold standard reinterpreted*, 2 vols. (New York, 1940).

Brusilov, A. A., *A soldier's note-book 1914–1918* (London, 1930).

Bucholz, Arden, *Hans Delbrück and the German military establishment: war images in conflict* (Iowa City, 1985).

—— (ed.), *Delbrück's modern military history* (Lincoln, Nebr., 1997).

—— *Moltke, Schlieffen, and Prussian war planning* (New York, 1991).

Buhrer, J., *L'Afrique orientale allemande et la guerre de 1914–1918* (Paris, 1922).

Bunselmeyer, Robert E., *The cost of the war 1914–1919: British economic war aims and the origins of reparation* (Hamden, Conn., 1975).

Burchardt, Lothar, *Friedenswirtschaft und Kriegsvorsorge. Deutschlands wirtschaftliche Rüstungsbestrebungen vor 1914* (Boppard am Rhein, 1968).

—— 'Walther Rathenau und die Anfänge der deutschen Rohstoffbewirtschaftung im Ersten Weltkrieg', *Tradition*, XV (1970), 169–96.

—— 'Zwischen Kriegsgewinnen und Kriegskosten: Krupp im Ersten Weltkrieg', *Zeitschrift für Unternehmensgeschichte*, XXXII (1987), 71–123.

Burdick, Charles B., *The Japanese siege of Tsingtau: World War I in Asia* (Hamden, Conn., 1976).

Burk, Kathleen, 'The diplomacy of finance: British financial missions to the United States 1914–1918', *Historical Journal*, XXII (1979), 351–72.

—— 'J. M. Keynes and the exchange rate crisis of July 1917, *Economic History Review*, 2nd series, XXXII (1979), 405–16.

—— *Britain, America and the sinews of war, 1914–1918* (Boston, 1985).

—— 'A merchant bank at war: the house of Morgan, 1914–18', in P. L. Cottrell and D. E. Moggridge (eds.), *Money and power: essays in honour of L. S. Presnell* (Basingstoke, 1988).

—— (ed.), *War and the state: the transformation of British government, 1914–1919* (London, 1982).

Burke, Edmund, 'Moroccan resistance, pan-Islam and German war strategy, 1914–1918', *Francia*, III (1975), 434–64.

Buse, D. K., 'Ebert and the coming of World War I: a month from his diary', *International Review of Social History*, XIII (1968), 430–48.

Busch, Briton Cooper, *Britain, India, and the Arabs, 1914–1921* (Berkeley, 1971).

Bussy, Carvel de (ed.), *Count Stephen Tisza, prime minister of Hungary: letters (1914–1916)* (New York, 1991).

Caesar, Rolf, 'Die Finanzierung des Ersten Weltkrieges und de Rolle der Sparkassen', *Zeitschrift für bayerische Sparkassengeschichte*, V (1991), 57–127.

Cailleteau, François, 'Le Commandement des armées françaises pendant la Grande Guerre', *Guerres mondiales et conflits contemporains*, 155, (juillet 1989), 3–24; 156, (octobre 1989), 3–24.

Cain, P. J., and A. G. Hopkins, *British imperialism: crisis and deconstruction 1914–90* (London, 1993).

Cairns, John C., 'Intellectuals, war, and transcendence before 1914', *Historical Reflections*, X (1983), 1–17.

Calkins, Kenneth R., *Hugo Haase: democrat and revolutionary* (Durham, NC, 1979).

Callwell, C. E., *Experiences of a dug-out 1914–1918* (London, 1920).

Camena d'Almeida, P., *L'Armée allemande avant et pendant la guerre de 1914–1918* (Nancy, 1919).

Carnegie, David, *The history of munitions supply in Canada 1914–1918* (London, 1925).

Cassar, George H., *Kitchener: architect of victory* (London, 1977).

—— *The tragedy of Sir John French* (Newark, 1985).

—— *Asquith as war leader* (London, 1994).

Castex, Raoul, *Théories stratégiques*, 5 vols. (Paris, 1927–35).

Cecco, Marcello de, *The international gold standard: money and empire*, 2nd edn. (London, 1984).

Cecil, Hugh, and Peter Liddle (eds.), *Facing Armageddon: the First World War experienced* (London, 1996).

—— and —— (eds.), *At the eleventh hour: reflections, hopes and anxieties at the closing of the Great War, 1918*, (Barnsley, 1998).

Chandler, Lester V., *Benjamin Strong, central banker* (Washington DC, 1958).

Charbonnet, Germain, *La Politique financière de la France pendant la guerre (août 1914–novembre 1920)* (Bordeaux, 1922).

Chapman, Guy, *A passionate prodigality* (London, 1933).

Charbonneau, Jean, 'La Grande Guerre sous l'équateur', *Revue militaire française*, 129, (1932), 397–420; 130 (1932), 80–99.

Charters, David A., Marc Milner, and J. Brent Wilson (eds.), *Military history and the military profession* (Westport, Conn., 1992).

Chi, Madeleine, *China diplomacy, 1914–1918* (Cambridge, Mass., 1970).

Chickering, Roger, *Imperial Germany and the Great War 1914–1918* (Cambridge, 1998).

Churchill, Winston S., *The unknown war: the eastern front 1914–1917* (London, 1941; first published 1931).

Cimbala, Stephen J., 'Steering through rapids: Russian mobilization and World War I', *Journal of Slavic Military Studies* IX (1996), 376–98.

Claus, Rudolf, *Die Kriegswirtschaft Russlands bis zur bolschewistischen Revolution* (Bonn, 1922).

Clayton, Anthony, *France, soldiers and Africa* (London, 1988).

Cochenhausen, Friedrich von, *Conrad von Hoetzendorf: eine Studie über seine Persönlichkeit* (Berlin., 1934).

Coetzee, Frans, and Marilyn Shevin-Coetzee (eds.), *Authority, identity and the social history of the Great War* (Providence, 1995).

Cohen, Stuart A., *British policy in Mesopotamia 1903–1914* (London, 1976).

—— 'The genesis of the British campaign in Mesopotamia, 1914', *Middle Eastern Studies*, XII (1976), 119–32.

Collyer, J. J., *The campaign in German South West Africa 1914–1915* (Pretoria, 1937).

—— *The South Africans with General Smuts in German East Africa 1916* (Pretoria, 1939).

Conrad von Hötzendorf, Franz, *Aus meiner Dienstzeit 1906–1918*, 5 vols. (Vienna, 1921–5).

Contamine, Henri, *La Révanche 1871–1914* (Paris, 1957).

—— *La Victoire de la Marne, 9 septembre 1914* (Paris, 1970).

Cooper, Caroline Ethel, *Behind the lines: one woman's war 1914–18*, ed. Decie Denholm (London, 1982).

Cooper, John Milton, 'The command of gold reversed: American loans to Britain, 1915–1917', *Pacific Historical Review*, XLV (1976), 209–30.

Corbett, Julian, *Some principles of maritime strategy*, ed. Eric Grove (Annapolis, 1988; first published 1911).

—— and Henry Newbolt, *History of the Great War: naval operations*, 5 vols. (London, 1920–31).

Cordonnier, Général, *Une brigade au feu (potins de guerre)* (Paris, 1921).

Cork, Richard, *A bitter truth: avant-garde art and the Great War* (New Haven, 1994).

Cornwall, Mark (ed.), *The last years of Austria-Hungary: essays in political and military history 1908–1918* (Exeter, 1990).

Corrigan, H. S. W., 'German–Turkish relations and the outbreak of war in 1914: a reassessment', *Past and present*, 36, (1967), 144–52.

Craft, Stephen G., 'Angling for an invitation to Paris: China's entry into the First World War', *International History Review*, XVI, (1994), 1–24.

Craig, Gordon, *The politics of the Prussian army 1640–1945* (London, 1955).

—— *Germany 1866–1945* (Oxford, 1981; first published 1978).

—— 'The Kaiser and the Kritik', *New York Review of Books*, 18 Feb. 1988.

Crampton, Richard J., *Bulgaria 1875–1918: a history* (Boulder, Col., 1983).

Cron, Hermann, *Geschichte des deutschen Heeres im Weltkriege 1914–1918* (Osnabrück, 1990; first published 1937).

Crook, Paul, *Darwinism, war and history: the debate over the biology of war from the 'Origin of the Species' to the First World War* (Cambridge, 1994).

Crouzet, François, 'Recherches sur la production d'armements en France (1815–1913)', *Revue historique*, CCLI (1974), 45–84.

Crow, Duncan, *A man of push and go: the life of George Macaulay Booth* (London, 1965).

Crowder, Michael, *Revolt in Bussa: a study of British native administration in Nigerian Borgu, 1902–1935* (London, 1973).

—— 'The First World War and its consequences', in A. Adu Boahen (ed.), *Africa under colonial domination 1880–1935*, vol. VII of *UNESCO General History of Africa* (London, 1985).

Crowe, J. H. V., *General Smuts' campaign in East Africa* (London, 1918).

Cruickshank, John, *Variations on catastrophe: some French responses to the Great War* (Oxford, 1982).

Cruttwell, C. R. M. F., *A history of the Great War 1914–1918*, 2nd edn. (Oxford, 1936).

—— *The role of British strategy in the Great War* (Cambridge, 1936).

Cutlack, F. M. (ed.), *War letters of General Monash* (Sydney, 1935).

Dahlhaus, Friedrich, *Möglichkeiten und Grenzen auswärtiger Kultur-und Pressepolitik dargestellt am Beispiel der deutschen–türkischen Beziehungen 1914–1928* (Frankfurt am Main, 1990).

Dallin, Alexander *et al.*, *Russian diplomacy and eastern Europe 1914–1917* (New York, 1963).

Daly, M. W., *Empire on the Nile: the Anglo-Egyptian Sudan 1898–1934* (Cambridge, 1986).

Danaïllow, Georges, *Les Effets de la guerre en Bulgarie* (Paris, 1932).

Daniel, Ute, *The war from within: German working-class women in the First World War* (Oxford, 1997; first published 1989).

Danilov, Youri, *La Russie dans la guerre mondiale (1914–1917)* (Paris, 1927).

Daunton, Martin, 'How to pay for the war: state, society and taxation in Britain, 1917–24', *English History Review*, CXI (1996), 882–919.

Davenport, T. R. H., 'The South Afrcian rebellion 1914', *English Historical Review*, LXXVIII (1963), 73–94.

David, Edward (ed.), *Inside Asquith's cabinet: from the diaries of Charles Hobhouse* (London, 1977).

Davis, Lance E., and Robert A. Huttenback, *Mammon and the pursuit of empire: the political economy of British imperialism 1860–1912* (Cambridge, 1986).

Davis, Shelby Cullom, *Reservoirs of men: a history of the black troops of French West Africa* (Geneva, 1934).

Deák, István, *Beyond nationalism: a social and political history of the Habsburg officer corps, 1848–1918* (New York, 1990).

Deauville, Max, *Jusqu' à l'Yser* (Paris, 1964; first published 1916).

Dedijer, Vladimir, *The road to Sarajevo* (London, 1967).

De Groot, Gerard J., 'Educated soldier or cavalry officer? Contradictions in the pre–1914 career of Douglas Haig', *War & Society*, IV (1986), 51–69.

—— *Douglas Haig, 1861–1928* (London, 1988).

—— *Blighty: British society in the era of the Great War* (London, 1996).

Deist, Wilhelm (ed.), *The German military in the age of total war* (Leamington Spa, 1985).

Delbrück, Clemens von, *Die wirtschaftliche Mobilmachung in Deutschland 1914* (Munich, 1924).

Delbrück, Hans, *Krieg und Politik 1914–1916* (Berlin, 1918).

Deppe, Ludwig, *Mit Lettow-Vorbeck durch Afrika* (Berlin, 1919).

Dereymez, Jean-William, 'Les Usines de guerre (1914–1918) et le cas de la Saône-et-Loire', *Cahiers d'histoire*, II (1981), 151–81.

Dewar, George A. B., *The great munitions feat 1914–1918* (London, 1921).

Dewey, P. E., 'Military recruiting and the British labour force during the First World War', *Historical Journal*, XXVII (1984), 199–223.

Dignan, Don, *The Indian revolutionary problem in British diplomacy 1914–1919* (New Delhi, 1983).

Digre, Brian, *Imperialism's new clothes: the repartition of tropical Africa 1914–1919* (New York, 1990).

Dirks, Uwe, 'Julian S. Corbett und die Britische Seekriegführung 1914–1918', *Militärgeschichtliche Mitteilungen*, 37 (1985), 35–50.

Dix, Arthur, *Wirtschaftskrieg und Kriegswirtschaft: zur Geschichte des deutschen Zusammenbruchs* (Berlin, 1920).

Djemal Pasha, *Memoirs of a Turkish statesman 1913–1919* (London, [1922]).

Djordjovic, Dimitrije, '"Vojovda" Radomir Putnik', in Bela K. Király and Albert A. Nofi (eds.), *East central European war leaders: civilian and military* (Boulder, Col., 1988).

Dockrill, Michael, and David French (eds.), *Strategy and intelligence: British policy and intelligence during the First World War* (London, 1996).

Doehring, Bruno (ed.), *Ein feste Burg: Predigten und Reden aus eiserner Zeit*, 2 vols. (Berlin, 1915).

Doerries, Reinhard R., *Washington–Berlin 1908/1917: die Tätigkeit des Botschafters Johann Heinrich Graf von Bernstorff in Washington vor dem Eintritt der Vereingten Staaten von Amerika in den Ersten Weltkrieg* (Dusseldorf, 1975); English edition, *Imperial challenge: Ambassador Count Bernstorff and German–American relations, 1908–1917* (Chapel Hill, 1989).

Doise, Jean, and Maurice Vaïsse, *Diplomatie et outil militaire 1871–1969* (Paris, 1987).

d'Ombrain, Nicholas, *War machinery and high policy: defence administration in peacetime Britain 1902–1914* (Oxford, 1973).

Douglas, Roy, 'Voluntary enlistment in the First World War and the work of the Parliamentary Recruiting Committee', *Journal of Modern History*, XLII (1970), 564–85.

Draeger, Hans (ed.), *Gouverneur Schnee: ein Künder und mehrer deutscher Geltung* (Berlin, 1931).

Droz, Jacques, *Les Causes de la première guerre mondiale* (Paris, 1973).

Dschawid-Bei [ie Djavid], *Türkische Kriegsfinanzwirtschaft. Budgetrede, gehalten in der türkischen Kammer am 3. März 1917* (Stuttgart and Berlin, 1917).

Dua, R. P., *Anglo-Japanese relations during the First World War* (New Delhi, 1972).

Dubail, Auguste, *Quatre ans de commandement 1914–1918*, 4 vols. (Paris, 1920).

Ducasse, André, Jacques Meyer, and Gabriel Perreux, *Vie et mort des français 1914–1918* (Paris, 1959).

Dülffer, Jost, 'Limitations on naval warfare and Germany's future as a world power: a German debate 1904–1906', *War & Society*, III (1985), 23–43.

Dunn, J. C., *The war the infantry knew 1914–1919: a chronicle of service in France and Belgium* (London, 1987; first published 1938).

Duroselle, Jean-Baptiste, *La France et les français 1914–1920* (Paris, 1972).

—— *La Grande Guerre des français: l'incomprehensible* (Paris, 1994).

Duus, Peter (ed.), *The Cambridge History of Japan*, 6 vols. (Cambridge, 1988–99).

—— Ramon H. Myers, and Mark R. Peattie (eds.), *The Japanese informal empire in China, 1895–1937* (Princeton, 1980).

Dyer, Gwynne, 'The origins of the 'nationalist' group of officers in Turkey 1908–18', *Journal of Contemporary History*, VIII (1973), 121–64.

—— 'Turkish "falsifiers" and Armenian "deceivers": historiography and the Armenian massacres', *Middle Eastern Studies*, XII (1976), 99–107.

Echenberg, Myron, *Colonial conscripts: the 'tirailleurs sénégalais' in French West Africa, 1857–1960* (Portsmouth, NH, 1991).

Echevarria, Antulio J., II, 'On the brink of the abyss: the warrior identity and German military thought before the Great War', *War & Society*, XII (1995), 23–40.

—— 'A crisis in warfighting: German tactical discussions in the late nineteenth century', *Militärgeschichtliches Mitteilungen*, 55, (1996), 51–68.

—— 'General staff historian Hugo Freiherr von Freytag-Loringhoven and the dialectics of German military thought', *Journal of Military History*, LX (1996), 471–94.

Edmonds, James E., *Military operations: France and Belgium*, 14 vols. (London, 1922–48).

Egger, Rainer, 'Heeresverwaltung und Rüstungsindustrie in Niederösterreich während des I. Weltkrieges', in Wilhelm Brauneder and Franz Baltzarek (eds.), *Modell einer neuen Wirtschaftsordnung. Wirtschaftsverwaltung in Österreich 1914–1918* (Frankfurt, 1991).

Ehlert, Hans Gotthard, *Die wirtschaftliche Zentralbehörde des deutschen Reiches 1914 bis 1919. Das Problem der 'Gemeinwirtschaft' in Krieg und Frieden* (Wiesbaden, 1982).

Eichengreen, Barry, *Golden fetters: the gold standard and the great depression, 1919–1939* (New York, 1992).

Eley, Geoff, 'The view from the throne: the personal rule of Kaiser Wilhelm II', *Historical Journal*, XXVIII (1985), 469–85.

Ekoko, Elango, 'British war plans against Germany in West Africa, 1903–14', *Journal of Strategic Studies*, IV (1984), 440–56.

Eksteins, Modris, *Rites of spring: the Great War and the birth of the modern age* (London, 1989).

Elango, Lovett, 'The Anglo-French "condominium" in Cameroon, 1914–1916: the myth and the reality', *International Journal of African Historical Studies*, XVIII (1985), 657–73.

Elgood, Peter, *Egypt and the army* (Oxford, 1924).

Ellinwood, DeWitt C., and S. D. Pradhan, *India and World War I* (New Delhi, 1978).

Elze, Walter, *Tannenberg. Das deutsche Heer von 1914. Seine Grundzüge und deren Auswirkungen im Sieg an der Ostfront* (Breslau, 1928).

—— *Der strategische Aufbau des Weltkrieges 1914–1918*, Berlin, 1933

Emin, Ahmed, *Turkey in the World War* (New Haven, 1930).

English, John A., *On infantry* (New York, 1981).

Epkenhans, Michael, *Die wilhelminische Flottenrüstung 1908–1914. Weltmachtstreben, industrieller Fortschritt, soziale Integration* (Munich, 1991).

—— 'Military–industrial relations in Imperial Germany', *War in History* (forthcoming).

Epstein, Klaus, *Matthias Erzberger and the dilemma of German democracy* (New York, 1971).

Erzberger, Matthias, *Die Rüstungsausgaben des Deutschen Reiches* (Stuttgart, 1914).

—— *Erlebnisse im Weltkrieg* (Stuttgart, 1920).

Evans, David C., and Mark R. Peattie, *Kaigun: strategy, tactics, and technology in the Imperial Japanese Navy, 1887–1941* (Annapolis, 1997).

Evans, R. J. W., and Hartmut Pogge von Strandmann (eds.), *The coming of the First World War* (Oxford, 1988).

Evans-Pritchard, E. E., *The Sanusi of Cyrenaica* (Oxford, 1949).

Fairbanks, Charles H., jr, 'The origins of the Dreadnought revolution: an historiographical essay', *International History Review*, XIII (1991), 246–72

Falkenhayn, Erich von, *General headquarters 1914–1916 and its critical decisions* (London, [1919]).

Falls, Cyril, *The First World War* (London, 1960).

—— *The History of the 36th (Ulster) Division* (Belfast, 1922).

Falzeder, Ernst, and Eva Brabant, *The correspondence of Sigmund Freud and Sándor Ferenczi*, vol. II, *1914–1919*, (Cambridge, Mass, 1996).

Farndale, Martin, *History of the Royal Regiment of Artillery: western front 1914–18* (Woolwich, 1986).

Farr, Martin, 'Reginald McKenna as chancellor of the exchequer 1915–1916', Glasgow University Ph.D. thesis, 1998.

Farrar, L. L., jr, *The short-war illusion: German policy, strategy and domestic affairs, August–December 1914* (Santa Barbara, 1973).

—— *Divide and conquer: German efforts to conclude a separate peace, 1914–1918* (Boulder, Col. 1978).

Farrar, Marjorie Millbank, 'Politics versus patriotism: Alexandre Millerand as French minister of war', *French Historical Studies*, XI (1980), 577–609.

—— *Principled pragmatist: the political career of Alexandre Millerand* (New York, 1991).

Farrar-Hockley, Anthony, *The death of an army* (London, 1967).

—— *Goughie: the life of General Sir Hubert Gough, GCB, GCMG, KCVO* (London, 1975).

Farwell, Byron, *The Great War in Africa 1914–1918* (London, 1987).

Fay, Sidney Bradshaw, *The origins of the world war* (New York, 1934).

Fayolle, Marie-Émile, *Cahiers secrets de la guerre*, ed. Henri Contamine (Paris, 1963).

Feldman, Gerald D., *Army, industry and labor in Germany 1914–1918* (Princeton, 1966).

—— 'The political and social foundations of Germany's economic mobilization, 1914–1916', *Armed Forces and Society*, III (1976), 121–45.

—— *The great disorder: politics, economics and society in the German inflation 1914–1924* (New York, 1993).

—— *Hugo Stinnes. Biographie eines Industriellen 1870–1924* (Munich, 1998).

Fendall, C. P., *The East African Force 1915–1919* (London, 1921).

Ferguson, Niall, 'Germany and the origins of the First World War: new perspectives', *Historical Journal*, XXXV (1992), 725–52.

—— 'Public finance and national security: the domestic origins of the First World War revisited', *Past and Present*, 142 (1994), 141–68.

—— *Paper and iron: Hamburg business and German politics in the era of inflation, 1897–1927* (Cambridge, 1995).

—— *The pity of war* (London, 1998).

Ferro, Marc, *The Great War 1914–1918* (London, 1973).

Ferry, Abel (ed.), *Les Carnets secrets (1914–1918)* (Paris, 1957).

Fewster, Kevin (ed.), *Gallipoli correspondent: the frontline diary of C. E. W. Bean* (Sydney, 1983).

Fiebig-von Hase, Ragnild, and Maria Sturm, 'Die transatlantischen Wirtschaftbeziehungen in der Nachkriegsplanung Deutschlands, der alliierten Westmächte und der USA, 1914–17', *Militärgeschichtliche Mitteilungen*, 52 (1993), 1–34.

Fischer, Fritz, *Germany's aims in the First World War* (London, 1967; first published 1961).

—— *World power or decline: the controversy over Germany's aims in the First World War* (London, 1974; first published 1965).

—— *War of illusions: German policies from 1911 to 1914* (London, 1975; first published 1969).

Fischer, H. C., and E. X. Dubois, *Sexual life during the world war* (London, 1937).

Fisk, Harvey E., *French public finance in the Great War and today* (New York, 1922).

Flood, P. J., *France 1914–1918: public opinion and the war effort* (Basingstoke, 1990).

Florinsky, Michael T., *The end of the Russian empire* (New Haven, 1931).

Foch, Ferdinand, *The memoirs of Marshal Foch* (London, 1931).

Foerster, Wolfgang, *Le comte Schlieffen et la guerre mondiale: la stratégie allemande pendant la guerre de 1914–1918* (Paris, 1929; first published 1921); English edition, *Count Schlieffen and the world war* (US Army War College, 1983).

—— and Helmuth Greiner (eds.), *Wir Kämpfer im Weltkrieg. Selbstzeugnisse deutscher Frontsoldaten in Feldpostbriefen, Kriegstagbüchern und Aufzeichnungen, vornehmlich aus dem Material des Heeresarchivs Potsdam* (Berlin, n.d.).

Foley, Robert T., 'Schlieffen's last Kriegsspiel', *War Studies Journal*, III (1998), 117–33; IV (1999), 97–115.

Fontaine, Arthur, *French industry during the war* (New Haven, 1926).

Fontana, Jacques, *Les Catholiques français pendant la grande guerre* (Paris, 1990).

Forbes, A., *History of the Army Ordnance Services: the Great War*, 2nd edn. (London, 1931).

Förster, Stig, *Der doppelte Militarismus. Die deutsche Heeresrüstungspolitik zwischen Status-quo-Sicherung und Aggression, 1890–1913* (Stuttgart, 1985).

—— 'Der deutsche Generalstab und die Illusion des kurzen Krieges, 1871–1914. Metakritik eines Mythos', *Militärgeschichtliche Mitteilungen*, 54 (1995), 61–95.

Forsyth, Douglas J., *The crisis of Liberal Italy: monetary and financial policy, 1914–1922* (Cambridge, 1993).

France—see Ministère de la Guerre

Frantz, Gunther (ed.), *Russland auf dem Wege zur Katastrophe. Tagebücher des Grossfürsten Andrej und des Kriegsministers Poliwanow. Briefe der Grossfürsten an den Zaren* (Berlin, 1926).

Fraser, Peter, 'The British "shells scandal" of 1915', *Canadian Journal of History*, XVIII (1983), 69–86.

Fraser, T. G., 'Germany and Indian revolution', *Journal of Contemporary History*, XII (1977), 255–72.

—— 'India in Anglo-Japanese relations during the First World War', *History*, LXIII (1978), 366–82.

Freedman, Lawrence, Paul Hayes, and Robert O'Neill (eds.), *War, strategy and international politics: essays in honour of Sir Michael Howard* (Oxford, 1992)

French, David, 'The military background to the "shells crisis" of May 1915', *Journal of Strategic Studies*, II (1979), 192–205.

—— *British economic and strategic planning 1905–1915* (London, 1982).

—— 'Sir Douglas Haig's reputation, 1918–1928: a note', *Historical Journal*, XXVIII (1985), 953–60.

—— *British strategy and war aims 1914–1916* (London, 1986).

—— 'The meaning of attrition, 1914–1916', *English Historical Review*, CIII (1988), 385–405.

French, John, Viscount, *1914* (London, 1919).

Freud, Sigmund, 'Thoughts for the times on war and death' (1915), in James Strachey (ed.), *The standard edition of the complete psychological works of Sigmund Freud*, vol. XIV (London, 1957).

Frey, Marc, 'Deutsche Finanzinteressen an der Vereinigten Staaten und den Niederlanden im Ersten Weltkrieg', *Militärgeschichtliche Mitteilungen*, 53 (1994), 327–53.

—— 'Trade, ships, and the neutrality of the Netherlands in the First World War', *International History Review*, XIX (1997), 541–62.

Fridenson, Patrick, *Histoire des usines Renault 1. Naissance de la grande enterprise 1898–1939* (Paris, 1972).

—— (ed.), *1914–1918: l'autre front* (Paris, 1977); English edition, *The French home front 1914–1918* (Providence, RI, 1992).

Friedman, Isaiah, *Germany, Turkey, and Zionism 1897–1918* (Oxford, 1977).

Fritzsche, Peter, *Germans into Nazis* (Cambridge, Mass, 1998).

Frothingham, Thomas, *The naval history of the world war*, 3 vols. (Cambridge, Mass., 1924–6).

Fuller, William C., jr, *Civil–military conflict in imperial Russia 1881–1914* (Princeton, 1985).

—— *Strategy and power in Russia 1600–1914* (New York, 1992).

Galet, Émile Joseph, *Albert king of the Belgians in the Great War* (London, 1931).

Galbraith, John S., 'British war aims in World War I: a commentary on statesmanship', *Journal of Commonwealth and Imperial History*, XIII (1984), 25–45.

Gall, Lothar, Gerald Feldman, Harold James, Carl-Ludwig Holtfrerich, and Hans E. Büschger, *The Deutsche Bank 1870–1995* (London, 1995).

Gamelin, Maurice, *Manoeuvre et victoire de la Marne* (Paris, 1954).

Ganz, A. Harding, 'Colonial policy and the imperial German navy', *Militärgeschichtliche Mitteilungen*, 21 (1977), 35–52

Garcia, Luc, 'Les Mouvements de résistance au Dahomey (1914–1917), *Cahiers d'études africaines*, X (1970), 144–78.

Garson, N. G., 'South Africa and World War I', *Journal of Imperial and Commonwealth History*, VIII (1979), 68–85

Gascouin, F., *L'Évolution de l'artillerie pendant la guerre* (Paris, 1920).

Gascouin, F., *Le Triomphe de l'idée* (Paris, 1931).

Gat, Azar, *The development of military thought: the nineteenth century* (Oxford, 1992).

Gatrell, Peter, 'After Tsushima: economic and administrative aspects of Russian naval rearmament, 1905–1913', *Economic History Review*, 2nd series, XLIII (1990), 255–70.

—— *Government, industry and rearmament in Russia, 1900–1914: the last argument of tsarism* (Cambridge, 1994).

—— and Mark Harrison, 'The Russian and Soviet economies in two world wars: a comparative view', *Economic History Review*, 2nd series, XLVI (1993), 425–52.

Gatzke, Hans W., *Germany's drive to the west (Drang nach Westen): a study of Germany's western war aims during the First World War* (Baltimore, 1950).

Gazin, F., *La Cavalerie française dans la guerre mondiale 1914–1918* (Paris, 1930).

Gehrke, Ulrich, *Persien in der deutschen Orientpolitik während des Ersten Weltkrieges*, 2 vols. (Stuttgart, 1960).

Geinitz, Christian, *Kriegsfurcht und Kampfbereitschaft. Das Augusterlebnis in Freiburg. Eine Studie zum Kriegsbeginn 1914* (Essen, 1998).

Geiss, Imanuel, 'The outbreak of the First World War and German war aims', *Journal of Contemporary History*, I (1966), 75–91.

—— *July 1914: the outbreak of the First World War: selected documents* (London, 1967).

Gemzell, Carl-Axel, *Organization, conflict, and innovation: a study of German naval strategic planning 1888–1940* (Lund, 1973).

Général ***, *Plutarque n'a pas menti* (Paris, n. d.).

Generalstabler, *Kritik des Weltkrieges. Das Erbe Moltkes und Schlieffens im Grossen Kriege* (Leipzig, 1920).

Genevoix, Maurice, *'Neath Verdun, August–October 1914* (London, 1916).

George, Mark, 'Liberal opposition in wartime Russia: a case study of the Town and Zemstvo Unions, 1914–1917', *Slavonic and East European Review*, LXV (1987), 371–90.

Germains, Victor Wallace, *The Kitchener armies: the story of a national achievement* (London, 1930).

Gershoni, Israel, and James P. Jankowski, *Egypt, Islam, and the Arabs: the search for Egyptian nationhood, 1900–1930* (New York, 1986).

Geyer, Dietrich, *Russian imperialism: the interaction of domestic and foreign policy 1860–1914* (Leamington Spa, 1987).

Geyer, Michael, *Deutsche Rüstungspolitik 1860–1980* (Frankfurt am Main, 1984).

Gifford, Prosser, and Wm. Roger Louis (eds.), *Britain and Germany in Africa: imperial rivalry and colonial rule* (New Haven, 1967).

Gilbert, Bentley Brinkerhoff, 'Pacifist to interventionist: David Lloyd George in 1911 and 1914. Was Belgium an issue?', *Historical Journal*, XXVIII (1985), 863–85.

—— *David Lloyd George: a political life. The organizer of victory 1912–1916* (London, 1992).

Gilbert, Charles, *American financing of World War I* (Westport, Conn., 1970).

Gilbert, Martin, *Winston S. Churchill*, vol. III, *1914–1916*, and companion volume (London 1971–2).

—— *First World War* (London, 1994).

Glaise von Horstenau, Edmund, *Ein General im Zwielicht. Die Erinnerungen Edmund Glaises von Horstenau. Band 1. K. u. k. Generalstabsoffizier und Historiker* (Vienna, 1980).

Gleason, William, 'The all-Russian Union of Zemstvos and World War I', in Terence Emmons and Wayne S. Vucinich (eds.), *The Zemstvo in Russia: an experiment in local self-government* (Cambridge, 1982).

Godfrey, John, *Capitalism at war: industrial policy and bureaucracy in France 1914–1918* (Leamington Spa, 1987).

Goebel, Otto, *Deutsche Rohstoffwirtschaft im Weltkrieg einschliesslich des Hindenburg-Programms* (Stuttgart, 1930).

Goldrick, James, *The king's ships were at sea: the war in the North sea August 1914–February 1915* (Annapolis, 1984).

—— 'Naval publishing the British way', *Naval War College Review*, XLV (winter, 1992), 85–99.

—— 'The battleship fleet: the test of war, 1895–1919', in J. R. Hill (ed.), *The Oxford Illustrated History of the Royal Navy* (Oxford, 1995).

—— and John B. Hattendorf (eds.), *Mahan is not enough: the proceedings of a conference on the works of Sir Julian Corbett and Admiral Sir Herbert Richmond* (Newport, RI, 1993).

Goldschmidt, Arthur, jr, 'The Egyptian nationalist party: 1892–1919', in P. M. Holt (ed.), *Political and social change in modern Egypt* (London, 1968).

Golovine, N., *The Russian army in the world war* (New Haven, 1931).

—— 'The battle of the Masurian lakes', *Journal of the United Service Institution of India* (Jan. 1932), 493–509; (Jan. 1933), 493–509.

—— *The Russian campaign of 1914: the beginning of the war and operations in East Prussia* (Fort Leavenworth, 1933).

—— 'La Bataille de Galicie', *Revue militaire française*, 158 (aôut 1934), 220–50; 159 (sept. 1934), 281–301.

Goltz, Colmar von der, *Denkwürdigkeiten* (Berlin, 1932).

Gooch, John, *The plans of war: the general staff and British military strategy c1900–1916* (London, 1974).

—— *The prospect of war: studies in British defence policy 1847–1942* (London, 1981).

Goodspeed, D. J., *Ludendorff: soldier, dictator, revolutionary* (London, 1966).

—— *The German wars 1914–1945* (London, 1978).

Gordon, Andrew, 'The crowd and politics in imperial Japan: Tokyo 1905–1918', *Past and Present*, 21 (1988), 141–70.

Gordon, Andrew, *The rules of the game: Jutland and British naval command* (London, 1996).

Gordon, Donald C., *The dominion partnership in imperial defense, 1870–1914* (Baltimore, 1965).

Gordon, Michael, 'Domestic conflict and the origins of the First World War: the British and German cases', *Journal of Modern History*, XLIV (1974), 191–226.

Gordon-Duff, Lachlan, *With the Gordon Highlanders to the Boer War and beyond* (Macclesfield, 1998).

Gorges, E. Howard, *The Great War in West Africa* (London, 1930).

Görlitz, Walter (ed.), *The Kaiser and his court: the diaries, note books and letters of Admiral Georg von Müller, Chief of the Naval Cabinet, 1914–1918* (London, 1961; first published 1959).

Gottlieb, W. W., *Studies in secret diplomacy during the First World War* (London, 1957).

Gourko, Basil, *Memories and impressions of war and revolution in Russia 1914–1917* (London, 1918).

Grady, Henry F., *British war finance 1914–1919* (New York, 1927).

Graf, Daniel W., 'Military rule behind the Russian front 1914–1917: the political ramifications', *Jahrbücher für Geschichte Osteuropas*, XXII (1974), 390–411.

Graham, Dominick, and Shelford Bidwell, *Coalitions, politicians and generals: some aspects of command in the world wars* (London, 1993).

Granier, Gerhard, 'Deutsche Rüstungspolitik vor dem Ersten Weltkrieg. General Franz Wandels Tagebuchaufzeichnungen aus dem preussischen Kriegsministerium', *Militärgeschichtliche Mitteilungen*, 38 (1985), 123–62

Gras, Yves, *Castelnau ou l'art de commander 1851–1944* (Paris, 1990).

Grasset, A., *Le 22 août au 4ᵉ corps d'armée: Virton* (Paris, 1922).

—— *Le 22 août au 4ᵉ corps d'armée: Ethe* (Paris, 1924).

Gratz, Gustav, and Richard Schüller, *Der wirtschaftliche Zusammenbruch Österreich-Ungarns* (Vienna, 1930).

Gray, Colin, *The leverage of sea power: the strategic advantages of navies in war* (New York, 1992).

Grebler, Leo, and Wilhelm Winkler, *The cost of the world war to Germany and Austria-Hungary* (New Haven, 1940).

Grieves, Keith, *The politics of manpower, 1914–1918* (Manchester, 1988).

—— *Sir Eric Geddes: business and government in war and peace* (Manchester, 1989).

—— 'Improvising the British war effort: Eric Geddes and Lloyd George, 1915–18', *War & Society*, VII (1989), 40–55.

—— '"Lowther's Lambs": rural paternalism and voluntary recruitment in the First World War', *Rural History*, IV (1993), 55–75.

Griffiths, Richard, *Marshal Pétain* (London, 1970).

Grigg, John, *Lloyd George: from peace to war 1912–1916* (London, 1985).

Groener, Wilhelm, *Der Feldherr wider Willen. Operative Studien über den Weltkrieg* (Berlin, 1930).

—— *Lebenserinnerungen. Jugend, Generalstab, Weltkrieg*, ed. Hiller von Gaertringen (Göttingen, 1957).

Groh, Dieter, 'The "unpatriotic socialists" and the state', *Journal of Contemporary History*, I (1966), 151–77.

Grove, Eric, 'The first shots of the Great War: the Anglo-French conquest of Togo, 1914', *Army Quarterly*, CVI (1976), 308–23.

Grove, Mark, 'The development of Japanese amphibious warfare, 1874 to 1942', in Strategic and Combart Studies Institute, *Occasional Paper*, 31 (1997).

Grundlingh, Albert, 'Black men in a white man's war: the impact of the First World War on South African blacks', *War & Society*, III (1985), 55–81

Gudmundsson, Bruce, *Stormtroop tactics: innovation in the German army, 1914–1918* (New York, 1989).

—— *On artillery* (Westport, Conn., 1993).

Guillen, P. (ed.), *La France et l'Italie pendant la première guerre mondiale* (Grenoble, 1976).

Guéno, Jean-Pierre, and Yves Laplume, *Paroles de poilus: lettres et carnets du front (1914–1918)* (Paris, 1998).

Guinn, Paul, *British strategy and politics 1914 to 1918* (Oxford, 1965).

Gullace, Nicoletta F., 'Sexual violence and family honor: British propaganda and international law during the First World War', *American Historical Review*, CII (1997), 714–47.

Guse, Felix, *Die Kaukasusfront im Weltkrieg bis zum Frieden von Brest* (Leipzig, 1940).

Güth, Rolf, 'Die Organisation der deutschen Marine in Krieg und Frieden 1913–1933', in Militärgeschichtliches Forschungsamt, *Handbuch zur deutschen Militärgeschichte 1684–1939. VIII. Deutsche Marinegeschichte der Neuzeit* (Munich, 1977).

Gutsche, Willibald, 'Die Entstehung des Kriegausschusses der deutschen Industrie und seine Rolle zu Beginn des ersten Weltkrieges', *Zeitschrift für Geschichtwissenschaft*, XVIII (1970), 877–98.

Hadley, Michael L., and Roger Sarty, *Tin-pots and pirate ships: Canadian naval forces and German sea raiders 1880–1918* (Montreal, 1991).

Hagen, Gottfried, *Die Türkei im Ersten Weltkrieg. Flugblätter und Flugschriften in arabischer, persischer und osmanisch-türkischer Sprache aus eines Sammlung der Universitätbibliothek Heidelberg eingeleitet, übersetzt und kommentiert* (Frankfurt am Main, 1990).

Halévy, Daniel, *L'Europe brisée; journal et lettres 1914–1918*, ed. Sébastien Laurent (Paris, 1998).

Haley, Charles D., 'The desperate Ottoman: Enver Pasha and the German empire', *Middle Eastern Studies*, XXX (1994), 1–51, 224–51.

Halpern, Paul, *The naval war in the Mediterranean 1914–1918* (London, 1987).

—— *A naval history of World War I* (London, 1994).

—— *Anton Haus: Österreich-Ungarns Grossadmiral* (Graz, 1998).

—— (ed.), *The Keyes papers: selections from the private and official correspondence of Admiral of the Fleet Baron Keyes of Zeebrugge*, vol. I, *1914–1918*, (London, 1972).

Hamilton-Grace, R. S., *Finance and war* (London, 1910).

Hamm, Michael F., 'Liberal politics in wartime Russia: an analysis of the progressive bloc', *Slavic Review*, XXXIII (1974), 453–68.

Hancock, W. K., *Smuts: the sanguine years 1870–1919* (Cambridge, 1962).

—— and Jean van der Poel (eds.), *Selections from the Smuts papers*, vol. III, *June 1910–November 1918* (Cambridge, 1966).

Handel, Michael I. (ed.), *Clausewitz and modern strategy* (London, 1986).

Hankey, Maurice, Lord, *Government control in war* (Cambridge, 1945).

—— *The supreme command 1914–1918*, 2 vols. (London, 1961).

Hanna, Martha, *The mobilization of intellect: French scholars and writers during the Great War* (Cambridge, Mass., 1996).

Hanssen, Hans Peter, *Diary of a dying empire*, ed. R. H. Lutz, M. Schofield, and O. O. Winther (Port Washington, NY, 1973; first published 1955).

Hardach, Gerd, *The First World War 1914–1918* (London, 1977; first published 1970).

Harper, R. W. E., and Harry Miller, *Singapore mutiny* (Singapore, 1984).

Harries, Meirion, and Susie Harries, *Soldiers of the sun: the rise and fall of the imperial Japanese army 1868–1945* (London, 1991).

Harris, Henry, 'To serve mankind in peace and the fatherland in war: the case of Fritz Haber', *German History*, X (1992), 24–33.

Harrison, Richard L., 'Samsonov and the battle of Tannenberg, 1914', in Brian Bond (ed.), *Fallen stars: eleven studies of twentieth-century military disasters* (London, 1991).

Hart, Basil H. Liddell, *Reputations* (London, 1930).

—— *A history of the world war 1914–1918* (London, 1934; first published as *The real war*, 1930; later editions, *History of the First World War*).

—— *Foch; man of Orleans*, 2 vols. (London, 1937; first published 1931).

—— *Through the fog of war* (London, 1938).

Harvey, A. D., *Collision of empires: Britain in three world wars, 1793–1945* (London, 1992).

—— 'The hand grenade in the First World War', *Journal of the Royal United Services Institute for Defence Studies*, CXXXVIII (Feb. 1993), 44–7.

Haste, Cate, *Keep the home fires burning: propaganda in the First World War* (London, 1977).

Hatry, Gilbert, *Renault: usine de guerre 1914–1918* (Paris, 1978).

Hatton, P. H. S., 'The Gambia, the Colonial Office, and the opening moves of the First World War', *Journal of African History*, VII (1966), 123–31.

Haupt, Georges, *Socialism and the Great War: the collapse of the Second International* (Oxford, 1972).

Hayashima, Akira, *Die Illusion des Sonderfriedens. Deutsche Verständigungspolitik mit Japan im ersten Weltkrieg* (Munich, 1982).

Haycock, Ronald, and Keith Neilson, *Men, machines, and war* (Waterloo, Ont., 1988).

Hayne, M. B., *The French foreign office and the origins of the First World War 1898–1914* (Oxford, 1993).

Haywood, A., and F. A. S. Clarke, *The history of the Royal West African Frontier Force* (Aldershot, 1964).

Hazlehurst, Cameron, 'Asquith as prime minister, 1908–1916', *English Historical Review*, LXXXV (1970), 502–31.

—— *Politicians at war, July 1914 to May 1915: a prologue to the triumph of Lloyd George* (London, 1971).

Headlam, John, *The history of the Royal Artillery from the Indian Mutiny to the Great War*, vol. II 1899–1914 (Woolwich, 1937).

Hecker, Gerhard, *Walther Rathenau und sein Verhältnis zu Militär und Krieg* (Boppard am Rhein, 1983).

Heichen, Walter, *Helden der Kolonien. Der Weltkrieg in unseren Schutzgebieten* (Berlin, n. d.).

Heine, Peter, 'Sâlih ash-Sharîf at-Tûnisi, a North African nationalist in Berlin during the First World War', *Revue de l'Occident Musulman et de la Mediterranée*, 33 (1982), 89–95.

Helfferich, Karl, *Der Weltkrieg* (Karlsruhe, 1925; first published 1919).

—— *Money* (New York, 1969; from the German edn. of 1923).

Heller, Joseph, *British policy towards the Ottoman empire 1908–1914* (London, 1983).

Henderson, W. O., *Studies in German colonial history* (London, 1962).

Hendrick, Burton J., *The life and letters of Walter A. Page* (London, 1930).

Hennig, Richard, *Deutsch-Südwest im Weltkriege* (Berlin, 1920).

Herbillon, Colonel, *Souvenirs d'un officier de liaison pendant la guerre mondiale: du général en chef au gouvernement*, 2 vols. (Paris, 1930).

Herrmann, David, *The arming of Europe and the making of the First World War* (Princeton, 1996).

Herwig, Holger H., 'Admirals versus generals: the war aims of the imperial German navy, 1914–1918', *Central European History*, V (1972), 208–33.

—— 'Clio deceived: patriotic self-censorship in Germany after the Great War', *International Security*, XII (1972), 5–44.

—— *The German naval officer corps: a social and political history 1890–1918* (Oxford, 1973).

—— *'Luxury' fleet: the imperial German navy 1888–1918* (London, 1980).

—— 'From Tirpitz plan to Schlieffen plan: some observations on German military planning', *Journal of Strategic Studies*, IX (1986), 53–63.

—— 'The failure of German sea power, 1914–1945: Mahan, Tirpitz and Raeder reconsidered', *International History Review*, X (1988), 68–105.

—— 'Disjointed allies: coalition warfare in Berlin and Vienna, 1914', *Journal of Military History*, LIV (1990), 265–80.

—— 'The German reaction to the *Dreadnought* revolution', *International History Review*, XIII (1991), 273–83.

—— *The First World War: Germany and Austria-Hungary 1914–1918* (London, 1997).

Herzfeld, Hans, *Der Erste Weltkrieg*, 7th edn. (Munich, 1985; first published 1968).

Hewins, W. A. S., *Apolgia of an imperialist: forty years of empire policy*, 2 vols. (London, 1929).

Hiery, Hermann, 'West Samoans between Germany and New Zealand', *War & Society*, X (1992), 53–80.

—— *The neglected war: the German South Pacific and the influence of World War I* (Honolulu, 1995).

Hiley, Nicholas, 'The failure of British espionage against Germany 1907–1914', *Historical Journal*, XXVI (1983), 867–89.

—— 'The failure of British counter-espionage against Germany, 1907–1914', *Historical Journal*, XXVIII (1985), 835–62.

—— 'Counter-espionage and security in Great Britain during the First World War', *English Historical Review*, CI (1986), 635–70.

Hindenburg, Paul von, *Out of my life* (London, 1920).

Hinsley, F. H., (ed.), *British foreign policy under Sir Edward Grey* (Cambridge, 1977).

Hirschfeld, Gerhard, '1986 regional conference: war and society in modern German history', *German History*, IV (1987), 64–91.

—— Gerd Krumeich, Dieter Langewiesche, and Hans-Peter Ullmann, *Kriegserfahrungen. Studien zur Sozial- und Mentalitatsgeschichte des Ersten Weltkriegs* (Essen, 1997).

Hirschfeld, Magnus, and Andreas Gaspar, *Sittensgeschichte des Weltkrieges*, 2 vols. (Leipzig, 1930).

Hirst, F. W., and J. E. Allen, *British war budgets* (London, 1926).

L'Histoire, 14–18: mourir pour la patrie (Paris, 1992).

Hobson, J. M., 'The military-extraction gap and the wary Titan: the fiscal sociology of British defence policy 1870–1913', *Journal of European Economic History*, XXII (1993), 461–506.

Hodges, G. W. T., 'African manpower statistics for the British forces in East Africa, 1914–1918', *Journal of African History*, XIX (1978), 101–16.

Hodges, Geoffrey, *The carrier corps: military labor in the East African campaign 1914–1918* (Westport, Conn., 1986).

Hoeppner, Ernst von, *L'Allemagne et la guerre de l'air*, (Paris, 1923; first published 1921).

Hoffmann, Max, *War diaries and other papers* (including *The war of lost opportunities*), 2 vols. (London, 1929; first published 1928).

Hoisington, Wiiliam A., jr, *Lyautey and the French conquest of Morocco* (Basingstoke, 1995).

Holmes, Richard, *The little field marshal: Sir John French* (London, 1981).

—— *Riding the retreat: Mons to the Marne 1914 revisited* (London, 1995).

Holmes, Terence M., 'The reluctant March on Paris: a reply to Terence Zuber's 'The Schreffen plan reconsidered', *War in History*, VIII (2001) (forthcoming).

Holtfrerich, Carl-Ludwig, *The German inflation 1914–1923: causes and effects in international perspective* (Berlin, 1986).

Hope, Nicholas, *German and Scandinavian protestantism 1700 to 1918* (Oxford, 1995).

Hopkirk, Peter, *On secret service east of Constantinople: the plot to bring down the British empire* (London, 1994).

Hordern, Charles, *Military operations: East Africa*, vol. I, (London, 1941; no more published).

Hörich, Gerhard, *Die deutsche Seekriegführung im ersten Weltkriegshalbjahr* (Berlin, 1936).

Horn, Martin, 'Alexandre Ribot et la coopération financière anglo-française 1914–1917', *Guerres mondiales et conflits contemporains*, 180 (October 1995), 7–28.

—— 'External finance in Anglo-French relations in the First World War, 1914–1917', *International History Review*, XVII (1995), 51–77.

Horne, John, 'Immigrant workers in France during World War I', *French Historical Studies*, XIV (1985), 57–88.

—— (ed.), *State, society and mobilization in Europe during the First World War* (Cambridge, 1997).

—— and Alan Kramer, 'German "atrocities" and Franco-German opinion, 1914: the evidence of German soldiers' diaries', *Journal of Modern History*, LXVI (1994), 1–33.

Hough, Richard, *The pursuit of Admiral von Spee* (London, 1969).

—— *The Great War at sea 1914–1918* (Oxford, 1986).

House, Jonathan M., 'The decisive attack: a new look at French infantry tactics on the eve of World War I', *Military Affairs*, XXX (1976), 164–9.

Hovanissian, Richard G., *Armenia on the road to independence 1918* (Berkeley, 1967).

Howard, Harry N., *The partition of Turkey: a diplomatic history 1913–1923* (New York, 1966; first published 1931).

Howard, Michael, *The continental commitment: the dilemma of British defence policy in two world wars* (Harmondsworth, 1974; first published 1972).

Huber, Wolfgang, *Kirche und Öffentlichkeit* (Stuttgart, 1973).

Hughes, Daniel J., 'Schlichting, Schlieffen, and the Prussian theory of war in 1914', *Journal of Military History*, LIX (1995), 257–78.

Hughes, Jackson, 'The monstrous anger of the guns: the development of British artillery tactics 1914–1918', Adelaide University Ph.D. thesis, 1992.

Huguet, Victor, *Britain and the war: a French indictment* (London, 1928).

Hull, Isobel V., *The entourage of Kaiser Wilhelm II 1888–1918* (Cambridge, 1982).

Humphreys, Leonard A., *The way of the heavenly sword: the Japanese army in the 1920s* (Stanford, 1995).

Hunt, Barry D., 'The outstanding naval strategic writers of the century', *Naval War College Review*, (Sept.–Oct. 1984), 86–107.

—— and Adrian Preston (eds.), *War aims and strategic policy in the Great War 1914–1918* (London, 1977).

Hüppauf, Bernd, 'Langemarck, Verdun and the myth of a "new man" in Germany after the First World War', *War & Society*, VI (1988), 70–103.

Hyam, Ronald, *The failure of South African expansion 1908–1948* (London, 1972).

Hynes, Samuel, *A war imagined: the First World War and English culture* (London, 1990).

Iklé, Frank W., 'Japanese-German peace negotiations during World War I', *American Historical Review*, LXXI (1965), 62–76.

Iliffe, John, *A modern history of Tanganyika* (Cambridge, 1979).

Ingram, Edward (ed.), *National and international politics in the Middle East: essays in honour of Elie Kedourie* (London, 1986).

Inostransev, M., 'L'Opération de Sarykamych (décembre 1914)', *Revue militaire française*, 164 (février 1933), 193–215.

—— 'La Première poussée allemande sur Varsovie (septembre-octobre 1914): étude stratégique', *Revue militaire française*, 143 (mai 1933), 274–98.

Ironside, Edmund, *Tannenberg: the first thirty days in East Prussia* (Edinburgh, 1925).

Isselin, Henri, *The battle of the Marne* (London, 1965; first published 1964).

Jack, J. L., *General Jack's diary 1914–1918: the trench diary of Brigadier-General J. L. Jack, D. S. O.*, ed. John Terraine (London, 1964).

Jacobsen, Irmgard, 'German attempts to influence the intellectual life in the Ottoman empire during World War I', *Revue d'histoire Maghrebine*, 59–60 (oct. 1990), 95–100.

Jahn, Hubertus F., *Patriotic culture in Russia during World War I* (Ithaca, 1995).

Jansen, Marius B., *The Japanese and Sun Yat-sen* (Cambridge, Mass., 1954).

Janssen, Karl-Heinz, *Der Kanzler und der General. Die Führungkrise um Bethmann Hollweg und Falkenhayn (1914–1916)* (Göttingen, 1967).

Jarausch, Konrad H., 'The illusion of limited war: Chancellor Bethmann Hollweg's calculated risk, July 1914', *Central European History*, II (1969), 48–76.

—— *The enigmatic chancellor: Bethmann Hollweg and the hubris of imperial Germany* (New Haven, 1973).

Jäschke, Gotthard, 'Der Turanismus der Jungtürken. Zur osmanischen Aussenpolitik im Weltkriege', *Die Welt des Islams*, XXIII (1941), 1–54.

—— 'Zum Problem der Marne-Schlacht von 1914', *Historische Zeitschrift*, CXC (1960), 311–48.

Jauffret, Jean-Charles, 'L'Organisation de la réserve à l'époque de la révanche, 1871–1914', *Revue historique des armées*, 174 (1989), 27–37.

Jeffery, Keith, *The British army and the crisis of empire 1918–22* (Manchester, 1984).

Jenkins, Roy, *Asquith* (London, 1964).

Jerabek, Rudolf, *Potiorek. General im Schatten von Sarajevo* (Graz, 1991).

Jèze, Gaston, and Henri Truchy, *The war expenditure of France* (New Haven, 1927).

Jindra, Zdenek, 'Die Rolle des Krupp-Konzerns bei der wirtschaftlichen Vorbereitung des Ersten Weltkrieges', *Jahrbuch für Wirtschaftsgeschichte* (1976), Teil 1, pp. 133–62.

Joffre, J., *Mémoires du Maréchal Joffre (1910–1917)*, 2 vols. (Paris, 1932).

Johnson, Elizabeth (ed.), *The collected writings of John Maynard Keynes*, vol. XVI, *Activities 1914–1919: the Treasury and Versailles* (London, 1971).

Johnson, Franklyn Arthur, *Defence by committee: the British Committee of Imperial Defence 1885–1959* (London, 1960).

Johnson, Jeffrey Allan, *The Kaiser's chemists: science and modernization in imperial Germany* (Chapel Hill, 1990).

Joll, James, *The Second International 1889–1914* (London, 1975).

—— *The origins of the First World War* (London, 1984).

Jones, A. Philip, *Britain's search for Chinese co-operation in the First World War* (New York, 1986).

Jones, Archer, and Andrew J. Keogh, 'The Dreadnought revolution: another look', *Military Affairs*, XLIV (1985), 124–31.

Jones, David, 'Nicholas II and the supreme command: an investigation of motives', *Sbornik*, XI (1985), 47–83.

—— (ed.), *The military-naval encyclopedia of Russia and the Soviet Union* (Gulf Breeze, 1978–).

Jones, Gareth Stedman, 'Working-class culture and working-class politics in London, 1870–1900: notes on the remaking of a working class', *Journal of Social History*, VII (1973–4), 460–508.

Jones, G. Gareth, 'The British government and the oil companies, 1912–1924: the search for an oil policy', *Historical Journal*, XX (1977), 647–72.

Jordan, Gerald (ed.), *Naval warfare in the twentieth century 1900–1945: essays in honour of Arthur Marder* (London, 1977).

Jose, Arthur W., *The Royal Australian Navy 1914–1918* (Sydney, 1935).

Jost, Walter, and Friedrich Folger (eds.), *Was wir vom Weltkrieg nicht wissen* (Leipzig, 1936).

Kaiser, David, 'Germany and the origins of the First World War', *Journal of Modern History*, LV (1983), 442–74.

Kakwenzaire, P. K, 'Sayyid Muhammad Abdille Hassan, Lij Yasu and the World War I politics: 1914–1916', *Transcaspian Journal of History*, XIV (1985), 36–45.

Kann, Robert, Bela K. Kiraly, and Paula S. Fichtner (eds.), *The Habsburg empire in World War I: essays on the intellectual, military, political and economic aspects of the Habsburg war effort* (New York, 1977).

Kaspi, André, 'French war aims in Africa, 1914–1919', in Prosser Gifford and Wm. Roger Louis (eds.), *France and Britain in Africa: imperial rivalry and colonial rule* (New Haven, 1971).

—— *Le Temps des Américains: le concours américain à la France en 1917–1918* (Paris, 1976).

Katzenellenbogen, S. E., 'Southern Africa and the war of 1914–18', in M. R. D. Foot (ed.), *War and society* (London, 1973).

Kautsky, Karl (ed.), *Die deutschen Dokumente zum Kriegsausbruch 1914*, 4 vols. (Berlin, 1922).

Kedourie, Elie, *England and the middle east: the destruction of the Ottoman empire 1914–1921* (London, 1956).

Keegan, John, *The mask of command*, (London, 1987).

—— *The First World War* (London, 1998).

Keiger, John F. V., *France and the origins of the First World War* (London, 1983).

—— 'Jules Cambon and Franco-German détente, 1907–1914', *Historical Journal*, XXVI (1983), 641–59.

Keithly, David M., 'Did Russia also have war aims in 1914?', *East European Quarterly*, XXI (1987), 137–45.

Kelly, R. B. Talbot, *A subaltern's odyssey: a memoir of the Great War 1915–1917* (London, 1980).

Kenez, Peter, 'A profile of the prerevolutionary officer corps', *California Slavic Studies*, VII (1973), 121–58.

Kennedy, Greg, and Keith Neilson (eds.), *Far-flung lines: essays on imperial defence in honour of Donald Mackenzie Schurman* (London, 1997).

Kennedy, Paul, *The rise of the Anglo-German antagonism 1860–1914* (London, 1980).

—— *The rise and fall of the great powers: economic change and military conflict from 1500 to 2000* (London, 1988).

—— (ed.), *The war plans of the great powers 1880–1914* (London, 1979).

Kent, Marian (ed.), *The great powers and the end of the Ottoman empire* (London, 1984).

Kielmansegg, Peter Graf, *Deutschland und der Erste Weltkrieg*, 2nd edn. (Stuttgart, 1980).

Killingray, David, 'Repercussions of World War I on the Gold Coast', *Journal of African History*, XIX (1978), 39–59.

—— 'Beasts of burden: British West African carriers in the First World War', *Canadian Journal of African Studies*, XII (1979), 5–23.

—— 'Labour exploitation for military campaigns in British colonial Africa 1870–1945', *Journal of Contemporary History*, XXIV (1989), 483–501.

Kimche, Jon, *The second Arab awakening* (London, 1970).

King, Jere Clemens, *Generals and politicians: conflict between France's high command, parliament and government, 1914–1918* (Berkeley, 1951).

Kiraly, Bela, Nandor F. Dreisziger, and Albert A. Nofi (eds.), *East Central European society in World War I* (Boulder, Col., 1985).

Kirby, David, *War, peace and revolution: international socialism at the crossroads 1914–1918* (Aldershot, 1986).

Kirkaldy, A. W. (ed.), *British finance during and after the war 1914–21* (London, 1921).

Kitchen, Martin, *The German officer corps 1890–1914* (Oxford, 1968).

—— *The silent dictatorship: the politics of the German high command under Hindenburg and Ludendorff, 1916–1918* (London, 1976).

Kiszling, Rudolf, *Österreich-Ungarns Anteil am Ersten Weltkrieg* (Graz, 1958).

Kjellen, Rudolf, *Die politischen Probleme des Weltkrieges* (Leipzig, 1916).

Klein, Fritz, *Deutschland im ersten Weltkrieg*, 3 vols. (Berlin, 1968).

Klein-Arendt, Reinhard, *'Kamina ruft Nauen!' Die Funkstellen in den deutschen Kolonien 1904–1918* (Ostheim/Rhön, 1996).

Klotz, L.-L., *De la guerre à la paix* (Paris, 1924).

Knauss, Robert, *Die deutsche, englische und französische Kriegsfinanzierung* (Berlin, 1923).

Knox, Alfred, *With the Russian army 1914–1917, being chiefly extracts from the diary of a military attaché*, 2 vols. (London, 1921).

Koch, H. W., (ed.), *The origins of the First World War: great power rivalry and German war aims* (London, 1972); 2nd edn. (1984).

Kocka, Jürgen, *Facing total war: German society 1914–1918* (Leamington Spa, 1984; first published 1973).

Koeltz, L., *La Guerre de 1914–1918: les opérations militaires* (Paris, 1966).

Koss, Stephen, *Asquith* (London, 1976).

Koss, Stephen E., 'The destruction of Britain's last Liberal government', *Journal of Modern History*, XL (1968), 257–77.

Kraft, Heinz, *Staatsräson und Kriegführung im kaiserlichen Deutschland 1914–1916. Der Gegensatz zwischen dem Generalstabschef von Falkenhayn und dem Oberbefehlshaber Ost im Rahmen des Bundniskreiges der Mittelmächte* (Göttingen, 1980).

Krauss, Alfred, *Die Ursachen unserer Niederlage. Erinnerungen und Urteile aus dem Weltkrieg*, 3rd edn. (Munich, 1923).

Kress von Kressenstein, Friedrich, *Mit dem Türken zum Suezkanal* (Berlin, 1938).

Kriegel, Annie, *Le Pain et les roses: jalons pour une histoire des socialismes* (Paris, 1968).

—— and Jean-Jacques Becker, *1914: la patrie et le mouvement ouvrier français* (Paris, 1964).

Krieger, Leonard, and Fritz Stern (eds.), *The responsibility of power: historical essays in honor of Hajo Holborn* (London, 1968).

Kroboth, Rudolf, *Die Finanzpolitik des deutschen Reiches während der Reichskanzlerschaft Bethmann Hollwegs und die Geld und Kapitalmarktverhältnisse (1909–1913/14)* (Frankfurt am Main, 1986).

Krohn, Claus-Dieter, 'Geldtheorien in Deutschland während der Inflation 1914 bis 1924', in Gerald D. Feldman, Carl-Ludwig Holtfrerich, Gerhard A. Ritter, and Peter-Christian Witt (eds.), *Die Anpassung an die Inflation* (Berlin, 1986).

Kronenbitter, Gunther, 'Die Macht der Illusionen. Julikrise und Kriegsausbruch 1914 aus der Sicht des deutschen Militärattachés in Wien', *Militärgeschichtliche Mitteilungen*, 57 (1998), 519–50.

Krumeich, Gerd, *Armaments and politics in France on the eve of the First World War: the introduction of three-year conscription 1913–1914* (Leamington Spa, 1984; first published 1980).

—— *Jeanne d'Arc in der Geschichte. Historiographie—Politik—Kultur* (Sigmaringen, 1989)

Kruse, Wolfgang, 'Die Kriegsbegeisterung im deutschen Reich zu Beginn des Ersten Weltkrieges', in Marcel van der Linden and Gottfried Mergner (eds.), *Kriegsbegeisterung und mentale Kriegsvorbereitung* (Berlin, 1991).

—— *Krieg und nationale Integration: eine Neuinterpretation des sozialdemokratischen Burgfriedensschlusses 1914/15* (Essen, 1993).

—— (ed.), *Eine Welt von Feinden. Der Grosse Krieg 1914–1918* (Frankfurt am Main, 1997).

Kuhl, Hermann, *Le Grand état-major allemand*, ed. Général Douchy (Paris, 1922; first published 1920).

Kühlmann, Richard von, *Erinnerungen* (Heidelberg, 1948).

Labbeke, W., 'The first three months: the campaign of the Belgian army in 1914', *Stand to!* 28 (spring 1990), 20–6.

Lackey, Scott W., *The rebirth of the Habsburg army: Friedrich Beck and the rise of the general staff* (Westport, Conn., 1995).

La Fargue, Thomas Edward, *China and the world war* (Stanford, 1937).

La Gorce, Paul-Marie de (ed.), *La Première Guerre Mondiale*, 2 vols. (Paris, 1991).

Laloy, Émile, 'French military theory 1871–1914 ', *The Military Historian and Economist*, II (1917), 267–86.

Lambert, Nicholas A., 'Admiral Sir John Fisher and the concept of flotilla defence, 1904–1909', *Journal of Military History*, LIX (1995), 639–60.

—— 'British naval policy, 1913–1914: financial limitation and strategic revolution', *Journal of Modern History*, LXVII (1995), 595–626.

—— ' "Our bloody ships" or "our bloody system"? Jutland and the loss of the battle cruisers, 1916', *Journal of Military History*, LXII (1998), 29–55.

Lambi, Ivo Nikolai, *The navy and German power politics, 1862–1914* (Boston, 1984).

Lampe, John R., *The Bulgarian economy in the twentieth century* (London, 1986).

Landau, Jacob M., *Pan-Turkism in Turkey: a study of irridentism* (London, 1981).

—— *The politics of pan-Islam: ideology and organization* (Oxford, 1990).

Langdon, John W., *July 1914: the long debate, 1918–1990* (New York, 1991).

L'Ange, Gerald, *Urgent imperial service: South African forces in German South West Africa 1914–1915* (Rivonia, 1991).

Lange, Karl, *Marneschlacht und deutsche Öffentlichkeit 1914–1939. Eine verdrängte Niederlage und ihre Folgen* (Dusseldorf, 1974).

Lange, Sven, *Hans Delbrück und der 'Strategiestreit': Kriegführung und Kriegsgeschichte in der Kontroverse 1879– 1914* (Freiburg, 1995).

Laqueur, Walter, *Young Germany: a history of the German youth movement* (London, 1962).

Larcher, M., *La Guerre turque dans la guerre mondiale* (Paris, 1926).

—— 'Données statistiques concernant la guerre 1914–1918', *Revue militaire française*, 140 (février 1933), 190–204; 141 (mars 1933), 291–303; 142 (avril 1933), 44–52.

—— 'Données statistiques sur les forces françaises', *Revue militaire française*, 155 (mai 1934), 198–223; 156 (juin 1934), 351–63.

Latzko, Andreas, *Men in battle* (London, 1930; first published 1918).

Lautenschlager, Karl, 'Technology and the evolution of naval warfare', *International security*, VII (1983), 3–51.

Laux, James M., 'Trucks in the west during the First World War', *Journal of Transport History*, 3rd series, VI (1985), 64–70.

Le Bon, Gustave, *The psychology of the Great War* (London, 1916).

Le Révérend, André, *Lyautey* (Paris, 1983).

Leslie, John Duncan, 'Austria-Hungary's eastern policy in the First World War, August 1914 to August 1915', Cambridge University Ph.D. thesis, 1975.

—— 'Österreich-Ungarn vor dem Kriegsausbruch. Der Ballhausplatz in Wien im Juli 1914 aus der Sicht eines österreicher-ungarischen Diplomaten', in Ralph Melville, Claus Scharf, Martin Vogt, and Ulrich Wengenroth (eds.), *Deutschland und Europa in der Neuzeit 2. Halbband* (Stuttgart, 1988).

—— 'The antecedents of Austria-Hungary's war aims: policies and policy-makers in Vienna and Budapest before and during 1914', *Wiener Beiträge zur Geschichte der Neuzeit*, XX (1993), 307–94.

Lettow-Vorbeck, Paul von, *My reminiscences of East Africa*, 2nd edn. (London, [1922]).

Lewis, Bernard, *The emergence of modern Turkey* (London, 1961).

Lewis, Geoffrey, 'The Ottoman proclamation of Jihad in 1914', in *Arabic and Islamic garland: historical, educational and literary papers presented to Abdul-Latif Tibawi* (London, 1977).

Liang, Hsi-Huey, *The rise of modern police and the European state system from Metternich to the Second World War* (Cambridge, 1992).

Lieven, D. C. B., *Russia and the origins of the First World War* (London, 1983).

—— *Nicholas II: emperor of all the Russias* (London, 1993).

Liman von Sanders, Otto, *Five years in Turkey* (Annapolis, 1927; first published 1920).

Lincoln, W. Bruce, *Passage through Armageddon: the Russians in war and revolution 1914–1918* (New York, 1986).

Lindsay, J. H., *The London Scottish in the Great War* (London, 1925).

Linke, Horst Günther, 'Russlands Weg in den Ersten Weltkrieg und seine Kriegsziele 1914–1917', *Militärgeschichtliche Mitteilungen*, 32 (1982), 9–34.

Linnenkohl, Hans, *Vom Einzelschuss zur Feuerwalze. Der Wettlauf zwischen Technik und Taktik im Ersten Weltkrieg* (Bonn, 1996).

Lobanov-Rostovsky, A., *The grinding mill: reminiscences of war and revolution in Russia, 1913–1920* (New York, 1935).

Longley, D. A., 'The Russian Social Democrats' statement to the Duma on 26 July (8 August) 1914: a new look at the evidence', *English Historical Review*, CII (1987), 599–621.

Lotz, Walther, *Die deutsche Staatsfinanzwirtschaft im Kriege* (Stuttgart, 1927).

Louis, Wm. Roger, *Ruanda-Urundi 1884–1919* (Oxford, 1963).

—— *Great Britain and Germany's lost colonies 1914–1919* (Oxford, 1967).

—— 'The origins of the "sacred trust"', in Ronald Segal and Ruth First (eds.), *South West Africa: travesty of trust* (London, 1967).

Lowe, Peter, *Britain and Japan 1911–1915: a study of British far eastern policy* (London, 1969).

Lübbe, Hermann, *Politische Philosophie in Deutschland. Studien zu ihrer Geschichte* (Munich, 1974; first published 1963).

Lucas, Charles (ed.), *The empire at war*, 5 vols. (Oxford, 1921–6).

Lucas, James, *Fighting troops of the Austro-Hungarian army 1868–1914* (Tunbridge Wells, 1987).

Lucas, [P. M. H.], *L'Évolution des idées tactiques en France et en Allemagne pendant la guerre de 1914–1918* (Paris, 1923).

Ludendorff, Erich, *My war memories 1914–1918*, 2 vols. (London, 1919).

—— *Urkunden der obersten Heeresleitung über ihre Tätigkeit 1916–18* (Berlin, 1920).

Lumby, E. W. R. (ed.), *Policy and operations in the Mediterranean 1912–14* (London, 1970).

Lutz, Ralph Haswell (ed.), *Documents of the German revolution: fall of the German empire 1914–1918*, 2 vols. (Stanford, 1932).

Luvaas, Jay, *The education of an army: British military thought, 1815–1940* (London, 1965).

Lyautey, Pierre, *Lyautey l'Africain: textes et lettres du maréchal Lyautey*, 4 vols. (Paris, 1953–7).

Lyon, James M. B., ' "A peasant mob": the Serbian army on the eve of the Great War', *Journal of Military History*, LXI (1997), 481–502.

Lyth, Peter J., *Inflation and the merchant economy: the Hamburg Mittelstand 1914–1924* (New York, 1990).

McCallum, Iain, 'Achilles heel? Propellants and high explosives, 1880–1916', *War Studies Journal*, IV (1999), 65–83.

Macdonald, Catriona M. M., and E. W. McFarland (eds.), *Scotland and the Great War* (East Linton, 1999).

McDonald, David MacLaren, *United government and foreign policy in Russia 1900–1914* (Cambridge Mass., 1992).

McEwen, John M., 'The national press during the First World War: ownership and circulation', *Journal of Contemporary History*, XVII (1982), 459–86.

Macfie, A. L., *The end of the Ottoman empire 1908–1923* (London, 1998).

McGibbon, Ian, *The path to Gallipoli: defending New Zealand 1840–1915* (Wellington, 1991).

McKale, Donald M., ' "The Kaiser's spy": Max von Oppenheim and the Anglo-German rivalry before and during the First World War', *European History Quarterly*, XXVII (1997), 199–219.

—— *War by revolution: Germany and Great Britain in the Middle East in the era of World War I* (Kent, Ohio, 1998).

McKean, Robert B., *St Petersburg between the revolutions: workers and revolutionaries, June 1907–February 1917* (New Haven, 1990).

Mackenzie, S. S., *The Australians at Rabaul: the capture and administration of the German possessions in the South Pacific* (Sydney, 1927).

McKercher, B. J. C., and Keith E. Neilson, ' "The triumph of unarmed forces": Sweden and the allied blockade of Germany, 1914–1917', *Journal of Strategic Studies*, VII (1984), 178–99.

McKibbin, Ross, *The evolution of the Labour party 1910–1924* (Oxford, 1974).

—— 'Why was there no Marxism in Great Britain?, *English Historical Review*, XCIX (1984), 297–331.

McLaughlin, Peter, *Ragtime soldiers: the Rhodesian experience in the First World War* (Bulawayo, 1980).

—— 'Victims or defenders: African troops in the Rhodesian defence system, 1890–1980', *Small Wars and Insurgencies* II (1991), 240–75.

MacMunn, George, *Turmoil and tragedy in India: 1914 and after* (London, 1934).

—— and Cyril Falls, *Military operations: Egypt and Palestine*, 2 vols. (London, 1928–30).

McNeill, William H., *The pursuit of power: technology, armed force, and society since A.D. 1000* (Oxford, 1983).

Maddox, Gregory, ' "Mtunya": famine in central Tanzania, 1917–20', *Journal of African History*, XXXI (1990), 181–97.

Mai, Gunther, *Das Ende des Kaiserreichs. Politik und Kriegführung im Ersten Weltkrieg* (Munich, 1987).

Maier, Charles S., 'Wargames: 1914–1919', *Journal of Interdisciplinary History*, XVIII (1988), 819–49.

Manchester, William, *The arms of Krupp 1587–1968* (London, 1969).

Mann, Thomas, 'Gedanken im Kriege', *Politische Schriften und Reden*, vol. II (Frankfurt am Main, 1960; first published November 1914).

Marder, Arthur J., (ed.), *Fear God and dread nought: the correspondence of Admiral of the Fleet Lord Fisher of Kilverstone*, 3 vols. (London, 1952–9).

Marder, Arthur J., *From the Dreadnought to Scapa Flow: the Royal Navy in the Fisher era, 1904–1919*, 5 vols. (London, 1961–70).

Marine-Archiv (ed.), *Der Krieg zur See 1914–1918. Der Krieg in der Nordsee*, by Otto Groos and Walter Gladisch, 7 vols. (Berlin and Frankfurt am Main, 1920–65).

—— (ed.), *Der Krieg zur See 1914–1918, Der Krieg in der Ostsee*, by Rudolph Firle, Heinrich Rollman, and Ernst von Gagern, 3 vols. (Berlin and Frankfurt am Main, 1922–64).

—— (ed.), *Der Krieg zur See 1914–1918. Der Kreuzerkrieg in den ausländischen Gewässern*, by E. Raeder and Eberhard von Mantey, 3 vols. (Berlin, 1922–37).

—— (ed.), *Der Krieg in den türkischen Gewässern*, 2 vols. (Berlin, 1928–38).

—— (ed.), *Der Krieg zur See 1914–1918. Die Kämpfe der kaiserlichen Marine in den deutschen Kolonien* (Berlin, 1935).

Marquand, David, *Ramsay MacDonald* (London, 1977).

Marquis, Alice Goldfarb, 'Words as weapons: propaganda in Britain and Germany during the First World War', *Journal of Contemporary History*, XIII (1978), 467–98.

Marrin, Albert, *The last crusade: the Church of England in the First World War* (Durham, NC, 1974).

Martin, Germain, *La Situation financière de la France 1914–1924* (Paris, 1924).

—— *Les Finances publiques de la France et la fortune privée (1914–1925)* (Paris, 1925).

Martin, Gregory W., 'Revolutionary projects and racial prejudices: non-military perceptions of the colonial manpower effort', unpublished paper.

Martin, Nicholas, 'Nietzsche under fire', *Times Literary Supplement*, 5 Aug. 1996.

Marwick, Arthur, *The deluge: British society and the First World War* (London, 1965).

Marwitz, Georg von der, *Weltkriegsbriefe*, ed. Gen. von Tschischwitz (Berlin, 1940).

März, Eduard, *Austrian banking and financial policy: Creditanstalt at a turning point 1913–1923* (London, 1984; first published 1981).

Materna, Ingo, and Hans-Joachim Schreckenbach, with Bärbel Holtz, *Dokumente aus geheimen Archiven. Band 4 1914–1918. Berichte des Berliner Polizeipräsidenten zur Stimmung und Lage der Bevölkerung in Berlin 1914–18* (Weimar, 1987).

Matthes, Kurt, *Die 9 Armee im Weichselfeldzuge 1914* (Berlin, 1936).

Matuschka, Edgar Graf von, 'Organisationsgeschichte des Heeres 1890–1918', in Militärgeschichtliche Forschungsamt, *Handbuch zur deutschen Militärgeschichte*, vol. V (Frankfurt am Main, 1968).

Maurer, John H., *The outbreak of the First World War: strategic planning, crisis decision making, and deterrence failure* (Westport, Conn., 1995).

Maurin, Jules, *Armée-Guerre-Société: soldats languedociens (1889–1919)* (Paris, 1982).

Maxon, Robert M., *Struggle for Kenya: the loss and reassertion of imperial initiative 1912–1923* (Cranbury, NJ, 1993).

May, Arthur J., *The passing of the Hapsburg monarchy 1914–1918*, 2 vols. (Philadelphia, 1966).

May, Ernest R., 'American policy and Japan's entrance into World War I', *Mississippi Valley Historical Review*, XL (1953–4), 279–90.

—— (ed.), *Knowing one's enemies: intelligence assessment before the two world wars* (Princeton, 1984).

Meaney, Neville, *The search for security in the Pacific, 1901–14* (Sydney, 1976).

Meinecke, Friedrich, *Strassburg/Freiburg/Berlin 1901–1919: Erinnerungen* (Stuttgart, 1949).

Meinertzhagen, R., *Army diary 1899–1926* (Edinburgh, 1960).

Meintjes, Johannes, *General Louis Botha: a biography* (London, 1970).

Melancon, Michael, *The Socialist Revolutionaries and the Russian anti-war movement, 1914–1917* (Columbus, Ohio, 1990).

Menning, Bruce W., *Bayonets before bullets: the imperial Russian army, 1861–1914* (Bloomington, 1992).

Mentzel, Heinrich, *Die Kämpfe im Kamerun 1914–1916. Vorbereitung und Verlauf* (Berlin, 1936).

Mentzel, Heinz, *Die Kämpfe in Kamerun 1914–1916*, *Münchener historische Abhandlungen: zweite Reihe: Kriegs- und Heeresgeschichte*, 1. Heft (Munich, 1932).

Menu, Ch., 'Les Fabrications de guerre', *Revue militaire française*, 149 (novembre 1933), 180–210.

Messimy, Adolphe, *Mes souvenirs* (Paris, 1937).

Meynier, Gilbert, *L'Algérie révelée: la guerre de 1914–1918 et le premier quart du XXe siècle* (Genève, 1981).

Meynier, O., 'La Guerre sainte des Senoussya en Afrique (1914–1918)', *Revue militaire française*, 131 (mai 1932), 176–204; 138 (decembre 1932), 412–32; 139 (janvier 1933), 121–44; 140 (février 1933), 244–54; 148 (octobre 1933), 120–42; 149 (novembre 1933), 336–53; 152 (février 1934), 214–37; 153 (mars 1934), 399–426.

Michalka, Wolfgang, (ed.), *Der Erste Weltkrieg. Wirkung, Warnehmung, Analyse* (Munich, 1994).

Michel, Bernard, 'L'Autriche et l'entrée dans la guerre en 1914', *Guerres mondiales et conflits contemporains*, 179 (juillet 1995), 5–11.

Michel, Marc, *L'Appel à l'Afrique: contributions et réactions à l'effort de guerre en A.O.F. (1914–1919)* (Paris, 1982).

—— *Gallieni* (Paris, 1989).

—— 'Le Cameroun allemand aurait-il pu rester unifié? Français et Britanniques dans la conquête du Cameroun (1914–1916)', *Guerres mondiales et conflits contemporains*, 168, (octobre 1992), 13–29.

Michelson, Alexander M., Paul N. Apostol, and Michael W. Bernatzky, *Russian public finance during the war* (New Haven, 1928).

Miller, Charles, *Battle for the Bundu: the First World War in East Africa* (London, 1974).

Miller, Geoffrey, *Superior force: the conspiracy behind the escape of 'Goeben' and 'Breslau'* (Hull, 1996).

—— *Straits: British policy towards the Ottoman empire and the origins of the Dardanelles campaign* (Hull, 1997).

Miller, Roger G., 'The logistics of the British Expeditionary Force 1914', *Military Affairs*, XLIII (1979), 133–8.

Miller, Steven E. (ed.), *Military strategy and the origins of the First World War* (Princeton, 1985).

Miller, Susanne, *Burgfrieden und Klassenkampf: die deutsche Sozialdemokratie im Ersten Weltkrieg* (Dusseldorf, 1974).

Millett, Allan R., and Williamson Murray (eds.), *Military effectiveness*, vol. I, *The First World War* (Boston, 1988).

Milner, Susan, *The dilemmas of internationalism: French syndicalism and the international labour movement, 1900–1914* (New York, 1990).

Ministère de la Guerre, État-Major de l'Armée—Service Historique, *Les Armées françaises dans la grande guerre*, 11 vols. (Paris, 1922–37).

Ministry of Munitions, *History of the Ministry of Munitions*, 12 vols. (London, 1922).

Miquel, Pierre, *La Grande Guerre* (Paris, 1983).

Mitchell, Allan, *Victors and vanquished: the German influence on army and church in France after 1870* (Chapel Hill, 1984).

Mitchell, Donald W., *A history of Russian and Soviet sea power* (London, 1974).

Mitchell, T. J., and G. M. Smith, *Medical services: casualties and medical statistics of the Great War* (London, 1997; first published 1931).

Moberly, F. J., *Military operations: the campaign in Mesopotamia*, 4 vols. (London, 1923–7).

—— *Military operations: Togoland and the Cameroons 1914–1916* (London, 1931).

Mollin, Volker, *Auf dem Wege zur 'Materialschlacht'. Vorgeschichte und Funktionen des Artillerie-Industrie-Komplexes im deutschen Kaiserreich* (Pfaffenweiler, 1986).

Mombauer, Annika, 'Helmuth von Moltke and the German general staff—military and political decision-making in imperial Germany, 1906–1916', Sussex University D. Phil thesis, 1997.

—— 'A reluctant military leader? Helmuth von Moltke and the July crisis of 1914', *War in History*, VI (1999), 417–46.

Mommsen, Wolfgang, 'Domestic factors in German foreign policy before 1914', *Central European History*, VI (1973), 3–43.

—— 'Society and war: two new analyses of the First World War', *Journal of Modern History*, XLVII (1975), 530–8.

—— *Max Weber and German politics 1890–1920* (Chicago, 1984; first published 1959).

—— *Imperial Germany 1867–1918: politics, culture, and society in an authoritarian state* (London, 1995).

Le Monde, La Trés Grande Guerre (Paris, 1994).

Monson, Jamie, 'Relocating Maji Maji: the politics of alliance and authority in the southern highlands of Tanzania', *Journal of African History*, XXXIX (1998), 95–120.

Moreman, T. R., *The army in India and the development of frontier warfare, 1849–1947* (Basingstoke, 1998).

Morgan, E. Victor, *Studies in British financial policy 1914– 25* (London, 1952).

Morgan, Kenneth O., *Lloyd George* (London, 1974).

Morgenthau, Henry, *Ambassador Morgenthau's story,* (New York, 1919).

Morris, A. J. A., *The scaremongers: the advocacy of war and rearmament 1896–1914* (London, 1984).

Moser, Otto von, *Feldzugsaufzeichnungen 1914–1918* (Stuttgart, 1928).

Moses, John A., 'The British and German churches and the perception of war, 1908– 1914', *War & Society*, V (1987), 23–44.

—— 'The Great War as ideological conflict—an Australian perspective', *War & Society,* VII (1989), 56–76.

—— 'The "ideas of 1914" in Germany and Australia: a case of conflicting perceptions', *War & Society,* IX (1991), 61–82.

Mosley, Leonard, *Duel for Kilimanjaro: an account of the East African campaign 1914– 1918* (London, 1963).

Moukbil bey, M., *Le Campagne de l'Irak 1914–1918: le siège de Kut-el-Amara* (Paris, 1933).

Moulton, H. Fletcher, *The life of Lord Moulton* (London, 1922).

Moyer, Laurence V., *Victory must be ours: Germany in the Great War 1914–1918* (New York, 1995).

Moyse-Barlett, H., *The King's African Rifles: a study in the military history of east and central Africa, 1890–1945* (Aldershot, 1956).

Mühlmann, Carl, *Deutschland und die Türkei 1913– 1914. Die Berufung der deutschen Militärmission nach der Türkei 1913, das deutsch–türkische Bündnis 1914 und der Eintritt der Türkei in den Weltkrieg* (Berlin-Grunewald, 1929).

—— *Das deutsch–türkische Waffenbündnis im Weltkriege* (Leipzig, 1940).

—— *Oberste Heeresleitung und Balkan im Weltkrieg 1914–1918* (Berlin, 1942).

Müller, Christian, 'Anmerkungen zur Entwicklung von Kriegsbild und operativ-strategischen Szenario im preussisch-deutschen Heer vor dem Ersten Weltkrieg', *Militärgeschichtliche Mitteilungen,* 57 (1998), 385–442.

Müller, Herbert Landolin, *Islam, Gihad ('Heiliger Krieg') und deutsches Reich. Ein Nachspiel zur wilhelminischen Weltpolitik im Maghreb 1914–1918* (Frankfurt am Main, 1991).

Müller, Stefan von, *Die finanzielle Mobilmachung Österreichs und ihr Ausbau bis 1918* (Berlin, 1918).

Murfett, Malcolm H. (ed.), *The First Sea Lords: from Fisher to Mountbatten* (Westport, Conn., 1995).

—— and John N. Miksic, Brian P. Farrell, Chiang Ming Shun, *Between two oceans: a military history of Singapore from the first settlement to British withdrawal* (Oxford, 1999).

Musil, Robert, *The man without qualities*, 3 vols. (London, 1979).

Myers, Ramon H., and Mark R. Peattie (eds.), *The Japanese colonial empire, 1895–1945* (Princeton, 1984).

Nasson, Bill, 'A great divide: popular responses to the Great War in South Africa', *War & Society*, XII (1994), 47–64.

—— 'War opinion in South Africa, 1914', *Journal of Imperial and Commonwealth History*, XXIII (1995), 248–76.

Naumann, Friedrich, *Werke*, vol. IV, *Schriften zum Parteiwesen und zum Mitteleuropaproblem*, ed. Theodor Schieder (Cologne, 1964).

Naveh, Shimon, *In pursuit of military excellence: the evolution of operational theory* (London, 1997).

Neilson, Keith, 'Russian foreign purchasing in the Great War: a test case', *Slavonic and East European Review*, LX (1982), 572–90.

—— *Strategy and supply: the Anglo-Russian alliance, 1914–17* (London, 1984).

—— 'Watching the "steamroller": British observers and the Russian army before 1914', *Journal of Strategic Studies*, VIII (1985), 199–217.

—— ' "My beloved Russians": Sir Arthur Nicolson and Russia, 1906–1916', *International History Review*, IX (1987), 521–54.

—— ' "That dangerous and difficult enterprise": British military thinking and the Russo-Japanese war', *War & Society*, IX (1991), 17–37.

—— *Britain and the last Tsar: British policy and Russia 1894–1917* (Oxford, 1995).

Nekrasov, George, *North of Gallipoli: the Black Sea fleet at war, 1914–1917* (Boulder, Col., 1992).

Nettl, J. P., 'The German Social Democratic Party 1890–1914 as a political model', *Past and Present*, 30 (1965), 65–95.

—— *Rosa Luxemburg*, 2 vols. (London, 1966).

Neulen, Hans Werner, *Feldgrau in Jerusalem. Das Levantekorps des kaiserlichen Deutschland* (Munich, 1991).

Nevakivi, Jukka, *Britain, France and the Arab middle east 1914– 1920* (London, 1969).

Newbury, Colin, 'Spoils of war: sub-imperial collaboration in South West Africa and New Guinea', *Journal of Imperial and Commonwealth History*, XVI (1988), 86–106.

Newell, Jonathan Quentin Calvin, 'British military policy in Egypt and Palestine, August 1914–June 1917', London University Ph.D. thesis, 1989.

Nish, Ian H., *Alliance in decline: a study in Anglo-Japanese relations 1908–23* (London, 1972).

—— *Japanese foreign policy, 1869–1942; Kasumigaseki to Miyakezaka* (London, 1977).

Nobécourt, R. G., *Fantassins du Chemin de Dames* (Paris, 1965).

Nogales, Rafael de, *Four years beneath the crescent* (London, 1926).

Northern Arts and Scottish Arts Council, *Futurismo 1909–1919: exhibition of Italian Futurism* (Newcastle and Edinburgh, 1972).

Nouailhat, Yves-Henri, 'Un emprunt français au États-unis en juillet 1916: l'emprunt de l'American Foreign Securities Company', *Revue d'histoire moderne et contemporaine*, XIV (1967), 356–74.

—— *France et États-unis août 1914–avril 1917* (Paris, 1979).

Noyes, Alexander D., *The war period of American finance 1908– 1925* (New York, 1926).

O'Brien, Phillips Payson, *British and American naval power: politics and policy, 1900–1936* (Westport, Conn., 1998).

—— (ed.) *Preparing for the next war at sea: technology and naval combat in the twentieth century* (London, 2001).

Occleshaw, Michael, *Armour against fate: intelligence in the First World War* (London, 1989).

Oelhafen, Hans von, *Der Feldzug in Südwest* (Berlin, [1923]).

Offer, Avner, 'The working classes, British naval plans and the coming of the Great War', *Past and Present*, CVII (1985), 204–26.

—— 'Morality and Admiralty: "Jacky" Fisher, economic warfare and the laws of war', *Journal of Contemporary History*, XXIII (1988), 99–119.

—— *The First World War: an agrarian interpretation* (Oxford, 1989).

—— 'Going to war in 1914: a matter of honor', *Politics and Society*, XXIII (1995), 213–41.

Olphe-Galliard, G., *Histoire économique et financière de la guerre (1914–1918)* (Paris, 1923).

Olson, William J., *Anglo-Iranian relations during World War I* (London, 1984).

Omissi, David, *The Sepoy and the Raj: the Indian Army, 1860–1940* (Basingstoke, 1994).

Österreichisches Bundesministerium für Heereswesen und vom Kriegsarchiv, *Österreich-Ungarns letzter Krieg 1914–1918*, ed. Edmund Glaise von Horstenau, 7 vols. (Vienna, 1931–8).

Osuntokun, Akinjide, *Nigeria in the First World War*, London, 1979).

Ott, Hugo, 'Kriegswirtschaft und Wirtschaftskrieg 1914–1918: verdeutlicht an Beispielen aus dem badisch-elsässischen Raum', in Erich Hassinger, J. Heinz Müller, and Hugo Ott (eds.), *Geschichte. Wirtschaft. Gesellschaft* (Berlin, 1974).

Overlack, Peter, 'Australian defence awareness and German naval planning in the Pacific 1900–1914', *War & Society*, X (1992), 37–51.

—— 'German interest in Australian defence, 1901–1914: new insights into a precarious position on the eve of war', *Australian Journal of Politics and History*, XL (1994), 36–51.

—— 'The force of circumstance: Graf Spee's options for the East Asia cruiser squadron in 1914', *Journal of Military History*, LX (1996), 657–82.

—— 'Australasia and Germany: challenge and response before 1914', in David Stevens (ed.), *Maritime power in the 20th century: the Australian experience* (St Leonards NSW, 1998).

—— 'Asia in German naval planning before the First World War: the strategic imperative', *War & Society*, XVII (1999), 1–23.

Overstraeten, R. von (ed.), *The war diaries of Albert I, king of the Belgians* (London, 1954).

Overton, John, 'War and economic development: settlers in Kenya, 1914–1918', *Journal of African History*, XXVII (1986), 79–103.

Owen, Gail L., 'Dollar diplomacy in default: the economics of Russian–American relations, 1910–1917', *Historical Journal*, XIII (1970), 251–72.

Oxford Faculty of Modern History, *Why we are at war: Great Britain's case*, 3rd edn. (Oxford, 1914).

Page, Melvin E., 'The war of *Thangata*: Nyasaland and the East African campaign, 1914–1918', *Journal of African History*, XIX (1978), 87–100.

—— '"With Jannie in the jungle": European humour in an East African campaign, 1914–1918', *International Journal of African Historical Studies*, XIV (1981), 466–81.

—— (ed.), *Africa and the First World War* (London, 1987).

Palat, Général [Pierre Lehautcourt], 'German military theory at the outbreak of the war', *The Military historian and economist*, II (1917), 357–71.

—— *La Grande Guerre sur le front occidental*, 14 vols. (Paris, 1917–29).

Panayi, Panikos, *The enemy in our midst: Germans in Britain during the First World War* (New York, 1991).

Panichas, George A. (ed.), *Promise of greatness: the war of 1914–1918* (London, 1968).

Pares, Bernard, *Day by day with the Russian army 1914–15* (London, 1915).

—— *The fall of the Russian monarchy: a study of the evidence* (London, 1939).

Paret, Peter (ed.), with Gordon Craig and Felix Gilbert, *Makers of modern strategy from Machiavelli to the nuclear age* (Oxford, 1986).

Parrini, Carl, *Heir to empire: United States economic diplomacy 1916–1923* (Pittsburgh, 1969).

Parry, Cyril, 'Gwynedd and the Great War', *Welsh History Review*, XIV (1988), 78–117.

Paskauskas, R. Andrew (ed.), *The complete correspondence of Sigmund Freud and Ernest Jones 1908–1939* (Cambridge, Mass., 1993).

Patterson, A. Temple, *Jellicoe: a biography* (London, 1969).

Pavlovich, N. B., *The fleet in the First World War*, vol. 1, *Operations of the Russian fleet* (New Delhi, 1979; first published, Moscow, 1964).

Pearson, Raymond, *The Russian moderates and the crisis of Tsarism 1914–1917* (London, 1977).

Pearton, Maurice, *The knowledgeable state: diplomacy, war and technology since 1830* (London, 1982).

Peattie, Mark R., *Nanyo: the rise and fall of the Japanese in Micronesia* (Honolulu, 1988).

Peball, Kurt, 'Der Feldzug gegen Serbien und Montenegro im Jahre 1914: Armee zwischen Tragik und Grösse', *Österreichische militärische Zeitschrift*, Sonderheft 1 (1965), 18–31.

—— (ed.), *Conrad von Hötzendorf. Private Aufzeichnungen: erste Veröffentlichungen aus den Papieren des k.u.k. Generalstabs-Chefs* (Vienna, 1977).

Pedroncini, Guy, *Les mutineries de 1917* (Paris, 1967).

—— 'Stratégie et relations internationales: la séance du 9 janvier 1912 du conseil supérieur de la défense nationale', *Revue d'histoire diplomatique*, XCI (1977), 143–58.

—— (ed.), *Histoire militaire de la France*. Tome III, *De 1871 à 1940* (Paris, 1992).

Pélissier, René, 'Campagnes militaires au Sud-Angola (1885–1915), *Cahiers d'études africaines*, IX (1969), 54–123.

—— *Les Guerres grises: résistance et révoltes en Angola (1845–1941)* (Orgeval, 1977).

—— *Naissance du Mozambique: résistance et révoltes anticoloniales (1854–1918)*, 2 vols. (Orgeval, 1984).

Perham, Margery, *Lugard: the years of authority 1898–1945* (London, 1960).

Perkins, Kenneth J., *Tunisia: crossroads of the Islamic and European worlds* (Boulder, Col., 1986).

Perrins, Michael, 'The council for state defence 1905–1909: a study in Russian bureaucratic politics', *Slavonic and East European Review*, LVIII (1980), 370–98.

Peters, John, 'The British government and the City–industry divide: the case of the 1914 financial crisis', *Twentieth Century British History*, IV (1993), 126–48.

Petit, Lucien, *Histoire des finances extérieures de la France pendant la guerre (1914–1919)* (Paris, 1929).

Petrovich, Michael Boris, *A history of modern Serbia 1804–1918*, 2 vols. (New York, 1976).

Pfeilschifter, Georg (ed.), *Deutsche Kultur, Katholizismus und Weltkrieg: eine Abwehr des Buches La Guerre allemande et le Catholicisme* (Freiburg im Breisgau, 1915).

Philbin, Tobias R., *Admiral von Hipper: the inconvenient hero* (Amsterdam, 1982).

Philpott, William J., 'The strategic ideas of Sir John French', *Journal of Strategic Studies*, XII (1989), 458–78.

—— 'Origines et signification de la stratégie britannique du "flanc nord"', *Guerres mondiales et conflits contemporains*, 180 (octobre 1995), 47–63.

—— *Anglo-French relations and strategy on the western front, 1914–1918* (Basingstoke, 1996).

Pick, Daniel, *War machine: the rationalization of slaughter in the modern age* (New Haven, 1993).

Pigou, A. C., *The political economy of war* (London, 1921).

Pitreich, Max von, *1914. Die militärischen Probleme unseres Kriegsbeginnes. Ideen, Gründe und Zusammenhänge* (Vienna, 1934).

Plaut, Paul, 'Psychographie des Kriegers', *Beihefte zur Zeitschrift für angewandte Psychologie*, XXI (1920), 1–123.

Pochhammer, Hans, *Before Jutland: Admiral von Spee's last voyage: Coronel and the battle of the Falklands* (London, 1931).

Pogge von Strandmann, Hartmut (ed.), *Walther Rathenau: industrialist, banker, intellectual, and politician. Notes and diaries 1907–1922* (Oxford, 1985; first published 1967).

Pokrowski, M. N. (ed.), *Die internationalen Beziehungen im Zeitalter des Imperialismus*, ed. Otto Hoetsch, series 1, ii (Berlin, 1933).

Pomiankowski, Joseph, *Der Zusammenbruch des Ottomanischen Reiches. Erinnerungen an die Türkei aus der Zeit des Weltkrieges* (Vienna, 1928).

Popovics, Alexander, *Das Geldwesen im Kriege* (Vienna, 1925).

Popplewell, Richard, 'British intelligence in Mesopotamia 1914–1916', *Intelligence and National Security*, V (1990), 139–72.

—— 'British intelligence and Indian subversion: the surveillance of Indian revolutionaries in India and abroad 1904–1920', Cambridge University Ph.D. thesis, 1988; published as *Intelligence and imperial defence: British intelligence and the defence of the Indian empire, 1904–1924* (London, 1995).

Porch, Douglas, *The march to the Marne: the French army 1871–1914* (Cambridge, 1981).

—— *The conquest of the Sahara* (London, 1985; first published 1984).

—— *The conquest of Morocco* (London, 1986; first published 1982).

—— 'The Marne and after: a reappraisal of French strategy in the First World War', *Journal of Military History*, LIII (1989), 363–85.

Poseck, M. von, *Die deutsche Kavallerie 1914 in Belgien und Frankreich*, 4th edn. (Berlin, 1930).

Pourcher, Yves, *Les Jours de guerre: la vie des français au jour le jour 1914–1918* (Paris, 1994).

Prasad, Yuvaraj Dera, *The Indian Muslims and World War I: a phase of disillusionment with British rule 1914–1918* (New Delhi, 1985).

Pressel, Wilhelm, *Die Kriegspredigt 1914–1918 in der evangelischen Kirche Deutschlands* (Göttingen, 1967).

Prete, Roy A., 'French strategic planning and the deployment of the B.E.F. in France in 1914', *Canadian Journal of History*, XXIV (1989), 42–62.

Prior, Robin, *Churchill's 'World Crisis' as history* (London, 1983).

—— and Trevor Wilson, *Command on the western front: the military career of Sir Henry Rawlinson 1914–1918* (Oxford, 1992).

Pugh, Martin, *The making of modern British politics 1867–1939* (Oxford, 1982).

Pürschel, Herbert, *Die kaiserliche Schutztruppe für Kamerun. Gefüge und Aufgabe* (Berlin, 1936).

Quinn, Frederick, 'An African reaction to World War I: the Beti of Cameroon', *Cahiers d'études africaines*, XIII (1973), 722–31.

Raithel, Thomas, *Das 'Wunder' der inneren Einheit. Studien zur deutschen und französischen Öffentlichkeit bei Beginn des Ersten Weltkrieges* (Bonn, 1996).

Ranger, T. O., 'Revolt in Portuguese east Africa: the Makombe rising of 1917', *St Antony's Papers*, 15 (1963), 54–80.

—— *Dance and society in eastern Africa, 1890–1970: the Beni 'Ngoma'* (London, 1975).

Raschke, Martin, *Der politisierende Generalstab: die friderizianischen Kriege in der amtliche deutschen Militärgeschichtsschreibung 1890–1914* (Freiburg, 1993).

Rathbone, Richard, 'World War I and Africa: an introduction', *Journal of African History*, XIX (1978), 1–9.

Rathmann, Lothar, *Stossrichtung Nahost 1914–1918: zur Expansionpolitik des deutschen Imperialismus im ersten Weltkrieg* (Berlin, 1963).

Ratinaud, Jean, *La Course à la mer de la Somme aux Flandres (14 septembre–17 novembre 1914)* (Paris, 1967).

Rauchensteiner, Manfred, *Der Tod des Doppeladlers. Österreich-Ungarn und der Erste Weltkrieg* (Graz, 1993).

Raynaud-Lacroze, E., *Méharistes au combat* (Paris, 1983).

Reader, W. J., *Imperial Chemical Industries: a history*, 2 vols. (London, 1970).

Reboul, C., *Mobilisation industrielle*. Tome 1, *Des fabrications de guerre en France de 1914 à 1918* (Paris, 1925).

Redlich, Joseph, *Austrian war government* (New Haven, 1929).

Regele, Oskar, *Feldmarschall Conrad. Auftrag und Erfüllung 1906–1918* (Vienna, 1955).

Reichsarchiv, *Der Weltkrieg, 1914 bis 1918*, 14 vols. (Berlin, 1925–44).

—— *Der Weltkrieg. Kriegsrüstung und Kriegswirtschaft*, 2 vols. (Berlin, 1930).

Reinharz, Jehuda, 'Science in the service of politics: the case of Chaim Weizmann during the First World War', *English Historical Review*, C (1985), 572–603.

Reith, John, *Wearing spurs* (London, 1966).

Reitz, Denys, *Trekking on* (London, 1933).

Renouvin, Pierre, *The forms of war government in France* (New Haven, 1927).

—— 'La politique des emprunts étrangers aux Etats–Unis de 1914 à 1917', *Annales: économies—societés—civilisations*, VI (1951), 289–305.

—— *La Crise européenne et la première guerre mondiale (1904–1918)*, 6th edn. (Paris, 1969).

Renzi, William A., 'Great Britain, Russia, and the straits, 1914–1915', *Journal of Modern History*, XLII (1970), 1–20.

—— 'Who composed "Sazonov's Thirteen Points"? A re-examination of Russia's war aims of 1914', *American Historical Review*, LXXXVIII (1983), 347–57.

[Repington, Charles à Court], *Essays and criticisms*, by the military correspondent of *The Times* (London, 1911).

Ribeiro de Meneses, Filipo, 'Too serious a matter to be left to the generals? Parliament and the army in wartime Portugal, 1914–18', *Journal of Contemporary History*, XXXIII (1998), 85–96.

Ribot, Alexandre, *Letters to a friend: recollections of my political life* (London, [*c.* 1925]).

—— *Journal d'Alexandre Ribot et correspondances inédites 1914–1922* (Paris, 1936), edited by A. Ribot.

Riedl, Richard, *Die Industrie Österreichs während des Krieges* (Vienna, 1932).

Riezler, Kurt, *Kurt Riezler. Tagebücher, Aufsätze, Dokumente*, ed. Karl Dietrich Erdmann (Göttingen, 1972).

Ringer, Fritz K., *The decline of the German mandarins: the German academic community, 1890–1933* (Hanover, NH, 1990; first published 1969).

Ripperger, Robert M., 'The development of the French artillery for the offensive 1890–1914', *Journal of Military History*, LIX (1995), 599–618.

Ritter, Gerhard, *The Schlieffen plan: critique of a myth* (London, 1958; first published 1956).

—— *The sword and the sceptre: the problem of militarism in Germany*, 4 vols. (London, 1970–3).

Rivet, Daniel, *Lyautey et l'institution du protectorat français au Maroc 1912–1925*, 3 vols. (Paris, 1988).

Robbins, Keith, *The First World War* (Oxford, 1984).

Robert, Jean-Louis, *Les Ouvriers, la patrie et la révolution: Paris 1914–1919* (Paris, 1995).

Roberts, A. D. (ed.), *The Cambridge History of Africa*, vol. 7, *1905–1940* (Cambridge, 1986).

Roberts, Richard, *Schröders: merchants and bankers* (Basingstoke, 1992).

Robinson, Ronald, and John Gallagher, with Alice Denny, *Africa and the Victorians: the official mind of imperialism* (London, 1961).

Rocolle, Pierre, *2000 ans de fortification française*, 2 vols. (Paris, 1973).

—— *L'hécatombe des généraux* (Paris, 1980).

Rodger, N. A. M. (ed.), *Naval power in the twentieth century* (Basingstoke, 1996).

Roesler, Konrad, *Die Finanzpolitik des deutschen Reiches im Ersten Weltkrieg* (Berlin, 1967).

Rogger, Hans, 'Russia in 1914', *Journal of Contemporary History*, I (1966), 95–119.

Rohkrämer, Thomas, *Der Militarismus der 'kleinen Leute'. Die Kriegsvereine im Deutschen Kaiserreich* (Munich, 1990).

Röhl, John C. G., 'Admiral von Müller and the approach of war, 1911–1914', *Historical Journal*, XII (1969), 651–73.

—— *The Kaiser and his court: Wilhelm II and the government of Germany* (Cambridge, 1994).

—— (ed.), *1914: delusion or design? The testimony of two German diplomats* (London, 1973).

—— (ed.), with Elisabeth Müller-Luckner, *Der Ort Kaiser Wilhelms II in der deutsche Geschichte* (Munich, 1991).

—— and Nicolaus Sombart (eds.), *Kaiser Wilhelm II: new interpretations* (Cambridge, 1982).

Rohrbeck, Major, *Taktik. Ein Handbuch auf Grund der Erfahrungen des Weltkrieges* (Berlin, 1919).

Rohwer, Jürgen (ed.), *Neue Forschungen zum Ersten Weltkrieg* (Koblenz, 1985).

Rommel, Erwin, *Attacks* (Vienna, Va. 1979; first published 1937).

Roosa, Ruth Amenda, 'Russian industrialists during World War I: the interaction of economics and politics', in Gregory Guroff and Fred V. Carstensen (eds.), *Entrepreneurship in imperial Russia and the Soviet Union* (Princeton, 1983).

Rosenberg, Arthur, *The birth of the German republic 1871–1918* (New York, 1962; first published 1931).

Rosenberger, Bernhard, *Zeitungen als Kriegstreiber? Die Rolle der Presse im Vorfeld des Ersten Weltkrieges* (Cologne, 1998).

Roskill, Stephen, *Hankey: man of secrets*, 3 vols. (London, 1970).

Roskill, Stephen, *Admiral of the Fleet Earl Beatty: the last naval hero: an intimate biography* (London, 1980).

Rothenberg, Gunther, *The army of Francis Joseph* (West Lafayette, 1976).

—— 'The Austro-Hungarian campaign against Serbia in 1914', *Journal of Military History*, LIII (1989), 127–46.

Rothwell, V. H., 'The British government and Japanese military assistance 1914–1918', *History*, LVI (1971), 35–45.

—— *British war aims and peace diplomacy 1914–1918* (Oxford, 1971).

Rouquerol, Gabriel, *Le Canon: artisan de la victoire* (Nancy, [*c.* 1920]).

Rubanowicz, Robert J., *Crisis in consciousness: the thought of Ernst Troeltsch* (Tallahassee, 1982).

Rumbold, Algernon, *Watershed in India 1914–1922* (London, 1979).

Rupprecht von Bayern, Kronprinz, *Mein Kriegstagebuch*, ed. Eugen von Frauenholz, 3 vols. (Munich, 1929).

Rürup, Reinhard, 'Der "Geist von 1914" in Deutschland. Kriegsbegeisterung und Idolisierung des Krieges im Ersten Weltkrieg', in Bernd Hüppauf (ed.), *Ansichten vom Krieg: vergleichende Studien zum Ersten Weltkrieg im Literatur und Gesellschaft* (Königstein, 1984).

Rustow, Dankwart A., 'The army and the founding of the Turkish republic', *World Politics*, XI (1959), 513–52.

Ryan, Stephen, *Pétain the soldier* (Cranbury, NJ, 1969).

Ryder, A. J., *The German revolution of 1918: a study of German socialism in war and revolt* (Cambridge, 1967).

Saatmann, Inge, *Parlament, Rüstung und Armee in Frankreich, 1914/18* (Dusseldorf, 1978).

Sackett, Robert Eben, *Popular entertainment, class, and politics in Munich, 1900–1923* (Cambridge Mass., 1982).

Samuels, Martin, *Command or control? Command, training and tactics in the British and German armies, 1888–1918* (London, 1995).

—— 'Directive command and the German general staff', *War in History*, II (1995), 22–42.

Sanborn, Josh, 'The mobilization of 1914 and the question of the Russian nation: a reexamination', *Slavic Review*, LIX (2000), 267–89.

Sanders, Michael, and Philip M. Taylor, *British propaganda during the First World War 1914–18* (London, 1982).

Santorini, Alberto, 'The first Ultra secret: the British cryptanalysis in the naval operations of the First World War', *Revue internationale d'histoire militaire*, 63 (1985), 99–110.

Sareen, Tilan Raj, *Indian revolutionary movements abroad (1905–1921)* (New Delhi, 1979).

Savage, Donald C., and J. Forbes Munro, 'Carrier corps recruitment in the British East Africa Protectorate 1914–1918', *Journal of African History*, VII (1966), 313–42.

Sayers, R. S., *The Bank of England 1891–1944*, 2 vols. (Cambridge, 1966).

Scham, Alan, *Lyautey in Morocco: protectorate administration, 1912–1925* (Berkeley, 1970).

Scheibe, Friedrich Carl, 'Marne und Gorlice: zum Kriegsdeutung Hans Delbrücks', *Militärgeschichtliche Mitteilungen*, 53 (1994), 355–76.

Scheler, Max, *Das Genius des Krieges und der Deutsche Krieg*, in *Politische-Pädagogische Schriften*, ed. Manfred S. Fring (Bern, 1982; first published 1915).

Schencking, J. Charles, 'Bureaucratic politics, military budgets, and Japan's southern advance: the imperial navy's seizure of German Micronesia in World War I', *War in History*, V (1998), 308–26.

Schindler, John, ' "There is no withdrawal": the Austro-Hungarian army in Serbia, 1914', *War in History*, forthcoming.

Schmidt, Martin E., *Alexandre Ribot: odyssey of a liberal in the Third Republic* (The Hague, 1974).

Schmidt-Richberg, Wiegand, 'Die Regierungszeit Wilhelms II', in Militärgeschichtliche Forschungsamt, *Handbuch zur deutschen Militärgeschichte*, vol. V (Frankfurt am Main, 1968).

Schnee, Heinrich, *Deutsch-Ostafrika im Weltkriege: wie wir lebten und kämpften* (Leipzig, 1919).

Schoen, Erich, *Geschichte des deutschen Feuerwerkswesens der Armee und Marine mit Einschluss des Zeugwesens* (Berlin, 1936).

Schöllgen, Gregor, *Escape into war? The foreign policy of imperial Germany* (Oxford, 1990).

Schorske, Carl E., *German social democracy 1905–1917: the development of the great schism* (New York, 1955).

Schubert-Weller, Christoph, *'Kein schönrer Tod...' Die Militarisierung der männlichen Jugend und ihr Einsatz im Ersten Weltkrieg 1890–1918* (Weinheim, 1998).

Schulte, Bernd F., *Die deutsche Armee 1900–1914: zwischen beharren und verändern* (Dusseldorf, 1977).

—— *Vor dem Kriegsausbruch 1914. Deutschland, die Türkei und der Balkan* (Dusseldorf, 1980).

—— *Europäische Krise und Erster Weltkrieg. Beitrage zur Militärpolitik des Kaiserreichs, 1871–1914* (Frankfurt am Main, 1983).

Schwabe, Klaus, *Wissenschaft und Kriegsmoral. Die deutschen Hochschullehrer und die politischen Grundfragen des Ersten Weltkrieges* (Göttingen, 1969).

Schwarte, Max, *Die Technik im Weltkriege* (Berlin, 1920).

—— (ed.), *Technik des Kriegswesens* (Leipzig, 1913).

—— (ed.), *Der Weltkrieg in seiner Einwirkung auf das deutsche Volk* (Leipzig, 1918).

—— (ed.), *Der Weltkampf um Ehre und Recht*, 10 vols. (Leipzig, 1921–33); first published as *Der grosse Krieg 1914/18* (Leipzig, 1921).

—— (ed.), *Die militärischen Lehren des grossen Krieges*, 1st edn. (Berlin, 1920); 2nd edn. (Berlin, 1923).

Schwarzmüller, Theo, *Zwischen Kaiser und 'Führer'. Generalfeldmarschall August von Mackensen: eine politische Biographie* (Paderborn, 1995).

Scott, Ernest, *Australia during the war* (Sydney, 1940; first published 1936).

Scott, J. D., *Vickers: a history* (London, 1962).

Scott, Peter T., 'Mr Stokes and his educated drain-pipe', *Army Quarterly*, CXI (1981), 209–28.

Seabourne, Teresa, 'The summer of 1914', in Forrest Capie and Geoffrey E. Wood (eds.), *Financial crises and the world banking system* (Basingstoke, 1986).

Sebald, Peter, *Togo 1884–1914. Eine Geschichte der deutschen 'Musterkolonie' auf der Grundlage amtlichen Quellen* (Berlin, 1988).

Seince, Pierre, 'La Veillée d'armes, 4 septembre 1914', *Revue historique des armées*, 172 (septembre 1988), 9–15.

Seitz, Theodor, *Südafrika im Weltkriege* (Berlin, 1920).

Self, Robert C. (ed.), *The Austen Chamberlain diary letters: the correspondence of Sir Austen Chamberlain with his sisters Hilda and Ida, 1916–1937* (Cambridge, 1995).

Seligmann, Matthew S., 'Germany and the origins of the First World War in the eyes of the American diplomatic establishment', *German History*, XV (1997), 307–32.

Semmel, Bernard, *Liberalism and naval strategy: ideology, interest, and sea power during the Pax Britannica* (Boston, 1986).

Seton-Watson, R. W., J. Dover-Wilson, Alfred E. Zimmern, and Arthur Greenwood, *The war and democracy* (London, 1915; first published 1914).

Shanafelt, Gary W., *The secret enemy: Austria-Hungary and the German alliance, 1914–1918* (Boulder, Col., 1985).

Shaw, Stanford J., and Ezel Kural Shaw, *History of the Ottoman empire and modern Turkey*, 2 vols. (Cambridge, 1976–7).

Sheehan, James J., *German liberalism in the nineteenth century* (Chicago, 1978).

Sheffy, Yigal, *British military intelligence in the Palestine campaign 1914–1918* (London, 1998).

Shepperson, George, and Thomas Price, *Independent African: John Chilembwe and the origins, setting and significance of the Nyasaland native rising of 1915* (Edinburgh, 1958).

Shevin-Coetzee, Marilyn, *The German army league: popular nationalism in Wilhelmine Germany* (New York, 1990).

Showalter, Dennis E., 'The eastern front and German military planning, 1871–1914—some observations', *East European Quarterly*, XV (1981), 163–80.

—— 'Even generals wet their pants: the first three weeks in East Prussia, August 1914', *War & Society*, II (1984), 60–86.

—— *Tannenberg: clash of empires* (Hamden, Conn., 1991).

Sieferle, Rolf Peter, 'Der deutsch–englische Gegensatz und die "Ideen von 1914"', in Gottfried Niedhart (ed.), *Das kontinentale Europa und die britischen Inseln: Wahrnehmungsmuster und Wechselwirkungen seit der Antike* (Mannheim, 1993).

Siegelbaum, Lewis H., *The politics of industrial mobilization in Russia, 1914–17: a study of the war-industries committees* (London, 1983).

Silberstein, Gerard E., *The troubled alliance: German–Austrian relations 1914 to 1917* (Lexington, 1970).

Simkins, Peter, *Kitchener's army: the raising of the New Armies, 1914–16* (Manchester, 1988).

Simon, Rachel, *Libya between Ottomanism and nationalism: the Ottoman involvement in Libya during the war with Italy (1911–1919)* (Berlin, 1987).

Simpson, Keith, *The old contemptibles: a photographic history of the British Expeditionary Force August–December 1914* (London, 1980).

Siney, Marion C., *The allied blockade of Germany 1914–1916* (Ann Arbor, 1957).

Sixsmith, E. K. G., *British generalship in the twentieth century* (London, 1970).

Skidelsky, Robert, *John Maynard Keynes*, vol. I, *Hopes betrayed 1883–1920* (London, 1983).

Smith, C. Jay, jr, 'Great Britain and the 1914–1915 straits agreement with Russia: the British promise of November 1914', *American Historical Review*, LXX (1965), 1015–34.

—— *The Russian struggle for power, 1914–1917: a study of Russian foreign policy during the First World War* (New York, 1969; first published 1956).

Smith, Leonard Vinson, 'Command authority in the French army, 1914–1918: the case of the 5ᵉ division d'infanterie', Columbia University Ph.D. *dissertation*, 1990; now published as *Between mutiny and obedience: the case of the French Fifth infantry division in World War I* (Princeton, 1994).

Smith, Paul, (ed.), *Government and the armed forces in Britain 1856–1990* (London, 1996).

Smith-Dorrien, Horace, *Memories of forty-eight years' service* (London, 1925).

Snell, John L., 'Socialist unions and socialist patriotism in Germany, 1914–1918', *American Historical Review*, LIX (1993), 66–76.

Snyder, Jack, *The ideology of the offensive: military decision-making and the disasters of 1914* (Ithaca, NY, 1984).

Soames, Mary (ed.), *Speaking for themselves: the personal letters of Winston and Clementine Churchill* (London, 1998).

Sombart, Werner, *Händler und Helden: politische Besinnungen* (Munich, 1915).

Soutou, Georges-Henri, *L'Or et le sang: les buts de guerre économiques de la première guerre mondiale* (Paris, 1989).

Spears, E. L., *Liaison 1914: a narrative of the great retreat* (London, 1930).

Spiers, Edward M., 'Rearming the Edwardian artillery', *Journal of the Society for Army Historical Research*, LVII (1979), 167–76.

—— *Haldane: an army reformer* (Edinburgh, 1980).

Spies, S. B., 'The outbreak of the First World War and the Botha government', *South African Historical Journal*, I (1969), 47–57.

Spitzmüller, Alexander, *Memoirs of Alexander Spitzmüller, Freiherr von Hammerstein (1862–1953)*, ed. Carvel de Bussy (New York, 1987).

Spring, D. W., 'Russia and the Franco-Russian alliance, 1905–1914: dependence or interdependence?', *Slavonic and East European Review*, LXVI (1988), 564–92.

Stamp, Josiah, *Taxation during the war* (London, 1932).

Stanley, William R., 'Review of Turkish Asiatic railways to 1918: some political-military considerations', *Journal of Transport History*, VII (1966), 189–204.

Stargardt, Nicholas, *The German idea of militarism: radical and socialist critics* (Cambridge, 1994).

Stegemann, Hermann, *Geschichte des Krieges*, 4 vols. (Stuttgart, 1918–21).

Steinberg, Jonathan, *Yesterday's deterrent: Tirpitz and the birth of the German battle fleet* (London, 1965).

Steiner, Zara, *Britain and the origins of the First World War* (London, 1977).

Stengers, Jean, 'L'Entrée en guerre de la Belgique', *Guerres mondiales et conflits contemporains*, 179 (juillet 1995), 13–33.

Stevenson, David, *French war aims against Germany 1914–1919* (Oxford, 1982).

—— *The First World War and international politics* (Oxford, 1988).

—— *Armaments and the coming of war: Europe, 1904–1914* (Oxford, 1996).

—— 'War by timetable? The railway race before 1914', *Past and Present*, 162 (1999), 163–94.

Stoecker, Helmuth (ed.), *German imperialism: from the beginnings until the Second World War* (London, 1986; first published 1977).

Stone, Jay, and Erwin A. Schmidl, *The Boer war and military reforms* (London, 1988).

Stone, Norman, 'Army and society in the Habsburg monarchy, 1900–1914', *Past and Present*, 33 (1966), 95–111.

—— 'Hungary and the crisis of July 1914', *Journal of Contemporary History*, I (1966), 153–70.

—— *The eastern front 1914–1917* (London, 1975).

—— *Europe transformed 1878–1919* (London, 1983).

Storz, Dieter, *Kriegsbild und Rüstung vor 1914. Europäische Landstreitkräfte vor dem Ersten Weltkrieg* (Herford, 1992).

Strachan, Hew, 'The First World War: causes and course', *Historical Journal*, XXIX (1986), 227–55.

—— *The First World War, New Appreciations in History*, no. 33, (London, [1993]).

—— 'Germany in the First World War: the problem of strategy', *German History*, XII (1994), 237–49.

—— 'The battle of the Somme and British strategy', *Journal of Strategic Studies*, XXI (1998), 79–95.

—— (ed.), *Oxford Illustrated History of the First World War* (Oxford, 1998).

Stromberg, Roland N., *Redemption by war: the intellectuals and 1914* (Lawrence, Kan., 1982).

Stubbs, John O., 'The impact of the Great War on the Conservative party', in Gillian Peele and Chris Cook (eds.), *The politics of reappraisal 1918–1939* (London, 1975).

—— 'The Unionists and Ireland 1914–1918', *Historical Journal*, XXXIII (1990), 867–93.

Student, Erich, *Kameruns Kampf 1914–16* (Berlin, 1937).

Stuermer, H., *Two war years in Constantinople* (London, 1917).

Stumpf, R., *The private war of Seaman Stumpf: the unique diaries of a young German in the Great War*, ed. Daniel Horn (London, 1969).

Suchomlinow [i.e. Sukhomlinov], W. A., *Erinnerungen* (Berlin, 1924).

Sulzbach, Herbert, *With the German guns: four years on the western front 1914–1918* (London, 1973; first published 1935).

Sumida, Jon Tetsuro, 'British capital ship design and fire control in the *Dreadnought* era: Sir John Fisher, Arthur Hungerford Pollen, and the battle cruiser', *Journal of Modern History*, LI (1979), 205–30.

—— *In defence of naval supremacy: finance, technology and British naval policy, 1899–1914* (Boston, 1989).

—— 'British naval administration and policy in the age of Fisher', *Journal of Military History*, LIV (1990), 1–20.

—— 'British naval operational logistics 1914–1918', *Journal of Military History*, LVII (1993), 447–80.

—— 'Sir John Fisher and the *Dreadnought*: the sources of naval mythology', *Journal of Military History*, LIX (1995), 619–37.

—— (ed.), *The Pollen papers: the privately circulated printed works of Arthur Hungerford Pollen, 1901–16* (London, 1984).

Summers, Anne, 'Militarism in Britain before the Great War', *History Workshop*, 2 (autumn 1976), 104–23.

—— *Angels and citizens: British women as military nurses 1854–1914* (London, 1988).

—— and R. W. Johnson, 'World War I conscription and social change in Guinea', *Journal of African History*, XIX (1978), 25–38.

Suren, Hans, *Kampf um Kamerun: Garua* (Berlin, 1934).

Swart, Sandra, ' "A Boer and his gun and his wife are three things always together": republican masculinity and the 1914 rebellion', *Journal of Southern African Studies*, XXIV (1998), 737–51.

Swietochowski, Tamusz, *Russian Azerbaijan, 1905–1920: the shaping of a national identity in a Muslim community* (Cambridge, 1985).

Sykes, Christopher, *Wassmuss: the German Lawrence* (London, 1936).

Tan, Tai-Yong, 'An imperial home-front: Punjab and the First World War', *Journal of Military History*, LXIV (2000), 371–410.

Tardieu, André, *Avec Foch (août–novembre 1914)* (Paris, 1939).

Taslauanu, Octavian C., *With the Austrian army in Galicia* (London, [1918]).

Taute, M., 'A German account of the medical side of the war in East Africa, 1914–1918', *Tanganyika Notes and Records*, 8 (Dec. 1939), 1–20.

Taylor, A. J. P., *Politics in wartime* (London, 1964).

—— (ed.), *Lloyd George: twelve essays* (London, 1971).

Teillard, Jean, *Les Emprunts de guerre* (Montpellier, 1921).

Teixeira, Nuno Severiano, *L'Entrée du Portugal dans la Grande Guerre: objectifs nationaux et stratgégies politiques* (Paris, 1998).

Terraine, John, *Mons: the retreat to victory* (London, 1960).

—— *Douglas Haig: the educated soldier* (London, 1963).

—— *The western front 1914–1918* (London, 1964).

—— *The Great War 1914–1918: a pictorial history* (London, 1965).

—— *The smoke and the fire: myths and anti-myths of war 1861–1945* (London, 1980).

Thomas, Roger, 'Military recruitment in the Gold Coast during the First World War', *Cahiers d'études africaines*, XV (1975), 57–83.

—— 'The 1916 Bongo "riots" and their background: aspects of colonial administration and African response in eastern upper Ghana', *Journal of African History*, XXIV (1983), 57–75.

Thompson, Wayne C., *In the eye of the storm: Kurt Riezler and the crises of modern Germany* (Iowa City, 1980).

Ticktin, David, 'The war issue and the collapse of the South African Labour party 1914–15', *South African Historical Journal*, 1 (1969), 59–80.

Townsend, Mary Evelyn *The rise and fall of the Germany's colonial empire 1884–1918* (New York, 1930).

Trachtenberg, Marc, '"A new economic order": Étienne Clémentel and French economic diplomacy during the First World War', *French Historical Studies*, X (1977), 315–41.

—— 'The coming of the First World War: a reassessment', in Trachtenberg, *History and strategy* (Princeton, 1991).

Travers, Tim H. E., 'The offensive and the problem of innovation in British military thought 1870–1915', *Journal of Contemporary History*, XIII (1978), 531–53.

—— 'Technology, tactics, and morale: Jean de Bloch, the Boer war, and British military theory, 1900–1914', *Journal of Modern History*, LI (1979), 264–86.

—— 'The hidden army: structural problems in the British officer corps, 1900–1918', *Journal of Contemporary History*, XVII (1982), 523–44.

—— *The killing ground: the British army, the western front and emergence of modern warfare 1900–1918* (London, 1987).

—— and Christon Archer (eds.), *Men at war: politics, technology and innovation in the twentieth century* (Chicago, 1982).

Trebilcock, Clive, 'The British armaments industry 1890–1914: false legend and true utility', in Geoffrey Best and Andrew Wheatcroft (eds.), *War, economy and the military mind* (London, 1976).

—— *The Vickers brothers: armaments and enterprise 1854–1914* (London, 1977).

—— *The industrialization of the continental powers 1780–1914* (London, 1981).

Trumpener, Ulrich, 'German military aid to Turkey in 1914: an historical re-evaluation', *Journal of Modern History*, XXXII (1960), 145–9.

—— 'Turkey's entry into World War I: an assessment of responsibilities', *Journal of Modern History*, XXXIV (1962), 369–80.

—— 'Liman von Sanders and the German–Ottoman alliance', *Journal of Contemporary History*, I (1966), 179–92.

—— *Germany and the Ottoman empire 1914–1918* (Princeton, 1968).

—— 'The escape of the *Goeben* and *Breslau*: a reassessment', *Canadian Journal of History*, VI (1971), 171–87.

—— 'War premeditated? German intelligence operations in July 1914', *Central European History*, IX (1976), 58–85.

Tuchmann, Barbara, *August 1914* (London, 1962).

Tunstall, Graydon A., jr, *Planning for war against Russia and Serbia: Austro-Hungarian and German military strategies, 1987–1914* (Boulder, Col., 1993).

—— 'The Habsburg command conspiracy: the Austrian falsification of historiography on the outbreak of World War I', *Austrian History Yearbook*, XXVII (1996), 181–98.

Turner, John, *British politics and the Great War: coalition and conflict 1915–1918* (New Haven, 1992).

—— (ed.), *Britain and the First World War* (London, 1988).

Turner, L. C. F., *Origins of the First World War* (London, 1970).

Tyng, Sewell, *The campaign of the Marne 1914* (London, 1935).

Uhle-Wettler, Franz, *Erich Ludendorff in seiner Zeit* (Berg, 1995).

Ullrich, Volker, *Kriegsalltag: Hamburg im ersten Weltkrieg* (Cologne, 1982).

Ulrich, Bernd, and Benjamin Ziemann (eds.), *Frontalltag im Ersten Weltkrieg: Wahn und Wirklichkeit* (Frankfurt am Main, 1994).

Unruh, Karl, *Langemarck: Legende und Wirklichkeit* (Koblenz, 1986).

Usborne, C. V., *The conquest of Morocco* (London, 1936).

Valiani, Leo, *The end of Austria-Hungary* (London, 1973; first published 1966).

Valone, Stephen J., ' "There must be some misunderstanding": Sir Edward Grey's diplomacy of August 1, 1914', *Journal of British Studies*, XXVII (1988), 405–24.

van Creveld, Martin, *Supplying war: logistics from Wallenstein to Patton* (Cambridge, 1977).

—— *Command in war* (Cambridge, Mass., 1985).

Vandenrath, Johannes, *et al.*, *1914: les psychoses de guerre?* (Rouen, 1985).

Veitch, Colin, ' "Play up! Play up! and win the war!" Football, the nation and the First World War 1914–15', *Journal of Contemporary History*, XX (1985), 363–78.

Verhey, Jeffrey Todd, 'The "spirit of 1914": the myth of enthusiasm and the rhetoric of unity in World War I Germany', University of California, Berkeley, Ph.D. dissertation, 1991; published as *The spirit of 1914: militarism, myth and mobilization in Germany* (Cambridge, 2000).

Vincent, C. Paul, *The politics of hunger: the allied blockade of Germany, 1915–1919* (Athens, Oh., 1985).

Vincent-Smith, John, 'Britain, Portugal, and the First World War, 1914–1916', *European Studies Review*, IV (1974), 207–38.

Vogel, Jakob, *Nationen im Gleichschritt: der Kult der 'Nationen in Waffen' in Deutschland und Frankreich, 1871–1914* (Göttingen, 1997).

Vogel, Renate, *Die Persien- und Afghanistanexpedition Oskar Ritter v. Niedermayers 1915/16* (Osnabrück, 1976).

Vogt, Adolf, *Oberst Max Bauer: Generalstabsoffizier im Zwielicht* (Osnabrück, 1974).

Walker, Eric A., *A history of southern Africa* (London, 1957).

Wallace, Stuart, *War and the image of Germany: British academics 1914–1918* (Edinburgh, 1988).

Wallach, Jehuda L., *Anatomie einer Militärhilfe. Die preussisch–deutschen Militärmissionen in der Türkei 1835–1919* (Dusseldorf, 1976).

—— *The dogma of the battle of annihilation: the theories of Clausewitz and Schlieffen and their impact on the German conduct of two world wars* (Wesport, Conn., 1986; first published 1967).

Walvé de Bordes, J. van, *The Austrian crown: its depreciation and stabilization* (London, 1924).

Wandruszka, Adam, and Peter Urbanitsch, *Die Habsburgermonarchie 1848–1918*, vol. I, *Die wirtschaftliche Entwicklung*, ed. Alois Brusatti (Vienna, 1973); vol. V, *Die bewaffnete Macht* (Vienna, 1987).

Wank, Solomon, 'Some reflections on Conrad von Hötzendorf and his memoirs based on new and old sources', *Austrian History Yearbook*, I (1965), 74–89.

War Office, *Statistics of the military effort of the British empire during the Great War* (London, 1922).

Warburg, Gabriel, *The Sudan under Wingate: administration in the Anglo-Egyptian Sudan 1899–1916* (London, 1971).

Warhurst, P. R., 'Smuts and Africa: a study in sub-imperialism', *South African Historical Journal*, XVI (1984), 82–100.

Watson, David Robin, *Georges Clemenceau: a political biography* (London, 1974).

Watt, Richard M., *Dare call it treason* (London, 1964).

Watts, Anthony J., *The imperial Russian navy* (London, 1990).

Weber, Eugen, *Action française: royalism and reaction in twentieth-century France* (Stanford, 1962).

Weber, Frank G., *Eagles on the crescent: Germany, Austria, and the diplomacy of the Turkish alliance 1914–1918* (Ithaca, NY, 1970).

Wegener, Wolfgang, *Die Seestrategie des Weltkrieges* (Berlin, 1929); English edn., *The naval strategy of the world war*, ed. Holger Herwig (Annapolis, 1989).

Wegs, James Robert, 'Austrian economic mobilization during World War I: with particular emphasis on heavy industry', Illinois University Ph.D. dissertation, 1970; published as *Die österreichische Kriegswirtschaft 1914–1918* (Vienna, 1979).

Wehler, Hans-Ulrich, *The German empire 1871–1918* (Leamington Spa, 1985; first published 1973).

Weir, Gary E., 'The imperial naval office and the problem of armor prices in Germany, 1897–1914', *Military Affairs*, XLVIII (1984), 62–5.

—— 'Tirpitz, technology,and building U-boats, 1897–1916', *International History Review*, VI (1984), 174–90.

Wells, H. G., *Mr Britling sees it through* (London, 1916).

Westwood, John, *Railways at war* (London, 1980).

Wette, Wolfram, 'Reichstag und "Kriegswinnlerei" (1916–1918): die Anfänge parlamentarischer Rüstungskontrolle in Deutschland', *Militärgeschichtliche Mitteilungen*, 36 (1984), 31–56.

—— (ed.), *Der Krieg des kleinen Mannes: eine Militärgeschichte von unten* (Munich, 1992).

Wheeler-Bennett, John W., *Wooden titan: Hindenburg in twenty years of German history 1914–1934* (London, 1967; first published 1934).

Whiting, R. C., 'Taxation and the working class', *Historical Journal*, XXXIII (1990), 895–916).

Wiedenfeld, Kurt, *Die Organisation der Kriegsrohstoff-Bewirtschaftung im Weltkriege* (Hamburg, 1936).

Wilcox, Craig, 'Relinquishing the past: John Mordike's *An army for a nation*', *Australian Journal of History and Politics*, XL (1994), 52–65.

Wild von Hohenborn, Adolf, *Briefe und Tagebuchaufzeichnungen des preussischen Generals als Kriegsminister und Truppenführer im Ersten Weltkrieg* (Boppard am Rhein, 1986).

Wildman, Allan K., *The end of the Russian imperial army: the old army and the soldiers' revolt (March–April 1917)* (Princeton, 1980).

Williams, Jeffrey, *Byng of Vimy: general and governor general* (London, 1983).

Williams, Rhodri, *Defending the empire: the Conservative party and British defence policy 1899–1915* (New Haven, 1991).

Williamson, D. G., 'Walter Rathenau and the K.R.A. August 1914–March 1915', *Zeitschrift für Unternehmensgeschichte*, XXIII (1978), 118–36.

Williamson, John G., *Karl Helfferich 1872–1924: economist, financier, politician* (Princeton, 1971).

Williamson, Samuel R., jr, *The politics of grand strategy: Britain and France prepare for war, 1904–1914* (Cambridge, Mass., 1969).

—— 'The origins of World War I', *Journal of Interdisciplinary History*, XVIII (1988), 795–818.

—— *Austria-Hungary and the origins of the First World War* (London, 1991).

—— and Peter Pastor (eds.), *War and society in East Central Europe*, vol. V, *Essays on World War I: origins and prisoners of war* (New York, 1983).

Wilson, Jeremy, *Lawrence of Arabia: the authorised biography of T. E. Lawrence* (London, 1989).

Wilson, Keith, 'The British cabinet's decision for war, 2 August 1914', *British Journal of International Studies*, I (1975), 148–59.

—— 'The Foreign Office and the "education" of public opinion before the First World War', *Historical Journal*, XXVI (1983), 403–11.

—— *The policy of the Entente: essays on the determinants of British foreign policy 1904–1914* (Cambridge, 1985).

—— 'Hankey's appendix: some Admiralty manoeuvres during and after the Agadir crisis', *War in History*, I (1994), 81–97.

—— 'Understanding the "misunderstanding" of 1 August 1914', *Historical Journal*, XXXVII (1994), 885–9.

—— (ed.), *The rasp of war: the letters of H. A. Gwynne to the Countess Bathurst 1914–1918* (London, 1988).

—— (ed.), *Decisions for war, 1914* (London, 1995).

Wilson, Trevor, *The downfall of the Liberal party 1914–1935* (London, 1966).

—— 'Britain's "moral commitment" to France in July 1914', *History*, LXIV (1979), 380–90.

—— 'Lord Bryce's investigation into alleged German atrocities in Belgium, 1914–15', *Journal of Contemporary History*, XIV (1979), 369–83.

—— *The myriad faces of war: Britain and the Great War 1914–1918* (Cambridge, 1986).

—— (ed.), *The political diaries of C. P. Scott* (London, 1970).

Wingate, Ronald, *Wingate of the Sudan: the life and times of General Sir Reginald Wingate, maker of the Anglo-Egyptian Sudan* (London, 1955).

Winkler, Wilhelm, *Die Einkommenverschiebungen in Österreich während des Weltkrieges* (Vienna, 1930).

Winter, Denis, *Death's men: soldiers of the Great War* (London, 1978).

Winter, J. M., *Socialism and the challenge of war: ideas and politics in Britain 1912–1918* (London, 1974).

—— *The Great War and the British people* (London, 1986).

—— *The experience of World War I* (Edinburgh, 1988).

—— (ed.), *War and economic development: essays in memory of David Joslin* (Cambridge, 1975).

Winter, Jay, and Blaine Baggett, *1914–18: the Great War and the shaping of the 20th century* (London, 1996).

Witkop, Philipp (ed.), *Kriegsbriefe gefallener Studenten*, 7th edn. (Munich, 1928).

Witt, Peter-Christian, *Die Finanzpolitik des Deutschen Reiches von 1903 bis 1913: eine Studie zur Innenpolitik des wihelminischen Deutschland* (Lübeck, 1970).

—— (ed.), *Wealth and taxation in Central Europe: the history and sociology of public finance* (Leamington Spa, 1987).

Wohl, Robert, *The generation of 1914* (London, 1980).

Wolff, Theodor, *Vollendete Tatsachen 1914–1917* (Berlin, 1918).

—— *Tagebücher 1914–1919*, ed. Bernd Sösemann, 2 vols. (Boppard am Rhein, 1984).

Woodward, Llewellyn, *Great Britain and the war of 1914–1918* (London, 1967).

Wright, Gordon, *Raymond Poincaré and the French presidency* (Stanford, 1942).

Wrisberg, Ernst von, *Heer und Heimat 1914–1918* (Leipzig, 1921).

—— *Wehr und Waffen 1914–1918* (Leipzig, 1922).

Wysling, Hans (ed.), *Letters of Heinrich and Thomas Mann, 1900–1949* (Berkeley, 1998).

Yates, Keith, *Graf Spee's raiders: challenge to the Royal Navy, 1914–1915* (Annapolis, 1995).

Yearwood, Peter J., 'Great Britain and the repartition of Africa', *Journal of Imperial and Commonwealth History*, XVIII (1990), 316–41.

—— '"In a casual way with a blue pencil": British policy and the partition of Kamerun, 1914–1919', *Canadian Journal of African Studies*, XXVII (1993), 218–44.

Yorke, Edmund James, 'A crisis of colonial control: war and authority in Northern Rhodesia, 1914–19', Cambridge University Ph.D. thesis, 1983.

Young, Francis Brett, *Marching on Tanga: with General Smuts in East Africa* (London, 1919; first published 1917).

Ypersele, Laurence van, 'Le 4 août en Belgique: naissance d'un mythe royal. Enquête dans la presse belge', *La Grande Guerre: pays, histoire, mémoire*, 8 (juin 1995), 7–10.

Zagorsky, S. O., *State control of industry in Russia during the war* (New Haven, 1928).

Zechlin, Egmont, 'Friedenbestrebungen und Revolutionierungsversuche: deutsche Bemühungen zur Ausschaltung Russlands im Ersten Weltkriege', *Aus Politik und Zeitgeschichte*, 20/61 (17 Mai 1961), 269–88; 24/61 (14 Juni 1961), 325–37; 25/61 (21 Juni 1961), 341–67.

Zeman, Z. A. B., *The break-up of the Habsburg empire 1914–1918: a study in national and social revolution* (London, 1961).

Ziemann, Benjamin, *Front und Heimat: ländliche Kreigserfahrungen im südlichen Bayern 1914–1923* (Essen, 1997).

Zilch, Reinhard, *Die Reichsbank und die finanzielle Kriegsvorbereitung 1907 bis 1914* (Berlin, 1987).

Zirkel, Kirsten, 'Military power in German colonial policy: the *Schütztruppen* and their leaders in East and South-West Africa, 1888–1918', in David Killingray and David Omissi (eds.), *Guardians of empire: the armed forces of the colonial powers c.1700–1964* (Manchester, 2000).

Zuber, Terence, 'The Schlieffen plan reconsidered', *War in History*, VI (1999), 262–305.

Zürcher, Erik Jan, *The Unionist factor: the role of the Committee of Union and Progress in the Turkish national movement 1905–1926* (Leiden, 1984).

Zweig, Stefan, *The world of yesterday* (London, 1943).

INDEX